The Encyclopedia of Religion

The Encyclopedia of Religion

Mircea Eliade

EDITOR IN CHIEF

Volume 7

MACMILLAN PUBLISHING COMPANY
New York
Collier Macmillan Publishers
London

MACMILLAN PUBLISHING COMPANY
866 Third Avenue, New York, NY 10022

Collier Macmillan Canada Inc.

Library of Congress Catalog Card Number: 86-5432

PRINTED IN THE UNITED STATES OF AMERICA

printing number
1 2 3 4 5 6 7 8 9 10

Library of Congress Cataloging-in-Publication Data

The Encyclopedia of religion.

Includes bibliographies and index.
1. Religion—Dictionaries. I. Eliade, Mircea, 1907–1986. II. Adams, Charles J.
BL31.#46 1986 200'.3'21 86-5432
ISBN 0-02-909480-1 (set)
ISBN 0-02-909780-0 (v. 7)

Acknowledgments of sources, copyrights, and permissions to use previously published materials are gratefully made in a special listing in volume 16.

Abbreviations and Symbols Used in This Work

abbr. abbreviated; abbreviation
abr. abridged; abridgment
AD *anno Domini,* in the year of the (our) Lord
Afrik. Afrikaans
AH *anno Hegirae,* in the year of the Hijrah
Akk. Akkadian
Ala. Alabama
Alb. Albanian
Am. *Amos*
AM *ante meridiem,* before noon
amend. amended; amendment
annot. annotated; annotation
Ap. *Apocalypse*
Apn. *Apocryphon*
app. appendix
Arab. Arabic
ʿArakh. *ʿArakhin*
Aram. Aramaic
Ariz. Arizona
Ark. Arkansas
Arm. Armenian
art. article (pl., arts.)
AS Anglo-Saxon
Asm. Mos. *Assumption of Moses*
Assyr. Assyrian
A.S.S.R. Autonomous Soviet Socialist Republic
Av. Avestan
ʿA.Z. *ʿAvodah zarah*
b. born
Bab. Babylonian
Ban. Bantu
1 Bar. *1 Baruch*
2 Bar. *2 Baruch*
3 Bar. *3 Baruch*
4 Bar. *4 Baruch*
B.B. *Bavaʾ batraʾ*
BBC British Broadcasting Corporation
BC before Christ
BCE before the common era
B.D. Bachelor of Divinity
Beits. *Beitsah*
Bekh. *Bekhorot*
Beng. Bengali
Ber. *Berakhot*
Berb. Berber
Bik. *Bikkurim*
bk. book (pl., bks.)
B.M. *Bavaʾ metsiʿaʾ*
BP before the present
B.Q. *Bavaʾ qammaʾ*
Brāh. *Brāhmaṇa*
Bret. Breton
B.T. Babylonian Talmud
Bulg. Bulgarian
Burm. Burmese
c. *circa,* about, approximately
Calif. California
Can. Canaanite
Catal. Catalan
CE of the common era
Celt. Celtic
cf. *confer,* compare
Chald. Chaldean
chap. chapter (pl., chaps.)
Chin. Chinese
C.H.M. Community of the Holy Myrrhbearers
1 Chr. *1 Chronicles*
2 Chr. *2 Chronicles*
Ch. Slav. Church Slavic
cm centimeters
col. column (pl., cols.)
Col. *Colossians*
Colo. Colorado
comp. compiler (pl., comps.)
Conn. Connecticut
cont. continued
Copt. Coptic
1 Cor. *1 Corinthians*
2 Cor. *2 Corinthians*
corr. corrected
C.S.P. Congregatio Sancti Pauli, Congregation of Saint Paul (Paulists)
d. died
D Deuteronomic (source of the Pentateuch)
Dan. Danish
D.B. Divinitatis Baccalaureus, Bachelor of Divinity
D.C. District of Columbia
D.D. Divinitatis Doctor, Doctor of Divinity
Del. Delaware
Dem. *Demaʾi*
dim. diminutive
diss. dissertation
Dn. *Daniel*
D.Phil. Doctor of Philosophy
Dt. *Deuteronomy*
Du. Dutch
E Elohist (source of the Pentateuch)
Eccl. *Ecclesiastes*
ed. editor (pl., eds.); edition; edited by
ʿEduy. *ʿEduyyot*
e.g. *exempli gratia,* for example
Egyp. Egyptian
1 En. *1 Enoch*
2 En. *2 Enoch*
3 En. *3 Enoch*
Eng. English
enl. enlarged
Eph. *Ephesians*
ʿEruv. *ʿEruvin*
1 Esd. *1 Esdras*
2 Esd. *2 Esdras*
3 Esd. *3 Esdras*
4 Esd. *4 Esdras*
esp. especially
Est. Estonian
Est. *Esther*
et al. *et alii,* and others
etc. *et cetera,* and so forth
Eth. Ethiopic
EV English version
Ex. *Exodus*
exp. expanded
Ez. *Ezekiel*
Ezr. *Ezra*
2 Ezr. *2 Ezra*
4 Ezr. *4 Ezra*
f. feminine; and following (pl., ff.)
fasc. fascicle (pl., fascs.)
fig. figure (pl., figs.)
Finn. Finnish
fl. *floruit,* flourished
Fla. Florida
Fr. French
frag. fragment
ft. feet
Ga. Georgia
Gal. *Galatians*
Gaul. Gaulish
Ger. German
Giṭ. *Giṭṭin*
Gn. *Genesis*
Gr. Greek
Ḥag. *Ḥagigah*
Ḥal. *Ḥallah*
Hau. Hausa
Hb. *Habakkuk*
Heb. Hebrew
Heb. *Hebrews*
Hg. *Haggai*
Hitt. Hittite
Hor. *Horayot*
Hos. *Hosea*
Ḥul. *Ḥullin*
Hung. Hungarian
ibid. *ibidem,* in the same place (as the one immediately preceding)
Icel. Icelandic
i.e. *id est,* that is
IE Indo-European
Ill. Illinois
Ind. Indiana
intro. introduction
Ir. Gael. Irish Gaelic
Iran. Iranian
Is. *Isaiah*
Ital. Italian
J Yahvist (source of the Pentateuch)
Jas. *James*
Jav. Javanese
Jb. *Job*
Jdt. *Judith*
Jer. *Jeremiah*
Jgs. *Judges*
Jl. *Joel*
Jn. *John*
1 Jn. *1 John*
2 Jn. *2 John*
3 Jn. *3 John*
Jon. *Jonah*
Jos. *Joshua*
Jpn. Japanese
JPS Jewish Publication Society translation (1985) of the Hebrew Bible
J.T. Jerusalem Talmud
Jub. *Jubilees*
Kans. Kansas
Kel. *Kelim*

Ker. *Keritot*
Ket. *Ketubbot*
1 Kgs. *1 Kings*
2 Kgs. *2 Kings*
Khois. Khoisan
Kil. *Kil'ayim*
km kilometers
Kor. Korean
Ky. Kentucky
l. line (pl., ll.)
La. Louisiana
Lam. *Lamentations*
Lat. Latin
Latv. Latvian
L. en Th. Licencié en Théologie, Licentiate in Theology
L. ès L. Licencié ès Lettres, Licentiate in Literature
Let. Jer. *Letter of Jeremiah*
lit. literally
Lith. Lithuanian
Lk. *Luke*
LL Late Latin
LL.D. Legum Doctor, Doctor of Laws
Lv. *Leviticus*
m meters
m. masculine
M.A. Master of Arts
Ma'as. *Ma'aserot*
Ma'as. Sh. *Ma'aser sheni*
Mak. *Makkot*
Makh. *Makhshirin*
Mal. *Malachi*
Mar. Marathi
Mass. Massachusetts
1 Mc. *1 Maccabees*
2 Mc. *2 Maccabees*
3 Mc. *3 Maccabees*
4 Mc. *4 Maccabees*
Md. Maryland
M.D. Medicinae Doctor, Doctor of Medicine
ME Middle English
Meg. *Megillah*
Me'il. *Me'ilah*
Men. *Menaḥot*
MHG Middle High German
mi. miles
Mi. *Micah*
Mich. Michigan
Mid. *Middot*
Minn. Minnesota
Miq. *Miqva'ot*
MIran. Middle Iranian
Miss. Mississippi
Mk. *Mark*
Mo. Missouri
Mo'ed Q. *Mo'ed qaṭan*
Mont. Montana
MPers. Middle Persian
MS. *manuscriptum,* manuscript (pl., MSS)
Mt. *Matthew*
MT Masoretic text
n. note
Na. *Nahum*
Nah. Nahuatl
Naz. *Nazir*
N.B. *nota bene,* take careful note
N.C. North Carolina
n.d. no date
N.Dak. North Dakota
NEB New English Bible
Nebr. Nebraska
Ned. *Nedarim*
Neg. *Nega'im*
Neh. *Nehemiah*
Nev. Nevada
N.H. New Hampshire
Nid. *Niddah*
N.J. New Jersey
Nm. *Numbers*
N.Mex. New Mexico
no. number (pl., nos.)
Nor. Norwegian
n.p. no place
n.s. new series
N.Y. New York
Ob. *Obadiah*
O.Cist. Ordo Cisterciencium, Order of Cîteaux (Cistercians)
OCS Old Church Slavonic
OE Old English
O.F.M. Ordo Fratrum Minorum, Order of Friars Minor (Franciscans)
OFr. Old French
Ohal. *Ohalot*
OHG Old High German
OIr. Old Irish
OIran. Old Iranian
Okla. Oklahoma
ON Old Norse
O.P. Ordo Praedicatorum, Order of Preachers (Dominicans)
OPers. Old Persian
op. cit. *opere citato,* in the work cited
OPrus. Old Prussian
Oreg. Oregon
'Orl. *'Orlah*
O.S.B. Ordo Sancti Benedicti, Order of Saint Benedict (Benedictines)
p. page (pl., pp.)
P Priestly (source of the Pentateuch)
Pa. Pennsylvania
Pahl. Pahlavi
Par. *Parah*
para. paragraph (pl., paras.)
Pers. Persian
Pes. *Pesaḥim*
Ph.D. Philosophiae Doctor, Doctor of Philosophy
Phil. *Philippians*
Phlm. *Philemon*
Phoen. Phoenician
pl. plural; plate (pl., pls.)
PM *post meridiem,* after noon
Pol. Polish
pop. population
Port. Portuguese
Prv. *Proverbs*
Ps. *Psalms*
Ps. 151 *Psalm 151*
Ps. Sol. *Psalms of Solomon*
pt. part (pl., pts.)
1 Pt. *1 Peter*
2 Pt. *2 Peter*
Pth. Parthian
Q hypothetical source of the synoptic Gospels
Qid. *Qiddushin*
Qin. *Qinnim*
r. reigned; ruled
Rab. *Rabbah*
rev. revised
R. ha-Sh. *Ro'sh ha-shanah*
R.I. Rhode Island
Rom. Romanian
Rom. *Romans*
R.S.C.J. Societas Sacratissimi Cordis Jesu, Religious of the Sacred Heart
RSV Revised Standard Version of the Bible
Ru. *Ruth*
Rus. Russian
Rv. *Revelation*
Rv. Ezr. *Revelation of Ezra*
San. *Sanhedrin*
S.C. South Carolina
Scot. Gael. Scottish Gaelic
S.Dak. South Dakota
sec. section (pl., secs.)
Sem. Semitic
ser. series
sg. singular
Sg. *Song of Songs*
Sg. of 3 *Prayer of Azariah and the Song of the Three Young Men*
Shab. *Shabbat*
Shav. *Shavu'ot*
Sheq. *Sheqalim*
Sib. Or. *Sibylline Oracles*
Sind. Sindhi
Sinh. Sinhala
Sir. *Ben Sira*
S.J. Societas Jesu, Society of Jesus (Jesuits)
Skt. Sanskrit
1 Sm. *1 Samuel*
2 Sm. *2 Samuel*
Sogd. Sogdian
Soṭ *Soṭah*
sp. species (pl., spp.)
Span. Spanish
sq. square
S.S.R. Soviet Socialist Republic
st. stanza (pl., ss.)
S.T.M. Sacrae Theologiae Magister, Master of Sacred Theology
Suk. *Sukkah*
Sum. Sumerian
supp. supplement; supplementary
Sus. *Susanna*
s.v. *sub verbo,* under the word (pl., s.v.v.)
Swed. Swedish
Syr. Syriac
Syr. Men. *Syriac Menander*
Ta'an. *Ta'anit*
Tam. Tamil
Tam. *Tamid*
Tb. *Tobit*
T.D. *Taishō shinshū daizōkyō,* edited by Takakusu Junjirō et al. (Tokyo, 1922–1934)
Tem. *Temurah*
Tenn. Tennessee
Ter. *Terumot*
Ṭev. Y. *Ṭevul yom*
Tex. Texas
Th.D. Theologicae Doctor, Doctor of Theology
1 Thes. *1 Thessalonians*
2 Thes. *2 Thessalonians*
Thrac. Thracian
Ti. *Titus*
Tib. Tibetan
1 Tm. *1 Timothy*
2 Tm. *2 Timothy*
T. of 12 *Testaments of the Twelve Patriarchs*
Ṭoh. *Ṭohorot*
Tong. Tongan
trans. translator, translators; translated by; translation
Turk. Turkish
Ukr. Ukrainian
Upan. *Upaniṣad*
U.S. United States
U.S.S.R. Union of Soviet Socialist Republics
Uqts. *Uqtsin*
v. verse (pl., vv.)
Va. Virginia
var. variant; variation
Viet. Vietnamese
viz. *videlicet,* namely
vol. volume (pl., vols.)
Vt. Vermont
Wash. Washington
Wel. Welsh
Wis. Wisconsin
Wis. *Wisdom of Solomon*
W.Va. West Virginia
Wyo. Wyoming
Yad. *Yadayim*
Yev. *Yevamot*
Yi. Yiddish
Yor. Yoruba
Zav. *Zavim*
Zec. *Zechariah*
Zep. *Zephaniah*
Zev. *Zevaḥim*

* hypothetical
? uncertain; possibly; perhaps
° degrees
+ plus
− minus
= equals; is equivalent to
× by; multiplied by
→ yields

I

(CONTINUED)

ICONOCLASM. The term *iconoclasm,* derived from the Greek *eikōn* ("image") and *klasma* ("broken thing"), refers to opposition to the veneration of images. It was a trend of thought that caused great disturbance in the religious life of the Byzantine empire between 724 and 843 and engendered debates that led to the clarification and elaboration of the theology of icons. [*See* Icons.]

Origins and Causes of the Movement. Distinct from the Christians of Syria and Armenia who, without rejecting sacred images, assigned to them a preponderantly didactic role as illustrations of biblical writings, Christians in the Greek-speaking areas of the Byzantine empire carried forward their pre-Christian traditions in which religious images played a significant part in divine worship and, therefore, venerated icons with a zeal that made them suspect of idolatry. Icons had been kissed, surrounded with burning incense and wick lamps, and made the object of other manifestations of devotion. The reservations about Greek culture held by Christians of eastern or Semitic traditions (and the emperors who opposed icons were precisely of such extraction) were further strengthened by the emergence and spread of Islam, which fundamentally abhorred anthropomorphic representations. Objections to the adoration of images by Christians activated the iconoclastic attitudes of the Byzantine emperors during the eighth and ninth centuries. The movement was also encouraged by the emperors' hostility to monasticism, a citadel of icon worship; by the triumph of monophysitism (which was essentially iconoclastic) in the eastern provinces of the Byzantine empire (these provinces were the main source of army recruits); and by the influence of Neoplatonic thinking.

Byzantine Emperors and the Church Councils. The unleashing of the iconoclastic movement is attributed to the steps taken in 725 and 726 by Emperor Leo III (r. 717–741); even two years earlier, however, he had supported the undertaking of two bishops from Asia Minor, Constantine of Nikoleia and Thomas of Claudioupolis, who voiced their opposition to the doctrine on images developed by Germanus I, patriarch of Constantinople (r. 715–730). Emperor Leo's iconoclastic policy was expressed first in the prohibition of image worship, then in his order to have all images destroyed, including a statue of Jesus Christ on the main gate of the imperial palace at Chalcedon, which had been raised by Constantine the Great. Leo III decreed two edicts against the veneration of icons (in 726 and 729) and forced Germanus to sign the latter edict and then, in 730, to resign. Opposition by the monks and members of the civil service of Constantinople brought in its wake a wave of persecutions, including banishment, confiscation, and some vilification. The newly appointed patriarch, Anastasius (730–741), and the higher clergy bowed to the emperor's orders, but the destruction of images was not effected with equal zeal in all parts of the empire. From abroad, John of Damascus, who served at that time as a high official at the court of Caliph Hishām (724–743) of the Umayyad dynasty, reacted by writing three apologies, together entitled *Defense of the Sacred Images.* Although the papacy was subject to the rule of the Byzantine emperor, popes Gregory II (715–731) and Gregory III (731–741) protested in writing the persecutions ordered by Leo III, which were also condemned by the Council of Rome (731). Leo's opponents emphasized the weaknesses of the emperor's policy, the theological substantiation for which was poor.

Emperor Constantine V Copronymus (741–775), a son of Leo III, developed his father's iconoclastic measures. As early as 752 he encouraged the elaboration of a doctrine that opposed image worship, and in 754 this doctrine was enforced by the Council of Hiereia, a council in which 338 theologians were forced to take part. While Leo III had justified his iconoclasm by strictly prohibiting the worship of whatever was made by the human hand, the theology developed by the Council of Hiereia had a christological dimension. To the supporters of image worship the iconographic representation of

Christ was a consequence and a demonstration of his incarnation. Iconoclastic theologians claimed that representing the Savior was tantamount to either separating his dual nature or limiting his person, which could not be circumscribed. They insisted rather on the essential indescribability of God. Their arguments helped to crystallize the theology of icons, since they compelled the supporters of image worship to justify their position by resorting to the entire Christian doctrine that had been elaborated in the third to the eighth centuries. The Council of Hiereia led in following years to savage repression against the monks, the principal opponents of both iconoclasm and the emperor's claim to secular as well as ecclesiastical supremacy. Many monasteries were destroyed and secularized, and many monks were killed, exiled, mutilated, or forced to marry and rejoin secular life. The harsh condemnation of that policy by the Eastern patriarchs outside Constantinople and by the papacy at the anti-iconoclastic Council of Rome (769) heralded the separation between Eastern and Western Christianity.

Solution of the Crisis. Following the death of the iconoclastic emperor Leo IV the Khazar (775–780) the cult of icons was temporarily restored by the emperor's widow, Irene, who until 790 assumed the regency on behalf of her son Constantine VI, then still a minor; she later forcibly prevented Constantine's succession and proclaimed herself "emperor" of Byzantium. Empress Irene came from the Greek region of the empire and favored the veneration of icons. In 784 she installed her own secretary, Tarasios, as patriarch of Constantinople, and in 787 she convened the Second Council of Nicaea. After nine metropolitans and two archbishops from Asia Minor had abjured the iconoclastic heresy, all iconoclastic bishops were admitted to the council, which endorsed the legitimacy of the veneration of images as "relative" worship, addressed through the mediation of icons to their divine prototype. The successful conclusion of the council, which was also attended by two legates of the pope, brought about a reconciliation of the Eastern and Western churches, allowed for the restoration of monastic life, and encouraged the definitive elaboration of the theology of icons with essential contributions by Theodore of Studios (759–826) and Nikephoros, patriarch of Constantinople (806–815).

Theodore and Nikephoros had to struggle against renewed iconoclasm after 813, however, when the army, which was hostile to image worship, brought Leo V the Armenian to the throne. The new emperor persuaded the Council of Hagia Sophia (815) to invalidate the decrees of 787 and recognize those of the Council of Hiereia. Nikephoros wrote several tracts against the council of 815, as did Theodore, but using different arguments: he emphasized the complete humanity assumed by Christ, which made possible the representation of his image. During the reigns of Leo V and his successors Michael II (820–829) and Theophilus (829–842), iconoclastic persecutions were resumed. In 843, soon after Theophilus's death, the regent-empress Theodora called another council at Constantinople, which restored image worship. Every year this event is celebrated on the first Sunday of Lent by the Eastern Orthodox church as "the Triumph of Orthodoxy," for the acceptance of the theology of icons is perceived as the ascendance of Christian doctrine.

BIBLIOGRAPHY

A general survey of the iconoclastic crisis is given in Edward J. Martin's *A History of the Iconoclastic Controversy* (New York, 1931) and André Grabar's *L'iconoclasme byzantin: Dossier archéologique* (Paris, 1984). For corrections and critical reservations concerning these works, see Jean Gouillard's review in *Revue des études byzantines* 16 (1958): 261–265. The present state of research and an extensive bibliography are to be found in Paul J. Alexander's *The Patriarch Nicephorus of Constantinople: Ecclesiastical Policy and Image Worship in the Byzantine Empire* (Oxford, 1958) and especially in *Iconoclasm: Papers Given at the Ninth Spring Symposium of Byzantine Studies, University of Birmingham, March 1975* (Birmingham, England, 1977), edited by Anthony Bryer and Judith Herrin.

VIRGIL CÂNDEA
Translated from Romanian by Sergiu Celac

ICONOGRAPHY. [*This entry comprises fourteen articles that discuss images and systems of images as sources of religious knowledge:*

Iconography as Visible Religion
Traditional African Iconography
Australian Aboriginal Iconography
Native American Iconography
Mesoamerican Iconography
Mesopotamian Iconography
Egyptian Iconography
Greco-Roman Iconography
Hindu Iconography
Buddhist Iconography
Taoist Iconography
Jewish Iconography
Christian Iconography
Islamic Iconography

The iconography of other religious traditions is discussed in Aegean Religions; Arctic Religions; Inca Religion; Iranian Religions; Jainism; Melanesian Religions; Neolithic Religion; South American Indians, *article on* Indians of the Andes; Vedism and Brahmanism; *and* Zoroastrianism. *For further discussion of visual dimensions of religious knowing, see* Dance *and* Drama.]

Iconography as Visible Religion

Iconography literally means "description of images," but it also refers to a research program in art history that exposes the different meanings of images vis-à-vis the beholder.

Words and Images. Religious iconography defines a relationship between word and pictorial scheme, each of which follows its own logic. Visual forms are not discursive: they do not represent their message sequentially but simultaneously. While the meanings given through verbal language are understood successively, those given through visual forms are understood only by perceiving the whole at once. Susanne Langer, who argues for such a distinction in her *Philosophy in a New Key* (1951, pp. 79–102), calls this kind of semantics "presentational symbolism," indicating that we grasp it not by reasoning but by feeling. From this basic difference it follows that word and image sometimes compete against each other and sometimes supplement each other. There is no universal law for this relationship; I shall illustrate some of the possibilities with examples from the history of ancient religions.

In ancient societies, the artist who shaped statues or carved stamps and seals was included among the artisans, a disparate group of producers who came to form a rank of their own. In Iran, as elsewhere, the three age-old social groups of priests, warriors, and peasants were joined in Parthian times (third century BCE–second century CE) by that of the artisans. But this new group was unable to elevate its status, as confirmed by the *Book of Ben Sira* (second century BCE). This text, which enumerates a list of craftsmen, acknowledges that without such skilled workers as the engravers of seals, the smith, or the potter, a city would have no inhabitants and no settlers or travelers would come to it. Yet, the writer points out, the artisans "are not in demand at public discussions or prominent in the assembly," since the assembly needs the wise men who are engaged in study rather than manual labor (*Ben Sira* 38:24–39:5).

The low reputation of the artisans is also reflected in the anonymity of their work. Artists working on behalf of a temple, a palace, or a private customer became alienated from their work. Although Greek vases were presumably signed by their painters for the first time about 700 BCE, the majority of artists were still unknown in later times and remained dependent on their patrons. The carvers of the Achaemenid rock reliefs (Iran, sixth–fifth century BCE), for example, relied completely on the political visions and models of the imperial court and were obliged to create a visual legitimation of Achaemenid kingship. (See Margaret Root's *The King and Kingship in Achaemenid Art*, Leiden, 1979).

Other trends of patronage can be observed with seals, stamps, amulets, and pottery. In Hellenistic Egypt, for example, the god Bes is represented in clay figures more often than the official and well-known Egyptian gods. The artisans in the provincial workshops obviously had to take into account the taste of private customers, who were looking for a deity able to avert evil powers and to protect men and women. The frightening appearance of Bes that the artisans shaped served as protection against such perils and met the demands of the laity (see Françoise Dunand in *Visible Religion* 3, 1985). The history of Greek vase paintings provides us with similar phenomena. While some paintings represent typically heroic attitudes toward dying, others display an unheroic, plebeian fear of death (see H. Hoffmann in *Visible Religion* 4, 1985/1986). Here the dependency on the court has been replaced by a dependency on citizens: the artisans were obviously serving civil demands and had to respond to changing social values. But in Egypt and Greece alike, the priests were scarcely able to control the artisans' relations with their customers. If there existed a market for religious objects and if there were influential lay employers, then priests could be expected to lose control of this part of religion. To make the point in positive terms: craft products sometimes reflect a popular comprehension of religion and thus can be used to trace the rulers' demands for political legitimation, on the one hand, and citizens' demands on the other. Yet, these materials have scarcely begun to be used for the study of political and civil conceptions of religion apart from the well-known priestly one.

Another factor should be noted: the scarcity of pictorial schemes. As there existed only a limited number of well-known stereotypes suitable for representing gods, we often find a certain break between image and inscription. A particularly dramatic example appears on a jar from Palestine (about 800 BCE; see figure 1), decorated with two figures similar to the Egyptian Bes (with feather crown, phallus, and crooked legs). An inscription declares: "I will bless you by Yahveh my [our] protector and his Ashera" (*Monotheismus im Alten Israel und seiner Umwelt*, edited by Othmar Keel, Fribourg, 1980, pp. 168–170). The pictorial representation of God of course violates the ban on images (*Ex.* 20:4), though this prohibition originally concerned cult statues *(pesel)* alone and was extended only later to a comprehensive ban on pictorial representation (Robert P. Carroll in

FIGURE 1. *Literary and Iconographic Incongruence.* Figures on a jar fragment; Palestine, c. 800 BCE. The inscription on the jar makes reference to the Israelite Yahveh, but the figuration is similar to that of the Egyptian Bes.

Studia theologica 31, 1977, pp. 51–64). Nor does the chosen pictorial scheme fit the official literary conceptions of Yahveh. But this incongruency does not prove that inscription and image are disconnected. There were only a small number of pictorial schemes appropriate for the representation of sky gods. In the second and first millennia BCE, three main schemes were used: the figure of a seated old man with a beard, dressed in a long garment with a horn-crown on his head; the figure of a standing young man with a club in his right hand (see figure 2); and the figure of a wild bull (Peter Welten in *Biblisches Reallexikon*, 2d ed., Tübingen, 1977, pp. 99–111).

Here we obviously touch on a characteristic of all traditional imagery: it tends toward the most simple schemes, which will be evident to almost all beholders. We know that ancient Jewish literature was aware of these schemes. The psalms refer to Yahveh as a smiting god (*Ps.* 29, for example; see Othmar Keel's *Die Welt der altorientalischen Bildsymbolik und das Alte Testament*, 2d ed., Zurich, 1977, pp. 184–197), while *Daniel* 7:9 refers to Yahveh as the old god. These schemes were welcome as textual symbols, but for visual form they were rejected by the priests and prophets. Nonetheless, images such as Yahveh as Bes may well have been a pictorial representation not admitted by priests and prophets, and in fact, the ban on images so poorly argued in the Hebrew scriptures should be carefully reviewed in this context of pictorial schemes.

Further examples will suggest other aspects of the relationship between word and image. In India the concretization of gods in images reduced their geographical universality and emphasized their local function (Heinrich von Stietencron in *Central Asiatic Journal* 21, 1977, pp. 126–138). In Greco-Roman religions, gods that originally belonged to the same tradition could be split by different representations (Hendrik Simon Versnel in *Visible Religion* 4, 1985/1986). These are only two instances where images have had an impact on the conceptual tradition. But we can also observe the contrary: a ban on images in the literary tradition can deeply affect the pictorial representation. Medieval and modern Shīʿī Muslim artists usually paint their holy imams as men without faces; the incomplete and mutilated human figures testify to an image-critical tradition. In other cases, as in Munich in 1534–1535, a ban on images could result in full-fledged iconoclasm (*Bildersturm*, edited by Martin Warnke, Munich, 1973). Yet a thorough analysis of iconoclasm must pay close attention to the different functions these images have had: a

FIGURE 2. *Image of Deity.* Palette of King Narmer; Hierakonpolis, Egypt, c. 2800 BCE. In the ancient Near East the sky god was often depicted as a youth with a club in his right hand.

political one in the case of state art, a civic one in the case of objects created by artisans for their fellow citizens, and finally, a sacerdotal one in the case of temple art. The destruction of rulers' emblems, the smashing of amulets, or the cleansing of the temple can all be justified by the same ban on images. But in fact each of these actions has its own rationale and must be described in separate terms.

Approaches to Iconography and Iconology. The study of iconography within the discipline of art history explores the symbolic references of pictorial representations. The first modern scholar to address such issues was Aby Warburg (1866–1929), who specialized in the art of the European Renaissance. Erwin Panofsky (1892–1968) proceeded to develop a comprehensive model for the description of pictorial arts based on three strata of meaning, each entailing particular analytical and terminological tools. According to Panofsky, the first level resides in the world of natural objects and events and is evident to every beholder. The second level, that of conventional meanings, can be detected in the motifs of works of art; it is the domain of iconography in the narrow sense of the word to identify these conventional meanings. Finally, there are underlying principles of *symbolic values,* in the sense defined by Ernst Cassirer, and he described the intuitive process of detecting them as *iconology* (see *Studies in Iconology,* pp. 3–31).

While Panofsky's design for reading images has been widely accepted, it has also been refined over time. Besides the Gestalt psychologists, the influence that Ludwig Wittgenstein (1889–1951) has exerted on the general theory of symbols has been felt in the field of iconology. In his *Philosophical Investigations* (1953), for example, Wittgenstein presents a figure that can be read as either a duck or a rabbit (see figure 3). What we see, he demonstrates, depends on our interpretation. In other words, there is no innocent eye; seeing is an active process, not a passive one. As recent research into pictorial representation emphasizes, the share of the beholder is decisive; the likeness between drawing and object is of minor importance. What might be called a critical rationalism of viewing dictates that when we read a drawing we are looking for stereotypes we have in mind already. This view, promoted most influentially by Ernst H. Gombrich (1977), implies that there is no clear-cut division between natural and conventional meanings as Panofsky maintained; reading images mainly involves the recognition of conventional schemes. Different cultures develop different schemes for identical objects; thus, we believe that we recognize likeness, but in fact we only recognize stereotypes well known in our own culture. Once the viewer's role is seen to be greater than Panofsky allowed, new problems are raised. How can we describe the way other people see their images? How do we distinguish between subjective association and objective perception? Where do we draw the line between true and false inference?

A second criticism of Panofsky's original scheme has been advanced by George Kubler, who reproaches the seeming preference for words over images in *The Shape of Time* (1962). Separating forms and meanings, he argues that artifacts have to be studied as forms of their own; their development must be traced regardless of the meanings connected with them. By including architecture and sculpture along with painting, Kubler has also conclusively extended the field. He reminds us that images and symbols are not free-floating but regularly connected with particular art forms and that, conversely, art forms have an affinal relationship with images and symbols. This phenomenon can be described in terms of iconological genres: images and symbols, like literary concepts, became institutionalized in genres (see Gombrich's introduction to *Symbolic Images,* 1972). The art form (a coin, for example, or a vase) is the place where an artisan combines a functional object with symbolic values. The study of continuity and variety in the designs of these art forms, therefore, yields insights into symbolic values. This analysis of iconological genres seems to offer a much more controlled approach to iconology than the intuition that Panofsky had in mind, since it allows us to discern between true and false implications.

It is evident that no verbal description can enter into details as much as a visual depiction. This means that each text leaves a certain free play to the imagination of the artist, and the manner in which artists have used this freedom is in no way accidental. To cite one example, the first Christian artists working in the Roman catacombs depicted Jesus as the Good Shepherd with a lamb on his shoulders, a motif obviously inspired by *Matthew* 18:12–14 and *Luke* 15:4–7. But there was a

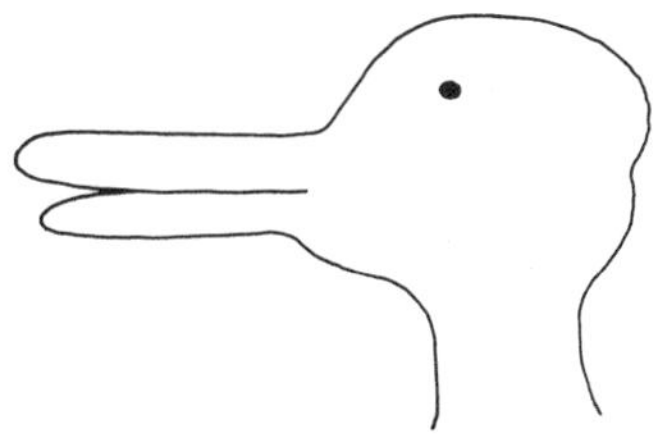

FIGURE 3. *Ambiguous Image.* This image, which can be seen as a duck or a rabbit, demonstrates the influence of interpretation on the act of seeing.

change in meaning: while the parables emphasize the concerns of the shepherd for the individual gone astray, the artists of the third century depicted Jesus with a lamb on his shoulders to emphasize the value of protection in the "age of anxiety." Later on, as social values changed, other motifs were demanded (see Moshe Barasch in *Visible Religion* 2, 1983). This episode neatly illustrates the subject of Panofsky's iconology: an image—in itself an illustration of a story—can be explained as a reflection of the symbolic value of an age, and therefore changes in the representation indicate changes in basic attitudes.

Panofsky himself perceived the risks connected with his approach. There is always the danger, he observed, that iconology, which should relate to iconography as ethnology relates to ethnography, will instead parallel the relationship between astrology and astrography (*Meaning in the Visual Arts*, p. 32). This danger of excessive interpretation is due to the very ambiguity of images and to the difficulty of comparing them. Every iconological statement must therefore be carefully argued and submitted to certain control. In the case of the history of Mediterranean religions and arts, two approaches appear to meet this fundamental demand, one focusing on styles, the other on the institutional function of images.

Changes of style. A comparison of art from early Egyptian and late Roman times immediately reveals certain changes in the means of depiction. The Egyptian mode, which Gerhard Krahmer has described as paratactical or pre-perspective (*Figur und Raum in der ägyptischen und griechisch-archaischen Kunst*, The Hague, 1931), can be seen on the famous Narmer Palette of about 2800 BCE (see figure 2). The details of the image are disconnected. Even the body is not a whole, for every part of it is depicted as an independent unit: head and legs are shown from the sides, eye and trunk from the front. The picture does not presuppose a spectator who perceives the depiction as a whole; rather, it tells a story by means of signs and symbols that are not interrelated. The visual and discursive systems of representation have not yet been separated: the visual does not evoke illusion, while the Egyptian system of writing represents discursive speech with pictorial symbols (see Herman te Velde in *Visible Religion* 4, 1985/1986). Only with classical Greek art does the depiction come to rely on an ideal beholder and deliberately evoke what we call illusion. These differences, of course, have nothing to do with skill or lack of it. More aptly, we should explain them in terms of a different *Kunstwollen*—a word used by Alois Riegl and only inadequately translated by "artistic intention" (Otto J. Brendel, *Prolegomena to the Study of Roman Art*, New Haven, 1979, p. 31). If one accepts the notion of *Kunstwollen*, however, the different artistic intentions remain to be explained.

At this point Panofsky again becomes useful because he looked for the symbolic values underlying artistic products. In this case, the change from paratactical to hypotactical (or perspectival) art can be analyzed as a change in worldview. By the fifth century BCE in Greece, an archaic conception of person and nature lacking the notion of organic coherence had been replaced by one stressing the organic interrelationship of different parts. Later on, in Hellenistic and Roman times, this organic conception of person and nature was replaced by yet another one stressing mechanical order. The individual object (a statue, for instance) then became part of a spatial scheme submitting different constructions and objects to a superior artificial order. The arrangements of space in late Roman art not only evoke military order but also reflect the values of a bureaucratic society that succeeded in crushing the civil structure of the *polis* (Hans Peter L'Orange, *Art Forms*, Princeton, 1965). There exist only a few of such large-scale comparisons of styles, but they are sufficient to prove the value of such an approach, and similar cases could be made for other cultures.

Genres. A second iconological approach describes and compares images as reflections of certain principles of decorum. Free-floating symbols can be assigned various meanings, but this variety will become more limited if symbols are regularly associated with specific art forms. The use of an object clearly influences the beholder's perceptions and associations: function guides the projection that the beholder makes. This phenomenon is also familiar from literature, where the reader's expectations are shaped by literary genre. The same holds true for visual representations: an image of a god on a coin evokes other associations than those summoned by the same image on an amulet: whereas the coin conveys political legitimacy, the amulet is associated with personal feelings of veneration. Thus, only by studying genres are we able to specify meanings, and only by studying institutional contexts can we discern between the true and false implications of images.

There are basically two theoretical models that can be invoked to explain the meaning of pictures: images can be read as elements of a structure, and they can be read as models of social reality. The two main theories of symbols, namely those of Claude Lévi-Strauss and Ernst Cassirer, are also used in the field of iconography. For Lévi-Strauss, the meanings of symbols are based on their own logical interrelationships, while for Cassirer, symbols provide a conceptual means to grasp reality.

[*See also* Images; Symbolism; *and the biography of* Cassirer.]

These approaches can be illustrated with recent scholarship on Greek material. Herbert Hoffmann has studied the paintings on Greek vases as structural codes. The scenes on the vases illustrate myths, but these illustrations can be read as paradigms referring to social values. Death, for example, is sometimes represented as the monster Gorgon whom the hero courageously encounters, and sometimes it is represented as an ugly demon pursuing human beings. Behind the choice of different mythological themes hide two distinct conceptions of death, one heroic and the other plebeian (*Visible Religion* 4, 1985/1986).

An approach more in the line of Cassirer is used in Wiltrud Neumer-Pfau's study of possible links between Hellenistic Aphrodite statues and the social position of women. Such links are not unlikely, because ancient physiognomic literature postulated a connection between body posture and the moral qualities of the person depicted. In fact, the posture of the Aphrodite statues changed in the course of time. In the early Hellenistic period the nude Aphrodite is shown reacting to an unseen beholder who has disturbed her; thus the spectator looking at the beautiful nude woman is freed from feeling any guilt. Later statues portray the nude goddess as less shy and modest: she allows the invisible beholder to admire her. Finally there are statues showing the goddess frankly exposing her nude beauty to the spectator. The moral qualities ascribed to the subject have gradually changed, and this change cannot be isolated from the fundamental impact that ancient Near Eastern culture had on the social and legal position of women in the Greek world. While women were under male tutelage in ancient Greek society, they enjoyed a certain independence in Egypt and the Near East. Thus the change of visual representation reflects the change of social reality. (See Neumer-Pfau, *Studien zur Ikonographie und gesellschaftlichen Funktion hellenistischer Aphrodite-Statuen*, Bonn, 1982).

These two theoretical models are valuable tools for enlarging scientific knowledge about past and foreign cultures. Iconography as a description of how other cultures read their images enables us to reconstruct hitherto undiscovered aspects of ethos and worldview.

[*See also* Aesthetics, *article on* Visual Aesthetics; Archetypes; Architecture; Colors; *and* Human Body, *article on* The Human Body as a Religious Sign.]

BIBLIOGRAPHY

Gail, Adalbert J., ed. *Künstler und Werkstatt in den orientalischen Gesellschaften.* Graz, 1982. A collection of essays dealing with the social status of artists and artisans in different ancient and modern societies of the East; a valuable survey.

Gombrich, Ernst H. "Aims and Limits of Iconology." In *Symbolic Images: Studies in the Arts of the Renaissance.* London, 1972. An introductory essay expounding the idea of genres and the institutional function of images.

Gombrich, Ernst H. *Art and Illusion: A Study in the Psychology of Pictorial Representation.* 5th ed. Oxford, 1977. An excellently written book with many interesting examples; the main thesis is that reading images means recognizing mental stereotypes.

Hermerén, Göran. *Representation and Meaning in the Visual Arts: A Study in the Methodology of Iconography and Iconology.* Stockholm, 1969. A sagacious analysis of the conceptual framework of iconography and iconology; the main thesis is similar to that of Gombrich—seeing is an active process, not a passive one—but the author elaborates this idea more systematically than Gombrich along the lines of philosophical theories of symbols.

Kaemmerling, Ekkehard, ed. *Ikonographie und Ikonologie: Theorien, Entwicklung, Probleme.* Cologne, 1979. A collection of first-class essays, including the basic texts of Panofsky that discuss the program of Warburg and Panofsky.

Keel, Othmar. *Die Welt der altorientalischen Bildsymbolik und das Alte Testament.* 2d ed. Zurich, 1977. A book full of pictorial schemes; it analyzes the imagery of Old Testament texts with regard to these schemes.

Kubler, George. *The Shape of Time.* New Haven, 1962. A contribution to a theory of iconological genres; he criticizes Panofsky for emphasizing meaning derived from texts and argues in favor of art forms that can be studied independently of meanings.

Langer, Susanne K. *Philosophy in a New Key: A Study in the Symbolism of Reason, Rite, and Art.* 3d ed. Cambridge, Mass., 1951. Especially important for iconography is the distinction she makes between discursive and presentational forms.

Panofsky, Erwin. *Studies in Iconology: Humanistic Themes in the Art of the Renaissance* (1939). Reprint, Oxford, 1972. The introductory chapter expounds his basic program.

Panofsky, Erwin. *Meaning in the Visual Arts* (1955). Reprint, Chicago, 1982. Further studies based on his methodological approach.

Riegl, Alois. *Spätrömische Kunstindustrie.* 2d ed. (1927). Reprint, Darmstadt, 1973. The well-known book of Riegl describes the history of art from early Egyptian to late Roman times as stages of ancient worldview; many descriptive terms.

Visible Religion: Annual for Religious Iconography. Edited by H. G. Kippenberg. Leiden, 1982–. An annual reconstructing how visual representations have been read by other cultures. Published to date: vol. 1, *Commemorative Figures* (1982); vol. 2, *Representations of Gods* (1983); vol. 3, *Popular Religions* (1984); vol. 4, *Approaches to Iconology* (1985–1986).

H. G. Kippenberg

Traditional African Iconography

Africa is enormous, and the diversity of peoples and complexities of cultures in sub-Saharan black Africa warn against generalizations, especially when discussing visual images, the significance of which is inextricably linked to local religious and aesthetic sensibilities. Hence, in order to understand the iconography of traditional African religions, one must use a comparative approach. Only by examining the religious iconography of a variety of cultures can one fully understand how visual images represent distinctive ways of experiencing the world for the peoples of sub-Saharan Africa.

Ancestors and Kings: Two Case Studies. On the granary doors of the Dogon people of Mali, rows of paired ancestor figures called Nommo stand watch over the precious millet stored within. Similar figures, at times androgynous, are placed next to the funeral pottery on ancestral shrines of families and on the shrine in the house of the *hogon,* the religious and temporal leader of a clan. Their elongated, ascetic bodies and proud, dispassionate faces image the Dogon's myths of origin, as well as their perception of themselves when life is filled with spiritual vitality, *nyama* (see figure 1).

Oral traditions recall a great drought in the fifteenth century that occasioned the migration of the Dogon in two successive waves from southwestern regions to the area of the Bandiagara cliffs and plateau. There they displaced the Tellem people, whose shrine sculpture they retained and used, and established themselves in small villages, often situated in pairs. In an environment largely devoid of permanent watercourses, the Dogon dug wells to great depths, cultivated subsistence crops of millet, and fashioned houses, shrines, and granaries of a mud-masonry architecture using the geometrical forms, such as cylinders, cones, and cubes, that can also be seen in Dogon wood sculpture.

FIGURE 1. *Dogon Primordial Couple, or Nommo; Mali.* Differentiation and complementarity as means of creation and order dominate Dogon iconography.

The Dogon trace their descent to the "four families" who made the legendary migration, but this history of origins is inextricably intertwined with an elaborate creation mythology, which profoundly informs their social and religious life. The variations in the myth, as in the sculptured forms expressing it, reflect the strong sense of individuality that each Dogon village possesses. It also permits the free play of the sculptor's imagination, whose work then generates new mythological interpretations. [*For further discussion of this creation myth, see* Dogon Religion.]

Dogon myth, ritual, and iconography express a view of life in which, through a process of differentiation and pairing of related beings, called Nommo, an ordered, fruitful world is to be created. But the creative process of complementarity or twinness contains within it the potential of opposition and conflict. The primordial being, or Nommo, who was a blacksmith, stole iron and embers from the sun and descended to earth within a well-stocked granary. It was he who led the descendants of the eighth Nommo in civilizing the earth. Thus creation involves human participation through ritual actions that restore life and maintain an ordered world. Among the materials of the ritual process are village shrines representing a set of twins; shrine sculpture, as well as granary doors with their bas-relief of paired figures, snakes and lizards, zigzag patterns, and female breasts, all symbolically associated with the creation myth; geometric patterns or "signs" on shrine walls, which refer to the basic ontological properties of the world; funerary masquerades and dances through which the deceased is transformed into a venerated ancestor; and secret languages through which the incantations and texts describing the creation of the world and the appearance of death are conveyed from one generation to another. These are the means by which the Dogon can act effectively in their world, strengthen the creative process, and at the very least provide a momentary stay against confusion.

Among the Edo people along the coastal forest of southeast Nigeria, the iconography of the Benin kingdom reflects a culture with a very different spirituality, one shaped by a monarchical tradition. The present dynasty traces its origins to the fourteenth century, beginning with Ọba Eweka I, who was fathered by Oranmiyan, son of Oduduwa (Odua), the Yoruba creator god and first king of Ifẹ (although, according to oral tradition, even before Eweka, the Benin kingdom was said to have been ruled by the Ogosi kings). Thus, for centuries the political and religious life of the Edo people has focused upon the person and powers of the *ọba*, or king.

The magnificently carved ivory tusks projecting from the top of the bronze memorial heads on the royal ancestral shrines (until the British punitive expedition of 1897) symbolized the powers of the king—his political authority and his supernatural gifts. While his authority depended upon statecraft and military conquest, it was by virtue of his descent from *ọba*s who had become gods and his possession of the coral beads, said to have been taken from the kingdom of Olokun, god of the sea, that the *ọba* had *aṣẹ*, "the power to bring to pass," the power over life and death.

Over the centuries the royal guild of blacksmiths created more than 146 memorial bronze heads of deceased *ọba*s, queen mothers, and conquered kings and chiefs; and the royal guild of carvers portrayed on 133 ivory tusks the king, his wives, chiefs, and retainers, as well as leopards and mudfish, emblems of his power over forest and water and of his ability to move across boundaries distinguishing disparate realms. Although the memorial heads and the carved tusks were created in honor of particular *ọba*s, and the rites that are performed before them are always in the name of an individual *ọba*, the bronze heads and carved figures do not portray the individuality of past *ọba*s in either form or expression. It is an aesthetic and a religious principle in Benin culture that the particular is subordinated to the general. The reigning *ọba* depends upon the collective royal ancestors and yields to their commands, and the same is true of the iconography of the ancestral shrines and ritual artifacts of the Edo people generally. Thus, the ancestral shrines and their sculptures are not merely memorials but serve as a means of communication with the living dead.

As in most other African religious traditions, the Edo distinguish between a high god, Osanobua, and a pantheon of deities that includes Olokun, god of the sea and bestower of wealth, Ogun, god of iron, and Ọṣun, god of herbal leaves, whose shrines and rituals articulate the religious life for king and commoner as one of response to the powers upon which individuals are dependent but over which they have relatively little control. However, in a monarchical society, with its divisions of labor among craftsmen, hunters, farmers, warriors, and traders (with the Portugese, Dutch, and British) and its high regard for individual enterprise and prowess, the Cult of the Hand, *ikegobo*, also known as *ikega*, provides a means for celebrating the ability of the individual to accomplish things and, within limits, to achieve new status. Containers for offerings to the Hand, crafted in bronze for kings and in wood for titled persons, bear images of power such as an *ọba* sacrificing leopards, a warrior holding the severed head of an enemy, Portugese soldiers with guns, or the tools and emblems of office for the blacksmith, carver, or trader. All shrines for the Hand bear the image of the clenched fist, showing the ventral side, with the thumb pointing upward and outward. The directness with which the ritual symbolism is expressed is unusual in African religious art but quite consistent with a ritual of self-esteem.

Form and Meaning. Notwithstanding the particularity of traditional African iconography, the general observation may be made that it is, in general, essentially conceptual and evocative. It is not representational and illustrative, and it is not abstract.

Although the principal subject of African art is the human figure, there is rarely any concern to portray individual likeness, even where a sculpture has been commissioned to commemorate a particular person, as in Akan funerary pottery, Yoruba twin figures, or, as noted above, the Benin bronze heads on royal ancestral shrines. And there is rarely any attempt to visualize in material form spiritual powers, although an elaborately constructed masquerade of cloth, wood, and raffia or a sculpted figure on a shrine may "locate" for ritual purposes the ancestral presence, the god, or the spirit. Rather, African iconography is primarily concerned with expressing the essential nature and status of those powers to which one must respond and with providing models of appropriate response to such powers.

Presence of power. Among the Igbomina Yoruba of southwestern Nigeria the costumes of the masquerades for the patrilineal ancestors, *egungun paaka*, combine materials of the forest with those of human manufacture, such as layers of richly colored cloths, bits of mirror, and beaded panels. The carved headdress portion will often meld animal and human features. Packets of magical substances will be secreted within the costume. It is the peculiar state of being of the living dead, who cross boundaries and move between two realms, who dwell in heaven yet profoundly affect the well-being of the living, that is materialized, for masquerades are created to reveal a reality not otherwise observable and to evoke an appropriate response, such as awe and dependency, on the part of the observer. Thus, among the Pende of Zaire the concept of *mahamba* signifies an object, such as a mask, or a ritual given by the ancestors to the living for the common good and through which

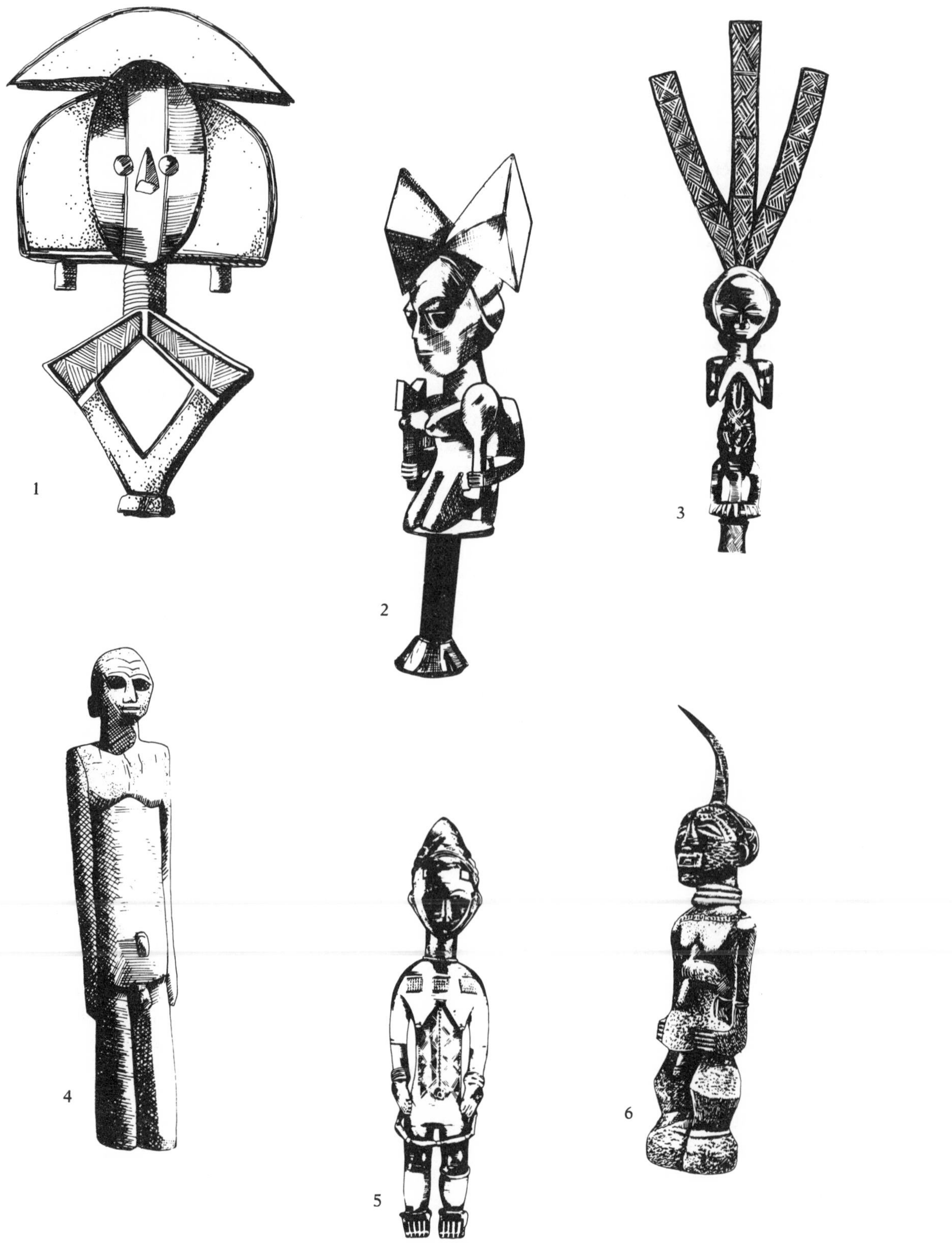

FIGURE 2. *African Figural Sculpture.* (1) Kota reliquary figure, or *mbulu-ngulu* ("image of the dead"); Gabon. (2) Yoruba dance wand, Ṣango cult; Nigeria. (3) Luba bow stand; Zaire. (4) Lobi spirit figure; Burkina Faso. (5) Baule spirit wife; Ivory Coast. (6) Songye power figure; Zaire. Along with dance and music, sculpture plays an important role in the religious life of Africans.

the ancestors periodically manifest themselves and communicate with their descendants.

A similar observation may be made about the reliquary figures of the Kota people of Gabon (see figure 2.1). Referred to as *mbulu-ngulu*, "image of the dead," the two-dimensional figures consist of a large ovoid head above a simple, diamond-shaped wooden base. On a shrine the sculptured form is seated in a bark container holding the bones of several generations of ancestors. The ovoid face and coiffure are created by applying thin sheets or strips of brass and copper to a wooden form in a variety of interrelated geometric patterns. In every case, it is the power of the eyes that holds and penetrates the beholder, expressing the bond between the living and the deceased and the protective power of the ancestors in and for the life of the extended family.

It is not only the reality of the ancestral presence that Africa's religious art presents. Among the Ẹgba, Ẹgbado, and Kẹtu Yoruba it is the power of "our mothers" that is celebrated in the spectacle of the Ẹfẹ/Gẹlẹdẹ festival of masquerade, dance, and song at the time of the spring rains. "Our mothers," *awọn iya wa*, is a collective term for female power, possessed by all women, but most fully by female ancestors and deities and by elderly women in the community who are thus able to sustain or inhibit the procreative process and all other human activities upon which the entire society depends. Balanced on the dancers' heads, for they always appear in pairs, are sculptures depicting the composed face of a beautiful woman above which there may be a dramatic scene of conflict between snakes and a quadruped (see figure 3.1) or scenes depicting domestic activities or social roles. The total sculpted image is perceived as a visual metaphor, often understood as having multiple levels of significance. Likewise, in the deliberate pairing of the delicate face masks and the massive forms and aggressive imagery of zoomorphic helmet masks of the Poro society among the Senufo people of the Ivory Coast (see figures 3.3 and 3.4) one also observes images that refer to the complementary roles of female and male, both human and spiritual, by which life is sustained. In these masquerades, as in Kuba helmet masks worn by the king, African artists are not concerned with the representational illusion entailed in copying nature. Rather, they concentrate on that which they know and believe about their subjects, and they seek to construct images to which the distinctive spirituality of a people can react.

This is also true of emblems of office, such as the beautifully carved bow stands owned by Luba chiefs in southeastern Zaire (see figure 2.3). The bow stands are considered sacred and are usually kept with ancestral relics, where only the chief and special caretakers are permitted to see them. The work images Luba political and spiritual power. It is through the maternal line that chiefs inherit their office. In the sculpted female figure at the top, woman as genetrix is conveyed in the lifting of the maternal breasts, the elaborately scarified abdomen, and the exposed genitals. The closed eyes of the serene face convey the inner, cerebral power that contrasts with the reproductive and nurturing power of her body. And the soaring three-pronged coiffure, express-

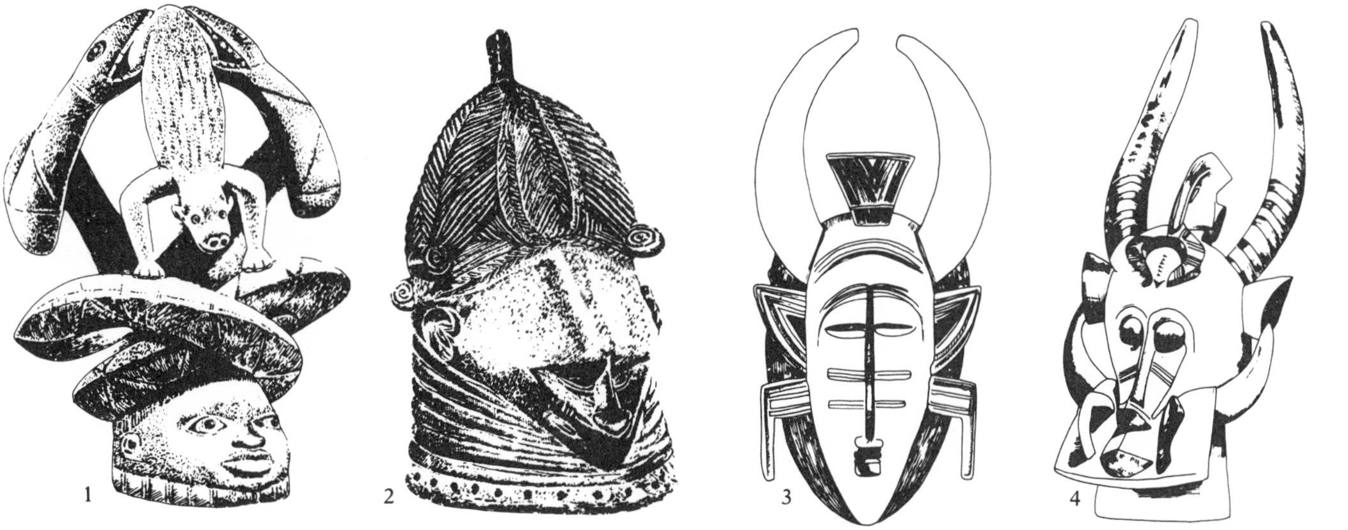

FIGURE 3. *Headdress and Masks.* (1) Yoruba headdress used in the Ẹfẹ/Gẹlẹdẹ festival; Nigeria. (2) Mende helmet mask of the female spirit Nowo; Sierra Leone. (3, 4) Senufo masks; Ivory Coast. Masks are used throughout Africa to embody the divine.

ing her status and beauty, repeats as an inverted pattern the sculptural treatment of the breasts and the legs, each of which frames a central vertical element. On ritual occasions, the chief's bow and arrows, signs of his political authority, would rest in her elaborate coiffure at the top of the staff. Below her, the metal tip of the staff is thrust into the earth, the realm of the ancestors. It is maternal power that provides the link with the ancestral power on which a Luba chief's power depends.

Models of response. Ritual sculpture provides not only images of the powers on which the living depend but models for appropriate response to gods and spirits. The naked male or female, arms at their sides or touching their abdomens, on Lobi shrines in Burkina Faso (see figure 2.4) as well as the figure of a kneeling woman with a thunder ax balanced upon her head and holding a dance wand for the Yoruba god Ṣango (see figure 2.2) are images of man and woman as devotees, as inspirited and powerful. They are images through which persons see their spirituality and by which their spirituality is deepened.

The distinction between imaging the nature and status of spiritual powers and imaging the religious self in the posture of devotion and power cannot in most instances be clearly drawn: much African iconography combines the two processes, less so perhaps where there are ancestral associations and more often where the reference is to gods and spirits. On the shrines of the Baule people of the Ivory Coast, men and women will place figures representing the spouse that they had in the other world before they were born (see figure 2.5). The figure is thus the locus for one's spirit spouse and the place where one attends to the claims of that other. But at the same time the sculptures—many of them carved with great skill—present idealized images of male and female, often in the maturity of life, the hair or beard carefully groomed, the body decorated with scarification patterns and adorned with beads, the face composed, the stance well balanced. Likewise among the Igbo people of southeastern Nigeria the tutelary gods of a town are imaged in wooden figures based upon an idealized human model, for the gods not only have life-giving powers but are also the guardians of morality. The sculptures, for they are often in groups, are looked upon as the "children" of the deity honored. Hence, in their presence the devotee is confronted with conceptions of the self that constrain him or her in thought and action to a deepened awareness of the self that that person is and is not.

Perhaps the most extraordinary images of self and of personal power are carvings that incorporate magical substances (in or on images) to the extent that they alter the human form of the image (see figure 2.6). They are found for the most part among the Songye and Kongo peoples of the lower Kongo (Zaire) Basin. Some figures have an antelope horn filled with "medicines" projecting from the head, others have nails and small knives pounded into the body or a magic-holding resin box imbedded in the belly. They are visualizations in the extreme of ritual action as manipulative power. Using such carvings in conjunction with words of invocation, the priest or owner of the image engages with the evil in the world, either to project or deflect its aggressive power.

Ritual Activity. It is evident from what has been said that the iconography of African peoples must be understood in the context of ritual activity where the world as lived and the world as imaged become fused together and transformed into one reality. There are essentially two types of rituals—those in which a person or group undergoes a change in status, usually referred to as rites of passage, and rituals of world maintenance through which a person or group affirms and seeks to secure in the words and actions of sacrifice a worldview.

Rites of passage. Among many African peoples the masquerade is associated with rites of passage, as, for example, the seasonal rituals of sowing, tilling, and harvesting among the Bwa and Bamana, the funeral rites of the Dogon and the Yoruba, and the rituals of initiation of youth into the societies of the Dan and Mende peoples of West Africa.

Among the Mende people of Sierra Leone, Nowo, a female spirit, appears in dance and masquerade to girls being initiated into the Sande (also known as Bundu) ceremonial society (see figure 3.2). As far as is known, it is the only female mask danced by a woman in Africa. While associated with the Sande society and thought of as the Sande spirit, Nowo appears in other ritual contexts. Her image is carved on the finial of the rhythm pounders used in the boys' initiation rites, on the staff carried by the leader of the men's Poro society, on the carved mace of the Mende king, as well as on divination implements, women's ritual spoon handles, and on weaving-loom pulleys. But it is only to the female initiates into Sande that Nowo appears in the fullness of the masquerade and the movements of the dance.

In the rituals, Nowo is a spiritual presence and images the beauty and power, the nobility, of woman. Thick, dyed-black fiber strands, suspended from a wooden helmet mask, cover the dancer's body. The carved headdress depicts a composed face with faintly opened eyes that see but may not be seen. The head is crowned with an elaborate coiffure into which are woven cowrie shells and seed pods, symbols of wealth and fertility. Black is said to be woman's color, the color of civilized life. The glistening black surface suggests the lustrous, well-oiled skin with which the initiates will reenter the world. Nowo thus provides an image of the physical beauty and the spiritual power of woman to those about to take their place as adults in Mende society.

World maintenance rituals. The role of iconography in Africa's rituals of world maintenance is no less important than in rites of passage. Among the Yoruba, to cite only one example, paired bronze castings of male and female figures joined at the top by a chain, *ẹdan*, are presented to an initiate into the higher ranks of the Ọṣugbo secret society, who worship Onile, "the owner of the house" (see figure 4). The house is the cult house, which is a microcosm of the universe. The secret, visualized in the linking of male and female, appears to refer to a vision of life in terms of its completion and transcendence of time.

The titled members of the Ọṣugbo society are the elders of the community. They are beyond the time of procreative concerns. For them sexual differentiation is no longer as important as it once was. Furthermore, kinship distinctions are secondary to the world of the cult house, since identification of person by patrilineage is replaced by an allegiance to the unity of all life in Onile. Thus, the Ọṣugbo participate in the settling of conflicts that divide the body politic. The sacred emblems of the society, the *ẹdan*, are placed on those spots where the relationships among men have been broken and blood spilled. Expressing the unity of male and female, they possess the power of reconciling and adjudicating differences and atoning through sacrifice for the violation of the "house."

The seated male and female figures present to the viewer the signs of their power and authority, *aṣẹ*. The female holds a pair of *ẹdan*, as she would twin children. The male figure, with clenched fists, makes the sign of greeting to Onile. Four chains with tiny bells are suspended from the sides of each figure's head. The number four, as well as multiples of four, are important in Ifa divination; Ọrunmila (also called Ifa), the divination god, knows the secret of creation and the sacrifices that will make one's way propitious. Above the spare, ascetic bodies, the heads of the paired figures radiate with their *aṣẹ*. Twelve chains are suspended from the plate below each figure. Twelve is a multiple of three and four, also numbers associated with Ọṣugbo and Ifa ritual symbolism. In their combination, there is completion and wholeness born of the secret knowledge of Ọṣugbo and Ifa, a secret readily revealed to the informed eye.

FIGURE 4. *Yoruba Ẹdan, Paired Bronze Castings of Male and Female Figures Coupled by a Chain; Nigeria.* Elder members of the Ọṣugbo society perceive in this sculpture the message of time's completion and transcendence.

BIBLIOGRAPHY

Biebuyck, Daniel. *The Arts of Zaire*, vol. 1, *Southwestern Zaire*. Berkeley, 1985.

Brain, Robert. *Art and Society in Africa*. New York, 1980.

Dark, Philip J. C. *An Introduction to Benin Art and Technology*. Oxford, 1973.

Drewal, Henry John, and Margaret T. Drewal. *Gèlèdé: Art and Female Power among the Yoruba*. Bloomington, Ind., 1983.

Fagg, William B., and John Pemberton III. *Yoruba Sculpture of West Africa*. Edited by Bryce Holcombe. New York, 1982.

Fernandez, James. *Bwiti: An Ethnography of the Religious Imagination in Africa*. Princeton, 1982.

Fischer, Eberhard, and Hans Himmelheber. *Die Kunst der Dan*. Zurich, 1976.

Glaze, Anita J. *Art and Death in a Senufo Village*. Bloomington, Ind., 1981.

Horton, Robin. *Kalabari Sculpture*. Lagos, 1965.

Imperato, Pascal Jaems. *Dogon Cliff Dwellers: The Art of Mali's Mountain People*. New York, 1978.

Lamp, Frederick. *African Art of the West Atlantic Coast: Transition in Form and Content*. New York, 1979.

Laude, Jean. *Les arts de l'Afrique noire*. Paris, 1966. Translated by Jean Decock as *The Arts of Black Africa* (Berkeley, 1971).

Maquet, Jacques. *Civilizations of Black Africa*. Revised and translated by Joan Rayfield. New York, 1972.

McCall, Daniel F., and Edna G. Bay, eds. *African Images: Essays in African Iconology*. New York, 1975.

Meyer, Piet. *Kunst und Religion der Lobi*. Zurich, 1981.

Rattray, R. S. *Religion and Art in Ashanti*. Oxford, 1927.

Siroto, Leon. *African Spirit Images and Identities*. New York, 1976.

Thompson, Robert Farris. *African Art in Motion.* Los Angeles, 1974.
Thompson, Robert Farris. *The Four Movements of the Sun: Kongo Art in Two Worlds.* Washington, D.C., 1981.
Vogel, Susan M., ed. *For Spirits and Kings: African Art from the Paul and Ruth Tishman Collection.* New York, 1981.
Vogel, Susan M. *African Aesthetics: The Carlo Monzino Collection.* New York, 1986.

JOHN PEMBERTON III

Australian Aboriginal Iconography

Art has a central place in Australian Aboriginal religion. The substance of Aboriginal ceremonies and rituals consists of enactments of events from the Dreaming, or ancestral past, events that are conserved in the form of the songs, dances, designs, and sacred objects that belong to a particular clan or totemic cult group. Such forms are referred to collectively by a word that can be translated as "sacred law," and it is as "sacred law" that art mediates between the ancestral past and the world of living human beings. Designs that were created in the Dreaming as part of the process of world creation are handed down from generation to generation as a means of maintaining the continuity of existence with the ancestral past. [*See* Dreaming, The.]

Designs can be referred to then as "Dreaming," and they are manifestations of the ancestral past in a number of senses. Each originated as a motif painted on an ancestral being's body, as an impression left in the ground by that being, or as a form associated in some other way with ancestral creativity. In many regions myths relate how ancestral beings gave birth to or created out of their bodies the sacred objects associated with particular social groups and land areas. The meaning of the designs on the objects often refers to the acts of ancestral creativity that gave rise to the shape of the landscape; in this respect, the designs can be said to encode Dreaming events. And finally, the designs can be a source of ancestral power. Paintings on the bodies of initiates are thought to bring the individuals closer to the spiritual domain; sacred objects rubbed against the bodies can have similar effect. In eastern Arnhem Land, upon a person's death, designs painted on his or her chest or on the coffin or bone disposal receptacle help to transfer the soul back to the ancestral world to be reincorporated within the reservoirs of spiritual power associated with a particular place. Art is linked in with the concept of the cycling of spiritual power down the generations from the ancestral past to the present that characterizes Aboriginal religious thought. The same design may later be painted on an initiate's chest, signifying what Nancy Munn refers to in *Walbiri Iconography* (1973) as the intergenerational transfer of ancestral power, which conceptually integrates the Dreaming with present-day experience.

Aboriginal art varies widely across the continent. Any similarities that exist tend to reside in the properties of the representational systems that are employed—the kinds of meanings that are encoded in the designs and the way in which they are encoded—rather than in the use of particular motifs. One notable exception appears to be what Munn refers to as the circle-line or site-path motif (0 = 0 = 0), which forms a component of designs throughout Australia. In such designs, the circles usually refer to places where some significant event occurred on the journey of a Dreaming ancestral being, and the lines refer to the pathways that connect the places.

Likewise, designs in Aboriginal art exist independent of particular media. The same design in Arnhem Land may occur as a body painting, a sand sculpture, an emblem on a hollow log coffin, or an engraving on a sacred object *(rangga)*. In central Australia the same design may be incised on a stone disc *(tjurunga)*, painted on the body of a dancer in blood and down, or made into a sand sculpture. Further, it is the design that gives the object its particular ancestral connection: the designs are extensions of ancestral beings and are sometimes referred to as their "shadows." Thus, they can be used in different contexts for different purposes. The same basic design may be used as a sand sculpture in a curing ceremony, painted on an initiate's body to associate him with particular ancestral forces or to mark his membership in a social group, or painted on a coffin to guide the dead person's soul back to the clan lands to be reincorporated within the ancestral domain.

Systems of Representation. Meaning in Aboriginal art is encoded in two distinct systems of representation, one iconic and figurative, the other aniconic and geometric. The iconography of Aboriginal religious art arises out of the interplay between these two complementary systems. This distinction extends outside the area of the visual arts to dance and ceremonial action, which involve some components and actions that are essentially mimetic and represent the behavior and characteristics of natural species as well as other components that are abstract and have a conventional and nonrepresentational meaning. The balance between the figurative and the geometric varies from one region to another. The art of central Australia, of groups such as the Walbiri, the Aranda, the Pintubi, and the Pitjantjatjara, is characterized by geometric motifs, whereas western Arnhem Land in contrast is associated with a highly developed figurative tradition. Nonetheless, there is a figurative component in central Australian art, and the *marayin* designs, clan-owned body painting designs used in certain western Arnhem Land initiation ceremonies, are largely geometric.

The forms of Aboriginal art are linked to its various functions in a systematic way. The figurative art presents images of the Dreaming that at one level can be readily interpreted as representations of totemic species and the forms of ancestral beings. The X-ray art of western Arnhem Land, for example, is a figurative tradition that creates images of totemic ancestors associated with particular places, thus linking them directly to the natural world. The figures are in part accurate representations of kangaroos, fish, snakes, and so on. But they are more than that. The X-ray component, representing the heart, lungs, and other internal organs of the animal, adds an element of mystery to the figures and differentiates the representations from those of ordinary animals. Moreover, the art includes representations that combine features of a number of different animals in a single figure. For example, the figure of the Rainbow Snake, an important mythical being throughout Arnhem Land, may combine features of a snake, a kangaroo, a buffalo, an emu, and a crocodile. Such figures in X-ray art, together with songs and dances associated with them, are part of a system of symbolism that decomposes the natural world into its elements, breaks the boundaries between different species of animals, and alludes to the underlying transforming power of the Dreaming. The western Arnhem Land X-ray figures are public representations of the ancestral world and, painted on cave walls, are projections of the ancestral past into the present in a fairly literal form. Their presence on rock surfaces acts as a sign of the ancestral transformations that created the form of the landscape and a reminder of the creative forces inherent in the land.

Much of the ceremonial art and most of the secret art of Australia is, however, geometric in form. The geometric art encodes meaning in a more elusive way, well suited to a system of esoteric knowledge in which some of the meanings of art are restricted to the initiated. Without some assistance its meaning will remain a mystery: in order to be understood it has to be interpreted and its meanings have to be revealed. Geometric art gives priority to no single interpretation, and as a person grows older he or she learns increasingly more about the meaning of particular designs. Thus, geometric art is potentially multivalent, and different meanings and interpretations can be condensed into the same symbol or design.

This property of geometric art enables it to encode the relationship between different phenomena or orders of reality. On one level, a circle in a design may represent a water hole, and the line joining it may represent a creek flowing into the water hole. On another level, the circle may be said to represent a hole dug in the ground and the line, a digging stick. On yet another level, the circle may be interpreted as the vagina of a female ancestral being and the line, the penis of a male ancestor. All three interpretations are related, for digging in the sand is an analogue for sexual intercourse, and the water hole was created through sexual intercourse between two ancestral beings in the Dreaming. The design of which the circle is a part may belong to a particular clan and be identified as such. The design as a whole thus represents ancestral beings creating features of the landscape in territory associated with a particular social group. It is this set of associations that characterizes the iconography of Aboriginal art: the designs mediate between the present and the ancestral past by encoding the relationship between ancestral being, people, and place.

The geometric art represents the ancestral world both semiotically and aesthetically, by expressing ancestral power in an artistic form. The Dreaming beings are often complex concepts, and their encoding in abstract representations provides one of the ways by which people develop shared understandings that help to order their collective experience of the ancestral past. For example, in the case of the Yiridja moiety of northeastern Arnhem Land, the Wild Honey ancestor consists of the whole set of things associated with the collection of wild honey: the hive, the bees, the honey; pollen and grubs; the paperbark tree where the hives are found and the swamps where the trees grow; the hunter, his baskets, and the smoke made by the fires he lights. All things associated with wild honey are attributes of the Wild Honey ancestor. In painting, the Wild Honey ancestor is represented by a complex diamond pattern representing the cells of the hive (see figure 1). The diamonds are crosshatched in different colors to signify different components of the hive: grubs, honey, pollen, and bees. The bars across some of the segments represent sticks in the structure of the hive, and the dots within the circles represent bees at its entrance. On another level, elements of the design signify smoke, flames, and ash from the hunter's fire, and on still another level, the diamond pattern represents the rippling of floodwater as it passes beneath the paperbark trees. The Wild Honey ancestor is all of those things and more.

Systems of Interpretation. As people go through life they learn the meanings of designs such as the Wild Honey pattern; they associate it with places created by the ancestral being and with ceremonies that celebrate that being's creative power. For the individual the design is no longer an abstract sign but a manifestation of

FIGURE 1. *Wild Honey Pattern.* Taken from a painting by Dula Ngurruwuthun of the Muwyuku clan of northeastern Arnhem Land, the design represents aspects of the story of the Wild Honey ancestor in the paperbark swamps. The diamond pattern represents the cells of the hive (and fresh flowing water). The elongated figure in the center represents a bark tree; the figures on either side represent entrances to hives.

the ancestral being concerned. Aesthetic aspects of the design reinforce this understanding. In northeastern Arnhem Land, body paintings convey a sense of light and movement through the layering of finely cross-hatched lines across the skin surface. Similar effects are created in central Australian painting through the use of white down and the glistening effect of blood, fat, and red ocher. These attributes of paintings are interpreted by Aboriginal people as attributes of the ancestral being: the light from the ancestral being shines from the painting as symbol or evidence of the power of the design.

Throughout much of Australia, rights to designs and other components of "sacred law" are vested in social groups that exercise some control over their use and have the responsibility to ensure that they continue to be passed down through the generations. Such rights are of considerable importance, as "sacred law" provides the charter for ownership and control of land. Hence designs not only represent sources of ancestral power but are politically significant in demonstrating rights over land and providing a focal point for group solidarity and identity. This dimension is reflected in the iconography insofar as designs often vary on the basis of group ownership, each group holding rights to a unique set of designs.

There is enormous regional variation in Australian Aboriginal art, and the specific symbolism of the designs can only be understood in their regional context. But everywhere the underlying principles of the art have much in common. Moreover, belief in the spiritual power and mediating functions of the designs is to an extent independent of knowledge of their meaning. For both these reasons, designs and other components of ritual can be passed on to other groups from neighboring or even from quite distant places and become part of those groups' ancestral inheritance. In this respect religious iconography is integral to the process of religious change, enabling religious ideas to be exchanged with other groups and hence to be diffused across the continent. Changes can also occur internally through the dreaming of new designs, thus allowing the iconographic system to adjust to sociopolitical reality, to the creation of new groups and the demise of existing ones. However, from the Aboriginal viewpoint such changes are always revelatory: they ultimately have a Dreaming reference and will always be credited to the past. The designs not only encode meanings that help endow everyday events and features of the landscape with cosmic significance but are themselves extensions of those Dreaming ancestors into the present.

[*See also* Tjurungas *and* Wandjina.]

BIBLIOGRAPHY

Berndt, Ronald M., ed. *Australian Aboriginal Art.* New York, 1964. A volume with essays by Ted Strehlow, Charles Mountford, and Adolphus Peter Elkin that provides a broad coverage of Aboriginal art and its religious significance.

Berndt, Ronald M., Catherine H. Berndt, and John E. Stanton. *Australian Aboriginal Art: A Visual Perspective.* Sydney, 1982. A comprehensive general survey of traditional, contemporary, and innovative Aboriginal art, with some detailed descriptions and analysis.

Cooper, Carol, et al. *Aboriginal Australia.* Sydney, 1981. The best general account of Aboriginal art, it contains chapters by Carol Cooper, Howard Morphy, Nicolas Peterson, and John Mulvaney as well as a catalog of 329 illustrated items.

Elkin, A. P., Ronald M. Berndt, and Catherine H. Berndt. *Art in Arnhem Land.* Melbourne, 1950. The pioneering work on Australian Aboriginal art, placing the art of Arnhem Land in its social and mythological context.

Groger-Wurm, Helen M. *Australian Aboriginal Bark Paintings and Their Mythological Interpretation.* Canberra, 1973. The best published account of northeastern Arnhem bark paintings, with detailed interpretations of their meanings.

Morphy, Howard. *Journey to the Crocodile's Nest.* Canberra, 1984. An account of the iconography of a mortuary ceremony in Arnhem Land, detailing the structure of the ceremony and the meaning of the dances and ritual action and their relation to the themes of the ritual.

Mountford, Charles Pearcy. *Art, Myth and Symbolism.* Records of the American-Australian Scientific Expedition to Arnhem Land. Melbourne, 1956. A comprehensive collection of paintings from western and eastern Arnhem Land and Groote Eylandt. The collection is extensively documented with accounts of Aboriginal myths. The documentation is somewhat general and not always accurate, but its coverage is excellent.

Munn, Nancy D. *Walbiri Iconography.* Ithaca, N.Y., 1973. A detailed account of the representational systems of the Walbiri of central Australia and the religious symbolism of the designs. This is the classic work on the geometric art of central Australia.

Ucko, Peter J., ed. *Form in Indigenous Art.* Canberra, 1977. A collection of essays presenting by far the most comprehensive review of Aboriginal art available, covering most parts of the continent. Chapters deal with both the formal properties of Aboriginal art systems and the function of art in ritual contexts.

HOWARD MORPHY

Native American Iconography

Iconography is a living force in North American Indian religious life, past and present. Rooted in mythical imagery, it informs the content of individual dreams and nourishes the themes of contemporary Indian art. A study of the iconography of a people provides a unique opportunity to gain insight into what Werner Müller calls the "pictorial world of the soul" (*Die Religionen der Waldlandindianer Nordamerikas,* Berlin, 1956, p. 57).

The following exposition of the major themes of religious iconography in North America is restricted to the evidence of the late-nineteenth and twentieth century of ethnographic research. As a result, the beautiful pottery and stone remains of the prehistoric peoples of the Southwest and Southeast are not represented here, nor are the remains of the Mound Builder cultures of the river regions.

The iconographical themes follow the general lines of myth and religious beliefs. As such, they can be cataloged in the following manner: the cosmos, supreme beings, tricksters/culture heroes, guardian beings, other mythic beings, astronomical beings, weather beings, animal beings, vegetation beings, human beings, geological beings, and abstract symbols. But it is not always the case that the verbal images of the myths are equivalent to iconographical images: one notorious example of divergence is the Ojibwa trickster, Rabbit, who, when pictured, is actually human in form.

Concerning the wide variety of media used, the following general distribution can be observed: in the Far North—ivory, bone, and stone; the Northeast and Southeast Woodlands—wood, bark, skin, quillwork, and beadwork; the Plains—skin, beadwork, pipestone, quillwork, and painting of bodies and horses; the Northwest Coast—cedar, ivory, argillite, blankets, and copper; California—baskets and some stone; the Southwest—sand painting, wood, stone, baskets, pottery, jewelry, and dolls.

The Cosmos. Cosmologies vary from tribe to tribe in both content and imagery. But whereas the mythical image of the universe (its cosmography) may be highly detailed, the iconographical rendering is necessarily restricted. The cosmos is most often graphically limited to those elements that characterize its basic nature and structure, including its nonvisual aspects.

The most widespread symbol of the whole cosmos is the ceremonial lodge, house, or tent. The fundamental idea of the ceremonial lodge, such as the Delaware *xingwikáon* ("big house"), is that all of its parts symbolize, and in ritual contexts actually are, the cosmos. Usually the realms of this cosmos are interconnected with a central post, which is conceived of as extending itself like a world tree up to the heavens. Renewing such a house constitutes the actual renewal of the cosmos.

Similar ideas are found among the Plains Indians, for whom the sacred camp circle constitutes an image of the world, and the central pole of the Sun Dance tipi, the whole cosmos. In fact the Crow call this tent the "imitation" or "miniature" lodge, a replica of the Sun's lodge.

Representations of the cosmos can refer to the more subtle manifestations of the world, as in the sand paintings of the Luiseño of California, but they can also approach the reality of topographical maps, as in the sand paintings of the neighboring Diegueño. In a completely different approach to the visualization of the cosmos, the well-known Navajo sand painting of Father Sky and Mother Earth illustrates the anthropomorphic representation of the cosmos.

Concerning nonvisual aspects of the cosmos, it is not uncommon that ethical ideals or holistic images of proper human life, which are extensions of the theological bases of many cosmologies, are also visualized iconographically. The most common image of this type is that of the right, or the beautiful, path. The Delaware big house has a circular path on its floor, which the visionary singers and other participants in the big house ceremony walk and dance upon. This path is called the

Good White Path, the symbol of the human life. It corresponds to the Milky Way, which is the path of the souls of the dead. The Ojibwa bark charts of the Midewiwin ceremony consist of illustrations of the degrees of initiation into the Mide secret society. All of the degrees are represented as connected by the path of the initiate's life, starting in the image of the primordial world and ending upon the island of direct communication with the supreme being. This path is pictured with many detours and dramatic occurrences.

Supreme Beings. Among the myriad images found in North American Indian iconography are certain divine beings whose representations cut across taxonomic groups; these include supreme beings, tricksters/culture heroes, guardian beings, and other mythical beings. Since the majestic, all-encompassing supreme being is difficult to visualize, its morphology is relatively simple. When not visualized as some object or animal intimately associated with the supreme being, its form tends to be anthropomorphic. For example, the Ojibwa song charts visualize the supreme being, Kitsi Manitu, with a pictograph of a human head, belonging to an initiate in the Mide secret society (see figure 1).

On the other hand, the all-pervasiveness of the supreme being among the Plains Indians can result in the use of symbols of lesser deities to represent it. Thus Wakantanka, of the Oglala Lakota, has various manifestations such as the Sun, the Moon, Buffalo, and so on, all of which are pictured on hides or, as with Buffalo, represented by a buffalo skull.

Tricksters/Culture Heroes. The most widespread iconographic trickster type is theriomorphic: Raven, Coyote, or Rabbit. The most well-known image is that of Raven among the Northwest Coast tribes, a character who encompasses all of the classical features of the trickster (see figure 2). He is pictured in raven-form on

FIGURE 2. *Kwakiutl House-Front Painting.* This image of Raven, the Kwakiutl trickster, appeared on both the right and, in reverse, the left of a house doorway.

virtually every object throughout the Northwest, usually in the context of a mythical event that somehow affected the ancestor of the house in which the object is found, be it house pole, settee, or some other form. As part of shamanic paraphernalia, his image imparts one of his main characteristics: that of transformation. Even though the trickster is an animal, in mythical thought he can change to human form, and this process is often reflected iconographically, as with the Navajo Coyote and the Delaware and Ojibwa Rabbit.

The culture hero is a divine or semidivine mythic figure who, through a series of heroic deeds—especially the theft of such an important item as fire or light—starts humanity upon its cultural road. When he is not the theriomorphic trickster, he is often simply visualized as a human being. [*See also* Tricksters, *article on* North American Tricksters.]

Guardian Beings. Guardian beings associate themselves most often on a personal level with single individuals, and they function as guardians who bring blessings to their human partners. In the Plains and Northern Woodlands cultures, to seek and receive a personal vision of just such a guardian is necessary in order to secure an individual's station in life. These guardians can appear in just about any form taken from the natural or the mythological world. Among the Oglala it may be necessary to paint a version of one's vision on the tipi in order to secure its validity, although generally images of the guardian are painted on shields.

In the cultures of the Far North and Arctic areas, the shaman and his guardians are a constant iconographic theme. His guardians are portrayed in several general ways: as diminutive human beings clustered near the shaman or as human faces clustered together, as a hu-

FIGURE 1. *Ojibwa Pictograph.* One of a series of ten pictographs appearing on the birchbark chart of a Mide priest, this pictograph provides mnemonic instructions for the first song of the day of the Mide initiation ceremonies. It simultaneously depicts both the singer and Kitsi Manitu, the supreme being. Voice lines denote intensity of accentuation and indicate that Kitsi Manitu is pleased.

man visage under an animal visage such as seen in Alaskan masks, as an animal form reduced in size and resting on the head or shoulders of the shaman, as birdlike shamans or shamans in transformation, as flying spirits being ridden by shamans, as an animal or human being with skeletal markings, or as flying bears or other usually flightless beasts (see figure 3). These images are portrayed in contemporary drawings, ivory sculpture, masks, stone sculpture, bone sculpture, drumsticks, shaman staff, and so on. Throughout North America the shaman also uses organic parts of his guardians in his ritual paraphernalia, or else he can use the entire skin of his guardian animal to transform himself.

Guardians appear in nonvisionary and nonshamanistic cultures as well. The Pueblo deities of the six world regions are considered to be guardians of humanity. Another type of guardian is Rainbow Serpent, pictured on almost all Navajo sand paintings. This figure encircles the entire painting but remains open toward the east. Its function is to keep the evil spirits out of the reinstated cosmic region.

Other Mythical Beings. Among the mythological figures who are pictured iconographically, one important group is that of monsters. The most common monster motif is an image of the primordial horned, flying serpent, the cause of floods and earthquakes. He is known all over the Americas and is generally pictured in exactly the form described. Another monster known all over North America is Thunderbird, usually pictured on shields, shirts, and beadwork as an eaglelike creature.

There is also a whole group of evil beings who, in one form or another, are believed to exercise a malignant and dangerous influence on humanity. Such creatures are usually theriomorphic but not necessarily so.

FIGURE 3. *Inuit Stonecut Stencil Design.* In this image from Baker Lake, an Inuit shaman takes flight, accompanied by his guardian spirits.

FIGURE 4. *Drawing of a Hopi Kachina Dancer.* As depicted in this Hopi artist's drawing, the impersonator of the sun god Taawa wears a rawhide mask decorated with radiating eagle-wing feathers.

Astronomical Beings. The sun, the moon, and the stars are pictured as beings throughout North America. The sun is portrayed most intensely where it is strongest, in southeastern and southwestern North America. The Hopi portray the Sun, Taawa, anthropomorphically but, in keeping with Hopi iconography, he wears a mask that consists of a circular disc fringed with radiating feathers and horsehair (see figure 4). This radial representation of the sun is the most common image known. The Ojibwa, on the other hand, have a completely different image, which is horned, winged, and legged.

The moon is usually represented in its quarter phase, although images of the full moon are sometimes found. The stars most often pictured are the Morning Star (Venus), the Pleiades, Orion, Altair, the constellation Ursa Major (which is invariably pictured as a heavenly bear), and the Milky Way. Stars are shown with four, five, and six points and are often associated with human figures.

Meteorological Beings. This group consists of Thunder, Wind, Rain, and Lightning. Thunder is often pictured as the Thunderbird, but other birds can also be used. Wind, on the other hand, is generally associated with the cardinal regions and therefore not visualized directly. Cultures with anthropocentric morphology, however, such as the Navajo and the Ojibwa, picture even this being in human shape.

Rain is usually illustrated as lines falling from cloud

symbols or as a being from which rain is falling. Lightning is always shown as zigzag lines regardless of the tribe in question. The lines usually end in arrowheads, for there is a conceptual link between lightning and arrows. Lightning and thunder are usually considered to be the weapons of the widely known Warrior Twins.

Animal Beings. There are a number of animals which are known and visualized throughout North America, such as the bear, the deer, and the buffalo. However, other animals peculiar to a particular region are the more common iconographical subjects, such as the whales and seals of the northern coasts, or the lizards and snakes of the desert regions. The general rule is that the animal is depicted in its natural form.

Representations of animals may signify the spirit or master of their species or the form of some deity, guardian being, or primordial creature, or they may indicate the totem animal. All animal images used in ritual contexts have religious significance. But the most common use of animal images occurs in heraldry, which casts some doubt on the exclusively religious significance of its use and meaning.

The Northwest Coast Indians are the most conspicuous users of totem symbols. These symbols are represented in literally every conceivable medium: poles, house fronts, hats, aprons, spoons, bowls, settees, boat prows, spearheads, fishhooks, dagger handles, facial painting, masks, speaker staffs, paddles, drums, rattles, floats, bracelets, leggings, pipes, and gambling sticks. The question of religious significance may be resolved by the fact that the totem animal is considered either a direct ancestor of the clan or somehow associated with an ancient human ancestor. Thus the symbol at least, if not its use, has religious meaning.

Vegetation Beings. Corn is the plant most commonly visualized. The representation can simply refer to the plant itself, but frequently a maize deity is being invoked. The latter is the case throughout the Southwest, whether among the Pueblo or the Athapascan peoples. The maize deity is usually clearly anthropomorphized. Hallucinogenic plants such as peyote, jimsonweed, or the strong wild tobaccos are more or less realistically pictured; such images refer to the deities of these potent plants. Others beings who somehow influence plant growth are also visualized iconographically; these include the Yuki impersonations of the dead, who have a decided influence on the abundance of acorns, or the Hopi impersonations of cultic heros and heroines whose rituals influence crop growth.

Human Beings. This category concerns not only human ancestors but also a miscellaneous collection of beings that have human form. The first type are effigies of once-living human beings. These are most commonly figured on Northwest Coast mortuary poles, but they are also found elsewhere: the Californian Maidu, Yokuts, Luiseño, and Tubatulabal, for example, all burn effigies of prominent people two years after their deaths.

Human images can also be material expressions of the ineffable. During the Sun Dance the Shoshoni and the Crow each bring out a stone image in diminutive human shape, which is then attached to a staff or the center pole of the tent. It is said to represent the spirit of the Sun Dance. Human images, such as dolls, can symbolize or are actually considered to be small sprite-like creatures who can have an array of functions and duties and who play a part in ceremonial contexts as well. Human representations can also signify the heroes or founders of cults; such is the case with many images on Pueblo altars and other representations on Northwest Coast poles.

Geological Beings. This category of images is based on a type of religious geomorphology. It is not a numerically dominant theme, but it is nonetheless of singular importance. The most prominent geological being envisioned is Mother Earth, although it is seldom that direct representations of it occur. In such anthropocentric iconographies as that of the Navajo, it is no problem to illustrate Mother Earth as a somewhat enlarged female human being. Usually, however, Mother Earth is symbolized by some fertility image, such as an ear of corn, or by a circle. Among the Delaware, the earth is symbolized by the giant tortoise who saved humankind from the flood and upon whose back the new earth was created by Nanabush (see figure 5). Sods of earth can also be used to represent Mother Earth, as in the Cheyenne buffalo-skull altar in the medicine lodge.

Another group of geological beings consists of images of mountains. Except for isolated pockets of flatlands and desert basins, most of North America is covered with mountains, and these are usually believed to be

FIGURE 5. *Delaware Pictograph.* Painted on one of a bundle of marked sticks that constitute the tribal chronicle of the Delaware, this pictograph shows the trickster Nanabush riding a great tortoise, symbol of Mother Earth.

alive or at least filled with life, that is, they are the abodes of the gods. This feature of mountains is highly important and is also recognized iconographically.

Finally, some mention should be made of stones and prehistoric implements. Animacy or power is attributed to implements such as ancient pipe bowls, mortars, and blades, any odd-shaped stones, and stones resembling animal, vegetable, or human outlines. Such stones symbolize whatever they resemble.

Abstract Symbols. The dynamic and highly stylized geometric patterns on Southwest Indian pottery, which represent categories already discussed (such as clouds, rain, lightning, the sun, and so on), also belong to the category of abstract symbols. Cultures with highly developed artistic iconographies, such as those of the Northwest Coast, the Southwest, and the Woodlands peoples with their birchbark illustrations, also develop series of signs referring to abstractions inherent to their systems. On the Ojibwa Midewiwin scrolls, for example, the symbol of bear tracks in a particular context represents a priest's four false attempts to enter the Mide lodge. These four false attempts can also be symbolized by four bars.

[*See also* North American Indians *and* Shamanism, *article on* North American Shamanism.]

BIBLIOGRAPHY

There is unfortunately no comprehensive work on the religious iconography of the North American Indians. Information about iconography is found in the original ethnographic data on various peoples published in the annual reports and the bulletins of the Bureau of American Ethnology. An ethnographic approach to art in North America, with emphasis on prehistoric art, can be found in Wolfgang Haberland's *The Art of North America,* translated by Wayne Dynes (New York, 1964). General works on the art of American Indians are numerous; the most comprehensive is Norman Feder's *American Indian Art* (New York, 1971). Another useful study is Frederick J. Dockstader's *Indian Art of the Americas* (New York, 1973).

For the Indians of the Far North, see Jean Blodgett's *The Coming and Going of the Shaman: Eskimo Shamanism and Art* (Winnipeg, 1979) and Inge Kleivan and Birgitte Sonne's *Eskimos: Greenland and Canada,* "Iconography of Religions," sec. 8, fasc. 1 (Leiden, 1984). Concerning the Northeast and Southeast Woodlands tribes, see Frank G. Speck's *Montagnais Art in Birch-bark, a Circumpolar Trait,* "Museum of the American Indian, Heye Foundation, Indian Notes and Monographs," vol. 11, no. 2 (New York, 1937), and *Concerning Iconology and the Masking Complex in Eastern North America,* "University Museum Bulletin," vol. 15, no. 1 (Philadelphia, 1950). For the Plains Indians, see Åke Hultkrantz's *Prairie and Plains Indians,* "Iconography of Religions," sec. 10, fasc. 2 (Leiden, 1973), and Peter J. Powell's *Sweet Medicine: The Continuing Role of the Sacred Arrows, the Sun Dance, and the Sacred Buffalo Hat in Northern Cheyenne History,* 2 vols. (Norman, Okla., 1969). For Indians of the Northwest Coast, see Charles Marius Barbeau's *Totem Poles,* 2 vols. (Ottawa, 1950–1951), and Franz Boas's *Primitive Art* (1927; new ed., New York, 1955). Concerning the Pueblo Indians of the Southwest, see my *Hopi Indian Altar Iconography,* "Iconography of Religions," sec. 10, fasc. 4a (Leiden, 1986), and Barton Wright's *Pueblo Cultures,* "Iconography of Religions," sec. 10, fasc. 4 (Leiden, 1985). For the Navajo Indians of the Southwest, see Sam D. Gill's *Songs of Life: An Introduction to Navajo Religious Culture,* "Iconography of Religions," sec. 10, fasc. 3 (Leiden, 1979), and Gladys A. Reichard's *Navajo Medicine Man: Sandpaintings and Legends of Miguelito* (New York, 1939).

ARMIN W. GEERTZ

Mesoamerican Iconography

Each major Mesoamerican culture developed its religious imagery in a distinctive fashion, although all were historically interlinked and drew from the common pool of Mesoamerican stylistic-iconographic tradition. This type of pictorialization was especially important in an area co-tradition that lacked fully evolved phonetic scripts. It constituted an effective technique of visually communicating in a standardized, codified manner the basic concepts of the religious-ritual systems that played such a crucial sociocultural role in pre-Hispanic Mesoamerica. [*See* Mesoamerican Religions, *especially article on* Mythic Themes.]

Issues of Interpretation. The Mesoamerican iconographic systems that were functioning at the time of the Spanish conquest in the early sixteenth century can be interpreted with the aid of a broad range of data, including written sources compiled in Spanish and in the native languages. The iconographies of the earlier cultures must be studied without the assistance of texts of this type and pose much greater interpretative difficulties. The technique most often employed has been to invoke similarities between the Conquest period images, whose connotations are reasonably well understood from ethnohistorical information, and those of the earlier traditions, assigning to the latter generally similar meanings. This procedure, employing the elementary logic of working from the known to the unknown, is often referred to as the "direct historical approach" or "upstreaming."

This technique has been criticized, particularly when long temporal spans are involved. Disjunctions between form and meaning in religious imagery, it has been pointed out, have been common in iconographic history (above all in the Western tradition with the sharp ideological breaks that accompanied the rise of Christianity and Islam). However, those who sustain the validity of the direct historical approach argue that no major disjunctions of the type that occurred in the West took place in pre-Hispanic Mesoamerica. They cite various examples of imagic continuity from Olmec to Aztec and suggest that Mesoamerica can be more fitly compared to pre-Christian Egypt or to India and China, areas well known for their long-term iconographic continuities of form and meaning. These disagreements among leading scholars indicate that considerable caution is advisable when appraising the accuracy of interpretations of religious images and symbols of the more ancient Mesoamerican cultures.

Olmec. Most archaeologists agree that the earliest sophisticated religious iconographic system in Mesoamerica was that of the Olmec, which flourished between about 1200 and 400 BCE (Middle Preclassic), and was centered in the Gulf Coast region of eastern Veracruz and western Tabasco. [*See also* Olmec Religion.] Olmec style, which conveyed religious concepts imaginatively and effectively, was one of the most striking and original esthetic expressions ever achieved in pre-Hispanic Mesoamerica. Unfortunately, accurately ascertaining the connotations of the intricate Olmec symbol system presents formidable difficulties, and interpretations of prominent students often differ radically.

A major characteristic of Olmec iconography is the blending of anthropomorphic and zoomorphic features. Much of the controversy surrounding the interpretation of Olmec iconography has focused on these fused images, which often exhibit additional overtones of infantilism and dwarfism. The most popular interpretation has been that they merge feline with human characteristics, and the term *were-jaguar* has become fashionable to refer to them. Frequently cited in support of this interpretation are two well-known Olmec monumental sculptures from two small sites near the great Olmec center of San Lorenzo, Veracruz, that supposedly represent a jaguar copulating with a human female, thus producing a hybrid feline-human race, the "jaguar's children." In this view, the composite creature, connoting rain and terrestrial fertility, constituted the fundamental Olmec deity, the archetypical ancestor of all later Mesoamerican rain-and-fertility gods. However, another interpretation would give preeminence to crocodilian rather than feline imagery; the rattlesnake and the toad also have their vigorous proponents.

Other Olmec composite beings are recognized, but opinions differ concerning the precise zoological identification of their constituent elements. A considerable case has been presented for the importance of a polymorphic, essentially saurian creature with various aspects. Called the Olmec Dragon, it has been postulated as the ancestor of a variegated family of celestial and terrestrial monsters prominent in later Mesoamerican iconography (see figure 1).

FIGURE 1. *Zoomorphic Figures.* (1) Olmec dragon, carved on a limestone sarcophagus from La Venta. (2) Olmec bird-monster, incised on an obsidian core found at La Venta.

To what extent Olmec religious imagery indicates the existence of discrete, individualized deities has also elicited considerable debate. Some scholars argue for a fairly sizable Olmec pantheon, often linking its members with prominent contact-period gods. Others view Olmec symbolism as connoting various generalized supernaturalistic concepts but not recognizable deities—which, in their opinion, did not emerge in Mesoamerica until much later. However, it seems likely that at least prototypical versions of various later deities were already being propitiated in "America's first civilization."

Izapa. A series of closely interrelated stylistic and iconographic traditions known as "Izapan," after the major site of Izapa, Chiapas, Mexico, flourished between about 500 BCE and 250 CE (Late Preclassic-Protoclassic) in the area flanking the Isthmus of Tehuantepec, concentrated in the Pacific slope region of Chiapas, Guatemala, and El Salvador. Izapan iconography bears a close relationship to Olmec, from which it partly derives, but its formats are generally somewhat more complex. The style is most typically expressed by low-relief carving, commonly on the perpendicular stone monuments known as stelae, which are sometimes fronted by plain or effigy "altars."

Izapan iconography frequently displays a narrative quality in its compositions, depicting a variety of ritual-mythic scenes, some of considerable complexity. These scenes are often framed by highly stylized celestial and terrestrial registers, interpreted as monster masks. As in Olmec, polymorphic creatures, ostensibly merging feline, saurian, and avian elements, are common. Even more than in the case of Olmec, identifying recognizable deities is difficult, but prominently featured in Izapan iconography is the profile mask of the "long-lipped dragon," depicted in numerous variants including the "scroll-eyed demon." Another significant Izapan composite creature was the "bi- and tricephalous monster," apparently with both celestial and terrestrial connotations. Also prominent on Izapan monuments are downward-flying, winged, anthropomorphic beings, downward-peering celestial faces, combat scenes (humanoid figures versus double-headed serpentine creatures), polymorphic bird monsters, cosmic trees with "dragon-head roots," and diminutive human ritual celebrants accompanied by various ritual paraphernalia. This region during the Late Preclassic and Protoclassic periods produced some of the most iconographically intriguing sculptures of Mesoamerica.

Classic Lowland Maya. The Izapan tradition led directly into the most sophisticated of all Mesoamerican iconographic and stylistic traditions, that of the Classic Lowland Maya (c. 25–900 CE) [*See also* Maya Religion.] As in the case of Izapan, which lies in its background, Maya art in general is essentially two-dimensional and painterly but is also more structured and mature in its expressive power than the earlier tradition. Nearly all of the most common Izapan iconographic themes were retained and often further elaborated. These included the bi- and tricephalous polymorphic celestial-terrestrial creature now frequently conceived as the "ceremonial bar" held by the rulers, the long-lipped dragon in numerous manifestations that eventually evolved into the long-nosed god of rain (Chac), celestial and terrestrial enclosing frames, cosmic trees, and avian composite creatures (serpent birds). Some deities that were clearly prototypical to those represented in the iconography of Postclassic Yucatán can be discerned in Maya religious art of the Classic period. Classic Maya stelae—accurately dated, erected at fixed intervals, and containing long hieroglyphic texts—display profile and frontal portraits of the great Maya dynasts. Their elaborate costumes are replete with religious symbols that invested them with the aura of divinity (see figure 2).

A particularly complex Lowland Maya iconography is portrayed on Late Classic painted ceramic vessels usually encountered in burials. An extensive pantheon of underworld supernaturals is featured in these scenes. It has been suggested that they frequently display connections with the Hero Twins of the *Popol Vuh,* the cosmogonical epic of the Quiché Maya of Highland Guatemala. The representations on these vessels were probably derived at least in part from painted screenfold paper books. Although no Classic period examples have been found, the surviving Postclassic specimens (known as Codex Dresden, Codex Paris, and Codex Madrid) provide some notion of the magnitude and importance of this lost Classic Maya "iconographic archive."

FIGURE 2. *Enthronement.* Representation of the enthronement of the Classic Maya ruler Chac Zutz in 723 CE. Accompanying hieroglyphic text records this event as well as the history of dynastic forebears. Tablet of the Slaves; Palenque, Chiapas.

The recent progress that has been made in the decipherment of Lowland Maya hieroglyphic writing has resulted in a considerably improved understanding of the meaning of the religious imagery so richly developed in this most spectacular of ancient New World cultures.

Monte Albán. Another major Mesoamerican cultural tradition, connected in its origins with Olmec and having some Izapan ties, was that of Monte Albán, so named from the huge site near the modern city of Oaxaca. Already well developed in Late Preclassic times (Monte Albán I–II, c. 600 BCE–100 CE), its full flowering occurred during the Classic period (Monte Albán IIIa–b, c. 100–700 CE). Monte Albán iconography is one of the richest and most structured in pre-Hispanic Mesoamerica. There is general agreement that a numerous pantheon of individualized deities was portrayed, especially in the famous funerary urns, theomorphic ceramic vessels placed in tombs. Many deities are identified by their "calendric names," the day in the 260-day divinatory cycle on which they were believed to have been born. Some can be tentatively connected with deities known to have been propitiated by the Zapotec-speakers who occupied most of the area around Monte Albán at the time of the Conquest, including the basic rain-and-fertility god, Cocijo. The walls of a few tombs at Monte Albán display painted images of deities or deity impersonators, some of them identical to those depicted on the ceramic urns. The hieroglyphic writing of Monte Albán is still poorly understood, but it has been of some aid in interpreting the iconography of one of the greatest of the Mesoamerican Classic civilizations.

Teotihuacán. Dominating the Classic period (c. 100–750 CE) in central Mexico—and spreading its influence throughout Mesoamerica—was the dynamic civilization of Teotihuacán, centered in the urban metropolis known by that name at the time of the Conquest and located about twenty-five miles northeast of Mexico City. Teotihuacán iconography, evidenced by a plethora of ceramic and stone pieces and numerous mural paintings, was one of the most intricate and variegated of ancient Mesoamerica. Symmetry and repetitiveness were hallmarks of Teotihuacán formats, which, particularly in the murals, include processions of ritual celebrants, frontal anthropomorphic and zoomorphic images flanked by profile figures, and complex scenes involving numerous personages engaged in a variety of activities. The dominant theme was clearly the promotion of fertility, featuring what appear to have been at least two major aspects of the preeminent rain-and-fertility deity that was prototypical to the Aztec Tlaloc (see figure 3). Aquatic and vegetational motifs are ubiquitous.

To what extent clear-cut deity representations are present in Teotihuacán iconography, as in the case of the earlier Mesoamerican traditions already discussed,

FIGURE 3. *Fertility Goddess.* Drawing after an aragonite plaque depicting in Teotihuacán style the image of a fertility goddess displaying the calendric name 7 *Reptile's Eye* on her chest. Ixtapaluca, Valley of Mexico.

has generated considerable differences of opinion. Various motif clusters have been defined, which some have suggested might have connoted distinct cults. Certain images have also been identified as discrete deities of the Aztec type, and they have often been labeled with Nahuatl names. They include Tlaloc, the rain-and-earth god; a female fertility deity who may be the prototype of various Aztec goddesses (Chalchiuhtlicue, Xochiquetzal, Teteoinnan, and others); an old fire god (Aztec Huehueteotl or Xiuhtecuhtli); the flayed god (Xipe Totec); a butterfly deity, the Fat God (possibly prototypical to Xochipilli/Macuilxochitl, the Aztec god of sensuality); and, perhaps, prototypes of Quetzalcoatl, the feathered serpent creator-and-fertility god; Xolotl, god of monsters and twins; and Tecciztecatl, the male lunar deity. As in earlier and contemporary Mesoamerican traditions, composite zoomorphic images are another hallmark of Teotihuacán iconography. Some, such as the feathered serpent, may have served as the "disguises" or avatars of various deities, as in the Aztec system.

Classic Veracruz. During the Early Classic period (c. 100–600 CE), after the fade-out of the Olmec tradition in the Gulf Coast region, a distinct regional stylistic and iconographic tradition emerged, climaxing during the Late Classic and Epiclassic periods (c. 600–900 CE). It was best expressed at the major site of El Tajín, in northwest Veracruz, where a sophisticated style of relief carving, featuring double-outlined, interlocking scroll motifs, decorates a number of structures; these include the famous Pyramid of the Niches, two ball courts with friezes portraying complex sacrificial rituals connected with the ball game (see figure 4), and even more complicated ceremonial scenes on a series of column drums in the Building of the Columns.

The most famous exemplars of Classic Veracruz iconography are the handsomely carved stone objects worn by the ball players or replicas thereof: yokes (ball game belts); *hachas*, thin stone heads; and *palmas*, paddle-shaped stones, the latter two objects attached to the yokes worn by the players. Sculptured on these pieces are various anthropomorphic and zoomorphic beings, especially a monstrous creature probably symbolizing the earth. A major tradition of ceramic sculpture also flouished in this region during the Classic period. Some examples appear to represent deities that were prototypical to those of Postclassic times. They include the Old Fire God; versions of Tlaloc and long-lipped beings probably related to the iconographically similar Izapan and Maya rain-and-fertility deities; male and female figures wearing human skins, evidencing rituals similar to those of the Aztec fertility deities Xipe Totec and Tlazolteotl/Teteoinnan; the Fat God; perhaps a proto-Ehé-

FIGURE 4. *Sacrificial Ritual.* Portrayal in classic Veracruz style of a human sacrifice performed in the playing alley of a ball court. South Ball-Court Panel 4; El Tajín, Veracruz.

catl (wind god); and a whole complex of smiling figures seemingly expressing aspects of a cult of sensuality—possibly involving the ritual ingestion of hallucinogens—similar to that of Xochipilli/Macuilxochitl of later times. Complex ceremonial scenes are also represented on mold-pressed, relief-decorated ceramic bowls.

Xochicalco. With its apparent *floruit* during the Epiclassic period (c. 750–900 CE), the extensive hilltop site of Xochicalco flourished in what is now the state of Morelos, Mexico, and gave rise to another distinctive stylistic and iconographic tradition, mainly expressed in relief sculpture. The greatest amount of sculpture decorated one remarkable structure, the Pyramid of the Feathered Serpent. Aside from huge, undulating representations of the feathered serpent, various cross-legged seated personages, reflecting Lowland Maya stylistic influence, are depicted, many identified with their name signs and in some cases, seemingly, place signs as well. Calendric inscriptions are also present, and some scholars have suggested that the carvings may commemorate a major gathering of priests to discuss calendric reform and other ritual-religious matters. Another possibility is that this conclave involved some important dynastic event, perhaps a royal coronation. Other Xochicalco monuments, such as three elaborate stelae now in the Museo Nacional de Antropología, feature hieroglyphic inscriptions and different deities, including a version of the rain god, Tlaloc, and a fertility goddess.

Toltec. At the outset of the Postclassic period a new political and cultural power arose north of the Basin of Mexico, at Tollan, modern Tula, in the state of Hidalgo. Flourishing between about 900 and 1200, Tollan was a major metropolis, capital of an extensive empire. Its stylistic and iconographic tradition was quite eclectic and represented an amalgam of various earlier traditions (Teotihuacán, Xochicalco, El Tajín, and others). [*See also* Toltec Religion.]

Toltec iconography is known primarily from relief sculpture, decorated ceramics, figurines, and some remarkable cliff paintings at Ixtapantongo, southwest of Tula in the Toluca Basin. The relief carvings frequently depict armed, elaborately attired personages on quadrangular pillars and, in processional files, on bench friezes. Some of these figures are identified with their name (or title) signs and seem to depict actual individuals. The militaristic flavor of Toltec imagery was also expressed by alternating representations of predatory animals and birds: jaguars, pumas, coyotes, eagles, and vultures. Recognizable deity depictions are rare in the reliefs but can be more readily identified in the ceramic figures and especially in the Ixtapantongo cliff paintings. Many appear to be prototypical forms of Aztec deities: Tlaloc, Quetzalcoatl, Xipe Totec, various fertility goddesses, pulque deities, solar and Venus gods, and others. Toltec iconography was particularly haunted by the feathered-serpent icon symbolizing Quetzalcoatl; the related "man-bird-jaguar-serpent" motif was also important.

Mixteca-Puebla and Aztec. During the Toltec period a new stylistic and iconographic tradition was apparently emerging to the southeast, centered in southern Puebla, Veracruz, and western Oaxaca (the Mixteca), which has been labeled "Mixteca-Puebla." During the Postclassic period its pervasive influence was felt throughout Mesoamerica, as a kind of final iconographic synthesis of the earlier traditions already described. In contrast to its predecessors, it was characterized by a greater depictive literalness, plus a particular emphasis on symbolic polychromy. An extensive pantheon of anthropomorphic and zoomorphic supernaturals was represented with relatively standardized identificatory insignia.

The Aztec sytlistic and iconographic tradition, which flourished in central Mexico during the last century or so before the Conquest, can be considered, from one aspect, a regional variant of Mixteca-Puebla. [*See also* Aztec Religion.] It differs principally in displaying an even greater naturalism in human and animal imagery. It also was expressed much more frequently in monumental three-dimensional stone sculpture, particularly deity images. Because of the wealth of available ethnohistorical documentation, the Aztec iconographic tradition can be interpreted with considerably more success than any other Mesoamerican system. Virtually all of its principal symbols have been correctly identified as well as the great majority of the numerous deity depictions, which include almost every member of the crowded pantheon mentioned in the primary sources. Those who advocate maximum utilization of the direct historical approach in the analysis of pre-Hispanic Mesoamerican iconography stress the importance of this extensive corpus of information concerning the Aztec system as a key point of departure for interpreting the much less well-documented pre-Aztec traditions.

[*See also* Temples, *article on* Mesoamerican Temples.]

BIBLIOGRAPHY

Acosta, Jorge R. "Interpretación de algunos de los datos obtenidos en Tula relativos a la epoca Tolteca." *Revista mexicana de estudios antropológicos* 14, pt. 2 (1956–1957): 75–110. A useful, well-illustrated summary of the archaeological aspect of Toltec culture by the principal excavator of Tula. Includes some discussion of the iconography.

Caso, Alfonso. "Calendario y escritura en Xochicalco." *Revista mexicana de estudios antropológicos* 18 (1962): 49–79. An important study of Xochicalco iconography, focusing on the hieroglyphic writing system and calendric inscriptions.

Caso, Alfonso. "Sculpture and Mural Painting of Oaxaca." In *Handbook of Middle American Indians,* edited by Robert Wauchope and Gordon R. Willey, vol. 3, pp. 849–870. Austin, 1965. Well-illustrated discussion of Monte Albán iconography through sculpture and wall paintings.

Caso, Alfonso. "Dioses y signos teotihuacanos." In *Teotihuacan: Onceava Mesa Redonda, Sociedad Mexicana de Antropología,* pp. 249–279. Mexico City, 1966. A broad survey of Teotihuacán iconography, extensively illustrated.

Caso, Alfonso, and Ignacio Bernal. *Urnas de Oaxaca.* Memorias del Instituto Nacional de Antropología e Historia, no. 2. Mexico City, 1952. The classic study of the effigy funerary urns of the Monte Albán tradition, illustrated with hundreds of photographs and drawings.

Coe, Michael D. *The Maya Scribe and His World.* New York, 1973. A beautifully illustrated catalog featuring principally Late Classic Lowland Maya painted ceramic vessels, with perceptive analyses of their complex iconographic formats and accompanying hieroglyphic texts.

Joralemon, Peter David. *A Study of Olmec Iconography.* Dumbarton Oaks, Studies in Pre-Columbian Art and Archaeology, no. 7. Washington, D.C., 1971. The most comprehensive study of Olmec iconography, profusely illustrated by line drawings. Includes "A Dictionary of Olmec Motifs and Symbols."

Kampen, Michael Edwin. *The Sculptures of El Tajín, Veracruz, Mexico.* Gainesville, Fla., 1972. An important monograph describing and analyzing the sculptural art of the greatest of the Classic Veracruz sites. Includes a catalog of all known Tajín carvings, illustrated with excellent line drawings.

Kubler, George. *The Iconography of the Art of Teotihaucan.* Dumbarton Oaks Studies in Pre-Columbian Art and Archaeology, no. 4. Washington, D.C., 1967. Significant pioneer discussion and analysis of Teotihuacán iconography, utilizing a linguistic model requiring that "each form be examined for its grammatical function, whether noun, adjective, or verb." Includes a table of approximately one hundred Teotihuacán motifs and themes.

Kubler, George. *Studies in Classic Maya Iconography.* Memoirs of the Connecticut Academy of Arts and Sciences, vol. 18. New Haven, 1969. Preliminary but broad-ranging consideration of Classic Lowland Maya iconography, with special attention to dynastic ceremonies, ritual images, and the "triadic sign."

Nicholson, H. B. "The Mixteca-Puebla Concept in Mesoamerican Archaeology: A Re-Examination." In *Men and Cultures,* edited by Anthony F. C. Wallace, pp. 612–617. Philadelphia, 1960. Discusses and defines the Postclassic Mesoamerican Mixteca-Puebla stylistic and iconographic tradition conceptualized as a "horizon style," with some consideration of its origins and the mechanism of its diffusion.

Nicholson, H. B. "The Iconography of Classic Central Veracruz Ceramic Sculptures." In *Ancient Art of Veracruz: An Exhibit Sponsored by the Ethnic Arts Council of Los Angeles,* pp. 13–17. Los Angeles, 1971. A concise discussion of the iconography of Classic Veracruz ceramic figures, with suggestions that some of them probably represent specific deities.

Nicholson, H. B. "The Late Pre-Hispanic Central Mexican (Aztec) Iconographic System." In *The Iconography of Middle American Sculpture,* pp. 72–97. New York, 1973. Summary discussion of the iconographic system of Late Postclassic central Mexico, with specification of its leading diagnostics.

Parsons, Lee A. "Post-Olmec Stone Sculpture: The Olmec-Izapan Transition of the Southern Pacific Coast and Highlands." In *The Olmec and Their Neighbors,* edited by Elizabeth P. Benson, pp. 257–288. Washington, D.C., 1981. Perceptive, well-illustrated discussion of the Izapan and related stylistic and iconographic traditions as manifested in the Pacific Slope region of Chiapas-Guatemala and adjacent highlands.

Quirarte, Jacinto. *Izapan-Style Art: A Study of Its Form and Meaning.* Dumbarton Oaks Studies in Pre-Columbian Art and Archaeology, no. 10. Washington, D.C., 1973. A significant pioneering attempt to define the leading formal and iconographic features of the Izapan stylistic and iconographic tradition; well illustrated with numerous line drawings.

Robicsek, Francis, and Donald M. Hales. *The Maya Book of the Dead: The Ceramic Codex; The Corpus of Codex Style Ceramics of the Late Classic Period.* Charlottesville, Va., 1981. Extensive album of photographs (including full-surface rollouts and color) of Late Classic Lowland Maya ceramic vessels with scenes and hieroglyphic texts related to the surviving ritual-divinatory paper screenfolds. Includes iconographic analysis and preliminary decipherment of the texts.

H. B. Nicholson

Mesopotamian Iconography

Any discussion of the religious iconography of ancient Mesopotamia is hampered by the fact that we have, on the one hand, religious texts for which we possess no visual counterparts and, on the other, representations—sometimes extremely elaborate ones—for which we lack all written documentation. Mesopotamia lacked raw materials such as stone, metal, and wood, and these had to be imported. As a result stone was often recut and metal was melted down; nor has wood survived. In time of war, temple treasures were carried off as booty, and divine statues were mutilated or taken into captivity, so that virtually none remains. Indeed we should know very little of Mesopotamian sculpture of the third and second millennia BCE were it not for the objects looted by the Elamites in the late second millennium BCE and found by the French in their excavations at Susa in southwestern Iran from 1897 onward. In time of peace the temples themselves frequently melted down metal votive objects in order to produce others. Occasionally a hoard of consecrated objects was buried near the temple, however, presumably to make room for others. The Tell Asmar and Al-'Ubaid hoards dating to the second quarter of the third millennium BCE are two examples of this practice. In only a few cases has fragmentary evidence survived to indicate how temples were decorated (the leopard paintings at Tell 'Uqair, for instance), but their elevations are often depicted on monuments and seals, and facades decorated with date-palm pilasters or water deities have been found. The decoration of secular buildings, among them the painted murals from the palace at Mari and the limestone reliefs that ornamented the palaces of the Assyrian kings, provide some evidence for religious iconography.

Our best sources for religious iconography are therefore the small objects that are more likely to have survived. Plaques and figurines made of local clay often illustrate a more popular type of religion. At certain periods painted pottery is the vehicle for representations that have religious significance. Decorated votive metal vessels, stone maces, and small bronze figures also occasionally survive. Without seals, however, our knowledge would be extremely scant. Prehistoric stamp seals were replaced during the second half of the fourth millennium by small stone cylinders that were used as marks of administrative or personal identification until the end of the first millennium BCE. These cylinder seals were carved with designs in intaglio and could be rolled across clay jar-sealings, door-sealings, bullae, tablets, or their clay envelopes so as to leave a design in relief. Such miniature reliefs are the vehicle for the most complex and tantalizing iconographic representations.

Early Imagery. Nude female figurines are among the earliest artifacts to which a religious significance can be attached. Among the prehistoric figurines of Mesopotamia are the tall, thin, clay "lizard" figures with elongated heads, coffee-bean eyes, slit mouths, and clay pellets decorating the shoulders (see figure 1). "Lizard" figurines have been found at southern sites in both male and female versions though the latter is dominant. Farther north, at Tell al-Sawwan, female figurines and male sexual organs were carved from alabaster. These figurines also have elongated heads and prominent eyes but are more rounded in shape. In the north, clay figurines often have abbreviated heads, and the emphasis is

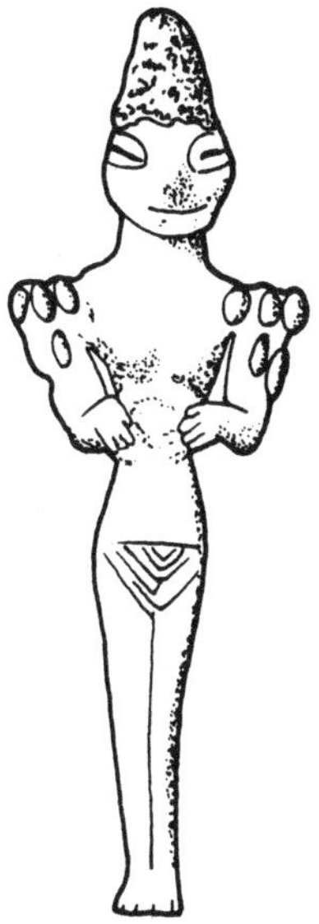

FIGURE 1. *Lizard-Woman.* Grave idol, Ubaid period; Ur, early fourth millennium BCE.

FIGURE 2. *Archer and Prey.* Detail of design on the interior of a painted pot, Halaf period; Tell Arpachiya, mid-fifth millennium BCE.

on a well-rounded, full-breasted body. An opposite trend is attested, however, at Tell Brak, where "spectacle" or "eye idols" were found in a late fourth-millennium temple. Here the eyes are emphasized to the exclusion of everything else, and there has even been debate as to whether they might not, in fact, represent huts. Although there is always a risk in attributing a religious significance to a figurine when there is no written evidence to corroborate this, it does seem likely that these figures had fertility connotations.

Animal combats. One motif that seems to have had a special significance throughout Mesopotamian prehistory and history shows a heroic male figure in conflict with wild animals. A pot of the Halaf period (c. 4500 BCE) shows an archer aiming at a bull and a feline (see figure 2). A figure traditionally known as the priest-king appears on a relief and a seal of the Uruk period (late fourth millennium) shooting or spearing lions and bulls, and the same theme reappears in the Assyrian reliefs of the ninth and seventh centuries BCE and forms the subject of the Assyrian royal seal. After the hunt the king is shown pouring a libation over the corpses, thus fulfilling his age-old function as representative of the god and protector of the country against wild cattle and lions. This function must have been particularly important when animal husbandry and agriculture were in their infancy but would have lost some of that immediacy in Assyrian times, when animals had become scarce and were specially trapped and released from cages for the hunt.

At certain periods the theme of animal combat became dominant in the iconographic repertoire. For several centuries during the third millennium, and at various times later on, heroes are shown protecting sheep, goats, and cattle from the attack of lions and other predators. Generally the heroes are either naked except for a belt, with their shoulder-length hair falling in six curls (see figure 3), or they are kilted and wear a decorated headdress. They are often assisted by a mythic creature who has the legs and horns of a bull and a human head and torso. Attempts have been made to equate the figures with the legendary king Gilgamesh and his wild companion Enkidu, but the evidence is lacking. We probably have here an extension of the theme already discussed, with the emphasis on the protection of domesticated animals from their aggressors. Prehistoric stamp seals showing figures who often wear animal masks and who are involved with snakes, ibex, and other animals probably reflect a more primitive animistic religious tradition.

Early urban imagery. The advent of an organized urban society in the second half of the fourth millennium led to the development of more varied vehicles for the transmission of iconographic concepts. Some examples of monumental sculpture have survived, among them an almost life-size female head which was probably part of a cult statue. The wig and the inlay that once filled the eye sockets and eyebrows have vanished and make this sculpture particularly attractive to modern Western aesthetic taste. Uruk, where the head was found, was the center of worship of the fertility goddess Inanna, and a tall vase is decorated with a scene where the robed goddess in anthropomorphic form, accompanied by her symbol, the reed bundle, receives offerings from a naked priest and a (damaged) figure who wears a crosshatched skirt; this latter is probably the priest-king mentioned above (see figure 4). In his role as *en* ("lord") he is depicted feeding flocks and cattle, engaging in ritual hunts, or taking part in religious ceremonies; in his role as *lugal* ("owner") he triumphs over prisoners. He too has survived in sculpture in the round, on reliefs, and on cylinder seals.

Other significant motifs are known only from their

FIGURE 3. *Animal Combat.* Detail from a cylinder seal, Akkadian period, c. 2300 BCE. A heroic figure struggles with a lion.

FIGURE 4. *Presentation of an Offering to Inanna.* Detail of design on an alabaster vase; Uruk, late fourth millennium BCE. The two figures standing behind the goddess Inanna, who is the robed figure, represent her symbol, the reed bundle.

impression on clay sealings. It seems that certain types of seals were used by particular branches of temple administration: boating scenes used by those connected with fishing and waterways, animal file seals for those dealing with herds. Certain designs, for instance those showing variations on a pattern of entwined snakes and birds, are more difficult to fit into this scheme of things. Other seals are squat, often concave-sided, and cut with excessive use of the drill to form patterns. These might have been used by an administration dealing in manufactured goods since potters and weavers are depicted. Some show a spider pattern, and it is tempting to associate these with the temple weavers, whose patron deity was the spider-goddess Uttu. Some more abstract patterns are difficult to interpret.

If we have dealt at some length with this early period it is because many of the iconographic concepts found later have their roots in the late fourth-millennium repertoire, including depictions of both the physiomorphic and the anthropomorphic form of deities, cult scenes with naked priests, the attitude of worship with hands clasped and large, inlaid eyes to attract the deity's attention, as well as the royal hunt, the sacred marriage, and banquet scenes. Even such quasi-abstract concepts as the rain cloud received its iconographic shape during this period, as testified by seal impressions showing the lion-headed eagle. Later he is shown on seals, vessels, reliefs, and particularly on a huge copper relief that adorned the temple at Al-ʿUbaid.

Later Developments. Banquet scenes were especially popular in Early Dynastic times (mid-third millennium) and are often associated with scenes of war: seals, plaques, and mosaic panels depict these ritual banquets, which are probably to be interpreted as victory feasts in some contexts and as marriage feasts in others. They are to be distinguished from later Neo-Hittite funerary meals, but the preparation of food for the gods is a favorite iconographic motif in the second half of the second and early first millennia BCE.

Deities and their attributes. The representation of deities developed slowly, though by the middle of the third millennium they were wearing horned headdresses as a means of identification. In Akkadian times (2340–2180 BCE) distinct iconographies were established for the more prominent deities, and their position facing left became fixed, though the detailed representations of myths on seals of this period are generally incomprehensible to us. The role of some deities can be identified by the attributes they hold, others by the sprigs of vegetation, streams of water, rays, or weapons which issue from their shoulders. Often these serve only to establish that the deity is, for instance, a vegetation or a warrior god without being more specific.

In fact, it is only a very few representations which can actually be identified with any degree of certainty. Plows are frequently depicted, especially on Akkadian seals, but this is not always a shorthand for Ninurta (who is, however, depicted in a chariot on the famous Stela of the Vultures). Warrior gods on Old Babylonian seals are probably also to be equated with him in many cases, and he appears on Assyrian reliefs. The temple of Ninhursaga at Al-ʿUbaid was decorated with friezes showing dairy scenes. There are clear representations of the water god Enki/Ea in his watery house or with water flowing from his shoulders on Akkadian seals. His Janus-faced attendant, Usmu, is also shown, as is the Zu bird who stole the tablets of destiny. Later the water god fades from the iconography and comes to be represented by a turtle. A Neo-Assyrian seal showing a divine figure running along the back of a dragon is often taken to represent the Babylonian god Marduk with the primeval monster Tiamat, but there is no proof that this is so.

The moon god Nanna/Sin was a major deity, but

there are surprisingly few representations of him. A stela from Ur and one of the wall paintings from the palace of Mari are perhaps the most convincing representations of this god, but where gods in boats can be identified with any certainty, they seem to be the sun god. The moon's crescent below the sun disk is also extremely common. The iconography of the sun god Utu/ Shamash is, however, well attested. He is frequently shown with rays rising from his shoulders, placing his foot on a mountain and holding the saw-toothed knife with which he has just cut his way through the mountains of the east (see figure 5). Often he is accompanied by his animal attribute, the human-headed bull (probably a bison), or by attendants who hold open the gates of dawn. Scorpions likewise can be associated with the sun god, but they are also symbols of fertility and attributes of the goddess of oaths, Ishara. A famous plaque shows the sun god seated in his temple in Sippar; he also appears as the god of justice, holding a symbolic rod and ring, on the law code of Hammurabi of Babylon.

From Old Babylonian times onward the storm god Adad occurs frequently, often standing on a bull and holding a lightning fork. His consort Shala may appear briefly, on seals and in the form of mass-produced clay figurines of the Old Babylonian period, as a nude goddess, shown frontally. Ishtar (Inanna), the Uruk fertility goddess, appears on Akkadian seals holding a date cluster, calling down rain, and often winged with weapons rising from her shoulders as goddess of war (see figure 6). It is this last aspect that becomes predominant, and the Old Babylonian representations are so standardized that it is tempting to see in them the depiction of a well-known cult statue. It may be her aspect as "mistress owl" which is shown on the famous Burney relief (on loan to the British Museum). Her earlier symbol, the reed bundle, is later replaced by a star. One early seal may show her consort Dumuzi (Tammuz) as a prisoner in the dock, but otherwise he is difficult to identify. Ningirsu is often identified as a lion-headed eagle or thunderbird. There are several representations of what is probably Nergal as a warrior god. The god in the winged disk on Assyrian reliefs has generally been identified as Ashur but is more likely the sun god Shamash. Amurru, the god of the Amorites, appears on Old Babylonian seals accompanied by a gazelle and holding a crook.

Unidentifiable figures. From the wealth of symbols which represent deities, many can only be tentatively identified. The Babylonian boundary stones show these symbols on podia and list names of deities, but there is often no correlation between image and text (see figure 7). This is also the case on Old Babylonian seals of the earlier part of the second millennium BCE where we have frequent representations of unidentifiable figures and a large number of inscribed seals mentioning divine protectors: the names do not generally have any bearing on the representation. It seems that the owners of the seals were "hedging their bets" and invoking some deities in pictorial form, others in written form, and still others by their symbols.

It has also been suggested that the deities invoked most frequently were those most likely to be depicted; again this cannot be so since Ishtar, for instance, is fre-

FIGURE 5. *Classic Representation of Shamash.* From a Babylonian cylinder seal, nineteenth–eighteenth century BCE.

FIGURE 6. *Classic Representation of the Warrior Goddess Ishtar (Inanna).* From an Old Babylonian cylinder seal.

FIGURE 7. *Symbolic Design.* From a Babylonian boundary stone, eighth century BCE. Some figures are unidentifiable.

quently depicted and is almost never mentioned in the inscriptions. It is likely that certain deities had a well-established iconography (like the popular saints of medieval Christianity), probably based on a commonly known cult statue or wall painting, while others were invoked by name because their iconography was not as immediately recognizable. The picture becomes even more complex in Neo-Assyrian times when demons played an ever-increasing part in religion: we have descriptions of the demons, but these are difficult to reconcile with the representations.

The rich and tantalizing iconography of Mesopotamia is also responsible for key images in the Judeo-Christian tradition. To cite only one example, the huge, winged, human-headed lions and bulls which decorated and protected the Assyrian palace entrances are the basis for Ezekiel's vision (*Ez.* 1:4–13) and by extension for the symbols of the four evangelists as we know them, combining human intelligence with the wings of the eagle and the strength of the bull or lion, the most powerful creatures in heaven and on earth.

[*See also* Mesopotamian Religions, *overview article.*]

BIBLIOGRAPHY

There is no recent study of Mesopotamian religious iconography. An early attempt at bringing order out of chaos is Elizabeth Douglas Van Buren's *Symbols of the Gods in Mesopotamian Art* (Rome, 1945). This is still a useful book but has been superseded to a large extent by Ursula Seidl's detailed study of the Babylonian boundary stones, *Die babylonischen Kudurru-Reliefs* (Berlin, 1968). The symbols which appear on these stones are analyzed, the various possible interpretations and identifications are discussed, and examples from all periods are listed.

Most studies on religious iconography have appeared in catalogs of cylinder seals, beginning with Henri Frankfort's pioneering attempt to relate the seal designs to the texts in his *Cylinder Seals* (London, 1939). Edith Porada's *Corpus of Ancient Near Eastern Seals in North American Collections,* vol. 1, *The Pierpont Morgan Library Collection* (Washington, D.C., 1948), is also a mine of information. The same author has more recently edited *Ancient Art in Seals* (Princeton, 1980), which includes an essay by Pierre Amiet relating the iconography of Akkadian seals to a seasonal cycle. In her introduction Porada summarizes the advances in glyptic studies which have taken place since Frankfort wrote. Many of the objects referred to here are illustrated in André Parrot's *Sumer* (London, 1960) and *Nineveh and Babylon* (New York, 1961) or in J. B. Pritchard's *The Ancient Near East in Pictures relating to the Old Testament* (Princeton, 1969).

DOMINIQUE COLLON

Egyptian Iconography

The principal iconographic sources for ancient Egyptian religion are the representations of scenes, both ritual and mythological, carved in relief or painted on the walls of Egyptian temples and tombs, as well as the numerous images and statues of gods and pharaohs. Additionally, there are many objects of ritual or practical function decorated with carved or painted religious motifs, and finally, numerous hieroglyphic signs belonging to the Egyptian writing system are representations of gods, religious symbols, and ritual objects. These types of sources remain constant throughout the more than three thousand years of ancient Egyptian history from the Old Kingdom to the Roman period (c. 3000 BCE–395 CE).

Egyptian gods were depicted both as human beings and as animals; a composite form combining a zoomorphic head with a human body enjoyed special popularity in relief and statuary alike (see figure 1). Anthropomorphic representations of Egyptian gods relate to their mythological functions and reveal narrative aspects of their relationships, whereas other forms may be defined as their "metamorphoses" or symbols, emphasizing one particular feature or event. In this symbolic realm one divinity could be represented by various animals or objects—for example, the cow, the lioness, the snake, and the sistrum (a musical instrument) are all manifestations of the goddess Hathor. Conversely, one animal could embody various gods; thus, the protective cobra that appears on the forehead of each pharaoh could be identified with almost all goddesses. The divine identity of an animal may differ in various local pantheons. Particularly numerous were iconographic variations of the sun god, which illustrate various phases of the sun's *perpetuum mobile.* Some male gods associated with generative powers (Min, Amun-Re, Kamutef) are depicted ithyphallically. A particular shape, that of a mummified human body, was attributed to Osiris, the god of the dead. This form also occurs in some representations of other gods, especially when they appear in the realm of the dead. Diads and triads of gods, frequent in Egyptian statuary, as well as larger

FIGURE 1. *Thoth Writing a Royal Name.* Drawing after a bas-relief from the Sanctuary of Queen Hatshepsut, Karnak; c. 1490–1468.

groups of divine beings represented in reliefs and paintings, are visual expressions of various relationships among numerous divinities. Syncretistic tendencies in Egyptian religion, popular after the Amarna period, take concrete form in the composite features that combine the iconographic features of different gods.

Scenes carved on the walls of tombs and temples as well as on furniture and ritual objects most frequently show the gods in the company of a king making offerings or performing other ritual acts (such as censing, purifying with water, or embracing the god). All representations of the king facing a divinity illustrate the ongoing relationship of reciprocity between them. In return for the precious object that he presents to the god, the pharaoh receives symbols of life, strength, stability, many years of kingship, and the like (see figure 2).

Statuary. Numerous Egyptian statues made of all possible materials, such as stone, wood, gold, bronze, and faience, represent one, two, or three gods often accompanied by a king. Both gods and king wear crowns and hold characteristic insignia, among which the most frequent are the sign of life *(ankh)* and various types of scepters. Many elements of the king's dress are identical with those of the gods, thus visualizing the divine aspects of the monarch's nature. The shape of their artificial beards is distinctive, however: the beard of the god is bent forward at the end, while that of the king is cut straight in its lower part.

The size of the statues varies according to their function. Small bronze statuettes of votive character were common, especially in the first millennium BCE. Many represent animals sacred to Egyptian gods; sometimes these figures are set on boxes containing mummies of the animals represented. The mummified bodies of larger animals, such as bulls, ibis, crocodiles, and cats, have been found buried within special necropolises near places connected with the cults of various gods.

Large stone statues served as cult objects in Egyptian temples. Pairs of colossal effigies of the seated king usually stood in front of the temple pylons. The sphinx, with its body of a lion and head of the king, was often placed in the front of the temple to symbolize the monarch's identity as solar god. Rows of sphinxes lined both sides of processional ways leading to the principal temple entrances.

Funerary Art. Another important part of our knowledge about ancient Egyptian iconography comes from the decoration of Egyptian tombs and coffins that comprises the great Egyptian religious "books"—literary compositions that combine spells of magical, mythological, and ritual character with pictures illustrating Egyptian visions of the netherworld. The most ancient of these "books" are the Pyramid Texts carved on the walls of some of the rooms inside the royal pyramids (Old Kingdom, c. 3000–2200 BCE). The illustrations accompanying this sort of text appear for the first time in the Book of Two Ways, which is part of the Coffin Texts (Middle Kingdom, 2134–1660 BCE) painted on the sides of wooden coffins.

Subsequent literary compositions of religious character are generally accompanied by elaborate tableaux, often in the form of vignettes drawn above a column of text written on papyrus. From the New Kingdom (1569–1085 BCE) on, the most popular of these "books" was the *Book of Going Forth by Day* (the so-called *Book of the Dead*), a copy of which was a necessary element of the funerary offerings of every noble. The visual aspects of royal eschatology are best known from a composition called *Amduat* (That Which Is in the Netherworld), which was painted or carved on the walls of royal tombs. Illustrations show the nightly wandering of the sun god through the netherworld. Beginning with the New Kingdom and continuing into the Roman period, fragments of these "books" also decorate many tombs, coffins, and ritual objects belonging to the nobles.

Temples. As the abode of the gods, Egyptian temples were accessible only to the kings and priests. The king, considered the mediator between the gods and the people, is usually shown in front of the gods in the ritual scenes that decorate the temple walls, although in reality it must have been the priests who performed the rituals in the king's name.

The sanctuary, usually situated at the far end of the

FIGURE 2. *King Amenophis III Making an Offering to a Djed Pillar, Symbol of Osiris.* Drawing after a mural in the Tomb of Kheruef, Thebes; c. 1405–1367.

temple along its axis, contained the sacred image of the god to whom the temple was dedicated. The statue of Amun-Re, the chief divinity of Thebes and the state divinity since the time of the New Kingdom, stood inside a shrine on a portable bark placed upon a sled. In Theban temples this effigy is often represented in connection with the Opet Feast or the Beautiful Feast of the Valley, during which it was transported along or across the Nile on a huge ceremonial boat adorned with reliefs and statues.

Narrative cycles. Many temple scenes form standardized sequences of pictures showing summarily, sometimes almost symbolically, successive episodes of mythicized rituals that often refer to important historical events, such as the miraculous birth of the king, his coronation, his victories over enemies, his jubilee, and the

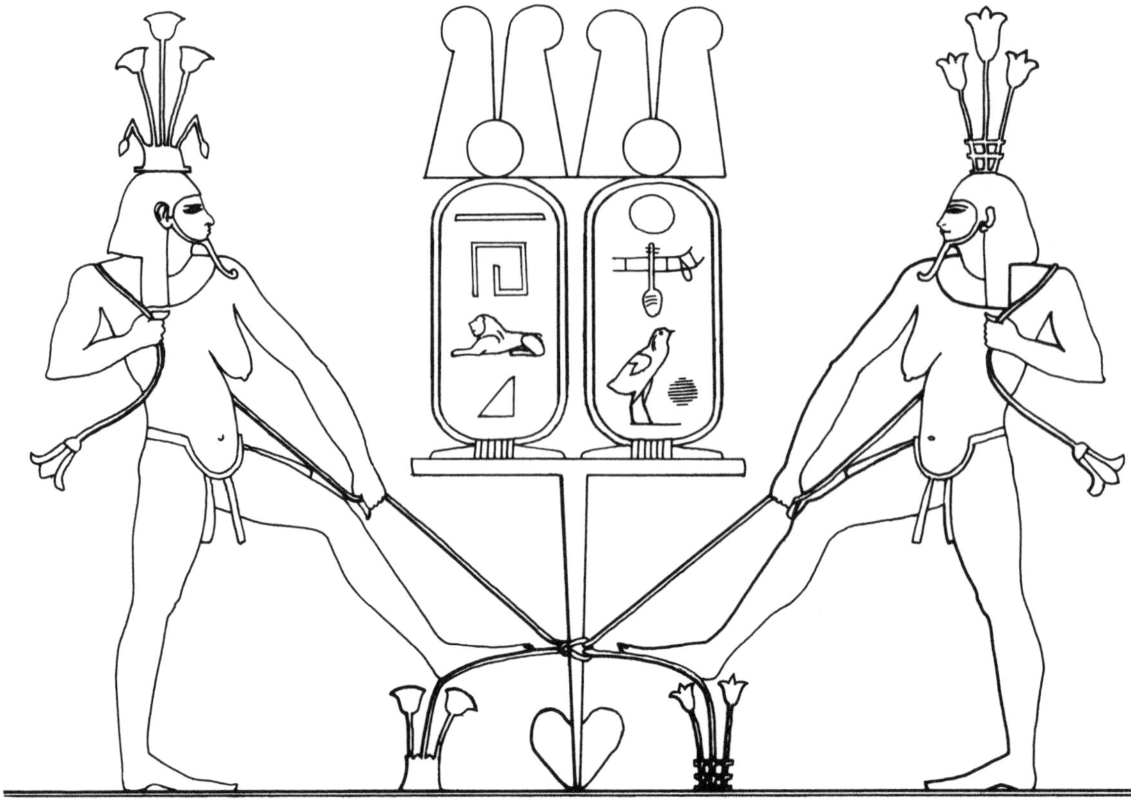

FIGURE 3. *Heraldic Symbol of Unity.* Two divine personifications of the Nile are shown binding together papyrus and bulrush plants, an action symbolic of the unification of Upper Egypt and Lower Egypt. Drawing after the Relief of Taharka; Gebel Barkal, c. 689–664.

founding of the temple. These representations appear in the inner parts of the temple, together with tableaux depicting the daily ritual performed before the statue of the temple's principal deity and scenes showing various offerings being made. Often the iconographic repertory of the decoration of the pillared hall—the central part of many temples—constitutes something of a "showcase," reviewing in abbreviated form all the important elements of the temple's relief decoration.

The interior of the walls enclosing the courts are often decorated with episodes of the most important feasts, while the grandiose tableaux found on the exterior of the walls and on the gates (frequently in the form of pylons) commonly illustrate the king's military achievements. Standard scenes on the pylon faces show the king smiting foreign captives, presenting them to a god, and images of the king offering a figure of the goddess Maat—the personification of truth, justice, and order—to the main divinity of the temple. Another iconographic pattern frequently occurring on the pylons and on the socle of royal thrones is the symbolic representation of subjugated peoples, the so-called ring-names, showing legless human figures, with hands bound, behind an oval ring containing the name of the foreign province. The facial features of these figures were meant to characterize the physiognomy of each particular people.

Symbolic motifs. In addition to these scenes referring to particular events, the temple walls are also decorated with numerous motifs of a more symbolic nature, which give visual form to religious, political, or geographical ideas. The so-called geographical processions, for instance, symbolize the provinces of Egypt in the form of hefty divinities personifying the Nile, each bearing offerings in their hands.

Various iconographic patterns invented by the Egyptians give shape to the idea of the unification of Lower and Upper Egypt. The central motif of a great number of them is the heraldic symbol called *sma-tawy,* which is composed of two plants, papyrus (for Lower Egypt) and a kind of bulrush (for Upper Egypt), bound together around the spinal cord and the lungs of an animal. Two divine personifications of the Nile—the motive power of this unification—are often shown holding and binding together the two plants (see figure 3).

Geographical and religious at the same time, the concepts of the country's division into two parts—either north and south or east and west—belong to the most important principles prevailing in Egyptian iconography. They find expression in symmetrical or antithetical compositions of scenes placed in the axial rooms of temples and tombs, as in the disposition of the various gods representing north and south or east and west, especially on the decoration of lintels, doorposts, and rear walls.

The netherworld. The Egyptian realm of the dead lay in the west. The best illustration of ancient Egyptian visual concepts of the netherworld appears in the decoration of New Kingdom royal and noble tombs situated in west Thebes; these iconographic patterns remained a favorite and repeated subject right up to the Roman period. Of the two principal groups of scenes depicted there, the first, usually found in the first room of the tomb, refers to various episodes in the earthly life of the deceased, including such religious ceremonies or feasts as the Beautiful Feast of the Valley, the royal jubilee, the New Year festival, or the harvest feast. Included in all these scenes are processions, offerings (including burnt offerings), incense burning, and performances with playing, singing, and dancing. Of special importance among Egyptian musicians was the harpist, who came to be represented by the squatting figure of a blind man shown in profile.

The other group of scenes, found in the inner room, illustrates various episodes of the funeral rites, such as the embalming ritual, the symbolic "pilgrimage to Abydos" by boat, and various processions with the mummy being dragged on sledges. The ritual of "opening the mouth" was one of the most important ceremonies of the long funeral cycle. Performed on the statue of the deceased or on his mummy, it was composed of episodes including censing, pouring libations, purifying, and "opening the mouth" with special instruments, all of which were intended to revive the spirit of the deceased.

Cult of the dead. Of particular importance in every tomb were the places intended for the cult of the deceased. These featured niches with statues of the dead person (and sometimes of members of his family), stelae often depicting the deceased adoring and making offerings to various gods or royal personages, and lastly, false-door stelae constituting a symbolic passage between the realm of the dead and the world of the living.

Enabling the deceased to enjoy the sight of the shining sun is another idea that predominates in the eschatological visions depicted and described on the walls of royal tombs. Such great religious compositions as the *Amduat*, the *Book of Gates*, and the *Book of Caverns* depict, among other things, the nightly journey of the sun god, who is often identified with the king. The monarch is thus endowed with the ability to reappear in the morning as a form of the solar divinity.

Most important in each tomb, however, was the burial chamber, commonly situated underneath the accessible rooms at the bottom of a deep vertical shaft. Here were contained the sarcophagus with the mummy of the deceased and all the funerary offerings, including the four Canopic jars for the viscera of the deceased, the mummiform figures known as *shawabti*s (*ushabti*s), a copy of the *Book of Going Forth by Day* written on papyrus, and various ritual objects. The sarcophagi and coffins, made of wood or stone, took the form of cubical or body-shaped cases decorated with painted or carved religious motifs. The four Canopic jars were associated with the four sons of the royal deity Horus, with the four cardinal directions, and with the four protective goddesses; they each had distinctive stoppers, often representing the heads of the four sons of Horus or simply anthropomorphic heads. Numerous *shawabti*s holding various objects, such as hoes, baskets, or religious symbols, and most frequently made of faience or stone, accompanied the deceased in his tomb in order to help him in the netherworld. In some tombs the number of these figures was considerable: more than one thousand were recovered in the tomb of King Taharqa (r. 689–664 BCE). Particularly rich were the grave goods of the royal tombs; the most complete version of such a funeral outfit has been found in the tomb of Tutankhamen (r. 1361–1352 BCE) located in the Valley of the Kings, the New Kingdom necropolis in west Thebes.

The evolution of iconographic patterns in the three-thousand-year course of ancient Egyptian history parallels general changes in religious concepts, which are themselves a function of political and social changes. A "democratization" of religious beliefs during the Middle Kingdom and the Second Intermediate period resulted, on the one hand, in the depiction of direct relations between gods and human beings and, on the other hand, in identifying the dead with the god Osiris. Religious conflicts during the eighteenth dynasty, probably reflecting political struggles and culminating in the "heresy" of Amenhotep IV-Akhenaton, led first to a disproportionate emphasis on solar cults and then to a development of religious concepts concerning the realm of the dead, with a dual focus on Osiris and the solar god. The union of these two once-competing deities occurs frequently after the Amarna period and contributes to a development of theological concepts as well as their iconographic renderings. This syncretism increases during the Third Intermediate period and generates an unparalleled variety of forms during the Ptolemaic period.

[*See also* Pyramids, *article on* Egyptian Pyramids, *and* Temple, *article on* Ancient Near Eastern and Mediterranean Temples.]

BIBLIOGRAPHY

The most complete and up-to-date compendium of information concerning the iconography of ancient Egyptian religion is *Egypt* (Leiden, forthcoming), volume 16 in the series "Iconography of Religions," edited by the Institute of Religious Iconography, Groningen. Each of the thirteen fascicles of this volume, arranged in chronological sequence, contains rich photographic materials and a detailed bibliography. Encyclopedic information on particular subjects can be found in Hans Bonnet's *Reallexikon der ägyptischen Religionsgeschichte*, 2d ed. (Munich, 1971), and in *Lexikon der Ägyptologie*, 6 vols., edited by Hans Wolfgang Helck, Eberhard Otto, and Wolfhart Westendorf (Wiesbaden, 1972–). Bonnet's *Ägyptische Religion* (Leipzig, 1924) may be consulted as a valuable complement to these publications. There is an amazing scarcity of scientific literature in English, but see Manfred Lurker's *The Gods and Symbols of Ancient Egypt*, revised by Peter A. Clayton (London, 1980).

KAROL MYŚLIWIEC

Greco-Roman Iconography

The religious structures of both Greeks and Romans conform to the typical patterns of divinity and belief found among the Indo-European peoples. Most notable of these is an organized pantheon of deities related by birth or marriage and presided over by a god of the sky who is both ruler and father (e.g., Zeus Pater and Jupiter). Nevertheless, although it is clear that such gods accompanied the movement of the Indo-Europeans into Greece and Italy, it is impossible to state with certainty what iconographic representation, if any, was used to worship them during this earliest period.

The attempt to discern early iconographic patterns is further hampered by the fact that both peoples were invaders whose later religious outlook was influenced by older, settled cultures. When the Greeks arrived at the beginning of the second millennium BCE, they found not only an indigenous population on the mainland (whom they called the Pelasgians) but also the flourishing civilization of nearby Crete, whose art and architecture show evidence of Egyptian and Near Eastern influences. Thus, not only all the gods who constituted the classical Greek pantheon but also their iconography must be considered the products of a long process of syncretism and synthesis of Indo-European, pre-Hellenic, Cretan, and Near Eastern concepts of divinity. Similarly, the Indo-European settlers in Italy mixed with a variety of peoples already well established on the peninsula. Therefore, any attempt to understand the development of the form and content of Greco-Roman iconography must necessarily entail a consideration of the often disparate parts of the traditions.

Minoan-Mycenaean Iconography (2000–1200 BCE). The study of Cretan (Minoan) religion may be compared to a picture book without a text. The two symbols of Minoan civilization, the double ax and the horns of consecration, clearly had religious significance, perhaps as tools of worship, but their function is not understood. From the archaeological evidence, however, which includes frescoes, seals, and figurines, one may conclude that the representation of the divine was both anthropomorphic and theriomorphic. Found are depictions of female deities encoiled by snakes or with birds perched upon their heads; these figures may explain the prominence of snakes in later Greek religion as well as the association of Greek deities with specific birds. In addition, animal-headed figures reminiscent of contemporaneous Egyptian material have been uncovered. One such type, a bull-headed male, may be the source for the Greek myth of the Minotaur. Also found are representations of demonlike creatures who appear to be performing various ritual acts; these have been cited as evidence of Mesopotamian influence. A number of seals portray the figures both of a huntress, who is called "mistress of the beasts" and whom the Greeks associated with Artemis, and of a male deity, who stands grasping an animal by the throat in each hand. Finally, the seals present strong evidence for the existence of tree cults and pillar cults, the survival of which perhaps may be seen in the Greek myths about dryads, the woodland spirits of nature who inhabit trees.

To what extent the traditions of Minoan iconography immediately influenced the Greeks can be explored through a consideration of Mycenaean remains. Indeed, although the Linear B tablets from Pylos have provided valuable linguistic evidence about the names of the earliest Greek deities, most of our information, as in the case of Crete, comes from archaeological sources. From the excavations at Mycenae have come a number of clay snakes, and at Tiryns a fresco depicts a crocodile-headed creature reminiscent of those seen on Crete. Persistence of the Minoan traditions may also be found in the Lion Gate of Mycenae, over which two lions, carved in relief and leaning on a central pillar, stand guard. Providing further evidence for the continuing influence of Minoan iconography are a number of Mycenaean seals, rings, and ornaments that display representations of sacred trees, bird-decorated shrines, and demons carrying libations. To what extent, however, the continuity of form indicates a continuity of content is difficult to determine.

In 1969, further excavations at Mycenae uncovered

the Room of the Idols, which contained a quantity of clay statues with arms either raised or outstretched. Although possessing only an approximation of human form, each has a distinctive individuality; it has been suggested they may be the earliest representations of those Olympian gods later described by Homer. However, perhaps most characteristic of Mycenaean religious iconography are the thousands of clay statuettes called *phi* and *psi* figurines (after their distinctive shapes). Although most are rendered recognizably female by the accentuation of the breasts, they do not necessarily portend future anthropomorphic representation. They are often found in graves, but there is no general agreement as to their function. It is possible that they once served as votive offerings but that, like much of later Greek art originally sacred in nature and function, they became separated from their original purpose.

Archaic and Classical Iconography. The difficulty of establishing the continuity of the iconographical tradition from the Mycenaean into the later periods of Greek history is illustrated by a comment of the historian Herodotus (fifth century BCE), who credits Homer and Hesiod with describing the gods and "assigning to them their appropriate titles, offices, and powers," but who concedes that the two poets had lived not more than four hundred years before him. Homer and Hesiod are in fact our earliest sources for the iconography of the Greek gods after the Mycenaean age. But another four hundred years separate the destruction of Mycenae and the life of Homer, and the poet's descriptions of the Olympian gods bear little resemblance to the representations of the divine found at Mycenaean sites.

Hesiod's account of the birth of the gods in his *Theogony* indicates that, while earlier generations of deities were often monstrous in appearance as well as behavior, the victorious Olympian gods, with Zeus as their ruler, were clearly anthropomorphic. Homer elaborates upon this concept, describing not only their very obviously human physical appearance but also their often all-too-human behavior. It has been suggested that the source for the relentlessly anthropomorphic quality of the Greek gods in both literature and art is a general rejection of the concept of an abstract deity. Despite criticism by philosophers such as the pre-Socratic Xenophanes, who commented rather cynically that "mortals consider that the gods are born and that they have clothes and speech and bodies like their own," or Plato, who banned poets from his ideal state because they told lies about the gods, the Greeks persisted in depicting their gods as human in form and action.

Nevertheless, there is a great deal of evidence to indicate that, in the conservative ritual of Greek religion, the older forms of representation of the divine persisted. Aniconic images of the divine, such as the *omphalos* at Delphi, provide proof of its survival. This stone, which in Greek myth was described as the one that Rhea gave to Kronos to swallow when he wished to devour his infant son Zeus, and that the ruler of the Olympians then placed at the center of the world, is clearly a baetyl, a sacred stone that contains the power of the divine. Similarly, the widespread appearance of the herm, a pillar on which was carved an erect phallus and that acted as an agent of fertility and apotropaic magic, points to the survival of earlier conceptions of the divine. Myth also provides a clear illumination of the remnants of a theriomorphic iconography: Zeus changes himself into a bull in order to rape Europa and into a swan in order to seduce Leda; Athena and Apollo metamorphose themselves into vultures to watch the battle between Hector and Ajax.

The amalgamation of a number of functional deities during the Archaic and Classical periods can be seen in the great variety of epithets by which each god was addressed. In the use of such epithets, we see once again the particularism of Greek religion. The disparate types, which link seemingly unconnected functions from both the world of nature and the world of humans in a single deity, are probably a result of the continuing processes of synthesis and syncretism described above. Owing to the conservative nature of Greek religion, no epithet was ever discarded. Thus, the most primitive expression of the power of nature embodied in the god as well as the most sophisticated conceptions of divine political power can be found in the iconography, but it is clear that not all aspects of a deity can be equally well expressed through the various cultic epithets.

Nevertheless, many of the epithets of the Olympians can be considered as proof of older iconographic substrata that reveal functions closely linked to the world of nature: horselike Poseidon, owl-eyed Athena, cow-eyed Hera, cloud-gathering Zeus. Although deities were often portrayed with their attributes of nature—the thunderbolt of Zeus, the trident of Poseidon—the connection between iconography and function may at times be difficult to establish because it is clear that many of the earlier "nature" functions of individual deities could not be expressed with clarity in the monuments.

The frequent dichotomy between mythic meaning and ritual function also presents one with difficulties in understanding the iconography of a particular god. In Greek myth, Poseidon is clearly the god of the sea, who appears in sculpture and vase painting brandishing his trident or rising from the sea in his chariot. Yet, Poseidon was also worshiped as a god of horses, and he is depicted on coins in the form of a horse. Likewise, the Artemis of myth is the eternal virgin, yet it is clear from both cult and iconography that she was worshiped as a goddess of fertility. It would seem that myth often serves to create a coherent portrait while religious ritual and practice see no such need. The medium, too, often shapes iconographic conceptualization: the narrative of myth can be more readily portrayed in vase painting and reliefs than through freestanding sculpture.

The evolution of the form and content of Greek iconography as a means of expressing spiritual ideals generally parallels that of Greek art, especially in sculpture. The earliest religious sculpture and architecture were executed in wood and have vanished; but in the the seventh century BCE we see the development of monumental stone architecture and sculpture. The most representative forms of sculpture are the *kouros* (male; see figure 1.1) and the *kourē* (female) figures that stand rigidly with stylized features and dress. Perhaps votive offerings, they have been variously identified as divine or human but may represent something in between: an idealized existence shared by gods and mortals alike. One cannot divorce iconography from the history of Greek art and architecture, for there is no such concept as purely hieratic art: the Classical Apollo, for example, is not only presented as the youthful god, naked and beardless, but comes to embody the idealization of youth (see figure 1.2). Similarly, a bronze statue of a muscular, bearded god with his left arm stretched out in front of him and his right arm extended behind as if to hurl something is identified as either Zeus or Poseidon; without lightning bolt or trident, it is impossible to distinguish between the spheres of sky and sea. Increasing emphasis on the beauty of the human form in repose and in action informs both Greek sculpture and the understanding of the divine. Furthermore, iconography is linked not only with the development of the artistic ideal but with that of the political as well.

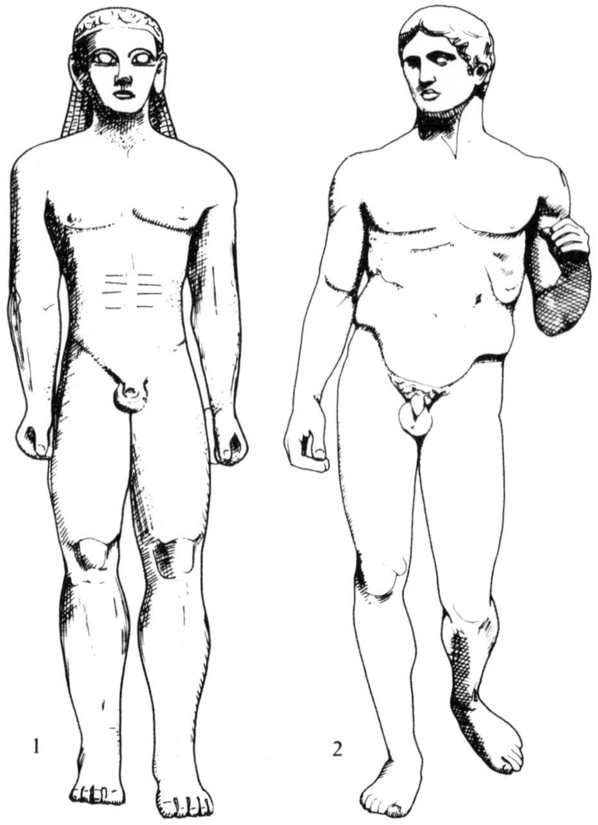

FIGURE 1. *Development of the Classical Ideal.* (1) The sixth-century Sunion Kouros epitomizes the rigid pose characteristic of Archaic figures. (2) The fifth-century Doryphorus of Polyclitus (shown here in a drawing after a Roman copy of the lost bronze original) exemplifies the fluid pose and anatomical precision of the Classical style.

As the institutions of the state evolved, the original gods of nature were made citizens of the polis and given civic functions as protectors and benefactors of the city. Thus, the gold and ivory statue of Athena in the Parthenon portrayed the armed goddess in full regalia as the protector and patron of Athenian civilization, the goddess who had led her people to victory against the Persians. The Parthenon itself is a symbol of the bond between Athena and her city, for the temple frieze depicts the procession of the Panathenaea, a festival held in honor of both the goddess and the powerful city that worshiped her, the pediment portrays scenes from the life of Athena, and the metopes record various victories of Greeks over barbarians.

Similarly at Olympia, which served as the religious and political center of Greece during the Classical period, the Phidian Zeus sat enthroned in the inner sanctuary of the great temple, the concrete expression of the god's power and majesty. Crafted of gold and ivory, nearly twelve meters high, the Lord of the Universe held in one hand a statue of Victory and in the other a golden scepter on which sat an eagle. Behind the throne were the Graces and Hours, goddesses of the seasons and regulators of nature. The worlds of nature and culture become one. Phidias himself reportedly said that he had meant to portray the king in his supremacy as well as in his magnanimity and nobility. The god may be seen as the source out of which all reality—sacred and profane—flows. The temple itself was also an expression of the all-encompassing might of Zeus: twenty-eight meters wide, sixty-nine meters long, and twenty meters high, its colossal size emphasized those attributes of power and universality that Phidias had sought to convey in his sculpture.

Hellenistic and Roman Iconography. The declining political fortunes of the Greek states after the Peloponnesian War paved the way for the rise of Macedon and the magnificent career of Alexander the Great. His military conquests produced a new cultural synthesis of East and West that radically altered the perception and portrayal of the divine; for although the Classical understanding of the nature of deity survived, it was now informed by new religious, social, and political ideals. Absolute monarchy, an altered concept of the divine as embodied in Eastern mystery cults, and the rise of a middle class eager to display its wealth all contributed to the development of different iconographic sensibilities.

Religious iconography in the Hellenistic period presents a curious admixture of Eastern and Western values, of monumentalism and individualism, of divine rationality and pathos, amalgams that expressed themselves in the formal magnificence of the tomb of Mausolus at Halicarnassus as well as in the representations of Aphrodite that emphasize her naked human beauty, in sleeping satyrs and playful cupids as well as in the struggling Laocoön doomed by the gods. The Great Altar of Zeus at Pergamum, with its wide monumental stairway, was encompassed by a frieze that, in depicting the ancient Greek myth of the war between the Olympians and the Giants, displays a remarkable range and intensity of human emotions. In a world where kings were hailed as living gods and apotheosis was a constant possibility, and where gods suffered and died, the division between sacred and profane iconography became even less distinct.

With the conquest of the Hellenistic kingdoms the Romans acquired the values that had informed later Greek religious art and architecture. Although the earlier Etruscan culture of Italy had been strongly influenced by Greek and Oriental ideologies, it shows evidence of a religious outlook distinct from both. Tomb paintings from the Archaic period, for example, portray lively Dionysian revels and rowdy funeral games that, while drawing on Greek sources, perhaps indicate a more optimistic view of the afterlife than that of the Greeks. Roman iconography, on the other hand, reflects the conscious choice of the Greek ideal.

Roman religion seems to have remained rooted in nature to a much greater extent than civic Greek religion had; the early anthropomorphic representations of Mars and Jupiter are exceptions, perhaps occasioned by their clear identification with the political rather than the agricultural life of the Roman people. Mars was the father of Romulus and Remus and thus the ancestor of the Roman people; but even so it was the she-wolf, nurse of the twin boys, who became the emblem of Rome's auspicious origins. Only when old Italic spirits of nature became identified with their anthropomorphic Greek counterparts did the Romans build temples as houses for their gods and represent them in human form. The conservative values of Roman religion not only inhibited the development of a distinctive iconography but at the same time led to the adoption of those elements in Hellenistic art that seemed best to reflect those values. Although Augustus's attempt to re-create the old Roman religious values through the resurrection of archaic rituals and priesthoods and the rebuilding of ancient temples and shrines was ultimately unsuccessful, his Altar of Augustan Peace (Ara Pacis) illustrates the Roman understanding of the connection between traditional expressions of piety and political success. One of its panels depicts Augustus offering solemn sacrifice; another reveals Mother Earth holding on her lap her fruitful gifts. The peace and prosperity of mortals and gods are attributed to Augustus's piety and devotion. More than three hundred years later, the Arch of Constantine was to reflect the same themes: celebrating the victory of the emperor over his enemies, its inscription attributes his triumph to the intervention of an unnamed divine power and his own greatness of spirit. Over three millennia, the iconography of Greek and Roman religion became increasingly concrete, locating the divine first in nature, then in objects, and finally within the human realm.

[*See also* Temple, *article on* Ancient Near Eastern and Mediterranean Temples.]

BIBLIOGRAPHY

Boardman, John. *Greek Art.* Rev. ed. New York, 1973. A useful and thorough survey of the development of Greek art forms from the Mycenaean age through the Hellenistic period.

Dumézil, Georges. *Archaic Roman Religion.* 2 vols. Translated by Philip Krapp. Chicago, 1970. An analysis of early Roman religion that depends primarily on a structural analysis of Indo-European religious institutions and mythologies.

Farnell, Lewis R. *The Cults of the Greek States* (1896–1909). 5 vols. New Rochelle, N.Y., 1977. Although lacking recent archaeological and linguistic evidence, this work remains the standard reference for ancient sources on Greek religion in all its forms.

Guthrie, W. K. C. *The Greeks and Their Gods.* London, 1950. A well-balanced view of the origins of each of the Greek gods, with detailed discussion of the multidimensional roles of the divine in Greek society.

Hauser, Arnold. *The Social History of Art,* vol. 1. New York, 1951. A combination of art criticism and social analysis, Hauser's work attempts to define the cultural forces that determine artistic sensibilities.

Nilsson, Martin P. *A History of Greek Religion* (1925). Translated by F. J. Fielden. 2d ed. Oxford, 1949. Emphasizes the continuity of tradition between Minoan and Mycenaean ritual and practice.

Nilsson, Martin P. *Greek Piety.* Translated by Herbert Jennings Rose. Oxford, 1948. This short work presents a thoughtful study of the various social, historical, and political forces that shaped Greek attitudes about the nature of the divine.

Peters, F. E. *The Harvest of Hellenism.* New York, 1970. A historical, cultural, and religious survey of the Greek and Roman world after Alexander.

TAMARA M. GREEN

Hindu Iconography

Viṣṇu, Śiva, and Devī are the basic visual images of Hinduism. Each of these deities is worshiped in a concrete image *(mūrti)* that can be seen and touched. The image is conceived in anthropomorphic terms but at the same time transcends human appearance. With certain exceptions, Hindu images have more than two arms. Their hands, posed in definite gestures, hold the attributes that connote the deity's power and establish its identity. While the images are concrete in their substantiality, they are but a means of conjuring up the presence of deity: this is their essential function. The image serves as a *yantra,* an "instrument" that allows the beholder to catch a reflection of the deity whose effulgence transcends what the physical eye can see. The divine effulgence is beheld in inner vision. As a reflection of this transcendental vision, the image is called *bimba.* This reflection is caught and given shape also by the *yantra,* a polygon in which the presence of deity during worship is laid out diagrammatically. The *yantra* is constructed with such precision that the "image" emerges in its unmistakable identity. [*See* Yantra.]

Deity, beheld by the inner eye, by an act of "imagination," is translated in terms of the image. In this respect the image is called *pratimā*—"measured against" the original vision of the deity as it arose before the inner eye of the seer. Iconometry in the case of the anthropomorphic three-dimensional image corresponds to the geometry of a linear *yantra.* Thus the anthropomorphic image is at the same time a reflection of a transcendental vision and a precise instrument for invoking the divine presence during worship in the man-made and manlike figure of the image. It has its place in the temple, where it is worshiped not only as a stone stela in high relief in the innermost sanctuary but also on the outside of the walls. There, a special niche or facet of the wall is allotted to each of the images embodying aspects of the image in the innermost sanctuary.

Viṣṇu, Śiva, and Devī (the Goddess) are represented in many types of images, for each of these main deities has multiple forms or aspects. These are carved in relief in niches on the outer side of the temple walls, each niche suggesting a sanctuary correlated in the main directions of space to the central image—or symbol—in the innermost sanctuary. While the images of Viṣṇu and Devī are anthropomorphic and partly also theriomorphic, the essential form in which Śiva is worshiped is in principle without any such likeness. [*See also* Mūrti.]

Śiva. The main object of Śiva worship is the *liṅga.* The word *liṅga* means "sign," here a sign in the shape of a cylinder with a rounded top. The word *liṅga* also means "phallus" however; some of the earliest Śiva *liṅgas* are explicitly phallus shaped. However, this sign is not worshiped in its mere anthropomorphic reference. It stands for creativity on every level—biological, psychological, and cosmic—as a symbol of the creative seed that will flow into creation or be restrained, transmuted, and absorbed within the body of the yogin and of Śiva, the lord of yogins. In its polyvalence the *liṅga* is Śiva's most essential symbol, while the images of Śiva, each in its own niche on the outside of the temple wall, are a manifestation of Śiva in a particular role offering an aspect of his totality (see figure 1).

The images of Śiva visualize the god's two complementary natures: his grace and his terror. Like all Hindu divine images, that of Śiva has multiple arms; their basic number, four, implies the four cosmic directions over which extends the power of deity in manifestation. Śiva's image of peace and serenity in one of its forms, Dakṣiṇāmūrti, is that of the teacher. Seated at ease under the cosmic tree, he teaches the sages yoga, gnosis, music, and all the sciences. In another image, standing as Paśupati, "lord of animals," Śiva protects all the "animals," including the human soul.

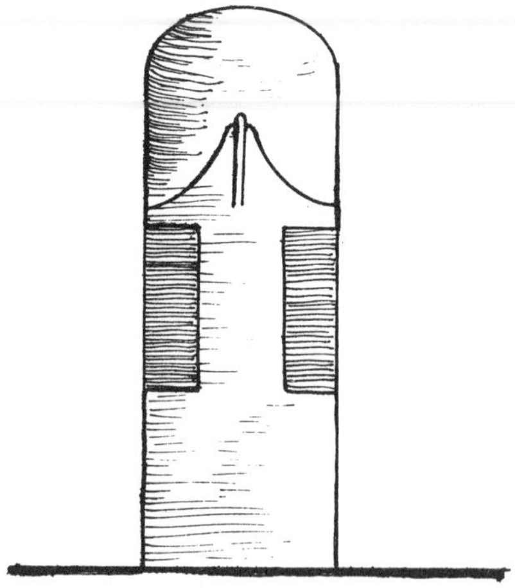

FIGURE 1. *Āḍhya ("Enriching") Liṅga.* The *liṅga,* (Skt., "sign" or "phallus"), the main object of Śiva worship, symbolizes biological, psychological, and cosmic creativity.

He is also the celestial bridegroom, Sundaramūrti, embracing his consort (Āliṅganamūrti) or enthroned with her (Umāmaheśvara), while as Somāskanda the seated image of the god includes his consort, also seated, and their dancing child. These images assure happiness within the human condition, whereas Ardhanārīśvara, the "lord whose half is woman," the androgyne god, his right half male and left half female, is an image of superhuman wholeness.

Myths and legends in which Śiva annihilates or pardons demons of world-threatening ambition are condensed in images of him as victor over destructive forces and death (Tripurāntaka, Kālāri). Another class of images visualizes the god as a young, seductively naked beggar (Bhikṣāṭana) and, in a later phase of the selfsame myth, as an image of terror, an emaciated, skeletal—or, as Bhairava, bloated—god who is sinner and penitent on his way to salvation. Bhairava is an image of the lord's passion on his way to release. There he dances as he danced on the battlefield in his triumph over fiends. Śiva's dance is the preeminent mode of the god's operation in the cosmos and within the microcosm, in the heart of man. The image of Śiva Nāṭarāja dancing his fierce dance of bliss subsumes ongoing movement and stasis in the rhythmic disposition of limbs and body as if the dance were everlasting: in his upper hands are the drum and flame, the drum symbolizing sound and the beginning of creation, the flame symbolizing the end of creation; one arm crosses over the body and points to the opposite, while his raised foot signals release from gravity and every other contingency in the world. The whole cycle of the eternal return is laid out in the *yantra* of Śiva's dancing image. In another image, that of the cosmic pillar, Śiva reveals himself to the gods Brahmā and Viṣṇu; an endless flaming pillar of light arises from the netherworld. The image of Liṅgodbhava shows the anthropomorphic figure of Śiva within the *liṅga* pillar bursting open.

The *liṅga* as both abstract symbol and partly anthropomorphic shape is the main Śaiva cult object. In some of the sculptures, a human head adheres to the cylinder of the *liṅga*, or four heads are positioned in the cardinal directions, implying a fifth head (rarely represented) on top. Five is Śiva's sacred number, and the entire Śaiva ontology—the five senses, five elements, five directions of space, and further hierarchic pentads—is visualized in the iconic-aniconic, five-faced *liṅga*. This concept underlies the image in the innermost sanctuary of the Caturmukha Mahādeva Temple in Nachna Kuthara, near Allahabad (sixth century), and that of Sadāśiva in the cave temple of Elephanta, near Bombay (mid-sixth century). These are ultimate realizations and constructs embodied in sculptural perfection. [*See* Yoni.]

The facial physiognomy of the image reflects the nature of the particular aspect or manifestation of the god. His calm, inscrutable mien as well as Bhairava's distorted countenance are shown with many nuances of expression that convey the significance of each particular manifestation, defined as it is by specific attributes and cognizances. The ornaments, however, the necklaces, belts, earrings, and so on, are not essentially affected by the specific manifestation. Likewise some of Śiva's attributes, particularly the trident, serpent, crescent moon, rosary, and antelope, are part of the god's image in more than one manifestation. Invariably, however, Śiva's crown is his own hair. He is the ascetic god, and his crown shows the long strands of the ascetic's uncut hair piled high on his head in an infinite variety of patterns, adorned by serpents, the crescent moon, and the miniature figure of the celestial river Gaṅgā (Ganges) personified. Lavish presentation here nonetheless constitutes iconographic economy, for each of the various symbols implies an entire myth, such as that of the descent from heaven of the river goddess Gaṅgā, whose impact would have wrought havoc on earth had not Śiva offered his hair as a temporary station for her.

An essential cognizance particular to Śiva among gods—though not present in every Śiva image—is the god's third eye (which also graces deities derived from the Śiva concept, such as Devī and Gaṇeśa). Vertically set in the middle of Śiva's forehead above sun and moon, his two other eyes, the third eye connotes the fire of the ascetic god. It broke out when Pārvatī, his consort, playfully covered the god's other eyes with her hands: darkness spread all over the cosmos. This fire also blazed forth to destroy the god Kāma, "desire," in his attempt to wound Śiva with his arrow.

Whether distinguished by one symbol only or by a combination of symbols, the identity of Śiva is unmistakable in his images. There is also no inconsistency if, for example, the crown of Śiva, lovingly enthroned with Pārvatī, is wreathed with skulls (Umā-Maheśvara from Belgavi, Karnataka, twelfth century). The total being of Śiva is present in the particular aspect.

Facing the *liṅga*, the image of Nandin, the zebu bull carved in the round and stationed in front of the entrance of the temple or in its hall, is at the same time the animal form of Śiva, his attendant, and conveyance (*vāhana*). In more than one respect, Nandin, the "gladdener," conveys Śiva. [*See* Śiva.]

Viṣṇu. The pervader and maintainer of the universe is represented by his anthropomorphic image in the innermost sanctuary. Invariably the image stands straight like a pillar, and its four arms symmetrically hold the god's main attributes: conch, wheel, mace, and lotus. The conch—born from the primordial ocean—

with its structure spiraling from a single point, is a symbol of the origin of existence. The wheel represents the cycle of the seasons, of time. The mace stands for the power of knowledge, while the lotus flower symbolizes the unfolded universe risen from the ocean of creation. According to their respective placement in the four hands of the Viṣṇu image, these four attributes define the particular aspect under which the god is worshiped according to the needs of the worshiper. Each of the twenty-four images—the total permutations of the four symbols in the four hands—has a name. The supreme god, Viṣṇu has a thousand names in which those of the twenty-four images are included.

In addition to the standing image in the innermost sanctuary—an anthropomorphic version of the concept of the cosmic pillar—Viṣṇu may assume two other positions, seated and recumbent. Indeed, no other Hindu god—except a Viṣṇu-derived allegory, Yoganidra—is shown recumbent, and together, these three positions render the mode of the god's pervasive presence in the cosmos and during its dissolution, when in yoga slumber Viṣṇu reclines on Śeṣa, the serpent whose name means "remainder," floating on the waters of the cosmic ocean. In South India each of the three types of images occupies its own innermost sanctuary, on three levels in three-storied temples. According to the needs of the worshiper, each of these three types of images fulfills four goals: total identification with the god, desire for wish fulfillment in worldly matters, desire for power, and desire for success by magic. According to their desired efficacy on these four levels, the images are more or less elaborate in the number of attendant divinities, with the images granting wish fulfillment on the worldly plane the most elaborate.

The twenty-four varieties of the four-armed, standing Viṣṇu image are emanations (*vyūhas*) of the supreme Viṣṇu. Four of the emanations, Saṃkarṣaṇa, Vāsudeva, Pradyuma, and Aniruddha, are considered primary, though their names occur as the thirteenth, fourteenth, fifteenth, and sixteenth in the list of twenty-four.

Theological doctrine and its supporting imagery each follow an inherent logic. The *vyūha* or emanation doctrine is as relevant to the twenty-four types of the Viṣṇu image as the *avatāra* or incarnation doctrine, according to which the supreme Viṣṇu was fully embodied in a specific shape, be it that of fish or boar or man or god. One or the other of these incarnate forms, however, including that of the dwarf (Vāmana) or of Kṛṣṇa, also figures among the twenty-four varieties of the main cult image of Viṣṇu.

Viṣṇu is also conceived in his five-fold aspect: as ultimate, transcendental reality *(para);* in his emanation *(vyūha);* in his incarnation *(vibhava);* as innermost within man *(antaryāmin),* the inner controller; and as *arcā* or consecrated image, this fifth instance being an *avatāra,* a "descent" into matter.

Each *avatāra* is assumed by the supreme Viṣṇu for a particular end, as the situation demands. Yet each *avatāra* or divine descent, though known to have come about at a definite time, remains valid for all times. The number of *avatāras* or incarnations (*vibhavas*) is generally accepted as ten, but twelve further *vibhavas* are also described. The ten shapes are those of the (1) fish (Matsya); (2) tortoise (Kūrma); (3) boar (Varāha); (4) man-lion (Narasiṃha); (5) dwarf and "[god who took] three strides" (Vāmana and Trivikrama); (6) Rāma with the ax (Paraśurāma), who reestablished the leading position of the brahmans; (7) Rāma, the ideal king; (8) Kṛṣṇa; (9) Buddha; and (10) Kalkin, the redeemer yet to come. In niches of the temple wall, the *avatāras* are imaged in anthropomorphic, theriomorphic, or combined anthropo-theriomorphic shapes.

The Matsya *avatāra* incorporates a deluge myth, tell-

FIGURE 2. *Viṣṇu Trivikrama.* Stone sculpture, Bengal. In his fifth incarnation, Viṣṇu spanned the cosmos in three strides and conquered the demon Bali.

ing how a grateful small fish saved by Manu in turn saved Manu, who became the founder of present-day mankind. The tortoise myth tells of the cosmic tortoise that lent its body as the firm support for the world mountain, which served as a churning stick at the churning of the primeval ocean. The third of Viṣṇu's descents similarly illustrates a creation myth out of the cosmic waters. While the Matsya *avatāra* establishes the existence of mankind on earth and the Kūrma *avatāra* guarantees the firmness of its support, the boar incarnation shows Viṣṇu as the savior who lifted the earth from the depth of the ocean waters to the light of the sun. In the man-lion incarnation, Viṣṇu assumes this combined shape, bursting out of a pillar in the demon king's palace in order to disembowel this fiend who had questioned Viṣṇu's omnipresence. The fifth incarnation, the dwarf, gained from the demon king Bali a foothold on which to stand and took the three-fold stride by which he traversed the cosmos (see figure 2). The four following *avatāras* appeared in the shape of man as hero or god. The images of Kṛṣṇa as the child of superhuman powers (Balakṛṣṇa) and as flute-playing young god have their own visual iconography, particularly in metalwork. Two forms of Kṛṣṇa are unlike other images of Hindu gods. The one is Jagannātha, "lord of the world," whose center of worship is in Purī, Orissa; the other is Śrī Nāthjī, whose center of worship is Nāthadvāra in Mewar, Rajasthan. Both these images are roughly hewn and painted wooden chunks only remotely anthropomorphic. From the sixteenth century on, Kṛṣṇa appears in miniature paintings incomparably more frequently than any other Hindu god. In front of Viṣṇu temples, the image in the round of Viṣṇu's partly anthropomorphic vehicle, the bird Garuḍa, is supported by a high pillar. [*See* Viṣṇu *and* Avatāra.]

Devī. The Great Goddess, Devī, represents the creative principle worshiped as female. She is Śakti, the all-pervading energy, the power to be, the power of causation, cognition, will, and experience. She is the power of all the gods; she wields all their weapons in her main manifestations or images. She is the origin of the world, the conscious plan of creation, the mother; she is the goddess Knowledge. Her main image is that of Durgā in the act of beheading the buffalo demon, the mightiest of the demons whom she defeats. This huge, dark, demonic animal, an embodiment of stupidity, is her archenemy. In her image as killer of the buffalo demon, the young and lovely goddess is accompanied by her mount, the lion (see figure 3).

In certain traditions the buffalo demon while still in human shape adored the goddess. In some of the sculptures of the goddess as slayer of the demon—his body that of a man, his head that of a buffalo—he ecstatically surrenders to her as she slays him. When not depicted in action but standing straight in hieratic stance, the goddess is supported by a lotus or a buffalo head.

FIGURE 3. *Durgā Killing the Buffalo Demon.* Stone sculpture, Bhubaneswar, Orissa. The main image of the Goddess, Devī, is that of Durgā manifesting her power as a conqueror of demons. She is accompanied here by her mount, the lion.

The Great Goddess has many forms. Like Śiva she has three eyes; like Viṣṇu, in her form as Yoganidrā, "yoga slumber," she is represented lying, an embodiment of Viṣṇu's slumber. Yoganidrā is most beautiful and has only two arms, whereas the Goddess displays from four to sixteen arms in her other images. Although the lion is the *vāhana* or vehicle of the Great Goddess, as Rambhā she rides an elephant; as Gaurī, the White Goddess—the aspect under which the gods contemplate her—she stands on an alligator. In her horrific, emaciated aspects, the owl is her vehicle. Like Śiva, the Goddess is seen in divine beauty or in a shape of horror as Kālī or Cāmuṇḍā.

When worshiped in her own image, the Goddess is the center of the composition, but as the *śakti* or creative power of a god she is figured by his side, smaller in stature, and with only two arms, for she is the god's consort. Pārvatī is Śiva's consort, whereas Bhūdevī and Śrīdevī—the goddess Earth (Bhū) whom Viṣṇu rescued in his boar incarnation, and the goddess Splendor (Śrī)—are shown by Viṣṇu's side.

If the images of these gods are cast in bronze, they are modeled in the round. These are processional images, meant to be visible from all sides, in contrast to the stone images in the innermost sanctuary or on the temple walls, where they confront the devotee as he or she approaches them. However, where the image of Devī is represented as the supreme goddess, she may be flanked or surrounded by smaller figures of gods and demons who play a role in the particular myth represented. Attendant divinities may further enrich the scene.

Devī is not only represented in her own right as supreme goddess or as the consort of one of the main gods, she is also embodied as a group, particularly that of the "Seven Mothers" (*saptamātṛkās*) where, as Mother Goddess, she is shown as the *śakti* of seven gods, including Brahmā, Viṣṇu, and Śiva. Brahmā, although the creator in ancient times, is rarely figured in the present-day Hindu pantheon and has but few temples of his own. In South India his image figures on the south wall of a Viṣṇu temple opposite that of Śiva Dakṣiṇāmūrti on the north wall.

Brahmā's consort Sarasvatī, the goddess of knowledge and speech, is worshiped in her own image to this day. The image of the "Seven Mothers" arrayed in one row are worshiped in their own sanctuary. Another assemblage of "group goddesses," though of lower hierarchical standing, is worshiped in hypaethral temples, which allow their total of sixty-four images to be worshiped separately. The iconography of the Goddess has its counterpoint in the (originally imageless) diagrams. Both these instruments of contemplation of the goddess—her image and the geometrical diagram—are man-made. The Goddess is also worshiped as a stone in its natural shape.

Stones in themselves are sacred. A *śālagrāma* stone, a fossilized ammonite embedded in dark stone, represents Viṣṇu, with the spiral of the fossil structure evoking Viṣṇu's wheel. The *śālagrāma* is worshiped in domestic rituals. Similarly another stone, the *bāṇaliṅga*, washed by the water of the river where it is found into *liṅga* shape, is sacred to Śiva. Among *liṅgas*, which can be made of any material, whether clay or precious stone, the *svayambhū liṅga*, a natural outcrop of rock like a menhir, has special sanctity.

Today most of the preserved images are made of stone or metal. The few paintings that have survived over the last four centuries are in watercolor on paper, as a rule small in size, and narrative rather than iconic. To this day the gods are painted in their iconographic identity on walls of houses and on portable paper scrolls. Color, according to ancient texts, was essential to the image: its use was primarily symbolic and expressive of the nature of the respective deities. However, different colors in different texts are prescribed for the same deity. [*See* Goddess Worship, *article on* The Hindu Goddess, *and* Durgā Hinduism.]

Gaṇeśa. Gaṇapati or Gaṇeśa, the lord of hosts and god of wisdom, who is also called Vighneśvara ("the lord presiding over obstacles"), has an obese human body topped by the head of an elephant. Worshiped throughout Hinduism, he is invoked at the beginning of any enterprise, for his is the power to remove obstacles but also to place them in the way of success. His shape is a symbol charged with meaning on many levels. His huge belly, containing the world, is surmounted by his elephant head, signifying the world beyond, the metaphysical reality. The head is maimed; it has only one tusk, thus signifying the power of the number one, whence all numbers have their beginning. Every part of Gaṇeśa's shape is a conglomerate symbol, and each is accounted for by more than one myth. According to one tradition, the dichotomy of Gaṇeśa's body resulted from Śiva's beheading of Vighneśvara, Pārvatī's son, in a fit of anger. Śiva then ordered the gods to replace Vighneśvara's head with that of the first living being they met. This was an elephant; they cut off its head and put it on Vighneśvara's body. According to another source, Gaṇeśa was the child Kṛṣṇa whose head was severed by Śani (Saturn) and replaced by that of the son of Airāvata, elephant of the god Indra.

In the *Ṛgveda* (2.23.1) Gaṇapati is a name of Bṛhaspati, the lord of prayer, the lord of hosts. From the fifth century CE, images of Gaṇeśa are numerous. An elephant-headed deity is shown on an Indo-Greek coin of the mid-first century CE. [*See* Gaṇeśa.] Today, Gaṇeśa is invoked at the beginning of all literary compositions and all undertakings. Every village, every house has an image of Gaṇeśa, seated, standing, or dancing—like Śiva. Some of his images have a third eye. In one of his (generally) four hands he holds the broken-off tusk. His vehicle is the mouse or the lion. In his form as Heramba, Gaṇapati has five heads; as Ucchiṣṭa Gaṇeśa, he is accompanied by a young goddess. He is red, yellow, or white in different varieties of his image.

[*See also* Maṇḍalas, *article on* Hindu Maṇḍalas, *and* Temple, *article on* Hindu Temples.]

BIBLIOGRAPHY

Banerjea, Jitendra. *The Development of Hindu Iconography.* 2d ed. Calcutta, 1956. A handbook particularly dealing with the beginnings and historical typology of Hindu images.

Coomaraswamy, Ananda K. *The Dance of Shiva* (1918). Rev. ed.

New York, 1957. Interpretation of an iconographic theme based on original sources.
Courtright, Paul B. *Gaṇeśa.* New York, 1985. The first comprehensive and insightful presentation of Gaṇeśa.
Eck, Diana L. *Banaras, City of Light.* New York, 1982. A topical study in depth, relating the icon to its setting.
Gopinatha Rao, T. A. *Elements of Hindu Iconography* (1914–1916). 2 vols. in 4. 2d ed. New York, 1968. The standard survey of Hindu iconography.
Kosambi, D. D. *Myth and Reality.* Bombay, 1962. An exposition of the roots of iconic and aniconic traditions.
Kramrisch, Stella. *The Hindu Temple* (1946). Reprint, Delhi, 1976. An exposition of architectural form in relation to the iconography of its images.
O'Flaherty, Wendy Doniger. *The Origins of Evil in Hindu Mythology.* Berkeley, 1976. A study in depth of the interrelation of gods and demons in Hindu mythology.
Shah, Priyabala, ed. *Viṣṇudharmottara Purāṇa.* 2 vols. Gaekwad's Oriental Studies, vols. 130 and 137. Baroda, 1958 and 1961. The most complete and ancient treatise (c. eighth century CE) of Hindu iconography.
Shulman, David D. *Tamil Temple Myths.* Princeton, 1980. An indispensable background study for South Indian iconography.
Sivaramamurti, Calambur. *The Art of India.* New York, 1977. The best-illustrated and best-documented presentation of Indian sculpture.
Zimmer, Heinrich. *Artistic Form and Yoga in the Sacred Images of India.* Translated and edited by Gerald Chapple and James B. Lawson. Princeton, 1984. A clarification of the function and relation of iconic, sculptural form and abstract, linear diagram.

STELLA KRAMRISCH

Buddhist Iconography

In the course of its development and diffusion, Buddhism has expressed itself through an abundance of visual forms, but in order to understand them, one has to take into account the profound evolution of Buddhist doctrine over time and space, notably the changes brought into the fundamental doctrines of early Hīnayāna ("lesser vehicle") Buddhism by the Mahāyāna ("great vehicle").

Śākyamuni Buddha. The fundamental image around which the cult has developed is that of its founder, the Buddha, represented in the essential moments of his religious career. These moments are often evoked solely through the language of gestures (*mudrās*) and postures (*āsanas*) devoid of all context. [*See* Mudrā.] Nonetheless, his image did not figure at all in the earliest, anecdotal presentations preserved on bas-reliefs. Because the Buddha as a personality was deemed to have passed outside of history altogether at his *parinirvāṇa*, or death, his presence was instead symbolized by such motifs as the rich turban of the prince Siddhārtha, the throne of the

FIGURE 1. *The Wheel of the Law.* One of the most ancient and ubiquitous of Buddhist motifs.

Blessed One, his footprints marked with the Wheel of the Law (see figure 1), the begging bowl *(pātra)*, or the Bodhi Tree (the Enlightenment). Similarly, the First Sermon among the monks in Banaras is evoked by the *triratna* ("three jewels," a three-pointed motif representing the Buddha, his Law, and his Community) surmounted by the Wheel (symbolizing by its movement the transmission of the dogma) and surrounded by deer. Most important of all, the *parinirvāṇa* of the Buddha is recalled by the stupa, the domical shrine believed to have contained the precious relics of the Master. Together with the image of the Buddha, the stupa, as an actual monument or an iconic representation (and through such transformations as the *dāgoba*, or step-pagoda, and the Tibetan *chorchen;* see figure 2) remains at the center of the cult and its visual imagery. [*See* Stupa Worship.]

From the outset of Indian Buddhist art (third–second centuries BCE), the legendary accounts of the Buddha's previous incarnations and earthly life *(jātaka* and *avadāna)* are reflected in sanctuary paintings and bas-reliefs representing the palace life of the young prince

FIGURE 2. *Stupa and Pagoda.* Figure shows (left to right) the development of the Indian stupa to the Chinese pagoda. The basic form develops into the more complex, multilayered stupa, which is further elaborated, in China, to become the multistoried pagoda. The drawing at far right depicts the northern Chinese pagoda design with wood and tiled roofs.

Siddhārtha. These depict scenes from the moment of his miraculous conception as a white elephant visiting Queen Māyā (his mother) to the time of his "Great Departure" from the life of a householder, mounted on his horse, Kaṇṭhaka. As the Buddha came to assume a supernatural aspect, the figure of the Great Departure sometimes appeared as an astral figure (clearly solar, as seen on the central medallion of the ancient sanctuary cupolas). Bedecked with princely garments, jewels, and an elaborate headdress, the future Buddha is often difficult to distinguish from other *bodhisattvas*, such as Maitreya.

The representation of the Buddha that rapidly became universal probably originated in Gandhāra or Mathurā between the first century BCE and the first century CE; it shows the monk wearing the robe and mantle of the *bhikṣu* (mendicant), with his head encircled by a nimbus, probably the result of Hellenistic influences. Among the thirty-two auspicious marks (*lakṣaṇas*) that designate a Buddha, the most characteristic ones are the *ūrṇā*, the circular tuft of hair on his forehead; the *uṣṇiṣa*, the bump in his skull that looks like a bun of hair; the distended earlobes; the wrinkles on his neck; his webbed fingers; and his gold skin coloring. His posture, the serenity of his features, and his half-closed eyes suggest the depth of his meditation and detachment from the exterior world. This body language rapidly became conventionalized (see figure 3), although, as seen especially in the *maṇḍalas* of the Esoteric (Vajrayāna) tradition in Tibet and East Asia, it hardly remained free of complexity.

FIGURE 3. *Seated Buddha.* This fifth-century sculpture from Sarnath, India, displays many of the iconographic elements that were carried through different regional traditions: the robe of the *bhikṣu;* the Lotus Position; the *mudrā*, here, the Dharmacakra Mudrā ("turning the wheel of the law," i.e., preaching); and the *laksana* ("auspicious marks"), including the *uṣṇiṣa*, the elongated earlobes, and the wrinkles in the neck.

Two of the major events following the Great Departure are the Buddha's Enlightenment under the Bodhi Tree and his First Sermon among the monks in the Deer Park in Banaras. But the ultimate evocation of his earthly life is the symbology of the *parinirvāṇa*, where the Master is shown lying on his right side upon a cushion in the presence of the Malla princes, the *bodhisattva* Vajrapāṇi, and his own disciples, all of whom are in mourning.

By the fifth century CE, representations of the Blessed One, standing, seated, or reclining as described above, attained colossal dimensions in a variety of media: chiseled in cliffs or modeled in clay, cut into stone or cast in bronze. From then on he is portrayed as monarch of the world *(cakravartin)*, with the "seven jewels" as his attributes (the attendant, the general, the beautiful woman, the horse, the elephant, the wheel, and the pearl or gem). This concept had been expressed earlier with images of the Buddha seated majestically on a lion throne, sometimes in the European fashion or wearing his royal attributes (crown, jewels, cloak with three points) over his monastic dress. Most often, however, he is shown seated in the Indian manner, his legs crossed more or less tightly, either on a "grass throne" (during the attack of Māra, the Evil One, immediately preceding his Englightenment) or on a stepped throne possibly symbolizing Mount Meru, axis of the world. Alluding to the Great Miracle of Śrāvastī, when the Buddha multiplied his presence in the form of little Buddhas seated on lotuses, he also appears, seated or standing, on a lotus base.

The Transcendent Buddha. With the Mahāyāna, the supernatural vision heralded in the Great Miracle of Śrāvastī culminates in the myriad Buddhas of the universe, which began to appear in the third and fourth centuries CE and were subsequently painted over and over on sanctuary walls and sculpted or modeled on temples and stupas. This concept of the Buddha's omnipresence is often combined with that of the lotus as cosmic image: each lotus petal constitutes a world, and each torus is occupied by one of the myriad Buddhas, evoking the universe past, present, and future.

The emphasis on this supernatural power manifested

itself concretely in both painting and sculpture with images of the Buddha Vairocana, monarch of the universe. These transcendent Buddhas, their bodies covered with images of Mount Meru, the stupa, the sun and moon, aquatic subjects and the lotus, the *vajra* (thunderbolt), wheel, *triratna,* and other signs and symbols, are encountered very early along the path of penetration of the Great Vehicle into China. The doctrine, once evolved, expresses itself in even more elaborate forms in Southeast Asia's mountain temples (Borobudur, Java) and in the temples of faces (Bayon of Angkor Thom, Cambodia). The human character of the Buddha, so evident in the older works, is totally overshadowed in the concept of his three bodies *(trikāya):* the formless body of the Law (*dharmakāya,* which is visually untranslatable); the pleasure body *(saṃbhogakāya),* or body of glory (supraworldly); the transformation, or human, body (*nirmāṇakāya;* i.e., the historical Buddha). From this point on, his retinue *(parivāra)* is enriched with a whole Buddhist pantheon. The eminent helping figures of this new religion of salvation, the Great Vehicle, are added to the monks, the holy patriarchs, the anonymous followers, and the princely donors: first the *bodhisattvas*, personalized as the Buddhas of the future, then the five Jinas ("victors") and their descendants, each one evoking an attitude of Śākyamuni Buddha.

Monks and Patriarchs. The monks are often dressed in the tattered monastic robes prescribed by the Buddha himself. The robe is attributed to certain of the ten disciples of Śākyamuni, among whom the youngest, Ānanda, and the oldest, Kāsyapa, often appear as acolytes in representations of the historical Buddha. The *arhat* (Chin., *lo-han*) are ascetics who have attained the highest degree of sanctification possible in Hīnayāna soteriology and are the designated protectors of the Law; they are portrayed as old men with pronounced features. Among the "eminent monks" and patriarchs, two groups are distinguished by their wild appearance, very close to that of the sorcerers: the five Masters of the Law as well as the *mahāsiddhas* ("perfected ones"), eighty-four of whom, according to Tibetan tradition, haunt the cemeteries where the adepts of Tantrism complacently thrive. The *bla-ma* (lama, teacher in the Tibetan tradition), by contrast, is depicted serenely.

Bodhisattvas and Minor Deities. The *bodhisattva* Maitreya has played a very significant role since the beginning of the Christian era, and for this reason he was rapidly designated in sculpture by specific attributes and often by his posture as well. Like the other *bodhisattvas* he wears the lavish garb of the Indian princes but frequently carries the water vase of the brahmans *(kamaṇḍalu)* in his left hand, while in his right hand he either holds the long-stemmed blue lotus or makes the gesture of instruction *(vitarka);* sometimes he carries a miniature stupa in his tiara and can be seated in European fashion, with his legs crossed in front of his chair. In painted sanctuary decoration he is often depicted enthroned in the Tuṣita Heaven, from which he must descend in order to reincarnate himself as Śākyamuni's successor.

The image of Avalokiteśvara (Kuan-yin in China, Kannon in Japan) also emerges early on, although his powers and therefore his iconography gain more precision with the texts of the Mahāyāna. At first he can be confused with Maitreya since they both carry a flask containing the elixir of life *(amṛtakalaśa)* and a lotus (see figure 4). His relationship with Amitābha Buddha is indicated by the presence of a little meditating Buddha in his tiara; as an assistant to Amitābha, he appears in the triad with the *bodhisattva* Mahāsthāmaprāpta and is included in the great painted scenes of the paradise of Amitābha. Avalokiteśvara is shown with little

FIGURE 4. *Avalokiteśvara.* Ink drawing on paper, Tunhuang, Kansu Province, China, tenth century CE. The *bodhisattva* is portrayed holding the flask and the willow branch, symbols of healing.

Buddhas of transformation in his aureole. According to the *Saddharmapuṇḍarīka Sūtra* he is the protector one invokes against the ten perils (snakes, ferocious beasts, robbers, poisons, storms, and so forth); these are often depicted with him on bas-reliefs and paintings.

Of the many forms he can take in both painting and sculpture, some, influenced by the Indian pantheon, are very particular: that of Avalokiteśvara "who faces all" with his eleven heads arranged in a pyramid above his shoulders in order to extend his protection to all directions (the towers of faces in Bayon at Angkor Thom convey the same concept). Reflecting another aspect of his multiple powers as Lord of the World (Lokeśvara), he is portrayed with four, six, or eight arms indicating a *mudrā*. The same aspect is summoned by Kuan-yin "of a thousand hands and a thousand eyes" that encircle him in an aureole; each hand, with an eye marked on the palm, holds a significant attribute: the stupa, rosary, jewel, flask, lotus, and so forth. In Far Eastern art, Kuan-yin comes to assume female forms.

With the diffusion of the Mahāyāna texts, other personalities of the *bodhisattvas* of salvation also appear as statues, on bas-reliefs, or in paintings decorating constructed and rock-cut sanctuaries, as well as in the illustrations of votive tablets and manuscripts. Mañjuśrī and Samantabhadra can often be identified by the animals they ride, generally the golden lion and the white elephant respectively. To the youthful Mañjuśrī one can attribute the book, as to the master of the word, with the gesture of instruction. Devotion to the *bodhisattva* Kṣitigarbha has widely diffused his image in art: as a monk, standing or seated with shawl, ringing stick (*khakkhara*), and pilgrims' bowl, he is enthroned, usually in the midst of the kings of the hells, as master of the six paths of rebirth.

Other Celestial Attendants. Vajrapāṇi, the faithful companion of the Blessed One, was present in all the scenes of the Buddhist legends of the Lesser Vehicle from the very beginnings of the religion. He rapidly abandoned the aspect of the Herculean athlete (the Gandhāra reliefs), however, for the costume and armor of a knight carrying the thunderbolt (*vajra;* see figure 5), the symbol of his protective power, received from Indra. The esoteric forms of Tantric Buddhism were to give Vajrapāṇi a terrifying aspect that multiplied itself into many ferocious *vajradhāras*. Alongside the Blessed One and presiding more or less visibly over his destiny are the titular divinities of Hinduism, Indra and Brahmā, one wearing his characteristic diadem, the other with his bun in a tiara. Later, with the evolution of the Mahāyāna, Śiva was to join them in his terrible aspect as Maheśvara.

The guardian-kings of the four directions (*lokapālas*) appear quite early in the entourage of the Master, in the episode of the offering of the four bowls after the Awakening. In the older paintings and reliefs they are often present up to the *parinirvāṇa,* shown in a princely aspect, with aureoles like the other figures of the Buddhist pantheon; soon, however, they appear as warriors wearing armor. The best known among them is Vaiśravana, guardian of the North and master of a host of animal-headed *yakṣas*. Dhṛtarāṣṭra, guardian of the East, leads the *gandharvas*, celestial musicians like the *kinnaras*, half-human, half-bird. In the same fashion Vrūpākṣa (West) and Virūḍakha (South) reign over the graceful flying Apsarasas and over the dwarf *gaṇas*, all of them celestial beings from Hinduism. They are often depicted as mounts or pedestals under the feet of the guardian-kings. The guardians of the doors (*dvārapālas*) were to retain their athletic physiques but rapidly took on the terrifying aspect commonly adopted by protective divinities to vanquish and convince, which was further accentuated by Tantrism. Also figuring among the supernatural spirits and guardians are the ten *devarājas*, or celestial kings, and the guardians of the Law, the most famous of which is probably Mahākāla, the "big black," who is shown in his monstrous Tibetan-Nepalese form with his lips curled back to show his menacing teeth.

Prajñā and Tārā, female counterparts of these divinities, soon made their appearance, and their powers were rapidly defined. Their complementary energies can often be seen in the representation of divine couples embracing on paintings and bas-reliefs, especially in

FIGURE 5. *Vajra.* This five-pronged *vajra* (Jpn., *kongōsho*) is one of several ritual objects (including one- and three-pronged *vajras* and a *ghanta,* or bell) employed in Japanese Tantrism. The five-pronged *vajra* represents the Five Wisdoms and the Five Buddhas.

Nepal and Tibet. Among the protective divinities, Dākiṇī and other tutelary goddesses with fierce aspects can be found on portable paintings (*tankas*); the terrifying Lha-mo appears on Tibetan bronzes, where she wears a necklace of skulls and rides on a bloody human corpse.

The ancient Hindu myth of the bird Garuḍa fighting the serpents to steal their soma, the elixir of life, has been adopted along with other Buddhist myths about hybrid beings as a theme of rebirth: Garuḍa can be an eagle, a falcon, a bird with a human head, or a man with a falcon's beak. The *haṃsa* (wild goose or duck) can evoke for the adept an intermediary state of the transmigrating soul. The Nāgarāja (king of the *nāgas*, or water serpents) in his princely aspect, his head capped or encircled by a hood of serpents, is found in all of the representations and legends dealing with the domain of the waters; in the Far East, the serpents become dragons.

Evocations of the Supernatural. As in the ancient religions, the representation of water, symbol of fertility, occupies an important place in iconography. Water bears the most expressive image of this fertility, the lotus, which appears everywhere, painted and sculpted on domes, walls, cupolas, and ceilings, to the point that it expresses the innumerable worlds of the cosmos. The lotus, also a symbol of purity, becomes the bearer of the most eminent figures of Buddhism as well as of the little reborn souls *(putti)* of the *bodhisattvas* of the Pure Lands. [*See* Lotus.]

It is through the theme of the waters peopled with aquatic figures, and through those of the flying musician spirits, that the artists have attempted to suggest supernatural visions and certain cosmic concepts: life-giving earth and elaborate heavens, which are, following sophisticated mental constructions, arranged in superimposed worlds. Mount Meru depicted as a conical pillar, as a stepped pyramid, or as an hourglass tied at the center with *nāgas*, constitutes the expressive symbol of the axis of the world plunging into the primordial ocean. Even the plan of the stupa, based on the square (earth) and the circle (heaven), with its structure combining the cube and the dome, develops into more and more elaborate buildings. Nonetheless, they always follow the rules inspired by the symbolism of forms and subject to an axial principle, the cosmic axis. This principle commands the elevation of multistory pagodas and is even found in the rock-cut sanctuaries, where the cult image of the Buddha is placed against the pillar of the encircling hall. In the decoration, the flying figures of the Apsarasas and the celestial musicians (*gandharvas*, *kinnaras*, or *kinnaris*) transpose these scenes to a supraterrestrial realm.

The evolution of the historical Buddha toward transcendence, already visualized in the multiplication of the Buddha images, was subsequently organized and systematized in the representation of the five transcendent Buddhas, the Tathāgatas or Jinas. Vairocana, the supreme Buddha, appears at the center, surrounded by the four cardinal points (this concept is found in the plan of certain sanctuaries or in *maṇḍalas*). Amitābha, the ruler of the West, was to achieve particular success in the Far East. His cult has produced numerous images, especially painted ones, where he is enthroned in the center of a multitude of *bodhisattvas* in his "Pure Land of the West," represented as a Chinese palace with terraces and a pond covered with lotuses, where the adepts hope to go through rebirth as pure souls. This paradise has its counterpart in the "Pure Land of the East" of the Buddha Bhaiṣajyaguru. The transcendental evocations are completed symmetrically with the representations of the Pure Land of Maitreya and that of Śākyamuni preaching on the Vulture's Peak.

The five Jinas appear together or separately on painted or sculpted images or on liturgical ornaments (the five-pointed tiara). Generally surrounded by attendants, they can be distinguished from one another by their specific ritual gestures, some of which are inherited from the *mudrā* tied to the principal events of the historical life of the Buddha Śakyamuni, and by the specific colors attributed to each of them and to their respective lineages.

In Esoteric Buddhism, the Jinas and the divinities can be represented by conventional symbols, such as the *vajra* in its diverse forms, by a Sanskrit formula, or even by a "seal" *(mudrā)*. The five Jinas each have ferocious aspects as counterparts, the "kings of sciences of great virtue" (*ming-wang* in Chinese, *myōo* in Japanese): surrounded by flames, they assume menacing postures, often have a number of faces with grimacing features, and brandish weapons and other symbolic attributes in their multiple hands.

With the widespread diffusion of these Esoteric forms, the more or less fantastic representations of the evolved Buddhist pantheon multiplied alongside the images of the serene Buddha. These fantastic forms appear not only as great cult images painted or sculpted in sanctuaries, on banners of silk or hemp in the Far East, and on Tibetan *tankas*, but also as small statues of painted wood, bronze, carved stone, or semiprecious materials (jade, amethyst, chalcedon, quartz) destined for offerings and domestic altars. Before the end of the first millennium CE, block prints contributed to the diffusion of the images of the most venerated figures in addition to manuscript illuminations. Even on the humblest of materials, such as the rough wood or modeled clay of Afghanistan or Central Asia, gold leaf is generally used along with paint, especially to cover the visible flesh of the Blessed One.

At this degree of complexity in the representations of Esoteric Buddhism, only the initiated could decipher the interpretation. For the majority of adepts, however, such doctrinal problems did not play a major role. The Chinese pilgrim I-ching reports that in India until the seventh century the institutional distinction between the adepts of the Hīnayāna and the Mahāyāna was not precise; the former recited the *sutras* of the Lesser Vehicle, the latter, those of the Great Vehicle, all in the same sanctuary. It is, however, through the concrete expressions of iconography as well as through the texts that we are able to trace the ascendancy and evolution of beliefs, beliefs that have been profoundly penetrated by the magic power of painted or sculpted images, for centuries objects of veneration for the faithful.

[*See also* Temple, *article on* Buddhist Temple Compounds.]

BIBLIOGRAPHY

Alfred Foucher's *L'art greco-bouddhique du Gandhāra*, 3 vols. (Paris, 1905–1923), remains one of the basic sources for the origins of Buddhist iconography. Foucher's *The Beginnings of Buddhist Art and Other Essays on Indian and Central Asian Archeology*, rev. ed. (Paris, 1917), may also be consulted. A different and complementary point of view is expressed in Ananda K. Coomaraswamy's *Elements Of Buddhist Iconography* (Cambridge, Mass., 1935). *The Image of the Buddha*, edited by David L. Snellgrove (Paris, 1978), is a collective work with broad coverage and abundant illustrations.

Étienne Lamotte's *Histoire du bouddhisme indien: Des origines à l'ère Śaka* (Louvain, 1958) provides a historical context for the religion. On the cosmology of the stupa from its origins to its most complex forms, see Paul Mus's *Barabudur* (1935), edited by Kees W. Bolle (New York, 1978). A good initiation into the Tantric pantheon is found in Marie-Thérèse Mallmann's *Introduction à l'iconographie du tântrisme bouddhique* (Paris, 1975).

For regional studies, see *Buddhism in Afghanistan and Central Asia*, by Simone Gaulier, Robert Jera-Bezard, and Monique Maillard, 2 vols. (Leiden, 1976), which analyzes the evolution of images along the Silk Route; E. Dale Saunders's *Mudrā: A Study of Symbolic Gestures in Japanese Buddhist Sculpture* (New York, 1960), which treats the symbolic language of ritual and iconography; and two museum catalogs: *Bannières et peintures de Touen-houang conservées au Musée Guimet*, 2 vols., compiled by Nicole Vandier-Nicholas et al. (Paris, 1974–1976), and Roderick Whitfield's *The Art of Central Asia: The Stein Collection in the British Museum*, vol. 1, *Paintings from Dunhuang*, 2 vols. (Tokyo, 1982–1983).

Simone Gaulier and Robert Jera-Bezard
Translated from French by Ina Baghdiantz

Taoist Iconography

The topic of Taoist iconography must be delimited arbitrarily, for there is still no definition of Taoism satisfactory to all scholars. Here it will be taken to mean a religion centered on attainment of a condition of immortal transcendency. It comes out of an ancient worldview, one that is not specifically Taoist, but more generally Chinese. Within this definition Taoist iconography symbolically expresses ideas concerning (1) the basic Chinese cosmology and mythology, (2) the Founders of the religion, (3) techniques of salvation, (4) those who have attained the goal, (5) immortality as a universal hope, and (6) Taoist concepts of, and relationships with, the numinous dimension and numinous beings.

Iconography and Worldview. The ancient worldview comprises both the impersonal forces of cosmology and the personalized beings of mythology. It long predates formation of any identifiable "Taoist religion" and is shared by the various schools of thought that developed in ancient China. Its most important cosmological agents are the Tao, *yin* and *yang*, and the Five Elemental Operative Qualities or Phases (*wu hsing*, often rendered as the Five Elements). The Tao, that ultimate reality underlying all, can only be represented by its derivative negative and positive forces or "Vital Breaths" *(ch'i)*, that is, *yin* and *yang* and their modes of being, the *wu hsing*. On the other hand, all creation may serve as tangible evidence of the Tao. In this sense landscapes, generally considered the most significant genre of Chinese painting during the past millennium, and landscape gardens, are representations of the Tao manifesting itself through the physical world. [*See also* Tao and Te *and* Yin-yang Wu-hsing.]

The most familiar symbol of the functioning of the Tao by means of its Vital Breaths is the ingenious design of the circle divided into two equal parts by a curving central line, one side of the circle representing the light of *yang* and the other side the darkness of *yin*, but with a bit of *yin* in the *yang* part and a bit of *yang* in the *yin* part (see figure 1). This expressive symbol is found on the liturgical robes of Taoists (a word we use to indicate professional clergy). The most sophisticated summary of the basic cosmology is the Diagram of the Ultimate *(t'ai-chi t'u)* devised by the eleventh-century philosopher Chou Tun-i, but it is not used iconographically.

The Eight Trigrams, each of which is formed from a combination of unbroken *(yang)* and broken *(yin)* lines, constitute another abstract symbol of common occurrence (see figure 1). These were in archaic times already invested with great significance as marks of the combi-

FIGURE 1. *Supreme Lord Lao-tzu.* Lao-tzu apotheosized, as shown in a popular print. He holds the cosmic diagram with the *yin* and *yang* symbol in the center surrounded by eight trigrams. The sun and moon are over his shoulders. Four peaches of immortality decorate his robe. His attendants carry, respectively, a palm-leaf fan of magical powers (particularly the ability to "resurrect the dead"—referring to the "liberation of the spirit of the corpse"—i.e., attainment of immortal transcendence) and a copy of the *Tao-te ching.* Stylized graphs for *shou,* or long life, decorate the skirt.

nations and permutations of those forces that produced the world and all beings in it. The classical exposition of the Trigrams appears in the ancient *Chou i* or *I ching* (Scripture of Change), a seminal source for Taoism as for all traditional thought. The Eight Trigrams are also embroidered on Taoist sacerdotal robes.

Mythological figures in human form include the traditionally accepted heroes of creation, cultural inventions such as cooking, housing, writing, and the calendar, and founders of the earliest polities, but while often encountered in Taoist iconography, they have little specifically Taoist meaning. In Taoism they have often been transmuted into deities of the numinous realm, about which we shall speak below.

Founders. One of these mythological figures has definitely retained his persona as a Taoist, along with his broader identification as a Chinese hero: Huang-ti, the Yellow Emperor. According to tradition he is the first ruler of a "Chinese empire." He is also given credit for invention of the calendar, musical scales, and the classical theories of medicine, and for other cultural innovations of basic importance. But to the Taoists he is especially the First Ancestor of Taoism, the man who first practiced Taoist techniques and attained immortal transcendency.

Two millennia later he was followed by the second Founder, Lao-tzu, supposedly a historical person somewhat senior to Master K'ung (Confucius) in the mid-sixth century BCE. After serving as archivist of the royal Chou court, he left China in despair over deteriorating political and social conditions. His legacy was the famous *Tao-te ching* (Scripture of the Tao and Its Virtues).

The third Founder is again only semihistorical: Chang Ling, or Chang Tao-ling, is presumed to have flourished around the end of the second century CE. He was not only a devoted practitioner of techniques for attaining immortal transcendency but also a charismatic faith healer whose followers established a sort of theocratic political entity in the far west of China (present-day Szechwan province). This cult was the first of many that, in the course of time, more or less coalesced to form "organized Taoism." Chang Tao-ling and his descendants developed an institutionalized religion known as T'ien-shih Tao (Way of the Celestial Masters), after the title (*t'ien-shih,* "celestial master") allegedly conferred on Chang Tao-ling by the deified Lao-tzu. The title, the texts, the rituals, and the prestige of the cult have come down to the present day in the tradition of the Perfect Unity, or Orthodox One (Cheng-i), Taoists.

All three of the Founders are represented in visual arts. Huang-ti, as an emperor, is depicted wearing a crown topped with a "mortar board" from the front and back of which hang the rows of jade tassels marking his exalted rank. Lao-tzu is most commonly shown as a snowy-bearded old gentleman riding an ox and holding a book, this memorializing the moment he rode off to the West after composing the *Tao-te ching* for the Chinese garrison commander at the frontier pass. Chang Tao-ling rides a tiger, or sits on a tiger throne, symbolizing the great spiritual powers attained during a lifetime of Taoist self-cultivation.

Techniques of Salvation. Salvation in Taoism is attained through various techniques—alchemical, yogic, dietary, sexual—and these are alluded to directly or indirectly in visual imagery. The caldron or mortar in which the elixir of immortality is prepared is a motif evoking the "alchemy of substances" *(wai-tan),* or preparation and ingestion of the elixir; the Chinese see a rabbit pounding the elixir in a mortar rather than a man in the moon. The most common dietary symbol is the *ling-chih* or "efficacious mushroom," a plant whose consumption produces longevity or even immortality. Aside from the preparation and consumption of substances, Taoists have always practiced what may be called "physiological alchemy" *(nei-tan),* in which the "caldron" is the body of the practitioner, and the ingredients of the elixir the elements of life: Spirit *(shen),* Generative Essence *(ching),* and, above all, Vital Breath *(ch'i).* Through elaborate techniques of yogic breath control and concentration the ingredients are mixed, the *ch'i* is circulated throughout the system, and (if properly performed) the process produces "a womb pregnant with an immortal transcendent" *(hsien-t'ai).* In illustrations, the astral body thus produced is depicted emerging from the top of the adept's head. [*See also* Alchemy, *article on* Chinese Alchemy.]

Whatever the technique employed, in the last analysis it is a matter of the proper intermingling of *yin* and *yang.* This is a common theme in the arts. It is most obviously expressed in sexual intercourse between man and woman (specific techniques of which constitute a form of Taoist cultivation), but the idea may be more obliquely shown in such motifs as dragons playing in the clouds, male and female *(yang* and *yin)* animals, and phallus- or vulva-shaped objects.

Those Who Have Attained. As a religion that has kept alive real hopes of immortality—or at least longevity—Taoism naturally has voluminous records of those who have attained the goal. The most common term for such adepts is *hsien,* a word whose graph suggests a person who has retired to the mountains—which was indeed the eremitic life recommended for the alchemist. As a type the *hsien* no doubt embodies common Chinese ideals: the genial eccentric in love with life, full of good humor and sagely wisdom, unhampered by the conventions of society, literally a free spirit. As a man he will likely be depicted in the ruddy good health of ageless age, dressed in flowing robes and a Taoist bonnet, leaning on a nobbly cane or holding the curving magic wand called *ru-i* (literally, "whatever you wish") that indicates his power to confer blessings on the deserving. If the *hsien* is a woman, she will on the contrary be young and beautiful, with an elegant, slim figure, typifying Chinese ideals of femininity. She will more than likely be floating in the air, demonstrating the form of locomotion favored by all *hsien.*

Out of the countless immortal transcendents in China's long past a few have naturally captured popular imagination. Outstanding among these is the group called the Eight Immortals, who are constantly depicted in all the arts as well as in literature. Among the eight, Lü Tung-pin, supposedly a historical figure of the eighth century, is foremost, as indicated by the fact that only he has his own temples in modern Taiwan. The story of his conversion to Taoism is a part of folklore, known to everyone as the "yellow millet dream"—in which Lü lived an entire lifetime of ups and downs during the few minutes it took his master-to-be to cook a pot of millet, thus awaking to the vanity of worldly ambitions. Lü Tung-pin and his companions communicate with their devotees through "spirit-writing" on the planchette.

Hsien may often be indicated simply by representation of their attributes. Thus, the Eight are denoted by sword, fan, flower basket, lotus, flute, gourd, castanets, and tube drum. The *ru-i* magic wand, the crooked cane, and the fly-whisk (a mark of spiritual attainment and authority taken over from Buddhism) are other common attributes of *hsien.* Perhaps the richest symbol is the gourd, which represents the alchemical caldron or its equivalent, the microcosm of the adept's own body, the universe, ancient notions of cosmogony, the dream of paradisiacal lands, and still other concepts. The paradisiacal lands, or abodes of *hsien,* are depicted very frequently. From ancient texts we learn that such places exist in the far western K'un-lun Mountains and in the oceanic islands off the eastern coast. The paradise in the West is the domain of Hsi Wang Mu, Royal Mother of the West, in whose garden grow the peaches of immortality. The islands in the Yellow Sea are called P'eng-lai, Fang-chang, and Ying-chou. Chinese literature and arts are full of images of these happy lands and their inhabitants. Among the earliest examples of the islands of the *hsien* are incense censers of the Han period (202 BCE–220 CE) that are cast in the shape of mountain peaks with tiny figures of *hsien* among them, and from whose insides curling smoke would have risen to represent clouds, that is, visible *ch'i.* Such was the powerful attraction of this image that it was even embroidered on official court robes. The mountain peak in the midst of ocean waves, home of the immortal transcendents, may be said to have remained the utopia wistfully hoped for by Chinese through the ages. [*See* Hsien.]

Immortality as a Universal Hope. Of course the goal of the Taoists is not their hope alone. Longevity, or even immortality, is one of the most conspicuously prayed-for desires of the Chinese. These desires are given visual form on the roofs of popular temples, where the ridge is lined with images of three star-gods, representing longevity, wealth and elite status, and many sons to carry on the family property and ancestral cult. The star-god of longevity, Shou Hsing, is of course shown as a *hsien.* His happy smile and rosy cheeks bespeak his healthy old age; his stout belly and bulging forehead indicate that he is an adept in cultivating his *ch'i,* and as he leans on his rough-hewn staff he holds a peach in his hand. The graph of longevity, *shou,* written in a hundred different ways, is a symbol in itself, omnipresent as a decoration on the products of art and craft (see figure 1). *Shou* is also the common euphemism for death, which, it is hoped, leads to immortality.

The decorative motifs of Chinese arts and crafts are in fact almost entirely expressive of the basic hopes, either by reference to their supposed characteristics, or by punning allusion (rebus). Longevity or immortality is symbolized by animals thought to be long-lived—crane, tortoise, deer, or stag—or plants that are similarly hardy—pine tree, bamboo, marigold (*wan-shou hua,* or "flower of immense longevity"), plum (*li,* the surname of Lao-tzu himself), and above all, the peach (see figure 1). In the sense that longevity is the underlying hope of Taoism, the religion may thus be said to have permeated the culture. Every Chinese understands the felicitous wish conveyed by pictures or vases or embroideries or jewelry bearing such motifs.

Taoism and the Numinous Dimension. The numinous realm of Taoism includes both macrocosm (the universe) and microcosm (the human body). Moreover, these two are essentially identical: the interior space corresponds with the exterior and is occupied by the same numinous beings.

This dichotomy that is at the same time no dichotomy is reflected in the praxis of the Taoist who simultaneously serves as community priest and seeks to cultivate personal immortality. By his possession and study of certain sacred texts and his ordination he receives appointment as an official in the spiritual realm, able to summon numinous beings, to have audience in the very Court of Heaven, and to promote the well-being of the community through negotiating pacts with the highest powers. Since the gods of popular religion are merely souls of the dead who have been promoted to high rank by the will of the people and the edicts of emperors, the Taoist has authority over them as well. As far as the interior realm is concerned, the numinous beings within the body that further the spontaneous workings of the Tao are in effect to be uninhibited by the adept so that his perfection of noninterference (*wu-wei*) will permit them to work for his salvation.

It is apparent then that most iconographic representations of spiritual beings fall under the category of popular religion rather than Taoism. It is perhaps the occasion of the rituals of the Chiao, the major liturgical performance of Taoists on behalf of the community, that most commonly shows Taoist concepts in anthropomorphic form. The Chiao serves nicely to set off Taoist icons from popular ones, insofar as during that great service the icons of the popular gods are relegated to a subsidiary, "guest" position within the sacred arena, while the Taoist officiants focus upon the "altar of the Three Pure Ones" (San Ch'ing), who represent different aspects of the Tao. Represented in iconic scrolls as venerable sages, they are the Heaven-Honored One of the Tao and Its Virtues (Tao-te T'ien-tsun), the Heaven-Honored One of the Primal Beginnings (Yüan-shih T'ien-tsun), and the Heaven-Honored One of the Spiritually Efficacious Treasure (Ling-pao T'ien-tsun). As hypostases of the Tao they may also be characterized as the "dharma-bodies" of Lao-tzu.

Hung at the same altar, in slightly subordinate positions to "stage left" and "stage right," are two other iconic portraits. On the left is that of the Supreme Emperor of Jadelike Augustness (Yü-huang Shang-ti), head of both the popular and the Taoist pantheons. On the offering table before him is the spirit tablet of the Lord of the Southern Bushel Constellation (Nan-tou-hsing Chün). The ensemble is called the Palace of the Jadelike Emperor (Yü-huang Kung). The portrait on the right is that of the Lord of the Northern Bushel Constellation (Pei-tou-hsing Chün), whose spirit tablet is on the offering table; the ensemble is called the Purple Forbidden Hall (Tzu-wei Tien). The Northern Bushel with its seven stars plays an important role in Taoist and shamanic ritual; the stars (depicted as dots connected by lines) are frequently seen on implements, banners, talismans, and so forth. Every person is born under the astrological influence of one of these stars. The Northern Pole Star itself has had special significance since most ancient times, representing (among other things) the ruler who remains quietly in his place while the accompanying stars revolve around him. In Taoist terms, this is the sovereign who rules simply by sitting with loose-flowing robes and folded hands—which is to say, who rules by nonaction or noninterference (*wu-wei*).

Subordinate to these last, but still connected with the altar of the Three Pure Ones, are two groups of iconic scrolls. At "stage left" are portrayed deities assigned to service at the Court of Heaven, deities responsible for the "aquatic country," and deities of the eastern and southern quadrants. At "stage right" are portraits of deities assigned to the "prefecture of Earth," the *yang* realm, and the northern and western quadrants.

Finally, Taoist iconography is associated with a special form of calligraphy, which originated in the belief that the Taoist has the power to command and control numinous beings. This calligraphy appears most commonly on charms or talismans *(fu)* that the Taoist issues to give spiritual protection from all sorts of harm. The efficacy attributed to such "official orders" written by Taoists is so impressive that lesser-ranked religious functionaries have long been accustomed to write them as well. In Taiwan one of the most common actions of a shaman is to cut himself with his sword and use the blood to confer even greater power upon a *fu*—something, however, that the Taoist, having authority over all the gods that work through shamans, need never stoop to do.

[*See also* Calligraphy, *article on* Chinese and Japanese Calligraphy, *and* Temple, *article on* Taoist Temple Compounds.]

BIBLIOGRAPHY

The problem with most treatments of Chinese symbolism and art is their failure to distinguish clearly between Taoism and popular religion. This limitation should be kept in mind when using a standard handbook such as C. A. S. Williams's *Encyclopedia of Chinese Symbolism and Art Motives* (New York, 1961), a reissue of *Outlines of Chinese Symbolism and Art Motives* (Shanghai, 1932). For the cosmological and religious ideas of Taoism that underlie its iconography, see Kristofer Schipper's *Le corps taoïste* (Paris, 1982). William Charles White's *Chinese Temple Frescoes: A Study of Three Wall-Paintings of the Thirteenth Century* (Toronto, 1940) shows unique examples of Taoist iconography from the Yüan period and gives extensive background and explanations of their meaning. Philip Rawson and Laszlo Legeza's *Tao: The Chinese Philosophy of Time and Change* (London, 1973) is a succinct but penetrating study of the *yin* and *yang* concept of Taoism; it is accompanied by many pertinent illustrations of art works that especially point up the sexual expressions of this concept. Legeza is also the author of *Tao Magic: The Chinese Art of the Occult* (New York, 1975), which treats the Taoist talismans *(fu)*, their religious symbolism, and their remarkable calligraphy.

Laurence G. Thompson

Jewish Iconography

Jewish iconography, whether actually represented in works of art or existing only as traditional imagery (and occasionally referred to in literature), was determined from the first by the biblical "prohibition of images." This prohibition, transmitted in the Bible in several versions, could be understood (1) as forbidding, in a religious context, all images, regardless of their subject matter (*Ex.* 20:4, *Dt.* 4:15–18), or (2) specifically forbidding the depiction of God and the ritual use of such a depiction as an idol (*Dt.* 27:15). While the first interpretation of the prohibition did not prevail (the Bible itself provides evidence of this in *1 Kgs.* 6:23–29, *Ez.* 8:5–12), the other was consistently implemented. Possibly the most striking feature of Jewish iconography throughout the ages is the systematic avoidance of any depiction of the figure of God. To a large extent this is also true for saintly personages: though hagiographical literature emerged in Judaism, it was not accompanied by any visual imagery of saints. From the beginning, then, Jewish religious iconography developed in marked contrast to the traditions predominant in the Christian West. Since the loss of political independence in 71 CE, Jewish imagery could not be formed within the framework of a state art and did not enjoy any official support for its symbols. As the art and imagery of a religious minority, however, it flourished in the Diaspora throughout the ages. The iconography that emerged within these limitations developed mainly in a few periods and thematic cycles.

FIGURE 1. *Wall Painting.* Dura Synagogue; Dura-Europos, mid-third century CE. This depiction of Ezekiel's vision of the resurrection of the dry bones (*Ez.* 37:1–14) is part of an extant cycle of fifty-eight figurative episodes in some twenty-eight panels.

Hellenism. The meeting between Judaism and the Greek world—a process that lasted from early Hellenism to late antiquity (roughly, second century BCE to fifth century CE)—resulted in a body of religious images. While the Mishnah and Talmud were being compiled (roughly second to sixth centuries CE) Jewish communities produced a large number of representations, which have been uncovered in Jewish remains (mainly synagogues and burial places) from Tunisia to Italy and eastward to the Euphrates; sites in Israel are particularly rich. [*See* Synagogue, *article on* Architectural Aspects.] Occasionally this imagery includes human figures, either in biblical scenes (see figure 1) or in pagan myths (frequently the image of Helios, the Greek sun god).

More often, however, these survivals show objects with definite ritual connotations (see figure 2). Most prominent are the seven-branched *menorah* (candelabrum), Aron ha-Qodesh (the Ark of the Covenant), *lulav* and *etrog* (palm branch and citron), and shofar (ceremonial animal horn). These objects (which reflect the crystallization of Jewish ritual) have no strict hierarchy, but the *menorah*, and the Ark of the Covenant, representing the law itself, are more important than the others. When both are shown together, they always occupy the central place. Besides such explicitly ritual objects, Jewish remains abound in artistic motifs, taken over from Hellenistic art, whose symbolic character is obscure. A good example is the vine, most likely derived from contemporary Dionysian imagery and often found in Jewish cemeteries. But whether in Jewish communities it carried the meaning of salvation that it had in the pagan world is a matter of dispute. Some modern scholars tend to see these motifs as "decoration" devoid of articulate symbolic meanings; others, especially Goodenough, attribute established symbolic meanings to them.

Middle Ages. In the European Middle Ages, especially between the thirteenth and fifteenth centuries, Jewish religious imagery developed further. The illumination of manuscripts is the central aesthetic medium of the period; of particular significance are the manuscripts produced in Spain, Italy, and Germany. All these manuscripts are of a ritual nature, the most important groups being the Haggadah for Passover and prayer books for the holidays, the *maḥzor*. The illuminations (and later, printed illustrations) represent many ritual utensils, but they also include, more often than in Jewish art of other periods and media, human figures, especially in biblical scenes (see figure 3). The iconographic repertoire is enlarged by mythical motifs, attesting to messianic beliefs. Among these motifs are the legendary beasts (such as the *shor ha-bar*, a kind of wild ox), on which the just will feast on the day of redemption; these are particularly prominent in manuscripts produced in Germany. The future Temple that, according to common belief, is to be built after the redemption, is another frequent mythical motif, especially in Spanish and German manuscripts; it is sometimes patterned after contemporary Christian models. Both the temple building and the ritual utensils (the

FIGURE 2. *Mosaic Floor.* Beit Alfa' Synagogue; Palestine, 518–527. At the top is the Ark of the Covenant (with eternal light above), lions, a seven-branched *menorah*, a *lulav*, an *etrog*, a shofar, and censers. In the middle appears a zodiac with the four seasons at the corners and the sun at the center. The bottom portion depicts the binding of Isaac, with the hand of God above and Abraham's servants and donkey at left.

FIGURE 3. *Illustrated Page from Printed Passover Haggadah.* Executed by Gershon Cohen; Prague, 1526–1527. Inset within the text is a picture of Elijah mounted on his donkey. The border contains representations of Judith carrying the head of Holofernes (left) and Samson with the gates of Gaza (right). Adam and Eve are above.

latter sometimes rendered on the opening folios of Bible manuscripts produced in Spain) may be taken as expressions of "the ardent hope and belief" to see the "restored Temple in the messianic future." In countries under Islamic rule, Jewish art readily adapted the aniconic attitude and the repertoire of decorative motifs common among the Muslims, although in literature, visual imagery continued to thrive in the form of metaphors and descriptions. [*See* Biblical Temple.]

Qabbalistic Symbolism. The qabbalistic tradition is a special field of iconographic creation. Qabbalistic literature abounds in visual metaphors, since the authors often tend to express (or to hide) their thoughts and mysteries in visual images and descriptions of supposed optical experiences. Since the beginnings of Jewish mysticism in late antiquity, a continuous tradition of visual symbols has persisted. Considerably enriched in the Middle Ages, and in the seventeenth century, this tradition remained unbroken up to, and including, Hasidic literature. The central image of qabbalistic symbolism is the Tree of Sefirot. The godhead is imagined as structured in ten spheres, each of them representing a "divine quality" (Heb., *sefirah*). The shape and place of the spheres, and the spatial relationships between them, are firmly established in the qabbalistic imagination. The overall pattern vaguely resembles a tree (hence the name), but the basic character of the image is abstract rather than figurative. Though the Tree of Sefirot has frequently been depicted (mainly in simple form, primarily in popular printed editions) and has exerted some influence on contemporary Jewish painters, the image is not primarily an artistic one; rather, it is still widely known from the literary sources.

Qabbalistic literature produced other visual symbols, among them the images of broken vessels, scattered sparks, Adam Qadmon (primordial man) as a figure of God, and so forth. Scholem has also shown that an elaborate color symbolism emerged in the qabbalistic literature. [*See* Qabbalah.] In modern civil societies, Jewish iconography is still in the process of formation and has not yet been properly studied.

BIBLIOGRAPHY

For the imagery of the Hebrew Bible (though not necessarily in art only) still useful is Maurice H. Farbridge's *Studies in Biblical and Semitic Symbolism* (1923; reprint, New York, 1970). Erwin R. Goodenough's *Jewish Symbols in the Greco-Roman Period,* 13 vols. (New York, 1953–1968), has a rich collection of photographs; the text is stimulating, albeit sometimes arguable. Mainly for the Middle Ages, see Jacob Leveen's *The Hebrew Bible in Art* (1944; reprint, New York, 1974). For early modern times, see *Beauty in Holiness: Studies in Jewish Customs and Ceremonial Art,* edited by Joseph Gutmann (New York, 1970), a catalog of Jewish artifacts from the Prague Museum shown at the Jewish Museum in New York.

Much can be learned from the discussion of single problems. See, for example, *The Temple of Solomon,* edited by Joseph Gutmann (Missoula, Mont., 1976). Another individual problem is discussed by Zofia Ameisenowa in "The Tree of Life in Jewish Ico-nography," *Journal of the Warburg and Courtauld Institutes* 2 (1938–1939): 326–345. Qabbalistic imagery is best discussed in Gershom Scholem's *Major Trends in Jewish Mysticism,* 3d rev. ed. (New York, 1954), esp. pp. 205–243. A highly interesting study of a particular subject in qabbalistic symbolism is Scholem's "Farben und ihre Symbolik in der jüdischen Überlieferung und Mystik," *Eranos Yearbook* 41 (1974): 1–49, *The Realms of Colour* (with English and French summaries).

MOSHE BARASCH

Christian Iconography

For the greater part of Christian history, the church's images have been drawn from its liturgical texts, scriptures, and pedagogy and rendered in the styles of the particular age and place the images served. In modern times, the sources for Christian iconography have expanded to include psychological, sociopolitical, and nontraditional elements.

The most distinctive characteristic of Christian iconography is its preoccupation with the person and role of Jesus Christ and his followers. The image of Christ as earthly founder and heavenly savior is central to the religion, especially insofar as the church defines itself as the body of Christ on earth. Thus the changing repertoire of images of Jesus and his followers reveals the nature of the religion in its many cultural and historical manifestations.

Early Christianity. Early Christian art surviving from the first half of the third century reflects the diversity of the Greco-Roman context from which it emerged. The earliest iconographic figures, borrowed directly from late antique conventions, were placed in new compositional and environmental settings on jewelry and other minor arts. For example, the common pose of the shepherd Endymion, a reclining male nude resting on one elbow with ankles crossed, was the type borrowed by artists to depict the Old Testament figure of Jonah resting under an arbor. For Christians, Jonah represented an image of resurrection and as such was used in funerary paintings and low-relief carvings on sarcophagi. Old Testament figures used in early Christian iconography appeared almost exclusively as typologies of Christ and his followers.

The earliest images of Christ were concerned with his person and role on earth and were borrowed from classical types of teaching figures, miracle workers, and heroes. Conventions for depicting divine attributes were missing, and there was no attempt at historical accuracy. Jesus did not look like an early first-century Jewish man from Palestine, but rather, like a Roman teacher-philosopher or like an Apollo-type mythic hero, such as the Christos-Helios figure in the necropolis of Saint Peter's Basilica in Rome. Frustration with the limitations of these typologies seems to have led to symbolic representations, such as the ubiquitous Christ as Good Shepherd (see figure 1) and the emblematic cross and wreath symbolizing the Trophy of Victory on sarcophagi. The Good Shepherd image was adapted from pagan culture, while the Trophy was the earliest representation of the cross (see figure 2).

Imperial Christianity. Following the adoption of Christianity as the state religion by the Roman emperor Constantine in the early fourth century, the figure of Christ as the imperial reigning Lord emerged. Jesus enthroned as the leader of the church, or in the heavens as an imperial judge, reflected the power the church had gained in that era (see figure 3). Within a hierarchically structured society, Jesus was depicted as a reigning philosopher-emperor who dispensed grace and judgment above all earthly power (see for instance the enthroned Christ in the apse mosaic of Santa Pudenziana in Rome).

Theological teachings and conciliar rulings are reflected in the Christian iconography that followed. From the fourth through the sixth century the figure

FIGURE 1. *The Good Shepherd.* From a fresco; Cyrene. An early symbolic representation of Christ.

FIGURE 2. *The Trophy of the Cross.* From a sarcophagus with scenes of the Passion; Rome, c. 350.

FIGURE 3. *Christ as Philosopher-Emperor.* From a terracotta relief showing a scene of the Last Judgment, interpreted according to Roman artistic conventions that depict the emperor distributing gold to the people.

of Jesus, elevated to a ruler over all, came to represent the power of the church over state and society. Christ seated in majesty above the heavens in the apse mosaic of the mausoleum of Santa Constanza in Rome (c. 350) or in the apse mosaic of the Church of San Vitale in Ravenna, Italy (c. 550), reflects christological formulations. Mary appears as an enthroned queen in the mosaics of Santa Maria Maggiore, Rome, after the Council of Ephesus in 431, which declared her *theotokos,* Mother of God. Two types of Christ figures occupy the twenty-six mosaic panels of the Christ cycle in San Apollinare Nuovo in Ravenna (c. 520). The figure in the scenes of Christ's ministry and miracles is an Apollo type—young, beardless, and dressed in royal purple—while the figure in the scenes of Christ's last days on earth is a philosopher type—older, bearded, also dressed in purple. These two figure types reflect Pope Leo the Great's late fifth-century theological treatise on the two natures of Christ.

Explicit representation of the crucifixion of Jesus is conspicuously absent from early Christian iconography prior to the fifth century. To the pagan world the mode of Jesus's death and resurrection was reserved for those who had been baptized. By the early fifth century, on rare occasions, crucifixion scenes appeared on liturgical objects and other church furnishings, such as the wooden doors of the Church of Santa Sabina in Rome. Nonetheless, the crucifixion is missing as an episode in the Christ cycle of the nave mosaics in the late fifth-century Church of San Apollinare Nuovo in Ravenna. Once the crucifixion came to be widely depicted, the preferred type in both East and West through the ninth century was a robed, open-eyed victorious Christ hanging on the cross, such as the ones in the illuminations of the Rabula Gospels from Mesopotamia (dated 586) or on the wall decorations of the Church of Santa Maria Antiqua in Rome.

From early Christian times to the ninth century, themes of rescue, delivery, and victory were dominant. Figures introduced as graced believers eventually became regal symbols of transcending powers. Mary, for instance, in third-century Roman fresco painting, was a Roman citizen; in the fourth century she acquired the dress of an aristocratic lady, and in the fifth, she was the queen of heaven. By the ninth century she was a reigning personification of the church.

Byzantine Art. Within the art of the Eastern Orthodox church, the image (as icon) relates to the liturgy in a manner distinguished from that of its Western counterparts. An icon can appear in a variety of media: painting, mosaic, sculpture, or illuminated manuscript. Its subject matter includes biblical figures, lives of the saints, scenes and narrative cycles that relate specifically to the liturgical calendar. To the present day, Byzantine tradition relies heavily on iconography in its worship. On the iconostasis, the screen extending across the front of the worship space, icons of Christ, Mary,

FIGURE 4. *Christ Pantocrator.* Painted icon of Christ as the Almighty. Saint Catherine Monastery; Sinai, sixth century.

and the saints appear as physical representations of the real spiritual presence of these figures for the worshipers, thereby creating the most integral and dynamic use of iconography in worship among all Christian traditions.

Over the centuries, rules for iconographers in the East were formalized, and copy books determined the style and subject matter of iconography. Paintings of the crucifixion in the Byzantine tradition, for example, often include the figures of Mary and Saint John at the foot of the cross in attitudes of grief, and the corpus traditionally hangs in a limp curve against the rigidity of the cross. This form then became popular in the West, especially in medieval Italy, and influenced painters such as Cimabue (d. 1302?).

Icons of the Madonna as the Blessed Virgin, Mother of God, emphasizing her role as mediator and eternal spirit of consolation and blessing, are numerous in Eastern iconography, but the single most imposing and austere composition in Byzantine iconography is the Pantocrator icon of Christ (see figure 4). The frontal presentation of this image emphasizes the presence of Christ as coeternal and coexistent with God the Father. Theologically, the Pantocrator gave visible form to the church's teachings on the consubstantiation of Father and Son, just as the Transfiguration icon visualized its teachings on the incarnation of God in Christ. The religious and social power of icons in society is reflected in the Iconoclastic Controversy of the eighth and ninth centuries, which produced a body of writings on the theology of iconography never again matched in Christian history. [*See* Icons; Iconoclasm; *and* Images, *article on* Veneration of Images.]

Middle Ages. While saints, heroes, and narrative episodes from scripture dominated medieval iconography, rich patterns of decoration and reference to everyday contemporary life worked their way into the art of the church in the West. Sculptural programs on church buildings and marginalia in illuminated manuscripts introduced genre scenes such as the symbols for the labors of the months and images for the seven liberal arts.

Christian iconography produced in the eighth and ninth centuries became regionally acculturated as its Roman origins disappeared from the face of indigenous expression. Elaborate decorated surfaces enclosed Christian symbols and figures, where, in the service of beautiful patterns, iconography became abstract and emblematic, especially on painted vellum in books (see figure 5).

During the ninth and tenth centuries a shift in emphasis from Christ the victor to Christ the victim took place in the thinking of the church; accordingly, images of the crucifixion with the victorious reigning Lord on

FIGURE 5. *The Mocking of Christ.* From the Book of Kells; County Meath, Ireland, c. 800.

the cross were replaced by those of the suffering human victim. The Gero Crucifix in the Cathedral of Cologne, Germany (c. 960), is one of the earliest representations of Christ as a suffering, dying figure (see figure 6). Under the influence of Anselm (d. 1109) the emphasis on the purpose of Christ's sacrifice shifted from the act necessary to defeat the devil to the act necessary to satisfy God on behalf of the world. Christian iconography of the crucifixion reflected that shift. Simultaneously, the role of Christ as a stern and eternal judge was emphasized in sculptural programs on the exterior of monastic churches such as those at Moissac and Autun in France. Images of Mary as mediator, together with the lives of the saints as models of virtue and fidelity, presented an array of images for instruction and contemplation.

By the twelfth century the decorative, narrative, and didactic role of the arts gave way to an explicitly sacramental function, one in which the imagery appeared in a context believed to be a model of the Kingdom of Heaven, the church building. Iconography in the church was believed capable of building a bridge that reached from the mundane world to the threshold of the divine spirit. Described in twelfth-century Christian literature as anagogical art, iconography served as an extension of the meaning of the mass. Visual images led believers from the material to the immaterial. (See *Abbott Suger, On the Abbey Church of St. Denis and Its Art Treasures,* ed. and trans. by Erwin Panofsky, 2d. ed., Princeton, 1979.) In a Gothic cathedral the sculptural programs

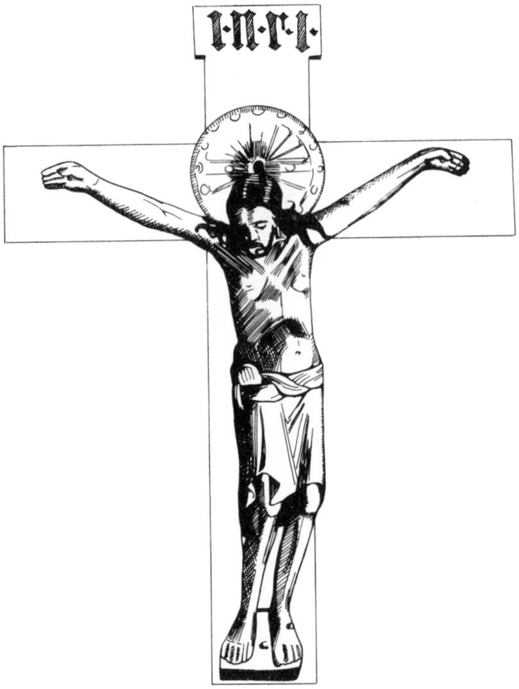

FIGURE 6. *Christ the Victim.* The Gero Crucifix, showing the suffering and dying Christ. Cologne Cathedral, c. 960.

(statue columns, tympana, archivolts, capitals, screens) and painted glass included figural compositions that narrated scripture, historical events, literature, and daily life, and all were considered to have an anagogical function.

In the Gothic era a proliferation of Old Testament imagery reflected renewed theological and political interests in manifestations of God working within and through royal hierarchies. During this period the suffering Christ of the Romanesque style became a more benign Savior. More types of Christ figures appear in the sculptural program and stained glass of Chartres Cathedral from the twelfth and thirteenth centuries than in the most elaborate Romanesque iconographic schemes. The quantity of figures was more important to the Gothic planners than to any of their predecessors, owing to the twelfth-century belief in the anagogical function of art.

In the late Gothic period, approximately the fourteenth and fifteenth centuries across northern Europe, the iconography of Christianity was populated with aesthetically appealing, elegant figures and decorative surfaces known in modern scholarship as the International Style. Attitudes, dress, and colors emphasized soft, flowing lines, gentle expressions, and rich textures.

Renaissance and Reformation. Christian iconography of the Renaissance in Italy acquired classically human characteristics as interest in Greco-Roman literature and art was revived. Jesus and his followers appeared in a human guise heretofore unknown. Scenes of biblical episodes and historically religious significance were given the illusion of three-dimensional settings that emphasized their reality in the natural world. Fifteenth-century Renaissance art reflected renewed interest in pagan mythology and Christian subject matter alike; therefore pagan iconography competed with traditional Christian iconography. Proportion, perspective, and human experience were new ingredients in the iconography of the Renaissance. For example, between 1495 and 1498 Leonardo da Vinci completed the *Last Supper* on the wall of the refectory of Santa Maria della Grazie in Milan, Italy. Leonardo's painting of the figures within a perspectival view of a room centered on Christ renders the moment as one of self-conscious and anxious questioning among the twelve apostles. In the twentieth century this painting has become the most popular and most often reproduced object of Christian iconography.

In an age in which "man was the measure of all things," the types of human figures ranged between idealized and ethereal images such as Raphael's *Madonna del Granduca* (1505) and the anxious and suffering figures in Michelangelo's Sistine Chapel *Last Judgment* (1536–1541). In the latter, terror lurks in the consciousness of the sinful, and the blessed rise passively to a severe and enigmatic Lord.

In northern Europe in the fifteenth and sixteenth centuries exaggerated realism in the treatment of subject matter and pre-Reformation currents of thought shaped Christian iconography. Matthias Grünewald's famous crucifixion panel in the Isenheim Altarpiece (1510–1512) presents Christ as a victim whose physical appearance betrays mutilation and disease and emphasizes divine participation on behalf of human suffering.

Specifically Reformation iconography illustrated biblical teaching by the reformers and liturgical practice. Lucas Cranach the Elder, a painter and a friend of Martin Luther, presented the subject matter of one of Luther's sermons in the figure of the crucified Christ in the Wittenberg Altarpiece of 1545, where Christ appears classically proportioned, alive, and without signs of maltreatment. Albrecht Dürer's engravings and woodcuts, known to a wide-ranging public, in some instances reflected contemporary religious thought as well. Whereas the old *Andachtsbild* (image for contemplation) tradition in medieval Christian iconography served prayer and meditation, many of Dürer's engravings engaged the intellect and gave focus to religious thought and theological propositions (see figure 7).

Reacting against "papist" imagery, Reformation iconoclasts destroyed vast amounts of iconographic imagery

FIGURE 7. *Theological Imagery.* Detail of woodcut of Christ on the Cross with angels by Albrecht Durer, c. 1524. Such images as this were printed and widely distributed.

and liturgical furnishings. For its part, the Roman Catholic church consciously appropriated iconographic programs in their churches in order to counteract the reforming movements. The Council of Trent, held in the middle of the sixteenth century, formulated instructions on the uses of iconography on behalf of the church. If the Reformation in some areas limited or forbade the use of images in the church, the Counter-Reformation encouraged a proliferation of them, thereby stimulating the expansion of the Baroque style of art. Eventually the church's use of Baroque forms extended beyond traditional sculptural programs and painted panels to wall surface decor, ceiling plaster, frescoes, elaboration of vestments and liturgical vessels, and extensive programmatic designs for altars and chapels. Dramatic highlighting, theatrical effects, and atmospheric illusions were used with iconographic programs to convince believers that the authentic home of spirituality and the true seat of the church's authority was in the Roman church.

Seventeenth and Eighteenth Centuries. Protestant iconography in the seventeenth century emphasized individual experience, and images of Jesus stressed his humanity and participation in the human condition. Rembrandt's portraits of Jesus, for example, show a thirty-year-old Jewish man; his *Deposition from the Cross* (1634) emphasized a Christ broken and dead. Roman Catholic iconography, by contrast, stressed the sacramental presence of a heroic Christ in programmatic sequences such as Peter Paul Rubens's early altarpieces and Nicholas Poussin's two series of paintings entitled *The Seven Sacraments* from the 1640s.

Eventually, architects created iconographic environments in church interiors that approximated a heavenly realm, decorated with ethereal figures of saints. As the German Rococo churches attest—see, for example, the Bavarian pilgrimage churches of Balthazar Neumann at Vierzehnheiligen and Dominikus Zimmermann at Wies—the setting for the sacrament was an integration of iconography and architecture that established a place separate from the natural world.

The New World. While the excesses of Rococo iconographic decoration engulfed worship spaces in eighteenth-century Europe, the New World seemed austere by contrast. Late seventeenth-century Christian iconography in North America consisted primarily of small, colorful panel paintings in the Southwest serving Spanish American communities (see figure 8) and of a con-

FIGURE 8. *Madonna.* Drawing after an American Indian hide-painting; New Mexico, c. 1675.

servative form of monochromatic portraiture on the East Coast. The art of the Southwest reflected a Spanish Roman Catholic culture with its indigenously adapted Baroque forms. By contrast, the arts introduced by the Puritans in New England were understated to the point of asceticism and iconoclasm. The elimination of imagery and decoration left a Christian iconography of simple abstract elements created by natural materials and excellent craftsmanship. Early American meetinghouse architecture symbolized a community's place of contact with itself and with God, specifically the word of God. Shaker communities, for instance, made a virtue of functional beauty and created a repertoire of objects that were revered for their clarity of form (see figure 9) and usefulness. Cemetery art in eighteenth-century New England relied on simple abstract symbols reduced to line drawings in stone, representing angels' heads or skulls with wings.

The earliest Christian imagery in North America as found in Western Hispanic communities and the Puritan centers in the East drew on separate European traditions and enjoyed no cross-fertilization. In the Southwest, images of Christ's crucifixion served Roman Catholic liturgical traditions public and private. In New England any iconography that suggested a Roman Catholic influence was considered "papist" and inappropriate. Not only were images of the crucifixion rare, but many churches refused to display the symbol of the cross in order to avoid appearing idolatrous.

FIGURE 9. *Tree of Life*. Symbolic emblem from a Shaker drawing; United States, nineteenth century.

By the late eighteenth century, the major trends in Christian iconography were competing with the secularization of Western culture and the impact of the Enlightenment. The American and French revolutions witnessed the destruction of institutional hierarchies and great Christian monuments associated with them. In France, for instance, the dismantling of the medieval monastery at Cluny and the destruction of royal imagery on Gothic churches at Nôtre-Dame and Saint-Denis in Paris demonstrated the negative power of Christian iconography that appeared to be royalist.

Nonetheless, during this period the private vision of artists dealing with Christian themes added an enigmatic dimension to religious iconography. For instance, William Blake's figures from the late eighteenth century combined traditional Christian subject matter with his own imaginative intuition (see figure 10). Whereas the human condition had always impinged upon and shaped the priorities of traditional Christian iconography, in the latter half of the eighteenth century personal insight shaped primary subject matter.

Nineteenth Century. Prior to the Enlightenment, the life of the Christian church, theologically and liturgically, influenced the images and forms of art directly: Christian iconography reflected the "mind" of the church. In the nineteenth century, Christian iconography served more private and artistically formal purposes. The recovery of historical styles in nineteenth-century art and architecture carried with it renewed interest in Christian iconographic themes. The English Pre-Raphaelites, for example, sought to recover the artistic values and qualities of the high Middle Ages. (See, for example, the Burne-Jones mosaic decoration for Saint Paul's Within-the-Walls in Rome, begun in 1881.) Generally speaking, nineteenth-century Christian iconography was created to celebrate a popular style, whereas in the past style had been shaped by its ecclesiastical settings and patrons.

Claims about the sublime as perceived in nature or in the depths of human consciousness created new aspects of religious iconography in the eighteenth and nineteenth centuries. After the Enlightenment, the canon of iconographic subject matter became open-ended. As the *formal* aspects of artistic production became foremost for artists who in previous centuries would have been concerned with narrative force and meaning, iconographic expression became more independent and individual. For instance, Vincent van Gogh (d. 1890), who in his early life had been a Christian missionary, created a personal iconography that eschewed for the most part any specifically Christian subject. Paul Gauguin's paintings of Old Testament subjects, the crucifixion, or religious imagery from life in Tahiti created a recogniz-

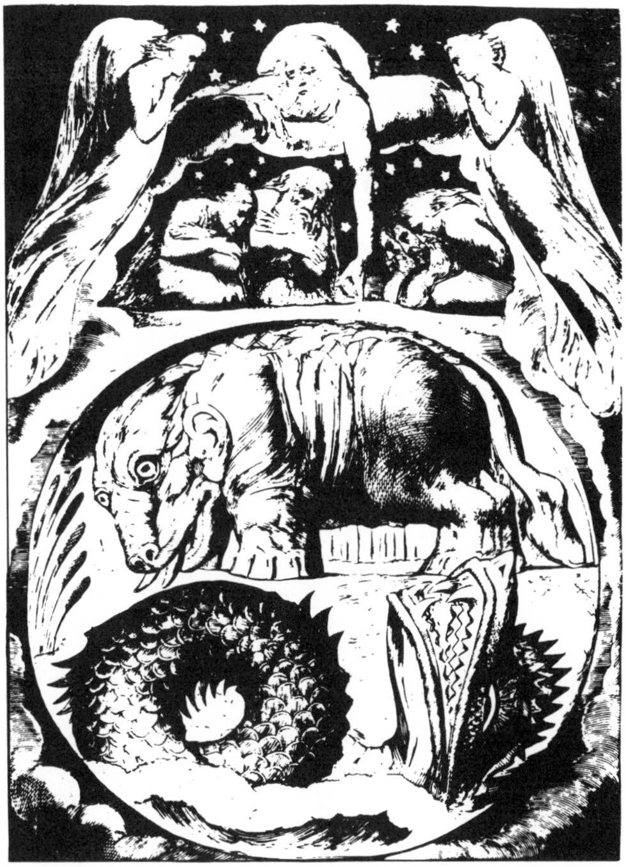

FIGURE 10. *Private Vision.* "Behold now Behemoth which I made with thee," from William Blake's *Illustrations of the Book of Job* (London, 1825).

able but private iconography that reflected individual interests and goals. The institutional church for the most part disengaged itself from major artists and movements. Under these circumstances, by the late nineteenth century a great part of Christian iconography had become copy work, sentimental and remote from the society at large.

Twentieth Century. A highly individualized Christian iconography has been shaped in the twentieth century by the religious consciousness of individual artists. The German Expressionists, for example, insisted upon interpreting and revealing their individuality. When Wassily Kandinsky (d. 1944) wrote *Concerning the Spiritual in Art,* what was revealed in the art included the feelings of the artist and the expressive properties of color. Emil Nolde's nine-part *Life of Christ* altarpiece (1911–1912) combined Nolde's interest in the impact of color with a traditional Christian format. George Rouault more than any other recognized twentieth-century artist sought to create compelling Christian imagery. His 1926 *Miserere* series compared Christ's suffering with twentieth-century experiences of human sufferings in war. Max Beckmann (d. 1950) equated Adam and Eve in the Fall with the grotesque dimensions of the human condition under fascism. In contrast, the most popular and most often reproduced image of Jesus in the United States in the first half of the twentieth century was W. H. Sallmon's *Head of Christ,* a sentimental figure with widespread influence.

Fantasy painters like Salvador Dali and Marc Chagall used Christian subject matter in a unique manner in order to suggest visions of the mind or vistas of a dream world fashioned out of the subconscious. Paintings such as Dali's *Sacrament of the Last Supper* (1955) and Chagall's *White Crucifixion* (1938) identify a private vision in which traditional Christian iconography is reinterpreted. Pablo Picasso's *Guernica* (1937) has been interpreted by some as Christian iconography although it has no traditional imagery, presumably because its reference to human terror and death suggest religious meanings.

Abstract art in the twentieth century has created the possibility of a broadly Christian iconography without recognizable subject matter. For instance, the purely abstract compositions of Piet Mondrian (d. 1944) were intended to provide an image of universal truths, religious in nature, that reflected theosophical beliefs.

Radical individuality and sociopolitical realities have influenced the content of Christian iconography in the twentieth century. Revolutionary movements have produced Christian iconography that places traditional religious figures in advocacy relationships with human beings suffering social and political injustice. In predominantly communist countries socialist realism that emphasizes the heroic stature of the worker or the revolutionary fighter has replaced Christian iconography. In other cultures indigenous forms have been integrated into Christian imagery. African sculpture, South American painting, and Asian graphics, for example, often provide indigenous twentieth-century iconography. One aspect of the Christian ecumenical movement around the world has been to encourage the diverse international community to reclaim and clarify their cultural heritages. Liturgical arts and iconography in non-Western cultures have emphasized their individual locales and traditions.

Following the lead of religious leaders such as the Dominican artist-priest M. A. Couturier (1905–1957) from France, who encouraged abstract and modern artistic treatment of Christian themes, various modern artists have entered the arena of religious art. In France, Matisse's windows and wall drawings at Vence, from the late 1940s, Le Corbusier's chapel at Ronchamp (1950–1955), the stained glass, tapestries, and altar cloth of

Léger at Audincourt (1951) all introduce Christian iconography in specifically twentieth-century forms.

In the United States, the work of the Abstract Expressionists from the early 1950s to the 1970s summarized much of the religious consciousness that had been expressed in modern art during the first half of the century by various abstract and expressionist movements. In works such as Robert Motherwell's *Reconciliation Elegy* (1962), Mark Rothko's chapel in Houston, Texas (1970), or Barnett Newman's *Stations of the Cross* (1958–1962), religious subject matter seemed identical with expressions of radical individuality. [*See* Modern Art.]

The twentieth century has also seen the emergence of Christian iconography in new media, notably film and electronic communications. Biblical stories presented in films with titles like *The Bible, The Ten Commandments, The King of Kings,* and *The Gospel According to St. Matthew* have engaged a public separate from the church. The mass media, which now include home video, have offered traditional Christian subject matter in extended narrative form as dramatic entertainment. Such presentations of Christian stories are a form of Christian iconography but in their cultural context appear to be no more than stories from one literary source among many, iconography for entertainment rather than worship. [*See* Cinema and Religion.]

The function of Christian iconography has varied in each generation. It has always been a living language of images invented by the religious consciousness of communities and individuals. Until the modern era the figures of Jesus and his followers were always central to iconographic programs, but during the twentieth century the focus shifted to the individual iconographer on the one hand and to major cultural presentations of the stories on the other. At the end of the twentieth century individual parishes and religious communities around the world are introducing indigenous imagery; therefore, in a manner similar to the origins of iconography in the early church, newly conceived Christian iconography is emerging.

[*See also* Aesthetics, *article on* Visual Aesthetics; Basilica, Cathedral, and Church; *and* Monastery.]

BIBLIOGRAPHY

Bottari, Stefano. *Tesori d'arte cristiana.* 5 vols. Bologna, 1956–1968. Excellent photoessays on major architectural monuments and their contents from early Christian times to the twentieth century. The principles of selection, however, are not clear, and the views printed are sometimes eccentric. Many color illustrations and ground plans.

Cabrol, Fernand, et al., eds. *Dictionnaire d'archéologie chrétienne et de liturgie.* 15 vols. Paris, 1909–1953. Essential material for the history of Christian iconography, architecture, and worship. Illustrations, although small in size and few in number, include good ground plans. A classic research and reference source.

Didron, Adolphe Napoléon. *Christian Iconography: The History of Christian Art in the Middle Ages* (1851–1886). 2 vols. Translated by Ellen J. Millington. New York, 1965. Organized thematically, with each essay treating historical sources in depth. Limited illustrations but valuable for theories concerning iconography.

Ferguson, George. *Signs and Symbols in Christian Art* (1954). New York, 1961. Remains the most reliable single-volume handbook on the subject.

Hall, James. *Dictionary of Subjects and Symbols in Art* (1974). Rev. ed. New York, 1979. Includes Christian subject matter.

Kirschbaum, Englebert, and Wolfgang Braunfels, eds. *Lexikon der christlichen Ikonographie.* 8 vols. Rome, 1968–1976. Volumes 1–4, *Allgemeine Ikonographie,* edited by Kirschbaum, present general articles on Christian iconography, alphabetically arranged; volumes 5–8, *Ikonographie der Heiligen,* edited by Braunfels, present the legends of the saints and their imagery in a separate alphabetical sequence. Both series of volumes include excellent bibliographies and summaries. Illustrations are relatively few in number and small in size.

Réau, Louis. *Iconographie de l'art crétien.* 3 vols. in 6. Paris, 1955–1959. Includes a historical overview (vol. 1), Old and New Testament iconography (vol. 2), and an iconography of the saints with legends and cult status (vol. 3). Very few illustrations.

Schiller, Gertrud. *Ikonographie der christlichen Kunst.* 4 vols. in 5. Gütersloh, 1966–1976. Offers excellent essay introductions to Christian themes in art and their sources, covering presentations of Christ (vols. 1–3), the church (vol. 4, pt. 1), and Mary (vol. 4, pt. 2). An exemplary study with many well-selected and clearly printed illustrations. The first two volumes have been translated by Janet Seligman as *The Iconography of Christian Art,* vol. 1, *The Incarnation and Life of Christ* (Boston, 1971), and vol. 2, *The Passion of Christ* (Boston, 1972).

JOHN W. COOK

Islamic Iconography

Islam is generally considered an iconoclastic religion in which the representation of living things has been prohibited from its very beginning. However, the Qur'ān nowhere deals with this problem or explicitly speaks against representation. Rather, the prohibition of pictorial activities was derived from certain *ḥadīth,* the traditions attributed to the prophet Muḥammad and his followers. It has often been argued that the development of figural painting in Iran was due to Iran's Shīʿī persuasion, which would have taken these *ḥadīth* less seriously, but this idea likewise is not in keeping with historical fact, since the Shīʿīs follow the tradition as strictly as the Sunnīs, and furthermore, Shiism was declared Iran's state religion only in 1501.

Islam's attitude toward representation is basically in tune with the stark monotheistic doctrine that there is no creator but God: to produce a likeness of anything might be interpreted as an illicit arrogation of the divine creative power by humans. Such an attitude may have hardened at the time of the Byzantine Iconoclastic Controversy; thus, in Persian poetical parlance, "pictures" are often connected with (Christian) "convents." Furthermore, the Islamic prohibition may have first been concerned primarily with sculpture, for sculptures—as they existed in the Kaʿbah in Mecca in pre-Islamic times—could lead mankind again into idolatry, and, indeed, hardly any sculptural art developed in Islam until recently.

Emerging Imagery. The feeling that representation was alien to the original spirit of Islam resulted in the development of abstract ornamental design, both geometric and vegetal, notably the arabesque as the endless continuation of leaves, palmettes, and sometimes animal-like motifs growing out of each other; it also gave calligraphy its central place in Islamic art. However, it would be wrong to claim that early Islam was without any pictures. In secular buildings such as palaces, there was no lack of representations of kings, musicians, dancers, and the like, and expressions in Persian poetry such as "like a lion painted in the bathhouse" point to the existence of wall painting (albeit with the additional, negative meaning of "something lifeless"). Decorative painting on ceramics includes not only more or less stylized animal or human figures as individual motifs but also scenes from (often unidentified) tales and romances. Although the Arabic and Persian texts scribbled around the rims of the vessels sometimes give a clue to the scene, little is known about such pictorial programs, which are found on metalwork as well. Theories about pre-Islamic (Sasanid or Turkic) or astronomical symbolism have been proposed. In the early Middle Ages, certain Arabic books were illustrated either for practical purposes, namely medical and scientific manuscripts, or for entertainment, as in the *Maqāmāt* (Assemblies) of al-Ḥarīrī or the animal fables known as *Kalīlah wa-Dimnah.*

New stylistic features came with the growing Chinese influence during the Mongol occupation of Iran in the late thirteenth century. (Persian literature speaks of China as the "picture house," where Mānī, the founder of Manichaeism, acts as the master painter.) Henceforward, illustrative painting developed predominantly in Iran, where the great epic poems (an art form unknown to the Arabs) inspired miniaturists through the centuries to the extent that the iconography of Firdawsī's *Shāh-nāmah* (Book of Kings) and Niẓāmī's *Khamsah* (Quintet) became almost standardized. Early historical works, such as the world history of Rashīd al-Dīn (d. 1317), were rather realistically illustrated. Human faces are clearly shown (and later sometimes mutilated by orthodox critics), and even the prophet Muḥammad appears with his face uncovered.

The same originally held true for a branch of painting that has continued from the fourteenth century to our day, namely, pictures of the Prophet's night journey *(isrā', miʿrāj)* through the heavens on the mysterious steed Burāq. In the course of time, Muḥammad's face was covered partly, then completely; at present, no representation of the Prophet is permitted at all: in the numerous popular pictures of the Miʿrāj, he is represented by a white rose or a cloud. Burāq, meanwhile, has become a centerpiece of popular iconography: pictures of this winged, donkey-shaped creature with a woman's head and a peacock's tail not only appear today on cheap prints but are also painted on trucks and buses, especially in Afghanistan and Pakistan, as a kind of protective charm.

Truck painting in these areas has developed into a new art form, and the religious and political ideals of the owners become visible in the pictorial and calligraphic decorations of their vehicles. Similarly telling are wall paintings in Turkish or Afghan coffee- or teahouses, where one may find realistic scenes from the *Qiṣaṣ al-anbiyā'* (Stories of the Prophets) or allusions to folk romances.

There was and is apparently no aversion to representing angels in Miʿrāj scenes, romances, or works on cosmology, or else as single figures, even in relief on walls. Their faces are always uncovered. Gabriel with his many enormous wings and Isrāfīl with the trumpet of resurrection are most prominent.

Islamic painting reached its zenith in Iran and India in the sixteenth and seventeenth centuries, when, partly under the influence of European prints, naturalistic portraiture was developed to perfection. The Mughal emperor Jahāngīr (r. 1605–1627) inspired the court painters to express his dreams of spiritual world-rule in his portraits by using the motif of the lion and the lamb lying together, or by showing him in the company of Ṣūfīs.

The Shape of Spirituality. Portraits of Ṣūfīs and dervishes are frequent in the later Middle Ages: many drawings capture the spiritual power or the refinement of a solitary Muslim holy man or illustrate the "sessions of the mystical lovers" *(majālis al-ʿushshāq).* Ṣūfīs are also shown as teachers or in their whirling dance. However, little has been done to identify them, although the color of their garments (or the shape of their headgear) sometimes betrays their affiliation with a certain Ṣūfī order (thus, a cinnamon- or rose-colored frock is typical of the Ṣābirī branch of the Chishtīyah). Colors are also used to indicate the spiritual state the mystic has reached.

Manuscripts of the Qur'ān and *ḥadīth*s were never illustrated but were written in beautiful calligraphy that sometimes assumes an almost "iconic" quality, as Martin Lings has pointed out. Qur'anic themes, however, as retold in the stories of the prophets or in poetry such as the *Yūsuf and Zulaykhā* by Jāmī (d. 1492), have developed a pictorial tradition of their own. Some mystical epics, especially 'Aṭṭār's *Manṭiq al-ṭayr* (The Conversation of the Birds), have inspired painters, but the few examples of Rūmī's *Mathnavī* with pictures, which date from fourteenth-century India to nineteenth-century Iran, lack any trace of Ṣūfī spirituality.

Sometimes seemingly simple motifs are interpreted mystically; my Turkish Ṣūfī friends explain the frequent use of tulips on the tiles in Turkish mosques with the fact that the word *lālah* ("tulip") has the same letters and thus the same numerical value as the word *Allāh,* that is, sixty-six. This is also true for the word *hilāl,* "crescent," and the *hilāl* has come to be regarded as the typical sign of Islam although its first appearance on early Islamic coins, metalwork, and ceramics had no religious connotations. It seems that in the eleventh century, when some churches (such as Ani in Armenia) were converted into mosques, their cross-shaped finials were replaced with crescent-shaped ones. A *ḥajj* ("pilgrimage") certificate of 1432 shows drawings of the sacred buildings in Mecca with such crescent finials. The Ottoman sultan Selim I (r. 1512–1520) used the *hilāl* on his flag, but only in the early nineteenth century was it made the official Turkish emblem, which appeared on postage stamps in 1863. Other Muslim countries followed the Turkish example, and now it is generally seen as the Islamic equivalent of the Christian cross (thus, the Red Crescent parallels the Red Cross).

There was no inhibition in representing pilgrimage sites in medieval guidebooks for pilgrims. In the late nineteenth century, photographs of the holy cities of Mecca and Medina became prized possessions of pilgrims and of those who were unable to perform the *ḥajj,* just as many Muslim homes now contain prints, posters, or wall hangings with representations of the Ka'bah and/or the Prophet's mausoleum.

While naturalistic representation of the Prophet and his family was increasingly objected to, other ways of presenting him developed. One might put a *ḥadīth* in superb calligraphy on a single page or write his *ḥilyah,* an elaboration of the classical Arabic description of his outward and inward beauty, in a special calligraphic style, as was done in Turkey from about 1600. The Prophet's footprints on stone, or representations of them, along with more or less elaborate drawings of his sandals, still belong to the generally accepted items in the religious tradition (see figure 1). One could also produce "pictures" of saintly persons such as 'Alī ibn Abī Ṭālib from pious sentences written in minute script (although in Iran quite realistic battle scenes showing the bravery and suffering of Ḥusayn and other members of the Prophet's family are also found in more recent times).

Calligraphic images have become more and more popular: the letters of the word *bismillāh* ("in the name

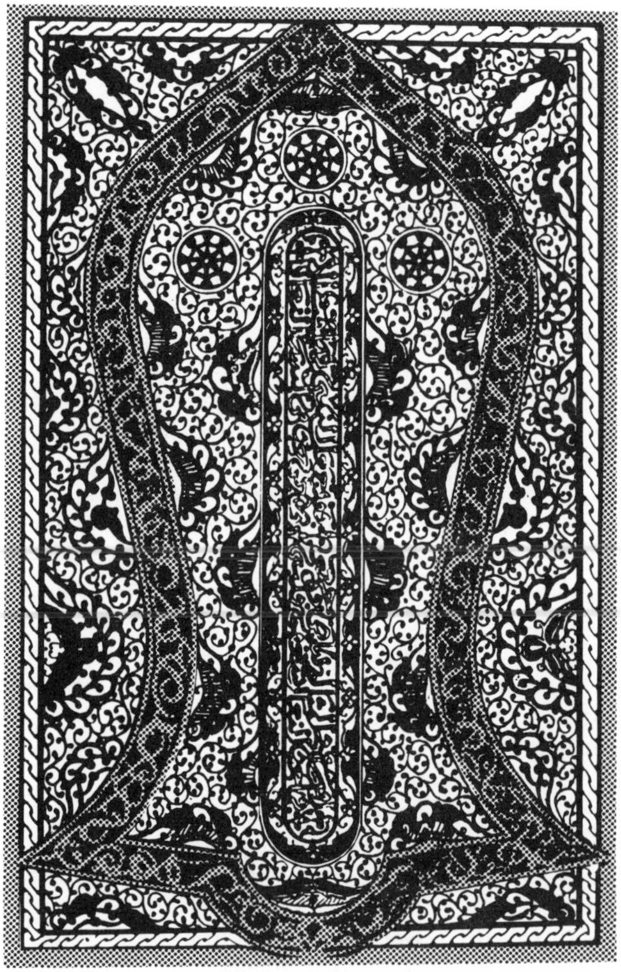

FIGURE 1. *Sandal of the Prophet.* Design from the Dhakhīra of the Sharqawa. Representations of the Prophet's footprints and of his sandals are images that are generally acceptable to Muslims.

of God") can be shaped into birds and beasts; Qur'anic passages of particular protective importance, such as the "throne verse" (surah 2:256), appear in animal shape; and whenever a calligraphic lion is found, it usually consists of a formula connected with ʿAlī, who is called the "Lion of God" (Asad Allāh, Ḥaydar, Shīr, and so forth). Most frequently used is the invocation "Nādi ʿAlīyan . . ." ("Call ʿAlī, who manifests wondrous things . . ."), which appears on many objects from Safavid Iran and Shīʿī India, as do the names of the twelve Shīʿī imams. The names of the Panjtan (Muḥammad, ʿAlī, Fāṭimah, Ḥasan, and Ḥusayn) combined with the word *Allāh* are used to form human faces, as in the Bektāshī tradition in Turkey. The names of protective saints such as the Seven Sleepers (surah 18) are also used as a calligraphic design (but their figures appear as well in Persian and Turkish painting, with their faithful dog Qiṭmīr or his name always in the center). Invocations of Ṣūfī saints may be written in the shape of a dervish cap (typical is that of Mawlānā Rūmī); other pious exclamations appear as flowers or are arranged in circular form.

Indeed, the most typical and certainly the most widely used means of conveying the Islamic message was and still is calligraphy. The walls of Persian mosques are covered with radiant tiles on which the names of God, Muḥammad, and ʿAlī in the square Kufic script give witness to the Shīʿī form of faith; Turkish mosques are decorated with Qur'anic quotations or with an enormous *Allāh*. In Turkey, various calligrams are based on the letter *w*, and the central statements of the faith are written in mirrored form.

Lately, under European influence, a very colorful popular iconography has developed in some parts of the Muslim world. On posters, religious motifs from various traditions are strung together in highly surprising form: Raphael's little angels appear along with the Lourdes Madonna around a deceased Muslim leader in a lush Paradise, or an apotheosis of Ayatollah Khomeini is coupled with the earthbound figure from Andrew Wyeth's *Christina's World.* (Here one is reminded of some pictures in the Indian Ismāʿīlī tradition that show ʿAlī as the tenth *avatāra* in the blue color of Kṛṣṇa, with Hanuman the "monkey-chief" carrying the royal umbrella over ʿAlī's white mule, Duldul.) Such syncretistic pictures are certainly not acceptable to the large majority of pious Muslims. On the other hand, the calligraphic traditions are gaining new importance from Morocco to Indonesia, and some attempts at producing a kind of Qur'anic scriptorial picture (thus Sadiqain and Aslam Kamal in Pakistan) are remarkably successful and deserve the attention of the historian of religion and the art lover.

[*See also* Calligraphy, *article on* Islamic Calligraphy, *and* Mosque.]

BIBLIOGRAPHY

Most histories of Islamic art deal with the topic of so-called iconoclasm in Islam. One of the latest publications is Mazhar Şevket Ipşiroğlu's *Das Bild im Islam: Ein Verbot und seine Folgen* (Vienna, 1971), which stresses the Ṣūfī influence on Islamic painting but is not completely convincing. The only scholar who has devoted a good number of studies to Islamic iconography is Richard Ettinghausen; out of his many valuable works I shall mention especially "Hilāl in Islamic Art," in *The Encyclopaedia of Islam,* new ed. (Leiden, 1960–), with a thorough historical survey; "Persian Ascension Miniatures of the Fourteenth Century," in *Oriente ed occidente nel medio evo* (Rome, 1957), which treats the early pictorial development of the ascension theme; and his religious interpretation of a Mughal painting of Jahāngīr preferring a Ṣūfī to worldly rulers, "The Emperor's Choice," in *De Artibus Opuscula XL: Essays in Honor of Erwin Panofsky,* edited by Millard Meiss (New York, 1961), vol. 1. See also Ettinghausen's *Islamic Art and Archaeology: Collected Papers,* prepared and edited by Myriam Rosen-Ayalon (Berlin, 1984). The volume dedicated to Ettinghausen, *Studies in Art and Literature of the Near East,* edited by Peter Chelkowski (Salt Lake City, 1974), lists more of his relevant works and contains some articles pertinent to the problem of iconography.

The best pictorial introduction to the *miʿrāj* miniatures is *The Miraculous Journey of Mahomet,* edited by Marie-Rose Séguy (London, 1977), based on a Uighur manuscript from the Timurid court at Herat. Popular painting has been dealt with in Malik Aksel's *Türklerde dinî resimler* (Istanbul, 1967), a delightful book with many examples of folk painting and calligraphic pictures from the Bektāshī tradition. A very useful introduction into Islamic iconography in Africa (a much neglected topic) is René A. Bravmann's *African Islam* (London, 1983). The calligraphic and iconographic aspects of the Qur'ān are lucidly explained in Martin Ling's *The Quranic Art of Calligraphy and Illumination* (London, 1976). A general survey of the calligraphic tradition in connection with the mystical and poetical expressions can be found in my *Calligraphy and Islamic Culture* (New York, 1984).

Annemarie Schimmel

ICONS. The term *icon* (from the Greek *eikōn,* "image") is applied in a broad sense to all sacred images worshiped by Christians in eastern Europe and the Middle East regardless of the image's media; thus icons may be mosaics, frescoes, engravings on marble or metal, or prints on paper. In its current use the term describes portable sacred images painted on wood, canvas, or glass.

Beginning and Growth of the Veneration of Icons. Portable icons first appeared in Egypt in the third century. The oldest works that have been preserved to this day bear a striking resemblance to the funeral portraits that replaced the masks on the anthropoid coffins of the Hellenistic period. The Judaic tradition, which relied on the biblical prohibition of the use of images in religious worship, was confronted in the eastern Mediterranean area with the Greek tradition, theoretically substantiated by Neoplatonism, according to which the material symbol is an expression of spiritual reality and the image has a didactic function. This latter tradition gained ground even in some Jewish communities; for example, frescoes based on biblical subjects were painted on the walls of the synagogue at Dura-Europos (present-day Salahiyeh, Syria) in the third century. It was the Greek tradition that caused the emergence as early as the second and third centuries of sacred imagery in the Christian church, which had originally used only symbols (e.g., the cross, lamb, fish, and dove). The didactic function of images was generally accepted throughout the Christian world, but the veneration of images did not spread to all areas: it remained a specific cult of Christianity in the Greco-Byzantine tradition.

The earliest icons, like the Hellenistic funeral portraits, originally had a commemorative value: they were representations of martyrs, apostles, the Virgin, and Jesus Christ. As early as the fourth century a typology of characters took shape, and their sacred nature was marked by a nimbus. The authenticity of portraits was an essential concern: the images of Christ and the Virgin were believed to be of miraculous origin, "made without hands" (Gr., *acheiropoiētos*); those of the saints were rendered according to descriptions preserved by traditional—oral or written—sources. The oldest icon representing the Virgin originated in Palestine and, with the exception of the visage, was attributed to the apostle Luke; the visage was said to have been painted miraculously, without the touch of the human hand. According to tradition, the representation of Christ relied on a portrait Jesus had sent to the king of Edessa, Abgar Ukkama, "the black" (d. 50 CE), and on the veil of Veronica, said to bear the imprint of the Savior's face (recent research suggests that the name Veronica derives from the Latin *vera icona*, "true face").

As Christian icon painting developed after the fourth century, themes relating to the historical cycles of Christ's mission (miracles, scenes from his life) and then events from the lives of saints and from the history of the Christian church were introduced. In the sixth century icon worship spread throughout the Byzantine empire. Icons were displayed to the faithful in churches or during processions, and they were also to be found in private homes. They were either in one piece or were combined from two or three pieces, forming, respectively, diptychs and triptychs. The strength of the development of icon worship, the miraculous powers attributed to certain icons, and the fact that in the minds of the faithful icons were identified with the character they represented, aroused, even from the beginning, opposition and hostility from some of the fathers of the church. This led in the eighth century to the iconoclastic crisis, which resulted in the destruction of a large number of icons, especially in areas under the direct authority of the Byzantine emperors. [*See* Iconoclasm.] Nevertheless iconoclasm was unable to prevent the further development of icon worship at the periphery of the empire; hence the oldest icons, dating from the fifth and sixth centuries, were preserved in Georgia (Transcaucasia), on Mount Sinai, and in Cyprus. With the official restoration of the veneration of icons in 843, the practice of veneration became generalized not only in the Byzantine empire but also in other regions where the Eastern Orthodox church had become predominant, such as the Balkan Peninsula and Russia.

Following the triumph of the doctrine claiming the legitimacy of icon worship many more wall icons were displayed in sanctuaries, and the iconostasis (Gr., *eikonostasis*, "support for icons") was introduced, a screen of icons that separated the altar from the nave of the church. The iconostasis apparently developed from the *templon*, a barrier made of stone, marble, or ivory that enclosed the main apse or chancel, where the sacred table was contained.

Theology of Icons. The final elaboration of the theology of icons resulted from the disputes caused by iconoclasm and the rules formulated by the Second Council of Nicaea (787). The earliest elements of the doctrine had already been enunciated in the second to the fourth centuries. Arguing against the Christian apologists who condemned idols as "devilish," such Neoplatonic thinkers as Celsus (latter half of the second century), Porphyry (c. 234–c. 305), and Emperor Julian the Apostate (d. 363) attempted to give a metaphysical justification of sacred images and statues as material symbols expressing external and spiritual realities and fulfilling at the same time a significant didactic function. According to Neoplatonists the relationship between image and prototype is not one of sameness: images serve only as vehicles by which to approach the divine prototype, which is hidden from humans because of the limitations of their corporeality. The arguments adduced by the Neoplatonists are to be found in subsequent developments of Christian theology. Thus, the concept according to which "sensible images are vehicles whereby we accede, as far as possible, to divine contemplation" was clearly stated by Dionysius the Areopagite (c. 500) in his treatise *Ecclesiastical Hierarchy* (1.2). The relationship between image and its divine prototype would be later clarified in the same vein in the writings of John of Damascus (c. 679–749) and other authors of the Eastern church.

The Christian authors of the eighth and ninth centuries who formulated the theology of icons relied on a belief that icon worship was a consequence of the incarnation of the Son of God. According to Germanus I, patriarch of Constantinople (r. 715–730), the Son could be portrayed because he "consented to become a man." An icon representing Christ is not an image of the "incomprehensible and immortal Deity" but rather that of the "human character" of the Logos (the Word) and serves as proof that "indeed he became a man in all respects, except for sin." Christ could be represented only "in his human form, in his visible theophany." John of Damascus, who wrote three treatises in defense of "sacred icons," gave the following definition of the painted image of the Deity: "I represent God the Invisible not as invisible but to the extent he became visible to us by partaking of flesh and blood."

John of Damascus and, especially, Theodore of Studios (759–826) and Nikephoros, patriarch of Constantinople (r. 806–815), further clarified the relationship between the sacred image, or icon, and its divine prototype. To them image is essentially distinct from the original: it is an object of relative veneration (Gr., *proskunēsis skhetikē*). Through the mediation of the icon the faithful actually address the prototype it represents, and so the relative veneration of the image becomes adoration (Gr., *latreia*) that is exclusively offered to the Deity. This distinction between adoration of the model and relative veneration of its image removed the danger of turning icons into fetishes, a danger that was inherent in their worship. Theodore of Studios emphasized that "veneration was not due to the essence of the image but rather to the form of the Prototype represented by the image . . . since matter cannot be subject to veneration."

These clarifications stressed the intimate connection between the theology of icons and the christological question posed by the heresy of Docetism, which questioned the real humanity of Christ and claimed that Christ's body was only apparent. In contradistinction, the icon was claimed to represent the image of an incarnation of the Son of God, thus, according to Germanus, "proving that he invested our nature by means other than imagination." Indescribable by his divine nature, Christ is describable by the complete reality of his historical humanity. [*See* Docetism.]

According to Theodore of Studios, "the fact that God made man after his likeness showed that icon painting was an act of God." The theology of icons confers upon icons an almost sacramental role. As the early painters saw it, their art did not belong to aesthetics but rather to liturgy. The perfection of form was no more than an adequate expression of the doctrine. The painter was not an artist in the modern sense of the word but a priest: his talent was a necessary, but not sufficient, condition. He was chosen and guided by a master; the beginning of his apprenticeship was marked by a ritual (e.g., prayer and benediction) quite similar to that of an initiation.

The earliest painters of icons never signed their works since their individuality was believed to be of no consequence. (The first icons to be signed, in the fifteenth and sixteenth centuries, signaled the beginning of decadence in the art of icon making.) Seen as mere interpreters of the truth, the painters of old had to follow strict rules: the subjects of their paintings could only be previously established models, scenes from the holy books, or, more rarely, acknowledged visions; they did their work after having fasted and received the Eucharist; and some even mixed holy water with their colors.

Diffusion of the Cult of Icons. After the conclusion of the iconoclastic crisis, icon painting in Byzantium, under the Palaeologus dynasty (1261–1453), witnessed a remarkable period in which artistic perfection was reached; that style further influenced the art of icon making down to our own time. In the Greek territories the main icon-producing centers were Mount Athos and the imperial workshops in Constantinople, Thessalonica, and, after the fall of Byzantium, Crete. Cretan painters, having remained outside the area of Ottoman domination between 1453 and 1669, produced a great many works that were disseminated throughout the Orthodox world. Their icons displayed a certain lavishness, to be explained by the comfortable conditions in which they were produced; they were increasingly influenced by the contemporary Italian painting not only in the rendering of human visages and bodies, and of space, but even in iconography.

In eastern and southeastern Europe the cult of icons was disseminated by the early missionaries and through contacts with Byzantium. At first icons were brought from the Byzantine territories, but later they began to be produced in local workshops: at Preslav and Veliko Tŭrnovo in Bulgaria; at the courts of Serbian kings and Romanian princes; in Walachia and Moldavia; and in major monasteries in all these countries. They were characterized by their faithfulness to the Byzantine prototypes, but starting in the eighteenth century, popular local tastes made an impact on the choice of colors, the design of costumes, and the decoration of space. The union of a part of the Eastern Orthodox Romanians in Transylvania with the church of Rome gave rise to a unique phenomenon in Eastern

Christian art: icons were painted on glass by peasant artists, producing works that strongly resembled naive folk painting.

Of the oldest icons imported to Russia after the baptizing of the Russians in 988, only works of Byzantine origin dating from the eleventh century have been preserved. In the same century the earliest local icon-making centers began to emerge, first in Kiev and then in Novgorod and Vladimir-Suzdal. The earliest masters were from Byzantium, but soon a specific Russian style took shape; it developed from a spiritualized and ascetic attitude to a search for artistic and didactic effects, a taste for minute detail, and naturalism. The Council of the Hundred Chapters held in Moscow in 1551 reacted against the penetration of Western elements into the art of icon painting and put down rigid, mandatory rules to be followed by painters. This led to a proliferation of handbooks that provided authorized versions (Ch. Slav., *podliniki,* "outlines") of the holy images; these guides were equivalent to the ones used in the Byzantine empire beginning in the eleventh century. The reforms enacted by Peter the Great (r. 1682–1725) inhibited the further development of icon painting, and the art subsequently lapsed into conservatism.

In the East after the Council of Chalcedon (451), the church (under the patriarchates of Antioch and Jerusalem) followed the orthodox doctrine upheld against monophysitism. In the seventeenth century the style of icon painting known as Melchite developed under new influences—Arabic, in terms of decoration; western European, in terms of subject matter.

[*For discussion of the importance of images in broad religious perspective, see* Images, *article on* Veneration of Images.]

BIBLIOGRAPHY

The scientific study of icons began in the latter half of the nineteenth century as part of the new discipline of Byzantology and enlisted especially Russian contributions; an essential bibliography is to be found in Oskar Wulff and Michael Alpatoff's *Denkmäler der Ikonenmalerei* (Leipzig, 1925), pp. 298–299. Earlier research included icons, described as "panel paintings" or "portable images," in studies on Eastern Christian iconography, among which the fundamental work remains Gabriel Millet's *Recherches sur l'iconographie de l'Évangile aux quatorzième, quinzième, et seizième siècles* (Paris, 1916). In western Europe and America icons were "discovered" as works of art and spiritual creations only after World War I, when the Christian Orthodox tradition was reassessed by Catholic and Protestant scholars; see David Talbot Rice's *Byzantine Art,* 2d ed., rev. & enl. (Baltimore, 1968). Most experts approach icons as works of art within the general framework of Byzantine or, particularly, Russian art—for example, André Grabar's *Byzantine Painting,* translated by Stuart Gilbert (New York, 1953), and Tamara Talbot Rice's *Icons,* rev. ed. (London, 1960). The theology of icons was systematically studied and clarified mainly by Western Orthodox authors during the past four decades; the most profound works are Leonid Ouspensky and Vladimir Lossky's *The Meaning of Icons,* translated by G. E. H. Palmer and Eugénie Kadloubovsky, rev. ed. (Crestwood, N.Y., 1982); and Leonid Ouspensky's *Essai sur la théologie de l'icone dans l'église orthodoxe* (Paris, 1960). Most writings about Eastern Orthodox Christianity contain pertinent chapters on icons: Timothy Ware's *The Orthodox Church,* rev. ed. (Baltimore, 1964); Paul Evdokimoff's *L'orthodoxie* (Paris, 1959); and John Meyendorff's *Byzantine Theology: Historical Trends and Doctrinal Themes* (New York, 1979). Photographs of the oldest, fifth- to sixth-century icons have been published in Georgios A. Sotiriou and Maria Sotiriou's *Icones du Mont Sinai/Eikonec the Monha Cina* (in Greek and French), vols. 1 and 2 (Athens, 1956–1958). New information about the role of icons during the posticonoclastic period is to be found in Manoles Chatzedakes's "L'évolution de l'icone aux onzième à treizième siècles et la transformation du templon," and Tania Velmans's "Rayonnement de l'icone à l'onzième siècle," in *Actes du quinzième Congrès international d'études byzantines,* vol. 1 (Athens, 1979), pp. 333–366, 375–419. For icons of the Middle East, see Sylvia Agémian's important study in my collection entitled *Les icones melkites* (Beirut, 1969).

VIRGIL CÂNDEA
Translated from Romanian by Sergiu Celac

IDEALISM. Idealism is the metaphysical view that reality is of the nature of mind. It stands in contrast with scientific philosophies, such as naturalism, realism, and pragmatism that assume that natural life in the natural world is philosophy's appropriate point of departure. [*See* Metaphysics; Naturalism; *and* Nature, *article on* Religious and Philosophical Speculations.] Idealism is not grounded in an empirical evaluation of fact. It is grounded in an intuitive evaluation of meaning. Since all philosophy presupposes that things have a meaning and that something, at least, of that meaning can be known, all philosophy has an idealistic element.

Idealism does not deny the reality of the physical world. It insists only that the apparent self-sufficiency of the natural world is deceptive. Nature seems to go its own way, to be self-sufficient, eternal, and operating on the basis of its own laws without need of a creator or outside force to initiate and sustain its motions, but idealism maintains that it relies on mind or spirit or idea for its forcefulness, purposiveness, and inherent meaning. Idealism therefore always distinguishes between appearance and reality, but its emphasis can either be objective or subjective. Subjective idealism sees the physical world as metaphysically insubstantial. Objective idealism regards physical substance as a necessary counterpart of mind.

Subjective Idealism. The doctrine of the world as *māyā* or illusion in Śaṅkara's Advaita Vedānta philosophy in India is the most systematic statement of subjective idealism, although George Berkeley's philosophy is the best-known statement of subjective idealism in the West. Berkeley observed that our visual perception of the physical world is one of shapes and colors, not of any substantial "thing." We project "physical substance" into the picture because we assume that there must be some "thing" that "has" these perceived qualities.

All we ever know, however, are the perceived qualities. Reality, therefore, is a perception on the part of a perceiver. Hence Berkeley's principle *esse est percipi* ("to be is to be perceived"). He pointed out that we seem to see distance; in fact, however, three-dimensional depth perception is a learned projection of the mind, not a physical reality that impinges directly on our senses. He added that the physical sciences are not concerned with some "substantial" reality of a physical object, but rather with those perceptions known to mind. To test a yellow metal to see if it is gold, for example, the chemist does not test "substance," but properties—solubility in different acids, combining proportions, and weight. The "substance" of gold is only a fact of experience that these properties bring together. Berkeley concluded that the distinction between what Locke had called primary qualities and secondary qualities—real "substance" as opposed to "appearances" (of color, shape, etc.)—was mistaken. Nature is, he insisted, whole. If space is mental, then all the other qualities of the natural object must also be mental. Reality is entirely an observer's perception.

But what of objects that are alone and unobserved by any human knower, like the tree in the deserted forest or the living-room furniture in the dead of night? Berkeley argued that natural laws hold for events past as well as future because there is an eternal mind to think them. The living-room sofa exists as an object in the eternal perception of the mind of God. God alone guarantees the eternal endurance and order of nature.

The most consistent subjective idealist in modern Western philosophy was G. W. Leibniz, who held that each self is a "monad" of self-enclosed experience. He accepted a plurality of worlds—my world must be different from yours—and solipsism, the view that each person is *solus ipse,* a "windowless monad."

Here subjective idealism runs afoul of the "ego-centric predicament." Confined to his or her own ideas, the self-confessed solipsist nevertheless assumes that he or she knows what it might be like *not* to be so confined; otherwise the assertion has no significance. Each self is conscious, necessarily, of what it is not, in order to know itself as a distinct and separate entity. Solipsism, therefore, is self-refuting.

Objective Idealism. Objective idealism, mindful of this pitfall, grants to naturalism that the physical world is given from "outside" ourselves, and must be received passively, but agrees with subjective idealism that our experience of this given world is, in large part, an interpretation shaped by our own minds. Both subjective and objective idealism are rooted in the intuition that reality is essentially mind. Objective idealism is distinguished by a nondual view in which the physical world shares metaphysical reality.

The historic relation between idealistic philosophy and religious reflection stems from this common concern for showing how an immaterial power gives the material world its reality and true being. The idealistic commitment to mind as ultimately real expresses, in the language of experience, a view that overlaps the religious commitment to spirit as the enabling power of being. This tradition in Western philosophy was first explored systematically by Plato, for whom reality lay in the eternal forms, or ideas, that were the meaning of any particular thing. These particulars, however, were always imperfect because they were necessarily material. Matter, for Plato, is an admittedly indispensable context for existence. More significantly, however, it is a hindrance to realization of the true meaning of things, which is their ideal form. Plato is unclear as to why nature should exist, and matter remains a dark and unresolved dilemma in his philosophy. Aristotle gave matter greater status by making it the counterpart of form or idea in any particular. Matter is therefore the possibility of a new form. Mind or spirit or form shapes matter, as the idea of a pot in the mind of a potter transforms a lump of clay into a utensil for human use.

Plato and Aristotle incline toward idealism but remain dualists. It was only after Immanuel Kant that idealism offered an integrated view of reality that did justice to natural fact. Beginning with the radical distinction between mind and matter with which René Descartes had first fashioned the modern mind, idealists argued that mind and matter are different but interdependent. J. G. Fichte argued that will is the essence of mind, and will requires the recalcitrant opposition of material stuff in order for work to teach us the moral lessons of industry, perseverance, and devotion to factual truth. For Fichte, nature is "the material for our duty, made sensible." For Friedrich Schelling and G. W. F. Hegel, nature is necessary in order that mind attain full self-awareness. Hegel argued that useful knowledge is always acquired through a double movement: first we gain an intimate knowledge of the particular thing, and then we learn something of what it is not. To know one's own language for what it truly is, for example, one must know something of a different language. So, to generalize from that experience, mind must know something that is not mind. It must wander in an alien world before it can return home to know itself truly for the first time. Nature, therefore, is the "otherness of spirit," the alien land in which the mind wanders in order to gain full possession of itself. Or, to put it less metaphorically, natural objects are the necessary content of mind. There is no thought without an object; one must think something. Whereas subjective idealism, in both the monadology of Leibniz and the Advaita Vedānta of Śaṅkara, argues that mind alone is the really real, objective idealism argues that objective nature is a necessary condition for the reality of mind. Reality is therefore not a univocal state; it is a dialectical process.

Idealist Ethics. Idealism also proposes an ethics, developed from its metaphysical view that mind or spirit constitutes an eternal and purposive transcendent order. As the metaphysical reality of any particular is derived from the idea that is its ultimate meaning, so the norms and values of human behavior are derived from the transcendent idea of love, power, justice, or so forth.

Unlike modern naturalisms, which regard ethical values as entirely relative to the social and psychological needs of natural groups, idealism holds that there are what Kant called categorical imperatives, or moral absolutes. Kant stated the foundational principle of all idealistic ethics, that we are to treat people always as ends in themselves and never as a means to some end; but his dogmatic categorical imperative lacks metaphysical justification. It was his successors who developed an independent metaphysics that could flesh out Kant's intuitive insight with a rational argument. Hegel supplemented the Kantian view with a dialectical interpretation of concrete freedom that seeks to ally itself with whatever is objectively rational and universal in the laws and institutions of one's community. This view turned idealism toward social realism. Josiah Royce later argued that the objective reason that Hegel sought in institutions could not be found there if, as Hegel himself noted, institutions rise and fall. Rejecting Hegel's conservatism, Royce argued that our loyalty is not just to the institutionalized rationality of the past but to the hoped-for rationality of the future. For Royce, therefore, our primary loyalty is not to institutions but to those creative causes that some institutions sometimes serve. There will be different interpretations as to what these causes should be, but the authentic common spirit of cause-servers everywhere will always be one of loyalty. Royce's categorical imperative is therefore that we should be loyal to loyalty wherever it is found.

Various forms of idealism were influential during the nineteenth and early twentieth centuries when there was confidence in reason and hope for the future. The prevailing spirit of the late twentieth century has become skeptical of rationalization and pessimistic about the future, so idealistic philosophy is less influential. However, when religious thinkers look for a rational and universal language of experience in which to articulate the dramatic, poetic, and mythological convictions of the great religions with their message of a divine *logos* that assures the ultimate fulfillment of a divine purpose, that language is inescapably some form of idealism.

[*See also the biographies of the philosophers mentioned herein.*]

BIBLIOGRAPHY

Plato's dialogues all focus on the idealist issue, and Plotinus's third century *Enneads* bears resemblance to the Advaita Vedānta philosophy in India, which Śaṅkara articulates in his ninth century *Commentary on the Brahma Sutra.* Kant's *Religion within the Limits of Reason Alone* (1793), translated by Theodore M. Greene et al. (New York, 1960), identifies mind and spirit in idealistic fashion, and Hegel's *Lectures on the Philosophy of Religion* (1832), 3 vols., translated by E. B. Speirs and J. B. Sanderson (London, 1895), is the first systematic statement of idealistic philosophy of religion in the West. Josiah Royce's *The Problem of Christianity,* 2 vols. (New York, 1913), and William Ernest Hocking's *The Meaning of God in Human Experience* (New Haven, 1912) are the best known systematic statements in the American philosophical tradition.

The best secondary sources on idealism are in the major histories of Western philosophy. For a technical discussion of philosophical ideas and their development, Wilhelm Windelband's *History of Philosophy,* translated by James H. Tufts (New York, 1893), is still unsurpassed. For idealism as an influential strand of modern intellectual culture, see John Herman Randall, Jr.'s *The Making of the Modern Mind* (New York, 1976) and Randall's two-volume *The Career of Philosophy* (New York, 1962–1965), especially volume 2, *From the German Enlightenment to the Age of Darwin.* The most recent significant interpretation of a major religious tradition in the light of an idealistic philosophy is Paul Tillich's three-volume *Systematic Theology* (Chicago, 1951–1963).

LEROY S. ROUNER

IDOLATRY. The word *idolatry* is formed from two Greek words, *eidōlon,* "image," and *latreia,* "adoration." Etymologically, *idolatry* means "adoration of images." Authors have given *idolatry* and *idol* widely differing definitions thereby revealing the complexity of the problem. Eugène Goblet d'Alviella uses the term *idol* to mean images or statues "that are considered to be conscious and animate" and sees idolatry in the act of "regarding an image as a superhuman personality" (Goblet d'Alviella, 1911, p. 126). In a relatively recent article, J. Goetz (1962), trying to get a better grip on the problem, establishes, first, that in the wake of etymology idolatry "designates the adoration of images by emphasizing the specific nature of the cult surrounding the objects, a cult of adoration, which strictly speaking expresses a feeling of absolute dependence, especially through sacrifice." He then states that the terms *idolatry* and *idol* remain inaccurate, and that "the authors who have tackled the problem of idolatry most often defined the idol as an object in anthromorphic form, intended to represent a spirit, the object of worship." [*See* Anthropomorphism.] Finally, venturing onto the terrain of religious phenomenology, he risks a definition of *idol:* "any material object that receives a form of worship more or less structured," idolatry being this form of worship.

The concept of idolatry originated in a very specific historico-religious context: the monotheism of Israel. Consequently, an authentic approach to the concept must refer to the Hebrew scriptures. In his research on the prophetic reaction to pagan religious concepts, Christopher P. North presents two ideas taken directly from the prophets. First, "Idolatry is the worship of the creature instead of the Creator and, to make matters worse, the creature is made by man, who is himself a creature" (North, 1958, p. 158). He then states: "Idolatry is the worship of what in modern terms we should call process, the 'life-force,' the *élan vital,* or what we will, instead of the Creator who transcends and is in some sort external to creation" (ibid., p. 159). Finally, here is another, more recently formulated definition: "Idolatry may be defined as the worship of an idol (*eidōlon,* image, portrait) considered as a substitute for the divine" (M. Delahoutre, "Idolâtrie," *Dictionnaire des religions,* Paris, 1984).

This brief survey should help situate our own research. The concept of idolatry originated in the application of the Second Commandment. It acquired definitive formulation in censure by the prophets of Israel of the pagan cults and their influence on the chosen people. This biblical heritage passed into the New Testament and early Christianity, blazing its way through the forest of pagan cults. The monotheism of Islam adopted this Judeo-Christian concept and made it one of the foundations of its beliefs and its faith.

Beginning with these notions formed with the help of the dogmatic thought as well as the polemic stance of the three great monotheisms, the historian of religions enlarges his vision of idolatry by studying this religious phenomenon through the behavior of *homo religiosus* in relation to the representation of divinity. However, this study becomes vast and includes other very important aspects: images for worship, symbolism in religions and cults, religious art, veneration of images, iconoclasm. The present study is limited to idolatry, which it will approach on two levels: on the one hand, the historico-religious fact that the three great monotheisms censured the worship of idols; and, on the other hand, the phenomenon of man's attitude of worship in the presence of a visible representation of divinity. The study of these two aspects is made with reference to the historical documentation left by the *homo religiosus* concerned.

Historical Semantics. In ancient Greek texts since Homer we rarely find the word *eidōlon.* Formed from *eidos* (n.), "aspect, shape," the word *eidōlon* has diverse meanings: "phantom, undetermined form, image reflected in a mirror or in water." It also means an image formed in the human mind. Thus in the ancient Greek world, *eidōlon* did not have a religious meaning.

We must therefore turn to the biblical Greek world, where we find *eidōlon* in the Septuagint. Used seventy times in the protocanonical texts, it translates sixteen different Hebrew words, as for example *aven,* vanity; *elil,* nothing; *gillulim,* excrement; *pesel,* carved statue; *tselim,* image. For these protocanonical texts the Vulgate uses *idolum* one hundred and twelve times and *simulacrum* thirty two times in order to translate fifteen Hebrew words. *Eidōlon* also appears many times in the apocryphal writings. The Hebrew Bible uses thirty different nouns in order to talk about idols and mentions forty-four pagan divinities. Thus *eidōlon* designates the false gods and does so with a scornful nuance, for they are vanity, lies, nothingness, vain images, molded metal, carved wood. It is therefore through choices made by Greek translators of the Bible that *eidōlon* acquired the religious sense of representing a pagan divinity considered to be a false god. Thus the Septuagint gave *eidōlon* a new pejorative and polemical meaning. (By extension, *eidōleion* means a temple in which idols are found.)

Eidōlon passed into the Greek New Testament. We do not find the word in the Gospels, but it appears elsewhere (*Acts* 7:41, 15:20; *Rom.* 2:22; *1 Cor.* 8:4, 8:7, 10:9, 12:2; *2 Cor.* 6:16; *1 Thes.* 1:9; *1 Jn.* 5:21; *Rev.* 9:20). The Vulgate sometimes translates it as *idolum* and sometimes as *simulacrum.* One passage (*1 Cor.* 7:10) has the word *eidōleion,* "temple of idols," which the Vulgate preserves, latinizing it as *idolium.* The New Testament passages show that in the eyes of the compilers, the pagan gods have no substance (*Gal.* 4:8). Behind their worship hides the work of demons (*1 Cor.* 10:19).

The word *eidōlon* passed into patristic terminology. Its usage is common from the second century on. In the

Epistle of Barnabas, the *eidōla* are the pagan gods to which the Hebrews turned in the desert. Justin Martyr (*1 Apology* 64.1) designates as an *eidōlon* a statue of Kore, who was considered to be the daughter of Zeus. In speaking of pagan gods, Clement of Alexandria made use of all the richness of Greek vocabulary of his time. Evidence of this can be found in chapter 4 of the *Exhortation to the Heathen,* devoted to statues of gods, *agalmata.* He calls them idols (4.53.1) and includes them among the demons (4.55.1), which are impure and base spirits. He invites his readers to approach these statues *(agalmata)* in order to uncover the error that they conceal: "Their exterior clearly shows the mark of your demons' inner dispositions" (4.57.1). Later he reproaches the Greeks for having given themselves models of sensuality in these idols (4.61.1). Justin proclaims that Christ came to liberate men from the domination of idols (*Dialogue with Trypho* 113.6). These pagan gods are only phantoms that take possession of the human spirit and give the pagans the illusion of divine worship (Athenagoras, *Libellus* 23). These few samples, taken from the arsenal of the polemic of the apologists and the Greek fathers, show how the meaning of *eidōlon* expanded in the Greek world during the first centuries of the common era.

The Latin fathers adopt the same vocabulary and an identical stance. Tertullian shows that the pagan gods have no substance (*Apologetics* 10.2); then he attacks the statues as inert matter, *simulacra* made of material related to that of vases and ordinary utensils (12.2). In a similar fashion, Firmicus Maternus speaks of the *imagines consecratas* of public pagan worship (*Octavius* 24.5). Augustine gives a definitive structure to this criticism of idolatry made by the Latin apologists. Speaking of the pagan gods, he shows the semantic relationship between *simulacrum* and *idolum: "simulacra,* which in Greek are called idols" (*Expositions on the Psalms* 135.3). In his eyes, the idol worshipers are *daemonicolae.* The idol lets the demon make his own revelation (Mandouze, 1958).

The words *eidōlolatria* and *eidōlolatrēs* are found neither in secular Greek texts nor in the Septuagint nor in the writings of Philo Judaeus. They are a specific contribution of the New Testament and Christian literature of the first Christian centuries. Paul considers idolatry a grave sin and puts it on the list of sins that Christians must avoid (*1 Cor.* 5:10–11, 6:9, 10:7, 10:14; *Gal.* 5:20; *Col.* 3:5; *Eph.* 5:5). The writer of *1 Peter* 4:3 speaks in analogous fashion of the worship of idols that ought to be rejected by Christians. The same idea appears in *Revelation* 21:8 and 22:15.

The use of the two words becomes constant in Greek patristic literature. Clement of Alexandria even leaves a definition of idolatry: "the extension to numerous divinities of what is reserved for the one true God" (*Miscellanies* 3.12). The Christian church opposed idols and condemned their manufacture. The second-century apologists left a veritable arsenal of arguments on which Christian polemicists would draw until the age of Augustine.

Idolatry and the Hebrew Scriptures. The formal condemnation of idolatry is found in *Exodus* 20:3–5. The biblical God (whose unvocalized name is YHVH) simultaneously forbids the worship of foreign gods and the making of images that claim to represent him, since it is impossible to represent the God of Israel. A confirmation and amplification of this commandment are found in *Deuteronomy* 4:12–19. The interdiction pertains to both theriomorphic and anthropomorphic images. It pertains also to symbolic animal representations of the divinity. Thus idolatry is vested with a double aspect: the idolatrous worship of Yahveh as well as the worship of false gods.

The Mosaic prohibition. The second commandment forbids the making of representations of the divinity (*Ex.* 20:4–6; *Dt.* 4:15–19 and 5:6–9; *Lv.* 26:1). A rigorous tendency took this Mosaic prohibition literally by banishing all ornamentation of religious buildings. This tendency, which became widespread among the Pharisees, insisted on the spiritualization of God and radically opposed the danger of idolatry. A more liberal tendency has always existed, however, as attested by the animal and human decoration of certain synagogues discovered by archaeologists. [*See* Iconography, *article on* Jewish Iconography *and* Synagogue, *article on* Architectural Aspects.]

Idolatrous worship of YHVH. Biblical texts refer to this worship on various occasions. The Hebrew tribes underwent the influence of Canaanite culture (*Jgs.* 3:5–6, *Dt.* 7:1–5). Micah of the tribe of Ephraim made a *pesel* and a *massekhah,* a carved image and idol of cast metal (*Jgs.* 17:1–13), perhaps an image of God. After his victory over Midian, Gideon made use of the gold taken from the enemy to make and set up an *efod* (*Jgs.* 8:22–27). Moreover, we have evidence of the tauriform cult of YHVH in the northern kingdom of Israel after the schism of 935 (*1 Kgs.* 12:26–32, *2 Kgs.* 15:24). In *1 Kings* 12:28, Jeroboam presents God, symbolized by the bull (Hadad and Teshub, fertility gods), as the liberator of Israel at the time of the flight from Egypt. The writer of *2 Kings* 15:24 speaks of the erection of statues of divine bulls. This is the religious tradition of the golden calf.

The prophets fought the use of images because they represented the danger of superstitition. *Hosea* 3:4 assails the stelae *(matstsebot)* erected next to the altars, the *efod,* which are either images or instruments for interrogating Yahveh, and the *terafim,* which closely resemble the *efod.* Thus, the prophet aims at the elimination of even the accessories to worship. Jeremiah went even further, proclaiming around 587 BCE that he would no longer speak of the Ark of the Covenant of Yahveh, which would be neither remembered nor missed, and which would never be built again (*Jer.* 3:16).

The prophetic argument is simple. It rejects all tangible representation of God as dangerous since the image is distinct from God. Hosea, moreover, refers to the past, to the youth of Israel, and to the flight from Egypt (*Hos.* 2:17). Thus, prophetic polemics find support in the Mosaic tradition. It is in this context that the incident of the golden calf (*Ex.* 32) must be understood and seen in terms of a protest against the worship of the tauriform Yahveh. Clearly, we are confronted here with a total rejection of the symbolism of the idol.

Idolatry as worship of false gods. The second aspect of idolatry holds a much larger place in the Bible; to understand it we must review the history of idolatry in Israel. The ancestors of the chosen people practiced polytheism. Joshua recalled this in his address to the assembly at Shechem: the father of Abraham and Nahor served other gods (*Jos.* 24:2, 24:14), and even in Egypt some Hebrews worshiped pagan divinities. Upon their return from Egypt, the seminomadic Hebrew tribes who settled in Canaan came under the influence of the surrounding pagan culture and were always tempted to adopt their gods (*Jgs.* 10:6; *1 Sm.* 7:4, 12:10). Furthermore, kings often advanced polytheism by the introduction of foreign wives who kept their gods (*1 Kgs.* 11:7, 11:33). Amos accuses his contemporaries of worshiping Sakkuth and Kaiwan (*Am.* 5:26), two astral divinities. The prestige of the Assyrian pantheon exercised a profound influence on the populations of Israel. During the reign of Manasseh (688–642 BCE) a serious religious crisis broke out. Shaken by the triumphs of the Assyrians and the Chaldeans, the faithful turned to the gods of the conquerors (*2 Kgs.* 21:1–9, 23:4–14). They worshiped the sun, the moon, the *baal*s, and the Astartes (*Jer.* 2:8, 7:9). Nergal and other divinities reigned in the sanctuaries (*2 Kgs.* 17:30–31). After 587 came the trial of exile, followed by a spiritual reform. The prophets' orations were beneficial for the piety of Israel, which regained consciousness of its monotheistic faith. Upon returning from exile, they were vigilant about keeping their distance from idolatry, which continued to threaten the people because of the populations that remained in Palestine, especially in Samaria. The reaction against idolatrous cults was especially characteristic of the syncretic attempts under Antiochus IV Epiphanes (*2 Mc.* 6:2). The entire Jewish nation drew tightly together around the faith in Yahveh.

The most formidable opponents of idolatry were the prophets and their prophecies. At the solemn unveiling of the golden calf at Bethel, a prophet appeared before Jeroboam and announced Yahveh's threat (*1 Kgs.* 13:1–32). Elijah and Elisha fought against the worship of Baal and his priests (*1 Kgs.* 18:22–40). Amos reproached his Judean compatriots for letting themselves be seduced by idols (*Am.* 2:4). Hosea spoke harshly also, because in his eyes the worship of Israel had become idolatry (*Hos.* 4:12–13). Isaiah attacked the idols and announced their fall (*Is.* 2:20, 17:7–8, 30:22).

One of the important themes of the prophetic polemic is the emptiness of false gods. Idols are nothing but stone and wood (*Jer.* 16:20). Hosea does not hesitate to liken idolatry to fetishism, for in his eyes the image is set up in place of God (*Hos.* 8:4–6). Isaiah writes veritable satires of the Babylonian gods, whom he compares to nothingness (*Is.* 44:14–17). These mindless gods are carried about by beasts of burden (*Is.* 46:1–2). The theme of the idol as vacuous will continue its march, to be exploited by subsequent prophets (*Bar.* 6, *Dn.* 13:65–14:42). Moreover, it will crystallize into an imposing number of ironic and scornful terms: *nothingness, insubstantial puff of wind, lie, corpse.* Ezekiel's favorite word is *gillutim* ("dunghill"). Derision of false gods is a biblical tradition antedating the prophets and continuing after the exile (Preuss, 1971).

The *Wisdom of Solomon,* written in Greek on the eve of the Christian era, holds a veritable trial of idolatry, especially in chapters 13–15. The author rejects the worship of nature, idolatry, and zoolatry (worship of animals). However, while remaining completely faithful to the biblical tradition, he reflects his time by paying homage to the beauty of nature and works of art. He attacks the Stoic conception of gods according to which Zeus was the ether, Poseidon the ocean, and Demeter the earth (*Wis.* 13:1–19). He attacks the dynastic cult of the Ptolemies (14:17–20) and the mystery religions (14:23). In his view, the adherents of zoolatry have completely lost their reason (15:18–19). It is in terms of an authentic Yahvism that he judges pagan religions. He considers idolatry a fundamental disorder because it gives the name of God to that which is not God (13:2, 14:15, 14:20). Furthermore, the faithful adore dead idols that are incompetent and powerless. This disorder, which comes from seduction, leads to a mental aberration that in the end produces a moral deficiency among the faithful, who fall into error if not into lechery. Yet even while condemning these mistaken ideas from which Abraham and the chosen people escaped, the author speaks of his admiration for art. The *Wisdom of Solomon* has left us a veritable synthesis of biblical polemics against idols, a synthesis into which certain ideas from the contemporary Greek world have already entered.

Idolatry and Christianity. The study of idolatry from the point of view of early Christianity is linked to problems of the birth of Christian art and the question of images, their worship, and the refusal to worship them. The attitude to adopt toward idols had been prescribed to the Christians from the first decades of the church. The Christians coming from Judaism had very strong traditions. Christians who converted from paganism radically separated themselves from idols and their worship. They all lived in the midst of pagan populations who had proliferated temples, altars, statues, sacrifices, processions, and festivals in Egypt, Greece, Rome, and the Middle East. The rapid expansion of Christianity into the provinces of the empire obliged the church to take very clear positions in regard to pagan cults.

The biblical heritage. Traces of the Old Testament opposition to idols are found in the New Testament, where *eidōlon* appears several times in the Pauline epistles. *Galatians* 4:8 takes up the common theme of pagan gods who have no substance. In *1 Corinthians* 10:19, Paul states that when one venerates idols, one is appealing to demons. This idea had already appeared in *Deuteronomy* 32:17 and was developed after the exile as a result of the success of demonology. The Pauline polemic revives the notion that the pagans offer sacrifices to demons. Demonolatry is also denounced in *Revelation* 9:20. The double biblical theme of the emptiness of idols and the demonic character of idolatry will be taken up later by the apologists and the church fathers. [*See* Devils.]

The biblical heritage concerning idols also reached Christians by a second route, namely that of Philo Judaeus. In *Allegory of the Law* Philo tries to differentiate the divinity from any human likeness, since "anthropomorphism is an impiety greater than the ocean" (*On the Confusion of Tongues* 27). In *On the Decalogue* (52–80) and *Of the Contemplative Life* (3–9), he writes two accounts of the pagan gods. Both follow the same five-point outline: (1) a critique of the deification of the elements (earth, water, air, fire); (2) a critique of the deification of the sun, the moon, and the cosmos; (3) a critique of the gods considered as actors in mythology; (4) an attack against idolatry; and finally (5) a critique of zoolatry. J. Schwartz (1971) has called this "the Philonian schema." It influenced the critique of idolatry by Greek and Latin apologists, who drew on it for part of their own polemical material. On the subject of the worship of statues and divine images, Philo writes, "Their substance is of rock and wood, which was completely formless just a little while before. . . . Fragments which were their brothers or their family have become vessels for bath water or foot-washing basins (*On the Contemplative Life* 7).

The Greek apologists and fathers. In his first *Apology* (9.1–5), Justin Martyr collects the principal themes of second-century polemics against idols: the human form is not suitable to divinity; idols have no soul and are made from a base substance; they are works of depraved artisans and bait for thieves; they bear the names of maleficent demons in whose appearance they are clothed. In his *Apology* Aristides of Athens has no sympathy for the idols of the Greeks. He severely condemns the sin of worshiping created things but is even harsher toward the barbarians, who revere earth, water, the sun, and the moon, and create idols they present as divinities. In his *Libellus*, another Athenian, Athenagoras, attempts to show that making statues of divinities is recent. All such statues are the works of men whose names we know. The artists have therefore made gods who are younger than their creators. In short, all these idols are no more than fragments of creation that the faithful adore in place of the creator. After this interpretation of idolatry in the sense of fetishism, Athenagoras explains the manipulation of idols by demons. The demons urge the faithful to block around the idols, then during the sacrifices they lick the blood of the victims. But all these gods had once been men. A heritage of the secularized Greek age of the centuries just prior to the Christian era, this theme of euhemerism was to be a weighty argument, one the Fathers would use continuously.

Clement of Alexandria wrote his *Protrepticus* in order to convince the worshipers of the gods of what he held to be the stupidity and baseness of pagan myths. He first tries to determine the origin and nature of idols. Blocks of wood and pillars of rock in ancient times, they became human representations thanks to the progress of art, of which the author gives a well-documented survey. Then Clement poses the fundamental question: where did the gods represented by idols come from? The historical response to this question, inspired by euhemerism, is the deification of human beings, of kings who have declared themselves divine, and of kings by their successors. Clement then gives a theological answer, partly inspired by Plato: the pagan gods are demons, shadows, infamous and impure spirits. Consequently,the error and moral corruption of idolatry becomes clear. The error is serious, for it leads the faithful to worship matter and demons as divine. The corruption of morals is a consequence of error: idols excite lust and sensuality, which were invented by demons. To idolatry, Clement opposes the adoration of the true God, who shows man his proper dignity. Clement indicates this path of happiness by invoking *Deuteronomy* (5:8), *Exodus* (20:4), the *Sybilline Oracles* (4:4–7, 24:27–30), and Christian doctrine (*1 Pt.* 2:9; *Rom.* 6:4; *Jn.* 8:23). Chapter 4 of the *Protrepticus* is a veritable synthesis of the Christian concept of idolatry at the end of the second century.

The Latin apologists. The position taken by the Latin apologists in regard to the pagan gods constitutes a final stage. Here we again find the Philonian schema of the *De vita contemplativa* (3–9). Yet, this schema is not a dead weight that condemns the argumentation of the Fathers to die-hard conservatism. Two facts emerge from the study of these documents: on the one hand, we are witnessing a permanent renewal of the antipolytheistic argument; on the other hand, the authors take into account changes in the pagan cults, especially the rise of the mystery cults with their new religiosity. The documents appear at intervals from the late second to the fourth century: *To the Nations, Apology,* and *On Idolatry* by Tertullian; *Octavius* by Minucius Felix; *To Donatus, To Quirinius, To Demetrianus, Quod idola di non sint* by Cyprian; *Divinae institutiones* and *Epitome* by Lactantius Firmianus; and *De errore profanorum religionum* by Firmicus Maternus.

The pagan gods are not idols, states Tertullian: "We stopped worshiping your gods once we realized they do not exist" (*Apology* 10.2). He first substantiates his statement through history, for it is known where these gods were born and where their tombs are. He reproaches the pagans for claiming that their gods became gods after death because of their merits in the service of men. After these considerations inspired by euhemerism, Tertullian tackles the question of *simulacra.* The statues are only inert matter, just like vases, dishes, and furniture. Insensitive to outrage or homage, these statues are given over to commerce if not to destruction. Tertullian treats these questions at greater length in *On Idolatry,* which undertakes to show that idolatry is the gravest sin, encompassing all others. He condemns painting, modeling, sculpture, and participation in public festivals, since idolatry hides beneath seemingly innocent actions. Furthermore, he forbids Christians to teach or to conduct business, for both pursuits require contact with idols. In short, all the powers and dignities of this world are alien to God; for this reason, Christians must likewise be forbidden the military life.

The Latin apologists also developed the idea that pagan gods are demons. Demonology held a place of honor at the beginning of the Christian era. Both Greek and Latin apologists transformed the false gods into demons. [*See* Demons.] The Fathers seized the opportunity to turn these demons, intermediary beings between man and divinity, into characters lurking in the shadows of idols. Minucius Felix explains that "the demons hide behind statues and sacred images and, by exhaling their breath," exercise their mysterious effects—spells, dreams, prodigies (*Octavius* 27.1–3). In *To the Nations* Tertullian speaks of the pagan gods represented by idols that the demons use as masks to deceive men, and in *On Idolatry,* he curses artists and workers who fashion these bodies for the demons. Minucius Felix does not hesitate to make the demons the beneficiaries of sacrifice. Taking up Tertullian's notion that the devil, in the mysteries of Mithra, mimics the Christian faith, Minucius Felix accuses the devil of having plagiarized Christian ritual in the religions of Mithra and Isis. Firmicus Maternus develops this theory further and discovers the devil everywhere in paganism—in idolatry, zoolatry, the deification of sovereigns, and astrology. Thus a shaken paganism faces a decisive condemnation of idolatry and idols.

Augustine. In his *Against the Pagans,* completed in 311, the convert Arnobius attacked paganism, denounced the anthropomorphism of the pagan cult, ridiculed the pagans' conception of the gods, censured their myths, and attacked the mystery cults. His disciple Lactantius, converted, like him, under the persecution of Diocletian, and began his *Divinae institutiones* in 304. Lactantius demonstrates that monotheism is the only form of belief in God consistent with truth and reason. Speaking of the general evil of polytheism, he explains it by euhemerism and by the ruse of demons who get themselves adored under divine names first in families and then in cities.

On 24 August 410 the hordes of Alaric entered Rome and subjected the city to pillage. The pagans accused the Christians of having destroyed the worship of the gods and thus chased away the city's protectors. Augustine's answer was the *City of God,* written between 413 and 426, whose twenty-two books constitute the last great apologetic work against ancient paganism.

The pagan gods were a prime target, but Augustine found himself confronting a paganism with multiple and contradictory aspects. Besides the divine populace of country rituals, there were the gods of the classical pantheon, deified men, and a Stoic pantheism that turned Jupiter into a world soul. Throughout the first ten books of *City of God,* Augustine launches a critique, in turn acerbic and ironic, of the Roman gods, polytheism, and mythology. To strike a fatal blow at the idols, he brings in Varro, Cicero, Seneca, Euhemerus, Apuleius, and Plato. He tries to fight Varro's theology with its false gnosis of etymologies of divine names and its tripartition of gods introduced by poets, philosophers, and heads of state. But Augustine knows that idols are not mere beings without substance, invented during the course of history. These idols are also in the hearts of men, for idolatry consists of worshiping creation or a part of it as God. This theme is developed in *On Christian Doctrine* and *On True Religion,* in which Augustine, not content with a critique of the idol, launches a critique of the idol's worshiper, whom he considers a devil worshiper.

Thus, an essential aspect of Augustine's criticism of idolatry is his study of demonology. After having reviewed some of the major themes of his predecessors, he virtually psychoanalyzes the work of demons in the life of idol worshipers. Evoked by men, demons take possession of idols. The *simulacra* become animate, and the work of demons can be achieved because the idol is no longer inert: an invisible *numen* is present. The idol serves as body for the demon. It receives life from the demon, to whom it lends itself. By this means, the demon accomplishes his revelation. For this reason, Augustine repeats incessantly, "The gods are demons, and worshipers of idols are worshipers of demons." Yet in book 8 of *City of God,* he diminishes the power of demons somewhat, since they are not gods. For Augustine, these false gods are lying angels who continue their struggle against the true God. The malice of the sin of idolatry is thus exposed.

Christianity since Augustine. Ever since the conversion of the empire to Catholicism, paganism had been in retreat. After one last revival under the emperor Julian, it found a tough opponent in Theodosius the Great (r. 379–395), who forbade idolatry as a crime of *lèse-majesté.* The fifth century witnessed the demolition of temples and idols; Augustine gave the final blow to pagan theology. But the church remained vigilant in order to uproot the last implantations of paganism and squelch its influence among the people. This preoccupation would be translated in three ways: penitential discipline enacted against the sin of idolatry; the teaching of morality, beginning with the writings of Tertullian; and the constant purification of Christian worship and vigilance regarding the veneration of saints. Several great controversies, especially iconoclasm and the Reformation, show that idolatry remained a preoccupation. In the sixteenth and seventeenth centuries, Protestants often accused the Catholic church of maintaining ceremonies and traditions tainted by idolatry. Recent discussions about the cult of the saints, the worship of images, and the origin of Christian worship show the historical and theological importance of the problem. [*See* Iconoclasm.]

Idolatry and Islam. An Arab proverb recorded by al-Maydānī says, "When you enter a village, swear by its god." On the eve of the Hijrah, Arab tribes venerated many gods. In his work *Kitāb al-aṣnām* (Cairo, 1914), Ibn al-Kalbi described the prosperity of the cult of idols in the pre-Islamic age (Jāhilīyah). These idols were *anṣāb,* or raised stones; *garis,* or stones upon which the blood of sacrifice was poured; sacred trees; and statuettes that were bought and sold at fairs and markets. Another word used by al-Kalbī, which we also find in the commentators of the Qur'ān, is *ṣanam* (pl., *aṣnām*), "an object venerated next to God." The word has a Semitic origin and seems close to the Hebrew *semel,* "representation." The word is found five times in the Qur'ān (6:74, 7:134, 14:38, 21:58, 26:1), designating the "idol" rejected by Muslims. In the pre-Islamic age *ṣanam* designated diverse objects: statues sculpted like the god Hubal, statues around the Ka'bah in Mecca, and sacred trees and stones. These stones, which received libations and became objects of worship, were *anṣāb* (sg., *nuṣub*); the Arabs carried them in their migrations. Therefore *ṣanam* does not mean "divinity."

Al-Azraqī says that in Mecca there was an idol in every house. Through this proliferation of idols, the Arab invoked divinity. The gods of this vast pantheon brought the divine into the everyday realities of existence. The distinctions between various epiphanies resided in the names given them and the numerous sanctuaries. Onomastic documentation takes us back to a distant age where these idols existed, epiphanies of the divine. In addition, Hellenism introduced into Arab paganism heroes, ancestors, and genies from Petra, Palmyra, and other Hellenistic cities.

Another word is *shirk (mushrikūn),* which designates the act of associating a person with divinity; it is the word for polytheism. In the Qur'ān the word appears in the Medina surahs, where its use is frequent in Muḥammad's attacks on the associators, the *mushrikūn* (surah 6:94, 10:19, 30:12, 39:4). Such persons are to be avoided by believers. One must not pray for them, even if they are relatives (9:114). Their sin will not be pardoned. The word *kāfir,* "unbeliever," is more general and includes both the associators and the possessors of scripture (Jews and Christians). In the Qur'ān *shirk,* "associator," is the opposite of *muslim,* "worshiper of God." *Shirk* retains this meaning in the *ḥadīth.*

Muḥammad's opposition to idolatry is a Judeo-Christian inheritance. Abraham becomes the prototype of the monotheistic faith that Muḥammad espouses. Abraham is to the prophets what the Arabs are to other Muslim peoples. Beginning with Abraham's revelation, Muḥammad goes on to see in Islam not only the true monotheism but primordial hanifism (from *ḥanīf,* one who follows the original and true monotheistic religion; a Muslim), which was transmitted by Abraham's son Ishmael, following in his father's footsteps. It is in this original path that we discover the Qur'ān's opposition to idolatry.

Idols are the enemies of God and his worshipers. Referring again to Abraham, the Qur'ān condemns them along with the whole Semitic ancestral tradition, which is the origin of their worship, a worship radically opposed to the worship of the one true God (26:69–83). The same idea is found in the text of surah 21:53/52 to 70, which tells how Abraham smashed the idols worshiped by his countrymen. These idols had no substance and were incapable of creating anything (25:3–5/4). Moses had to intervene against the sons of Israel who, after their flight from Egypt, began to worship the idols that they made for themselves (7:134/138). Thus Muḥammad orders his followers to avoid the stain of idolatry and to serve God in complete fidelity (22:31/30).

Throughout the whole Qur'ān we find opposition to idols and idolatry. One must turn away from them (15:94) for they bring unhappiness to their worshipers (41:5/6), who are nothing but liars upon whom God will inflict torment after torment (16:88/86–90/88). The idolators' error is a grave one because they have no faith in God (12:106), to whom they compare mere creatures (30:30). A terrible punishment awaits them: they will be treated like their idols (10:29/28), who will abandon them to their sad fate when they stand before the fire (6:23–29). Because of the seriousness of this error, the law of the Qur'ān demands that Muslims neither marry a woman idolator nor give their daughters to idolators in marriage (2:220–221). The Qur'ān makes a distinction between idolators (associators) on the one hand, and possessors of scripture on the other, that is to say, Jews and Christians. However, the two categories of non-Muslims are guilty of infidelity in respect to God, as emphasized in surah 98. In surah 22:17 (evidently a later text), we see the opposition between Muslims on the one hand, and Jews, Christians, Sabaeans, and Zoroastrians on the other. The Qur'ān demands that Muslims fight idolators (9:36).

Idolatry consists of associating a god or gods with God (51:51, 50:25–26). This idea keeps recurring; it is the Qur'ān's definition of idolatry, whence the word for associators. Idolatry is an insult to God, since honors reserved for him alone are bestowed on false gods. Surah 17:111 shows that there are three degrees of association: children, associates in kingship, and protectors (sg., *walī*). The idea of the protector is found several times in the Qur'ān. In surah 39:4/3, saints are divinities that the faithful worship because they consider them intermediaries who will bring them closer to God. From the beginning, in Islam, fear of idolatry led to the suppression of all mediation between the faithful and God. Association in kingship consists of putting false gods on an equal footing with the one and only God (14:35/30, 26:92, 26:98). It involves an actual insult to God, for the power of the Creator is given to beings who have no substance (32:3/4, 40:69/67, 29:41/42). These idols are only names (12:40); God is the sole master of the world and men. A third means of association consists of attributing children to God (43:81), an idea that appears repeatedly in diverse forms. The Qur'ān is undoubtedly alluding to polytheistic myths and statues of divinities in temples. Surah 23:93/91 tells of the quarrels of the gods who claim to be superior to each other. There is also mention of goddesses, daughters of God (43.15, 52:39). The most famous passage is surah 53:19–21, satanic verses about the three goddesses of the Ka'bah. These goddesses were highly honored in the pre-Islamic Arab world, with great financial returns for the tribe of Quraysh. At the beginning of his preaching, the Prophet did not dare touch them. After the seizure of Mecca in 630, however, he had all the idols of the Ka'bah destroyed in his presence.

The essence of idolatry resides in the insult to God by the associators, who confer on mere creatures the honors and worship reserved for the Unique, the Creator, the Master of the World. Like the apologists and the Fathers of the church, the Qur'ān insists on the work of the demon who impels men toward idols. Abraham asks his father not to worship Satan (19:45/44), who turns men away from the worship of God (27:24). The demon is the patron of idolators (16:65/63) and as such is opposed to God (4:118/119). Consequently, idolatry becomes the demon's auxiliary (25:57/55). In surah 4:117, the Qur'ān says that idolators pray only to females, or to a rebellious demon.

Allāh is the creator God, judge, dealer of retribution, unique and one in himself, all-powerful, and merciful. He reveals himself through his prophets. He does not show himself, but man recognizes him in the signs of the universe, in the signs of God, *āyāt Allāh*. He can be known only by his word, his names, his attributes, and his deeds. In any case, he cannot be represented by an image or a representation. Islam is a religion without icons.

Idolatry and Homo Religiosus. Idolatry is a historical-religious concept that finds expression in the response and behavior of the three great monotheisms when confronted with the beliefs and the practices of the polytheistic religions they encountered along their way. This concept was developed in the course of discussions and confrontations with these monotheisms:

three religions of the Book, depositories of a revelation, animated by prophecy and doctrines of salvation—religions that join man to a personal God who appears in history. olatry means divine worship of beings who are not God in the eyes of those who have defined worship as idolatrous. The word has a negative and pejorative connotation because to the faithful of a monotheistic religion, attitudes, behaviors, and rites that should be strictly reserved for the true God are turned by the idolator toward false gods. Thus, idolatry is a fundamental religious disequilibrium due to two paradoxical facts: on the one hand a divine cultus, on the other a substitute for the divine that is not God.

Fetishism is a historical-religious concept developed in the modern age by ethnologists and historians of religions, with a view to explaining the creeds of primal black peoples of western Africa. [*See* Fetishism.] In *Du culte des dieux fétiches* (1760), Charles de Brosses tried to apprehend man in his archaic state of raw nature. He observed that ancient peoples worshiped animals, trees, plants, fountains, lakes, seas, stars, and rivers as contemporary primitives still do. To this worship, de Brosses gave the name *fetishism,* a term formed from the Portuguese *feitiço* ("witchcraft, bewitched subject"). Man sees an active presence in the fetish, which provokes in him fear and the need for protection. He obtains protection through the observance of rites. Thus, the fetishist worships the object directly, unlike in polytheism, which de Brosses viewed as a more structured religion in which symbols are characterized above all by the image and the statue.

Research has made the notion of fetishism more precise. Fetishism is the belief in the existence of a power, concentrated in beings or objects, that man must harness for his own well-being. This power is obtained by means of individual or collective rites. The beneficial result will be a function of the force obtained; therefore man uses a whole web of rituals in order to increase the force and then capture it. We are still in the context of worship, but one in which ritual receives the greatest emphasis.

This parallel between two phenomena of worship, idolatry and fetishism, will allow us to better situate idolatry as a religious phenomenon perceived by the historian of religions. In this view, idolatry is the worship of a divinity represented by a substitute for the divine, called an idol. To grasp the different dimensions of this worship, the historian of religions centers his research on *homo religiosus* at work in the exercise of this worship. He seeks to understand man's behavior through his rites and in the implementation of his symbolic system.

In the Greco-Roman world, voices were raised against the adoration of divinity in human form by Heraclitus, Xenophanes, Pythagoras, Euripides, Diogenes and the Cynics, and Stoics such as Zeno and Seneca. Reflecting on the divinity, these thinkers tried to establish themselves as intermediaries between the philosophers' religion and that of the people. In this area, Plutarch's thought becomes apparent. Seeking to avoid the two extremes of superstition and atheism, he emphasizes that divine life and intelligence are not subordinate to men. Likewise, he refuses the application of gods' names to insensate natures or inanimate objects (*De Iside* 66–67). In Egypt, he confronts zoolatry, which may lead to repugnant aberrations because of the worship of sacred animals. However, observing that the Egyptians were extraordinary inventors of symbols and emblems, Plutarch accepts the symbolism of the divine manifested in the life of beings. Consequently, he approves of those for whom these beings are an occasion to worship the divine.

During the first century of the common era, Dio Cocceianus (Chrysostomos) of Prusa, writing an apology for Greek art, affirmed: "We invest God with the human body since it is the vessel of thought and reason. In the complete absence of a primitive model we seek to reveal the incomparable and the invisible by means of the visible and the comparable, in a higher manner than certain barbarians who, in their ignorance and absurdity, liken the divinity to animal shapes." For Dio, plastic beauty expresses the divine. A century later the eclectic Platonist Maxim of Tyre treated the question of the legitimacy of portraying the gods. He notes that the Persians adored the divinity in the ephemeral image of fire; that the Egyptians contemplated their gods in objects and beings worthy of scorn; and that though the images may vary, the essential thing is to worship divinity: "God, the father of all things and their creator, existed before the sun and is older than the sky. . . . Since we cannot grasp his essence, we seek help in words, names, animal shapes, figures of gold, ivory, and silver" (*Philosophumena* 2.10).

Augustine leaves numerous allusions to the allegorical interpretation of idolatry by pagan authors. In *Expositions on the Psalms* 113 he speaks of certain people who claim that their worship does not really address itself to the elements themselves but to the divinities who are their masters. The same idea is found elsewhere in the same work (96), where the idolator declares that he worships the statue he sees, but submits to the god he does not see; the statue is only a substitute for the divinity. The pagan authors targeted by Augustine are perhaps the emperor Julian, Porphyry, and Varro.

The history of religions approaches idolatry in terms

of those four fundamental aspects of religious belief and practice that *homo religiosus* has been evolving from prehistoric times down to our own days: the sacred, myth, rite, and symbol. The idol represents a hierophany in which man perceives a manifestation of the sacred that clothes the object in a new dimension. [*See* Hierophany.] This dimension is obtained by means of rites consecrating the objects of worship, altars, divine statues, and temples: sacral presence and sacred space are indispensable. Through consecration, the image or object now belongs to the divinity and can no longer serve a secular use. The Egyptian rituals for opening the mouth, eyes, nose, and ears of a statue made to represent a divinity attest to a theology of the sacred in which the idol is an incarnation of power and life, a personification; it evokes the greatness of the god. Greek art tried to render this sacral dimension through the whiteness of marble or through protective coatings applied to the idols. Worship reactualizes myths that put the worshiper in contact with primordial time and furnish him models for his life. Thanks to this celebration, man again becomes contemporary with the primordial event, which awakens and maintains his awareness of a world distinct from the secular world.

This mythical behavior of *homo religiosus* is likewise found in Christian worship, but with an essential difference: the return to a primordial event is not a return to mythical time, but to the historical time of the life of Christ. The Incarnation is effected in a historical time: the Christian who celebrates the mysteries of Christ knows that he is simultaneously attaining the historical time of Jesus and the transhistoric time of the Word of God.

Idolatry is the area in which rites and symbols are multiplied. For man, it is a matter of transcending his human condition through contact with the sacred. His reference point remains the archetype. This is the role of ritual. Religions have left us extraordinary documentation on the rites of celebration, as for instance the sacrificial rites of ancient Greece and Rome, as well as sacred meals with mystical participation of the gods through statues led in procession; rituals of sacrifice with three fires in the Indo-European world; rites of *soma* in India and of *haoma* in Iran; the symbolism of the cults of Cybele and Mithra; the rites of daily worship in Egyptian temples; the power of the rite and of the word in the imitation of the primordial gesture of the god Thoth, creator of the cosmos; funeral rituals of embalming in ancient Egypt, linked to the Osiris myth; and the symbolism of the altar and of gestures in Hindu temples. Incorporated in the life and existence of *homo religiosus*, the symbolism of worship has the function of revelation, for it is the language of hierophany. It reveals a dimension that transcends the natural dimension of life. Consequently, it introduces a new significance into the life of man and society. In the celebration of worship, such sacred symbolism, myths, and rites help man to penetrate the mystery of salvation, a mystery that is represented for him by the holy history of his religion and culture.

[*For an understanding of the religious role of images, apart from theological interpretations of monotheism,* see Images.]

BIBLIOGRAPHY

Barthélemy, Dominique. *God and His Image.* New York, 1966.

Baumer, Iso, Hildegard Christoffels, and Gonsalv Mainberger. *Das Heilige im Licht und Zwielicht.* Einsiedeln, Switzerland, 1966.

Baynes, Norman H. "Idolatry and the Early Church." In *Byzantine Studies and Other Essays,* pp. 116–143. London, 1955.

Bevan, Edwyn Robert. *Holy Images: An Inquiry in Idolatry and Image-Worship in Ancient Paganism and in Christianity.* London, 1940.

Campenhausen, Hans von. "Die Bilderfrage als theologisches Problem der alten Kirche." In *Tradition und Leben,* edited by Campenhausen, pp. 216–252. Tübingen, 1960.

Clerc, Charly. *Les théories relatives au culte des images chez les auteurs grecs du deuxième siècle après J.-C.* Paris, 1915.

Dubarle, A. M. *La manifestation naturelle de Dieu d'après l'écriture.* Paris, 1976.

Duesberg, Hilaire. "Le procès de l'idolâtrie." In *Les scribes inspirés,* vol. 2. Paris, 1939. Second edition (1966) written in collaboration with Frarsen Irénée.

Gelin, Albert. "Idoles, idolâtrie." In *Dictionnaire de la Bible, supplément,* vol. 4. Paris, 1949.

Gilbert, Maurice. *La critique des dieux dans le Livre de la Sagesse.* Rome, 1973.

Goblet d'Alviella, Eugène. "Les origines de l'idolâtrie." In *Croyances, rites, institutions,* vol. 2, pp. 125–147. Paris, 1911.

Goetz, J. "Idolâtrie." In *Catholicisme hier, aujourd'hui, demain,* vol. 5. Paris, 1962.

Mandouze, André. "Saint Augustin et la religion romaine." In *Recherches augustiniennes,* vol. 1, pp. 187–223. Paris, 1958.

Marion, Jean-Luc. *L'idole et la distance: Cinq études.* Paris, 1977.

Michel, A. "Idolâtrie, idole." In *Dictionnaire de théologie catholique,* vol. 7. Paris, 1921.

North, Christopher P. "The Essence of Idolatry." In *Von Ugarit nach Qumran,* edited by Johannes Hempel and Leonhard Rost, pp. 151–160. Berlin, 1958.

Prat, Ferdinand. "Idolâtrie, idole." In *Dictionnaire de la Bible,* vol. 3. Paris, 1912.

Preuss, Horst Dietrich. *Verspottung fremder Religionen im Alten Testament.* Stuttgart, 1971.

Sauser, Ekkart. "Das Gottesbild: Eine Geschichte der Spannung von Vergegenwärtigung und Erinnerung." *Trierer Theologische Zeitschrift* 84 (1975): 164–173.

Schwartz, J. "Philon et l'apologétique chrétienne du second siècle." In *Hommages à André Dupont-Sommer,* edited by André Caquot and M. Philonenko, pp. 497–507. Paris, 1971.

Vermander, Jean-Marie. "La polémique des Apologistes latins contre les Dieux du paganisme." *Recherches augustiniennes* 17 (1982): 3–128.

Will, Robert. *Le culte: Étude d'histoire et de philosophie religieuses.* 3 vols. Paris, 1925–1935.

Julien Ries
Translated from French by Kristine Anderson

IGBO RELIGION. The Igbo are the largest ethnic group of southeastern Nigeria, numbering about ten million people in 1982. Until recently the overwhelming majority of Igbo were farmers, raising yams as their staple crop. Traditionally, the Igbo lived in villages or village-groups surrounded by their farms. The village-group was the primary unit of political authority; there was no sustained tradition of centralized states within Igbo society. Rather, there were strong ties to the village community, the extended family system, age-group associations, and the various religious organizations that were important in community life. The Igbo have been exposed to Christian missionary activity since 1857, when a mission was opened at the important town of Onitsha along the Niger River. By the mid-twentieth century most Igbo had adopted Christianity, though Igbo traditional religion still has millions of devotees.

Igbo religion distinguishes between three types of supernatural beings: God, the spirits, and the ancestors. Igbo believe that there is only one supreme being, Chukwu, who created the world; he lives above the world and upholds it. He is said to be the one who is known but never fully known. Igbo parents honor Chukwu by naming their children in praise of his power: Chukwudi ("God lives"), Chukwu nyelu ("God gave"), Chukwuneke ("God creates"), Chukwuma ("God knows"), Chukwuka ("God is greater"), Ifeanyichukwu ("nothing impossible with God"), Chukwuemeka ("God has been very kind"), Kenechukwu ("thank God"), Ngozichukwu ("blessing of God"), Chukwumailo ("God knows my enemies"), Chukwujioke ("God is the sharer").

Chukwu is seen as a power for good who provides people with the gifts of rain and children and is merciful toward them. Every morning the father of the family offers prayers to the supreme being. Chukwu does not intervene in the minor details of human existence, however. Such matters he leaves to the spirits and ancestors, who are often described as his messengers.

The spirits *(alusi)* are powerful beings who are quite distinct from both God and humans. Some of these spirits are regarded as the personification of phenomena such as rivers, hills, lightning, and farms. There is also a spirit associated with each day of the Igbo four-day week. An individual's personal destiny is associated with a type of spirit called *chi*. One of the most important spirits in Igbo religion is the earth spirit, Ani, who is worshiped throughout the Igbo region. These spirits are regarded as benign and have shrines, priests, and religious festivals as part of their worship. There are also wicked spirits who bring trouble to the community. They receive no regular cultic activity, but when active they receive joyless sacrifices in which the supplicant asks to be left alone.

The Igbo believe in judgment after death. Those who lived well on earth and who had the final funeral rites performed for them enter into a new spiritual existence as ancestors. The ancestors retain a close relationship to their living descendants. They are invoked during prayers and sacrifices and there is a yearly feast celebrated in honor of all the ancestors. Major ancestors have statues, which recall their spiritual power, located at a family shrine. Before drinking palm wine, the Igbo pour out a few drops in honor of the ancestors. The ancestors are believed to help the living reap a good harvest, have many children, and protect the family from misfortunes. Ancestors may also be reincarnated among the children of their descendants.

Acts of religious worship permeate daily life and are often conducted on behalf of family or village groups. A father's morning prayer to Chukwu is offered on behalf of his entire family. Individuals will invoke the name of a spirit or even that of Chukwu when they sense danger or have cause to rejoice and when they sneeze or approach a spirit's shrine. Prayers also accompany ritual sacrifice. They are offered to God, the spirits, and the ancestors and can be prayers of petition, praise, or thanksgiving. Each major stage of an individual's life is celebrated by a religious festival. Thus there are birth rituals, naming ceremonies, puberty rites, marriage rites, and funerary rites, all of which are designed to ensure a safe passage into the next stage of existence.

Sacrifice is central to Igbo religious life. Sacrifices are offered for the expiation of sins, for protection from misfortune, to petition for assistance, and to offer thanks. Most are offered to spirits and ancestors, but in certain cases sacrifices of white chickens are offered directly to Chukwu. Sacrifices at family shrines are performed by the senior man of the family. Each spirit has its own priests who perform sacrifices at its shrine. Offerings include eggs, chickens, fruits, goats, cows, and (in a few rare cases of community sacrifices) human beings. Sometimes the victim, either an animal or a person, was offered to a spirit and a little blood was shed as a sign of an offering, but the victim was allowed to live as a devotee who is consecrated to the spirit.

Other ritual specialists were less concerned with sacrifice than with resolving spiritually anomalous situations. Thus diviners used a variety of techniques to discern the spiritual cause of a particular malady or misfortune. They could discern whether a particular problem was caused by a violation of Igbo moral duties, an offense against a spirit, or a bad personal fate *(chi)*. Itinerant priests from the town of Nri specialized in the cleansing of pollution caused by the commission of heinous acts, such as incest or suicide, or unnatural acts, such as dying unattended or in the bush.

Igbo moral codes are firmly rooted in their religion. This is stressed by the Igbo use of the term *omenani* ("what happens on our land") for what would be described in English as religion, etiquette, law, and custom. Theft is regarded as a particularly grievous sin, especially when it is directed against farmers. The economic survival of the community is threatened when a farmer no longer feels that his yam fields are protected. Igbo will go to certain shrines and request that spirits or ancestors punish an undetected thief. Igbo ideas of right and wrong are not clearly referred to the supreme being. Rather, the earth spirit and the ancestors are regarded as guardians of morality. The most serious crimes are abominations committed against the earth spirit. They include patricide, suicide, incest, theft of crops or livestock, giving birth to twins, and the killing of sacred animals. Such acts require special sacrifices of expiation.

BIBLIOGRAPHY

Arinze, Francis A. *Sacrifice in Igbo Religion.* Ibadan, 1970.
Henderson, Richard N. *The King in Every Man: Evolutionary Trends in Onitsha Ibo Society and Culture.* New Haven, 1972.
Ilogu, Edmond. *Christianity and Igbo Culture.* New York, 1974.
Ottenberg, Simon. "Ibo Oracles and Intergroup Relations." *Southwestern Journal of Anthropology* 14 (1958): 295–317.

FRANCIS A. ARINZE

IGNATIUS LOYOLA (c. 1491–1556), author of *Spiritual Exercises*, founder and first superior general of the Jesuits, Christian saint. Iñigo López de Loyola was born to noble, wealthy Basque parents in the castle at Loyola, near Azpeitia, Guipúzcoa province, in northernmost Spain. Beginning in the mid-1530s he more and more frequently called himself Ignatius, although he also used his baptismal name Iñigo (Enecus in Latin). Up to 1521 his career gave no premonition of his subsequent development into one of the most influential religious figures of the sixteenth and later centuries.

Early Life and Education. In the patriarchal family in which Iñigo spent his boyhood, loyalty to Roman Catholic doctrines was unquestioning, and observance of religious practices and moral standards was about average for its social class. At about the age of twelve Iñigo received the tonsure; but his father may well have intended this not to mark the start of a clerical vocation, but merely to be the means of procuring the income from a local benefice at his disposal.

A momentous change in the youngster's life occurred when he was between twelve and sixteen years of age. His father (who died in 1507, long after his wife) accepted the invitation of Juan Velázquez de Cuéllar to receive the boy into his home at Arévalo in Castile, and there raise him as if he were his own son, while preparing him for a career in politics, public administration, and arms. The wealthy and famous Velázquez would act as the boy's patron at the royal court, while utilizing his services as a page. Velázquez was the master of the royal treasury and a confidant of King Ferdinand the Catholic; his wife was an intimate friend of the queen. Baldassare Castiglione's famous *Book of the Courtier* (1528), a manual for the training of the polished gentleman and model courtier, details the type of education furnished to the young page, with emphasis on courtly manners and conversation, proficiency in music and dancing, fastidiousness about dress and personal appearance, devotion to the ruler, and skill in arms. Iñigo's literary schooling proved superficial, consisting mainly of avid reading of tales of chivalry, then very popular. As he later admitted, his mind was filled with the military and amorous adventures of Amadis of Gaul and other fictional heroes. These novels proved an important formative influence, however, for they fired an ambition to gain fame by great feats of arms.

As Iñigo developed into manhood—short (about five feet, two inches tall) but robust, well-formed, fair-haired with long locks—his activities included gaming, dueling, and amorous affairs. In 1515 he and his brother Pero, a priest, were hailed before a secular court for some unspecified deeds of premeditated violence perpetrated at night during the carnival at Azpeitia. They escaped sentence by appealing to an ecclesiastical court, whose judgment remains unknown. Another revealing incident took place a few years later in Pamplona. While Iñigo was walking along a street, a group of men headed in the opposite direction shoved him against a wall. Drawing his sword, he chased them and would have run them through had he not been restrained.

When Velázquez died in 1517, his page promptly entered the service of the duke of Nájera, viceroy of Navarre, as a courtier, with obligations to military duty if needed. During the revolt of the Comuneros, Iñigo fought in the forefront of the duke's forces in the victorious storming of Nájera (September 1520), but he refused to participate in the customary sack of the town as an act unworthy of a Christian or a gentleman. When the French invaded Navarre in 1521 and attacked Pamplona, its capital, the townsfolk surrendered without a struggle. Almost alone at a council of war, Iñigo advocated resistance to death in the fortress above the city. In the absence of a priest, he prepared for the end by following a medieval custom of confessing his sins nonsacramentally to a comrade-in-arms. During the six-hour bombardment of the citadel on 21 May, a cannon ball struck Iñigo, injuring his left leg and breaking his right one below the knee. This calamity moved the small garrison to surrender; it also effected a metamorphosis in the wounded man's life.

Chivalrously but inexpertly, the French tended Iñigo's injuries and then permitted their vanquished enemy to be carried back to his family home on a litter. In resetting the limb there, the surgeon shortened the broken leg and left a large, unsightly protrusion on the kneecap. Impelled by vanity, by a determination to return to his former lifestyle, and by romantic notions about impressing a lady of very high, perhaps royal, lineage, whose name is still the subject of conjectures and who may have been an imaginary figure, Iñigo insisted on further surgery. The lump was sawed off and the leg was stretched almost to normal length. During all these excruciatingly painful operations, performed without anesthesia, the iron-willed patient voiced no complaint.

To while away the tedium of convalescence, the sick man turned to reading. Since the meager family library lacked his preferred tales of chivalry, he accepted Spanish versions of Ludolph of Saxony's life of Christ and Jacobus de Voragine's *Golden Legend,* a collection of saints' lives. As he kept rereading and reflecting on these two famous works of edification, Iñigo developed an aversion for his worldly ideals and ways. He resolved to serve and imitate Christ alone and to emulate the deeds of the saints, although in a manner as yet undetermined.

Spiritual Life and Leadership. Early in 1522 Iñigo left home and started on a pilgrimage to the Holy Land. Soon he took a vow of perpetual chastity, dismissed his two servants, and disposed of all his money. At the Benedictine monastery of Montserrat on 22–25 March, he gave away his mule and his fine clothes, donning a coarse pilgrim's garb of sackcloth. Then he made a knightly vigil of arms, praying all night before the altar of Our Lady, where he discarded his sword and dagger. From Montserrat he proceeded to the nearby town of Manresa, where his stay, originally intended to last only a few days, extended to eleven fateful months. At Manresa, the pilgrim, as he now termed himself, refused to divulge his true identity. He led a life of great austerity and underwent bodily penances so severe that they permanently impaired his rugged constitution. Unkempt in appearance, he obtained food and lodging by begging, a practice he was to follow for years. At times he dwelt in a cave. Besides devoting seven hours daily to prayer on his knees, he read pious books, especially the *Imitation of Christ,* and performed works of charity.

At Manresa Iñigo also composed the substance of *Spiritual Exercises,* although he continued revising and expanding the text until 1541. In its opening paragraph the slender book describes spiritual exercises as "every method of examination of conscience, of vocal and mental prayer, and of other spiritual activities that will be mentioned later . . . to prepare and dispose the soul to rid itself of all inordinate attachments; and after their removal, to seek and find God's will concerning the disposition of one's life for the salvation of the soul." Along with a number of annotations, rules, and notes, the text proposes points for methodical meditations and contemplations on various Christian doctrines and on some key topics original to the author, but mostly on incidents in the life of Christ.

Divided into four stages, called weeks, the exercises in their fullness are meant to occupy the memory, imagination, understanding, and will of a retreatant, under a director and secluded from temporal affairs, for thirty days, although considerable elasticity in length is permitted. Primarily the book is a manual of practical directives for a retreat director. Highly compressed and lacking in literary embellishments, the text is not designed for continued pious reading in the usual sense. The book was mainly the product of the author's own experiences within himself and with others. It soon won acclaim as a spiritual masterpiece, original, unified, outstanding for its sound religious psychology and pedagogy, and remarkably well organized. Its contents manifest the essence of Ignatian and Jesuit spirituality, and it has exerted an enormous influence throughout the Catholic world down to the present day. As early as 1548, Paul III's *Pastoralis officii* gave what has been termed the most explicit and honorable papal approval ever accorded a book. A long list of popes have added their own commendations, culminating with Pius XI, who in 1922 officially designated Ignatius as the patron saint of spiritual exercises.

From Manresa the pilgrim traveled by foot and by ship to Jerusalem, arriving on 4 September 1523 by way of Barcelona, Gaeta, and Rome and Venice. Only because he was denied permission to reside permanently in the Holy City, where he had hoped to spend his days visiting the sacred places and evangelizing, did he decide to return to Spain. He set sail for Venice on 3

October 1523 and arrived in Barcelona in February 1524.

Study, motivated by a desire to help souls, preoccupied the next eleven years. After applying himself to Latin in Barcelona (1524–1526), Iñigo undertook university courses in philosophy at Alcalá (March 1525–June 1527) and Salamanca (July–September 1527). Extracurricular apostolic activities won the student a number of followers, mostly women, and aroused official suspicions regarding his apparent adherence to the heretical Alumbrados. During their investigations, diocesan officials at Alcalá imprisoned the uncomplaining suspect for forty-two days and those at Salamanca for an additional twenty-two, but in both cases Iñigo was exonerated. To escape the restrictions attached to his freedom, he migrated to the University of Paris (1528–1535), where he gained a master of arts degree in philosophy in 1534 and then studied philosophy for a year and a half.

In Paris, new followers were attracted by Iñigo's spiritual exercises. On 15 August 1534, in a chapel on Montmartre, he and six companions vowed to dedicate their lives to the good of their neighbors, while observing strict poverty, and to journey to Jerusalem on pilgrimage or, if this proved impossible (as it did because of war), to place themselves at the disposal of the pope. Three others joined in the renewal of this vow a year later, bringing to ten the original membership of the as yet unforeseen Society of Jesus.

Heading for Jerusalem, Ignatius traveled in December 1535 to Venice, where his nine companions joined him in January 1537. He and six of the nine were ordained priests there the following June. After long deliberations with the whole group, Ignatius resolved to make their association a permanent, structured one, to be called the Society of Jesus. His First Formula of the Institute, a brief draft of a constitution, received solemn confirmation from Paul III on 27 September 1540, canonically establishing it as a religious order. The new order aimed at the salvation and perfection of its members, popularly known as Jesuits, and of all humankind. To this end it incorporated a number of innovations in its organization, manner of life, and scope of ministries.

In 1541 the other nine cofounders of the Society of Jesus unanimously elected Ignatius superior general for life. Under his leadership, membership increased rapidly, reaching about 940 at the time of his death, on 31 July 1556. Members dispersed throughout Europe and penetrated Africa, Asia, and the Western Hemisphere. They engaged in numerous pastoral, educational, and missionary labors, while moving to the forefront of the work of the Catholic revival and Counter-Reformation. As head of the highly centralized society, Ignatius played the key role in all this activity, as well as in the internal development of the order. He it was who devised, organized, supervised, or at least approved all these ministries, keeping in close contact with them through an enormous correspondence; some seven thousand of his letters have since been published. Besides admitting new members, choosing superiors, and regulating the spiritual life of his fellow religious, he composed the Jesuit Constitutions, along with other religious instructions and rules. In Rome he founded the tuition-free Roman College (now the Gregorian University) and the German College to train priests for Germany. In addition he founded and won support for several charitable institutions.

Because of his rare combination of talents, Ignatius influenced modern religious life as few have done. He was at once a man of prayer, a contemplative, a mystic who reported many visions, a man of action, and a born leader not only in individual spiritual direction but also in practical projects of great magnitude. He was zealous in promoting the greater glory of God, and he was a sharp judge of persons and events: reflective, imperturbable, prudent, decisive, and wise in adjusting means to ends. His mode of government, while stressing obedience, was paternal, not at all military, as is sometimes argued. In personal contacts he was inevitably courteous, tactful, grave but pleasant and genial. He was beatified in 1609 and canonized in 1622.

[*See also* Jesuits.]

BIBLIOGRAPHY

For editions of the writings by Ignatius in their original languages and in translations, as well as for the enormous secondary literature about him, see *Bibliographie ignatienne* (1894–1957), edited by Jean-François Gilmont, S.J., and Paul Daman, S.J. (Paris, 1958), containing 2,872 entries; *Orientaciones bibliográficas sobre San Ignacio de Loyola*, edited by Ignacio Iparraguirre, S.J., vol. 1, 2d ed. (Rome, 1965), with 651 items; and *Orientaciones bibliográficas sobre San Ignacio de Loyola*, edited by Manuel Ruiz Jurado, S.J., vol. 2 (Rome, 1977), adding another 580 items (both volumes contain evaluative comments and references to important book reviews). Complete annual bibliographies appear in *Archivum Historicum Societatis Iesu*, published since 1932 in Rome. An important source, although incomplete, brief, and ending in 1538, is *The Autobiography of St. Ignatius Loyola, with Related Documents*, translated by Joseph F. O'Callaghan and edited with an introduction and notes by John C. Olin (New York, 1974). Ignatius's best-known work is available in several English translations; a particularly good version is *The Spiritual Exercises of St. Ignatius* by Louis J. Puhl, S.J. (Westminster, Md., 1952), reprinted many times. *The Constitutions of the Society of Jesus* has been translated, with an introduction and commentary by George E. Ganss, S.J. (Saint Louis, Mo., 1970). The best biography available in English is by Paul Dudon, S.J.: *St. Ignatius of Loyola* (Milwaukee, 1949). *Saint Ignatius Loyola: The Pilgrim Years* (London, 1956), by James Brodrick, S.J., covers the years 1491–1538 only and is written by a superior stylist. *The Jesuits, Their Spiritual Doctrine and Practice: A Historical Study* (Chicago, 1964), by Joseph de Guibert, S.J., is an authoritative study.

JOHN F. BRODERICK, S.J.

IGNATIUS OF ANTIOCH (c. 35–c. 107), bishop and Christian saint, martyred in Rome. His name may be derived from the Latin *ignis,* which means "fire," but we know nothing of his origins. Origen informs us that Ignatius was the second bishop of Antioch after Peter, but Eusebius of Caesarea writes that he was the third bishop of Antioch after succeeding Peter and Euodius (d. around 69) and thus the predecessor of Heron of Antioch (70–107). He may have met the apostles and most probably John and Paul, but there is no confirmation of this. In his letter to the Ephesians (9.2), he calls himself *theophoros,* that is, "God-bearer," a man who bears in himself God and Christ. Indeed, his letters show him to be an exceptional man with an exceptional faith in Christ.

Although Ignatius lacked formal education, his rule as bishop was an illustrious one. During the persecutions of Emperor Trajan he was arrested, condemned, and ordered to be executed at Rome. Because of his high reputation, his execution in Rome would provide an example to the growing numbers of Christians in the East and at the same time an entertainment for the Romans, who delighted in witnessing the execution of prominent Christians. On his way to Rome, Ignatius was taken under the guard of ten soldiers to Smyrna, whence he wrote letters to the Christians of Ephesus, Magnesia Tralles, and Rome. From Troas he wrote letters to the churches in Philadelphia and Smyrna and to Polycarp, bishop of Smyrna. Apparently, throughout the long and exhausting journey, he was received by the Christian communities with great respect and reverence. Finally he was executed in the Colosseum of Rome. Another tradition, originating in Antioch and recorded in the sixth century by John Malalas, holds that Ignatius suffered martyrdom in Antioch, but such information is without any historical foundation. The Eastern church commemorates Ignatius's name on 20 December and the Western church on 1 February.

Most patrologists today accept the authenticity of seven letters of Ignatius. Because of Ignatius's emphasis on the importance of the office of bishop, a dispute arose among patristic scholars during the fifteenth and then during the sixteenth centuries concerning the authenticity of the letters. Although there are four versions of these letters, the dispute has settled on the authenticity of the so-called long recension and short recension. The first contains thirteen letters and the second only three (those to the Ephesians, Romans, and Polycarp). Through vigorous discussion and debate by John Pearson (1672), Joseph B. Lightfoot (1885), and others, the authenticity of the seven letters has been accepted. Most recently, J. Rius-Camps (1980) advanced the theory that a forger, availing himself of the genuine ending of the letter to the Ephesians, and through a process of interpolation and plagiarism, composed three spurious letters to the churches of Philadelphia and Smyrna, and to Polycarp. The chief motive of the alleged forger, according to Rius-Camps, was to emphasize church unity and absolute obedience to the bishop. Such an elaborate hoax cannot be proved beyond dispute. The seven letters of Ignatius can still claim credibility and acceptance.

Although not a man of secular erudition, Ignatius, with his simplicity of style, his biblical language and idioms, and his emotional and passionate devotion to Jesus Christ, is one of the most attractive of the early church fathers. His great faith, humility, and willingness to suffer martyrdom for Christ are reflected movingly in his letters, which emphasize three central themes: Christ, the unity of the church under the bishop, and the Eucharist. He is probably the first father of the church to emphasize in clear terms both the divinity and the humanity of Christ: "There is only one physician—of flesh yet spiritual, born yet unbegotten, God incarnate, genuine life in the midst of death, sprung from Mary as well as God, first subject to suffering then beyond it—Jesus Christ our Lord" (*Letter to the Ephesians* 7.2). He is ready to die for Christ and only for him. "Of no use to me will be the farthest reaches of the universe or the kingdoms of this world. I would rather die and come to Jesus Christ than be king over the entire earth" (*Letter to the Romans* 6.1).

Ignatius is the first Christian writer to use the term *catholic* for the church, and he insists on the unity of the church under the auspices of the bishop. In his letter to the church at Smyrna he says

> You should all follow the bishop as Jesus Christ did the Father. Follow, too, the presbytery as you would the apostles; and respect the deacons as you would God's law. Nobody must do anything that has to do with the Church without the bishop's approval. You should regard that Eucharist as valid which is celebrated either by the bishop or by someone he authorizes. Where the bishop is present, there let the congregation gather, just as where Jesus Christ is, there is the Catholic Church. (8.1–8.2)

Other letters declare the bishop to be *tupos*, or likeness, of God the Father and charge that nothing should be done "without the bishop." This unity under the bishop must have practical applications. To the Magnesians he writes, "Hence you must have one prayer, one petition, one mind, one hope, dominated by love and unsullied joy—that means you must have Jesus Christ. . . . Run off—all of you—to one temple of God, as it were, to one altar, to one Jesus Christ, who came forth from one Father, while still remaining one with him, and returning to him" (7.1–2).

Ecclesiastical unity should be expressed most especially during the Eucharist. Ignatius admonishes the Ephesians to

> assemble yourselves together in common, every one of you severally, man by man, in grace, in one faith and one Jesus Christ, who after the flesh was of David's race, who is Son of Man and Son of God, to the end that you may obey the bishop and the presbytery without distraction of mind; *breaking one bread, which is the medicine of immortality and the antidote that we should not die but live for ever in Jesus Christ.* (20.2)

To the Philadelphians, he writes: "Be careful, then, to observe a single eucharist. For there is one flesh of our Lord, Jesus Christ, and one cup of his blood that makes *us* one, and one altar just as there is one bishop along with the presbytery and the deacons, my fellow slaves" (4.1). The message is clear: one God the Father, one Jesus Christ, one Holy Spirit, one church, one eucharist, one altar, one bishop. Only through this kind of unity will the Christians prove themselves real disciples of Christ and will Christ dwell in them.

The impact of Ignatius's letters was great. He dispelled the notion that the new religion offered a magical way of salvation and propagated the teaching that only through real unity in the life of the church and in the sharing of the corporate eucharistic life will Christians taste the joy of salvation and become members of the kingdom of God.

BIBLIOGRAPHY

A complete bibliography is available in Johannes Quasten's *Patrology*, vol. 1 (Utrecht, 1950), pp. 63ff. Texts of the letters can be found in *The Apostolic Fathers*, edited and translated by Joseph B. Lightfoot (1956; reprint, Grand Rapids, Mich., 1973); *The Epistles of Saint Clement of Rome and Saint Ignatius of Antioch*, edited and translated by James A. Kleist, S.J., "Ancient Christian Writers," no. 1 (Westminster, Md., 1946); and *Early Christian Fathers*, edited by Cyril C. Richardson, "The Library of Christian Classics," vol. 1 (Philadelphia, 1953). Especially valuable discussions of the letters are found in John Romanides's "The Ecclesiology of Saint Ignatius of Antioch," *The Greek Orthodox Theological Review* 7 (Summer 1961–Winter 1962): 53–77; and in J. Rius-Camps's *The Four Authentic Letters of Ignatius, the Martyr*, "Orientalia Christiana Analecta," no. 213 (Rome, 1980).

George S. Bebis

IGNORANCE. *See* Knowledge and Ignorance.

IʿJĀZ is the concept of the "miraculousness of the Qur'ān." That the Qur'ān is the miracle of Muḥammad is an Islamic doctrine of the utmost importance because it is held to prove the divine source of the holy Book, and hence its authority, as well as the authenticity of the Prophet to whom it was revealed. But what constitutes this miracle is a subject that has engaged Muslim thinkers for many generations. By the early part of the third century AH (ninth century CE), the word *iʿjāz* had come to mean that quality of the Qur'ān that rendered people incapable of imitating the Book or any part thereof in content and form. By the latter part of that century, the word had become a technical term, and the numerous definitions applied to it after the tenth century have shown little divergence from the key concepts of the inimitability of the Qur'ān and the inability of human beings to match it even when challenged.

The idea of the challenge is based on several verses of the Qur'ān: in surah 52:33–34 there is a challenge to produce a discourse resembling it; in surah 17:88, to bring forth a like of it; in surah 11:13, to contrive ten surahs similar to it; in surahs 10:38 and 2:23–24, to compose only one surah matching it, the latter surah adding, "and you will not." The Qur'ān declares also that even if men and *jinn* were to combine their efforts, they would be incapable of producing anything like it (17:88) or even like one surah of it (10:38).

The argument, as in *Ḥujaj al-nubūwah* (Proofs of Prophethood) of al-Jāḥiẓ (d. AH 255/869 CE), that Muḥammad's pagan Arab contemporaries failed to take up the hallenge to discredit him, although they were masters of rhetoric and strongly motivated by opposition to Islam and by tribal pride, led some Muslim thinkers to associate the miracle with the Qur'ān's sublime style. Others supported this argument by reference to the contents of the Qur'ān, highlighting its information about the distant past, its prophecies of future and eschatological events, its statements about God, the universe, and society—all of which were beyond an unlettered man like Muḥammad.

Early in the theological discussion, al-Naẓẓām (d. 846) introduced the concept of the *ṣarfah* ("turning away") and argued that the miracle consisted in God's turning the competent away from taking up the challenge of imitating the Qur'ān, the implication being that otherwise the Qur'ān could be imitated. This notion was acceptable only to a few, such as Hishām al-Fuwaṭī (d. 833?), ʿAbbād ibn Sulaymān (ninth century), and al-Rummānī (d. 996). On the whole, the Muslim consensus continued to hold to the stylistic supremacy of the Qur'ān. In his systematic and comprehensive study entitled *Iʿjāz al-Qur'ān,* al-Bāqillānī (d. 1013) upheld the rhetorically unsurpassable style of the Qur'ān, but he did not consider this to be a necessary argument in favor of the Qur'ān's uniqueness and emphasized instead the content of revelation. On the other hand, al-Qāḍī ʿAbd al-Jabbār (d. 1025) insisted on the unmatchable quality of the Qur'ān's extraordinary eloquence and unique stylistic perfection. In volume 16 of his extensive *Al-mughnī* (The Sufficient Book), he argued that eloquence *(faṣāḥah)* resulted from the excellence of both meaning and wording, and he explained that there were degrees of excellence depending on the manner in which words were chosen and arranged in any literary text, the Qur'ān being the highest type.

The choice and arrangement of words, referred to as *naẓm,* have been treated in several books entitled *Naẓm al-Qur'ān,* such as those by al-Jāḥiẓ, now lost, al-Sijistānī (d. 928), al-Balkhī (d. 933), and Ibn al-Ikhshīd (d. 937). Al-Rummānī offered a detailed analysis of Qur'anic style in his *Al-nukat fī iʿjāz al-Qur'ān* (Subtleties of the Qur'ān's Inimitability) and emphasized the psychological effect of the particular *naẓm* of the Qur'ān without, however, disregarding other elements of content that render the Qur'ān inimitable. His contemporary al-Khaṭṭābī (d. 998) argued in his *Bayān iʿjāz al-Qur'ān* (Clarification of the Qur'ān's Inimitability) that the source of *iʿjāz* is the insuperable manner in which Qur'anic discourse binds meaning and wording, using various styles that combine literary qualities characteristic of the Qur'ān alone and that are conducive to a special psychological effect.

The author who best elaborated and systematized the theory of *naẓm* in his analysis of the *iʿjāz* is ʿAbd al-Qāhir al-Jurjānī (d. 1078) in his *Dalā'il al-iʿjāz* (Indicators of Inimitability). His material was further organized by Fakhr al-Dīn al-Rāzī (d. 1209) in his *Nihāyat al-ījāz fī dirāyat al-iʿjāz* (Extreme Concision in the Comprehension of Inimitability) and put to practical purposes by al-Zamakhsharī (d. 1144) in his exegesis of the Qur'ān entitled *Al-kashshāf* (The Elucidator), rich in rhetorical analysis of the Qur'anic style.

Hardly anything new has been added by later writers on *iʿjāz.* In modern times, Muṣṭafā Ṣādiq al-Rāfiʿī (d. 1937) emphasized two points in explaining the sources of *iʿjāz* in his *Iʿjāz al-Qur'ān wa-al-balāghah al-nabawīyah* (Cairo, 1926), namely, the insufficiency of human capabilities to attempt an imitation and the persistence of this inability throughout the ages. A more recent writer, ʿAbd al-Karīm al-Khaṭīb, offers four points in the same vein in his two-volume study *Iʿjāz al-Qur'ān: Dirāsah kāshifah li-khaṣā'iṣ al-balāghah al-ʿarabīyah wa-maʿāyīrihā* (An Elucidating Study of the Characteristics of Arabic Rhetoric and Its Criteria; 2d ed., Beirut, 1975), namely, the absolute truth of the Qur'ān; its authoritative, all-knowing tone of speech; its beautiful *naẓm;* and its spirituality, which derives from the spirit of God.

[*See also* Qur'ān *and, for discussion of Qur'anic interpretation,* Tafsīr.]

BIBLIOGRAPHY

Abdul Aleem's article "'Ijazu'l-Qur'an [*sic*]," *Islamic Culture* 7 (1933): 64–82, 215–233, surveys the development of the *iʿjāz* doctrine and the major works on the subject. A shorter survey can be found in the introduction to *A Tenth-Century Document of Arabic Literary Theory and Criticism,* edited by G. E. Von Grunebaum (Chicago, 1950), which also contains a well-annotated English translation of the sections on poetry of Muḥammad ibn al-Tayyib al-Bāqillānī's *Iʿjāz al-Qur'ān.* J. Bouman's *Le conflit autour du Coran et la solution d'al-Bāqillānī* (Amsterdam, 1959) analyzes the theological discussions on *iʿjāz* in their historical background and presents al-Bāqillānī's in detail. John Wansbrough argues in his *Quranic Studies: Sources and Methods of Scriptural Interpretation* (Oxford, 1977), pp. 77–83 and 231–232, that the dogma of *iʿjāz* developed more as an assertion of the Qur'ān's canonical status within the Muslim community than as evidence of Muḥammad's prophethood.

ISSA J. BOULLATA

ĪJĪ, ʿAḌUD AL-DĪN AL- (AH 680?–756/1281?–1356 CE), Muslim theologian and jurist of the Il-khanid period. He originated from a well-to-do family of notables and judges living in the town of Īg in the province of Shabānkārah, near the strait of Hormuz in the Persian Gulf. As a young man, he tried to make a career at the court of the Mongol dynasty reigning in Iran, the Il-khanids in Tabriz, and succeeded in winning the favor of the powerful vizier Rashīd al-Dīn Faḍl Allāh, a Jew who had converted to Islam when the Mongols themselves finally gave up their inherited shamanist or Buddhist convictions. Rashīd al-Dīn gave him a teaching post at a mobile "university" that accompanied the Il-khanid ruler Öljeitu during his campaigns, but since al-Ījī was a Sunnī, his position may have become precarious when Öljeitu turned to Shiism in 1310. In the long run, he seems to have returned to Shabānkārah, where, after the death of his father in 1317, he had to administer large estates that secured the wealth of his family in the form of a charitable trust *(waqf)*. When Rashīd al-Dīn was executed in 1318, al-Ījī severed his relations with the court and returned only when Rashīd al-Dīn's son Ghiyāth al-Dīn managed to take over the vizierate in 1327; he then became chief judge of the empire. However, with the end of the Il-khanid dynasty in 1335, he moved to Shiraz where he found the protection of the provincial ruler Abū Isḥāq Injü and became chief judge of the town. His salary was much lower than before, but he enjoyed the atmosphere of an art-loving court and the company of poets such as Ḥāfiẓ Shīrāzī (d. 1390?). This phase of quiet life lasted for almost twenty years until, in 1354, al-Ījī's patron was driven out of Shiraz by Mubāriz al-Dīn, a rival ruler whose sphere of influence also included Shabānkārah. Al-Ījī therefore prudently knotted secret connections with the new man and escaped to his native town shortly before Shiraz was captured. His treason did not, however, go unnoticed. Apparently at the initiative of a former adherent of Abū Isḥāq Injü, he was imprisoned in a fortress near Īg and died there in 1356.

Al-Ījī was a prolific writer. Many of his works are dedicated to Ghiyāth al-Dīn or Abū Isḥāq. Intended as systematic handbooks for teaching in high schools, they have no claims to originality, but they are well structured and reflect the long scholarly tradition of the Muslim East, which had never been completely interrupted by the Mongol invasion. They cover the disciplines of scholastic theology, jurisprudence (according to the Shāfiʿī school), Qur'anic exegesis, rhetoric and dialectics, ethics, and, to a certain extent, historiography. Their popularity is attested by the great number of commentaries on them. Some of them are still used in religious universities such as al-Azhar in Cairo. They have, however, been almost completely neglected in Western scholarship. The most important work among them is the *Kitāb al-mawāqif* (Book of Stations), a concise *summa theologica* that, after the example of Fakhr al-Dīn al-Rāzī, explains traditional Ashʿarī doctrine in philosophical terms borrowed from Ibn Sīnā (Avicenna). It consists of six books, of which only the last two deal strictly with theological problems, which are subdivided into matters depending on reason (the essence of God and his attributes) and on revelation (eschatology, belief and sin, and so forth). The first four books are concerned with the general conceptual framework of theological discourse: epistemology, philosophical principles (such as necessity, possibility, eternity, and contingence), accidents, and substances.

BIBLIOGRAPHY

Further biographical information can be found in my article "Neue Materialien zur Biographie des ʿAḍudaddīn al-Īğī," *Die Welt des Orients* 9 (1978): 270–283. The *Kitāb al-mawāqif* was first analyzed in Louis Gardet and Georges C. Anawati's *Introduction à la théologie musulmane* (Paris, 1948). I have translated and commented upon the first chapter of the *Kitāb al-mawāqif*, on epistemology, in my *Die Erkenntnislehre des ʿAḍudaddīn al-Īcī* (Wiesbaden, 1966).

JOSEF VAN ESS

IJMĀʿ. The Arabic term *ijmāʿ*, which means "agreement" or "consensus," becomes in Islamic jurisprudence the designation for one of the four sources of law posited by classical Sunnī theory, namely the consensus of the Muslim community. This consensus ranks as the third of the four sources, the first, second, and fourth of which are the Qur'ān, the *sunnah* (custom) of the Prophet Muḥammad, and analogical reasoning *(qiyās)*. For the majority of Sunnī legal theorists, the work of constructing legal rules is carried on by qualified scholars, called *mujtahid*s, on behalf of the community as a whole. Whatever these scholars agree upon is therefore constitutive of the consensus of the community, and it is not necessary for them to take into account the views of an unqualified laity. The majority of theorists further hold that an authoritative consensus is fully constituted at the very moment when the community's living scholars agree unanimously on a rule of law; it is not necessary to allow additional time for individual scholars to reconsider their decisions or to wait until the entire body of scholars involved in the consensus has passed away, thus eliminating any possibility of reconsideration. Once constituted, a consensus is irrevocable. It represents, in the view of all Sunnīs, an infallible and immutable statement of the divine law, or *sharīʿah*. As such, it is worthy to be made the basis of further legal constructions by individual scholars through either interpretation or analogical deduction. It is for this reason that *ijmāʿ* is included among the sources of law.

Sunnī theorists agree that the authority of consensus must rest upon revealed declaration and that all attempts to base that authority upon purely rational considerations are futile. The only self-constituted authority is that of the Creator-Lord; the authority of consensus can be nothing more than its derivative. However, the search for a clear-cut divine endorsement for the authority of consensus has been one of the most arduous tasks undertaken by classical Islamic jurisprudence. The various *loci classici* employed in this search have all proved to be in some degree problematic: the relevant Qur'anic passages allow diverse interpretations, and the relevant dicta of the Prophet (as recorded in *ḥadīth*, the literary embodiment of the *sunnah*) are not only open to differing interpretation (despite their being in some cases more precise than the Qur'ān in their support of the authority of consensus, as in the case of the well-known dictum, "My community will never agree upon an error") but are also fraught with text-critical uncertainties. Scholarly opinion has therefore been divided as to whether or not the textual evidence for the authority of consensus is entirely conclusive. Among those who acknowledge that it is not, compensation for the resulting element of uncertainty is found in the principle that on issues relating to human conduct, an authority need not be conclusively grounded in the texts in order to acquire validity, so long as there is sufficient textual evidence to make the legitimacy of that authority more likely than its nonlegitimacy. In this view, the case for the authority of consensus thus rests upon the principle of the sufficiency of probable textual evidence.

While a few Sunnī theorists have conceded to the consensus the privilege of engendering rules that have no demonstrable textual basis, the great majority have restricted its role to granting finality to rules constructed on the basis of the texts. Accordingly, the consensus must emerge from the exegetical deliberations of individual scholars. Individuals *qua* individuals can at best, according to the general view, produce only probable constructions of the law; their exegesis can never be more than tentative. This exegesis is in fact called *ijtihād* ("exertion," whence the term *mujtahid*) precisely because of its tentative character. The exegetes, as fallible mediators of the divine law, exert themselves in the effort to achieve, through philological procedures and analogical reasoning, the most accurate construction of that law possible *for them*. When the results of their efforts are confirmed by the consensus of their contemporaries, then, and only then, do these results acquire the stature of an infallible and immutable pronouncement. This confirmation may take the form of either explicit espousal or silent consent. The theorists differ, however, as to the value of the latter. The confirmation must, furthermore, be unanimous; a consensus cannot be constituted by a mere majority.

Since the Islamic tradition does not provide for the public certification or official convening of legal scholars and since unanimity on a scale vast enough to embrace the entire Muslim world would be difficult to achieve in the best of circumstances, the consensus, as conceived in the classical theory, has been virtually unrealizable throughout the greater part of Islamic history. While few theorists have accepted the view of Dā'ūd al-Ẓāhirī (d. AH 270/884 CE) and his followers, which restricted the prerogative of consensus making to the first generation of Muslims who were still alive after the Prophet's death, it is not surprising that the classical theorists have generally drawn their examples of consensus from that generation. In so doing, they have implied that only in the earliest period of Islam, when those Muslims who had been in sufficient contact with the Prophet to be deemed authorities ("Companions of the Prophet") were still concentrated in one locality, did the circumstances required for the constitution of a true consensus exist and that thereafter the consensus has remained more a theoretical possibility than a historical actuality. The notion that the consensus is identifiable with Muslim public opinion is distinctly modern.

In Shī'ī theory, consensus is reckoned among the sources of law, but it cannot, according to that theory, be regarded as properly constituted unless the divinely appointed leader, the imam, is present within the community. Since the word of the imam is considered infallible apart from the consensus, the consensus is deprived of the role it occupies in Sunnī theory as the infallible finalizer of rules of law and becomes, in effect, the community's affirmation of solidarity with the imam, such that its teaching and his are one and the same. Thus, from the Shī'ī point of view, the consensus may be deemed a source of law only by special license, and this status is granted only insofar as the consensus is presumed identical with the doctrine of the imam.

BIBLIOGRAPHY

There is as yet no monograph in a Western language devoted specifically to *ijmā'*. For a more extensive survey of the subject than the above, see the article "Idjmā'" by Marie Bernand in *The Encyclopaedia of Islam*, new ed. (Leiden, 1960–). On the controversies over the authority of consensus, see George F. Hourani's "The Basis of Authority of Consensus in Sunnite Islam," *Studia Islamica* 21 (1964): 13–60. The standard Islamicist view of *ijmā'* and its historical development can be found within the pages of Joseph Schacht's *An Introduction to Islamic Law* (Oxford, 1964). For a French translation of the writing of an important classical author, Abu'l Ḥusayn al-Baṣrī, on *ijmā'*, see Marie Bernand's *L'accord unanime de la communauté comme fondement des statuts légaux de l'Islam* (Paris, 1970).

BERNARD G. WEISS

IJTIHĀD. The Arabic word *ijtihād*, which in ordinary usage means "strenuous endeavor," has become in the Muslim scholarly tradition a technical term for the endeavor of an individual scholar to derive a rule of divine law *(sharī'ah)* directly from the recognized sources of that law without any reliance upon the views of other scholars. Since these sources consist preeminently of texts, namely the Qur'ān, the *ḥadīth* (narratives recording the divinely sanctioned custom of the Prophet), and dicta expressing the consensus of Muslim scholars, *ijti-*

hād is a fundamentally text-related activity embracing two principal tasks: the authentication of texts and the interpretation of texts. These entail not only deliberation upon actual texts but also the working out of appropriate methodological principles. In carrying on *ijtihād,* a scholar, while not relying for final answers upon other scholars, does interact with scholars holding contrary opinions in a setting of a highly formalized process of disputation. The rules of law that the great scholars of the past have arrived at through *ijtihād* are recorded in the literature of *fiqh,* whereas the methodological principles of *ijtihād* are set forth in the literature of *uṣūl al-fiqh.* [*See* Uṣūl al-Fiqh.]

The Tasks of Ijtihād. The text-critical tasks entailed in *ijtihād* relate mainly to *ḥadīth* and, to some extent, to historical material used to determine the existence of a consensus in an earlier generation. The Qur'ān itself is considered by Muslim scholars to be of incontestable authenticity and therefore not in need of attestation through formal text-critical procedures. The focus of attention in all Muslim text criticism is upon the "chain of transmitters" *(isnād),* rather than upon the contents of the texts themselves. The examination of these chains itself entails a complex methodology, which is explored at length in the *uṣūl al-fiqh* literature. Considered as a purely individual scholarly activity, this transmission-criticism claims to be able to establish, at the very most, the *probable* authenticity of a text, although the degree of probability may—as in the case of "sound" *(ṣaḥīḥ) ḥadīth*—be very high. Once the degree of probability of a text's authenticity has been determined, the scholar faces yet another task before he may proceed to interpret the text: he must determine whether or not, during the course of the Prophet's lifetime, the text was abrogated by some other text, for only if it was not may he endeavor to derive a rule from it.

The process of deriving rules from the texts entails two distinct activities: (1) the determination of rules that lie within the meaning of the text, and (2) the determination of any additional rules that may be deemed analogous to these rules. The first of these activities constitutes a derivation of rules from the texts in the sense that it brings to light rules that are not immediately obvious from any particular text taken in isolation. One seldom encounters in the texts legally precise statements of rules, that is to say, statements having a form such as "*x* is obligatory upon all Muslims without exception" (*x* representing an unambiguous reference to a human act considered as a class or category). Such statements, which are necessary to the development of law in Islam, must therefore be extrapolated from the texts by scholars. In carrying on this task, scholars must deal with a host of problems relating to the language of the texts. A good example of these problems is the imperative form of the verb, which appears frequently in the sorts of texts that Muslim legal scholars tend to focus upon. One may not assume from the presence of an imperative in a text such as *aqīmū al-ṣalāt* ("Perform the prayer," surah 2:43 and elsewhere) that an obligation is intended, for imperatives are used not only to impose obligations but also to invite, exhort, warn, permit, and so on. If, therefore, an obligation is intended, this can be known, according to the majority of Muslim scholars, only from the context. This context need not consist of the larger passage immediately surrounding the text in question, since *any* text within the corpus of recognized texts may shed light on any other text. This being the case, each text must be interpreted in the light of the entire corpus of texts, since virtually no text is free of some degree of ambiguity, vagueness, or generality. As the corpus of texts is vast and the greater part of it—namely, the *ḥadīth*—is subject, in greater or lesser degree, to text-critical problems, the work of Muslim legal scholars is perceived by the scholars themselves to be extremely demanding, and we can thus readily appreciate why they chose to call it *ijtihād.*

The use of analogical reasoning *(qiyās)* to deduce further rules from rules established through exegesis of the texts has been a matter of considerable controversy among Muslims. The main living adversaries of this method are the Twelver Shīʿī scholars. Among Sunnīs of all four surviving schools of law, the method is universally accepted, although an earlier school, namely that of Dā'ūd al-Ẓāhirī (d. 884), rejected it, and there is some evidence of its having been rejected by some scholars within earlier "traditionist" circles out of which the Ḥanbalī school arose. In any case, *ijtihād* is clearly not to be identified solely with *qiyās,* as some Western writers have been wont to do, since *ijtihād* has been as vigorously undertaken by opponents of analogical reasoning as by its partisans. In place of analogical reasoning, some Twelver Shīʿī scholars have espoused certain more strictly rational operations as valid methods of legal inquiry, which they have subsumed under the heading of *ʿaql* ("reason"). [*See* Qiyās.]

In consideration of the enormity of the text-critical, interpretive, and deductive tasks just described, the Sunnī scholarly tradition acknowledges that certainty about rules of divine law is rarely possible and that the formulations of rules that emerge out of *ijtihād* represent the opinions *(ẓann)* of scholars, not hard knowledge *(ʿilm).* That this is so is especially evident in the face of differences of opinion that arise among scholars. On the other hand, the exegetical tentativeness of the rules constructed by scholars is deemed among Sunnīs to be no barrier to the validity and binding character of these rules. If the *ijtihād* of a scholar is truly representative of his very best efforts, then the opinions emerging from it are binding upon the scholar himself and upon all less qualified persons (*muqallid*s, lit., "imitators") who choose to follow his teaching.

The practice of following the opinion of a scholar in preference to engaging in *ijtihād* on one's own is called, in Arabic, *taqlīd* ("imitation"). Through the *taqlīd* of the majority of Muslims, the *ijtihād* of scholars, whose number must necessarily be relatively small, is able to acquire authority within society at large and thus to engender law as a social force. The Shīʿī tradition recognizes both *ijtihād* and *taqlīd* but allows less scope for variation of opinion, emphasizing its preference for knowledge over opinion.

Mujtahids. Since the law of God comprehends, in principle, the whole of life, it must be continually expounded as novel life situations present themselves. Consequently, the exercise of *ijtihād* is not a right but a responsibility, one that rests in every age upon the community as a whole. As with all communal responsibilities, it is discharged by the few (that is, the appropriately qualified scholars) on behalf of the many and could in principle be discharged by a single scholar. Those who engage in *ijtihād* bear the title of *mujtahid,* which, though in form a participle, becomes thus denotative of a status. While the claim to this status is theoretically a matter of individual conscience, any such claim becomes effective only after it has veen validated by a substantial number of scholars. The validity of such a claim is considered to be contingent upon the satisfaction of certain requirements, which are discussed at length in the *uṣūl al-fiqh* literature. These fall into two general categories: (1) mastery of the belief system of Islam and of its rational basis and (2) mastery of the rules of legal interpretation, text criticism, and (among Sunnīs) analogical deduction.

Eventually Muslim scholarship drew distinctions between different ranks within the general status of *mujtahid,* the highest being that of the "unrestricted *mujtahid*" *(mujtahid muṭlaq),* whose holders are free to engage in *ijtihād* within any field of law and to disregard the established doctrine of any school. *Mujtahids* in the various subordinate ranks, on the other hand, were bound to the general doctrine of a particular school and permitted to explore only those questions that had not been fully resolved within that school or were restricted to certain fields of law. The rigor of the scholarly qualifications varied from rank to rank.

Muslim jurisprudents debated the issue of whether it was possible for the Muslim community to exist in any age without the presence of at least one *mujtahid* (a situation commonly referred to in later Muslim literature as "the closing of the door of *ijtihād*"), but a consensus seems never to have been reached on this matter. The general presumption of Muslim scholarship down to the modern age seems, in any case, to have been that *ijtihād* is, at least in its restricted forms, an ongoing process, even if it be on occasion temporarily interrupted. The requirements for the rank of *mujtahid muṭlaq,* however, were regarded as so demanding as to render the claim to this high rank extremely rare. Muslim jurisprudence has generally shown great deference for the great *mujtahid*s of the early centuries of Islam, especially the founders of the schools of law. In Shīʿī Islam, this deference is intensified by the fact that the founders of Shīʿī law were none other than the infallible imams.

In the modern age, the concept of *ijtihād* has sometimes been applied, in an entirely unprecedented manner, to reformist legislation introduced by, or at least subject to the ratification of, elected parliamentary bodies. It has also been adopted by a variety of reform-minded Muslim thinkers, both "modernist" and "fundamentalist," as a rationale for programs calling for fundamental social change or intellectual reorientation.

BIBLIOGRAPHY

While virtually every general work on Islam or Islamic law—for example, Joseph Schacht's *An Introduction to Islamic Law* (Oxford, 1964)—deals to some extent with the subject of *ijtihād,* there is as yet no major scholarly monograph in a Western language on the scholarly activities that constitute *ijtihād.* For a cursory discussion, see my "Interpretation in Islamic Law: The Theory of *Ijtihad,*" *American Journal of Comparative Law* 26 (1978): 199–212, and Abdur Rahim's *The Principles of Muhammadan Jurisprudence according to the Hanafi, Maliki, Shafii and Hanbali Schools* (1911; reprint, Westport, Conn., 1981), pp. 69–115, 137–192.

BERNARD G. WEISS

IKHWĀN AL-MUSLIMŪN, AL-. *See* Muslim Brotherhood.

IKHWĀN AL-ṢAFĀʾ (Brethren of Purity) is a pseudonym assumed by the authors of a well-known encyclopedia of the philosophical sciences who described themselves as a group of fellow-seekers after truth. Members of a religio-political movement, they deliberately concealed their identity so that their treatises, entitled *Rasāʾil Ikhwān al-Ṣafāʾ* (Epistles of the Brethren of Purity), would gain wider circulation and would appeal to a broad cross-section of society.

Authorship and Dating. Over the centuries, the authorship of the *Epistles* has been ascribed to the Muʿtazilah, to the Ṣūfīs, to Imam Jaʿfar al-Ṣādiq, and to the great astronomer and mathematician al-Majrīṭī. The assertion of Abū Ḥayyān al-Tawḥīdī (d. 1023) that the treatises were composed by a group of learned men in Basra during the middle of the tenth century was widely accepted. Al-Qifṭī (d. 1248), the famous biographer of physicians and philosophers, expressed his skepticism of al-Tawḥīdī's attribution by acknowledging the prevalence of the belief that the treatises were composed by an ʿAlid imam. In 1932 Ḥusayn Hamdānī stated that the Ismāʿīlī Mustaʿlī-Ṭayyibī tradition attributes the *Epistles* to the hidden imam Aḥmad. He also pointed out marked features of the treatises that are manifestly Ismāʿīlī in character.

The Ismāʿīlī character of the *Epistles* is therefore no longer in dispute. What is yet to be determined is the precise identity of their authors within the Ismāʿīlī movement. Zāhid ʿAlī and Wilferd Madelung consider the authors to have been Qarāmiṭah from Basra. On the basis of al-Tawḥīdī's comments and certain information provided by another contemporary Muʿtazilī author, al-Qāḍī ʿAbd al-Jabbār (d. 1025), S. M. Stern also implies that the authors were Qarāmiṭah from Basra. Yves Marquet affirms the Ismāʿīlī authorship of the *Epistles* and suggests that the composition might have begun under the hidden imams and that the authors mentioned by al-Tawḥīdī might have been later editors.

Recently Abbas Hamdani has pointed out the weaknesses in al-Tawḥīdī's assertion and the untrustworthiness of his report and has published the earliest reference to the *Epistles* found in the Ismāʿīlī literature. He therefore rejects the Qarmaṭī authorship of the *Epistles* and argues that they were compiled by the Ismāʿīlīyah as an ideological spearhead before the establishment of the Fatimid state in North Africa in 909.

Contents of the Epistles. *Rasā'il Ikhwān al-Ṣafā'* consists of fifty-two philosophical treatises arranged in four groups, a compendium (*Al-risālah al-jāmiʿah*, ed. Jamīl Ṣalībā, Damascus, 1949), and a compendium of the compendium (*Risālat jāmiʿat al-jāmiʿah*, ed. ʿĀrif Tāmir, Beirut, 1959). The four sections are (1) "The Mathematical Sciences," fourteen treatises on numbers, geometry, astronomy, music, geography, theoretical and practical arts, morals, and logic; (2) "The Physical and Natural Sciences," seventeen treatises on physics, generation and corruption, mineralogy, botany, the nature of life and death, the nature of pleasure and pain, and the limits of human beings' cognitive ability; (3) "The Psychological-Intellectual Sciences," ten treatises on the metaphysics of the Pythagoreans and of the Brethren themselves, the intellect, the cycles and epochs, the nature of love, and the nature of resurrection; and (4) "The Divine Religious Sciences," eleven treatises on beliefs and creeds, the nature of communion with God, the creed of the Brethren, prophecy and its conditions, actions of the spiritual entities, types of political constitutions, providence, magic, and talismans.

The Brethren attempted to popularize learning and philosophy among the masses. Appealing to a multiplicity of races and religions, they developed a strong strain of interconfessionalism. Their attitude toward other religions is therefore strikingly liberal. They argued that religious differences stem from accidental factors such as race, habitat, and time and do not affect the unity and universality of truth.

The complete text of the *Epistles* was first published in 1305–1306/1887–1889 in Bombay, then in 1928 in Cairo (ed. Ziriklī), and most recently in 1957 in Beirut. However, a critical, reliable edition based on the widely scattered original manuscripts of the treatises has yet to be compiled.

Sources of the Epistles. The *Epistles* draw on a variety of sources. The Greek element has been dominant throughout; for example, Ptolemy in astronomy, Euclid in geometry, Hermes Trismegistos in magic and astrology, Aristotle in logic and physics, Plato and Neoplatonists in metaphysics. Another pervading influence is that of the Pythagoreans, especially in arithmetic and music. Of the Neoplatonists, Plotinus and Porphyry exercised the strongest influence. In astrology there are traces of Babylonian and Indian elements. There are also stories of Indian (Buddhist) and Persian (Zoroastrian and Manichaean) origin, and quotations from the Bible. Despite these diverse sources the authors have achieved a remarkable overall synthesis.

Parables and the Animal Story. The Brethren employ fables, parables, and allegories to illustrate and prove their doctrine while concealing their own identities; as a result, much of their doctrine remains hidden from the careless reader. The reason they give for hiding their secrets from the people is not their fear of earthly rulers, but a desire to protect their God-given gifts. To support their contention they invoke Christ's dictum not to squander the wisdom by giving it to those unworthy of it.

The dispute between humans and animals (part of the twenty-second epistle, entitled "On How the Animals and Their Kinds Are Formed") is an allegorical story in which the animals complain to the just king of the *jinn* about the cruel treatment meted out to them by human beings. In the course of the debate, the animals refute man's claim of superiority over them by denouncing the rampant injustice and immorality of human society. This fable is a good example of the Brethren's sociopolitical criticism of Islamic society couched in animal characters. The most severe criticism is leveled against the wealthy (who go on amassing fortunes without caring for the needy), the privileged, and the ruling classes. The point is rendered more explicitly in the compendium *(Al-risālah al-jāmiʿah),* wherein it is stated that the animals in the story symbolize the masses who blindly follow their rulers, and the men represent "the advocates of reasoning by analogy" (those who deduce legal prescriptions from the Qur'ān and the *sunnah* by reasoning and by analogy), the disciples of Satan, the adversaries of the prophets, and the enemies of the imams.

The story enjoyed wide popularity among the masses. It was translated into Hebrew during the fourteenth century and was rendered into Urdu-Hindustani by Mawlavī Ikrām ʿAlī (Calcutta, 1811). In modern times it was translated into English by L. E. Goodman as *The Case of the Animals versus Man before the King of the Jinn* (Boston, 1978).

Philosophical System. The philosophical system of the *Epistles* is a synthesis of reason and revelation wherein the cosmos is viewed as a unified, organic whole. The philosophical structure and the cosmology are derived from Neoplatonism and Neo-Pythagoreanism. Eclectic in nature, the system draws on various faiths and philosophies, with a strong undercurrent of rationalism. The Brethren offered a new political program under the aegis of an ʿAlid imam, and their utopia, referred to as *al-madīnah al-fāḍilah al-rūḥānīyah* ("the spiritual, virtuous city") or *dawlat ahl al-khayr* ("the government of virtuous people"), was to be governed by a lawgiving philosopher-prophet. The organization and arrangement of the *Epistles* and their classification of the sciences reflect this ultimate objective.

God is described as absolutely transcendent, beyond all thought and all being. He is the One, the originator and the cause of all being. He is unique in every respect, and nothing can be predicated of him. The universe, which is quite distinct from the divine unity, is related to God by its existence *(wujūd),* permanence *(baqā'),* wholeness *(tamām),* and perfection *(kamāl).* The universe is derived by emanation *(fayḍ),* whereas creation, when it is spoken of, is understood as a form of adaptation to theological language.

The superstructure of the hierarchy of beings originates with the intellect emanating from God. The intellect, therefore, is described as the first existent being that emanates from God's munificence *(jūd).* It is a simple spiritual substance with the qualities of permanence, wholeness, and perfection. It contains the forms of all things and is in fact the cause of all causes. Second in the hierarchy is the soul, which emanates from the intellect. It is a simple spiritual substance with the qualities of permanence and wholeness but lacking the quality of perfection. Third in the hierarchy is prime matter, which emanates from the soul. It is a simple spiritual substance that has permanence but lacks wholeness and perfection. It is also susceptible to form.

The cause of the intellect's existence is God's munificence, which emanates from him. The intellect accepts God's munificence and virtues (permanence, wholeness, and perfection) instantaneously, without motion, time, or exertion, on account of its proximity to God and its utmost spirituality. Because of its perfection it overflows with munificence and virtues into the soul. But as its existence is through the intermediacy of the intellect, the soul is deficient in receiving the virtues, and thus its status is below that of intellect. To procure goodness and virtue, it turns sometimes to intellect and at other times to matter. Consequently, when it turns to intellect for goodness, it is distracted from doing good to matter, and vice versa. Being imperfect, the soul becomes attached to matter, which lacks not only the virtues but also the desire to receive them. The soul, therefore, turning to matter, takes special care in its advancement by acting on the matter and by making manifest the virtues inherent in it. Hence the soul is afflicted with exertion, hardship, and misery in reforming and perfecting matter. When matter accepts the virtues, it attains wholeness, while the soul achieves its own perfection. When the soul turns to the intellect, is attached to it and united with it, it attains tranquillity.

The process of emanation terminates with matter. As the soul acts on matter, the matter receives its first form—the three dimensions (length, breadth, and depth)—and thereby becomes absolute body *(al-jism al-muṭlaq)* or universal matter *(hayūlā al-kull).* Thenceforth begins the realm of the composite *(ʿālam al-murakkabāt).* Next, absolute body takes its first form, which is circular because that is the best form. Thus, the spheres and the stars are formed from absolute body. Subsequently come the nine spheres beginning with the outermost sphere, which encompasses all spheres. Next to it is the sphere of fixed stars, followed by the spheres of Saturn, Jupiter, Mars, the sun, Venus, Mercury, and the moon. The higher the position of the sphere, the purer and finer its matter. The spiritual force that directs and manages each sphere is called the particular soul of that sphere.

Under the sublunar world comes the physical matter *(hayūlā al-ṭabīʿah)* of the four elements, fire, air, water, and earth. The earth, being farthest from the One, is the coarsest and darkest kind of physical matter. The active force of the soul that operates on the four elements through heat, cold, dryness, and wetness is known as "the nature of generation and corruption." It moreover produces the generated beings that form the three kingdoms of minerals, plants, and animals. The active force operating on each of these generated beings is called the particular soul. Thus, the process wherein the soul mixes the elements to various degrees and thereby produces the generated beings terminates with man, who is the culmination of that process. Humanity is therefore the noblest of all creation, and the rest of the three kingdoms have been made subservient to it. The unity and complexity of the human being's soul and body make him or her a microcosm. Humans, by virtue of their position, are the central link in the long chain of beings; below them is the animal kingdom and above them is the world of angels, and they are connected to both. In the Perfect Human Being, who has realized his divine origin, the process of generation in descending order comes to an end and the reverse journey in ascending order starts. The human being, therefore, fulfills the purpose of creation.

The *Epistles* occupy a unique position in the history of Islamic thought and exercised a great influence on the Muslim elite. The existence of a large number of manuscript copies of the text scattered throughout the Muslim countries is an eloquent witness to their popularity and influence.

BIBLIOGRAPHY

To the extensive bibliography provided by Yves Marquet in his article "Ikhwān al-Ṣafā'," in *The Encyclopaedia of Islam*, new ed. (Leiden, 1960–), the following studies should be added: Abbas Hamdani's "Abū Ḥayyān al-Tawḥīdī and the Brethren of Purity," *International Journal of Middle East Studies* 9 (1978): 345–353, and "An Early Fāṭimid Source on the Time and Authorship of the *Rasā'il* Ikhwān al-Ṣafā'," *Arabica* 26 (February 1979): 62–75; Hamid Enayat's "The Political Philosophy of the *Rasā'il Ikhwān al-Ṣafā'*," in *Ismā'īlī Contributions to Islamic Culture*, edited by Seyyed Hossein Nasr (Tehran, 1977); and Ian R. Netton's *Muslim Neoplatonists* (London, 1982).

ISMAIL K. POONAWALA

IKKYŪ SŌJUN (1394–1481), poet, calligrapher, Zen eccentric, revitalizer of the Daitokuji line of Rinzai Zen. Ikkyū was likely, as legend suggests, the unrecognized son of the hundredth emperor of Japan, Gokomatsu (1377–1433; r. 1392–1412), by a rather low-ranking court lady. At an early age, perhaps for lack of any other option, his mother placed him in the Gozan temple of Ankokuji, in Kyoto. He spent the rest of his childhood in Ankokuji and in Tenryūji, yet another Gozan establishment. A quick student, Ikkyū was precocious in both scriptural studies and in the literary arts that had become a focus of the aesthetically oriented Gozan movement.

In 1410 Ikkyū left Tenryūji to live in the streetside hermitage of the eremetic monk Ken'ō Sōi (d. 1414). Ken'ō belonged to the Daitokuji-Myōshinji lineage of Rinzai. Since these two temples had long been out of the Gozan orbit patronized by the shoguns, and since Ken'ō lacked formal certification of enlightenment from his own master, Ikkyū's decision to take him as spiritual master left the young monk doubly removed from the orthodox Zen establishment and clearly illustrates his desire to reach the substance of the Zen tradition rather than grasping for the formal honors offered by the power brokers of his day.

Ikkyū's devotion to the rigors of meditative life in preference to the aesthetic glory and institutional pomp of establishment Zen led him, after Ken'ō's death in 1414, to leave Kyoto to join the circle of the demanding master Kasō Sōdon (1352–1428), twenty-second abbot of Daitokuji, at his small hermitage at Katada on the shores of Lake Biwa. There, in 1420, Ikkyū attained *satori* but following the example of his early master, Ken'ō, refused to accept Kasō's certification.

Shortly thereafter, apparently following an extended squabble with Kasō, Ikkyū left Katada to spend several years in Sakai, a booming port town on the Inland Sea. There he gained a reputation for wild eccentricity, in part due to his repeated bouts of tavern and brothel hopping. These establishments, he claimed, were far better sources of enlightenment than the corrupt temples of Kyoto and Kamakura. Even Daitokuji came under his criticism, and although he was briefly appointed abbot of Daitokuji's Nyoi-an subtemple in 1440, he soon stormed out in disgust at the temple's general pretentiousness and in particular at the role taken there by Kasō's chief disciple, Yōsō Sōi (1376–1458).

By the 1440s Ikkyū had once again taken up practice of the arts. He was eventually to become known for his unconventional poetry and his powerful, at times even unsettling, calligraphy. He was, as well, the confidant and friend of a number of key figures in the development of the new urban middle-class arts—the *nō* playwright Komparu Zenchiku (1405–1468); the early tea master Murata Shukō (1427–1502); the painters Bokkei Saiyo (dates unknown) and Motsurin Shōtō, also known as Bokusai (d. 1492), who wrote the earliest biography of Ikkyū; and the *renga* poet Sōchō (1448–1532)—and was thus an important conduit for Zen ideas and attitudes geographically outward from Kyoto and socially downward to the largely *nouveau riche* audience for these emerging arts.

In his later years, Ikkyū made peace with the hierarchy of Daitokuji and was appointed abbot of the temple in 1474, at a time when the temple was but a shell, its buildings having been almost entirely destroyed in the early battles of the Ōnin War (1467–1477). It was, indeed, in no small part Ikkyū's connections with the upwardly mobile merchant class of Sakai that provided the funds for the rebuilding and revitalization of Daitokuji and laid the foundation for it and its sister temple, Myōshinji, to fill the spiritual vacuum left by the intertwined collapse of the Ashikaga shogunate and the Gozan establishment. Ikkyū's final years were also marked by his famous autumnal affair with a blind woman singer called Mori. He died in 1481 at the age of eighty-eight. Popular fiction of the Tokugawa period made much of Ikkyū's eccentricities and transformed him from a serious historical figure into an amusing, but stereotypical, folk image, an image whose most recent manifestation was as the hero of a cartoon show on Japanese television.

Several literary works are attributed to Ikkyū. The most important of these are his collection of over a thousand poems, the *Kyōunshū* (Crazy-Cloud Anthology), and the related collection the *Jikaishū* (Self-Admonitions). He was also the author of six prose works on Buddhist themes: the prose poem *Gaikotsu* (Skeletons); *Amida hadaka* (Amida Laid Bare); *Bukkigun* (The War of the Buddhas and Demons); *Mizu-kagami menashi gusa* (Mirror for the Sightless), which includes the sometimes separated *Futari bikuni* (Two Nuns); *Kana hōgo* (A Vernacular Sermon); and *Maka hannya haramitta shingyō kai* (Explication of the Heart Sutra). Two *nō* librettos, *Yamamba* (Old Woman of the Mountains) and *Eguchi*, are also ascribed to Ikkyū, but these attributions are doubtful. A fair number of examples of his extraordinary calligraphy survive, as do a number of forgeries.

[*See also* Calligraphy *and* Gozan Zen.]

BIBLIOGRAPHY

The fullest, though by no means either complete or perfect, treatment of Ikkyū in English is my own *Zen-Man Ikkyū* (Chico, Calif. 1981). Also useful are Donald Keene's biographical sketch, "The Portrait of Ikkyū," most easily available in his *Landscapes and Portraits* (Tokyo and Palo Alto, Calif., 1971), Sonja Arntzen's annotated translations of several dozen poems from the *Kyōunshū, Ikkyū Sōjun: A Zen Monk and His Poetry* (Bellingham, Wash., 1973), and her *Ikkyū and the Crazy Cloud Anthology* (New York, 1986). The best study of Bokusai's critical biography of Ikkyū is Hirano Sōjō's *"Ikkyū oshō nempu" no kenkyū* (Kyoto, 1977), which includes the whole of Bokusai's original text. The best, though still incomplete, study of Ikkyū's poetry is Hirano's *Kyōunshū zenshaku*, 2 vols. (Tokyo, 1976–). Ikkyū's prose pieces can be found in *Ikkyū oshō zenshū*, edited by Mori Taikyō (Tokyo, 1913). The fullest representation of his calligraphy is Tayama Hōnan's *Zenrin bokuseki kaisetsu* (Kamakura, 1965) and *Zoku Zenrin bokuseki kaisetsu* (Kamakura, 1965). Serviceable modern biographies on Ikkyū in Japanese include Furuta Shōkin's *Ikkyū* (Tokyo, 1946), Ichikawa Hakugen's *Ikkyū: Ransei ni ikita zenja* (Tokyo, 1971), and Murata Taihei's *Ningen Ikkyū* (Tokyo, 1963). For general background on the age in which Ikkyū lived, *Japan in the Muromachi Age*, edited by John Whitney Hall and Toyoda Takeshi (Berkeley, 1977), and Martin Collcutt's fine *Five Mountains: The Rinzai Zen Monastic Institution in Medieval Japan* (Cambridge, Mass., 1981) are especially valuable.

JAMES HUGH SANFORD

ILLUMINATIONISM. *See* Ishrāqīyah.

ILMARINEN. According to the list of pagan Finnic gods compiled in 1551 by Michael Agricola, who introduced the Reformation to Finland and established the Finnish literary language, Ilmarinen was the creator of both wind and calm weather and controlled travel on water. There is no evidence that Ilmarinen was ever worshiped, but what is probably the oldest stratum of *Kalevala*-type poetry concerning the exploits of Ilmarinen connects him with various cosmogonic acts. Elias Lönnrot's redaction of the *Kalevala* includes material from this ancient folk tradition but increases the number of his appearances, featuring him in twenty-seven out of the fifty divisions of the epic. Lönnrot also enhances Ilmarinen's personality with a human dimension.

The name *Ilmarinen* is probably derived from the Finno-Ugric word *ilma*, meaning "air," and, by extension, "weather" and "world." The Udmurts (Votiaks), distant relatives of the Finns and inhabitants of the region northeast of Moscow between the Kama and Vyatka rivers, called their sky god Ilmar or Inmar. A famous Saami (Lapp) witch drum, presented in 1692 as an exhibit in court, depicts a god named Ilmaris as having the power to raise and calm storms at sea.

Among the epithets applied to Ilmarinen in the epic tradition is "shaper of the mysterious, luck-bringing *sampo*." *Sampo* is a difficult term, and scholarly research has produced more than sixty definitions for it, but according to the most widely held view, the *sampo* is a support of the world. A close derivative of the term is *sammas*, meaning "statue." A frequent substitute or parallel for the term is *kirjokansi*, meaning "brightly worked cover," which in other contexts stands for the sky. Certain Saami cult images in stone and wood are believed to be late representations of the *sampo*.

One folk poem places the forging of the *sampo* shortly after the genesis of the sky, earth, sun, moon, and stars, all of which, the poem claims, were formed by the breaking of an eagle's (in some versions, a waterfowl's) egg. The poem, which goes on to relate how Ilmarinen and his brother Väinämöinen steal the *sampo*, resembles the ancient Nordic sagas. But the epithet "shaper of the mysterious, luck-bringing *sampo*" refers to the tradition in which Ilmarinen creates the *sampo* himself, as in the episode in which, as a result of this act, he wins a competition against his brother for the beautiful maid of Pohjola. Together, Väinämöinen and Ilmarinen strike the primeval spark in the upper aerial regions.

Ilmarinen is also credited with forging a golden maid, who eventually proves no match for a real woman. Ilmarinen as smith-god later developed into a culture hero who makes useful objects for people and takes part in various adventures, including love-quests.

[*See also* Finnic Religions; Väinämöinen; *and* Lemminkäinen.]

BIBLIOGRAPHY

Fromm, Hans. *Kalevala.* Munich, 1967. See the index, s.v. *Ilmarinen.*

Honko, Lauri. "Ilmarinen." In *Wörterbuch der Mythologie,* edited by H. W. Haussig, vol. 1, *Gotter und Mythen im Vorderen Orient,* pp. 309–311. Stuttgart, 1965.

Krohn, Kaarle. *Kalevalastudien,* vol. 3, *Ilmarinen,* and vol. 4, *Sampo.* Folklore Fellows Communications, nos. 71–72. Helsinki, 1927. Krohn's six-volume work, although partially outdated, still gives the most thorough summary of the sources of the *Kalevala.*

Matti Kuusi

IMAGES. [*To explore the role of images in various religious traditions and their connection to the realm of the imagination, this entry consists of three articles:*

Veneration of Images
Images and Imagination
The Imaginal

The first article presents an overview of religious practices that involve images. This is followed by a historical survey of Western theories of the imagination and the role of sacred images in religious experience. The third article is a discussion of Henry Corbin's theory of "the imaginal." For discussion of the role of visual images in particular religious traditions, see Iconography.]

Veneration of Images

The veneration of images (statues, paintings, and other representations of gods, saints, heroes, etc.) has been a widespread phenomenon in the history of religions, but it has not been featured equally in the various religious traditions of the world. Some scholars have tried to place the major historical religions along a sort of spectrum ranging from those traditions that are aniconically inclined (Islam, prophetic Judaism) to those in which images have flourished (Mahāyāna Buddhism, Hinduism). At appropriate intervals between these extremes, they have located Vedism, Protestantism, Shintō, ancient Buddhism, Jainism, Roman Catholicism, Eastern Orthodoxy, and the religions of ancient Egypt and Greece, to mention only a few. Occasionally, they have tried to insert primitive religions at various places as well.

Such a scheme, however, is misleading. Though perhaps useful in giving an overall picture of the importance of images in different traditions, it presents a simplistic and superficial view of the matter. A number of factors make the picture more complicated.

First of all, historically, the attitudes of many religions toward images have by no means been uniform. Hinduism and Buddhism both started out aniconically and only gradually accepted images into their worship. Christianity did the same, but then vacillated with regard to their acceptability. We must therefore examine the history of images in individual traditions, before generalizing about their veneration.

Second, what a tradition or an individual may say or think about the veneration of images does not always correspond to what is actually done or felt in front of a real image. In Theravāda Buddhism, for example, those who venerate an image of the Buddha may not say that he is present in his statue or that he is able to respond in any way to their offerings or praise, but they sometimes behave as though he were. Much the same thing could be said about the veneration of images in many other traditions.

Third, at any given period even within a single tradition, several different attitudes toward images are likely to be expressed. The Chinese Zen master, for example, who burned a statue of the Buddha when he needed firewood, had different things to say about it than a fellow monk who was horrified by his action. More generally, the extent to which venerated images are actually thought to embody the divine or the supernatural may vary considerably. Some people—for example, iconoclasts—think that images do not or should not have any relationship with divinity at all. Others, however, hold more positive views. There is, for example, what Albert C. Moore calls the "thoroughgoing image-worshipper" who "as he enters the temple . . . sees the central icon as a living embodiment of the god" (Moore, 1977, p. 32). This does not quite mean that for him the god *is* the image. In fact, that degree of idolatry is usually found only in the misguided pronouncements of monotheists or missionary ethnographers against "heathen" tribes who supposedly worship "sticks and stones." But for such a worshiper the image may well be divine—that is, there may be a permanent and intimate relationship between the god and the image, in which the deity can always be found. The fifth-century BCE citizens of Athens who banished their compatriot Stilpo for claiming that Phidias's statue of Athena was not the goddess herself must have been of this type. So too was the South Indian devotional mystic Āṇḍāl, who married an image of Viṣṇu and was then miraculously absorbed in his embrace.

On the other hand, there is the devotee who views the god as somehow present in the image, but only for the duration of a ritual. In fact, in many cases, the rites themselves are believed to bring about or affirm this presence. The divinity is invited to come to the ritual or is awakened at its beginning, and is then dismissed or put to rest at the end of the ceremony. Thus each morning, in temples throughout ancient Egypt, the high priest would open the doors of the temple chamber, take the statue of the god down, change its clothes, cleanse it, feed it, and adorn it, before retiring to leave it in darkness.

Finally, there is the person who thinks that images are helpful foci for veneration, but that ultimately they are only reflections and reminders of the deity's characteristics. Such individuals do not actually worship the image but worship before the image, which is seen as an effective channel for prayer, devotion, or meditation. Thus J. B. Pratt tells in *The Religious Consciousness* (New York, 1920) of a Hindu who explained that the image he was worshiping was not Śiva (who was in Heaven), but that it nonetheless enabled him to pray to Śiva.

Prehistoric and Primitive Evidence. The origins in time of the veneration of images are rather difficult to ascertain. Some scholars have suggested that certain Paleolithic remains—such as the sculpted female figure known as the Venus of Willendorf, or the so-called Dancing Sorcerer found painted on the walls of a "sanctuary" in the cave of Les Trois Frères in southern France—constitute early examples of an image cult. But prehistoric art is notoriously difficult to interpret. [*See* Paleolithic Religion.]

Other scholars have turned instead to instances of image worship among nonliterate, or primitive, societies, arguing or implying that if Africans, Oceanians, and Native Americans venerate images, it must be an ancient practice. But here too there are difficulties, for even if one can accept such evidence as relevant to the question of historical origins, the ethnographic data are mixed: some tribes venerate images, whereas others do not. Moreover, the debate is further complicated by another question: images of whom? Many primal cultures do not represent the figure of their high god or supreme being, but may well venerate images of various lesser divinities, spirits, or ancestors. For example, the Maori do not represent their high god Io but place strikingly carved images of lesser spirits in their ancestral shrines. Similar evidence can be adduced from Africa and the Americas.

It should also be pointed out that contact with the Western world has often strongly affected indigenous imagistic traditions. Maori teachings about Io, for example, may well have been a response to Christian doctrines about God. Similarly, when the people of Tonga were converted to Christianity in the nineteenth century, they destroyed virtually all of their "idols," except for a few that, ironically, were saved by a missionary for a museum. Alternatively, the Asmat of New Guinea did not start making and venerating images until the turn of the twentieth century, when, partly in response to Western demands for primitive art, they found they could file down (imported) iron nails and use them as small chisels to create images.

The veneration of images in primal cultures thus escapes any easy generalizations, complicated as it is by inadequacies of reliable information and by questions of theological, cultural, and even technological contexts.

Hinduism. For centuries, the Hindu tradition was essentially aniconic. The various deities of the Vedic pantheon were not represented, at least not anthropomorphically, and the ritual sacrifices involving them stressed the importance not of the divine form per se, but of sacred sound (*mantra*s), the fire, and the sacrificial altar.

Only with the freezing of the sacrificial tradition, the growing use of temples, and the rise of devotional movements *(bhakti)* did images of the gods become a prominent feature of Hinduism. [*See* Mūrti.] Viṣṇu, Kṛṣṇa, Śiva, Kālī, and other gods and goddesses all came to be represented in their various forms in statues and paintings and were venerated in temples and homes throughout India.

The general pattern of Hindu image veneration can be seen in the domestic rite of *pūjā*. This may take place several times a day, but it is typically done in the morning. The devotee first ritually purifies himself by bathing, changing his clothes, and so forth, so that he can approach the god. He then makes offerings to the image, including flowers, incense, praise, perfumes, lights, water, a bath, fresh ornaments, and food and drink. In other words, the image is treated as though it were an honored guest. Indeed, *pūjā* replicates for the god the common Indian acts of hospitality; it is a way of making the god present, or at home in an especially honored way in one's own house or temple.

Two important gestures connected with *pūjā* are *praṇāma* and the eating of *prasāda*. *Praṇāma* refers to prostration or bowing or any equivalent salutation of respect. It is made not only to images of the gods but to great persons. As in many other traditions, it expresses one's subordination, and especially one's relative impurity vis-à-vis the deity. Honor is paid by placing the purest part of one's own body, the head, below the most impure part of the god's body, his feet.

Prasāda, on the other hand, is the food that has been offered to the deity and is then distributed to the devotees. The consumption of such food—found in many sacrificial traditions throughout the world—is often interpreted as an act of communion or commensalism with the god. In Hinduism, however, it is a further act of veneration. The devotee does not really share in the god's meal; he eats after him. *Prasāda* represents the god's leftovers—which, in the Hindu context, would be thought of as highly polluting if they came from another human being. In thus consuming the deity's scraps, the devotee once again symbolically asserts his own relative impurity and the god's divinity. [*See* Pūjā.]

Buddhism. It is a well-known fact that Buddhism, founded in the sixth century BCE, did not see the first image of its founder until around the first century CE. Early Buddhist bas-reliefs represent the Buddha aniconically. Other figures—devotees, disciples, and divinities—are physically depicted, but not the Buddha, whose presence is asserted only through a variety of symbols such as footprints, trees, wheels, stupas, and empty thrones. These symbols, however, were themselves already objects of a veneration very much like what was later directed toward images of the Buddha. In other words, though Buddhism did evolve from an aniconic to an iconic stage, acts of veneration in Buddhism may not have changed much in the process. The image was just another symbol of the Blessed One.

Art historians have much debated the origin of the Buddha image. Some claim that it first arose from indigenous Indian depictions of local divinities (*yakṣas*); others, that it was inspired by the importation of Hellenistic imagery and artists into northwestern India. Be this as it may, it was not long before Buddhist texts began to espouse a definite stance on the veneration of images. The second-century-CE *Aśokāvadāna*, for example, states that it is acceptable to venerate an image of the Buddha, provided one remembers the Buddha and does not focus on the wood or clay of which his statue is made.

However, the veneration of images in Buddhism—at least in the Theravāda tradition—has been complicated by the doctrine of the Buddha's *parinirvāṇa*. According to this, the Buddha is dead and gone: his power has become a thing of the past; he has done all that he needed to do. He is thus incapable of being prayed to, of receiving offerings, or of responding to his devotees. Theravādins are cognizant of this doctrine, yet, as Richard Gombrich (1971) has pointed out, affectively they sometimes sense that the Buddha is present, that his image is in some way alive, and hence make *pūjā* offerings to it of flowers, incense, lights, and even food and drink. This does not, however, make the Buddha a god in the Hindu sense. It is noteworthy that in Sri Lanka the food offerings made to images of the Buddha are not then eaten as *prasāda* by his devotees. They cannot be shared or returned, so they are thrown away or fed to the dogs or given to Tamil (Hindu) beggars.

The offerings themselves, however, create a mood, or perhaps better a milieu, in which the Buddha and his teachings can be contemplated. For example, in presenting a flower to a Buddha image, the devotee often recites a verse that makes him reflect on the doctrine of impermanence: "Just as this flower fades, so my body goes towards destruction" (Gombrich, 1971, p. 116). And on lighting a lamp, he contemplates the Buddha himself, "the truly enlightened lamp of the three worlds" (p. 117). The veneration of a Buddha image, therefore, whatever the ontological status of the Buddha, is also an act of meditation.

At the same time, of course, it is a soteriologically oriented act. Though the Buddha, at the end of his one-way street, cannot come back, Buddhist devotees can make progress toward him. Usually they express their aims quite clearly in making offerings to Buddha images, seeking thereby to acquire merit so as to gain a better rebirth and eventual enlightenment as well.

China and Japan. Once the idea of the Buddha image and its veneration was established in India, it flourished impressively and contributed to the development of a whole pantheon of enlightened beings. The veneration of celestial Buddhas such as Amitābha, and of *bodhisattvas* such as Avalokiteśvara and Mañjuśrī, became one of the hallmarks of Mahāyāna Buddhism.

Buddhist images, in fact, were an important means of spreading the faith and a stimulus to the development of iconic traditions in the whole of East Asia. China, during the first millennium BCE, appears to have been basically uninterested in representing and venerating its gods anthropomorphically. (One of its early, legendary sage-kings, for instance, is reputed to have ordered his soldiers to fight with the statues of various deities; when his soldiers won, he proclaimed the superiority of man and the folly of worshiping gods made of clay.) The introduction of Buddhism in the first century CE, however, transformed the Chinese outlook. Even official Confucianism eventually allowed for images of Confucius (though this decision was later reversed by a return to simple wooden ancestral tablets to represent the departed master).

In Taoism and folk religion, however, a whole pantheon of popular divinities, inspired by Buddhist imagery, came to be depicted and worshiped. Some figures such as Mi-lo, the so-called Laughing Buddha, were clearly the result of syncretism. Others, such as Kuan-ti, the god of war, were apotheosized heroes. Many Chinese homes had their doors guarded by images of the gate gods, and their kitchens looked over by paper prints of Tsao-wang, the god of the hearth. Tsao-wang's cult, in fact, reflects what has been called the Chinese "down-to-earth sense of the presence of the deity in the image" (Moore, 1977, p. 180). At the end of each year, when he was thought to leave his post in the kitchen to report to the Jade Emperor on everything that had transpired in the household during the past year, he was given especially fine offerings as a bribe. His image was then removed, and the few days of his absence in heaven were a time of unsupervised relaxation, until a new image was set up at the New Year to indicate his return.

In Japan too the veneration of images was imported with the introduction of Buddhism. Early Shintō used a variety of symbols or natural objects to represent the presence of sacred powers *(kami)*, but did not usually attempt to depict these directly. Even today this Shintō reticence continues: shrines rarely contain statues or paintings, even though occasional depictions of individual *kami* can be found.

But with the importation of Buddhism beginning in the sixth century CE, the Mahāyāna's impressive and influential iconography soon became established. Some Buddhas and *bodhisattvas* continued to be venerated much as they had been in China. The cults of others, however, took off in new Japanese directions. Thus Dainichi Nyorai (Vairocana), the Great Sun Buddha, came to play an important role in the formation of a Japanese national ideology. Fudō (Acala), never popular in Indian or even Chinese Buddhism, became in Japan the object of a flourishing cult with esoteric overtones. And the veneration of the *bodhisattva* Jizō (Kṣitigarbha), the wayside guardian of travelers and children and the consoler of beings in hell, syncretized a number of disparate elements (including Japanese phallicism), so that his image became one of the most popular ones at the local level.

Ancient Greece. In the Western world, the veneration of anthropomorphic images of deities made its appearance in ancient Greece much earlier than in India or East Asia. Some scholars have suggested that Greek anthropomorphism only gradually emerged out of aniconic forms, pointing to images such as the herms (stone pillars showing only the head and phallus of Hermes) as halfway marks in this process.

Greek mythology, however, had long had an anthropomorphic understanding of the gods, so that already in the seventh century BCE images of deities as athletic and physically perfect specimens began to appear. This anthropomorphism reached its climax, perhaps, with the work of Phidias (fifth century BCE), the sculptor who worked on the Parthenon and on various colossal statues of individual gods such as Athena and Zeus.

Images typically were housed in temples where they were the objects of petitions, prayers, and sacrifices. Altars were erected before them either inside or outside the temple proper, and on these the offerings were placed. These could be either bloodless offerings of cereals, vegetables, or fruits, especially at harvesttime, or animal sacrifices that required a fire. Only parts of the victim were burned for the deity; the rest was cooked for a communal feast.

Such veneration of anthropomorphic images, however, was not without its perennial critics in Greece, especially among the intelligentsia. Thus the pre-Socratic philosopher Heraclitus (fifth century BCE) is said to have likened prayers made to images of the gods to one's attempting to converse with a building. And Xenophanes (sixth century BCE) is well known for his declaration that, if horses and cows could make images, they would represent their gods in equine and bovine forms; anthropomorphism was thus, in his view, man's misguided attempt to limit essentially nonphysical forces.

Christianity. In the Christian tradition, Christ was at first represented aniconically by various symbols such as the fish or the lamb, or by sacred monograms such as the combined Greek letters chi-rho (for *Christos*). Images per se—of Christ and the saints, since the Christian tradition has always been somewhat reluctant to depict God the Father—did not appear until the fourth century, and their veneration did not really flourish until the second half of the sixth.

At first, images may have served primarily didactic and decorative purposes; at least, they were defended on such grounds. But soon they came to fill admittedly devotional functions. This was especially true of the icons that became a prominent feature of Eastern Orthodoxy. Deliberately nonnaturalistic, these images of Christ, the Virgin, and the saints were supposed to reflect the other world and avoid the recollection of this one. They came, indeed, to be viewed as direct mirrors or impressions of the figures they represented, akin to the imprint made by a stamp or seal. They were thus thought to be filled with sacred and potentially miraculous power and accordingly became effective foci for prayer and veneration. [*See* Icons.]

Various reasons have been given for the rise of the veneration of images in Christianity. Peter Brown (1973) sees in it a continuation of the piety that was directed toward saints and holy men. Ernst Kitzinger (1976) has emphasized its relationship to the Roman cult of the imperial portrait, a practice that continued even after the triumph of Christianity under Christian emperors. It is, in fact, one of the ironies of the early fifth century that a Christian might well venerate the statue of Constantine in Rome with candles, incense, and prayers, but not (or at least not yet) a statue of Christ.

Once established, however, the veneration of images soon became subject to aniconic tendencies. In the eighth century, the Iconoclasts, with the support of Byzantine emperors, proclaimed and maintained for more than a century a ban on all representations of Christ except the cross and the alpha and omega monogram. They argued that images were prohibited in the Bible, that iconic representations of Christ denied his divinity, and that their veneration was reversion to pagan idolatry. They may also have had political motivations.

In 787, however, the Second Council of Nicaea sought to restore and justify the place of images in Christian devotion. The council proclaimed that, though true worship was reserved only for God, honors could legitimately be rendered to images and were, in fact, effective, since they were passed on to the person portrayed. Veneration was not to be directed to the image of Christ or the saints, but to Christ or the saints in their image.

Not everyone immediately accepted the council's declaration. There continued for a while to be iconoclastic emperors in the East, and Charlemagne in the West resisted it as well. Nevertheless, the council's basic position became that of the church in the Middle Ages, at least as it was popularly understood, although more sophisticated formulations of it (such as that of Thomas Aquinas) realized the need for further distinctions between images of saints, which reflected the gift of grace, and images of Christ, which reflected his incarnation.

Yet attitudes within Christianity continued to vary. Bernard of Clairvaux (1090–1153), for example, wary of the effect of images on monks, banned carvings, paintings, mosaics, and stained glass from all Cistercian churches. And starting in the sixteenth century, during the Prostestant Reformation and its various aftermaths, images were occasionally smashed or more often simply removed from churches in German, Swiss, and English towns.

Judaism and Islam. The same sort of vacillation between iconoclasm and iconolatry can be found, albeit in a rather different context, in Judaism. The Decalogue's ban on graven images and on likenesses of anything that is in heaven or on earth or in the waters under the earth (*Ex.* 20:4; but see also 20:23), must be contrasted with the praise given to the "desert artist" (*Ex.* 31:1–5) and the extensive use of art in Solomon's temple. Although God was not usually portrayed, other figures such as cherubim were. Moreover, the repeated denunciation of the worship of idols by various Old Testament prophets (Hosea, Isaiah, Micah, Jeremiah, Ezekiel, etc.) is generally taken as evidence of the ongoing popularity and veneration of images, if not always publicly, at least in private homes.

It is also possible that prophetic iconoclasm was not always religiously motivated. As Joseph Gutmann has pointed out, in ancient Israel, "prophetic preaching was iconoclastic for political reasons. It was not . . . a return to the demand for aniconic worship in so-called 'official normative Yavism.' The prophets . . . . were deliberately mocking images [because these] symbolized the values of the hated upper classes in their most sacred form" (Gutmann, 1977, p. 8).

The situation in Islam is at once simpler and more complicated. That tradition's general opposition to the representation of all living beings is well known, but clear statements of that opposition (such as that of the Decalogue) are difficult to find in early Islamic sources. Certain passages in the Qur'ān (e.g., 5:92, 6:74) denounce the worshiper of idols, but almost in passing. Others (e.g., 34:12–13, 3:43) indicate that God alone is the creator of living forms.

While these texts hardly amount to a blanket condemnation of all artistic representations of animate beings, they do point to an overriding Muslim concern that God should have no competition whatsoever. It is not art per se that is frowned upon, but its veneration and especially its creation, since creation is the prerogative of God. Thus, in the *ḥadīth,* it is not images that are condemned but the image-makers, who by creating potentially animate forms are seen as aping God.

While such views obviously abetted the development in Islam of nonfigurative arts such as calligraphy and the beautiful geometric ornamentations that adorn so many mosques, they did not put an end to images altogether. Later legalistic traditions, in fact, sought to specify ways in which images could be used; they were permitted in hallways, on floors, or in baths—that is, in places where their veneration was not likely.

Moreover, as Islam moved out of Arabia and sought to popularize itself in new lands, it sometimes tended to be more liberal in its attitudes toward images. In

Persia, for instance, illustrated books depict heavenly beings and the prophet Muḥammad himself, while in parts of West Africa, despite occasional iconoclastic outbursts, syncretic tendencies have allowed some converts to keep images of traditional African divinities who have been incorporated into the spiritual world of orthodoxy.

The Venerability of Images. Enough has been said to give an idea of the history and veneration of images in a variety of religious traditions. A number of issues, however, have been left untouched. These revolve primarily around the questions of why and how images become sacred—that is, worthy of veneration—in the first place, and why and how certain images become more venerated than others.

Generally speaking, religious images are man-made objects. They are produced in workshops by artisans whose livelihood or duty it is to meet the demand for them. There is thus no reason, at least from this perspective, why they should be thought to embody the divine any more than anything else.

This problem has been dealt with in several ways by the various traditions we have been considering. One solution has been simply to deny that certain images were actually man-made. The many stories of sacred images that were miraculously or accidentally discovered, buried in the ground or hidden in a cleft in the rocks, may reflect this kind of claim. More explicitly, in Hinduism, certain images of Kṛṣṇa or Śiva are thought to have grown naturally, or to have been self-made by the deity. In ancient Greece, certain statues (such as that of Artemis at Ephesus) were likewise thought to be of divine origin, rained down from heaven by Zeus. And in Christianity, the tradition developed of *acheiropoiētai*, images "not made by human hands" and thus infused with venerability from the start. The most famous of these, perhaps, was the mandylion, an image of Christ's face that he is said to have imprinted miraculously upon a cloth and sent to King Abgar of Edessa. It was much copied in the Byzantine world, and reproductions of it were thought to be only slightly less infused with power than the original.

The same notion of an image as a direct imprint of its archetype may be found in a number of other traditions as well. The Buddha, for example, is said to have left a reflection or shadow of himself in a cave in Northwest India, and this too was much reproduced, especially in Chinese Buddhist art. Similarly, according to an Australian Aboriginal tradition, the Wandjina (creative beings of the Dreaming) were thought to have entered certain caves long ago, where they simply became the paintings on the walls and as such are still venerated today.

Alternatively, certain images owed their charisma to their reputation as having been painted by direct contemporaries of their subject. Thus they were man-made but reliable replicas that captured something of the presence of the saint or holy person depicted. Moreover, the artists making such portraits were often thought to be saints themselves. The apostle Luke was said to be the maker of one of the most famous ancient images of the Virgin. And according to at least one tradition, the renowned Sandalwood First Image of the Buddha, commissioned by King Udyāna, was carved by artists who were sent to the heaven where the Buddha was spending the rains retreat.

Miraculous Images. It is understandable that such images, as a further enhancement of their venerability and of their close relationship with the divine, should also be thought capable of producing miracles. Alexander Soper (1959) has studied stories of miraculous images in both Eastern and Western traditions and has found in them certain remarkable consistencies, even as to details. Throughout India, China, the Greco-Roman world, and the whole of Christendom, tales are told of images bleeding, weeping, sweating, growing hair, emitting light, moving or refusing to move, and otherwise giving signs that warned or reassured their devotees. Some images were felt to be especially potent defenders of their churches or cities and were venerated with that in mind. A famous example from the Christian tradition was the aforementioned mandylion that saved Edessa from a Persian siege. Others were used offensively in war as palladia for armies. Some were venerated as rainmakers or used as personal amulets or talismans. And in all traditions, many were famous for their medicinal and curative powers. The practice of rubbing or touching the part of a saint's image corresponding to the part of one's own body that one wishes to cure is found in both Christianity and Buddhism.

Occasionally, of course, images were thought to fail in effecting cures or offering divine protection. In such instances, they might actually be punished or destroyed. In times of drought or disaster, the Chinese, for example, have been known to flog the statues of local earth deities who were thought to be failing to carry out their duties, and in Siena, Italy, in the fourteenth century, a recently discovered nude statue of Venus was set up in the town square, only to be blamed for the plague of 1348 and disposed of by the city government.

The Consecration of Images. Not all images, however, were miraculous by nature or had their reputations enhanced by myths and legends. A more common way of making images venerable depended on ritual. Ceremonies of consecration could transform an essentially inert statue or painting into a vitalized image of a deity.

In ancient Egypt, the ceremony to animate the image was performed while it was still in the sculptor's workshop. This was the ritual of the "opening of the mouth," whereby the heretofore inert stone was infused with the divinity's life force *(ba)*. The same ceremony was performed, incidentally, on mummies, and has obvious connections with the Old Testament story in which man, made in the image of God, is animated by the divine breath. In a curious iconoclastic reversal, in Islamic tradition it is said that artists will be exposed and mocked on Judgment Day by being asked—and shown to be unable—to breathe life into their works.

From Sri Lanka to Japan, Buddhist consecration ceremonies attained their climax with the painting in or insertion of the eyes of the image, whereby it became a sacred and venerable object. As one early observer of the ceremony in Sri Lanka put it: "Before the eyes are made, it is not accounted a God, but a lump of ordinary metal, and thrown about the shop with no more regard than anything else. . . . The eyes being formed, it is thenceforwards a God" (Gombrich, 1971, p. 114). At such times, it is understandably thought to be dangerous to gaze directly into the eyes of the Buddha, so the artist carrying out the ritual must work from the side or through a mirror.

In Chinese Buddhism and folk religion, in addition to the painting in of the eyes, various objects representing internal organs may be placed inside the image to add to its lifelike character. Alternatively, relics (as sometimes in Christian practice) or copies of Buddhist texts might be put inside statues to enhance their venerability.

Conclusion. In his recent study *Man's Quest for Partnership* (Assen, 1981), Jan van Baal has hypothesized that every ritual act of veneration has two aspects: "the one is turned to the realization of contact and communication with the supernatural, the other to the expression of awe by the observance of a respectful distance" (p. 163).

Although we have seen enough examples of the veneration of images to know that things are sometimes more complex than this, there is a certain usefulness in this easy formulation. The observance of a respectful distance can be emphasized in a variety of ways. Physically, images usually have their own space and may be further separated from devotees by a curtain or a screen, or kept altogether hidden. In addition, a buffer zone may be created by certain individuals (priests) who alone may be allowed or capable of approaching them. Furthermore, preliminary rites of purification (bathing, changing clothes, fasting, etc.), certain physical stances (kneeling, bowing, prostration), and certain taboos (not touching an image, not gazing directly at it) may serve to express this feeling of awe and distance. But perhaps the most radical expression is found in the aniconic and iconoclastic views adopted by a number of traditions.

Contact with the supernatural, on the other hand, may also be asserted in various manners. Prayers for assistance or benefits of some kind usually assume that some form of communication with the divine is taking place. So too, generally speaking, do acts of praise and offerings, whether these be simple candles lit before an icon, or a gift of flowers to adorn a statue of the Buddha, or live animals sacrificed to an image of an Olympian god, or the full daily toilet of a Hindu or Egyptian deity. In all these instances, the sacred is somehow embodied in the image itself, and the gap between it and the profane has been bridged.

[*For theologically negative views of images and their veneration, see* Fetishism *and* Idolatry.]

BIBLIOGRAPHY

By and large, discussions of the veneration of images must be gleaned from the works of art historians, anthropologists, and historians of religions, since there are very few general comparative discussions of this topic. Useful surveys, however, may be found in Albert C. Moore's lucid and helpful *Iconography of Religions: An Introduction* (Philadelphia, 1977) and in the series of articles entitled "Images and Iconoclasm" in the *Encyclopedia of World Art* (New York, 1963). The essays under "Images and Idols" and under "Worship" in the *Encyclopaedia of Religion and Ethics*, edited by James Hastings, vols. 7 and 12 (Edinburgh, 1914 and 1921), vary greatly in quality. Some are now seriously dated; others are still useful.

For Hinduism, reference should be made to Lawrence A. Babb's chapter on "Puja" in his *The Divine Hierarchy: Popular Hinduism in Central India* (New York, 1975), pp. 31–68, and for purely descriptive purposes, to Sivaprasad Bhattacharyya's "Religious Practices of the Hindus" in *The Religion of the Hindus*, edited by Kenneth W. Morgan (New York, 1953), pp. 154–205.

For Buddhism, a fine place to start is Richard F. Gombrich's discussion of "The Buddha as Worshipped: Man or God?" in his *Precept and Practice: Traditional Buddhism in the Rural Highlands of Ceylon* (Oxford, 1971), pp. 103–143. Of more specialized interest are his often cited "The Consecration of a Buddhist Image," *Journal of Asian Studies* 26 (November 1966): 23–36, and his less well-known but important translation of the text recited during the eye-painting ceremony in Sri Lanka, "Kosala-Bimba-Vaṇṇanā," in *Buddhism in Ceylon and Studies on Religious Syncretism in Buddhist Countries*, edited by Heinz Bechert (Göttingen, 1978), pp. 281–303. A rich source of information on the veneration of Buddhist images in China as well as India is Alexander Coburn Soper's *Literary Evidence for Early Buddhist Art in China* (Ascona, Switzerland, 1959).

For two authoritative studies of images in early Christian worship, see Ernst Kitzinger's "The Cult of Images in the Age before Iconoclasm," in his *The Art of Byzantium and the Medieval West* (Bloomington, 1976), pp. 90–156, and Peter Brown's "A Dark-Age Crisis: Aspects of the Iconoclastic Controversy," *English Historical Review* 88 (January 1973): 1–34. A useful discussion of Muslim attitudes toward images may be found in Oleg Grabar's *The Formation of Islamic Art* (New Haven, 1973), chap. 4. Finally, for a series of fascinating studies of iconoclasm and image veneration in Judaism, Islam, and early, medieval, and reformed Christianity, see *The Image and the Word*, edited by Joseph Gutmann (Missoula, Mont., 1977).

JOHN S. STRONG

Images and Imagination

The topic "imagination" is very much in vogue these days, but its popularity often appears to be in inverse proportion to the clarity of its treatment. Traditional wisdom warns against imagination as being mere fantasy, distraction, or delusion; yet such admonitions are disregarded by certain of its contemporary advocates who invoke imagination as the locus of our creative impulses and/or our psychological well-being. At the same time, there is also evident in current religious and philosophical circles a more thoughtful reappraisal of the received understanding of imagination. Several participants in this reappraisal coexist in a state of wary vigilance of one another, as each perspective has its own prescription for righting the perceived imbalance in Western treatment of imagination. All of these approaches are appealing in that they refuse to relegate imagination to a subordinate role in an epistemological framework. But from this point on they part company. The resulting different models for the reintegration of imagination within a philosophical and religious structure provide the basis of the present ambiguity in scholarship whenever the term *imagination* is used.

As a circumspect approach to this complex and extensive topic, the work of four contemporary thinkers—Gilbert Durand, C. G. Jung, Mircea Eliade, and Paul Ricoeur—will provide the focus of this discussion. While this selection has its obvious advantages, it does not leave sufficient space in which to delineate the similarities and differences these theories share with non-Western theories of the imagination. The place and role of imagination in Hinduism and Buddhism is particularly problematic, as there is no exact translation in these traditions for the way the word is used by the abovementioned thinkers. For example, the place of image worship in Hinduism rests on the acceptance of the devotees' belief in the indwelling presence of the god or goddess, which is in no way related to a philosophy of imagination. The concept of the *pratibhā*, or intuitive faculty, is perhaps the closest Sanskrit equivalent, but it is also extremely different in various ways and is dealt with solely within aesthetic theory. Thus, this discussion will have a Western theoretical orientation.

The Platonist View of Imagination in the Work of Gilbert Durand. The first of the four contemporary thinkers to be discussed is Gilbert Durand, a French anthropologist and philosopher. His major works, *Les structures anthropologiques de l'imaginaire* (Paris, 1963), *L'imagination symbolique* (Paris, 1968), and *Science de l'homme et tradition* (Paris, 1975), remain untranslated into English. The theory of imagination advocated by Durand is located within a Platonist worldview that emphasizes an esoteric and revelatory dimension inherent in words and symbols. In his view, all words originally had a capacity to convey this deeper level of knowledge (that is, all language formation was originally symbol naming). He argues that this ability of words to disclose an inner depth of meaning has been distorted by what he identifies as a Western rationalist and scientific insistence on univocal statements of fact. Durand observes that only poetic language now retains that original evocative power, but he hopes, by his portrayal of imagination, to redress this deficiency.

A coterie of thinkers subscribe to a similar worldview, although each has his own unique vocabulary to describe an appropriate model of the imagination and its workings. In the work of C. G. Jung, Ananda Coomaraswamy, Owen Barfield, and Mircea Eliade, there are essential underlying presuppositions that resemble Durand's depiction of imagination within a Platonist and monistic framework.

In his theory and model of imagination, Durand uses the French word *imaginal*—after the work of Henri Corbin—instead of *imaginatif* ("imaginative," with its connotations of fantasy) to call attention to imagination's properties as a vehicle of a special type of knowledge. *Imaginal*, in Durand's lexicon, also helps to distinguish imagination from those traditional, suspect connotations associated with it—fancy, distraction, error, and the like. Durand places this view of imagination within a Platonist structure where the idea of soul, in a tripartite division of body-soul-spirit, mitigates the "soulless" dualism of body-spirit, subject-object. Within this setting, the soul is regarded as coterminal with, if not identical to, imagination.

Durand is somewhat evasive as to the ultimate grounding of this theory of imagination. He leaves its ontologial status in an ambiguous position, a characteristic ploy of most thinkers who subscribe to this model. It is difficult to determine whether Durand's use of the Platonist structure is merely a convenient appropriation of a triadic format, wherein imagination functions as an intermediary in a type of transcendental capacity, or whether he regards imagination as actually the means of access to union with the Ultimate. In his care to avoid overtly traditional religious terminology and connections, Durand is perhaps deliberate in this lack of precision. In any case, it is worth a short historical excursion to establish the background of this particular understanding of imagination.

Most thinkers tend to relegate a spiritual or inspirational conception of the imagination to a variant of the Romantic idealist worldview. Recent Renaissance studies, however, particularly those of Daniel P. Walker and Frances Yates, point to an earlier lineage. The worldview of Renaissance Platonism was a syncretic complex. By medieval times, the original Platonic insight and its strictures against images had been modified, not only by currents from other philosophic orientations, such as those of Plotinus, Proclus, and the Stoics, but also by subtle religious variations from Christian, Jewish, and Islamic sources. (According to the pristine Platonic theory, all images—mental or material—are to be regarded as inferior reflections, as it were, of eternal, abstract, ideal Forms or Ideas. The latter constitute the essence of any idea or object and can never themselves be represented.) What occurred was that certain apocryphal treatises from the second and third centuries CE, which had a strong magical component and which had been variously attributed to Zarathushtra, Hermes, and Orpheus, had also been accepted as authentic. Walker is credited with coining the term *theologia prisca* to refer to "a certain tradition of Christian apologetic theology which rests on misdated texts" (Walker, 1969, p. 1). During the centuries that these writings, with their potent mixture of magical formulas, mysticism, and Platonist symbolic systems, were deemed genuine, Plato's own low estimation of the power of imagination was reversed.

Renaissance Platonists such as Marsilio Ficino (1433–1499) embellished the elaborate system (first described in the early apocryphal works) of magical correspondences of a macro-microcosmic nature and attributed to the *vis imaginativa,* "the fundamental and central force," the role of a medium connecting the material and spiritual parallels of the diverse realms. It must be observed, however, that this usage was confined to Ficino's treatises on magic, specifically *De vita caelitus comparanda,* in contrast to his epistemological works (e.g., *Platonic Theology*). In the latter, his usage of the concept of imagination did not differ from established categories of the time and indeed reflected their somewhat wary attitude toward purely personal imaginings as distinguished from spiritual emanations.

While Ficino's Christian orthodoxy remained unquestioned, later adherents of this tradition, such as Giordano Bruno (1548–1600), Cornelius Agrippa (1486–1535), and Paracelsus (1493–1541), developed their interpretations of magic and imagination in a much more humanist direction. The general shift in emphasis in their work was one from an accepted theurgic relationship, wherein a magus figure was initiated as a hierophant into divine mysteries, to a system in which the magus himself became divorced from divine connections and celebrated as the source of his own power. As this humanist thread developed, the powers of inspiration and creativity were no longer attributed solely to a transcendent entity or deity to whom a human being related by means of rituals, incantations, and talismans. This extraordinary creative potential was now regarded as residing in each individual, and the locus of this creative autonomy was none other than the imagination itself.

Since the Renaissance, then, this Platonist understanding of imagination has had a type of dual heritage that can be looked at from either a spiritual or a secular perspective. Thus, imagination is at times extolled as the divine spark and presence in human beings, while at others it becomes the ultimate vindication of human potential and the apex of human aspiration. The backdrop for both versions is monistic and idealistic; the scenario depends on the variations in vocabulary evoked by the adherent's symbolic system and its ultimate referent.

Within this context, however, the matter of reconciling the Platonist model and its transcendent referent with humanity's autonomous, creative powers still remains. This can be problematical for those who wish to sustain a vision of a creative imagination within a Christian setting. This situation has been addressed by Owen Barfield, a twentieth-century English scholar who does not hesitate to identify imagination with the Christian soul. The humanist variant, however, eschewing even Heidegger's noncommittal stance of poetic "disclosure" *(alēthia)* of Being, regards human beings as the source of their own imaginative productions, postulating a type of world soul, or collective unconscious, as the repository of symbolic material.

Nevertheless, it would appear that, even with its divided allegiances, this Platonist understanding of imagination fulfills a need in contemporary consciousness. On the one hand, it can serve those who, like Barfield, are quite content with the more "orthodox" Platonist convention, where imagination is equated with soul as the agency of divine illumination and communication. On the other hand, it can accommodate those such as Durand, who subscribe neither to the tenets of Christianity in its doctrinal or creedal formulations nor to the tradition of ascetic contemplation of the Forms advocated by Plato as a way to the Absolute. The principal reason that both groups favor the Platonist model of imagination is that they detect in the "unconscious," or psyche, and its symbolic representations a vision of the human being that is not reduced to dualist and materialist formulas. The unconscious, the psyche, the soul, imagination, are all variations of a position that seeks to avoid the theoretical reduction of human beings to mere constructs of mind and matter.

This model is also appropriated because Durand and others wish to assert that imaginative constructions have equal standing with rational and reflective procedures. In their estimation, neither realist nor critical (dare one mention analytical?) philosophies provide structures that support their position. It is only within the Platonist model that they find vindication of their appreciation of humanity's creative and dynamic processes.

C. G. Jung and the Imagination. Although the imagination is never thematized in a developed manner in his work, Swiss analytical psychologist C. G. Jung's ideas on this topic bear a remarkable similarity to those of Durand in a number of respects. Jung understands imagination as disclosing itself in symbols that occur principally in dreams. Certain of these symbols he names archetypal symbols, acknowledging their source in a domain he calls the collective unconscious, as distinct from the personal unconscious—the former being the source of primordial images, at once the most universal and enduring of symbolic forms, as old as humanity itself. For Jung, the human mind, or psyche, is divided into the unconscious and conscious areas—the imagination functions as a symbolic intermediary between the two.

Both Durand and Jung understand the archetype not as an original image but as a type of patterning of fundamental experience, rooted in instinctual and affective forces, the meaning of which finds expression in iconic rather than verbal form. [*See* Archetypes.] The archetypal symbol thus functions as the "substantification" of these tendencies, giving them a particular form and image. For example, the Shadow, manifested by such symbols as a devil, a dragon, a witch, and so forth, is the archetypal embodiment of evil for Jung. These archetypes are presented as virtually genetically based, emotionally related symbolic translations of spontaneous activity on the part of what Jung calls the psyche, and Durand, the imagination. And it is this specific symbolic activity to which both Jung and Durand refer with the interchangeable adjectives "spiritual" and "psychic."

In Jung's theory, the "transcendental function" would appear to be the agent at work in the personal constellation and appropriation of archetypal symbols. It is by attempting to be aware of the particular meaning of these symbols that a person initiates the psychic process of individuation. For Jung, *individuation* is a term used to describe the end product of a therapeutic analysis that involves this conscious "negotiation" with particular, personal dream images. Individuation per se should be regarded not as a normative state, that is, maturity, but rather as the realization of a full psychic identity, or "wholeness," that Jung posited as realizable for most human beings. Durand is not concerned with this personal aspect of individuation; rather, he is concerned with a restoration of balance to be brought to the Western rationalist bias by a reevaluation of, and emphasis on, imaginative productions.

Jung's description of the soul is remarkably similar to Durand's depiction of the imagination. Were Jung and Durand content to remain at the level of empirical study, as both claim to do, such descriptions, though problematical in terminology, would fit into a three-tiered model of human consciousness in which the imagination (or soul) performs a mediating function between the two other domains, the conscious and the unconscious.

Jung, however, remains enigmatic as to the final grounding of his theory, allowing that, psychologically, we can finally establish only the presence of certain conscious contents of the psyche, which are conventionally categorized as spirit and matter or mind and body, respectively. With Jung, the problem ultimately is to ascertain whether he is speaking as an empirical psychologist or as one who believes that the contents of myths, symbols, and images are of divine origin.

Imagination in the Work of Mircea Eliade. It is within this Platonist tradition, yet with its own distinctive emphasis on the concept of a sacred cosmos permeated by images and symbols, that the work of Romanian-born Mircea Eliade finds its place. Although he never systematically developed its configurations, the central dynamic of Eliade's worldview is indeed the imagination. In *Images and Symbols* he states, "All that essential and indescribable part of man that is called *imagination* dwells in realms of symbolism and still lives upon archaic myths and theologies" (Eliade, 1961, p. 19).

Even if people living in the twentieth century may be alienated consciously from such symbolic manifestations, Eliade points to dreams, daydreams, and nostalgic longings as vestiges of a part of human consciousness that has become submerged by modern materialism. Even in the distortions and vulgarizations of modern media Eliade discerns remnants of these once-vibrant and -energizing powers. His vision is that, by means of our imagination, we can discover the true source of our being and once again live, not as truncated, monochromatic ciphers in a programmed universe but in harmony with the rhythms of a sacred cosmos.

Essential to Eliade's prognosis is the vital role of archetypes—images or exemplary models, as he variously refers to them. These images, which recall the time of human beginnings, "the paradisiac stage of primordial humanity," are vehicles that can recharge our dormant sensibilities. In this sense, his usage of the term *archetype* is different from that of Durand and Jung. The *uroboros*, the *axis mundi*, and the Great Mother are oft-cited examples of images; it is useless to enquire into their origins, for they are as old as consciousness itself, evading conceptual encapsulation of any kind. For Eliade, these original images embody, as do all images and symbols, the inherent paradoxical and multivalent nature of the world of our experience. Their plurivocity at once evokes and respects limitless vistas of possibility—past, present, and future.

As a historian of religions, Eliade has been an itinerant connoisseur and recorder of the images that constitute our heritage, but he would probably not regard this labor as merely an encyclopedic testimony to the vagaries of the human imagination. It is in and through the restorative agency of the imagination and its symbolic energy, he urges, that the modern world can be restored to full participation in symbolic enactments and visions. All too often, this legacy has become vitiated and hackneyed through meaningless and unimaginative repetition. Eliade maintains that the imagination has a double agenda in modern times: the revitalization of dormant symbols from our ageless heritage and the reawakening of our innate capacity to perceive all reality as charged with sacred and symbolic force. Indeed, Eliade understands the history of religions, with imagination at its core, as a maieutic discipline able to provide exemplars and sources for such a regeneration. Its mandate, he says, is that of rescuing our late twentieth-century world from its literalness, secularism, and probable extinction.

Ananda Coomaraswamy and His Work. At this stage, brief mention should be made of the hybrid scholarship of Ceylonese-born, American-domiciled Ananda Coomaraswamy (1877–1947). His studies of Eastern and Western art and religion depend on an implicit view of the imagination that is very much in harmony with those discussed above. For Coomaraswamy, the primary act of imagination in all art is that of placing the individual in harmony with the divine spirit of inspiration that reveals the essential ideas to be expressed. In his belief that all religions and religious manifestations are but diverse ways of seeking the one, eternal Absolute, Coomaraswamy is just one of a number of adherents of a theosophic and esoteric *philosophia perennis* (other notable participants are René Guenon, René Daumal, Frithjof Schuon, and Huston Smith, all of whose views on imagination, though not always explored in such detail as in Durand's work, would be sympathetic to the Platonist approach). It is this universalist and essentialist modality that has lent itself to explorations and comparisons of both Eastern and Western symbol systems, with imagination invoked as the underlying and authenticating principle. These excursions, however, have not always met with approbation by Christian, Hindu, Buddhist, or Muslim scholars.

It should also be observed that all of the discussed theories above that adhere to a Platonist model sustain an innate dualism. Though imagination is recognized as equal, if not superior, to the enterprise of reason, the two are juxtaposed as separate spheres of activity. Preeminent in support of this oppositional mode is Gaston Bachelard, Durand's *maître*, who has written what could be described as virtually an invocation in *The Poetics of Reverie* (Boston, 1971): "Perhaps it is even a good idea to stir up rivalry between conceptual and imaginative activity. In any case, one will encounter nothing but disappointments if he intends to make them cooperate" (p. 52).

Paul Ricoeur's Theory of Imagination. Another, different approach in contemporary religion and philosophy to the role of imagination is that of the French philosopher Paul Ricoeur, who is a frequent guest professor at North American universities. His monumental effort to wed "poetics" (here understood as having wide-ranging application to all creative acts, including those of knowledge) to the structures of intentional consciousness has preoccupied him for approximately thirty years. His voyage from eidetics through empirics to the hermeneutics of text and discourse has been variously documented. The shift from static epistemological categories to a participatory ontological mode of consciousness and action is inherent in this development. Though Ricoeur's struggle to define the workings of the imagination has not yet culminated in an articulated philosophy, the theme has permeated his work virtually from its inception.

Originally, it seemed that Ricoeur sought, within the bounds of a self-confessed post-Hegelian Kantian framework, to locate imagination in those structures of intentional consciousness that allowed symbolic forms to be incorporated within a traditional epistemological framework. But as he came to appreciate the dynamic qualities of imaginative productivity, Ricoeur began to express a growing dissatisfaction with Kant's treatment of the productive imagination, particularly his conservative reworking of the topic in the second edition of the *Critique of Reason.* This deficiency prompted Ricoeur to search for a more congenial form that permitted an autonomous, innate dimension of a creative imagination.

At the same time, Ricoeur became increasingly aware, in his explorations of symbolic material, that hermeneutics, as traditionally understood in its role of interpretation, was at a methodological impasse between the approaches of explanation and understanding and that the process itself could be reductive in its application. From this latter perspective, hermeneutics did not automatically encourage an undistorted interpretation of human experience and its resultant modes of expression (be they words or symbols) but rather could reinforce the viewpoint of the inquirer. In response, Ricoeur undertook an optimistic search for a hermeneutic method that would be both heuristic and corrective and would acknowledge imagination.

In *The Rule of Metaphor* (Toronto, 1977) and in various articles, Ricoeur maps out a proposed agenda for his own solutions to these two dilemmas. Although the exposition of this resolution is still in the formative stage, Ricoeur lays the groundwork in these writings for a creative imagination that, thus far, finds its most efficacious expression in a dynamic hermeneutics. Ricoeur's revision of the role of imagination entails, at the same time, a reconstitution of the hermeneutic task. To arrive at this revised understanding of imagination Ricoeur adroitly weaves together several strands of thought that permit him to focus on metaphor as the paradigmatic moment exemplifying the creative dynamics of imagination. In so doing, Ricoeur broadens the scope of his vision, perceiving hermeneutics as part of a wider spectrum of creative acts of knowledge by which we understand ourselves in the realm of Being within a spectrum of a "poetics of experience." Ricoeur's method, however, is not without a hermeneutic of suspicion that strives to eliminate historical and personal distortions of symbols that have resulted in misguided theological declarations.

Ideally, the imagination, for Ricoeur, would also have a catalytic effect, provoking the depiction and aiding, through imaginative representations, the appropriation of new ways of being in the world. It is in imagination that this new way of being is brought to our attention. Thus, imagination has the power not only to generate meaning but ultimately to change the world—that is, the world of experience, as we live and understand it. This world, for Ricoeur, is grounded ultimately within a Christian vista of promise and hope. So it is that imagination can deepen our appreciation of the mysteries of faith.

Ironically, it would seem that for Durand, Jung, Eliade, and Ricoeur, imagination is, in some form, the agent of revelation. But while Ricoeur's interdependent model allows imagination free play in the fields of ontological exploration, it does not give imagination the last word (in the way that the other thinkers seem to do). For Ricoeur, any increment in knowledge results from an interaction of the imagination with reflective and critical modes of knowing, prior to any final incorporation into our present worldview.

Conclusion. It should be added that William Blake (1757–1827), Søren Kierkegaard (1813–1855), and John Henry Cardinal Newman (1801–1890) all dealt with the imagination in their discussions of religion, although the concept was central only to Blake's work. Apart from Blake's own writings, a splendid appreciation of his visionary exaltation of the imagination as the locus of divine inspiration is found in the work of Northrop Frye.

It should be noted that although the contemporary theories of imagination discussed above have essentially different emphases, they all signal a remarkable change in attitude on the part of Western religious and philosophical tradition toward the place and the role of imagination. Such a change reflects the transition in contemporary scholarship from an exclusive emphasis on logical, propositional, or dogmatic formulations as the sole criteria of truth. There is increasing acknowledgment of an existential and experiential notion of truth that refers to a sense of ontological self-awareness and responsibility, which permeates all that we are and do. In this process, imagination has an integral role to play as the agency of all those exploratory experiences that initially pose their insights in imagistic form. These images can both resonate with the cherished vestiges or dormant aspects of our past and delight us with the vibrancy of unexplored dimensions that, as human beings, we have not yet even begun to grasp. In the world of religious experience, this movement is at once the inspiration and the sustenance of our very being.

[*See also* Soul *and* Symbolism; *for the role of imaginative experience in revelation, see* Inspiration.]

BIBLIOGRAPHY

An intriguing discussion of Plato's unsympathetic treatment of images and the inconsistency in his view is presented by Irish Murdoch in *The Fire and the Sun* (Oxford, 1977). The development and elaboration of Plato's original theories are described by Raymond Klibansky in *The Continuity of the Platonic Tradition during the Middle Ages* (1939; reprint, New York,

1982), an excellent work. Renaissance views of imagination as well as the relation of magic to imagination are treated by Daniel P. Walker in *Spiritual and Demonic Magic from Ficino to Campanella* (London, 1958). Gnostic and theosophic notions are expertly detailed in Frances A. Yates's *Giordano Bruno and the Hermetic Tradition* (London, 1964). On modern European views, see James Engell's *The Creative Imagination: Enlightenment to Romanticism* (Cambridge, Mass., 1981), a thorough and extremely well informed description of the general cultural background (as opposed to specifically religious concerns) and changes in attitude toward the imagination.

Although it is difficult to locate a specific and succinct source for each author whose ideas are discussed in this article, the following works can be profitably consulted. Gilbert Durand's most comprehensive work on imagination is *L'imagination symbolique*, 2d ed. (Paris, 1968), as yet untranslated. For C. G. Jung's view, three volumes of *The Collected Works of C. G. Jung* are apposite: volume 7, *Two Essays on Analytical Psychology*, 2d ed. (Princeton, 1966); volume 8, *The Structure and Dynamics of the Psyche*, 2d ed. (Princeton, 1969); and volume 13, *Alchemical Studies* (Princeton, 1967). Mircea Eliade's theoretical position on the imagination finds its most explicit expression in *Images and Symbols: Studies in Religious Symbolism* (New York, 1961). For an impression of the depth and scope of Eliade's knowledge of religious symbols and images and their historical significance, see *A History of Religious Ideas*, vol. 1, *From the Stone Age to the Eleusinian Mysteries* (Chicago, 1978). Owen Barfield's appropriation of the Platonist model to a Christian setting is admirably and concisely presented in "Matter, Imagination, and Spirit," *Journal of the American Academy of Religion* 42 (December 1974): 621–629. The most accessible formulation of Ananda K. Coomaraswamy's ideas is his *Christian and Oriental Philosophy of Art* (New York, 1956), in which see especially chapter 2, "The Christian and Oriental, or True, Philosophy of Art." As yet, Paul Ricoeur's theory of imagination awaits a detailed presentation. His ideas, in inchoate yet distinctly adequate form, are published in two articles: "The Metaphorical Process as Cognition, Imagination, and Feeling," *Critical Inquiry* 5 (Autumn 1978–1979): 142–159, and "Imagination in Discourse and Action," *Analecta Husserliana* (Dordrecht) 7 (1978): 3–22. For an excellent, if controversial, treatment of William Blake's idiosyncratic vision of the imagination, see Northrop Frye's *Fearful Symmetry: A Study of William Blake* (Princeton, 1947).

MORNY JOY

The Imaginal

The relationships between imagery and religion are complex. On the one hand, every religion intent on transcending the ephemeral and the apparent distrusts imagination, which here more than elsewhere is "mistress of error and falsity," and which is at the very least grounded in appearance. Religions, and particularly the great world religions, are always potentially iconoclastic. Theologies often recoil from visions and theophanies. On the other hand, the most elementary process of the human imagination, by which it relates an image to a concrete but currently absent perceptual experience, seems to be characteristic of all religious thought: religion relates the world as it is perceived, remembered, or imagined back to its origin, to its creative and justifying principle. Thus all religion is symbolic, if we mean by *symbol* some thing that, by means of its present qualities, allows us to recall something absent, something "symbolized."

Even while it distrusts imagery, therefore, religion nonetheless bases its beliefs on a system of signs symbolizing what cannot be directly shown. Religions accordingly, in their use of imagery, range between two extremes: one a radically apophatic and iconoclastic attitude, a sort of infrared in the religious spectrum that refuses to relativize the Absolute or to mold it into imaginal incarnations; the other a pantheistic extreme, like an ultraviolet at the opposite end of the spectrum, which multiplies symbolic signs to infinity, losing them in allegory and suppressing the fundamental theological divergence between immanence and transcendence. The use of the religious image ranges therefore between radical iconoclasm and a generalized pantheistic idolatry. Because such images cannot be understood as purely psychological phenomena, some specialists prefer to use the technical term *imaginal* in referring to their particular domain.

In theory, the imaginal provides the possibility of returning to an intuition of the divine, if not of divinity itself, by way of images and thus without succumbing to apophatism. At the same time, it distinguishes itself from the profane realm of imagery, where significations are multiplied to such a degree that they no longer mean anything. It is important to note that we owe this distinction, which authenticates the imaginal as a mode of the specifically religious imagination, to the great scholar of Islam Henry Corbin. For Islam, of all the "religions of the Book," is rightly considered the most iconoclastic, refusing any mixture whatsoever of earthly appearance with divinity, and for this reason rejecting such Christian doctrines as the Trinity or divine incarnation. I shall return shortly to the paradoxical valorization of imagination in iconoclastic Islam.

My overall aim, however, will be to try to show how the world of the imagination, under the rubric *imaginal*, emerges supreme in religious experience and in the very definition of the religious process. This holds both for the apophatic iconoclasm dear to a certain radical rationalist theology and for the idolatry that profanes because it submerges transcendence—which is necessary to the definition of the sacred—in profane immanence.

Iconoclasm and the Imaginal. We could just as easily have chosen one of the great iconoclastic religious traditions as the first seat of the imaginal, for instance Judaism—the wellspring of all Western monotheisms—or Buddhism. In Buddhism, the world of images has a close link to *māyā,* the world of false appearances. The essential Buddhist exercise of purification through emptiness must grapple first of all with the obstacles posed by the imagination.

Almost from its inception, however, Buddhist apophatism, which borders on atheism, developed under the impact of the symbolic and mythical figures it encountered during the course of its spread through Indochina, China, Tibet, Mongolia, Korea, and Japan. From the death of Śākyamuni Buddha (480 BCE) onward, the Buddhist *saṃgha* was split between two currents: the "ancients" and the "moderns"—the Sthaviravāda and the Mahāsāṃghika. Paradoxically, the innovations of the second of these, the Mahāsāṃghikas, would introduce iconic elements that would flourish in the Mahāyāna some centuries ahead. With the Mahāsāṃghika, as with the Mahāyānists later, the Buddhist ethic was not only theologized but theophanized. The rights of the imaginal were restored.

Then came an invasion by the figures of multiple Buddhas and *bodhisattva*s, under the influence of Tibetan, Korean, Tonkinese, Annamese, Chinese, and Japanese cultural traditions. Parent-child relationships interconnected Buddhas and *bodhisattva*s, as for example in the association of the *bodhisattva* Avalokiteśvara with the great Buddha Amitābha. In China, Avalokiteśvara was assimilated to Kuan-yin, an indigenous fertility goddess, and became revered in Chinese Buddhism as the embodiment of compassion. Thus from the eighth century on, the *bodhisattva* became "the childbearing lady," sometimes represented alone and sometimes carrying a little child. "In these various forms, the resemblance to our madonnas is often striking," writes Henri de Lubac (*Amida,* Paris, 1955).

A mystical fondness for iconography burgeoned in Japan, multiplying and feminizing the divine figure. This is especially true at the Kyoto Hōjōji, the Temple of a Thousand Buddhas, and at the Shizuoka sanctuary, a temple containing 3,000 statues of the Buddha Kannon. Not only did the originally apophatic tradition of Buddhism express itself in feminine figures fifteen centuries after its founding (the 1,001 Hōjōji statues were sculpted by Ensei in 1103 CE), it was flooded with representations as exuberant as any that Indian polytheism had ever known. We find Kannons with six, eight, twenty, or a thousand arms brandishing symbolic emblems of mercy; Kannons with three, nine, eleven, or thirty-six heads.

We could likewise analyze how numerous figures were introduced into the strict iconoclastic monotheism of Judaism to support the "spiritual exercises" of religious practice. Such is the function of the images of the *merkavah* and the ten *sefirot* represented in the qabbalistic tree. Beginning in the first century BCE, Ezekiel's famous vision of the chariot, or divine throne—the *merkavah*—became a central subject of meditation among Jewish mystics. As Gershom Scholem writes, "Without doubt the earliest Jewish mysticism is the mysticism of the throne . . . the preexisting throne of God that contains and illustrates all the forms of Creation" (*Les grands courants de la mystique juive,* Paris, 1960). Let us recall that the "four beings" supporting the divine throne would later give rise to the Christian iconography of the tetramorph.

It is interesting to see theriomorphic figures, which Mosaic monotheism seemed to have violently excluded, reintroduced into the heart of imaginal Jewish mysticism. The qabbalistic vision progressed quite naturally from the "four beings" to the ten *sefirot* (emanations and manifestations of the godhead), grouped in three columns, one of which represents rigor (or firmness) and another mercy (or love). Scholem writes that these ten figures "together form the unified universe of the life of God, the world of Union. . . . They are the faces of the King." Here the unknowable Absolute is molded into a plurality of figures variously synthesized: whether by a tree (preferably upside down, that is, with its roots in the heavens), by the perfect man, or by divine speech (the Word).

What is more, a feminine "face" of God appeared in the mysticism of the *Zohar.* It shows first in the *sefirah* Binah, "the heavenly mother" whose "maternal breast" lets the seven days flow out, as Scholem writes, following ʿAzri'el of Gerona. But it emerges above all in the tenth *sefirah,* Malkhut, or the Shekhinah, who definitely typifies the people of Israel and yet is the figure of the queen, the matron, the princess, or the wife. Avraham ha-Levi in the sixteenth century saw her as a "woman dressed in black weeping over the husband of her youth." This feminine figuration of divinity surfaced against opposition from the Talmudists, of course. As Scholem emphasizes, "If this idea was accepted despite the obvious difficulty of reconciling it with the concept of the absolute unity of God, and if no other element of qabbalism acquired such a degree of popular approval, it proves that this duality responded to a deeply rooted religious need."

We see, thus, that even among religions with an iconoclastic calling, Buddhism and Judaism, religious need gives rise to a proliferation of symbols and to the appearance of feminine, or indeed animal, figures that give expression to something elemental in religious experience.

Islam. It is in the profound iconoclasm of Islam, however, that Henry Corbin uncovers not only figurative formations similar to those of Buddhism and Judaism, but also a veritable philosophy, if not theology, of the creative imagination and of the function of the *mundus imaginalis,* or world of the imaginal. Quite paradoxically, the awareness of the theophanic role of the image, of its sacredness, has been keenest in the midst of Islam's strictly observed iconoclasm, while despite Christianity's tolerance—even conciliar recommendation—of the cult of icons, religious discourse there concentrated on the abstract demonstrations of scholasticism rather than on a theory of the image.

During Islam's first centuries, a feminine figure suddenly emerged in the midst of patriarchal, male-dominated Arab culture as forcefully as one had among the Mahāyāna and the *merkavah* mystics, or in the Qabbalah. The figure had as important a theological function as the Buddhist representation of compassion, the Jewish Shekhinah, or the Christian Virgin Mary. This was the personage of Fāṭimah, daughter of the prophet Muḥammad, wife of ʿAlī, the first imam, and mother of the two young imams martyred at Karbala, Ḥusayn and Ḥasan.

These five figures—"the five of the mantle," or those to whom the prophetic mantle gives privileged protection—constitute more than a moving "holy family" centered on the daughter of the Prophet and the mother of an imam lineage. Fāṭir, "Fāṭimah the dazzling," is the creator, and according to Ṣūfī and Shīʿī theology she is indispensable to the radiation of the light of Muḥammad. In the Muslim system Fāṭimah is as indispensable a person as the Prophet himself for the fulfillment of Islam. Like the Virgin Mary among Christians, she is invested with the title and role of the "portal" *(bāb)* of heavenly light. She is the "major sign," the "sign among signs" of which the Qur'ān speaks (74:35–39). Accordingly, the prophets themselves are "below the rank of Fāṭimah-Sophia." Moreover, her creative femininity permeates the lineage of the imams, husbands and sons, since they are "wives" of the Prophet.

But this retrieval of figures as intermediaries in the midst of Islamic monotheism, thus applied to the later tradition through the imaginal promotion of the lineage of the imams, was also applied to the earlier tradition. Thus mystical theosophy such as that of ʿAlā' al-Dawlah al-Simnānī (1261–1336) identified the seven great prophets of Islam (Adam, Noah, Abraham, Moses, David, Jesus, and Muḥammad) as the visionary "stations" or subtle organs of the self. One could develop a fruitful rapprochement between this inward imaginal pilgrimage to the seven stations of the soul and the various Christian "spiritual exercises" (at Carmel or in the *Exercises* of Ignatius Loyola), and especially with "those who descend toward the *merkavah" (yordei merkavah),* a descent through seven heavenly palaces guarded by "porters," themselves comparable to the archons of pagan gnosticism. Scholem remarks that as "the voyage advances, the dangers become progressively greater."

In al-Simnānī's Sufism, the imaginal intuition of the prophetic stations is accompanied by colored visions. Thus "black light" appears in the ascent to the first station (Adam) and in the next-to-last phase (Jesus). I need not comment here on the mystical meaning of this darkening that shadows and frames the supreme revelation of "emerald" (Muḥammad); suffice it to say that a colored vision emanates from each station.

Therefore, in the quasi-hagiographic sacralization of the lineage of Fāṭimah's sons, as much as in the hierarchy of the "prophets of your soul," Muslim iconoclasm led to the reintroduction of the role of imaginal figures or "faces," just as Jewish mysticism and the Mahāyāna religious experience had done. For the imaginal figures are the necessary "intermediaries" between the unknowable call of divine transcendence (the "hidden treasure" in Islam) and the believer's earthly experience of faith.

Henry Corbin's studies of the works of Islam's two most important philosophers, Ibn ʿArabī and Ibn Sīnā, reveal the unfolding in Islam of a theory of the creative imagination that is highly significant in a paradoxical way. The theory of the theophanic imaginal rests on two essential notions: *ta'wīl* and *ʿālam al mithāl.* Whereas *tanzīl* is the transmission of revelation of the higher world to the voice or pen of the proclaiming prophet and is therefore the foundation for positive religion, revealed exoterically, *ta'wīl* is the inverse process by which each soul traces the prophetic word back to its esoteric sense. Etymologically, *ta'wīl* means "to take back to." As the Muslim philosopher Kalami Pir puts it, "He who practices *ta'wīl* is thus one who turns the expression away from external appearance [exoteric appearance, *ẓāhir*] and makes it return to its truth [*ḥaqīqah*]," that is, to its hidden, esoteric meaning *(bāṭin).*

This turning away is in no way a transgression. On the contrary, the esoteric word, which is pure metaphor *(majāz),* is a transgression of the true idea *(ḥaqīqah).* "To put it briefly," writes Corbin, "in the three pairs of terms mentioned, *majāz* goes with *ḥaqīqah, ẓāhir* with *bāṭin,* and *tanzīl* with *ta'wīl* in the relationship of symbol and symbolized" (1954). In contrast to an allegory, which is an arbitrary sign, a representation of an abstraction that can be made in many other ways, a symbol *(mithāl)* is the unique and irreplaceable expression of the symbolized "as a reality that thereby becomes wholly clear to the soul but that in itself transcends all expression" (ibid.). Indeed, the symbol is the *only* expression of the signified source that it symbolizes. Therefore, penetrating its meaning by *ta'wīl* in no wise corresponds to making it superfluous or eliminating it.

Thus, between the realities of the revealed word and the knowledge of what it reveals, there is a world of symbols *('ālam al mithāl)* that is both necessary and unique, a world of the imaginable universe "where spirits take on body and bodies take on spirit." This world is at once the reality of the intermediary faces or figures (angels) and of each soul's spiritual activity: the *imaginatio vera,* the "creative imagination," a kind of personal Paracletic guarantee, an absolutely natural grace that every Adamic psyche is endowed with. It is a world of angels/souls typified, in the revealed writings, by the image of the East to which the *cognitio matutina* aspires and which is nothing other than an exodus.

If I have dwelt at some length on the fundamental notions that constitute the theory of the creative imagination and of the *mundus imaginalis,* it is because they seem to form a theory and a conceptualization that are unsurpassed in the West and that our psychoanalytical and psychological probings of human depths have barely caught up with over the last half century. Islamic philosophy especially, on the subject we are considering, proposes a conceptual and experimental approach to religious imagination, an exegetical operation of the creative imagination, that is indispensable to conceptions of religious experience in even the most monotheistic dogmatics. In this, Islam runs counter to the whole stream of Western philosophy, which has minimized the role of imagination in general and of theophany in particular—and for good reason: because of progressive profanation.

In science as in religious experience, it is necessary to postulate a world of intermediary images or symbols and an exegetical and gnostic faculty of imagination. The iconoclastic mistrust inherent in all strictly monotheistic orthodoxy begins and ends with this necessary postulate, as we have seen. Here lies "the paradox of monotheism," which proposes to affirm the unity of the unique and at the same time the unicity of each soul's imaginal experience, composing what Corbin calls a kathenotheism, a theology of the unique for each of us. For knowledge of the "hidden treasure" in every apophatic formulation must, like all desire for knowledge, create a world. "I was a hidden treasure, I desired to be known, I created the world. . . ."

The Imaginal and Allegory. I said at the beginning that the second barrier that blocks religious consciousness—or, failing that, absorbs it—is pantheism's profusion of metaphors. Now that we have examined the *imaginatio vera* and the imaginal, it will be easier to see how religious imagination disarms the temptation toward what Corbin calls allegory. For allegory is the impetus behind idolatry. I agree with Corbin that allegory partakes of that arbitrariness of signs dear to philosophers since de Saussure. It is thus totally literal, both because it can replace its signal with another signal or by a play on words, and because what it signifies, being knowable in another way, is radically transparent to knowledge. Allegory is without mystery and needs no exegesis.

This is indeed the case with the subreligious category of the idol. Just as apophatic iconoclasm is a snare for all monotheism, idolatry is a snare for all polytheism. If the danger for monotheism lies in the apophatism of theologies that so separate God from the world, make such an abstract idea of him that nothing can be rendered unto him or asked of him, the danger for polytheism, in contrast, is that of turning even a likeness struck on a coin into a little god, of rendering everything unto Caesar and asking everything of the world and its princes.

Let us take, for example, the limit Christianity sets for the religious imagination. For Christianity's dogmatic belief in the incarnation of a divine person—and, *a fortiori,* the dogma of the Trinity—marks an approach to polytheism. This is more or less strongly evidenced by the proliferation of Christian hagiography. The saints are indeed the successors of the pre-Christian gods. It is also shown, in inverse fashion, both by the different iconoclastic vectors in the Eastern church and in Western Calvinism and by theological quarrels that reopened the dogma of the Trinity to question, such as those that arose around docetism or Arianism. Within the Christian churches of the West and the East, the pendulum swings continually: between a fondness for icons bordering on idolatry at one extreme, and a puritanical iconoclasm in violent reaction against it on the other. This means that the problem of the image and its degree of spiritual reality is constantly present.

Christianity stands dogmatically and scripturally in the interstice, so to speak, between the ethical monotheism of the Pharisees and the polytheism of the gentiles. Jesus Christ is at bottom a concrete, incarnate figure, bringing to actuality the prophetic metaphors of the Old Testament. As Bernard Morel (1959) says so well, "The Christ is the unique and perfect sign, the sign *par excellence.*" He possesses to the highest degree that apparitional power that he will manifest especially after his resurrection, a power that will later be shared by the Virgin and by some saints. The Son of man represents *in concreto* the perfection of man, created "in the image and likeness of God."

In addition, Christ made abundant use in his preaching of a quite special genre, the parable. Its originality consists in taking everyday objects and acts, the most commonplace perceivable world, and relating them back to the exemplifications of the Kingdom: "The kingdom of heaven is like. . . ." There is a resemblance between this process and the Muslim *ta'wīl,* with the important difference that *ta'wīl,* like a certain type of Jewish qabbalistic exegesis, relates the word of the text back to its esoteric sense, whereas the parable relates every profane *eidōlon* back to a sacred exemplification. What the great Christian poets retain from the Bible is the *Song of Songs,* which is already the mystical parable *par excellence:* carnal love typifies the mystical union.

In Christianity, where all painting is profusely iconic, the point of departure is creation, the world of creatures that *Genesis* calls good. Pictorial representation of holiness was accompanied very early with pictorial renderings of utensils, emblems, clothing, and landscapes that underscore the hagiographic purpose. Christian imagery is thus pictorial in the strongest sense of the word. This can be seen clearly in a comparison of Western Christian painting, from the Gothic miniature to at least the nineteenth century, with Muslim or Buddhist painting—even with Muslim figurative painting, like the Mughal miniature. The Christian image is parabolic, maintaining a minimal realism that in some cases has verged on profanation (as in sixteenth-century works that overwhelm the subject with Baroque landscape, fabric, and decor) or even on idolatry (as for example in Baroque statuary and Sulpician neoclassicism). For Christians, because of belief in incarnation, this world is at least redeemable, if not redeemed. Hence Christianity's enormous capacity to absorb and use the objects and figures of the profane world.

But as regards this sacral restoration that Christianity constantly produces, there is no religion—even one as polytheistic as Hinduism or one of the African or Kanakan totemisms—that does not demonstrate this same operation in the midst of its proliferation of images. For the ancient Romans, as Georges Dumézil has so often shown, as well as for many African peoples, the imaginary pantheon is organized in functional and hierarchical structures that rearrange the seeming dispersion of religious images as triads or tetrads within a *plērōma* (spiritual cosmos), even within actual sacred histories. The obliging complexity of idols always refers back to a unifying religious intention, which is ultimately monotheistic. As a keystone there always exists what the monotheisms would call a God of gods.

Thus every religious people, even those caught up in the profane world of space (like the agricultural world of the Dogon or of the ancient Romans) or of time (like Christian incarnationism), saves the holy image from the simplistic reductions of profane meanings and restores its symbolic power.

Images: A Typology. Monotheistic theology therefore must create images in order to function truly as a religion. Conversely, the ascription of value to the objects and actions of the profane world must be metaphorical if they are to attain the status of religious parable. In both cases, we see that in every religion there is a necessary theophanic dimension that is expressed in visions of an imaginal world. There is furthermore a valorization of the human faculty that is capable of making this imaginal return, the creative imagination. It is necessary now to draw up a classification of these symbolic realities that compose the very heart of *religare,* the bond between the immanence of the vision and the transcendence of what is signified.

One can distinguish four major groups of symbolic images in the operation of every religion: iconic figures, mythic figures, liturgical or sacramental figures, and apparitional figures. Images that can be so grouped take on varying importance in one or another religion. Sometimes iconic representation prevails over apparitional expression, as in Hinduism; sometimes the essential form is the liturgical and sacramental image, as in Catholicism; and sometimes it is myth, like the sacred history of some Protestant faiths. Then too, there is a close interpenetration among these four categories, which I shall analyze here briefly.

A religion makes its first impressions on an outside observer by its iconic representations: sculpture, painting, architecture, collections of symbolic objects, and so forth. Christianity in general, and especially Catholicism since the Reformation, gives iconic representation a preferential place, of which we have already spoken. Beings, objects, and religious locales are not only depicted but gain a degree of sacredness by the very fact of their representation. John of Damascus won a decisive victory for the notion of the holy image over the Iconoclasts in the great crisis of 726. The icon, or statue of God or of a saint, carries within itself the germ of the symbolized being because of the latter's figurative presence. It is at least the seed of the creative religious imagination, and in numerous societies the iconic image is an actual consubstantial double of its model. Every kind of what we call magic also uses this vicarious power of the iconic image.

Mythic imagery in its various forms, including sacred history, is the root of all oral or written literature, as Dumézil has clearly shown, and it exerts a more subtle attraction than iconic figures because it allows the individual creative imagination a more active role. Hence the importance of sacred accounts and texts in the great religions such as Buddhism, Islam, Christianity, Judaism, and Zoroastrianism. Generally, in the religious traditions that are iconoclastic in the strict sense of the term—those that reject iconic images—mythic imagery is the base for image-centered meditation; this is so in Judaism and Islam, in their inexhaustible bodies of exegesis.

The third category, liturgical figures, are symbols—originally profane objects (a cup, water, bread, wine, a spouse, a king)—or movements and spoken or sung formulas that initiate the imaginal return. As Bernard Morel puts it, the sacramental figure is the "analogic signal of the mystery." Priestly religions like Catholicism and Christianity generally, the religions of ancient Rome, Egypt, or Assyria, and that of the Aztec, among others, as a rule place great importance on at least symbolic rituals, if not on sacramental representations.

Finally, there are apparitional figures. Here value is accorded either to natural visions (as in the analysis of dreams among Muslims and among most Africans but also in the Greco-Roman tradition of dream interpretation) or to visions induced by ritual (in Haitian Voodoo or Afro-Brazilian Candomblé) or by drugs (among the Guayaquil Indians). I have already referred to Henry Corbin's book on the technique of the "visionary recital" in Islam. Let us also note that Christianity, so circumspect about apparitions that are alien to those related in the Gospels, has integrated willy-nilly the frequent apparitions of the Virgin (at Lourdes, Pontmain, and La Salette in the nineteenth century and at Fatima in the twentieth) into the canonical cult.

We must note, however, that these four groups of symbolic images in the experience and the institution of religion span the whole field of the manifestations of religiosity. We should not be surprised therefore to find that, over the last half century, developments in the exploration of imagery resulting from Freudian psychoanalysis and Jungian depth psychology have converged with a new orientation of the old history of religions discipline. Thus, with Mircea Eliade, Henry Corbin, and Georges Dumézil—to cite only a few authors—reflections on the phenomenon of religion have broken away from etiological reductions within purely historical, social, even graphic or meteorological contexts to enter the territory of a more anthropological field—one centered on the properly religious function of the creative imagination and on consideration of the effectiveness of images and their synchronic regroupings.

[*See also* Symbolism *and the biography of Corbin.*]

BIBLIOGRAPHY

Corbin, Henry. *Avicenna et le récit visionnaire.* 2 vols. Tehran, 1954.

Corbin, Henry. *Ombre et lumière: La physiologie de l'homme de lumière dans le soufisme iranien.* Paris, 1960.

Corbin, Henry. *Terre céleste et corps de résurrection.* Paris, 1961.

Corbin, Henry. *The Creative Imagination in the Sufism of Ibn 'Arabī.* Princeton, 1969.

Dumézil, Georges. "Preface." In *Traité d'histoire des religions,* by Mircea Eliade. Paris, 1949.

Durand, Gilbert. *L'imagination symbolique.* Paris, 1964.

Eliade, Mircea. *Images and Symbols: Studies in Religious Symbolism.* New York, 1961.

Eliade, Mircea. *Myths, Dreams and Mysteries: The Encounter between Contemporary Faiths and Archaic Realities.* New York, 1961.

Guardini, Romano. *Sacred Signs* (1927). Saint Louis, 1956.

Morel, Bernard. *Le signe sacré.* Paris, 1959.

GILBERT DURAND
Translated from French by Sally Gran

IMAGINATION. *See* Images, *article on* Images and Imagination; *see also* Aesthetics.

IMAMATE. The Arabic term *imām* means in general "leader" or "master." In nontechnical usage it is often applied to a leading authority in a field of scholarship or to the leader of a community. As a technical term in Islamic law and theology, it refers to the legitimate supreme leader of the Muslim community and also to the leader of the ritual prayer *(ṣalāt).* The imamate, as the office of imam, will be dealt with here in these two technical senses.

Supreme Leadership of the Muslim Community

The question of leadership, in theory and practice, has historically evoked different responses within the different branches of Islam.

The Sunnīs. Representing the great majority of Muslims, the Sunnīs have generally viewed the historical caliphate as the legitimate leadership of Islam after the prophet Muḥammad. For them, the imam is thus identical with the ruling caliph. Actual rule, even if reduced to a minimum, is indispensable for the legitimacy of the imam. [*See* Caliphate.] Throughout history, however, the Sunnīs were primarily concerned with preserving the unity and solidarity of the Muslim community under a single imam and were prepared to compromise on the ideal of his legitimacy and justice. Sunnī theory generally held that the true and exemplary caliphate, meaning the vicegerency of prophecy *(khilāfat al-nubū-*

wah) was restricted to the first four, or "Rightly Guided" (Rāshidūn) caliphs, Abū Bakr, ʿUmar, ʿUthmān, and ʿAlī. This view was embodied in a well-known *ḥadīth* attributed to Muḥammad, according to which the caliphate was to last for only thirty years after his death and to be followed by mere autocratic kingship *(mulk)*. Sunnīs considered the first four caliphs to be the most excellent of humankind after Muḥammad and thus entitled to his succession as leaders of the community.

This judgment did not apply, however, to the later caliphs, many of whom were seen as unjust and impious. While the later caliphate was thus recognized to be imperfect, Sunnī doctrine viewed it still as a divinely sanctioned and indispensable institution and stressed the obligation of every Muslim to obey and actively support the established imam, be he just or oppressive, pious or immoral, except in violation of the religious law. Conservative traditionalist opinion, especially that of Ḥanbalī jurists, virtually equated power and legitimacy, affirming the validity of the imamate gained by usurpation. In their view, the imamate could become binding without any act of recognition by the Muslim community. The only prerequisite for the rightful imam was that he be a Muslim of the Quraysh, the tribe of Muḥammad.

A less radical view of the caliphate was taken by another current of Sunnī thought, represented in particular in the legal school of al-Shāfiʿī. The Shāfiʿī jurists did not confine the legitimate imamate to the most excellent of the community and allowed that a less excellent candidate might be chosen, especially in order to avoid discord. They considered the later caliphate essentially as a legitimate continuation of the ideal rule of the four Rightly Guided caliphs, to be judged by the standards they had set. On this basis they elaborated a comprehensive legal doctrine concerning the qualifications, election, rights, and duties of the imam. Their activity reached its peak with al-Māwardī (d. 1058), whose book *Al-aḥkām al-sulṭānīyah* (The Statutes of Government) came to be widely regarded as an authoritative statement of classical Sunnī teaching on the imamate.

Classical theory. Classical Sunnī theory considered the imamate as an institution necessary for the legitimacy of all acts of government. Thus it held that the Muslim community was under the obligation to set up an imam as its supreme head at all times. It allowed for only a single imam at any time and considered rival caliphs, even if they were in clear control of part of the Islamic world, to be illegitimate. The imam was to be of Qurayshī descent, male, major, free, physically fit, and capable to execute the political and military duties of the office. He was to have the knowledge of the religious law required for the judgeship and probity as required for legal testimony. The imam could be either appointed by his predecessor or elected. These alternative modes of investment were based on the fact that the second caliph, ʿUmar, was appointed by his predecessor, Abū Bakr, but, before his death, set up an electoral council *(shūrā)* of six prominent companions of the Prophet to choose his successor. The later caliphs in most instances appointed their successors, commonly their sons.

In the case of election, the law considered any Muslim of probity, discernment, and with knowledge about the nature of the office qualified to act as an elector. The number of electors required to make the election binding on the whole Muslim community was generally held to be small, and a common view considered a single elector sufficient. The legal doctrine here reflected the fact that in the absence of an appointed successor a handful of powerful men were usually able to impose a successor of their choice. The election was not intended to be a free choice between candidates, but a selection of the "most excellent" in religious terms. The election of the "less excellent" was viewed as permissible only for proper cause.

The imamate became legally invalid through loss of liberty and of mental or physical fitness. Many Shāfiʿī authorities also held it to be forfeited by loss of probity through immoral conduct, injustice, or heterodoxy; this view was denied, however, by others and by Ḥanbalī and Ḥanafī opinion in general. In practice there was no way to apply this rule. Sunnī law defined the duties of the imam as: guarding the faith against heresy, protecting the peace in the territory of Islam, defending it against external enemies, conducting *jihād* against those outside the territory of Islam resisting its supremacy, enforcing law and justice between disputants, administering punishments *(ḥudūd)* under the religious law, collecting legal alms and other taxes and the fifth of war booty due to the imam, spending revenue according to the provisions of the law, and appointing trustworthy and qualified officials in delegating his authority.

Subsequent developments. The overthrow of the Abbasid caliphate in Baghdad by the Mongols in 1258 confronted Sunnī legal theory with a new situation. The Abbasid shadow caliphate set up by the Mamluk sultans in Cairo was generally ignored. After the Ottoman conquest of Egypt in 1516, the claims of the Ottoman sultans to the caliphate gained some popular support. Sunnī jurists, however, mostly considered the imamate to be in abeyance. Relying on the legal principle of necessity *(ḍarūrah),* they maintained that since the actual exercise of power was essential to the imamate, its functions had devolved upon the rulers of the Muslim world, whoever they were. The formal abolition of the Ottoman sultanate (1922) and caliphate (1924) by the Turkish National Assembly has led to a renewed interest in the question of a supreme and universal leader of Islam. Although some modernists have denied the need for the imamate, others among them, as well as fundamentalists, have advocated its restoration. Here the ideal model is the caliphate of the four Rightly Guided caliphs rather than the later dynastic caliphate. Modernists have stressed in particular the principle of rule by consultation *(shūrā),* often seen to imply the need for an elected parliamentary council to advise the supreme ruler, and the principle of election rather than appointment by the imam's predecessor.

The Shīʿah. While Sunnī Muslims were essentially motivated to back the actual holder of supreme power as the guarantor of the unity of the Muslim community, the Shīʿah have primarily emphasized the principle of legitimacy of the imam, which they see vested in the family of the prophet Muḥammad. The majority of Shiʿī imams, except among the Zaydīyah, never held political power, though the Shīʿah considered them solely entitled to the supreme leadership of the Muslim community and viewed the historical caliphs, with the exception of ʿAlī, as illegitimate usurpers. Partly as a result of their lack of political power, the Shiʿah have tended to endow their imams with great religious authority and to place the imamate at the center of religion.

Twelvers. Twelver Shiʿī doctrine bases the imamate on the permanent need for a divinely guided, infallible ruler and teacher of religion. This need was recognized through human reason rather than revelation. After the age of the prophets had come to a close with Muḥammad, these divinely guided leaders were the imams, beginning with Muḥammad's cousin and son-in-law, ʿAlī. They were, like the prophets, fully immune from sin and error and shared the same function and authority, though they would not bring a new divine scripture since the Qur'ān was final. The imamate thus assumed the same religious significance as prophecy. Ignorance or disobedience of any of the imams constituted infidelity equal to ignorance or disobedience of the Prophet. For the Twelvers, the imamate is handed down by divinely directed designation *(naṣṣ)* of the successor. Thus the great majority of the companions of Muḥammad and the Muslim community at large had become apostates when they recognized Abū Bakr as the imam in place of ʿAlī, who had been publicly designated by Muḥammad as his successor. After Ḥasan and Ḥusayn, the grandsons of Muḥammad, the imamate was to be transferred only from father to son among the descendants of Ḥusayn.

In 874 the death of the eleventh imam without apparent son caused a crisis which was eventually resolved by the affirmation that a son had been born to him and continued to live on earth, though in concealment *(ghaybah)* from humankind. The twelfth imam was identified with the eschatological Mahdi or Qā'im who is expected to appear before the end of the world and to rule it in glory. Since the twelfth imam is present on earth and may show himself to some of the faithful in person or in a dream, he is held to be essentially still able to fulfill his supreme function of conveying infallible divine guidance. His more practical legal duties and rights have either been assumed gradually by the Shīʿī *ʿulamā'* (religious scholars), who claim a general deputyship of the imam during his concealment, or remain in abeyance. [*See* Ghaybah.]

Twelver Shīʿī tradition ascribes to the imams numerous miracles and supernatural powers. They are described as having complete command of all crafts and languages, including those of animals. Though they are not endowed with a natural knowledge of the hidden, God gives them knowledge of anything they wish to know: "what has been and what will be." Because they inherit the knowledge of the prophet Muḥammad, they are perfectly informed of both the outer (exoteric) and the inner (esoteric) meaning of the Qur'ān. They are in possession of all revealed scriptures as well as books containing secret knowledge, including the *Saḥīfah, Jafr, Jāmiʿah,* and the *Muṣḥaf* of Fāṭimah. They receive divine guidance from an angel who speaks to them and informs them, though unlike the messenger prophets, they do not see him.

The imams are endowed with the Holy Spirit. In numerous passages of the Qur'ān they are evoked by terms such as "the light of God," his "witnesses," his "signs," those "firm in knowledge." They are the "vicegerents" of God on earth and the "gates" through which he may be approached. In popular piety the privilege of the imams to intercede with God for the sinners of their community has always loomed large and has inspired the frequent pilgrimages of the faithful to their tombs. Later esoteric Twelver Shīʿī teaching, influenced by Ṣūfī and Ismāʿīlī thought, defined the permanent essence of the imamate as *walāyah,* the quality of a *walī,* "friend of God," and as the esoteric aspect of prophecy. The imam was viewed as the initiator to the mystical truths. [*See* Walāyah.]

Ismāʿīlīyah. When, after the sixth imam, Jaʿfar al-Ṣādiq, the Ismāʿīlīyah separated from the group developing into the Twelver Shīʿah, they retained the idea of a permanent need for a divinely guided, infallible leader and teacher but developed from it a cyclical view of the history of the true religion. For the Ismāʿīlīyah, prophetic revelation progresses through seven eras. Each of the first six is inaugurated by a "speaker prophet," who brings a scripture with a law and is followed by a "silent fundament." The fundament reveals the esoteric truth concealed in the scripture and is followed by seven imams in sequence, the seventh of whom rises in rank to become the speaker of the following era. The imam takes the place of the speaker prophet in guarding and applying the literal aspect of the revealed law, while his *ḥujjah* ("proof"), representing the rank below the imam in the hierarchy, succeeds the fundament in revealing the esoteric truths to the initiate.

In the sixth era, that of Muḥammad and Islam, ʿAlī was the fundament and Jaʿfar al-Ṣādiq's grandson Muḥammad ibn Ismāʿīl the seventh imam from Ḥasan. As such he was expected, after his imminent advent from concealment, to rise in rank to become the seventh speaker prophet, who was identified with the Mahdi and Qā'im. This early Ismāʿīlī expectation was modified in the tenth century by the rise of the Fatimid caliphs, who claimed to be imams. Some Ismāʿīlī backers of the Fatimid caliphate recognized the first Fatimid caliph as the Mahdi, while others continued to expect the early return of Muḥammad ibn Ismāʿīl and considered the Fatimids his lieutenants. As Fatimid rule continued, however, these eschatological expectations receded, and the Fatimid caliphs were viewed as a continuous line of imams within the era of Islam.

After the fall of the Fatimid dynasty, the Ismāʿīlīyah survived mainly in two branches. The Ṭayyibīyah recognized al-Ṭayyib, an infant son of the Fatimid caliph al-Āmir about whose fate nothing is known, as their imam and denied his death. They hold that al-Ṭayyib, though in concealment, remains in touch with his community and will return. He is not identified, however, with the eschatological Qā'im. In later Ṭayyibī gnostic thought, the imam is described as having both a human nature *(nāsūt)* and a divine nature *(lāhūt)*. His human, physical nature, also called the "camphoric figure," is composed of the vapors that arise from the souls of the faithful three days after their death. The divine nature is described as a light temple formed by the assembly of light points of the souls of the faithful and the teaching hierarchy. This light temple will, after the death of the imam, rise to the horizon of the Tenth Intellect, the demiurge, where it will assemble with the temples of the other imams to form the immense light temple of the Qā'im.

The Nizārī branch recognized Nizār, a son of the Fatimid caliph al-Mustanṣir, as their imam and has continued to adhere to a line of present imams leading, for the great majority, to the Aga Khans. [*See* Aga Khan.] The proclamation of the Resurrection *(qiyāmah)* in 1164 and the subsequent return to an age of concealment brought major reforms of the esoteric doctrine of the imamate. The imams were now raised in rank above the prophets. As a potential Qā'im, each imam was held to have the authority to suspend or apply the religious law as the circumstances required. The imam was in his spiritual essence defined as a manifestation of the divine word or command, the cause of the spiritual world. The faithful attain spiritual birth, or resurrection, through recognition of the essence of the imam. In the era of concealment, spiritual union with the imam was restricted to his *ḥujjah,* who was his gate for the faithful and the sole dispenser of spiritual truth.

Zaydīyah. Unlike other Shīʿī Muslims, the Zaydīyah do not consider their imams divinely protected from error and sin and do not recognize a hereditary line of imams. They hold that after the first Shīʿī imams, ʿAlī, Ḥasan, and Ḥusayn, who were appointed by the prophet Muḥammad through a descriptive designation, the imamate belongs to any qualified descendant of Ḥasan or Ḥusayn who rises against the illegitimate rulers. Apart from his descent, the legal qualifications of the imam are substantially the same as in Sunnī law. Special emphasis is placed, however, on religious learning, competence to render legal judgment, moral integrity, and courage. Zaydī imams have generally been scholars of rank and authors of the most authoritative Zaydī religious works. The imamate becomes legally binding upon the issuance of a formal call to allegiance *(daʿwah)* and rising against illegitimate rule, not through election or appointment by a previous imam. After his call to allegiance, recognition and active backing of the imam is incumbent upon every believer. The imamate is forfeited by loss of any of the qualifications, in particular by moral offenses. According to the prevalent doctrine, only the most excellent claimant is entitled to the imamate, and if a more excellent candidate arises to claim it, the excelled imam must surrender it to him. This has been disputed, however, by some later authorities. In practice rival claims to the imamate have often divided the allegiance of the Zaydī communities, both in Yemen and in the coastal regions south of the Caspian Sea.

Although in Zaydī legal theory there must always be a qualified candidate for the imamate, the Zaydī imamate has often been in abeyance for prolonged periods. The list of recognized imams has never been definitely fixed, though there is consensus on many of them. Many Zaydī ʿAlid rulers did not claim the imamate or were not recognized as imams by later Zaydī opinion because they did not fulfill the requirements, especially that of religious learning. These were often considered as "restricted" imams, or "summoners" *(du'āt)*, with limited authority.

Khārijīs. Whereas the Shī'ah historically based their repudiation of the Sunnī caliphate on the principle of legitimacy, the Khārijīs founded their opposition on an uncompromising concept of the justice and moral integrity of the imam. In Khārijī doctrine the imam loses his legitimacy by any violation of religious law and must be removed, by force if necessary. The unjust or immoral imam and his supporters are to be treated as infidels unless they repent. 'Uthmān and 'Alī are viewed as initially legitimate imams who became infidels by their illicit acts and thus were rightfully murdered. Any Muslim who does not dissociate himself or herself from them and their supporters shares their state of infidelity. Likewise any Muslim who does not affirm solidarity with just imams like Abū Bakr and 'Umar is an infidel. The Khārijīs also unanimously rejected the elitist Sunnī doctrine restricting the imamate to the Quraysh. They held that any qualified Muslim, even of non-Arab and slave origin, was eligible. An exceptional view extended this egalitarian principle to women as well. The other qualifications and functions of the imam were similar to Sunnī doctrine, with special emphasis on the Qur'anic duty of "commanding what is proper and prohibiting what is reprehensible" and on the imam's leadership of the *jihād* against non-Khārijī Muslims.

Only the most moderate sect of the Khārijīs, the Ibāḍīyah, survived the first centuries of Islam. The Ibāḍīyah took a more accommodating view toward non-Khārijī Islam at large, and their doctrine came to recognize different types of imams corresponding to the four states in which the community of the faithful could face its enemies. These include the state of manifestation, when the community was strong enough to overcome the opponent; the state of defense, when it could merely hope to ward off the enemy; the state of self-sacrifice, when a small group of the faithful seeking martyrdom would choose to attack a powerful enemy; and the state of concealment, when the faithful were forced to live under the rule of the opponent and to practice dissimulation. Only the imam of the state of manifestation was entitled to exercise all the functions of the imamate.

Leadership of the Ritual Prayer

The ritual prayer, which is obligatory for every Muslim five times daily, may be performed individually or in group with a leader who is called the imam. The same applies to several special prayers, which are merely recommended, on the occasion of festivals and solar or lunar eclipses, prayers for rain, and supererogatory and funeral prayers. In most of these cases group prayer, preferably in a mosque, is the recommended form whenever possible. The congregational Friday prayer, which is generally obligatory for those in easy reach of a congregational mosque *(jāmi')*, can only be performed in group with an imam.

The imam must face the *qiblah*, the direction toward Mecca. In the mosque he stands in front of the *miḥrāb*, or prayer niche, which indicates this direction. In the early time of Islam a staff or lance was placed in the ground before him. The congregation stands in rows behind the imam; no one is permitted to be in front of him. If there is only a single worshiper following the prayer, he may stand at the imam's right, and a second one may stand at his left. The members of the congregation must strictly follow the imam in every movement and recitation. While the imam recites in a loud voice, however, they should generally not be heard. If the congregation is too large for everyone to see and hear the imam, special "conveyors" (sg., *muballigh*) may be employed to repeat his *takbīr*s, marking the transition to the next phase of the prayer, for the worshipers in the back rows or outside the mosque.

The obligation to imitate strictly the movements of the imam applies even if a worshiper belongs to another legal school prescribing different prayer rituals. While this rule has been generally accepted among the four Sunnī schools, there have at times been problems. Some Ḥanafī authorities held that raising the hands during the bowing *(rukū')* and lifting the head, as practiced by the Shāfi'īyah and others, invalidates the prayer and ruled that a Ḥanafī must not pray behind a Shāfi'ī imam. This matter provoked friction between the two schools for centuries.

A group praying outside a mosque may generally choose its own imam. Preferably he should be the most worthy among them, with particular consideration given to probity, knowledge of Qur'anic texts for recitation during prayer, knowledge of the ritual, and freedom from speech defects. While a woman may act as prayer leader only for other women, the imam may be a minor boy, a slave, or a moral offender among men and women alike. Prayer led by an imam with a speech defect is invalid. In a private home, the owner is most entitled to lead the prayer even if otherwise more worthy men are present.

Mosques have generally appointed official imams. Whenever the official imam or a substitute appointed by him is present, he is entitled to lead the prayer. In the congregational mosques or others maintained by the caliph, his governors, or, in modern times, the government, the imam is appointed by them. In private mosques maintained by individuals or local communities, the imam is chosen by the neighborhood. Once chosen he cannot be removed except for cause. The imam has usually the right to choose and direct the muezzin, who makes the call to prayer.

The imam of the Friday congregational worship may be appointed separately from the imam of the daily prayers. He is normally also the preacher *(khaṭīb)*, who delivers the official sermon *(khuṭbah)* with the prayer for the ruler before the Friday prayer. In early Islam the Friday congregational prayer in particular was led by the caliph himself in the capital and by his governors in the provincial capitals. Later they generally deputed imams. The Friday prayer remained closely associated with government authority, however, and some of the legal schools held it to be invalid without the presence of the supreme imam (caliph) or his appointed representative. In Twelver Shiism, for instance, the Friday worship has been generally held to be in abeyance in the absence of the rightful supreme imam. Only when the Safavids established a Shīʿī regime in sixteenth-century Iran did the matter become controversial, and some Shīʿī jurists maintained that Friday worship was obligatory in the presence of a qualified legal scholar. Today the Friday prayer is performed among the Twelver Shīʿah, though not as widely as among Sunnīs. Sunnī concern for maintaining the unity of Islam by backing the established rulers, whatever their moral failings, found expression in the affirmation contained in many Sunnī creeds that every Muslim must "pray behind every imam, be he righteous or immoral." The Shīʿah and Khārijīs generally reject this attitude and prohibit prayer behind an imam who is known to be either immoral or heterodox. [*See also* ʿIsmah *and* Nubūwah.]

BIBLIOGRAPHY

There is no comprehensive study of the imamate. The institutional development of the caliphate is analyzed by Thomas W. Arnold in his *The Caliphate* (Oxford, 1924); the second edition contains a chapter on the abolition of the caliphate and its aftermath by Sylvia G. Haim (New York, 1965). See also Emile Tyan's *Institutions du droit public musulman* (Paris, 1954–1957), volume 1, *Le califat*, and volume 2, *Califat et sultanat*. The most authoritative medieval treatise on the Sunnī (Shāfiʿī) legal doctrine of the imamate, al-Māwardī's *Kitāb al-ahkām al-sulṭānīyah*, has been translated into French by Edmond Fagnan, as *Les statuts gouvernementaux* (Algiers, 1915). Modernist views are discussed by Malcolm H. Kerr in this *Islamic Reform: The Political and Legal Theories of Muḥammad ʿAbduh and Rashīd Riḍā* (Berkeley, 1966) and by Henri Laoust in the introduction to his *Le califat dans la doctrine de Rašīd Riḍā* (Beirut, 1938), which contains the translation of a major work on the subject by a conservative modernist.

Twelver Shīʿī doctrine is described by Dwight M. Donaldson in *The Shi'ite Religion* (London, 1933), and later esoteric teaching by Henry Corbin in *Histoire de la philosophie islamique*, vol. 1 (Paris, 1964), pp. 53–109. For Ṭayyibī esoteric doctrine, see the analysis and annotated translation of a typical Ṭayyibī treatise on the subject in chapter 4 of Henry Corbin's *Trilogie ismaelienne* (Tehran, 1961). Nizārī doctrine after the *qiyāmah* is described by Marshall G. S. Hodgson in *The Order of Assassins* (1955; reprint, New York, 1980), pp. 160–175. Rudolf Strothmann's *Das Staatsrecht der Zaiditen* (Strasbourg, 1912) discusses Zaydī legal doctrine and practice. Khārijī doctrine is analyzed by Elie Adib Salem in *Political Theory and Institutions of the Khawārij* (Baltimore, 1956), especially in chapter 4. For details of the legal rules concerning the imamate of the ritual prayer, see chapter 9 of al-Māwardī's work cited above and *Nawawī, Minhaj et Talibin: A Manual of Muhammadan Law according to the School of Shafi*, translated by E. C. Howard (1914; reprint, Lahore, 1977), pp. 42–69.

WILFERD MADELUNG

ĪMĀN AND ISLĀM. *Islām*, a noun derived from the verb *aslama* ("to submit or surrender [to God]"), designates the act by which an individual recognizes his or her relationship to the divine and, at the same time, the community of all of those who respond in submission. It describes, therefore, both the singular, vertical relationship between the human being and God and the collective, horizontal relationship of all who join together in common faith and practice.

In its communal aspect *islām* has come to be the commonly accepted term for the religion of the followers of the prophet Muḥammad and today claims many millions of adherents. As the personal act of response to the oneness of God and his commands *islām* often has been viewed as coordinate with another term basic to Muslim theology. This is *īmān*, most commonly understood as faith, from the verb *āmana* ("to be secure, to place one's trust [in God]"). While *islām* as a verbal noun appears only eight times in the Qur'ān, *īmān* is found over five times as often in the sacred scripture.

Qur'anic context. The Qur'ān as understood by Muslims is not a theological document per se, although it does reveal something of the being and will of God. It is rather a record of the revelations to the prophet Muḥammad that details the ways in which men and women of faith are to respond to the fact of divine oneness. It also sets forth the specific ways in which they are to conduct their daily lives in preparation for the reality of the final day of judgment and recompense. Terms such as *islām* and *īmān* therefore are not defined and analyzed in the Qur'ān. In some instances they are apparently interchangeable in meaning, and in others Qur'anic usage seems to suggest that the two have different emphases, particularly as they relate to works. In one place only (surah 49:14) is a clear discrimination between *islām* and *īmān* implied. Here a distinction is drawn between the verbal acknowledgment of *islām* by the tongue and the *īmān* that has entered the heart. The suggestion that *islām* is the outward sign and *īmān* the inward, however, runs counter to the general understanding of the Qur'ān that they are essentially synonymous and that they both designate the religious response by which one heeds the message of God's oneness and thereby escapes the eternal retribution of the Day of Resurrection.

Ḥadīth. Many kinds of references to *islām* and *īmān* are to be found in the collections of *ḥadīth,* the narratives or "traditions" that record the community's memory of the sayings and actions of the prophet Muḥammad and his companions. Individual traditions often fail to suggest a distinction between *islām* and *īmān.* The Prophet is sometimes quoted as having indicated that the essentials of *islām* are the *Shahādah,* the twin testimonies to the oneness of God and the prophethood of Muḥammad, as well as the other duties constitutive of formal *islām,* with no specification of the components of faith. More often, however, the reports seem to imply that the terms connote at least different aspects of the same response, if not two separate kinds of responses.

One particularly interesting narrative found in a range of renditions presents the Prophet defining *islām* as clearly distinct from *īmān.* In the best-known version the story is told about a stranger with a beautiful face, black hair, and a white robe (usually understood to be the angel Gabriel) who joins the Prophet and a group of his companions and asks "What is *islām?*" (or, in other versions, "Tell me about *islām*"). The Prophet answers that *islām* is the performance of certain duties. The specifics of these duties differ in the various renditions of this *ḥadīth,* but the most commonly cited are witnessing that there is no god but God and that Muḥammad is his Messenger *(shahādah),* submitting to God with no association of anything else, performing the prayer ritual *(ṣalāt),* paying the alms tax *(zakāt),* observing the Ramaḍān fast *(ṣawm),* and making the pilgrimage *(ḥajj).* If the first two of these are combined, the list then reflects the elements that commonly have been accepted in Islam as the five duties that constitute the "pillars" *(arkān)* of the individual Muslim's religious responsibilities.

After this enumeration the stranger assures the Prophet that the definition is correct. He then goes on to ask about *īmān* and is told that it consists of faith in the following (again differing somewhat according to the several versions): God, his angels, his books (or book), his messengers (or messenger), the resurrection, the garden and the fire, and other eschatological realities. Though less commonly classified than the *arkān,* the elements in this list generally are identified as the key components of the creeds that have been developed by members of the Muslim community. Several versions indicate that after thus defining *islām* and *īmān* the stranger asks the Prophet, "If I do that am I a *muslim* and a *mu'min?*" to which the Prophet responds "Yes."

The continuation of the story includes commentary on *iḥsān,* a third element beyond *islām* and *īmān,* which the Prophet says is the state of being perfected and serving God as if he were always before your eyes. From the structure of the narrative it is clear that the discussion was intended to suggest degrees of religious response, with *islām* as the first and most basic and *iḥsān* as the last and highest. This kind of ranking is supported by another commonly cited narrative in which the Messenger of God says that *islām* is external while *īmān* belongs to the heart. For reasons that are not entirely clear, scholastic theology *(kalām)* did not generally develop the concept of *iḥsān* but centered its subsequent discussions primarily on the first two terms.

Other *ḥadīth*s seem to suggest that faith is a component element of *islām.* When asked about *islām* on one occasion the Prophet is said to have replied, "Witness that there is no god but God and that I am the Messenger of God, and have faith in all foreordinations, their good and evil, their sweetness and bitterness." On another occasion, the Prophet says that the more virtuous *islām* is *īmān,* which consists of faith in God, his angels, his books, his messengers, and the resurrection. Here *īmān* becomes a kind of subdivision of *islām,* with the most virtuous *īmān* said to be the emigration (Hijrah) and so on through a series of subcategories. In several traditions *islām* seems to consist of *īmān* plus works, as when the Prophet says that one should say "I have faith" and walk the straight path.

Theology. The respective definitions of *islām* and *īmān* became increasingly important in the early Muslim community as the nation of Islam grew through great numbers of conversions, and its members early on began to struggle with the question of who was or was not a Muslim. In a variety of ways, and for political as well as theological reasons, sects, schismatic groups, individual thinkers, and schools of theology adopted positions by which they tried to determine membership in the Islamic community. To this end clearer and firmer distinctions came to be drawn between *islām* and *īmān,* and the various groups in the young Muslim community often defined their positions according to those distinctions.

Khārijīs. Theological speculation is often said to have begun with the political movement of the Khārijīs, the earliest of the Muslim sects. It was, however, a movement not of passive reflection but of active involvement in the effort to purify Islam. As decades passed after the death of the Prophet, some began to feel that those in power were betraying the basic understanding of the faith. All the members of the community were being called *mu'minūn* ("persons of faith") regardless of the degree of their piety and their adherence to the essentials of Islam. The Khārijīs, in their zeal to ensure that the Muslim community was led by those most qualified in matters of faith and obedience, focused attention on the question of who is a true *muslim/mu'min* and who is a *kāfir* (best defined not as unbeliever or infidel but as one who actively rejects the will of God). *Īmān* and *islām* were seen by the Khārijīs as essentially synonymous: both include verbal and intellectual assent as well as works and are in absolute opposition to *kufr* ("rejection"). Rather than trying to define the *muslim/mu'min* the Khārijīs concentrated on the *kāfir* and adopted often ruthless means of condemning and in fact excommunicating such a person from the community.

Murji'ah. The sect known as the Murji'ah (lit., "those who postpone [judgment]") was politically and, on this issue, theologically opposed to the Khārijīs. This group felt that it is wrong to condemn a member of the community as a *kāfir,* no matter what his or her actions. Judgment of human conduct and final determination of one's state of punishment or felicity must be left in the hands of God, they said, postponed until the Day of Resurrection.

Gradually, however, this doctrine came to mean for them not simply the postponement of judgment. In addition, they gave works a place of secondary importance behind faith by saying that good works are not a necessary indication of faith. This was in distinction to the Khārijīs, who stressed the importance of outward acts of piety in conformity with God's laws. The Murji'ah thus became the first in the Muslim community specifically to address the question of the internal structure of *īmān.* While there clearly were different schools of Murji'ah (al-Khaṭīb al-Baghdādī breaks them into three main groups, and al-Ashʿarī identifies twelve different strands), their overall contribution to Islamic theology was in their identification of the nature of faith as separate from works and in their assurance for the *mu'min* of a place in paradise despite his or her failure to observe the laws of God.

Virtually all of the succeeding theoretical discussions about the nature of faith took as their starting point the issues and problems raised by the various schools of the Murji'ah. There was general acceptance of the Murji'ī thesis that the main elements to be considered in the understanding of *īmān* are affirmation *(taṣdīq)* and verbal acknowledgment *(iqrār)* of that affirmation. (While most later thinkers stressed the primary significance of *taṣdīq* as heartfelt affirmation, however, the Murji'ah rather understood affirmation as intellectual assent or knowledge.) While they assented to the importance of *taṣdīq* and *iqrār* as necessary constituents of *īmān,* the Murji'ah clearly rejected works.

As a consequence of this doctrine the Murji'ah, in clear opposition to the Khārijīs, did not believe that the quality of one's faith could be determined by the commission of sins, even major or grave sins. One school of the Murji'ah, the Karrāmīyah, went so far as to maintain that *īmān* consists strictly of the saying of the two *shahādah*s, the testimony of the oneness of God and the prophethood of Muḥammad, and involves neither affirmation nor works.

Later discussion. The debates between sects such as the Khārijīs and the Murji'ah were based on crucial questions of membership in the Muslim community and were therefore far from strictly intellectual issues. They were, in fact, quite often matters of life and death. As time passed, however, and the community began to stabilize after its initial growth, a stage was reached in which these kinds of questions were seen less as issues requiring decisive action and more as matters of intellectual engagement and decision. Thus the nature of *islām* and *īmān* continued to be discussed by the leading thinkers of the community.

One way of treating the relationship of, or distinction between, submission and faith is to consider which is the broader category under which the other is subsumed. Not surprisingly, different Muslim interpreters and schools of theology have reached different conclusions, often based on traditions from the Prophet such as those cited above.

If one understands *islām* as consisting of the five pillars or duties (the testimony, prayer, fast, alms tax, and pilgrimage) it is possible to argue that the first of these, witnessing to God's oneness and the prophethood of Muḥammad, can be considered an act of faith. In that way *īmān* is part of the larger category of *islām.* Thus Ashʿarī theologians such as al-Bāqillānī (d. 1013), for example, concluded that all *īmān* is part of *islām,* but not all *islām* is part of *īmān.* Al-Ashʿarī (d. 935) himself said that *islām* is wider than *īmān* and that therefore not all the former is part of the latter.

The later Ḥanbalī thinker Ibn Taymīyah (d. 1328) carefully developed another way of seeing this relationship in his analysis of the *ḥadīth* in which the Prophet seems to rank *islām, īmān,* and *iḥsān.* Because of the very ranking, he said, *iḥsān,* while characteristic of the most select number of the faithful, in fact connotes the most inclusive definition. That is, the person of faith *(mu'min)* must by definition be a submitter *(muslim)*, and the person of perfection *(muḥsin)* must therefore be both of the former. *Īmān*, therefore, contains *islām*. Ibn Taymīyah's conclusion was more than academic. It is clear, he felt, that *islām* is an external act while *īmān* is a matter of the heart. For Ibn Taymīyah the Ash'arī conclusion that *islām* is wider than *īmān* implies that while all those who submit are persons of faith, not all who profess faith are *muslims*, a conclusion with which he totally disagreed. And in fact the majority Ash'arī view was that although faith can exist without *islām*, failure to do the works characteristic of *islām* is a grave sin. For Ibn Taymīyah, to have faith but not to do works of obedience is an impossible contradiction.

While some in the Muslim community continued to debate these and other theological issues, others turned to the task of systematizing the conclusions reached by thinkers within the various schools into creedal formulations. One of the most popular of the creeds over the centuries has been the *Sharḥ al-'aqā'id* of the Ḥanafī jurist al-Nasafī (d. 1143). The creed was later commented on by the Ash'arī scholar al-Taftāzānī (d. 1367). *Īmān*, said al-Nasafī, is affirmation *(taṣdīq)* of that which the Prophet brought from God and confession *(iqrār)* of it. While acts of obedience may increase, faith neither increases nor decreases. Then, in a very interesting conclusion, he declares that *īmān* and *islām* are one; they are so, al-Taftāzānī explains, because obedience *(idh'ān)* is the essence of both *islām* and *taṣdīq*, which, in al-Nasafī's definition, is *īmān*.

Despite the common element of obedience, al-Taftāzānī did not completely identify the terms but rather said that one cannot exist without the other. In the Ḥanafī creed *Fiqh akbar* II (Greater Understanding II), attributed to Abū Ḥanīfah (d. 767) but probably written in the tenth century, *īmān* and *islām* share the common ingredient of submission and overlap so much that they are essentially interchangeable.

Qur'ān commentators analyzing the eight verses in which *islām* is mentioned all have stressed the essential component of submission, usually in relation to God's initiative. To the extent to which they have dealt with faith in relation to submission they have made it clear that *īmān* (most commonly defined as *taṣdīq* and *iqrār*) is identified in some clear ways with *islām*. The degree to which they have equated the terms, however, has varied considerably. In his monumental commentary on the Qur'ān, *Jāmi' al-bayān 'an ta'wīl āy al-Qur'ān*, al-Ṭabarī (d. 923) suggests a kind of bipartite *islām*. On one level is the verbal acknowledgment of submission by which one becomes part of the community of Islam, and on a deeper level is that *islām* that is in fact coordinate with the act of faith *(īmān)* and that involves the complete surrender of the body, the mind, and the heart. Fakhr al-Dīn al-Rāzī (d. 1209), in the *Mafātīḥ al-ghayb* (Keys to the Mystery), insists that while the two are different in generality they are one in existence. If *islām* is not of the heart, he said, it cannot be called *islām*. Muḥammad Rashīd Riḍā, the twentieth-century Egyptian author of the *Manār* commentary, suggested a similar interpretation when he said that the true meaning of both *islām* and *īmān* is what he calls *īmān khāṣṣ*, interiorized faith, which is the only means of salvation. In this understanding *islām* and *īmān* converge in a single reality *(ḥaqīqah)*.

Most Qur'ān commentators through the centuries, however, have seen *islām* and *īmān* as more distinct than al-Ṭabarī, al-Rāzī, or Rashīd Riḍā have. They admit that *islām* can have a purely external meaning, while *īmān* always involves confirmation of the heart. Although they differ in their attempts to interpret the distinctions between the terms, in no instance have they seen them as irreconcilable. And despite the variety of responses reflected in the works of theology, general usage of the terms *islām* and *īmān* has revealed some common understanding both of their respective definitions and of the ways in which these terms together express the totality of the Muslim's response to the being and will of God.

[*See also* Ummah *and the biographies of the principal scholars mentioned herein.*]

BIBLIOGRAPHY

Works in Arabic. For a full collection of traditions from the prophet Muḥammad in which the terms *islām* and *īmān* are used, see Ibn Ḥanbal's *Musnad*, 6 vols. (1895; reprint, Beirut, 1969). The earliest extensive Qur'ān commentary that analyzes the relation of the terms in their scriptural usage is Abū Ja'far Muḥammad al-Ṭabarī's *Jāmi' al-bayān 'an ta'wīl āy al-Qur'ān*, 30 vols. in 12 (Cairo, 1954–1968). Of the several creedal formulations dealing the the juxtaposition of faith and submission in the thinking of the early Muslim community, one of the most popular is 'Umar ibn Muḥammad al-Nasafīyah's *Sharḥ al-'aqā'id*, with commentary by Sa'd al-Dīn al-Taftāzānī (Cairo, 1974). A rich treatment of the meaning of faith and its relation to submission is found in the *Kitāb al-īmān* of the fourteenth-century theologian Ibn Taymīyah (Damascus, 1961).

Works in Western Languages. Such basic works as A. J. Wensinck's *The Muslim Creed* (1932; reprint, New York, 1965) and Louis Gardet and M. M. Anawati's *Introduction à la théologie musulmane*, 2d ed. (Paris, 1970), are helpful for a general understanding of the significance of the *īmān/islām* discussions in the development of Islamic theology. More specific treatments such as Helmer Ringgren's *Islam, 'aslama, and muslim*, "Horae Soederblomianae," vol. 2 (Uppsala, 1949), and "The Conception of Faith in the Koran," *Oriens* 4 (1951): 1–20, analyze Qur'anic usage of the terms. Toshihiko Izutsu provides an extensive study of the interpretation of *īmān* in the history of Islamic thought, with a chapter on its relation to *islām*, in *The Concept of Belief in Islamic Theology* (Tokyo, 1965).

JANE I. SMITH

IMMANENCE. *See* Transcendence and Immanence.

IMMERSION. *See* Baptism.

IMMOLATION. *See* Sacrifice.

IMMORTALITY. The concept of immortality can be understood and expanded upon on three levels. In its first sense, immortality is the quality attributed to divine beings, mythical or angelic, who by their very nature are not subject to death. The second sense concerns those heroes who have attained a divine status that they share with the gods. In its third sense, the concept of immortality has to do with the human being who enters upon a new form of eternal and incorruptible existence after death. The present article will deal only with immortality in this third sense, treating the permanence of the human being beyond the phenomenon of death.

Human life is recognizable in the animation produced by life-giving breath, and it is likewise attested to by a whole series of expressions and activities. It may also be defined, following Aristotle's use of the word *organon,* as that which is organized and self-organizing. Whether understood as organization, animation from without, or expression and activity, human life is subject to the final wearing away that is death. Hence, immortality, in the third sense given above, is the infinite prolongation of human existence and of the human personality beyond death. Life is then followed by another form of organization, the afterlife. Other concepts, such as eternity, paradise, hell, and transmigration, are then associated with the afterlife. These, however, will not be discussed in this article.

Approaches to Popular Belief. Two fundamental approaches to an examination of conceptions of immortality as found in popular belief must consider (1) the celebration of death as a transition to the afterlife and (2) the traditions and texts of the various cultures and religions. The first has to do with the attitude of the living in the presence of death and the dead, including appropriate actions, behavior, rituals, prayers, treatment of the corpse—in short, a vast symbolic network. Thus, archaeology and history reveal various methods of handling the body of the deceased: burial, embalming, mummification, exposure, and cremation. In addition to these activities there is the environment created for the deceased: the type, materials, and decoration of the grave, the covering of the corpse, funeral furnishings and offerings, and the presence of signs and symbols. Mention must also be made of funerary ritual: rites of opening of the mouth, eyes, ears, and nose, purification rituals, rites to celebrate the funeral ceremonies, and postmortem rites—all are indicative of beliefs.

The study of written documents and oral traditions allows us to comprehend the meaning of these beliefs directly, and thus to begin to interpret the symbolism of the rites. In this approach via documents and oral traditions we make use of three types of information. First there are the written texts of the world's various religions, then come myths and folk tales, with the material added by cultural tradition, and finally we have the texts of funerary rituals.

Prehistoric Peoples. The people who lived during the two million years before 9000 BCE have left us broken messages and mute testimony: bones, skulls, stone tools, grave furnishings, wall carvings, and cave and rock paintings. Analysis of these records reveals that early *Homo sapiens* was also a *homo religiosus.* Aside from the symbolic interpretation of cannibalism as a reembodiment of the dead person by the living (Louis-Vincent Thomas, *Le cadavre: De la biologie à l'anthropologie,* Brussels, 1980, p. 169), we possess early Neanderthal graves (80,000 BCE), with funerary deposits, orientation of the body, supine and fetal burial positions, and red ocher. Grave VI at Shanidar in Iran (50,000 BCE) shows that the body was laid on a litter of flowers. Upper Paleolithic sculptures (35,000 to 9000 BCE) show numerous ornamental objects and the importance of red ocher as funeral makeup, a substitute for blood. Paleolithic strata continually yield deposits of bones and skulls that have been manipulated or arranged according to a deliberate plan. In Upper Paleolithic wall art, symbols like the rainbow and the earthly bridge suggest connection with the world beyond.

Mesolithic and Neolithic periods. Funerary records become more plentiful in Mesolithic and Neolithic times. In the ancient Near East, the funeral practices at the Natufian (7800 BCE) seem to reveal a "cult of the dead." At Jericho, skulls have been found arranged in a circle, looking inward, as have three groups of three skulls each, all facing in the same direction. The Neolithic city of Çatal Hüyük in central Anatolia (6500-5600 BCE) has yielded numerous shrines whose plaster walls are decorated with paintings referring to death and skulls adorned and surrounded with everyday objects. The civilization of Lepenski Vir, on the southern bank of the Danube in eastern Serbia, has enriched our knowledge of Neolithic burial practices, including inhumation under or near houses and, in the center of the house, a rectangular hearth with a decorated altar or an egg-shaped stone behind it; skulls and long bones were buried between the hearth and the altar. For two millennia following 5800 BCE, megalithic tombs covered northern and western Europe, extending to the Mediterranean. In these collective tombs are found bodies with grave goods, decorative objects, offerings of food, cultic objects, and reliefs on the walls. In the course of the third millennium the image of a protector-goddess of the dead appeared.

The dawn of historical time. The Bronze Age sees the birth of spirit worship at Carnac, France, at Stonehenge, England, and in Egypt and Mesopotamia. In the late Bronze Age the collective ossuary and the individual tumulus give way to "urnfields." Cremation destroys the corpse in order to free the spirit through fire, which becomes the vehicle of the soul. Cremation takes its accustomed place in the Uranian religions and in astral cults. Urnfields from western Europe and stelae from Valcamonica, Tyrol, and the upper Adige take on new significance in light of the great discoveries of Georges Dumézil concerning ancient Indo-European ideology. From the Neolithic period on, belief in an afterlife is clearly demonstrated in the context of cosmic religions and the worship of the mother goddesses.

Nonliterate Peoples. Having considered the beliefs in immortality of early prehistoric man, we go on to the study of such beliefs in traditional societies, that is, in nonliterate cultures. Our primary reason for this is that such research permits us to discover the symbolic value of the beliefs and rites practiced by primitive peoples, most specifically in the area of the encounters of the living with the dead. The study of this symbolism affords insight into a number of the living values of these peoples, their relations with their ancestors, their initiation rites, their sense of time, and their eschatological myths, and in this way we arrive at a better comprehension of the basic patterns of the activity of *homo religiosus.* A second point of interest for our investigations, one especially conspicuous in the works of Mircea Eliade, is that through the study of the beliefs and rituals of traditions that have survived into the contemporary era, we gain a comparative perspective that enables us to understand more deeply the records left behind by prehistoric man.

Sub-Saharan Africa. A discussion of traditional beliefs in Africa presents a number of difficulties, given the variety and nature of the ethnological evidence, much of which is drawn from an oral tradition of myths and proverbs, as well as from personal inquiries and testimony. Moreover, sub-Saharan Africa contains more than two thousand ethnic groups separated by pronounced specific differences, so that any discussion of traditional beliefs necessarily presupposes a great many choices and omissions.

One element of African beliefs in immortality arises from eschatological concerns. For the African there are two kinds of time: mythical time, the time of the eternally valid group and its continuity, and real time, in which the life of the individual and the discontinuity of death take place. Between these two times lies the symbolic mediation of funeral rites, through which the deceased leaves contingent time and passes into mythical time, the time of the pyramid of beings. The funeral rites are the collective response to the death of an individual; they allow the group to endure. This conception of the immortality of the ethnic group, coupled with the dual reality of time, is found in most African cosmogonies.

Alongside this vision of the undying ethnos exists the belief in the deathlessness of the personal being, indispensable for the continuity of the group. Among the Bobo of Burkina Faso, real time lies under the sign of Dwo, an unchanging divinity who rules over spirits and genies, the life force *(nyama),* and the ancestors. Also in Burkina Faso, in the eschatology of the Dagaï, a cyclic conception of time is accompanied by the notion of the reincarnation of the deceased—all new births arise from the transformation of the ancestors. After death, the deceased passes first to the land of the spirits, either to become an ancestor or to be reincarnated in the body of a totemic animal. Among the Luba and other Bantu-speaking peoples of Zaire, the *muntu,* the essence of each person's being, goes after death either to the world of the ancestors or to that of the shades. Whenever a birth occurs, the ancestor invests the infant with his own life force. The Samo teach that the *mere,* the immortal double of the dead person, passes initially to a first village of the dead and then, after another death, to a second village. At the end of this double life-death operation, the *mere* takes up residence in a tree, and when the tree is destroyed it enters another tree of the same species. In Yoruba belief, *emi* ("breath"), the life force, leaves the body and passes into the abode of the blessed ancestors, where it becomes one with *ori* ("head"), its tutelary spirit. But in all African cultures, the evil dead, whose life energy has been banished from society, wander about in the air and become imprisoned by the forces of evil. In Africa, immortality is marked by a reference to the past, through which the dead play an important role in the society of the living. Reincarnation symbolically returns the dead to the circle of the living, so that the invisible living exist side by side with the visible living (Thomas, 1982, pp. 122–136).

A second basic aspect of immortality is the belief in the ancestors. There are two classes of ancestors, those who are mythical and primordial and those who have entered this state after their life on earth. Ancestor worship holds a most important place in African belief and ritual. The conception of the ancestor is made up of two components: on the one hand, the purity of the social and religious ideal, and on the other, a concern with the continuity and identity of the community. Together the two components form the concept of individual and collective immortality. The ancestor represents the symbolic transposition of the human condition to a numinous plane while continuing to be a part of the world of the living. It is in the role of ancestor that the most important stage of one's destiny after death is realized. A true solidarity binds together the dead who have attained ancestral status and the living who remain in communion with them so as to live according to the exemplary past, the highest ideal of life. The organization of the ancestral world is ruled by a complex hierarchy, one both social and familial, based on descent and function. There are close or immediate ancestors, those who have died recently, and distant ancestors, who make up a faceless crowd. The more eminent among the dead are watchful ancestors, while others are ordinary dead people who never leave the mass of collective anonymity. To the African mind, the ancestors are ranked according to the strength of their life force, for example Bantu-speaking peoples distinguish the *vidye,* spiritual beings who take an active part in the life of the community, from the *fu,* the ordinary dead. Among the latter are the ghosts, who must be appeased by the living with offerings and sacrifices.

The ancestors provide more than a personal and ethnic immortality, however. The hierarchical ancestral community is the repository of the accumulated knowledge of successive generations, and in this sense it is the memory of the ethnic group, the product of its origins and its past. It represents the law of the fathers, and it exercises a permanent regulatory function over the life of the group. This explains the importance of cult and ritual in African society.

Before they can attain a final, lasting rest, the dead undergo profound changes. This rest depends partly on the remembrance of the living and their ability to keep alive the memory of those who have gone before. As long as their descendants honor and pray to them, they remain among the "living dead," but as soon as they fall into oblivion they enter a collective afterlife. According to the Bambara of Mali, the most perfect of the ancestors are allowed to gaze upon God. In any case, the world of the ancestors provides the community with a model, a tradition of norms, and the assurance of its continuity. Ancestrality and immortality are bound together.

Another aspect of ancestral immortality is found in African beliefs in reincarnation. Ethnologists have emphasized the complexity of the idea that the person is composed of multiple elements (see Zahan, 1963). One can say that it is the person's life force that is reincarnated, but the actual conditions of reincarnation depend upon many variables or choices, including those of sex, time, the will or condition of the deceased, and that of the group. Reincarnation brings about a reactualization of the deceased that partially interrupts his postmortem fate. Reincarnation implies that the returning ancestor is recognized and present in the memory of the living, and it can only occur in a child of the same lineage and sex. The ancestor transmits a portion of the genetic inheritance, which is why the various ethnic groups attach so much importance to respect for the body and its preservation at death and in the funeral ceremony. The ancestor also transmits the spiritual elements: the *kili,* in the belief of the Serer of Senegal, the *ri,* or "thought," among the Samo of Burkina Faso. But the reincarnated ancestor continues to live in the beyond. "The belief in reincarnation serves to bring back the dead, to return him, symbolically at least, to the circle of the living" (Thomas, 1982, p. 135).

In all cultures, funeral rituals serve as primary expressions of belief in immortality while at the same time serving as instruments that help to make it real by symbolically absorbing the shock caused by a death. Like the rites of birth and initiation, they effect a passage that is at once a separation and a coming together. In all African communities, funeral rites mark out the successive stages traversed by the deceased. The actors are many: the deceased, the master of the ceremony, gravediggers, bier-builders, family, clan, the deceased's stand-ins, priests, and chiefs. In the performance of the ritual due emphasis must be laid on the sonorous background of chants and cries, which are thought of as a collective release but also as a symbol of fertility; also to be considered are the purification of the corpse, a plentiful supply of speech-making and food, rituals making light of death, burial of the corpse, and in some cases a second funeral, in which the bones are retrieved from the grave, washed, adorned, and placed on the altar of the ancestors. The Fali of Cameroon ritually prepare the skull, place it in an urn, and replace it in the grave.

In the rites of revitalization performed on the deceased we perceive the beliefs concerning their transformation with a view to their new life. The preparations are conducted with care so as not to bruise the body and to protect its appearance, like the bathing of a newborn. The ritual continues with makeup and adornments involving ashes, kaolin (fine white clay), red ocher, and gold dust. Kaolin is the symbol of life, and it is used in fertility rituals for sprinkling on seeded fields. The priest and the initiate are covered with it in initiation ceremonies. Applied to the corpse, white kaolin signifies rebirth and life. Red ocher is commonly used as facial makeup. The sacrifices and funeral meals make up the provisions needed for the journey, and the dead person's escort is represented by metal and carnelian jewelry and figurines of birds, snakes, and crocodiles, symbolizing eternity. The rites of separation and completion set the deceased on the road to the beyond through graduated stages extending through time. The rites that follow the death ensure passage from one stage to the next. The family altar, masks, and icons will evoke the presence of the ancestors; the *ases*, or metal family trees, found in Benin are another symbolic support for this presence. In Gabon, the Mpongwe keep relic chests in which the red-painted skulls lie on a bed. Identical customs are found among the neighboring Mitsogo and Fang tribes. The arrangement of African funeral rituals helps to maintain the balance between the two elements which make up society, the living and the dead.

The perception of time, ancestorism, and funeral rites are three essential features of culture and religion in sub-Saharan Africa. They offer an impressive convergence of facts and symbols that shed light on the dual conception of immortality, that of the ethnic group and that of the individual. Time is the pillar of generations. Past, present, and future, the three instants of duration, can only be thought of in human terms, but they must be viewed in their relation to the world of the ancestors, the ideal world of the living. Thus immortality is linked to the past and to ancestral tradition. This tradition is the attainment of successive generations; it is the sum total of the wisdom and the fundamental value of life. Through the experience of the deceased and the ever-growing ancestral community, the living unceasingly enrich their spiritual wealth. Linear time and cyclic time intersect each other to form the axis of immortality. The other world is associated with the notions of rest, tranquillity, and peace, a paradise toward which the society of the living progresses so long as it lives in conformity with tradition. It is by way of the ancestral community and worship of the ancestors that the African reaches immortality.

Australia. In 1770, the explorer James Cook arrived in Australia, claiming it for England. By 1788 around five hundred Aboriginal groups had been counted, each one comprising a group of individuals linked by a common descent. Numerous ethnological studies have been devoted to these peoples, who are known especially for their totemic practices and their systems of kinship classification. Australian myths, the subject of particular study in recent decades, refer to supernatural creator beings who fashioned the world out of a preexisting cosmic substance. The appearance of man in his present form is placed in the Dreaming, a primordial era called *alchera* or *alcheringa* by the Aranda, a central Australian people who are especially interesting for their social and religious life, and who are very well known thanks to the studies of Carl Strehlow, Baldwin Spencer, and F. J. Gillen. The creation myths revolve around the great gods and the civilizing heroes, so that primordiality is fundamental. The cosmogonic and primordial myths play a pivotal role because all the rites of initiation, reproduction, and fertility are reenactments of these myths. In sum, "all of the Australian's religious acts can be thought of as so many means, different yet related, of reestablishing contact with the Supernatural Beings and reentering the sacred Dream Time" (Eliade, 1973).

As a single cell of the sacred universe created by the supernatural beings, a cell that has become profane by being born, each individual must rediscover his spiritual origin through rites of initiation: circumcision, which is a symbolic killing amid the howls of the bull-roarers and anointing with blood; rites of purifying and spiritualizing fire; the rite of water-purification; and the ritual return of the *alcheringa*. The Aranda word *alcheringa (churinga, tjurunga)* means "mythical time, dream time"; it refers to both the ancient times and the hero-ancestors. In the form of a material object, a stone or a piece of wood, the *tjurunga* is given back to the initiate as an effective symbol of his recovered spiritual being. Through the *tjurunga* the initiate is put back in touch with the primordial Dreaming—he becomes *altjira*, "sacred." The sacred symbols are of prime importance for the life of the individual and the tribe, for they enable one to achieve contact with primordial time and to relive the ancient events through myths, rites, visitation of sacred places, and contact with the God of heaven and the Dreaming. An extraordinary abundance of objects created by native art allows us to realize the coherent functioning of this symbolism.

Death is a shock to the tribe and is felt as a disruption of the collective life, hence the cries and wailing, the mourning rituals, the rhythmic chanting, and the search to discover the evil spirit who caused this death. But the Australians believe that death is the final rite of passage that leads one from the profane world to the sacred universe. Man has two souls. The true self, the primordial and preexistent spirit, comes from heaven, the totemic center. At death, the true soul leaves the body and goes back to live forever in the eternal Dreaming, where it was before the individual's birth, while the other soul remains on earth, taking up residence in another person and moving about among the living. Eliade believes that death is thought of in Australia as an ecstatic experience, patterned after the first journey of the supernatural beings and the mythic ancestors (Eliade, 1973). The soul does what was done at the very beginning. All Australian tribes profess a belief in the indestructibility of the human soul, a spiritual entity that has its origin in the Dreaming.

The funeral rites take various forms. The body is treated in different ways by different tribes—buried, mummified, cremated, exposed on a platform with delayed burial, or deposited in the crotch of a tree. Double funerals, with an intervening period of mourning, are very common. Mummification is intended to help separate the body from the spirit, for the mummy is burned at the end of the mourning period, and the cremation frees the soul completely. The combination of funeral rituals must bring about this separation so that the spirit can return to its primordial home among the civilizing heroes. Through the funeral rites, the preexisting spirit regains its spiritual domain, sometimes thought of as the primordial totemic center. A whole ritual symbolism punctuates this journey, for example the occasional placing of bones within a totemic coffin. Beliefs in reincarnation, however, are rare and confused. For human beings the life cycle is simple: from the preexisting spirit, birth into a body and entry into the profane world, to the first stage of reintegration into the Dreaming via initiation, and finally the return to the original state through funeral rites.

The Americas. We come now to American Indian beliefs in immortality, as they are found outside the more advanced American civilizations. These are forms of religion that have survived through the post-Columbian era and still exist in some areas of North and South America. The belief in a life beyond the grave seems to have been firmly established in Indian thought in early times, to judge from their conception of the world and of life, from ancestral traditions, and from the testimonies of seers. These seers are sometimes persons who undergo dreamlike experiences, and sometimes medicine men who travel, in their imagination or in trance, to the borders of the realm of the dead. Funeral rituals also constitute a valuable source of knowledge about beliefs in an afterlife.

Among the American Indian peoples we find a conception of the soul that forms the basis of their beliefs in immortality. In North America the idea of a double soul is extremely widespread. The corporeal soul gives life, consciousness, and the faculty of movement to the body, whereas the dream soul is separate from the body and can move about in space and go to distant places. Death occurs when the separate soul becomes trapped in the realm of the dead. Then the corporeal soul is also detached from the body. Among the Inuit, the corporeal soul, called *tarneg,* survives after death, keeping the form of the deceased in the realm of the dead. The Yuchi and Sioux tribes speak of four souls, splitting the notion of a double soul to bring it into accord with the sacred number four. In South America, the same dichotomy is found in the case of the Mundurucú, but the Waica of the upper Orinoco and the Jivaroan people of Ecuador appear to have no concept of a separate soul.

In *The Religions of the American Indians* (Berkeley, 1979), Åke Hultkrantz makes two important observations. First, in both North and South America, the great civilizations share a monistic conception of the soul, a fact which may be attributed to the decline of shamanism in these cultures. Second, the belief in two souls, one of which can be separated from the body even during life, could have been motivated by shamanistic experiences of the journey of the soul. Indeed, the wanderings of the shaman and other people in dreamlike trances provided abundant information about journeys to the realm of the dead. In North and South America these tales report obstacles set up in the soul's way: curtains of fire, expanses of water, and monsters who threaten the traveler and try to make him lose his mind. The Ojibwa and Choctaw of North America speak of the slippery pine-trunk joining the banks of a rushing stream which the soul must get across. In South America, the Manacica believe that the deceased begins the journey to the realm of the dead as soon as the funeral is over. The medicine man guides him through virgin forests, seas, swamps, and mountains to the river that separates the land of the living from that of the dead. He has only to cross the bridge joining the two, which is guarded by a divinity.

In the American Indian conception of immortality, the Milky Way occupies a special place. It is also likened to the rainbow; the Kwakiutl of Vancouver Island think of it as the *axis mundi.* In British Columbia, the path of souls is the world tree. The *axis mundi,* the world tree, the road linking earth and sky, and shamanism are features of the mythic context of ecstasy and immortality. The Indians believe that the soul goes to the region of the dead, which is known through myths and tales to be patterned after the world of the living. Thus in North America it is sometimes called the "happy hunting ground." The Plains tribes imagine the dwelling place of the dead as a wide rolling prairie with feasting and dancing, whereas east of the Mississippi River and in South America, the cultivation of maize and agrarian festivals color the images of this realm. The afterlife of immortality is a reflection of earthly life.

The location of the land of the dead varies widely. For the Cubeo of the Amazon Basin, the country of the ancestors lies close by the villages of the living; the Blackfeet of Montana and Alberta speak of the "sandy hills" a few days' walk from the camps of the living, most of the Amazonian tribes think of a place beyond the setting sun, and the Pueblo Indians imagine it underground, an uncommon idea among American Indians since most of them locate the soul in a brightly lit place. Indian thought is marked by an ancient dualism: the "evil ones" and those who have died "badly" are doomed to a wandering life as ghosts, for the realm of the dead is open only to those who, after normal death, have received funeral rites.

These rites provide us with some valuable data. There are various methods of entombment: inhumation in South America, and in Canada placement of the body on a platform, in a tree, or on the ground. There is also incineration. Among the Iroquois, the Algonquians to the south of the Great Lakes, there are second funerals, involving the burial of the disinterred bones in a common grave or funeral urn. The provision of grave goods—food, drink, weapons, clothing, and jewelry—is widespread in the Andean region. The occasional addition of mummification in this practice allows us to speak of the "life of the corpse." In Colombia, archaeologists have discovered funeral wells, symbols of the afterlife, as well as traces of human sacrifices and anthropophagy. The Waica of the Amazon Basin practice cremation of the corpse, believing that the soul of the dead person, called *nobolebe* ("cloud"), rises to the sky where it is joined by *nonish,* the shadow soul. The funeral rites are intended to facilitate the deceased's journey to the region of the dead and to prevent his return. Belief in reincarnation is present both in the South and in the North, especially among the Inuit. The extent of ancestor worship is not so great; we find it in particular among the Zuni of New Mexico, in the Andes, and in the West Indies among the Taino. H. B. Alexander has emphasized the "wanderings of the soul" that appear in various initiation ceremonies, such as those of the Great House of the Delaware tribe and the Midewiwin of the Algonquian tribes (*The World's Rim: Great Mysteries of the North American Indians,* Lincoln, Nebr., 1953). Such initiations are meant to enable the initiate to grasp the meaning of life, which begins in this world and continues in the other world after death.

Inner Asia and the Finno-Ugric peoples. A great similarity in beliefs concerning the soul can be noted on both sides of the Urals. The Khanty (Ostiaks) and Mansi (Voguls), Ugrians from the Ob River region, believe in the existence of a double soul comprising the breath or bodily soul and the shadow or dream soul, which is free and quite incorporeal but is tied to the dead person after death. Thus, after the person's death, the soul that was free and immaterial in life takes on a bodily form because of its ties to the corpse. Corpse and soul together stand for the complete, personal identity of the deceased person. Thus while the body is in the grave, it is also somewhere else thanks to its soul. The Khanty and Mansi believe that the free soul enters a subterranean realm where it represents the deceased and his personality. The same idea is found among the Samoyed of Europe and Siberia: the free soul survives, allowing the dead to lead lives in the underground world comparable to those which they lived on earth. In the dualistic eschatology of the Tunguz of the Yenisei River region, the free soul goes after death to the celestial land of the souls, along "the upper course of the tribal river," to heaven, where it becomes an *omi,* an "infant soul," so that it can be reincarnated. The body and soul that sojourned in the body go to the subterranean world, and the free soul, becoming an infant soul, remains in heaven until it is reborn. The Yukagir, who occupied Siberia before the Tunguz and the Yakuts, also have a twofold conception of the soul: man possesses a free soul, which has its seat in the head and which goes to the realm of the dead after death, plus bodily souls located elsewhere in the body.

Finnic pneumatology is identical to that of the northern Eurasian world. The free soul (image soul, shadow soul) is the extracorporeal manifestation of the person, which can become separated from the body even during life, in dreams, ecstasy, or trance. The corporeal soul, bound to the body, animates physical and psychic life. This dualism has faded under the influence of Christianity, but has left numerous traces in religious practices. The Mari (Cheremis), a Finnic people studied by Harva, say that after death, *ört,* the free soul, remains near the corpse and follows it to the grave. During the memorial ceremonies a feast is given in its honor, after which it is led back to the grave. The corporeal souls have ceased to exist, while the free soul continues to represent the human being. Thus throughout northern Eurasia death is conceived of as twofold: there is the corpse, abandoned by the corporeal souls, and then there is the soul of the deceased that continues to prolong the person's life. This dual status of the dead explains the funeral rites and the concept of the afterlife. The family handles the corpse with care, washing and dressing it and providing it with funeral furnishings and gifts for the other deceased members of the family. The Finns believe that the living and the dead form a family that is cemented together at the funeral and the memorial services. To discourage the soul from coming back into the house, the corpse is taken out through a hole cut in the wall. The grave is sacred, and it is located in a pleasant and picturesque spot, since it is the deceased's home; the cemetery is the "village of the dead." However, the Finnish language also carries traces of ideas about an underground abode of the dead and the dead person's continuing his work. Finnic eschatology, like that of all northern Eurasian cultures, is focused on the present, and conceives immortality not as an eternity, but as a present. The Finns continue to recognize this "presence" of the dead through feasts and memorial ceremonies. Many such rituals have been retained even after the conversion of these populations to Christianity.

Summary. To complete this brief overview of the beliefs in immortality among the preliterate populations of Africa, Australia, America, and Asia, a few further details must be mentioned. I have touched only in passing on the important area of reincarnation as a realization of the afterlife. Further, I have stressed the fact that immortality is linked to ancestor worship on the one hand and to the worship of the dead on the other. It should of course be noted that there is a difference between these two types, for not every dead person becomes an ancestor. If ancestor worship represents an important datum for the understanding of immortality in African thought, it must nevertheless always be distinguished from the veneration of the dead. The latter forms part of postmortem rituals, whereas ancestor worship is among the basic elements that make up certain archaic religions. Such a distinction takes on great importance in primitive religions such as the tribal cults of Indonesia: the ancestors worshiped there are a select group who have played a pivotal role in the life of the people. The creation of an ancestor is the work of the whole society, performed in a solemn initiation festival. In such a case we turn from the study of the worship of the dead to that of the worship of kings.

The study of immortality among American Indian and Eurasiatic peoples has revealed the existence of the "road of the dead." Study of these routes of the deceased is of value for our knowledge of these peoples' beliefs in immortality. They are of two principal kinds. The first is the heavenly road, reserved for chiefs, initiates, and those among the moral elite. The second is underground, or horizontal; it is the normal road leading to the world of the dead, or quite simply to the deceased's familiar haunts. In the "discovery" of the roads of the dead, a major role has been played by shamanism, for it is through the shamans' journeys to the transcendental world that the living have been informed about the paths to the beyond. By his ability to make such journeys the shaman has helped to etch in the memories of many peoples the landmarks of the funerary landscape and the road of the dead. Moreover, because this "revelation" is instructive for the life of archaic peoples, we should emphasize one idea that dominates these myths and rituals: "Communication between Heaven and Earth can be accomplished—or could be *in illo tempore*—by some physical means (rainbow, bridge, stairway, liana, rope, 'chain of arrows,' mountain, etc.). All the symbolic images dealing with the connection between Sky and Earth are merely variations on the World Tree or the *Axis Mundi*" (Eliade, 1964). The road of the dead, shamanism, and immortality bring us back to the basic realities for *homo religiosus:* the symbolism of the center, the cosmic tree, and the primordial time when contacts between heaven and earth were normal. The belief in immortality has led various archaic peoples to the discovery of the mythic, paradisiacal moment before the fall and the loss of contact between heaven and earth.

Mesoamerican Religions. The Mesoamerican cultural and religious complex includes various civilizations dating from 3500 BCE to the Spanish conquest in the sixteenth century CE. There are three major periods: the Preclassic concludes in the third century CE, and the Classic era extends from that time to the year 1000, followed by the Postclassic era. I shall consider here only the last period, for which we have relatively abundant archaeological and historical records.

The Aztec. The religion of the Aztec—the dominant people in Mexico at the time of the conquest—is a syncretic one in which three principal gods are found: the sun god Huitzilopochtli, the rain god Tlaloc, originally from Teotihuacán, and Quetzalcoatl, the feathered serpent of the Toltec, the culture hero and cosmic embodiment of wisdom. For the Aztec, the present world—which has already been preceded by four others—has the shape of a cross whose northern end is the land of darkness, the abode of the dead. It was created by Quetzalcoatl, who wrested the bones of the dead from the underworld and restored them to life by sprinkling them with his blood. This world is threatened with a calamity that can only be averted by means of human blood, and this is why there are wars, which are necessary for finding prisoners for sacrifice.

After death, people are subject to different fates, according to the choice of the gods. Stillborn children go to the thirteenth heaven, where the "tree of milk" is found that provides them with nourishment for an eternal infancy. Warriors slain on the battlefield and all those who have been sacrificed on an altar, as well as traders who have died on their journeys, become companions of the Sun, who has chosen them to take part in the cosmic salvation. Cremation prepares them for this solarization: the corpse is adorned with precious materials, the face covered with a mask, the head decorated with plumes, and the legs and arms are bound. Before consigning this mummy to the flames, it is provided with a precious stone, *chalchihuitl*, meant to take the place of its heart in the afterlife. Warriors, sacrificial victims, and tradesmen become the "companions of the eagle," *quauhteca*, accompanying the Sun from his rising until he reaches the zenith. Women who have died in childbirth are ranked with the warriors. They accompany the Sun from noon until sunset, carrying him on a litter of quetzal plumes. Thus there is immortality for this select group, and the warriors are reincarnated after four years.

The second category of the deceased is made up of men and women chosen by Tlaloc, those killed by drowning, lightning, and marsh fevers. These are buried, and go to the eastern abode, to the gardens of the god. The agrarian creed of Tlaloc envisages for them a happy life ever after amid luxurious vegetation—immortality in the paradise of Tlaloc. A fresco from Teotihuacán depicts this tropical garden and the elect who sing of their happiness there.

All other dying people go to the northern realm, the land of night. Their bodies are burned together with those of dogs, their companions on the road of the dead, a route beset with dangers—eight steppes and nine rivers. At the end of a four-year journey, during which their families carry out funeral ceremonies, they reach the underworld of the god Mictlan, who will annihilate them.

The Maya. Maya religion is known through the discovery of great cities such as Tikal, Copan, Palenque, and Uxmal. The period of its highest attainment extends from the third to the tenth centuries. In its funeral practices we find again three categories of the dead. The privileged groups are warriors who fall in battle, women dying in childbirth, priests, and suicides by hanging. These are immortal and enjoy eternal gladness in the Maya paradise beneath the sacred ceiba, the tree that crosses all the celestial spheres. This is the "tree of the beginning," Yache, which creates the junction between heaven and earth. The recent discovery of the tomb of Pacal, the king of Palenque from 615 to 633, offers irrefutable evidence of the Maya belief in immortality: the deceased falls into the mouth of the setting sun and, transformed into the bird Mohan, the symbol of immortality, rises into the sky again with the rising sun. The cross-shaped cosmic tree sends its roots into the world below and spreads its branches into the heavens. The *Book of the Dead* of the Maya religion also expands on the doctrine of reincarnation.

Inca Religion. At a time when various civilizations shared the Andean region (Peru, Bolivia, and Ecuador), new populations came on the scene. Chief among these were the Inca, named after their founding tribe, who settled the town of Tiahuanaco and the area around Lake Titicaca around 1445. Their empire would last only a century, crumbling under the impact of the Spanish invasion.

The highest god in the Inca pantheon was the Sun, the creator god, called by the name Viracocha in the mountains and Pachacámac in the coastal areas. The chiefs of the country were the "sons of the Sun." Alongside the worship of the sun (solar temples which were built in all the great cities), there was also the worship of Pachamama, the earth goddess, the embodiment of fertility.

Various witnesses of the Spanish conquest left accounts of Inca religion, all of which agree that the Inca believed in immortality and imagined the afterlife as a continuation of the present life. The evidence found in Peru attests to funeral customs such as the preservation of the corpse, the giving of a deceased ancestor's name to a newborn child, and the placing of the body in a fetal position in the grave or funeral jar. The belief in an afterlife accounts for the care devoted to the arrangement of graves, the embalming of the bodies of princes, and the strict punishment for any violation of graves. For the funeral of the ruler, the ritual prescribed embalming, special treatment of the face and eyes, the sacrifice and embalming of his wives and servants, and the placing of his furniture and possessions in the tomb.

Religions of China. The discovery of the Yang-shao culture in 1921 provided the first data on the early Chinese Neolithic period (4115 or 4365 BCE) and revealed something of early Chinese conceptions of sacred space, fertility, and death. Belief in the afterlife of the soul is attested by the placing of tools and foodstuffs in graves. The funeral urns of children were furnished with an opening at the top that allowed the soul to go out and to return. The funeral urn, the deceased's home, attests to the worship of ancestors. Red decoration in three motifs—triangle, checkerboard, and cowrie—forms a complex symbol of life, afterlife, and rebirth. These houses for the soul, which are numerous in Chinese prehistory, are the precursors of the ancestral tablets. Under the Shang dynasty (1751-1028 BCE), there are an increasing number of Bronze Age oracular inscriptions incised on bones and oyster shells that reveal the dialectic of the opposites (the *coincidentia oppositorum*, which foreshadows the doctrines of Taoism) and conceptions of the renewal of time and spiritual regeneration. Sacrifices to the supreme god Ti and to the ancestors make their appearance, and the royal graves have revealed animal and human sacrifices meant to accompany the ruler in his afterlife.

The year 1028 BCE marks the beginning of the Chou dynasty, which ruled China until 256 BCE. From its earliest days, the fundamental feature of the country's organization is lordship founded upon the family group and the possession of manorial land, thus the religion rests on the twin bases of the ancestors, who make up the divinized family, and the god of the earth, the apotheosis of lordship. Every family has its ancestors, who act as its protectors, and the king's forefathers are the guardians of the entire country. The funeral rites demonstrate a belief in the afterlife of souls, but this belief is somewhat inconsistent with regard to the fate of the dead. To begin with it must be recognized that every person was supposed to have multiple souls. The abode of the dead can be either the grave, the Yellow Springs, ruled by the earth god, the celestial world of Shang-ti ("lord on high"), or the ancestral sanctuary. The correct observance of the funeral rites is an essential condition for the afterlife.

Under the Chou dynasty, from the eighth to the third centuries BCE, Chinese civilization was transformed and expanded, and philosophical thought reached a high point. The celestial god T'ien ("heaven"), or Shang-ti, was all-knowing and all-seeing but impersonal; this "omniscient heaven" tradition was inherited by the philosophers. In the worship of the ancestors, the urn-house was replaced by the depositing of a tablet in the temple. The pattern of macrocosm-microcosm in the oppositional cycle of *yang* and *yin* was also integrated into Chinese thought, as the ancient symbolism of polarity and alternation underwent a remarkable development to become a system of cyclic totality, involving cosmic alternations and ritual separation of the sexes, the ordering principle upon which the philosophy of the Tao was based. According to Eliade, this is an archaic cosmogonic vision of the original unity-totality: "For Lao-tse, 'One,' the primitive unity/totality, already represents a step toward 'creation,' for it was begotten by the mysterious and incomprehensible principle of the Tao" (Eliade, 1982). The Tao exists before heaven and earth; it is a primordial wholeness, living and creative, and also a paradisiacal state.

The attempts of Taoist adepts to reintegrate this paradisiacal state constitutes their search for immortality, an exaltation of the primordial human condition. The attempt of Confucius (K'ung-tzu) was similar to that of Lao-tzu, in that both were based on ancient fundamental ideas—the Tao as the principle of wholeness, the *yin-yang* alternation, and the application of the analogy between macrocosm and microcosm to all levels of existence. Lao-tzu and his followers sought out the original unity within their own lives; Confucius looked for it in a balanced and just society. Lao-tzu was in search of the Tao, the ultimate, mysterious, unfathomable reality underlying all existence, seeking out the living wholeness through a reconciliation of the opposites and a return to the beginnings. Confucius (551–479) rejected neither the Tao, nor the god of Heaven, nor the veneration of ancestors. For him, the Tao was a decree from Heaven. He recommended a system of education that could transform the ordinary individual into a superior person, so that society might become an embodiment of the original cosmic harmony.

China did not produce a hierarchical classification of its beliefs about the fate of the dead. Most of them were destined for the kingdom of the Yellow Springs, while the kings and princes ascended to be near the Lord on High. The lords lived out their afterlives in the temples of the family ancestors, near their graves. This ancient agrarian religion dissolved along with the early social structure once the Han dynasty came to power, beginning in 206 BCE. Taoism then developed spectacularly, reaching its peak under the Six Dynasties, from the fourth to the sixth centuries of our era. As a religion of salvation, it had to offer an afterlife, and as the human being was thought to have many souls, but only one body for them to live in, it was along these lines that thinkers sought immortality. Some envisioned a melting pot of souls, out of which the deceased would receive an undying body, provided that the living were assiduous in practicing the funeral rites. But most tended to the view that the living body was preserved and became an immortal one. To this end they felt one should develop certain organs to be substituted for the corporeal ones. This gave rise to various practices to which the adepts, *tao-shih*, applied themselves in the desire to ensure the immortality of the living (body)—dietary practices to kill demons and maintain bodily vigor, embryonic circular breathing to induce ecstatic experiences, and sexual practices involving a mixing of the semen with the breath in order to stimulate the brain (Henri Maspero, *Taoism and Chinese Religion*, Amherst, 1981). Spiritual techniques such as insight, meditation, and mystical union came to be added to these physical ones. Between the second and sixth centuries, these techniques were supplemented by ceremonies for the dead, rites intended to melt the souls in a fire that would transform them into immortals *(hsien)*.

Ancient Egypt. At the center of the Egyptian belief in immortality lies the theme of life. The whole history of Egypt—its architecture, its art, its writings, its religion—proclaims the joy of life. From the deepest antiquity the *ankh* appears, a symbol of life, a symbol that even the Christians adopted as a precious legacy of three millennia of Egyptian religious tradition.

From the time of the Old Kingdom, the Egyptians envisaged a complex spiritual pattern, modeled on the divine life and made up of three elements necessary for life to exist. *Akh* is divine energy. *Ba* is the faculty of movement, human consciousness, and the ability to take various shapes. The divine breath and support of all created beings, *ka,* is the collection of qualities of divine origin that give eternal life; it is the life force connected with Ptah and Re, and it is the divine, living part of man. When the *ka* becomes separated from the body, it disintegrates, and the person must then be re-created through mummification and funeral rites if an afterlife is to be possible.

The Pyramid Texts, from the Old Kingdom, deal solely with the fate of the pharaoh. They assert that the dead king flies or climbs heavenward, to become a star or a companion of Re, the sun god, on his daily journey. In fact, we see that the deceased pharaoh has a dual destiny. Becoming one with Osiris, he returns to life through mummification, which gives him an everlasting body that must be fed and clothed by means of offerings, after which he goes to the realm of Re to live in the celestial world. The synthesis of this double doctrine of the pharaoh's assimilation to both Osiris and Re, which took place during the fifth dynasty, forms the foundation of the ancient Egyptian belief in immortality.

The mastabas, erected by their eventual occupants during their lifetimes, give an idea of the nature of Old Kingdom beliefs. Everything in these structures speaks of life as if in a house, for the afterlife is an extension of life beyond death. To go on living is to go on eating, so the walls of the mastabas are covered with bearers of offerings, funerary meals, and scenes of everyday life. A false door allows the deceased to come and go symbolically between the worlds of the dead and the living. The funeral scenes pictured in the mastabas show the two goddesses Isis and Nephthys, the sisters of Osiris, accompanying the deceased. The notion of rebirth in Osiris is current among the people already in the Old Kingdom. The earliest depiction of the afterlife is an image of the deceased sitting at his table, but the luxuriance of decoration down to the smallest detail shows that every aspect of immortality was already being imagined.

In the second millennium BCE, the Middle and New Kingdoms left behind a codification of their beliefs in the Coffin Texts and the *Book of Going Forth by Day.* Alongside older ideas recast in a somewhat democratic mold, new beliefs appear. The *ba,* the life force connected with Ptah and Re, is the dead person's soul. It remains near the mummy, but can also enter the *tuat,* the increasingly important realm of the dead, where Osiris reigns beneath the earth. The *ba* can also rise up to heaven, but its greatest joy lies in leaving the tomb during the day to move among human beings. Thanks to the *ka,* the soul can assume different shapes. Placing incantations from the *Book of Going Forth by Day* on the mummy's heart allowed the *ba* to go out in the daytime and do what the living do, returning to the tomb at night.

The *Book of Going Forth by Day* represents a confluence of various doctrines concerning immortality—mummification, psychostasia, or weighing of the *ba,* the judgment of the dead, the kingdom of the dead, the freedom of the *ba,* and the happy fate of those who have led their lives in accord with Maat. These seemingly contradictory features can be reconciled in terms of the trial of the soul before Osiris and his court. Mummification was intended to bind the *ba* to the body of the deceased and to this world. After vindicating himself before Osiris, the blessed one, *maa kheru,* was free to move about among the gods and spirits of the *tuat.* Meanwhile he also maintained ties with the world of the living, a world of joy in Egyptian eyes. Although Egyptians observed the Osirian funeral, the dependence of immortality on the preservation of the mummy need not be overemphasized. Even if the disintegration of the mummy broke the connection between the *ba* and the world, the deceased who had been consigned to the *tuat* continued to live happily in the Field of Reeds. The happy lot of the just person living in the boat of the Sun was reserved for those who were too poor to secure an Osirian funeral. The vast world of the immortals in the Middle and New Kingdoms was composed of Osirian immortals tied to their preserved mummies, and thus free to move about in the beyond and in this world of the living, Osirian immortals whose mummies had been destroyed but who were still happy in the *tuat* kingdom, where they were constrained to stay, and solarized, blessed immortals in the boat of the Sun. Their happy everlasting life had been prepared for by an ethical life in conformity with Maat ("justice") by the arrangement of the tomb and mummification, and all that went into the construction of the eternal home. The necropolises are testaments to life. Such a conception of immortality is further clarified by the illustration of the weighing of the *ba* and the trial of Osiris. The presence of the monster who devours the dead person seems to refer to a second death for the evildoer, and perhaps his total destruction.

In Hellenistic and Roman times the religion of Isis was to undergo a great expansion. Although immortality remains centered around the theme of life, water also assumes great symbolic importance. Life-giving, purifying, a symbol of rejuvenation, water is "the identification of the Nile and Osiris," which the goddesses Isis, Nephthys, or Nut procure for the deceased. In imperial times the "fresh water of the dead" is mentioned. According to Françoise Dunand, the dead person who receives the life-giving water of Osiris wins immortality, for by drinking the water he absorbs the strength of the god (*Le culte d'Isis,* vol. 3, Leiden, 1973, p. 212). In addition, the god Anubis opens up the roads to the otherworld and becomes himself a solar god. Plutarch makes Osiris the god of the celestial world, a pure and invisible world that the deceased enters after being transformed into Osiris, and in this context the rite of initiation takes its place as a doctrine of salvation and a path to immortality.

India. In all three of the great directions in Indian religious thought—Vedic, Brahmanic, and *bhakti*—the belief in immortality is clear and constant.

Vedic India. The Sanskrit word *amṛta* (Pali, *amata*) is formed from privative *a* plus *mṛta* ("death") and means "nondeath." Related are the Greek *am(b)rotos* ("immortal") and *ambrosia* ("elixer of immortality"); the Avestan *Ameretāt,* the name of an abstract divine entity meaning "deathlessness, immortality"; and the Latin *immortālitās.* Thus our word *immortality* is of Indo-European origin and means literally "nondeath." As Georges Dumézil showed in the early days of his studies on comparative Indo-European mythology (*Le festin d'immortalité,* Paris, 1924), *amṛta* is an essential concept in Indo-European thought. In the Vedic texts, particularly in sacrificial contexts, *amṛta* appears together with *soma. Amṛta* is the heavenly elixir of immortality, as *soma* is a sacrificial libation offered to the gods by the priests. *Amṛta* is the drink of immortality of gods and men; *soma* is the elixir of life that has come from heaven to bestow immortality *(amṛtam).* Both words contain the idea of the winning of immortality, conceived as a perpetual renewal of youth and life.

In the *Ṛgveda* a distinction is made between the body and the invisible principle of the human being, designated by the words *asu,* the life force or breath, and *manas,* the spirit, the seat of intellect and internal feelings, located in the heart. The nature of the soul can be seen in the Vedic attitude toward death, for the dead are simply the shadows of the living. What survives is the individuality, the essence of the human person, which becomes immortal by being indefinitely prolonged in time, as part of a perfectly ordered cosmos. Immortality is a perpetual remaking in accord with universal law, and consists in being born everlastingly. The Ṛgvedic hymn 10.129.1–3 speaks of "the One that was before being and nonbeing, before death and nondeath." Nondeath is understood in relation to both the birth of organized time and the womb that is synonymous with death and renewal.

The Vedic sacrificial symbolism through which the belief in immortality is affirmed revolves around the sun, *soma,* and *agni* ("fire"). The motion of the sun and the cosmic drama in which it is destroyed only to be restored again are deeply ingrained in Vedic India. The sun appears as the substance of rejuvenation and the prototype of the sacrificial fire. The fire is the god Agni, ever renewed and hence forever young (*Ṛgveda* 3.23.1), the navel of immortality, whose eternal youth lies in his ability to be reborn. The immortality symbolized by *agni,* the divine fire, and *soma,* the drink of life, is perpetual rebirth. Agni, the golden embryo, the sun, *soma,* and the celestial tree (the *Ficus religiosa*) are all symbols of immortality. The immortal world is *sukṛta,* "well-made," and *saṃskṛta,* "perfected," and within its dynamically interwoven patterns lies the basis of immortality. For the *Ṛgveda,* "to be born limitlessly is deathlessness, and those who are born, the sun and fire, are also immortals, the very guardians of the immortality that they obtain for man (Lilian Silburn, *Instant et cause: Le discontinu dans la pensée philosophique de l'Inde,* Paris, 1955, p. 45).

Brahmanic India. By laying stress on perpetual renewal, the Brāhmaṇas deepen and systematize this idea of the infinite extension of the cosmic order. Their foundation is threefold: fire, the sacrificial altar, and Prajāpati. Already present in the *Ṛgveda* as the patron of reproduction, Prajāpati becomes the central figure of the Brāhmaṇas. The thirty-fourth god, beside the thirty-three Vedic divinities, he is the creative force, the concentrated spiritual act preceding creation, the energy that is scattered about in creating the world in all its multiplicity and that must reassemble and lead to the unity of the beginnings. Prajāpati is the sacrifice, an earthly copy of the great cosmic drama. The cyclic rhythm of the cosmos is repeated in that of the sacrificial ritual, a replica of the cycle of the sun and its alternation without beginning or end. The ritual must restore the lost unity, it must reassemble it and provide structure and continuity. Thus the ritual becomes a transcendence of death.

The symbolism of immortality in the Brāhmaṇas goes beyond the Vedic symbolism. The sacrifice confers long life and immortality, symbolized by the cosmic year; the days and nights are symbols of human lives, of mortal, transient time. The seasons make up the year in its real sense, a limitless rebirth; the year is the symbol of divine life and immortality, and Prajāpati is the year. The sacrificial altar is constructed in the course of a year using 10,800 bricks, each one representing an hour. The *gārhapatya* fire represents a womb, into which a special *mantra* inspires the breath of life. Through the *āhavanīya* fire the sacrificer rises to heaven, to be born a second time and attain immortality. Thus the sacrifice constitutes the transcendence of death by means of ritual.

With the Upaniṣads India enters a period of deep reflection on consciousness and liberation. The concept of the *ātman,* or self, comes to the fore: it is thought of as the undying basis of man, whose task is to free itself from the human body to attain perfect oneness with *brahman.* The *ātman* is unchanging, immortal *(amṛta),* indestructible, eternal, imperishable. *Brahman* is the creative principle, the phenomenal reality and totality of the universe, the sacred principle.

Upaniṣadic thought takes India out of its Brahmanic ritualism and confers a new importance on human action, attributing to it an energy that will continue to bear fruit until it is spent. Under the influence of *karman* with its doctrine of retribution of acts through reincarnation, the *ātman* will experience a continual unfolding of existence beyond death. Here we become involved more deeply in the idea of deliverance, which can proceed via two possible routes. The first is a return to a body, a reincarnation, and the second is the route of the gods, the royal road, the development of the metaphysical and mystical consciousness needed to discover the *ātman,* the *brahman,* and the identity of *brahman-ātman.* This quest for the Absolute is the search for immortality, the *tat tvam asi,* "thou art that." Immortality is the absorption of the individual in *brahman;* it is attained by seeing the underlying oneness of things. To the ritualism of the Vedas and the Brāhmaṇas, the Upaniṣads oppose a release from rebirths through the knowledge that unites man once and for all with *brahman.*

Bhakti. In the last centuries before the common era, a religious current known as *bhakti* spread across India. It was a form of Hinduism that implies a relationship between God and his creatures based on grace, and conversely one of total devotion to God on the part of his creation. *Bhakti* is a loving devotion that gives the believer a greater knowledge of the Lord (Kṛṣṇa or Īśvara) than any meditation or reflection, and it is a divine gift given only to those who have prepared themselves by a loving attitude. Within the wider context of the transmigration of souls, the *bhakti* movement affirms a monotheistic tendency and an emphasis on salvation. Devotion should be accompanied by knowledge, but it is superior to knowledge, as two stanzas from the *Bhagavadgītā* will illustrate: "I will reveal that which is to be known and by knowing which, eternal life is gained. / It is the Supreme *brahman,* who is without beginning and who is said to be neither being nor nonbeing" (13.12). Along with this knowledge, utmost devotion to the Lord is necessary: "And whoever, at the time of death, gives up this body and departs, thinking of Me alone, he comes to My status (of being)" (8.5; trans. Radhakrishnan, New York, 1948). *Bhakti* takes the place of the elixir of life, conferring eternal life with Kṛṣṇa. A number of texts emphasize the destiny of the *bhakta,* who is *siddha* ("perfect"), *amṛta* ("immortal"), and *tṛpta* ("happy").

Summary. As we have seen, although the forms taken by the Indian belief in immortality are diverse, they are linked together by a rich and overlapping symbolism with many points in common. In this symbolism we touch on a subject that has been strongly emphasized by Eliade (1969): the techniques for the winning of immortality. I have already referred to symbolism such as that of Agni and the sacrificial fire, the mystic flame produced by *tapas,* the bridge leading to the supreme *brahman,* the great journey reminding us of the importance of reincarnation, the master charioteer, the sun and the cosmic wheel, the celestial tree, and *soma.* Eliade has also stressed two further aspects of this long development of Indian philosophy, namely yogic practices, already apparent in the Upaniṣads, and the tendency, incipient in the Vedas and firmly established in the Brāhmaṇas and the Upaniṣads, to assert the existence of several layers of reality. In the quest for complete reintegration, the ultimate aim of existence, transmigration too is described in very lively terms.

In the symbolism of *amṛta,* funerary worship holds pride of place. In the Vedic ritual the dying person is laid in a purified place, the head turned toward the south, the direction of the land of the dead. After death, the corpse is scrupulously prepared for the cremation. Gold pieces, symbols of deathlessness, are placed on the facial openings. The fire is carried at the head of the funeral procession, always in new vessels. The cremation place is selected carefully, near the water, with a pleasant view to the west. On the spot where the pyre will be built a gold piece is laid. The pyre is lit from three sacrificial fires, symbolized by three layers of grass, for the cremation is considered a sacrifice. After the body is consumed by the fire, the bones are cleansed, reassembled, and placed in an urn or a grave. In household rites, an offering of rice is made, representing an offering to the fathers and a meal for the dead. Several kinds of Vedic and Brahmanic rituals have been observed for millennia, and all are symbolic enactments of the fundamental tenet of India, expressed in the words of the *Bṛhadāraṇyaka Upaniṣad:* "Lead me from death to nondeath" (1.3.28).

Buddhism. The Upaniṣads taught that there exists within every person an *I*, the *ātman*, an enduring and eternal entity, an immutable substance underlying the ephemeral world of phenomena. Hence the way to immortality was easily found. The *ātman*, they said, becomes immortal not through sacrifice or ritual or ascetic discipline, but by taking possession of the immortal, the *brahman*. For the Upaniṣads, it is the identification of *ātman* and *brahman* that bestows immortality. The Buddha denied the existence of the *ātman*, teaching instead the doctrine of *anātman*, or "noself," in which every person is a collection of aggregates, a functioning whole for which ceaseless change is the true reality. The Buddha replaced the vital principle of *ātman* with these "aggregates," or *skandha*s, and by the "chain of being," *santāna*, whose links are related by cause and effect. He recognized the act and its fruit but not the actor, believing that there is no *sattva*, or independent self that can be reincarnated. But the whole functions, the "contingent self" exists from moment to moment, laden with its previous actions and carrying with it the potential for unceasing rebirth. Death marks the instant when retribution for another set of actions must begin; it is a rebirth, but not a transmigration. The individual is an unceasingly renewing flow, for he has within him, in his actions and desires, the seeds of his continued existence.

The belief in an afterlife and immortality is not ignored by the Buddha. Like the brahman, the yogin, and the mendicant, he seeks "that which endures," "deliverance," and "what is undying." "The first words of Śākyamuni on becoming Buddha are to proclaim that he has attained the Immortal, and has opened the gates of the Immortal" (Louis de La Vallée Poussin, *Nirvâna*, Paris, 1925, p. 50). "The inexpressible Immortal is the goal of the holy man, because it means release from birth and death" (ibid.). This goal is called *nirvāṇa*. The Buddha did not define *nirvāṇa;* we know it by its attributes: unshakeable happiness and blessedness, unborn, unproduced, undone, unconditioned, perfect, unconstructed gladness. *Nirvāṇa* is release, an unseen dwelling, immortal, never returning to the world below. Speaking of the saint who has attained perfect enlightenment in this world, one text says: "The *arhat*, already in this life, restrained, having attained *nirvāṇa (nibbāna)*, feeling happiness within him, passes his time with *brahman*" (*Aṅguttara Nikāya* 2.206). To arrive at *nirvāṇa*, and thus immortality, one must follow the method and the way of the Buddha. La Vallée Poussin and Eliade have stressed the yogic nature of this path to deliverance.

A discussion of the debates concerning *nirvāṇa* among the various schools of the great movements of historical Buddhism—Hīnayāna, Mahāyāna, Tantric, and Pure Land—is outside the scope of this article. Let us cast a brief glance, however, at Tibet, for the tradition of Tibetan Buddhism constitutes a unique synthesis of the ancient Bon religion and highly fragmented Buddhist doctrines. The Tibetan *Book of the Dead* is an invaluable source for our knowledge of the journey of the soul. By reciting the texts at the dead person's bedside, the lama is supposed to restore the life force, *bla*, to the deceased's body for its journey of forty-nine days through the intermediate stage between death and rebirth. If this rebirth does not occur, the deceased appears before the god of the dead to be judged. (Several details indicate an Iranian influence.) Giuseppe Tucci (*The Religions of Tibet*, Berkeley, 1980) emphasizes among other ceremonies the various rites performed around the *maṇḍala* especially constructed for the funeral. After a purification ritual, a piece of the dead person's bone *(rus)* or a piece of paper or wood with his name written on it is placed on the *maṇḍala;* the bones are the supports of the deceased and the seat of his soul. The ceremony is meant to induce rebirth, but it is reminiscent too of the journeys of the soul in the world of the shaman. The Tibetans have retained their belief in a direct link between earth and the paradisiacal spheres of heaven. They also believe that in eternity, the deceased keeps the appearance he had when living on earth. Carried in a fabric sling, the symbol of his meritorious deeds, he can rise to the celestial regions, in an ascension ritual revealing the shamanistic influence of Inner Asia.

Celts, Germans, Scandinavians, Thracians, and Getae. The work of Georges Dumézil has pioneered the discovery of the tripartite organization, based on sovereignty, force, and fertility, of ancient Indo-European religious ideology. Thanks to this insight, the study of the religion of the Indo-European peoples has been made considerably easier by revealing both the consistency of Indo-European thought and the importance of the Indo-European inheritance. These factors prove to be invaluable in the study of peoples who have left behind only scattered remains, in archaeological records and epigraphy, eyewitness accounts handed down by neighboring peoples, and mythological remants.

A firm belief in an afterlife is attested by the funerary practices of the Celts, Germans, and Scandinavians. Archaeological evidence is abundant, including megalithic tombs, dolmens, and individual burials in coffins marked with solar symbols, and cremation is known from the urnfields as early as 1500 BCE. Everything in these graves speaks in the symbolic language of the afterlife: the preservation of skulls, the location of graves near the living, bodies turned to face the house, and the inclusion of the dead person's possessions. The widespread nature of cremation around the middle of the second millennium BCE (a practice finally prohibited by Charlemagne) points to an Indo-European presence.

The belief in the soul's immortality among the Celts and the Gauls is attested by numerous early witnesses. Caesar (*Gallic Wars* 6.14) says that the druids asserted that souls are immortal, that after death they pass into another body, and that this belief explains the reckless fearlessness of their warriors. For the Germans, the soul is reborn within the *Sippe* (the clan). Diodorus Siculus speaks of the Gaulish custom of throwing letters addressed to the deceased onto the funeral pyre. Various Celtic traditions give accounts of an *aes sídh*, or "paradise of the dead," an open world connected by a bridge to the land of the living, sometimes also appearing as an island in the ocean. Eggshells found in graves are an especially important symbol; the broken egg is a sign of newly born life.

In Germanic religion, Valhǫl (Valhalla) is a lodging reserved for warriors who have fallen on the field of battle, and for all those who have died a heroic death. It is the home of the *einherjar*, the heroes who pass a pleasant life there; part of their time is taken up with the feast of immortality, in which the flesh of the wild boar Sæhrímnir is recovered intact every night so that the banquet can go on the next day, and the sacred mead is served by the *valkyrjar* (valkyries). Another symbol of the Germanic world is the tree Yggdrasill, which stands at the center of the world, sending one root into the land of the dead, another into that of the giants, and a third into the world of men. It symbolizes fate, the link between the living and the dead, as well as the continual rebirth of life.

The cult of Zalmoxis among the Thracians and the Getae (Herodotus, 4.94–95) also entails the belief in the deathlessness of the soul, obtained through an initiation ritual that belongs among the mystery cults of the Mediterranean world, particularly those having to do with the preparation for a happy existence in the other world.

Religions of Ancient Iran. Turning to Iran, we do not leave the Indo-European world. In fact, we enter an area heavily indebted to the inheritance of Indo-European trifunctional religious thought, as Dumézil has shown. However, the theme of immortality here has to be examined from a new angle, since the religious reform of Zarathushtra (Zoroaster) had a profound effect on Iranian thought.

In the *Gāthās*, the opposition between body and spirit is everywhere, for the human soul is complex. *Vyana* is the breath-soul, the spiritual self. *Manah* is mind, the activity of consciousness, thought, and memory. *Urvan* is the part of the personality that deals with the spiritual and religious domain; it corresponds to the Indian *ātman*. *Daēnā* is the religious intelligence that allows for knowledge of the revelation. The *Gāthās* lay great stress on the spiritual part of the human being.

The word *fravashi*, absent from the *Gāthās*, is of pre-Zoroastrian origin, being derived from *fravarti* ("protector, guardian"), according to Söderblom (1901). It is used elsewhere in the Avesta; *Yasna* 23.1 says, "I call to the sacrifice all the holy *fravashi*s, whoever they are, who are on the earth after their death," recalling the Indo-European notion of the "fathers," the "ancestors," or spirits of the dead. Söderblom thinks that the *fravashi*s go back to pre-Avestan popular beliefs and worship of the dead. There are traces of a vague notion of the continuation of the dead person's life near the house, and hence the idea of a preexisting soul that survives death. At the end of the year, the *fravashi*s of the dead come to earth to ask for food and clothing from the living, in exchange for their protection.

Priest and prophet, Zarathushtra brought about a profound religious reform. Departing from Indo-Iranian polytheism, he conferred the status of supreme god on Ahura Mazdā, the creator of light, living creatures, and mental faculties. An all-knowing god and lord of wisdom, Ahura Mazdā lives in a realm of light, surrounded by his celestial court, who are six trifunctional Indo-Iranian gods transposed into archangels (Dumézil). Three are on his right side: Vohu Manah ("good thought"), Asha ("justice"), and Khshathra Vairya ("strength"). Three are on the left: Ārmaiti ("piety"), Haurvatāt ("wholeness, health"), and Ameretāt ("immortality"). These divine entities arose from Ahura Mazdā. In creation, energy and activity are the privilege of two spirits: Spenta Mainyu ("good spirit"), who is very close to Ahura Mazdā, acts as his deputy in the creation, and is charged with bestowing health and immortality; and Angra Mainyu ("evil spirit"), the creator of nonlife and sower of disorder. Man must choose between the two. The choice between good and evil is paramount, since eternal happiness depends on it.

The ancient Indo-European belief in immortality takes on a new aspect, as the theistic and mystical conception is succeeded by one of a religion of salvation. Beside the universal eschatology, the *Gāthās* propound an individual soteriology. Thus immortality results from the salvation of the soul, which is realized after death on the basis of merit gained through the choices made in life. Salvation depends upon judgment, and it is Ahura Mazdā who bestows immortality. In this area we find a very rich symbolic background, as in descriptions of the passage between earth and heaven via the Chinvat Bridge (*Yasna* 46.10–11; 32.13). Whoever does not cross this bridge successfully ends up in the house of *druj*, the hell of damned souls. The journey of the soul and the crossing of the bridge reveal a shamanistic influence, recalling the soul's ecstatic journey to the sky and its journey to heaven after death. Zarathushtra thus spiritualized Iranian eschatology and the Indo-European concept of the afterlife. The reward is an immortal life, a life of eternal happiness, a transfiguration and rejuvenation. There is no question of the Indian *saṃsāra* or of cyclic time; immortality is final after death, new youth being bestowed by Ahura Mazdā himself. Haurvatāt and Ameretāt, material and spiritual happiness, are part of this reward. The soul finds itself in the house of Ahura Mazdā, amid fields of justice and mercy (*Yasna* 33.3).

Zarathushtra's revelation had a definitive influence on the Zoroastrian belief in immortality. The most indicative of the later Avestan texts is undoubtedly the *Hadhōkht Nask;* dating in its present form from the Sasanid period, it describes the vicissitudes of the soul's journey after death. For the first three nights the soul remains near the body. The just person's soul sings the praises of Ahura Mazdā; that of the evildoer cowers in anguish. At the end of the third night, the soul of the righteous person feels the coming of a bracing, sweet-smelling breeze from the south, bringing to it its own *daēnā*, in the form of a radiant young girl. Who is this *daēnā?* For H. S. Nyberg (*Die Religionen des alten Iran*, Osnabrück, 1966) it is a luminous virgin who represents the celestial realm of the Zoroastrian community. Geo Widengren (*Die Religionen Irans*, Stuttgart, 1965) sees in it the heavenly counterpart of the soul. *Urvan* and *daēnā* are the two parts of the soul, and the *daēnā*, the celestial part, is conditioned by the person's earthly life. In *Zarathustras Jenseitsvorstellungen und das Alte Testament* (Vienna, 1964), after analyzing the *urvan*'s conversation with its *daēnā*, Franz König discusses the eschatological doctrine of these twins: by its thoughts, words, and deeds in this life, the *urvan* creates its heavenly *daēnā*, a mirror image of its earthly life. Immortality begins with the reconciliation of the *urvan* and the *daēnā*. Thereupon the righteous soul crosses three heavenly spheres before appearing at the entrance to the kingdom of light, where it receives the "butter of spring," followed by its judgment and entry into heaven, Asan or Asman, "the radiant world above, which rises over the earth" (*Yashts* 13.2). There it meets the two divine entities Haurvatāt and Ameretāt. The evil soul is thrown into a cavern.

Thus it may be seen that although the popular religion of the Zoroastrian community introduced some substantial new elements, the broad outlines of Zarathushtra's doctrine of immortality were preserved.

Mesopotamia. Through scraps of texts, archaeological records, funerary rituals, and other hints we are able to recover a few features of the Mesopotamian concept of the afterlife. A pair of myths provide some details about the search for immortality, and show that this was a question that preoccupied the thinkers of the time. The myth of the sage Adapa recounts how he was summoned before the court of Anu for having broken the wings of the south wind. Adapa admits what he has done, but he refuses to eat the "bread of life" or drink the "water of life" that the god has offered to him, and thus he loses his chance to become immortal. Another myth concerning the quest for immortality is the epic about Gilgamesh, the ruler of Uruk. This epic, written in Akkadian, tells of the defeat of a hero who tries to overstep the human condition. Although Gilgamesh fails to pass the initiation test, which requires him to go without sleep for six days and seven nights, Utanapishtim reveals to him the secret of the gods, the whereabouts of a youth-restoring plant. Gleefully Gilgamesh descends to the bottom of the sea and harvests the sweet-smelling plant. On the return route he stops to bathe, and a snake takes advantage of this to rob him of the plant that would confer immortality.

In Mesopotamia, death is seen as the universal and inescapable fate. The body becomes a corpse and disintegrates, leaving behind two elements. The first of these is the skeleton of the human being—hence the great respect accorded the tombs in which the dead lie—and the second is the "ghost," or shade, attested around 2500 BCE in the Sumerian word *gedim*. The afterlife of the deceased is spent down below, in the lower hemisphere beneath the land of the living, which explains the funeral rites in which bodies were placed in the ground, in pits, graves, or caves. As a rule there is neither exposure of the corpse nor cremation. The world below was also inhabited by the *anunnakis*, divinities of the lower world.

Entry to the world of the dead was gained through the grave or through the west, where the sun sets in the evening. There is thus a road of the dead, an entry into the domain of the dead, an enormous dark cave. The question of whether there was a postmortem trial among the Assyro-Babylonians is still open, but in any case the journey is one of no return. Inequalities in the fates of the dead, attested in various records, are to be understood primarily in terms of the attitudes taken toward them by the living. The dead were interred, preferably under the house, their grave goods comprising a dish, ornaments, tools, weapons, and toys. Because the dead had to receive food and drink, water was poured into the grave through a tube. At the end of the lunar month, the memory of the dead and the ancestors was celebrated in order to help them and to turn their wrath away from the living. In short, what is known for certain about the Assyro-Babylonian world is that there was an afterlife and the dead descended to the realm below and lived an unhappy life there.

The Hebrew Scriptures. From remotest times the Hebrews practiced inhumation, placing various objects, weapons, and provisions in the grave for the use of the dead, gestures which seem to constitute at least one facet of a *votum immortalitatis.* The Hebrew Bible sees the human being as a composite of flesh *(basar),* the breath of life, or soul *(nefesh),* and spirit *(ruaḥ). Basar* is functionally equivalent to *caro,* and *nefesh* to *anima,* as *ruaḥ* is to *pneuma* (Lat., *spiritus*). The hierarchic structures of this triad reveal a dualistic trend of *soma* versus *psuchē;* the Septuagint, a Greek version of the Bible, uses the word *psuchē* about a thousand times to refer to *nefesh,* and it is quite clear that Palestinian Judaism, just as much as the Greek version, assimilated a view of man on the pattern of body and soul (see Albert Descamps, "La mort selon l'écriture," in Ries, 1983, pp. 52–55).

After death, people go to She'ol—an immense, underground place, deep, dark, and bolted shut, the abode of shadows—to lead lives that are shadows of their lives on earth, and according to *Job* 7:9–10, this life is one of no return. This idea contrasts with the archaic concept of the "afterlife" of a corpse that makes use of objects and food, and is undoubtedly later. She'ol is not to be confused with the grave, the habitat of the corpse. The shade in She'ol is not the remnant of the mortal being in the grave, it is a "double"; She'ol is an extension of the grave.

The doctrine of She'ol was of popular origin and remained quite vague, but it demonstrates a spiritualistic tendency in the belief in an afterlife found in the Hebrew scriptures. References to an afterlife are found in the Bible. The human being is not destroyed after death, but is reunited with his ancestors. The miracles performed by Elijah and Elisha (*1 Kgs.* 17:17–24, *2 Kgs.* 4:31–37) show that life can be restored to the body. Moreover, the evocation of the dead, characteristic of popular beliefs in an afterlife, shows that the living attempted to get in touch with the deceased. According to *Genesis* 2 and 3, man was immortal (by nature or through grace) in God's original plan, but showed himself to be unworthy of this fate. The story reflects man's refusal to accept death, the deep desire to live unendingly in a long and happy life. This is the theme of the earthly paradise, the *votum immortalitatis* in which man partakes of the divine *ruaḥ* (*Gn.* 1:26–27, 5:1, 9:6). This participation vouchsafes to man, after the Fall, the afterlife of She'ol. The faith of Israel admits of no failure of Yahveh in regard to She'ol.

The *refa'im* of She'ol are the biblical forerunners of immortal souls. Several passages in *Job* and *Psalms* allude to a union with God that death will not destroy. During the persecutions of Antiochus Epiphanes, the fate of the dead is foremost among Israel's preoccupations; the vision of dry bones in *Ezekiel* 37:1–14 serves as the basis of a meditation on resurrection and God's power to bring his believers out of She'ol. In the *Book of Daniel* 7:9, the motif of the "book of life" marks a gradual shift toward individual judgment, and the faith in individual eschatological resurrection is clearly attested in both *Daniel,* which dates from 165 BCE (*Dn.* 11:40–12:13), and in *2 Maccabees* (chaps. 7, 9, 11), written in Greek sometime after 124 BCE.

In the *Wisdom of Solomon,* written in Greek around 50 BCE, the concept of the afterlife is rendered for the first time by *aphtharsia,* "immortality" (1:11–15, 2:23–25), and the immortality of the souls of the righteous is clearly affirmed. They are in the hand of God (3:1–4), and their souls enjoy a never-ending life with God in peace, rest, love, grace, and mercy (3:9, 4:7, 5:15). After the destruction of the Temple in the year 70 CE, a doctrine of resurrection for everyone—not only the righteous but also for nonbelievers—appears within the circle of the tannaim.

The Qumran Texts. The Essenes, as described by Josephus Flavius, believed in the immortality of the soul and its future life freed from bodily ties, hence their renunciation of even the most legitimate of the pleasures of this world. As for the Qumran texts, the *Manual of Discipline* says that those who let themselves be guided and inspired by the spirits of truth and light will be blessed in this world and will enjoy eternal gladness in a world without end. The wicked will be punished in the darkness of an everlasting fire (2.8, 4.7–8). The community forms an eternal alliance with God in this world and beyond, so that the immortality of the souls of individual members is closely bound up with that of the community, envisaging a home in the world of light above, the world of God and his angels (J. P. M. van der Ploeg, "L'immortalité de l'homme d'après les textes de la Mer Morte," *Vetus Testamentum* 2, 1952, p. 173). Psalm 3 seems to refer to a resting place for the blessed, an unending height or a vast plain, in a symbolism matched by expressions in *Psalms* 16:9–10 and 73:23–28. Belief in a happy future life appears to be common in the thinking of the composers of these psalms.

The Greco-Roman World. The imagination of the ancients endowed the land of Greece with many mouths of the underworld, called the "gates of Hades." For some, these were the paths through which people vanished after death, for others they were the wombs of perpetual rebirth; the Greeks were divided over these two views of the afterlife (André Motte, *Prairies et jardins de la Grèce antique,* Brussels, 1973, p. 239). This phenomenon accounts for one of the earliest notions of the afterlife in the Greek world, the idea of a cycle of successive deaths and rebirths. In Homer the belief in the beyond is marked by a deep-seated pessimism. Hesiod is more optimistic, speaking of the islands of the blessed where the dead carouse. The theme of immortality, barely outlined in Homer and Hesiod, begins to gain ground from the sixth century on. Thus the works of Pindar are permeated by a deep longing for immortality. One particular religious movement, Orphism, came to play a decisive role in the diffusion of doctrines of immortality.

Orphism. Monuments to Orpheus are found as early as the sixth century BCE, and allusions to his descent into the underworld appear in the fifth century. Priests who preach salvation in the name of Orpheus and promulgate an initiation that sets people free for their lives in the next world are reported in Classical times. In the Hellenistic period references to Orpheus become more frequent, and Orphism finds fertile ground in Ptolemaic Egypt, where it encounters the cult of Osiris.

From the confused obscurity of a mixture of traditions, Eliade has unraveled the important fact that Orpheus is a founder of initiations and mysteries, a religious figure of a type formally parallel to Zalmoxis, the culture hero of the Getae, the Thracians who believed themselves to be immortal. Certain elements also recall shamanistic practices. Introducing a religious message predating Homer, Orpheus makes inroads into the Olympian religion. He extols vegetarianism, asceticism, purification, and initiation; herein lies the conjunction with Apollo and Dionysos.

The Orphic anthropogony is a dualistic one, and the early records are corroborated by the recently discovered Derveni Papyrus. It refers to the myth of the Titans, who were burned to ashes by Zeus's thunderbolt in punishment for the murder of Dionysos. From these ashes arose the human race, composed of Titanic matter and the pure soul that stemmed from the blessed race of the undying gods, which was sent forth as a falling star to earth, where it was united with a body and became subject to fate. Hence the present race of men carries a dual inheritance, from both the gods and the Titans. The evidence of gold lamellae found in graves in Italy and Crete is invaluable, providing references about the journey of the soul of the dead extending from the second to the fourth century CE.

In contrast with Homeric thought, which was oriented toward earthly pleasures and very little concerned with the next world, Orphism professes the belief in a happy afterlife. The seed of salvation is within man, since his immortal soul is a piece of the divine stuff, and the purpose of life on earth is to come to a permanent choice. The Orphic doctrine of purification allows for the reincarnation of souls. We know from Plato that the Orphians offered rather gloomy descriptions of the torments of the guilty soul and the evils awaiting the damned, plunged into a pool of mud (*Republic* 2.363d). The disciple's initiation and asceticism and the permanent change in his behavior were meant to prepare him for a happy eternity, the future life about which the golden plates furnish some details. A plate from Petilia in northern Italy pictures the soul coming to two springs, one near a cypress tree and the other near the Lake of Memory. It drinks from the second spring and rediscovers its divine origin. A lamella from Thurium in Italy shows the soul, freed from its bodily prison, hearing these words: "O happy and fortunate one, you will be a god and not a mortal" (Guthrie, 1952). Another has the soul say, "I have lost myself in the bosom of the Queen." In such an apotheosis, Persephone carries out the mystical act of divine filiation, and the initiate becomes once more divine and immortal.

Early Pythagoreanism. Pythagoreanism stands out against a background of dualistic doctrines. Settling in Magna Graecia in the second half of the sixth century, Pythagoras founded at Croton a brotherhood shrouded in secrecy, which introduced its followers to a new kind of life meant to point the way that led to salvation. In religious matters Pythagoras espoused Orphic views and brought about, as Eliade (1982) has indicated, a large-scale synthesis of archaic elements (some of them "shamanistic") and bold reevaluations of ascetic and contemplative techniques. The Orphic and Pythagorean doctrines regarding the soul display many features in common: immortality, transmigration, punishment in Hades, and the soul's eventual return to heaven. Pythagoreanism, however, developed its teaching independently, in a closed society. For Pythagoras the human soul is immortal; it is held within the body as if in a prison and can live independently of the body. After death, the soul passes into Hades to be purified, and to the extent that it is not completely cleansed it must return to earth and seek a new body. The soul's journey back to the celestial world is made possible by many incarnations and after a life of ascetic discipline marked by purifying ceremonies. The goal of human life is to withdraw the soul from earthly existence so as to restore its freedom as a divine being.

Plato. To understand Plato's conception of the immortality of the soul one must begin with his theory of Ideas, or Forms, which are thought of as a reality separate from the objects of the senses. The highest principle of the universe is the Idea of the Good. Starting from the Ideas, or Forms, the Demiurge creates the visible world and thus disrupts their original oneness. The world is built on the model of the Ideas, and is alive thanks to the soul that confers order and harmony on it. Plato uses myths to outline his approach to the concept of the world soul and the souls that are divine sparks or pieces of it, thus prolonging the old doctrine of archetypal patterns.

At the beginning of the myth of the winged chariot in the *Phaedrus*, immortality is declared to be the original condition of the soul, as it was in the beginning, leading an ideal life absorbed in contemplation of the Forms and enjoying immortality as a dynamic principle. Thus the soul is seen as a purely spiritual and incorporeal celestial body (*Phaedrus* 245d, 247b) and the source, ground, cause, and origin of life, unbegotten, incorruptible, and undying.

The human soul is a combination of three constituents. The first of these is the *nous*, the rational soul, a remnant of the material of the world soul created by the Demiurge. It contemplates the world of Forms and is immortal. Incarnated in a body, it falls into its prison, with modifications introduced by the other two (mortal) elements, the *thumos* ("heart, spirit, passion") and *epithumētikos* ("desire"). The symbolic illustration of the chariot is expressive: the charioteer is the *nous*, the head and driver of the chariot, the immortal part of the soul, which aims toward its original state of connaturality with the Forms. The two horses are the *thumos* and the *epithumia*. The wings of the chariot are the urge toward spiritual reality.

Once incarnated in a body, this immortal soul will have to free itself through multiple reincarnations, and the first of these has very important consequences for those that follow. If it becomes a philosopher, the *nous* keeps the soul very close to the contemplation of the Forms, its celestial immortality is not far off, and its liberation will come soon. Plato proposed a scheme involving nine incarnations. Thus reincarnation is only a conditional immortality, and true immortality is the prerogative of the incorporeal soul, the celestial body. The doctrine of the tripartite nature of the soul condemns the two lower constituents to the dissolution common to all matter. Only the immortal part will finally escape the cycle of reincarnation, for it is a divine spark. Souls are immortal and are as old as the universe, endlessly migrating through a succession of living mortals; a divine lineage underlies the Platonic view of the immortality of the soul.

The Platonic doctrine had a profound influence in the Mediterranean world during the Hellenistic age. The church fathers readopted it, but in a radically altered form. Both Platonists and Christians agreed on the word *immortality*, but they were deeply divided over its nature and that of the soul. For the Platonists, the soul was supraindividual, and as such it was immortal because it remained within the universal Soul after its final liberation. For the Christians each soul was created immortal and individual by God, committing it irrevocably to the afterlife. A different disagreement separates Platonism from the views of the Stoics, who also saw man as a composite of soul and body, but for whom the soul too is material. For the Stoics the soul survives the body in a temporary and limited afterlife, and thus Stoicism takes an intermediate position between the Platonic conception of immortality and the Epicurian denial of it.

Summary. The Orphic, Pythagorean, and Platonic doctrines thrived and soon found a new area of expansion in the opening of the Orient after the conquests of Alexander. The Mediterranean world in Hellenistic times was a place of great ferment of religious ideas, as Mediterranean man was in quest of salvation. Mystery cults, Osirism, Hermetism, and the teachings of the magi came to the aid of those who saw themselves as strangers in this world, and it is into this milieu that Christianity would come in full bloom to play the role of catalyst. The Oriental gods found in Greece and Rome are savior gods. All eyes are turned toward heaven, the dreamt-of place of salvation, as solar theologies and astral religions add their own prescriptions. Gnosticism and Mithra worship put themselves forward as rivals of the salvation offered by Christianity.

Franz Cumont, in *Lux perpetua* (Paris, 1949), coined the apt phrase *celestial immortality* to identify the common denominator of the various currents of thought regarding immortality in the Hellenistic world. In pharaonic Egypt, Minoan Crete, Vedic India, and Avestan Iran alike, man's gaze was raised toward an eternal life in the glow of the heavens. The teachings of Zarathushtra added important details to this idea of immortality in the divine light, and were taken up by the magi, who added many Babylonian features to it and circulated it throughout the Near East. We know for certain that Pythagoreans and magi had contacts with one another, and astronomy too came to the support of theology. The popular notion of the *fravashi*s and the Platonic theory of the preexistent soul also had an impact on the thinking of Hellenistic man.

Rome fell in early with this syncretistic trend. Pythagoreanism won full citizenship there and was soon established as both a church and a school. Some of the elements that account for its success in Rome are its rules of strict observance, meditation, music, its effectiveness as a celebrational ritual, and its funeral rites in which the white shroud symbolizes the immortal soul. With Posidonius, astrological doctrines took on a religious and mystical tinge. Cicero, following his example, adopted the mystic quality of astral eschatology in the *Dream of Scipio;* in *De Senectute* he sums up the traditional proofs of immortality and shows the aspiration toward a divine congregation of light.

The astral concept of immortality retrieved old mythological material concerning the relationships of souls with heavenly bodies, thereby forming a learned doctrine that would serve as a foundation for the pagan mysticism of the first centuries of our era. The Pythagoreans thought that the space between the earth and moon was filled with souls on their way toward their destiny. The eclectic Stoics also cast a sidelong glance at the stars. The crescent moon appeared often on Roman funeral monuments, but solar cults also developed, and in imperial times the sun became more and more usual as the god of the dead.

Although the creed of solar immortality claimed many followers, the astrology of the planets was also not abandoned. The sequence of seven gates in the mysteries of Mithra indicates the extent of the syncretism possible within the context of celestial immortality. Thus the Mediterranean world in late antiquity was dominated by the concept of man's immortality in the radiance of the world beyond, a world of repose in eternal light. The Christians expanded on this while rejecting pagan astrology and introducing the doctrine of the eternal contemplation of God.

Gnostic Religion. The central element in gnostic philosophy is a dualistic teaching that the human being possesses a divine spark that originated in the world above but has fallen into the lower material world and is held captive there. This divine spark—the soul—has to regain the knowledge of its heavenly origins, escape the material world, and return to its native home. Each sect of this gnostic religion, with its own creed and method of salvation, teaches and practices the release of souls in its own way. Gnosis implies the identity of three factors—the knower, the celestial substance, and the means of salvation. This threefold assimilation makes it a transforming faith reserved for a select group of initiates. To the transitory material world of birth and death, gnosticism opposes the higher world, the world of life, permanence, incorruptibility, and immutability. The gnostic thinks of himself as a complete stranger to the world—he is "allogenous," of another race. He rejects the world, feeling that empirical existence is evil and opposed to the only true, transcendent reality.

Thus the gnostics viewed man as a combination of matter and spirit and saw the body as the prison which holds the soul after its fall. Within this mixture, the soul, an aeon of the same substance as the celestial world, remains intact, for it is incorruptible. The technical term *aphtharsia* ("incorruptibility") is part of the theological vocabulary of all gnostic systems. Incorruptibility is part of the soul's makeup because of its divine origin and is the essence of its immortality, even though by being imprisoned in the body the soul has become steeped in matter.

Salvation consists in the liberation of the soul. A heavenly savior intervenes to stir the captive soul's memory, to remind it of its origin and make it recognize its true "self." This revelation is made through a series of initiatory trials, by the end of which the soul has discovered a luminous vision of its own essence; the vision awakens in it a burning desire to return to its home. Then begins the second stage, that of the return to the "realm of life." The description of this ascension (or *Himmelsreise*) is found in the texts of all the sects; it includes deprivation and release from material bonds, a path passing through many dangers, the presence of a heavenly guide, and a triumphant entry into celestial Paradise for an immortal destiny amid the blessed light. The gathering of all the souls that have been held in bodies reconstitutes the Pleroma.

Manichaeism. Within the wide range of gnostic sects, Manichaeism holds a special place. Mani wished to establish a universal, definitive religion that would bring together all the previous revelations. It is based on a radical dualism of two eternal realms that stand opposed to one another from *Urzeit* to *Endzeit,* representing light and darkness, matter and spirit, body and soul, a dualism that pervades cosmology, anthropogony, soteriology, and eschatology. Claiming to possess the most perfect gnosis, Manichaeism divides mankind into the two categories of pneumatics and hylics and further divides its own church into elect and catechumens.

In the Manichaean scheme, man is a mixture of light and darkness. His body is the work of the archons, but his soul is a divine spark, a portion of the eternal realm of light that has fallen into the material world and been imprisoned in the body by birth. The saving element in the earthbound soul is the *nous,* while the *psuchē* is the part that must be saved; this is the task of Gnosis, a hypostatic divine entity from the realm of light. The gnostic message awakens the *psuchē,* makes it aware of its divine origin, and stirs in it the desire to return on high. This awakening of the soul is the beginning of salvation. The gnostic strives to realize the separation of light and darkness within himself. By an unceasing choice he carries out a *katharsis* within himself, a preliminary salvation that will take full effect after death, in a final liberation of the radiant and eternal soul.

The body is mere matter, destined for destruction as in Zoroastrianism, and is abandoned to the darkness from which it arose. The soul can regain the paradise of light, but if it is not reinstated at the hour of death, it remains enslaved to the archons and will have to continue its existence by being reincarnated into another body. In contrast, the souls of the elect are completely free to begin their triumphant ascension to the realm of light. The Coptic hymns of Medinēt Mādi give numerous examples of this ascension. It is the hour of final victory, completed by the bestowing of a crown (254.64.10–11). Stamped with the seal of purity, the elect join the angels in the shining city (254.64.14–15). Jesus himself, as the spouse of the perfected soul, awaits it and ushers it into the nuptial chamber where it becomes a holy bride of light (265.81.13–14). Three angels come toward it to present it with the crown, the trophy, and the robe (267.84.17–20), as trumpets sound in joyful welcome of the one who will forevermore taste of plenty and rest in the city of light (261.75.11–16).

In the *Fihrist* of the Arabic chronicler al-Nadīm (d. 995), it is the Primordial Man who sends a guide of light to the soul, accompanied by three angels bearing a crown of water, a robe, a diadem, and a crown and band of light. A virgin, the replica of the elect's soul, comes out to meet it, echoing the symbol of the *daēnā* that comes to meet the *urvan*, the earthly part of the soul, in the Avestan *Hadhōkht Nask*. The fate of the souls of the Manichaean *auditores* is not the same as for those of the elect. For them purification in the cycle of reincarnations is required, to enable them one day to follow in the footsteps of eternal salvation of the elect. There is also a third category of people, the sinners who have rejected the gnostic message. For them there is no escape; they are doomed eternally to make up the *massa damnata* of the realm of darkness.

Islam. The proclamation of the Day of Judgment comes at the beginning of the Qur'ān, and it is seen from the standpoint of the resurrection, *qiyāma*. On that day all the race of Adam will be gathered together, each one to receive judgment and everlasting retribution according to his deeds. Fear of the Last Day and of the punishment of Hell is a fundamental feature of the Prophet's teaching. The chosen ones on the right, the believers, will be called to enjoy Paradise, while the unbelieving will be condemned to torture. This preaching of Muḥammad's left its traces in every surah of the Qur'ān and gave rise to various systematizations within the currents of Islamic thought. Tradition has never ceased to enliven and enrich this central theme, and it is from this starting point that the elements that make up the common belief in immortality can be brought together.

Islamic anthropogony. The Islamic view of the nature of man is not particularly clear. The word *rūḥ* means *pneūma*, "breath"—the subtle breath that comes from the brain, that is, the mind. In some traditions it dies with the body only to be brought back to life with it. This is the spiritual part of the human being. There is also the *nafs* (Heb., *nefesh*), commonly translated as "soul," the carnal breath that comes "from the viscera." The philosophical debates of Islamic scholars show the influence of Iran and Greece in the argument that *rūḥ* or *pneuma*, is the truly spiritual part of the human being, the immortal element destined for the afterlife. Various Ṣūfī traditions distinguish between *nafs* as the seat of lust and *rūḥ* as the spiritual breath that can communicate with God.

The spiritualist doctrine of Shiism views the *rūḥ* as the pure breath of all matter, a spiritual substance that is immortal by nature. In this perspective man is not a body with a soul, but a spirit which temporarily inhabits a body as its instrument. Only on leaving the body does it find its true nature, for it is made to live independently; the soul's pleasure lies in the spiritual world. This tradition sees the spirit as a celestial, radiant substance, imperishable and immortal.

As against the spiritualistic tendency of Shiism, the traditional Sunnī theologians held that man is rather a compound of substances, body and soul, and entirely material. The central question is this: what happens at the moment of death? For those who take man to be a material composite of body plus soul, the soul "disappears" at death and is brought back to life on the last day, while those who see in the body only a temporary instrument of the soul believe the human soul to be made for the spiritual life, even after its separation from the body. In the first case the resurrection of the body is indispensable, whereas in the second the afterlife can do without it. As may be seen, the possible viewpoints can differ sharply.

After death. The early tradition of the Sunnī faith, based on surahs 40:45–46 and 40:11, holds that the body and spirit both die but that God resuscitates them in the grave for a brief afterlife and a judgment followed by a second death, the latter being abrogated for those who have been killed in the cause of God (3:169–170). The short afterlife in the grave, which has been extensively embellished by popular imagery, is devoted to a personal judgment and settling of individual accounts, with a cross-examination by two angel assessors and the divine judge. Islamic scholars wondered about a death of the body and soul at the time of this second death, but no clear answer to this question was ever arrived at, although some insisted that the soul must have an afterlife because it is inherently immortal.

Spiritualist trends discarded the afterlife of the grave, claiming that the human spirit is immortal and can begin to live its own life from the moment of death. From then on the souls of believers who love God join him in a spiritual, radiant world, where they live until the day of the resurrection. After their bodies arise and are given back to them for the judgment, they enter Paradise once and for all. The wicked and the unbelieving remain in unhappiness and suffering until the last day, when they will be reunited with their bodies for an everlasting punishment.

Resurrection. The resurrection of the body is an essential article of Islamic faith. The usual term used to refer to it is *ba'th* ("awakening"). Where the Qur'ān speaks of *qiyāmah*, theologians often use *ma'ād* ("return"), referring to the return of the being who has ceased to exist. The word *yawm* ("day") appears 385 times in the Qur'ān to designate the end of the present world, the resurrection of the dead, and the universal judgment followed by the beginning of the torments of Hell for unbelievers and a new life in Paradise for the faithful. On this promised day, awful and inescapable, the dead will rise to their feet as God grants them life. (A second creation is also alluded to in surah 22:5.) Details about the ceremony are not lacking: two books are brought forth, one for the unbelievers and one for the pure, and witnesses are present. Every person is introduced to a new life, in Hell or in Paradise, that must go on forever. For the believers Paradise awaits, where they will live in divine reward *(riḍwān)*, while Hell is reserved for unbelievers, polytheists, and detractors of the Prophet.

The descriptions of this afterlife are plentiful and make use of a rather remarkable symbolism. As Louis Massignon has shown, surah 18 of the Qur'ān speaks of a future life parallel to the present one, to be led in accordance with the will of God, and also lays stress on the submission of man to God and his ardent desire for justice that will blaze forth at the final resurrection. It is recited at the mosque on Friday, and expresses the central theme of immortality in the Qur'ān, the belief that the end of humankind on the final day of resurrection will allow true life to burst forth.

Christianity. In order to understand the Christian doctrine of immortality, the message of the New Testament must be located within its twofold setting in the biblical tradition of Israel on one hand and the context of religious beliefs and philosophical ideas of the Greco-Roman world on the other. At the time of the birth of Christianity, the Platonic doctrines of the human composite of *soma* and *psuchē*, the dissolution of this composite by death, and the immortality and afterlife of the *psuchē*, were widely held in Mediterranean thought. With this in mind, the central question concerns not the immortality of the soul as such but the originality of Christian revelation concerning the immortality of man, as he is created in the image of God and redeemed by Christ. Such a problem calls for an examination of the two aspects of Christian immortality, the resurrection of the body and the afterlife of the spirit.

The hope of resurrection. As we have seen, the faith in an individual and eschatological resurrection is clearly attested in the *Book of Daniel* and in the *Second Book of the Maccabees*, in the second century BCE. But where did the idea of bodily resurrection fit into the eschatological thought of Jesus? In an early presentation, Jesus affirms that those who enter the kingdom will receive a share in a life of unending peace and happiness, a point of view both communal and personal. The divine gift of eternal life is one of a spiritual nature; whosoever will enter the kingdom easily will be transformed (*1 Cor.* 15:51). This presentation ends by proclaiming the Messiah's passage through death and the reopening of his kingdom after it. This is the idea behind the earthly pilgrimage of the church, through which Jesus shared his own victory over death with his disciples (*1 Cor.* 15:20).

How did apostolic Christianity interpret the resurrection of Christ? After living first in the hope of the Lord's coming (*1 Cor.* 16:22), the apostles focused on the message of resurrection. Jesus is resurrected as the first fruit of the believers who die before his second coming. Later the church gradually accorded more importance to resurrection for all. As Albert Descamps notes in "La mort selon l'Écriture" (in Ries, 1983, p. 46), "Always sustained by the Jewish hope of the resurrection of the body, and even more by the memory of a Paschal event that is taken as a model, the faith in resurrection will become the Christians' main response to the problem of the other world, a resurrection expected by virtue of Christ's own and somehow understood as being in its image (*1 Thes.* 4:14; *Rom.* 6:5; *1 Cor.* 15:20, 15:23; *Col.* 1:18; *John* 11:24)." This doctrine, for nineteen centuries the central belief of Christianity, fulfills the biblical Jewish hope in an eschatological resurrection and replaces it with the inclusion of all Christians within the resurrection of Christ. For this reason the resurrection of non-Christians and sinners is devoid of Paschal glory (*1 Thes.* 4:14).

Afterlife of the soul. The immortality of the souls of the righteous is clearly affirmed fifty years before the common era in the *Wisdom of Solomon* (1:15, 3:9, 5:15). The setting of the biblical text is a world under the influence of Platonism, with the addition of traditional ideas from Israel. The place of the immortal soul in the teaching of Jesus is evident in his proclamation of the kingdom. It offers eternal life, which implies the expectation of a spiritual afterlife as suggested by the *Gospel of Matthew* 10:28. But the disciples' questions would be answered by apostolic Christianity, beginning with Paul (*2 Cor.* 4:7–5:10), who felt that existence after death is independent of the body. In the *Letter to the Philippians* 1:19–26, where Paul affirms even more clearly his certainty that he will never be separated from Christ (cf. *Rom.* 8:37–39, 14:7–12). Here we see the revival and christianization of Hellenistic Judaism and Greek wisdom, the Christian evaluation of the doctrine of Plato's *Phaedo:* the presence within man of a basic and incorruptible spiritual principle. The reflection of this Greek view of man appears also in the confirmation of an afterlife of the soul in *Matthew* 10:28, and in the parable of the evil rich man and Lazarus the beggar in *Luke* 16:19–31 the same idea is developed in popular terms. Jesus' answer to the second criminal on the cross (*Lk.* 23:43) openly declares the certainty of an immediate afterlife in the spirit.

In the light of the texts of the New Testament, the belief in immortality is an affirmation of the eschatological resurrection as a consequence of that of Christ and his presence on earth during the intermediate period after his death. This belief is the culmination of a millennium of earlier biblical reflection and piety, and has for nineteen centuries been the basis of the theology and faith of Christian believers.

Conclusion. The course of our research into beliefs in immortality, spanning the wide cultural and religious range of humanity from prehistory up to the great monotheistic systems, has uncovered several essential traits in the character of *homo religiosus.* Thrown into a universe to which he attempts to give some order, in search of a direction that will enable him to know where he is going, man discovers a dimension that transcends his earthly life. Through his day-to-day experiences, he ponders the mysterious phenomenon in which all his actions and all his behavior are rooted—the phenomenon of life. Such reflection marks the beginning of an unceasing quest into the nature and the density of life, which is revealed as a hierophany. The recognition of a sacred dimension in his own existence impels man to seek out the origin of life and to return to it. His ceaseless encounter with death all around him intensifies his questioning, and it is in this "nostalgia for the beginnings" that the search for immortality and the never-ending effort to transcend the human condition take root.

Our survey has revealed a *homo symbolicus,* for indeed it is through a symbolic language that man attempts to express his perception of the mystery of life, a life which he tries to comprehend as something absolute. The combination of this symbolic language with the efforts that have been made to solve the mystery of life is the source of an impressive fund of cultural and religious wealth in the form of art, literature, and ritual. The spirit attempts to approach the mystery of life and the afterlife through a series of universal symbols: the tree as a symbol of life and as *axis mundi,* the water that heals, rejuvenates, fertilizes, and becomes *soma;* the fire, the youth-restoring *ignis divinus* that can transform the body and become a divine messenger; the symbolism of ascension in the flight of birds; the sun and moon, signs of resurrection and guidance; and the rainbow, the link between heaven and earth.

Ritual symbolism too represents an important aspect of the efforts of *homo religiosus* to comprehend and realize his afterlife, as seen in such details as the fetal position of the corpse; the preparation and decoration of the tomb; the special attention given to the skull; funeral furnishings and offerings; stelae recalling the memory of the deceased; red ocher as a substitute for blood; inhumation, cremation, and mummification; gold foil on the funeral pyre; postmortem rituals for accompanying the soul on its journey; rites of opening the mouth, nose, ears, and eyes; and the placing of a book of the dead in the grave. What is most striking is the similarity between the rites for birth, initiation, and funerals. *Homo religiosus* believes that his life does not end, for death is a birth into a new life and an initiation into the afterlife.

Sacred, symbolic, and ritual converge in peoples' beliefs in immortality, and myths that underlie these beliefs are also numerous. The phoenix, for example, appears often in the mythic structure of immortality; Herodotus and Plutarch present this legendary bird in unequaled splendor. As the hour of its death nears it builds itself a nest of aromatic branches, and is consumed by a fire kindled by its own heat, after which it is reborn from the ashes. In ancient Egypt, it was associated with the daily cycle of the sun and the annual flooding of the Nile, and in pharaonic funerary symbolism, after the weighing of the soul, the deceased became a phoenix. In India it stands for Śiva, and in Greece it was a substitute for Orpheus. From Origen on, Christians took the phoenix as a sign of the triumph of life over death, and it is a symbol of Christ's resurrection throughout the Middle Ages.

[*See also* Soul; Afterlife; *and* Resurrection.]

BIBLIOGRAPHY

Alger, W. R. *A Critical History of the Doctrine of the Future Life.* New York, 1981.

Anati, Emmanuel, ed. *Prehistoric Art and Religion: Valcamonica Symposium 1979.* Milan, 1983.

Beier, Ulli. *The Origin of Life and Death.* London, 1966.

Bianu, Zeno. *Les religions et la mort.* Paris, 1981.

Camps, Gabriel. *La préhistoire: À la recherche du paradis perdu.* Paris, 1982. See pages 371–445 for a remarkable synthesis on prehistoric religious man.

Choisy, Maryse. *La survie après la mort.* Paris, 1967.

Cullman, Oscar. *Immortality of the Soul or Resurrection of the Dead? The Witness of the New Testament.* London, 1958.

Cumont, Franz. *Lux perpetua.* Paris, 1949.

Dumézil, Georges. *Le festin d'immortalité.* Paris, 1924.

Edsman, Carl-Martin. *Ignis divinus: Le feu comme moyen de rajeunissement et d'immortalité; Contes, légendes, mythes et rites.* Lund, 1949.

Eliade, Mircea. *Shamanism: Archaic Techniques of Ecstasy.* Rev. & enl. ed. New York, 1964.

Eliade, Mircea. *Yoga: Immortality and Freedom.* 2d ed. Princeton, 1969.

Eliade, Mircea. *Australian Religions: An Introduction.* Ithaca, N.Y., 1973.

Eliade, Mircea. "The Religions of Ancient China." In his *A History of Religious Ideas,* vol. 2, *From Gautama Buddha to the Triumph of Christianity.* Chicago, 1982.

Fröbe-Kapteyn, Olga. "Gestaltung der Erlösungsidee in Ost und West." In *Eranos Jahrbuch 1937.* Zurich, 1938.

Goossens, W. "L'immortalité corporelle." In *Dictionnaire de la Bible: Supplement,* vol. 4. Paris, 1949.

Guiart, Jean, ed. *Les hommes et la mort: Rituels funéraires.* Paris, 1979.

Guthrie, W. K. C. *Orpheus and Greek Religion.* 2d ed., rev. London, 1952.

Heiler, Friedrich. *Unsterblichkeitsglaube und Jenseitshoffnung in der Geschichte der Religionen.* Basel, 1950.

Heissig, Walther. *The Religions of Mongolia.* Translated by Geoffrey Samuel. Berkeley, 1980.

James, William. *Human Immortality* (1898). 2d ed. New York, 1917.

Klimkeit, Hans J., ed. *Tod und Jenseits im Glauben der Völker.* Wiesbaden, 1978.

La Vallée Poussin, Louis de. *Nirvâna.* Paris, 1925.

Lemaitre, Solange. *Le mystère de la mort dans les religion de l'Asie* (1943). 2d ed. Paris, 1963.

Parrot, André. *Le refrigerium dans l'au-delà.* Paris, 1937.

Pfannmüller, Gustav. *Tod, Jenseits, und Unsterblichkeit.* Munich, 1953.

Preuss, K. T. *Tod und Unsterblichkeit im Glauben der Naturvölker.* Tübingen, 1930.

Ries, Julien, ed. *La mort selon la Bible, dans l'antiquité classique et selon le manichéisme.* Louvain-la-Neuve, 1983.

Silburn, Lilian. *Instant et cause: Le discontinue dans la pensée philosophique de l'Inde.* Paris, 1955.

Söderblom, Nathan. *La vie future d'après le mazdéisme à la lumière des croyances parallèles dans les autres religions.* Paris, 1901.

Stendahl, Krister, ed. *Immortality and Resurrection.* New York, 1965.

Stephenson, Günther. *Leben und Tod in den Religionen.* Darmstadt, 1980.

Théodoridès, A., P. Naster, and Julien Ries, eds. *Vie et survie dans les civilisations orientales.* Louvain-la-Neuve, 1983.

Thomas, Louis-Vincent. *La mort africaine: Idéologie funéraire en Afrique noire.* Paris, 1982.

Tucci, Giuseppe. *The Religions of Tibet.* Translated by Geoffrey Samuel. Berkeley, 1980.

Wenzl, A. *L'immortalité: Sa signification métaphysique et anthropologique.* Paris, 1957.

Zahan, Dominique, ed. *Réincarnation et vie mystique en Afrique noire.* Strasbourg, 1963.

Julien Ries

Translated from French by David M. Weeks

IMPURITY. *See* Purification.

INANNA, the Sumerian astral deity representing the planet Venus, was known throughout the Mesopotamian world; the Akkadians (and later the Assyro-Babylonians) called her Ishtar. For both the Sumerians and the Akkadians, she was the principal goddess in their respective pantheons. Inanna-Ishtar's closest counterparts to the west are the Canaanite Astarte and the later goddesses of Greece and Rome, Aphrodite and Venus.

When the Semitic Akkadians settled in the lower Tigris-Euphrates Basin, they assimilated the preexisting, predominantly Sumerian culture. Comparative Semitic evidence suggests that the Akkadian Venus deity was originally masculine but became completely feminized when identified with the female Sumerian deity Inanna. Because of the eventual syncretism of the Sumerian and Akkadian pantheons, the traditions concerning Inanna-Ishtar are extremely complicated. By one such tradition she is the daughter of the sky god An, by another the daughter of the moon god Nanna-Sin (and thereby the sister of the sun god Utu-Shamash), and by still another, the daughter of Enlil or Ashur. Similarly, Inanna-Ishtar was associated with more than one consort, alternately Zababa of Kish, Ashur, An, and Dumuzi (called Tammuz by the Akkadians). Although her main cult center was Uruk, she was worshiped in many other localities, each of which gave her rather diverse epithets and characteristics.

A very large corpus of Sumerian and Akkadian cuneiform literature is extant in which Inanna-Ishtar is prominent. The primary image that emerges from these texts, in addition to her as the embodiment of Venus, is that of a goddess of love and sexuality, but in some she is instead a goddess of warfare. The Code of Hammurabi, for example, calls her "the lady of battle and conflict."

One of the most important myths about Inanna-Ishtar concerns her relationship to the shepherd god Dumuzi-Tammuz, who is probably a divinization of an actual early ruler of Uruk. Although the myth has many variations, its basic outline can be reconstructed from the Sumerian *Inanna's Descent to the Netherworld,* the Akkadian parallel *Ishtar's Descent,* and recently translated fragments of the *Death of Dumuzi,* as well as various laments for Dumuzi and a large set of *Sacred Marriage* texts.

According to these sources, Inanna and Dumuzi have a passionate love affair and marriage. Subsequently the goddess wants to visit the underworld, ruled by her enemy and sister, Ereshkigal, probably to try to rule there as well as in heaven. After bedecking herself with jewels and finery, Inanna descends and is met at the gate by a servant of Ereshkigal, who at various stages removes her garments. Finally she approaches her sister naked and humiliated. Ereshkigal fastens on her the "eyes of death," turns her into a corpse, and hangs her body on a stake.

Inanna's servant, worried after three days of her absence, fashions creatures who descend with revivifying materials. They bring her back to life and she reascends to earth, accompanied by frightening demons who wander with her from city to city in Sumer. When she returns to Uruk she finds her lover Dumuzi not bewailing her plight in the underworld, but actually celebrating it. She sets after him the demons, who after a long chase overtake and torture him and drag him down to the underworld.

There are many variations of this myth, but its importance lies in the love affair between Dumuzi-Tammuz, who comes to represent the annual dying and regenerated vegetative cycle, and Inanna-Ishtar, the embodiment of the generative force in nature. In their intercourse she fecundates the growth cycle of spring.

This came to be ritualized in an annual ceremony in which the king, representing Dumuzi-Tammuz, entered into a *hieros gamos,* a sacred marriage, with a sacred temple prostitute, representing Inanna-Ishtar, and thus sympathetically brought regeneration to the land. Their intercourse was, in a sense, the resurrection of the dead god, and lamentation was turned into rejoicing. The popularity and geographical spread of this myth and its ritualization are attested in *Ezekiel* 8:14, where the prophet condemns the practice followed by some Jerusalem women of lamenting the death of Tammuz.

In the *Epic of Gilgamesh* Ishtar becomes infatuated with the hero Gilgamesh and tries to seduce him. He rejects her, pointing out the shabby treatment she has given her former lovers, including Tammuz: "For Tammuz, the lover of your youth, you decreed a yearly lament. Having loved the dappled shepherd-bird, you smote him, breaking his wing." Enraged at this, Ishtar goes to her father An to seek vengeance. The incomplete text is not clear, but apparently the death of Gilgamesh's friend Enkidu is part of this chain of events.

A rather unexpected aspect of Inanna is revealed in the Sumerian myth *Inanna and Enki.* Inanna wishes to benefit Uruk, of which she is patroness, by making it the center of the civilized world. To do this she goes to the ancient city of Eridu to visit Enki, the lord of wisdom, plotting to finagle from him the divine decrees that govern every aspect of human civilization. Enki greets her warmly and has a banquet prepared to welcome her. Amid the glow of good food and drink he gives her the decrees and she departs, but afterward Enki realizes he has made a terrible mistake and sends a messenger, accompanied by various monsters, to overtake Inanna and retrieve the decrees. They do not succeed, however, and Inanna enters Uruk in jubilation with the precious decrees.

There are several hymns to Inanna-Ishtar, including one in which she praises herself as queen of the heavens and omnipotent among the gods. Another, the *Hymnal Prayer of Enheduanna,* addresses Inanna as "queen of the divine decrees, radiant light, life-giving woman, beloved of heaven and earth, supreme one." This remarkable hymn, reputedly written by the daughter of Sargon the Great, touches on virtually every aspect of Inanna.

BIBLIOGRAPHY

Translations of the major texts involving Inanna-Ishtar can be found in *Ancient Near Eastern Texts relating to the Old Testament,* 3d ed. with supplements, edited by J. B. Pritchard (Princeton, 1969). Samuel Noah Kramer's *The Sumerians: Their History, Culture, and Character* (Chicago, 1963) provides access to the story line of partially published texts, and situates Inanna within the broader aspects of Sumerian life and religion. Most recent are two articles, "The Descent of Inanna as a Ritual Journey to Kutha?" by Giorgio Buccellati, which suggests that the tale may involve a ritual procession of a statue of Inanna from southern to northern Babylonia, and "A Catalog of Near Eastern Venus Deities," by Wolfgang Heimpel, which compares and contrasts Inanna with parallel Near Eastern goddesses. Both are in *Syro-Mesopotamian Studies* 4 (December 1982): 3–7, 9–22.

William J. Fulco, s.j.

INAW are carved wooden wands used by the Ainu in rituals. They are whittled so that shavings, often very curly, remain attached to the stick. Although there is no controversy as to the recent use of the *inaw* as offerings to the deities, their use and meaning in the distant past are not altogether clear. Chiri Mashio maintains that these sticks were used to expel evil spirits and demons, while Neil Munro claims that they represented stylized human effigies that were at the same time considered receptacles for the souls of the ancestors. The *inaw* are essential in Ainu rituals as offerings to mediate between the Ainu and their deities, but are taboo items during funeral rites. Because they are sacred objects, only men, and not women, may carve them.

Approximately six types of *inaw* may be distinguished, each used for certain occasions and for certain deities. There are about fifteen species of trees used for *inaw*. Trees considered auspicious by the Ainu, including the willow, elder, walnut, and ash, are used for *inaw* for good deities, whereas trees considered to have an "offensive" odor, such as the *maackia amurensis* (*chikupe-ni* in Ainu) and the bird-cherry (*kiki-ni* in Ainu), and thorn-bearing trees are used in making *inaw* for evil deities. The *inaw* are placed both inside and outside the house. A special *inaw* for the fire goddess (Iresu-Huchi), for example, is placed at the hearth in the center of a one-room Ainu house, and an *inaw* for the deity of the house is placed at the northeastern corner of the house where the treasures, which are considered offerings to the deities, are enshrined. A cluster of *inaw* forming a fence-like structure is called *nusa* and such clusters are placed at various locations outside the house. Most importantly, a *nusa* is constructed at an altar a short distance from the sacred window, located on the northeastern side of the Ainu house. This altar serves as the place for most important religious ceremonies. It is considered that the souls of the deities rest at the *inaw* fence, where they listen to the Ainu pleas and also communicate through the sacred window with the fire goddess inside the house, who mediates between the Ainu and other deities. When rituals are held, the Ainu offer libations to the deities at the *nusa*, who join in the festivities with them. The *inaw* fences are also made at such places as the high-water mark for the deity who protects boats, at harbors for the deity in charge of the harbors, and at locations that symbolically represent the residences of important deities.

Some *inaw* bear incised signs or designs. Some of these are markers for the male ancestral lines and some are signs for the settlements of the *inaw* makers, whereas the meaning of others is not known among the Ainu themselves.

[*See also* Ainu Religion.]

BIBLIOGRAPHY

Ainu minzokushi. 2 vols. Tokyo, 1969. Sponsored by Ainu Bunka Hozon Taisaku Kyōgikai. See pages 634–645.

Chiri Mashio. *Bunrui Ainugo jiten.* Tokyo, 1953. *Inaw* are discussed on pages 119–120 of volume 1.

Munro, Neil G. *Ainu Creed and Cult.* New York, 1963. See especially pages 28–29.

EMIKO OHNUKI-TIERNEY

INCANTATION. The practice of incantation (Lat., *incantatio,* from *incantare,* "to chant a religious formula") differs considerably from culture to culture. For the purposes of this cross-cultural overview, however, incantation can be understood as the authorized use of rhythmically organized words of power that are chanted, spoken, or written to accomplish a desired goal by binding spiritual powers to act in a favorable way.

Since incantation uses words to move spiritual powers and accomplish a desired result, this practice is related to other uses of sacred language such as prayer, invocation, blessing, and cursing. Verbal formulas associated with prayer beseech the spiritual powers for certain actions or maintain communication by praise and submission. However, verbal formulas associated with incantation are designed to perform the desired result by "obliging" (Lat., *ob-ligare,* "to bind") spiritual powers. Invocation, blessing, and cursing are used with both prayer and incantation.

The Power of Incantation. Even though practices of incantation differ widely from culture to culture, its validity or efficacy appears to depend on cultural consensus about a number of primary factors, namely, the power of the chanted verbal formula, the authority of the incantor, the receptivity of spiritual forces both good and evil, the connection with the religious or mythological tradition, and the power of the accompanying ritual.

The power of the formula. Societies that use incantations understand them to be performative, that is, they accomplish what they say. The act of chanting the verbal formula itself has power. Scholars have put forth a variety of explanations concerning the effect incantations have for people. Older theories considered incantation to be a form of magic, an attempt to control and manipulate the forces of nature. More recent theories have suggested that incantations are expressive of needs and wishes or symbolize a desired result, or that they have the psychological effect of restructuring reality in the minds of people. Although these explanations may provide certain insights into the meaning of incantation, it must be remembered that, to the people involved, the proper chanting of the formula itself has performative power. To them it does not express or symbolize some other action—it *does* it. When, for example, the incantation experts of the Trobriand Islanders chant over the newly planted yam vines, "Raise thy stalk, O taytu. Make it flare up, make it lie across!" (Malinowsky, 1935, vol. 1, p. 146), the people know that the "hearing" of these commands by the tubers is what makes them sprout and grow.

It is not, however, just any words that have such power. Incantations are special verbal formulas that in a variety of ways, depending upon the particular cultural tradition, tap into sacred power. They may, for example, contain powerful scriptural expressions, *mantras*, or sacred names. [*See, for example,* Mantra *and* Names and Naming.] They are usually rhythmically organized and chanted repeatedly. They may use special devices such as foreign or unintelligible words, "abracadabra" nonsense phrases. The Anglo-Saxon medical-incantation treatise *Lacnunga* provides an example, using powerful names and impressive nonsense words:

> Sing this prayer over the black blains nine times: first, Paternoster. "Tigath tigath tigath calicet aclu cluel sedes adclocles acre earcre arnem nonabiuth aer aernem nidren arcum cunath arcum arctua fligara uflen binchi cutern nicuparam raf afth egal uflen arta arta arta trauncula trauncula. [In Latin:] Seek and you shall find. I adjure you by the Father, Son, and Holy Spirit that you grow no larger but that you dry up. . . . Cross Matthew, cross Mark, cross Luke, cross John." (Grattan and Singer, 1952, p. 107; my trans.)

It should be noted that, although the primary power of an incantation resides in its oral presentation, once these formulas could be written down, the chirographic (handwritten) text itself contributed to the potency of the incantation. From before 600 CE come Jewish-related Aramaic incantation texts written by experts on bowls and designed to ward off various sorts of evil. Such power could now be extended even into the realm of the dead, as in the case of Middle Kingdom Egyptian incantations inscribed on the inside wall of coffins, by which the various gods and demons encountered by the soul would be bound to act beneficially.

The chanter's authority. Closely connected to the power of the verbal formula is the authority of the incantors. These may be experts in terms of learning or ecclesiastical authority, like Taoist priests or Christian monks; they may be people who have been specially initiated into the use of such power, like various kinds of shamans; they may be charismatic holy ones who keep certain special observances or practices that sanction their authority. In the incantation itself, the chanter often clothes himself in the aura of divine authority and power. A Malay shaman, drawing authority from both Hinduism and Islam, outroars a thunderstorm:

> Om! Virgin goddess, Mahadewi! Om!
> Cub am I of mighty tiger!
> ʿAli's line through me descends!
> My voice is the rumble of thunder, . . .
> By virtue of my charm got from ʿAli
> And of Islam's confession of faith.
> (Winstedt, 1925, p. 59)

Receptivity of the spiritual forces. The power of the incantation further derives from the people's shared understanding of the nature and receptivity of the spiritual powers to be moved and bound by the powerful words. That spiritual entity may be simply an object or person that is to perform in a certain way. At other times, the incantation invokes, with careful mention of names, spirits, or gods who control aspects of nature and life, empowering or binding them to act beneficially. Ritual specialists of Java, when burying the umbilical cord of a newborn baby, intone the following words: "In the name of God, the Merciful, the Compassionate! Father Earth, Mother Earth, I am about to leave in your care the birthcord of the baby. . . . Don't bother the baby. This is necessary because of Allah. If you do bother him, you will by punished by God" (Geertz, 1960, p. 46).

A great many incantations are addressed to evil spirits or demons, conjuring them to leave or stay away. It is extremely important that the incantor name and identify the origin and characteristics of the evil power in order to bind it. Pre-Spanish Maya incantations, for example, list detailed knowledge about the evil spirit of the disease, recounting its parentage, its lustful impulses that inspired its shameful birth, and all its characteristics; they then proceed to consign the spirit to the foul-smelling underworld or to cast it into the wind to fall behind the sky. An Aramaic incantation becomes very specific in naming one of the many demons: "I adjure you, Lilith Ḥablas, granddaughter of Lilith Zarnai, . . . the one who fills deep places, strikes, smites, casts down, strangles, kills, and casts down boys and girls, male and female foetuses," while another text conjures by name nearly eighty demons and spirits of evils or sicknesses (Isbell, 1975, pp. 61, 121–122), showing that, occasionally, an incantation will name a whole series of evil spirits and demons—just to be sure that the right one is included.

Connection of the chant with tradition. The successful operation of the incantation depends on its connection with the religious or mythological tradition of the people. In one way or another, the incantation fits the specific human circumstance into the larger pattern of sacred existence and power as known in the religion of the people. Incantations in which such patterns are made explicit can be called narrative incantations. For example, Scottish incantations are regularly grounded in stories or legends about Christ and his disciples, as in this example: "Christ went on an ass, / She sprained her foot, / He came down / And healed her foot; / As He healed that / May He heal this, / And greater than this, / If it be His will to do" (Carmichael, 1928, vol. 2, p. 17). An ancient Egyptian narrative incantation, relating at great length how Isis rescued her son Horus from a scorpion's bite, concludes with the main point: "It means that Horus lives for his mother—and that the sufferer lives for his mother likewise; the poison is powerless!" (Bourghouts, 1978, pp. 62–69).

The accompanying ritual actions. While incantations can be used alone without any accompanying actions, in most cultures the chanting of incantations is usually associated with the power of other ritual actions. The incantation may be related to a ritual object that it empowers with sacred force. For treating a child with worms, the Javanese doctor chants over a special herb: "In the name of God, the Merciful, the Compassionate! Grandmother spirit, Grandfather spirit. . . . The harmful worms—may they all die. The good worms—may they stay for the whole length of the child's life" (Geertz, 1960, p. 93). Cherokee specialists almost always chant their incantations over tobacco, "remaking" or empowering the tobacco to perform the desired benefit. A Taoist priest chants this incantation over a small puppet as he rubs it over a patient: "Substitute, be thou in place of the fore part of the body, . . . be thou in place of the back parts, . . . be thou in place of the left side, that health may be ensured to him for year upon year" (de Groot, 1967, vol. 6, p. 1260). Incantation texts are often accompanied by directions for ritual actions. For example, an ancient Mesopotamian incantation for potency commands: "Let the ass swell up! Let him mount the jenny! Let the buck get an erection! Let him again and again mount the young she-goat!"; then the ritual directions follow: "Pulverized magnetic iron ore you put [into] puru oil; you recite the incantation over it seven times; the man rubs his penis, the woman her vagina with the oil, then he can have intercourse" (Biggs, 1967, p. 33). Incantation and ritual together accomplish the desired result.

Forms of Address. Within the great diversity of forms taken by the incantation formulas in different cultures and even within the same culture, a number of standard types can be discerned in the way spiritual powers are addressed. Many operate with the command form, using imperatives or statements of obligation to bind the spiritual powers to the desired action. Other incantations use the declaratory mode to establish the hoped-for result. And there are other incantations that approach the prayer mode, beseeching or charming the spiritual powers to take the beneficial action. Many times, of course, incantations use a combination of these three forms.

The command form, at its simplest, consists in naming the spiritual power and binding it to the desired action with an imperative. The High German "Pro Nessia" incantation from the ninth century AD, driving out the worm spirit that causes disease, is pure command:

> Go out, nesso,
> with the nine little ones,
> out from the marrow into the veins,
> from the veins into the flesh,
> from the flesh into the hide,
> from the hide into this arrow.
> Three paternosters.
> (Hampp, 1967, p. 118; my trans.)

In Burma, an exorcist addresses many powers of the supernatural world in a general incantation in order to focus his powerful command on the *ouktazaun* (minor spirit) that is possessing his client: "To all the *samma* and *brahma devas* of the sky heavens; to all the ghosts, monsters, and other evil creatures; to the ogres of the earth; to the master witches and the wizards; to the evil nats and the *ouktazauns:* I command you to leave. I command you by the glory of the Triple Gems [Buddha, Dhamma, and Sangha]" (Spiro, 1967, p. 177).

Very often incantations use a declaratory mode to perform the intended result of binding evil forces or compelling the good, declaring the desired state to be a reality in the present or the future. A Cherokee incantation designed to break up a happily married couple, for the benefit of a forgotten lover, simply declares the result to be so:

> Now! Very quickly pillow your head upon the Soul of the Dog, outside, where there is loneliness!
> Your name is ________.
> In the very middle of your two bodies loneliness has just come to think.
> You are to be broken in the Pathway.
> Now! Where the joining is has just come to be divided.
> Your two souls have just come to be divided somewhere in the Valley.
> Without breaking your soul, I have just come to stupefy you with the Smoke of the Blue Tobacco.
> (Kilpatrick and Kilpatrick, 1965, pp. 139–140)

When the Trobriand sorcerer tours the gardens with their budding leaves, he intones, "The yam rises and swells like a bush-hen's nest. The yam rises and swells like a baking-mound. . . . For these are my yams, and my kinsmen will eat them up. My mother will die of surfeit, I myself will die of repletion" (Malinowsky, 1935, vol. 1, p. 146). It is in this declaratory mode that blessings and curses are often formulated, focusing on the person or thing to be involved and declaring the favorable or unfavorable state to be a reality.

A third mode of expression in many incantations is that of beseeching or charming the sacred powers to act benevolently. This form approaches that of prayer and, at times, is indistinguishable from it. Yet the typical expressions, "May you," "Let God," "I ask you," and the like, can also be understood as compelling or binding the spiritual powers, not just beseeching them. A Burmese doctor chants a prayer-spell over a sick girl, repeating it three times as he empowers many spiritual beings for action: "May the five Buddhas, the nats, and the Brahmas rest on the forehead [of the patient]; may Sakka rest on the eyes and ears, Thurasandi Devi on the mouth, and Matali on the hands, feet, and body, . . . and may they guard and protect me" (Spiro, 1967, p. 152). And the Malay incantor turns even to Iblīs (Satan) and the other spirits and devils and firmly requests direct action on behalf of his lovesick client:

> In the name of God, the Merciful, the Compassionate!
> Friend of mine, Iblis!
> And all ye spirits and devils that love to trouble man!
> I ask you to go and enter the body of this girl,
> Burning her heart as this sand burns,
> Fired with love for me. (Winstedt, 1925, p. 165)

Purposes of Incantation. Purposes for the use of incantation differ widely and cover the whole gamut of life needs of individuals and societies. It is possible, however, to classify incantations, according to their purpose, into three broad categories: defensive, productive, and malevolent.

Defensive incantations. Among defensive incantations, a major purpose is prophylactic or apotropaic, that is, warding off evil spirits and their troubles, especially in the critical passages of life. Classic among apotropaic incantations are those widespread in the ancient Near East, directed against demonic powers called liliths—ghostly paramours of men, who attack women during their periods and at childbirth and who devour children. An incantation bowl binds these demons:

> I adjure you, every species of lilith, in the name of your offspring which demons and liliths bore. . . . Woe, tramplers, scourgers, mutilaters, breakers, disturbers, squeezers, muzzlers, and dissolvers like water. . . . You are fearful, terrified, and bound to my exorcism, you who appear to the sons of men—to men in the likeness of women and to women in the likeness of men—you who lie with people during the night and during the day. (Isbell, 1975, pp. 17–18)

Vedic incantation from ancient India is directed against the fiends who cause pregnant women to abort: "The blood-sucking demon, and him that tries to rob health, Kanva, the devourer of our offspring, destroy, O Prisniparni [medicinal plant], and overcome!" (*Atharvaveda* 2.25.4, as cited in Bloomfield, 1964, p. 22). The Egyptian Coffin Texts testify to the need for incantations to ward off the evil powers who feast on the soul in the passage of death.

The other major use of defensive incantations is for the expulsion of evil powers that have taken up abode. A Malay Muslim shaman exorcises the demon of disease, reciting first the creation story and then chanting,

> Where is this genie lodging and taking shelter?. . .
> Genie! if thou art in the feet of this patient,
> Know that these feet are moved by Allah and His prophet;
> If thou are in the belly of this patient,
> His belly is God's sea, the sea, too, of Muhammad. . . .
> (Winstedt, 1925, pp. 62–63)

Sickness can also be seen as the result of attack by rival humans, and then the appropriate measure is a counter-incantation. The Atharva priest of ancient India chants over a special ritual plant: "The spell which they skillfully prepare . . . we drive it away! . . . With this herb have I destroyed all spells. . . . Evil be to him that prepares evil, the curse shall recoil upon him that utters curses: back do we hurl it against him, that it may slay him that fashions the spell" (*Atharvaveda* 10.1.1, 4–5, as cited in Bloomfield, 1964, p. 72).

Productive incantations. A second purpose of incantation is beneficial, that is, it promotes growth, health, and happiness either by urging on the responsible inherent powers or by causing beneficial interference by divine powers. A curer in Java uses a massage and a spitting ritual with this incantation:

> In the name of God, the Merciful, the Compassionate!
> May the Prophet Adam repair [the person],
> May Eve order [the person].
> Untangle the tangled veins,
> Right the dislocated bones,
> Make the fluids of the body feel pleasant, . . .
> Health falls with my white spittle,
> Well, well, well, by the will of God.
> (Geertz, 1960, p. 94)

A great many incantations of the productive type have to do with love and sexual attraction, marriage, home and family, potency, successful birth, and the like. The Cherokee, for example, have a large variety of love incantations, for creating loneliness in the desired person, for retaining affection of a wandering mate, for acclimatizing a newlywed wife, or compelling a runaway spouse to return. Cherokee men and women can use incantations to "rebeautify" themselves and thus become attractive to a potential mate:

Now! I am as beautiful as the very blossoms themselves!
I am a man, you lovely ones, you women of the Seven Clans! . . .
All of you have just come to gaze upon me alone, the most beautiful.
Now! You lovely women, already I just took your souls!
I am a man!
You women will live in the very middle of my soul.
Forever I will be as beautiful as the bright red blossoms!
(Kilpatrick and Kilpatrick, 1965, pp. 86–87)

At times, productive incantations are needed to bring about pregnancy, as this one from ancient India: "Into thy womb shall enter a male germ, as an arrow into a quiver! May a man be born there, a son ten months old!" (*Atharvaveda* 3.23.2, as cited in Bloomfield, 1964, p. 97).

Malevolent incantations. A third purpose of incantation is related to the need to harm, punish, or take revenge on enemies or rivals. A jilted woman can target her erstwhile lover with this fierce imprecation:

> As the best of the plants thou art reputed, O herb; turn this man for me today into a eunuch that wears his hair dressed! . . . Then Indra with a pair of stones shall break his testicles both! O eunuch, into a eunuch thee I have turned; O castrate, into a castrate thee I have turned!
> (*Atharvaveda* 6.138.1–3, as cited in Bloomfield, 1964, p. 108)

The Cherokee bent on revenge learns from the shaman to recite the name of his adversary, repeating the following incantation four times and blowing his breath toward him after each rendition: "Your Pathways are Black: it was wood, not a human being! Dog excrement will cling nastily to you. You will be living intermittently. . . . Your Black Viscera will be lying all about. . . . Your Pathway lies toward the Nightland!" (Kilpatrick and Kilpatrick, 1967, p. 127).

Conclusion. Incantations, as rhythmic or formulaic words of power used to accomplish a desired goal by binding spiritual powers, have sometimes been considered as magic rather than religion, or as a form of religious practice lower than prayer. It is true that incantations oblige the powers to perform the action rather than prayerfully request them for it. And it is also true that incantations have to do with self-interest, sometimes at the expense of others. Yet they do represent a religious mode of being in the world, albeit a mode of aggression rather than simple submission to spiritual powers. The power of chanted words fits the events of human life into the pattern of the sacred realities that underlie and support human existence. Far from being trivial, incantations provide help for whatever deeply troubles or concerns humans: health, birth, love, marriage, family, prosperity, death. Human existence is understood as a drama involving the interaction of many spiritual powers, and, through the power of the chanted formula, a restructuring of these powers is performed so that life can become more healthy, secure, prosperous, and happy.

[*See also* Magic *and* Spells.]

BIBLIOGRAPHY

Among the many works that include incantations from all over the world, the following provide a representative survey from ancient, medieval, and modern cultures.

Biggs, Robert D. *Šà.zi.ga: Ancient Mesopotamian Potency Incantations.* Locust Valley, N.Y., 1967. Translations and textual studies of incantations used in Mesopotamian society for this universal sexual problem.

Bloomfield, Maurice, trans. and ed. *Hymns of the Atharva-Veda.* Delhi, 1964. Reprint of "Sacred Books of the East," vol. 42 (Oxford, 1897). Translations and interpretations of the most important incantations and hymns of the fourth Veda from ancient India by one of the outstanding American Sanskritists of the nineteenth century.

Borghouts, J. F., trans. *Ancient Egyptian Magical Texts.* Leiden, 1978. Translations of a representative range of incantations from ancient Egypt, dealing with concerns of everyday life, mostly from the Middle Kingdom and later.

Carmichael, Alexander. *Carmina Gadelica: Hymns and Incantations,* vol. 2. Edinburgh, 1928. Various incantations collected orally in the highlands and islands of Scotland and translated into English.

Geertz, Clifford. *The Religion of Java.* Glencoe, Ill., 1960. Extensive information about incantations in this important study of the Javanese religious system, which combines Islam and native spirit beliefs.

Grattan, J. H. G., and Charles Singer. *Anglo-Saxon Magic and Medicine.* Oxford, 1952. Some incantations and healing rituals especially from the semipagan text *Lacnunga,* translated into modern English.

Groot, J. J. M. de. *The Religious System of China* (1892–1910). 6 vols. Reprint, Taipei, 1967. Especially volume 6 of this multivolumed work contains traditional Chinese rituals and incantations against specters.

Hampp, Irmgard. *Beschwörung, Segen, Gebet: Untersuchung zum Zauberspruch aus dem Bereich der Volksheilkunde.* Stuttgart, 1961. A rich sourcebook for incantations from German cultures, providing also a study of types and purposes.

Isbell, Charles D. *Corpus of the Aramaic Incantation Bowls.* Missoula, Mont., 1975. Texts and translations of all the published Aramaic texts inscribed on incantation bowls, from Jewish-related societies in Babylon.

Kilpatrick, Jack Frederick, and Anna Gritts Kilpatrick. *Walk in Your Soul: Love Incantations of the Oklahoma Cherokees.* Dallas, 1965. Incantations used in situations of love and marriage among the Cherokee.

Kilpatrick, Jack Frederick, and Anna Gritts Kilpatrick. *Run to-*

ward the Nightland: Magic of the Oklahoma Cherokees. Dallas, 1967. Incantations of the Cherokee for use in various situations.

Malinowski, Bronislaw. *Coral Gardens and Their Magic.* 2 vols. London, 1935. Texts of many incantations interspersed with descriptions of the Trobriand Islanders to the east of New Guinea, with important interpretations by this famous anthropologist.

Roys, Ralph L., trans. and ed. *Ritual of the Bacabs.* Norman, Okla., 1965. Translations of healing incantations from the pre-Spanish Maya culture.

Spiro, Melford E. *Burmese Supernaturalism: A Study in the Explanation and Reduction of Suffering.* Englewood Cliffs, N.J., 1967. A careful study of the Burmese spiritual world, including translations of incantations used in this Buddhist culture.

Winstedt, R. O. *Shaman, Saiva and Sufi: A Study of the Evolution of Malay Magic.* London, 1925. Includes translations of many incantations in a study of religious practices in Malay culture, which mixes Islamic, Hindu, and indigenous religious influences.

THEODORE M. LUDWIG

INCA RELIGION. The pre-Columbian Andean cultures, of which the Inca empire was the final heir, extended over a geographical area that the Inca believed corresponded to the four quarters *(tahuantinsuyu)* of the world. At the time of the Inca empire's fall to Spanish forces under Francisco Pizarro in 1532, the Inca occupied large portions of present-day Ecuador, Peru, Bolivia, and Chile. The great Andean civilizations flourished in this setting of contrasting ecosystems (coastal desert ribbed with fertile valleys, arable highlands at altitudes of more than four kilometers, Amazonian and montane rain forests) that offered resources for pursuing a variety of means of subsistence, including fishing, hunting and gathering, agriculture, and the herding of llamas, guanacos, and alpacas.

Historical Background. The great pre-Inca civilizations that flourished in what is now Peru were the Chavín (after about 800 BCE), the Nazca and Moche (c. 100–800 CE), the Tiahuanaco (c. 200–1000), the Huari (c. 800–1200), and the Chimu (c. 1200–1400). None of these cultures, the Inca included, appears to have possessed a written language, though this function was filled, to some extent, by the use of *quipus*, or knotted strings. [*See* Knots.] (The geometric plastic arts of the ancient Andean peoples may one day be shown to comprise a system of ideograms.) Aside from scattered archaeological evidence—including figurative and abstract images on stone and wood, funerary pieces, and some fresco fragments—we possess documents (written in Spanish and, less frequently, in Quechua) that were composed during the years following the Conquest and that detail the religious practices of indigenous Andean peoples. (The Inca were reported to have painted mythological scenes on canvas and wood, but these are now lost.)

Despite their separation in time and the contrasts between their ecological milieus, the Andes high cultures and their religious systems manifested a common spirit. Religious practices permeated all aspects of public and private life. These religions for the most part included cults of the dead, of ancestors, of a founding culture hero, and of a divine king. Offerings and sacrifices (often human) were performed, and reflected beliefs in the needs of the "living corpse" and in the exigencies of the cosmic powers on which the cycles of nature depended. These deified powers were portrayed as monstrous beings that combined human, animal, and vegetable traits. The images of the principal deity throughout these cultures were basically variations on constant themes. This deity, which in images is variously characterized as an anthropomorphized feline (a puma or jaguar), a one- or two-headed serpent, a condor, or an ear of maize, is often portrayed brandishing weapons or other instruments.

The temples of the urban centers of these civilizations were built either in the form of truncated, stepped pyramids or as series of enclosures. Some possessed underground vaults, with or without labyrinths. In some locations, temple architecture is suggestive of the structure of the cosmos, comprising three vertical levels. Elsewhere, rows or circles of stones testify to astral observations and to cults connected to the organization of sacred time and space, in which the movements of the sun, moon, and stars, the alternations of day and night and dry and rainy seasons, the cycles of the earth and sea, and human, animal, and vegetable fecundity all seem to play a role. Calendars were based on the cycles—individually or in combinations—of the sun, the moon, the planet Venus, and the Pleiades. The Sun and Moon pair of deities and the pair composed of this couple's sons (often seen as enemy twins) were important pan-Andean deities. Among coastal groups, the Moon, represented in bird form and associated with the sea and the dead, was the preeminent deity. Divine symbols and religious rites were not, however, always directly related to the ecosystem within which the particular culture flourished, as is evident when one compares pre-Inca iconography with Inca mythology and with the myths of present-day Amazonian peoples.

Inca Cosmology. The Inca religious system is usually attributed to either the Inca Tupac Yupanqui or his predecessor, the Inca Pachacuti, and dates to at most one hundred years before the European conquest. The expansion of Cuzco, the Inca capital, was carried out in the name of the superiority of its gods over those of other peoples who, once they were assimilated into the empire, left their principal idol (or its replica) in the Inca capital. The colonization, or federation, was founded on a system of reciprocity overseen by Cuzco. Certain cults and temples were richly endowed by the Inca (the title given the head of the empire); others were suppressed. The great social and religious leaders of the empire went regularly to the capital city, and the Inca brought colonies of collaborators *(mitima)* to the temples of the empire and sometimes had himself named priest of honor. The sanctuaries of the provinces paid tribute in kind to Cuzco, contributing, for example, young children to be sacrificed during the Capacocha ceremony, which was held to ensure the Inca's health and prosperity. Rites of communion were held periodically to ensure the political and religious cohesion of the empire. Generally, these rites took place at the Temple of the Sun, in the center of the *tahuantinsuyu,* which center was located at the junction of the two rivers of Cuzco. Slow processions or rapid messengers departed from and returned to this center, traveling along the roads that divided the empire into four regions (*chinchaysuyu* to the northwest, *antisuyu* to the northeast, *contisuyu* to the southwest, and *collasuyu* to the southeast) or along the forty-one *ceque* (theoretical lines radiating from the center, on which 428 shrines were placed), and returned. Although the Inca authorized the conservation of certain regional religious structures in the cities of the empire, they also reproduced Cuzco's geometrical organization of sacred space and built replicas of the capital's principal temples in all the ceremonial centers. The bipartition of villages and adjacent territories—the distribution in halves—was common throughout the Andes. In Cuzco these halves were called *hanan* (which roughly means "high, superior, right, masculine") and *hurin* ("low, inferior, left, feminine"). Other categories of opposition and complementarity could intersect or be superimposed over this base, determining various socioreligious complexes. Such halves (or moieties) were linked respectively with the cosmic powers of the lower and upper worlds, and with two cardinal points.

The inhabitants of the Andean region worshiped a great number of gods, idols, and spirits, which were designated by the generic name *huaca,* a term that was also applied to the shrines. The oral traditions frequently related the adventures of the great *huacas* (gods or parents of gods), their births and metamorphoses; the magical creation of wells, lakes, and irrigation canals; hunts, rivalries, wars, and conquests of lands, waters, and women who were captured by force or trickery; and the powers of the *huacas* over men and men's duties toward them. All this took place "in the time when the *huacas* were men . . . afterward they were turned into stone." Each family—and, at the higher level, each village and province—claimed to descend from a given *huaca* (a particular man-god, conquering ancestor, founder, or civilizer), who represented a cosmic power and whom they venerated in the form of a mummy, a stone, an animal, or a constellation of stars. The codification of these beliefs was founded on the oppositions and complementaries of nature—binary or ternary (e.g., man-woman, the head and the two arms), biological and parental, or cultural (conqueror-conquered, interior-exterior, etc.)—expressed in the representation of cosmic forces. Similarly, certain numbers, probably the results of astronomical calculations, gave order to the sacred.

Inca Gods. The kings of Cuzco, reputed to be sons of the Sun, formed a religious, cosmic, and territorial imperial structure in which the Sun reigned over the Andean highlands and the heavens and the god Pachacamac ruled over the lowlands and the underworld.

The Coricancha, the great Temple of the Sun in Cuzco, was flanked by two golden pumas and its walls were covered with gold and silver plaques. The halls contained statues and cosmic representations, and the mummies—or their replicas—of earlier kings and queens. There were three sculptural triads of the Sun; each included a father and two sons, each triad symbolizing, respectively, the heavenly body, its light, and its vital warmth. One of these statues, Punchao, depicts two pumas between whom is seated a man with serpents at his waist and rays emanating from his shoulders. It contained a reliquary filled with a powder made from the entrails of dead kings. The temple sheltered a large number of priests (the first priest was a close relative of the Inca) and the "virgins of the Sun" *(aclla),* who dedicated themselves to making cloth and corn beer for the cult of the Sun, and who also served as concubines to the Inca (who was himself the manifestation of the Sun) or to dignitaries.

From the dark bowels of the cosmos, Pachacamac caused earthquakes and sent pestilence. With his wife Pachamama ("mother of the earth"), he ruled the waters of the underworld, and, with his daughters, he controlled the depths of the sea. His temple was located at the seacoast. Although represented by a golden fox, he was also worshiped in the form of a wooden pillar, which was sculpted in a dark chamber atop a truncated adobe pyramid.

Illapa, who represented thunderbolts, lightning, rain, hail, snow, and frost, was venerated by a large cult in the highlands. He was conceived of as a triad (father, brother, and son). One of the three was represented by a man holding a club in one hand and a sling in the other. It was said that the *huacas*, sons of Illapa from whom various tribes were descended, had been thrown off a mountaintop and were raised by men. They were identified with the mountain and became masters of its animals and plants. The mountains were personified and arranged hierarchically and were the object of a cult.

The serpent Amaru represented the striking thunderbolt and also the animal or monster who, according to the myths, rose from the lake and moved toward the upper world. With one head at each of his extremities, Amaru symbolized communication between the upper and lower parts of the cosmos.

Women were the principal participants in the cult of Quilla, the Moon, who was the sister and wife of the Sun. The Coya ("queen") was believed to be the daughter of the Moon, just as the Inca was believed to be the son of the Sun. The anthropomorphic statues of Quilla were silver, while those of the Sun were gold. A lunar calendar was used along with a solar calendar. [*See* Calendars, *article on* South American Calendars.] Quilla was associated with the earth and the dead. Traditionally, she pursued dead thieves into the underworld at night. One month of the year was especially sacred to her. Men also worshiped her, in Cuzco and elsewhere, particularly in the temple of Nusta, which was located on an island in Lake Titicaca.

When they were not visible, the stars, like the sun and the moon, were believed to go under the earth. The Milky Way—thought of as two rivers—may have inspired the construction of the Coricancha at the junction of the two rivers of Cuzco. Among the constellations, that of the llama, visible during the dry season, was of special importance to cattle raisers. The Pleiades were associated with the rainy season. If they appeared clearly at the end of May, a good harvest was augured.

After death, one of the two souls that were attributed to a man returned to its place of origin, either before or after a journey strewn with obstacles, and dwelt in the land of the souls, which was not unlike the world of the living. The kind of afterlife enjoyed by this soul was conditional on the type of death, social rank, and virtues of the dead. The other soul remained in the body, which had to be preserved intact, and which had the same needs as the living person. The bodies of nobles, kings, and queens were mummified, kept by their families, and often moved about. The mummies of ancient kings—or their replicas—were set out hierarchically in parallel series *(hanan* and *hurin)* of four. At the head was the common founding ancestor, theoretically androgynous, of whom the first was Manco Capac. The ancestors, associated with the netherworld and germination, were considered oracles of the past, the future, and distant events, and they were consulted by expert priests.

Viracocha was the supreme god of the Inca. The Spanish missionaries—monotheists and monogenists—would have liked to make him or perhaps Pachacamac into a creator god who was unique, abstract, and infinite. But in Andean thought, each tribe had been transformed (rather than created) from water, earth, animals, and so forth, by a particular god at the beginning of a cosmic cycle, and the role of all deities was to have given, and to continue to give, the breath of life and strength *(cama)* to man and to nature.

Viracocha was one of these personified gods. He was also a complex deity and was thought of as both one and many, the principle of transformation. Two others of his names were Con-Ticsi-Viracocha and Pachayachachic ("he who gives order to the world") and he had a large family with several sanctuaries. Viracocha was associated with water and the foam of Lake Titicaca, whence he had come, and with the foam of rivers and the surface of the ocean, where, according to some myths, he (in human form) disappeared to the northwest, walking on the waves. These attributes associated him with the rainy season, and others made him the representative of the fire of the heavens and of the triumphant Sun. Under the name of Huari Viracocha (an androgynous being) he was able to draw to himself all the cosmic functions of the upper and lower worlds. He had created the sun, the moon, the stars, and the prototypes of the Andean tribes—including the Inca—thus separating night from day and ushering in the solar cosmic cycle, which he entrusted to the Inca Manco Capac. The latter, accompanied by his brothers and sisters (the Ayars), was plunged into the earth by Viracocha and reemerged from the central window of Pacaritambo, to the south of Cuzco, at dawn, in order to reflect the first appearance of the sun. Viracocha's sons, Imaymana and Tocapu, taught the Andeans the names and virtues of the flora and fauna. Their travels, like Viracocha's, may have corresponded to astronomical observations.

Some prayers to Viracocha have been preserved. Around 1575, a number of prayers were recorded by Fray Cristóbal de Molina (collected in *Las crónicas de los Molinas,* Lima, 1943). The first of these may be rendered in English as follows:

> O Creator, you who are at the ends of the earth, peerless, who has given being and force to men, who has said, "Let this one be man and that one be woman." You made them, you gave them shape, you gave them being. Let them live in health, free from danger, in peace. Wherever you may be, whether up in the heavens, below with Thunder, or with the

clouds of the storm, listen to me, answer me, grant me my prayer, give us eternal life. Keep us forever in your hand. This offering, receive it, wherever you are, O Creator.

Inca Rites. The Inca was considered to be the son of the Sun and the Earth, Viracocha's chosen one and equal. In this world, between the two vertical halves of the cosmos, he was the synthesis of their opposition, acting as center and mediator. A *huaca* himself, he had ambiguous powers over the *huaca*s, with whom he either negotiated or made war. He contributed to the upkeep and vigor of the cosmic cycle in which he lived by seeing that the order of Pachayachachic was respected. Specialized priests (for such matters as divination, interpreting oracles, making sacrifices, hearing confessions, etc.) conducted the rites that measured the cycles of agriculture and husbandry, which were spread throughout the year, and which corresponded to the solstices and equinoxes, the alternation of rainy (October to March) and dry seasons, and the alternation of day and night. Each month a particular segment of Cuzco society dedicated itself to the prevailing cult. One of the most important festivals was Hanan Raymi (held at seedtime in December), during which the initiation rites of the young nobility took place, and after which the Citua was celebrated to expel the illnesses brought on by the rains. Another important ceremony was Inti Raymi, which took place at harvest time in June.

The great religious ceremonies were publicly celebrated in Cuzco. The sacrifices were designed to nourish and placate the gods, and offerings were selected from the great complementary ecosystems of nature (plants, birds, shells, the blood of animals—particularly llamas—and men) and culture (maize, coca, pepper, corn beer, cloth, statuettes). At the center of the ceremonial place was the *usnu*, a small edifice on which the Inca sat enthroned and that was pierced at its base by underground canals leading to the temples of Viracocha, the Sun, and Illapa. Here the Sun was given "drink," which acted to placate and balance the powers of the lower and upper worlds. The *usnu* may also have served as an astronomical observatory. The golden statues of Viracocha, the Sun, and Illapa, the silver statue of the Moon, and the mummies of dead sovereigns—or their replicas—were set out on ceremonial occasions.

The performance of these ritual duties was also intended to ward off cataclysms *(pachacuti)*, especially those caused by excessive heat ("suns of fire") or water (floods). Such cataclysms were believed to result from the dissatisfaction of the cosmic powers of the upper and lower worlds. They were believed to have occurred before, ushering in new cycles, and it was thought that they could happen again. These ideas, which were based on the observation of the movements of the sun and moon and the oppositions of day and night, dry and rainy seasons, and fire and water, were projected through time to construct an explanation of the history of the world. In any case, the important Quechua word *pacha* means both "time" and "space."

Conclusion. It is impossible to show in this short essay the wealth and the complexity of the official Inca religion, which was itself superimposed over the no less rich religions of the conquered provinces. Religion imbued and governed all private and public activities of the Andean people. Daily tasks and major undertakings alike were performed with equal passion and competitive spirit, for the dualism of the religion imparted its dynamism to society. The great ritual festivals of participation and communion involved the population from the capital as well as that from the countryside, thus assuring the cohesion of the social and ethnic groups of the empire. The deification of power guaranteed its intangibility and the stability of the social order. Finally, we know that piety was general, and that members of the elite did not hesitate to offer their children for sacrifice.

To be sure, no Andean religious books exist. But there is much to discover in the colonial documents. Recent years have seen considerable progress, especially in scholarly knowledge of Andean astronomy. Religion, culture, and philosophy were built around several fundamental ideas: the opposition of contraries, the search for their conciliation in a harmonious equilibrium, and concern for the natural and human laws, which religion had as its object to predict and to regulate.

But this religion also had its failings in regard to the social order, owing especially to the importance attributed to the oracles and to the divinization of the Inca, factors that certainly facilitated the conquest of the empire by the Spaniards. Given the present state of Andean studies, it is difficult to talk about theology in connection with Inca religion. One can, however, speak of a complex metaphysic in connection with the major god Viracocha, the conception of whom was forced to enrich and complexify itself during the final days of the empire.

The religious spirit of the Andeans revealed its full intensity after the Spanish conquest, especially in the cruel but vain attempts to make the indigenous priests confess the locations of hidden treasures. After the official religion had been forbidden and destroyed by the invaders, after it had disappeared with the empire, the rural religions, which in general antedated the Inca conquest, continued to be practiced secretly despite the fierce assaults of the itinerant Inquisition upon the Indians. During the colonial centuries, the indigenous religions formed the core around which crystallized the spirit of resistance and the preservation of the cultural identity of the Andeans.

BIBLIOGRAPHY

Duviols, Pierre. *La lutte contre les religions autochtones dans le Pérou colonial: "L'extirpation de l'idolâtrie" entre 1532 et 1660.* Lima, 1971. A history of the itinerant Inquisition (called "the extirpation of idolatry") against the Indians, its methods and the reactions of the indigenous peoples.

Duviols, Pierre. "Punchao, ídolo mayor del Coricancha: Historia y tipología." *Antropología andina* 1 (1976): 156–182. Shows the continuity in one of the representations of the Andean solar god.

Duviols, Pierre. *La destrucción de las religiones andinas: Conquista y colonia.* Mexico City, 1977. Studies the means used to suppress the Andean religions and the efforts to replace them with Christianity.

Lumbreras, Luis G. *The Peoples and Cultures of Ancient Peru.* Washington, D.C., 1974.

Mariscotti de Görlitz, Ana María. *Pachamama Santa Tierra.* Berlin, 1978. Monograph on this topic.

Murra, John V. *The Economic Organization of the Inca State.* Greenwich, Conn., 1980. Numerous references to the economics of religion.

Pease, Franklin. *El pensamiento mítico.* Lima, 1982. Anthology of ancient Andean myth, preceded by a study.

Platt, Tristan. "Symétries en miroir: Le concept de *yanantin* chez les Macha de Bolivia." *Annales, economies, sociétés, civilisations* 33 (1978): 1081–1107. Analysis of the concepts of reflection and the double among the Macha of Bolivia.

Rostworowski de Diez Canseco, María. *Estructuras andinas del poder: Ideología religiosa y política.* Lima, 1983. Study of a large number of current works, focusing on the theme of dualism.

Rowe, John Howland. "The Origins of Creator Worship among the Incas." In *Culture in History: Essays in Honor of Paul Radin,* edited by Stanley Diamond, pp. 408–429. New York, 1960.

Taylor, Gerald. "*Camay, Camac,* et *camasca* dans le manuscrit Quechua de Huarochiri." *Journal de la Société des Americanistes* 63 (1974–1976): 231–244. Analyzes an important concept in Andean thought.

Urbano, Henrique. *Wiracocha y Ayar: Héroes y funciones en las sociedades andinas.* Cuzco, Peru, 1981. Anthology of ancient Andean myths, preceded by an attempt at interpretation using the trifunctional model of Georges Dumézil.

Urton, Gary. *At the Crossroads of the Earth and Sky: An Andean Cosmology.* Austin, 1981. Analysis of contemporary Andean astrological beliefs in terms of pre-Columbian Andean astronomy.

Zuidema, R. Tom. *The Ceque System of Cuzco: The Social Organization of the Capital of the Inca.* Leiden, 1962. Analyzes the geometrical and arithmetical organization of the sacred space of Cuzco.

Zuidema, R. Tom. "Mito e historia en el antiguo Perú." *Allpanchis* (Cuzco) 10 (1977): 15–52.

Zuidema, R. Tom. "Hierarchy and Space in Incaic Social Organization." *Ethnohistory* 30 (1983): 49–75.

PIERRE DUVIOLS
Translated from French by Erica Meltzer

INCARNATION. The concept of incarnation (Lat., *incarnatio,* "being in flesh") has been applied in the Christian community to the mystery of union between divinity and humanity in the person of Jesus Christ. More generally, the concept has been extended to take into account a variety of forms of incarnation that the history of religions has described in various lands and among different peoples. The term *incarnation* is broadly defined here as the act or state of assuming a physical body (as a person, an animal, a plant, or even an entire cosmos) by a nonphysical entity such as the soul, the spirit, the self, or the divine being.

Typologically speaking, there are two sharply contrasting evaluations of incarnation. One of them is a tragic view, according to which the union of the soul, the spirit, or the self with the world of matter, hence with the physical body, is interpreted as a fall from its proper place into an alien abode, an imprisonment, or an enslavement. Salvation consists, according to this view, in the soul's escape from the world into which it has fallen by dissociating and liberating itself through purifications, rites of initiation, or meditation, from the chains of its captivity. There is, on the other hand, a positive interpretation of incarnation, which sees the assumption of a bodily form by the soul, the spirit, or the divine being as occurring for the purpose of saving or sanctifying the phenomenal world. This type of bodily manifestation is seen, for example, in the leaders of small tribal communities, the founders of religions, and the heads of theocratic states. In a certain sense, the history of religions has been the history of persistent battles fought between these two distinctive visions of the incarnation.

The "Primitive" Tradition. The belief in the divine incarnate can be attested as early as the late Paleolithic period, in a considerable number of pictures of human beings in animal forms, often in dancing posture. Among the best known is a figure of the "great sorcerer" in a Trois Frères cave, sporting a deer's head crowned with huge antlers. The same cave has also preserved the portrayal of a dancer disguised as a bison, playing a bow-shaped instrument, possibly a kind of flute. It is certain that the early hunters wore masks and skins of animals for the celebration of their magico-religious ceremonies. These masked figures and many parallel examples were probably believed to be the incarnations of spirits or divine beings akin to the Lord of the Animals.

Wearing masks has been one technique for incarnating souls or spirits in premodern societies. [*See* Masks.] In Inner Asia, for example, a shaman's mask symbolizes the incarnation of a mythical personage (ancestor, mythical animal, or god). For its part, the costume transforms the shaman into a spiritual being. In Polynesia and Melanesia, the souls or spirits of dead ancestors are believed to come from the land of the dead at certain fixed times, especially when the old year passes into the new year. They appear in disguise, wearing terrifying masks and strange costumes; the "dead" call on villagers, praising them for their good conduct and rebuking them severely for any wrongdoing they have committed. The "dead" also perform the rites of initiation for young novices. Finally, they give blessings for a good crop in the coming months and, after receiving hospitality from the villagers, return to their homeland far across the sea. In fact, the spirits of the dead are impersonated by members of secret societies (e.g., the Dukduk of the Bismarck Archipelago, the Arioi of the Marquesas Islands), but these awe-inspiring "sacred visitors" wield such terror over the noninitiated that they are truly believed to be the incarnations of the ancestral spirits. Significantly, the arrival of the spirits from the world beyond announces the renewal of time, the advent of the new year, and the renovation of the entire universe. A similar belief in the sacred visitors *(marebito)* is also attested in Japan.

The belief in the preexistence and incarnation of souls is abundantly documented in the "primitive" world. According to the Caribou Inuit (Eskimo), for example, the immortal soul of a dead person leaves his body, ascending to the supreme being Pinga in heaven who receives it. If the person lived properly according to the rules of life, Pinga lets the soul assume a bodily form, human or animal. Such a belief is also widespread among the North American Indians. Especially noteworthy is the belief found among the Aranda in central Australia, according to which every human being has two souls: the mortal soul, which comes into being with the fetus as a result of intercourse between the parents, and the immortal soul, which predates and really creates man's entire personality. More concretely, the immortal soul is a particle of life of the totemic ancestor who unfolded his sacred history in the beginning of mythical time; every individual is what he is today because of the incarnation in him of the immortal soul, a spark of his primeval ancestor's life. The Aranda becomes aware of this mystery of life as he undergoes the rites of initiation, in which he learns the sacred history of his ancestors. It is a sort of anamnesis, a remembering of the preexistence of his immortal soul in the mythical sacred history—a recollection accompanied by the acute realization of the immortal soul's involvement in temporary, phenomenal existence.

Greece, India, Iran. The ancient Greek doctrine of metempsychosis presupposes the incarnation of preexistent and immortal souls in successive bodies, human and animal, and even in inanimate substances. Pythagoras certainly believed in the transmigration of souls (Xenophanes, frag. 7); according to him, the human soul, despite its immortality, has been imprisoned in the body and condemned to a cycle of reincarnation due to the fall from its original state of bliss. A similar idea was held by Empedocles: man's immortal soul has fallen from its proper abode into the world, into the physical body, due to its primal sin. Condemned to the physical world, the fallen soul is destined to wander through a series of incarnations until it is restored to the primeval state of bliss from which it has fallen. Plato contrasts the immortal part of the soul, which the Demiurge has created, with the mortal part, including perception, which is added by the created deities at the moment of union with the body (e.g., *Timaeus* 69c–d). Immediately before incarnation, the immortal soul drinks from the waters of Lethe ("forgetfulness"); "burdened with a load of forgetfulness and wrongdoing," the soul "sheds her wings and falls to the earth" (*Phaedrus* 248c), that is, it falls into the physical world, into the body which is a "tomb" (*Gorgias* 493c), imprisoned by the cycle of becoming and incarnation. But, it is still possible for the immortal soul to *learn*, to recall its extraterrestrial experience of the perfect condition that existed prior to the fall (cf. especially *Meno* 81c–d). For Plato, to live fully and meaningfully is, after all, to remember a discarnate, purely spiritual existence; it is an anamnesis of the soul's true identity, that is, a re-cognition of its heavenly origin.

This Greek mythology of the soul, more or less hostile to the world of matter and the physical body, was incorporated into gnosticism, a set of doctrines characterized by anticosmic dualism. Man, as viewed by the gnostics, is constituted by three components: the self, the soul, and the body. The physical body belongs to the deficient world of nature *(phusis)*, but the soul is also part of this evil world. Man's psychic activities arise from and are limited by the continual flux of natural events. It is only the self that transcends the evil world. It is divine in nature, hence not subject to time and change; it is indestructible. Where is the original home of the divine self, the spiritual part of man? The gnostic myth narrates, with manifold variations, the fate of the self, its origin in the world of light, its tragic fall into the alien world, and its imprisonment in the physical body. Salvation consists, in the last analysis, in the emancipation of the self from the dark world of matter and the physical body and its return to its genuine home, the world of light.

India presents us with a doctrine similar to gnosticism, namely, Sāṃkhya-Yoga, whose central message may be summed up as follows: (1) man's destiny in the world is conditioned by the mysterious interplay between the self *(puruṣa)*, which is indestructible, eternal, and not subject to change, and matter *(prakṛti)*, which is subject to time and transformation and which constitutes man's psychophysiological complex; (2) the self is essentially a stranger to the world of matter, into which for unknown reasons it has fallen and been enslaved, resulting in the oblivion of its original, true identity; and (3) deliverance *(mokṣa)* begins when the self remembers its eternal freedom and tries to dissociate itself through the practice of yoga from the world of matter.

However, in India the tragic view of the incarnation coexists peacefully with another, more positive view. The Hindu god Viṣṇu, out of his profound concern for the welfare of the universe, has frequently embodied himself wholly or partially in the phenomenal world. According to one of the earliest versions of the doctrine contained in the *Bhagavadgītā*, he incarnates himself in the person of Kṛṣṇa, but he is also able to manifest himself in other bodily forms, human and animal. "Whenever the law of righteousness withers away," Viṣṇu declares, "I come into being age after age for the protection of the good, for the destruction of evildoers, and for the setting up of the law of righteousness" *(Bhagavadgītā* 4.7–8). While Hindu myths and rituals have concentrated attention on Viṣṇu's ten primary incarnations, in some formulations four saviors appear as his *avatāra*s, or incarnations, each ushering in one of the four cosmic ages constituting a *mahāyuga*, a complete cosmic cycle. In the *kṛtayuga*, which lasts 4,800 divine years (with one divine year corresponding to 360 human years), Viṣṇu makes his appearance as the sage Kapila, while in the *tretāyuga*, lasting 3,600 divine years, he appears as the universal monarch Cakravartin. In the third cosmic age, *dvāparayuga*, of 2,400 divine years, the supreme being incarnates himself as the sage Vyāsa, and in the final cosmic age, *kaliyuga*, lasting 1,200 divine years, he will manifest himself as Kalki, a sort of messianic figure who will come in glory to establish the golden age, judging the wicked, rewarding the virtuous, and ruling over the entire universe in peace and prosperity.

The ancient Iranians of the Parthian period had an ardent hope or expectation for Mithra incarnate, who would come at the end of the world as the great universal monarch and savior. This king and savior will descend on the Mount of Victories in the form of a column of light or a shining star to be born in a cave. He will be given birth by a human mother, but in truth he is of heavenly origin; he descends from above with the light, that is, he is the child of light. There were, in fact, magi who lived near the Mount of Victories; every year, at a certain fixed date, they climbed the mountain in which there was a cave, and quietly prayed to the heavenly god for three days, waiting for the appearance of the star.

Kings, Emperors, Imams. The status of kings was often defined in terms of God incarnate. In ancient Egypt, for example, the king was believed to be divine in essence. His coronation, usually celebrated at the beginning of the new year, signified not an apotheosis but an epiphany, a self-manifestation of the god. As long as he ruled, the king was identified with the god Horus; in fact, he was Horus incarnate in his earthly existence, but upon his death he was mystically assimilated to Osiris, the god of rebirth and immortality. [*See* Kingship.]

The Greco-Roman world generally dissociated itself from the notion that the king was the incarnation of a certain god, despite the fact that royal titles such as *The Young Dionysos* and *Epiphanes* were often used by kings in the Hellenistic period. According to Arthur Darby Nock, the only exception was Ptolemy XIII of the mid-first century BCE, who demonstrably considered himself to be Dionysos incarnate, probably under the influence of the pharaonic conception of the king as Horus incarnate.

While the Chinese emperor was generally called Son of Heaven *(t'ien-tzu)* and as such was considered the earthly representative of Heaven or heavenly will, some emperors were regarded as incarnations of the Buddha. For example, the founder of the Northern Wei dynasty (386–534), T'ai-tzu, was regarded by the eminent monk Fa-kuo as the Tathāgata in person, an incarnation of the Buddha. This idea was iconographically represented in the caves of Yün-kang to the west of Ta-t'ung, the capital of the empire until 494. Moreover, toward the end of the seventh century the Empress Wu Chao, who was a strong supporter of Buddhism, was considered to be the incarnation of Maitreya, the future Buddha. Among the Tibetans, the Dalai Lama has been accepted as an incarnation of the bodhisattva Avalokiteśvara.

In ancient Japan, the emperor was explicitly called the *akitsumi kami* ("manifest *kami*"), that is, the god who manifested himself in human form in the phenomenal world. The essential part of the Japanese conception of sovereignty was the belief in the emperor's heavenly origin, and this belief was clearly expressed in the myths of Ninigi, the grandson of the sun goddess Amaterasu. Ninigi is born in the heavenly world and then descends onto the summit of Mount Takachiho, carrying the three items of the sacred regalia as well as the heavenly mandate guaranteeing his eternal sovereignty on earth. The emperor was identified with this mythic figure at the annual harvest festival as well as on the occasion of his enthronement festival.

In Islam, more particularly among the Shīʿah, the imam enjoyed a truly exalted and significant status; while among the Sunnīs an imam is no more than a leader of congregational prayer at a local mosque, among the Shīʿah the imam was endowed with a power at once political and religious. Like the caliph, he was one who ruled the community in mercy and justice, but unlike the caliph, who had no legal authority, the imam was empowered to interpret the *ḥaqīqah,* or esoteric meanings of the Qurʾān and Islamic law. This power was based on the Shīʿah conviction that Muḥammad's charisma, or spiritual gift, which he received from God, would be transmitted genealogically only within his household. It was natural that the imam became the central focus of Shīʿah faith to such an extent that he was believed to be the embodiment of the divine light. Some extreme sects of the Ismāʿīlī movement went even further in believing that the imam was the incarnation of the godhead itself. The Druze of the Lebanon Mountains hold the Caliph Ḥākim (r. 996–1021) of the Fatimid dynasty in Egypt to be the incarnation of the godhead, now in concealment but with the promise of a return.

Buddhism. Buddhism was founded by Siddhārtha Gautama of the Śākya clan in India, who left his home in quest of truth, devoted himself to the practice of meditation, and finally attained enlightenment. Hence he is also called the Buddha, the Enlightened One. During the early centuries of the history of Buddhism, this historical Buddha commanded the primary attention of Buddhists.

However, as a new trend of the Buddhist movement called the Mahāyāna developed in the course of the second century BCE, a shift occurred in Buddhology; emphasis was now placed less on the historical Buddha than on the Eternal Buddha. This Eternal Buddha is transcendent, absolute, and infinite, embodying the universal and cosmic truth. Hence he is called the *dharmakāya* ("body of the law"), the essential Buddha who is the ultimate reality as viewed by Mahāyāna Buddhism. The Eternal Buddha does not wish, however, to hold himself aloof from the phenomenal world; out of his deep compassion for mankind in pain and suffering he has incarnated himself in the person of Siddhārtha Gautama, as the *nirmāṇakāya* ("body of transformation").

This doctrine is elaborated, for example, in the *Saddharmapuṇḍarīka Sūtra,* also known as the *Lotus Sutra.* The scripture presents the Buddha in two aspects: his absolute aspect in the form of the Eternal Buddha, which is dealt with in the section following chapter 15, while the section preceding this chapter is concerned with his relative aspect in the person of the historical Śākyamuni Buddha, who assumed human form for the sake of benefiting all sentient beings. According to the doctrine of the "Tendai school" in medieval Japan, the absolute and the relative are in essence qualitatively equal; they represent the two different aspects of the Buddha but, in reality, are one and the same.

Japanese Buddhism, more particularly, the Shingon school of Buddhism, has also unfolded what may be called a cosmotheism, a fascinating conception of the cosmos as the embodiment of the Buddha Mahāvairocana. The place of central importance in Shingon Buddhism is occupied no longer by the historical Buddha but rather by the Cosmic Buddha Mahāvairocana (Jpn., Dainichi, "great sun"); just as the sun is the source of light, illuminating the whole universe and giving life to all forms of existence, so Mahāvairocana is the Great Illuminator of all existence, both animate and inanimate. He is transcendent, absolute, and eternal because he is identified with the *dharmakāya.* However, Mahāvairocana is not only transcendent but also immanent in the universe. This Buddha is cosmic in nature because, according to Shingon Buddhism, he embodies himself in the six great elements constituting every form of existence in the universe: earth, water, fire, wind, space, and mind. These six elements are interfused and in a state of eternal harmony. In fact, the whole universe is viewed as the "*samaya* (symbolic) body" of the Buddha Mahāvairocana. When the universe is referred to as the Buddha's *samaya* body, it means two things at the same time: first, the cosmos symbolizes and points to the ultimate reality, Mahāvairocana identified with the *dharmakāya;* and second, while the ultimate reality embodies itself in the cosmos, for its part the cosmos participates substantially in the ultimate reality itself. Accordingly, the cosmos is a sanctified world endowed with the quality of the sacred, assuming profound soteriological value.

Christianity. That God was incarnated in the person of Jesus of Nazareth in order to save mankind is a basic tenet of Christianity. One of the earliest confessions of faith pronounced by the primitive church (*Phil.* 2:6–2:11) speaks of the preexistent divine figure Christ Jesus, who condescended to take on human form, won victory in his death over the cosmic forces of evil, and reigns now with God in heaven. In the *Gospel of John*, dating from the end of the first century, Christ Jesus is presented as the incarnate Word (Logos) of God (*Jn.* 1:1–1:14). In sharp contrast to the portrait of the life of Jesus in the synoptic Gospels, John identifies him as the preexistent divine being who, descending from heaven, moves mysteriously through human life, proclaiming heavenly messages and working miracles, and who even foretells his ascension to heaven following his impending suffering and death. John's language may sound preeminently gnostic, but the content of his central message, namely, that the divine Logos had become human flesh, was certainly antignostic.

Christian gnostics accepted the belief that Christ was the divine Logos, the chief intermediary between God and man. However, they rejected the idea that the Logos took on human flesh, since to them the flesh was both evil and insubstantial. Characteristically, they denied the reality or historicity of the incarnation: the human life of Christ was spiritual but not material; Christ hovered over mortal life, never really participating in the birth, suffering, and death of the historical Jesus. [*See* Docetism.] The Christian church set itself against this docetic view in such affirmation of the Apostles' Creed as "God the Father Almighty, creator of heaven and earth." By implication this was an affirmation of the goodness of all God's creation, material as well as spiritual. Similar affirmations concerning Jesus' birth, suffering, and death were directed against the gnostic denial of the incarnation of Jesus Christ. Moreover, the assertion in the Apostles' Creed of the resurrection of the dead affirmed the salvation of the whole person and not merely the discarnate soul, spirit, or self. It is thus significant that Christian orthodoxy affirmed the humanity of Christ and the goodness and reality of the cosmos against gnosticism and any form of the gnostic view of man and the universe. "After the Incarnation," Mircea Eliade states in his *Myth and Reality* (p. 172), "the World has been reestablished in its original glory." The phenomenal world, our world, the world as it is, is a *sanctified* cosmos because Jesus Christ the Savior has dwelt in it.

The Christian church attempted to articulate the nature of the person of Jesus Christ as God incarnate at the First Council of Nicaea (325). It adopted a creed that included such phrases to define Christ as "begotten not made," "begotten before all ages," and "of one essence with the Father." Thus Christ was declared to be *homoousios*, "consubstantial," with God the Father, a doctrine that was to be formulated later by Augustine as *una substantia tres personae* ("one substance in three persons"); Christ was essentially divine without being a kind of "second God." Once this result was generally accepted, a further question arose: how are the divine and human elements related to each other in the person of the historical Jesus? After apparently endless debates and anathemas, the orthodox view was formulated at the Council of Chalcedon (451): two natures of Christ, divine and human, are perfectly blended in one person; Jesus Christ is *vere Deus vere homo* ("truly God and truly man").

Twentieth-Century Views. While the affirmative view of incarnation has apparently won the victory, the tragic view of the destiny of the soul, as it was classically expressed by Plato, gnosticism, and Sāṃkhya-Yoga, is far from dead; on the contrary, it has often asserted itself ever since. In fact, as Martin Buber has aptly stated, man's self-understanding has gained "depth" in those crisis periods in history when man has felt homeless in the physical world in which he lives, becoming aware of his acute alienation from it. Our century, one such crisis period, has shown a keen interest in the gnostic outlook on life and the universe, as it is reflected in the writings of C. G. Jung, Hermann Hesse, and Martin Heidegger. For Heidegger, for example, the world is no longer a home for modern man but an alien realm; we are homeless in the world. Moreover, we live in a period of cosmic night, and the darkness of this cosmic night is to continue for some time. According to him, our soul is not in its proper place in this evil world; here, it is a stranger, imprisoned in the physical body. The soul is destined to leave this world behind and, becoming "a blue soul," to set out for the dark wandering, journeying toward the land of the evening.

[*For a discussion of incarnation in Indian religions, see* Avatāra. *See also* Soul *and* Reincarnation, *which treats the topic within the conceptual framework of repeated incarnations.*]

BIBLIOGRAPHY

There is no single book dealing with the problem of incarnation in the general history of religions. On masks and their religious meaning in prehistory, see Johannes Maringer's *Vorgeschichtliche Religion: Religionen im steinzeitlichen Europa* (Einsiedeln, Switzerland, 1956), pp. 184ff., edited and translated by Mary Ilford as *The God of Prehistoric Man* (New York, 1960), pp. 146ff.

Hutton Webster offers us basic information on the periodic return of the ancestral spirits in Polynesia and Melanesia in his

Primitive Secret Societies (New York, 1980). On the Aranda conception of the immortal soul, there is a fascinating account in Mircea Eliade's *Australian Religions: An Introduction* (Ithaca, N.Y., 1973), pp. 44–59.

The incarnation of the soul in the Greek philosophical tradition has been competently discussed by W. K. C. Guthrie in *The Earlier Presocratics and Pythagoreans* (pp. 306ff.) and *The Presocratic Tradition from Parmenides to Democritus* (pp. 249ff.), volumes 1 and 2 of his *A History of Greek Philosophy* (Cambridge, 1962 and 1965). The best single book on the gnostic view of the destiny of man and his immortal soul in the world remains Hans Jonas's *The Gnostic Religion*, 2d ed., rev. (Boston, 1963). On Sāṃkhya-Yoga, there is a concise account in Robert C. Zaehner's *Hinduism* (London, 1962), pp. 67ff. Focusing his attention on the fate of the immortal self in the world, Mircea Eliade has compared gnosticism with Sāṃkhya-Yoga in his essay "Mythologies of Memory and Forgetting," now included in his *Myth and Reality* (New York, 1963), pp. 114–138. There is a fine comparative study of the avatar beliefs of India and the Christian doctrine of the incarnation in Geoffrey Parrinder's *Avatar and Incarnation* (New York, 1970).

The eschatological expectation of the birth of the savior Mithra in ancient Iran has been elucidated by Geo Widengren in his *Iranisch-semitische Kulturbegegnung in parthischer Zeit* (Cologne, 1960), pp. 62–86. See also Mircea Eliade's *Méphistophélès et l'androgyne* (Paris, 1962), pp. 60ff., translated by J. M. Cohen as *The Two and the One* (Chicago, 1965), pp. 51–55.

Major problems of Greco-Roman kingship have been discussed authoritatively by Arthur Darby Nock in volume 1 (pp. 134ff.) and volume 2 (pp. 928ff.) of his *Essays on Religion and the Ancient World* (Cambridge, Mass., 1972), with an introduction by Zeph Stewart. On the conception of kingship in ancient Japan, see my article "Sacred Kingship in Early Japan: A Historical Introduction," *History of Religions* 15 (1976): 319–342.

Mahāyāna Buddhism has attempted to explain the historical Buddha Śākyamuni as an incarnation of the Eternal Buddha. See, in this connection, a brief but illuminating account of the doctrine of the "three bodies" *(trikāya)* of the Buddha by T. R. V. Murti, *The Central Philosophy of Buddhism*, 2d ed. (London, 1970), pp. 284–287. On the conception of the cosmos as the embodiment of the Buddha Mahāvairocana, see *Kūkai: Major Works*, translated, with an account of Kūkai's life and a study of his thought, by Yoshito S. Hakeda (New York, 1972), pp. 76ff.

On the history of the Christian doctrines of the incarnation, there is an admirable account by Jaroslav Pelikan in *The Emergence of the Catholic Tradition, 100–600*, volume 1 of his *The Christian Tradition* (Chicago, 1971).

MANABU WAIDA

INCENSE. The term *incense* (from Latin *incendere*, to burn or kindle) has the same meaning as the word *perfume*, i.e., the aroma given off with the smoke *(per fumar)* of an odoriferous substance when burned. Incense may then be associated with the perfume arising from the burning of substances that produce a pleasant odor. Aloe, camphor, cloves, sandalwood, myrrh, frankincense, cedar, juniper, balsam, galbanum, and turpentine have been used as incense. Since ancient times incense has been an important part of religious rites and practices in various regions of the world. Incense has been used to appease the gods, sanctify a place or an object, display reverence and respect, honor commitments, tie bonds, and seal promises and friendships. Valued as a precious commodity, it was offered as a gift to honored personages: frankincense and myrrh were two of the gifts the wise men of the East brought to the infant Jesus.

In association with concepts of purity and pollution, incense plays a major role in purification rites and customs. Incense smoke is used for these purposes because of the transforming powers of fire, as well as the seemingly purificatory powers of sweet smells. Because its fragrance is thought to be pleasing to the gods, incense has played an important role in worship and is used in ceremonies of offering, prayer, intercession, or purification. It is used to attract the attention of, or establish a connection with, a deity and is also used to exorcise evil or harmful forces.

The Far East and India. In Chinese, the word *hsiang* can mean both "aromatic" and "incense." In China incense was sometimes burned in conjunction with aesthetic enjoyments like reading, writing compositions, or performing music; in Japan it was an important part of the tea ceremony. In Chinese Taoism, incense was used to disperse evil and to appease the gods; it was also employed in rituals for the cure of disease. Considered a punishment for evil deeds committed by the sufferer himself or by an ancestor, illness was regarded as a punishment by the San Kuan (Three Officials), the judges and officials of the dead. During the rituals for curing sickness, a formal appeal was made to mitigate and revoke the officials' judicial severity. Using the rising flame and smoke from the incense burner in the center of the oratory to transmit a message borne by spirits exteriorized from within his own body, the Taoist libationer submitted petitions *(chang)* to the appropriate bureau of the Three Heavens (San T'ien), where officials pronounced judgment on the appeal and marshaled celestial forces against the offending demons responsible for the illness. Incense played a major role in another Taoist ritual for fending off disease, the Mud and Soot Retreat or Retreat of Misery. The ritual was usually performed outdoors at a specially delimited sacred area, or altar *(t'an)*. It was a ceremony of collective contrition where the combined effects of clouds of incense, the light of many lamps, and the sound of the chanted liturgy produced a cathartic experience in the participants.

Incense is also central to the Taoist Chiao liturgy, which renews the community through communication with the gods. Chiao rites may be held for the ordination of priests or the birthdays of gods or may be held to ward off calamities. For the Chiao ritual, a village feast is held outside the temple, and an esoteric liturgy is performed inside the closed temple. In the temple ritual the main incense burner, the central object in the temple, is the focus of the rite. A symbolic incense burner is "lighted" inside the body of the main priest, whose meditation transforms him into a mediator with the divine and makes possible the efficacy of the rite. Incense is employed for the ecstatic symbolic journey to heaven performed inside a sacred area demarcated by five buckets of rice. Together with the burning incense, a document is burned ("sent off to heaven") as a "memorial to the throne" *(chang)*, which announces to Heaven the performance of the liturgy.

Incense also forms an important part of the Buddhist ritual ceremonies in Korea. When taking the vows of Buddhist priesthood, young initiates undergo a rite called Pul-tatta, or "receiving the fire." In this ceremony a moxa, or cone of burning incense, is laid upon the arm of the novice after the hair has been shaved off; the ignited cone is then allowed to burn slowly and painfully into the flesh. The remaining scar is considered a mark of dedication and holiness and commemorates the ceremony of initiation. Incense is used in ancestor worship as well; tablets containing the names of the departed written in gilt and black characters are placed on every household altar, where sacrifices are offered and incense burned.

At least until the late nineteenth century, incense timekeepers were used in Japanese Buddhist temples to mark the intervals at which the priest struck the great bell to call the people to prayer. The use of incense to measure time was an idea borrowed from China, and so in Japan these sticks were called "Chinese matches." In China the first literary mention of incense being used as a time indicator appears in the sixth century, although it may have been used much earlier. It was widely used from the tenth century on. To make the timekeepers, hardened-paste incense was prepared in sticks or spiral coils and marked into hourly intervals. Depending on the season, the burning time of the sticks was usually between seven to eleven *k'o*, one *k'o* being equivalent to about a half an hour of modern time. Sometimes a continuous trail of powdered incense was marked off into equal lengths and burned to indicate how much time had passed. The legacy of using incense sticks as timekeepers has been transferred to Hawaii, where many Japanese and Chinese have migrated.

In India, incense is used in both Hindu and Buddhist rituals. In Hindu rites it is offered in temples as an act of homage before the statue of the deity; in the *arati* ceremony, for instance, the incense censer or stick is rotated before the image of the deity in order to make an offering and evoke blessings. Fragrant incense was also used to waft prayers to the gods and to drive off foul-smelling demons.

The Ancient Near East. In ancient Egypt, incense was frequently used in cultic rituals. According to Plutarch, the Egyptians burned incense to the sun three times a day; Herodotus recounts that incense was daily burned before an image of a cow. Sacrifices were offered to the pharaoh, and incense was burned before him in the coronation procession. The importance of offering incense is evident from the title of a courtly official, the "Chief of the House of Incense." It was also an important element of funerary practices, since the soul of the dead was considered to ascend to heaven by the smoke of the burning incense.

Incense also figures in Mesopotamian mythology. In the Mesopotamian *Epic of Gilgamesh,* Gilgamesh's mother Ninsuna supplicated the gods, asking them to protect and befriend her son. She burned incense and offered it to the god of creation, Shamash, to show her reverence and receive his blessings. As Gilgamesh embarked on his mission to kill the Evil One, Huwawa, he heard the words of his mother and remembered the fragrant aroma of the incense.

Judaism, Christianity, Islam. According to the Hebrew scriptures, in ancient Israel incense was considered a holy substance and was reserved for Yahveh; it was included with the bread offered to him on the Sabbath (*Lv.* 24:7). Incense was placed in the Tent of Meeting (*Ex.* 30:34) and was used in the offerings of the first fruits (*Lv.* 2:15–16); it was offered in censers on the Day of Atonement when the high priest appeared before the mercy seat (*Lv.* 16:12ff.). Its use as a perfume is indicated in *Song of Songs* 3:6, which states that it was used to scent Solomon's couch. In Psalm 141 incense is likened to prayer.

Until the time of Constantine, incense was not used in public worship ceremonies of the Christian church. Its use as an offering was severely condemned by the early Fathers (e.g., Cyril of Alexandria and John Chrysostom) because of its association with pagan practices. Christians were identified by their refusal to burn incense before a statue of the emperor; Saturninus and Sisinnius were martyred for their refusal to do so. Those Christians who capitulated in order to escape death were known as *turificati,* or burners of incense. However, by the ninth century incense was used in some churches for the dedication and consecration of the altar. Incense was later incorporated into the liturgical services of both the Eastern Orthodox and Western churches.

In the Islamic tradition, incense is burned to create a pleasant aroma in places of worship, although it does not have any specific religious significance. The Muslims of India burn incense sticks on auspicious occasions such as weddings, births, or religious festivals. Incense is frequently offered at the tombs of saints, which people visit in order to obtain blessings. In the Ṣūfī *samāʿ* incense is often burned as the *dhikr* is chanted.

BIBLIOGRAPHY

Atchley, E. G. C. F. *A History of the Use of Incense in Divine Worship.* London, 1909.

Lucas, A. "Cosmetics, Perfumes and Incense in Ancient Egypt." *Journal of Egyptian Archaeology* 16 (May 1930): 41–53.

Schoff, Wilfred H. "Aloes." *Journal of the American Oriental Society* 42 (1922): 171–185.

Smith, G. Elliot. "Incense and Libations." *Bulletin of John Rylands Library* 4 (September 1917–January 1918): 191–262.

Van Beek, Gus W. "Frankincense and Myrrh." *Biblical Archaeologist* 23 (September 1960): 70–95.

HABIBEH RAHIM

INCUBATION. *See* Dreams; *see also* Asklepios.

INDIAN PHILOSOPHIES. The origin of all Indian philosophical systems may be traced to the *Ṛgveda,* traditionally regarded as the oldest and most important of the four Vedas. The relationship of the philosophical systems to this Veda is either a direct one, manifested as interpretations, explanations, and justifications of the Vedic texts by independent arguments—as in the six Vedic systems, or *darśanas*: Sāṃkhya, Yoga, Pūrva Mīmāṃsā, Vedānta, Nyāya, and Vaiśeṣika—or an indirect and essentially "protestant" one—as in the non-Vedic systems: Jainism, Buddhism, and the Cārvāka school. In addition to surveying the religious and philosophical issues raised by these traditions, I shall also refer, albeit briefly, to Tantric thought, traditionally considered to have developed independent of Vedic authority.

The *Ṛgveda* provides abundant evidence of a continuous struggle ranging over several centuries between two peoples, perhaps of two different ("Aryan" and "non-Aryan") races. Theirs was a struggle not only for military but also for cultural supremacy. The Aryans worshiped Indra as the king of the gods, and their mode of worship was the offering of sacrifices to Indra and the other gods. The non-Aryans, naturally, did not worship Indra, nor did they believe in sacrifice as a method of worship. Eventually, the non-Aryans were subjugated and integrated into a broader cultural pattern. It is interesting to note that the Upaniṣads, traditionally regarded as the "end of the Vedas" *(vedānta),* themselves came to abandon worship of the gods through sacrifice and developed instead a system of contemplation and meditation on the inner reality hidden behind the "world appearance" *(māyā).* [*For discussion of how the Vedic sacrifice was transformed in the Upaniṣads, see* Vedism and Brahmanism.]

This broadening of the cultural and philosophical outlook in order to accommodate conflicting theories and ways of life into one integrated whole, present only in a rudimentary form in the *Ṛgveda,* became a fundamental concern of later philosophical systems. Jainism and Buddhism, the most important of the nonorthodox schools, each eventually devised new logics and ontologies in order to accommodate all philosophical systems, both Vedic and non-Vedic. The Vedic schools, in order to integrate and reconcile opposing theories and ways of life, employed a method of gradation whereby philosophical schools were categorized in graded degrees of superiority or inferiority to each other. Both Vedic and non-Vedic schools also followed the usual methods of refuting the claims of rival schools in order to establish their own teachings. Hence it is usual in Indian philosophy to distinguish between (1) philosophical theories themselves and (2) their evaluation on a metaphilosophical level.

The Buddhist thinker Nāgārjuna (c. 150–250), for example, used a method of *reductio ad absurdum* to show that all philosophical theories current at his time were equally untenable. To avoid the charge of self-refutation, Nāgārjuna explicitly stated that his interpretation of Buddhism was not itself a philosophical theory *(dṛṣṭi).* The Jains, on the other hand, developed a logic of relative truths *(syādvāda)* and an ontology of manifold reality *(anekāntavāda)* to argue that all contemporary philosophical theories were equally tenable, though only from their own respective points of view. For the Jains (as for, in a modified form, Nāgārjuna's Mādhyamika philosophy) the absolute truth was that the truth of any one philosophical position was relative to a particular point of view, and that *this* absolute truth was not itself a relative truth. Thus, from the very beginning of philosophical thinking in India, a major concern of both theory and practice was to preserve the oneness of a culture that comprised so many competing and conflicting worldviews and ways of life. The task of reconciling rather than refuting other philosophies in one's culture was never of such vital concern to Western philosophers; indeed, this constitutes one of the main points of divergence between the philosophical traditions of India and the West.

That Indian philosophy as a whole has many unique features is principally due to a historical accident, namely, that during its formative period it was never influenced by the traditions of other cultures (although various Indian philosophies, especially Buddhism, developed new forms in cultures outside that of their origin). With the sole exception of the Cārvāka school, all Indian philosophical systems, Vedic and non-Vedic, accepted certain basic ideas on which they formulated their theories: (1) the law of *karman,* (2) the belief in the process of rebirth, and (3) an emphasis on mystic experience as the panacea for all evils. Even such familiar concepts as "body" and "mind" have meanings very different from those in the West. Despite these differences, Indian philosophies, like their Western counterparts, remain essentially rational justifications of experience, both mundane and mystical.

Epistemologies: Theories of Cognition. Although the Sanskrit word *jñāna* is philologically cognate with the English word *knowledge* through the Greek *gnosis,* *jñāna* is used in Indian philosophy in a different sense. The main points of difference are as follows.

1. *Jñāna* is always used only in the episodic sense to denote an occurrence of a cognitive act, never in the dispositional sense. The term *saṃskāra* is used for disposition in general, both in a physical and mental sense. In the context of cognition, *saṃskāra* denotes dispositional traces, usually unconscious, which, when stirred up or activated, produce conscious memory cognitions. I shall use "act" solely as an abbreviation of "actual mental state," not to refer to any activity or action.
2. *Jñāna* is used to denote not only propositional cognitive acts such as judging, believing, disbelieving, doubting, assuming, inferring, remembering, introspecting, or perceiving but also nonpropositional states such as sensing. *Jñāna* is therefore identical with awareness (of facts, objects, sensory qualities, mental states, and so forth).
3. *Jñāna* may be either true, false, or doubtful and therefore cannot be translated as *knowledge* in the sense in which it is employed in Western epistemology. For this reason, we shall use the term *cognition* as a translation of *jñāna.* [*See also* Jñāna *and* Vijñāna.]

Classification and definitions of cognition. Cognitions are classified first as informative (giving new information) and as recollective (as in memory, providing no new information). Second, cognitions are classified as either true or nontrue. Advaita Vedānta includes novelty (i.e., new information) in the very definition of true cognition and classifies recollective cognitions as untrue. Nyāya, on the other hand, classifies only informative cognitions into true and nontrue cognitions, recollective cognitions being true or nontrue depending on the truth (or nontruth) of the original informative cognition. Nyāya therefore does not include novelty in the definition of true cognition, which is cognition corresponding to its object. Nontrue cognitions, according to Nyāya, are again classified into doubt (without belief) and false cognitions (with belief).

Cognition is conceived of as being produced under certain conditions, and one of the main problems of Indian epistemology is to determine the different instrumental causes of the various forms of cognition. Every effect has an instrumental cause, which is roughly that by means of which the effect is produced. In the case of perceptual cognition, for example, the relevant sense organs are the instrumental causes. For the cognition of an inference, the sense organs cannot be instrumental causes, for inference is mediate cognition produced by the cognition of the premises. According to Nyāya the cognition of the universal major premise produces the cognition of the conclusion in very much the same manner as the sense organs produce perceptions. In many systems, specially the Nyāya and the Vaiśeṣika, cognitions are classified into perception, inference, and so forth by their instrumental causes. In other systems, such as the Advaita Vedānta of Śaṅkara, cognitions are classified by their intrinsic properties. Perception, for example, is defined as direct knowledge of objects; it does not matter if this direct cognition (knowledge) is not produced by the sense organs. The stock example is that of the person who forgets to count himself when counting persons present. If someone then tells him, "You are the tenth man," this sentence produces the direct cognition (knowledge) of himself being the tenth man; this is therefore to be counted as perceptual cognition even though not produced by the senses. The Jains and the Buddhists classify cognitions by their objects. Perception, for the Jains, is the cognition of the particularities of the object in detail, whereas inference is the cognition of the general features of objects. According to Buddhists like Dharmakīrti, perception is cognition of the particular object (with or without universals), and inference is cognition only of universals. Thus fire, when perceived and when inferred, is not cognized in the same way: In perception we cognize a particular fire; in inference we cognize a fire on the perception of smoke.

Sources of true cognition (knowledge). The instrumental causes of cognition are often regarded as sources of cognition. The usual practice is to consider the sources only of true cognitions, that is, knowledge in the Western sense. Different philosophical systems admit different sources of knowledge.

1. Jayarāśi, the only skeptic in India whose work is still available, examines the so-called sources of knowledge and concludes that there can be no knowledge, as the sources are all inadequate.
2. The Cārvāka philosophers (the materialists) hold that sense perception is the only source of knowledge; inference is impossible, involving as it does a knowledge of a universal relation between the major term and the middle term, for knowledge of this universal relation cannot be justified, although inference is useful in practical life.
3. Buddhist logicians like Dharmakīrti admit both perception and inference as sources of knowledge at the empirical level. They argue against the Cārvāka philosophers that causal relation, for example, logically justifies the knowledge of the universal relation needed for inference.
4. Sāṃkhya admits three sources, two being those of the Buddhists, and the third being sentences of any authoritative person. The Vedas, being revealed, are sources of infallible knowledge of the supramundane realm.
5. Nyāya adds a fourth source—analogy. Knowledge derived from this source is that of the meaning of a word based on known similarity. Thus, when a person has heard that a *gavaya* is like a cow, and has then perceived a *gavaya* by perceiving its similarity to a cow, he comes to know that this animal is called a *gavaya;* that is, he knows the meaning of the word *gavaya.*
6. Pūrva Mīmāṃsā and Advaita Vedānta add two further sources to the Nyāya list—nonperception and postulation. Nonperception is a special way of knowing negative facts, and postulation is a way of knowing by resolving contradiction. If, for example, someone knows that Caitra (a person) is fat but does not eat anything in the day, he knows by postulation that Caitra must be eating at night, for this is the only way of resolving the contradiction in the known facts.

Cognition of cognition. According to Nyāya, a cognition is the awareness of the object (fact) and nothing more. When one cognizes, for example, that the table is brown, one states, "The table is brown." If one wants to cognize this cognition, one has to perform a second-order cognitive act of introspection that has the first-order act as its object. This second-order introspective cognition is expressed in language as "I cognize that the table is brown."

Buddhist, Jain, Sāṃkhya, and Advaita Vedānta philosophers hold that when one cognizes an object, one cognizes in the same act also the act of cognizing. According to the Prabhākara school of Pūrva Mīmāṃsā, all three elements of cognition—the subject, the object, and the act of cognition—are cognized in every cognition. Thus, when one cognizes that the table is brown, one expresses this cognition in "I cognize that the table is brown."

Metaphysics. Indian systems differ in their ontologies in various ways. Cārvāka philosophers are materialists, and as they accept only perception as the source of knowledge, perceptible matter of four kinds—earth, water, fire, air—is reality. Consciousness, mind, self, and so on, are just by-products of matter. Nyāya-Vaiśeṣika philosophers admit eternal material atoms of four kinds—earth, water, air, and fire, plus ether (or space)—as well as a material inner sense *(manas)* of atomic size, space, time, an infinite number of eternal individual selves, and a God who fashions the universe out of preexistent matter in accordance with the merits and demerits of the individual selves. Apart from these "substances," these philosophers admit six categories of real entities: attributes, movement, universals, ultimate differentia of eternal entities, inherence as a relation, and negative objects such as absence or difference. In their theory of selves, these philosophers come close to the Cārvāka philosophers, for selves are essentially unconscious; consciousness belongs to them only when they are related to the body and the inner sense, which are both material. The world as we know it is real.

Jain philosophers, like Nyāya-Vaiśeṣika philosophers, admit both matter and self to be real, but unlike Nyāya-Vaiśeṣika, the self in this theory is essentially conscious. Many Jain philosophers do not postulate any God.

Buddhists may be classified into two groups according to their ontological theories. First, the Vaibhāsikas and the Sautrāntikas are realists, believing in the reality of an external material world over and above subjective ideas. Second, the Yogācāra and Mādhyamika philosophers are idealists and admit momentary ideas as the only reals. These four schools of Buddhism agree in denying any permanent reality, material or mental, simple or complex, particular or universal. All Vedic philosophies and Jainism hold that the ultimate reality is, by definition, that which is, was, and will be—that is, it must be eternal without beginning or end. The Buddhists are the only philosophers in India who deny this basic doctrine of all other systems.

The Advaita Vedānta of Śaṅkara upholds a form of extreme monism and idealism that denies the reality of multiplicity. Thus matter and consciousness cannot both be real; matter, being the principle of change, cannot be real. Thus consciousness, impersonal and infinite, devoid of attributes, relations, and actions, is the only reality. This reality cannot be identified with God, who is a person and is the creator of the universe. Yet the world, with its infinitely many objects and finite selves, cannot be wholly unreal, like the son of a barren woman, for the world is perceived and the unreal in the sense of the impossible cannot be perceived. Thus the world cannot be real, but cannot be unreal either; it is an appearance, *māyā,* in the technical sense of being incapable of description either as real or as unreal. [*See* Māyā.]

The monistic theory of the grammarians *(śabdādvaita),* as propounded by Bhartṛhari and his school (the Śabdādvaita), emphasizes the role that language plays in man's existence. Advaita Vedānta emphasizes the dualism between the subject and the object of knowledge, whereas Bhartṛhari emphasizes the dualism between words and the objects they denote. The ultimate reality is the subject, but the subject is not consciousness pure and simple. Consciousness is essentially speech, and the world emerges from consciousness only via speech; the world is founded in consciousness only as speech, not as the subject of knowledge. In empirical consciousness this creativity is not manifest, for speech at this level consists solely of uttering words—producing sounds but not the objects that the words denote. Yet when one goes deeper into one's consciousness, this semantic relation is seen to be founded in a more intimate and ultimately inseparable relationship. At the deepest level of consciousness, speech and the world melt into one unity, into an undifferentiated consciousness.

The Body and the Self. Problems concerning the nature of body and mind in Indian philosophies have no parallel in Western philosophy because most systems of Indian philosophy postulate the existence of *manas* and also a subtle body, neither of which corresponds to any concept in Western philosophy. This is surprising, for one would expect such a common, vitally important concept as "the body" to be formulated in more or less the same manner everywhere. I shall give here an exposition of the Sāṃkhya theory because it represents the dominant trend in this area.

Sāṃkhya distinguishes between the gross physical body and the subtle body. The gross body is that which comes into existence at the time of conception and goes out of existence at the time of death. Hence this body is said to be impermanent, unstable, and unchanging. But the subtle body—which comprises the sense organs (*indriyas*), the inner sense *(manas),* the ego *(ahaṃkāra),* and representations and ideas *(buddhi)*—survives the death of the gross body. This subtle body has all the psychological states described by Western philosophy. The individual self passes through a cycle of births and deaths until it attains liberation. The individual self is beginningless, just as the nescience that lies at the root of the individuality of the self consists of the element of pure consciousness together with the subtle body. It is the subtle body that determines the family in which the individual will be born in his next birth, the type of the gross physical body he will have, and so on. Thus the subtle body cannot come into being at the time of conception of the gross body.

The empirical subject is the subject known in introspection. It is that which knows objects (near or far; present, past, or future), performs actions (moral or immoral), and feels pleasure or pain. It is the principle of unity that runs through all types of objective knowledge, actions, and feelings of an individual. The empirical subject, in the context of knowledge, can be analyzed as a composite structure of four elements: consciousness, representation, the ego, and an instrument of deliberation. That the empirical subject involves consciousness is regarded as self-evident, but this element of consciousness is not, by itself, "I-consciousness"; rather, it is consciousness pure and simple.

The basic nature of cognitive consciousness is that it can have representations. Objects can be represented to consciousness only through mental states. Since the pure consciousness and the material objects cannot be directly related, Sāṃkhya philosophers postulate a reflecting plastic material element that relates consciousness on the one hand and the material object on the other. This element reflects the inner light of pure consciousness and thus becomes luminous itself, by borrowed light. External objects leave their impressions on this material through the sense organs. Being plastic, this material element assumes the shapes of the material objects, which are called representations of the material object. This luminous plastic material element is the *buddhi.* Knowledge of objects is not possible unless consciousness and object are somehow related. As there cannot be any direct relation between them, *buddhi* mediates between them by mirroring objects on the one hand and consciousness on the other.

The third element in the structure of the empirical subject is the ego *(ahaṃkāra),* which is responsible for I-consciousness. It also has the functions (1) of owning all mental states and acts of the individual, (2) of organizing and systematizing all contents of the *buddhi* into a unity (and hence it is ontologically dependent on the *buddhi*), (3) of restricting the person and separating him or her from other persons and objects, (4) of being the center around which all thoughts, actions, dreams, and desires revolve, of usurping all functions of the pure consciousness as the foundation of the person, (5) of being the principle of personal identity and, for ordinary (nonliberated) persons, of identifying itself with the body-mind complex.

The fourth element in the empirical subject is the *manas,* which is responsible for deliberation in the context of cognition and determination in willing. Sometimes there is conscious vacillation, as in a state of doubt that is resolved only by a deliberate act, which is different from mere representation. The ontological principle responsible for this act of resolving doubt is the *manas.*

These three ontological principles of *buddhi, ahaṃkāra,* and *manas* are not to be identified with faculties recognized in Western psychology, for in Sāṃkhya these principles are different elements (*tattva*s) and have different ontological status, *buddhi* being the primary of this triad, *ahaṃkāra* being an evolute of *buddhi,* and *manas* being an evolute of *ahaṃkāra.* This evolution of *tattva*s, which is not a temporal but an ontological process, is due to an ontological necessity of the empirical subject as a knower of objects. The empirical subject cannot function at all as a knower of objects without representations of objects, without the ego, and without the element that resolves doubt.

The Advaita Vedānta of Śaṅkara adds a fourth ontological element, *citta,* to explain memory, but combines all four as different functions of the inner sense *(antaḥkaraṇa),* thus coming closer to the psychological faculties noted by Western philosophers. The word *antaḥkaraṇa* is used in different senses in different systems of Indian philosophy. We have already seen that according to Nyāya, *antaḥkaraṇa* is identical with *manas.* But in Sāṃkhya and Advaita Vedānta, the word *antaḥkaraṇa* represents a triad: it is used to mean not merely the *manas* but also the *buddhi* and the ego. In Yoga, *antaḥkaraṇa* is called *citta.*

Incarnation and Liberation: Tantra Philosophy. Problems of mind-body relation become, at their deepest metaphysical level, problems of incarnation (associating consciousness with a body) and liberation (dissociating consciousness from body). Problems of incarnation may be of two types: general problems of how consciousness can have any body at all, and special problems of how a particular self or center of consciousness can have the particular body that is its own body. Problems of liberation are problems of explaining how the reverse process of dissociating from (ceasing to have) a body can be intelligible and shown to be possible. In both types of incarnation, and in liberation, the crucial problem is to understand the meaning of "consciousness having a body." Different Indian philosophies have different solutions to these problems, but I shall explain only the solution of Tantra philosophy, especially of Abhinavagupta, who discusses the subject in detail. [*See also the biography of Abhinavagupta.*]

The first point to be noted in connection with the analysis of "consciousness having a body" is that all individual selves are not at the same level of spiritual, moral, intellectual, or emotional perfection; all selves therefore do not "have" their bodies in the same sense. This is because their bodies do not have the same value, the same importance, the same function for them. For ordinary people, those living a life of self-interest, to have a body is to be identified with it. This is true of almost all children, for they are openly, shamelessly selfish. We may thus say that man is born with this attitude, that this is the original, natural attitude of man. Many people never grow out of it in their lives. A person at this level of life is just a conscious, living body, which he feels to be as one with himself. It is a mistake to say "my body" or that "I am the body" at this level. For everyone (at whatever level of perfection) always says, "I am myself"—that is, "I am I"—and never "I am the body," especially at the first level of existence, for the concept of the body as distinct from "myself" has not yet emerged. When, at whatever level of spiritual or moral development one says "my body," there is a separation, experiential or at least conceptual, between the body and its owner. But when the body (that is, what *we* call the body) is immediately felt as the ego, it is the owner, the "myself." This is because the ego is the owner of all mental states and also of the body. But if the body is identified with the ego (i.e., experienced as "myself"), then it cannot have another owner. Hence locutions like "my body" will mean "my I," which is, of course, nonsense.

We should explain here more fully what we mean by identifying the ego with the body. First, it is not the whole body, nor everything in the body that is immediately felt as "I." Leaving aside such outer growth as hair and nails, with which the ego does not identify itself, there are millions of living organisms within the body (e.g., blood corpuscles) that are not felt as "I" or as part of "myself." These organisms, though essential for the existence of the body, still have their separate lives; they live and propagate, fight and die, within the body, yet they are never felt as "myself." The ego identifies itself with the body only through the nervous system. Consciousness spreads itself all over the body through the afferent and efferent nerves (*agni* and *vāyu*).

Second, although consciousness is felt as spread over the body, and it is the body as a whole (though not the whole body) that is felt as "I," the ego at this stage of human existence is rooted in the lowest part of the spinal cord. The point of view of the ego is that of the crudest form of self-centeredness. That there is such a thing as the location of the ego in some portion of the nervous system that becomes its standpoint is experienced in suitable circumstances. Thus, when one trips or is suddenly without support, one has a feeling of emptiness in the pit of the stomach. This sickening feeling of emptiness, of being unsupported, also comes when one unexpectedly confronts grave personal danger for which one was not prepared at all, when one's very existence is threatened. Only in such times of crisis do we have immediate and overwhelming experience of ourselves being located in a part of the body. [*See also* Cakras.]

Development of spiritual, moral, intellectual, and emotional life is, again, the same as identifying oneself with the higher centers of the autonomous nervous system. The ego is lifted gradually to the level of the heart, the throat, the brain, and finally, at liberation, it goes beyond the body and is identified experientially with the whole universe and even transcends it. The upward movement of the ego, which is really just the broadening of the point of view, releases the individual from his narrow self-centeredness and opens him up to refined stimuli. An individual at higher levels of existence can perceive minute details and finer qualities, say, of music, of color, and even in the taste of food. He is genuinely concerned about everything, not merely human, not merely animate, but also about inanimate objects. He shrinks from wanton destruction of things, of plants, of animals, as much as from that of fellow human beings. He will be at peace with himself, that is, with the whole universe. [*See also* Jīvanmukti.] He also has a clearer intelligence and is a better seeker of truth, being devoid of all prejudices and personal preferences, and is wholly impersonal. This is the way of liberation, of freeing oneself from the limitations of thought, feeling, and action that characterize lower forms of human existence.

[*For individual discussions of the six systems of classical Hindu philosophy, see* Sāṃkhya; Yoga; Mīmāṃsā; Vedānta; Nyāya; *and* Vaiśeṣika. *For non-Vedic Indian philosophies, see* Jainism; Buddhist Philosophy; *and* Cārvāka. *Many of the figures and technical terms mentioned herein are the subjects of independent entries.*]

BIBLIOGRAPHY

Primary Sources

Bhatta, Kumaril. *Ślokavārtikavyākhyā*. Edited by S. K. Ramanatha Sastri. Madras, 1940.

"Bṛhatī" of Prabhākara Misra. 2 vols. Edited by S. K. Raghunatha. Banaras, 1906–1908.

Gautama's Nyāya Sūtras. Edited and translated by Ganganatha Jha. Poona Oriental Series, no. 62. Poona, 1939.

Īśvarakṛṣṇa. *The Tattva-kaumudi: Vacaspati Misra's Commentary on the Samkhya-Karika.* Translated and revised by Ganganatha Jha. Poona Oriental Series, no. 10. Reprint, Poona, 1957.

The Principal Upaniṣads. Edited and translated by Sarvepalli Radhakrishnan. New York, 1953.

Rig-Veda Sanhitā: A Collection of Ancient Hindu Hymns of the Rig-Veda. 6 vols. Edited and translated by H. H. Wilson. Reprint, Delhi, 1977–1978.

The Vedānta Sūtra, with the Commentary by Śaṅkara. Translated by George Thibaut. Reprint, New York, 1962.

Viśvanātha Nyayapancanana Bhattacarya. *Bhāṣā-pariccheda with Siddhanta-muktavali.* Translated by Swami Madhavananda. Calcutta, 1940.

The Yoga-system of Patañjali. Translated by James Haughton Woods. Harvard Oriental Series, vol. 17. 3d ed. Delhi, 1966. A translation of the *Yoga Sūtra.*

Secondary Sources

Bhattacharyya, Sibajiban. "The Middle Term." *Notre Dame Journal of Formal Logic* 9 (1968): 229–232.

Bhattacharyya, Sibajiban. "Some Principles and Concepts of Navya-Nyāya Logic and Ontology." *Our Heritage* (Calcutta) 24 (1976): 1–16; 25 (1977): 17–56.

Conze, Edward. *Buddhist Thought in India* (1962). Reprint, Ann Arbor, 1970.

Dasgupta, Surendranath. *A History of Indian Philosophy.* 5 vols. London, 1922–1955.

Kalupahana, David J. *Causality: The Central Philosophy of Buddhism.* Honolulu, 1975.

Radhakrishnan, Sarvepalli. *Indian Philosophy.* 2 vols. London, 1923.

Sastri, Gaurinath. *The Philosophy of Word and Meaning: Some Indian Approaches, with Special Reference to the Philosophy of Bhartṛhari.* Calcutta, 1959.

SIBAJIBAN BHATTACHARYYA

INDIAN RELIGIONS. [*This entry provides an introduction to the indigenous religious traditions of India. It consists of four articles:*

An Overview
Rural Traditions
Mythic Themes
History of Study

For treatment of nonindigenous traditions, see Islam, *article on* Islam in South Asia; Judaism, *article on* Judaism in Asia and Northeast Africa; *and* Christianity, *article on* Christianity in Asia.]

An Overview

The Indians, anthropologically a mixture of immigrant Aryans and partly autochthonous peoples, gradually elaborated a many-sided, highly developed culture rooted in the archaic structure of the human mind. This culture is characterized by an often almost complete integration of heterogeneous elements, by unity in diversity, by homogeneity despite the utmost variety and complexity of its ethnic and social composition, by a multitude of languages and different cultural patterns, and by a great diversity in mental character and socioreligious customs, cults, beliefs, practices, and ways of life varying widely both regionally and, within the same region, from class to class. Indian culture gives free scope to the emotional and imaginative sides of human nature, to speculative, more or less visionary thinking and modes of apprehension, and it has long preserved the cohesion of its provinces: religion, art, literature, and social organization.

Vedism. The religious life reflected in the oldest Indian literature in preclassic Sanskrit, the Veda (from about the thirteenth century BCE), is that of a predominantly ritual and sacrificial system (Vedism) developing, almost in seclusion, at first in the Punjab, later in the Ganges Plain, among the immigrant Aryans (Indo-Europeans), whose ideas and representations of the divine constitute an almost unified synthesis embodied in an elaborate mythology partly paralleled by ritual equivalences. Vedic thought was based on the belief in an inextricable coordination of nature, human society, ritual, and the sphere of myth and the divine; it was also founded on the belief that these spheres influence one another continuously and that men have, by means of ritual, an obligatory part to play in the maintenance of universal order and the furtherance of their common interests. In later times also, Indians have constantly sought correspondences between objects and phenomena belonging to distinct spheres of nature and conceptual systems. Many hymns and individual stanzas of the oldest literary corpus (the *Ṛgveda Saṃhitā*, an anthology drawn from family traditions) were intended for the cult and used in the liturgy of spectacular solemn *(śrauta)* ceremonies, which gradually increased in number, length, and complexity. These ceremonies were to ensure the orderly functioning of the world for the benefit of noble or wealthy patrons. The rites were performed in the open on a specially prepared plot—there were no temples or idols—by specialized officiants. Part of this literature was employed, along with texts from the *Atharvaveda Saṃhitā*, in the domestic or magic ritual performed by a householder or single priest to ensure an individual's health, safety, success, prosperity, and longevity. These texts and the ritual formulas of the *Yajurveda*, which invariably fulfill some ritual function, are collectively called *mantra*s. They are believed to be revelations of aspects of the divine, the product of the exalted experiences of sages (*ṛṣi*s) and hence constitute sacred and inherently powerful verbal formulas for producing a desired result. Some Vedic *mantra*s remained in Hinduist rites, which, however, generally require other ones.

No definite chronology can be established for Vedic literature or the development of religious ideas and ritual practices. We do know that the collections of hymns were succeeded by the Brāhmaṇas, texts that discuss rites and rituals and explain their origin, meaning, and validity. These sacral acts, being the counterpart of the cosmic drama, are in fact also the symbolic expression of speculations about the origin and functioning of the universe and the significance, activity, and operation of the powers, personal and impersonal, presiding over its provinces and manifesting their presence and influence. Thus the ceremonious construction of a special place for the ritual fire is believed to reintegrate the creator god, enabling him to continue his creative activity and to bring about a transformation and higher existence of the patron of the sacrifice, who in and through this ritual is identified with the creator and delivered from death. Mainly based on the Brāhmaṇas are the Śrautasūtras, manuals in which the rites are for practical purposes systematically and authoritatively described. No information is given on the earlier, prehistoric cult, which cannot be reconstructed. These works arrange the solemn rites in three classes: the partly inherited bloodless sacrifices, the more elaborate animal sacrifices, and the typically Indian soma ceremonies. In the course of time these elite *śrauta* rituals fell largely into disuse and were superseded by Hinduist rites performed at the expense of and for the benefit of much larger parts of the population. [*See also* Vedas *and* Brāhmaṇas and Āraṇyakas.]

Hinduism. Some prehistoric forms of Hinduism—the civilization of the Hindus, consisting of their beliefs, practices, and socioreligious institutions—must have existed at the Vedic period, especially in the unrecorded religion of the lower classes, and probably earlier. Domestic ritual, which is entirely different from the solemn rites, consists of many rites that, though described and systematized by brahman authorities in the Vedic Gṛhyasūtras, are in essence not typically Vedic, or rather constitute Vedic varieties of widespread rites of passage, rites of appeasement, cult of the dead, and so on. Later chapters of this literature show markedly non-Vedic and post-Vedic influences, such as strong leanings toward Vaiṣṇava ritualism, which attest to the gradual incorporation of non-Vedic rites and substitution of extra-Vedic elements for those recognized by the original compilers of Hindu rites and practices. Gradually these elements became more prominent.

Non-Aryan influences. How much influence was exerted by the religions of the non-Aryan inhabitants of India on the formation and development of Hinduism is a matter of dispute. Although aborigines may have contributed some elements, their religion is generally different in many respects (e.g., they do not venerate the cow, and they allow their widows to remarry). The Vedic religion had no demonstrable relation with the great civilizations of Harappa, Mohenjo-Daro, and vast regions to the east of the Indus Valley (c. 2500–1500 BCE). As long as the graphic symbols on seals from these sites are not convincingly deciphered and the language is not identified (that it was Dravidian—the name of non-Aryan languages of southern India—is still unproved conjecture), most of the conclusions drawn from archaeological material and argumentation regarding links with elements or characteristics of older and even contemporary Hinduism remain as speculative as the hypothesis of a predominantly influential Dravidian substratum. Do the clay figurines of women really attest to some form of worship of a mother goddess that continued in the historical period, or to the existence of a prehistoric Śaiva *śakti* cult? Is the figure of a male dancer identical with the dancing Śiva? The wide distribution in various countries of, for instance, objects that may have been amulets or votive offerings should prevent us from hastily regarding their occurrence in Hinduist religions as an uninterrupted continuance of a function supposedly attributed to certain Indus objects. [*See also* Indus Valley Religion.]

General characteristics. The main current of Hinduism, the so-called great tradition, is a remarkably continuous whole. The tendency to maintain continuity has always been deep-rooted but did not exclude the constant accretion and integration of further elements derived from non-Aryan peoples, extraneous sources (invaders on the northwestern frontier may have contributed to the custom of *satī*, the self-immolation practiced by widows, for example), and the activities of individual religious leaders. While continuity and change have been the prevailing patterns, incorporation and synthesis between the new and the traditional usually were more obvious than the often almost imperceptible elimination of those elements that no longer had a useful and recognizable function. Nevertheless, it is more common to draw upon the past than to invent anew, and apparently original ideas may be foreshadowed by concepts apparent centuries earlier. Thus many features of Hinduism have their roots in the Vedic past, and some characteristic ideas inherited from that past and developed in a few main currents—primarily doctrines of salvation—have up to the present largely determined the Indian view of life and the world.

The older Upaniṣads are the first recorded attempts at systematizing Indian philosophical thought. They are esoteric supplements to the Brāhmaṇas, intended for advanced pupils with a bent for reflection, abstract speculation, and philosophical discussion rather than ritual theory, and therefore answering the needs of ascetics and anchorites. Few Indians are inclined to reject the contents of these Upaniṣads, with which every subsequent philosophy had to show itself in accord. While emphasizing the philosophical value of the Vedic tradition, they are essentially concerned with describing the nature of what is alternately called *brahman* (the Absolute) or *ātman* (universal soul), and its relation with the individual soul (often called *jīva*). The realization of the identity of the latter with the former came to be substituted for the ritual method of conquering death and attaining integral life, the ultimate goal of all speculation. Being compilations, the Upaniṣads do not present a homogeneous philosophical theory, but there was a move to reconcile the references to the dualistic and evolutionistic doctrines of what was to become the influential Sāṃkhya school of philosophy with the prevailing monistic doctrines. Hinduism, directed by these works toward monism, has largely sought its inspiration in them.

There are a number of more or less constant elements of Hinduism. The central focus of India's spiritual life is the belief in and search for an uncreated eternal, fundamental principle *(brahman)*, the ultimate source and goal of all existence. *Brahman* is the One that is the All and the sole reality, which transforms itself into the universe, or causes all existence and all beings to emanate from itself, and which is the self *(ātman)* of all living beings. *Brahman* may also be conceived of as a personal "high god" (usually as Viṣṇu or Śiva), characterized by sublime and adorable qualities. Further elements are the confidence that one's own existence and the culture of one's community are founded on an eternal and infallible basis, and the craving for building one's life and ideals on this firm foundation; the recognition of a pristine body of religious literature (the Veda) as an eternal and absolute authority considered to be *brahman* appearing as words, however unknown its contents; and acknowledgment of the spiritual supremacy by birth of the brahmans, another manifestation of *brahman*, who are regarded as representing the norm of ritual purity and who enjoy social prestige. The keystone of Hinduist ethics is the belief in the unity of all life and its corollary respect for life and fellow feeling with all living beings *(ahiṃsā)*; the doctrine of transmigration and rebirth (*saṃsāra*, a post-Vedic term), first adumbrated in one of the oldest Upaniṣads (c. 600 BCE), and its complement, the belief

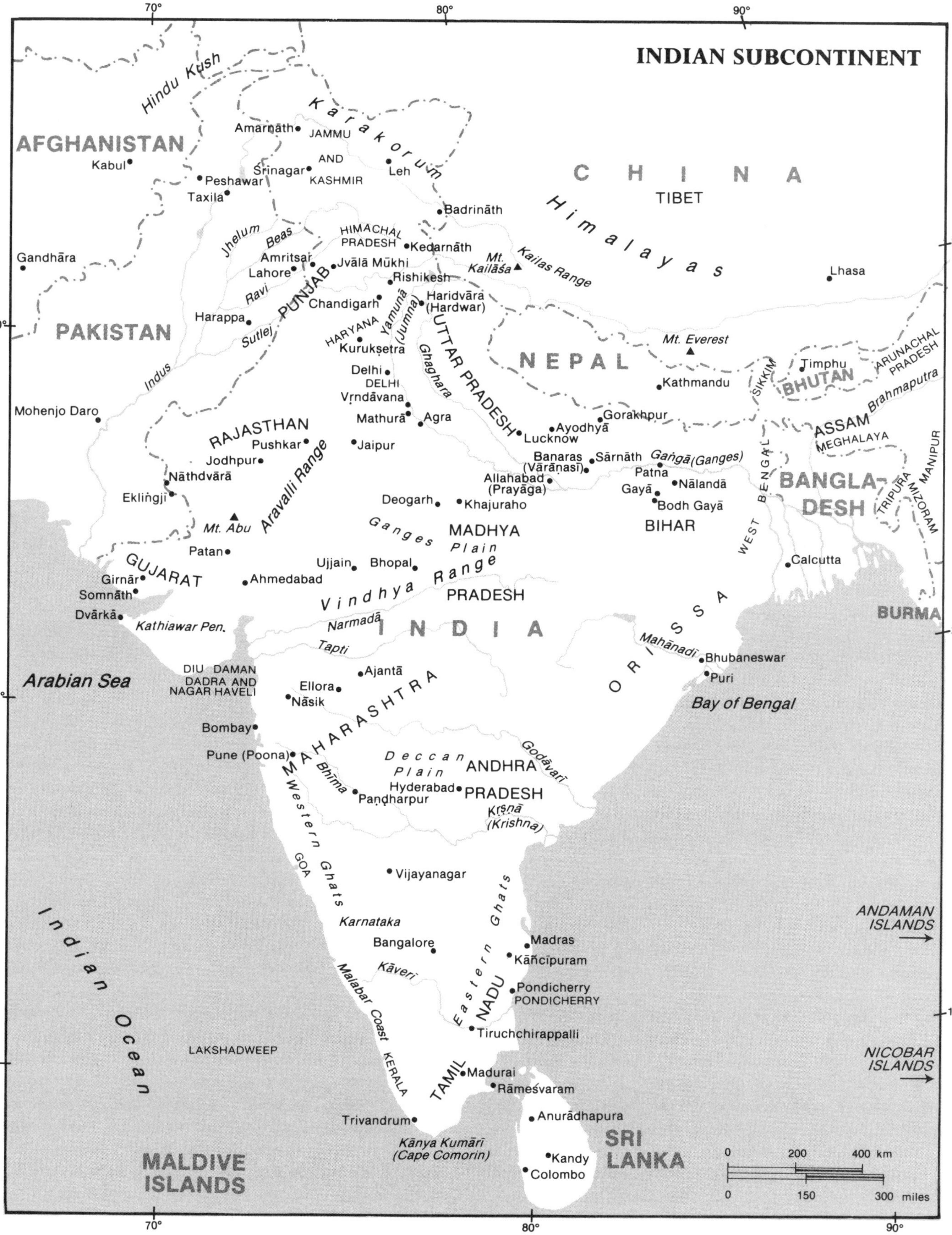
INDIAN SUBCONTINENT
AFGHANISTAN
PAKISTAN
CHINA
TIBET
NEPAL
BHUTAN
BANGLA-DESH
BURMA
INDIA
SRI LANKA
MALDIVE ISLANDS
Hindu Kush
Karakorum
Himalayas
Kailas Range
Mt. Kailāśa
Mt. Everest
Kabul
Peshawar
Taxila
Gandhāra
Amarnāth
JAMMU AND KASHMIR
Srinagar
Leh
Badrināth
HIMACHAL PRADESH
Kedarnāth
Jvālā Mūkhi
Rishikesh
Amritsar
Lahore
Jhelum
Beas
Ravi
Sutlej
PUNJAB
Chandigarh
Haridvāra (Hardwar)
Harappa
HARYANA
Kurukṣetra
Yamunā (Jumna)
UTTAR PRADESH
Ghaghara
Indus
Delhi
DELHI
Vṛndāvana
Mathurā
Agra
Lhasa
Timphu
ARUNACHAL PRADESH
SIKKIM
Kathmandu
Brahmaputra
ASSAM
MEGHALAYA
MANIPUR
Gorakhpur
Ayodhyā
Lucknow
Mohenjo Daro
RAJASTHAN
Pushkar
Jaipur
Jodhpur
Nāthdvārā
Ekliṅgji
Mt. Abu
Aravalli Range
Banaras (Vārāṇasī)
Sārnāth
Gaṅgā (Ganges)
Patna
Allahabad (Prayāga)
Nālandā
Gayā
Bodh Gayā
BIHAR
WEST BENGAL
TRIPURA
MIZORAM
Deogarh
Khajuraho
Ganges Plain
MADHYA PRADESH
Patan
GUJARAT
Girnār
Somnāth
Dvārkā
Kathiawar Pen.
Ahmedabad
Ujjain
Bhopal
Vindhya Range
Narmadā
Tapti
Calcutta
ORISSA
Mahānadī
Bhubaneswar
Puri
Bay of Bengal
Arabian Sea
DIU DAMAN
DADRA AND NAGAR HAVELI
Ajantā
Ellora
Nāsik
MAHARASHTRA
Bombay
Pune (Poona)
Deccan Plain
ANDHRA PRADESH
Godāvarī
Bhīma
Hyderabad
Pandharpur
Kṛṣṇā (Krishna)
Western Ghats
GOA
Vijayanagar
Eastern Ghats
Karnataka
Indian Ocean
Bangalore
Madras
Kāñcīpuram
Kāverī
Malabar Coast
TAMIL NADU
Pondicherry
PONDICHERRY
Tiruchchirappalli
LAKSHADWEEP
KERALA
Madurai
Rāmeśvaram
Trivandrum
Kānya Kumārī (Cape Comorin)
Anurādhapura
Kandy
Colombo
ANDAMAN ISLANDS
NICOBAR ISLANDS
0 200 400 km
0 150 300 miles
70°
80°
90°
30°
20°
10°

in *karman* (previous acts) as the factor determining the condition into which a being is reborn, a consequence of a cyclic view of all worldly processes and existence. These doctrines encourage the opinion that mundane life is not true existence (the so-called Indian pessimism) and hence relate to the conviction that human endeavor should be directed toward final emancipation *(mokṣa)* from the mechanism of *karman* and transmigration, the only goal of this effort being the One *(brahman)* that is beyond all phenomenal existence. In view of the above, Hinduism exhibits a natural tendency to speculation hand in hand with religion as well as to a monistic philosophy and mysticism that has left intact traditional mythology and common beliefs. Finally, it is characterized by a complex polytheism subsumed in a fundamental monotheism and by a propensity to ascribe the attributes of other gods to the deity one is worshiping.

Early history. The history proper of Hinduism begins with the emergence of the great works on *dharma,* the totality of traditional custom and behavior that, agreeing with standards considered to derive their authority from the Vedas, manifests and maintains order and stability. This is also the age of the epics, especially the *Mahābhārata* (c. 300 BCE–300 CE), that "encyclopedia of Hinduism" that shows, even then, what appears to be a varied and confused conglomerate of beliefs and practices. However, there are two main currents, soteriologies when viewed from their doctrinal aspect and religions from the viewpoint of their adherents: Vaiṣṇavism and Śaivism. Neither current is in itself a unity. Yet all Vaiṣṇavas are essentially monotheistic, believing in Viṣṇu as their immanent high god (Īśvara), although in many contexts he appears as one of the divine polytheistic figures *(devas*). In the Vedas, Viṣṇu represents universal pervasiveness; his beneficent energy, in which all beings abide, reaches the world through the *axis mundi,* the central pillar of the universe. Vaiṣṇavas often worship him through his manifestations or incarnations (*avatāras*), such as Rāma or Kṛṣṇa. These and other originally independent figures had fused with Viṣṇu mainly as a result of the tendency to identify the various representatives of the Highest Person with the Primeval Person (Puruṣa), whose self-limitation, according to a Ṛgvedic hymn, inaugurated the era of creation. Preference for an *avatāra* is mainly traditional; in the North, Kṛṣṇa is more often worshiped; in the South, it is Rāma, Viṣṇu himself, or Viṣṇu's consort, Śrī. In many myths the versatile Viṣṇu performs, often in well-known Indian places, great and miraculous deeds to confirm the *dharma,* protect humanity, and preserve the world. The *Bhagavadgītā,* an episode of the *Mahābhārata* and the most seminal of all Vaiṣṇava works, founded Vaiṣṇava ethics: fulfilling their duties disinterestedly, men should realize God's presence in themselves, love him and their fellow beings devotedly, and dedicate all their actions to him so as to earn the prospect of final emancipation.

The Hinduist worship, in many different groups and currents, of Śiva in his various manifestations results from a complex development to which the often malevolent outsider god Rudra of the Vedas has contributed much. (There may also have been Dravidian influences.) Rudra, primarily representing the untamed aspects of uncultivated nature, was called Śiva ("the mild one") when the benevolent and auspicious aspects of his nature were emphasized. Śaivism is an unsystematic amalgam of pan-Indian Śaiva philosophy, local or folk religion, mythological thought, and popular imagery. Śiva's many-sided character, to which accreted features of great gods as well as demoniac powers, is split up into many partial manifestations representing aspects of his ambivalent nature. As Īśvara he is the unique and almighty Supreme Person, representing an abstract, sole principle above change and variation, less human than Viṣṇu, and much less active, although elsewhere, in his role as Naṭarāj the dancer, he originates the eternal rhythm of the universe. He is both mild and terrible, a creator and destroyer, an ascetic and a sexualist. Thus Śiva represents a composite god who is a unity to his devotees, and he plays many apparently contradictory roles in myths, which, on various levels, resolve logically irreconcilable contradictions.

Buddhism and Jainism. The same period saw the spread of two heterodox soteriologies, heterodox because they reject the authority of the Veda and the social prejudices of the brahmans, although they scarcely attack the fundamentals of Hindu belief and practices. The way in which the early Buddhists presented their doctrines has much in common with the oldest Upaniṣads, which must antedate the spread of the Aryan culture to the south and the activity of Gautama (c. 560–480 BCE). Gautama, the Buddha, first gave an exposition of his basic doctrine in Banaras. He taught that those who wish to be delivered from *saṃsāra* and the automatism of *karman,* which does not rely upon a permanent transmigrating soul (whose existence the Buddha denied), should realize four basic truths: (1) earthly existence is pain; (2) the cause of pain is craving for existence, leading to rebirth; (3) cessation of that craving is cessation of pain; (4) an eightfold path leads to that cessation. Final deliverance is realized only in an ascetic and monastic life by those who, after having successfully observed definite rules of life and reached complete meditation *(samādhi),* experience the undefinable state of *nirvāṇa,* the cessation of all becoming. The daily activities of Buddhist monks were recitation, meditation, instruction, and collecting alms from the laity (who largely continued adhering to Hindu belief and observing Hindu practices). As the number of adherents increased, the Buddhist order received large gifts that led to the establishment of monasteries. The multiplying order spread to different parts of India, including the south and Sri Lanka (third century BCE). In the beginning of the fourth century BCE the community began to be split by successive schisms, each of which made its own collection of canonical texts. After about 500 CE, Indian Buddhism began to decline.

The Buddha was not the only illuminated teacher who, after renouncing the world, organized his initiates into a community. In Bihar one of his contemporaries, Vardhamāna Mahāvīra, reformed an existing community and founded the predominantly monastic Jainism, which spread to northern and central India, Gujarat, and the Deccan, and in the last few centuries BCE split into two groups, not on philosophic disagreement but on points of rules for the monks. Jainism is systematic and has never changed in its basic ideology. Its philosophy is dualistic: it posits nonliving entities (including space and time) pervaded by (partly transmigrating, partly emancipated) immaterial and eternal souls; the world, eternal and changeless, is not governed by a supreme being; the system is characterized by the absence of gods (*devas*); *karman* is the central power that determines the destiny of unemancipated souls. Man has to perfect his soul and that of his fellow creatures; *ahiṃsā* and universal tolerance are the main duties and cardinal virtues. Whereas the adherents of Buddhism were from a variety of social classes, Jainism attracted the wealthy and influential. The Jains erected beautiful temples with statues of their perfect souls (*siddhas*) and produced an enormous body of moral and narrative literature. Nowadays they often tend to return to Hinduism, against whose social order they have never revolted.

Hinduism after about 300 BCE. When Buddhism and Jainism enjoyed royal protection, they could extend their influence. However, the masses doubtless always remained Hinduist, even under the Maurya dynasty (c. 326–c. 187 BCE), from which time the epigraphical records left by kings create the impression of a Buddhist supremacy, and in the first and second centuries of the common era, when foreign rulers accorded Buddhists protection. Until the fourth century, inscriptional and numismatic evidence of Vaiṣṇavism and Śaivism is scanty, but the period of the Gupta dynasty (320–c. 500 CE), which patronized the brahmans and the Hinduist communities, saw the full development of classical Sanskrit and the rise of a non-Buddhist architectural style. The construction of a temple, a rite based on mythical reality, a sacrifice leading to a higher level of self-realization for the builder, is, like the construction of the great Vedic sacrificial fire-place (usually, though inaccurately, called "fire altar"), always the material expression of the doctrine of reintegration. At the temple the god is worshiped through his image *(mūrti)*, whose beauty contributes to its force as a sacred instrument. In elaborate ceremonies the god, as an exalted personage and royal guest, is offered food, flowers, and incense. His iconography, consecration (introduction of the god's spirit), and installation, as well as the *mantras* used, the significance of the material and requisites, and the spirit animating the execution of temple and images, are all meticulously described. This daily worship *(pūjā)* probably continues many non-Aryan elements that were gradually received by the higher classes and incorporated into the Brahmanical literature. *Pūjā* is also performed at home by the householder. As far as the uncomplicated older private cult survived, it was supplemented by the traditional *(smārta)* cults of Viṣṇu, Śiva, and other gods, morning and evening rites, oblations in the consecrated fire, recitation, and mental adoration.

During many centuries after about 300 CE there arose an enormous body of mainly Vaiṣṇava and Śaiva literature. The Purāṇas, stemming from various circles and regions, but significantly all attributed to the redactor of the Vedas and the *Mahābhārata* and claiming to be inspired, deal with cosmogony, cosmology (the universe exists cyclically, its eternal return implying the eternal return of souls to bondage and suffering), mythology and legends, principles and philosophy, religious practices and ceremonies, local cults and sanctuaries, sacred rivers and places of pilgrimage. The many, still-influential Āgamas, also in Sanskrit, mainly teach the practical realization of religious truths, while largely governing temple and household ritual and the traditional religious life and behavior of Hindus. Their subject matter is theoretically divisible into four categories: higher knowledge, which gives access to final emancipation; physical, mental, and psychic concentration, that is, complete control of all corporeal and mental functions, leading to the same goal (yoga); meritorious works; and rites, including the many socially and religiously important festivals that are believed to stimulate and resuscitate the vital powers of nature. The Āgamas favor various philosophical doctrines. A feature of the Vaiṣṇavāgamas, usually called Saṃhitās, is *bhakti*, "participation (of the soul in the divine)," devout and emotional worship and adoration of a personal deity in a spirit of deep affection, amounting to surrender to God. Since these works also teach non-Vedic tenets, they are often considered heterodox, in that they deviate from the Hindu *dharma*. Some religions, such as the northern Śaiva Pāśupatas, have propagated consciously divergent rites and practices. Most Vaiṣṇavas, among them the Pāñcarātras, however, deny that they deviate from the generally accepted tradition; many southern Śaivas regard their Āgamas (although with no certain proof) as the sanskritization of an originally Dravidian tradition; some assume the influence of oral esoteric doctrines. In fact, numerous elements are, notwithstanding argumentation to the contrary, non-Brahmanical in origin.

Śaiva Religions and Tantrism. Some religions of India do deviate from common Hinduist traditions and institutions. In contrast to the Śaiva Siddhāntins of the Tamil-speaking South—who, basing themselves also on the mysticism of the Śaiva Tamil saint-poets (Nāyaṉārs), teach that God in the shape of a spiritual guide, or *guru*, graciously permits himself to be realized by the purified soul—the Vīraśaivas, or Liṅgāyats, in southwestern India (not mentioned before the twelfth century) abandon many traditional elements (e.g., caste, image worship). Doctrinal dissent is always possible. The religio-philosophic idealist and monist Kashmir school of Śaivism disagrees in certain important respects with the teaching of Śaṅkara (eighth century), the founder of Advaita monism, derived from the Upaniṣadic Vedānta as a system of absolute idealism that is mainly followed by the intellectual elite. Śaṅkara, a native of Malabar who resided in Banaras and traveled throughout India, was a superb organizer; he established a monastic order and monasteries (*maṭhas*), which, like the many hermitages (*āśramas*) and the great shrines, became centers of religious activity and contributed to the realization of his ideal of Hindu unity.

From about 500 CE, Tantric ritual and doctrines manifest themselves more or less frequently in Buddhism, Śaiva Siddhānta, and Pāñcarātra. Tantrism, primarily meant for esoteric circles, yet still an important aspect of Hinduism, is a systematic quest for spiritual excellence or emancipation through realization of the highest principle, the bipolar, bisexual deity, in one's own body. The possibilities of this microcosmos should be activated, sublimated, and made to exert influence on the macrocosmos, with which it is closely connected (physiological processes are thus described with cosmological terminology). Means to this end, partly magical, partly orgiastic, include recitation of *mantras*, contemplation of geometrical cosmic symbols (*maṇḍalas*), leading the performer of the rites to the reintegration of consciousness; appropriate gestures (*mudrās*), and meditation. Tantric *pūjā* is complicated and in many respects differs from conventional ceremonies. Especially in Bengal, Tantrism has tended to merge with the Śākta cult. The term *Tantra* commonly applies to Śaiva or Śākta works of the Tantric tradition. Śāktism, not always clearly distinguishable from Śaivism, is the worship of the Supreme as divine creative energy *(śakti)*, a female force that creates, regulates, and destroys the cosmos; when regarded as a person, she usually is Śiva's spouse, often the dreadful goddess Durgā or Kālī. In contrast to the so-called right-hand Tantrists, who emphasize yoga and *bhakti*, the left-hand Tantrists seek to realize the union of the male and female principles in the One by combining control of the senses with the sexual act; in addition, they make sacramental use of what is forbidden (e.g., meat) to the brahmans.

Vaiṣṇava Religions and Bhakti. Although Vaiṣṇavism, less coherent than Śaivism, had, in the sixth century, spread all over India, it reached predominance in Tamil Nadu, which became the cradle of important schools and movements that still have many adherents. The tradition known as the Śrī Vaiṣṇavas was inaugurated between about 900 and 1130 by Yāmuna, the first apologist of Vaiṣṇava theology, and consolidated by the great philosopher Rāmānuja (c. 1050–1137). The Śrī Vaiṣṇavas introduced into their temple ceremonies the recitation of Tamil hymns of the Āḻvārs, which evince a passionate belief in and love of God. Considering these poets and their great teachers (*ācāryas*) integral parts (*aṃśas*) of God's nature, they often worship images of them in their temples. According to Rāmānuja, *brahman* is as a "person" *(puruṣa)* the sole cause of his own modifications (emanation, existence, and absorption of the universe), immaterial, perfect, omnipotent, the soul of all being, the ultimate goal of all religious effort, to which God induces the devotee who wishes to please him. The purificatory significance of the ritual, meritorious works, disinterested discharge of duties, and *bhakti* are emphasized.

The influential *Bhāgavata Purāṇa* (c. 900?), also composed in Tamil Nadu, teaches that God through his incomprehensible creative ability *(māyā)* expands himself into the universe, which is his outward appearance. On the basis of this teaching, Bengal Vaiṣṇavism developed the theory of a relation of inconceivable difference in identity and identity in difference between God and the world, as well as the belief that God's creative activity is his sport *(līlā)*. The emotional and erotic description of young Kṛṣṇa's sport with the milkmaids (*gopīs*), who represent souls pervaded by *bhakti* who yearn for God, enjoys lasting popularity. In this Purāṇa, *bhakti* religiosity was expanded, deepened, and stimulated by singing, meditation, and looking at Kṛṣṇa's image. As the safest way to God, *bhakti*, a mystical attitude of mind involving an intuitive, immediate apprehension and loving contemplation of God, often overshadows the devotee's aspirations to final emancipation and assumes a character of uncontrollable enthusiasm and ecstasy, marked by tears, hysteria, and fainting.

In northern and central India the *bhakti* movement flourished from the thirteenth to the eighteenth century, producing a vast and varied literature in vernacular languages. Even today these areas feel the influence of a long succession of saint-poets, passionate itinerant preachers (among them Caitanya, in Bengal, 1485–1533), and *gurus*. These mystics and religious (rather than social) reformers propagated public singing of their devotional songs and *kīrtana* (the praise of God's name and glory), and preached a nonextremist way of life. While so addressing the masses, *bhakti* influenced almost all religious communities and contributed as a unifying force considerably to a revival of Hinduism.

Reaction to Foreign Religions. The revival of Hinduism in the south and the spread of the *bhakti* movement also prepared the Indians to withstand the proselytizing of external religions, particularly Islam. From 1000 CE onward, the Muslims conquered the Northwest, made Delhi their capital, and extended their influence to Bengal, the Deccan, and the South, destroying temples and idols and making many converts, particularly among the untouchables. But Islam scarcely affected the Hindu way of life; rather, it provoked a counterreaction in the form of increased adherence to the Hindu *dharma* and the Hindu religions and stricter observance of rites and ceremonies. Nevertheless, the presence of Islam in India involved an age-long conflict between strict monotheism and the various manifestations of Hinduism. In one field, however, Islam and Hinduism could draw near to each other: Muslim and Hindu mystics have in common the idea of an all-embracing unity. To be sure, the Ṣūfīs made this idea a channel of islamization, but some Indian spiritual leaders tried to bridge the gulf between Islam and Hinduism. Kabīr (c. 1440–1518), an itinerant ascetic, mystic, and strictly monotheist poet and eclectic teacher and preacher, rejected traditional ritual and Brahmanical speculation but retained the belief in basic concepts such as *karman* and *saṃsāra*. In the course of time his syncretistic religion became largely hinduized. Nānak (1469–1539) was likewise a strict monotheist who stated that any pluralistic and anthropomorphous idea of the Supreme should dissolve in God's only form, the really existent. An opponent of caste and idolatry, he organized his followers, the Sikhs, in an exclusive community, an amalgam of Islam and Hinduism, which gradually was transformed into an armed brotherhood hostile to Islam but separated from the Hindus. Supreme authority resides in their holy scripture *(Granth)*, the reading of which is their main form of worship.

India's contact with the West, Christianity, and modern life since the early nineteenth century has led to the emergence of many new religious movements and spiritual groups, as diverse in their principles, ideals, and reactions to foreign influences as the personalities of their founders; most distinguish themselves from traditional devotional movements by a more pronounced interest in ethical, social, and national issues. The extent of their influence in India has, however, often been exaggerated in the West, for the beliefs and customs of the Indian masses are still largely traditional.

The first product of this cultural encounter, the Brāhmo Samāj, a partly social, partly religious organization, was founded by the Bengali brahman Ram Mohan Roy (1772–1833), who, using modern vehicles of propaganda such as the press, advocated social reform and a reformation of Hinduism, which, if purged of abuses and with its monotheistic features underscored, might become the foundation of a universal religion. Schisms resulting mainly from the activities of the *bhakti* mystic Keshab Chandra Sen (1838–1884) led to the coexistence of various small groups of differing aims and ideals. In the second half of the nineteenth century, anti-Muslim and anti-Western ideas as well as religious nationalism led to movements of reformation and modernization or to the propagation of what was considered the essence of traditional Hinduism. One such reformation movement representing the former tendency is the Ārya Samāj, founded in 1875 by Dayananda Sarasvati (1824–1883). Sarasvati advocated absolute adherence to the religion of the Vedic hymns, which he regarded as a continually misinterpreted source of pure monotheism, moral and social reform, and guidance toward the right way to salvation; however, most of the doctrines Sarasvati accepted (e.g., *karman*) were post-Vedic. Opposed to foreign religions, the Ārya Samāj propagates a refined nationalist and democratic Hinduism without symbols and local cults but including the worship of God with praise, prayer, meditation, and daily ceremonies. The main object of Ramakrishna (1836–1886), perhaps the best-known modern Hindu saint, was the propagation of the Vedānta as a superior and comprehensive view of life that synthesizes all faiths on a higher level of spiritual consciousness. A devotee of Rāma and later of Kṛṣṇa, he practiced the Vaiṣṇava form of love; convinced that Hinduism, Islam, and Christianity all lead to the same God, he also adopted Christian methods.

Under his disciple Vivekananda (1862–1902), who turned the trend of Vedānta philosophy toward new values, the Ramakrishna Mission (founded 1897) became, in India, an important force for spiritual regeneration and unification.

[*For discussion of specific traditions, see* Hinduism; Vedism and Brāhmaṇism; Vaiṣṇavism; Śaivism; Durgā Hinduism; Gāṇapatya Hinduism; Kṛṣṇaism; *and* Saura Hinduism. *For discussion of specific; nonorthodox traditions, see* Buddhism; Jainism; Cārvākas; Ājīvikas; Sikhism; *and* Parsis. *On the Indo-European components of Vedic religion, see* Indo-European Religions, *overview article. For surveys of regional religious traditions in India, see* Bengali Religions; Hindi Religious Traditions; Marathi Religions; Tamil Religions; *and* Sinhala Religion. *Much of the religious literature and many of the technical terms, philosophical systems, deities, and historical figures mentioned in this article are the subjects of independent entries.*]

BIBLIOGRAPHY

Carman, John Braisted. *The Theology of Rāmānuja: An Essay in Interreligious Understanding.* New Haven, Conn., and London, 1974.

Eliot, Charles. *Hinduism and Buddhism: A Historical Sketch* (1921). 3d ed. 3 vols. London, 1957.

Embree, Ainslie T., ed. *The Hindu Tradition: Readings in Oriental Thought.* New York, 1966.

Gonda, Jan. *Aspects of Early Viṣṇuism* (1954). 2d ed. Delhi, 1969. A third edition is forthcoming.

Gonda, Jan. *Change and Continuity in Indian Religion.* The Hague, 1965. A series of essays and monographs aiming at a fuller appreciation of the many difficulties with which the historian of the Indian religions is confronted.

Gonda, Jan. *Viṣṇuism and Śivaism: A Comparison.* London, 1970. The Jordan Lectures for 1969.

Gonda, Jan. *Medieval Religious Literature in Sanskrit.* Wiesbaden, 1977.

Gonda, Jan. *Die Religionen Indiens.* 2 vols. Vol. 1, *Veda und älterer Hinduismus,* 2d rev. ed. Vol. 2, *Der jüngere Hinduismus.* Stuttgart, 1978, 1963. Comprehensive, detailed, and well-documented histories of all aspects of Vedism and Hinduism. Translated into French as *Les religions de l'Inde,* 2 vols. (Paris, 1962–1965) and into Italian as *Le religioni dell'India,* 2 vols. (Milan, 1981).

Gonda, Jan. *Vedic Ritual: The Non-Solemn Rites.* Leiden and Cologne, 1980.

Gupta, Sanjukta, Dirk Jan Hoens, and Teun Goudriaan. *Hindu Tantrism.* Leiden, 1979.

Keith, Arthur Berriedale. *The Religion and Philosophy of the Veda and Upanishads* (1925). 2 vols. Reprint, Westport, Conn., 1971.

Moore, Charles A., ed. *The Indian Mind: Essentials of Indian Philosophy and Culture.* Honolulu, 1967.

O'Flaherty, Wendy Doniger. *Śiva: The Erotic Ascetic.* London, 1981. Reprint of *Asceticism and Eroticism in the Mythology of Śiva* (1973). An original discussion of various aspects of Śaivism and Indian mythology in general.

Renou, Louis. *Religions of Ancient India.* London, 1953. The Jordan Lectures for 1951.

Renou, Louis, and Jean Filliozat. *L'Inde classique: Manuel des études indiennes.* 2 vols. Paris, 1947–1953.

Zaehner, R. C. *Hinduism.* London, 1962.

Jan Gonda

Rural Traditions

The religious beliefs and practices of rural India reflect the influence of three general cultural traditions that throughout history have mingled and mixed in varying degrees. Grouped generally, these traditions are those of agricultural cultures, food-gathering communities, and nomadic societies.

Since the third millennium BCE the most stable groups within these three traditions have been those of the agricultural cultures, which are typified by their development of written script and by their emergent sophistication in the production of artifacts reflecting a pervasive consciousness of the earth and its vegetation. The myth-bound lives of people in these cultures have long been linked to the cycles of time experienced in the circular movement of the seasons and in the resulting change in the earth's character. The fundamental energy that gave life to sprouting seeds was commonly understood to be feminine and was represented in female images—although a variety of icons, figurines, and magical geometric drawings painted on home floors and walls also reveal a pervasive worship of the sun, water, grain, and other natural phenomena. Possessed of an archaic knowledge of tools and agricultural methods, these people were India's first inventors and creators and have given as their cultural inheritance to India agrarian technologies that until recently remained unchanged for five thousand years.

A second general cultural stream arose from the archaic food-gatherers living in India's forests and mountain regions and whose myths reflect the notion that they are the firstborn of the earth. Made up mostly of tribal societies with a remote past and no recorded history, these groups established kingdoms and ruled large areas of the vast interior of India, but then disappeared again into the wilderness, where they lived in caves, hunted animals, and collected wild foodstuffs from the dark and pathless forests. These peoples, too, experienced life as power and developed magical and sacerdotal means by which they could please or combat the intensely felt but unseen and terrible potencies of the natural world. Like the ancient agriculturalists, they also felt kinship with the earth but in their case revered the animals and wild plants of the forest rather than of the domestic arena. They, too, knew the earth intimately and understood her to whisper her secrets to them as long as they did not wound her breasts with the plough.

The third cultural stream was comprised of nomadic peoples, wanderers across the lands who have bequeathed to their descendants a racial memory of ancient migrations across wild deserts, over rugged mountains, and through lush valleys. These were cattle herders and horse riders who first entered India, the land of rivers, seeking water for their stock. They had a penetrating visual vocabulary based on an astute appreciation of color and light. Their rituals and art forms share in this vibrant experience of the world. Their bards and dancers were vigorous drinkers who lived a free and spontaneous life full of the passion of war and love.

India's rural religious traditions arose from the confluence of these three cultural streams. These ancient societies are the predecessors of the rural people today whose farming techniques, arts, and rituals give form to primordial tribal myths. When women today paint ceremonial drawings, when artisans create fecundative images, when singers and performers tell of epic conquests, they concretize the legends and mysteries of these ancient groups. From this archaic unconscious come rural myths of cosmic power, of cyclical destruction and creation, of natural processes in which human beings live their lives.

Women of today's higher castes in northern Mithila recount a myth that is identical both in form and meaning to a legend sung by autochthonous women of the deep south who worship the goddess Pedammā. The long history of the myth indicates a substratum of powerful and energetic female memories, the unconscious source of which is transmitted through feminine culture and given form in the act of communication between mother and daughter. In this myth are to be found remnants of ancient wisdom regarding creative power that carries the germ of its own destruction. Out of this tradition arises values that are deeply understood by the women of Mithila, who say with great simplicity that "these insights come from a time without beginning; we carry this wisdom in our wombs."

Candrakālā Devī, a traditional artist of Mithila, narrates the following myth:

> First there was Ādi Śakti ("primordial power"), another name for whom was Mahāmāyā ("great creator"). She was the one, alone. She desired [a partner] and, displaying her *māyā*, created the manifest world out of the void. A cosmic egg appeared and the new male gods Brahmā, Viṣṇu, and Śiva emerged when it hatched. As these gods grew to young manhood, Ādi Śakti turned with fiery passion to Brahmā and sought to marry him. Brahmā recoiled, saying, "You are our mother!" The goddess laughed at him and reduced him to ashes. The same thing happened to Viṣṇu: he, too, retreated, filled with horror and he, too, was consumed by fire. The luminous goddess then approached Śiva, the young, beautiful, long-limbed youth who, hearing her demands, smiled and accepted her as his bride.

The story's versions as told in the South and the North are the same to this point. But now they diverge. In the legend as told in Mithila (in the North), Śiva responds to the goddess Ādi Śakti by asking her to accept him as her disciple. She agrees to his request, and Śiva learns from her the secrets of life and various incantations for raising the dead. Having mastered these mysteries and ancient secrets of power, Śiva then destroys the primordial Ādi Śakti by engulfing her with flame and reducing her to ashes, promising to her as he does so that he will marry her again after many aeons when she is reborn as Satī, the daughter of Dakṣa. The story acknowledges that this second marriage did, indeed, eventually take place.

The Dravidian variant—one in which passionate youth is said to lead irrevocably to old age and decrepitude—is darker and more archaic. As in the northern version, Śiva agrees to marry Ādi Śakti after the goddess has reduced Brahmā and Viṣṇu to ashes for refusing to do so. In the southern account Śiva is then said to ask Ādi Śakti if he may have as a gift from her the brilliant jewel that shines as brightly as ten thousand suns and that rests on her forehead. Infatuated, she agrees to the request and hands the jewel to her young lover. As he takes it from her hand the goddess ages frightfully, as if centuries had just elapsed in the moment's duration. Formerly a beautiful goddess who lived unhindered by time, she is now suddenly a bent and undesirable old woman. Time, the devourer of all things, has entered the world. Śiva merely smiles; for he is Kāla, the lord of time. With this action, the new gods have taken over. The primordial primacy of female power is reduced to ashes, its brilliance usurped. The female takes second place in the Puranic pantheon to the male.

Candrakālā Devī molds images of Ādi Śakti out of clay and paper pulp to which has been added *methi* (cumin seed), ground to a paste. The image of the goddess has many arms, an elongated body, and hollow eyes. She is reminiscent of the ancient and universal Mātalas, the earth mothers. Their gaunt, passionless, masklike faces have crater-deep eyes, stark with the secrets of death and life.

Images of Ādi Śakti, the primeval mother, are made at harvest time. Also known as Aṣṭabhuja ("eight-armed"), she holds in her hands the cosmic egg as well as a cup that holds the seed or blood to fertilize the fields; she also holds the sun and moon, the earth (depicted as a flat plate and covered with grass and sprouts of other plants), two bullocks pulling a plow, a plowshare, a flower, and a sword.

By the beginning of the second millennium (no one knows exactly how early), groups of peoples migrated into India from the Northwest. They were not of one tribe, nor had they all reached the same levels of cultural development or of artistic abilities. The best-known of these migrating groups were the Vedic Aryans. Strong, heroic, and proud of their identity, these people had wandered the steppes for generations, never settling long enough to establish any cities.

The Vedic Aryans were warriors who brought with them into the river valleys of northern India the songs and poems that came to be included in the *mantras* (hymns) of the Vedic religious textual tradition. Their songs were robust, loud, and full of life: hymns to the awesome processes of nature; invocations to Aditya, the sun god; praises to Vāyu, the wind, and to Uṣas, the maiden of the dawn. Moving into the decaying or destroyed Harappan urban areas, the Vedic Aryans introduced to those agricultural peoples the instruments of war, new dimensions of language, new volumes of sound, new relationships with nature, and pulsing vitality.

In successive waves through the centuries the Vedic Aryans moved on their horse-driven chariots along the densely forested banks of the Indus, Ganges, and Yamunā rivers. It took a thousand years for them to reach the Narmada River in central India (in modern Madhya Pradesh), by which time they had merged into the cultures of the vast hinterland through intermarriage and by adopting local customs, skills, and tools.

It is likely that the Vedic Aryans found the original inhabitants of India living at various levels of technological culture, those groups living within the walled cities of Mohenjo-Daro and Harappa contrasting vividly with the Paleolithic societies living in the dense forests along the banks of the Ganges or in the caves of the Vindhya Mountains. Five-thousand-year-old ruins scattered throughout the Harappan sites indicate that the people of the Indus Valley had established a highly developed society: they had discovered the wheel, with which they transformed their methods of transportation and increased the sophistication with which they molded their clay pots; they had developed simple tools with which they could measure angles and with which they could build structures with precision and accuracy; they had learned to grow and spin cotton, to weave and dye cloth, to mold clay, and to cast bronze into figurines. [*See* Indus Valley Religion.]

Intense intellectual and psychological activity accompanied the tremendous revolution in technology and the production of tools brought about by these early city dwellers. They had developed a script to illumine their pictographs, and they practiced yoga and other meditative techniques to expand their minds.

With the fall of the cities to natural and martial forces, large numbers of people took refuge in the wilds of central India, traveling all the way to the banks of the Narmada and Tapti rivers and even farther south. They carried with them into the inner lands of the subcontinent their knowledge of agriculture, technology, ritual, and magic. The influence of these urban skills and perceptions appear in their symbols, worship, and magical practices.

The migrations of nomadic peoples onto the fertile plains of India were to continue through the centuries. One of the most important of these tribes to the development of Indian culture and its rural traditions were the Ahirs, who came to be known in the epic *Mahābhārata* as the "snake-loving" Abhiras.

The figure of Kṛṣṇa also was known as Māyōṉ or Māyavan in ancient Tamil *samgam* literature; the dark-skinned, non-Aryan god emerged in the culture of Mathurā and reflects a mixture of elements from Ahir and tribal backgrounds. The name itself, *Kṛṣṇa* ("dark one"), is pregnant with early Aryan scorn; but it was Kṛṣṇa who was to supply the generative vitality that transformed Indian arts and culture. [*See* Kṛṣṇa.]

Stories about the personalities and affairs of Kṛṣṇa, of the Goddess, and of other local heroes were collected by the compilers of the epic poems the *Mahābhārata* and the *Rāmāyaṇa*. These tales, as well as myths and legends recounted in the various Purāṇas, traveled by word of mouth through the vast lands of India. Transmission of these stories was enhanced by their widespread multifaceted use of song, dance, mime, drama, and iconography. These various media allowed all kinds of people, particularly members of those tribal groups living outside the mainstream of society, to experience the sensory nature of the divine presence and to express the immediacy of that presence through an active, personal, and contemporaneous participation. [*See* Mahābhārata; Rāmāyaṇa; *and* Purāṇas.]

Rural painters and balladeers drew their inspiration and source material from Ahir love songs, accounts of brave and victorious heroes, and tales of the Puranic gods and their erotic adventures. The most famous of these ballads was the *Lorikagan*, which was composed in Avadhi (a dialect of Hindi) and which recounts the love held by Lorik, an Ahir from the Mithila country, for Chaṇḍa, the wife of Śrīdhara. According to the tale, Śrīdhara had become impotent as a result of a curse placed on him by the goddess Pārvatī. Chaṇḍa then fell in love and eloped with Lorik. Śrīdhara searched for the couple, only to be killed by Lorik when he found them. The young couple then approached the master gambler Mahāpatra Dusadh and engaged him in a game of dice. Lorik lost Chaṇḍa and all his wealth to Mahāpatra Dusadh. But Chaṇḍa argued with Dusadh that the stakes involved in the game did not include her clothing and demanded that the gambling continue. On resumption of the game she sat down in front of Dusadh and exposed her beautiful body. Intoxicated by the sight of Chaṇḍa's nakedness, Dusadh lost control of the game and was defeated by Lorik, who later killed him. This legend finds expression in paintings, theater, and song.

The tribal kings of central India also had an ancient bardic tradition. The Gond *rājas* included in their courts official tribal genealogists and musicians known as Pardhans, who recounted to the royal household the ancient stories of the Gond hero-kings and warriors. Serving also as priests and diviners, in time the Pardhans absorbed Hindu legends, gods, and even ethics into their tribal epics, ballads, and other expressions of folklore.

A Pardhan today worships his musical instrument, the *bana*, as the god Bara Pen. "As his sacred books [are] to a Brahmin, as his scales [are] to a Bania, as his plough [is] to a Gond, so is the bana to the Pardhan" (Hivale, 1946, p. 66).

It is said that the original Pardhan was timid when he first played his wonderful new music in the house of the Gond brothers. But he played so divinely that all those residing in the heavenly as well as earthly worlds were enchanted. Even the supreme god, Nārāyaṇ Deo, stood watching in amazement. Then the Pardhan forgot his shyness and completely lost himself in his music. He danced ecstatically with his *bana*, with which he produced sounds the world had never heard before. On that day, it is said, three new *pars* (sounds or combination of sounds) known as Sarsetī Par, Nārāyaṇ Par, and Pujan Par were first created.

Pābujī is a folk hero who is especially popular among the Bhils, a tribal group living in Rajasthan. According to legend, Pābujī was suckled as an infant by a lioness and grew to be a brave warrior. He was given a powerful black mare named Kāḷmī by Devaḷ, a *cāraṇ* woman of a pastoral community. In return for this gift Pābujī promised to protect Devaḷ's life and cattle, and he eventually died in the attempt to keep his promise. Among the Bhils are a group of bardic musicians (*bhopās*) who travel through the countryside with a fifteen-foot long painted scroll known as the Pābujī-kā-Pad. (Pābujī's scroll). In its center lies the main figure, a portrait of Pābujī himself, painted in vibrant red, black, olive, and yellow ocher. Surrounding this main figure are depictions of warriors engaged in battle, images of horses, lions, and tigers, and scenes of heroic incidents that serve to illustrate the legend of Pābujī. Performers reenact stories based on that legend at night. The scroll is stretched out, oil lamps are lit, and the *bhopā* sings his story. As he sings, a woman lifts the lamp to the cloth in order to illumine for the crowd the figures of warriors on horseback, animals, birds, and other elements of the tales. She joins with the *bhopā* in singing the refrain and, at times, dances.

The bards of the Santals in Bengal and Bihar are known as *jādu paṭuā* ("magic-painters"), who carry from village to village their painted *paṭs* depicting scenes from the Pūraṇas as well as their own tribal cosmogonic and anthropogonic myths.

The fundamental assumptions of male supremacy in Brahmanic culture were established by the time of the classical law books such as the *Manusmṛti* (c. 200 BCE–100 CE) and the various Dharmaśāstras. [*See also* Śāstra Literature.] According to these and other texts, a girl was dependent on her father and then, as a woman, was inferior to her husbands and sons. Such ideals of Indian womanhood as obedience and faithfulness to the male were embodied in the images of the goddesses Sītā and Savitrī.

Vedic learning was closed to women by the time of the *smṛti* ("remembered") literatures. However, in the vast and flat countryside that encircled the cities and in the rural life of the village and fields surged a powerful, flexible, ancient, and secret undercurrent among women, wandering yogins, Tantric adepts, and magician-priests, who focused their religious sensibilities on the primeval female, Śakti, and on Śiva, the mysterious god of the autochthonous tribes. [*See* Śiva.]

The earliest, almost primordial, images of the earth mother glorified a feminine creative principle made manifest by the image itself, which often celebrated the secrets of birth and death. The dark earth-bound goddess was a mother, yet a virgin, for "no father seemed necessary to the society in which she originated" (Kosambi, 1962, p. 90). Originally represented aniconically through hieroglyphs and vegetation symbols, through the centuries the primeval mother came to be represented in animal and finally in anthropomorphic images of Śakti, who had a thousand names and forms. Potent with the energy of life itself, and holding within herself the essence of her earlier incarnations, she had the capacity to heal and transform. Such earlier forms find expression in the hieroglyphic triangle resting on her heart or generative organs. Her vegetal nature appeared in the plants she held in her hands. Her animal incarnations were transformed into the various beasts on which she rode. As the primary physical and spiritual essence of the universe, Śakti was alive in the experience of color, form, taste, and fragrance. In her final form she was Durgā—the holder of all life, brighter than a thousand suns.

Tantric texts describe Durgā's symbols: "The Goddess of renowned form assumes in times of protection the form of a straight line. In times of dissolution, she takes the form of a circle. Similarly for creation she takes the brilliant appearance of a triangle" (Sastry, 1906, p. 280).

A new priesthood and new relationships with the gods became inevitable with the rise of the male godhead into the Puranic pantheon. The emergent potent male deity was known as the *kṣetrapal* (guardian of the field and womb), Thakur Dev. The *kṣetrapal* protected and fecundated the earth and field, the body of the goddess. In the religious rites the people expressed their search for cosmic transformation, embodied in the act of sexual union between the God and Goddess. Agricultural magic fused with alchemical and Tantric practices. [*See* Alchemy, *article on* Indian Alchemy.]

Either the aboriginal magician-priest known as the *baiga* or a priest from the potter, the barber, or the *camār* community presided at ceremonies worshiping trees and river-washed stones held at the village or forest shrines honoring the primeval mother, the Goddess, various deities, or the tribal hero. The potency of his magic was recognized and accepted by the villagers and householders living in the sheltered rural societies. The Tantric doctrines outlined in the Āgama and Nigama textual traditions, the frenzied ecstatic worship of Śakti through ritual performance and *mantra*-recitation, had pervaded the Indian psyche to the depths of the cultural subconscious. In prosperous villages the Puranic gods were worshiped; but along with this praise, and at a deeper level, a worship of the pre-Vedic deities continued and the practice of Tantric rituals remained. [*See also* Tantrism.]

One of the attributes of the Goddess was *jāgaritṛ* (wakefulness). Through practicing such *vrata* ("vow") rites as fasting, meditative concentration, and other observances, the woman votary directly invoked the power of the goddess by awakening her power *(śakti)* inherent in various symbols, stones, trees, and water pots. She drew geometric shapes (*maṇḍalas*) on the ground and on the wall of houses, worshiped the interlocking triangle known as the *yantra* dedicated to the Goddess, and performed in the darkness various rituals accompanying the sprouting of corn. Songs, dance, and image-making flourished as part of the ceremonies. The worshiper hoped through creative expression, *vrata*, and ritual song and dance to awaken *śakti* and to ensure that, once awakened, that primal energy was not dissipated or dispersed. [*See* Maṇḍalas, *article on* Hindu Maṇḍalas, *and* Yantra.]

Unlike the temporary clay images of the *grāma mātṛkās* ("village mothers"), which have mysterious links with the earth and its cyclical patterns of creation and destruction, the images of the *vīras* (deified "heroes") and the *kṣetrapal*s are shafts embodying virility and power carved in stone and wood. Rising as pillars to the sky and toward the sun and yet rooted in the earth, the harsh simplicity of the flat visual planes thus gives to the images a heroic dimension representing the sanctity of the immovable and the eternal divine presence.

The term *vīra* ("hero") is often used to refer to the valiant ancestors killed in battle while protecting women, fields, and cattle. It also is used to describe the alchemists, yogins, magicians, and enlightened ones who gained control over and conquered the ways of their bodies and minds. Both types of *vīra*s were deified and worshiped in the form of the *vīrakaḷ* and *pāḷiā* stones. The *vīra* cult itself is an ancient one that centers on an admixture of ancestor worship, veneration of the heroic protectors and guardians as well as of magicians and seers, and praise of such figures as the Hurā Purā (deified heroes) or the Āyi Vaḍil (deified ancestors) of the Bhil tribes. The cult also includes the worship of a wonderfully rich symbolic complex associated with the *yakṣas*, spirits of the forests and rivers known by the compilers of the *Atharvaveda* and the Purāṇas. Depicted as having tall male bodies (which they are mysteriously able to transform), the *yakṣa*s were regarded at first as malevolent beings, but underwent a significant change at some point when they became associated and identified with the *kṣetrapal*s and the *vīra*s, with whom they protected and watched over the welfare of the earth and the Goddess.

India's most powerful symbol of the hero is a rider on a horse. Carved in memorial stones or cast in metal icons and amulets, the image displays the vitality and energy of the heroic male. [*See also* Horses.]

Elements of the *vīra* cult evolved through time into the worship of Śiva, the supreme god of rural India. Śiva is described as late as the third century CE as a *yakṣa* who is to be propitiated in the wild regions beyond the village walls. Rural customs still exist in India that reflect Śiva's autochthonous origins. In the Punjab and in Himachal Pradesh, for example, women are not permitted the worship of Śiva. Women in Uttar Pradesh can worship Śiva in the form of the *liṅga*, but they must carry their offerings to the god in the corner of their *sārīs* and must never allow their hand to touch the phallic form as they circumambulate it.

The tribal Bhils worship Śiva as their first ancestor. The Gonds of Bastar sing an epic, *Lingo pen*, in which they describe the appearance of Śiva in human form:

> There the God Mahadev was ruling from the upper sea to the lower sea. What was Mahadev doing? He was swimming like a rolling stone, he had no hands, no feet.
>
> He remained like the trunk [of a tree]. Then Mahādev performed austerities for twelve months.
>
> And Bhagavān [i.e., Śiva] came and stood close to Mahādev and called to him.
>
> "Thy devotion is finished, emerge out of the water."
>
> He said, "How shall I emerge? I have no hands, no feet, no eyes."
>
> Then Mahādev received man's form. Thus man's form complete was made in the luminous world.
>
> (Hislop, 1866, pp. 2–3)

Next to their drawings of the corn goddess the Warlis of Maharashtra often display an image known as Pāñc Siryā Dev, a headless male figure with five sheaves of sprouting corn emerging from his body. Among the Bhils of Gujarat a five-headed figure with an erect penis is cast in metal and is called Pāñc Mukhi Dev. Both images are linked to Śiva and to cultic fertility rites.

In some regions of West Bengal the roles and personalities of Śiva and the sun god fuse into the worship of Dharma Thākur. The *maṇḍala* (village headman) performs rituals centered on the marriage of Śiva and Gaurī at which Kalighat painters used to congregate in order to sell their paintings to pilgrims.

At the Nīla Gajan or Gambhira festivals Śiva is worshiped as Nīlakaṇṭha (*nīla* is an indigo cloth worn by low-caste devotees of Śiva who worship the planets and for whom the Gambhira is a key harvest ritual). Singing abounds in these rites. One song describes Śiva as a cultivator of cotton and as one who loves Koch tribal girls:

> The month of Baisakh came,
> The farmer ploughed the field;
> The month of Āṣāḍh came,
> God Śiva planted cotton seeds,
> As the planting was over,
> Śiva went to the quarter of the Koch women.
> He stayed and stayed on there,
> Until he knew that cotton had grown.
> Śiva returned to gather cotton,
> He placed the stuff in the hands of Gaṅgā,
> She spun yarn out of it.
> Śiva wove a piece of cloth,
> The washerwoman Netā washed it clean,
> She washed it by water from the ocean of milk.
>
> (Bhattacharya, 1977, pp. 60–61)

Having become the central deity in rural areas, Śiva then became the figure from which all of the minor rural gods emerged. The elephant-headed Gaṇeśa ("lord of the folk"), for example, is regarded as the son of Śiva, though no legend specifically relates the nature of his birth. Originally worshiped as a malevolent spirit and the creator of obstacles, Gaṇeśa underwent a transformation during the time of the composition of the Purāṇas and assumed the role of protector of the people and the remover of obstacles. Hanumān (or Maruti), the devotee of Rāma, is also known to be an incarnation of Mahābhairav, who, in turn, is one of Śiva's many manifestations. No forest or village masculine deity is free of an intimate association with Śiva, the central personality of the cosmos and locus of the processes of creation and destruction.

Deep within the religious practices and ideologies of rural India lie the recognition of cosmic transformation marked by the flexive flow of creation and destruction, the appreciation of the vital forces of life, and the longing to be protected from the powers of the physical and spiritual worlds. The gods fuse and merge, or they are transformed, or they vanish with the receding forests and disappearing tribes. New gods come into being and new rituals emerge, bringing with them changes in the form and content of religious expressions. But the sacredness and the mystical power of rural religious sensibilities survive the many changes in deities and rituals throughout history.

[*For further discussion of the mythology of rural India, see* Purāṇas. *See also* Goddess Worship, *article on* The Hindu Goddess. *For related discussions of specific areas, see* Bengali Religions; Hindi Religious Traditions; Marathi Religions; *and* Tamil Religions. *Many of the deities mentioned in this article are the subjects of separate entries.*]

BIBLIOGRAPHY

Archer, William G. *The Vertical Man: A Study in Primitive Indian Sculpture*. London, 1947.

Bhattacharya, Asutosh. *The Sun and the Serpent Lore of Bengal*. Calcutta, 1977.

Dasgupta, Sashibhushan. *Obscure Religious Cults*. Calcutta, 1962.

Elmore. W. T. *Dravidian Gods in Modern Hinduism*. Lincoln, Nebr., 1915.

Elwin, Verrier. *The Baiga*. London, 1939.
Hislop, Stephen. *Papers relating to the Aboriginal Tribes of the Central Provinces*. Nagpur, 1866.
Hivale, Shamrao. *The Pardhans of the Upper Narbada Valley*. Oxford, 1946.
Jayakar, Pupul. *The Earthen Drum: An Introduction to the Ritual Arts of Rural India*. New Delhi, 1980.
Kane, P. V. *History of Dharmaśāstra*. 2d ed., rev. & enl. 5 vols. in 7. Poona, 1968–1975.
Kosambi, D. D. *Myth and Reality*. Bombay, 1962.
Kramrisch, Stella. *Unknown India: Ritual Art in Tribe and Village*. Philadelphia, 1968.
Oppert, Gustav. *On the Original Inhabitants of Bharatavarṣa or India* (1893). Reprint, Delhi, 1972.
Reeves, Ruth. *Cire Perdue Casting in India*. New Delhi, 1962.
Shamasastry, R. *The Origin of the Devanagari Alphabets*. Varanasi, 1973.

PUPUL JAYAKAR

Mythic Themes

India, like other civilizations, has myths that deal with themes shared by all human beings—the great themes of life and death, of this world and the world beyond—which she inflects with her own personal colorations and thus makes different from the myths of other civilizations. Moreover, Indians have been inspired to create myths on themes that have not appealed to other civilizations with the same intensity, or on themes that simply do not exist outside of India. We can go further in laying out this spectrum of the general and the particular, beginning with the universals and moving through large shared cultures (such as the Indo-European) down through India as a whole until we reach the many particular, local traditions within India. This approach views myths on the analogy of languages (as F. Max Müller taught us to do), which can be broken down into language families (again, the Indo-European), languages, dialects, and regional dialects. Indeed, if we wish, we can go still further, until we reach, in India, at least one language (or dialect) that is said to be spoken by only one person. So, too, at the end of the line (and perhaps at the beginning of the line too, *in illo tempore*), each myth exists in a unique version in the mind of the individual who knows it.

In attempting to present an overview of Indian mythic themes, I have chosen to begin with the great universal themes as they appear in their Indian incarnations (primarily Hindu forms, though with some passing references to the Buddhist variants of the pan-Indian themes) and to move through the narrower Indo-European functions of the myths in India to variants that are uniquely Indian. There I shall perforce stop; it would be impossible to trace the regional subvariations in an essay of limited size and wide range, and of course the subsubvariations in the minds of all the individual myth-knowers are infinite. But we must never forget that these subvariations do exist (and have been recorded in some of the books listed in the bibliography attached to this article) and that, moreover, they flow not only downstream (from the pan-Indian to the local) but upstream, from the local to the pan-Indian, in a cybernetic process that lends the great myths much of their particular flavor, texture, and vivid detail.

Animals. Although it is no longer believed, as it once was, that all mythology is somehow connected with totemism, it is certainly still true that you cannot have a mythology without animals. Animals and gods are the two communities poised on the frontiers of the human community, the two "others" by which we define ourselves. And though all animals can be mythical, certain animals tend to be more mythical than others, more archetypal, if you will. Birds and snakes recur throughout the mythologies of the world, both individually and as a matched pair. Individually, birds (and eggs) are symbols of creation; their wings make them part of the kingdom of heaven, where they come to function as symbols of God (in Christianity) or of the magic woman from the other world (the swan-maiden of European folklore). Snakes slough their skin to become symbols of rebirth, or bite their tails to become symbols of infinity (the Uroboros); they bring about the loss of innocence (as in the *Book of Genesis*) or the loss of immortality (as in the *Epic of Gilgamesh*). Together, birds and snakes symbolize the elements of air and subterranean water, spirit and matter, good and evil, or simply the principle of opposition, through the observed natural enmity of the two species.

All of this symbolism is found in Indian mythology, together with more narrowly Indo-European themes: the killing of the dragon-serpent (Indra killing Vṛtra, Kṛṣṇa subduing Kāliya); the battle between birds and snakes (the quarrel between Vinatā, the mother of snakes, and Suparṇā, the mother of birds, in the opening books of the *Mahābhārata*). We also find in the *Mahābhārata* traces of the more subtle Indo-European theme of the battle between the snake and the horse (of which we also find echoes in paintings of Saint George, always mounted on his white horse, killing the dragon): in the course of the quarrel between Vinatā and Suparṇā, the black snakes form the hairs of the tail of the sacred horse, a trick that leads eventually to a great sacrifice in which snakes are killed in place of the usual stallion. But as might be expected in a country as snaky as India, snake symbolism is more luxuriant than it is elsewhere. The *nāgas*, half serpent, half deity, who inhabit the waters of the lower world, participate in many myths and adorn most temples; Viṣṇu sleeps on Ananta, the serpent of eternity, and Śiva wears snakes for his bracelets, his necklaces, his sacred thread, and (with occasionally embarrassing results) his belt. Birds of a rich mythological plumage are equally pervasive; Viṣṇu rides on the *garuḍa* bird (a descendant of the Vedic sun-bird), Skanda on a peacock (an appropriate emblem for the general of the army of the gods), and Brahmā on a royal goose or swan (the *haṃsa* that is also a symbol of the transmigrating soul). [*See also* Birds; Snakes; *and* Nāgas and Yakṣas.]

Another important Indo-European pair of animals, the horse and the cow, remain essential to the mythology of the Vedas and to that of later Hinduism. The stallion loses in India some of his ancient power as a symbol of royal, martial, and fertile functions (the Indo-European triad), although he remains an important figure on the local, village level, where one still encounters many minor horse deities and equine heroes, as well as charming terra-cotta horses, some of enormous size. The mare became in India a symbol of the voracious female who must be tamed (like the submarine fire in the form of a mare held in check by the waters of the ocean, until the moment when she will emerge at doomsday to destroy the universe). [*See also* Horses.] But the animal who truly usurped the stallion's place of honor is the cow, which became symbolic of all the values of the society of the newly settled Ganges Valley (in contrast with the nomadic, warring Indo-European society that was so well symbolized by the stallion); the cow represented motherhood, nourishment, chastity, and noninjury (the cow being an animal able to furnish food without having to be slaughtered). The bull plays a relatively minor role, primarily as Nandi, the vehicle of Śiva.

A more purely Indian symbol is the elephant, representing royalty, power, wisdom, fertility, longevity, and much else. The mother of the future Buddha dreamed, upon conceiving him, that a white elephant had entered her womb; Lakṣmī, the goddess of good fortune, is lustrated by two elephants; elephants support the earth and the quarters of the sky; the god Gaṇeśa, patron of scribes and of all enterprises, has the head of an elephant, the source of his cunning and of his ability to remove obstacles. [*See also* Elephants.] At the other end of the Indian animal spectrum is the dog, already maligned in Indo-European mythology (Kerberos, the dog of Hades, appears in the *Ṛgveda* as the two Sārameyas, the four-eyed brindled dogs of Yama, the king of the dead). In India, the dog became a vehicle for all the negative values of the caste system; he was regarded as unclean, promiscuous both in his eating habits and in his (or, more often, her) sexual habits; dogs are said to be the food of untouchables (who are called "dog-cookers," *śvapaka*s, in Sanskrit). Yet Yudhiṣṭhira, the righteous king in the *Mahābhārata,* refused to enter heaven until the gods allowed to enter with him the dog that had followed him faithfully through all his trials, a dog who turned out to be none other than the god Dharma himself, incarnate.

In addition to these individual animals, Indian mythology teems with animals of a more miscellaneous sort. Every Indian god has an animal for his vehicle *(vāhana).* This association means not only that the god is literally carried about on such an animal (for the elephant-headed Gaṇeśa is awkwardly mounted on a bandicoot, or large rat) but also (and more importantly) that the animal "carries" the god in the way that a breeze "carries" perfume, that the god is always present in that animal, in all of its manifestations (the bandicoot, for example, shares Gaṇeśa's nimbleness of wit and ability to get past anything, and so is indeed an appropriate vehicle for the god). This is the only sense in which animals (including cows) are sacred in India; the tendency not to kill them (which does not, unfortunately, generally extend to a tendency not to ill-treat them) arises from something else, from the concept of noninjury *(ahiṃsā)* that discourages the taking of any life in any form. In addition to these official vehicles, many gods appear in theriomorphic or semitheriomorphic forms; Viṣṇu becomes incarnate as the man-lion Narasiṃha, but he also is often represented with the head of a boar and the body of a man in his *avatāra* as the boar. When Śiva makes war on Viṣṇu the boar, he takes the form of a *śarabha,* a beast with eight legs, eight tusks, a mane, and a long tail.

More generally, whether or not people get the gods they deserve, they tend to get the gods that their animals deserve; the natural fauna of any country has a lot to do with the ways in which the people of that country perceive their gods. For example, two animals that play an important role in Indian mythology are the monkey and the tiger. Although neither of these animals is the vehicle of a god, the monkey is a cousin of Hanuman, the monkey ally of Rāma, the divine hero of the *Rāmāyaṇa,* and the tiger sometimes replaces the lion as the vehicle of the goddess Devī (especially in places where lions have long been extinct). But the influence of monkeys and tigers extends far beyond their recorded roles in the mythology. The ingenious mischievousness of the monkey and the uncanny cruelty and beauty of the tiger are qualities that have found their way into the images of many Hindu gods and goddesses. If Judaism has a mythology of lions, and Christianity a mythology of sheep, India has a mythology of monkeys and tigers. [*See also* Monkeys.]

The Tree and the Mountain at the Center of the Earth. Many, if not all, of the mythologies of the world have located a tree or a mountain, or both, at the center of the world. In India, the sacred mountain is Mount Meru, the golden mountain, wider at its peak than at its base. The sacred tree, too, is inverted, the banyan with its roots in the air. The particularly Indian variants of this myth begin in the *Ṛgveda,* where the sacred *soma* plant, which bestows immortality on the gods, functions as the *axis mundi,* or cosmic pillar, in propping apart heaven and earth. The same *soma* plant is said to have been stolen from heaven by Indra, mounted on an eagle, who carried the plant down to the mountains of earth. This is the Indian variant of the Indo-European myth of the theft of fire; Prometheus carried fire down to earth in a hollow fennel stalk, while Indra (who also embodies the lightning bolt) carries the fiery liquid of *soma* in its own hollow stalk. The association of the mountain, the sacred plant, and the theft continued to produce offshoots in later Hindu mythology. In the *Rāmāyaṇa,* Hanuman is sent to fetch a magic plant that will revive the fallen hero; he flies to the magic mountain and, unable to decide which plant it is that he wants, uproots the entire mountain and brings it to the battlefield. Elsewhere in the *Rāmāyaṇa,* and in the *Mahābhārata,* the gods and demons join forces to use the sacred mountain Mandara as a churn with which they churn the waters of the ocean to obtain the *soma.* As soon as they get it, the demons steal the *soma* from the gods, and the gods steal it back again.

Snakes are also associated with the mountain and the magic plant (as is the serpent in Eden) and with the cosmic waters: when the serpent Vṛtra has wrapped himself around a mountain, holding back the waters (which are homologous both with the *soma* juice that Indra loves and with the rains that he controls), Indra pierces him so that the waters flow again; it is a snake, Vasuki, who is used as the rope for the churn when the gods and demons churn the ocean for *soma*; and when Viṣṇu sleeps on the serpent of eternity in the midst of the cosmic ocean, a lotus plant grows up out of his navel—the navel of the universe. This web of associations forms the framework for the many local myths about particular trees (banyan trees, coconut palms, the sacred mango tree in the temples of South India) and particular plants sacred to particular gods (the *tulsī* of Viṣṇu, the *rudrākṣa*s of Śiva).

Cosmogony, Theogony, and Anthropogony. Most Indian mythologies seem to agree about the way in which the universe is arranged: it has a sacred mountain in the center, and concentric oceans and continents around the center; the sacred mountain connects the earth with heaven above and the underworld below. This is the basic Indian cosmology. But there are many different explanations of how the universe came to be the way that it is; these are the Indian cosmogonies. Our earliest source, the *Ṛgveda,* refers glancingly to many different theories of creation. Sometimes the world is seen as the result (often apparently a mere by-product) of a cosmic battle, such as the victory of Indra over Vṛtra, or as the consequence of the seemingly unmotivated act of separating heaven and earth, an act that is attributed to several different gods. These aspects of creation are woven in and out of the hymns in the older parts of the *Ṛgveda* (books 2–9). But in the later, tenth book we encounter for the first time hymns that are entirely devoted to speculations on the origins of the cosmos. Some of these hymns seek the origins of the existence of existence itself, or of the creator himself, the golden womb or golden embryo (later to become the golden egg or the golden seed of fire in the cosmic waters). Other hymns speculate upon the sacrifice as the origin of the earth and the people in it, or upon the origins of the sacrifice itself. Sacrifice is central to many concepts of creation, particularly to those explicitly linked to the sacrificial gods or even sacred speech itself, but it also appears as a supplement to other forms of creation, such as sculpture or the spreading out of dirt upon the surface of the waters.

In more anthropomorphic conceptions, creation takes place through a primeval act of incest. In the Brāhmaṇas, the incestuous father is identified as Prajāpati, the lord of creatures; his seed, cast into the fire in place of the usual oblation of clarified butter or *soma* juice, was distributed into various life forms, ritually creating the living world. Later Indian cosmogonies in the epics and Purāṇas continue to combine the abstract with the anthropomorphic. Sometimes the universe is said to arise out of the waters of chaos, from a flame of desire or loneliness that expresses itself in the creation of living forms as well as such abstract entities as the year, logic, grammar, and the thirty-six musical scales. Sometimes a single god (Brahmā, the creator, or Śiva or Viṣṇu, according to the sectarian bias of the text, or even an undifferentiated sort of Vedantic godhead) arises out of the primeval waters and begins to create, more precisely to emit, the world from within himself; this emission *(prasarga)* is the act of projecting his mind onto formless chaos to give it the form that is its substance. In this latter case, the god usually continues to create by taking the form of an androgyne or by producing a woman out of his own body. From there creation proceeds through anthropomorphic methods, often by a combination of sexual intercourse and the generating of ascetic heat, or *tapas.*

The link between abstract cosmogony and highly inflected anthropogony is made explicit in the Purāṇas, which are traditionally expected to deal with five basic topics: the primary creation (of the universe) and the secondary creation (of gods and men and all the other living creatures); the dynasties of the sun and of the moon (that trace their lineage back to those divine celestial bodies and forward to the rulers at the time of the recension of the text that contains the list); and the ages of the Manus or ancestors of man, generally said to be fourteen, of which we are now in the seventh. A different sort of cosmogony-cum-anthropogony begins back in the *Ṛgveda*. This is the Indo-European theme of the dismemberment of a cosmic giant or primeval man (Puruṣa), a theme that also appears, outside of India, as the dismemberment of the primeval androgyne. In the *Ṛgveda*, this man is the victim in a sacrifice that he himself performs; the moon is born from his mind, the sun from his eye, the gods from his mouth, and so forth. Moreover, from this dismemberment there arise the four classes, or *varṇa*s, of ancient Indian society: the brahmans from his head, the rulers and warriors from his chest, the workers from his arms, and the servants from his feet. The Indian text thus extends the three original Indo-European functions that Georges Dumézil has taught us to recognize (priest-kings, warriors, and producers of fertility) by adding a fourth class that is "outside" the original three, for these three alone receive the epithet "twice-born" (that is, reborn at the time of initiation) throughout Indian social history. [*See also* Varṇa and Jāti.]

But the myth of the dismembered man says little about theogony, and the *Ṛgveda* contains no systematic narration of the birth of the gods as a whole, although the births of various gods are described in some detail: Indra, kept against his will inside his mother's womb for many years, bursts forth out of her side and kills his own father; Agni, the god of fire, is born of the waters; and so forth. One important late hymn does speak of the birth of the gods in general, from a female called Aditi (Infinity), who is more particularly the mother of the sun and who remains the mother of the solar gods or *āditya*s (who are contrasted with the *daitya*s, or demons, the sons of Diti) throughout later Indian mythology.

In the epics and Purāṇas, the creation of the gods (and, in turn, of mankind and the animals) is usually attributed to whichever god is regarded by the text in question as the supreme god; thus the Vedic tendency to worship several different gods, but to regard the god one is addressing at the moment as God (a kind of theological serial monogamy that F. Max Müller dubbed henotheism or kathenotheism, "one god at a time") continues into post-Vedic theogonies and anthropogonies.

Eschatology and Death. At the end of each aeon comes doomsday, or *pralaya,* when the universe is destroyed by a combination of fire and flood until at last the primeval waters of chaos close back over the ashes of the triple world. In anthropomorphic terms, this is regarded as the moment when God, whose waking moments or whose dream has been the source of the "emission" of the universe from his mind, falls into a deep, dreamless sleep inside the cosmic waters. And at the end of that sleep, at the end of the period of quiescence, the universe, and the consciousness of the god, is reborn once more out of the waters of chaos.

Thus, eschatology is necessarily the flip side of cosmogony; the wave set in motion by the act of creation is already destined to end in a certain kind of dissolution. The particular Indian twist on the Indo-European model, which added a fourth class to the original three in the anthropogony, places its stamp on the Indo-European eschatology, with its twilight of the gods. First of all, India developed, like Greece, a theory of four ages of declining goodness; where the Greeks named these ages after metals, the Indians called them after throws of the dice, the first and best being the *kṛtayuga,* which is followed by the *tretā,* the *dvāpara,* and finally the present age, or *kaliyuga* (the equivalent of snake-eyes in dice). The choice of the metaphor of dice, with its implication of a fortuitous, impersonal controlling mechanism (which is, moreover, a negative one: the house always wins), is not itself fortuitous; it expresses a basic Indian belief in the inevitable loss of goodness and happiness through the fault of no conscious agent, but just "through the effects of time." The Indian version of the loss of Eden (which appears in Buddhist and Jain as well as Hindu texts) further emphasizes a change in quality between the first three ages and the fourth: the first three are the mythic ages, while the last is real, the time we live in now. And the "end" that comes after the fourth age is not the end at all; the linear decline is combined with the circular pattern of cosmogony and eschatology that we have already seen, and the end becomes the beginning. Time spirals back in on itself like a Möbius strip.

This eternal circularity of time is further developed in India within the context of the unique Indian mythology of *karman,* according to which there is a substance that is intrinsic to all action (*karman,* from the Sanskrit verb *kṛ,* cognate with the Latin *creo,* "to do, to make") and that adheres to the transmigrating soul throughout its life and across the barrier of death, determining the nature of the next rebirth. There are many assumptions embedded in this theory: that there is a transmigrating soul; that one's positive and negative actions are tallied up and carried across the bottom of the ledger page at the end of each life. But the mythology of *karman* reveals a hidden ambivalence in the values expressed by the theory of *karman*. That is, in many myths of *karman*, people want to go on being reborn, in better and better conditions of life, and ultimately in the heaven of the gods. These are the myths within the Vedic and Puranic corpus that exalt *pravṛtti*, or active involvement in worldly life *(saṃsāra)*. But there are many other myths in which people want to escape from the wheel of rebirth, to cease from all activity *(nivṛtti)*, to find release *(mokṣa)*; these are myths influenced by Vedānta and by Buddhism and Jainism. In this latter view, the universal eschatology is replaced by the individual eschatology (or soteriology), the ultimate dissolution of the individual soul *(ātman)* in its final release from the universe itself. [*See also* Karman.]

A parallel development took place in the mythology of death. In the *Ṛgveda*, death is vaguely and uneasily alluded to as the transition to a place of light where the ancestors live, a place ruled by Yama, the primeval twin and the first mortal to die. Much of the subsequent mythology of the Brāhmaṇas is an attempt first to explain the origin of death and then to devise means by which death may be overcome, so that the sacrificer will be guaranteed immortality. The Upaniṣads then begin to speak of the terrors of re-death, and to begin to devise ways of obtaining not immortality but release from life altogether, *mokṣa*. And in medieval Hinduism, *bhakti*, or the passionate and reciprocated devotion to a sectarian deity (Śiva, Viṣṇu, or the Goddess), was thought to procure for the worshiper a kind of combination of the Vedic heaven and the Vedantic release: release from this universe into an infinite heaven of bliss in the presence of the loving god. In this way, the mythology of *bhakti* resolved the conflict between the Vedic desire for eternal life and the Vedantic desire to be free of life forever. [*See also* Cosmology, *article on* Hindu and Jain Cosmologies.]

Householder and Renouncer, Dharma and Mokṣa. A similarly irreconcilable conflict of values is addressed in the Hindu mythology of the householder and the ascetic. Again, one can, if one wishes, see this simply as the Indian version of the widespread theme of the conflict between involvement in the world and a commitment to otherworldly, spiritual values, the conflict between God and mammon. But we can still view the development of this theme within the particular context of Indian intellectual history, more particularly as another instance of the pattern that adds a (transcendental) Indian fourth to an older, Indo-European societal triad. Originally, there were three stages of life, or *āśramas*, in ancient India: student, householder, and forest dweller. That this was in fact the original triad is substantiated by the three "debts" that all Hindus owe: study (the first stage), the debt owed to the Vedic seers, or *ṛṣis*; the oblation (performed by all married householders) to the ancestors; and sacrifice (offered by the semirenunciatory forest dweller) to the gods. And there were three goals of life for a man (*puruṣārthas*): success *(artha)*, social righteousness *(dharma)*, and pleasure *(kāma)*. At the time of the Upaniṣads and the rise of Buddhism, Jainism, and other cults of meditation and renunciation, a fourth stage of life was added, that of the renouncer *(saṃnyāsin)*, and a fourth goal, *mokṣa*. Although these fourth elements were basically and essentially incompatible with the preceding triads, revolutionary negations of all that they stood for, the dauntless eclecticism of Hinduism cheerfully embraced them as supplements or complementary alternatives to the other three. (Similarly, the *Atharvaveda*, a text wholly incommensurate to the other three Vedas in style and purport, was tacked on as the fourth Veda during roughly the same period.) This conjunction of opposites inspired many ingenious responses in the mythology. In some myths, the covert, ancient, antiascetic bias of worldly Hinduism was expressed through tales of hypocritical, lecherous, and generally carnal renouncers; in others, the self-deceptive aspirations of otherworldly householders were dashed or ridiculed. In yet others, the uneasy compromise of the forest dweller—half householder, half renouncer, and the worst half of both—was exposed as a double failure; the myths in which Śiva mocks the sanctimonious sages of the Pine Forest and their sex-starved wives, or the myths in which the impotent and jealous sage Jamadagni curses his lubricious wife, Reṇukā, are important examples of this genre. [*See also* Saṃnyāsa.]

The mythology of renunciation, particularly as it interacted with the mythology of the ancient, nonrenunciatory orthodox caste system, gave rise to an important cycle of myths about kings and untouchables. Even in the Vedic period, the ritual of royal consecration included a phase in which the king had to experience symbolically a kind of reversal, renunciation, or exile before he could take full command of his kingdom. In the later mythology of the epics, this theme is crucial: both the heroes of the *Mahābhārata* and Rāma in the *Rāmāyaṇa* are forced to dwell in exile for many years before returning to rule their kingdoms. In several of the early forms of this myth, the period of exile is spent in association with untouchables; thus Hariścandra, Viśvāmitra, and other great kings are "cursed" to live as untouchables among untouchables before being restored to their rightful kingship. In terms of world (or at least Indo-European) mythology, we can see this theme as the Indian variant of the motif of the true king who is kidnapped or concealed for his own protection at the time of his birth (the slaughter of the innocents) and raised among peasants before returning to claim his throne. This theme is well known to us through such figures as Moses, Jesus, Oedipus, Romulus, or even Odysseus, and, in India, Kṛṣṇa. But the particularly Indian aspect of this theme emerges from two special applications of the phenomenon of renunciation or exile.

First, this experience happens not only to kings but also to brahmans, many of whom are cursed or otherwise condemned to live as untouchables for a period before they are ultimately restored to their brahmanhood. This adventure is neither politically necessary nor psychosexually expedient (in the Freudian mode); it is simply an aspect of the initiation into suffering and otherness that is essential for the fully realized human being in Indian myths. For the king, at the top of the political scale, the experience among the untouchables is a descent from power to impotence; for the brahman, at the top of the religious scale, it is a descent from purity to defilement. The experience of impotence is regarded as just as essential for the wise execution of power as the experience of defilement is essential for the dispassionate achievement of purity.

Second, the Indian development of the myth of renunciation and exile does not always end with the resumption of political power. The most famous example of this alternative denouement is the myth of Gautama, the Buddha Śākyamuni, who dwelt among the Others not by actually leaving his palace to live as an untouchable but by seeing and empathizing with the quintessential "other" from the standpoint of a young king who had been sheltered from every form of weakness or sadness: the vision of an old man, a sick man, a dead man, and a renouncer. As a result of this vision, the Buddha left his palace, never to return again. This myth served as a paradigm not only for many Buddhist (and Buddhist-influenced) myths of renunciant kings but also for many local, sectarian myths about saints and the founders of heterodox traditions, who left the comfort of orthodoxy to dwell among the Others—not necessarily true untouchables, but non-brahmans, even women, people who did not know Sanskrit and had no right to sacrifice—and who never returned.

A final cycle within the corpus of myths of renunciation is the series of myths in which "good" demons "renounce" the canons of demonality in order to become ascetics or devotees of the sectarian gods. The myth of the demon Prahlāda, who loved Viṣṇu and was saved from the attacks of his truly demonic father by Viṣṇu in the form of the man-lion, is the most famous example of this genre. One could view these myths as covert attacks on the threat posed by the ideal of asceticism to the worldly basis of conventional Hinduism: anyone who strove for renunciation, instead of remaining within the bourgeois, sacrificial Hindu fold, was "demonic." To this extent, the myths of good demons can with profit be related to other, non-Indian myths about conscientious devils and saintly witches, myths in which religious innovators or inspired misfits are consigned by the religious establishment to the ranks of the ungodly. But, as always, the Indian variant is peculiarly Indian; here, these myths become myths about caste, and although there are many systems that may resemble caste, there is nothing outside India that duplicates the caste system.

The myths of the good demon are myths in which the overarching, absolute, pan-Indian values of universal *dharma* (*sanātana dharma,* which includes truthfulness, generosity, and noninjury) are pitted against the specific, relative, mutually contradictory, and localized values of "one's own *dharma*" *(svadharma),* which is peculiar to each caste. Thus, some castes may be enjoined to kill animals, to kill people in battle, to execute criminals, to carry night soil, or even to rob. As the *Bhagavadgītā* tells us, it is better to do one's own duty well (even if it violates absolute *dharma*) than to do someone else's duty (even if it does not violate absolute *dharma*). The good demon—good in relativistic, demonic terms—would be good at killing and raping, not good at telling the truth. Thus, in the mythology of orthodox Hinduism, the gods send Viṣṇu in the form of the Buddha to corrupt the "good" demons, to persuade them (wrongly) to give up Vedic sacrifices in favor of noninjury and Buddhist meditation. Stripped of their armor of absolute goodness, the demons are destroyed by the gods, while the demons who remain safely within the fold of their relative goodness survive to contribute their necessary leaven of evil to the balance of the universe. In the later mythology of *bhakti,* however, which successfully challenged caste relativism, the "good" demons are not destroyed; on the contrary, they are translated out of the world entirely, forever absolved of the necessity of performing their despicable duties (despicable in absolute terms), to dwell forever with the God for whom caste has no meaning.

These myths may also express the conflict between life-affirming Vedic values (which, traditionally, have included killing one's enemies in battle as well as killing sacrificial animals) and life-renouncing Vedantic values (of which *ahiṃsā,* the ideal of noninjury, is the most famous if not the most important). They may also be viewed as conflicts between contradictory cosmogonies. The traditional Hindu universe, or "world egg," was closed; those who died must be reborn in order to allow life to recirculate; those who were virtuous had to be balanced by others who were evil in a world of limited good. This reciprocity was further facilitated by the *karman* theory, which held that one's accrued good and bad *karman* could be transferred, particularly through exchanges of food or sexual contact, from one person to another; if one gained, the other lost. Thus, if there are to be saints, there must be sinners. Nor may the sinners refuse to sin, or the demon to rape and pillage, if the saint is to be able to bless and meditate. (Or, in another part of the forest, the householder must not refuse to sacrifice and produce food if the renouncer is to be able to remain aloof from sacrifice and yet to go on eating.) Yet the renouncer wished, ideally, to leave this universe altogether; the good demon wished to abandon demondom forever. The *bhakti* mythology of good demons was thus inspired to create a series of liminal heavens in which the devotee, or *bhakta*, demonic or human, could satisfy the absolute demands of universal *dharma* while disqualifying himself from, rather than defying or explicitly renouncing, the demonic demands of his own *svadharma*. [*See also* Dharma, *article on* Hindu Dharma.]

Gods versus Demons. But it is a mistake to view demons as merely the symbolic expression of certain human social paradoxes. Demons *exist,* and are the enemies of the gods. Indeed, in India that is what demons primarily are: non-gods. In the earliest layer of the *Ṛgveda,* which still shares certain important links with Avestan mythology and looser ties with the Olympian gods and Titans, gods and demons were not different in nature or kind; they were brothers, the children of Prajāpati, the lord of creatures. The demons were the older brothers, and therefore had the primary claim on the kingdom of heaven; the gods were the usurpers. The gods triumphed, however, and post-Vedic mythology (beginning with the Brāhmaṇas) began to associate the divine victors with a cluster of moral virtues (truthfulness, piety, and all the other qualities of universal *dharma*) and the demonic losers with the corresponding moral flaws. The "good" demons of the medieval pantheon, therefore, were not so much upstarts as archconservatives, reclaiming their ancient right to be as virtuous as the gods of the arriviste establishment.

These palace intrigues in heaven had interesting repercussions on earth, in the relationship between men and gods. In the *Ṛgveda,* men and gods were pitted against demons. Men and gods were bound to one another by the mutually beneficial contract of sacrifice: the gods kept men prosperous and healthy in return for the offerings that kept the gods themselves alive and well and living in heaven. The demons were the enemies of both gods and men; the major demons or *asura*s (the ex-Titans) threatened the gods in heaven, while the minor demons, or *rākṣasa*s (more like ghouls or goblins), tormented men, both in their secular lives (killing newborn children, causing diseases) and in their sacred offices (interfering with the sacrifices that maintained the all-important bond between heaven and earth).

But with the rise of the ideal of renunciation as a challenge to the sacrificial order, these simple lines were broken. For demons might offer sacrifice, but if they sacrificed to the gods they strengthened their enemies, which went against their own interests, while if they offered the libations into their own mouths (as they were said to do in the Brāhmaṇas) they exposed their innate selfishness, and the powers of truth and generosity abandoned them, taking with them their power to overcome the gods in battle. But if demons amassed ascetic power they could not be faulted on traditional moral grounds—for they had, in effect, renounced traditional moral grounds—and their power could not be neutralized by the powers of the gods. In this situation, demons were like human ascetics, who could bypass the entire Brahmanic sacrificial structure and strike out as religious loners, outside the system, with powers that, although gained by nonsacrificial methods, could nevertheless challenge the sacrificial powers of the gods on equal grounds, since the heat *(tapas)* generated by the ascetic was of the same intrinsically sacred nature as the heat generated by the sacrificial priest. In the myths, this challenge is expressed by the simple transfer of heat: the *tapas* generated by the demonic or human ascetic rises, as heat is wont to do, and heats the throne of Indra, the king of the gods; Indra immediately recognizes the source of his discomfort (for it recurs with annoying frequency) and dispatches from heaven a voluptuous nymph (an *apsaras*) to seduce the would-be ascetic by siphoning off his erotic heat in the form of his seed. In this middle period, therefore, the epic period in which Indra ruled in heaven, men and demons could be pitted against the gods. [*See also* Tapas.]

A further realignment took place with the rise of the great sectarian gods, Viṣṇu and Śiva. The mythology of the "good" demon brought into play a mythology of the "good" untouchable or the good non-brahman in local and vernacular traditions; we have seen one aspect of this development in the myths of the king among the untouchables. For in *bhakti* mythology the devotional gods are on the side of good men and good demons alike; they are against only evil men and evil demons. The straightforward lines of Vedic allegiance are thus sicklied o'er with the pale cast of morality. While in classical orthodox Hinduism, it was one's action that mattered (ortho*praxy*), now it was one's thought that mattered (ortho*doxy*). Thus, devotional Hinduism can be generous to untouchables, and even to Buddhists and Muslims, whose ritual activities made them literally anathema to orthodox Hinduism, but it can be bitterly intransigent toward wrong-thinking Hindus (and, of course, to wrong-thinking Muslims, Buddhists, and untouchables), no matter how observant they might be of caste strictures governing behavior. In this view, what one is (demon or untouchable) or what one does (kill, tan leather) is not so important as what one thinks, or, even more, feels (love for the true God). [*See also* Bhakti.]

Illusion. This emphasis on what is thought or felt in contrast with what is done or brought into existence is basic to all of Indian mythology. Its roots go back to the Vedas, where the gods use their powers of illusion *(māyā)* not merely to delude the demons (themselves masters of illusion) but to create the entire universe. The Upaniṣadic doctrine that the state of unity with the godhead is closer to dreaming sleep than it is to waking life (and closest of all to dreamless sleep) paved the way for the concept, already encountered in the myths of cosmogony, that the universe is merely a projection or emanation from the mind of a (sleeping) god, that we are all merely a dream of God. The belief that we see the gods most closely in our dreams is encountered widely outside of India and accounts, in part, for the universal value set on premonitory dreams. But just as Indian philosophy, particularly Mahāyāna Buddhist philosophy, developed the doctrine of illusion to a pitch unknown in other forms of idealism, so too Indian mythology played countless imaginative variants on the theme of dreams and illusion.

In its simplest form, the theme could transform any myth at all into a myth of illusion: at the end of any number of complex adventures, the god appears *ex machina* to say that it was all nothing but a dream. All is as it was at the beginning of the story—all, that is, but our understanding of what the situation *was* at the beginning of the story. This is a motif that is known from other cultures (although not, I suspect, from any culture that could not have borrowed it from India). But in its more complex form, the theme of illusion is combined with the folk motif of the tale within a tale, the mechanism of Chinese boxes, with the peculiar Indian Möbius twist: the dreamers or tellers of tales are dreaming of one another, or the dreamer of the first in a series of nested dreams, one within the other, turns out to be a character inside the innermost dream in the series. Ultimately, the worshiper is dreaming into existence the god who is dreaming him into existence. [*See also* Māyā.]

The Pantheon. I have left until last the theme that is usually regarded as the meat and potatoes of mythology: the pantheon of gods and goddesses. These will all be treated separately elsewhere in this encyclopedia, so it remains for me only to remark upon their interrelationships and the patterns of their interactions. The basic structure of the Indian pantheon might be viewed, appropriately enough in the home of *homo hierarchicus,* in terms of a decentralized hierarchy. At the center of the pantheon is a single god, or a godhead, recognized by most Hindus. They may refer to it (him/her) as the Lord (Īśvara), the One, the godhead *(brahman),* or by a number of other names of a generally absolute character. This godhead is then often identified with one of the great pan-Indian gods: Śiva, Viṣṇu, or the Goddess (Devī). The concept of a trinity consisting of Brahmā the creator, Viṣṇu the preserver, and Śiva the destroyer is entirely artificial, although it is often encountered in the writings of Hindus as well as Western scholars. If there is any functional trinity, it is the triangle of Śiva, who is married to Devī, who is the sister of Viṣṇu.

On the third level of differentiation, Viṣṇu may be worshiped in the form of one of his *avatāra*s (of which Rāma and Kṛṣṇa are by far the most popular), and Śiva may be worshiped in one of his "manifestations" or "playful appearances" on earth. [*See* Avatāra.] Devī is often identified with a local goddess who brings as her dowry her own complex mythology. In general, local gods are assimilated to the pan-Indian pantheon through marriage, natural birth or adoption, or blatant identification: Durgā marries Śiva; Skanda is the natural son of Śiva; the demon Andhaka becomes Bhṛṅgin, the adopted son of Śiva; and Aiyanar *is* Skanda, a god by another name. These assimilations work in the upstream direction as well; the pan-Indian concept of the dancing Śiva probably originated in South India, and the erotic liaison of Kṛṣṇa and Rādhā in Bengal. Such cross-fertilizations result in gods and goddesses who are truly and literally multifaceted; their many heads and arms reflect not merely the many things that they are and can do, but the many places they have come from—and are heading toward.

At this point, the pantheon splinters into a kaleidoscope of images and tales that demonstrate how the one God became manifest right here, in Banaras or Gujurat or Madurai, how this particular temple or shrine became the center of the earth. For, like a hologram, the entire Indian mythological panorama is always present in its entirety in every single spot in the Indian world.

[*Many of the deities, mythic figures, and technical terms mentioned in this article are the subjects of independent entries. See also* Mahābhārata; Rāmāyaṇa; *and* Purāṇas.]

BIBLIOGRAPHY

There are several good introductory collections of Indian myths. Both my own *Hindu Myths* (Harmondsworth, 1975) and Cornelia Dimmitt and J. A. B. van Buitenen's *Classical Hindu Mythology* (Philadelphia, 1978) give translations of selected central texts. The latter inclines more to folkloric and localized Sanskrit traditions; the former leans more toward the classical themes and includes a detailed bibliography of primary and secondary sources. The available surveys are useful as reference works: Sukumari Bhattacharji's *The Indian Theogony* (Cambridge, 1970), Alain Daniélou's *Hindu Polytheism* (London, 1964), V. R. Ramachandra Dikshitar's *The Purāṇa Index* (Madras, 1955), E. Washburn Hopkins's *Epic Mythology* (1915; reprint, New York, 1969), A. A. Macdonell's *Vedic Mythology* (1897; reprint, New York, 1974), Vettam Mani's *Purāṇic Encyclopaedia* (Delhi, 1975), and Sören Sörensen's *An Index to the Names in the Mahābhārata*, 13 pts. (London, 1904–1925).

Most of the primary sources for Indian mythology in Sanskrit are now available in English translations of varying reliability. For the *Ṛgveda*, see my *The Rig Veda* (Harmondsworth, 1982); for the Brāhmaṇas, see Arthur Berriedale Keith's *Aitareya and Kauṣītaki Brāhmaṇas* (Cambridge, Mass., 1920); Julius Eggeling's *The Śatapatha Brāhmaṇa*, 5 vols., "Sacred Books of the East," vols. 12, 26, 41, 43, and 44 (Oxford, 1882–1900; reprint Delhi, 1966); Willem Caland's *The Pañcaviṃśa Brāhmaṇa* (Calcutta, 1931); and A. A. Macdonell's *The Bṛhaddevatā Attributed to Śaunaka* (Cambridge, Mass., 1904). The *Mahābhārata* has been completely if awkwardly translated by Pratap Chandra Roy and K. M. Ganguli, 12 vols. (1884–1896; 2d ed., Calcutta, 1970); a fine new translation by J. A. B. van Buitenen, terminated by his death when he had completed only five of the eighteen books (Chicago, 1973–1978), is in process of completion by the University of Chicago Press at the hands of a team of translators. The *Rāmāyaṇa* has been completely if clumsily translated by Hari Prasad Shastri, 3 vols. (London, 1962), and is now being properly translated by Robert P. Goldman and others and published by Princeton University Press.

The Purāṇas, which are the main sources for the study of Hindu mythology, are now becoming available in English translations in several different series: "Ancient Indian Tradition and Mythology" (AITM), published by Motilal Banarsidass in Delhi; the "All-India Kashiraj Trust" (AIKT), in Varanasi; and two older series that have recently been resurrected, the "Chowkhamba Sanskrit Series" (CSS), in Varanasi, and the "Sacred Books of the Hindus" (SBH), originally published in Allahabad and now republished in New York by AMS Press. These are the Purāṇas that have emerged so far:

Agnipurāṇam. 2 vols. Translated by M. N. Dutt. CSS, no. 54. Calcutta, 1901; reprint, Varanasi, 1967.

Bhāgavata. 4 vols. Translated by Ganesh Vasudeo Tagare. AITM, nos. 7–10. Delhi, 1976.

Brahmāṇḍa. 5 vols. Translated by Ganesh Vasudeo Tagare. AITM, nos. 22–26. Delhi, 1983.

Brahma-vaivarta Purāṇam. 2 vols. Translated by Rajendra Nath Sen. SBH, no. 24. Allahabad, 1920–1922; reprint, New York, 1974.

Śrīmad Devī Bhāgavatam. Translated by Swami Vijnanananda. SBH, no. 26. Allahabad, 1922–1923, issued in parts; reprint, New York, 1973.

Garuḍapurāṇam. Translated by M. N. Dutt. CSS, no. 67. Calcutta, 1908; reprint, Varanasi, 1968.

Kūrma Purāṇa. Translated by Ahibhushan Bhattacharya and edited by Anand Swarup Gupta. Varanasi, 1972.

Liṅga Purāṇa. 2 vols. Edited by Jagdish Lal Shastri and translated by a board of scholars. AITM, nos. 5–6. Delhi, 1973.

Mārkaṇḍeya Purāṇa. Translated by F. Eden Pargiter. Bibliotheca Indica. Calcutta, 1888–1904, issued in parts; reprint, Delhi, 1969.

Matsya Purāṇam. 2 vols. Translated by a *taluqdar* of Oudh. SBH, no. 17. Allahabad, 1916–1919.

Śiva Purāṇa. 4 vols. Edited by Jagdish Lal Shastri and translated by a board of scholars. AITM, nos. 1–4. Delhi, 1970.

Vāmana Purāṇa. Translated by Satyamsu M. Mukhopadhyaya and edited by Anand Swarup Gupta. Varanasi, 1968.

Viṣṇu Purāṇa. Translated by H. H. Wilson. London, 1940; 2d ed., Calcutta, 1961.

For a complete list of Sanskrit editions of the Purāṇas, see my *Hindu Myths*, cited above.

There are also several useful studies of selected Indian mythic themes. Still the best introduction is Heinrich Zimmer's *Myths and Symbols in Indian Art and Civilization*, edited by Joseph Campbell (1946; reprint, Princeton, 1972). Also helpful is Arthur Berriedale Keith's *Indian Mythology*, vol. 6, pt. 1, of *The Mythology of All Races*, edited by Louis H. Gray (1917; reprint, New York, 1964). There are also a number of books devoted to particular gods or mythic themes: for Tamil mythology, David Dean Shulman's *Tamil Temple Myths* (Princeton, 1980); for gods and demons, my *The Origins of Evil in Hindu Mythology* (Berkeley, 1976); for cosmology, Richard F. Gombrich's "Ancient Indian Cosmology," in *Ancient Cosmologies*, edited by Carmen Blacker and Michael Loewe (London, 1975); for Kṛṣṇa, John Stratton Hawley's *Krishna, the Butter Thief* (Princeton, 1983) and *At Play with Krishna* (Princeton, 1981); for Śiva, my *Śiva, the Erotic Ascetic* (Oxford, 1981); for Devī, *The Divine Consort: Rādhā and the Goddesses of India*, edited by John Stratton Hawley and Donna M. Wulff (Berkeley, 1982) and my *Women, Androgynes, and Other Mythical Beasts* (Chicago, 1980); for the myths of illusion, my *Dreams, Illusion, and Other Realities* (Chicago, 1984). Finally, no study of Indian mythology can fail to take into account the writings of Madeleine Biardeau, particularly her *Clefs pour la pensée hindoue* (Paris, 1972); *Études de mythologie hindoue*, 4 vols. (Paris, 1968–1976); and her essays in the *Dictionnaire des mythologies*, edited by Yves Bonnefoy (Paris, 1981).

WENDY DONIGER O'FLAHERTY

History of Study

As is the case with other great traditions, the study of and interest in Indian religions cannot be described in terms of academic research alone; nor is it confined to the accumulation of factual information. It also involves questions of motivation, hermeneutic conditions, religious commitment, philosophical reflection, and interaction and dialogue between India and the West. It reflects the work and attitudes of missionaries and philologists, travelers and philosophers, anthropologists and theologians. It has roots and repercussions in the general trends and developments of Western science, religion, and philosophy. Its impact upon Indian as well as Western self-understanding is undeniable and still growing. More than other religions, Indian religions and specifically Hinduism are integrated into the totality of forms of culture and life, and to that extent, Indian studies in general have a direct or indirect bearing upon the religion of Hinduism. In such broad and comprehensive application, the term *religion* itself has become subject to questioning and reinterpretation.

Beginnings of Indological Research. Although institutionalized Indological research and systematic and organized study of Indian religions are not older than two centuries (initiated in part by the foundation in 1784 of the Asiatic Society of Bengal and by the establishment in 1814 of the first chair for Indian studies at the University of Paris), the Western encounter with the Indian religious tradition was by no means an unexpected and unprepared event. Since the days of classical Greece, and in particular since the Indian campaign of Alexander the Great (327–325 BCE), there has been interest in and speculation about Indian wisdom and religion. On the one hand, such interest was nurtured by the idea that the origins of the Greek religious and philosophical tradition were to be found in the East; on the other hand, it may also have reflected a search for alternatives and correctives to the Greek tradition. In spite of this interest, however, verifiable contacts between West and East were rare; the linguistic and cultural barriers were usually insurmountable. Even Megasthenes, the Greek ambassador at the Maurya court in Pāṭaliputra (today Patna, Bihar) from 302 to 291 BCE, was unable to explore Indian religion in its original textual sources. The rise of the Sasanid empire and then of Islam virtually precluded direct contacts between India and Europe for many centuries, and there was little more than a repetition and rearrangement of the materials inherited from Greek and Roman antiquity. However, a highly original and thorough study of India, based upon textual sources as well as travel experiences and accompanied by an unprecedented hermeneutic awareness, was produced in Arabic by the great Islamic scholar al-Bīrūnī (973–1048). But his work remained unknown in contemporary Europe, and even in medieval Islam it was a unique and somewhat isolated phenomenon.

The Portuguese explorers who reopened direct Western access to India (a development marked by Vasco da Gama's arrival in 1498 in the South Indian port city of Calicut) were motivated not by any interest in Indian religion or philosophy but by trade and missionary interests. Yet, the urge to teach and to proselytize turned out to be a powerful incentive to explore the contexts and conditions for spreading the Christian message. For several centuries, missionaries were the leading pioneers in the study of Indian languages and of Indian religious thought. Their greatest representative, Roberto de Nobili (1577–1656; active in Madurai, South India), learned Tamil and Sanskrit and acquired and unequaled knowledge of the Indian tradition. But his writings remained unpublished during his lifetime and were only recently rediscovered. The work of another missionary, Abraham Roger's Dutch-language *De opendeure tot het verborgen heydendom* (The Open Door to the Hidden Heathendom), published in 1651, was translated into other European languages and widely used as a sourcebook on Indian religion. The works of travelers like François Bernier and Jean Baptiste Tavernier provided additional information.

The ideological movements of Deism and the Enlightenment opened new perspectives on India and on non-Christian religions in general. One characteristic argument (used, for example, by Voltaire) was that the basic ideas concerning God and religion are older, more original, and less deformed in the ancient cultures of Asia than in the Christian West. Similarly, a certain deistic openness toward a universal religion can be found in the works of two eighteenth-century British pioneers of the study of Hinduism, Alexander Dow and John Z. Holwell. Like them, the French scholar A. H. Anquetil-Duperron (1731–1805) did not have direct access to Sanskrit; instead, his Latin version of fifty Upaniṣads, published in two volumes in 1801–1802 under the title *Oupnek'hat* and of seminal importance for the appreciation of Indian religious thought in continental Europe, was based upon a Persian translation (*Sirr-i Akbar,* 1657). Even William Jones (1746–1794), founder of the Asiatic Society of Bengal and one of the most influential pioneers of modern Indology, initially studied Persian before gaining access to the Sanskrit language. Charles Wilkins (1749–1836), the first English translator of the *Bhagavadgītā* (1785), and Henry Thomas Colebrooke (1765–1837), whose wide-ranging studies set new standards for Indian studies, continued the work of Jones. The general British attitude toward India was, however, under the impact of more practical interests, and, accordingly, it viewed Indian religion most often in its association with social, administrative, and political issues.

The situation was significantly different in continental Europe, and specifically in Germany, where the Romantic movement produced an unparalleled enthusiasm for ancient India, celebrated as the homeland of the European languages and of true religion and philosophy. German scholars contrasted the original spiritual purity and greatness of India with a progressive degeneration and obscuration in more recent times. In several cases, this enthusiasm led to a serious study of the original sources and to a more sober assessment; a certain disenchantment, for example, is documented in Friedrich Schlegel's classic *Über die Sprache und Weisheit der Indier* (On the Language and Wisdom of the Indians, 1808). August Wilhelm Schlegel, who shared his brother's early enthusiasm, became the first professor of Indology in Germany (at the University of Bonn in 1818) and a pioneer in the philological treatment of Indian texts. The Romantic influence persisted to the time of F. Max Müller (1823–1900), a German-born leader of nineteenth-century Indology and at Oxford University an influential advocate of comparative religion and mythology. In general, the discovery of the Indian materials had a special, often decisive impact upon the development of comparative studies in the humanities.

Classical Indology. Textual and historical scholarship of the nineteenth century has laid the foundations for our present access to ancient and classical Indian sources. Dictionaries prepared during this period as well as catalogs of manuscripts and editions and translations of religious texts are still considered indispensable. Throughout the nineteenth century there was a particular fascination with the Vedas, the oldest religious literature of Hinduism, and especially with the *Ṛgveda*. The first complete editions of the *Ṛgveda* were prepared by F. Max Müller (1849–1874) and Theodor Aufrecht (1861–1863). Müller saw in it the origins and early developments of religion as such; his contemporary Rudolf Roth took a more philological approach. Interest in the vast ritualistic literature of the Brāhmaṇas remained more limited, and pioneering work was done by Albrecht Weber (1825–1901) and Willem Caland (1859–1932). For earlier scholars the Vedas had been primarily a record of Indo-European antiquity, and at the core of its religious impulse they had seen a mythology of natural forces. Subsequently, other dimensions of the Vedas were emphasized, and they were interpreted more specifically in their Indian context and with reference to later developments. Moreover, Western interest in the Vedic and Upaniṣadic texts further enhanced their reputation in India. Between 1816 and 1819 the Bengali reformer Ram Mohan Roy published Bengali and English translations of some of the Upaniṣads, which in Anquetil-Duperron's Latin version had already impressed European thinkers, most conspicuously Arthur Schopenhauer; Roy is an early example of an Indian author who contributed to the modern exploration and dissemination of ancient Indian religious documents. Toward the end of the nineteenth century, Schopenhauer's admirer Paul Deussen (1845–1919) made further significant contributions to the study of the Upaniṣads and to the Vedānta system, which is built upon the interpretation of the Upaniṣads.

The great epics the *Mahābhārata* and the *Rāmāyaṇa* were studied as both religious and literary documents. In particular, the most famous episode of the *Mahābhārata*, the *Bhagavadgītā*, which was first translated into English by Charles Wilkins (1785) and has since appeared in numerous new translations and editions, has become in our time the most popular piece of Indian religious poetry in the West. The Purāṇas, by contrast, attracted much less interest in spite of the outstanding efforts of H. H. Wilson (whose English translation of the *Viṣṇu Purāṇa* was published in 1840) and Eugène Burnouf (whose edition and French translation of the *Bhāgavata Purāṇa* was published 1840–1847; a French version based upon a Tamil version had been published in 1788). A full exploration of this vast literature has begun only in the twentieth century. Serious scholarly work on the Tantras has lagged behind still farther and is still in its infancy. The collection and description of Tantric manuscripts begun by Rajendralal Mitra and others, and the editions and studies done in this area by John George Woodroffe (pseudonym, Arthur Avalon), the chief justice of Bengal, broke new ground. R. G. Bhandarkar's *Vaiṣṇavism, Śaivism and Minor Religious Systems* (1913) gave an authoritative summary of the information on sectarian Hinduism available at the time it was written.

Apart from his extensive Vedic studies and his contributions to other fields such as Brahmanic literature, Albrecht Weber laid the foundations for modern Jain studies, an area in which he was followed by scholars like Georg Bühler and Hermann Jacobi, who established the distinctive and extra-Vedic character of the Jain tradition. Another representative Indologist of the nineteenth century, Monier Monier-Williams (1819–1899), tried to combine textual learning with an understanding of living Hinduism and of practical missionary and administrative problems; this effort was visible, for example, in his work *Modern India and the Indians* (1878). By and large, popular Hinduism and the practical, institutional, or social dimensions of Indian religions were not among the topics of classical Indological research. Up to the beginning of the twentieth century, these phenomena were recorded principally by missionaries in accounts such as the controversial yet very influential report of Jean-Antoine Dubois entitled *Hindu Manners, Customs and Ceremonies* (1816, a translation of a French manuscript completed in 1805–1806). Further valuable information on social and religious life was provided by various gazetteers of India. Missionaries or scholars with missionary background also contributed richly to the study of religious literature in vernaculars, especially in South India, where they compiled most of the early dictionaries of Dravidian languages; and they produced as well the first accounts of the tribal religions of India, which are more or less outside the great scriptural traditions. The missionary J. N. Farquhar covered the whole range of Hindu religious literature in his still useful *Outline of the Religious Literature of India* (1920); his *Modern Religious Movements in India* (1915) is one of the first surveys of Neo-Hinduism and related phenomena.

Philosophical Approaches to Indian Religions. The results of Indological research have affected the thought of various Western theologians and philosophers. In turn, Western systems of thought have provided motivations and interpretive frameworks for the study of Indian religions or have even influenced Indological research directly. These influences are exemplified by three important nineteenth-century philosophers, namely, G. W. F. Hegel (1770–1831), Arthur Schopenhauer (1788–1860), and Auguste Comte (1798–1857).

Hegel rejects the Romantic glorification of India. Nonetheless, he is a careful witness of the beginnings of Indological research and deals with Indian religious thought and life in considerable detail. In Hegel's view, the way of the *Weltgeist* ("world spirit") leads from East to West. Eastern and in particular Indian thought represents an introductory and subordinate stage of development that has been transcended (*aufgehoben,* i.e., canceled, conserved, and exalted all at once) by the Christian European stage. The inherent and distinctive principle of Indian religion and philosophy (systems that Hegel sees as inseparable) is the orientation toward the unity of one underlying "substance." God is conceived of as pure substance or abstract being *(brahman),* in which finite beings are contained as irrelevant modifications. The individual human person has to subdue and extinguish individuality and return into the one primeval substance. In this light, Hegel tries to give a comprehensive and coherent interpretation of all phenomena of Indian life and culture and to establish the basically static, ahistorical character of the Indian tradition. Whatever the deficiencies of this interpretation may be, it has had a significant impact upon the treatment of India in the general histories of religion, and it has largely contributed to the long-lasting neglect of Indian culture in the historiography of philosophy.

Schopenhauer's association with Indian thought is much more familiar to Western readers than that of Hegel, and his attitude is conspicuously different. He does not accept any directedness or progression in history, and he can recognize insights and experiences of foreign and ancient traditions without having to subordinate them to the European standpoint. In the religious metaphysics of Vedānta and Buddhism he rediscovers his own views concerning the "world as will and representation" and the undesirability of existence, and he claims these traditions as allies against what he considers to be the errors and evils of the Judeo-Christian tradition, such as the belief in historical progress and in the uniqueness of the human person. He sees the Old Testament as a worldly book without the genuine sense of transcendence and of final liberation that he discovers in the Indian religious documents. In the New Testament he finds more to appreciate; his speculations that its teachings were influenced by Indian sources are not uncommon in the nineteenth century. He hopes that the Indological discoveries will initiate a "New Renaissance." While in fact this may not have happened, Schopenhauer's ideas nevertheless have stimulated much interest in Indian and comparative studies, though largely outside the academic world. Among the followers of Schopenhauer who contributed to the textual exploration of Indian religion and philosophy Paul Deussen remains the most outstanding example.

Comte does not show any noticeable interest in Indian thought, but his conception of "positive philosophy" and his programmatic ideas about transforming philosophy into sociology and anthropology (i.e., the systematic study of the human phenomenon) have set the stage for important developments in European, specifically French intellectual and scholarly life, such as the work of Lucien Lévy-Bruhl, Émile Durkheim, and Marcel Mauss in ethnology, sociology, and religious studies. In general, these writings have provided a broad ideological background for the anthropological and sociological study of religion. Paul Masson-Oursel's *La philosophie comparée* (1923; translated as *Comparative Philosophy,* 1926) reflects this tradition in its own way. By juxtaposing and comparing the "facts" of philosophical and religious thought in India, China, and Europe, Masson-Oursel tries to explore the full range of human potential and to discover the basic regularities of its development. Indeed, he presents himself as a disinterested cartographer of the human mind, an observer no longer attached to one particular cultural tradition or metaphysical viewpoint.

The three approaches just outlined remain exemplary and influential. There are, of course, numerous variants, as well as other, genuinely different approaches. Among the latter is a wide spectrum of attempts to find a common core or horizon of religiosity or a "transcendent unity of religions" (as proposed by Frithjof Schuon) or to approach the Indian tradition in the name of "religious experience" or "comparative mysticism" (as proposed by Rudolf Otto); another approach, with a psychological and agnostic emphasis, was taken by William James. Again, instead of Hegel's European self-confidence or the rigid Christian absolutism of such theologians as Karl Barth, we now find a variety of more or less far-reaching ideas about encounter and dialogue, adaptation, and even synthesis. Among Catholic theologians, Karl Rahner has set new standards of openness toward other religions. Psychological or psychoanalytic methods and viewpoints have repeatedly been applied to the study of Indian religions, most conspicuously and influentially in the works of C. G. Jung and some of his followers. Other methodologies or ideologies, too, have had an explicit or implicit bearing upon the study of Indian religions; in particular, structuralist orientations have gained momentum. A Marxist interpretation of the Indian tradition exists as well, represented by Walter Ruben and others.

Scientific Contributions. The study of Indian religions by anthropologists and other social scientists is largely a phenomenon of the period after 1945. These studies rely principally on field investigations of living communities to generate their descriptions and models of Indian religions, and only indirectly on historical works or classical textual sources.

From their predecessors in the study of Indian religions, social scientists have inherited the following major questions about Indian religions. What is the nature and structure of the dominant religious traditions of India? What is the relationship between the legacy of norms, concepts, and beliefs contained in the great textual traditions of India and the day-to-day religious lives of its people? In what way does religion in India affect social structure (and, in particular, the caste system)? To what degree do the religions of India inhibit its economic development and vigor? Social scientists have inherited also a tendency to focus on Hinduism, the majority religion of the subcontinent, so that minority religions, including Islam, have till recently not been the focus of sustained research except insofar as they support or refute ideas about Hindu social forms.

In the period since 1945, social scientists trained principally in India, England, France, and the United States have translated these overarching questions into a series of more manageable ones about the functioning of religion at the village level of Indian society, addressing the following subjects: the ritual aspects of hierarchy in village life; the structure of the village pantheon; the links between social mobility and changed religious practices; the Hindu grammar of purity and pollution; indigenous ideas about power and authority; Indian explanations of fate, misfortune, and determinacy; and Hindu conceptions of space and time, death and liberation. Although much of this investigation has been conducted and communicated within the village framework, there has been throughout this period a concomitant countertradition of synthetic works that aim to capitalize on and generalize from these many local studies. The four decades since 1945 can, for expository convenience, be divided into three phases, which are sequentially discussed below. The following discussion focuses on major or representative works, approaches, and authors, rather than on more specialized, peripheral, or transient trends.

The first phase, which began in 1945, was dominated by the publication of *Religion and Society among the Coorgs of South India* by M. N. Srinivas (1952). In this study, Srinivas used the term "Sanskritization" to characterize a general mobility strategy that enabled Coorgs, and many other groups, either to enter the social fold of Hinduism or to rise within its hierarchy. This concept, which has been much invoked, debated, and refined since then, rested on the assumption of a critical historical, linguistic, and conceptual gap between local religious beliefs and customs and those of what Srinivas called "Sanskritic Hinduism," that is, the Hinduism of esoteric texts, literate priests, and cosmopolitan centers. This approach dovetailed very fortuitously with the ideas of the American anthropologist Robert Redfield regarding the difference between "great" and "little" traditions in peasant civilizations. Subsequently, an influential group of anthropologists centered at the University of Chicago set themselves to refining, synthesizing, and operationalizing the ideas of Redfield and of Milton Singer as they applied to Indian religions and society. A collection of essays edited by McKim Marriott and titled *Village India* (1955) signals the beginning of this trend, and Singer's *When a Great Tradition Modernizes* (1972) marks its zenith. This latter work also contains the most thorough anthropological critique available of Max Weber's influential thesis about the antagonism between caste ideology (with its Hindu assumptions) and modern capitalistic enterprise. This first phase, rooted in the empirical study of village religion, was dominated by the problem of reconciling village-level diversities with what were perceived as pan-Indian uniformities in religious belief and practice.

In the second phase, inaugurated by the publication of *Homo Hierarchicus: The Caste System and Its Implications* by Louis Dumont (1966; first English translation, 1970), this problem was largely replaced by a concern to analyze the conceptual core of Hinduism. Dumont, whose intellectual starting point was the opposition of pure and impure in Hindu thought (an opposition first remarked by Celestin Bougle, 1908), denied the conceptual gap between "great" and "little" traditions on the grounds of a shared conceptual scheme that animated Indian religious systems at all levels. He argued that the Hindu religious understanding of hierarchy was the philosophical basis of the caste system, and suggested that there was a radical incompatibility between approaches appropriate to the analysis of Western societies, which assume the axiomatic importance of equality and the individual, and those appropriate to the study of Indian society, with its cultural axiom of hierarchy—based on religiously defined purity—and its assumption of the priority of the social group. Dumont's work, in spite of its controversial qualities, has generated two decades of anthropological and sociological writing on India characterized by a concern with hierarchy, an almost exclusive focus on Hinduism, and a tilt toward the conceptual rather than the behavioral aspects of religious life in India.

Starting approximately in 1975, there has been a turning away from some of these larger debates and a return to more focused ethnographic and thematic investigations. Recent approaches have included anthropological analysis of both specific Hindu texts and textual traditions in an effort to learn of their cosmological assumptions; more systematic effort to investigate the local incarnations and involutions of dominant civilizational concepts; and a rediscovery of oral traditions, which, together with local performance genres, reveal important variations on civilizational themes and motifs. This most recent phase continues to explore traditional problems in the study of Indian religions, but makes more explicit and self-conscious use of methods and theories developed recently in folklore, linguistics, and philosophy. But perhaps the most promising recent trend has been the turn toward historical analyses of religious institutions, processes, and symbolic forms, a shift that has involved renewed dialogue between historians and anthropologists. This trend has produced a number of studies reminding us that Indian religions are not unchanging ways of expressing timeless truths.

Recent Trends and Developments. There is no single spectacular work separating modern from traditional Indology; instead, there is continuation and expansion, combined with gradual changes in orientation. The tradition of classical Vedic scholarship has been continued by Heinrich Lüders, Louis Renou, Jan Gonda, and others; these scholars have also reexamined the problems of continuity and change between Vedic and Hindu India. The quantity of available source materials has increased rapidly, and more scholars of different geographical, cultural, and religious origins and disciplinary backgrounds participate now in the process of research, which is no longer a primarily European affair. In the United States, the tradition of classical Indology (first represented by scholars like William Dwight Whitney and Maurice Bloomfield) continues to some extent; but the study of Indian religion is pursued more vigorously in the context of other disciplines and of so-called area studies in the university curriculum. In Japan, which adopted Western academic institutions and methods of research in the late nineteenth century, research interests have focused on Buddhism, but much significant work has been done also on the other religious traditions of India, primarily in the field of textual studies (by Ui Hakuju, Nakamura Hajime, and others). From the beginning of modern Indology, the participation of Indians as collaborators in the process of research and as interpreters of their own tradition has been indispensable. In the twentieth century, particularly since India's independence (1947), their role has become more active, and their growing presence at Western universities, specifically in North America, has had a significant impact upon the exploration and teaching of Indian religions. Indian scholars have not traditionally been attracted by historical and philological methods; yet certain massive projects necessitating such methods could be executed properly only in India. Such a project was the critical edition of the *Mahābhārata,* which was inspired by Western philologists but actually produced in India (by V. S. Sukthankar and others). More recently, Indians have begun a systematic textual exploration of the Purāṇas, Āgamas, and Tantras, and of the vast devotional and philosophical literature of the sectarian movements. Still, there is on their part some reluctance to devote serious scholarly attention to religious literature considered to have lesser theoretical status (such as the *māhātmya* literature) or written in a vernacular language. The wide field of connections between religious texts on the one side and art, architecture, and iconography on the other also remains an important area for further studies; scholars like Ananda K. Coomaraswamy and Stella Kramrisch have made stimulating, though to some extent controversial, contributions in this area.

Much work remains to be done in the study of Indian religions. A new area of research (and speculation) was opened during the 1920s by the archaeological discovery of the pre-Vedic Harappan civilization; the religious practices of this civilization and its connection with Vedic India are still open to question. The Vedas themselves are being approached in new and unorthodox ways, for example, in the *soma* studies of R. Gordon Wasson. The vastness of classical and later Sanskrit materials available for study is made evident by the *New*

Catalogus Catalogorum (edited since 1949 by V. Raghavan, continued by K. Kunjunni Raja), a comprehensive listing of extant Sanskrit texts. In addition, the materials in Prakrit (specifically in Jainism) and numerous South and North Indian vernaculars still await comprehensive cataloging and exploration. These are particularly relevant for the study of sectarian and theistic movements, such as the South Indian Śaiva Siddhānta or Śrī Vaiṣṇava traditions; moreover, the increasing awareness of the details and inner differentiations of the Hindu tradition leads to new questions concerning its identity and coherence and its manifold and ambiguous relations to Buddhism and Jainism, but also to Islam, which has been present in India for more than a thousand years, and finally to Christianity. This emergent complexity has been an occasion for discussions concerning the meaning and applicability of the idea of tolerance in the Indian context. Furthermore, because of the pervasive role of religion in India, its study has to be based upon a wide variety of sources, including, for example, the Dharmaśāstras (law books); the work of such Dharmaśāstra scholars as P. V. Kane is immediately relevant for the study of Indian religion. More specifically, philosophical literature supplements religious literature because it is, with few exceptions, built upon religious foundations or motivated by religious goals; it also provides religious practices and ideas with a theoretical framework that at times challenges conventional Western understanding of such theological concepts as revelation, grace, or creation. Such interdependence gives the work of historians of Indian philosophy—for example, Surendranath Dasgupta—obvious importance for the study of Indian religion.

In the past few decades, the relationship of textual norms and theories to actual religious life has become an increasingly significant issue. A variety of nontextual approaches have been suggested to correct or supplement the understanding that can be gained from the texts alone. Combinations of textual and nontextual methods have been applied to such topics as the caste system, world renunciation, religious devotion *(bhakti),* and the doctrine of *karman* and rebirth in order to clarify not only their theoretical meaning but also their practical functions in the life of the Indian people. By means of such combined methods, local cults are correlated and contrasted with the standards of the great traditions; precept and practice, text and social context are investigated in their mutual relations. The pioneering works of Max Weber (1864–1920) continue to have an impact upon the sociological study of Indian religion. Anthropologists and other specialists have tried to construe theoretical frameworks to be applied to the textual-contextual continuum and to provide heuristic models for further research in this direction.

In a general and inevitably simplifying sense, it may be said that three basic attitudes dominate the current study of Indian religion:

1. the historical and philological approach, which derives its data and its direction from the Indian texts themselves and is primarily interested in historical reconstruction;
2. the sociological and anthropological approach, which tries to understand religious life in a functional manner, with reference to—or even directly in terms of—social, economic, ethnographic, political, and behavioral phenomena; and
3. the more existentially or ideologically involved approaches, which find in the Indian religious tradition a genuine religious, philosophical, or theological challenge and which respond to it in the name of specific worldviews or religious convictions.

These three approaches are not mutually exclusive; they can be and have been combined with one another. Still, they represent clearly distinguishable types of scholarly interest and orientation.

Finally, the development of Indological studies in the West has had a remarkable influence on India's interpretation of its own traditions. Not only do Indians now participate in the Western study of their religious past, but they also respond to it and to the challenge of Western thought in general, thus opening a religious dialogue with potentially far-reaching implications. Traditional Indian thought had not previously sought such dialogue or shown interest in non-Indian traditions, and yet it has produced a rich heritage of debate and refutation, as well as of coordination and harmonization of different standpoints. But foreign religions, including Islam and Christianity, did not become part of this process until the beginning of the nineteenth century, when Hinduism opened itself to the impact of Western ideas and entered into a fundamentally new relationship with the non-Indian world. At that time, Ram Mohan Roy (1772–1833) and others initiated a movement of reform and modernization of Hinduism that combines apologetics and self-affirmation with reinterpretation, adaptation, and universalization.

Thus, Western ideas and terms have been used not only to interpret the Indian religious tradition to foreigners but also to articulate a new Indian self-understanding. Modern reinterpretations of such key concepts as *dharma* exemplify the ambiguity of India's reaction to the Western challenge and specifically to the Christian notion of religion. In response to missionary activities, Christianity and other religions have been readily incorporated into traditional Hindu schemes of concordance, where they appear as different approaches to the same goal or as preliminary stages on a path often seen as culminating in the philosophical religion of Advaita Vedānta. In this context, "comparative religion" has found many advocates in India; similarly, against the Hegelian subordination of Asian thought to that of the West, Brajendranath Seal (1864–1938) formulated his program of "comparative philosophy." In general, there has been a tendency to respond to science and technology and to Western political domination by invoking religion and spirituality, which have been presented as genuinely Indian phenomena by such successful advocates of Neo-Hinduism as Vivekananda (1863–1902; represented Hinduism at the World Parliament of Religions, Chicago, 1893). The concept of religious experience plays a crucial role in the modern self-presentation of Hinduism in the West. In increasing numbers, Indian scholars, teachers, gurus, and founders of syncretistic movements have come to the West and contributed to a growing awareness of the Indian religious tradition. At the same time, these developments are themselves continuations and transformations of the tradition, and they are a legitimate topic of study and research. Among those who have contributed to the scholarly and critical evaluation of Neo-Hinduism, Paul Hacker (1913–1979) ought to be mentioned especially.

The hermeneutic and religious position of Neo-Hinduism is still problematic and tentative and has had difficulties in finding an adequate language for presenting the Indian religious tradition to the modern world. Accordingly, the situation of the religious dialogue between India and the West is still precarious. Nonetheless, the fact that the Indian religious tradition is no longer just an object of Western study but now speaks back to the West, questioning some of the very basic presuppositions of Western historical research, is in itself a highly significant event. It affects not only the modern Western perception of India but also the religious and philosophical situation of the modern world.

BIBLIOGRAPHY

Dandekar, R. N., and V. Raghavan, eds. *Oriental Studies in India.* New Delhi, 1964. A survey of Asian, primarily Indian, studies with sections on Vedic, Dravidian, and Islamic studies, philosophy and religion, archaeology, and so on, including a list of centers of teaching and research in India.

Dell, David, et al. *Guide to Hindu Religion.* Boston, 1981. A generously annotated bibliography of studies of Hinduism, covering such areas as history of Hinduism, religious thought, sacred texts, rituals, sacred locations, soteriology; emphasis on more recent contributions; not always fully reliable.

Gonda, Jan, et al. *Die Religionen Indiens.* 3 vols. Stuttgart, 1960–1963. One of the most comprehensive surveys of research on the religions of India, primarily from the standpoint of textual and historical studies. This survey is further extended in Gonda's *Viṣṇuism and Śivaism: A Comparison* (London, 1970).

Hacker, Paul. *Kleine Schriften.* Wiesbaden, 1978. A comprehensive collection of articles in German and English by a scholar whose studies of Indian religion combine a thoroughly philological orientation with theological and philosophical commitment; important methodological discussions and references to Neo-Hinduism.

Halbfass, Wilhelm. *Indien und Europa: Perspektiven ihrer geistigen Begegnung.* Basel, 1981. A study of the intellectual and spiritual encounters between India and Europe, of the patterns of mutual understanding in the areas of religion and philosophy, and of the beginnings of Indological research.

Holland, Barron. *Popular Hinduism and Hindu Mythology: An Annotated Bibliography.* Westport, Conn., 1979. A useful bibliographical guide (including sections on "sacred literature," etc.), although the annotations are extremely short and often not very helpful.

Mandelbaum, David G. *Society in India.* 2 vols. Berkeley, 1970. This general introduction to the anthropological study of Indian civilization also contains (in chapters 28–31 of volume 2) the best introduction, for the nonspecialist, to the social and historical dynamics of Indian religions.

O'Flaherty, Wendy Doniger, ed. *Karma and Rebirth in Classical Indian Traditions.* Berkeley, 1980. A collection of essays, by authors with varied backgrounds, on one of the most fundamental ideas in Indian religious thought.

Otto, Rudolf. *Mysticism East and West: A Comparative Analysis of the Nature of Mysticism* (1932). New York, 1960. Although somewhat obsolete, still an exemplary approach to the Indian religious tradition by a liberal Christian theologian.

Radhakrishnan, Sarvepalli. *The Hindu View of Life* (1927). London, 1968. Not a contribution to the academic study of Hinduism, but one of the most eloquent and successful statements of Neo-Hinduism, exemplifying its basic patterns of reinterpretation and modernization.

Renou, Louis. *Bibliographie védique.* Paris, 1931. An exemplary bibliography of scholarly literature on the Vedas. A sequel to this work is R. N. Dandekar's *Vedic Bibliography,* 3 vols. (Bombay and Poona, 1946–1973).

Schwab, Raymond. *La renaissance orientale.* Paris, 1950. Translated by Gene Patterson-Black and Victor Reinking as *The Oriental Renaissance* (New York, 1984). A comprehensive and richly documented account of the seminal period between 1770 and 1850, when the foundations were laid for modern Indology and for a new appreciation of Indian religion and philosophy; equally detailed on academic and nonacademic developments; analyzes thoroughly the intellectual background of Indian and Oriental studies. The translation is not always reliable.

Smith, Bardwell L., ed. *Hinduism: New Essays in the History of Religions.* Leiden, 1976. A collection of eight contributions, exemplifying recent approaches to the study of Hinduism, including structuralism.

Windisch, Ernst. *Geschichte der Sanskrit-Philologie und indischen Altertumskunde.* 2 vols. Strasbourg, 1917–1920. Though incomplete, somewhat obsolete, and not extending beyond 1900, this remains the most thorough and comprehensive survey of the history of Indology and of the textual exploration of Indian religion.

Zimmer, Heinrich. *Myths and Symbols in Indian Art and Civilization* (1946). Edited by Joseph Campbell. Princeton, 1972. A somewhat idiosyncratic, yet stimulating and influential study of Hindu religion and mythology, with particular reference to its visual illustrations.

WILHELM HALBFASS and ARJUN APPADURAI

INDO-EUROPEAN RELIGIONS. [*This entry concerns the religions of peoples whose languages are classified in the Indo-European language family. It consists of two articles:* An Overview *and* History of Study. *For discussions of specific Indo-European traditions, see* Albanian Religion; Armenian Religion; Baltic Religion; Celtic Religion; Etruscan Religion; Germanic Religion; Greek Religion; Hittite Religion; Indian Religions; Iranian Religions; Roman Religion; Slavic Religion; *and* Thracian Religion.]

An Overview

The study of Indo-European religion has a relatively recent origin, for the very existence of the Indo-European language grouping was not recognized until a celebrated lecture given by Sir William ("Oriental") Jones in 1786. Speaking to the Royal Asiatic Society of Bengal, Jones first observed that there were striking philological similarities between Greek, Latin, Sanskrit (the ancient language of India), and Persian, too numerous and precise to be explained by simple borrowing or chance. Going further, he suggested that the Celtic and Germanic languages exhibited many of the same features and argued that all of these geographically and historically far-flung languages were best understood as separate derivates of a common parent language, a language nowhere preserved in written form, but which might be reconstructed through systematic comparison of the derivate stocks.

Later research has confirmed the relations among these languages, adding not only Germanic and Celtic firmly to the family now known as Indo-European but also Baltic, Slavic, Armenian, Albanian, Anatolian (chiefly Hittite), and Tokharian (an obscure language found in western China and Turkistan). Rigorous and systematic comparison of words in these various languages has permitted scholars to posit numerous prototypes as a means to explain the systematic resemblances that have been adduced. As a simple example of how this is done we might consider certain words for "god," assembling a set of correspondences (to which other reflexes might be added) as shown in table 1.

From these correspondences, along with the knowledge of Indo-European phonetics gained from hundreds of other such comparisons, linguists can reconstruct a prototype **deywo-s* (the asterisk denotes a reconstructed form unattested in any written source), which means "god, deity." Phonetic rules explain the various sound shifts in each language, but one must also note semantic changes in certain stocks, each of which is instructive for the history of the corresponding religion. Thus, for instance, the old word for "god" has become the most important word for demonic beings in Avestan (the Iranian language in which the most ancient Zoroastrian scriptures were composed), a transformation that seems to originate in the prophet Zarathushtra's renunciation of the old Indo-Iranian pantheon.

The Greek reflex of **deywo-s* has also lost its sense as "deity," being replaced in this usage by *theos.* The older term survives as an adjective, however, which reveals one of the fundamental attributes of deity in Indo-European thought: gods are celestial beings, characterized by light, for the word **deywo-s* (whence the Greek *dios,* "celestial") is derived from a verb that means "to shine." In contrast, one of the most important words for "human" identifies people as "terrestrial" beings (note the relation of the Latin *homo,* "man," and *humus,* "soil"), while humans and deities are further contrasted in other terminology that identifies them as "mortals" and "immortals" respectively.

This relatively simple example reveals some of the possibilities and some of the pitfalls of research into Indo-European religion. Careful examination of lexical items gives us insight into the nature of thought on religious topics. But each of the separate Indo-European families differs from the other families in important re-

TABLE 1. *Indo-European Words for "God"*

LANGUAGE	PHONETIC FORM	SEMANTIC SENSE
Latin	*deus*	"deity"
Lithuanian	*diẽvas*	"deity"
Greek	*dios*	"celestial"
Hittite	*ᵈŠiuš*	"deity"
Sanskrit	*deváḥ*	"deity"
Avestan	*daēva*	"demon"

gards, and just as Latin phonology differs from Iranian phonology for all that they are related (to cite but one example), so Roman religion is not identical to Iranian: a *deus* is not the same thing as a *daēva*.

Reconstruction that proceeds along linguistic lines is relatively safe, however, compared to research that seeks out correspondences in the myths, rituals, laws, cosmologies, and eschatologies of the various Indo-European peoples and that attempts to recover their hypothetical antecedents. Such research is possible, to be sure, but in all instances it is extremely risky and difficult, involving the adducement of parallel phenomena (usually called "correspondences" or "reflexes") attested in the religions of several different Indo-European families; the study of each reflex in its cultural specificity; the isolation of those features that the scattered reflexes hold in common; the explanation of those features that diverge (often called "transformation"); and the positing of a hypothetical prototype that is capable of accounting for evident similarities, along with a train of historical development that explains the forces producing each transformation. Finally, the reconstructed prototype ought to be set within a plausible set of assumptions regarding the nature of Indo-European culture in general.

Based on linguistic and archaeological research, the ancient Indo-European peoples are generally considered to have been semisettled pastoralists, whose wealth consisted of relatively large herds, including domesticated sheep, pigs, goats, and, most important, cattle. Horses were also highly significant, especially when yoked to chariots and used in warfare, but cattle remained the normal draft animals for peaceful purposes, the source of most foods, and the fundamental measure of wealth. Some agriculture seems to have been practiced, although this was much less important and prestigious an activity than herding or war. The pursuit of warfare, especially the raiding of livestock from neighboring peoples, was facilitated not only by use of chariots but also by an elaborate weaponry built on a single metal, probably copper or bronze.

Linguistic data are insufficient to posit the existence of either a homeland or a proto-Indo-European community, and it is possible to view the similarity of the various Indo-European languages as the cumulative result of complex borrowings, influences, and cultural interrelations between multiple social and ethnic groups over many centuries. Some scholars have sought to employ archaeological evidence to demonstrate a specific point of origin for proto-Indo-European society. Of such theories, the most widely accepted is that of Marija Gimbutas, who has delineated what she calls the Kurgan culture, dating to the middle of the fifth millennium BCE and located in the southern Russian steppes, in the area that stretches from the Urals to the land north of the Black Sea, and including such groups as the Jamna culture of the Ural-Volga region north of the Caspian and the Srednii Stog II culture north of the Black Sea.

Mythic Legitimations of Society, Economy, and Polity. Comparison of texts in which are described the patterns of social organization among the Indian, Iranian, and Celtic peoples reveals a common structure, which is also preserved in the ideal republic envisioned by Plato. This system is characterized by the distinction of three hierarchically differentiated classes—or "functions," as they are called by Georges Dumézil (1958), who was first to recognize their importance. Moreover, it is possible to reconstruct a number of myths that describe the origin of these classes, their nature, and their sometimes problematic interrelationships.

Most important of these is the creation myth, a complex, polyphonic story that told how the world was created when the first priest (often bearing the name Man, *Manu) offered his twin brother, the first king (often named Twin, *Yemo), in sacrifice, along with the first ox. From Twin's body, the world was made, in both its material and social components. Portions of two reflexes of this myth may conveniently be cited: the first, from the Indic "Song of Puruṣa" (*Ṛgveda* 10.90.11–14) dates to about 900 BCE; the second, the Old Russian *Poem on the Dove King*, is mentioned in sources dating to the thirteenth century CE and was still circulating orally in the nineteenth century:

> When they divided Puruṣa, how many pieces did they prepare?
> What was his mouth? What are his arms, thighs, and feet called?
> The priest was his mouth, the warrior was made from his arms;
> His thighs were the commoner, and the servant was born from his feet.
> The moon was born of his mind; of his eye, the sun was born;
> From his mouth, Indra and fire; from his breath, wind was born;
> From his navel there was the atmosphere; from his head, heaven was rolled together;
> From his feet, the earth; from his ears, the directions.

> Our bright light comes from the Lord,
> The red sun from the face of God,
> The young shining moon from his breast,
> The bright dawn from the eyes of God,
> The sparkling stars from his vestments,

The wild winds from the Holy Spirit.
From this our little Tsars are on earth—
From the holy head of Adam;
From this princes and heroes come into being—
From the holy bones of Adam;
From this are the orthodox peasants—
From the holy knee of Adam.

Although we shall return to the cosmic dimensions of this myth, it is its social contents that concern us now. Among these, the following four should be noted:

1. Society consists of vertically stratified classes, with priests or sovereigns in the first position, warriors in the second, and commoners—those entrusted with the bulk of productive labor—in the third. To these, a fourth class of relative outsiders—servants, or the like—was sometimes added, as in the Indian example cited above.
2. The characteristic activity of each of these classes is explained and chartered by the part of Twin's body from which they originated. Thus, the intellectuals who direct society by exercise of thought and speech come from his head; those who defend society by their physical prowess come from his chest (heart) and arms; those who produce food, reproduce, and provide material support for the other classes come from the lower body, including belly, loins, legs, and feet.
3. The priest, following the model of Man, has as his prime responsibility the performance of sacrifice, sacrifice being the creative act *par excellence*.
4. The king, following the model of Twin, combines within himself the essence of all social classes and is expected to sacrifice himself for the good of the whole.

Another myth, which has as its central character the first warrior, whose name was Third (*Trito), provided an analysis of the warrior class. Within this story, it was related that cattle originally belonged to Indo-Europeans but were stolen by a monster, a three-headed serpent who was, moreover, specifically identified as a non-Indo-European. Following this theft, it fell to Third to recover the stolen cattle, and he began his quest by invoking the aid of a warrior deity to whom he offered libations of intoxicating drinks. Having won the god's assistance, and himself fortified by the same intoxicant, Third set forth, found the serpent, slew him, and recovered the cattle, which had been imprisoned by the monster.

This myth, which is attested in more reflexes than any other (its traces are still apparent in countless fairy tales), speaks to the eternal themes of wealth and power. It asserts, first, that cattle—the means of production and of exchange in the most ancient Indo-European societies—rightly belong exclusively to Indo-Europeans, falling into other hands only as the result of theft. Theft is condemned here because of its reliance on stealth and treachery, and it is set in contrast to raiding, which—far from being condemned—is heartily endorsed. Raiding emerges as a heroic action sanctioned by the gods, hedged with ritual, and devoted to regaining what rightfully belongs to the Indo-European warrior or his people. Throughout Indo-European history, Third in his various reflexes has remained the model for warriors, who repeatedly cast themselves in his image—raiding, plundering, and killing their non-Indo-European neighbors, convinced all the while that they were engaged in a sacred and rightful activity.

Yet another myth emphasized the importance of the commoner class to the social totality, although no individual heroic figure was provided as a model for commoners. Rather, the myth begins with separation and even hostility existing between the generalized representatives of the upper classes and those of the commoners. After an inconclusive struggle, however, members of all classes recognize their need for one another, and they merge into a larger, all-encompassing society. Thereafter the classes are expected to cooperate and live harmoniously, although the commoners continue to occupy a subordinate position, a considerable portion of their labor being diverted for the support of the noble classes of priests, warriors, and kings. At the level of mythic ideology, however, if not of actual social process, commoners were assured of their superiority to even the most privileged members of society, for an important set of myths, recently studied by Cristiano Grottanelli, focused on the conflict of a humble woman who was the mother of twins (thus signifying abundant reproductive power) with a king's horses (the emblem of martial and royal power), in which the lowly woman emerged victorious.

Cosmology and the Gods. While Georges Dumézil and his followers have consistently argued that the Indo-European pantheon mirrored the organization of social classes, other scholars have at times been skeptical of this view. Chief among its difficulties is the fact that Dumézil's proposals include none of the gods for whom names can be linguistically reconstructed, all of whom are personified natural phenomena—Shining Sky (*Dyeus), Sun (*Swel), Dawn (*Ausos), and so forth—while reconstructible names exist for none of the deities he proposes.

In general, as noted above, deities were characterized as radiant celestial beings. In addition to the **deywo-s*, however, there was another class of divinities associated with the waters beneath the earth's surface and with darkness. These deities—whose names were regularly formed with the preposition signifying downward motion (*ne-, as in Latin *Neptunus*, Greek *Nēreus*, Germanic *Nerthus*, Sanskrit *Nirṛti*)—figure in myths that are nothing so much as meditations on the interconnections between "above" and "below," involving immergence into and emersion out of the world ocean, as has recently been demonstrated by Françoise Bader.

Speculation on the nature of the cosmos also forms an important part of the creation myth, the social contents of which we touched on above. It must be noted, however, that beyond this social discourse, the myth established a series of homologic relations between parts of the human body and parts of the physical universe—that is to say, an extended parallelism and consubstantiality was posited between the microcosm and the macrocosm. Many texts thus tell of the origin of the sun from the eyes of the first sacrificial victim, stones from his bones, earth from his flesh, wind from his breath, and so forth, while others invert the account—as for instance, in the following medieval accounts, the first Germanic and the second Slavic:

> God made the first man, that was Adam, from eight transformations: the bone from the stone, the flesh from the earth, the blood from the water, the heart from the wind, the thoughts from the clouds, the sweat from the dew, the locks of hair from the grass, the eyes from the sun, and he blew in the holy breath. (from the Old Frisian *Code of Emsig*)

> And thus God made man's body out of eight parts. The first part is of the earth, which is the lowliest of all parts. The second is of the sea, which is blood and wisdom. The third is of the sun, which is beauty and eyes for him. The fourth is of the celestial clouds, which are thought and weakness. The fifth is of the wind—that is, air—which is breath and envy. The sixth is of stones, that is, firmness. The seventh is of the light of this world which is made into flesh, that is humility and sweetness. The eighth part is of the Holy Spirit, placed in men for all that is good, full of zeal—that is the foremost part. (from the Old Russian *Discourse of the Three Saints*)

In these and other texts the elements of the physical universe are converted into the constituent parts of a human body, as cosmogony (a story of the creation of the cosmos) becomes anthropogony (a story of the creation of man). In truth, cosmogony and anthropogony were regarded as separate moments in one continuous process of creation, in which physical matter eternally alternates between microcosmic and macrocosmic modes of existence. Bones thus become stones and stones become bones over and over again, matter and change both being eternal, while the body and the universe are only transient forms, alternate shapes of one another.

Ritual Action. The myths that we have considered were closely correlated with and regularly re-presented in numerous ritual forms. Thus, the creation myth was inextricably connected to sacrifice, the most important of all Indo-European rites. Insofar as the first priest created the world through the performance of a sacrifice in which a man and an ox were the victims, so each subsequent priest re-created the cosmos by sacrificing men or cattle. This was accomplished through manipulation of the homologies of macrocosm and microcosm, such that when the victim was dismembered, its material substance was transformed into the corresponding parts of the universe. Thus, for example, an Indic manual of ritual practice, the *Aitareya Brāhmaṇa* (2.6), provides instructions for the sacrificial dismemberment of an animal victim in terms drawn directly from the creation myth:

> Lay his feet down to the north. Cause his eye to go to the sun. Send forth his breath to the wind, his life-force to the atmosphere, his ears to the cardinal points, his flesh to the earth. Thus, the priest places the victim in these worlds.

Without this matter drawn from the bodies of sacrificial victims all the items of the material world—earth, stones, sun, wind, water, and the like—would become depleted; it is only because they are replenished in sacrifice that the cosmos continues to exist.

If sacrifice is thus a sort of "healing" of the cosmos based on principles articulated in the creation myth, medical practice was also based on the same principles and bears a curious relation to sacrifice. For if in sacrifice the priest shifted matter from the body to the universe, then in the healing of a broken limb—as attested in the famous Second Merseberg Charm and corresponding materials throughout the Indo-European world—the healer took matter from the universe and restored it to a broken body, creating new flesh, bones, blood, and the like out of earth, stones, and water.

Royal investiture was based on yet another elaboration of ideas contained within the creation myth, as is suggested by the researches of Daniel Dubuisson. Investigating accounts of ancient "coronation" rituals in Ireland and India, he has shown that a king was ritually constructed by having the essential properties of the three Indo-European social classes placed within his body, symbolic gifts, clothing, unctions, and the like being employed toward this end.

Other rituals were closely related to the myth of Third. Embarking on cattle raids—which were raised to the status of a sacred act as a result of this mythic charter—Indo-European warriors invoked the assistance of martial deities, poured libations, partook of intoxicating drinks, and aspired to states of ecstatic frenzy. Moreover, each young warrior had to pass through certain initiatory rituals before he attained full status as a member of the warrior class. Regularly his first cattle raid was something of a rite of passage for the young warrior, and other initiations were consciously structured on the myth of Third and the serpent. It appears that in some of these, a monstrous tricephalous dummy was constructed, and the initiand was forced to attack it. If able to summon up the necessary courage to do so, he discovered that his seemingly awesome opponent was only a joke, with the implicit lesson that all of his future enemies, however fearsome they might seem, would be no more formidable than this dummy. Those enemies, of course, were to be cast in the role of the serpent—a monster, a thief, and, what is most important, an alien (i.e., a non-Indo-European)—the plunder and murder of whom was established by myth as not only a rightful but also a sacred act.

While the use of intoxicants was an important part of warrior ritual, these had other applications as well. The oldest Indo-European intoxicating beverage was mead, later followed by beer, wine, and a pressed drink known as *soma* to the Indians and *haoma* to the Iranians; the symbolism and ideology surrounding all of these remained relatively constant. In all instances, the drink appears as a heightener of abilities and activities. When consumed by a priest, it increases his powers of vision and insight. Similarly, it makes a poet more eloquent, a warrior more powerful, a king more generous and just.

A large group of rituals served to forge bonds of community and to cement important social relations. Extremely important in this regard were certain formalized reciprocal obligations, including hospitality and gift exchange, whereby individuals, lineages, and even larger units were brought into repeated contact and friendly interchange. Marriage also must be considered as a prolonged exchange relationship between social groups, given the predominant preference for exogamy. An individual marriage was thus as much a part of an ongoing exchange between lineages or clans as it was a permanent bond between two individuals.

Verbal rituals—including those of vow, oath, and treaty—played a highly important part in the establishment and preservation of social bonds; accordingly, truth and fidelity were cardinal virtues. Initially, this must be related to the lack of literacy among the most ancient Indo-European peoples, a state of affairs that also contributed to the high development of verbal art (epic poetry, for instance) and mnemonic techniques. But even after the introduction of writing among the scattered Indo-European peoples, a marked preference for the oral transmission of religious lore remained, for the spoken word was perceived as a live vehicle, in contrast to the dead written letter, and was preferred accordingly.

If verbal rituals could serve to establish social connectedness, they could also be used to sunder unwanted connections, as is attested in a formula of outlawry that survives in Hittite and Germanic reflexes, the former dating to 1600 BCE. Here, particularly disreputable individuals (an abductor and murderer in the first instance, a grave robber in the second) are told "You have become a wolf" and "May he be a wolf" respectively, the wolf being the most feared predator of pastoral societies, a dangerous outsider ever to be kept at bay. Ironically, however, it was not only outlaws who were regarded as wolves, for Indo-European warriors also styled themselves wolflike beings, as is attested by the many ethnic names derived from the word for "wolf" (thus the Luvians, Lykians, Hirpini, Luceres, Dacii, Hyrcanii, and Saka Haumavarka), personal names so formed (Wolfram, Wolfhart, Wolfgang), and the Greek term *lussa* ("rabies, wolfish rage"), which denotes the highest pitch of fury attained by heroes such as Achilles and Hector in the *Iliad.* Apparently what legitimated the wolfish violence of these heroes is that it was directed outside the community of Indo-Europeans, in contrast to that of outlaws, which was directed internally, an inference which is supported by the fascinating name of a heroic warrior attested in the *Ṛgveda:* Dasyave Vṛka, "wolf to the Dasyu," that is, to the non-Indo-European.

Death, Resurrection, and Eschatology. A central issue in Indo-European religions, as in most religions, was what becomes of an individual after death. Although several scholars have devoted attention to certain details of funerary ideology, the full nature of Indo-European thought on this topic remains to be worked out. Among the major contributions thus far are the studies of Hermann Güntert (1919), who showed that there was a goddess *Kolyo ("the coverer") whose physical form incarnated the mixture of fascination and horror evoked by death, for she was seductively beautiful when seen from the front, while hiding a back that was repulsive—moldy and worm-eaten—in the extreme. Paul Thieme (1952) has also contributed an important study of the view of death as a reunion with departed ancestors, and Kuno Meyer (1919) has shown that in Ireland as in India it was the first mortal (*Yemo, the twin) who founded the otherworld.

If ideas regarding the fate of the soul are unclear—no reconstructible word approximates the semantic range of the English *soul,* the nearest equivalent being a term for "life-breath"—those on the fate of the body are extremely precise and reveal a remarkable religious content. For death is seen as the last sacrifice that an individual can offer, in which his or her own body is itself the offering. Moreover, that body is transformed into the elements of the physical universe, just as were those of Twin at the time of creation, each death being not only a sacrifice but a re-presentation of the cosmogonic sacrifice. Such a view is preserved, for instance, in Euripides' *The Suppliant Women:*

> Let the corpses now be covered with the earth,
> From which each of them came forth to the light
> Only to go back thither: breath to the air
> And body to earth. (531–534)

Or in the funeral hymn of the *Ṛgveda:*

> Your eye must go to the sun. Your soul must go to the wind. You must go to the sky and the earth, according to what is right.
> Go to the waters, if you are placed there. You must establish the plants with your flesh.
> (10.16.3)

This is not a final fate, however, for it would seem that nothing within the cosmos was perceived as final. Just as cosmogony was seen to alternate with anthropogony, so also death and resurrection. That matter that assumes its cosmic form when one specific human body dies will once again assume bodily form when that specific cosmos itself dies, as must inevitably happen. Greek, Germanic, and Indo-Iranian evidence permits reconstruction of a temporal scheme involving four world ages, the first of which is most pure and stable, followed by ages in which human virtue and the very order of the cosmos gradually break down. At the end of the fourth world age, there is an apocalyptic collapse, followed by the creation of a new, pure, and regenerated world. One of the cardinal features of the eschatological destruction of the cosmos, however, is the resurrection of the dead, their bodies being formed out of the material substance freed when the cosmos falls apart. The new creation that follows is then in most versions accomplished with an initial act of sacrifice. Descriptions of the resurrection are preserved, *inter alia,* in the *Pahlavi Rivāyat Accompanying the Dādistān ī dīnīg,* a Zoroastrian text of the ninth century CE, and in Plato's *Politicus:*

> [In order to accomplish the resurrection] Ōhrmazd summons the bone from the earth, the blood from the water, the hair from the plants, and the life from the wind. He mixes one with the other, and in this manner, he keeps on creating.
> (*Pahlavi Rivāyat* 48.98–107)

> When the transition of the old people to the nature of a child is completed, it follows that those lying [dead] in the earth are put back together there and brought back to life, the process of birth being reversed with the reversal of the world's rotation. (*Politicus* 271b)

Behind these formulations stand several very simple, yet very profound, principles: (1) matter is indestructible; (2) matter is infinitely transmutable; (3) living organisms and the physical universe are composed of one and the same material substance; (4) time is eternal. While change is thus constant, it is also meaningless, for nothing that is essentially real is ever created or destroyed. Worlds come and go, as do individuals of whatever species, but being—material being—is always there.

The gods are also subject to the same rhythms of dissolution and reemergence, but in truth the gods seem to have been of much less concern than mythic ancestors such as Man, Twin, and Third. We must now, however, correct certain statements made above in light of what has just been said about the nature of time and the cycles of creation and destruction. For whereas we initially called these figures the "first" king, priest, and warrior respectively, we must now conclude that they were merely the first of the current world age, time and the world receding infinitely into the past as well as stretching eternally into the future.

BIBLIOGRAPHY

Among the most interesting and important general studies of Indo-European religion are (in chronological order): Joseph Vendryes's "Les correspondances de vocabulaire entre l'indo-iranien et l'italo-celtique," *Mémoires de la Société de Linguistique de Paris* 20 (1918): 265–285; Hermann Güntert's *Der arische Weltkönig und Heiland* (Halle, 1923); Paul Thieme's *Mitra and Aryaman* (New Haven, 1957); Georges Dumézil's *L'idéologie tripartie des Indo-Européens* (Brussels, 1958); Émile Benveniste's *Indo-European Language and Society,* translated by Elizabeth Palmer (Coral Gables, Fla., 1975); Franco Crevatin's *Ricerche d'antichità indeuropee* (Trieste, 1979); and my own *Priests, Warriors, and Cattle: A Study in the Ecology of Religions* (Berkeley, 1981).

Specialized studies of particular merit are Marija Gimbutas's numerous articles on the archaeological record of the Indo-Europeans, most complete of which to date is "An Archaeologist's View of PIE in 1975," *Journal of Indo-European Studies* 2 (Fall 1974): 289–308; Georges Dumézil's three-volume *Mythe et épopée* (Paris, 1968–1973), in which he demonstrates the ways in which many myths were transformed into epic, pseudohistory, and other genres; Stig Wikander's *Der arische Männerbund* (Lund, 1938) and Lily Weiser's *Altgermanische Jünglingsweihen und Männerbunde* (Baden, 1927) on warriors; Wilhelm Koppers's "Pferdeopfer und Pferdekult der Indogermanen," *Wiener Beiträge zur Kulturgeschichte und Linguistik* 4 (1936): 279–411, and Kasten Rönnow's "Zagreus och Dionysos," *Religion och Bibel* 2 (1943): 14–48, on sacrifice (both to be used with caution, however); Daniel Dubuisson's "Le roi indo-européen et la synthèse des trois fonctions," *Annales économies sociétés civilisations* 33 (January–February 1978): 21–34, on kingship; Hermann Güntert's *Kalypso* (Halle, 1919); Kuno Meyer, "Der irische Totengott und die Toteninsel," *Sitzungberichte der preussischen Akademie der Wissenschaften* (1919): 537–546; and Paul Thieme's *Studien zur indogermanischen Wortkunde und Religionsgeschichte* (Berlin, 1952) on death and the otherworld; and my own *Myth, Cosmos, and Society: Indo-European Themes of Creation and Destruction* (Cambridge, Mass., 1986) on the creation myth.

Two papers presented at a panel on Indo-European religion held during the Ninth International Congress of Anthropological and Ethnographic Sciences (Vancouver, 1983) were of considerable importance, and publication is forthcoming in the *Journal of Indo-European Studies* 14 (1986). These are Françoise Bader's "Une mythe indo-européene de l'immersion-émergence" and Cristiano Grottanelli's "Yoked Horses, Twins, and the Powerful Lady: India, Greece, Ireland and Elsewhere."

On the problems and insecurities of research in this area in general, see Ulf Drabin, "Indogermanische Religion und Kultur? Eine Analyse des Begriffes Indogermanisch," *Temenos* 16 (1980): 26–38; Jean-Paul Demoule, "Les Indo-Européens ont-ils existé?" *L'histoire* 28 (1980): 108–120; and Bernfried Schlerath, "Ist ein Raum/Zeit Modell für eine rekonstruierte Sprach möglich?" *Zeitschrift für vergleichende Sprachwissenschaft* 95 (1981): 175–202.

BRUCE LINCOLN

History of Study

Strictly speaking, the history of comparative Indo-European studies begins in the late eighteenth century as a direct result of the momentous discovery that the ancient languages we now classify as "Indo-European" (e.g., Latin, classical Greek, Sanskrit, Old English, Old Persian, Old Icelandic, Old Church Slavonic, Old Irish, Hittite, etc.) all stemmed ultimately from a common source, that is, Proto-Indo-European. As we shall see, it soon became apparent that the speakers of these languages, which can be considered along with their progeny as members of a grand "family" of languages, shared more than simply a common linguistic heritage, and that among the most important features of this extralinguistic, Indo-European heritage was a common body of religious beliefs and practices.

To be sure, the taproots of the discipline can be traced back to classical antiquity, to the theories of Euhemerus (fl. 300 BCE) and other Greek and Roman scholars who attempted to come to grips with the origin and meaning of myth. It is also possible to trace the immediate source of the ideas that flowered in the nineteenth century to the ideas of such eighteenth-century precursors as Bernard de Fontenelle (1657–1757), Giovanni Battista Vico (1668–1744), and Charles de Brosses (1709–1777), who first suggested that a search for natural metaphors might be preferable to the traditional euhemeristic and allegorical approaches that had heretofore been the rule. These ideas may also be traced as well to that curious (albeit all-pervasive) philosophical, literary, and artistic movement called Romanticism, adumbrated in the works of J. G. Herder (1744–1803), which profoundly influenced most of the scholars who first began to conceive of a distinctly Indo-European religious tradition in the early nineteenth century. But these ideas belong properly to the general history of comparative mythology and religion; for the purposes of this article, I begin my survey with the discovery of the Indo-European language family.

Discovery of the Indo-European Language Family. Until the last quarter of the eighteenth century, most theories about the nature and origin of language were grounded in philosophical speculation, much of it centering on the idea of degeneration. Thus, the primordial language was often held to be Hebrew, since it must have been spoken in the garden of Eden. Following the ancient notion of degeneration from an assumed "golden age," many writers on the subject maintained that Greek was a degenerate form of Hebrew, Latin a degenerate form of Greek, and that the modern languages of Europe were all degenerate offspring of Latin.

However, thanks to the voyages of discovery and the rapid expansion in European awareness of the range and diversity of human languages, and impelled by the romantic emphasis on national origins, which effectively precluded the notion that all languages were necessarily descended from Hebrew, scholars had begun to suspect that the degeneration hypothesis, whether secular or religious, was inadequate to explain the historical relationships among languages. Nowhere was this more obvious than in India, which, by the latter part of the eighteenth century, had become in effect the private preserve of the British East India Company. As European awareness of this vastly complex region deepened, it became clear that Sanskrit, the ancient language of the Hindu sacred texts, occupied a position in religious and literary affairs similar to that occupied by Latin in Europe during the Middle Ages. Indeed, several scholars, beginning with Filippo Sassetti in 1600, had remarked on the curious similarities between Latin and Sanskrit, but these similarities defied explanation in terms of the "degeneration hypothesis," as Sanskrit was patently as ancient as either Latin or classical Greek.

Furthermore, the modern languages of North India—Hindi, Bengali, and the rest—seemed to bear the same immediate relationship to Sanskrit as French, Spanish, Italian and other members of what later came to be called the Romance languages did to Latin.

The problem was finally solved in 1786 by William Jones (1746–1794), who is generally considered the founder of scientific linguistics. An amateur philologist (he was reputed to have been fluent in some twenty-two languages), Jones had recently been appointed chief justice of the East India Company's establishment at Calcutta, and in his off-hours he immediately set about learning Sanskrit. In September 1786, at a meeting of the Royal Asiatic Society of Bengal, he gave an after-dinner speech in which, for the first time, the idea of the language family was first clearly articulated. As Jones saw it, the relationship among Sanskrit and the ancient languages of Greece and Rome, as well as those spoken by the ancient Germans and Iranians, was that of a set of orphaned siblings: all were descended from a common parent language that had long since disappeared. That parent language, however, might be reconstructed by rigorously comparing the grammars and lexicons of these attested languages. The whole ensemble could be described as a family tree, one to which Hebrew, Arabic, and other Semitic languages did not belong, for they were members of another, wholly distinct language family.

Thus was born both comparative philology and the idea of the Indo-European language family. Although Jones himself never followed up his monumental discovery, others soon did, and by the beginning of the third decade of the next century the science of comparative philology, together with the discipline we now refer to as comparative Indo-European religious studies, was well under way.

Almost from the outset, the practitioners of this new science, almost all of them steeped in romantic idealism, found themselves confronted by more than simply a set of linguistic similarities. The primary source materials—the *Ṛgveda,* the *Mahābhārata,* the *Iliad,* the Iranian Avesta, the Icelandic Eddas, and so forth—were religious and/or mythological texts, and it soon became apparent that the gods, heroes, rituals, and events described in these texts could be compared using the same basic methodology that Jones and others had developed, that is, the *comparative method,* which is predicated on the assumption that anterior stages and/or prototypes can be systematically reconstructed from attested evidence, linguistic or otherwise. Thus, comparative mythology, and especially comparative Indo-European mythology, rapidly took its place as a sister discipline of comparative philology. [*See* Comparative Mythology.]

Early Nineteenth Century. As might be expected, many early nineteenth-century scholars, even those who were not directly concerned with Indo-European linguistic studies, had something to say about various aspects of the newly discovered parallels among the several Indo-European pantheons. This was especially true in Germany, where romantic concern with the origins of the *Volk* (German and otherwise) had become almost a national passion. Thus, Karl O. Müller (1797–1840) and G. F. Creuzer (1771–1858) drew heavily, albeit selectively, upon the linguistic evidence in their attempts to reconstruct the prototypes of Greek and other Indo-European gods and heroes. Even the philosopher G. W. F. Hegel (1770–1831), in whose works Romantic idealism reached the apex of its development, seems to have been strongly influenced by the new comparativism, and, as Richard Chase puts it, "longed for a 'polytheism in art' and imagination, a plastic and mythological philosophy" (*Quest for Myth,* 1949, p. 39).

Most of the pioneer philologists, among them Franz Bopp (1791–1867), Friedrich Schlegel (1772–1829), and Rasmus Rask (1787–1832), also made important contributions to comparative Indo-European mythological and religious studies. In many respects, the most distinguished member of this group was Jakob Grimm (1785–1836), who, with his brother Wilhelm (1786–1859), was responsible for amassing the great collection of tales that bears their name. However, Jakob Grimm was more than a mere collector of folk tales; he was also a preeminent philologist, and in 1823 he articulated the principle that later came to be known as "Grimm's law," which firmly established the phonological connections among Latin, Greek, and the ancient Germanic languages. His most important single contribution to Indo-European religious studies was a two-volume work entitled *Deutsche Mythologie* (1835). In it he developed the thesis that the *Märchen* he and his brother had collected were the detritus of pre-Christian Germanic mythology. This argument is bolstered by a host of etymologies, as well as comparisons to other Indo-European traditions. A good example of the latter is Grimm's suggestion that the ancient Scandinavian account of a war between the gods (Óðinn, Vili, and Vé) and an earlier generation of giants (Ymir et al.) is cognate to the Greek Titanomachy, or the war between the Olympians and the Titans (that is, between Zeus and his siblings and the supernatural beings of the previous generation, led by Kronos).

Elsewhere in Europe and in America interest in mythology, if not exclusively Indo-European mythology, also ran high. In Britain, for example, most of the Romantic poets—Wordsworth, Coleridge, Blake, Shelley, Keats, Byron, and others—drew extensively upon mythological themes; and Thomas Bulfinch's *The Age of Fable* (1855) popularized the study of mythology like no other work before it. Thus, by the middle of the nineteenth century, the science of comparative philology had reached maturity, interest in mythology and the history of religions had become widespread, and the stage was set for the appearance of the first grand paradigm in the history of Indo-European religious studies.

The First Grand Paradigm: F. Max Müller and the Naturists. In his seminal book, *The Structure of Scientific Revolutions* (1970), the eminent philosopher of science Thomas S. Kuhn makes a persuasive case for the proposition that all scientific knowledge expands in what amounts to an ascending and ever-widening spiral. In its earliest stages a new discipline necessarily finds itself groping for a central focus, for an overarching model in terms of which theories can be generated. Eventually, however, thanks to the efforts of a few scholars, a breakthrough is made, and there emerges a grand paradigm, which not only organizes the knowledge heretofore gained, but by its very nature generates a host of new discoveries and/or interpretations. The emergence of such a paradigm is revolutionary in its impact, and constitutes a quantum leap forward in the history of a discipline.

Kuhn, of course, focuses his attention upon the growth of the physical sciences, which so far have known at least two grand paradigms—Newtonian mechanics and quantum mechanics/relativity—and which may well be on the verge of a third. But the model applies generally. For example, in the history of linguistics, William Jones's discovery led to that discipline's first grand paradigm, which indeed precipitated the study of Indo-European religions. However, it was not until the 1850s, almost sixty years after Jones's death, that Indo-European religious studies finally achieved its own grand paradigm.

The man most responsible for this "revolution" was F. Max Müller (1823–1900), a German-born Sanskrit scholar, philologist, and student of Indian religions who had studied with Bopp and the eminent French Sanskritist Eugène Burnouf. Shortly after completing his formal studies, Müller accepted a position at Oxford University as a lecturer in Sanskrit and Indian religions; as it turned out, he spent the rest of his career there, eventually becoming one of the Victorian era's most distinguished men of letters.

In 1856, seven years after arriving at Oxford, Müller published a long essay entitled simply "Comparative Mythology" (published in *Oxford Essays*, 1856), and the revolution was launched. Although he went on to publish a veritable library of books, as well as innumerable collections of essays, articles, introductions, and so forth, most of his basic ideas were laid out in "Comparative Mythology."

Solar mythology and the "disease of language." First and foremost among Müller's ideas was the notion that the gods and heroes of the "Aryan" (i.e., Indo-European) peoples were basically metaphors for the sun, in all its aspects. To be sure, this was not a brand-new idea. In 1795, Charles-François Dupuis (1742–1809) had suggested that Jesus Christ was a solar metaphor and that the twelve apostles could be interpreted as the signs of the zodiac. But it was Müller who escalated the notion into a full-blown paradigm, one that had special relevance to the ancient Indo-European-speaking domain. Moreover, as a philologist, Müller insisted that the key to understanding these solar metaphors lay in the etymologies of divine names.

Müller asserted that language, including Proto-Indo-European, which he identified in effect with the earliest form of Sanskrit, was in its pristine state eminently rational. Objects such as the sun, the moon, stars, and other natural phenomena were labeled without reference to any divine beings or concepts, as the earliest dialects were incapable of expressing abstractions. But as time went on, Müller concluded, a curious malady set in, a "disease of language," the prime symptom of which was metaphor. What had begun as simple, descriptive terms gradually evolved into increasingly complex and abstract metaphors, and these in turn came to take on a life of their own. In short, by the time the earliest religious texts (e.g., the *Ṛgveda* and Hesiod's *Theogony*) were composed, the "disease of language" had become terminal; myth and religion had replaced reason and rationality. By judicious use of the comparative method, however, one could cut through the layers of metaphoric accretion and arrive at the root meanings underlying divine and heroic names. Thus, for example, the equation between Zeus and the Indian figure Dyauḥ, which clearly stemmed from a Proto-Indo-European conception of the sky god, could be traced back to a series of abstract conceptions relating to light, brightness, dawn, and so on, which, in turn, ultimately derived from metaphors for various solar attributes. Although he admitted that other natural phenomena play a part in generating mythical metaphors, Müller constantly emphasized the sun as the prime source of Indo-European religious inspiration: "I am bound to say that my own researches have led me again and again to the dawn and the sun as the chief burden of the myths of the Aryan race" (*Lectures on the Science of Language*, 1864, p. 520).

Müller's solar mythology rapidly began to gain adherents, both in Great Britain and abroad. Perhaps the most important of these was the English classicist George W. Cox (1827–1902), author of *The Mythology of the Aryan Nations* (1887). Despite his obsession with "pan-Aryanism" and with solar and other natural metaphors, Cox added a new and important dimension to comparative Indo-European mythology through his emphasis upon structural as well as etymological equations. As we shall see, this prefigured more recent theories about the nature of the Indo-European religious tradition. Another major disciple was the Semitist Robert Brown (b. 1844), who extended the paradigm far beyond the Indo-European domain and used it to explain the ancient Near Eastern divinities as well as those of the *Ṛgveda*. Two American scholars, John Fiske (1842–1901) and Daniel G. Brinton (1837–1899), also made significant contributions to the literature of solar mythology. In *Myths and Mythmakers* (1888) Fiske attempted to reconcile the meteorological and solar varieties of naturism, and Brinton, in *The Myths of the New World* (3d ed., 1896), sought to demonstrate the parallels between North American Indian and Indo-European mythological figures.

It should be pointed out that Müller's was by no means the only naturistic school of comparative Indo-European mythology to flourish in the late nineteenth century. Indeed, the "first paradigm," as we have termed it, actually included several rather distinct subparadigms, all of which shared essentially the same methodology and basic assumptions. For example, in 1859 Adalbert Kuhn (1812–1881) published his famous *Die Herabkunft des Feuers und des Göttertranks*, in which thunderstorms and their attendant bolts of lightning, rather than the sun, were conceived to be the prime source of Indo-European (and other) mythological and religious metaphors. Kuhn's most famous onomastic equation, later shown to be totally incorrect, was the assumed etymological connection between Prometheus and the Indian figure Pramantha. Both were seen as archetypal "fire bringers," and Kuhn and his followers were as assiduous in discovering other Indo-European fire gods as Müller and others were in discovering their solar divinities. Another prominent naturist was the Italian philologist Angelo de Gubernatis (1840–1913), who emphasized animal metaphors; thus, where Müller and Kuhn saw the sun and the lightning bolt, Gubernatis saw wild beasts, especially beasts of prey. Still others sought to find lunar and/or stellar metaphors in the Indo-European and other ancient mythological traditions.

Collapse of the first paradigm. While Müller, Kuhn, Cox, and the rest were developing their naturistic models, another scholarly approach to myth and religion per se was quietly taking a shape that would ultimately prove to be the undoing of these models. This approach was fostered by the pioneer anthropologists, such as E. B. Tylor (1832–1917), John Lubbock (1834–1913), and John McLennan (1827–1881), who, as might be expected, came to focus their attention not on the Indo-European tradition, but rather on the vast corpus of data that had come to light relative to the beliefs and practices of contemporary "primitive" peoples. In his *Primitive Culture* (1871), for example, Tylor laid the foundations for the theory of animism, that is, the notion that all religious beliefs are rooted in the concept of the human soul. The anthropologists were for the most part not trained philologists—although they did, of course, make use of the comparative method in its broadest sense—and therefore were not as attuned to etymologies and the metaphoric significance of names. The result was a profoundly different conception of the origin and evolution of man's religious beliefs.

By the late 1880s the naturists and the anthropologists found themselves on a collision course. The anthropological attack was led by a brilliant and iconoclastic Scotsman, Andrew Lang (1844–1912). A sometime disciple of Tylor, Lang set about to destroy naturism in general and the theories of Max Müller in particular. In a series of books, essays, and popular articles he hammered at Müller's assumptions and etymologies, and by the end of the century had effectively demonstrated the weaknesses in the naturistic paradigm so effectively that it did not long survive the death of its chief proponent in 1900.

It would be impossible here to trace all of the thrusts and counterthrusts that marked this famous scholarly debate, but Lang's principal objections can be summed up as follows: (1) Müller's theory—and, by extension, the theories of Kuhn, Cox, Fiske, and the rest—was implicitly based on the fallacious linkage of "degradation" to Original Sin, which, although the chosen people in this instance were the so-called Aryans (i.e., Indo-Europeans) rather than the Jews, was modeled on traditional Judeo-Christian historiography and did not take into account the comparative data from contemporary non-Western cultures; (2) too much emphasis was placed upon language and linguistic processes, especially metaphor and etymology, and too little on the differential effects of the social, cultural, and physical setting wherein myths and religious concepts originated; and (3) there was too much concern with origins and not enough with the historical development of myths and mythmaking, nor was enough attention paid to the universal, evolutionary stages evident in the Indo-European tradition. Needless to say, Müller attempted to answer these charges as best he could, and indeed his criticisms of unilineal evolutionism are remarkably similar to those of later critics. But in the end Lang was triumphant, and solar mythology, together with the other varieties of naturism that had flourished since the middle of the century, went into a permanent eclipse.

Empirical Reaction and Emergence of New Models: 1900–1920. Thus passed the first grand paradigm in comparative Indo-European religious studies. As the new century dawned, the majority of scholars working in the field—classicists, Indologists, Germanists, Celticists, and so forth—rapidly abandoned the naturistic/etymological approach in favor of more intense efforts to explain the various Indo-European religious traditions on their own terms. As in other disciplines at this time, including anthropology, a new spirit of empiricism came to the fore, marked by a growing distrust of comparativism. Most of these specialists, as they may be termed (e.g., the Celticist Joseph Vendryes), relied heavily on the methods of textual criticism, phrasing their analyses in terms of new translations, new specific etymologies, and the like. Indeed, save for the purposes of linguistic reconstruction, the idea of a common Indo-European religious and/or mythological heritage was rarely mentioned in the first two decades of the twentieth century.

At the same time, unrelated, for the most part, to Indo-European studies, several new theoretical models for the study of religion emerged, two of which were to have an important impact on the future development of this discipline. In his massive survey of primitive religion, *The Golden Bough* (3d ed., 12 vols., 1911–1915), James G. Frazer (1854–1941) came to the conclusion that religion everywhere was rooted in magic, and that all belief systems, including those of the ancient Indo-European-speaking communities, were predicated on a sacrificial ritual wherein a god was killed and replaced so as to renew the world. Among Frazer's prime examples was the death of Baldr, the Apollo-like son of the chief Norse god, Óðinn, who, thanks to the machinations of Loki, was unintentionally killed at the peak of his youthful vigor by his sibling, the blind god Hǫðr. Thus, through a form of "sympathetic magic" the gods, and the forces they incarnated, were periodically manipulated so as to keep them perpetually vigorous and fertile. Although largely rejected by subsequent generations of anthropologists, Frazer's influence lingered on in the so-called ritualist school of mythology associated with Jane E. Harrison, Francis M. Cornford, Jessie L. Weston, Gilbert Murray, F. R. S. Raglan, and H. J. Rose, all of whom drew heavily on Greco-Roman beliefs and practices in the formulation of their theories (indeed, most were classicists by academic training).

A second theoretical development occurred in France under the aegis of Émile Durkheim (1858–1917), one of the founding fathers of contemporary social science. In 1903, in collaboration with his principal student and disciple, Marcel Mauss (1872–1950), Durkheim published a short monograph entitled "De quelques formes primitives de classification: Contribution à l'étude des représentations collectives" (*Année sociologique* 6, 1903, pp. 1–72), which argued that social classification systems are necessarily "collectively represented" in a society's belief systems. This was followed in 1912 by his *magnum opus, Les formes élémentaires de la vie religieuse* (translated as *The Elementary Forms of the Religious Life,* 1917), in which he persuasively demonstrated that society itself is the stuff of the divine and that man necessarily fashions his gods as collective representations of fundamental "social facts." To be sure, Durkheim's prime examples were drawn from the belief systems of the Australian Aborigines, but the implications for the study of religion per se were clear: a new primary source of religious metaphors had been identified, and the immediate implications for the study of Indo-European belief systems were also clearly present from the outset, as Durkheim's ideas themselves were in some measure influenced by the demonstration (1907) of Antoine Meillet (1866–1936) that the Iranian god Mithra (equivalent to the Vedic god Mitra) was the personification of the idea of "contract." Indeed, as we shall shortly see, Meillet, perhaps the most eminent Indo-European philologist of his time, had more than a little to do with the development of the second grand paradigm in Indo-European studies.

Neo-Comparativists and the Search for a New Paradigm: 1920–1938. Although comparative Indo-European religious studies suffered a marked decline in the generation following Müller's death, the basic questions he and his colleagues had addressed regarding the fundamental similarities among the several ancient Indo-European pantheons remained, and in the early 1920s the pendulum began to swing once again in the direction of what can best be labeled neo-comparativism. For example, Albert Carnoy began to speak in no uncertain terms about a "religion indo-européenne," and shortly thereafter, although they differed widely in inspirations and orientation, a number of German scholars, among them Walter F. Otto, Hermann Güntert, Friedrich Cornelius, and F. R. Schroeder, came to the same general conclusion: that it is impossible to understand any single ancient Indo-European religious system without reference to a common set of deities, rituals, and myths, and that it is indeed possible to conceive of such a common Indo-European tradition without reference to the discarded theories of Müller and Kuhn. Another driving force in this new effort was provided by Meillet, who, although he himself never attempted with Indo-European mythological materials the kind of broad synthesis that characterizes his *Introduction à l'étude des langues indo-européennes* (1922), encouraged his students to undertake such studies. One of these students was Georges Dumézil (b. 1898), a young philologist and historian of religions who took his doctorate under Meillet in 1924.

Like the other neo-comparativists, Dumézil sought to find a viable theoretical basis upon which to build a new paradigm for comparative Indo-European mythology. In his early studies, for example, *Le festin d'immortalité* (1924), *Le crime des Lemniennes* (1924), and *Le problème des Centaures* (1929), which focused on what he came to call the "ambrosia cycle," that is, the common Indo-European traditions surrounding the preparation and consumption of a deified beverage (*soma*, mead, ambrosia, and so forth), he drew heavily on Frazer's theory of death and rebirth and of the ritual sacrifice of the king. But as he himself later observed, the Frazerian model ultimately proved to be insufficient for his purposes; it simply could not explain the multitude of common motifs that pervaded the several Indo-European traditions.

After a decade of grappling with the problem, Dumézil took an extended leave from his academic duties in the early 1930s and undertook the study of ancient Chinese religion under the guidance of Marcel Granet (1884–1940), an eminent Sinologist who had also been one of Durkheim's most devoted disciples. Yet although the project began as an attempt to gain a perspective on the Indo-European tradition by coming to grips with a wholly different ancient belief system, it ended by providing Dumézil with the framework he had been searching for and that he came to call *la méthode sociologique*. Thus, in 1938, not long after he had completed his studies with Granet, Dumézil achieved the breakthrough he had been seeking, and the second grand paradigm in Indo-European studies was born.

The Second Grand Paradigm: Dumézil and the New Comparative Mythology. Although the breakthrough itself came in 1938, the first hint of what Dumézil now refers to as the tripartite ideology actually surfaced shortly before he began his Chinese studies. In 1930 he published an article comparing the three divisons of ancient Scythian society—the "Royal Scyths," the "Warrior Scyths," and the "Agricultural Scyths," each of which was believed to have descended from one of the sons of the primeval figure Targitaus (Herodotus, 4.5–4.6)—with the three *varṇas*, or classes of Vedic India: the *brāhmaṇas* (priests), the *kṣatriyas* (warriors), and the *vaiśyas* (cultivators). He also recognized that the sovereignty of the Royal Scyths was based on the myth that their ancestor, Targitaus's youngest son, had managed to recover three fiery golden objects, a cup, an ax, and a yoked plow, each symbolic of one of the social divisions, that had fallen from the sky, although the full import of this symbolism did not become apparent until the new paradigm had fully crystallized. Two years later, in 1932, the linguist Émile Benveniste arrived independently at a similar conclusion relative to the parallels not only between the Scythian and Indian situations, but also among these two and the social classes of ancient Iran. However, all of the societies concerned belonged to the Indo-Iranian substock, and at the time there seemed to be no reason to conclude that this tripartite hierarchy of priests (or priest-kings), warriors, and cultivators was necessarily pan-Indo-European.

Nevertheless, in the years that followed, Dumézil began to pick up hints of an analogous structure in the Roman tradition (see, for example, *Flāmen-Brahman*, 1935), especially in the makeup of the most ancient of the Roman priestly colleges, the *flamines maiores*. Could the distinctions between the *flamen Dialis*, or chief priest of Jupiter, the *flamen Martialis*, who presided over the cult of the war god Mars, and the *flamen Quirinalis*, who served the popular divinity Quirinus, an incarnation of the mass of Roman society, reflect the same structure he and Benveniste had discovered in the Indo-Iranian tradition, especially in light of the probable etymological connections between the two terms *flamen* and *brahman*? It was not until he had focused his attention upon the ancient Germanic pantheons in the course of giving a series of lectures at the University of Uppsala in Sweden in the fall of 1938 that he finally came to the realization that this threefold hierarchy was in fact pan-Indo-European, and that it was reflected in both the structure of the pantheons and the structure of society itself, especially in the system of social stratification. And here, of course, his recent exposure to Durkheimian theory in the course of his studies with Granet served him well. The Old Norse gods Óðinn, Þórr, and Freyr reflected the same basic type of social organization, even though the priestly, or brahmanic, level had long since disappeared as a viable social entity by the time the myths were transcribed by Snorri Sturluson and Saxo Grammaticus. Óðinn (Odin), like Jupiter and the Vedic god Varuṇa, was a collective representation of ultimate sovereignty; Þórr (Thor) was the incarnation of the warrior stratum and thus was cognate to Mars and Indra; while Freyr (together with his father Njǫrðr), like Quirinus and the Vedic Aśvins ("divine horsemen"), represented the producing classes, that is, the herders and cultivators upon whom the other two classes depended for nourishment.

Dumézil's discovery was in large measure confirmed by his Swedish colleague Stig Wikander's conclusive demonstration that among the most prominent features of ancient Indo-European social organization was the *comitatus* ("war band"), which typically formed itself around the person of a chief. According to Wikander, the *comitatus* was mythologically reflected by such otherwise diverse phenomena as Indra and his Marut (i.e., the Rudriyas) and the war bands that followed Irish heroes like Cú Chulainn and Finn (see *Der arische Männerbund,* 1938). Thus, thanks to Wikander, who became one of Dumézil's earliest and most productive supporters (see below), a major piece of the puzzle had fallen into place.

A preliminary statement of the new model appeared in *Les dieux des Germains* (1939), which was based on the lectures Dumézil had given in Sweden, and for the next decade the discoveries came thick and fast. Dumézil rapidly came to the conclusion that the sovereign level, shortly to be labeled the "first function," was in fact represented by two complementary divinities: Varuṇa, Jupiter, and Óðinn were primarily concerned with the maintenance of cosmic order (e.g., the Vedic concept of *ṛta*), while Mitra, Týr, and the otherwise obscure Roman divinity Dius Fidius were concerned with social and juridical sovereignty. This idea of the "joint sovereignty" formed the major focus of *Mitra-Varuṇa: Essai sur deux représentations indo-européennes de la souveraineté* (1940). The first comprehensive statement of the new paradigm appeared a year later in a book entitled *Jupiter, Mars, Quirinus* (1941). Although Dumézil here focuses on Rome and its mythological origins, this book spelled out in detail for the first time the concept that came to be known as the "three functions" of social organization, that is, the "first function" (cosmic and juridical sovereignty in all its manifestations), the "second function" (the exercise of military prowess), and the "third function" (the provision of nourishment, health, physical well-being, wealth, the welfare of the masses, etc.).

In short, by the end of the 1940s, in a remarkable series of books, monographs, and shorter works, Dumézil had fully articulated the basic elements of the second grand paradigm in comparative Indo-European religious studies. The Iranian and Celtic traditions had been brought into the picture, and a great many secondary themes had been discovered; for example, the recognition that the juridical sovereign (e.g., Mitra and Týr) typically had two ancillary manifestations, each of whom was concerned with an aspect of this function. In the Vedic texts, these were the figures Aryaman and Bhaga, who represented, respectively, the Aryan community itself, along with its most basic social relationship, marriage; and the equitable distribution of goods and rewards. This idea was first enunciated in *Le troisième souverain* (1949).

In his first articulations of the new paradigm Dumézil had relied heavily on the previously mentioned Durkheimian proposition that "social facts" give rise to "supernatural facts," or "collective representations." However, as he himself observed, around 1950 his orientation began to shift, and he took what amounted to a long step beyond strict Durkheimianism and "la méthode sociologique." Adopting what in retrospect may be called a more structuralist perspective, he began to conceive of the three functions as expressions of a deep-seated, tripartite ideology that was manifest in both social and supernatural contexts, but which ultimately lay outside either sphere. Thus, the functions were gradually redefined as "un moyen d'analyser," a method of analysis, and this revised orientation is, in some respects, not dissimilar to the structuralist vision espoused by Claude Lévi-Strauss (b. 1908). There is, however, a major difference between the two French scholars: Lévi-Strauss (in such works as *Le cru et le cuit,* 1964) is concerned primarily with the "deep structure" of the human mind per se, while Dumézil remains committed to the proposition that the tripartite ideology is uniquely Indo-European, and that other major language families, such as the Sino-Tibetan, the Hamito-Semitic, and the Uto-Aztecan, are probably characterized by their own unique ideologies. Perhaps the best way to describe this approach is to label it "structural relativism."

In the course of the next three decades more important discoveries were made, not only by Dumézil himself, but also by the scholars who have come to adopt the paradigm. One of the earliest of these was Stig Wikander, who in 1947 demonstrated the extent to which the heroes of the *Mahābhārata* (Yudhiṣṭhira, Arjuna, Bhīma, Nakula, and Sahadeva) were at bottom transpositions of the major Vedic divinities (Mitra, Varuṇa, Indra, and the Nāsatya) and showed that the tripartite ideology could be detected at the epic as well as the mythological level. Other early followers of Dumézil were Lucien Gerschel, Jan de Vries, Edgar Polomé, Robert Schilling, Jacques Duchesne-Guillemin, François Vian, and Marie-Louise Sjoestedt.

In the late 1950s and early 1960s a new generation of scholars was attracted to the Dumézilian model, including Jaan Puhvel, Donald J. Ward, Françoise Le Roux, and myself, and the paradigm was extended even more broadly. Among the major subthemes discovered by Dumézil and his colleagues over the years, in addition to Wikander's 1947 breakthrough, were (1) the "three sins of the warrior," that is, the recognition that Indo-European warrior figures (e.g., Indra, Herakles, and the Norse figure Starkað) typically commit three canonical "sins," one against each of the functions, and (2) the "war between the functions," manifested principally in the Roman and Germanic traditions, wherein representatives of the first two functions defeat representatives of the third and incorporate them into the system, rendering it complete (e.g., the Sabine war and the conflict between the Æsir and Vanir).

In the early 1970s Dumézil pushed the paradigm in yet another important direction (see *Mythe et épopée*, vol. 2, 1971, especially "L'enjeu du jeu des dieux: Un héros") through his discovery that Indo-European warrior figures such as the Vedic character Śiśupāla are in the final analysis but counters in a game played by the gods, and that the gods themselves can be sorted into "dark" and "light" categories—that is, those who represent the chaotic forces of nature and those who seek to control these forces. In the Indian tradition this dichotomy is reflected in the difference between the "dark" divinity Rudra and the "light" divinity Viṣṇu; in ancient Scandinavia it appears in that between Óðinn and Þórr. The full implications of this discovery are being probed by several of Dumézil's disciples, among them Udo Strutynski and myself.

In the course of the last decade or so, in what may be termed his *phase de bilan,* Dumézil's remarkable scholarly output has continued unabated. Among his more recent books are a reexamination of the Indo-European concept of sovereignty (*Les dieux souverains des Indo-Européens,* 1977) and a disquisition on Indo-European attitudes toward marriage (*Mariages indo-européens,* 1979). He has also published several collections of earlier writings, all of which bear on one or another aspect of the tripartite ideology. Dumézil's career was capped in 1979 when he was elected to the Académie Française.

This is not to imply that the "new comparative mythology" is now universally accepted by Indo-Europeanists. Indeed, almost from the outset it has been the subject of intense and persistent criticism from a variety of scholars, many of whom have suggested that Dumézil has imposed the tripartite model on the data, and that it has no existence save in the minds of the researchers concerned. Among the most persistent of these critics was Paul Thieme, an Indologist, who asserted on numerous occasions that Dumézil's interpretation of the Indic pantheon, especially the role played by the god Aryaman, was wholly incorrect. Thieme interpreted the Sanskrit root *ari-* to mean "stranger" rather than "the people" (or "the shining ones"), the common meaning of most ethnic self-identification terms, modern as well as ancient—for example, Hopi, Diné (Navajo), and so forth. Other prominent critics have included H. J. Rose (who took Dumézil to task for ignoring the "manaistic" basis of Roman religion), Jan Gonda, Angelo Brelich, the Germanist E. A. Philippson, and John Brough, a Sanskrit scholar who claimed to have discovered the tripartite ideology in the Bible and therefore asserted that it was not uniquely Indo-European.

Dumézil has vigorously responded to these and other criticisms, and to date no single critic has emerged as a potential "Andrew Lang" as far as this paradigm is concerned. Indeed, it is fair to say that the majority of contemporary scholars in the field of comparative Indo-European mythology and religion continue to make effective use of the general theoretical and methodological framework developed by Dumézil and his colleagues in the course of the last four decades. A good example is Joël Grisward, whose brilliant analysis of the medieval French legends of Aymeri de Narbonne and the extent to which they have Indo-Iranian counterparts (see his *Archéologie de l'épopée médiévale,* 1982) is, as Dumézil himself noted, perhaps the most important contribution to the new comparative mythology since Wikander's discovery of epical transposition in 1947. Another excellent example can be seen in Udo Strutynski's convincing demonstration that the English weekday names, at least from Tuesday through Friday, and their cognates in other modern Germanic languages, represent a persistence of a tripartite ideological formula—that is, "Týr's day," "Óðinn's day," "Þórr's day," and "Frigg's day" (see his "Germanic Divinities in Weekday Names," *Journal of Indo-European Studies* 3, 1975, pp. 363–384).

It would be impossible in the space of this brief article even to mention, let alone discuss in any detail, all of the significant research that has been pursued since the late 1960s by specialists in comparative Indo-European religion and mythology who have oriented their work around the Dumézilian paradigm. For example, Atsuhiko Yoshida, a Japanese Hellenist who studied with Dumézil for the better part of a decade, has demonstrated the strong probability that the development of Japanese mythology was profoundly influenced, either directly or indirectly, by Indo-European themes in the late prehistoric period (that is, the fourth and fifth centuries CE), and that the most likely source of this influence was one or another tribe of North Iranian–speaking steppe nomads (Scythians, Alans, etc.) that managed to reach East Asia during this period (Yoshida, 1977). Ōbayashi Taryō, an anthropologist at the University of Tokyo, and I subsequently joined Yoshida in this effort. Bruce Lincoln has published a book comparing Indo-Iranian and contemporary East African religious attitudes toward cattle (*Priests, Warriors, and*

Cattle, 1981). David Cohen has expanded our understanding of the "three sins" typically committed by the Indo-European warrior (see above) in a penetrating analysis of the Irish hero Suibhne ("Suibhne Geilt," *Celtica* 12, 1977, pp. 113–124).

In France, Daniel Dubuisson, who took his doctorate under Dumézil in 1983, has attempted to develop a quasi-mathematical approach to Indo-European myth, based in large part on his Indological research, while Bernard Sergent has illuminated the dual kingship at Sparta by judicious application of the Dumézilian paradigm ("La représentation spariate de la royauté," *Revue de l'histoire des religions* 189, 1976, pp. 3–52). And in 1984 D. A. Miller investigated the trifunctional implications of the "three kings" in Sophocles' *Oedipus at Colonus* from what can best be termed a neo-Dumézilian standpoint. Other scholars who have extended the paradigm in a variety of new and potentially important directions include Steven O'Brien, Miriam Robbins, Alf Hiltebeitel, David B. Evans, and Jean-Claude Rivière.

Some Recent Developments. Like all grand paradigms that have been pushed to their effective limits, the Dumézilian paradigm is fraying a bit at the edges, and several of the most important recent advances in Indo-European religious studies have involved matters that transcend the tripartite ideology. One of these is the matter of "dark" and "light" divinities mentioned earlier. Indeed, Dumézil himself has suggested that this dichotomy cuts across the three functions, and perhaps reflects a more fundamental binary structure that underlies social and supernatural tripartition. If this proves to be the case, it may well be that the ideological model Dumézil first detected some forty-odd years ago is but a special case of a broader and more deep-seated mental template, as it were, that is shared by *homo religiosus* as a whole. Such a template, if it exists, would closely parallel the presumably universal "deep structure" of the human psyche posited by Lévi-Strauss.

Another extremely significant development involves the matter of a common Indo-European cosmology, something Dumézil never really came to grips with and which, heretofore, had defied all attempts at elucidation via the tripartite ideology. In 1975, Puhvel and Lincoln, working independently, reached compatible conclusions; they agreed that the elusive cosmology was in fact embedded in a theme, present in the Roman, Indo-Iranian, and Norse traditions, wherein a primeval being kills his twin and makes the world from the latter's remains. This theme closely approximates the nearly universal concept of what Adolf E. Jensen calls the "*dema* deity," that is, a sacrificial victim whose body parts provide the *materia prima* of either the world itself or some important part thereof (as in the Ceramese myth of Hainuwele; see Jensen, *Myth and Cult among Primitive Peoples,* 1963).

For Puhvel, the point of departure was the pseudo-historical account of Romulus and Remus, in which the latter is killed shortly after the founding of Rome. Underlying the names *Romulus* and *Remus,* Puhvel suggests, are **Wironos* ("man") and **Yemo(no)s* ("twin"), to which may be compared *Yama* (Skt.), *Yima* (Av.), and *Ymir* (ON), as well as *Mannus* and *Tuisto,* mentioned in Tacitus's *Germania.* Although Romulus/*Wironos did not explicitly "make the world" from Remus/*Yemos's remains, Remus's death seems clearly to have been somehow essential to the building of the city, like a sacrificial offering, and the fact that Remus's "crime" consists of jumping over the newly dug foundation for the city wall implies that the victim's essence was in one way or another mixed with the mortar that eventually filled the ditch. Lincoln's point of departure was the Indic manifestation of the theme and its implications as they relate to the *dema*-deity concept, that is, the account in *Ṛgveda* 10.90 wherein Manu (i.e., "man") sacrifices Yama (or Puruṣa, as he is called in the Vedic text) and creates the world from his corpse. (Unlike Remus/*Yemos, Puruṣa was a willing victim, and Manu is credited with originating the institution of religious sacrifice; however, the basic context of the two accounts is remarkably similar.) As luck would have it, Lincoln sent a draft of his manuscript to Puhvel for comment and criticism, and the result was a pair of seminal articles that in 1975 appeared back-to-back in *History of Religions.*

The paradigmatic implications of this discovery are still under investigation, and various questions have been raised by scholars. Does the ideology itself spring from this primordial sacrifice? Is it possible that the account of Romulus and Remus, who began life as the foster children of a shepherd, became warriors, and finally went off to found a city, is a euhemeristic survival of an ontological myth wherein the three functions emerge successively after a primeval fratricide? And is there a connection between the *dramatis personae* of this primeval drama and the dark/light dichotomy (see above)? Or does the theme in question lie totally outside the parameters of the paradigm? As yet no clear answers have been provided to these questions.

In sum, as the field of Indo-European religious studies approaches its bicentennial, it remains a vigorous and intellectually viable discipline. In the course of the last two hundred years it has managed to develop and then transcend one grand paradigm (naturism) and is currently dominated by a second (the new comparative mythology). How long this second paradigm will continue to reign is uncertain; as has been indicated, there are already signs that it may have begun to outlive its usefulness. But whatever may be the ultimate fate of the Dumézilian model—and I suspect that it will eventually become a "special case" of a much broader paradigm, the outlines of which cannot yet be clearly perceived—the discipline itself will almost certainly persevere, and will continue to contribute important insights not only into a fundamental aspect of the heritage shared by all Indo-European speakers, but also into the nature of religion per se.

BIBLIOGRAPHY

Dorson, Richard. "The Eclipse of Solar Mythology." In *Myth: A Symposium,* edited by Thomas A. Sebeok, pp. 25–63. Bloomington, Ind., 1965. The definitive study of the Müller-Lang controversy.

Dumézil, Georges. *L'idéologie tripartie des Indo-Européens.* Brussels, 1958. Remains the most succinct overview of Dumézil's thesis.

Dumézil, Georges. *Camillus.* Berkeley, 1980. A translation by Annette Aronowicz and Josette Bryson of the "Camillus" sections from *Mythe et épopée,* vol. 3 (Paris, 1973) and related passages from *Fêtes romaines d'été et d'automne* (Paris, 1975). Includes a definitive introduction by Udo Strutynski.

Dumézil, Georges. *The Stakes of the Warrior.* Berkeley, 1983. A translation by David Weeks of the "L'enjeu du jeu des dieux: Un héros" section of *Mythe et épopée,* vol. 2 (Paris, 1971). Includes a masterful introduction by Jaan Puhvel, which puts the "dark/light" dichotomy into its proper perspective.

Feldman, Burton, and Robert D. Richardson, eds. *The Rise of Modern Mythology, 1680–1860.* Bloomington, Ind., 1972. A comprehensive anthology of the major eighteenth- and early nineteenth-century contributions to comparative mythology, from Vico and Fontenelle to F. Max Müller.

Larson, Gerald James, C. Scott Littleton, and Jaan Puhvel, eds. *Myth in Indo-European Antiquity.* Berkeley, 1974. A symposium on various aspects of the Dumézilian model and related subjects. Includes papers by Littleton, Puhvel, Strutynski, David Evans, Mary R. Gerstein, Steven E. Greenebaum, Edgar Polomé, Marija Gimbutas, Jeannine Talley, Matthias Vereno, and an essay by Dumézil entitled " 'Le Borgne' and 'Le Manchot': The State of the Problem." This essay concerns yet another Indo-European subtheme: the loss of an eye and a hand, respectively, by the cosmic and juridical representatives of the first function: for example, Óðinn, who gives up an eye in exchange for wisdom, and Týr, who loses a hand while swearing what amounts to a false oath, as well as the Roman figures Horatius Cocles, who is one-eyed, and Mucius Scaevola, who also loses a hand while swearing falsely.

Lincoln, Bruce. "The Indo-European Myth of Creation." *History of Religions* 15 (1975): 121–145. A seminal contribution to the understanding of the Indo-European cosmogonic myth; see the article by Puhvel listed below.

Littleton, C. Scott. *The New Comparative Mythology: An Anthropological Assessment of the Theories of Georges Dumézil.* 3d ed. Berkeley, 1980. A comprehensive review of the origins and current state of the "second paradigm," that is, the Dumézilian model. Includes a discussion of the major criticisms that have been directed against the model, as well as an essay comparing Dumézil and Lévi-Strauss, and an extensive bibliography of works by Dumézil and other contributors to the new comparative mythology.

Meillet, Antoine, "Le dieu indo-iranien Mitra." *Journal asiatique* 9 (1907): 143–159. A seminal article on the Vedic god Mithra and the extent to which he is a "collective representation" of the idea of "contract"; had an impact on Durkheim and later on the development of Dumézil's theory.

Puhvel, Jaan, ed. *Myth and Law among the Indo-Europeans.* Berkeley, 1970. A symposium on the new comparative mythology. Includes papers by Puhvel, Littleton, Strutynski, Donald Ward, Jacques Duchesne-Guillemin, Edgar Polomé, Calvert Watkins, James L. Sauvé, Robert L. Fisher, and Stephen P. Schwartz.

Puhvel, Jaan. "Remus et frater." *History of Religions* 15 (1975): 146–157. Reprinted in Puhvel's *Analecta Indoeuropaea* (Innsbruck, 1981), pp. 300–311. Together with the article by Lincoln listed above, this paper probes the Indo-European cosmogonic myth and concludes that it is based on a primeval sacrifice of "Twin" by "Man." An extremely significant contribution to the new comparative mythology.

Rivière, Jean-Claude, ed. *Georges Dumézil à la découverte des Indo-Européens.* Paris, 1979. A symposium marking Dumézil's election to the Académie Française in 1979. Includes essays by several of his colleagues and former students, including Rivière, Robert Schilling, François-Xavier Dillmann, Jean Varenne, Joël Grisward, Georges Charachidzé, and Alain de Benoist, editor of *Nouvelle école.* Original versions of some of these essays were published, together with other materials, in a 1973 issue of *Nouvelle école* devoted to Dumézil.

Vries, Jan de. *Perspectives in the History of Religions.* Translated by Kees W. Bolle. Berkeley, 1977. A succinct survey of the history of religious and mythological thought from classical antiquity to modern times. De Vries was an early disciple of Dumézil, and he includes an interesting section on his theories (pp. 182–186).

Ward, Donald. *The Divine Twins: An Indo-European Myth in Germanic Tradition.* Berkeley, 1968. An important contribution to the study of the "third function" and the role played in dioscurism in the Indo-European ideology.

Wikander, Stig. "Pāṇḍava-sagan och Mahābhārata's mytiska förutsättningar." *Religion och Bibel* (Lund) 6 (1947): 27–39. Demonstrates that the heroes of the *Mahābhārata* reflect the tripartite ideology and were derived from the Vedic divinities. Wikander's essay was a major step forward in the development of the new comparative mythology.

Yoshida, Atsuhiko. "Japanese Mythology and the Indo-European Trifunctional System." *Diogenes* 98 (1977): 93–116. Summarizes the evidence suggesting that Japanese mythology, as expressed in the *Kojiki* (712 CE) and the *Nihonshoki* (720 CE), was influenced by the tripartite Indo-European ideology at some point in the late prehistoric period.

C. SCOTT LITTLETON

INDRA. In India the worship of the god Indra, king of the gods, warrior of the gods, god of rain, begins properly in the *Ṛgveda,* circa 1200 BCE, but his broader nature can be traced farther back into the proto-Indo-European world through his connections with Zeus and Wotan. For although the *Ṛgveda* knows a sky father called Dyaus-pitṛ, who is literally cognate with Zeus-patēr and Ju-piter, it is Indra who truly fills the shoes of the Indo-European celestial sovereign: he wields the thunderbolt, drinks the ambrosial *soma* to excess, bestows fertility upon human women (often by sleeping with them himself), and leads his band of Maruts, martial storm gods, to win victory for the conquering Indo-Aryans.

In the *Ṛgveda,* Indra's family life is troubled in ways that remain unclear. His birth, like that of many great warriors and heroes, is unnatural: kept against his will inside his mother's womb for many years, he bursts forth out of her side and kills his own father (*Ṛgveda* 4.18). He too is in turn challenged by his own son, whom he apparently overcomes (*Ṛgveda* 10.28). But the hymns to Indra, who is after all the chief god of the *Ṛgveda* (over a quarter of the hymns in the collection are addressed to him), emphasize his heroic deeds. He is said to have created the universe by propping apart heaven and earth (as other gods, notably Viṣṇu and Varuṇa, are also said to have done) and finding the sun, and to have freed the cows that had been penned up in a cave (*Ṛgveda* 3.31). This last myth, which is perhaps the central myth of the *Ṛgveda,* has meaning on several levels: it means what it says (that Indra helps the worshiper to obtain cattle, as he is so often implored to do), and also that Indra found the sun and the world of life and light and fertility in general, for all of which cows often serve as a Vedic metaphor.

It was Indra who, in the shape of a falcon or riding on a falcon, brought down the *soma* plant from heaven, where it had been guarded by demons, to earth, where it became accessible to men (*Ṛgveda* 4.26–27). Indra himself is the *soma* drinker *par excellence;* when he gets drunk, as he is wont to do, he brags (*Ṛgveda* 10.119), and the worshiper who invites Indra to share his *soma* also shares in the euphoria that *soma* induces in both the human and the divine drinker (*Ṛgveda* 9.113). But Indra is a jealous god—jealous, that is, of the *soma,* both for lofty reasons (like other great gods, he does not wish to allow mortals to taste the fruit that will make them like unto gods) and for petty reasons (he wants to keep all the *soma* for himself). His attempts to exclude the Aśvins from drinking the *soma* fail when they enlist the aid of the priest Dadhyañc, who disguises himself with a horse's head and teaches them the secret of the *soma* (*Ṛgveda* 1.117.22).

But Indra's principal function is to kill enemies—non-Aryan humans and demons, who are often conflated. As the supreme god of the *kṣatriya*s or class of royal warriors, Indra is invoked as a destroyer of cities and destroyer of armies, as the staunch ally of his generous worshipers, to whom Indra is in turn equally generous (Maghavan, "the generous," is one of his most popular epithets). These enemies (of whom the most famous is Vṛtra) are often called Dāsas or Dasyus, "slaves," and probably represent the indigenous populations of the subcontinent that the Indo-Aryans subjugated (and whose twin cities, Mohenjo Daro and Harappā, in the Indus Valley, may have been the citadels that Indra claims to have devastated). But the Dāsas are also frequently identified with the *asura*s, or demonic enemies of the gods themselves. The battles thus take place simultaneously on the human and the divine levels, and are both political and cosmogonic.

Indra's reputation begins to decline in the Brāhmaṇas, about 900 BCE, where his supremacy is preempted by Prajāpati, the primordial creator. Indra still drinks the *soma,* but now he becomes badly hungover and has to be restored to health by the worshiper. Similarly, the killing of Vṛtra leaves Indra weakened and in need of purification. In the epics, Indra is mocked for weaknesses associated with the phallic powers that are his great glory in the *Ṛgveda.* His notorious womanizing leads, on one occasion (when the sage Gautama catches Indra in bed with Ahalyā, the sage's wife), to Indra's castration; though his testicles are later replaced by those of a ram (*Rāmāyaṇa* 1.47–48); in another version of this story, Indra is cursed to be covered with a thousand *yoni*s or vaginas, a curse which he turns to a boon by having the *yoni*s changed into a thousand eyes. When Indra's excesses weaken him, he becomes vulnerable in battle; often he is overcome by demons and must enlist the aid of the now supreme sectarian gods, Śiva and Viṣṇu, to restore his throne. Sometimes he sends one of his voluptuous nymphs, the *apsarase*s, to seduce ascetic demons who have amassed sufficient power, through *tapas* ("meditative austerities"), to heat Indra's throne in heaven. And when the demon Nahuṣa usurps Indra's throne and demands Indra's wife, Śacī, the gods have to perform a horse sacrifice to purify and strengthen Indra so that he can win back his throne. Even then Indra must use a combination of seduction and deceit, rather than pure strength, to gain his ends: Śacī goads Nahuṣa into committing an act of hubris that brings him down to a level on which he becomes vulnerable to Indra.

Old Vedic gods never die; they just fade into new Hindu gods. Indra remains a kind of figurehead in Hindu mythology, and the butt of many veiled anti-

Hindu jokes in Buddhist mythology. The positive aspects of his person are largely transformed to Śiva. Both Indra and Śiva are associated with the Maruts or Rudras, storm gods; both are said to have extra eyes (three, or a thousand) that they sprouted in order to get a better look at a beautiful dancing *apsaras;* both are associated with the bull and with the erect phallus; both are castrated; and both come into conflict with their fathers-in-law. In addition to these themes, which are generally characteristic of fertility gods, Indra and Śiva share more specific mythological episodes: both of them seduce the wives of brahman sages; both are faced with the problem of distributing (where it will do the least harm) certain excessive and destructive forces that they amass; both are associated with anti-Brahmanic, heterodox acts; and both lose their right to a share in the sacrifice. And just as Indra beheads a brahman demon (Vṛtra) whose head pursues him until he is purified of this sin, so Śiva, having beheaded Brahmā, is plagued by Brahmā's skull until he is absolved in Banaras. Thus, although Indra comes into conflict with the ascetic aspect of Śiva, the erotic aspect of Śiva found new uses for the discarded myths of Indra.

[*See also* Vedism and Brahmanism; Prajāpati; *and* Śiva. *For further discussion of Indra's Indo-European cognates, see* Jupiter.]

BIBLIOGRAPHY

For a detailed summary of the mythology of Indra, see pages 249–283 of Sukumari Bhattacharji's rather undigested *The Indian Theogony* (Cambridge, 1970). For a translation of a series of myths about Indra, and a detailed bibliography of secondary literature, see pages 56–96 and 317–321 of my *Hindu Myths* (Harmondsworth, 1975). For the sins of Indra, see Georges Dumézil's *The Destiny of the Warrior* (Chicago, 1970) and *The Destiny of the King* (Chicago, 1973), and my *The Origins of Evil in Hindu Mythology* (Berkeley, 1976). For the relationship between Indra and Śiva, see my *Śiva: The Erotic Ascetic* (Oxford, 1981), originally published as *Asceticism and Eroticism in the Mythology of Śiva* (1973).

WENDY DONIGER O'FLAHERTY

INDUS VALLEY RELIGION is the goddess-centered religious system of the urban civilization that emerged in the Indus Valley of western India around 2500 BCE and declined into a series of successor posturban village cultures after 1750 BCE. The antecedents of this religion lie in the village cultures of Baluchistan and Afghanistan, which were part of a larger regional cultural system in western Asia that also included the village cultures of southern Turkmenistan and the Elamite culture of southwestern Iran. Common religious patterns within this larger region continued into the early stages of urbanization in Elam, Turkmenistan, and the Indus Valley, after which the unification of the local regions and subsequent historical changes led to separation: Elam was drawn into the orbit of Sumerian and Akkadian culture; Turkmenistan was settled by new groups from the northern steppes; and Indus settlement shifted eastward into the Ganges-Yamunā Valley in the North and Gujarat and the Deccan Plateau in the South as the original cities in the Indus Valley were abandoned. After the entry of Aryan tribes into northern India around 1500 BCE, the continuity of Indus Valley religion is found mainly in the Dravidian cultures of South India, although various elements were also preserved in the village cultures of North India and in the synthesis of Aryan and non-Aryan cultures that marked late Vedic and post-Vedic developments in the Ganges-Yamunā Valley.

The Western Asian Setting. The evolution of the Neolithic cultures of western Asia that preceded the Indus civilization cannot yet be reconstructed in detail, but a pattern is emerging from current evidence that sheds new light on the basic features of the Indus Valley religious system. Archaeological research in southern Turkmenistan has revealed a continued sequence of village cultures north of the Kopet Dagh Mountains from a least 6000 BCE onward, culminating in a regional urban culture at Namazga and Altin around 2500 BCE. Research on the Proto-Elamite and Proto-Dravidian languages points to a common proto-Elamo-Dravidian ancestry among a pastoral people moving southward from Central Asia into Iran sometime between 8000 and 6000 BCE, combining the herding of goats, sheep, and cattle with the cultivation of wheat and barley, and gradually separating into two branches: a proto-Dravidian branch that settled eastward in Afghanistan and Baluchistan, and a proto-Elamite branch that continued westward across southern Iran to the Zagros Mountains. The broadly based set of common cultural features established throughout western Asia in this early period and reinforced by later interregional contacts is reflected in similar patterns of proto-urban development and urbanization between 3500 and 2500 BCE in the various localized regions.

Since the Indus civilization's script has not been deciphered, the proto-Dravidian identification of the Indus language remains uncertain. There is broad scholarly consensus, however, that a form of Proto-Dravidian was the dominant language of the Indus urban culture, and this is substantiated by parallels between cultural and religious features of the Indus civilization and later Dravidian village culture. These parallels, in conjunction with the pre-urban cultural affinities with Elam and Turkmenistan, provide a framework for interpreting the evidence from village and urban sites in the Indus Valley region and constructing a hypothetical picture of Indus Valley religion.

The single most significant religious feature in all of the western Asian village cultures is the importance of female powers or goddesses, as evidenced by stylized clay and terra-cotta female figurines in a variety of types that appear—often in conjunction with figurines of bulls or rams—from the early levels of village culture on into the urban periods in Turkmenistan, Elam, and the Indus Valley. Whether they represent specific goddesses or powers is impossible to determine without more information, and the villages are mute. Evidence of coherent mythologies only appears in the richer range of artifacts at the urban level, and by then, in all of the urban regions, clearly defined goddesses had become part of complex urban cultic systems that reflect at least in part differences in regional urbanization. Enough affinities remain, however, to provide clues to the Indus Valley system.

Turkmenistan, where extensive excavation has been carried out, provides a valuable point of reference for parallel developments in Afghanistan, Baluchistan, and the Indus Valley. Turkmenistan village sites show four millennia of clay and terra-cotta goddess figurines and figures of male animals, most often rams and bulls. The goddesses appear in a variety of styles and are often marked with painted stripes, dot-centered circles, or clusters of pocked depressions; most have concentrated attention on the breasts, thighs, and buttocks, and they often have either no arms or vestigial stumps. One distinctive type, the so-called foot profile style, shows the truncated legs and torso of a female in a semi-reclining posture.

Evidence from early sites indicates that special areas were set aside as shrine rooms for a likely domestic cult. Enclosed village shrines appear by the fifth or fourth millennium along with a new type of Namazga III "foot profile" figurines with elaborate hairdos. The Bronze Age Namazga IV culture, concurrent with developments in early Elam and the pre-Indus village cultures of Baluchistan and Afghanistan, has evidence of more elaborate shrines and a range of figurine types. Finally, around 2500 BCE, a full urban culture appeared in the Namazga V period that was contemporary for several centuries with the early phases of the Indus cities.

Urbanization in Turkmenistan brought not only greater complexity but also dramatic new religious forms. A massive brick platform, with three stepped tiers reaching forty feet in its final height, was built on the edge of the Namazga V site of Altin. This was certainly a center for public rituals, and implies a class of professional priests or priestesses. A richly endowed burial of a woman holding two female figurines in her hands has been tentatively named a "priestess's grave." Namazga V figurines are in a new and highly abstract style: flat fiddle-shaped cutouts with no legs, stylized triangular arm extentions, pinched masked-like faces usually without a mouth, conical breasts, and a stippled pubic triangle with a vaginal line. There is evidence of a more standardized iconography and a clearer identification of individual figurines, including the use of different hair styles and engraved markings that resemble signs found in the Elamite and Indus writing systems.

Goddess worship in Turkemenistan clearly survived the transition from Neolithic to Bronze Age culture and subsequent urbanization. The styles of representation changed, the identities and meanings of individual goddesses may have varied, and the form of cultic practice certainly differed dramatically at the urban level from that in early villages, but the goddesses and their powers remained the central focus of religious life throughout the millennia. Much the same pattern can be seen also in the Elamite culture of southwestern Iran.

The foundation of Elamite culture was laid by Proto-Elamite-speaking settlers who brought wheat and barley cultivation and the herding of sheep, goats, and cattle into the southern Zagros Mountain region of Iran sometime after 7000 BCE. By 4000 BCE, cultivation had been carried into the lowlands of Khuzistan at the western base of the Zagros, providing an agricultural base for urbanization. Sumer, across the Tigris in southern Mesopotamia, achieved urbanization around 3500 BCE. By 3200 BCE, Khuzistan and the Zagros highlands had been united in the rival urban civilization of Elam, with a highland capital at Anshan near later Persepolis and a lowland capital at Susa. Within the next two centuries, a Proto-Elamite script had been developed and Elam had extended its influence eastward along a trade network that passed through Tepe Yahya in southern Iran as far as the Nal village culture of southern Baluchistan.

The expansion of Elamite urban culture was limited to the early third millennium, and its eastern trading centers had been abandoned several centuries before the first Indus cities emerged. The similarity between the later Indus script and the Proto-Elamite script provides circumstantial evidence for the transfer of writing during this period, since the Proto-Elamite script had been replaced by cuneiform by the middle of the third millennium; there is, however, no evidence of direct Elamite influence on Indus urbanization. Yet if Elam cannot be assigned a significant causal role in the creation of Indus civilization, it nonetheless provides an important model for understanding Indus Valley religion because of the many evident parallels between the two traditions.

Pre-urban cultural levels at Persepolis and Susa reveal a familiar pattern of female figurines and goddess worship, and painted pottery at these sites reveals a related concern for serpents as objects of religious veneration—a combination found also in the Dravidian villages of South India, and further evidence for an earlier common culture. Terra-cotta female figurines from Susa and other sites in the early third millennium show that goddess worship survived the transition from agricultural villages to urbanization in Elam as in Turkmenistan. The religious data from urban proto-Elamite sites such as Susa, however, is much richer than that of Turkmenistan, and it reveals not only the importance of goddesses in urban religious life but also an elaborate system of myths, symbols, and cultic practices.

Cylinder seals in a distinctive proto-Elamite style provide the most valuable evidence for the symbolism of this period. Many of the motifs in the proto-Elamite seals can be traced back to painted designs on earlier village pottery, but the more elaborate seal designs reflect a new urban sophistication: complex mythic or ritual scenes; symbolic designs involving mountains, trees, and animals (bulls and rams most often, but also lions and other felines); and an androgynous bovine in a variety of humanlike poses characteristically found in the figurines of goddesses. This latter figure is most likely the animal form or surrogate of the main Elamite fertility goddess, a moon goddess who was born from the Primeval Bull and was both the protector and soul of cattle—roles certainly consistent with the symbolism of the seals. None of the other figures can be identified with any certainty, and the meaning of individual symbols and scenes remains obscure in the absence of explanatory myths. In general, however, the symbolism reflects a developed fertility religion with its roots in the village past—probably a mountain past—but with new dimensions and new meanings in the urban culture: a religion in which the village goddesses have become patron deities of the city as well.

Cylinder seals, supplemented by other data, allow at least a partial reconstruction of proto-Elamite cultic practices. One seal shows a goddess or priestess being drawn in procession in a chariot flanked by moon symbols and horned cattle; another shows a tree in procession in a similar chariot, also with horned cattle and moon symbols; another shows an image or shrine on a palanquin flanked by attendants carrying moon symbols and what are either snakes or snake symbols in their hands. The goddess being honored in all of these scenes is almost certainly the moon goddess, whose connection with trees, serpents, and horned animals is indicated on a seal from the late third millennium that shows priests wearing belts or girdles of snakes around their waists and a device on their heads that combines the symbolism of crescent-shaped horns and trees.

Ritual processions and pilgrimages to sacred sites were apparently important features of Elamite religion. Elamite reliefs from around 2000 BCE depict long lines of worshipers in procession, confirming the evidence from earlier proto-Elamite seals. Sumerian texts from the same period describe similar practices associated with the moon goddess Inanna, whose characteristics closely match those of the main Elamite goddess with whom she was later assimilated. A hymn to Inanna vividly describes a parade of priestesses, musicians with harps, drums, and tambourines, and a priest who sprinkles blood on the goddess's throne, and notes that men in the procession "adorn their left side with women's clothing" while women "adorn their right side with men's clothing" (Wolkstein and Kramer, 1983, p. 99).

The centers of Elamite worship were the shrines and temples erected for the goddess, usually in high places and with an associated sacred grove. In Susa, temples to the major deities were located on an elevated sacred area on the western edge of the city between the river and the royal establishment. The main ritual activity in the temples was animal sacrifice, and raised altars with drains attest to the emphasis on blood in these sacrificial rites. The major sacrificial festival to the goddess at Susa was descriptively called a "day of the flowing sacrifice" in tribute to the quantity of blood offered on this occasion. [*For further discussion of ancient western Asian religions, see* Iranian Religions *and* Prehistoric Religions, *article on* The Eurasian Steppes and Inner Asia.]

The Elamo-Dravidian Pattern. The significance of these features of Elamite religion for comparative purposes is the light they shed on those aspects of Indus Valley religion for which there is no available Indus evidence. Indus seals and votive figurines, for example, suggest that Indus religion was based on some form of animal sacrifice centered around goddesses, but there is no direct evidence of ritual practice. Indus stamp seals, however, depict goddesses, trees, tigers, and horned animals such as rams, bulls, and water buffaloes in various combinations in mythic or cultic scenes. In other symbolic settings snakes appear as sacred animals. One scene portrays a line of androgynously appareled worshipers parading before a buffalo-horned goddess in a tree. This is the same basic set of symbols—goddesses, trees, lions/tigers, horned animals, snakes, and androgynous figures—found on Elamite cylinder seals, and indicates a significant body of shared religious concepts that reflect the common proto-Elamo-Dravidian ancestry and presuppose a common ritual practice. The relevant ritual in Elamite religion was blood sacrifice to the goddess, as it was also, along with many of the same symbols, in later Dravidian village religion. It is thus highly likely that Indus Valley religion followed the same Elamo-Dravidian pattern.

This is not a case of wholesale borrowing of Elamite religion or of basing Indus urban culture on external models. There are well-documented influences from Turkmenistan for at least a millenium prior to urbanization in the Indus Valley, and there must have been some degree of contact with Elam during the late stages of Indus urbanization to account for the similar scripts. Indus urbanization may have been stimulated by these contacts, just as trade and interregional contacts stimulated urbanization throughout western Asia. The similarities between Indus urban culture and other western Asian cultures, however, were general family resemblances, like those between the Elamite and Dravidian language systems. Indus urban culture was both unique and uniquely Indian, as much a product of the regional setting as of the common western Asian heritage, with characteristic features that were deeply rooted in the pre-urban cultures of Afghanistan and Baluchistan.

The groundwork for Indus urbanization was laid by a series of village cultures in the highlands west of the Indus Valley, the earliest of which dates from around 6000 BCE. Archaeological research since the 1950s has revealed several early aceramic settlement sites with subsequent pottery development and domestication of local plants and animals, proving that the Indus region contributed to the Neolithic revolution and was not just a recipient of imported culture. By the early fourth millennium local village cultures had been established in northern and central Baluchistan, and by the mid- to late fourth millennium these cultures had been linked by trade with the Namazga III culture of southern Turkmenistan.

By around 3000 BCE, when Elam was extending its influence eastward, the Nal culture had emerged in southern Baluchistan and the Nal-related Amri culture had expanded into the southern Indus Valley. By early in the third millennium another related culture known as Kot Dijian had expanded northward along the Indus from the region of later Mohenjo-Daro as far as the later sites of Harappa and Kalibangan. These new developments laid the foundation for urbanization.

Goddess worship was an integral part of Indus village culture, as can be seen from the example of Mehrgarh, the oldest known continuous settlement site within India proper. Discovered in the 1970s at the eastern end of the Bolan Pass, Mehrgarh spans the range from aceramic settlement around 6000 BCE to the brink of urbanization around 2600 BCE. Goddesses in the form of female figurines appear at every cultural level, and their evolution is intertwined with the development of the Indus region.

The earliest figurines from Mehrgarh date from the sixth and fifth millennia, a period when pottery was being developed, cultivation was expanding, and local animals—especially humpbacked cattle (zebus)—were being domesticated to replace the earlier reliance on hunting. The style of these first Indian village goddess figurines was the "foot profile" style found also in Turkmenistan, and this style continued essentially unchanged down to around 3000 BCE. At that point, reflecting Mehrgarh's greater involvement in regional trade, there was a convergence toward the pinched-faced, goggle-eyed "Zhob mother goddesses" from the Zhob culture in northern Baluchistan. During the village's final century, from 2700 to 2600 BCE, nude goggle-eyed female figurines were being produced commercially by the thousands at Mehrgarh and are for the first time in a standing position like Zhob figurines. Nude male figures, also standing, with shoulder-length hair and Zhob-like goggle eyes, suggest for the first time the possibility of a divine couple.

The end of Mehrgarh's final century marks the beginning of urbanization. As in Turkmenistan, the new iconography of female figurines and the appearance of male figurines coincided with the building of monumental ritual platforms. At Mehrgarh, the platform was a massive structure of brick faced with plaster with a colonnade of square mud-brick columns in front. This was contemporary with others in the larger contiguous area, one of which, near Quetta, had drains in the center and a stone-built hollow containing a jawless human skull, perhaps evidence of a "building sacrifice" in the platform's construction. Near this platform were found figurines of females and cattle with painted stripes.

Other platform structures of note belonged to the Kulli culture, which gradually replaced the Nal culture in southern Baluchistan after about 3000 BCE and was still flourishing when the Indus civilization emerged on its eastern boundaries about five centuries later. Near the fertile stretches of the Porali River elaborate ceremonial centers were built on a new vast scale: at one typical site are two stone-built platforms about thirty feet high with ramps to the top and, nearby, a complex of over forty buildings. [*For further discussion of ritual platforms, see* Altar.] The Kulli ceremonial centers are set apart from the nearby agricultural villages with which they share common artifacts such as pottery and figurines. As the latter include both goddess figurines and striped cattle, it is likely that the cattle were votive offerings to the goddess. The whole combination, with platforms, wells, and drains, clearly suggests a ritual pattern involving sacrifice and ablution. The goddess figurines show a combination of originally Elamite postures with other styles (Zhob, Mehrgarh) developed regionally in western India. Although the Indus Valley civilization synthesizes elements from all these cultural styles, Kulli figurines and ceremonial centers provide its most direct prototypes.

Harappa and Mohenjo-Daro. The Indus civilization has been widely noted for its rapid development and continued stability over a seven-hundred-year period from around 2500 to 1750 BCE. Over an estimated 500,000 square miles, the same basic cultural features recur from the cities to the several hundred towns and villages so far discovered. Such uniformity is striking, since unlike the concentrated settlement patterns in Mesopotamia, Indus sites were often well over fifty miles apart. It was the long-established base of village agriculture—wheat and barley cultivation along with cattle herding—that by the mid-third millennium provided the base for urbanization. The new cities, however, also broke with traditional village cultural patterns, and imposed new developments upon them. The two largest, Harappa and Mohenjo-Daro, both seem to go back to the civilization's beginnings. Their founding was no doubt decisive in setting the new political, economic, and religious styles. To the north, Harappa was built over an earlier Kot Dijian farming village, while to the south, Mohenjo-Daro's new urban culture dominated and soon replaced the neighboring village of Kot Diji and the local culture of Amri farther south. Similarly, at the smaller Indus city of Kalibangan further east, the imposition of the new urban culture included construction of an Indus style ritual platform on the mound of an earlier fortified Kot Dijian agricultural settlement.

Mohenjo-Daro and Harappa were both built on a similar plan, one that smaller sites replicate. The cities were divided into two basic components: a lower city, about three miles in circumference with rectangular grid streets, and an upper area on each city's western edge formed by a brick-walled platform on an artificial mound that leveled some twenty feet above the surrounding plain. The massive exterior walls of the two major cities, over 40 feet thick at the base, served to protect against flooding: Mohenjo-Daro from the Indus River, Harappa from the Ravi. Mohenjo-Daro was the larger of the two, and in most matters preserves the best evidence, as most of the Harappa mound was destroyed either by erosion or by its dismantling in 1856 by British engineers to provide ballast for a railroad. It was not until the early 1920s that the antiquity of Indus sites was recognized.

The lower city's residential and commercial character is evident at Mohenjo-Daro. The exterior baked brick walls lining the main street were for the most part without adornment or direct street access. Residences range from barracklike dwellings to multistoried complexes, two of which have been dubbed a palace or hostel, but the typical residence was of a still common South Asian type: small rooms around a central courtyard. Interspersed among residences were various shops and ateliers, and a large area with threshing floors has been found at Harappa. The lower city shows no clear evidence of dominant religious structures. In continuation of village patterns, there probably was a domestic cult centered in the home, perhaps connected with the teracotta female figurines and the elaborate drainage system that suggests a concern for hygiene and purity. But for the culture's larger religious patterns one must turn elsewhere, and first of all to the raised platform mound on the western edge of the urban complex.

The standardization of the urban plan suggests that dominant political and religious sanctions lay behind the civilization's conservatism. It is noteworthy that the two major cities show none of the gradual growth that occurred in Mesopotamian cities, but were built from the very beginning with their dominant platform mounds. One may assume from this that the civilization's basic values were set and preserved by those who established these structures, and that their functions were connected with the architectural eminences they created.

These platform structures—often misleadingly called citadels—did not have a primarily defensive purpose. Though the heavily walled mounds at some of the more decentralized locations like Harappa and Kalibangan may have been used defensively, and the Mohenjo-Daro platform had watchtowers fortified with pellets, it is noteworthy that at a time when Mesopotamian rulers had for several centuries raised large armies to extend their power, the Indus cities leave no traces of arrows, spears, or swords.

Rather than citadels, the monumental platforms are thus no doubt continuations of the structures found at pre-urban village sites, but on a far grander scale, with a surface area large enough for several big buildings. With such structures, they differ from unoccupied platforms elsewhere (most notably Altin in Turkemistan). But they bear a resemblance to the "acropolis" at Elamite Susa, also on the west of the city, and the purpose is clearly similar: to give prominence to the institutions and activities set apart and above. It is even possible, with the Kulli culture as an intermediary, that Elam provided the model for the Indus platforms, as for its script. But in specific features the Indus platform reflects an independently emergent tradition with its own cultural dynamics.

Most of the structures on the Mohenjo-Daro mound have been variously identified. A large columned building was probably an assembly hall; another has been dubbed a college. Definite is a granary; with grain as the primary measure of wealth and medium of exchange, the control of grain distribution was tied to civic authority. Yet most distinctive was a structure called the Great Bath.

The Great Bath itself was both literally and no doubt also symbolically the center of this complex. A large rectangular bitumen-lined tank in a colonnaded courtyard, it had steps leading down into its water from both ends. Clearly the steps were for bathing, and possibly for crossing from one end to the other. Moreover, the trouble taken to build such an *elevated* bath probably reflects an intensified concern for purification already evident in the lower city. In later Indian notions, higher waters are purer. Quite likely the whole complex—with wells, bathing rooms, and bath—served for the performance of purification rites supervised or enacted by priests. And because it was situated adjacent to the granary, such concerns probably also tied in conceptually with an interest in agricultural fertility.

In all this we are faced with a combination of concerns similar to those that underlay the practices connected with the platform mounds of pre-Indus villages. There is a new assertion of political, economic, and religious authority in the building of such massive structures in the heart of the riverine plain. The platforms themselves, however, must have been more than *assertions* of power by a new urban elite; they must also have been intended as *sources* of power: not because they were dominant physically, but because they provided a stage for rituals that would bring the ascendant cultural forces into harmony with the divinely empowered order of nature so evident in the nearby rivers, herds, and fields of grain.

One representation of divinity in Indus sites has been met: the terra-cotta female figurine, a surviving type from pre-urban village cultures, with the closest analogues being from Kulli and Zhob. Similar figurines also reappear in classical periods of Hinduism and serve as models for the *yakṣīs* on early Buddhist stupas. [*See also* Nāgas and Yakṣas.] The basic Indus type has bare breasts, tapered or full-length legs, a girdle, heavy pendant necklaces, and an elaborate hairdo. Whether one or more goddesses is represented is uncertain, but parallel evidence from Elam suggests an iconographic differentiation. A few male figurines have also been found. While human figurines are predominantly female, animal figurines are invariably male. Most common are various bovines: zebu, short-horned bulls, and water buffalo. Most likely different kinds of potency were represented: that of the female in the form of the anthropomorphic goddess, that of the male in animal form, perhaps linked with symbols of civic power.

Indus Valley Seals. For further insights into the religious conceptions of the Indus Valley civilization, however, one must turn to a new iconography that has no precedent in the pre-urban village cultures. This comes from the controversial evidence of the Indus Valley seals. Here again, however, one must reckon with prior developments in Sumer and Elam, which produced cylinder seals earlier than the flat steatite (soapstone) stamp seals—measuring about ¾–1¼ inches per side—of Indus sites. Although Elamite seals are linked typologically to Sumer, their subjects are distinctively Elamite, and in certain cases present images with Indus counterparts, indicating the likelihood of iconic cross-fertilization. Thus, two cylinder seals from Susa seem to draw on familiar Indus motifs: one a series of bulls eating from a manger, and the other a composite bull-antelope with long wavy horns facing a stylized peepul tree.

It is not, however, only the older urban civilizations that shed light on the Indus seal iconography, but also the likely continuities from Indus urban culture to the Dravidian village culture of South India. For not only is there the likelihood of linguistic continuities, but there is also archaeological evidence of cultural continuities from the Indus civilization, through Gujarat, to the Dravidian culture of the Deccan Plateau. Moreover, the urban models that the Indus cities provided during the Indus period not only reshaped village life in Indus times, but transmitted patterns that long outlived the Indus cities.

The Indus Valley stamp seals, found by the hundreds, confirm impressions gained from the terra-cotta figurines, most notably the tendency to accentuate female power in human form and male power through animal forms. But the situation with the seals is also more complex, as there are also humanized males and human-animal and even human-animal-plant composites of apparently both genders. Of single animals, many are drawn from nature: short-horned bulls, zebu, buffaloes, rhinoceroses, tigers, elephants, antelopes, crocodiles. Composite human-animal forms reach such complexity as one with tiger hind quarters, ram forepart, bull horns, elephant trunk, and human face. Others show animal heads radiating from a central trunk.

The most frequently depicted seal animal is a "unicorn" bull or ox of generalized bovine traits with a single erect horn that faces an apparently sacred object, perhaps a brazier or incense burner. The unicorn's horn is sometimes shown as a thin curved shaft crossed by lines that taper toward the tip, suggesting an affinity between animal and plant forms. Some of the naturally drawn animals also sometimes face simpler brazier or manger type objects. It is thus likely that "real" animals were linked with ritual symbols as well, and mythologically marked no less than the more clearly "mythic" figures like the composites, multicephalics, and unicorns.

It is the seals with humanoid figures, however, that take one beyond the general sense of mythic and ritual markers to evidence for a cult with a complex of sacrificial symbols. Females appear in various such scenes, but the most important are a series of scenes that portray a recurring ensemble involving goddesses, trees, tigers, and water buffaloes. Three seals show these interrelationships most dramatically. In one, a slender goddess with a crescent-shaped headdress kneels on a branch of a neem (margosa) tree, her arm outstretched toward a tiger below that turns its neck around to face her. The goddess's position replicates a worshiping pose in other seals and suggests that she beckons the tiger with her outstretched arm. In the second seal, the goddess, now descended from the neem tree, stands behind the tiger about to seize it from the back. Yet both goddess and tiger are strikingly transformed. The goddess has assumed multiple traits of the water buffalo: along with filling out the stylized crescent horns, her legs and feet have become flanks and hoofs and her ears pointed and flapped. Meanwhile, the tiger has sprouted horns that replicate the serrated V branch and leaf pattern of the neem, which now stands behind the goddess.

These two seals seem to suggest that the goddess has her primary affinity with the buffalo, and an opposition to the tiger. But a third seal shows a fusion of the goddess and the tiger, joined together so that the goddess retains a standing human form as the forepart of a tiger's body that extends back from her hips and rear. Here, where the goddess's affinity is with the tiger, she has wavy ram's horns rather than buffalo-like horns. There is thus the suggestion that while the goddess has affinities with both the tiger and the buffalo, the two animals themselves remain in an oppositional and unfused tension.

This sense of a tiger-buffalo opposition is further reinforced in the so-called proto-Śiva seal from Mohenjo-Daro. But before discussing this seal, we should observe the primary seal evidence for a connection between the transformational themes that link the goddess to these and other animals and to a sacrificial cult. Clearest in this regard is the so-called ritual seal from Harappa depicting a goddess in the U-shaped twin branches of a stylized peepul tree, which rises from a circular platform base or altar. The goddess has crescent buffalo-like horns and a pony tail like the goddess who descends toward the tiger from the neem. But her horns have a third central peak, and she does not have the hind legs or hoofs of the buffalo. Standing at rest, her bangled arms loose at her sides, she observes a horned and pony-tailed figure much like herself kneeling at the base of the peepul in the same "suppliant" posture that the goddess in the neem adopts toward the tiger. The kneeling suppliant has led before the goddess in the peepul a composite animal with buffalo hind quarters, ram horns and forepart, and a large masklike human face. Seven figures in thigh-length tunics, single backward-curving horns, pigtails, and bangled arms stand or possibly file before this scene, which clearly depicts the essentials of a sacrifice. The horned goddess is the recipient of an offering, its composite nature no doubt representing something of the range of victims she receives: the ram, buffalo, and the human face. Whether all are real offerings, or the human face solely symbolic, we cannot say.

The kneeling figure making the offering in the "ritual seal" has an intermediate status between the horned goddess whose dress he affects and the composite human-animal he offers. The precise nature of his sacrificial role eludes us. But it is striking that the combination of elements that the seals configure remain coherent in the setting of still current South Indian village rituals. In that Dravidian context, the neem, a female tree, is itself a form of the goddess. It is linked to her fierce side, and more specifically to the forms she takes to "cool" and thus overcome violent forces like smallpox, fevers, and various demons. The peepul, on the other hand, is the male tree the goddess marries, so the two trees will be planted to actually intertwine. It is highly suggestive that while the seal goddess on the neem branch descends to overcome the fierce and *wild* tiger, the goddess in the peepul stands tranquilly in a position to receive as a sacrifice the composite of human and *domesticated* animals that would seem to reflect the range of her regular cult.

Since the discovery of the Indus civilization, the one seal most central to a succession of different interpretations of the religion has been the so-called proto-Śiva seal from Mohenjo-Daro. This designation, however, now appears to have been based on a combination of misattributions: most notably the "three heads" that actually outline the dewlap of a buffalo face, and the "trident" headdress that actually consists of buffalo horns enclosing a central fan-shaped and stylized tree or sheaf of grain reminiscent of the tree-and-horns headpiece worn by Elamite and Sumerian priests. Moreover, above this "mitre" is what looks like a stylized peepul tree. The main figure is thus a humanlike water buaffalo with a buffalo head and horns, axially centered on representations of a plant and/or tree. He sits with his knees out to the side and his feet drawn in below an erect phallus. The posture has usually been identified as yogic, though it is also reminiscent of the posture of the androgynous bovine seated in the pose of the goddess on an Elamite seal. Possibly the series of V-shaped stripes that end at his waist—sometimes regarded as necklaces—represent tiger stripes, making him a figure in whom the tiger-buffalo tension finds a resolution in a yogic or more likely regally dominant self-discipline.

The central buffalo figure in the "proto-Śiva" seal seems to be the male counterpart to the goddess, who herself combines both tiger and buffalo attributes in various transformational modes. But in this male figure, what remains tense and dynamic in the goddess seems to find poise, dominance, and resolution. This is especially suggestive in view of the four animals that surround him, for the tiger and buffalo appear among these along with the elephant and rhinoceros. By analogy with later Indian iconographies, the four together are likely to have had a directional symbolism: the elephant linked with the east, the rhino with the west, the tiger with the north, and the buffalo with the south. Most strikingly, while the elephant and rhinoceros apper indifferent to each other, both facing east, the tiger and buffalo, which most directly flank the buffalo-man's horns, face each other in a state that has the look of combative arousal. Furthermore, a stick figure appears over the back of the charging tiger: possibly a form of the goddess herself.

Of the four "wild" animals on the seal, two—the elephant and water buffalo—are susceptible to some degree of domestication even though they retain their "wild" traits. There is some evidence that elephants were captured and trained for heavy forest work during the Indus period, and it is likely that domestication of the water buffalo for agricultural use in the river valley was one of the major achievements of the Indus civilization, complementing the village cultures' earlier domestication of the zebu in the highlands. It is significant that the water buffalo played the main symbolic role in Indus urban culture instead of the zebu, despite the latter's longstanding economic importance. This suggests that the buffalo had a critical role in the riverine agriculture on which the Indus system was based, and that it symbolized the control of both nature and culture that made urban civilization possible.

The central water buffalo figure on the proto-Śiva seal seems to have the same general symbolic meaning of power-under-control as does the bull in Mesopotamian symbolism, and like the latter it probably also represents the king or ruling authority. Since the figure is male, we may assume that the Indus rulers also were male, as the few examples of protrait sculpture at Mohenjo-Daro suggest. There is little doubt, however, that the Indus people considered the goddess to be the real power and the ruler only her surrogate, empowered by her and thus responsible to her and for her. This is certainly consistent with the symbolism of the seal, where the central figure seems to bring into a regulated and authoritative image the various forces that the goddess oversees: agriculture, animal sacrifice, and the dangerous forces associated with the truly wild regions beyond the domain of civilization.

What kind of authority—priestly, political, economic—this figure represented still remains uncertain. The urban background of the ritual complex on the platform mound leaves all these possibilities open, and the distinctively Indian features of Indus symbolism make it risky to explain the Indus civilization on the basis of other urban cultures, even the closely related proto-Elamite culture. There is little doubt, however, that Indus Valley religion played a major role in establishing and maintaining that authority, and there is even less doubt that sacrifices to the goddess were the primary form of cultic practice. All of the external evidence—earlier village cultures, contemporary and related western Asian urban cultures, and later Dravidian culture—points to this conclusion, and the Indus evidence seems to confirm it.

Concluding Observations. Taking the evidence as a whole, we can construct a model of Indus Valley religion that explains its major known features and its place in the Indus civilization. The central element was certainly worship of the goddess at both the domestic and public levels, with corresponding levels of cultic practice. At the domestic level, votive sacrifices involving figurines were the likely form of worship, with a related emphasis on bathing and ritual purity. At the public level, represented by the raised platform mounds, worship must have involved more powerful blood sacrifices.

Mohenjo-Daro seems to have been the major cultic center for the system as a whole and the site for the most important sacrifices. Indus symbolism and later Dravidian practice point toward water buffalo sacrifices as the most important cultic rituals. The buffalo is the husband of the goddess in Dravidian cult sacrifices, and on Indus seals he appears as both the goddess's surrogate and the symbol of centralized rule; it is likely that

Indus cultic practice involved these elements, at least on major ceremonial occasions, but there is no direct evidence for how this might have been conceptualized.

The interpretation of Indus Valley religion cannot proceed beyond such speculation at the present time. Much has been learned about the Indus civilization since its discovery in the 1920s, and the pattern of Indus Valley religion is beginning to emerge from the growing body of data, but there are still many gaps to fill. The major task, moreover, has hardly begun: to trace the contributions of the Indus system to later Indian religious developments and to understand the place of the Indus system in the larger pattern of religious history.

[*For specific discussion of Indus Valley religion within the greater context of later Indian religions, see* Hinduism. *For further discussion of ancient Dravidian religion, see* Tamil Religions. *Themes common both to Indus Valley and later Indian religions are discussed in* Goddess Worship, *especially the overview article and the article on* The Hindu Goddess, *and* Indian Religions, *especially the articles on* Mythic Themes *and* Rural Traditions. *Sacrifice in ancient India is further discussed in* Vedism and Brahmanism.]

BIBLIOGRAPHY

The most useful single source on village cultures and urbanization in Turkmenistan and western India is S. P. Gupta's *Archaeology of Soviet Central Asia and the Indian Borderlands*, vol. 2 (Delhi, 1979), which presents a judicious overview of the archaeological evidence and current interpretive theories. An assessment of the archaeological data from Turkmenistan sites is provided by the Soviet prehistorians V. M. Masson and V. I. Sarianidi in *Central Asia: Turkmenia before the Achaemenids* (London, 1972), edited and translated by Ruth Tringham and published initially in English as volume 79 of the *"Ancient Peoples and Places"* series. The best and most comprehensive survey of cultural development in India from earliest times through the establishment of Indus urban culture is Walter A. Fairservis, Jr's. *The Roots of Ancient India*, 2d rev. ed. (Chicago, 1975), which examines the relevant evidence from all of the regional village cultures, discusses the factors that led to urbanization, and describes the basic features of the Indus civilization. The most accessible summary of the evidence from Mehrgarh is Jean-François Jarrige and Richard H. Meadow's "The Antecedents of Civilization in the Indus Valley," *Scientific American* 243 (August 1980): 122–133.

A variety of data on proto-Elamite religion is available in *A Survey of Persian Art*, edited by Arthur U. Pope and Phyllis Ackerman (1938–1939; reprint, London, 1964–1965), especially in the sections by Phyllis Ackerman on cult figurines and early seals (vol. 1, chaps. 11 and 14, and accompanying plates in vol. 7). A summary of Elamite history, culture, and religion is provided in Walther Hinz's *The Lost World of Elam: Recreation of a Vanished Civilization* (New York, 1973). Diane Wolkstein and Samuel Noah Kramer's *Inanna: Queen of Heaven and Earth* (New York, 1983) supplements what is known of Elamite goddesses with a comprehensive portrait of the closely related Sumerian goddess Inanna. The argument for a common origin of the proto-Elamite and proto-Dravidian languages is presented in David W. McAlpin's *Proto-Elamo-Dravidian: The Evidence and Its Implications* (Philadelphia, 1981). The significance of the Elamite trading center at Tepe Yahya for understanding interregional contacts in West Asia is discussed in Carl C. Lamberg-Karlovsky and Martha Lamberg-Karlovsky's "An Early City in Iran," *Scientific American* 224 (June 1971), and in Carl C. Lamberg-Karlovsky's "Trade Mechanisms in Indus-Mesopotamian Interrelationships," *Journal of the American Oriental Society* 92 (1972).

Data from the early excavations at Mohenjo-Daro are contained in John Marshall's *Mohenjo-daro and the Indus Civilization*, 3 vols. (London, 1931), and E. J. Mackay's *Further Excavations at Mohenjo-daro*, 2 vols. (New Delhi, 1938). A valuable synthesis and interpretation of Indus evidence is presented in Mortimer Wheeler's *The Indus Civilization*, 3d ed. (Cambridge, 1968), and in his *Civilizations of the Indus Valley and Beyond* (London, 1966). A survey of Indus data up to the mid-1970s is provided in Walter A. Fairservis, Jr's. *The Roots of Ancient India* (Chicago, 1975), supplemented by his *Allahdino I: Seals and Inscribed Material* (New York, 1976). Many of the most important contributions to the ongoing study of the Indus civilization are found in two volumes edited by Gregory L. Possehl: *Ancient Cities of the Indus* (New Delhi, 1979) and *Harappan Civilization: A Contemporary Perspective* (New Delhi, 1982). Possehl's own initial work on Indus culture in Gujarat is presented in his *Indus Civilization in Saurashtra* (Delhi, 1980).

Understanding Indus Valley religion has been a concern of investigators since Marshall and Mackay offered their first tentative interpretations, and the issue receives significant attention in the cited works by Wheeler and Fairservis. Indus seals in particular have been studied for clues to Indus religious concepts, with the so-called proto-Śiva seal receiving the greatest interest. A major new interpretation of the symbolism on this seal is found in Alf Hiltebeitel's "The Indus Valley 'Proto-Śiva,' Reexamined through Reflections on the Goddess, the Buffalo, and the Symbolism of *vāhanas*," *Anthropos* 73 (1978): 767–797. Earlier interpretations of this seal and of other supposedly related Indus data are challenged in Doris Srinivasan's "Unhinging Śiva from the Indus Civilization," *Journal of the Royal Asiatic Society* (1984 pt. 1): 77–99. New insights into the meaning of Indus seals, especially those dealing with goddess-and-tiger motifs, are presented in Pupul Jayakar's *The Earthen Drum: An Introduction to the Ritual Arts of Rural India* (New Delhi, 1980), a beautifully illustrated book that interprets Indus religious data by drawing comparisons with the art and religious practices of later Indian folk traditions.

THOMAS J. HOPKINS and ALF HILTEBEITEL

INGEN (1592–1673), more fully Ingen Ryūki (Chin., Yin-yüan Lung-ch'i); Buddhist master from China who established the Ōbaku school of Zen in Japan. Ingen was born in Fukien Province in southeast China and was ordained there at the Zen monastic complex on Mount Huang-po in 1619. Huang-po had been an important Zen center in earlier periods, but by Ingen's time it had fallen into decline. In 1639 Ingen resolved to revive the fortunes of the monastery, and by 1651 he had rebuilt it into a vibrant religious community with over a thousand monks in residence during its summer meditation retreats. From that time Ingen emerged as one of the foremost Buddhist figures in southern China. His renown spread even to immigrant Chinese living in Japan, who had fled China during the political upheaval at the end of the Ming dynasty (1368–1644). These overseas Chinese invited Ingen, as well as other Buddhist masters, to serve in their temples, and at the age of sixty-two Ingen answered their call. In 1654 he sailed to Nagasaki accompanied by some twenty disciples.

In Japan Ingen quickly rose to prominence. During his first year he remained with the Chinese community in Nagasaki, but after that he moved to temples near Osaka and Kyoto. In 1658 Ingen was granted an audience with the shogun Tokugawa Ietsuna (1641–1680), and three years later received permission to build his own temple at Uji, south of Kyoto, on land that the shogun donated. Ingen named it the Manpukuji after his home temple on Mount Huang-po. The Manpukuji was patterned after the Zen monasteries of Ming dynasty China both in architecture and in religious practice. The form of Zen that Ingen taught there differed markedly from the Rinzai (Chin., Lin-chi) and Sōtō (Chin., Ts'ao-tung) traditions of Japan. His teachings contained elements of Pure Land Buddhism, such as meditating on the Pure Land Buddha Amida (Skt., Amitābha) and chanting Amida's name as a means of awakening the mind to enlightenment. This practice, known as the *nembutsu kōan,* reflects the separate course of development that Zen took in China and Japan. Because of these differences, Ingen and his following could not be absorbed into Japan's existing traditions, even though he represented the mainstream of Rinzai in China. The Manpukuji therefore emerged as the head temple of its own school of Zen, called Ōbaku, the Japanese pronunciation of Huang-po. Ingen's brand of Zen was faithfully preserved at the Manpukuji, and for most of the next century Chinese Zen masters were brought from the mainland to serve as its abbots.

Despite the discord that existed between Ingen's teachings and Japanese Zen, his presence in Japan worked as a catalyst for religious reform. Buddhism had fallen into a state of turmoil during the seventeenth century, partly because of internal laxity and partly because of strictures placed on it by the government. In this context the Zen community at the Manpukuji served as a model for renewal and reform. Ingen's adoption of strict monastic rules—specifically, an amalgamation of rules drawn from earlier Zen collections and compiled under the title *Ōbaku shingi*—and his insistence on qualified "dharma heirs" *(hassu)*—that is, disciples properly trained to carry on their master's teachings—inspired Sōtō and Rinzai leaders to confront abuses in their own traditions within these areas. Ingen also established a new ordination platform at the Manpukuji and instituted a three-stage ordination procedure that included novice precepts *(shamikai),* full clerical precepts *(bikukai),* and *bodhisattva* precepts *(bosatsukai).* This helped revive interest in the clerical precepts among Japanese Buddhists, and it contributed to a growing movement aimed at rectifying the conduct of the clergy. In Ingen's wake the Manpukuji produced several priests of national stature such as Tetsugen (1630–1682), who organized and supervised the first printing of the Buddhist canon in Japan. All of these events bespeak the far-reaching influence that Ingen exerted on Japanese Buddhism. In recognition of his contributions, Retired Emperor Gomizuno-o (1596–1680) bestowed on him the honorary clerical name Daikō Fushō Kokushi in 1673. The day after receiving this title Ingen died at his hermitage in the Manpukuji. He was eighty-one years old (eighty-two by traditional Chinese reckoning).

[*For further discussion of the Ōbaku sect, see* Zen.]

BIBLIOGRAPHY

There are no accounts in Western languages of Ingen's life and thought except for brief passages in general works such as Heinrich Dumoulin's *A History of Zen Buddhism,* translated by Paul Peachey (New York, 1963). In Japanese there are numerous books and articles concerning Ingen. The most popular biography is Hirakubo Akira's *Ingen,* "Jinbutsu sōsho," no. 96 (Tokyo, 1962). Another important study describing the impact of Ingen's teachings on Japanese Buddhism is Furuta Shōkin's *Nihon Bukkyō shisōshi no shomondai* (Tokyo, 1964). In the Taishō edition of the Buddhist canon, *Taishō shinshū daizōkyō,* vol. 82, three works of Ingen's are included: *Fushō Kokushi goroku* (T.D. no. 2605), *Fushō Kokushi hōgo* (T.D. no. 2606), and *Ōbaku shingi* (T.D. no. 2607).

JAMES C. DOBBINS

INITIATION. [*This entry surveys the phenomenon of initiation in three articles:*

An Overview
Men's Initiation
Women's Initiation

For further discussion from other perspectives, see Rites of Passage *and* Secret Societies.]

An Overview

The term *initiation* in the most general sense denotes a body of rites and oral teachings whose purpose is to produce a radical modification of the religious and social status of the person to be initiated. In philosophical terms, initiation is equivalent to an ontological mutation of the existential condition. The novice emerges from his ordeal a totally different being: he has become "another." Generally speaking, there are three categories, or types, of initiation.

The first category comprises the collective rituals whose function is to effect the transition from childhood or adolescence to adulthood, and which are obligatory for all members of a particular society. Ethnological literature terms these rituals "puberty rites," "tribal initiation," or "initiation into an age group."

The other two categories of initiation differ from puberty initiations in that they are not obligatory for all members of the community; indeed, most of them are performed individually or for comparatively small groups. The second category includes all types of rites of entering a secret society, a *Bund,* or a confraternity. These closed societies are limited to one sex and are extremely jealous of their secrets. Most of them are male, constituting secret fraternities *(Männerbünde),* but there are also some female societies. However, in the ancient Mediterranean and Near Eastern world, such sites, or "mysteries," were open to both sexes. Although they differ somewhat in type, we can still classify the Greco-Oriental mysteries as secret confraternities.

Finally, there is a third category of initiation, the type that occurs in connection with a mystical vocation. On the level of archaic religions, the vocation would be that of the medicine man or shaman. A specific characteristic of this third category is the importance of personal experience. Initiation in secret societies and those of the shamanic type have a good deal in common. What distinguishes them in principle is the ecstatic element, which is of greatest importance in shamanic initiation. Despite their specialized uses, there is a sort of common denominator among all these categories of initiation, with the result that, from a certain point of view, all initations are much alike.

Puberty Rites. The tribal initiation introduces the novice into the world of spiritual and cultural values and makes him a responsible member of society. The young man learns not only the behavior patterns, techniques, and institutions of adults but also the myths and the sacred traditions of the tribe, the names of the gods, and the history of their works; above all, he learns the mystical relations between the tribe and supernatural beings as those relations were established at the beginning of time. In a great many cases, puberty rites, in one way or another, imply the revelation of sexuality. In short, through initiation, the candidate passes beyond the "natural" mode of being—that of the child—and gains access to the cultural mode; that is, he is introduced to spiritual values. Often, on the occasion of the puberty rites the entire community is religiously regenerated, for the rites are the repetitions of operations and actions performed by supernatural beings in mythical time.

Any age-grading initiation requires a certain number of more or less dramatic tests and trials: separation from the mother, isolation in the bush under the supervision of an instructor, interdiction against eating certain vegetable or animal foods, knocking out of an incisor, circumcision (followed in some cases by subincision), scarification, and so forth. The sudden revelation of sacred objects (bull-roarers, images of supernatural beings, etc.) also constitutes an initiatory test. In many cases, the puberty initiation implies a ritual "death," followed by a "resurrection" or a "rebirth." Among certain Australian tribes the extraction of the incisor is interpreted as the neophyte's "death," and the same significance is even more evident in the case of circumcision. The novices isolated in the bush are likened to ghosts: they cannot use their fingers and must take food directly with their mouths, as the dead are supposed to do. Sometimes they are painted white, a sign that they have become ghosts. The huts in which they are isolated represent the body of a monster or a water animal: the neophytes are considered to have been swallowed by the monster, and they remain in its belly until they are "reborn" or "resuscitated." The initiatory death is interpreted either as a *descensus ad inferos* or as a *regressus ad uterum,* and the "resurrection" is sometimes understood as a "rebirth." In a number of cases, the novices are symbolically buried, or they pretend to have forgotten their past lives, their family relations, their names, and their language, and must learn everything again. Sometimes the intiatory trials reach a high degree of cruelty.

Secret Cults. Even on the archaic levels of culture (for example, in Aboriginal Australia), a puberty initiation may entail a series of stages. In such cases sacred history can be revealed only gradually. The deepening of the religious experience and knowledge demands a special vocation or an outstanding intelligence and willpower. This fact explains the emergence both of the secret cults and of the confraternities of shamans and medicine men. The rites of entrance into a secret society correspond in every respect to those of tribal initiations: seclusion, initiatory tests and tortures, "death" and "resurrection," bestowal or imposition of a new name, revelation of a secret doctrine, learning of a new language. A few innovations are, however, characteristic of the secret societies: among these are the great importance attached to secrecy, the particular cruelty of initiatory trials, the predominance of the ancestors' cult (the ancestors being personified by masks), and the absence of a supreme being in the ceremonial life of the group. In the *Weiberbünde,* or women's societies, the initiation consists of a series of specific tests, followed by revelations concerning fertility, conception, and birth.

Initiatory "death" signifies both the end of the "natural," acultural man and the passage to a new mode of existence, that of a being "born to the spirit," that is, one who does not live exclusively in an immediate reality. Thus the initiatory "death" and "resurrection" represent a religious process through which the initiate becomes "another," patterned on the model revealed by gods or mythical ancestors. In other words, one becomes a real man to the extent that one resembles a superhuman being. The importance of initiation for the understanding of the archaic mind centers essentially in the fact that it shows that the real man—the spiritual one—is not automatic, is not the result of a natural process. He is "made" by the old masters, in accordance with the models revealed by divine beings in mythical times. These old masters form the spiritual elite of archaic societies. Their main role is to transmit to the new generations the deep meaning of existence and to help them assume the responsibility of real men, and hence to participate actively in the cultural life of the community. But because culture means, for archaic and traditional societies, the sum of the values received from supernatural beings, the function of initiation may thus be summarized: it reveals to every new generation a world open to the transhuman; a world, one may say, that is transcendental.

Shamans and Medicine Men. As for shamanic initiations, they consist in ecstatic experiences (e.g., dreams, visions, trances) and in an instruction imparted by the spirits or the old master shamans (e.g., shamanic techniques, names and functions of the spirits, mythology and genealogy of the clan, secret language). Sometimes initiation is public and includes a rich and varied ritual; this is the case, for example, among the Buriats of Siberia. But the lack of a ritual of this sort in no way implies the absence of an initiation; it is perfectly possible for the initiation to be performed in the candidate's dreams or ecstatic experiences. In Siberia and Central Asia the youth who is called to be a shaman goes through a psychopathic crisis during which he is considered to be tortured by demons and ghosts who play the role of the masters of intiation. These "initiatory sicknesses" generally contain the following symbolic elements: (1) torture and dismemberment of the body, (2) scraping of the flesh and reduction to a skeleton, (3) replacement of organs and renewal of blood, (4) a sojourn in the underworld and instruction by demons and the souls of dead shamans, (5) an ascent to heaven, and (6) "resurrection," that is, access to a new mode of being, that of a consecrated individual capable of communicating personally and directly with gods, demons, and souls of the dead. A somewhat analagous pattern is to be found in the initiations of Australian medicine men. [*See* Shamanism.]

The little we know about Eleusis and the initiations in the Hellenistic mysteries there indicates that the central experience of the initiand *(mustēs)* depended on a revelation concerning the death and resurrection of the divine founder of the cult. Thanks to this revelation, the *mustēs* acceded to another, superior mode of being, and concurrently secured for himself a better fate after death. [*See* Mystery Religions.]

The Meaning of Initiatory Ordeals. In many puberty intiations, the novices must not go to bed until late in the night (see some examples in Eliade, 1958, pp. 14–15). This initiatory ordeal is documented not only among nonliterate cultures (e.g., Australia, coastal California, Tierra del Fuego) but even in highly developed religions. Thus, the Mesopotamian hero Gilgamesh crosses the waters of death to find out from Utanapishtim how he can gain immortality. "Try not to sleep for six days and seven nights!" is the answer. But Gilgamesh at once falls asleep, and Utnapishtim wakes him on the seventh day. Indeed, not to sleep is not only a victory over physical fatigue but is above all a demonstration of will and spiritual strength; to remain awake is equivalent to being conscious, present in the world, responsible. [*See* Ordeal.]

Another puberty initiation ordeal is the interdiction against eating for a few days, or against drinking water except by "sucking it through a reed" (Australia, Tierra del Fuego). Among some Australian tribes, the dietary prohibitions are successively removed as myths, dances, and pantomimes teach the novices the religious origin of each kind of food. But most puberty ordeals are cruel and terrifying. In Africa, as in Australia, circumcision is equivalent to death; the operators, dressed in lion and leopard skins, attack the novices' genital organs, indicating that the intention is to kill them. In the Kongo or the Loango coast, boys between ten and twelve years old drink a potion that makes the unconscious. They are then carried into the jungle and circumcised. Among the Pangwe, the novices are taken to a house full of ants' nests and are badly bitten; meanwhile, their guardians cry, "You will be killed; now you must die!"

(See examples in Eliade, 1958, pp. 23ff., 30ff.) Excesses of this kind sometimes result in the death of the boy. In such cases the mother is not informed until after the period of segregation in the bush; she is then told that her son was killed by the spirit, or that, swallowed by a monster with the other novices, he did not succeed in escaping from its belly.

The assimilation of initiatory tortures to the sufferings of the novices in being swallowed and digested by the monster is confirmed by the symbolism of the cabin in which the boys are isolated. Often the cabin represents the body or the open maw of a water monster, a crocodile, for example, or of a snake. In some regions of Ceram the opening through which the novices pass is called the snake's mouth. Being shut up in the cabin is equivalent to being imprisoned in the monster's body. On Rooke Island (Umboi), when the novices are isolated in a cabin in the jungle, a number of masked men tell the women that their sons are being devoured by a terrifying, demonic being. In New Guinea, the house built for the circumcision of the boys has the form of the monster Barlun, who is believed to swallow the novices; that is, the building has a "belly" and a "tail." The novice's entrance into the cabin is equivalent to entering the monster's belly. Among the Nor-Papua the novices are swallowed and later disgorged by a spirit whose voice sounds like a flute. The initiatory cabin represents not only the belly of the devouring monster but also the womb. The novice's "death" signifies a return to the embryonic state.

It is in the interval between initiatory "death" and "resurrection" that the Australian novice is gradually introduced to the sacred history of the tribe and is permitted to witness, at least in part, its pantomimes and ceremonial dances. Learning the myths of origins, that is, learning how things came into existence, the novice discovers that he is the creation of supernatural beings, the result of a specific primordial event, the consequence of a series of mythological occurrences, in short, of a sacred history. Such revelations, received through the ordeals of a ritual "death," characterize most of the age-grading initiations. The "resurrection," or "rebirth," proclaims the coming into being of a new person: an adult aware of his religious condition and of his responsibilities in the world.

From Tribal Intiation to Secret Cult. Female puberty initiations are less widespread than boys' initiations, although they are documented in the ancient stages of culture (Australia, Tierra del Fuego, and elsewhere). The rites are less developed than those for boys' initiations. Furthermore, girls' initiations are individual; that is, they begin with the first menstruation. This physical symptom, the sign of sexual maturity, compels a break—the young girl's separation from the community. The length of the girl's segregation varies from culture to culture: from three days (in Australia and India) to twenty months (New Zealand), or even several years (Cambodia). Consequently, in many parts of the world, the girls do in the end form a group, and then their initiations are performed collectively, under the direction of their older female relatives (as in India) or of other old women (Africa). These tutors instruct them in the secrets of sexuality and fertility and teach them the customs of the tribe and at least some of its religious traditions—those accessible to women. The instruction is general, but its essense is religious: it consists in a revelation of the sacrality of women. The girl is ritually prepared to assume her specific mode of being, that is, to become a "creator of life," and at the same time is taught her responsibilities in society and in the world—responsibilities that are always religious in nature.

Among some peoples, there are several degrees of female initiation. Thus, among the Yao of Thailand initiation begins with the first menstruation, is repeated and elaborated during the first pregnancy, and is only concluded with the birth of the first child. There are also a number of women's cult associations, most probably created under the influence of the male secret societies. Some African female secret associations include masculine elements (for instance, the directress, symbolizing a leopard, attacks and "kills" the novices; finally they "kill" the leopard, and free the novices from its belly). Among the Mordvins of Russia there existed a secret women's society whose emblem was a hobbyhorse and whose members were called "horses." But such masculine influences have been exercised chiefly on the external organization of female societies. (On female intiations, see Eliade, 1958, pp. 44ff., 78ff., and especially Lincoln, 1981.)

The morphology of men's secret societies is extremely complex, and their origin and history are still obscure. But there is a continuity between puberty rites and rites of initiation into men's secret societies. Throughout Oceania, for example, both initiations of boys and those requisite for membership in the men's secret societies involve the same ritual of symbolic death through being swallowed by a sea monster, followed by resurrection—which indicates that all the ceremonies derive historically from a single center. In West Africa, we find a similar phenomenon: the secret societies derive from the puberty initiations. (For other examples, see Eliade, 1958, pp. 73ff., 153.)

The socioreligious phenomenon of secret male cults and masked confraternities is especially widespread in Melanesia and Africa. As in the tribal initiations, the rites for entrance into men's secret cult societies present the well-known pattern: seclusion, initiatory ordeals and tortures, revelation of a secret doctrine, bestowal of a new name, instruction in a special language.

In the two American continents, the climbing of a tree or a sacred pole plays an important role not only in puberty initiations (as, for example, in the north of the Gran Chaco, and among the Mandan, the Kwakiutl, and the Pomo) but also in public festivals (the Festival of the Sun held by the Ge; various festivals among the Tupi, the Plains Indians, the Salish, the Delaware, the Maidu), or in the ceremonies and healing séances of shamans (Yaruro, Araucanian, Maidu). The climbing of the tree or of the sacred pole has the same goal: to meet with the gods or heavenly powers in order to obtain a blessing, whether a personal consecration, a favor for the community, or the cure of a sick person.

Martial and Heroic Initiations. In ancient Greece, some heroic scenarios can be identified in the saga of Theseus; for example, his ritual descent into the sea (an ordeal equivalent to a journey into the beyond) or his entering the labyrinth and fighting the monster. Other initiatory ordeals survived in the famous Spartan discipline of Lykurgos, under which an adolescent was sent away to the mountains, naked, to live for a full year on what he could steal, being careful to let no one see him. In other words, Lacedaemonian youths led the life of a wolf for a whole year.

Among the ancient Germans, a young man had to confront certain ordeals typical of the initiations of warriors. Tacitus tells us that among the Chatti the candidate cut neither his hair nor his beard until he had killed an enemy. A Taifali youth had to bring down a boar or a wolf; among the Heruli, he had to fight unarmed. Through these ordeals, the young man took to himself a wild animal's mode of being; he became a dreaded warrior in the measure in which he behaved like a beast of prey. Such warriors were known as berserkers, literally, "in shirts *(serkr)* of bear," or as *úlfheðnar*, "men with the skin of a wolf." They thought that they could metamorphose themselves into wolves by the ritual donning of a wolfskin. By putting on the skin, the initiand assimilated the behavior of a wolf; in other words, he became a wild-beast warrior, irresistible and invulnerable. "Wolf" was the appellation of the members of the Indo-European military societies. [*See* Berserkers.]

The martial initiatory ordeal *par excellence* was the single combat, conducted in such a way that it finally roused the candidate to the "fury of the berserkers." The ancient Germans called this sacred force *wut*, a term that Adam of Bremen translated as *furor;* it was a sort of demonic frenzy, which filled the adversary with terror and finally paralyzed him. The Irish *ferg* (lit., "anger") is an almost exact equivalent of this same terrifying sacred experience, specific to heroic combat. [*See* Frenzy.]

The initiation of the youthful hero Cú Chulainn admirably illustrates such tumultuous and burning "fury." While still a little boy, Cú Chulainn asked his uncle, the king of Ulster, for arms and a chariot, and set off for the castle of his uncle's three famous adversaries. Although those heroes were supposed to be invincible, the little boy conquered them and cut off their heads. But the exploit heated him to such a degree that a witch warned the king that if precautions were not taken, the boy would kill all the warriors in Ulster. The king sent a troop of naked women to meet Cú Chulainn, and the lad hid his face, that he might not see their nakedness. Thus they were able to lift him from the chariot and place him in successive vats of cold water to extinguish his wrath *(ferg)*. The first vat burst its staves and its hoops; the next boiled with big bubbles; "the third vat into which he went, some men might endure it and others not. Then the boy's *ferg* went down, and his garments were put on him" *(Táin Bó Cuailnge,* trans. Joseph Dunn, London, 1914, pp. 60–78).

Initiation in the Christian and Western World. Initiatory scenarios can be recognized in many medieval and postmedieval religious, mystical, and esoteric groups, some, but not all of them, considered heretical by the ecclesiastical authorities. The matter is too complex, and as yet insufficiently researched, to permit a brief summary. Still, throughout almost all of rural Europe, and down to the end of the nineteenth century, the ceremonies marking the passage from one age class to the next still reproduced certain themes characteristic of traditional puberty initiations. Furthermore, the symbols and rituals of a secret society can be recognized in the military organizations of youth: the ordeals of their entrance, their peculiar dances (for example, the Scottish sword dance), and even their costumes. Also, the ceremonial of the artisans' guilds has an initiatory pattern, especially among the blacksmiths and masons. Finally, the closed milieus of the alchemists contained many recognizable elements; indeed, the *opus alchymicum* implies the well-known pattern of initiation: tortures, "death," and "resurrection" (Eliade, 1978, pp. 142ff.).

It is significant that in medieval and postmedieval times, some initiatory patterns were conserved in the oral as well as written literatures, for instance, in folk tales, in the Arthurian cycle, in the neo-Greek epic *Digenis Akritas*, in the ecstatic poems of *Fedeli d'amore*, and even in certain children's games (see some examples in Eliade, 1958, pp. 124ff.; Eliade, 1969, pp. 120ff.). No less significant is the survival of initiatory scenarios in many pre-Romantic and Romantic novels, from Goethe's *Wilhelm Meister* to Balzac's *Séraphita*. With regard to the initiatory rituals practiced by the various secret associations of the same period, only that of Freemasonry seems to prolong an authentic tradition. Most other secret groups are recent creations, and their initiation rites were either constructed by their founders or inspired by certain esoteric literature. The same phenomenon of improvising secret associations with more or less complicated initiatory ordeals continued into the twentieth century (see Eliade, 1976, pp. 58ff.).

But such pseudo-initiatory improvisations have a religious significance. In recent times, literary critics have recognized initiation themes in much modern European and American literature; Nerval *(Aurélia)*, Jules Verne *(Voyage au centre de la terre, L'île mystérieuse)*, T. S. Eliot *(The Waste Land)*, and many other contemporary writers, such as Sherwood Anderson, F. Scott Fitzgerald, Thomas Wolfe, and William Faulkner, have made use of this notation (see Eliade, 1969, pp. 123ff.). Other authors have deciphered initiatory scenarios in contemporary plastic arts and especially in cinema. Thus, in the modern Western world, initiatory symbols have survived on the unconscious level (i.e., in dreams and imaginary universes). It is significant that these survivals are studied today with an interest difficult to imagine sixty or seventy years ago. In the desacralized Western world, the sacred is present and active chiefly in the realms of the imaginary. But imaginary experiences are part of the total human being, no less important than his diurnal experiences. This means that the nostalgia for initiatory scenarios, a nostalgia deciphered in so many literary and artistic creations, reveals modern man's longing for a total and definitive renewal, for a *renovatio* capable of radically changing his existence.

BIBLIOGRAPHY

The important critical literature published through the late 1950s is noted in my *Birth and Rebirth: The Religious Meanings of Initiation in Human Culture* (London, 1958), pp. 137ff., reprinted under the title *Rites and Symbols of Initiation* (New York, 1965). See also the more recent critical bibliographies cited in "Initiation and the Modern World" in my *The Quest: History and Meaning in Religion* (Chicago, 1969), pp. 112–126.

Angelo Brelich's *Paides e parthenoi* (Rome, 1969) is invaluable for its rich documentation and insightful analyses. Frank W. Young presents a sociological interpretation in his *Initiation Ceremonies: A Cross-Cultural Study of Status Dramatization* (Indianapolis, 1965). The best monograph on female initiation is Bruce Lincoln's *Emerging from the Chrysalis: Studies in Rituals of Women's Initiation* (Cambridge, Mass., 1981).

On secret cults, see M. R. Allen's *Male Cults and Secret Initiations in Melanesia* (London, 1967), an exemplary analysis of initiation ceremonies in New Guinea; *Secret Societies*, edited by Norman MacKenzie (New York, 1967); *Classes et associations d'âge en Afrique de l'Ouest*, edited by Denise Paulme (Paris, 1971); and Robert S. Ellwood, Jr.'s *Religious and Spiritual Groups in Modern America* (Englewood Cliffs, N.J., 1973). On the initiation pattern among alchemists, see my *The Forge and the Crucible*, 2d ed. (Chicago, 1978). For a discussion of initiatiory ordeals among secret societies improvised in this century, see my *Occultism, Witchcraft, and Cultural Fashions: Essays in Comparative Religions* (Chicago, 1976).

MIRCEA ELIADE

Men's Initiation

The word *initiation* implies a new beginning, as the Latin *initium* suggests. By means of a rite of passage or transition, a person is separated from one social or religious status and incorporated into another. From a religious perspective, initiation may be seen as an encounter with the sacred. The transition is therefore a profound one, with the initiand emerging from the passage changed not only socially but existentially and spiritually as well. This radical transformation is almost universally symbolized by images of death and rebirth. One is not simply changed; one is made new.

The study of initiation in general, particularly in primitive society, has been almost synonymous with the study of men's initiation in particular. This situation exists, in part, because the vast majority of ethnologists, anthropologists, and even untrained observers were male and, therefore, had greater access to the secret rituals of their own sex. More germane, however, is the fact that male initiations are frequently given more importance, both social and religious, than female initiations. They are, in any event, usually more elaborate and therefore more conspicuous than their female counterparts. Men's initiation may be divided into three categories: puberty rites; specialized initiations into secret societies or confraternities; and specialized initiations into religious vocations or mystical careers.

Primitive Puberty Rites: Methodological Approaches. These invariably obligatory rituals effect the transition from childhood or adolescence to manhood. The boy is separated, often quite literally, from the world of women and children, emerging from his seclusion a man in the company of men. For the male, the arrival of biological puberty is not as punctuated an event as it is for the female. Male initiations are therefore largely cultural rather than biological transitions. Relatedly, boys are usually initiated in groups.

The nature and purpose of male puberty rites have been interpreted from three primary perspectives: history of religions, anthropology, and psychoanalytically oriented schools of psychology. Although they emphasize different aspects of the ritual, these approaches often complement rather than conflict with one another.

Historians of religion, most notably Mircea Eliade, are essentially concerned with interpreting the meaning of the ritual, particularly its symbols of transformation, such as death and rebirth. Historians of religion seek to make intelligible the existential moment experienced by the initiand himself. Their inquiry ranges well beyond primitive society in general and puberty rites in particular in an effort to discern universal patterns in initiation per se. As a consequence this approach is more concerned with cross-cultural symbols than it is with either the varying social frameworks in which those symbols appear or the structure of the rite as such.

By comparison, structure is a primary concern for the anthropologist. Beginning with Arnold van Gennep's *Rites of Passage* (1909), the "career" of the initiand has been analyzed from the perspective of its three basic stages: "separation" from one social status, "transition," and "incorporation" into another social status. Like Eliade, van Gennep clearly recognized the religious dimension of initiation in primitive society. Developing the views of van Gennep and Bronislaw Malinowski, contemporary anthropology concerns itself primarily with how the rite "functions" in primitive society. Its emphasis is, therefore, on how rites reinforce social values, maintain social stability, promote group solidarity, and provide needed instruction and psychological support for the individual.

Unlike Eliade and van Gennep, however, the contemporary social sciences regard initiation as an essentially secular activity. Concerning themselves almost exclusively with male initiation, they suggest that adolescent boys, because of their increasing prowess, strength, and sexual capacities, threaten the order of society and its social equilibrium. Puberty rites help socialize these individuals, thereby allaying their socially disruptive potential. Although theories that stress group solidarity are applicable in a primitive context, they often shed little light on individual initiations in postprimitive society.

Psychoanalytically oriented schools of psychology have shown great interest in men's puberty rites. In fact, it is only this particular aspect of primitive society that has attracted their attention. Using Freudian theory, particularly oedipal conflict and castration anxiety, as a starting point, most exponents of these schools concern themselves not with puberty rites in general but rather with ritual details such as circumcision.

Puberty Rites: Patterns and Issues. From a cross-cultural standpoint, three comprehensive traits characterize male puberty rites in primitive society. First, as noted, is the structure of separation, transition, and incorporation. This scenario is frequently correlated with images of death and rebirth. Second is the disclosure of sacred knowledge, particularly mythical paradigms. Third is the performance of ritual operations on the body and the often related presence of ordeals.

Separation and incorporation / death and rebirth. As illustrated by Eliade, separation from childhood and the female realm is often dramatic and symbolized by death. In Australia, for example, mythical beings in the form of masked men snatch the boys from their mothers and "devour" them. The mothers mourn for the novices just as one mourns for the dead.

The transitional period between separation and incorporation is often prolonged, particularly in the elaborate rituals afforded the male. This period, referred to as one of "liminality," has attracted increasing attention. The social anthropologist Victor Turner draws particular attention to the "liminal persona" as one that is neither this nor that, neither here nor there, but rather betwixt and between. The period of liminality is one of ambiguity and paradox. The initiand may be seen as neither living nor dead, but as both at the same time. Much of the symbolism accompanying this rite is accordingly bivalent. The hut in which the secluded initiand dwells, for example, symbolizes both devouring monster and generative womb, that is, both death and rebirth. During this period, the initiand is seen as pure possibility or primal totality. Males are often dressed as females, thus representing androgyne. Again, they are neither male nor female, but both. The liminal persona is in many ways "invisible," living beyond the norms and categories of society. Traditional taboos and moral injunctions do not apply to him. Liminal personas are sacred, even dangerous. It is therefore often necessary that they be purified before reentering society.

Disclosure of knowledge and mythical paradigms. Some scholars, particularly the psychoanalytically oriented, have suggested that little, if any, significant knowledge is imparted during initiation. Most other scholars, however, suggest that instruction is, in fact, central to the primitive rite. A more significant issue concerns the type of knowledge imparted. Sociologists emphasize instruction in behavior that will be appropriate to the new social status of the person. Historians of religion tend to emphasize the revelation of sacred myths and the true meaning of ritual objects. To a certain degree these two forms of knowledge are interrelated; it is through the myth that the initiand learns who he is and what he is to be. It is, however, the revelation of sacred myth and, relatedly, divine-human relations that require the ritual to be kept secret from women and the uninitiated. Almost always, it is the men only who receive instruction in these matters. Male initiation frequently takes place on a secluded and sacred ground to which women have no access. According to the myths in many cultures, it is on this very ground that the first initiation took place. Among the Kamilaroi of Australia, the sacred ground is the first camp of the All-Father, Baiame. The novices not only learn of mythical events, they reexperience them, returning to the primordial time when the first initiation took place.

Ritual operations and ordeal. Ritual operations on the body are widely performed during primitive puberty rites. The body may be cut, scarred, pierced, branded, or tattooed in innumerable ways, often with great ingenuity and artistic skill. The operation symbolizes differentiation from uninitiated individuals as well as permanent incorporation in a new group. Particularly painful operations, along with harsh treatment, tests of endurance, and other imposed hardships are common in all but the most archaic of male initiations. Invariably, such an ordeal symbolizes ritual death and has a mythological model. [*See* Ordeal.]

Although van Gennep regarded genital operations as simply another form of bodily modification with no unique significance, circumcision in particular has attracted uncommon interest and generated great controversy. Circumcision of males at puberty is a widespread, if not universal, practice among archaic tribes. [*See* Circumcision.] Many societies see it as equivalent to initiation itself and regard uncircumcised men as children. Mythologies and rituals of circumcision are generally dramatic; death symbolism is often conspicuous. The masters of initiation frequently portray mythical animals that seize and symbolically destroy the genitals of the novice. Like Freud himself, many psychoanalytically oriented scholars see in male puberty rites a ritual confirmation of Freudian theory. They regard circumcision as a symbolic form of castration and a primary means of generating castration anxiety within the adolescent male. The ritual act is seen as an ongoing repetition of a primal punishment imposed by a primal father on his rebellious sons. The ritual produces submission to the father's will and reinforces the taboo against incest. Adherents of this school regard ordeal as the essential aspect of the ritual and see instruction as insignificant or peripheral.

Far less prevalent than circumcision is the practice of subincision, whereby the undersurface of the penis is slit open. The initial cut is made some time after circumcision, but may be subsequently lengthened until the incision extends along the entire penile urethra. The wound is periodically opened and blood is drawn. Various explanations and interpretations have been offered. In certain cases, particularly where the incision is explicitly equated with a vulva, the intent of the rite is apparently to provide the male, in symbolic fashion, with both sex organs. The initiand takes on a bisexual or androgynous character, thereby emulating a divine totality. Relatedly, the blood periodically drawn from the reopened wound may symbolize menstrual blood. In Australia and elsewhere, blood is sacred, and males are often anointed with it during the initiation ritual. [*See* Blood.]

The psychologist Bruno Bettelheim offers interpretations of both circumcision and subincision in primitive society. He observes that adolescent boys experience anxiety because they lack a clear biological confirmation of sexual maturity such as the female's first menstruation. Departing from mainstream Freudian theory, Bettelheim sees circumcision as a means of allaying rather than increasing anxiety. Circumcision, in effect, demonstrates to the boys their sexual maturity. Subconsciously at least, they desire it. Their anxiety alleviated, they can more easily adjust to their new social roles. Subincision, for Bettelheim, is rooted in the male's subconscious envy of the female, her sexual organs, and her reproductive ability. Such envy may be seen as the male counterpart of "penis envy" experienced by females, according to Freudian theory. The ritual of subincision creates a vagina; its periodic opening re-creates menstruation; and the ritual, according to Bettelheim, helps the male master his envy of the opposite sex.

Despite evident differences, ritual homologues of the primitive puberty rite are found in every major religion: confirmation in Christianity, Upanayana in Hinduism, and *bar mitsvah* in Judaism, to name a few. This last-named rite will serve as a representative illustration. Properly speaking, the term *bar mitsvah* refers not to the ritual but rather to the initiand. [*See* Rites of Passage, *article on* Jewish Rites.] On the day following his thirteenth birthday, the Jewish male becomes a "son of the commandments," as the term suggests. Separated from religious and moral childhood, he is incorporated into a life of ethical responsibility and ritual obligation. He is incorporated, too, into the *minyan*, the ten persons necessary for the recital of public prayer. Of great importance is the first public reading of the Torah (the Pentateuch) by the initiand. This simultaneously demonstrates his religious knowledge and his place in the adult world. In many communities an examination was given prior to the ceremony. In certain traditional communities the boy is expected to present a *derashah*, or scholarly discourse on the Talmud (the collection of Jewish law and tradition), at the celebration that follows. The initiand's investiture with sacred objects is also central to the rite, as it was for the primitive youth.

Having become a *bar mitsvah,* the male is obligated and permitted to wear the *tefillin,* two cubical leather boxes containing four biblical passages, expressing four basic precepts. The two containers, connected to leather thongs, are ritually bound to the arm and the forehead during recitation of the morning prayers. These boxes contain passages from the Pentateuch (*Dt.* 6:4–9; 11:13–21) requiring the Jew to "bind" the Law as a sign between the eyes and on the hand (arm). This the *bar mitsvah* now does literally and for the first time.

Specialized Initiations. Religious man (*homo religiosus*) seeks an ever-increasing participation in the sacred. Initiations of a specialized nature are therefore appropriate. These rites are invariably voluntary. Particularly in primitive society, puberty rites enable the novice to fully enter the human condition. Specialized initiations, by comparison, enable the individual to transcend that condition. In primitive, classical, and modern society, specialized initiations for men may be divided into two categories: (1) initiation into secret societies or male confraternities and (2) initiations into religious vocations or mystical careers. These specialized initiations are morphologically similar to puberty rites. Patterns and motifs characteristic of primitive puberty rites reappear in specialized initiations, even those in classical and modern society.

Initiation into secret societies. Initiations into primitive secret societies or male confraternities tend to be more selective, more severe, more dramatic, and more secretive than puberty rites. [*See* Secret Societies.] Again, however, we find the ubiquitous symbols of death and rebirth or resurrection. The "mystery" cults of the ancient Greco-Roman world may clearly be regarded as secret societies. The Greek word *mustērion* indicates a rite performed only for initiates. Unlike the formalized state religions of the time, the "mysteries" afforded the worshiper a highly personal experience. Invariably the mysteries promised a resurrection or rebirth beyond the grave. This posthumous resurrection found its temporal equivalent and precondition in ritual rebirth. It was, in fact, at a highly secret initiation during which sacred objects were revealed that this rebirth took place. Invariably, too, the triumph or rebirth of the initiand found its model in the paradigmatic victory of a god or celestial hero.

Although most Hellenistic "mysteries" were open to both sexes, there was one major exception. Mithraism, the secret cult surrounding the celestial Mithra, was open only to men. [*See* Mithraism.] This confraternity, with its evidently masculine and austere emphasis, had a particular appeal for the soldiers of Rome. The paradigmatic myth relates how the lord Mithra sacrificed the primal bull. From its dying body and shed blood issued the bread and wine of a fecund earth. Plants and animals, too, sprang forth as new life issued from death. Relatedly, at the initiation rite, the new member was baptized in the blood of the dying bull, after which he shared a sacred meal of bread and wine. This ritual feast found its model in the original banquet celebrated by Mithra after the ritual slaying.

Just as Mithra ascended to heaven, passing through the seven planetary spheres, so too does the initiand pass through seven stages or grades of initiation. The seven ritual grades correspond also to the planetary journey of the initiand's own soul after death, winning for him immortality beyond the grave.

The initiatory process was characterized by test and ordeal, befitting the military and austere constituency of the confraternity. Although information here is obscure, it appears that the initiand was branded, subjected to extremes of heat and cold, and, with hands bound, possibly hurled across a pit. The use of crypts and tombs as sites of initiation clearly reinforced the death imagery. Initiation at the mysteries, including the Mithraic rite, was essentially concerned with effecting a personal transformation of the initiand rather than simply imparting information.

In the modern world, initiations into secret societies have become semireligious vestiges of their archaic counterparts. Although the actual experience of transcendence, sacrality, and renewal has become rare, the desire for it often remains. This is clear in modern Freemasonry. Initiation to the level of Master Mason will serve as a representative example. Although Freemasonry began as an institution in the seventeenth century, it has generated a mythology, or legendary history, according to which its origins are to be found in the biblical reign of Solomon and the building of his temple. According to this mythology, the master architect, Hiram Abiff, was slain by assailants just before the completion of the temple, because he refused to divulge the secrets of a Master Mason. His actions at that time constitute the paradigmatic gestures now reiterated and explained during the ritual of initiation. As he died, so now dies the initiand. A coffin, an open grave, or the depiction of a grave on the floor make this symbolically clear, as do the skull and crossbones surrounding it. The initiand is "lowered" into the grave from which he is, however, "resurrected," symbolizing his rebirth and incorporation into the circle of Master Masons who assist in the resurrection. The ordeal accompanying the ritual is essentially symbolic rather than real. Just as Hiram Abiff refused to divulge the secrets of a Master Mason to the uninitiated, so does the initiand now swear himself to secrecy under penalty of death. Not only are his knowledge of myth and symbol tested at this level, but higher levels of knowledge and interpretation are disclosed. The tools of the stonemason assume a sacred significance as ritual objects. Their symbolic significance, which invariably contains a moral message, is now disclosed.

Initiation into a religious vocation. A representative illustration is afforded by the Buddhist monk. Prior to the ordination proper, initiation into a probationary period takes place. This step, the *pravrajyā,* or "going out," literally implies a "departure" or separation from the normal world. This initiation often takes place at the age of eight and, like the Upanayana in Hinduism, is a homologue of primitive puberty rites. In some Buddhist countries of Southeast Asia, the novice is sometimes so cut off from the world that no woman, not even his mother or sister, may approach him. Having attained the age of twenty and completed the probationary period, the novice undergoes ordination proper, or *upasaṃpadā.* Here again, separation from the world and symbolic death are evident. In Laos, the women of the house ritually weep on the eve of the ordination, reminiscent of primitive practice. It is frequently the Buddha himself, leaving behind his world of pleasure, who provides the mythical and paradigmatic model for the ritual activity. In Cambodia, for example, the future monk, dressed in princely robes to represent the Buddha's preascetic life, rides toward the monastery amid the joyous cries of friends and relatives who represent the gods in their praise of the future Buddha. Others attempt to hinder the initiand's progress, just as Māra, the Buddhist devil, attempted to impede the future Buddha.

Ordination, or *upasaṃpadā* is, however, literally an "arrival." The initiand is very clearly "incorporated" into the body of monks, the Buddhist order, as is evident at the completion of the rite when the monks surround the newly ordained member, symbolizing refuge in the Buddha, his teachings, and the order itself. The exact moment at which the monks close in around the novice is carefully recorded, as his rebirth takes place and his new life begins at this time. The assumption of a new name is commonplace.

Many of the ordination activities find their model in the events that transpired at the council of Rājagṛha shortly after the Buddha's death. The participants at this council and their activities demonstrate a mythical quality. Just as Ānanda, the Buddha's favorite disciple, was tested by the early *arhat*s or "enlightened ones," so now is the novice tested and subjected to ordeal. Just as Ānanda did then, so must the initiand now confess his sins, be banished from the gathering, and then be permitted to return. In Tibet and elsewhere the initiand is presented with certain sacred objects such as robes and books.

The Roman Catholic rite (sacrament) of ordination to the priesthood also illustrates many traditional initiatory motifs. The rite is, however, public, as are its ritual equivalents (e.g., Buddhist ordination) in most modern religions. After a period of candidacy, the ordinand is examined, declared worthy, and presented to the bishop for election. Just as Jesus selected priests for his ministry, so is the ordinand now selected. The paradigmatic Jesus serves as model throughout the rite. He is referred to not only as teacher and shepherd, but also as priest. His paradigmatic death and rebirth-resurrection are continually evident. The bishop states in the revised rite: "In the memorial of the Lord's death and resurrection, make every effort to die to sin and to walk in the new life of Christ."

Central to the rite is the "laying on" or "imposition of hands" by the bishop. Already in the Old Testament (*Nm.* 8:5–11), the tribe of Levi is "set apart" for service to God by this gesture. As the Latin *ordo* (a social body separate from the people at large) originally made clear, the priest is set apart or separated from the people by this rite. Yet, following the laying on of hands by the bishop, all the priests present lay their hands upon the ordinand. This ancient ceremonial is a symbol of incorporation, homologous to the Buddhist monks surrounding their new member. Like the Buddhist initiand, the Roman Catholic ordinand is "received into" an order.

After being anointed on the palms, the new priest is empowered to offer Holy Communion (the Eucharist) for the first time. The sacred objects are given him: a chalice of wine and a paten (silver plate) with the host (bread). Just as Jesus offered bread and wine, so now does the ordinand. In the Mass they become the body and blood of Christ; thus the Last Supper becomes a contemporary event and the Lord's death and resurrection are shared by the congregation.

BIBLIOGRAPHY

A pioneering work, now dated but still useful and interesting as an introduction, is Arnold van Gennep's *Les rites de passage* (Paris, 1909), translated by Monika B. Vizedom and Gabrielle L. Caffee as *The Rites of Passage* (Chicago, 1960). Hutton Webster's *Primitive Secret Societies,* 2d ed., rev. (1932; reprint, New York, 1968), is also a pioneering work, first published in 1908. It views secret societies from the perspective of their political power. Written by the noted historian of religions, Mircea Eliade, *Rites and Symbols of Initiation: The Mysteries of Birth and Rebirth* (New York, 1958) is the best overview of initiation in general and male initiation in particular. It confines itself largely but not exclusively to primitive society. *Initiation*, edited by C. Jouco Bleeker (Leiden, 1965), is a collection of essays in several European languages, including English. It represents various methodological approaches and deals with ritual in numerous religious traditions. The article by Eliade contains an excellent, even if now slightly dated, bibliography. John W. M. Whiting, Richard Kluckhohn, and Albert Anthony's "The Function of Male Initiation Ceremonies at Puberty," in *Readings in Social Psychology*, edited by Eleanor E. Maccoby et al. (New York, 1958), is a frequently cited and stimulating article combining sociological and psychological theory. Frank W. Young's *Initiation Ceremonies: A Cross-cultural Study of Status Dramatization* (Indianapolis, 1965) views the primitive rite from the perspective of its social function. Michael Allen's *Male Cults and Secret Initiations in Melanesia* (Melbourne, 1967) combines sociological and psychological perspectives and sees the rite as a means of reinforcing sexual identity. Bruno Bettelheim's *Symbolic Wounds: Puberty Rites and the Envious Male* (Glencoe, Ill., 1954) is a little classic. It is readable, controversial, even provocative, and in many ways superior to the sociological and psychological works that have followed it. For further information on Buddhist initiation, see Paul Lévy, *Buddhism: A "Mystery Religion"?* (New York, 1968).

WALTER O. KAELBER

Women's Initiation

Although rituals of women's initiation resemble in numerous ways those celebrated for men, there are also highly significant differences that reflect the biological and—more importantly—the social distinctions between men and women. For instance, it has often been noted that whereas males are usually initiated as a group, women's initiation is quite frequently performed separately for each individual. In part, this may result from the fact that a dramatic individual physiological event—the onset of menstruation—marks the moment at which women's initiation is to take place in many cultures. But one should also note that whereas strong sociopolitical solidarity is established among those males who are initiated together as a corporate group or age-set, the isolation of women in initiation reflects and helps perpetuate a situation in which females are not integrated into any broad-based, powerful, or effective sociopolitical unit.

The task of initiatory rituals is the making of an adult: the transformation of a child into a productive, responsible member of society, prepared to assume the rights and obligations of the particular status marked out for him or her by tradition. Within any ritual of women's initiation, one may thus expect to find encoded the expected norms of female existence as defined by a given society, for it is in that ritual that girls are led to adopt those norms, or—to put it differently—that those norms are imposed on each girl by society as a whole. Here, the observations of Simone de Beauvoir in *The Second Sex* (New York, 1961) are particularly appropriate: "One is not born, but rather becomes, a woman. No biological, psychological, or economic fate determines the figure that the human female presents in society; it is civilization as a whole that produces this creature, intermediate between male and eunuch, which is described as feminine" (p. 249).

Although women's initiation is widely practiced—statistical studies show it to be current among more of the world's peoples than its male counterpart—it has rarely received the degree of attention directed toward men's corresponding rituals. In part, this unfortunate state of affairs may exist because male fieldworkers have been unable to gain admission to these ceremonies, or they may simply have been uninterested in making the attempt. Thus, only a few examples have been reported in any real detail, and still fewer subjected to thorough analysis. Some attempts have been made to draw conclusions from statistical surveys based on the Human Relations Area Files (New Haven), but the findings proposed—correlating performance of women's initiation with matrilocal residence patterns, for instance—have been called into serious question. The field remains largely unexplored, and more work is urgently needed.

Among the examples that have been most thoroughly reported and studied is the Nkang'a ritual of the Ndembu, witnessed by Victor and Edith Turner. This ceremony, which is performed for each Ndembu girl at the time when her breasts begin to develop, but before her menarche, consists of three stages that lead up to the initiand's marriage. The first of these phases, Kwing'ija ("causing to enter"), begins when the prospective bridegroom of the initiand exchanges arrows with the mother of his bride-to-be and also gives an arrow to a specially selected woman who will serve as the girl's instructress and who presides over her initiation. On the next day, dances are held for the girl by the women of her village (men being for the most part excluded) at a consecrated *mudyi* tree just outside the village. The *mudyi* tree, which is the focus of this day's rituals, has strong symbolic associations to numerous referents; among these are the central Ndembu principle of matrilineal descent, the relation of mother and child, female breasts and their milk, and, more broadly, life, learning, the tribe as a whole, and tribal custom in general. Throughout the day's dancing, the initiand lies motionless and naked in a clear *regressus ad uterum*, tightly wrapped within a blanket. Meanwhile, another important symbolic item is introduced to the ceremonial apparatus: after the bridegroom's (phallic) arrow has been inserted into the roots of the *mudyi* tree, a string of white beads, representing the emergent fertility of the initiand, the children she will bear to her husband, and the continuity of her matrilineage, is draped over the arrow. Shortly before this, the women sing:

> They are giving you Nkang'a.
> You have grown up, my child,
> When you have passed puberty you will be pregnant.

Late in the day, a seclusion hut is prepared for the initiand on the side of the village opposite the *mudyi* tree; at sunset she is taken there, carried through the village on the back of the instructress. Here she will spend some weeks or even months, in the second stage of the rite, Kunkunka ("seclusion in the hut"). During this time, she is subjected to numerous ritual interdictions and is given detailed instruction, primarily in dance and in sexual technique. Men may not enter the seclusion hut, with one significant exception: when the girl is first placed within, her future bridegroom enters to light a new fire for her, representative of their impending marriage. The white beads with which the initiand was earlier presented are now wrapped around a miniature bow (the female counterpart to the male arrow) and placed at the apex of the seclusion hut, where an arch is formed of two poles from the *mudyi* tree, symbolic of the female thighs spread in the position of intercourse. The apex thus represents the genitals, and the beads, once again, the children the initiand will bear. Throughout her period of seclusion, however, the initiand is forbidden to look up and see this mystery that rests over her.

The final phase of the ritual, Kwidisha ("bringing out"), begins with a number of mock confrontations between the kinship group of the initiand and that of her bridegroom, in which the latter group is expected to prevail. At dawn, after a night of dancing, the initiand, once again wrapped in a blanket, is carried from her seclusion hut to a place outside the village. There she is washed, shaved, rubbed with oil and red earth, adorned with rattles, and dressed in a skirt, although her now more fully developed breasts remain exposed. Most importantly, her hair is carefully coiffed, leaving a central part into which the string of white beads is placed. The entire coiffure is then covered with densely packed oil and earth. Many of the women present also remove their beads and place them on the head and shoulders of the novice, so that she bears upon her the fertility of all womankind while hiding her own personal fertility as a secret within.

Once adorned, the initiand is led to the village dance place, where she dramatically exhibits the dance skills she has acquired while in seclusion, receiving compliments and gifts from all assembled. In these dances, she is at the height of her power, as is evident from the fact that at a certain moment she is given the eland-tail switch, emblem of the village headman's authority, to carry. Shortly thereafter, however, she must kneel before the drums of the men of the village, dance kneeling, and then spit before the drums "in blessing and thanksgiving." When the dance is concluded, the initiand is led to her bridegroom's hut, where the marriage is consummated. If all goes well, on the following morning the newly married woman, her initiation complete, washes and takes the white beads from her hair in the presence of her husband, shaking the red earth—perhaps signifying the blood of parturition or menstrual blood—from her hair. The beads are then carried to her mother, who will keep them until the rituals for her daughter's first pregnancy are performed, at which time the beads are returned to her.

In assessing this complex and fascinating ritual, Victor Turner (1968) has called attention above all to the way in which it serves to adjust the Ndembu social field when it has been temporarily disrupted by the emergence of a female member from childhood to adult status. This transition calls into focus the deep-seated contradiction in Ndembu social organization between matrilineal descent and virilocal residence: when a girl reaches maturity and marries, she is lost to her lineage, the very lineage that she is expected to perpetuate through the birth of her children. Thus, in the ritual she is first systematically separated from her mother and then gradually handed over to her husband through the intermediary of the instructress; at the same time, the mother is reassured that her daughter's children—represented by the string of white beads—will be returned to her and will ensure the continuity of her matrilineage, as well as the continuity of the Ndembu people as a whole.

Beyond this, one must also consider the effects of the Nkang'a ritual on the initiand herself, for her fertility—what makes her a woman and no longer a girl—is symbolically and ceremonially created within the course of the ritual through her association with the *mudyi* tree, with the apex of the seclusion hut, and, above all, with her string of white beads. But for all that a woman's creative power in fertility is celebrated, her position of sociopolitical subordination is also unambiguously asserted: after a brief flirtation with power as she carries the eland-tail badge of authority, she is quickly forced to kneel before the men's drums.

The ways in which traditional social definitions of ideal female nature are effectively impressed upon successive generations of women through initiation rituals are given striking expression in the Kinaaldá ("first menstruation," or perhaps "house sitting") ceremony of the Navajo, as reported by Charlotte Johnson Frisbie (1967) and others. A major part of this four-night, five-day ceremony is the repeated massaging of the initiand by older women of known good character. Known as "molding," this practice has as its explicit goal the definitive reshaping of an individual woman, both in terms of bodily form and moral character: for it is stated that at the time of her initiation, a girl's body becomes soft again, as it was at birth, so that she is susceptible to the pressures exerted on her by the hands, minds, and speech of those around her.

The events of the Kinaaldá are all patterned upon the first Kinaaldá, performed for the goddess Changing Woman (also known as White Shell Woman), recounted at length in the Blessingway, one of the longest and most important of Navajo sacred chants. The initiand is dressed as Changing Woman, and she is systematically identified with her through sacred songs, just as the girl's family dwelling, where the ritual is celebrated, is identified with that occupied by the goddess at the dawn of time.

Changing Woman, in the opinion of many the most important of Navajo deities, is an enormously complex figure who defies easy categorization. In part the paramount representative of the abstract principle *hózhǫ́* (lit., "beauty," but also "harmony," "balance," "goodwill," etc.), the Navajo *summum bonum,* she is also identified with the earth, vegetation, fertility, growth, abundance, and ideal womanhood. Moreover, as recounted in the Blessingway, having become pregnant by the Sun, she gave birth to the twin culture heroes of Navajo mythology, who rid the world of monsters and established civilization as we know it.

For the first four days of the Kinaaldá, the initiand's actions are quite restricted. Most of her time must be spent in the family hogan grinding corn, and through her vigorous labor at this time it is expected she will come to be industrious—industry being a highly prized female virtue for the Navajo—for the rest of her life. Repeatedly she is "molded," and three times each day she must run eastward from the hogan in pursuit of the Sun. Ultimately, this pursuit seems to be successful, and it is implied that the initiand will conceive by the Sun, as did Changing Woman. But this will not happen until the initiand is thoroughly assimilated to the goddess in the course of an all-night sing held for her on the fourth night of the ritual. In the songs chanted at that time, the family hogan is identified with that of Changing Woman, located at Gobernador Knob, the sacred mountain where she was born out of the union of Sky and Earth. Further, all those who attend the sing take on the identity of the gods who participated in the initiation of Changing Woman; most important, the initiand is herself thoroughly identified with the goddess, as in the following song:

> I am here; I am White Shell Woman, I am here.
> Now on the top of Gobernador Knob, I am here.
> In the center of my white shell hogan I am here.
> Right on the white shell spread I am here.
> Right at the end of the rainbow I am here.

At dawn on the fifth day, as an all-night sing comes to a close, the initiand runs to the east for the last time, toward the rising sun that has just cast its light on her through the hogan's eastern door. Shortly thereafter, the participants in the sing move outside to eat a sweet circular corn cake that has been baking in an earth oven overnight. Compressed within this cake are symbols of the sun and earth, male and female, vegetation, pregnancy, birth, the four cardinal points, and the zenith and nadir. All partake of this cake except the initiand, who offers it to the others as if she herself has given birth to it and to all it represents. The Kinaaldá is expected to ensure universal rebirth consequent upon a woman's initiation, for as Changing Woman was told at the first such ritual, as a result of its proper performance, "there will be birth. Vegetation, as well as all without exception who travel the surface of the earth, will give birth; that you will have gained."

Emergent sexuality is celebrated as the means for the renewal of life, society, and the cosmos in both the Kinaaldá and the Nkang'a rituals, although ceremonies of female initiation celebrated within cultures that hold a more ambivalent attitude toward sex can be expected to treat things quite differently. Thus, for example, as Audrey I. Richards reported in her 1956 study of the Bemba of Northern Rhodesia, among the Bemba sexual intercourse is considered a "hot" activity that can pollute domestic and ritual fires by which approach ought be made to the ancestral spirits central to all cultic activity. Only if a man and wife purify themselves after sex, using a small secret pot conferred upon the wife at the time of her initiation (Chisungu), may these dangers be avoided. The Chisungu—which is somewhat unusual in that it is a corporate ritual in which a group of girls are secluded together for a month or more—thus involves considerable instruction in the mysteries of sexuality, pollution, and purification. By the application of those principles that are learned during initiation, and through the pot that is conferred only upon those who have been initiated, women are able to bring the dangers of sexuality under control. But the tensions, anxiety, and aggression implicit in male-female relations are emphatically dramatized in the culminating acts performed on the final night of the ceremony, when mock bridegrooms appear at the Chisungu hut, singing loudly, "I have tracked my game, / Now I have speared my meat," after which they symbolically carry off their "brides."

Such ambivalence toward emergent female sexuality is not particularly common among agricultural populations, who regularly associate a woman's fertility with the desired fertility of the land. But among peoples whose means of subsistence is hunting and/or fishing, the situation is different, for there it is often perceived that an excess of human fertility results in overpopulation that threatens a fragile ecosystem. Such considerations clearly affect the cultural norms of ideal womanhood as they are transmitted—or better, continually recreated—in initiatory rituals. Thus, for instance, the initiand in the Tucuna Festa das Moças Novas (Festival of the New Maiden) is menaced by a variety of demons (the *noo*) who, according to the myths of this fishing people of the northwest Amazon, avenge themselves mercilessly on those who disrupt the delicate balance of humans and game. Isolated within the large familial residence *(maloca)* in a chamber that bears the name of the underworld of the *noo*, the initiand is told these spirits will kill her, suck the viscera from her body, and carry off her empty corpse, should she violate any of her ritual prescriptions; each night she hears the "voices" of the *noo* in the form of sacred trumpets hidden from women's view by men. Upon emerging from her seclusion chamber—like a butterfly from a cocoon, according to Tucuna metaphor—the initiand is again assaulted by the *noo*, now represented by a host of masked dancers, who only in the course of a wild night of drink and dancing shed their costumes and resume human identity. Should the girl survive this ordeal, she is taken on a symbolic tour of heaven, earth, and multiple underworlds, and is finally bathed in a contraceptive solution passed upward from her feet to her head, "to prevent her becoming prematurely pregnant." Only when these magico-ritual checks upon her potentially excessive fertility have been established is the Tucuna woman accorded adult, marriageable status.

In general, specialized initiatory rites for women tend to disappear in urban and later in industrial societies; often they blend into marriage ceremonies or into those lacking gender specificity, such as graduation from school. Still, it is sometimes possible to recognize the traces of older women's initiation rituals within a new context and dramatic program. Thus, for example, such scholars as Angelo Brelich and Walter Burkert have been able to show how, within the Greek *polis*, broader rituals of women's initiation came to be narrowed so that only a few individuals, drawn always from wealthy, prominent families, passed through a series of initiatory schemata, serving perhaps as representatives of all women in general. In his *Lysistrata* (lines 641ff.), Aristophanes preserves a list of the age-grades through which these women passed: *arrēphoros, aletris, arktos,* and *kanēphoros*, each status conferred by ritual means. While the details of each grade are complex, we may note briefly that the last two of these were celebrations and consecrations of a young girl's virginity prior to marriage: as an *arktos* (lit., "bear") she took up residence with Artemis in the wilds; as a *kanēphoros* she carried a basket holding sacred objects for the Panathenaia festival celebrated in honor of Athena. (Artemis and Athena were the goddesses most protective of virgins and virginity.) Having played the role of *kanēphoros,* however, a girl was considered eligible for marriage; in myths such as that of Oreithyia women are abducted and raped while or shortly after appearing as *kanēphoros*.

Although they may appear in combination in any specific ritual complex, four general "ideal types" of women's initiation have been recognized. These are (1) rituals of bodily mutilation, involving such operations upon the initiand's physical self as tattooing, scarification, clitoridectomy, or other genital surgery as well as such processes as the Navajo "molding"; (2) rituals involving identification with a mythic heroine, whether goddess, culture heroine, primordial ancestress, or some other prototypical figure; (3) rituals involving a cosmic journey, in which the initiand is symbolically conveyed to heavens, underworlds, the four quarters, and other places of cosmologic significance, as a means of lifting her beyond her normal locus and identity; (4) rituals focused upon the play of opposites, wherein such normally exclusive categories as male/female, human/divine, above/below, right/left, black/white, and wild/tame are somehow united within the initiand, establishing her as a being who transcends the dualities of fragmented mundane existence.

In all of these types, three interrelated levels of transformative action are regularly claimed to be accomplished. First, it is claimed that rituals of women's initiation transform a girl into a woman, conferring upon her marriageable status. Second, it is claimed that they renew society, providing it with new members ritually empowered to play productive and reproductive roles for the good of the social totality, whether lineage, tribe, or other corporate entity. Third, it is claimed that they renew the cosmos, by virtue of the homology between the initiand's fertility and that of nature at large. This last claim is the most audacious and fascinating of all.

It must be emphasized, however, that in contrast to

male initiations, women's rites do not usually advance those who have completed them toward political offices of power and prestige. For while the status of a woman may be ritually changed from that of child to adult (from unmarriageable to marriageable or even married), the woman's sphere of influence and activity has been restricted in virtually all human societies to the home. In light of this, it appears a reasonable hypothesis that the exorbitant claims of cosmic transformations wrought by women's initiation and of the cosmic significance of an adult female life offer a form of false consciousness that deflects women's attention and lives from the sociopolitical arena, offering a religio-cosmic ground of meaning and action in place of the sociopolitical one reserved—and preserved—for men.

[*See also* Feminine Sacrality.]

BIBLIOGRAPHY

The chief attempts to draw theoretical generalizations regarding rituals of women's initiation are D. Visca's "Le iniziazioni feminili: Un problema da riconsiderare," *Religioni e Civiltà* 2 (1976): 241–274; my *Emerging from the Chrysalis: Studies in Rituals of Women's Initiation* (Cambridge, Mass., 1981); and Judith K. Brown's "A Cross-Cultural Study of Female Initiation Rites," *American Anthropologist* 65 (1963): 837–853. The last of these, however, has been subjected to severe criticism by Harold E. Driver in his "Girls' Puberty Rites and Matrilocal Residence," *American Anthropologist* 71 (1969): 905–908.

Among the finest anthropological case studies of specific data are Victor Turner's *The Drums of Affliction: A Study of Religious Processes among the Ndembu of Zambia* (London, 1968), pp. 198–268; Charlotte J. Frisbie's *Kinaaldá: A Study of the Navaho Girl's Puberty Ceremony* (Middletown, Conn., 1967); Audrey I. Richards's *Chisungu: A Girls' Initiation Ceremony among the Bemba of Northern Rhodesia* (London, 1956); Kathleen E. Gough's "Female Initiation Rites on the Malabar Coast," *Journal of the Royal Anthropological Institute* 85 (1955): 45–80; and Judith Modell's "Female Sexuality, Mockery, and A Challenge to Fate: A Reinterpretation of South Nayar *talikettukalyanam*," *Semiotica* 50 (1984): 249–268. Classicists have also made considerable progress in the reconstruction of women's initiations as practiced in the ancient world. Among the best of these studies are Angelo Brelich's *Paides e Parthenoi* (Rome, 1969) and Walter Burkert's "Kekropidensage und Arrephoria: Vom Initiationsritus zum Panathenäenfest," *Hermes* 94 (1966): 1–25.

BRUCE LINCOLN

INNER ASIAN RELIGIONS. Inner Asia, essentially a historical concept, was that great land mass surrounded by the civilized worlds of Rome, Greece, Arabia, Persia, India, and China. Central Eurasia, the more scholarly term for the region, should not be confused with Central Asia, which, in the strict sense, comprises the modern-day Uzbek, Turkmen, Kirghiz, Kazakh, and Tajik republics in the Soviet Union; or, in a broader sense, adds Chinese Turkistan (Sinkiang). Until modern times, the boundaries that separated Inner Asia from the rest of the Eurasian land mass were in constant flux, expanding or contracting according to the relations of the peoples within Inner Asia toward the surrounding sedentary states.

Inner Asia is a vast area with a multitude of peoples, speaking a variety of languages, possessing distinct religious practices, yet culturally united in a unique civilization. The languages spoken in Inner Asia belong to a number of linguistic families, the largest of which is Altaic (comprising the Turkic, Mongol, and Tunguz languages), followed by Uralic (the Finno-Ugric and Samoyed languages), Paleosiberian or Paleo-Asiatic, Indo-Iranian, and the isolated languages of the Caucasus. The noninstitutionalized forms of religion in Inner Asia, as reported by early travelers and recorded by historians, were most evident in their myths of origin, in the ceremonial activities present in daily life, such as rituals performed before hunting or connected with funerals, and in art. Tolerance of outside religions was the norm, rather than the exception, and Buddhism, Islam, and Christianity all exerted great influence on the region.

Ecologically, Inner Asia is divided into four great longitudinal belts: the tundra in the far north, the forest (taiga), the steppe, and finally the desert in the south. The existence of these four separate zones has led to the inaccurate stereotyping of the economic activity practiced in the north by the Finno-Ugric, Samoyed, and Tunguz peoples as hunting, fishing, and gathering, and that practiced in the south by the Turkic and Mongol peoples as exclusively nomadic herding. However, just as hunting and limited agriculture were a part of Turkic and Mongol economies, so was animal husbandry a part of the economy of the more northern peoples. The prevailing climatic conditions severely limited agricultural potential without man-made changes in the environment, giving rise to one of the most important unifying features of Inner Asia: the relationship between horse and pasture. As the mainstay of Inner Asian economy, the horse, dependent only on pasture, was either traded for basic necessities, particularly armaments that could only be manufactured by the surrounding sedentary civilizations, or used for military conquest. It thus became the key to the rise of the great nomadic civilizations.

Major problems arise in dealing with the history of Inner Asia. Indigenous written material is extremely scant, existing only from the eighth century CE. Much of the Inner Asian tradition was preserved only orally, transmitted by storytellers, singers, shamans, and priests. Most often the early history of Inner Asia was

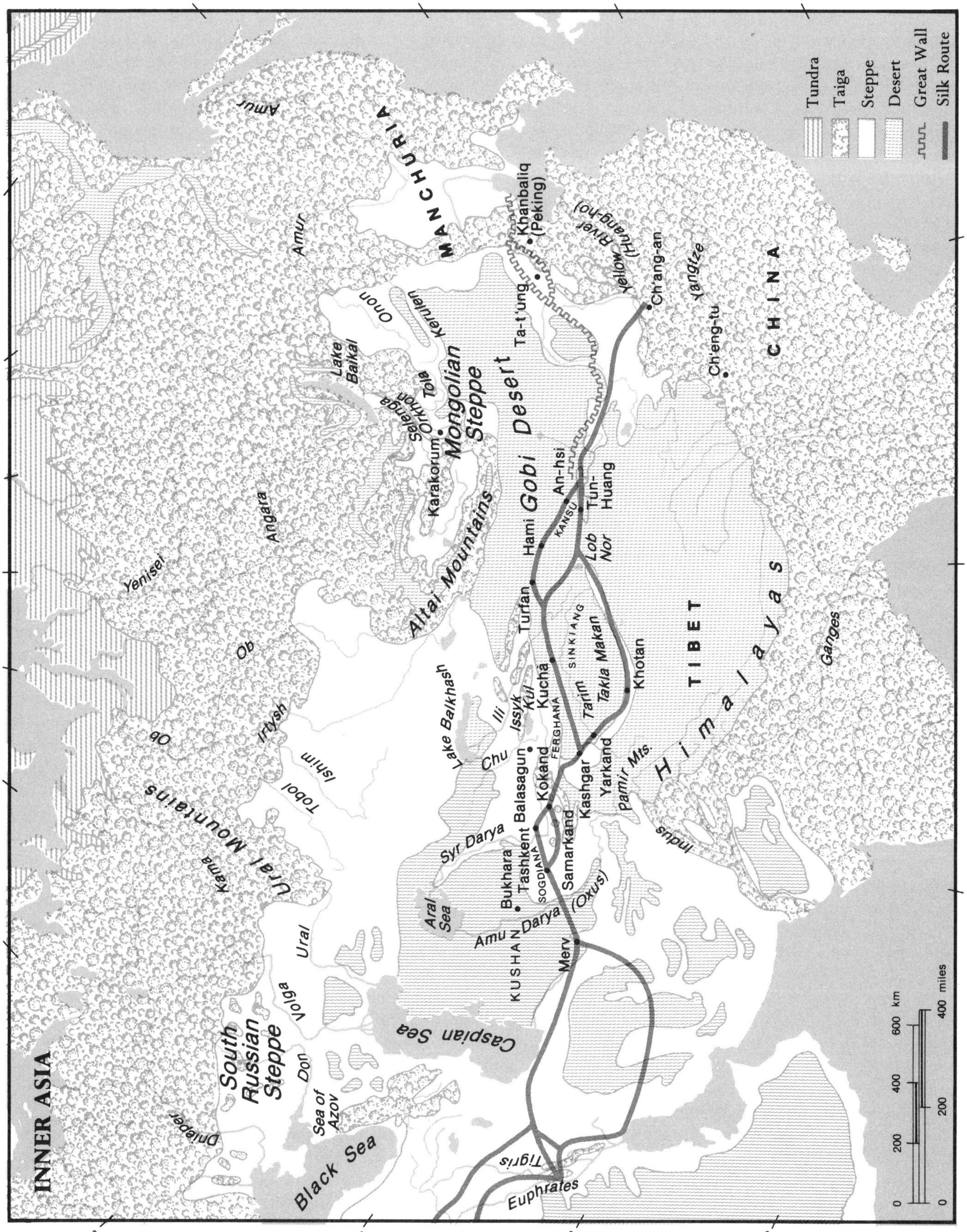
INNER ASIA
Tundra
Taiga
Steppe
Desert
Great Wall
Silk Route
0 200 400 600 km
0 200 400 miles
MANCHURIA
Mongolian Steppe
Gobi Desert
Altai Mountains
Ural Mountains
South Russian Steppe
TIBET
CHINA
Himalayas
Lake Baikal
Lake Balkhash
Aral Sea
Caspian Sea
Black Sea
Sea of Azov
Amur
Onon
Kerulen
Tola
Orkhon
Selenga
Angara
Yenisei
Ob
Irtysh
Ishim
Tobol
Ural
Volga
Don
Dnieper
Kama
Syr Darya
Amu Darya (Oxus)
Chu
Ili
Issyk Kul
Tarim
Indus
Ganges
Yangtze
Yellow River (Huang-ho)
Tigris
Euphrates
Khanbaliq (Peking)
Ta-t'ung
Ch'ang-an
Ch'eng-tu
Karakorum
An-hsi
Tun-Huang
KANSU
Hami
Lob Nor
Turfan
SINKIANG
Takla Makan
Khotan
Kucha
FERGHANA
Balasagun
Kokand
Kashgar
Yarkand
Pamir Mts.
Tashkent
Samarkand
Bukhara
SOGDIANA
Merv
KUSHAN

recorded by the surrounding civilizations, eager to protect their own ways of life and highly critical of different customs and manners. Because the written records are in a variety of nonindigenous languages, the correct identification of names in Inner Asia presents problems. Ethnonyms and toponyms, not to mention personal names and titles, that appear, for example, in Chinese sources are extremely difficult to equate with names or terms given in Greek or Arabic sources. When a name such as *Scythian* or *Hun* or *Turk* first appeared, it meant a specific people; later, the name would often become a generic term applied to any barbarian people. Imprecise geographical knowledge only added to the problems; distances were exaggerated, and few people from the surrounding sedentary civilizations had actually visited Inner Asia. The history of the region therefore must be filtered from ideas and ways hostile to its peculiar civilization and drawn from the precious scraps of indigenous material—written fragments, archaeological data, art—often literally scraped out of the desert sands or the frozen soil of the tundra.

To most peoples of the so-called civilized world, Inner Asia was seen as one vast zone. The world, from the time of Homer (c. tenth century BCE) until the beginning of the Russian expansion into Asia in the late sixteenth century, saw Inner Asia as a land shrouded in mystery and myth, defined only by its barbarousness. It was the inhospitable land of the north, unfit for man or beast.

Ancient Views of Inner Asia. Early Chinese and Classical Greek sources spoke of Inner Asia, but many of the peoples mentioned were imaginary and showed the civilized world's lack of real knowledge about the region. To the Greeks these were the peoples who inhabited such places as the City of Perpetual Mist or the Rhipaean Mountains. These regions and the peoples who lived there were removed, beyond the pale of Greek civilization, their barbarous nature, according to Hippocrates (460?–377? or 359?), directly determined by the environment in which they lived. The Greek geographer and historian Strabo (c. 63 BCE–23 CE) reminded his readers that before the Black Sea was navigable the barbarous tribes surrounding it as well as the fierce storms on it caused it to be called Axine ("inhospitable"); not until the Ionians established cities on its shores did it become known as Euxine ("hospitable"). This case is an example of one of the myths perpetuated about Inner Asia by external historians: the lack of cities was equated with a lack of civilization. On the other side of Inner Asia, the Chinese held similar views. The Inner Asian lived in the "submissive wastes," the "great wilderness," the region of the "floating sands," in the barren lands "where frost came early." The "five grains" would not grow there. Chinese emperors were often challenged by their ministers on the wisdom of trying to expand Chinese territory into these wastelands. This attitude perpetuated another myth: the lack of agriculture meant the people were uncivilized.

Early Medieval Judaic, Christian, and Islamic Views. In the Judeo-Christian and Islamic traditions, the peoples of Inner Asia had been driven into the barren, desolate lands of the north, to the hidden, dark regions of the world—to the land of Gog and Magog. When Jeremiah was asked by the Lord what he saw, he answered, "I see a seething pot; and the face thereof is toward the north" (*Jer.* 1:13). Within this "seething pot" were the unknown kingdoms of the north, which, at the end of time, would rise and the contents spill upon the land, bringing death and destruction. Classical Arab and Persian geographers (ninth to eleventh century) located Gog and Magog in the fifth and sixth climes and warned of their cold, bestial nature, but others recognized their brave, warrior-like qualities. To al-Kashgārī (fl. eleventh century) they were an army, the army of the prophet Muḥammad, to be sent out when he was angry with a people. This army, called Turk, would come at the end of time. The fear that medieval man had regarding the peoples of the north was also manifest in the *Roman d'Alexandre,* in which the hordes of Gog and Magog are sealed off behind an iron gate.

The armies of Inner Asia did not exist in myth alone; the fears of medieval man had been justified by repeated invasions from the steppe lands. Walls—such as the Roman *limes* or the Great Wall of China—were monuments of the civilized world's futile attempt to contain the encroaching and often unknown peoples from Inner Asia. When the hordes of Inner Asia broke through, they did bring death and destruction with a terrible swiftness. It was because of such invasions that the peoples of Inner Asia first entered recorded history in some detail and accuracy.

The History of Inner Asia. The peoples of Inner Asia who lived in the tundra and taiga were widely dispersed in small communities and posed no threat to their neighbors. It was the peoples of the steppes, formed in large tribes with vast herds of sheep, goats, camels, cattle, and horses, who were highly mobile and had the organizational ability to lead military excursions against their sedentary neighbors. When these peoples first appear in historical sources, they come from two great steppe regions: the south Russian (or Pontic) steppe and the Mongolian steppe.

Scythians. The first important Inner Asian people, the Indo-Iranian Scythians, appeared on the south Russian steppe in the eighth century BCE and began to fade out of the historical scene around 175 BCE, although some remnants survived until the third century CE. While little is known about their origin, a detailed description of their mode of life and some remarks on their history are given by Herodotus (c. 480–420 BCE) in book 4 of his *Histories*. The Scythians were the first historically known people to use iron, and having defeated the Cimmerians, they assumed full command of the south Russian steppe. Their greatness as steppe warriors was recognized when Darius I (r. 521–486 BCE), king of Persia, led a campaign against the Scythians north of the Black Sea from 516 to 513. These Scythian mounted archers soon frustrated Darius by seemingly fleeing before him, attacking when and where he least expected, all the while drawing him farther and farther into their land. In the end, Darius was forced to retreat to Persia. This type of warfare and the ability of the skilled horseman to turn and shoot behind him—the Parthian shot—became a trademark of the Inner Asian warrior.

In Persian sources these people were called Saka, and three kinds were enumerated: the Saka beyond the sea, the pointed-hat Saka, and the Saka who revered Hauma. The Scythians of Herodotus lived north of the Black Sea, while the Saka of Persian sources lived beyond the Oxus River (the modern Amu Darya) and south of this area in Iran. The social structure of the Scythians was tripartite: agriculturists, warriors, and priests. They had cities, centers of metallurgy, and a highly developed, stylized animal art.

Animals, particularly horses and cattle, as well as humans were sacrificed as offerings to the gods. Herodotus listed the Scythian gods with what he thought were their Greek equivalents, the supreme deity being Tabiti (Vesta). Images, altars, and temples were used. Scythian soothsayers were called into service when the king was ill; Enarees, womenlike men among the Scythians, practiced divination; elaborate funeral and burial rites, a strong will to protect the tombs of their ancestors, and prescribed ceremonies for oath taking existed. By the late second century BCE, the ethnically and linguistically related nomadic tribes of the Sarmatians began to replace the Scythians, who had reached a degree of civilization perhaps unparalleled by any other Inner Asian empire. [*See also* Scythian Religion *and* Sarmatian Religion.]

Hsiung-nu. On the eastern edge of Inner Asia, the Hsiung-nu were the first clearly identifiable and important steppe people to appear on the borders of China, constantly menacing the frontier with raids that sometimes penetrated deep into Chinese territory. Their center of power was the Mongolian steppe. Appearing in Chinese sources around 230 BCE, an account of the Hsiung-nu was provided by the grand historian of China, Ssu-ma Ch'ien (c. 145–86 BCE). By about 56 BCE internal revolts had begun to rack the Hsiung-nu empire and some tribes moved to the west; in 48 CE the Hsiung-nu finally split into two major groups: the Southern Hsiung-nu and the Northern Hsiung-nu. The former continued to be a serious threat to China and finally faded from the historical scene around 400 CE, while the Northern Hsiung-nu remained on the original homeland of the Mongolian steppe. The Northern Hsiung-nu never regained their former power, however, and about 155 CE they were destroyed by another steppe people, the Hsien-pei.

The language of the Hsiung-nu is unknown. Long thought to be Mongol or Turkic, more recent studies seem to indicate that it comprised some elements of the Yenisei branch of the Paleosiberian languages. Since the eighteenth century, it has been popular to equate the Hsiung-nu of the east with the Huns of the west: at best the theory is controversial.

The military power of the Hsiung-nu, like that of the Scythians, lay in their remarkable skill as highly disciplined mounted archers. In fact, Ssu-ma Ch'ien considered warfare their main occupation. Made up of numerous tribes, the Hsiung-nu confederation was most highly organized in its relations with foreign states, depending upon the horse for both military superiority and for economic gain. The Chinese set up border markets in an attempt to weaken the Hsiung-nu by supplying them with luxuries and fostering a dependence on Chinese goods. Even though there was a hereditary aristocracy within the Hsiung-nu confederation, internal organization was loose, each tribe having its own pastures. A son would marry his stepmother when his father died; a brother would marry a deceased brother's widow—both practices aimed at preventing the extinction of the clan.

At set times of the year, sacrifices were offered to ancestors, gods, heaven and earth, while auspicious days were chosen for major events, and the stars and moon were consulted for military maneuvers. Burials were elaborate, particularly for the ruler, with many of his concubines and loyal ministers following him in death. Although condemned by the Chinese for lacking in morals, not understanding court ritual, and not showing respect for the aged, the Hsiung-nu had laws, customs, and manners of their own that contradicted the ethnocentric views of the Chinese.

Yüeh-chih, Wu-sun, and Kushans. The Hsiung-nu greatly affected the history of Inner Asia to the west and south of their domains where, in 160 BCE, they inflicted a terrible defeat on the Yüeh-chih, an Indo-European people located on the Chinese border of modern Kansu Province. This caused the Yüeh-chih to divide; the Lesser Yüeh-chih moved to the south while the Greater Yüeh-chih began moving west. As the latter migrated through the Ili River valley, they abandoned the Mongolian steppe to the complete control of the Hsiung-nu, while they themselves displaced the Sai (or Saka) tribes. The majority of the Yüeh-chih continued to move west into the Greek state of Bactria. At about the same time, the Chinese emperor Wu-ti (r. 140–87 BCE) sent Chang Ch'ien to the Greater Yüeh-chih to form an alliance against the Hsiung-nu. Leaving in 139, Chang Ch'ien had to pass through Hsiung-nu territory, where he was detained and held prisoner for more than ten years. Chang Ch'ien's account, made to the Chinese emperor on his return, brought the first real knowledge of the western regions to China, information that would allow China to expand westward and become actively involved in Central Asia. Although his mission to the Yüeh-chih failed, he was sent again in 115 to try to form a different alliance against the Hsiung-nu, this time with the Wu-sun, another people probably of Iranian origin, who accepted the gifts that Chang Ch'ien brought as well as an imperial princess to become the wife of their ruler, but who also refused to cooperate. It was not until the Hsiung-nu empire was disintegrating that the Wu-sun inflicted serious defeats on them.

The Yüeh-chih tribes that settled in Bactria were later united under one tribe, the Kushans, probably in the first century BCE. Besides Bactria, their kingdom included extensive domains in Central Asia and large portions of Northwest India, where centers of Greco-Buddhist art were established at Gandhāra and Mathurā. The Kushan period is extremely controversial, and the dates and order of kings are widely disputed. But it was during the reign of Kaniṣka, a patron of Buddhism, that this Indian religion began to spread into Central Asia and China, heralding a new era for the region. Chinese monks began to travel to India and Sri Lanka to obtain the Buddhist *sūtras*, passing through Tun-huang, Khotan, and Turfan on the edge of the Tarim Basin, as well as Ferghana and Sogdiana. Most notable are the accounts left by the monks Fa-hsien (traveling from 399 to 413 CE) and Hsüan-tsang (traveling from 629 to 645). Buddhist texts had to be translated into Turkic languages; the routes used by pilgrims were destined to become active trade routes, linking east and west. [*See also* Missions, *article on* Buddhist Missions, *and* Buddhism, *article on* Buddhism in Central Asia.]

Huns. With the appearance of the Huns toward the end of the fourth century CE, a new movement began on the south Russian steppe. Rumors of invasions spreading fear and panic reached Jerome (c. 311–420) in Palestine, where he wrote that these "wolves of the north"—the Huns—"spared neither religion nor rank nor age." It was with this turmoil on the steppe north of the Sea of Azov that the *Völkerwanderung*, or migration of the peoples, began. The name *Hun* first appears in the writings of Ptolemy (fl. second century CE), but later historians of the Huns such as Ammianus Marcellinus (c. 322–400), Priscus (fl. fifth century), and the less reliable Jordanes (fl. sixth century) portray a culture typical of Inner Asian society and very different from Roman civilization. Aided by civil wars in Italy that occupied the Roman army, some Hun tribes had established themselves by 409 on the Roman *limes* and in the Roman province of Pannonia (on the right bank of the Danube). When, in 434, a Hun king named Rua died, he was succeeded by his nephews, Bleda and Attila.

Hun penetration into Europe and the displacing of existing tribes were instrumental in the formation of modern Europe. Aetius, the great fifth-century general and power broker of the Western Roman Empire, provoked some Hun tribes to attack the Burgundians in 437 in order to shatter Germanic power and to strengthen Roman rule in Gaul. The Visigoths, who had been pushed from the east into the Toulouse area, forced the Vandals into Spain and North Africa, an event that caused great consternation to the entire Roman empire. However, Aetius's attempt to use the Huns to defeat the Visigoths failed in 439. Turmoil continued, this time in the Eastern Roman Empire with the Persian decision to attack Byzantium; at the same time, Attila attacked the Byzantines from the north, gaining new treaty concessions. Then in 445 Attila murdered Bleda, thus becoming the sole ruler of the Hun tribes of Pannonia. In the end, a nervous Aetius allied himself with the Visigoths to meet Attila in the Battle of the Catalaunian Plain (451) near Troyes, France, where the Visigoth king Theodoric II lost his life and the Romans withdrew in a battle that left neither Hun nor Roman the victor. With Attila's death in 453, Hun influence on Europe rapidly crumbled.

Where the Huns had originated is unknown, but written sources leave no doubt on their physical appearance, which was clearly mongoloid. No text in the Hun language has been found; archaeological finds from Hun areas remain controversial. What is certain is that despite their impact on the formation of Europe, the Huns never attained the power of the great Inner Asian states such as those of the Türks or the Mongols. [*See also* Hun Religion.]

Hsien-pei and Juan-juan. As already mentioned, the Northern Hsiung-nu state was replaced around 155 CE by that of the Hsien-pei, who probably spoke a Mongol language. Through this victory, the Hsien-pei became the dominant tribal confederacy on the Mongolian steppe. With other nomadic peoples, including the Southern Hsiung-nu and the Wu-huan, they continued attacks on China but were repulsed, particularly by the famous Chinese general Ts'ao Ts'ao. When the Hsien-pei first appeared, during the Wang Mang interregnum (9–23 CE), they had no supreme ruler; unified leadership is not ascribed to them until just before their defeat of the Hsiung-nu. Oral tradition embellished this first leader, T'an-shih-huai (d. between 178 and 183), with a "miraculous birth," heroic qualities, and the wisdom to be a chief, yet the Hsien-pei failed to create a lasting empire in this fragmented period of steppe history.

From approximately 400 to 550 a new power emerged on the Mongolian steppe: the Juan-juan (or Jou-jan). Their origins are uncertain but future research may clarify their relation to the Hua and to the Avars who appeared in Europe in the fifth century. According to a widely accepted but yet unproven theory, the Juan-juan in the east are identified with the Avars in the west. Personal names, as given in Chinese, do not appear to be either Turkic or Mongol, but it is with the Juan-juan that the title *kaghan* is first used for the ruler. In 546 the last ruler, A-na-kui, was approached by a man named Bumin (T'u-men), whom he called a blacksmith slave, and who had the audacity to request the hand of one of A-na-kui's daughters. He was rudely refused—so the story goes—whereupon Bumin and his followers revolted, overthrew the Juan-juan, and established their own Türk empire.

Türk. The appearance of the Türk—the first Inner Asian people whose language is known and the first also to use with certainty a Turkic idiom—marks a turning point in the history of the steppe. According to Chinese sources they were metallurgists employed by the Juan-juan, but it is not clear whether the revolt led by Bumin (d. 552) was social in character or a minority uprising. After Bumin's death the empire split, one group, led by his son, establishing itself on the Mongolian steppe, while the other group, under the leadership of his brother Ishtemi, ruled over the more western part of the empire. They encountered the Ephthalites (or White Huns) on the borders of Persia. The Türk made an alliance with Sasanid Persia (226–655), encircled and destroyed the Ephthalites, establishing thereby a common border with Persia, but also obtaining control of the lucrative silk trade. Because of its commercial interests—represented mainly by Sogdian merchants—the Western Türk empire then found itself embroiled in the conflict between Persia and Byzantium. Persian attempts to stop silk from reaching Byzantium forced the Türk to go directly to Byzantium by a northern route. It was for this reason that embassies were first exchanged between Türk and Byzantium, opening up entire new horizons for Romans as well as for the Chinese. The first Türk embassy, headed by a Sogdian named Maniakh, reached the court of Justin II (r. 565–578) in 567. The Türk embassy remained in Constantinople, then part returned to the Türk with the Byzantine ambassador Zemarkhos. A later Greek ambassador arrived at a Türk camp at the death of the ruler and witnessed the funeral rites, which included laceration of the faces of the mourners and the sacrifice of horses and servants. The Western Türk empire disintegrated around 659.

The Eastern Türk empire, in a semipermanent state of war with China and plagued by internal dissension, was finally defeated in 630. Chinese rule then lasted until 682 when the Türk revolted and again seized power, forming a second Türk empire that was overthrown in 743 by the revolt of three Turkic tribes: the Basmil, the Karluk, and the Uighur. It was from the period of the second Türk empire that the first indigenous texts from Inner Asia—as stated above, written in a Turkic language—have been found. The most famous of these are funeral-stela inscriptions written in a runiclike alphabet found in the area of the Orkhon River and dedicated to the Türk ruler, Bilge Kaghan (r. 716–734), his brother Kül Tegin, and the prime minister Tonyuquq. These texts give not only a history of the Türk people but also provide valuable insight into Türk society and customs, including their belief in *tengri* ("heaven, sky"), in the sacred mountain of Ötükän, and in the erection of *balbal* (stone pillars) on the tomb of a warrior inscribed with the name of an enemy he had killed. [*See* Tengri.] Chinese sources recorded three Türk legends of origin quite different from one another: the child raised by a wolf, the child born of the spirit of wind and rain, the child born of the spirit of the lake. Such a multiplicity of ancestral traditions would suggest that the Türk empire was most likely a confederation of tribes of diverse origin.

Avars, Khazars, and Bulgars. The Greek historian Priscus wrote of a migration of peoples taking place from 461 to 465 on the south Russian steppe. An embassy from the Oghur, Onoghur, and Saroghur had arrived in Byzantium, reporting that they had been pushed by the Sabir, who in turn were being displaced by a people in Central Asia called Avar. For almost a century there was no news of them, but in 558 the Avars, now in the Caucasus, sent an embassy to the Byzantine emperor Justinian I (r. 527–565) requesting land in exchange for military protection. Fleeing from the Western Türk, the Avars were given asylum in the Byzantine empire by Justin II, an act that infuriated the Türk, who considered the Avars their own, fugitive subjects. It is a well-documented Inner Asian concept that ruling tribes owned the peoples whom they had conquered. Settled in the Carpathian Basin, the Avars remained there for some two and a half centuries, becoming an effective wedge between the northern and southern Slavs. When they had arrived in the Carpathian Basin, the Avars found two Germanic tribes, the Gepids, whom they destroyed, and the Lombards, who fled and settled in northern Italy. The Avars also menaced the Byzantines and the Franks. In 626 the Avars and the Persians jointly attacked Constantinople and were defeated only when the Byzantine forces destroyed the Persian fleet as it attempted to cross the Bosphorus.

Meanwhile, the south Russian steppe continued to be a place of turmoil. The Turkic-speaking Khazars became increasingly powerful with the weakening of the western Türk, and by the mid-seventh century achieved independence. Christian and Islamic missionaries had already had some influence among the Khazars, but in 740 the Khazar ruler and his entourage adopted Judaism. Not an empire bent on conquest, but practicing a settled, mixed economy based on cattle breeding, agriculture, and trade, the Khazars nevertheless caused some movement on the steppe and prevented Arab and Islamic penetration into eastern Europe. Pushed by the Khazars, the Bulgars (a Turkic-speaking people who had lived on the Pontic steppe from the late fifth century) split around 680. One group, moving north to the Volga-Kama region, was, in 921, visited by an Arab embassy described by one of its members, Ibn Faḍlān, who left an invaluable account of both the Khazars and the Volga Bulgars. A Christian Bulgar prince, Kovrat, and his son Asparukh led other Bulgar tribes, mostly Turkic, to the lower Danube region where Asparukh created a Bulgar state between 679 and 681. Some of the Bulgars settled with the Avars in the Carpathian Basin, but the formation of this Bulgar buffer state between the Avars and Byzantium effectively ended Avar-Byzantine relations by 678. As a result, the Avars led a reasonably quiet life for over a century until they were attacked and greatly weakened (although not defeated) in 791, 795–796, and 803 by Charlemagne. The Avars slowly disappeared over the next eighty years until Hungarian (Magyar) tribes filled the vacuum and maintained the non-Slavic wedge in central Europe. [*See also* Hungarian Religion.]

Uighurs. The final blow to the Türk empire was delivered by the Uighurs who, as we have seen, had been a part of the Türk confederacy. Their language was basically the same as that of the Türk, with some of their texts written in runic script and some in a script borrowed from the Sogdians, one that would become a major script used in Inner Asia. Unlike the Türk, whom they overthrew in 743, the Uighurs often allied themselves with China; thus, during the reign of Mou-yü the Uighurs helped China to quell the An Lu-shan rebellion (755–757). When Mou-yü visited Lo-yang in 762–763, he was converted to Manichaeism, which had been propagated in China by the Sogdians. A description of his conversion appears on the trilingual inscription (in Uighur, Sogdian, and Chinese) of Karabalghasun, the Uighur capital city. When Mou-yü returned home he took Manichaean priests with him and made Manichaeism the state religion. [*See* Manichaeism, *overview article*]. Thus, the Uighurs became the first Inner Asian people to adopt an institutionalized, major religion. Many Uighurs disliked the influence gained by Sogdians in Uighur affairs and an anti-Sogdian faction, led by the uncle of Mou-yü, revolted and killed the kaghan and his family. There followed a succession of rulers embroiled in family intrigues, plagued by assassinations and suicide. Even so, Sogdian and Manichaean influence remained in a kingdom dominated by Buddhism. An Arab traveler, Tamīm ibn Baḥr, visited Karabalghasun in 821 and left an account of what he saw. Of particular interest are his remarks about the flourishing town of Karabalghasun and other small settlements, located in richly cultivated areas. The picture he draws contradicts the stereotyped image of the incompatibility of Inner Asian civilization and urban development. In 840 the Uighurs were attacked by a new Turkic power, the Kirghiz, who lived north and west of the great Mongolian steppe.

Not absorbed into the new ruling Kirghiz confederacy, the Uighurs moved. Some went to China, settling in today's Kansu Province, where some of their descendants can still be found; the majority moved to the Tarim Basin and created a new state centered on the city of Kocho (850–1250), where a sophisticated, multilingual, and multiethnic civilization developed. A cultured leisure class in the refined society supported Buddhism, Manichaeism, the arts and letters, and lavish entertainments. Here, the Uighurs adopted a completely sedentarized life based on agriculture supported by extensive irrigation works. As Kocho was a main stop on the east-west trade route, economic prosperity played a major role in the growth of Uighur civilization. When the Kitans, a Mongol people who overthrew the Kirghiz in 924, offered to let the Uighurs return to their former steppe lands, the Uighurs declined to move, preferring their life in Kocho. In 1250, the kingdom of Kocho voluntarily submitted to the Mongols. Uighur script was adopted by the Mongols and many Uighur scribes became skilled administrators for the Mongols. The famous German Turfan expeditions of 1902–1903, 1904–1905, and 1905–1907, led by A. Grünwedel and Albert von Le Coq, unearthed from the dry sands of the Tarim Basin the glories of the kingdom of Kocho: unparalleled art treasures including Manichaean and Buddhist frescoes and manuscripts in many languages, illuminating the splendor of Uighur civilization.

Mongols. The rise of Mongol power and the domination of the Chinggisid states brought unification to Inner Asia in a way that had not existed since prehistoric times.

Central Asia before the Mongol conquest. Arab penetration into Central Asia began in 652 and culminated in the Battle of Talas (751), thus permitting the spread of Islam into Central Asia. Wars with the Uighurs had forced the Karluk west and in 999 they seized Bukhara, an act that brought strong Turkic influence to the region. Farther to the west on the steppe north of the Black and Caspian seas lived the Turkic tribes of the Kipchaks (known also as Cumans or Polovtsy), whose move to these regions is shrouded in mystery. To the south of them, the Oghuz tribes—mentioned in the Orkhon inscriptions—were steadily moving westward, into Anatolia, where they were to form the basis of the Ottoman state.

The rise of Inner Asian powers in Manchuria. A mixture of forests rich in game, agricultural land made fertile by abundant rainfall, and pastures suitable for horse and cattle breeding determined the basic economy of Manchuria. The settled way of life also made pig raising an important feature of all Manchurian civilizations. In the fourth century, the Mongol-speaking Kitan began to gain dominance in the region, entering into relations with China in 468, but by the sixth century, they came under Türk domination. A new Kitan rise to power was signalled by their attack and defeat of the Kirghiz ruling over the Mongolian steppe in 924; they then expanded their rule over North China, adopting the Chinese dynastic title of Liao (927–1125). In 1125 Kitan domination was replaced by that of the Jurchen, a Tunguz-speaking Manchurian people who had been Kitan subjects. The Jurchen assumed the Chinese dynastic title of Chin (1125–1234) and maintained their rule over northern China until the Mongol conquest. When the Jurchen moved into North China, some Kitan tribes, with the permission of the Uighurs, moved west across the Tarim Basin through the kingdom of Kocho to Central Asia, where a third Kitan state was founded (after those of Manchuria and China), that of the Karakitai (Black Kitan or Kitai) centered at Balasagun in the Chu River valley.

Chinggis Khan and the Mongol conquest. Between Central Asia and Manchuria, two major mongolized Turkic tribes, the Naiman and the Kereit, were vying for power in the eleventh century. Both tribes had been strongly influenced by Nestorianism; the conversion of the Kereit around 1000 was related by the Syriac chronicler Bar Hebraeus (fl. thirteenth century). [*See also* Nestorian Church.] The first united Mongol kingdom ended in the late eleventh century, followed by a period of internecine warfare between Mongol tribes and against the neighboring Tatar tribes. It was not until Chinggis (known as Temüjin before he was elected khan) had defeated all of his rivals that a new and powerful Mongol state emerged. These events, chronicled in *The Secret History of the Mongols* (mid-thirteenth century), were only the first shadows of what was to come as the Mongol empire spread over the Eurasian continent.

Chinggis, angered by the Naiman leader Küchlüg, who had defeated the Karakitai in Central Asia, began the great push west, defeating the Naiman in 1218, and then led a punitive campaign against Khorezm aimed at avenging the murder of Mongol envoys. Before Chinggis's death in 1227, Central Asia had been devastated, and the campaigns of the famous Mongol generals Jebe and Sübetei had spilled into Georgia, across the Caucasus, and into Russian territory, where the Russian forces and their Cuman allies were defeated in the Battle of Kalka in the late spring of 1223. The Mongols advanced as far as the city of Bulgar where they were turned back at the very end of the year 1223. With the death of Chinggis, the Mongol empire was to be divided among his four sons. But the eldest son, Jochi, predeceased Chinggis and his appanage of the westernmost Mongols, the so-called Golden Horde, went to his son, Chinggis's grandson, Batu. Of the remaining sons, Čagadai's domains were in Central Asia, Tolui remained on the homeland, and Ögedei was elected great khan in 1229. (See figure 1.) [*See also the biography of Chinggis Khan.*]

The Mongols in Europe. Defeating Bulgar in the winter of 1237–1238, the Mongols then swept into eastern and central Europe with a great offensive begun in the winter of 1239–1240: Kiev fell on 6 December 1240, German forces were defeated at the Battle of Liegnitz on 9 April 1241, and the Hungarian army fell two days later. Suddenly, in 1242, the Mongols withdrew from Europe and returned to the rich pastures of the south Russian steppe. All of Europe now accepted the Mongol threat as real, however, an attitude that opened a period of rapprochement in Mongol-Western relations, begun by Pope Innocent IV (r. 1234–1254) at the Council of Lyons (June 1245). Three groups of papal emissaries were sent to the Mongols: the Dominican Ascelinus, the Dominican Andrew of Longjumeau, and the Franciscan Giovanni da Pian del Carpini, who brought back the first extensive accounts of the Mongols, as did the later

FIGURE 1. *Genealogy of the House of Chinggis*

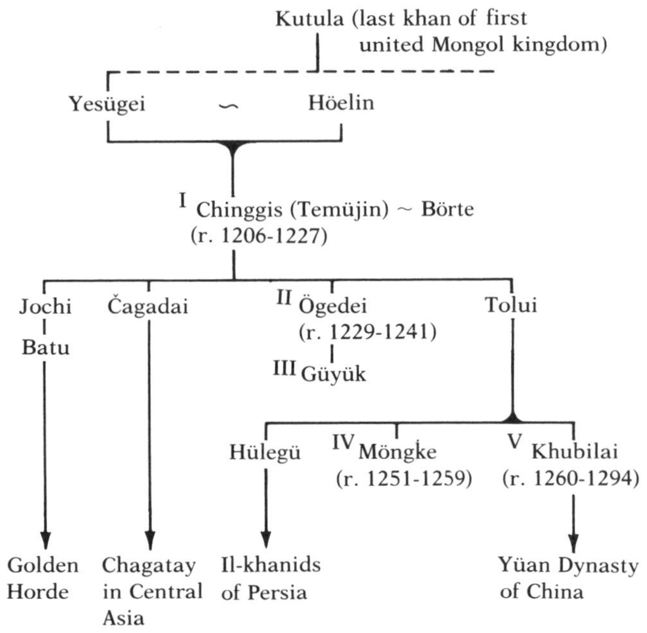

FIGURE 2. *Genealogy of the Golden Horde*

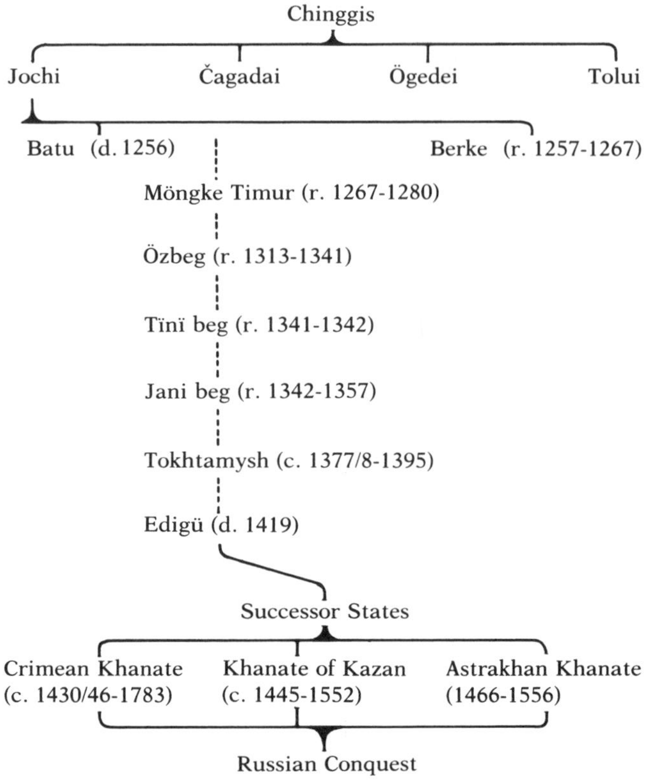

Franciscan missionary William of Rubruck, who journeyed to the Mongols from 1253 to 1255.

The Golden Horde and the Il-khanids. With Batu's death in 1256, his brother Berke (r. 1257–1267) became ruler of the Golden Horde. He converted to Islam, thus placing the Golden Horde at odds with the Il-khanids of Persia. The Il-khanids came to power under Hülegü, who sacked Baghdad in 1258 and ended the Abbasid caliphate. The Mamluk sultan Baybars (r. 1259–1277), powerful foe of the Crusaders but also of the Mongols, defeated the Il-khanid forces in the Battle of Ain Jalut (1259), thereby stopping the Mongol conquest of the Arab world. During the reign of the Il-khan Arghun (r. 1284–1291), Buddhism was declared the state religion and close contact was maintained with Europe, particularly with the Vatican and the kings of France and England. Under severe economic pressure, Il-khanid Persia declined and religious tension forced Gazan (r. 1295–1304) to proclaim Islam the official religion. With the death of Abu Saʿīd in 1335, Il-khanid Persia fragmented. (See figure 2.) Meanwhile, the power of the Golden Horde reached its apogee under Özbeg (r. 1313–1341), but attempts to expand its territory brought it into military conflict with ambitious Muscovite princes and the great military leader Timur (Tamarlane; 1336–1405) in Central Asia. Finally, the Golden Horde split into three successor states: the khanates of Kazan, Astrakhan, and the Crimea. (See figure 3.)

The Mongols in China. It was Khubilai (r. 1260–1294), the last great Mongol khan, who brought China under Mongol rule (the Yüan dynasty, 1264–1368). With the extended visit of Marco Polo to Khubilai's court (1271–1292) the first reliable information about China came to the West. After the death of Khubilai, Mongol rule in China began to weaken until they were overthrown in 1368 by the Chinese. What remained of Mongol power returned to the steppe where the western Mongols (Oirats, Dzungars, Kalmuks) became a factor in Central Asia, with two successive Oirat states menacing the territory between the western Mongolian steppe and the Caspian Sea from the mid-fifteenth century until their final defeat in 1758 at the hands of the Chinese.

With the decline of the Mongol empire, the patterns of Inner Asian civilization were well established. The development of firearms eliminated the advantages of the Inner Asian warrior: the economic structure of Inner Asia could not technologically advance. The change from land routes to sea routes considerably diminished Inner Asia's role as an intermediary between east and west. Even though the last Chinese dynasty, the Chʻing (1644–1911) was Manchu, founded by Tunguz-speaking peoples from Manchuria, it rapidly became sinicized, losing much of its Inner Asian character at a very early date. The simultaneous penetration by Russia and

FIGURE 3. *Genealogy of the Il-khanids of Persia*

Chinggis
- Jochi
- Čagadai
- Ögedei
- Tolui
  - Hülegü (r. 1258-1265)
    - Abagha (r. 1265-1282)
    - Arghun (r. 1284-1291)
    - Gaykhatu (r. 1291-1295)
    - Gazan (r. 1295-1304)
    - Öljeitü (r. 1304-1316)
    - Abu Sa'id (r. 1316-1335)
  - Möngke
  - Khubilai

China had profoundly changed the structure of Inner Asian civilization. The history of these later periods, not typically Inner Asian, does not shed light on what made the civilization of Central Eurasia unique.

[*See also* Turkic Religions; Mongol Religions; Islam, *article on* Islam in Central Asia; *and* Prehistoric Religions, *article on* The Eurasian Steppes and Inner Asia.]

BIBLIOGRAPHY

The classic definition of Inner Asia can be found in Denis Sinor's "Central Eurasia," in *Orientalism and History*, 2d rev. ed., edited by Denis Sinor (Bloomington, Ind., 1970), pp. 93–119, and expanded in textbook form in his *Inner Asia: History, Civilization, Languages; A Syllabus* (Bloomington, Ind., 1969). Sinor's *Introduction à l'étude de l'Eurasie Centrale* (Wiesbaden, 1963) is the basic bibliographic work for the study of Inner Asia and is invaluable for the author's opinion on research in a field dominated by French, German, Russian, and Hungarian scholarship. Other histories of Inner Asia that can be consulted with profit include René Grousset's *The Empire of the Steppes: A History of Central Asia*, translated by Naomi Walford (New Brunswick, N.J., 1970); Wilhelm Barthold's *Turkestan down to the Mongol Invasion*, 3d ed. (London, 1968); and the collection of essays in the *Handbuch der Orientalistik*, vol. 5.5, *Geschichte Mittelasiens*, under the general editorship of Bertold Spuler (Leiden, 1966). *The Cambridge History of Inner Asia*, under preparation by its editor, Denis Sinor, will bring the scholarship on Inner Asia up to date.

For the art of Inner Asia, Karl Jettmar's *The Art of the Steppes*, translated by Ann E. Keep (New York, 1967), provides an excellent introduction plus ample illustrations both in black and white and in color. The best book on the epic in Inner Asia is Nora K. Chadwick and Victor Zhirmunsky's *Oral Epics of Central Asia* (Cambridge, 1969), but it concerns only the Turkic-speaking peoples.

For a discussion of the early Arab penetration into Inner Asia, which opened the region to Islam, H. A. R. Gibb's *The Arab Conquests in Central Asia* (London, 1923) remains a useful account. In a similar vein, Owen Lattimore's *The Inner Asian Frontiers of China* (New York, 1940) and *Studies in Frontier History: Collected Papers 1928–1958* (Oxford, 1962) are unique in that much of Lattimore's life has been spent in the region.

The most extensive portrayal of the life of the Scythians can be found in Ellis H. Minn's *Scythians and Greeks: A Survey of Ancient History and Archeology on the North Coast of the Euxine from the Danube to the Caucasus* (Cambridge, 1913). The most detailed account of the Huns is J. Otto Maenchen-Helfen's *The World of the Huns: Studies in Their History and Culture*, edited by Max Knight (Berkeley, 1973). Annemarie von Gabain's work on the Uighur kingdom of Kocho, *Das Leben im uigurischen Königreich von Qočo: 850–1250*, in "Veröffentlichungen der Societas Uralo-Altaica," vol. 6 (Wiesbaden, 1973), is unparalleled. There is no good history of the Türk empire, a gap that will be filled by *The Cambridge History of Inner Asia.*

For the Mongols, however, there is an abundance of material. René Grousset's *Conqueror of the World*, translated by Denis Sinor in collaboration with Marian MacKellar (Edinburgh, 1967), is the best book on the life of Chinggis. For the Mongol Il-khans and the Golden Horde, Bertold Spuler's *The Muslim World: A Historical Survey*, vol. 2, *The Mongol Period* (Leiden, 1960); *Die Goldene Horde: Die Mongolen in Russland, 1223–1502*, 2d ed. (Wiesbaden, 1965); and *Die Mongolen in Iran* (Leipzig, 1939) are by far the most useful in this complex period of Mongol history.

RUTH I. MESERVE

INNOCENT I, bishop of Rome (401–417). We know nothing about Innocent's early life save the fact that, according to Jerome, he was the son of his predecessor, Anastasius I (r. 399–401). His episcopacy took place during the period of Rome's decline and witnessed some important events, namely, the displacement of Milan by Ravenna as the seat of imperial administration in the West (c. 404) and the sack of Rome in 410 by Alaric the Goth. Only thirty-five of Innocent's letters survive, in a variety of sources. A few are short administrative documents, but others are more personal and reveal a vigorous personality with decided views. The severe proscriptions against heretics issued at Rome in 407 by the emperor Flavius Honorius and later incorporated into book 16 of the Theodosian Code were probably inspired by Innocent.

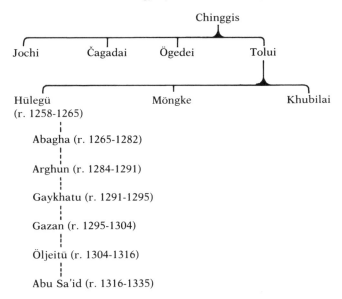

In ecclesiastical matters Innocent took a strong stand with regard to the prerogatives of his see, which he viewed as the ultimate court of appeal in all important ecclesiastical cases, claiming Roman supremacy over church councils and church courts. Through his letter to Decentius, bishop of Gubbio, Innocent was the first pope to voice such a claim of dominion in the realm of liturgy as well. The church at Gubbio was considering using some liturgical rites (probably deriving from Gaul) that deviated from Roman practice. Innocent asserted that Decentius should not depart from the Roman norm—an understandable attitude, since Gubbio was a suffragan see—but went on to censure all other churches in the West (Spain, Gaul, Sicily, and Africa) for not following Roman usage. This stand of Innocent's was without precedent. The letter to Decentius remains a precious historical source on the Roman liturgy of this period.

Innocent's letters to Victricius and Exsuperius, bishops of Rouen and Toulouse, deal with numerous points of ecclesiastical discipline. His statement (to Exsuperius) that marital relations are forbidden to married men from the time of their ordination may indicate that his own birth occurred early in the career of his father, Anastasius I. Other groups of letters show Innocent's involvement with events in Africa and the East. His correspondence with the bishops of Africa deals with the Pelagian controversy; five bishops, including Augustine, had appealed to Innocent for a condemnation. He denounced the error but did not contest the decision of the Palestinian bishops, who had pardoned Pelagius. In the East, Innocent intervened as a supporter of John Chrysostom, the persecuted and exiled bishop of Constantinople, and of Jerome in his struggle with John, bishop of Jerusalem. Innocent also brought the churches of eastern Illyria, which had been part of the Eastern Empire since 388, back into Western jurisdiction.

The principles and precedents established by Innocent became the foundation for many of the claims later made by the medieval papacy. Innocent's policies reflect both his own strong personality and the ecclesiopolitical situation of the time, when the ascendancy of a new Rome at Constantinople, and the decline of the old Rome, helpless before Alaric, invited the consolidation and assertion of power by the incumbents of the see of Peter, the only apostolic see in the West.

BIBLIOGRAPHY

Innocent I's letters can be found in J.-P. Migne's *Patrologia Latina*, vol. 20, *Epistolae et decreta* (Paris, 1845), cols. 457–637. Not all are genuine; see Eligius Dekkers's *Clavis Patrum Latinorum* (Bruges, 1961), vol. 1, no. 1641. Only the letter to Decentius exists in a good critical edition, with commentary: *La lettre du pape Innocent Premier à Décentius de Gubbio, 19 mars 416*, edited and translated by Robert Cabié (Louvain, 1973). On the emergence of new papal claims and Innocent's role in that development, see Myron Wojtowytsch's *Papsttum und Konzile von den Anfängen bis zu Leo I, 440–461: Studien zur Entstehung der Überordnung des Papstes über Konzile* (Stuttgart, 1981), especially pages 205–264. Wojtowytsch (p. 205, n. 1) stresses that a new study of Innocent I is needed, although Erich Caspar's chapter on Innocent in his *Geschichte des Papsttums*, vol. 1, *Römische Kirche und Imperium Romanum* (Tübingen, 1930), pp. 296–343, still remains important. Gerald Bonner's review of Wojtowytsch's *Papsttum und Konzile* in the *Journal of Ecclesiastical History* 34 (July 1983): 451–453 suggests some added reasons for the fourth-century shifts in papal attitudes.

For Jerome's letter identifying Anastasius I as Innocent's father, see Epistle 130, sec. 16, of Isidor Hilberg's edition in *Corpus Scriptorum Ecclesiasticorum Latinorum*, vol. 56 (Vienna, 1918), p. 196.

PAUL MEYVAERT

INNOCENT III (Lothar of Segni, 1160?–1216), pope of the Roman Catholic church (1198–1216). Innocent was the son of Trasimund of Segni, a count of Campagna, and Clarissa Scotti, daughter of a distinguished Roman family. He was educated first in Rome, possibly at the Schola Cantorum; then in Paris, where he studied theology; and finally in Bologna, where he probably studied law for a short time. Clement III elevated him to the cardinal diaconate of Saints Sergius and Bacchus in 1190. Before becoming pope, Innocent was active in the Curia Romana and took part in a number of legal cases as an auditor. As cardinal, he wrote three theological tracts, *De miseria humane conditionis* (Misery of the Human Condition), *De missarum misteriis* (Mysteries of the Mass), and *De quadripartita specie nuptiarum* (Four Typologies of Marriage), in addition to sermons. *Mysteries of the Mass* and *Misery of the Human Condition* enjoyed enormous popularity until the sixteenth century. Innocent was not a profound theological thinker. His thought was derivative and conventional, even a little old-fashioned.

When Innocent became pope in January 1198, the political situation in Italy and the German empire was very unstable. Emperor Henry VI had died in 1197 after subjecting most of the Italian Peninsula to imperial authority. He left a young son, the future Frederick II, and two rival claimants for the imperial throne, his brother, Philip of Hohenstaufen, and Otto of Brunswick. Innocent skillfully extracted promises from both candidates that they would respect the integrity of the papal states. He regained control over the city of Rome and gradually reasserted papal hegemony over the Patrimony of Saint Peter. Although he eventually turned to Henry VI's young son Frederick in 1212, Innocent used the rivalry of Philip and Otto to establish the pope's right to judge a disputed imperial election in an important decretal, *Venerabilem*. He also indicated the importance of imperial affairs for the church by entering many letters, papal and secular, in a special register, the *Regestum super negotio imperii*.

Lack of imperial leadership during his pontificate permitted Innocent to strengthen papal prerogatives outside the papal states and inside the church. He received the kingdom of Sicily as a fief and was regent to young Frederick. In the Roman church he reorganized the Curia and managed the complex administrative and judicial affairs with consummate skill. He developed a new vision of papal monarchy, using earlier traditions, but with a powerful change of emphasis. An ingenious biblical exegete who cleverly used the Bible to support his vision of papal monarchy, he exalted the pope and his authority within the church as no earlier pope had done, and also attempted to mediate the affairs of secular rulers. He extolled the pope's status as Vicar of Christ, placing him above man but below God. The pope exercised divine authority granted by Christ only to him and held fullness of power *(plenitudo potestatis)* within the church.

Innocent formulated most of his ideas about ecclesiastical government early in his pontificate. His theories had practical consequences of strengthening the judicial hierarchy of the church, underlining the pope's position of supreme judge, and, at the same time, fundamentally destroying the last vestiges of the decentralized church of the early Middle Ages. He demanded the subordination of the bishops to the pope and insisted that all episcopal translations, resignations, and depositions fall entirely under papal jurisdiction. His anonymous biographer and other chroniclers drew a picture of a pope with enormous capacity and skill in judicial affairs, who frequently participated in the cases before the papal court and enjoyed the exercise of authority.

During Innocent's pontificate, law became a central concern of ecclesiastical government. He authenticated a collection of his decisions and sent them to the law school in Bologna in 1209–1210. This collection, the first officially promulgated code of canon law, signaled Innocent's awareness that the papacy was an institution with many of the same concerns as secular states. He heard appeals from all parts of Christendom, issued rulings on disputed points of law, and established a professional cadre of trained men in Rome to carry out his policies.

Crusades. Innocent called for a new, papally led crusade in August 1198 and imposed a special tax on the clergy to support it. Although the Fourth Crusade (1202–1204) lacked strong leadership and sufficient money, Constantinople, capital of the Byzantine empire, was successfully assaulted in 1204. Innocent hoped that the conquest of Constantinople would result in the reunification of the Latin and Greek churches, but his hopes were in vain.

In 1218 he summoned another crusade, for which he made final arrangements at the Fourth Lateran Council (1215). Although he died before the Fifth Crusade (1217–1221) departed, it bore his imprint. Financed by the church and directed by the papacy, this crusade was a more sophisticated attempt to elaborate the policies Innocent had conceived in 1198. It was the last attempt of the papacy to organize a crusade without strong secular leadership.

Innocent also turned his attention to the proliferation of heretics, especially in the papal states. In 1199 he issued *Vergentis*, which decreed that condemned heretics should be dispossessed of their lands because heresy is treason. In effect, he defined the church as a state that the heretics had betrayed. This new conception of heresy led to his calling a crusade against the heretics of southern France, the Albigensian crusade (1208–1229). An army was gathered together under the leadership of a papal legate, Arnold Amalric, and at a heavy cost in lives the crusade was successful in extirpating heresy in Languedoc.

Pastoral Care and Reform. Innocent exalted the authority of the pope but also had a profound understanding of his pastoral duties. His ability to balance power and solicitude marks him as the greatest pope of the Middle Ages. In November 1215, some 412 bishops convened in Rome to take part in the Fourth Lateran Council. The council's seventy-one canons reflect Innocent's concerns. Heresy and the crusade were important items on the agenda—canon 8 established the foundations for the Inquisition—but the canons covered a wide range of other topics. Canon 18 forbade the participation of clerics in ordeals, which necessitated changes of judicial procedure in secular courts; canon 21 dictated that all Christians should confess their sins and receive Communion once a year; canon 50 changed the limits of consanguinity and affinity for marriage from seven to four degrees. Innocent also promulgated a number of canons regulating the lives of the clergy and the administration of churches.

The Fourth Lateran Council was the most important general council of the Middle Ages and provided a fitting end to Innocent's pontificate. Its canons are a measure of Innocent's strengths and serve as a guidepost for his policies. Innocent may have, in the words of the thirteenth-century Franciscan, Salimbene, involved the church too much in worldly affairs, but he was a militant pastor and a great monarch.

BIBLIOGRAPHY

Ernest F. Jacob's chapter on Innocent in the *Cambridge Medieval History,* vol. 6, edited by J. R. Tanner et al. (1929; reprint, Cambridge, 1957), pp. 1–43, though dated, is still readable and full of insights. For a longer treatment, Helene Tillmann's *Pope Innocent III* (1954), translated by Walter Sax from the German (New York, 1980), is sympathetic but not uncritical, and sprinkled with keen observations. Christopher R. Cheney's *Pope Innocent III and England,* "Päpste und Papsttum," vol. 9 (Stuttgart, 1976), is a brilliant study, the sum of a lifetime's work, and broader than its title might indicate. Three German scholars have recently discussed Innocent's thought and policies: Helmut Roscher's *Papst Innocenz III. und die Kreuzzüge* (Göttingen, 1969) examines all aspects of Innocent's crusades; Manfred Laufs's *Politik und Recht bei Innocenz III.* (Cologne, 1980) describes the dispute between Philip of Hohenstaufen and Otto of Brunswick, and Innocent's handling of this complex problem; Wilhelm Imkamp's *Das Kirchenbild Innocenz' III., 1198–1216,* "Päpste und Papsttum," vol. 22 (Stuttgart, 1983), explores the theological basis of Innocent's ecclesiology. Brian Tierney gives a masterful analysis of Innocent's ideas on the relationship of church and state in "'Tria quippe distinquit iudicia. . . .': A Note on Innocent III's Decretal *Per venerabilem,*" *Speculum* 37 (1962): 48–59. Innocent's vision of papal monarchy is studied in my book *Pope and Bishops: The Papal Monarchy in the Twelfth and Thirteenth Centuries* (Philadelphia, 1984). Editions of Innocent's works cited at the beginning of the article can be found in Cheney and Imkamp.

KENNETH PENNINGTON

INNOKENTII VENIAMINOV (John Popov Veniaminov, 1797–1879), known in English as Innocent; Russian Orthodox missionary to Alaska, bishop of Siberia and Alaska, metropolitan of Moscow. Born into a poor clerical family in the village of Anga, near Irkutsk (south-central Siberia), John Popov received his early education from his father, the church sacristan. From 1806 to 1818 he attended the seminary in Irkutsk, where he was an outstanding student. During this period, his surname was changed to Veniaminov.

After his marriage, Veniaminov served as a priest in Irkutsk. When the Russian-American Company called for volunteers to serve as missionary priests, he at first refused, but changed his mind after hearing of the zeal of the Aleuts for the Christian message. In 1823 he set out with his wife, son, brother, and mother for the fourteen-month journey to Unalaska in the Aleutian chain. His first task there was to build his own house and a church.

Veniaminov studied the Aleutian language, creating an alphabet and teaching the Aleuts to read and write. One of the books he wrote in Aleut, *A Guide to the Way to the Heavenly Kingdom,* was translated into Russian and went through forty-six editions. Veniaminov was also an outstanding scientist and anthropologist. A series of his articles, published in Russia, aroused so much interest that they also were published in French and German journals. His three-volume *Notes on the Islands of the Unalaska District* remains a basic reference work. Veniaminov's main interest, however, was in the conversion of the Aleuts. His careful work in evangelism and teaching left an established church.

After ten years in the Aleutians, Veniaminov was transferred to Sitka in southeast Alaska and commenced work among the Tlingit, a tribe previously hostile to both Russian culture and religion. Upon completing fourteen years of missionary service, he returned to Russia to oversee the printing of his Aleutian translations. When his wife died, he entered the monastic ranks, taking the name Innokentii. He was then made bishop of the newly created Diocese of North America and Kamchatka (1840).

Innokentii returned to Sitka in 1841, but was not content to direct affairs from his episcopal residence. He traveled widely over his scattered diocese, visiting areas that had rarely seen a priest. He changed his episcopal residence three times to be on the front line of the missionary expansion of his diocese. As the result of his efforts, the synod enlarged his diocese and elevated him to archbishop in 1850.

In 1868, at the age when he normally would have retired to a monastery, Innokentii was elected primate of the Russian church. This honor was truly a crown to his life's work, as it enabled him to submit new plans and to press for reforms in the Orthodox church. The most far-reaching project was the establishment of the Orthodox Missionary Society (1870), which put Russian missionary activity on a sound financial footing for the first time. The society was an attempt to mobilize the whole church by the formation of local diocesan committees, and its work continued into the twentieth century.

Innokentii's influence extended beyond his own dioceses. He encouraged Nikolai Kassatkin, Orthodox chaplain to the Russian consulate in Hakodate, Japan, to learn Japanese. Kassatkin credited Innokentii's advice and example as part of the impetus that resulted in the establishment of the Japanese Orthodox church. Innokentii worked toward the establishment of an independent Diocese of North America with the episcopal see to be located in either San Francisco or New York. He was canonized on 6 October 1977 by the Holy Synod of the Church of Russia and honored with the title Evangelizer of the Aleuts and Apostle to America.

BIBLIOGRAPHY

Innokentii's writings and a biography are available in seven volumes in *Innokentii Mitropolit Moskovskii i Kolomenskii, Tvo-*

reniia (Writings) and *Pis'ma* (Letters), edited by I. P. Barsukov (Moscow, 1883–1888; Saint Petersburg, 1897–1901). The only full-length biography in English is Paul D. Garrett's *Saint Innocent, Apostle to America* (Crestwood, N.Y., 1979). Valuable information is found in Josef Glazik's *Die russisch-orthodoxe Heidenmission seit Peter dem Grossen* (Münster, 1954), Hector Chevigny's *Russian America: The Great Alaskan Venture, 1741–1867* (New York, 1965), and Gregory Afonsky's *A History of the Orthodox Church in Alaska, 1794–1917* (Kodiak, Alaska, 1977). Two articles in *Saint Vladimir's Theological Quarterly* refer to materials in the U. S. Library of Congress: Vsevolod Rocheau's "Innocent Veniaminov and the Russian Mission to Alaska, 1820–1840," 15 (1971): 105–120; and Dmitry Grigorieff's "Metropolitan Innocent: The Prophetic Missionary," 21 (1977): 18–36; they are excellently researched introductions.

James J. Stamoolis

INQUISITION, THE. The Inquisition of medieval Europe was a special tribunal established under ecclesiastical and civil authority to contend with the extraordinary problems of authority created by the growth of Christian heresies. It originated between the late twelfth and mid-thirteenth centuries, but its theoretical roots lay as much in classical Roman law as in the theology of the Middle Ages. In the late Roman empire the maintenance of social order required prohibition of what were viewed as antisocial activities, such as sorcery, sacrilege, and treason, all of which were punishable by death. The emperor Diocletian (d. 313) issued an edict against the Manichaeans, "Oriental" dualists, who were to be burned along with their writings. Other intrusive sects, such as Christians, were subject to control and on occasion to capital punishment. However, with the advent of toleration in the reign of Constantine (d. 337), roles were reversed and Christian leaders were faced with the need to formulate policy regarding the conversion of pagans and the elimination of unorthodox Christian beliefs. Most early church fathers specified that blood was not to be shed in the pursuit of religious uniformity, but some, such as Augustine of Hippo (d. 430), confronted by the threat of religious rivalry in Donatism, held that coercion would be appropriate in some cases, a sentiment echoed later in the imperial legislation of the codes of Theodosius (fifth century) and Justinian (sixth century). [*For further discussion, see* Persecution, *article on* Christian Experience, *and* Heresy, *article on* Christian Heresies.]

After the fall of the Western Empire in the fifth century, the political fragmentation of Europe undermined church organization. Henceforth, the task of church leaders would be limited to maintaining episcopal continuity while attempting to convert the pagans and Arian Christians of the so-called barbarian kingdoms. By the time of Charlemagne (d. 814), the church in most of Europe, while enjoying the protection of secular powers, lacked organizational and doctrinal unity. In these circumstances, the problem of heresy was dealt with on an *ad hoc* basis. In any event, the heresies of the period before about AD 1000 in Europe did not present a serious threat, since they were limited to the writings of a few intellectuals or to the desultory activities of groups of peasants swayed by the rantings of semiliterate preachers. Such sporadic outbursts were controlled by secular, episcopal, or papal means.

The Early Medieval Inquisition. During the eleventh century, western European society began a metamorphosis that led to great cultural and social achievements during the twelfth and thirteenth centuries. The church found strong leadership in the reformers who had brought institutional and doctrinal innovations to the eleventh-century papacy. Monastic reform, exemplified by Cluny, provided centers of spiritual and liturgical power throughout the West, while the laity discovered a new consciousness of social cohesion through the Peace and Truce of God movements, church-sponsored attempts to control noble and knightly ravages. In the midst of eleventh-century social and economic expansion, a sense of spiritual unity was born: Europe had become Christendom. At the end of the century, this spiritual unanimity shared by laity and clergy alike manifested itself in the First Crusade, called in 1095.

Long before the First Crusade, however, this new sense of Christian unity was evident in reactions to heretics, who now seemed, to townspeople and rulers alike, to threaten society itself: hence the public burning of a dozen or so heretics at Orleans in 1022, at the command of King Robert and with public approval. In addition, the three-year-old corpse of a heretic was exhumed and ejected from its Christian burial ground. Heretics were burned by popular demand at Milan about 1028, while Henry III of Germany allowed the hanging of purported Cathari at Goslar in 1052. In most cases of executions by mobs or lay rulers, the church was not involved; although it wished to curtail heresy and bring heretics to repentance, it did not condone their execution.

In the twelfth century, antiheretical activities on the part of church and lay princes accelerated. The dualist Cathari—some of whom may have been victims of eleventh-century popular violence—were expanding into western Europe from eastern Europe, particularly into regions where secular authority was weak or fragmented by competing powers, as in southern France (Languedoc) and northern Italy (Lombardy). In these areas, Cathari and other sects (such as the Waldensians) were able to establish themselves in the midst of relatively tolerant Roman Catholics; it was more difficult for the heretics elsewhere. Mobs and secular authorities continued to put heretics to death, as at Soissons, Cologne, and Liège, and the king of Aragon officially decreed burning as the penalty for heresy in 1197. [*See also* Cathari *and* Waldensians.]

The church dealt with heresy in several twelfth-century councils (Toulouse, 1119; Second Lateran, 1139; Reims, 1157; Tours, 1163), prescribing as punishments excommunication, confiscation of property, and imprisonment. The church still did not recognize death as a proper penalty. The secular arm of Christendom was asked to help in the apprehension of heretics; and, on occasion, lay powers turned to the church for assistance. Count Raymond V of Toulouse requested more Cistercian preachers to combat heresy in southern France; as a result, a papal legate and others came to Toulouse in 1178, but their efforts had little effect. The following year, at the Third Lateran Council, Pope Alexander III, with this failure in mind, called attention to the need to quell the Cathari of Languedoc and to confiscate their lands, and again he requested aid from secular lords. The earlier conciliar legislation had had limited effect, however, and in 1184 Pope Lucius III, in association with Emperor Frederick Barbarossa (d. 1190), issued more specific orders. In the bull *Ad abolendam,* Lucius regularized the episcopal inquisition, requiring bishops to visit their parishes and ascertain, through witnesses, who was engaged in heretical activity. The accused were to be apprehended and examined. If the charges were proven, but the accused refused to accede to ecclesiastical authority, they were to be handed over to the secular power for due punishment *(animadversio debita).* The punishment, however, was not specified by the pope.

The use of the inquisition *(inquisitio)* in criminal cases was well known in later Roman law (along with *accusatio* and *denuntiatio*), and general inquests into criminal matters were already familiar to many twelfth-century European secular powers. Lucius formally attempted to apply this procedure, in which accuser and judge tended to merge, in actions against heretics. By 1184, the church had developed a coherent system of canon law, to a large extent founded upon Gratian's *Decretum* of the 1130s. In addition, the twelfth-century revival of the study of Roman law influenced the canonists. By the end of the century an intelligible program was evolving in the church's battle against heresy on the theoretical level. In 1199 Pope Innocent III (d. 1216), following the lead of earlier canonists, equated heresy with treason, in the bull *Vergentes in senium.* The obstinate were to be handed over, as traitors to God, to the secular powers for (unspecified) punishment, and their lands were confiscated. Roman concepts of *lèse-majesté,* and appropriate procedures and punishments, were beginning to be absorbed into canonical forms and penances.

The battle against heresy (especially Catharism) during the thirteenth century grew more rigorous and determined under the leadership of powerful popes. Innocent III commissioned Cistercian monks to preach and stir up antiheretical sentiment in Languedoc from 1203 to 1208; he also called upon the French king, Philip II, to mount a crusade against the Cathari in the south. Little was accomplished, however, until after the murder of a Cistercian preacher in 1208, for which the count of Toulouse (Raymond VI), as local ruler, was held responsible. Innocent's repeated call to crusade, with confiscation of heretics' lands, was answered by the barons of northern France. The Albigensian crusade, led by Simon de Montfort, lasted for some twenty years. Many Cathari, and orthodox Christians as well, were killed by the Crusaders, who invaded Languedoc for material as well as spiritual motives. Innocent III repeated earlier antiheretical canons in 1215 at the Fourth Lateran Council, encouraging episcopal inquisitions and calling upon the secular powers to aid the church. These canons were incorporated into imperial legislation by Frederick II (d. 1250) at his coronation in 1220; in addition, he explicitly equated heresy with treason. The emperor followed this up in 1224 when he decreed that, in his realm of Lombardy, relapsed heretics were to be burned at the stake; lesser offenders were to lose their tongues. In 1226, King Louis VIII of France, though not prescribing execution, ordered the confiscation of heretics' property.

In the later 1220s, the papacy experimented with a variety of antiheretical procedures. A Dominican assisted the priest Conrad of Marburg, who held inquisitions in Germany until his assassination in 1233; in Italy, Pope Gregory IX (d. 1241) commissioned the Dominican prior of Florence to prosecute a notorious heretic in 1227. Thus the new orders of friars (including, in later years, the Franciscans) were enlisted by the papacy. However, other agents continued to be used as inquisitors: at the Council of Toulouse (1229), teams of laymen, together with the parish priest, were ordered to seek out and denounce heretics to the bishop; at the end of the council, the papal legate himself held an inquisition. Elsewhere the episcopal inquisition still functioned, albeit somewhat ineffectively.

In the aftermath of the Albigensian crusade, many Cathari returned to Languedoc, but they were far more secretive: they had been driven underground, but not exterminated. Pope Gregory IX was determined to put an end to the heresy and in 1230 he began to enact severe legislation against it. Besides sending out friars as inquisitors, by 1231 he had adopted the canons of the Council of Toulouse (1229) and the punishment of death by fire prescribed by his enemy Emperor Frederick II (in 1224). In 1233 the pope established a tribunal at Toulouse, staffed by legatine-controlled Dominicans, who were to cooperate with the bishop in prosecuting heretics. The popular outcry caused by this inquisition—for its policy of exhuming the corpses of purported heretics, for example—was chronicled by William Pelhisson, one of the Dominican inquisitors assigned to the area. Other Dominicans operated elsewhere, such as the fanatical Robert le Bougre, who worked in northern France until the pope ordered him imprisoned for life. Although Gregory faced difficulties in securing the cooperation of many northern Italian cities, and for political reasons had to suspend the inquisition of Toulouse in 1238 (later reinstated), he had established the Inquisition in its basic outlines. In later decades its powers and procedures were to increase in extent and complexity.

The Cathari of Languedoc suffered a major setback—one from which they never really recovered—when their castle of Montségur was stormed in 1244, following the murder of a party of local inquisitors in 1242. More than two hundred Cathar leaders, known as the *perfecti*, were said to have been burned after the lengthy siege. The count of Toulouse (Raymond VII), hitherto negligent in pursuing heretics, burned eighty Cathari at Agen in 1249, the same year in which he himself died. Pope Innocent IV (d. 1254), as enthusiastic in his antiheretical activities as Gregory IX, applauded such developments.

In the late 1240s Innocent commissioned the first handbook of inquisitorial procedure, which was drawn up by two inquisitors of Languedoc. Such manuals continued to be compiled until the end of the Middle Ages. More significantly, in the bull *Ad extirpanda* (1252), Innocent ordered that heretics handed over to the secular arm should be executed within five days, and he ordained that torture could be used to elicit information for inquisitorial courts. In doing so, Innocent brought the special tribunal of the Inquisition into line with criminal procedure already followed by thirteenth-century lay governments. Not only the revival of Roman law (with its *inquisitio* and use of torture) but also the abolition of the ordeal and other divine aids encouraged a more rigorous application of human agencies to prove guilt in both secular and inquisitorial courts. During the Inquisition, hidden matters of conscience—normally revealed only to a confessor—were the central issue; extraordinary procedures were thought necessary to bring these to light. And, just as secular courts punished treason with death, the Inquisition allowed the same punishment for those suspected guilty of treason to God.

Inquisitorial Procedure. Between the mid-thirteenth century and the time of the inquisitor Bernard Gui (d. 1331), author of a well-known manual of practice in the early fourteenth century, a certain procedural sequence seems to have developed, although individual inquisitors altered their routines to fit local circumstances. In general, a place reputed to harbor heretics was visited by an inquisitor who, in a sermon that all were required to attend, preached about the iniquities of heresy and invited anyone who might have heretical tendencies, or who knew of others of such disposition, to appear before him and report these. A grace period of up to thirty days was allowed, after which the inquisitor began to summon those who had not voluntarily appeared but who were suspected (by local clergy or trusted laity) of heretical leanings. The inquisitor sent his summons with a cleric and witnesses to the suspect's house or, if it were thought appropriate, seized and placed him or her temporarily in the inquisitorial or civil prison. At the hearing, a suspect was questioned by the inquisitor or his deputy in the presence of two witnesses and a notary or scribe, who prepared a written summary of the proceedings. According to Gui, the suspect was presented with the depositions of the accusers but their names did not appear on those documents. Only two accusers were necessary, and the suspect had but one defense: if he could name his enemies (and sometimes he had to present his own witnesses to prove enmity), and the inquisitor saw that such an accuser had brought the charge because of enmity, the suspect could be freed. Otherwise, the suspect had the choice of either admitting heresy or denying it. If he admitted heresy, the suspect would be given the appropriate penance; if he denied it, according to Gui, he was returned to prison, which would "help" the suspect to discover his heresy; if imprisonment failed to bring about a confession, torture would be applied. Returned to the tribunal, the suspect would then confess his errors and be given penance. In some cases, suspects refused altogether to confess. They, and confessed heretics who had relapsed into their old beliefs, were liable to be handed over to the secular arm for punishment at the stake—although this did not invariably occur.

After all the suspects of a given locality had been investigated in this manner, including those *in absentia* who were automatically excommunicated, the inquisitor, after consultation with legal advisers, announced the sentences in a sermon *(sermo generalis)*. He began with the lightest penances and ended with release to the secular arm (which meant death) and the exhumation of the dead. The penances—known as such because technically the Inquisition did not "punish"—included attendance at masses and the taking of Communion, scourging by the clergy, pilgrimages, wearing of yellow crosses, seizure of property, destruction of heretics' houses, and imprisonment, technically for life, either in an "open prison" *(murus largus)* or chained into cells *(murus strictus)*. Exemptions, commutations, and bribery often reduced prison terms, however. When the secular power executed a heretic and confiscated his or her property (part of which went to the Inquisition), the heretic's progeny were disinherited and debarred from public office for two generations. The same consequences befell the heirs of a person who was posthumously found to be a heretic and whose corpse had been exhumed and burned. Heretics who abjured as they were led to the stake were sent to perpetual imprisonment, if their conversion seemed genuine; if not, their pleas were ignored. Appeals to the pope could be made only before sentencing, but not many could afford this; on the other hand, inquisitors were often willing to reduce sentences. When the inquisitor moved on, he took with him carefully collated notarial records that contained all the names and sentences dealt with; when he or his successor returned, perhaps years later, this incriminating material would be used again.

The Later Medieval Inquisition. The heresy of the Cathari, which had helped to bring the Inquisition into being, declined in Languedoc (after a brief revival in the early fourteenth century) and throughout western Europe; by the mid-fourteenth century it had virtually disappeared. At the same time, however, the Inquisition continued to develop in other areas of Europe along procedural lines laid down in the thirteenth century. Under papal leadership it spread into eastern Europe and Germany, though in the latter, local bishops sometimes resisted papal interference. England never accepted the institution, whereas by the later fifteenth century, it had been absorbed into the political machinery of Castile and Aragon and would result in the infamous Spanish Inquisition. The Spanish monarchs Ferdinand and Isabella used the inquisitorial machinery for their own political as well as religious ends. Their attempts to expand their authority through persecution of Moriscos and Marranos were guided by the Grand Inquisitor Tomás de Torquemada (1420–1498). [*See* Marranos *and the biography of Torquemada.*] In Italy, though Cathari were no longer a problem, the Waldensians continued to interest inquisitors, whose tasks were made more difficult by political rivalries among Italian city-states, and between these states and the papacy. During the sixteenth-century Counter-Reformation, the Inquisition, or Holy Office, underwent reorganization and centralization at Rome.

Political complications are also evident in France, where King Philip IV (d. 1314), in his conflict with the papacy, was sympathetic toward complaints levied against the Inquisition. By 1307, with a compliant pope, the king had turned the Inquisition against the Order of the Knights Templar, which was dissolved at the Council of Vienne (1312). From the mid-fourteenth century, the Parlement and University of Paris tended to exercise inquisitorial powers. Indeed, throughout its history the Inquisition was rivaled by local ecclesiastical and secular jurisdictions. No matter how determined, no pope ever succeeded in establishing complete control of the institution in western Europe: princes, bishops, civil authorities, and kings vacillated between acceptance and resistance.

Inquisitors in the fourteenth century continued to find heresies to occupy their attention, such as those of the heterogeneous, mystically inspired, and anticlerical groups known generally as the Brethren of the Free Spirit, who are often associated with the Beghards and the Béguines. The Spiritual Franciscans (Fraticelli) were subjected to inquisitorial tribunals in the fourteenth and even fifteenth centuries. By the end of the fifteenth century, a new, ominous aspect began to unfold, with prosecutions of sorcery and witchcraft, best illustrated in the witch-hunters' handbook of 1486, *Malleus maleficarum.* [*See* Witchcraft, *article on* Concepts of Witchcraft.]

Historical judgments on the medieval Inquisition have varied from absolute condemnation to qualified approval of at least some of its characteristics. Only a small portion of those who appeared before the Inquisition were sent to their deaths, and in this respect, it was more lenient than violent mobs or contemporary secular criminal courts; yet even in the thirteenth century, some, such as the lawyers who cautioned against the unrestricted use of torture, doubted whether this ecclesiastical tribunal, with its distinctive procedures, served the interests of Christendom.

BIBLIOGRAPHY

A brief, valuable introduction to the Inquisition is Bernard Hamilton's *The Medieval Inquisition* (London, 1982), with a bibliography of recent as well as older, standard works. Walter Ullmann's historical introduction to Henry C. Lea's *The Inquisition of the Middle Ages* (London, 1963) provides a good overview of historiographical changes since the late nineteenth century, when Lea wrote. Elphège Vacandard's *The Inquisition* (London, 1908), though somewhat erratic, is a general survey that also contains extensive excerpts from contemporary documents. The crucial twelfth and thirteenth centuries are well analyzed by Christine Thouzellier in "La répression de l'hérésie et les débuts de l'inquisition" in *Histoire de l'Église,* vol. 10, by Augustin Fliche and others (Paris, 1950). Henri Maisonneuve's

Études sur les origines de l'inquisition, 2d ed. (Paris, 1960), with full bibliography, is especially interesting in chapters 5 and 6, which set the Inquisition in broad historical context and explore the contrasts between northern and southern European attitudes toward it. A very useful research tool, listing nearly two thousand titles on the late medieval and postmedieval Inquisition, is E. van der Vekene's *Bibliographie der Inquisition: Ein Versuch* (Hildesheim, 1963). See also parts 8 and 9 of Herbert Grundmann's *Bibliographie zur Ketzergeschichte des Mittelalters, 1900–1966* (Rome, 1967), listing twentieth-century works, and Carl T. Berkhout and Jeffrey B. Russell's *Medieval Heresies: A Bibliography, 1960–1979* (Toronto, 1981), particularly part 17, "Repression." Much has been written about the Inquisition in southern France, such as Walter L. Wakefield's *Heresy, Crusade and Inquisition in Southern France, 1100–1250* (Berkeley, 1974), with extensive bibliography, and E. Le Roy Ladurie's *Montaillou: Cathars and Catholics in a French Village, 1294–1324,* translated by B. Bray (London, 1978), which provides an intimate look at how the Inquisition affected peasant life in a specific region. A good idea of contemporary procedure in Languedoc can be gained from Bernard Gui's *Manuel de l'inquisiteur,* 2 vols., translated by G. Mollat (Paris, 1926–1927), a practical guide for heretic hunters. Heretics and the Inquisition in southern France are the subjects of several issues of *Cahiers de Fanjeaux: Collection d'histoire religieuse du Languedoc au treizième et au début du quatorzième siècles* (Toulouse, 1966–). An example of recent historical studies outside this region is *Quellen zur Böhmischen Inquisition im 14 Jahrhundert,* edited by Alexander Patschovsky (Weimar, 1979), with a detailed introduction to over 150 pages of contemporary documents, including notarial registers. Interesting essays on heresy and its repression in general are R. I. Moore's *The Origins of European Dissent* (New York, 1977) and Edward Peters's *The Magician, the Witch and the Law* (Philadelphia, 1978), both containing astute observations on the legal and sociological aspects of repression.

R. C. FINUCANE

INSECTS appear in mythology not only as the gods, often as the creators of the world, but also as messengers to the gods. They serve sometimes as the agents of creation and frequently function as symbols of the human soul. Moreover, some insects, such as cicadas, beetles, and scarabs, often symbolize rebirth, resurrection, or eternal life.

According to the Lengua, a South American tribe of the Gran Chaco, a god in the shape of a huge beetle created the world and peopled it with mighty spirits. He holds aloof, however, from his creation and is not invoked in prayer. The butterfly is often worshiped as a god, sometimes as the creator. In Madagascar and smong the Naga of Manipur, some trace their ancestry to a butterfly. According to the Pima of North America, at the time of beginning the creator, Chiowotmahki, assumed the form of a butterfly and flew over the world until he found a suitable place for mankind.

It is, however, the spider that plays a prominent part in the myths of North American Indians; it appears as the creator (e.g., among the Sia Pueblo Indians) or culture hero, or at least as the trickster (among the Dakota Indians). The Jicarilla Apache believe that at the time of beginning, when creatures lived in the underworld, the spider spun a web in the hole leading up to the earth and, together with the fly, came up on it before the people emerged. The spider and the fly were told by the Holy Ones to make a web and extend it to the sky in order to bring down the sun. According to the Navajo, Spider Man and Spider Woman are supernatural beings who instructed their mythical ancestors in the art of weaving and established the four warnings of death. The spider is also conspicuous in West African myths. In some myths, he is creator of the world; in others, he plays the role of culture hero, as in the stories in which he steals the sun. However, his usual role is that of a crafty and cunning trickster who prospers by his wits. [*See* Tricksters.]

In Hindu mythology, ants are compared to a series of Indras. One day Indra in his palace receives a visit from a boy dressed in rags, who is Viṣṇu in disguise. While the boy speaks of the innumerable Indras who people the innumerable universes, a procession of ants appears in the great hall of the palace. Noticing them, the boy suddenly stops and bursts into laughter. "What are you laughing at?" asks Indra. The boy replies, "I saw the ants, O Indra, filing in long parade. Each was once an Indra. Like you, by virtue of pious deeds each one ascended to the rank of a king of the gods. But now, through many rebirths, each has become again an ant. This army is an army of former Indras."

In West Africa, ants are often viewed as the high god's messengers. In the Romanian creation myth, the bee serves as God's messenger. It also helps God to complete his creation with advice that it overhears from the hedgehog. Although the angry hedgehog puts a curse on it, condemning it to eat only ordure, God blesses the bee so that the filth it eats may become honey.

The bee is still an important symbol in Islam. The Qur'ān explicitly mentions it as a model of an "inspired" animal, and both Muḥammad and, even more, ʿAlī are connected in folklore with the pious and useful bee. Honey becomes sweet, it is said, because the bees hum blessings for the Prophet as they go about their work.

In some earth-diver myths, which speak of the origin of the earth from the primordial waters, insects serve as agents of creation. According to the Garo of Assam, the goddess Nosta-Nōpantu was to carry out the work of creation on behalf of the god Tattaro-Robuga. To get a particle of soil from the bottom of the primeval ocean, she sent in turn a large crab, a small crab, and a dung beetle. Only the dung beetle succeeded in bringing up a little clay, and from this Nosta-Nōpantu formed the earth. The Semang Negritos of the Malay Peninsula (such as the Menik Kaien, Kintak Bong, and Kenta tribes) similarly believe that the earth was brought up from the primeval ocean by a dung beetle, although in this version the insect seems to have dived on its own initiative. Among the Shan of Burma, the divers are ants. In North America, too, insects are known as earth divers among the Cherokee. In contrast to earth-diver myths are stories that speak of the celestial origin of the earth—as in the Indonesian and Micronesian cosmogonies—and in these myths, too, insects play an important role. The Toba and the Batak of Sumatra, for example, have preserved the tradition that a swallow and a large dung beetle brought down a handful of earth from the sky.

While bees, ants, and dragonflies often symbolize the souls of the dead, the image of the butterfly as the human soul is widely diffused in Europe, Asia, and the Pacific islands. The early Greeks sometimes depicted the soul as a diminutive person with butterfly wings, and later as a butterfly. A similar belief was shared by the Romans. The Maori of New Zealand believe that the soul returns to earth after death as a butterfly, and in the Solomon Islands a dying person, who has a choice as to what he will become at death, often chooses to become a butterfly. In Japan, the motif has been incorporated into *nō* dramas, and in the world of Islam, it is one of the favorite images of Sufism: the moth that immolates itself in the candle flame is the soul losing itself in the divine fire.

The cicada, on account of its metamorphosis, was well known in ancient China as a symbol of rebirth or renewal of life. According to the Arawak of Guyana, at the time of beginning the creator came down to earth to see how mankind was getting along. But men were so wicked that they tried to kill him; so he deprived them of eternal life and bestowed it instead on animals that renew their skin, such as serpents, lizards, and beetles. In ancient Egypt the scarab, a beetle of the Mediterranean region, was identified with the sun god Khepri and thus became a symbol both of the force that rolled the sun across the heavens and of the rising sun, self-generated. Scarab amulets made of green stone set in gold were placed over the heart of the dead during the funeral ceremony as a sign that just as the sun was reborn, so would the soul of the man be born again.

Insects are not always viewed as beneficent creatures. According to Northwest Coast Indians such as the Tlingit, the Haida, and the Tsimshian, mosquitoes are pests that originated from the ashes of an ogre's burned body. The same motif is found among the Ainu and in southern China. In Japanese mythology, spiders appear as a symbol of the evil forces that were subjugated by the heavenly gods before the imperial dynasty—and with it, Japan—was established.

BIBLIOGRAPHY

On insects playing a role in cosmogonic myths, see Mircea Eliade's *Zalmoxis, the Vanishing God: Comparative Studies in the Religions and Folklore of Dacia and Eastern Europe* (Chicago, 1972), pp. 76–130. See also Charles H. Long's *lpha: The Myths of Creation* (New York, 1963), pp. 44ff. There is a fine study of scarab symbolism in the Greco-Roman world in *Fish, Bread, and Wine*, volume 5 of Erwin R. Goodenough's *Jewish Symbols in the Greco-Roman Period* (New York, 1956), pp. 172ff. Schuyler Cammann discusses the symbolism of the cicada in his very useful essay "Types of Symbols in Chinese Art," in *Studies in Chinese Thought*, edited by Arthur F. Wright (Chicago, 1953). On the origin of mosquitoes, see Gudmund Hatt's *Asiatic Influences in American Folklore* (Copenhagen, 1949), pp. 89–90. On the Islamic symbolism of insects, there is an admirable study in Annemarie Schimmel's *The Triumphal Sun: A Study of the Works of Jalaloddin Rumi*, rev. ed. (London, 1980), pp. 108ff.

MANABU WAIDA

INSPIRATION. As it appears in the general history of religions, *inspiration* may be defined very broadly as a spiritual influence that occurs spontaneously and renders a person capable of thinking, speaking, or acting in ways that transcend ordinary human capacities. Taken in this general sense, the term refers to a form of religious experience that is widely distributed and found in a great variety of forms. Taken more narrowly, the actual term (which derives from the Latin *inspirare*, "to blow or breath upon") implies the existence of a *spiritus*, or "breath," that is breathed into the soul and enlivens it. Although inspiration may often be conceived in this way, its specificity as a religious phenomenon should not be located in an explicit notion of spiritual breath or divine spirit, since such a notion may be absent in cases where we would still wish to speak of inspiration. In such cases, inspiration may be attributed to the direct action of a god, or even to the effects of a particular kind of food or drink. What is common to most forms of inspiration is its efficacy as an influence that motivates or facilitates action, very often in the form of inspired speech or song. An understanding of inspiration is thus closely related to questions of human agency and its transcendence.

The use of the term *inspiration* should probably be restricted to those cases where human agency is transformed but not totally displaced. This would make it possible to contrast inspiration with trance, since in the latter, human agency is simply canceled out, to be replaced in most cases by the action of a possessing god, spirit, or ancestor. The notion of possession itself, however, which need not always imply a state of trance, can sometimes be used to account for particularly intense experiences of inspiration. The essential point is that inspiration never leads to a state of complete dissociation of the personality and subsequent amnesia, as is the case with trance. [*See also* Spirit Possession.]

One of the earliest historical forms of inspiration is that experienced by the *ṛṣi*s, or poet-seers, of the *Ṛgveda*. In composing their liturgical hymns, the *ṛṣi*s often invoked their gods to inspire their songs. The gods Mitra and Varuṇa, the Aśvins, and in particular the god Agni were asked to stimulate the visions of the seers, to animate or impel their speech, and to set their songs in motion. The verbs used in these contexts convey a sense of power: *cud-* ("to impel, animate"); *tuj-* ("to strike, instigate"); *hi-* ("to set in motion, urge on"). One of the most famous verses in the *Ṛgveda* (3.62.10), the so-called Gāyatrī, is in fact a prayer addressed to the god Savitṛ, asking for such inspiration, a verse that is recited daily by traditional Hindus. This example of the inspiration of the Vedic seers may be taken as representative of the phenomenon of inspiration among the ancient Indo-European peoples generally. This is illustrated most clearly by the Indo-European root **vat-* ("to blow," or more figuratively, "to inspire"). This root not only appears in the names *Ṛgveda* and *Avesta* but also underlies the Latin word *vates* ("seer, prophet, poet") and the Old Irish term *fáith* ("prophet, seer").

The Vedic seers also sought inspiration by drinking a special beverage called *soma*, which was used in the Vedic sacrifice. Here again one finds Indo-European parallels, both in the *haoma* found in ancient Iran, and in the legendary mead of the ancient Scandinavians, a drink that was believed to make anyone who drank it a poet or a visionary. [*See* Beverages.]

Whatever its exact source, inspiration is experienced as an impulse that either comes from without, or, if it arises within, does so spontaneously, in independence of the individual's will. In principle this trait distinguishes it from the ecstatic experience that is the defining characteristic of shamanism, since once initiated the shaman is capable of acting on his own and controlling the inhabitants of the spirit world for his own ends. [*See* Shamanism.] This autonomy is what gives shamans their importance as "technicians of the sacred." The inspired person is by contrast much more dependent upon a continuing source of inspiration.

In classical India an experience of spontaneous inspiration was sometimes referred to as *pratibhā*, a "flash" of insight that arose in an inexplicable way, free of any intentional cognitive act on the part of the subject. In Indian poetics, *pratibhā* became a common term for poetic inspiration. In early Mahāyāna Buddhism, it took on a distinctly religious value, referring to the inspired speech uttered spontaneously by a disciple in praise of the Buddha. It is, however, in later Hindu devotionalism *(bhakti)* that we find the most striking Indian examples of inspiration. In inspired states that are often hard to distinguish from states of possession, the devotees of Viṣṇu and Śiva (the Āḻvārs and Nāyaṉārs) composed thousands of hymns in honor of their god. One of the greatest of these, the Vaiṣṇava poet-saint Nammāḻvār (9th–10th century CE), spoke of being taken over by Viṣṇu, such that Viṣṇu himself sang through his mouth (*Tiruvāymoḻi* 7.9.1).

The connection of inspiration with poetry and song was also recognized in ancient Greece, where poets sought the inspiration of the Muses, much as their Indian counterparts might pray to Sarasvatī, the goddess of eloquence. Plato describes the inspiration of the Muses as a form of *mania* ("madness or frenzy") and makes the poet's art wholly dependent upon it. It is because the poet's mind is "taken away" by the gods that we know that it is the gods who speak and not the poet himself. Poets are "simply inspired to utter that to which the Muse impels them" (*Ion* 534).

Poetic inspiration was not the only type of *mania* that Plato recognized, however. In the *Phaedrus* (265a–b) he distinguishes four different types: besides the poetic *mania* of the Muses there are also prophetic, telestic (ritual), and erotic forms of *mania*. All save the telestic are described as forms of inspiration *(epipnoia)*. In many respects the most important of these was prophetic or mantic inspiration, the type given by Apollo for purposes of divination, and most important in connection with the Delphic oracle. Although the famed "frenzy" of the Pythia at Delphi has been shown to be largely a product of the literary imagination (Lucian's in particular), there is no doubt that she was at all periods believed to be genuinely inspired by the god Apollo. [*See* Oracles.] Mention should also be made of those enigmatic, quasi-legendary figures of antiquity, the sibyls. Their inspired oracles were collected and consulted at Rome, while many later Christians looked upon some of them as pre-Christian prophecies of Christ [*See* Sibylline Oracles.]

The fact that Plato classified both poetic and prophetic inspiration as forms of madness is indicative of the Greek tendency to view inspiration in terms of possession, a tendency we have already noted in South India, and which is very widespread among tribal cultures the world over. Inspiration as a form of *mania* is conceived of as a manifestation of *enthousiasmos,* literally the presence of a god within the inspired person, that is, possession. [*See* Enthusiasm.] We shall see that this theory exerted an important influence on some early Jewish and Christian theories of inspiration, only later to be rejected.

In the ancient Near East inspiration was closely associated with the phenomenon of prophecy. In its earliest form, the Near Eastern prophet served primarily as a counselor of the chief or king, giving advice in the form of inspired oracles. His role was distinguished from that of the cultic priest by the fact that the latter employed technical means of divination while the prophet relied primarily on inspiration. The more familiar figure of the prophet as the inspired critic of both king and cult derives from the later history of prophecy in Israel, where the prophet became the divinely elected spokesman of Yahveh. The ecstatic behavior and utterances of prophets such as Saul, Elijah, and Elisha were the effect of the powerful spirit *(ruaḥ)* of God. In the later, so-called classical prophets the experience of inspiration is less violent and takes on the character of a close personal encounter.

In general the role of the prophet in this more familiar noncultic sense and the nature of inspiration as a religious phenomenon seem to be very intimately connected. The spontaneity and dynamism that characterizes inspiration achieve an almost paradigmatic realization in the figure of the itinerant prophet, who feels free to confront the established centers of power in the name of his god. It is surely not by chance that some of the clearest instances of inspiration among the peoples of Africa are found among the African tribal prophets who have appeared since the end of the last century in struggles against foreign domination. Prophetic inspiration, in one form or another, has historically been an important factor in a large number of nationalistic, nativistic, and resistance movements. [*See* Prophecy.]

The experience of inspiration in the early Christian communities was interpreted as the outpouring of the Spirit predicted by the prophet Joel, and was dramatically symbolized by the descent of the Holy Spirit in a rush of wind and in tongues of fire at Pentecost (*Acts* 2). The inspiration of the Spirit brought with it a variety of ecstatic experiences, which included speaking in tongues and a revival of prophecy. [*See also* Glossolalia.] In the light of such experiences, and given the Christian belief in the divinity of the Holy Spirit, it is not surprising that some early Christians found theories of inspiration congenial that were hardly distinguishable from theories of possession. Thus the apologist Athenagoras could say that the Spirit made use of the prophet as a flute player makes use of a flute. Justin Martyr also seems to have had a "mantic" view of inspiration. Such theories may well have derived from Philo Judaeus, who explicitly ascribed scriptural prophecy to divine possession, in this undoubtedly being influenced by Plato. As a whole, however, the Christian tradition resisted such notions, and from the time of Origen on affirmed the importance of the active involvement of the inspired subject.

The Christian theological concept of the Holy Spirit as a divine person gave the concept of inspiration a theological importance that it could not have in either Judaism or Islam, where the strong sense of divine immanence implied in such a notion was viewed with suspicion. This is made clear by the role ascribed to inspiration in the constitution of the scriptures of these three religions. While affirming the supreme authority of the Torah, the rabbis denied that it was inspired. Rather it was given directly to Moses by God verbatim. The intervention of an inspired author would have served only to weaken its authority. Only the Prophets and the Writings could properly be described as inspired. Similarly in Islam, a clear distinction is drawn between revelation *(waḥy),* which is applied to the *verbatim* transmission of the Qur'ān to Muḥammad through the angel Gabriel, and inspiration *(ilhām),* which is restricted to the inspiration of individuals on matters that are of primarily personal concern. In Christianity, by contrast, it is precisely the concept of inspiration that is traditionally invoked to account for the authoritativeness of scripture.

This should not be taken to mean, however, that the concept of inspiration is unimportant in either Judaism or Islam. The rabbinical notion of the *ruaḥ ha-qodesh* (lit., "holy spirit"), while not to be confused with the Christian notion, nevertheless fulfills some of the same functions. It was used by the rabbis to explain prophetic inspiration, and was also believed to be present to holy souls, and in particular to those who taught the Torah in public. According to a Midrash, "All that the righteous do, they do with the power of *ruaḥ ha-qodesh*" (*Tanḥuma' Va-yeḥi* 13).

In Islam the fact that the revelation made to Muḥammad is distinguished from the inspiration received by the individual believer should not prevent us from recognizing in Muḥammad an inspired prophet. Nor can we fail to note the similarity between the oracular structure of some of the earliest surahs of the Qur'ān and the inspired oracles encountered elsewhere in the history of religions, in particular among the *kāhin,* or soothsayers, of pre-Islamic Arabia.

The later Ṣūfīs recognized the validity of another type of ecstatic utterance, called *shaṭḥ,* which they believed to be divinely inspired. The saying of al-Hallāj, "Anā al-ḥaqq" ("I am the Truth"), is probably the most famous of such utterances, but one which unfortunately encouraged misunderstandings that eventually led to his death. Inspiration did not always take such a dramatic form, however. The experience of *ilhām* remained an essentially inner experience that was believed to be authoritative only for the saintly soul who received it as a gift from God.

These few examples must suffice to illustrate the variety of ways in which inspiration has been experienced from the earliest times down to our own day. Throughout human history we find such examples of men and women who are open to a form of experience that ultimately defies our attempts to explain, or even understand. Friedrich Nietzsche put it beautifully, in describing his own personal experience of inspiration: "One hears—one does not seek; one takes—one does not ask who gives: a thought suddenly flashes up like lightning, it comes with necessity, unhesitatingly—I have never had any choice in the matter" (Nietzsche, 1954).

BIBLIOGRAPHY

A broad view of inspiration in its variety of forms in the history of religions is provided by N. Kershaw Chadwick's *Poetry and Prophecy* (Cambridge, 1942) and Edwyn Robert Bevan's *Sibyls and Seers: A Survey of Some Ancient Theories of Revelation and Inspiration* (London, 1928). A recent work by Gilbert Rouget, *Music and Trance: A Theory of the Relations between Music and Possession* (Chicago, 1985), while dealing primarily with possession trance, does have some interesting things to say about inspiration and is to be recommended.

Much information on inspired poets among Indo-European peoples can be found in *Indogermanische Dichtersprache*, edited by Rüdiger Schmitt (Darmstadt, 1968), although this book is aimed at the trained philologist. For a more accessible sampling of the hymns of the Vedic *ṛṣis*, see Wendy Doniger O'-Flaherty's *The Rig Veda* (Harmondsworth, 1981). The inspired speech of the Mahāyāna Buddhists is discussed by Graeme MacQueen in "Inspired Speech in Early Mahāyāna Buddhism," *Religion* 11 (1981): 303–319 and 12 (1982): 49–65. On Nammāḻvār, see A. K. Ramanujan's *Hymns for the Drowning: Poems for Viṣṇu by Nammāḻvār* (Princeton, 1981), especially the very helpful afterword.

For a general view of inspiration among the Greeks, see E. R. Dodds's *The Greeks and the Irrational* (Berkeley, 1951). A more recent work by Joseph Fontenrose, *The Delphic Oracle* (Berkeley, 1978), proposes a fundamental revision of traditional views of the inspiration of the Pythia at Delphi. On the inspiration of the Muses, one may consult Eike Barmeyer's *Die Musen: Ein Beitrag zur Inspirationstheorie* (Munich, 1968).

A wealth of information on inspiration among the Greeks, Hebrews, and early Christians can be found in the article on *pneuma* in the *Theological Dictionary of the New Testament*, edited by Gerhard Kittel (Grand Rapids, Mich., 1968). Johannes Lindblom's *Prophecy in Ancient Israel* (Philadelphia, 1962) is also a rich resource. Johannes Pedersen's short study, "The Role Played by Inspired Persons among the Israelites and the Arabs," in *Studies in Old Testament Prophecy* (Edinburgh, 1950), is helpful for the attention it gives to early Arabic sources. For rabbinical theories of inspiration, see Paul Billerbeck's "Der Kanon des Alten Testaments und seine Inspiration," excursus 16 of the *Kommentar zum Neuen Testament aus Talmud und Midrasch*, by Hermann L. Strack and Paul Billerbeck (Munich, 1928). For inspiration in Islam, see Fazlur Rahman's *Prophecy in Islam: Philosophy and Orthodoxy* (London, 1958), Annemarie Schimmel's *Mystical Dimensions of Islam* (Chapel Hill, N.C., 1975), and the articles on *waḥy*, *ilhām*, and *shaṭḥ* in the *Shorter Encyclopaedia of Islam*, edited by H. A. R. Gibb and J. H. Kramers (Leiden, 1974).

Friedrich Nietzsche's account of his own experience of inspiration while engaged in writing his *Thus Spake Zarathustra* was included by his sister in her introduction to that work and is reproduced in the Modern Library edition of Nietzsche's major works, *The Philosophy of Nietzsche* (New York, 1954), pp. xix–xxxiii.

DAVID CARPENTER

INTELLECTUALS are persons who produce or intensively study intellectual works. Intellectual works are coherent complexes of symbolic configurations that deal with the serious or ultimately significant features of the cosmos, the earth, and human beings. An intellectual work is unified by logical connectedness and the substantive identity of its subject matter, and it is set forth in a conventional form.

Religious intellectual works are those that deal with transcendent powers and their verbal, physical, and inspirational manifestations. They deal with the relations of transcendent powers to texts that are regarded as sacred, and with the influence of transcendent powers in the genesis and working of the cosmos, in human life and destiny, and in the norms that guide human action.

Religious activities, both intellectual and practical (i.e., religious practices), have as their objective the engendering or maintaining of a state of belief that comprises a relationship to transcendent powers. Religious intellectual activities, embodying this particular state of mind or belief, aim at attaining and transmitting knowledge or understanding of transcendent powers and their manifestations. The attainment of a religious state of mind encompasses practices such as the performance of prescribed rituals, the incantation of sacred songs, the reiteration of sacred words, and the ingestion, handling, and bearing of sacred objects. Such practical religious activities are infused with symbolic components and are hence intimately related to the intellectual religious activities that have constructed their underlying symbolic configurations. The intellectual elucidation of the meaning of practical religious activities and objects creates an intimate bond between the intellectual and practical spheres of religious activity.

Bodies of religious beliefs and practices differ, however, in the degree to which beliefs and practices have been elaborated and rationalized. Religions that are built around sacred texts are more susceptible to an elaborate variety of interpretations than are those that have no sacred texts. These elaborate interpretations are possible only on the basis of prolonged and intensive study by religious intellectuals who study the religious intellectual works that are central to the complex of beliefs espoused by the religious community and who produce works of their own.

"Primordial" and "World" Religions. Not all religious communities, that is, communities with common religious beliefs and practices, cultivate or depend upon intellectuals. The majority of these religions without intellectuals are primordial religions, that is, the religions of societies that define themselves by locality and lineage and in which no written texts contain their fundamental ideas. Such religions have beliefs and ritual practices, but they do not have doctrines. Their religious beliefs remain centered on local, occasional, and functional deities. Their rituals often have been codified, as was the case with Roman religion, and they sometimes have developed priesthoods as distinct professional strata; but, having no sacred books, they generally have no religious intellectuals to construct doctrines that could become integrally connected with their ritual observances. The larger, differentiated, and literate societies that continue to adhere to their primordial religions have produced intellectuals, including religious intellectuals, but the latter have had no ecclesiastical role. In these societies, such as those of ancient Greece and Rome, the construction of theological-philosophical theories has been left to laymen whose theories remained outside the realm of religious practice and influence.

Both in theory and in fact, however, the line dividing primordial religions from "world" or "universal" religions, that is, doctrinal religions that have acquired their doctrines through the work of religious intellectuals, cannot be precisely delineated. A primordial religion could in principle acquire an intellectual constituent. Its mythological pantheon could be rationalized and its rituals given a more pronouncedly transcendent reference; its magical procedures could be given a more explicit symbolic interpretation. World religions contain much that has been taken from the primordial religions that were indigenous to the territories from which they emerged or into which they entered. Yet no primordial religions that were indigenous to the territories from which they emerged or into which they entered can be turned into world religions without sacred or canonical texts and without intellectuals to construct doctrine from these texts.

Doctrine. The world religions have been primarily doctrinal religions in which articles are defined and ritual observances prescribed; belief and observance are required of members. Buddhism, Christianity, and Islam are unqualifiedly such religions. Confucianism has no primordial qualifications: it is open to all who can study the classical texts. In Hinduism, one is in principle a Hindu by being born into a Hindu caste, but it is also a religion centered around sacred writings and the rituals prescribed in the sacred writings. In this respect, Judaism is also in a marginal position. It is certainly a religion of doctrines insofar as it has a tradition contained in a sacred text and elaborated by commentary, but it is also a primordial religion: a Jew is one who is born of Jewish parents. Nevertheless, both of these world religions, despite this primordial element, have allowed prominent places to religious intellectuals.

Although the world religions, once established, recruit their members from among the offspring of their existing members, in order for transmission and expansion to occur, there must be a doctrine that is susceptible to simplification and exposition. Even if the founder of the religion is, in Max Weber's terms, an "exemplary" rather than an "ethical" prophet, this exemplification has to be transformed into expoundable and teachable doctrine as a condition of its expansion. The doctrine is precipitated into intellectual works; the construction of this doctrine is the accomplishment of religious intellectuals.

Primordial religions have expanded territorially with the movement of their adherents, but they have not expanded to become the religions of entire societies to which they were not indigenous. Having no doctrines, they could not become world religions.

The combination of the written works, commentary, and systematic speculations of religious intellectuals has given to the world religions an influence in world history that the fragmentary, unwritten, and inchoate beliefs of the devotees of primordial religions could not achieve. The self-confidence of the propagators of the world religions within and outside the societies of their origin has rested, in part, on the collective consciousness of participation in a system of beliefs that answers urgent ultimate questions. It was difficult for the devotees of doctrineless religions to stand up against the forceful proclamations and denunciations of a world religion that possessed an elaborated and rationalized doctrine. To the charismatic force of the prophetic founder and his sacred text was added the derivative charismatic force of an elaborated doctrine that expanded the concentrated and intense charisma of the founder. Local primordial religions fell before the expansion of the world religions pushing outward from their centers of origin.

In contrast, world religions have been resistant to one another's expansion. The Chinese, for example, were fortified by the intellectually elaborated outlooks of Confucianism and Buddhism against the intellectual argument of Christian missionaries. The expansion of world religions has been made primarily at the expense of primordial religions that have had no significant intellectual rationalization to resist attacks from an intellectually elaborated world religion. As world religions have expanded, the primordial religions, as visible collective entities, have been all but obliterated. They have survived within this expansion only through their unacknowledged assimilation. Their traditions were powerful enough to survive in fragmentary form, but they were not sufficiently rationalized to be able to survive as recognizable wholes.

Tradition and Originality. An affirmative attitude towards a particular tradition is inherent in the activities of religious intellectuals, since they claim to carry forward sets of beliefs that rest on the revelations of a founder, or a divinely engendered sacred text, or both. Religious intellectuals are committed to a tradition that continues, with some attenuation, the sacrality of the founding moment or period in the past. All subsequent truths must be demonstrably continuous with that sacred past event or sequence of events.

Originality in the world religions is admitted only for the founder of the religion or for the sacred scriptures in which the founder serves as the voice of a transcendent power. This conception of the originating sacredness of a body of scriptures does not acknowledge any subsequent originality by the religious intellectuals who take upon themselves the responsibility for expounding and interpreting them.

Prophetic—charismatic, founding, and renewing—originality is acknowledged in most world religions. Interpretative rationalizing originality is not acknowledged as originality. Yet originality does occur within the traditions of Buddhism and in the work of Jewish rabbis, Roman Catholic and Protestant theologians, Islamic theologians and Hindu philosophers. It is not, however, regarded as originality. It is treated either as clarification of unchanging doctrine or it is rejected as heretical. In addition to rationalizing interpretative originality, there is in the world religions the originality of the mystic who, while affirming his acceptance of the most fundamental objects of the religion, breaks out of the constraints of rationalized theological doctrine and routine ritual.

Religious intellectuals are not less creative or less original than secular intellectuals who produce works of science, literature, and art that are appreciated for their creativity or originality. Since the meaning of a sacred text is not self-evident, interpretation is necessary. Interpretation is intended to discern the "true," or preexistent, meaning of a sacred text. The successful discovery of this "true" meaning is perceived to be not an addition to existing knowledge but a reassertion and confirmation of an already existent truth. Nevertheless, a considerable degree of originality within the tradition might in fact be attained.

When intellectuals elaborate doctrines that are based on inherently problematic sacred texts, divergent and hence conflicting doctrinal currents of belief appear. Such conflicts have occurred in every world religion and have led to intense disputes until one current has become prevalent over the others and has been established as the orthodox position. There is, however, an important difference between a prevailing doctrine that is orthodox solely through a substantial intellectual consensus and a prevailing doctrine that is promulgated as orthodox by an authoritative institution. An authoritatively promulgated doctrine is a dogma. Where there is dogma, heterodoxies are proscribed, and their intellectual proponents are suppressed.

The authorities that the religious intellectuals must confront are the authority of the sacred writings and the doctrines formed from them, the authority of the religious intellectual community, and that of ecclesiastical institutions. In principle, the authority of the sacred writings is inviolable. In fact, however, the authority of these writings is the authority of the prevailing doctrinal tradition and of those who espouse it within the institution. Critical interpretation of sacred texts is thus perpetually a potential threat to the effective "official" authority of the religious institution.

Within more complex societies, even those of very restricted literacy, there have been some self-taught laymen different in their occupation and status from the majority of religious intellectuals in their society. They may be called lay or amateur religious intellectuals. Sometimes they have been merchants or craftsmen, sometimes scribes, officials, or soldiers. These laymen have studied the texts zealously and sometimes arrived at conclusions different from the prevailing doctrines. They have also resented the pretensions of the officially acknowledged and self-assertive priestly, academic, or monastic religious intellectuals. Their dissenting interpretations of sacred writings have occasionally broken into passionate public dissent from the prevailing doctrines and from the priestly and academic representation of those doctrines. These autodidactic intellectuals, sometimes reinforced by renegades from the more established stratum of religious intellectuals, have often furiously denounced the main body of the priesthood as departing fundamentally from the "true" meaning of the sacred texts. The priests, and especially the higher level of the priestly hierarchy, have been accused of excessive subservience to the ruling house and to the powerful landowning families.

Heterodox or dissenting doctrines have occasionally been the work of intellectuals within the priesthood itself. Such interpretations at first lived an "underground" life. Some of them were cultivated in seclusion by dissenting, autodidactic religious intellectuals. The latter have often been subtle, learned, and ingenious.

Among the greatest of these intellectuals who were critical of the priestly or orthodox interpretation have been those prophets who were founders of new religions, that is, religions that declared themselves to be distinct from the hitherto prevailing body of religious belief and its proponents. The Buddha, Jesus, and Muḥammad were such prophets. They were the beneficiaries of new revelations or illuminations.

Jesus said he was divinely chosen to fulfill the mission of earlier prophets. The Buddha was a profoundly original prophet, but he too was a continuator of Hinduism. Muḥammad claimed to be not only the recipient of a new revelation but to have realized more truly the religion of Abraham and Jesus. In contrast, Confucian scholars in China claimed no authority from revelation, and they did not bring forth prophets from their ranks.

There have also been prophets who have claimed to realize the true intentions of long-accepted doctrines against those who had falsified them. The Hebrew prophetic intellectuals did not claim at any time to found a new religion. They demanded the restoration of the religion of the Jews to its prior condition of purity. Martin Luther, John Wyclif, and the monastic reformers of Christian religious orders must be placed in the same category as the prophetic intellectuals who thought that their religious community had departed from its original meaning and had succumbed to the ways of the earthly world.

Religious intellectual traditions alter as they pass from region to region and from generation to generation. The world religions—Hinduism, Buddhism, Confucianism, Judaism, Christianity, and Islam—have experienced numerous doctrinal vicissitudes and variations. They have survived largely because their doctrines have been received and retransmitted with modifications and increments by religious intellectuals. Without the constant reaffirmation and modifications of doctrinal traditions by religious intellectuals, there could be no religious communities with more or less uniform practices and beliefs over extended periods and large geographical areas.

Secular and Religious Intellectual Activities. In no large societies have religious intellectual activities been the only intellectual activities. Yet except in ancient Greece and Rome, most intellectual activities in the societies of the ancient world were carried on by religious intellectuals. In the modern age, the increased volume of intellectual works, the increased differentiation of objects of intellectual activity, and the increased specialization of intellectuals in dealing with aspects of the world (which is now thought to be relatively independent of transcendent powers) have been associated with a great increase in the proportion of secular intellectuals and a recession of the jurisdiction of religious intellectuals.

In territories where autonomous intellectual traditions—both religious and secular—were well developed, religious intellectuals often assimilated intellectual traditions that lay outside their own religious tradition. This occurred, for example, in Christianity and later in Islam when they became established in the territory of Hellenistic civilizations. Christian intellectuals found affinities between their own Christian beliefs and Platonic, and later Aristotelian, philosophy. Islamic intellectuals quickly absorbed the Hellenistic philosophical and scientific knowledge that had been cultivated in Syria and other parts of the Middle East under the Seleucids and the Romans. By the end of the European Middle Ages, Christian religious intellectuals drew knowledge directly from ancient secular Western sources. By the seventeenth century, both the quantity and the intellectual authoritativeness of secular intellectual works gained the ascendancy. Religious intellectuals absorbed some of this secular knowledge and attempted to render it compatible with Christian belief.

The humanistic intellectuals of the Renaissance, taking up the traditions of the secular cultures of Greece and Rome, continued to be Christians, but their attention moved toward the study of earthly things. After the Reformation this differentiation and multiplication of secular intellectuals continued. Religious intellectuals also declined more and more in status in comparison with secular intellectuals.

Religious intellectuals now constitute a small minority of the intellectuals of European and American societies. Many of them have made very far-reaching concessions to the substantive and technical standards of secular intellectuals. They have accepted the findings of the research of physical and biological scientists and the approaches and analyses of secular historians and social scientists.

In modern times, religious intellectuals have confined their intellectual activities to religious objects in a restricted sense: theological studies, textual and historical analysis of sacred writings and their commentaries, the archaeology of sacred sites, church history and the history of religious doctrines, and closely related topics. But even within some of these restricted spheres of religious study, a secular criterion of validity has prevailed. Secular modes of study in the analysis of religious phenomena have become predominant, and in certain fields, such as church history, the history of doctrines, and the sociological and anthropological study of religion, the techniques of research and the interpretations of secular intellectuals have come to predominate.

For centuries, religious intellectuals were an integral part of the political life of their respective societies. The earthly centers of power could not claim the legitimacy of their ascendancy without its attestation by religious intellectuals. It was thought that social order could be assured only if the earthly center was properly aligned with the transcendent center. The earthly centers called upon religious intellectuals for administrative services. The education of young persons and children was entrusted to religious intellectuals. There was, by and large, a relationship of mutual support between religious intellectuals, princes, and great landowners. In the bourgeois age, religious intellectuals became more critical of the new plutocratic elite and of the bourgeois order of society. In Western European countries and North America religious intellectuals increasingly joined with secular intellectuals in oppositional political activities.

In the once-colonial territories, now sovereign states, "traditionalistic," revivalistic religious intellectuals have become more active. In these countries, during the period of foreign rule, traditional religious intellectuals had been mainly passive toward the foreign rulers. Indigenous rulers enjoyed the same submission of intellectuals in Asian societies that remained independent. Such passivity among traditional religious intellectuals is no longer so common. In Iran, for example, they have succeeded in establishing a theocracy. In a few other Islamic countries, they have been influential enough to compel secular military and civilian rulers to designate their states as "Islamic" and to install "Islamic constitutions." Christian religious intellectuals in the formerly colonial societies have not been so active politically; in their religious intellectual activities, they have sought to overcome their "alien" situation by reinterpreting Christianity to render it compatible with indigenous cultural traditions.

In Western countries in the twentieth century religious intellectuals have narrowed their intellectual activities in accordance with the prevailing tendencies toward specialization and professionalization. At the same time, they have acquired many of the scientific, cultural, moral, and political traditions of the secular intellectuals. In many respects, religious intellectuals in Western countries have become very much like secular intellectuals.

BIBLIOGRAPHY

Arnold, Thomas W. *The Caliphate.* 2d ed. Oxford, 1965.

Baron, Salo W. *The Jewish Community: Its History and Structure to The American Revolution.* 3 vols. Philadelphia, 1942.

Burkert, Walter. *Greek Religion.* Cambridge, Mass., 1985.

Eliot, Charles. *Hinduism and Buddhism.* 3 vols. 3d ed. London, 1957.

Gibb, H. A. R., with Harold Bowen. *Islamic Society and the West,* vol. 1, *Islamic Society in the Eighteenth Century.* Oxford, 1950.

Goldziher, Ignácz. *Die Richtungen der islamischen Koranauslegung* (1920). Leiden, 1952.

Harnack, Adolf von. *The Constitution and Law of the Church in the First Two Centuries.* London, 1910.

Hooke, S. H. *Prophets and Priests.* London, 1938.

James, E. O. *The Nature and Function of Priesthood.* London, 1955.

Le Bras, Gabriel. *Institutions ecclésiastiques de la chrétienté médiévale.* Paris, 1959.

Moore, George Foot. *Judaism in the First Centuries of the Christian Era, the Age of the Tannaim.* 3 vols. Cambridge, Mass., 1927–1930.

Marrou, Henri Irénée. *A History of Education in Antiquity.* New York, 1956.

Nilsson, Martin P. *Geschichte der griechischen Religion.* 2 vols. 3d ed. Munich, 1967–1974.

Ryan, John. *Irish Monasticism: Origins and Early Development.* Dublin, 1931.

Schacht, Joseph. *The Origins of Muhammadan Jurisprudence.* Oxford, 1950.

EDWARD SHILS

INTERLACUSTRINE BANTU RELIGIONS.

The term *interlacustrine Bantu,* as used here, encompasses a variety of peoples who live between the Great Lakes of east-central Africa and speak closely related Bantu languages. Their territory includes some of the most densely populated regions of Africa, consisting of all of Uganda south of the Victoria Nile, the states of Rwanda and Burundi, and a substantial portion of northwest Tanzania. Before independence, most of the area was divided into a number of traditional kingdoms, the largest of these being Rwanda and Burundi in the south and the four Uganda monarchies of Buganda, Bunyoro, Toro, and Ankole in the north. There were also about a dozen smaller but structurally similar units in the Tanzanian sector. The mass of the people are agriculturalists, but in many areas a cattle-owning minority, called Huma, or Hima, in the north and Tutsi in the south, formed a dominant and hereditary upper class.

Today most of the people of the region are at least nominally Christians; there is also a substantial minority of Muslims. But the indigenous cults are still widespread and are remarkably similar throughout the area.

The Spirit Powers. All the peoples of the area have the idea of a supreme being, known as Imana in the south, Ruhanga in the Nyoro-speaking north, and Katonda in Uganda; the last two names mean "creator." In some myths the hierarchical class structure mentioned above is ascribed to him, which to a certain degree may have sanctioned its acceptance by the less privileged. But, in a familiar pattern, the creator god, having made the world, was disappointed by it and withdrew from active participation in human affairs. Shrines are not made for him, nor are sacrifices offered as they are to the other gods (though here Buganda seems to have been an exception). In contrast to the lesser spirit powers, no mediumship cult is dedicated to the supreme being. He is, however, thought to be generally well disposed toward humans, and brief prayers and thanks may be offered up to him on a casual basis.

Far more significant in everyday life are the powerful spirits known as *embandwa* or *emandwa*. The most important of these form a group of hero-gods, whose names are well known throughout the area. They are linked in the south with a quasi-mythical ruler called Ryangombe and in the north with a shadowy ruling dynasty whose members are called *cwezi*. These heroic figures are the subject of a rich mythology; sometimes they are represented as the earliest descendants of the creator, sometimes as having come from a distant country. In either case they were great warriors, larger than life, and the doers of marvelous deeds. They were accompanied by retinues of kin and servants, and their women are included among their number. Like the Greek gods, some are identified with particular features of the environment; thus Wamara is associated with rain and rivers, Kagoro with thunder and lightning, Mulisa with cattle and cattle herding, Mugasa with the Great Lakes, and so on.

Eventually this heroic race vanished from the world: some say that the *cwezi* disappeared into one of the lakes in the area; Ryangombe is said to have been killed by a wild buffalo while hunting. But whatever their fate, it is believed that they left the institution of spirit mediumship behind for the benefit of their successors. This institution involved both possession and mediumship; it is believed that the possessing spirit, while "in the head" of its medium, may enter into communication with the living within an accepted framework of values and beliefs. Traditionally, these cults focused especially on the hero-gods who were, and still are, regarded as primarily beneficial, concerned especially with human fecundity. In Bunyoro and some neighboring areas the *cwezi* are known as the "white" *embandwa;* the color white signifying purity and blessing. These traditional cults, centered on the *cwezi* in the north and on Ryangombe and his associates in the south, may be said to form the core of interlacustrine Bantu religions.

There are many other spirits of nonhuman and sometimes of foreign origin that can be approached through mediumship ritual. These are sometimes known in the northern areas as the "black" *embandwa,* and they include spirits associated with the bush, with certain illnesses, and with some neighboring countries. In the interlacustrine area (as elsewhere in Africa) more recent spirits have come to represent new and formidable forces of all kinds, such as hitherto unknown illnesses, manifestations of Western power such as motorcars, airplanes, and even army tanks, as well as such abstract qualities as "Europeanness." All these elements and a great many more have been readily incorporated into the mediumship cults.

In addition to the high god and the wide and growing variety of *embandwa* spirits, there are the ghosts of the dead. Ghost cults are not necessarily ancestor cults. An ancestor cult is concerned with the deceased forebears of a lineage, who are usually conceived as a collectivity and are believed to be directly interested in the well-being of their descendants. Though traces of such a cult are still found in parts of the interlacustrine area, it has none of the importance of such fully developed cults as have been described among, for example, some West African peoples.

But the cult of ghosts is important throughout the region. It is believed that ghosts are left by people after they die; diffused like the wind, such ghosts are sometimes associated with a shadowy underworld, and it is thought that they may bring death, illness, or other calamity on those who have injured or offended them while they were alive. Ghosts are not necessarily kin or affines of their victims, though very often they are. Disputes are especially likely to arise within a person's circle of relatives, and it is believed that these may readily take the form, postmortem, of ghostly vengeance. Anyone, relative or not, who dies with a grudge against another may "leave a ghost" to obtain revenge.

Throughout the interlacustrine area, ghosts are seen as malevolent rather than benevolent, more concerned to punish than to reward. They are feared rather than revered, though if they cannot be exorcised it is desirable to remain on good terms with them. In either case, recourse must be had to the possession cults.

Cults. Generally people have recourse to the cults as a response to some misfortune, and when things go wrong, the first step is to consult a diviner. He, or possibly she, using one of a wide variety of techniques, is likely to ascribe the client's trouble to an *embandwa* spirit, an offended ghost, or sorcery. If the responsible agent is found to be an *embandwa* spirit or a ghost there are two possibilities. If the ghost is that of a stranger (or of a very distant relative) or if the affliction is attributed to a minor spirit such as might be sent by a sorcerer, then there are special ritual techniques for exorcising it and either destroying it or turning it away from its intended victim forever.

But the more important *embandwa,* and the ghosts of closely related kin or affines, cannot be dealt with so summarily. The afflicted person must become initiated into the mediumship cult as the spirit's human medium. This establishes an enduring relationship between person and spirit, a relationship which should be sustained from time to time by further possession ritual. In the course of these séances the possessing power is believed to be able to communicate with the living through its medium, who is supposed to be in a state of trance while this is happening. The spirit may begin by announcing its identity, and then greet and be greeted by all present. It may go on to explain what offended it and ask for food and drink—an offering that should be given to it there and then while it is "in the medium's head." Or it may demand the sacrifice or dedication to it of a cow or a goat, or the building for it of a spirit hut. And it may, if it is the ghost of a close kinsman, ask for the reconciliation of quarreling family members. Before it "leaves the head" of its medium, a spirit, if it is mollified, is likely to bless all present and to promise them good fortune, and especially more children, in the future. Séances are dramatic occasions, involving drumming, dancing, and the singing of special songs, and mediums may assume the language and gestures appropriate to their possessing spirits.

While possessed, mediums appear to be in a state of trance and may claim afterward that they have no recollection of what happens to them when they are possessed. But evidence from several parts of the area indicates that complete dissociation is seldom, if ever, achieved; generally, the medium is "putting on an act." But this does not mean that they are fraudulent; the play they are performing is a religious one, a "liturgical drama" in Luc de Heusch's phrase. And, in addition to providing a ritual means of influencing powers over which there are no other means of control, the mediumship cults are also a source of dramatic entertainment in their own right.

Admission to the cults requires a complex (and expensive) cycle of initiation ritual, often lasting for several days and culminating in the possession of the novice by the spirit concerned. The pattern of cult initiation is broadly similar throughout the area. First, the initiate's change of status is stressed. He, or more probably she, is reborn into a new family, that of her fellow mediums, and this rebirth may be symbolically enacted. Second, the secrets of cult membership have to be learned; in particular, the novice may be told how to simulate possession and mediumship even though she does not actually achieve these states. Threats of the fearful consequences of disclosure confirm the candidate's commitment to secrecy. And third, the process of initiation puts the aspirant in a condition of ritual impurity, needing special ritual to remedy it.

Social Context. Important throughout much of the area was the role of the household medium, in the Nyoro-speaking region called *omucwezi w'eka* or, if female, *nyakatagara.* One member of the family, usually female and preferably initiated while still a child, links the domestic group with one of the traditional *embandwa* spirits as its medium: this spirit is supposed to have a special concern for the well-being of the family members. Here especially the purity and auspiciousness of the traditional cults are stressed; for only a gentle and well-mannered child is acceptable to the spirits as a household medium. In some areas there is, in addition, a broader association between particular traditional spirits and particular clans, but generally this does not involve any special ritual over and above the "domestic" cults just mentioned.

The relationship between the *embandwa* cults and the traditional kingships was commonly one of implicit or explicit opposition. In several kingdoms, most notably those of Bunyoro and Rwanda, members of the royal clan (including the king himself) were debarred from participation in the mediumship cults. Kings in the interlacustrine region were not priests. Instead, they maintained priests at court—professional mediums who, like everyone else, were subject to the royal authority. Among the larger kingdoms it was only in Buganda, by far the most politically centralized of the interlacustrine states, that the royal line was closely identified with the mediumship cult. The official Ganda cult centered on the ghosts of former kings, whose tombs, carefully maintained, provided the locus for state ritual. But even here it was the *lubale* (i.e., *embandwa*) "priests," and not the king, who were the mediums for the royal ancestors.

In the twentieth century the opposition between religion and state is exemplified in the rise and decline of the Nyabingi cult. This cult focused on a powerful female *embandwa* called Nyabingi and her associates, whose cult has been ascribed to various sources but may have originated in northern Rwanda, whence it spread rapidly into southwest Uganda. It appears to have begun as a reaction both against the traditional Ryangombe cults and against Rwanda's ruling class, the pastoral Tutsi. But with the coming of European colonial power, the cult became a protest movement against all governmental authority. In the 1920s a revolt by Nyabingi adherents against the local administration was crushed by military force, though the cult survived in attenuated form for many years.

It is not surprising that the *embandwa* cults found themselves in opposition to the Christian mission churches, which, with only very limited justification, regarded them as being involved with witchcraft. Since the traditional cults were generally seen as beneficent and as being especially concerned with childbearing, attempts by government officials and missionaries to eradicate them were readily interpreted by the traditionally minded as aimed, in the long term, at the elimination of the indigenous peoples themselves. Mention should also be made here of the revivalist and fundamentalist Balokole ("the Saved Ones") movement within the Anglican church. Although this movement affected only a small minority of Christians, its uncompromising evangelism brought it into conflict not only with the *embandwa* cults—with which it had certain things in common, for example, the notion of being "born again"—but also with the secular authorities.

How, finally, is one to explain the continued survival of the cults, old as well as new, throughout much of the area? Some of the reasons are implicit in what has been said above. But among the most important of them is the cults' eclecticism. Inimical aspects of the environment, and in particular the disruptive effects of social change, are not denied or rejected; rather they are assimilated and dealt with through dramatic ritual. To give concrete expression to the forces which shape human lives (even if this is done in symbolic form) provides the interlacustrine Bantu with one basis for coping with these forces.

[*For further discussion of the religions of closely related peoples, see* East African Religions, *article on* Northeastern Bantu Religions.]

BIBLIOGRAPHY

Three works adopt a comparative approach. In his *Entre le Victoria l'Albert et l'Édouard: Ethnographie de la partie anglaise du Vicariat de l'Uganda* (Rennes, 1920), the missionary P. Julien Gorju gives a good account of the cults and of initiation into them in the Uganda kingdoms. Luc de Heusch's *Le Rwanda et la civilisation interlacustre: Études d'anthropologie historique et structurale* (Brussels, 1966) contains a comprehensive analysis of the Ryangombe cult in Rwanda, taking account also of comparable data from neighboring areas. And Iris Berger's *Religion and Resistance: East African Kingdoms in the Precolonial Period* (Tervuren, Belgium, 1981), although largely concerned with historical reconstruction, includes an up-to-date review and assessment of current information on the cults over the whole area as well as a useful bibliography. Berger notes in particular the important role played in the cults by women.

There are several brief accounts of the religious beliefs and rituals of particular peoples in the area; see, for example, Lucy P. Mair's "Religion and Magic," chapter 9 of her book on the Ganda, *An African People in the Twentieth Century* (1934; New York, 1965); J. J. Maquet's "The Kingdom of Ruanda," in *African Worlds*, edited by Daryll Forde (London, 1954); and John Beattie's "Spirit Mediumship in Bunyoro," in *Spirit Mediumship and Society in Africa*, edited by John Beattie and John Middleton (New York, 1969). A monograph by a Norwegian anthropologist, Svein Bjerke, *Religion and Misfortune: The Bacwezi Complex and the Other Spirit Cults of the Zinza of Northwestern Tanzania* (Oslo, 1981), provides a detailed account, based on field research, of the cults among one of the less well known peoples of the region. Relevant to the study of religion in its political context is Elizabeth Hopkins's "The Nyabingi Cult of Southwestern Uganda," in *Protest and Power in Black Africa*, edited by Robert I. Rotberg and Ali A. Mazrui (Oxford, 1970), a history of the rise and influence of an anticolonial spirit cult. Finally, for an African academic's view of his own traditional religion, see Abel G. M. Ishumi's "Religion and the Cults," chapter 6 of his *Kiziba: The Cultural Heritage of an Old African Kingdom* (Syracuse, N.Y., 1980).

JOHN BEATTIE

INTERMEDIATE BEINGS. *For a general discussion of beings whose nature is intermediate between deity and humanity, see* Demons. *For discussions of specific kinds of demonic beings, see* Angels; Devils; Fairies; Ghosts; *and* Monsters.

INTERNATIONAL SOCIETY FOR KRISHNA CONSCIOUSNESS (ISKCON) is the missionary form of devotional Hinduism brought to the United States in 1965 by a pious devotee of Kṛṣṇa who wanted to convert the English-speaking world to "God-consciousness." In less than two decades ISKCON became an international movement with more than two hundred centers worldwide (sixty-one in the United States).

The founding *guru,* A. C. Bhaktivedanta Swami Prabhupada, was born Abhay Charan De in 1896 in Calcutta. Educated in a Vaiṣṇava school and later in Scottish Church College, he was a sporadically successful businessman in the pharmaceutical industry. However, after he was initiated in 1922 by Bhaktisiddhanta Saraswati, a Gauḍiya (Bengali) Vaiṣṇava in the line of the sixteenth-century saint and reformer Caitanya, he began increasingly to invest time and money in his religious interests. In 1944 Bhaktivedanta established the magazine *Back to Godhead,* and in 1952 he formed the Jhansi League of Devotees. He gave up his life as a householder *(gṛhasthin)* in 1954 and in 1959 took the formal vows of an ascetic *(saṃnyāsin).*

In September 1965, at the age of sixty-nine, Bhaktivedanta arrived in New York City with a suitcase full of his translations of the *Śrīmad Bhāgavatam* and less than ten dollars in his pocket. He lived with various Indian and American supporters in Manhattan, where he set out daily to chant and sing the praises of Kṛṣṇa to anyone who would listen. Bhaktivedanta's lectures and devotional services slowly attracted a following, primarily counterculture youths, and preaching centers were eventually established in Los Angeles, Berkeley, Boston, and Montreal. By the late 1960s Los Angeles had become the headquarters of ISKCON and home of its publishing office, which has printed more than fifty different volumes of translations and original works by Bhaktivedanta.

From the earliest years of the movement, Bhaktivedanta's disciples have been known for their public chanting *(saṅkīrtan)* of the Hare Kṛṣṇa *mantra* and their distribution of *Back to Godhead* as well as Bhaktivedanta's books. Like his Indian predecessors, Bhaktivedanta believed that the recitation of God's name was sufficient for salvation. Further, his *guru* had instructed him to make known "Krishna consciousness" to the English-speaking world. Consequently, the "Hare Krishnas" in India and America have been both visible and very missionary-minded.

In July 1970, Bhaktivedanta formed a Governing Body Commission of twelve advanced devotees to administer an ever more widespread and complex ISKCON and to allow him to spend his time preaching and translating. Around the same time, he instituted a series of standardized practices that had the effect of making ISKCON devotees more like their Indian counterparts. Every male devotee who entered the temple had to wear the traditional saffron dress of the monastic novice and shave his head; women wore traditional Indian saris. All temples were to follow a daily regimen of rising at 3:30 A.M. for morning devotional services *(pūjā),* chanting sixteen rounds of the Kṛṣṇa *mantra* on 108 prayer beads, and attending a lecture on a scriptural passage. A clear distinction was made between *brahmacārin* or "student" devotees who intended to take the four monastic regulative principles (no meat eating, no intoxicants of any kind, no sexual activity of any kind, and no gambling) and *gṛhasta* or "householder" devotees who intended to live in marriage outside the temple and who might also take a modified version of the four vows.

Throughout the 1970s, ISKCON became ever more conscious of its Indian roots at the same time as it was expanding to every continent on the globe. Bhaktivedanta returned frequently to India from 1970 until his death there in Vṛndāvana in 1977. He received a hearty welcome from most Indians, who jokingly called his devotees "dancing white elephants." He established temples and preaching centers near Bombay, in Vṛndāvana (the birthplace of Kṛṣṇa), and in Māyāpur (the birthplace of Caitanya). By the early 1980s, the Bombay temple had more than six thousand Indian "lifetime" members and the Vṛndāvana temple was included in most Kṛṣṇa pilgrims' circuits.

Bhaktivedanta circled the globe several times in his twelve years of missionary activity and established temples in England and continental Europe. Just before his death, he appointed eleven disciples as initiating *gurus* to keep the Caitanya chain of disciples unbroken and to missionize the rest of the world. (In 1982 the number was expanded to thirteen.) By the early 1980s his disciples had established forty-five temples or farms in Europe, ten in Africa, thirty-five in Asia, and forty in South America. Whereas the full-time membership of the American temples remained fairly constant after 1977, ISKCON branches grew rapidly overseas, where they often found more tolerant environments.

ISKCON has encountered opposition from anticult groups such as the Citizens Freedom Foundation, but the movement has also experienced challenges from within. In 1970 a group of devotees questioned Bhaktivedanta's disciplic authority, and in 1982 one of his appointed successors left the organization to follow another *guru.* The movement's practices and techniques of book distribution and proselytizing have most often been at the heart of both external and internal criticism. Yet these practices shaped by the unbounded enthusiasm and organizational inconsistencies of the early years of ISKCON are now, in the mid-1980s, being molded by processes of institutionalization and accommodation that are well under way in ISKCON throughout the world. In the absence of the founding *guru,* it is the Governing Body Commission and the appointed *gurus* who will determine the viability of this Indian tradition on foreign soil.

[*See also* New Religions, *articles on* New Religions and Cults in the United States *and* New Religions and Cults in Europe. *For discussion of the theology of Kṛṣṇa worship, see* Kṛṣṇaism *and* Vaiṣṇavism. *See also the biography of Caitanya.*]

BIBLIOGRAPHY

J. Stillson Judah's study of California devotees, *Hare Krishna and the Counterculture* (New York, 1974), is now dated, but its emphasis on ISKCON's origin as a religious alternative to and embodiment of countercultural values and attitudes is still instructive. The glossary includes most major terms and names of persons associated with Kṛṣṇa devotion. An anthropological study that focuses on the Boston, New York, London, and Amsterdam temples is Francine Jeanne Daner's *The American Children of Kṛṣṇa* (New York, 1976). Daner also places the rise of ISKCON in the context of "counter-culture religions" as well as in the framework of Erik Erikson's identity theory of personality development. My own study, *The Dark Lord* (Philadelphia, 1985), is based on more than one hundred interviews of Kṛṣṇa devotees from fourteen temples throughout America and presents the various aspects of the American Kṛṣṇa faith in the framework of anticult criticisms and a history of religions response to those criticisms.

LARRY D. SHINN

INTI was the Inca sun god, worshiped in the Andes at the time of the Spanish conquest in the first half of the sixteenth century. The Sun was the Inca's dynastic ancestor and imperial god. The Inca ruler was believed to be the son of the Sun; his commands were divine oracles. According to one variant of the Inca creation myth, the Sun, having been created by the god Viracocha on a sacred island in Lake Titicaca (on the Bolivian-Peruvian Altiplano), rose over the lake and spoke to the first Inca ruler, Manco Capac, to whom he gave instruction in Sun worship. The Sun was the most important sky god, with Thunder (or Weather), Moon, and the star deities trailing in rank. There may have been a tripartite division of the Sun, but this is not clear. As was often true in New World religions, the Sun had various aspects or names. Inti was the royal deity; he was also identified with Punchao, the Sun of the day—that is, daylight. There may also have been specifically identified Suns of solstices or other astronomical events.

Inca sun worship was intimately integrated with the growing of maize. The sun was of vital importance in an expanding agricultural society mostly situated in hail-ridden altitudes with frequent frosts. The sun also regulated planting times. In the Inti Raymi ("sun festival"), held at the winter solstice (June), priests made a pilgrimage toward the east, and a ceremony took place in which the Inca ruler lifted a cup of *chicha* (a fermented maize drink) to the Sun, then sprinkled the liquid on the ground. There were sacrifices to the Sun on neighboring hills.

The legend of the founding of Cuzco, the capital city, indicates the agricultural basis of Inca religion. The wandering Inca, led by Manco Capac, were told to establish the city in a place where a gold rod given to them by the Sun would sink into the earth with one blow, indicating good planting ground. The Coricancha ("golden enclosure"), begun by Manco Capac as a humble shrine on the spot where the rod sank, was later expanded into the Temple of the Sun, an impressive structure of finely worked stone buildings around a courtyard; the facade was decorated with sheets of gold that reflected sunlight. (Manco Capac had originally presented himself to the Cuzco Valley people dressed in sun-catching gold ornaments.)

The Coricancha was the primary religious center, a place of pilgrimage, and a model for other Sun temples throughout the vast Inca empire. The priests of the Sun were of the highest rank (the chief priest was a relative of the Inca ruler), and there were many of them. At the Coricancha lived the "chosen women," wives of the Sun, who performed ritual duties including the preparation of ceremonial maize and *chicha* and the weaving of fine cloth to be offered to the Sun. At Inti Raymi, maize was specially prepared by them because it was thought to be a gift from the Sun. During several festivals only maize could be eaten. It was grown in the garden of the Coricancha, and three times a year, during festivals, maize plants fashioned of gold were displayed there. The best lands and largest herds of llamas belonged to the Sun, who also received the finest offerings, including pure-white llamas and objects of gold.

[*See also* Manco Capac *and* Viracocha.]

BIBLIOGRAPHY

Bernabé Cobo's *History of the Inca Empire* (Austin, 1979) is a valuable early source on myth and rite. Burr C. Brundage's *Lords of Cuzco* (Norman, Okla., 1967) includes a description of Inti Raymi, and J. H. Rowe's *An Introduction to the Archaeology of Cuzco* (Cambridge, Mass., 1944) includes a detailed section on the Coricancha.

ELIZABETH P. BENSON

INTOXICANTS. *See* Beverages *and* Psychedelic Drugs.

INTUITION. The term comes from the Latin *intuitio,* which is derived from *intueri,* meaning to look at attentively (with astonishment or admiration), gaze at, contemplate, or pay attention to. At first confined to direct visual experience, the term came to denote the process of insight as well as its object. Intuition in this first sense is a direct "look" at a particular thing that shows itself immediately in its concrete fullness without the mediation of any other knowledge, procedure, or content. The roots of this meaning lie in the visual character of the Greek, Arabic, and Hebrew mentalities as reflected in the Platonic-Augustinian tradition. In the later and wider sense, the word designates the direct apprehension of an object in its present, concrete reality through either sense perception (including memory and imagination) or the intellect. *Intuition* is today almost exclusively understood in a metaphorical sense; the word designates the human capacity for instant and immediate understanding of an object, a person, a situation, and so forth. The immediacy of intuition sets it in opposition to the discursive function of the intellect, which is mediated by concepts and propositions. In this sense, intuition entails the direct, nonmediated presence of the object to the knowing faculty; it sometimes extends to a partial or total fusion of subject and object. Knowledge of this kind excludes all rational, gnoseological, or even psychological analysis or justification.

The many, sometimes divergent, uses of the word can be classified into several distinct types: (1) sensory (aesthetic) or empirical intuition is a nonconceptual, nonrational grasp of reality; (2) intellectual, logical, or mathematical intuition is the self-evident grasp of fundamental ideas, axioms, principles, or truths; (3) essential intuition is a grasp of the inner essence of a thing, a being, a cause, a situation; and (4) spiritual intuition is the immediate contemplation of the highest order of things, an insight gained neither through the senses nor through intellectual reflection, but stemming from the "inner man" and akin to the receiving of a revelation.

The Philosophical Tradition. In Plato's works, especially the dialogue *Phaedrus,* with its myth of the soul that contemplates the heavenly ideas before its embodiment, intuition is of these eternal essences, which are visible only to the intellect. In Plotinus, for whom the *nous* is able to apprehend the true world in itself, and the Neoplatonic mystics, the role of intuition in the spiritual sense looms large. Aristotle recognized the existence of intuitive knowledge (*Posterior Analytics* 1.9.76a21) in relation to the first principles, which are not in need of any demonstration. Augustine of Hippo, who believed that "the truth lies in the inner man," considered intuition a form of mental contemplation. Thomas Aquinas attributed to God the veritable creative intuition; he defined human intuitive cognition as "the presence, in some way, of the intelligible to the intellect" (*Commentaries on the Sentences* 1d3.94a5). The medieval scholastics used "intuitive cognition," as opposed to "abstractive cognition," to designate knowledge in which the object is delivered directly to the senses. For Descartes, intuition constitutes each successive link in a chain of deductions that are noninferential concepts of the "pure and attentive mind." For Spinoza, it is the third and highest degree of cognition. Kant recognized only sensible intuition. The German Idealists (Schelling, Fichte, Schopenhauer) and Husserlian phenomenologists viewed intellectual intuition as a deep and instantaneous understanding of things, essences, and situations given in perception. For Henri Bergson, intuition signifies an immediate awareness akin to instinct and sympathy, capable of penetrating its object while unfolding in the unique, qualitative time ("duration") of each living being. Bergson opposed intuition to intelligence, the proper dimensions of which are geometrical space and mechanical clock-time; for him, intuition alone is capable of grasping the dynamic nature of things in its original simplicity.

Religious Intuition. In religion, the term *intuition* functions on several levels; the specific meanings are mostly variants of the spiritual intuition defined previously. The following aspects of religious intuition may be distinguished: (1) the understanding of divine commands; (2) the perception of the divine in religious or numinous experience, in the sense of a peering into the mysterious elusive presence of the transcendent in ways simultaneously sensory (seeing, hearing, or "smelling" divinity), intellectual, and suprasensory; (3) the illuminating understanding of the meanings hidden in metaphors and other literary tropes of sacred writings; and (4) the means of communicating and communion among believers.

All forms of mysticism and gnosticism rely on intuition in the formulation of cognitive claims regarding the ineffable understanding of religious mysteries. The highest states of mystical contemplation may be conceived as uninterrupted chains of intuitive acts. The experience of nonduality in Advaita Vedānta, for example, is based on the insight of oneness and the disappearance of the distance between subject and object. "Suchness" *(tathatā)* in Mādhyamika Buddhism may be called an intuition of the ultimate as the invisible reality underlying all things. The Buddha's enlightenment constitutes an intuitive peak—the highest form of mystical contemplation. Zen Buddhism, with its abhorrence for the discursive intellect, emphasizes *satori* as the immediate grasp of the Buddha nature. The crux of Zen meditational disciplines, whether of gradual enlightenment (in the "*zazen* only" Sōtō school) or of sudden enlightenment (the *kōan*-solving Rinzai school), lies in the all-pervading illumination of the mind, an insight that reaches into that which is beyond any subjectivity or objectivity.

In Jewish mysticism, the secret contents of the Qabbalah are considered highly intuitive, obtained by a form of supernatural illumination. The poverty of ordinary human faculties does not allow proper cognition; intuition alone, tantamount in its "fine points" to divine inspiration, can create a felicitous "science of God" that reasoning is incapable of encompassing. Hence the claim, characteristic of Jewish mysticism, that true tradition and true intuition coincide, a tenet that plays an important part in the history of Qabbalah, that of maintaining the balance between tradition and innovation.

In Islam, intuition plays a role in connection with *al-ʿaql,* a cognitive faculty often mentioned in the Qur'ān that binds man to God (the root *ʿql* means literally "to bind"). Religious knowledge is participatory knowledge, higher than rational yet not opposed to the intellect. Direct vision by a "third eye," as opposed to the indirect knowledge yielded by intellectual ratiocination, is emphasized. In Islamic theology and philosophy, but especially in Ṣūfī mysticism, where the heart is traditionally considered the locus of intelligence and spirituality, the actually intuitive "knowledge of the heart" is connected with the creative imagination of the perfected universal man; such knowledge alone counts before the divine and is essential for salvation. In the esoteric tradition, some commentators of the Qur'ān considered the intuitive faculty a gift of revelation by the Holy Spirit (the archangel Gabriel), an illumination received by the intellect.

In Taoism, the doctrine of "no knowledge" or "ignorance" is aimed at obtaining true wisdom or intuition. Creativity is unconscious of accumulated technical knowledge, but it relies on the certainty and precision of intuitive knowledge.

[*See also* Knowledge and Ignorance.]

BIBLIOGRAPHY

Bahm, A. J. *Types of Intuition.* Albuquerque, 1960.

Bergson, Henri. *Introduction à la métaphysique.* Paris, 1903.

Hadamard, Jacques. *Subconscient, intuition, logique dans la recherche scientifique.* Paris, 1947.

Husserl, Edmund. *Ideas: General Introduction to Pure Phenomenology* (1913). Translated by W. R. Boyce Gibson. London, 1931.

Lévinas, Emmanuel. *Théorie de l'intuition dans la phénoménologie de Husserl.* New ed. Paris, 1963.

Lonergan, Bernard J. F. *Insight: A Study of Human Understanding.* London, 1957.

Nasr, Seyyed Hossein. "Intellect and Intuition: Their Relationship from the Islamic Perspective." *Studies in Comparative Religion* 13 (Winter–Spring 1979): 65–74.

Palliard, Jacques. *Intuition et réflexion.* Paris, 1925.

Penzo, Giorgio. "Riflessioni sulla intuitio tomista e sulla intuitio heideggeriana." *Aquinas* 9 (1966): 87–102.

Pritchard, Harold Arthur. *Moral Obligation.* Oxford, 1949.

Schuon, Frithjof. *L'œil du cœur.* Paris, 1950.

Stace, W. T. *Mysticism and Philosophy.* Philadelphia, 1960.

Thompson, D. G. "Intuition" and "Inference." *Mind* 3 (1878): 339–349, 468–479.

Verdú, Alfonso. *Abstraktion und Intuition als Wege zur Wahrheit in Yoga und Zen.* Munich, 1965.

Ileana Marcoulesco

INUIT RELIGION. The Inuit (Eskimo) live in the vast Arctic and sub-Arctic area that stretches from the eastern point of Siberia to eastern Greenland. Of the approximately 105,000 Inuit, 43,000 live in Greenland, 25,000 in Arctic Canada, 35,000 (plus 2,000 Aleut) in Alaska, and 1,500 (plus a small number of Aleut) in the Soviet Union. Language has been used as the basic criterion for defining the Inuit as an ethnic group. The "Eskimo languages" (as they are invariably referred to) are divided into two main branches, Inuit and Yupik. Inuit is spoken from northern Alaska to eastern Greenland, forming a continuum of dialects with mutual comprehension between adjacent dialects. Varieties of Yupik are spoken in Siberia and in southern Alaska as far north as Norton Sound.

The word *Eskimo* seems to be of Montagnais origin and has been erroneously believed to mean "eater of raw meat." The word *Inuit* means "people." *Inuit* as a self-designation is used primarily in Canada and, to some extent, in Greenland (where the more common self-designation is *Kalaallit*). *Yupik* means "a real person," just as *Inupiat,* which is the self-designation in northern Alaska, means "real people." *Inuit,* however, is the common term used to designate themselves collectively by the members of the Inuit Circumpolar Conference, an organization established in 1977 by representatives from Greenland, Canada, and Alaska.

Traditionally the Inuit are divided into many geographic groups. The members of each group, or band, were connected through kinship ties, but the band was without formal leadership. The nuclear family was the most important social unit, but the extended family often cohabited and worked cooperatively. Dyadic relationships, such as wife-exchange partners and joking partners, were also common.

Today, most Inuit live in the so-called Arctic area, north of the treeline and the 10°C July isotherm. The Inuit were hunters who adapted to the seasonal availability of various mammals, birds, and fish. Hunting sea mammals with harpoons was characteristic, but hunting inland during the summer was also part of the subsistence pattern of many Inuit. A few groups in northern Alaska and in Canada have spent the entire year inland, hunting caribou and fishing for arctic char. In southern Alaska, the wooded valleys along the long rivers were inhabited by Inuit who relied upon the great run of the fish as well as the migrations of sea mammals and birds.

Most Inuit in Canada lived in snow houses during the winter; others settled in winter houses built of stone and sod or wood. Stone lamps that burned blubber were used for heating, lighting, and cooking. Skin boats and, except in southern Greenland and Alaska, dog sledges were used for transportation; kayaks were used for seal hunting and large, open umiaks for whale hunting. Although some Inuit are still hunters and fishermen, today's Inuit societies are modernized. Money economy has replaced subsistence economy; modern technology and education have been introduced; television plays an important role; and so on. Except for the small population in Siberia, the Inuit have become Christians, and even the Inuit in Siberia no longer observe their religious traditions.

Historically, the Inuit held many observances to insure good hunting, and in the small and scattered hunting and fishing communities many local religious practices were observed. Generally, ritual life was more elaborate in Alaska than in Canada and Greenland. In Alaskan settlements there were usually one or more big men's houses, called *qarigi* among the Point Barrow Inuit and *qasiq* among those of the Bering Sea, where people gathered for social and religious feasts. In Canada, the Inuit built temporary festival snow houses, but no eyewitness accounts exist of festival houses in Greenland.

Relations between Men and Animals. According to eastern Inuit religious tradition, each animal had its own *inua* (its "man," "owner," or "spirit") and also its own "soul." Within the western Inuit religious tradition, the *inua* seems to have been identical to the soul. The idea of *inua* was applied to animals and implements as well as to concepts and conditions (such as sleep). Lakes, currents, mountains, and stars all had their own *inua*, but only the *inua* of the moon, air, and sea were integral to the religious life of the Inuit.

Since the Inuit believed that the animals they hunted possessed souls, they treated their game with respect. Seals and whales were commonly offered a drink of fresh water after they had been dragged ashore. Having received such a pleasant welcome as guests in the human world, their souls, according to Inuit belief, would return to the sea and soon become ready to be caught again, and they would also let their fellow animals know that they should not object to being caught. When the season's first kill of an important species of seal was made, the meat was distributed to all of the inhabitants of a settlement. This practice divided the responsibility for the kill among the entire community and increased the possibility of good hunting.

Inuit rituals in connection with the polar bear are part of an ancient bear ceremonialism of the circumpolar regions of Eurasia and North America. In southern Greenland, for example, the head of a slain polar bear was placed in a house facing the direction from which the bears usually came so that the bear's soul could easily find its way home. During the five days that the soul was believed to require to reach its destination the bear was honored: its eyes and nostrils were closed so that it would not be disturbed by the sight and smell of human beings; its mouth was smeared with blubber; and it was given presents. [*See also* Bears.]

Whaling was of great social, economic, and ritual importance, especially among the North Alaska Inuit. In the spring, all hunting gear was carefully cleaned, and the women made new clothes for the men. The whales would not be approached until everything was cleaned. During the days before the whaling party set out, the men slept in the festival house and observed sexual and food taboos. The whaling season terminated with a great feast to entertain the whales.

Taboos, Amulets, and Songs. Unlike cultic practices in connection with the deities, which had relatively minor significance, taboos, amulets, and songs were fundamentally important to the Inuit. Most taboos were imposed to separate the game from a person who was tabooed because of birth, menstruation, or death. A separation between land and sea animals was also important in many localities, reflecting the seasonal changes in hunting adaptation. An infringement of a taboo might result in individual hardship (for example, the loss of good fortune in hunting, sickness, or even death), but often, it was feared, the whole community would suffer. Usually a public confession under the guidance of the shaman was believed sufficient to reduce the effect of the transgression of a taboo.

Amulets, which dispensed their powers only to the first owner, were used primarily to secure success in hunting and good health and, to a lesser degree, to ward off negative influences. Parents and grandparents would usually buy amulets for children from a shaman. Amulets were usually made up of parts of animals and birds, but a wide variety of objects could be used. They were sewn on clothing or placed in boats and houses.

One way to increase the effect of the amulets was

through the use of food totems and secret songs. Used primarily to increase success in hunting, secret songs and formulas were also used to control other activities and were often associated with food taboos. Songs were either inherited or bought. If a song was passed on from one generation to the next, all members of the family were free to use it, but once it was sold it became useless to its former owners.

Rites of Passage. In many localities in Canada and Alaska, women had to give birth alone, isolated in a small hut or tent. For a specified period after the birth, the woman was subjected to food and work taboos. Children were usually named after a person who had recently died. The name was regarded as a vital part of the individual, and, in a way, the deceased lived on in the child. The relationship resulted in a close social bond between the relatives of the deceased and the child.

The family celebrated particular stages in a child's development, especially in connection with subsistence activities. For example, when a boy killed his first seal, the meat was distributed to all the inhabitants of the settlement, and for each new important species a hunter killed, there was a celebration and ritual distribution.

Death was considered to be a passage to a new existence. There were two lands of the dead: one in the sky and one in the sea (or underground). The Inuit in Greenland considered the land in the sea more attractive because people living there enjoyed perpetual success in whale hunting; those in the sky, on the other hand, led dull existences. It was not the moral behavior of the deceased that determined the location of his afterlife, but rather the way in which he died. For example, men who died while whaling or women who died in childbirth were assured of an afterlife in the sea. Conceptions of the afterlife, however, differed among the Inuit. The Canadian and Alaskan Inuit believed the most attractive afterlife was found in the sky. Some Inuit had either poorly conceptualized beliefs in an afterlife or no beliefs at all.

While death rituals usually included only the nearest family members and neighbors, the Great Feast of the Dead, celebrated in the Alaskan mainland from the Kuskokwim River to the Kotzebue Sound, attracted participants even from neighboring villages. The feast was given jointly, and the hosts' social status was demonstrated by the quantity of food, furs, clothing, and implements that were given away.

The Bladder feast, an important calendar feast celebrated in Alaska from Kodiak Island to Point Hope, was held in midwinter. At this feast, the bladders of all the seals that had been caught during the previous year were returned to the sea in order that their souls might come back in new bodies and let themselves be caught again. The skins of all the small birds and animals that the boys had caught were displayed in the festival house, and gifts were given to human souls, to the souls of the seals, and to those who were present.

Shamans. In Greenland and Canada, the shaman *(angakkoq)* played a central role in religion. In Alaska, however, where it was common for an individual to become a shaman as the result of a calling, many rites did not demand the expertise of the shaman. Prospective shamans often learned from skilled shamans how to acquire spirits and to use techniques such as ecstatic trances. In Greenland and Labrador, the apprentice was initiated by being "devoured" by a polar bear or a big dog while being in trance alone in the wilderness. After having revived, he was ready to become master of various spirits.

Shamans in Greenland always used a drum to enter a trance. Masks were also instrumental, especially in Alaska, both in secular and religious connections. The shaman might summon his familiar spirits to the house where a séance was taking place, or he might go on a spiritual flight himself. The Canadian shaman might, for example, go down to the *inua* of the sea, that is, the Sea Woman, to get seals. In Alaska, a shaman on Nunivak Island would go to the villages of the various species of animals in the sea. In the Norton Sound area he would go to the moon to obtain animals for the settlement.

Although shamans were the principal revealers of unknown things, some other people could also acquire information from the spirits by using a simple technique called *qilaneq*. It required that an individual lift an object and then pose questions, which were answered affirmatively or negatively according to whether the object felt heavy or not.

Shamans also functioned as doctors. For example, they would suck the sick spot where a foreign object had been introduced or try to retrieve a stolen soul. Sorcerers—often believed to be old, revengeful women—were also common, and shamans were sometimes called to reveal them. There were instances, however, in which the shaman himself was accused of having used his power to harm someone; in such cases the shaman could be killed.

The Deities. The Inuit of Canada and Greenland believed that the *inua* of the sea, the Sea Woman, controlled the sea animals and would withhold them to punish people when they had broken a taboo. Franz Boas (1888) transcribed the name given to her by the Inuit on Baffin Island as *Sedna*, which probably means "the one down there." [*See* Sedna.]

The Inuit of eastern Baffin Island ritually killed

Sedna during a feast that was held when the autumn storms came and whose purpose was to make sealing possible again. The Sedna ceremony included, *inter alia,* a ritual spouse exchange and a tug-of-war, the result of which predicted the weather for the coming winter.

While Sedna represented the female principle of the world, the *inua* of the moon, Aningaaq, represented the male principle. An origin myth tells how he was once a man who committed incest with his sister. She became the sun, he the moon. Otherwise the sun played no part in the religion of the Inuit, but the moon was associated with the fertility of women. He was recognized as a great hunter, and some Alaskan Inuit believed that the moon controlled the game. [*See* Aningaaq.]

The air was called Sila, which also means "universe" and "intellect." The *inua* of the air was a rather abstract but feared figure; if it was offended when taboos were broken, it would take revenge by bringing storms and blizzards.

The Raven appeared, primarily in Alaska, as a creator, culture hero, and trickster in a cycle of myths that included those of the earth diver and the origin of the light. The Raven, however, played a negligible role in religious practices. [*See* Tricksters, *article on* North American Tricksters.]

The differences between and sometimes vagueness in Inuit religious ideas may be related not only to their wide and scattered distribution but also to the fact that their societies had a loose social organization and were without a written language before contact with the Europeans. For all Inuit, however, a close and good relationship with the animals on which they depended for their survival was believed to be of vital importance.

BIBLIOGRAPHY

An excellent survey of Inuit culture from prehistoric to modern times is given in the *Handbook of North American Indians,* vol. 5, edited by David Damas (Washington, D.C., 1984). The best survey of Inuit religion is Margaret Lantis's article "The Religion of the Eskimos," in *Forgotten Religions,* edited by Vergilius Ferm (New York, 1950), pp. 311–339. Lantis is also the author of *Alaskan Eskimo Ceremonialism* (New York, 1947). This well-documented book is based primarily on literary sources, but it also contains Lantis's field notes from Nunivak. A review of the religion of the Inuit in Canada and Greenland has been written by Birgitte Sonne and myself as an introduction to a collection of plates that illustrate the religious life of these people in *Eskimos: Greenland and Canada* (Leiden, 1985), vol. 8, pt. 2, of the series "Iconography of Religions." A strong visual impression of the Bering Sea Inuit culture in the nineteenth century is found in William W. Fitzhugh and Susan A. Kaplan's *Inua: Spirit World of the Bering Sea Eskimo* (Washington, D.C., 1982). This is a fascinating book that examines how the spirit world manifests itself in all areas of the life of these Inuit. A study of the religion of two Inuit groups in Canada is given in J. G. Oosten's *The Theoretical Structure of the Religion of the Netsilik and Iglulik* (Mappel, Netherlands, 1976). Information that has been gathered on rituals in connection with animals is presented in Regitze Søby's article "The Eskimo Animal Cult," *Folk* (Copenhagen) 11/12 (1969–1970): 43–78. The position of the Inuit shaman has been analyzed by Birgitte Sonne in "The Professional Ecstatic in His Social and Ritual Position," in *Religious Ecstasy,* edited by Nils G. Holm (Stockholm, 1982), pp. 128–150, and by Daniel Merkur in his *Becoming Half Hidden: Shamanism and Initiation among the Inuit* (Stockholm, 1985).

Among the many valuable and often quoted books by Knud Rasmussen is *The Netsilik Eskimos: Social Life and Spiritual Culture* (Copenhagen, 1931). This book presents material that Rasmussen collected from various groups of Inuit who had had limited contact with the Euro-American world. Among the many valuable studies on the Alaskan Inuit, two should be mentioned: Robert F. Spencer's *The North Alaskan Eskimo: A Study in Ecology and Society* (Washington, D.C., 1959) and Ann Fienup-Riordan's *The Nelson Island Eskimo: Social Structure and Ritual Distribution* (Anchorage, Alaska, 1983).

An extensive bibliography for Inuit religion is given by John Fisher in his article "Bibliography for the Study of Eskimo Religion," *Anthropologica,* n.s. 15 (1973): 231–271.

INGE KLEIVAN

IOANN OF KRONSTADT (Ivan Il'ich Sergeev, 1829–1908), also known as John of Kronstadt; Russian Orthodox priest. Ioann was born in the village of Suro in the Arkhangelsk province of Russia and at the age of ten was sent to the parochial school in Arkhangelsk. He later entered the seminary there, finishing at the top of his class in 1851. He then enrolled in the Theological Academy of Saint Petersburg, one of the four graduate faculties of theology in the empire. High-strung, physically weak, overworked, and radically committed to his life of study, prayer, ascetic discipline, and spiritual struggle, Ioann suffered greatly during these academic years. An added burden was the constant necessity to support himself by outside work. He finished the academy near the bottom of his class in 1855, was ordained deacon on 11 November of that year, and priest on the very next day.

Before accepting priestly ordination, Ioann dreamed of becoming pastor of Saint Andrew's Cathedral in the port city of Kronstadt, a naval base and penal colony on the island of Kotlin in the Gulf of Finland near Saint Petersburg. Kronstadt, teeming with outcasts and criminals, was notorious as a place of dirt, darkness, and sin. Since parish priests as a rule could not be celibate, Ioann married Elizaveta Nesvitskii, the daughter of Saint Andrew's retiring pastor, but he never consummated the marriage, a fact that has caused much debate since it remains unclear whether the bride had consented to such an arrangement.

Ioann served as pastor of the Kronstadt church until his death on 20 December 1908 at the age of eighty-one. His priestly career was distinguished by numerous acts of social, charitable, and educational work, both personal and institutional. Ioann established philanthropic agencies such as the Home for Constructive Labor, which provided free schools, workshops, training centers, libraries, counseling services, medical care, and food, for people of all ages. He also taught religious classes in the parish school for thirty-two years, not freeing himself from this obligation until 1889.

Ioann's greatest fame, however, was not as a philanthropist or a pedagogue but as a man of prayer. He was sought by people of all classes and religions from all parts of the Russian empire and beyond as an intercessor before God. From early in his priestly career he began the unprecedented practice, even for monastics, of celebrating all of the Orthodox church services every day, including the eucharistic liturgy. He did so with great fervor and devotion, spending long hours at the altar praying for those who begged his intercession. He often added his own words to the official church prayers and always insisted that the thousands of people who thronged to his church each day participate fully in the worship by receiving Holy Communion. To make this radically innovative practice possible, Ioann further instituted public confession whereby the crowds of penitents openly acknowledged their sins before all while the praying priest walked about the church bestowing absolution and offering counsel.

Ioann, who had come to be known as the "all-Russian pastor," was violently attacked by his detractors for his radical practices, and only the protection of the tsar kept him from becoming the object of punitive action. His spiritual diary, *My Life in Christ,* is a classic of contemporary Russian Orthodox spirituality.

BIBLIOGRAPHY

Ioann of Kronstadt's spiritual diary, *Moia zhizn' vo khriste* (My Life in Christ), is available in the original Russian (Moscow, 1892), and in English translation by Ernest E. Goulaeff (1897; reprint, Jordanville, N.Y., 1971). English excerpts from this work can be found in *The Spiritual Counsels of Father John of Kronstadt,* edited by W. Jardine Grisbrooke (London, 1967; Greenwood, S.C., 1983), and G. P. Fedotov's *A Treasury of Russian Spirituality* (1950; reprint, Belmont, Mass., 1975). A two-volume work in Russian analyzing Ioann of Kronstadt's life and work, containing letters, photographs, and a church service in his honor, is I. K. Surskii's *Otets Ioann Kronshtadtskii* (Father John of Kronstadt), 2 vols. (Forestville, Calif., 1979–1980). The best work in English is *Father John of Kronstadt: A Life,* by (Bishop) Alexander Semenoff-Tian-Chansky (Crestwood, N.Y., 1979).

THOMAS HOPKO

IPPEN (1239–1289), also known as Chishin; a Japanese holy man, founder of the Jishū, an order of Pure Land Buddhist itinerants. Ippen was born in the province of Iyo (modern Ehime Prefecture) to a long-powerful military clan, the Kōno, which had recently suffered a serious defeat in the Jōkyū War of 1221. Ippen's grandfather died in exile, and Ippen, three of his brothers, and his father all became monks. At the age of twelve, Ippen was sent to Kyushu to study the doctrines of the Seizan branch of the Jōdo (Pure Land) sect. Upon the death of his father in 1263, he returned to household life in Iyo. Perhaps because of intraclan strife, he left home again eight years later, and spent the rest of his life on the road as a holy man *(hijiri).*

Ippen initially went on pilgrimages to the great Buddhist temples and Shintō shrines and underwent austerities in the mountains of Shikoku. While on a pilgrimage to Kumano in 1274, he had the climactic experience of his life. The Shintō deity *(kami)* of the main shrine, believed to be a manifestation of Amida Buddha, appeared before him and commanded him to distribute to all people, regardless of their belief or unbelief, purity or impurity, paper talismans *(fuda)* on which were printed the words "Namu Amida Butsu" ("Homage to Amida Buddha"). This Ippen did for the rest of his life, traveling throughout the Japanese archipelago.

By 1278, Ippen had attracted a small group of followers that he called the Jishū, or "time group," referring to its chanting of Amida's name at all times. Before his death, this group numbered perhaps over two hundred men and women, and Ippen had established rules for group poverty and incessant wayfaring. In addition, he had enrolled 251,724 names in a register of lay supporters.

In 1279, this Jishū began its distinctive dance *(odori nembutsu)* celebrating the instantaneous salvation available in Amida's name. Originally spontaneous and ecstatic, the dance became a regularized performance by members of the Jishū on the grounds of shrines and temples, and in other public areas such as beaches and markets. After being brutally driven out of Kamakura, the shogunal capital, in 1282, Ippen led his Jishū to the provinces around the imperial capital (modern Kyoto). Here he met with great success and was even invited to many notable temples and shrines. In 1288, Ippen led his group to his home in Iyo and then back across the Inland Sea, where he died in 1289. He is buried near the modern city of Kobe.

Ippen interpreted the Pure Land *sūtras* to mean that Amida's enlightenment and the rebirth *(ōjō)* of all beings into Amida's Pure Land were precisely the same event. Since Amida's enlightenment had occurred ten *kalpas* ago, so too must have the rebirth of all beings. Both, furthermore, had their origin in "Namu Amida Butsu," the "six-character name" established through the vows Amida had made while still a *bodhisattva*. For this reason, the name alone was sufficient to effect the rebirth attained ten *kalpas* ago and to obliterate the distinctions between then and now, between this world and the Pure Land, and indeed between all beings and Buddhahood. Ippen's paper talismans, therefore, immediately saved all who received them, regardless of their faith, practice, or morality. The dance served as a celebration of this absolutely universal salvation.

Ippen's thought was largely derived from that of the Seizan branch of the Jōdo sect, itself strongly influenced by Esoteric *(mikkyō)* Buddhism. His originality lay in using these ideas to employ for Buddhist salvation existing popular traditions of shamanistic holy men and magic. The Jishū became the largest itinerant order of medieval Japan, absorbing earlier, similar groups, and several of its members were important in the literature and arts of the Muromachi period (1338–1573). Many samurai supported the Jishū, attracted by its endorsement of Shintō, and used its members both as a cultural entourage and as participants in funeral and memorial services. The fortunes of the order declined dramatically, however, with the turmoil that swept the country at the end of that period, and the Jishū continues today as only a minor Buddhist sect with headquarters in the city of Fujisawa.

Nevertheless, the practices and beliefs of the Jishū were widely diffused among the Japanese during the medieval period. Ippen's dance, for example, continues as a feature of folk Buddhism in several regions and is tied to the legendary founding of the *kabuki* theater. The *Ippen hijiri e* (Illustrated Life of the Holy Man Ippen), a work of twelve scrolls completed in 1299, is one of the masterpieces of Japanese painting and the single most important source for studying popular life in thirteenth-century Japan.

[*See also* Nien-fo.]

BIBLIOGRAPHY

A 1756 collection of Ippen's sayings, letters, and verse has been translated and annotated by Dennis Hirota and serialized as "The Records of Ippen" in six issues of *The Eastern Buddhist*, n.s. 11 (May 1978): 50–65 and (October 1978): 113–131; 12 (May 1979): 130–147; 13 (Spring 1980): 104–115; 14 (Spring 1981): 94–112 and (Autumn 1981): 95–120. The only other substantial work on Ippen in English is my "Ippen and Popular Buddhism in Kamakura Japan" (Ph.D. diss., Stanford University, 1977). In Japanese, the two best works are Ōhashi Toshio's *Ippen: Sono kōdō to shisō* (Tokyo, 1971) and Kanai Kiyomitsu's *Ippen to Jishū kyōdan* (Tokyo, 1975).

JAMES H. FOARD

IQBAL, MUHAMMAD (1877–1938), influential Muslim poet-philosopher of the Indian subcontinent. Born at Sialkot (presently a Pakistani town on the border of India), Iqbal received his early schooling in his native town and his college education at Lahore (where he studied philosophy with the British Islamicist T. W. Arnold). In 1905 he went to Europe, where he followed M'Taggart's lectures in philosophy, took his doctorate from Munich with a thesis on the development of metaphysics in Persia, and was called to the bar from Lincoln's Inn in London in 1908. In the same year he returned to Lahore where he taught for a while at the Government College and pursued a hectic but unsuccessful law practice. He was knighted in 1922 for his contributions to poetry (about 60 percent of which is in Persian and 40 percent in Urdu). In 1927 he was elected to the Punjab Legislative Assembly, and in 1930 he gave the historic presidential address to the annual session of the Muslim League at Allahabad, wherein he suggested that the solidly Muslim areas of northwest India might be given autonomy so that Muslims could run their affairs according to Islamic norms, the idea that later took the shape of Pakistan. During his last years he was often ill and did not appear in public after April 1936. He died on 21 April 1938 and was buried in the complex of the Imperial Mosque of Lahore. Iqbal's commitment to the creation of Pakistan was a direct result of his philosophic thought, which was so powerfully expressed in his poetry.

Iqbal had displayed his unusual talent as a moving and eloquent poet with a "grand style" even in his college days. Before going to Europe he had been a Platonic idealist, an Indian nationalist, and a romanticist of the past who sang hymns to the Himalayas, to intercommunal understanding, and to universal love. In Europe, he discovered Islam with a vengeance, having been shocked by his experience of the European double standards that combined liberal morality and democracy at home with colonial exploitation abroad and, even at home, with the capitalistic exploitation of the working classes. Coupled with this disillusionment he saw the increasing dilapidation of human values in the machine age and the decline of the family institution. But looking at the Eastern and particularly the Muslim societies, he found them in deep somnolence. At this point, he discovered the "true Islam" of the Qur'ān and of Muḥammad, an Islam that was dynamic and not static; in its dynamism he discovered a creative impulse that directed the raw materials of history into a positive moral channel. The modern West, unlike the world of Islam, was industrious enough, but it lacked a positive moral direction for the uplift of humanity; it was inventive but not creative and was, in fact, destructive to the human moral fiber. Henceforth, he invited the whole world, both Muslim and non-Muslim, to join this energizing and ethically positive Islam.

In the development of this dynamic philosophy, which is expressed in Bergsonian vitalistic terms (although unlike Bergson, Iqbal regards God as being outside the process of history), the key role is played by the twin terms *khudī* ("self") and *ʿishq* ("absorbing love," or *élan vital*). The goal of this ethical dynamism is to expand and fortify the self (which is the only way to individual survival after death), since only when an enlarged and fortified self is realized can a meaningful community of the faithful be launched on earth as the prophet Muḥammad was able to do. Although in the early years of his intellectual development after his discovery of Islam Iqbal was not optimistic about a similar reawakening on the part of the Muslim community at large, he did eventually come to place his faith in such a development. Through both his poetry and his major prose work, *The Reconstruction of Religious Thought in Islam* (chapter 5), he tried to urge Muslims to create a new future through *ijtihād*, literally "exerting oneself," a Muslim legal term for independent reasoning, which Iqbal used to describe the exercise of new creative thought within the framework of Islam.

Iqbal, who had been known as a good poet in Urdu early on, first indicated his concern with the Muslim cause in the two great poems *Shikwah* (Complaint) and *Jawāb* (Answer, that is, God's response to the complaint), but he subsequently turned to Persian in order to reach a larger group of educated Muslims. His *Asrār-i khudī* (Secrets of the Self), first published in 1915, speaks of that individual human core that should be strengthened until it reaches its highest fulfillment. The duties of this "self" in the community were discussed two years later in the *Rumūz-i bīkhudī* (Mysteries of Selflessness). The Persian collection *Payām-i mashriq* (Message of the East) acknowledges Iqbal's spiritual debt to Goethe, who was his Western guide as much as Mawlānā Rūmī was his Eastern master. His major Persian work is the *Jāvīd-nāmah* (Jāvīd's Book), written for his son in 1932. In this spiritual journey through the spheres in Rūmī's company, he discusses religious, political, and social problems with Muslim and non-Muslim poets and thinkers alike. Among his Urdu poetry, *Bāl-i Jibrīl* (Gabriel's Wing) is outstanding.

The titles of Iqbal's work point to his understanding of himself: he wanted to use "the rod of Moses" *(ẓarb-i kalīm)* and assumed the role of "the sound of the camel-bell" *(bāng-i darā)* that had led the Muslims in the caravan of the Prophet back to Mecca. The general impression among Westerners that Iqbal indulged in romanticization of the past glory of Islam is not correct. While he did show romanticizing tendencies before his "conversion," after his discovery of the dynamic nature of Islam, he was anything but a romanticist of the past. He continually called for the creation of a new future, although he singled out, for the sake of inspiration, certain past achievements of the Muslims, as, for example, in his poem *The Mosque of Cordoba*, which appears in *Bāl-i Jibrīl.*

BIBLIOGRAPHY

Iqbal's collected persian poetic works have been published in Tehran (1964) and in Pakistan (1973), while his collected Urdu poetic works were published in Pakistan in 1975 and reproduced in India in 1980. *The Reconstruction of Religious Thought in Islam* has had (like his poetic works) a number of printings, including a recent one from Lahore in 1960. A major part of his Urdu poetry has been translated into English by V. G. Kiernan under the title *Poems from Iqbal* (London, 1955); some of his Persian poetic works have been translated by Reynold A. Nicholson and A. J. Arberry, although several still await translation.

Translations into German by Annemarie Schimmel include *Payām-i Mashriq* as *Botschaft des Ostens* (Wiesbaden, 1963); *Jāvīd-nāmah* as *Das Buch der Ewigkeit* (Munich, 1967); and *Muhammad Iqbal, Persischer Psalter* (Cologne, 1968), with selected poetry and prose. Iqbal's Urdu poetry has also been translated into German by Johann Christoph Bürgel as *Steppe im Staubkorn* (Bern, 1983). Italian translations by Alessandro Bausani include "Il 'Gulšan-i raz-i ǧadid' di Muhammad Iqbāl," *Annali Istituto Universitario Orientale di Napoli*, n.s. 8 (1958): 125–172; *Il poema celeste* (Rome, 1952); and *Poesie di Muhammad Iqbal* (Parma, 1956). There are also French, Czech, Dutch, Arabic, and Russian translations available, and much of his work has been translated into the regional languages of Pakistan.

There has been a plethora of works on Iqbal, not all of good quality. The following three should give a comprehensive introduction to Iqbal's thought as well as his biography and bibliographies: Syed Abdul Vahid's *Iqbal: His Art and Thought* (Lahore, 1944); Annemarie Schimmel's *Gabriel's Wing: A Study into the Religious Ideas of Sir Muhammad Iqbal* (Leiden, 1963); and *Iqbal: The Poet-Philosopher of Pakistan*, edited by Hafeez Malik (New York, 1971).

FAZLUR RAHMAN

IRANIAN RELIGIONS. Because of the scarce and fragmented data in our possession, we do not know the religions of ancient Iran, other than Zoroastrianism, as organic systems endowed with a specific pantheon, a mythology, particular creeds, cosmogonic and cosmological ideas, and precise eschatological notions. We can postulate the existence of other religions only through a careful analysis of those elements contained within Zoroastrianism that can be linked to a pre-Zoroastrian paganism and through an Indo-Iranian comparison. That is to say, we have no sources, other than the Zoroastrian, for any Iranian religion. Some scholars have viewed as testimony of a non-Zoroastrian cult those few religious references found in the royal Achaemenid inscriptions (sixth to fourth century BCE), as well as Herodotus's mention of "the Persian religion" (1.131–132), although, as is well known, Herodotus never refers to Zarathushtra (Zoroaster). Given these meager materials, we cannot be sure that the cults referred to were not affected in some way or at some time by the Zoroastrian "reform." In fact, it is probably most prudent to consider the religion of the Achaemenids—whose inscriptions also never mention Zarathushtra—as belonging to the Zoroastrian tradition and as a stage in its troubled and complex historical development.

Having said this, it is nonetheless possible to reconstruct a few essential elements of ancient Iranian religions through traces of ideas and beliefs that appear to be independent of the Zoroastrian tradition. Some of these are completely original, but most are held in common with ancient, especially Vedic, India. Such elements pertain mainly to rituals, the pantheon, concepts of death and the afterlife, and cosmology.

Rituals included libations *(zaothra),* offered both to Āpas ("water") and to Ātar ("fire"). The latter was called Agni by the Indians. The libations offered to water were a blend of three ingredients: milk and the juice or leaves of two plants. Those offered to fire were also a blend of three ingredients: dry fuel, incense, and animal fat. In both the libations to water and fire, called *āb-zōhr* and *ātakhsh-zōhr* in late Zoroastrian literature, we find the symbolism of the number three, which also occurs in a number of Brahmanic practices, as well as the blending of ingredients from the animal and vegetable worlds.

These offerings to water and fire, typical of a daily and familiar ritual, were also at the heart of the priestly ritual called the Yasna by the Iranians and Yajña by the Indians, from the root *yaz* ("sacrifice, worship"). Animal sacrifice was certainly practiced in the oldest Yasna and was accompanied by prayers that made it sacred and justified it as a religious act through which the spirits of the household animals being sacrificed became absorbed into a divine entity called Gēush Urvan, the "soul of the bull." Herbs also played an important role in the Yasna, and the priest who carried out the sacrifice held a bundle of herbs in his left hand, called a *baresman* by the Iranians. In time the bundle of herbs was discarded in favor of a bundle of consecrated twigs.

Undoubtedly, *haoma* (*soma* in Sanskrit) constituted a central element in the cult. The offering made to the waters at the conclusion of the Yasna was prepared by blending milk, the leaves of a plant, and the juice squeezed from the stems of a different plant. The substance's name, *haoma,* applied to both the sacrificial matter and its *yazata,* that is, the "being worthy of worship," or deity, whom it represented. *Haoma,* which was endowed with hallucinogenic and stimulating properties and was seen as a source of strength for warriors, inspiration for poets, and wisdom for priests, was extracted in a stone mortar during a preparatory ritual, after which the consecrated substance was consumed by the priests and by those taking part in the ceremony. [*See* Haoma *and* Yazatas.]

The premises, the instruments, and the ingredients for the ceremony were purified with water in a meticulous and careful way. Purifying and disinfectant properties were also attributed to cattle urine *(gōmez),* a substance that played an important role in the Zoroastrian ritual of the Great Purification, Bareshnūm, as well as in the initiation of priests and corpse-beares, in accordance with practices and notions that were certainly Indo-Iranian in origin.

Libations offered to water and fire, essential components in the ceremonial aspects of the cult, cannot be understood without an awareness of the complex symbolism linked to those two elements, both in Zoroastrian and pre-Zoroastrian Iran, as well as in ancient India. The Indo-Iranian background is particularly evident in the symbolism of fire: in the three ritual fires and in the five natural fires found in Iranian and Indian thought. We can trace the concept of the three fires, those of priests, warriors, and farmers, as well as the concept of five fires burning before Ahura Mazdā, in the bodies of men, animals, plants, clouds, and the earth, respectively, to the Indo-Iranian background. Two *yazatas,* Apąm Napāt ("grandson [or son] of waters") and Nairyōsanha ("of manly utterance"), are linked to fire and have Indian counterparts in Apāṃ Napāt and Narāśaṃsā, an epithet for Agni, whose name also belongs to a different god in the Vedas.

Concerning the pantheon, an Indo-Iranian comparison provides considerable help in reconstructing the pre-Zoroastrian religious environment in Iran. There are many divine entities that derive from a common cultural heritage, although they do, at times, present significant differences. Particularly important in such comparisons is the section of the Avesta known as the *Yashts,* or hymns to the various *yazata*s, which mostly perpetuate the worship of gods from an ancient, pre-Zoroastrian cult through a veil of zoroastrianization after the fact. Worthy of mention, in addition to the cult gods Āpas, Ātar, Gēush Urvan, and Haoma, are the nature gods, such as Asman ("heaven"), Zam ("earth"), Hvar ("sun"), Māh ("moon"), and the two winds, Vāta and Vāyu. A juxtaposition with the Vedic religion clarifies many aspects of an ancient theology dating back to a period that we can definitely call proto-Indo-Iranian. According to some scholars, a few of these divine beings, as well as others well known to the Zoroastrian tradition, such as Zrwan (Zurwān) and Mithra, were originally high gods of Iranian religions other than the Zoroastrian and were thus in competition with Ahura Mazdā, the creator god of Zoroastrianism. [*See* Ahura Mazdā and Angra Mainyu.] Apart from a few specific details in the theories propounded by various scholars (H. S. Nyberg, Stig Wikander, Geo Widengren), and apart from the complex question of the so-called Zurvanist heresy, it is hard not to recognize a certain degree of verisimilitude in their reconstructions, as we find embedded in the Zoroastrian tradition, and not only in the *Yashts,* clear traces of a plurality of heterogeneous elements gradually absorbed and modified.

The Iranian pantheon, like the Indian, was subdivided into two main groups of divine beings, *ahura*s and *daiva*s, although there exists sufficient evidence to hold that in Iran the latter word at one time indicated the gods in general. This can be inferred from the Avestan expression *daēva/mashya,* analogous to the Vedic *deva/martya,* to which correspond the Greek *theoi/andres (anthrōpoi)* and the Latin *dii/hominesque,* all of which mean "gods and men." *Daiva*s, as gods of an ancient polytheism condemned by Zarathushtra, acquired negative connotations only with the Zoroastrian reform. This happened also with some of the Indo-Iranian gods, such as Indra, Saurva (Śarva in India), and Nānhaithya (Nāsatya in India). The term *ahura* ("lord"; *asura* in India), on the other hand, maintained its positive connotations and became part of the name of the supreme god of Zoroastrianism, Ahura Mazdā, as well as being attached to the name of some of the ancient gods from the Indo-Iranian pantheon, such as Mithra (Mitra in India) and Apąm Napāt. [*See* Ahuras *and* Daivas.]

We are not able to establish whether, behind the image of Ahura Mazdā, which was probably created by Zarathushtra himself, there lies the Vedic Indian god Varuṇa or an Indo-Iranian god named Ahura or Asura. This problem, however, is not critical, for even if Zarathushtra's god were a sublimation of the ancient Varuṇa by the Iranian prophet's great religious reform, Varuṇa would certainly have already attained a higher status than that of other gods, such as Mitra or the other sovereign gods of the Indo-Iranian pantheon (Dumézil, 1968–1973).

If the Iranian Mithra corresponds to the weaker Indian Mitra, then Anāhitā, the other great divine being of the triad mentioned in the Achaemenid inscriptions, corresponds to the Indian Sarasvatī, through the Avestan Aredvī Sūrā Anāhitā. [*See* Anāhitā.] The latter, however, presents some very complex problems. Most likely, this ancient Indo-Iranian goddess was subject at an early date to the influence of religious concepts belonging to the Anarian substratum of the Iranian world. Even Herodotus (1.131), speaks of an "Assyrian" and an "Arabian" origin of the great goddess, who certainly shows traits typical of the Great Goddess of the most ancient settled civilizations of the Near and Middle East. In fact, in attempting to reconstruct Iranian religions other than Zoroastrianism, one must rely heavily on elements obtained through an investigation of the Indo-Iranian background. One must, however, try to ascertain, with the help of archaeological findings, what part was played by the Anarian substratum, from the Elam civilization to the so-called Helmand civilization, which came to light in the 1960s during excavations at Shahr-i Sokhta, in Iranian Seistan. A thorough investigation into more recent times is also necessary in order to see whether there are to be found, among the religions of the Hindu Kush, between Nuristan and Dardistan, any fossilized remains of ancient proto-Indo-Aryan religions (Jettmar, 1975; Tucci, 1977).

An Indo-Iranian comparison also provides many other elements pertaining to the pantheon, as well as mythical figures and epos. The latter has been the object of particularly detailed study in recent decades (Dumézil, 1968–1973; Wikander, 1949–1950; Molé, 1953). In this context, we find cast in a leading role the Iranian god Verethraghna, whose Indian name, Vṛtrahan ("slayer of the dragon Vṛtra"), is an epithet of the god Indra. Behind the sacred figure of Verethraghna, who represented victory in the Zoroastrian tradition, was, most likely, the idea of overcoming an obstacle to the activity of the cosmos, which is manifest through the flow of waters.

In the cosmogony of pre-Zoroastrian Iran, we find signs of a myth of separation of heaven and earth, in which the figure of Vāyu, the god of wind and of the atmosphere, the intermediate zone, must have played an important role. It is likely also that the doctrine of seven consecutive creations, of the sky, of water, earth, vegetation, animal life, man, and fire, which we find in late sources, in fact dates from very ancient times.

Essential elements are also provided by an Indo-Iranian comparison in matters pertaining to cosmology. Both Iranians and Indians believed that the world was divided into seven regions, whose Avestan name was *karshvar* (Pahl., *kēshwar;* Skt., *dvīpa*), and that it was surrounded by a mountain range. The central region was called Khvaniratha in Iran and Jambūdvīpa in India, and at its center was a high mountain, called Mount Harā in Iran and Meru or Sumeru in India. South of the mountain was the Tree of All Seeds, just as, in Indian cosmography, we find the Jambū Tree south of Mount Meru. The Tree of All Seeds was thought to be at the center of the great sea Vourukasha, to the south of the mountain standing at the center of the world, also called, in Avestan, Hukairya ("of good activity") or, in Pahlavi, Hukar and Cagād i Dāidīg ("the lawful summit"). [*See also* Cosmology, *article on* Hindu and Jain Cosmologies.]

The views of death and of the afterlife in the most ancient Iranian religions, before the Zoroastrian reform, seem to have included the survival of the soul *(urvan).* After wandering around the earth for three days, the soul was thought to enter a gray existence in a subterranean world of shadows, ruled by Yima, the first king, or king of the Golden Age, and the first man ever to have died. (The figure of Yima seems to correspond, although not without some question, to the Indian Yama.) There also appears to have been a notion of survival of a sort of "double" of the soul, the *fravashi,* linked to a concept of immortality typical of an aristocratic and warrior society, in which were present the values of the Indo-Iranian *Männerbund* (Wikander, 1983). [*See* Fravashis.] There was, as well, the idea of a terrible trial to be overcome by the dead man's spirit: the crossing of Chinvat Bridge, a bridge that could become wider or narrower, to the width of a razor's edge, depending on whether the dead man had been just *(ashavant)* or evil *(dregvant).* There was probably a test, analogous to this trial after death, used in initiation rites (Nyberg, 1966). [*See* Chinvat Bridge.]

Traces of a common concept of initiation can be found in both Iran and India. It is related to the basic Indo-Iranian religious idea of *asha* (in the Avesta) or *ṛta* (in the Vedas), which remained central even in Zarathushtra's reform, although modified by partly new and different aspects. If we compare the Indian and the Iranian ideas, we can see clearly that a vision of *asha* (or of the sun, which, in turn, is the visible manifestation of the Vedic *ṛta*), was considered by both as a step in the spiritual fulfillment of the believer, who thus became *ashavan* (Av.; OPers., *artāvan*), that is, a participant in the supreme state of possessing *asha/ṛta.* In fact, the Indo-Iranian concept, which the Zoroastrian tradition transformed into one of the Amesha Spentas, contained various positive meanings, from that of truth (its exact translation) to that of a cosmic, ritual, and moral order. The Iranian *ashavan* (Pahl., *ahlaw/ardā[y]*) and the Indian *ṛtāvan* stood, although with different shades of meaning, for "the initiate" and, more generally, for those who, alive or dead, would succeed in penetrating a dimension of being or existence different from the norm.

The idea of the need for an initiation in order to achieve the supreme state of *asha/ṛta,* held in common by the ancient Indo-Iranian world and by what we may call "Aryan mysticism" (Kuiper, 1964), was also linked to the experience of illumination and of the mystic light. The blessed state of *asha* manifests itself through light (*Yasna* 30.1), and *asha* is to be found in "solar dwellings" (*Yasna* 53.4, 32.2, 43.16). The initiate is, then, first of all a "seer," one who has access to the mysteries of the otherworld and who can contemplate a luminous epiphany.

The experience of a mystical light and a complex symbolism connecting spirit, light, and seed form part of a common Indo-Iranian heritage and constitute, therefore, specific elements of an ancient Iranian religion that precedes Zarathushtra's reform. It may not be pure coincidence that we find in the *Gāthās* no mention by Zarathushtra himself of the concept of *khvarenah* ("splendor"), which was a notable aspect of Iranian religious thinking; yet we see it becoming part of the Zoroastrian tradition, as, for example, in *Yashts* 19. Khvarenah is a luminous and irradiating force, a sort of igneous and solar fluid (Duchesne-Guillemin, 1962), that is found, mythologically, in water, in *haoma,* and (according to an anthropological concept found in the Pahlavi tradition) in semen. [*See* Khvarenah.]

Khvarenah is an attribute of Mithra, of royalty, of divine and heroic figures belonging to a national and religious tradition, of Yima, of Zarathushtra, and of the Saoshyant; it does not have an exact Indian counterpart but is found in a context that, both literally and in terms of mythological structure, is strictly analogous to the Indian. [*See* Saoshyant.] In the Indian tradition, we find concepts concerning light—its splendor, its activity, its energy, and its effects—such as *ojas* (Av., *aojah*), *varcas* (Av., *varecah*), and *tejas,* meaning, respectively, "strength," "energy," and "splendor," concepts that closely resemble some in Iranian anthropology. The same adjective is used to describe "splendor" in both Iran and India: *ughra* (Av.) and *ugra* (Skt.), meaning "strong."

The Iranian religions other than Zoroastrianism, can, as we have seen, be partially reconstructed, not as organic systems, but rather in some of their particular and characteristic elements: cult and pantheon, cosmogony and cosmology, individual eschatology, anthropology, and psychology, as well as a concept of the experience of initiation substantially common to the entire ancient Indo-Iranian world. Such a common heritage was handed down in ancient Iran by schools of sacred poetry, which left their mark both on Zarathushtra's *Gāthās* and on the *Yashts* of the Younger Avesta.

[*For discussion of Iranian religions in broader context, see* Indo-European Religions. *For discussion of particular Iranian religions, see* Magi; Manichaeism; Mazdakism; Mithraism; Zoroastrianism; *and* Zurvanism. *See also the biographies of Mani and Zarathushtra.*]

BIBLIOGRAPHY

Preeminent among general reference works on Iranian religions is H. S. Nyberg's monumental *Irans forntida religioner* (Stockholm, 1937), translated by Hans H. Schaeder as *Die Religionen des alten Iran* (1938); 2d ed., Osnabrück, 1966. Among other invaluable references are Geo Widengren's *Stand und Aufgaben der iranischen Religionsgeschichte* (Leiden, 1955); Jacques Duchesne-Guillemin's *La religion de l'Iran ancient* (Paris, 1962), translated as *Religion of Ancient Iran* (Bombay, 1973); Geo Widengren's *Die Religionen Irans* (Stuttgart, 1965), translated as *Les religions de l'Iran* (Paris, 1968); and Mary Boyce's *A History of Zoroastrianism*, vol. 1 (Leiden, 1975).

On particular aspects of Iranian religions, the following works are recommended. On ceremonials, see Mary Boyce's "*Ātaš-Zōhr* and *Āb-Zōhr*," *Journal of the Royal Asiatic Society* (1966): 100–118. For a discussion of the Iranian pantheon and an Indo-Iranian comparison, see Émile Benveniste and Louis Renou's *Vṛtra et Vṛthragna* (Paris, 1934) and Stig Wikander's *Vayu* (Uppsala, 1941). On epos, see Stig Wikander's "Sur le fonds commun indo-iranien des épopées de la Perse et de l'Inde," *La nouvelle Clio* 1–2 (1949–1950): 310–329; Marijan Molé's "L'épopée iranienne après Firdōsī," *La nouvelle Clio* (1953): 377–393; and Georges Dumézil's *Mythe et épopée*, 3 vols. (Paris, 1968–1973). On the religions of the Hindu Kush, see Karl Jettmar's *Die Religionen des Hindukush* (Stuttgart, 1975) and Giuseppe Tucci's "On Swāt: The Dards and Connected Problems," *East and West*, n.s. 27 (1977): 9–103.

For discussion of the common Indo-European background of some concepts of the most ancient cosmography, see G. M. Bongard-Levin and E. A. Grantovskii's *De la Scythie à l'Inde: Énigmes de l'histoire des anciens Aryens*, translated by Philippe Gignoux (Paris, 1981). On the concept of the Iranian *Männerbund*, see Stig Wikander's *Der arische Männerbund* (Lund, 1983) and my "Antico-persiano *anušya-* e gli immortali di Erodoto," in *Monumentum Georg Morgensterne*, vol. 1, "Acta Iranica," no. 21 (Leiden, 1981), pp. 266–280. For discussion of the concept of *asha* and Aryan mysticism, see F. B. J. Kuiper's "The Bliss of Aša," *Indo-Iranian Journal* 8 (1964): 96–129.

On initiation, see Jacques Duchesne-Guillemin's "L'initiation mazdéenne," in *Initiation: Contributions to the Theme . . .* edited by C. Jouco Bleeker (Leiden, 1965), pp. 112–118, and on the common Indo-Iranian background of initiation through possessing *asha* and the experience of light, see, in particular, my "Ašavan: Contributo allo studio del libro di Ardā Wirāz," in *Iranica*, edited by me and Adriano V. Rossi (Naples, 1979), pp. 387–452.

For comparison of the Indo-Iranian notions of *ojas/aojah, varcas/varecah*, and so on, see Jan Gonda's *Ancient-Indian 'ojas', Latin '*augos', and the Indo-Iranian Nouns in -es/-os* (Utrecht, 1952), pp. 57–67, and my "Licht-Symbolik in Alt-Iran," *Antaios* 8 (1967): 528–549. On the ancient Iranian tradition of sacred poetry, which was Indo-Iranian (and, more generally, Indo-European) in origin, see the various contributions by J. Wackernagel, Hans H. Schaeder, and Paul Thieme to *Indogermanische Dichtersprache*, "Wege der Forschung," vol. 165, edited by R. Schmitt (Darmstadt, 1968).

GHERARDO GNOLI
Translated from Italian by Ughetta Fitzgerald Lubin

IRENAEUS (c. 130–c. 200), bishop of Lyons (177/178–c. 200), theologian and antiheretical writer. Claimed by both Roman Catholics and Protestants as their progenitor, Irenaeus framed the catholic concept of authority that helped to pull diverse churches together in a period of identity crisis created by gnosticism, Marcionism, and other movements. Opposing the radical accommodation of Christian thought to Hellenistic culture, he pointed to canon and creed as interpreted by bishops in churches of apostolic foundation. Until the discovery of a gnostic library at Nag Hammadi (modern-day Chenoboskion, Egypt) in 1945, Irenaeus's treatise *Against Heresies* also supplied the main and most reliable information on gnostic thought.

Life. Nothing is known of Irenaeus's ancestry or of the date or place of his birth. He grew up, however, in Smyrna, where he sat at the feet of Polycarp, the distinguished bishop martyred about 155, who, according to Irenaeus, had known the apostles, specifically John, in Asia. From Polycarp perhaps he drew his penchant for biblical theology, for, he observed, Polycarp "related all things in harmony with the scriptures," which he then noted "not on paper, but in my heart." Irenaeus witnessed Polycarp's debate with Anicetus in Rome about 155 and studied in Justin's school, gaining much from Justin's apologetic methods but diverging sharply from him in his partiality for a biblical theology rather than for Platonism. After 164 he went to Lyons, where he was ordained a presbyter. He narrowly missed the pogrom that took place in Lyons and Vienne in 177, when Pothinus, the nonagenarian bishop of Lyons martyred in the persecution, sent him to Rome with a letter for Eleutherius (pope, 175–189) in which Pothinus characterized his protégé as "zealous for the covenant of Christ" and "among the first as a presbyter of the church."

On returning to Lyons, Irenaeus succeeded Pothinus

as bishop. When Victor, bishop of Rome (189–199), rashly excommunicated the Christians of Asia because they observed Easter according to the Jewish Passover, whatever day of the week that might fall on, and not always on a Sunday, as in Rome, Irenaeus intervened with a stern rebuke. Writing in the name of "the brethren in Gaul," he pointed out that although variety of practice was customary among Christians from ancient times, they had always lived in peace with one another. Victor's predecessors in Rome, he added, all adhered to the Roman custom but did not excommunicate the Asians on account of a different practice. Anicetus and Polycarp once had a direct confrontation; although neither could persuade the other to change, they remained in communion with each other. Apart from his writing activities, little more is known about Irenaeus's career as bishop of Lyons. About 576 Gregory of Tours reported that Irenaeus was martyred in the persecution under Septimius Severus, but the lateness of the account makes this unlikely.

Writings. Two major works of Irenaeus—*Refutation and Overthrow of Knowledge Falsely So-called* (usually referred to as *Against Heresies*) and *Proof of the Apostolic Preaching*—have survived. In addition, three letters—one to Blastus, *On Schism;* a second to Florinus, *On Monarchy* or *That God Is Not the Author of Evil;* and a third to Victor on the Easter controversy—are quoted partially or wholly in the *Church History* of Eusebius. Other works have survived only in fragments or not at all, including a treatise against Valentinian gnosticism entitled *On the Ogdoad;* an apology, *On Knowledge, against the Greeks;* and comments on scriptures under the title *Dissertations*. Irenaeus's works, especially the treatise *Against Heresies*, circulated widely and exerted a widespread influence on Christian theology in subsequent centuries, particularly in the West.

Composed at the request of a friend and usually dated 185–189, *Against Heresies* is somewhat repetitious and disjointed. In book 1 Irenaeus outlines the gnostic system of Valentinus and his pupil Ptolemaeus and refutes it briefly on the grounds of inconsistency and diversity, especially in handling scriptures (in contrast to the unity of the catholic church's teaching); in a similar way he sketches and refutes the practices and thought of the Marcosians; and he gives thumbnail sketches of the variegated teachings of other heretical teachers or sects: Simon Magus (the archheretic, according to Irenaeus), Menander, Saturninus, Basilides, Carpocrates, Cerinthus, the Ebionites, the Nicolaitans, Cerdo, Marcion, Tatian, and the Encratites, Barbeliotes, Ophites, Sethians, and Cainites. In book 2 Irenaeus undertakes a more detailed rational refutation of the Valentinian system with its elaborate cosmology. In book 3 he constructs his famous argument for catholic teaching based on scriptures and tradition. In book 4 he pursues the refutation of Marcion (d. 160?) that he begins at the end of book 3. Following in the train of his teacher Justin, whose treatise *Against Marcion* is no longer extant, Irenaeus argues from scriptures the oneness of the God of the Old Testament and the God who had disclosed himself in Jesus of Nazareth. Christ bore witness to the God of the Old Testament; the scriptures of the Old Testament bore witness to the Christ of the New. In book 5 Irenaeus sustains chiefly the Christian doctrines of resurrection of the flesh, incarnation, and last things against gnostic "spiritualizing." Like his teacher Justin, Irenaeus adopts the eschatology of the *Revelation to John* with its expectation of the millennial reign of Christ.

The *Proof of the Apostolic Preaching*, long lost but rediscovered in an Armenian translation in 1904, is a catechetical treatise, addressed to a certain Marcianus, that Irenaeus describes as "a manual of essentials." Basically a summary of salvation history, the first part focuses on theological matters (divine monarchy, Trinity, baptism) and the second on christological matters (Jesus as Lord, Son of David, Christ, Son of God; the glory of the Cross; the kingdom of God). "Proofs" for various doctrines come principally from the Old Testament.

Thought. Irenaeus, responding to gnostics and Marcionites rather than presenting an apology to gentiles, rejected Justin's concept of the Seminal Logos who illuminated the minds of both Jews and Greeks. Although he could praise Plato faintly, he had few compliments for nonbiblical writers and writings. He placed his confidence, rather, in the Old Testament and in writings beginning to be collected into a New Testament. Against Marcion and some of the gnostics, he asserted vigorously that one and the same God inspired both. In his understanding of inspiration he came closer to the rabbinic concept of the spirit indwelling an individual who faithfully adheres to the established tradition of truth than to the Greek mantic theory, but he never denied the latter. He regarded the Old Testament in the Greek Septuagint as canonical in its entirety. Although the limits of his New Testament canon are not clear, he left no doubt that it included at its core the four Gospels and thirteen letters of Paul.

In his polemic against the gnostics Irenaeus criticized especially their use of allegorical exegesis, but he himself resorted freely to this method even in interpretation of the New Testament, the first orthodox writer to do so. He struggled to solve problems posed by the Old Testament by way of a theory of progressive education of the human race; but, although biblical, he lacked historical sensitivity in treating of the Old Testament. In the final analysis, Irenaeus saw the basis of religious authority as the tradition committed to the churches by the apostles, as a collective and not as an individual witness. The "living voice," a continually renewed understanding of the church's heritage, was his actual authority.

Irenaeus's theology reflected throughout a strong biblical and especially Pauline slant. Against gnostic and Marcionite dualism he affirmed Jewish monotheism. One God, the creator, created *ex nihilo* and not through emanations (as in Valentinian gnosis). To prove at once the immanence and the transcendence of God, Irenaeus developed the distinctive doctrine of "the two hands of God." Through the Son and the Holy Spirit (or the Word and Wisdom), God acted directly in creation, not through intermediaries, and God continues to act in inspiration or revelation. Scholars have often tried to decide whether Irenaeus held to an "economic," or "modalist," concept of the Trinity (that God appeared at one time as Father, at another time as Son, at a third time as Holy Spirit), but the "two hands" doctrine is scarcely compatible with such a concept. For Irenaeus, God is the living God of the Old Testament. Although he counterbalanced this understanding with ideas drawn from the philosophical leanings of earlier apologists, he always leaned heavily toward the biblical side. Whereas Justin thought of the Logos as the hypostatized Divine Reason, for example, Irenaeus conceptualized the Logos as the Word of God depicted in *John* 1:1–14. Also, whereas Justin could call the Logos a "second God" *(deuteros theos)*, a part of God, for Irenaeus the Logos is God—God self-disclosed.

Unlike his precursor Justin, Irenaeus was also profoundly biblical and Pauline in his doctrine of redemption. According to his famous recapitulation theory, Jesus traversed the same ground as Adam but in reverse. Through his obedience he overcame the powers that hold humankind in thrall—sin, death, and the devil. To establish his theory, Irenaeus contended that Jesus experienced every phase of human development—infancy, childhood, youth, mature adulthood—sanctifying each by obedience. On the basis of a comment in the *Gospel of John* ("You are not yet fifty," *Jn.* 8:57), he argued that Jesus lived to age fifty. To be sure, alongside the motif of Christus Victor in his recapitulation theory, Irenaeus also gave attention to the Greek concept of divinization by way of the vision of God in the incarnate Son. "He became man," said Irenaeus, "in order that we might become divine." This idea, however, did not dominate his theology as did that of recapitulation. As Irenaeus used it, moreover, it had both Pauline and Johannine roots. Thus, although nodding to Hellenism, Irenaeus did not depart from a strong biblicism.

There has been much debate among Protestant scholars about Irenaeus's emphasis on free will. In opposition to the gnostic division of humankind into three groups—material, psychic, and spiritual—he insisted on the survival of freedom even after the Fall. Distinguishing "image" *(eikōn)* and "likeness" *(homoiōsis)* in the *Genesis* account of creation, as did Valentinus, he held that the Fall affected only the "likeness." The "image," the whole bodily and spiritual nature with no added supernatural gift, was unaffected. Loss of the divine "likeness," however, resulted in a disordered human nature, death, and enslavement to Satan. Thus every person is born in sin, but this does not mean, as it did to Augustine, inheritance of guilt. Realizing that moral responsibility necessitates freedom of choice, Irenaeus viewed sin as wrong moral choice by a responsible agent. Although this meant that he sometimes minimized the need for grace, he was far from being a forerunner of Pelagius (fl. 410–418), who emphasized "natural grace" almost to the exclusion of supernatural. The Fall, Irenaeus would say, attenuated free will, although it did not obliterate it.

In his understanding of the church Irenaeus again reproduced much of Paul's thought. The church is Israel under a new covenant, the true Israel, the priestly people of God. Although he believed in a universal priesthood, Irenaeus nevertheless lacked Paul's concept of the church as the body of Christ. He understood the church rather as a corporation composed of individuals and seldom spoke of being "in Christ" or "in the Spirit."

Irenaeus did not comment at length on the sacraments. Baptism, according to him, is a sign of faith and marks the beginning of the Christian life. He presupposed adult baptism, although one allusion connected with his recapitulation theory has often been pressed in support of infant baptism. The Eucharist, or Lord's Supper, played a minor role in his thinking. With Ignatius he could designate it "the antidote of life," or with Justin he could say the elements were "no longer common bread." Yet he preferred the phrase "the new oblation of the new covenant." Rich as his writings were in the formation of catholic theology, however, he did not approach the medieval idea of transubstantiation. The Eucharist is a "sacrifice" of praise symbolic of the recapitulating death of Christ; it proclaims and sets forth Christ's saving truth, the *raison d'être* of the church.

Irenaeus's understanding of ecclesiastical authority has evoked fierce debate between Protestants and Roman Catholics, for the meaning of a crucial statement is uncertain. Citing Rome as an example of an "apostolic" church, "founded and organized by Peter and Paul," and possessed of a reliable succession of bishops,

Irenaeus added, "Ad hanc enim ecclesiam propter potiorem principalitatem necesse est omnem convenire ecclesiam." Roman Catholics have preferred to translate this sentence as "For it is necessary that every church agree with this church on account of its more powerful authority"; Protestants as "For it is necessary that every church come together with this church on account of its greater antiquity." Lack of a Greek original makes certainty impossible.

In eschatology, Irenaeus followed in the footsteps of his mentor Justin. Indeed, he was more rigorous than Justin in demanding adherence to millenarian beliefs. Countering the gnostics' dualism, he attached great importance to the idea of general resurrection, and he insisted on a resurrection of the flesh. Curiously, unlike Justin, he expected the general resurrection and the Last Judgment of both human beings and fallen angels to precede the millennium. Citing Papias (c. 60–130), bishop of Hierapolis, he believed the devil and his angels (demons) would be consigned to an everlasting fire while the saints would reign with Christ during the millennium. This millennial vision capped Irenaeus's theory of the evolution of religion.

Influence. Irenaeus's integration of biblical and Hellenistic thought, more cautious than that of his predecessor Justin or his contemporary Clement of Alexandria, was to have a significant impact in subsequent centuries. Eastern theology adopted his Christus Victor motif and his idea of the perfectibility of human nature consummated in immortality. A strong emphasis on free will in Eastern thinking probably also has its roots in Irenaeus. In the West both Roman Catholics and Protestants have claimed Irenaeus and Augustine as their leading mentors. Roman Catholics have cited Irenaeus on authority, Protestants on the Bible. Neither, however, has felt entirely at ease with the bishop of Lyons. Although Irenaeus came up with a "catholic formula" for truth, he left much uncertainty about Rome's place in safeguarding it. Similarly, although he was basically a biblical theologian, the Protestant reformers felt uncomfortable with both his idea of authority and his "Pelagian" tendencies. In the present ecumenical climate, fresh studies of Irenaeus are aiding in the reexamination of theology that must inevitably accompany progress toward Christian unity.

BIBLIOGRAPHY

The standard text of Irenaeus's treatise *Against Heresies* is *Sancti Irenaei libros quinque adversus haereses*, 2 vols., edited by W. W. Harvey (Cambridge, 1857). A complete English translation can be found in volume 1 of *The Ante-Nicene Fathers*, edited and translated by Alexander Roberts and James Donaldson (1867; reprint, Grand Rapids, Mich., 1975). Irenaeus's catechetical work appears in two English translations: *The Demonstration of the Apostolic Preaching*, translated by J. Armitage Robinson (London, 1920), and *Proof of the Apostolic Preaching*, translated and annotated by Joseph P. Smith, S.J. (Westminster, Md., 1952) for the series "Ancient Christian Writers." The standard English biography of Irenaeus is F. R. M. Hitchcock's *Irenaeus of Lugdunum* (Cambridge, 1914). Valuable comprehensive studies of Irenaeus's theology include John Lawson's *The Biblical Theology of Saint Irenaeus* (London, 1948) and Gustaf Wingren's *Man and the Incarnation: A Study in the Biblical Theology of Irenaeus*, translated by Ross Mackenzie (Edinburgh and Philadelphia, 1959).

E. GLENN HINSON

IRESU-HUCHI is the Ainu goddess of fire. Variously called Kamuy Huchi ("elderly woman deity"), Abe Kamuy ("fire deity"), and Unchi Ahchi ("fire grandmother"), she is perhaps the most important deity in the Ainu pantheon, although it is difficult to determine her importance relative to that of the bear, the animal on which much of Ainu ritual is centered. [*See* Ainu Religion.] Envisioned as an elderly woman, the goddess Iresu-Huchi resides in the hearth, considered a microcosm of the Ainu universe and located at the center of the Ainu house. The crucial importance of the deity derives from her role as the exclusive mediator between the Ainu and all other deities. Therefore, not only in the formulaic prayers dedicated to the deities by male elders during major rituals, such as the bear ceremony, but also in prayers during shamanistic rituals, one must first address her to ask her to deliver messages to the deities concerned. Without her mediation, humans have no means of communication with the deities. At times of emergency, the goddess is also addressed for her own direct intervention.

The hearth as the residence of the goddess is sacred space, where impurity is never allowed to enter. Thus, the Ainu must ensure that their firewood is free not only from contamination by human and animal excreta but also from pollution incurred by death in the family. From time to time, especially after the death of one of its members, a family must renew the life of the goddess by renewing the ash through a ritual. During the ritual, old ash is carefully moved to a special ash pile outside the house and fresh sand from the beach is placed in its stead.

Among the Hokkaido Ainu, it is said that the goddess originally gave Ainu women instructions on how to make their "sacred girdles," which they wear under their clothing and never show to others. Because every woman inherits from her mother a specific type of girdle with a prescribed design and shape, each type is worn only by matrilineally related women. No women may marry a man whose mother has the same type of girdle as herself.

There are various accounts of the origin of the goddess. Many link her with the sky and with the deities related to the sky, such as the deity of thunder and lightning.

BIBLIOGRAPHY

Munro, Neil G. *Ainu Creed and Cult.* New York, 1963. See pages 17–18.

Ohnuki-Tierney, Emiko. *The Ainu of the Northwest Coast of Southern Sakhalin.* Prospect Heights, Ill., 1984. See pages 89–90.

EMIKO OHNUKI-TIERNEY

IROQUOIS RELIGION. The League of the Iroquois consisted, at the time of contact with Europeans, of five "nations" (the Mohawk, Oneida, Onondaga, Cayuga, and Seneca). In 1724, these groups were joined by the Tuscarora to form the Six Nations of the Iroquois. These tribes form part of a larger complex of Iroquoian-speaking peoples. The northern language group of which the members of the league are a part also includes the Saint Lawrence Iroquois, Huron, Wyandot, Susquehanna, Nottoway, Erie, Wenro, and Neutrals. The Cherokee form the southern language group. The separation between the northern and southern groups probably occurred between three and four thousand years ago, with further dialects developing over time.

Geographically, the early-seventeenth-century Iroquois inhabited the area from 42° to 44° north latitude and from 74° to 78° west longitude. In the late seventeenth century, the League of the Iroquois controlled territory from the Mohawk Valley in the east to Lake Erie in the west, and from Lake Ontario in the north to the mountains of western and south-central New York State and northwestern Pennsylvania in the south.

At contact the Iroquois were a matrilineal and matrilocal people living in clusters of longhouses situated on hilltops. The villages were usually palisaded and semipermanent. The men involved themselves in hunting, fishing, and making war; the women took care of the fields and gathered berries, nuts, and roots. The clan mothers elected the fifty sachems, or chiefs, who guided the external policies of the league from Onondaga.

Cosmology. The cosmological structuring of space into three tiers provides the Iroquois with the basic categories with which to interpret human experience. The sky world and the underworld represent extremes of both a spatial and an existential nature. The sky world is order, goodness, warmth, light, and life. The underworld is chaos, evil, coldness, darkness, and death. In the in-between world—the world of ordinary human experience—the qualities of both worlds are intertwined in a myriad of ways. One of the ways is cyclical, as when night follows day; another is antagonistic, as when good struggles with evil.

Mythically, this world was the creation of two twins, one good and the other evil. The former, the Master of Life, was the creator of flora and fauna. He held the sky world in mind at all times while creating living things, and he gave customs to humans modeled after those of the sky world. His brother tried to imitate his creative acts, but what issued instead were all of the nasty, noxious, and monstrous forms of life. The evil twin is described as cold and hard, like ice and flint, and his influence is believed to infect all areas of existence. Each of the twins left behind spirit-forces and other manifestations of his orientation and power. The general thrust of Iroquois religion is toward increasing and renewing the power of those forces that sustain life and reducing or eliminating those forces that diminish life, such as disease and pain.

Community Rituals. To live in harmony with the spirit-forces is the essential requirement of Iroquois religion. These fundamental relationships that sustain community life are renewed, intensified, and celebrated in the calendrical cycles of the Longhouse religion. This final form of the Iroquois ceremonial cycle crystallized in the nineteenth century under the influence of the Seneca prophet Handsome Lake (1735–1815). [*See the biography of Handsome Lake.*] The Longhouse religion, as it is practiced today, is a synthesis of elements from the hunter-gatherer traditions of the Middle Woodland and early Late Woodland periods (300–1000 CE) and the agricultural complex that gradually took hold during the Late Woodland period (1000–1500 CE).

The fundamental attitude of the Iroquois community toward the benevolent spirit-forces of the universe is thanksgiving. Thus all Iroquois ceremonies begin and end with a thanksgiving address, a paean to all the forces of earth, sky, and the sky world that create, support, and renew life. The address is divided into three main parts. The first part includes prayers of thanksgiving for the earth, waters, plants and trees, animals, birds, and the "three sisters" (the staple Iroquois foodstuffs—maize, beans, and squash). The second section gives thanks to those spirit forces that have greater power: wind, thunder, sun, moon, and stars. The final section gives thanks to the spiritual guides of the Iroquois: Handsome Lake, the creator, and the Four Beings (protectors of humans and messengers from the creator to Handsome Lake).

The epitome of the synthesis represented by the Longhouse religion is the Midwinter festival. Concentrated into its eight days are all of the major themes and components of Iroquois ceremonialism. The first half of the Midwinter rite is the older and contains many elements from the hunting-forest complex that centered on shamanic practices. It is given over to the symbolic expulsion of the old year through rites of confession, ashes-stirring, and dream fulfillment, as well as medicine-society curing ceremonies, False Face society rituals, and the White Dog sacrifice (no longer practiced). These expiatory and cathartic rituals clear the path for the new year and for the second half of the festival, whose structure largely reflects the farming-village complex. The "four sacred rituals"—a feather dance, a skin (or drum) dance, a personal chant, and a bowl game—are considered the gifts of the creator, modeled after ceremonies in the sky world. A tobacco invocation, a kind of thanksgiving address, beseeches all of the spirit-forces to bless the people during the coming year. Both the Our Sustenance Dances and the performance by the Husk Faces anticipate a fruitful agricultural season. The yearly ceremonial cycle unfolds from the Midwinter festival and returns to it.

While the ceremonial cycle may vary slightly from longhouse to longhouse, a representative list would include the Midwinter festival, the Bush Dance, and the Thanks-to-the-Maple, Seed Planting, Strawberry, Raspberry, Green Bean, Thunder, Little Corn, Green Corn, and Harvest ceremonies.

Medicine Societies. Not only has Iroquois religion been concerned with affirming and intensifying life, it has also been concerned with countering those things that diminish life. The spirit-forces that assist humans in this battle revealed themselves long ago and entered into covenants with individuals, families, and societies. Through fasting, dream-visions, and ecstatic states, the ancient shamans sought to divine the causes of illness, pain, famine, and sudden or widespread death. Other shamanic specialists had their own ceremonies and skills that brought healing power. At times groups of shamans who possessed similar secrets joined together into sodalities. With the demise of individual shamanism, these "medicine societies" grew in importance in Iroquois life and became the preserver of the ancient shamanic traditions.

The significance of medicine society rituals in Iroquois life differs from that of the communal ceremonies. The latter are thanksgiving-celebrative, follow the agricultural cycle, are directed toward the major spirit-forces, and are held in the longhouse. The former are power-evocative and occasional, invoke the tutelary spirit of the particular medicine society, and are usually conducted in private homes. Membership in a society is generally limited to those who have been cured by one of that society's rituals. The medicine societies have their own myths, songs, dances, prayers, costumes, and ritual paraphernalia. A listing of Iroquois medicine societies and their major characteristics follows.

1. *The Society of Medicine Men* (also known as Shake the Pumpkin) is the largest medicine society. Most members of the other societies also belong to it. The society began with a covenant relationship between the medicine animals and its founders. In return for feasts offered in their honor, the animals promised to cure diseases, ease pain, and get rid of bad luck. Practices of this society, such as juggling red-hot coals and wearing masks without eye holes, are quite ancient.

2. *The Company of Mystic Animals* includes the Buffalo, Otter, Bear, and Eagle societies. In varying degrees the members imitate their tutelary animals in their dances, songs, and practices. They continue the shamanic tradition in which humans and animals communicate with, and can be transformed into, one another.

3. *The Little Water Medicine society*, like its ally in the Eagle society, was originally associated with war and the healing of wounds received in war. The Iroquois say that its medicine, concocted from parts of animals, birds, and plants, is the most potent made by any society. Ceremonies are held at night, several times a year, to renew the medicine.

4. *The Little People society* (also known as Dark Dance) also holds its ceremonies at night. This society fosters a good rapport with the *jo-ga-oh* ("little people"), elflike spirits who help humans in a variety of ways and who adopt many different forms for mischievous purposes.

5. *The False Face society* is the favorite of the Iroquois. The wooden masks worn by its members are filled with power. Reverence and ritual surround both their carving and their care. The most common practices of the Faces today were noted among the Huron by seventeenth-century observers: blowing ashes, handling hot coals, imitating hunchbacks, and carrying sticks. It is quite possible that the Faces came to the Iroquois from the Huron. The False Face society holds rites for cleansing the community of disease in the spring and fall. It sponsers rites at Midwinter both for its own members and for the broader community in the longhouse and performs individual curing rites when needed.

6. *The Husk Faces* are dedicated to the agricultural spirits. They also cure by blowing ashes and handling hot coals. During Midwinter they burst into the longhouse and announce that they are going to the other side of the world to till the crops.

7. *The Towii'sas society* is a woman's society honoring corn, beans, and squash. It participates in the Green Corn ceremony and also has its own curing ceremonies.

8. *The Ohgiwe society* conducts ceremonies for people who have been dreaming of ghosts. A feast is held to feed the ghost and to dissuade it from bothering the living. Just as the sharing of food brings harmony into human relationships, so does it harmonize relations between living and dead. The Iroquois both respect and fear the dead and therefore conduct a number of feasts for them. In addition to the feasts conducted by the Ohgiwe society, there is a community Feast of the Dead (also called Ohgiwe) that is held annually or semiannually. All souls, but especially those of the recently deceased, are invited. Songs and dances are performed, and a post-midnight feast is held. There are also frequent family feasts for the dead during the winter months. These celebrations both fulfill the family's obligations to the dead and serve as a means of bringing together relatives of the deceased.

The Individual. In traditional (i.e., pre-nineteenth-century) Iroquois lore, access to the power and guidance of the spirit-forces was not limited to the community (through its collective ceremonial life) nor to the curing societies. The individual Iroquois had an array of spiritually vital allies, including charms, medicine bundles, guardian spirits, and his or her own soul.

The most common medium for communication with these forces was the dream-vision. During puberty rites or shamanic training a guardian spirit would reveal itself to the individual through the dream-vision. The spirit could take the form of a human being, or animal, or a bird such as a raven or crow. An intimate and powerful relationship was established between the person and the guardian spirit. A person who had such a friendship had greater inner power and confidence than one who did not. The guardian spirit revealed its desires in dreams. To ignore this ally or to fail to understand its desires could result in illness. Such an illness signified a dangerous disruption of the relationship between spirit-forces and humans. Should someone become ill, his dreams would be consulted to ascertain what the guardian spirit desired. Sometimes the efforts of everyone in the community would be needed to fulfill the dream. They willingly undertook this.

Similarly, an alienation could occur between a person's ego and soul. The Iroquois believed that the soul was the source of biological as well as mental well-being. Dreams were its language. To lose touch with or deny the desires of the soul could cause it to revolt against the body. Dreams were carefully investigated in order to avoid such a possibility or to remedy it when illness occurred. The dream-guessing rite that even today forms a part of the Onondaga Midwinter festival was performed quite frequently by the seventeenth-century Huron. The ill person's soul's desire would be given in riddle form; whoever guessed it correctly had to fulfill the desire. This might involve an object, a feast, the performance of a particular ritual, or any of a number of other actions.

Dreams were also thought to contain warnings about future events—events whose actual occurrence might be prevented by acting out the dream and thereby fulfilling it. Thus, a warrior who dreamed that he had been captured, bound, and tortured by an enemy might, upon waking, ask his fellow tribesmen to tie him up and make cuts or burns in his flesh in order that the greater pain and shame predicted by the dream might be avoided. Dreams also affected hunting, fishing, military, and political plans.

There was no aspect of life among the ancient Iroquois and Huron that was not touched by the dream. Religiously it played both a conservative and an innovative role. That is, it confirmed within an individual's experience the culturally transmitted religious system while also initiating changes in the beliefs and rituals that constituted this system. It would not be going too far to say that most of Iroquois religion was constructed of dream material. Through this building process, the individual hierophany became symbolized and available to all. The last series of significant changes introduced into Iroquois life by the dream resulted from the revelations given to Handsome Lake, which were eventually institutionalized into the present-day Longhouse religion.

Today the majority of Iroquois live on reservations in Canada and New York State. Perhaps one-fourth of the approximately twenty thousand Iroquois adhere to the traditionalist Longhouse religion. In addition to the ceremonies described above, they perform partial recitations of the *Gaiwiio* ("good word") of Handsome Lake on the first mornings of both the Midwinter festival and the Green Corn ceremony. This formalization of the dream-vision revelations received by the prophet from 1799 until his death in 1815 provides the moral, ceremonial, social, and theological context in which followers of the Longhouse religion live. A complete recitation by an authorized preacher may occur every other fall at a meeting of the Six Nations, depending upon which longhouse is sponsoring the meeting.

BIBLIOGRAPHY

The main source for information on seventeenth-century Huron religion, which also provides some insight into Iroquois life, is *The Jesuit Relations and Allied Documents*, 39 vols. (1896–1901), edited by Reuben Gold Thwaites (New York, 1959). The nineteenth century marked the beginning of modern studies on Iroquois religion. Midcentury produced Lewis H. Morgan's classic *The League of the Ho-de-no-sau-nee, or Iroquois* (1851; reprint, New York, 1966). The most complete collection of Iroquois cosmological stories is found in J. N. B. Hewitt's "Iroquois Cosmology," which was published in two parts in the *Annual Report of the Bureau of American Ethnology* 21 (1899–1900) and 43 (1925–1926). An excellent, thorough study of the Midwinter festival is found in Elisabeth Tooker's *The Iroquois Ceremonial of Midwinter* (Syracuse, 1970). For an introduction to and translation of a thanksgiving address, see Wallace L. Chafe's "Seneca Thanksgiving Rituals," *Bureau of American Ethnology Bulletin* 183 (1961). A much more thorough, if complex, comparison of several thanksgiving addresses along with a study of other events in the ritual cycle is M. K. Foster's *From the Earth to Beyond the Sky: An Ethnographic Approach to Four Longhouse Speech Events* (Ottawa, 1974). Valuable information on the medicine societies, along with the only full translation at present of "The Code of Handsome Lake" (i.e., the *Gaiwiio*), is found in a collection of Arthur C. Parker's writings, entitled *Parker on the Iroquois*, edited by William N. Fenton (Syracuse, 1968). Fenton has done this century's most important work among the Iroquois. Among his numerous articles, special mention should be made of "An Outline of Seneca Ceremonies at Coldspring Longhouse," *Yale University Publications in Anthropology* 9 (1936): 3–22; and "Masked Medicine Societies of the Iroquois," in the *Annual Report of the Smithsonian Institution* (Washington, D.C., 1940), pp. 397–430. An indispensable collection of articles on the Iroquois and their neighbors can be found in the *Handbook of North American Indians*, vol. 15, *Northeast* (Washington, D.C., 1978).

DONALD P. ST. JOHN

IRVING, EDWARD (1792–1834), controversial Scottish minister associated with the founding of the Catholic Apostolic church. Born in Annan, Dumfriesshire, Irving was educated at the University of Edinburgh. After serving as a schoolmaster at Haddington in 1810 and Kirkcaldy in 1812, he was licensed to preach in the Church of Scotland in 1815. He became Thomas Chalmers's assistant at Saint John's, Glasgow, in 1819 but left Scotland in 1822 to become pastor of Caledonian Chapel, a small, struggling congregation in Hatton Garden, London. His dynamic preaching drew such large crowds that a new church had to be built at Regent Square in 1827.

Avowal of controversial doctrines soon undercut Irving's popularity. In the mid-1820s, Irving became a millenarian through the influence of James Hatley Frere, Henry Drummond, and Drummond's Albury Circle. He published *Babylon and Infidelity Foredoomed of God* (1826), in which he predicted the second coming of Christ in 1864; translated *The Coming of Messiah in Glory and Majesty* (1827), a millenarian work by the Spanish Jesuit Manuel Lacunza; lectured on the *Book of Revelation* at the University of Edinburgh (1828); and was a regular contributor to Drummond's prophetic journal *The Morning Watch* (1829–1833).

Citing his *The Doctrine of the Incarnation Opened* (1828) and *The Orthodox and Catholic Doctrine of Our Lord's Human Nature* (1830), the London Presbytery in 1830 charged Irving with teaching the sinfulness of Christ's human nature. He vigorously denied the charge, arguing that though Christ shared humanity's weak and infirm nature, his reliance on the Holy Spirit kept him without sin. Further, Irving refused to recognize the presbytery's authority.

Irving also believed in the continuation of the charismata of apostolic times and urged his congregation to pray for their outpouring. In the fall of 1831, glossolalia, faith healing, and prophetic visions broke out at Regent Square. As a result, Irving was deposed from the church in 1832 and excommunicated by his Scottish presbytery in 1833. He then became a wandering preacher, while several hundred of his London parishioners established the sacramental, millenarian, and charismatic Catholic Apostolic church. Eventually Irving was ordained a deacon in the new church, but he never assumed any significant leadership role. He died at Glasgow and was buried in the cathedral there.

Always the controversialist, Irving attacked the cold and somewhat complacent spirit of orthodoxy in the Church of Scotland. Through his adoption of millenarian and charismatic views, he became an early shaper of those movements in British and American evangelicalism.

BIBLIOGRAPHY

Irving's works are found in *The Collected Writings of Edward Irving*, 5 vols. (London, 1864–1865), edited by Gavin Carlyle. For studies of Irving's life, one may consult H. C. Whitley's *Blinded Eagle* (London, 1955), the work of an unabashed admirer, and Margaret Oliphant's *The Life of Edward Irving*, 2 vols. (London, 1862), a fine example of Victorian biography. A helpful examination of Irving's associations is Andrew L. Drummond's *Edward Irving and His Circle* (London, 1938). Irving's theology is analyzed in C. Gordon Strachan's *The Pentecostal Theology of Edward Irving* (London, 1973).

TIMOTHY P. WEBER

ISAAC, or, in Hebrew, Yitsḥaq; the second of the biblical patriarchs and the only son of Abraham and Sarah. Although not known from elsewhere, the name *Yitsḥaq* conforms to a well-known Northwest Semitic type and means "may God smile"; Ugaritic texts from the thirteenth century BCE refer to the benevolent smile of the

Canaanite god El. The Bible, however, ascribes the laughter to Isaac's mother, who was amazed to learn that she would have a child despite her advanced age.

Isaac is the only patriarch whose name was not changed. The Bible treats him primarily as Abraham's son or the father of Jacob and Esau. He was the first ancestor of the Israelites to be circumcised on his eighth day in accordance with God's command (*Gn.* 17:12). At an unspecified age he was taken to be sacrificed in order to test Abraham's faithfulness; however, Isaac himself did little except ask why his father had not brought an animal for the offering. His later marriage to Rebecca, a cousin, was arranged by Abraham and provided comfort to Isaac after his mother's death. In his old age, Isaac was deceived into giving Jacob the blessing intended for the older Esau.

Isaac's only independent actions are found in *Genesis* 26, in which he tells King Abimelech that Rebecca is his sister, a story reminiscent of one told twice about Sarah and Abraham. The same chapter mentions his involvement in agricultural activities and his resolution of a dispute over water rights between his shepherds and those of Abimelech. Isaac died at the age of 180 and was buried alongside Rebecca at Machpelah.

Postbiblical Jewish interpretations focus largely on the story of Abraham's intended sacrifice of Isaac, called the *ʿaqedah* ("binding"), and often elaborate his role beyond the biblical description. According to one version he actually died and was then revived. Christian tradition, perhaps attested as early as the writings of Paul (*Rom.* 8:32), views this incident as prefiguring the Crucifixion. Paul contrasted Isaac, representing Christianity, with Ishmael, the rejected older son who symbolizes Judaism (*Gal.* 4:21–30).

BIBLIOGRAPHY

An excellent survey of modern scholarly insights into the patriarchal narratives is Nahum M. Sarna's *Understanding Genesis* (New York, 1972). Rabbinic legends are collected in Louis Ginzberg's *The Legends of the Jews*, 7 vols., translated by Henrietta Szold et al. (Philadelphia, 1909–1938). Shalom Spiegel's *The Last Trial*, translated by Judah Goldin (New York, 1967), summarizes a vast array of postbiblical legends pertaining to the binding of Isaac (*Gn.* 22).

FREDERICK E. GREENSPAHN

ISAAC THE SYRIAN (d. AD 700?), also known as Isaac of Nineveh; bishop in the ancient Nestorian church of Syria, monk, recluse mystic, and creative writer whose discourses have had widespread influence on Christian and, some think, Ṣūfī spirituality. The English world at first greeted his work, originally written in Syriac, with culture-bound coolness, but has eventually come to recognize him as one of the most sublime and original mystic writers of the Christian East.

Little is known about Isaac's life. Born in a region around the Persian Gulf, he became a monk and for a time the bishop of Nineveh (modern Mosul), an office he resigned after only five months. He then withdrew to one of the monasteries in the mountains of Huzistan (southwestern Iran), where he practiced strict solitude (hesychasm) as a way of pursuing unceasing communion with God. In order not to break the rule of solitude, as Isaac himself relates in a stirring personal account, he refused to go to the deathbed of his brother, a monk in another monastery. Toward the end of his life a burning love led Isaac to write a profusion of illuminating discourses on Christian perfection—the fruit of his assiduous study of scripture, his reading of Christian authors, and his own experiences, about which he is discreetly modest.

Isaac's writings were translated into Greek, Coptic, and Arabic, and became influential from Byzantium to Ethiopia. Later Latin and Spanish translations made him known to the West. The Greek translation (ninth century) was printed in a partly critical edition by Nikēphoros Theotokēs (1770), and this edition was in turn the basis of a Russian translation by Feofan the Recluse (nineteenth century), excerpts of which were rendered into English by Eugénie Kadloubovsky and G. E. H. Palmer in *Early Fathers from the Philokalia* (1954). Earlier, A. J. Wensinck, working on Paul Bedjan's critical edition of the original Syriac discourses (1909), had published his English translation of *Mystic Treatises by Isaac of Nineveh* (1923), valuable but unfortunately inadequate in correctly rendering key patristic terminology derived from the Greek Fathers. A new translation, *The Ascetical Homilies of St. Isaac the Syrian*, based on the Greek and Syriac, is in preparation by the Holy Transfiguration Monastery, Brookline, Massachusetts.

Only the earnest student will be rewarded by reading Isaac's work in English; wide cultural differences, the sublimity of Isaac's thought, and the fact that it is addressed principally to other solitaries, not ordinary Christians, add to other problems of translation. Although he cites Evagrios of Pontus, Theodore of Mopsuestia, and others who are in some respects suspect to orthodox theology, there is nothing specifically Nestorian about Isaac's Christology. Isaac strictly avoided dogmatic disputations and was completely grounded in the traditions of Eastern Christianity's piety and spirituality. He frequently quoted not only the Old and New Testaments but also the ascetics of Egypt and eminent church fathers such as Ephraem of Syria, Athanasius, Basil of Caesarea, Gregory the Theologian, and Chrysostom. Isaac was interested primarily not in mysticism but in God; his originality lies in his luminous descriptions of the deep stirrings of the Holy Spirit in the heart, the new birth, the gift of tears, and profound stages of prayer leading to ecstasy. For him the goal of Christian perfection is the love of God, of "the food of angels . . . which is Jesus."

BIBLIOGRAPHY

Bejan, Paul, ed. *Mar Isaacus Ninivita de perfectione religiosa.* Paris, 1909.

Kadloubovsky, Eugénie, and G. E. H. Palmer, trans. *Early Fathers from the Philokalia.* London, 1954.

Theotokēs, Nikēphoros. *Isaak tou Syrou Eurethenta Askētika* (1770). Reprint, Athens, n.d. (1960s).

Wensinck, A. J., trans. and ed. *Mystic Treatises by Isaac of Nineveh.* Amsterdam, 1923.

THEODORE STYLIANOPOULOS

ISAIAH (fl. 740–701 BCE), or, in Hebrew, Yesha'yahu or Yesha'yah; Hebrew prophet. Isaiah, son of Amoz, prophesied during the reigns of Uzziah, Jotham, Ahaz, and Hezekiah, kings of Judah (see *Is.* 1:1). He was a contemporary of the prophets Micah and Hosea and lived soon after Amos. (Amos and Hosea were active in Israel, or Ephraim, while Micah prophesied in Judah.) This was the period of the Syro-Ephraimite war (734/3–733/2 BCE), in which these kingdoms to the north of Judah surrounded Jerusalem, threatening to replace the house of David (*Is.* 7:1–6 [verse citations are according to the English version]). It was also the time of the Assyrian invasions, a chain of military campaigns that caused the fall of the northern kingdom of Israel in 722 and made Judah a vassal of the Assyrian empire. During this stormy political period, Isaiah addressed the political elite and the people of Jerusalem, delivering God's word, which often did not correspond with the rulers' political views. He repeatedly criticized the rulers for the prevailing social injustices.

Composite Nature of the Book of Isaiah. *Isaiah* contains sixty-six chapters and is the largest prophetic book in the Hebrew Bible. The existing structure had appeared by the beginning of the second century BCE. *Ben Sira* apparently knows *Isaiah* as a whole (*Sir.* 48:17–25), and the Dead Sea Scrolls, as well as the New Testament, regard the entire sixty-six chapters as a single composition. There are, indeed, certain stylistic usages that are common to the entire book, such as the combination "Holy of Israel" (*Is.* 1:4, 5:16, 5:19, 5:24, 6:3, 10:20, 12:6, 30:11, 30:12, 30:15, 31:1, 41:14, 41:16, 41:20, 43:3, 43:14, 45:11, 47:4, 48:17, 49:7, 54:5, 55:5, 60:9, 60:14) and the expression "Thus says God," in the imperfect tense instead of the usual perfect, "said" (*Is.* 1:11, 1:18, 33:10, 41:21, 66:9; cf. 40:1, 40:25).

Contrary to these early sources, however, modern scholarship on *Isaiah* generally differentiates between chapters 1–39 of the book and chapters 40–66, treating them as distinct major works by different authors. The first 39 chapters of *Isaiah* bear the title "The Vision of Isaiah the Son of Amoz" (1:1); chapters 40–66 are ascribed to an anonymous prophet to whom scholars refer as "Second Isaiah," or "Deutero-Isaiah." Some scholars also recognize the existence of a "Third Isaiah," or "Trito-Isaiah," the author of chapters 56–66, since the tone and approach of these chapters is more critical and condemning than that of chapters 40–55.

The division of the *Book of Isaiah* into two sections follows from the fact that the two parts are concerned with two distinct historical periods, the Assyrian and the Persian, and different political situations during these periods, which are reflected in the different topics and particular prophetic themes of the book. The author of the first part is concerned with social problems and concentrates on the moral and ethical misconduct of the rulers of Jerusalem, while the author of the second part responds to the national religious crisis of the exiled Jewish community in Babylonia. Accordingly, speeches of judgment distinguish the first part, while words of encouragement and oracles of salvation characterize the second. The prophet of the second part anticipates the collapse of Babylon in 539 BCE and the triumph of Cyrus II (558–529), the founder of the great Persian empire. He knows about the destruction of the Temple in Jerusalem (587/6 BCE), and assigns Cyrus the task of building the new temple (*Is.* 44:28, 45:1; cf. 52:5, 52:11). Historical evidence thus dates the second part of *Isaiah* to the second half of the sixth century BCE, approximately two centuries later than the first part. The division in *Isaiah* was already recognized in the twelfth century CE by the Hebrew commentator Avraham Ibn 'Ezra (in his commentary on *Is.* 40:1), and the literary-thematic distinction has recently been confirmed by a computer analysis (Y. T. Radday, *The Unity of Isaiah in Light of Statistical Linguistics,* Hildesheim, 1973).

But how were these distinct compositions tied together? We can only speculate. Perhaps it was just a technical matter in which a shorter scroll was attached to a longer one for preservation, and the origin of the work as two separate manuscripts was later forgotten. Or perhaps the combination was intentional, the product of a school of religious thought that sought to create a continuous ideological composition in which the period of judgment had been fulfilled, thus confirming the old Isaian prophecies and pointing out the validity of the new ones concerning the new era of salvation. Or perhaps the composer of the second book considered himself Isaiah's faithful disciple. This hypothesis may explain the lack of superscription in the second part as well as the similarity of idioms and phrases in the two parts. For example, in a rare passage in which Second Isaiah refers to himself, he describes God's word as *limmudim,* "teaching" (*Is.* 50:4), language that resembles that of Isaiah (*Is.* 8:16). Isaiah's spiritual disciple responds to his teacher's feeling of "distress and darkness" (*Is.* 8:22), which caused the master to seal his testimony (*Is.* 8:16–17). The disciple feels that times have changed. He notices that God again reveals himself (*Is.* 40:5), and he considers himself the one who bears the leader's testimony.

The First Isaiah. It appears that Isaiah, the son of Amoz, was from Jerusalem (unlike his contemporary Micah, who grew up outside the city). He was familiar with city life (see, e.g., *Is.* 3:16–23), and Jerusalem was the center of his activity. He married a woman whom he called "the prophetess" (*Is.* 8:3). They had at least two sons, whose names are associated with their father's prophetic message (cf. *Hos.* 1:3–9): Shearjashub (lit., *She'ar yashuv,* "a remnant shall return"; *Is.* 7:3) and Maher-shalal-ḥash-baz (lit., "pillage hastens, looting speeds"; 8:3). Isaiah may have had a third son, 'Immanu'el ("God is with us"; 7:14; cf. 8:18), whose name refers to trust in God even in moments of political despair. Isaiah is rarely mentioned outside of his book, but is referred to in *2 Kings* 19–20 and *2 Chronicles* 26:22, 32:20, and 32:32, where he appears not just as a prophet but as the king's healer and the court chronicler. All the sources indicate that Isaiah was closely associated with King Hezekiah, especially during the Assyrian siege of Jerusalem. He had access to the king (*Is.* 7:1ff.) and was the king's political counselor (37:1ff.). He makes frequent reference to the forms and vocabulary of the wisdom literature and is clearly familiar with the scribal profession (30:8; cf. *2 Chr.* 26:22). [*See* Wisdom Literature, *article on* Biblical Books].

There are a number of traditions about Isaiah's role and activities that make it difficult to reconstruct the "real" Isaiah. His close ties with Hezekiah as portrayed in the narrative (*Is.* 36–39, *2 Kgs.* 19–20) may create the impression that he functioned as a court prophet, but his confrontation with King Ahaz (*Is.* 7) depicts him as an independent prophetic figure. The portrayal of Isaiah as a healer in *Kings* 20:1–7 is significant—"And Isaiah said: bring a cake of figs. And let them take and lay it on the boil, that he may recover" (*2 Kgs.* 20:7)—and is repeated in the appendix of the *Book of Isaiah* (*Is.* 38:1–8). That *Isaiah* inserts this deed of healing at the end of Hezekiah's poem as an excursus may reflect a tendency to minimize Isaiah's role as a healer and portray him instead in the role of God's messenger, who does not perform miracles in the tradition of the earlier prophets (such as that of Elisha, described in *2 Kgs.* 2–5). Note, however, that even in chapters 1–35, which deal directly with Isaiah's prophecy, the prophet does not appear only as God's messenger but performs symbolic acts in the tradition of the earlier prophets, such as Elijah. For example, he walks barefoot and naked in Jerusalem for three years as a symbol of the fate that would overtake Egypt and its ally Ethiopia at the hands of Assyria (*Is.* 20:1–6). We must keep in mind, however, that this is but a single episode.

Speeches and additional material. The major critical issue surrounding the book of Isaiah is the determination of his original speeches. We have noted that even chapters 1–39 do not constitute a single composition. The poetic, oratorical language is replaced in chapters 36–39 with a historical narrative (as well as Hezekiah's prayer in 38:10–20). The *Book of Isaiah* seems to have a long literary history. Rabbinic sources hint at an editorial process in which it was not Isaiah himself who wrote the book but later scribes (Hezekiah and his school). Modern criticism attempts to establish clear criteria for the distinction between the authentic and the added material. Some scholars distinguish between oracles of judgment and prophecies of salvation, with the latter, reflecting the days to come, considered a later theological addition. Style is another criterion for analyzing the editorial process. Isaiah is regarded as a poet. Thus some hold that only the material in verse is authentic. Accordingly, passages such as 1:18–20, which breaks the poetic structure, and 4:2–6, a prosaic text differing from the poetic material surrounding it, are considered late. Similarly, this view does not regard texts such as 2:2–4/5 and 11:1ff., which are prophecies of salvation, as Isaiah's compositions. It has also been suggested that verses referring to the fall of Assyria (e.g., 8:9–10, 10:16–19, 10:20–23, 10:24–27, 10:33–34) are the product of an "Assyrian redaction" added in the period of Josiah's territorial expansions and Assyrian decline, toward the end of the seventh century BCE. The goal of the redactor, in this view, was to update Isaiah's original prophecy and show how it was fulfilled through God's determination of political events. Thus there is a complete theological paradigm: first God appears as the accuser and punisher of Israel, and later he reveals himself as Israel's savior. Scholars of the redactional school such as Barth, Clements, and Kaiser assume that Isaiah was not a prophet with a complete political vision, but merely a deliverer of judgmental oracles.

It is the opinion of this author, on the other hand, that Isaiah had a politico-religious worldview that was not limited to contemporary conditions. As a man of vision, he had a total religious concept which looked beyond the day of judgment which was imminent. Isaiah was not just a social critic and man of protest; his proclamation of judgment led to his prophetic outlook for the future as well. There is neither stylistic nor philological evidence that the oracles designed for the days to come (included in chapters 1–35) are products of later hands, unless one imposes on the text specific external critical theories (for certain exceptions, see below). Rather than regarding style (verse versus prose) as the criterion for distinguishing between the original and added text, one should consider that stylistic variations and mixing of styles may be the function of the subject matter and may have been intentional in a particular prophetic message. Subject and function determine Isaiah's style; the question of how it has been said is related to the issue of what has been said. Isaiah employs a significant variety of stylistic forms: *mashal* ("parable"; 5:1ff.), comparison (1:2–3), vivid description (1:4–9), polemic discourse (1:10–17), lament (1:21), satire (3:4ff.), vision (6:1ff.), prediction (7:7–9), and narrative (7:11ff., 8:1ff.), among many others.

The rich language and varied stylistic modes reveal that the prophet was not a narrator who merely reported events. Isaiah sought to appeal to his audience by the force of his language, a goal that, in light of the prophetic office, requires the use of religious language. This language uses metaphor and an imaginative style to create an array of sensory impressions. For example, the description of the foreign influence in Judah is hyperbolic: "Their land is filled with silver and gold, and there is no end to their treasures; their land is filled with horses, and there is no end to their chariots" (2:7). The prophet's stylistic technique creates a vivid and dynamic word picture. The poem of the vineyard in 5:1ff. aims to illustrate a specific aspect of the people's misconduct. The use of a parable, that is, the rhetorical description of the situation in a different context, enables Isaiah to focus his audience's attention and get their sympathy. If he had presented his criticism directly, it might have been rejected by the hostile audience. Another illustration of this technique is the vision of the future in 4:2–6, written in a prose style and following the description, in vivid imagery, of the corrupted daughters of Zion (3:16ff.). The present reality is described in verse in order to stir the emotions and move the audience. However, in this context if a description of the future were delivered in verse, it might have been received as an imaginative discourse having nothing to do with the present reality. Isaiah therefore employs a prosaic style, the language of historical fact, and the address, though it refers to the days to come, seems to have an air of reality.

Chronological order of the speeches. The speeches of chapters 2–5 (as well as those of 1:21–31) differ thematically from the material of 7:1ff., and it has been suggested that each topic mirrors a different political era. The sharp social criticism is replaced by political addresses. The first cycle of speeches (chaps. 2–5 is assigned to the days of Uzziah (c. 787–c. 736), a time of political stability, security, and economic prosperity (see *2 Kgs.* 15:1–7, *2 Chr.* 26:1–23). The social and political elite of Jerusalem regained their strength, creating severe social tension in Judah that affected the poor. Isaiah criticizes the rulers for oppressing their citizens. The speech of 7:1ff. refers to the days of Ahaz (who became king probably in 741 and was coregent until 725), during the Syro-Ephraimite war. Here Isaiah is responding to political developments rather than to the domestic situation. This historical reconstruction of Isaiah's activity assumes, however, that 1:4–9, which describes a major war that has endangered Jerusalem, is either not in order or that the whole of the chapter is an introduction to Isaiah's prophecy and does not belong to his early activity in the days of Uzziah. However, if we do not ignore 1:4–9 and read chapters 1–5 chronologically in their existing order, they reflect a period of war that had gravely threatened Jerusalem. Isaiah is concerned here with the cause of the military disaster. He indicates that corrupt domestic conditions are the reason for the political and military defeat and the people's suffering, which are God's punishment. In chapters 7–8 however, he focuses on King Ahaz's foreign policy. Isaiah's major thrust is directed not toward Uzziah's time but Ahaz's.

Isaiah's prophecy is thus a series of responses to specific political and domestic situations that, in his view, are mutually related. He reveals his deep involvement with and specific viewpoint regarding these political events and offers his unique prophetic interpretation of the political situation through a series of speeches that attempt to persuade. Isaiah does not speak as a political analyst or as a political philosopher; he uses rhetoric or any other means of appeal to reach his audience (see, e.g., 7:10ff.). Accordingly, the various speeches must be analyzed as a whole, and each speech or vision studied in light of Isaiah's thematic prophetic ideology and not as a separate entity. Prophecies of salvation follow from oracles of judgment, and both are integrated into Isaiah's prophetic worldview.

Political context and arrangement of the speeches. The book deals with two major political events that shocked Judah: the Syro-Ephraimite war and the Assyrian threats (734–701). Isaiah's prophecy is presented in light of his overall prophetic conception, which does not see the actual events as mere politico-military developments, although they shaped the prophet's political views. In the Syro-Ephraimite war the kings of Aram (Syria) and Ephraim (Israel) sought to fight against Assyria and needed Judah's active support. Ahaz, the Judahite king, refused, and as a result the northern coalition launched a military attack meant to replace Ahaz with their favorite, who was not a descendant of the house of David (see *Is.* 7:1–6). God's sacred promise to David and his house of an eternal throne in Jerusalem (see *2 Sm.* 7:1–17) was thus endangered. The sacred status of the house of David is the starting point of Isaiah's prophetic responses. It forces him to deal with the cause of the problem, which was, in his view, the social and ethical misconduct of the rulers (see 1:4–5, 1:10–17, 1:21–23, 3:14–15, 3:16ff., 5:1ff.). The war is God's punishment (see 1:4–9). At the last moment (1:9) the city will be purified, and justice will be restored (1:25–27, 2:2–4/5, 4:2–6; hence the above-mentioned connotation of the name of Isaiah's son Shearjashub, "a remnant shall return." This teleology, the faith that God will interfere on behalf of the people and for the sake of Jerusalem, leads Isaiah to oppose Ahaz's political attempts at saving himself by means of the foreign powers of Assyria or Egypt (7:18–25), and to assure the king that the enemies of the north will collapse (7:5–9). Furthermore, a series of speeches delivered by Isaiah emphasize the continuity of the Davidic dynasty (9:1–6, 11:1ff.). Chapters 10–11 should be read with the implications of the Assyrian threat in mind. Aram and Ephraim, Judah's enemies, had collapsed, and Judah itself was powerless against Assyria. The new political development invited the prophet's interpretation, and Isaiah delivers a series of speeches that interpret the meaning of the situation. Again, he points to moral and ethical misconduct as the cause of the military threat (10:1–4). God's response is direct: Assyria is his means of punishment (10:5–6), but that empire overestimates its power and will be punished (10:7ff.).

It has been suggested that the collection of oracles against the nations in chapters 13–23 may include material that is not Isaian (particularly chapters 13–14 and perhaps also chap. 23). The collection, which includes a prophecy against Judah concluding with a personal attack on two officers (22:1ff.), is an integral part of Isaiah's prophetic ideology. The structure of this collection resembles the work of Amos, who starts with a series of oracles against the nations and climaxes with a prophecy against Israel (1:2–2:16), his major point. The common theme in Isaiah's prophecies against the nations is that they will suffer military defeat. Isaiah repeatedly reveals his basic religious and political belief that the international political situation does not exist in a vacuum but is determined by God, who does not exclude Judah. Consequently, Judah's efforts to protect itself through military and political means will fail (22:1ff.).

The visions of chapters 24–35 abstractly summarize once again Isaiah's prophetic ideology: God's absolute universal domination and his punishment for misbehavior in the form of military defeat (24:1–5, 24:21–23, 28:14–22, 29:13–14, 30:1–3, 34:1ff.). Isaiah, a master of language, moves from visionary to more concrete speech and characteristically, concludes with an optimistic vision of the future (35:1ff.). It is unnecessary, therefore, to regard chapters 34–35, with their enthusiastic tone, as part of Second Isaiah's prophecy, as a number of scholars suggest.

Such a thematic reading of Isaiah's speeches raises the question of the place and function of chapter 6, which is regarded by many as Isaiah's call, his "inaugural vision." Was it originally placed at the beginning of the book? If so, why would the message of the vision be to harden the hearts of the people (6:9, 6:10)? Perhaps this is, in fact, a response to the people's stubbornness and their denial of Isaiah's earlier comments on their political and military troubles. In this light the vision of chapter 6 would seem to be in its correct chronological setting, reflecting Isaiah's despair over the people's unresponsiveness.

Alternatively, those who read *Isaiah* as a series of discrete speeches of judgment have suggested that the book's editors intended its literary structure to reflect a specific theological view that incorporated the late prophecies of salvation. For example, the literary passage 5:25–30 may be read together with a group of invective threats in 9:8–21, and the *hoy* ("woe") oracle of 10:1–4 may be associated with a series of *hoy* oracles in 5:8–24. It has been suggested as well that these two series of threats and *hoy* oracles were broken apart and rearranged in a chiastic order. The intent was to frame Isaiah's actual encounter with Ahaz in a way that would recall the fall of Israel and would also warn seventh-century Judah (the time of Josiah) by recalling the realization of Isaiah's words. Thus, in this view, the prophecies were rearranged, and the book was edited in light of the political climate of Josiah's times.

"Second Isaiah." The Babylonians exiled the social and political elite of Judah (see *2 Kgs.* 24:12–26, *Jer.* 52:16–30) to Babylonia. Evidence suggests that many of the Jews in exile preserved their national and religious identity. The Sabbath emerged as the expression of the covenant between God and the Jewish people, a view which has distinguished the Jews since the exilic period (see *Is.* 56, 58:13–14). The exilic period is also noted for its nationalistic-religious literary activity. The masterpiece of biblical historiography, the Deuteronomist work, was developed and shaped in this period. Nevertheless, there was a feeling of despair in the exiled Jewish community. The prophet Ezekiel asked hopelessly, "How are we to go on living?" (*Ez.* 33:10; see also 37:11). *Lamentations* repeatedly conveys a feeling of pessimism: "There is no one to comfort me" (*Lam.* 1:2, 1:16, 1:17, 1:21). Psalm 137 also reflects a hopeless situation, and Second Isaiah himself struggles with an attitude of religious and national despair: "A voice says: 'cry'! And I said: 'What shall I cry?' All flesh is grass and all its beauty is like the flower of the field" (*Is.* 40:6; RSV). The people felt the fall of Jerusalem, the destruction of the Temple in 587/6 BCE, and then the exile to be a hopeless situation that resulted from God's disappearance from the political stage. The exiles were indifferent to the momentous developments that were occurring on the international scene. The sensational victories of Cyrus I, king of Persia, did not affect the pessimistic religious attitude of the Jewish community in Babylonia. In 539 BCE, however, Babylonia surrendered to Cyrus II, and in 538 Cyrus announced his famous declaration allowing the Jewish community in exile to return to Jerusalem and restore the Temple (*Ezr.* 1:3–5 [*2 Chr.* 36:23], 6:3–5).

An important issue in the interpretation of Second Isaiah's prophecy is thus whether he addressed the exiles before or after the fall of Babylonia. Cyrus's edict is not quoted in Second Isaiah's speeches, and in light of his struggle with his audience's skepticism about God's control of contemporary political events, the speeches would sound inappropriate if Cyrus had already publicly granted permission to rebuild the Temple in Jerusalem. We should also take into account that Second Isaiah's description of the fall of Babylonia is not realistic. In contrast to inscriptions that report that the city fell peacefully, Second Isaiah describes Marduk, Babylon's god, being carried into captivity (46:1–2), which suggests that the prophet prophesied prior to 539 BCE.

The unknown prophet, the so-called Second Isaiah, was aroused by these significant political developments and considered that his prophetic goal was to persuade the exilic community that the immediate future held great promise and new hope. He considered the great king, Cyrus II, to be an agent of God, "who says of Cyrus: 'He is my shepherd. And he shall fulfill all my purpose,' saying of Jerusalem; 'she shall be built,' and of the Temple, 'your foundation shall be laid' " (44:28; see also 45:12–13). He rejected the spiritual crisis of the exiles and proclaimed two major themes: that God is not hidden from the Jewish people and that God is directing the new political events on their behalf. But first, Second Isaiah had to struggle with and reject the basis of the religious crisis. The cry "there is no one to comfort me" (*Lam.* 1:21) was replaced with "Comfort, comfort my people, says your God" (*Is.* 40:1). Furthermore, there was no reason for the people's feeling of guilt that they suffered because of their forefathers' sins; a new spiritual and religious era has begun: Jerusalem's warfare has ended and she has been pardoned (40:12). This explains the absence of threat, so characteristic of the biblical prophets, in Second Isaiah's speeches and sheds light on his style. His aim was to persuade, to appeal to his audience through words of comfort and encouragement, not by means of threat and judgment.

The major issue in research on Second-Isaiah is the demarcation of the prophetic speech. There are almost no formal indications of the beginning or end of the address. In general, two opposite approaches have been taken. The first considers the book to be a product of planned literary activity and regards Second Isaiah's work as composed of large units. The second approach argues that Second Isaiah delivered his speeches orally, and that the book is a collection of a number of short, distinct oracles. This approach raises the issue of the arrangement of the material and the editorial principles behind it. It has been suggested that the short, independent oracles were arranged mechanically according to a principle of keywords or similarity of theme, with each speech placed on the basis of its association with the preceding unit. One should note, however, that the question of defining the individual speech depends on the function of Second Isaiah's prophecy, which was to change his audience's religious attitude. He thus appealed to his audience by employing numerous means of persuasion; he thus relies on argument and style. Second Isaiah paid close attention to the organization of his addresses; each emerged from and is a response to a particular situation. An analysis of the text in light of the prophet's rhetorical goal and his efforts to effect his listeners reveals that his speeches are not short thematic oracles but are relatively long, thus enabling him to develop his argument at some length.

Second Isaiah was a master of language and employed his skill to stress his point and attract the attention of his audience. He often repeats himself to emphasize a certain point. On the other hand, he often varies his style by using a colorful and rich vocabulary to create an aesthetic effect. He is very flexible in his use of language and often employs unusual words or phrases with the intention of providing variety and avoiding clichés.

The beginning of Second Isaiah's prophecy, 40:1–2ff., is a good illustration of his style. His first announcement, "Comfort, comfort my people" is brief and clear. The entire section, verses 1–2, is explicit in structure, with no coloration or figures of speech, and is designed to express clearly and straightforwardly his primary announcement. But the audience may miss a message delivered in such an unadorned style. Therefore, Second Isaiah uses the stylistic device of repetition and repeats the key word of his message, *comfort*. The reiteration of the word is intended to make a deep impression on the audience. The verb *comfort* in the form used here was coined by Second Isaiah based upon the lament "no one comforts her" (*Lam.* 1:2). Yet Second Isaiah uses it in a positive sense, to stress the motif of rejoicing, while in *Lamentations* the expression connotes religious despair. Thus at the beginning of his address, Second Isaiah employs a familiar expression in a way that changes its meaning. By using a familiar expression in an unexpected manner, he attracts attention and also cancels its earlier, negative meaning. In addition, verse 1 reverses the normal order and places the opening formula, "says your God," at the end. Since Second Isaiah wants to convey his message's immediacy, he has adjusted the formula accordingly. In addition, as is well known, rhyme is not highly developed in biblical prosody. In order to unify the various elements in a verse, the biblical poets developed the literary device of the sound effect. Sound plays an important role in this verse. *Alliteration* holds the verse together and focuses attention on the consonant *ḥeit(ḥ)* in the opening words *"naḥamu, naḥamu."* The sound is then repeated at the end of verse 2 *(ḥaṭṭo'teikhah)* thus binding the entire statement into a whole.

The songs of the "servant of the Lord [ʿeved YHVH]" have received special attention from scholars. There are four poems that speak about the servant (42:1–4, 42:5–7, 49:1–6, 50:4–9) and an additional two poems which may be related to them (50:10–11, and 52:13–53:12). These poems share a common theme: their subject, the servant, suffers when he is ignored by the people who surround him. In the future, however, the servant will be recognized as God's servant, who has a mission to restore justice, which will be fulfilled. The poems occupy a distinct place in the history of sacred interpretations and have theological significance in the histories of Jewish and Christian religious interpretation. The major critical issue for Second Isaiah is whether to isolate the poems from their context or to consider them as an integral part of his prophecy. There is the further question of the identity of the servant, with scholars divided between an individual and a collective identity. Thus there have been various attempts to identify the servant as a specific public or historical figure, such as Jeremiah, Josiah, Zerrubbabel, or even the prophet himself. Second Isaiah makes other allusions to the servant of God, however (41:8ff., 41:13, 42:19, 44:1–2); and in light of the frequent references to Israel as God's servant (see, e.g., 49:3), it has been suggested that the servant be seen as the people of Israel, sympathetically portrayed by Second Isaiah to arouse hope and a feeling of mission and fulfillment as well as to convey the message that the current suffering has not gone unnoticed. Another view holds that the servant is neither a particular figure nor a group, but the combination of a mythological cultic and royal figure.

"Third Isaiah." Concerning chapters 56–66, it has already been mentioned that these may constitute a separate collection by another anonymous prophet, called Third Isaiah, or Trito-Isaiah, who was active after Second Isaiah, during the time of Ezra and Nehemiah, in the fifth century BCE. Third Isaiah is no longer located in Babylonia but is based in Judah. His prophecies presuppose the existence of the Temple in Jerusalem (which was dedicated in 515). There is no clear thematic line in this work as we find in the speeches of Second Isaiah. The collection of Third Isaiah emphasizes ritual requirements. It starts with words of encouragement to those who observe the Sabbath, including the eunuchs, and stresses the importance of Sabbath worship (56:1–8). It continues with a critique of the leaders (56:9–12), a short lament on the death of the righteous (57:1–2), a stormy attack on foreign cults (57:3–13), a prophecy of comfort (57:14–19), and a criticism of those who fast ritually without thought (58:1–7). Chapters 60–61 contain another prophecy of salvation in the style of Second Isaiah. In 63:7–64:11 there is a communal lament, and 66:1–4 rejects both the building of the Temple and the sacrificial cult. This attitude reflects a view opposite that held by the prophets Haggai and Zechariah, who encouraged and supported the rebuilding of the Temple. It has been suggested that Third Isaiah was a disciple of Second Isaiah and his redactor as well. Another view holds that Second Isaiah returned to Jerusalem following Cyrus's edict and continued his prophetic activity there. His prophecies in Judah would then constitute chapters 49–66, in which Zion is the background for the speeches (see 49:14ff., 51:17–23, 54:1ff., 60:1ff., 62:1–9).

Texts of Isaiah Found at Qumran. The scrolls found in 1947 on the northwestern shore of the Dead Sea reveal two almost complete manuscripts of the entire *Book of Isaiah*, dated to the second or first century BCE. [*See* Dead Sea Scrolls.] As a rule, the scrolls of *Isaiah* reflect the Masoretic text. Of the two scrolls, one (found in Cave I) shows certain corrections and interlineations from a more popular edition, but these are mainly matters of spelling and stylistic characteristics rather than important editing. This scroll shows indications that it may actually have been composed of two manuscripts: there is evidence that the existing chapter 34 was started on a new sheet of leather, which may mean that it was a new manuscript. This may have influenced the modern critical division of the book into Isaiah of Jerusalem and Second Isaiah (and the remainder of the book).

BIBLIOGRAPHY

Isaiah 1–39

Barth, Hermann. *Die Jesaja-Worte in der Josiazeit.* Neukirchen, 1977.

Clements, R. E. *Isaiah 1–39.* Grand Rapids, Mich., 1980.

Kaiser, Otto. *Isaiah 13–39.* Translated by R. A. Wilson. Philadelphia, 1974.

Kaiser, Otto. *Isaiah 1–12.* 2d ed. Translated by R. A. Wilson. Philadelphia, 1983.

Wildberger, Hans. *Jesaja.* 3 vols. Neukirchen, 1972–1983.

Isaiah 40–66

Elliger, Karl. *Jesaja II.* Neukirchen, 1970–.

Gitay, Yehoshua. *Prophecy and Persuasion: A Study of Isaiah 40–48.* Bonn, 1981.

Kaufmann, Yeḥezkel. *History of the Religion of Israel,* vol. 4, *From the Babylonian Captivity to the End of Prophecy.* Translated by Clarence W. Efroymsen. New York, 1977.

Muilenburg, James. "Isaiah 40–66 (Introduction and Exegesis)." In *The Interpreter's Bible,* vol. 5, pp. 381–419, 422–773. New York, 1956.

Westermann, Claus. *Isaiah 40–66: A Commentary.* Translated by David M. G. Stalker. Philadelphia, 1969.

YEHOSHUA GITAY

ISHIDA BAIGAN (1685–1744), Japanese philosopher of the Tokugawa period (1603–1868) who developed the concept of a moral or ethical philosophy known as Shingaku. Ishida was born on 15 September 1685 in the village of Tōge in Tamba Province (modern Kameoka City, Kyoto Prefecture), the second son of a farmer. At the age of ten (eleven by Japanese count) he was sent to Kyoto as a merchant's apprentice. There he spent his leisure time studying Shintō doctrine and attending lectures by local Confucian scholars, Buddhist monks, and experts on the Japanese classics.

When Ishida reached the age of about thirty-five he began to feel an inner restlessness; he felt that he did not know the nature of human beings. In his search for a guide or a direction, he met a Buddhist monk, Ryōun, who led him to an awakening of the spirit such as that described by the Chinese founder of Taoism, Lao-tzu. It was then that Ishida realized that man's true nature was egoless. In his writings, he pointed out that once one understood this aspect of human nature, one's life would automatically coincide with what he called the "universal principle" and one's *kokoro* ("soul" or "spirit") would be content and at peace. Ishida believed it would be possible to reach an egoless, natural state and to acquire instinctive knowledge by meditative restraint of the senses. In accordance with his convictions, he lived as a celibate ascetic, although he acknowledged that social responsibilities were also inherent in his view of human nature.

In 1727 Ishida left the service of the Kyoto merchant; two years later, he began to conduct lectures at his home in Kyoto. At these lectures, which were free and open to all, Ishida encouraged his listeners to seek individual awakening through meditation. To make learning accessible to all, Ishida distributed simplified manuscripts of his interpretations of Chinese and Japanese classical literature. He repudiated the critiques of scholars, whom he believed were interested only in the meanings of words. Ishida strove instead to capture the essence of the classics as he understood them, although his views did not always agree with the original intent of the authors.

In his search for a fundamental principle, Ishida believed that the first and last step in the learning process was to understand the human heart and thereby gain insight into human nature. He adopted the term *jinsei,* which refers to the total capacity of the mind, from the Chinese Confucian thinker Meng-tzu. According to Ishida, one must utilize all one's spiritual and mental capacity to overcome desires. Only when one's *kokoro* is empty and free of human desires is it possible to unite with the universal spirit. Overcoming the ego and its desires will enable one to carry out one's duty in life. One can then develop a spirit of self-sacrifice toward one's ruler, be properly filial toward one's parents, and discover one's proper vocation in life.

BIBLIOGRAPHY

A number of works have been published on Ishida Baigan and his philosophy of Shingaku, or practical ethics. Robert Bellah's *Tokugawa Religion: The Values of Pre-Industrial Japan* (Glencoe, Ill., 1957) clarifies the religious morals of the Tokugawa period, morals that had their origin in Ishida's concept of ethics and that played a part in the modernization of Japan. Readers of Japanese will want to consult a translation of this seminal work, *Nihon kindaika to shūkyō rinri* (Tokyo, 1981), translated by Hōri Ichirō and Ikeda Akira. Ishikawa Ken's *Shingaku, Edo no shomin tetsugaku* (Tokyo, 1964) discusses Ishida's philosophy and its applicability to the common people. Sakasai Takahito focuses on Ishida's conversion to popular morality in "Sekimon shingaku no igi to genkai, sono tsūzoku dōtoku e no tenraku ni tsuite," *Rikkyō keizaigaku kenkyū* 18 (February 1965). Another work that deals with Ishida's ethics is *Sekimon shingaku,* edited by Shibata Minoru (Tokyo, 1971), in volume 42 of "Nihon shisō taikei." Finally, Takenaka Yasukazu's *Sekimon shingaku no keizai shisō* (Tokyo, 1962) emphasizes the economic aspects of Ishida's ethical philosophy.

HAGA NOBORU
Translated from Japanese by Irene M. Kunii

ISHMAEL, or, in Hebrew, Yishma'e'l; eldest son of Abraham. Ishmael's mother was Hagar, an Egyptian slave girl whom Sarah gave to Abraham because of her own infertility; in accordance with Mesopotamian law, the offspring of such a union would be credited to Sarah (*Gn.* 16:2). The name *Yishma'e'l* is known from various ancient Semitic cultures and means "God has hearkened," suggesting that a child so named was regarded as the fulfillment of a divine promise.

Ishmael was circumcised at the age of thirteen by Abraham and expelled with his mother at the instigation of Sarah, who wanted to ensure that Isaac would be Abraham's heir (*Gn.* 21). In the New Testament, Paul uses this incident to symbolize the relationship between Judaism, the older but now rejected tradition, and Christianity (*Gal.* 4:21–31).

In the *Genesis* account, God blessed Ishmael, promising that he would be the founder of a great nation and a "wild ass of a man" always at odds with others (*Gn.* 16:12). He is credited with twelve sons, described as "princes according to their tribes" (*Gn.* 25:16), representing perhaps an ancient confederacy. The Ishmaelites, vagrant traders closely related to the Midianites, were apparently regarded as his descendants. The fact that Ishmael's wife and mother are both said to have been Egyptian suggests close ties between the Ishmaelites and Egypt. According to *Genesis* 25:17, Ishmael lived to the age of 137.

Islamic tradition tends to ascribe a larger role to Ishmael than does the Bible. He is considered a prophet and, according to certain theologians, the offspring whom Abraham was commanded to sacrifice (although surah 37:99–111 of the Qur'ān never names that son). Like his father Abraham, Ishmael too played an important role in making Mecca a religious center (2:127–129). Judaism has generally regarded him as wicked, although repentance is also ascribed to him. According to some rabbinic traditions, his two wives were Aisha and Fatima, whose names are the same as those of Muḥammad's wife and daughter. Both Judaism and Islam see him as the ancestor of Arab peoples.

BIBLIOGRAPHY

A survey of the Bible's patriarchal narratives can be found in Nahum M. Sarna's *Understanding Genesis* (New York, 1972). Postbiblical traditions, with reference to Christian and Islamic views, are collected in Louis Ginzberg's exhaustive *The Legends of the Jews,* 7 vols., translated by Henrietta Szold et al. (Philadelphia, 1909–1938).

FREDERICK E. GREENSPAHN

ISHMAEL BEN ELISHA. *See* Yishma'e'l ben Elisha'.

ISHRĀQĪYAH, from *ishrāq* ("illumination"), is the name of a school of esoteric philosophy in Islam. The two major currents of thought in the development of Islamic philosophy, one exoteric and the other esoteric, are known respectively as *falsafah* ("scholastic philosophy," derived from Aristotle and Plato) and *'irfān* (a special type of philosophy derived from a metaphysical experience of Being through spiritual realization). Introduced into the West from the twelfth century onward through numerous translations from Arabic to Latin, it was *falsafah* that almost exclusively came to constitute "Islamic philosophy" in the West, while the other important tradition, that of *'irfān,* was left in complete obscurity. But *'irfān* has always been a creative force in Islamic spirituality, and as such it has produced a type of philosophy that is quite different from, and in many respects sharply opposed to, *falsafah.* [*See* Falsafah *for further discussion of this current.*]

Imaginal Thinking. The word *philosophy* tends to suggest the inner act of thinking as a logical outcome of reason. One has to be reminded, however, that philosophic thought is not necessarily activated only on the level of pure reason. Because human consciousness is extremely complicated and multilayered, various forms of thinking can be realized at different levels of the mind. "Imaginal" thinking is one of them.

"Imaginal" thinking, also known as "mythopoeic thinking" or "mythopoesis," is a peculiar pattern of thinking that evolves through interconnections and interactions among a number of archetypal images in a particular depth-dimension of consciousness. In the technical terminology of Islamic *'irfān,* this depth-dimension is called the *'ālam al-mithāl,* meaning literally the "world of symbolic images." The type of philosophy produced by this kind of thinking naturally manifests remarkable differences from philosophy as a product of pure reason.

Imaginal thinking is not confined to Islamic *'irfān.* Quite the contrary; many different systems of philosophy that have come into being in various Asian regions reflect self-expressions of "imaginal" consciousness. The "illuminationism" *(ishrāqīyah)* of Suhrawardī represents one case, the "unity of being" *(waḥdat al-wujūd)* of Ibn ʿArabī another. Complicating the matter with regard to the Islamic variety of "imaginal" or esoteric philosophy, however, is the fact that the majority of the first-rate thinkers in this domain were also great masters of scholastic, exoteric philosophy, so that both the "imaginal" and the rational modes of thinking appear in subtle entanglements on the textual surface of their works. This is notably the case with men like Suhrawardī and Ibn ʿArabī. [*See the biography of Ibn al-ʿArabī.*]

Suhrawardī, in particular, is known to have written three voluminous books on scholasticism, *Kitāb al-talwīḥāt, Kitāb al-muqāwamāt,* and *Kitāb al-muṭāraḥāt,* the famous trilogy attesting to his rarely surpassed accomplishment as an exoteric philosopher, prior to embarking upon the production of his major work on Illuminationism, *Ḥikmat al-ishrāq* (Theosophy of Illumination). As indicated by the title, this is essentially a product of imaginal thinking, representing a peculiar kind of esoteric philosophy based on a metaphysical experience of light. Yet it begins with a sober exposition of the principles of Aristotelian logic before gradually becoming an "imaginal" presentation of the hierarchic structure of the angels of light. It is important to note that this seemingly odd combination of the exoteric and esoteric modes of thinking, together with the very conception of *ishrāq,* can be traced back to Ibn Sīnā (Avicenna).

Ibn Sīnā and "Oriental Philosophy." In a number of respects, and particularly with regard to the idea of *ishrāq,* Ibn Sīnā may be considered an important precursor of Suhrawardī. Quite characteristically, however, in Ibn Sīnā's work the rational and "imaginal" modes of thinking are still consciously and methodically separated from one another, so that *falsafah* and *ʿirfān* are conceived as two independent and essentially different types of philosophy (although in the process of the structuralization of Ibn Sīnā's symbolic narratives, we sometimes notice technical concepts of Aristotelianism creeping into the "imaginal" space of *ʿirfān*).

It is important to note that of the two types of philosophy Ibn Sīnā himself laid greater weight on the imaginal (i.e., esoteric) than on the rational (i.e., exoteric). At the outset of his *magnum opus,* the famous *Kitāb al-shifāʾ* (Book of Remedy, known in the West in Latin translation as *Sufficientia*), which is a huge systematic exposition of Peripatetic philosophy, Ibn Sīnā declares that what he is going to write does not represent his personal thought but is intended to acquaint the students of philosophy with the thought-world of the ancient Greeks, Aristotle in particular.

As for his own "true thought," he seems to have long cherished the idea of giving a direct expression to it in a completely different book, *Al-ḥikmat al-mashriqīyah* (Oriental Philosophy), of which the now extant *Manṭiq al-mashriqīyīn* (The Logic of the Orientals) is only the introductory part. Whether completed or not, the book itself has not come down to us. Besides this work we have a few short treatises of esotericism and some symbolic tales from his own pen.

Ibn Sīnā's use of words meaning "Orient" and "Oriental" is significant here, for the word *mashriq* ("Orient"), from the root *shrq,* literally means the "place *(ma-)* where what is designated by the root *shrq* becomes activated," that is, the original point of "illumination" *(ishrāq).* The "Orient," in other words, is not a geographical notion, but a term designating the East in a mythopoeic or spiritual geography.

The "Orient" in this particular context is the sacred locus from which the divine light makes its appearance, illuminating the whole world of being, "the place where the sun rises," the ultimate origin of all existence. In the Persian commentary on Ibn Sīnā's mythic-symbolic tale, *Ḥayy ibn Yaqẓān* (a proper name, literally "Living, son of Wakeful"), one of his disciples (Abū ʿUbayd al-Juzjānī?) explicates the symbolism of "Orient" and "Occident" in the following manner. Utilizing in his own way the Aristotelian theory of the distinction between "form" and "matter," he begins by stating that matter in and by itself has no existence, whereas form is the source of existence. Matter, in other words, is pure nonexistence. But his Iranian frame of reference naturally and immediately translates this proposition into another, namely, that matter in itself is sheer darkness. And he assigns matter (as darkness) to the Western region of the cosmos in the "imaginal" map of his symbolic geography.

The implication of this position is clear. Ibn Sīnā defines the Orient as the original abode of form (light), and thus symbolically as the world of "forms," or existential light, while the Occident is the world of "matter," that is, of darkness and nonexistence.

Matter turns into existence only by the influx of the all-existentiating luminous energy of form, coming from the divine Orient through the intermediary of ten angels—the number limited to ten in conformity with the ten celestial spheres of Hellenistic astronomy. Directly reflecting the divine light, the angels embody the highest degree of existential luminosity, while all other beings and things that become luminous (i.e., existent) through the illuminating activity of the angels are less bright (i.e., less densely existent). The existential luminosity naturally grows less and less intense as the rays of the divine light go down the scale of being (i.e., become further and further removed from its original source), until they merge almost totally into the darkness of matter when they reach the lowest stage of being.

As long as they do exist factually, the "things" in the empirical world are not sheer darkness. They are shadowy existents, faint reflections of the divine light. But since it is matter that is overwhelmingly dominant in this domain, the empirical world is "imaginally" represented as a world of darkness. In some privileged cases (notably the prophets), however, the human consciousness may suddenly flare up in glorious light under the influence of the Active Intellect (Gabriel, the angel of revelation), illuminating the world of darkness in which the souls of ordinary human beings are imprisoned—a typical theme of gnosticism.

Such, in brief outline, is the general plan of the "Oriental philosophy" of Ibn Sīnā. Underlying it is clearly a vision of the cosmos as the interplay of light and shadow, a vast "imaginal" field in which the divine light appears in infinitely various and variegated forms, determining itself in accordance with various degrees of interfusion with material darkness through the light-transmitting activity of the angels. It is a gnostic vision of the world permeated with the "imaginal" presence of the angels of light. [*See also the biography of Ibn Sīnā.*]

Suhrawardī, Founder of the Ishrāqī School. The esoteric worldview manifested in Ibn Sīnā's philosophy, with its strong gnostic influences, was inherited in turn by Shihāb al-Dīn Yaḥyā ibn Ḥabash ibn Amīrak al-Suhrawardī (1153–1191), the real founder of the Illuminationist school in Iran. Significantly enough, Suhrawardī, who has come to be known by the honorary title Shaykh al-Ishrāq, "master of illumination," traces the "tradition" of his Illuminationist philosophy back to Hermes Agathodaemon (who appears in Islam under the figure of the prophet Idrīs). It must be remembered that long before the rise of Islam, the Mediterranean school of Hermetism had established itself in Alexandria, and from this center it had infiltrated into the wide domain of the Middle East. There, in the city of Harran, the "followers of the prophet Idrīs," the Sabaeans who venerated the *Corpus Hermeticum* as their scripture, cultivated the esoteric learning of Hermetism and propagated it in various directions. Through one of these it must have reached Suhrawardī.

In the "imaginal" dimension of Suhrawardī's consciousness, however, the history of Illuminationism (which he straightforwardly identifies with the history of philosophy in general) takes on a remarkably original and peculiar form. Ishrāqī wisdom as the only authentic actualization of the "perennial philosophy" (*ḥikmah ʿatīqah*) of mankind has its ultimate origin in the divine revelations received by the prophet Idrīs, that is, Hermes, who thereby became the forefather of philosophy. This Hermetic wisdom was transmitted to posterity through two separate channels: Egyptian-Greek and ancient Iranian. The first branch of Hermetic wisdom, after flourishing in ancient Egypt, went to Greece, where it produced such gnostic sages as Pythagoras, Empedocles, Plato, and Plotinus. The tradition was maintained in Islam by some of the eminent early Ṣūfīs, including Dhū al-Nūn (d. 859) and Abu Sahl al-Tustarī (d. 896).

The second branch of Hermetism, represented in ancient Iran by the mythical priest-kings Kayūmarth, Farīdūn, and Kay Khusraw, developed into the Sufism of Bāyazīd al-Basṭāmī, generally known in the West as al-Bisṭāmi (d. 874), and Manṣūr al-Ḥallāj (d. 922).

Suhrawardī considered himself the historical point of convergence between the two traditions, unifying and integrating into an existential, organic whole all the important elements of the Hermetic wisdom elaborated in the long course of its historical development. And to the integral whole of gnostic ideas thus formed Suhrawardī gave a peculiar philosophical reformulation, structured in terms of the Zoroastrian symbolism of light and darkness—the term *Zoroastrianism* here understood in the sense of the spiritual, "esoteric" teaching of Zoroaster as distinguished from the "exoteric."

East–West symbolism. In approaching Suhrawardī's Illuminationist philosophy, the first thing we must pay attention to is the symbolism of East and West. *Qiṣṣat al-ghurbah al-gharbīyah* (The Narrative of the Occidental Exile), which he composed in Arabic—most of his symbolic tales or narratives are in Persian—makes it clear that he attaches the same "imaginal" meanings to "Orient" and "Occident" as did Ibn Sīnā. Thus, the Orient for him too means the Orient of lights, the sacred place in which divine light originates, the source of spiritual as well as cosmic illumination, whereas the Occident is the abyss of material darkness, in which the human soul is imprisoned and from which it must set itself free so that it may go back to its real home, the Orient.

Hierarchy of lights. Rejecting (or radically modifying) the Aristotelian doctrine of hylomorphism, which explains every existent in terms of a conjunction of matter and specific form, Suhrawardī employs a completely different ontology, of gnostic origin, explaining all things as degrees of light (or as various mixtures of light and darkness); the Aristotelian "form" thereby appears metamorphosed into an angel as a luminous being. Suhrawardian philosophy thus turns out to be an ontology of light, with varying degrees of intensity, in a hierarchical order.

Light, says Suhrawardī, is that which illuminates itself, and by so doing illuminates all other things. Light, otherwise expressed, is that which exists by and in itself (i.e., light *is* existence) and by its own existence brings into existence all things. Light thus defies definition, while all other things can and must be defined in reference to it. Light, in short, is nothing other than the ontological "presence" *(ḥuḍūr)* of the things; it is the ultimate source of all existence. It follows, therefore, that the whole world of being must be realized as a grandiose hierarchy of lights, beginning with the absolute light in the highest degree of luminosity and ending with the weakest lights just about to sink into the reign of utter darkness *(ghasaq),* that is, absolute nonexistence.

What stands at the top of this cosmic hierarchy of light is the "light of lights" *(nūr al-anwār),* which, in the terminology of Islamic theology, is God. Beneath it, spreading down to the domain of the densely dark bodies in the physical world, are various degrees of light (existence), which, in Suhrawardī's system, characteristically appear in the guise of angels who govern the world of being.

Unlike Ibn Sīnā's angelology, which is Neoplatonic, Suhrawardī's is fundamentally Zoroastrian. Rather than being limited to ten (corresponding to the ten heavens of Ptolemy), the number of angels is innumerable. Their function, moreover, is not limited to the Neoplatonic angels' triple intellection of their origin, of themselves, and of those that come out of them. As a result, the hierarchy of Suhrawardī's angelology is far more complicated than that of Ibn Sīnā. There are, to begin with, two different basic orders of angels, "longitudinal" *(ṭūlī)* and "latitudinal" *(ʿarḍī),* with regard to their successive generations, their spatial disposition, and their functions.

Longitudinal and latitudinal order. The longitudinal order of angels lays the primary foundation of the world of being in its entirety as a "temple of light," or rather, a dazzling complex of "temples of light" *(hayākil al-nūr;* sg., *haykal al-nūr),* radiant with angels reflecting the "light of lights" and mutually reflecting each other. Their procession is described by Suhrawardī in the following manner.

From the "light of lights," representing the highest and ultimate point of cosmic-metaphysical luminosity, proceeds the archangel Bahmān, who is the "nearest light" *(nūr aqrab).* Directly contemplating his own origin, the "light of lights," the archangel Bahmān reflects it without any intermediary. And this immediately brings into being another light-entity, or archangel, which is doubly illuminated, receiving as it does illumination directly from the "light of lights" and from the first light from which it has arisen. The double illumination of the second light immediately generates the third light, which is now illuminated four times, once by the "light of lights," once by the first light, and twice by the second light (the second light being, as we have just seen, itself doubly illuminated). And so continues the downward procession of the archangels, resulting in the constitution of the "longitudinal" order of lights. Each one of these angelic lights is called in Suhrawardī's technical terminology a "dominating light" *(nūr qāhir),* with "forceful domination" *(qahr)* one of the basic principles determining the activity of these angels.

This longitudinal order of archangels of light has in itself two mutually opposed aspects, the masculine and the feminine, from the former of which issues an essentially different order of angels, the latitudinal. Unlike the archangels of the longitudinal order, the latitudinal angels do not generate one another, but simply coexist horizontally, positioned side by side, thus constituting the world of eternal "archetypes" that are "imaginal" equivalents of the Platonic ideas. Suhrawardī calls them in this capacity the "lords of the species" *(arbāb al-anwāʿ;* sg., *rabb al-nawʿ).* Every thing in the empirical world specifically stands under the domination of a lord of the species; in other words, every individual existent in our world has its corresponding metaphysical archetype in the angelic dimension of being, somewhat like the ontological relationship between the individual and universal realms in Platonic idealism. Each existent in the empirical world is technically called the "talisman" *(ṭilasm)* of a particular angel governing and guarding it from above. And the angel in this capacity is called the "lord of the talisman" *(rabb al-ṭilasm).*

As for the feminine aspect of the longitudinal order of angels, it primarily has to do with such negative attributes as being dominated, being dependent, being receptive to illumination, being remote from the "light of lights," nonbeing, and so on. The fixed stars and the visible heavens come into being from it as so many hypostatizations of the luminous energies of the archangels. And this marks the ending point of the Orient and the beginning point of the Occident.

The latitudinal order of angels gives rise to still another order of angels, whose basic function is to govern the species in the capacity of vicegerents of the "lords of the species." These deputy angels are called by Suhrawardī the "directive lights" *(anwār mudabbirah;* sg., *nūr mudabbir).* Using the characteristic Persian word *ispahbad,* meaning "commander-in-chief," Suhrawardī calls them also "light-generalissimos" *(anwār isfahbadīyah).* These are the angels who are charged with maintaining the movement of the heavens, and who, as the agents of the "lords of the species," govern all the species of the creatures in the physical world, including human beings, whose shared "lord of the species" is the archangel Gabriel (Jibrīl). The "deputy governor" (*ispahbad*, the "light-generalissimo") of Gabriel resides in the inmost part of the soul of each human being, issuing directions concerning his or her internal and external acts.

As will be clearly observable even from this very brief, and necessarily incomplete, exposition, Suhrawardī's Illuminationist worldview is fundamentally mandalic in nature. The world of being in its entirety is conceived or imaged as a vast cosmic mandala composed of innumerable angels of light spreading out in geometric designs along longitudinal and latitudinal axes. Here we have a typical product of mandalic consciousness completely self-realized in the form of a vision of the whole world of being appearing as an "imaginal" space saturated with light.

Post-Suhrawardian Developments. Suhrawardī's life was extremely short; in the citadel of Aleppo where he was imprisoned as a propagator of anti-Islamic "new ideas" he was murdered at the age of thirty-eight in the year 1191. But after his death the influence of his Ishrāqī teaching grew stronger in the Islamic world, particularly in Iran, where it exercised the greatest influence on the historical formation of the philosophy of Shiism.

The long chain of followers of the Master of Illumination begins with Shams al-Dīn Shahrazūrī (thirteenth century), who studied personally under Suhrawardī or under one of his direct disciples. He wrote the first systematic and most extensive commentary on the *Ḥikmat al-ishrāq*, thereby preparing the ground for subsequent interpretations of this fundamental work of Illuminationism. It was, as a matter of fact, in complete reliance on this commentary that Quṭb al-Dīn Shīrāzī (d. 1311) composed his famous commentary on the *Ḥikmat al-ishrāq*.

Shahrazūrī was in reality a far more original thinker than Quṭb al-Dīn Shīrāzī, and his commentary was far more important and interesting than Quṭb al-Dīn's, which is now known to be an abbreviated version. Quṭb al-Dīn's fame, however, soon overshadowed that of his great predecessor, so that his commentary came to be regarded as virtually *the* commentary on the *Ḥikmat al-ishrāq;* thus from the early fourteenth century until today almost all those who have been interested in Suhrawardian Illuminationism have read or studied the book mainly through the interpretation given by Quṭb al-Dīn.

The historical importance of Quṭb al-Dīn lies in the fact that besides being an ardent propagator of Illuminationism, he was also a disciple of Ṣadr al-Dīn Qūnawī (or Qunyawī), a personal disciple of Ibn ʿArabī and his son-in-law, and that through this channel he was well versed in the *waḥdat al-wujūd* type of philosophy. In fact, Quṭb al-Dīn is counted among the greatest expositors of Ibn ʿArabī's ideas. Combining thus in his own person these two important currents of the post-Avicennian Islamic philosophy, Quṭb al-Dīn fundamentally determined the subsequent course of the development of the Ishrāqī school. Indeed, after Quṭb al-Dīn, Suhrawardian Illuminationism quickly assimilated into its structure the major ideas of the "unity of existence" that had been independently developed by the school of Ibn ʿArabī.

The work of integration reached its first stage of completion in the Safavid period in Iran. The two centuries of the Safavid dynasty (1499–1720), during which the city of Isfahan was the political and cultural center and Twelver Shiism was the recognized form of Islam, realized what is often called the "renaissance of Islamic [Shīʿī] culture." It was in the flourishing city of Isfahan that the intellectual heritages of Ibn ʿArabī and Suhrawardī were harmoniously integrated into an organic whole through the works of generations of outstanding thinkers. These thinkers are now referred to among historians of Islamic philosophy as the "school of Isfahan," the greatest figure in which is uncontestedly Ṣadr al-Dīn Shīrāzī (popularly known as Mullā Ṣadrā, 1571–1640). [*See the biography of Mullā Ṣadrā.*]

Mullā Ṣadrā's philosophy is a colossal and complicated system, synthesizing ideas derived from various sources in conjunction with his own quite original thoughts. As regards Illuminationism, Mullā Ṣadrā made thoroughly explicit what had from the beginning been implicit (and occasionally explicit), namely, the complete identification of "light" with "existence." In this way, "existence" became totally synonymous with "luminosity." The existence of each thing is in the metaphysical-"imaginal" vision of Mullā Ṣadrā nothing other than a degree of light, a luminous issue or illumination from the "light of lights." The "light of lights" itself is completely identified with what is referred to in Ibn ʿArabī's *waḥdat al-wujūd* system as the "one," that is, existence in its primordial state of absolute undetermination, but ready to start determining itself in an infinity of different ontological self-manifestations.

[*For discussion of related topics, see* Hermeticism; Images, *article on* The Imaginal; *and* Nūr Muḥammad.]

BIBLIOGRAPHY

Works by Suhrawardī in Translation. Shihāboddīn Yahyā Sohravardī's "L'archange Empourpré," translated by Henry

Corbin, in *Documents spirituels,* vol. 14 (Paris, 1976), is a collection of symbolic narratives and short essays of Suhrawardī, translated into French from Persian and Arabic, with copious notes. It is indispensable for all those seeking initiation into the mystical world of the Master of Illumination. A French translation, also by Henry Corbin, of *Ḥikmat al-ishrāq,* the basic text of Illuminationism, is now in preparation.

Works on Suhrawardī and Illuminationism. Seyyed Hossein Nasr's "Shihāb al-Dīn Suhrawardī Maqtūl," in *A History of Muslim Philosophy,* edited by M. M. Sharif (Wiesbaden, 1963), vol. 1, pp. 372–398, is by far the best introductory exposition of the Illuminationism of Suhrawardī. See also his "The School of Iṣpahān," in the same source, vol. 2, pp. 904–932, and "The Spread of the Illuminationist School of Suhrawardī," *Islamic Quarterly* 14 (July–September 1970): 111–121, a short but important paper that traces the historical development of Illuminationism in Iran, India, and Turkey down to modern times. See also Henry Corbin's *Sohrawardî et les platoniciens de Perse,* vol. 2 of *En Islam iranien* (Paris, 1971), one of the most important works on Suhrawardī.

TOSHIHIKO IZUTSU

ISHTAR. *See* Inanna.

ISIDORE OF SEVILLE (560–636), bishop of Seville (603–636), proclaimed "eminent teacher and an honor to the church" by the Council of Toledo of 653. Member of an eminent Andalusian family, Isidore was prepared to inherit the see of Seville by his older brother Leandro, also bishop of Seville. In his youth the king, Leovigild (r. 569–586), was able to stabilize the Visigothic kingdom, in which a minority of Visigoths (Germanic peoples who entered the Iberian peninsula in the fifth century) and a vast majority of ancient inhabitants (the Hispano-Romans) coexisted. Under Reccared (d. 601) the Goths abjured the Arian doctrine and embraced the catholic faith (c. 589). In 614 the Jews were forced by Sisebut to convert to Christianity.

Through his pastoral leadership, Isidore imbued the Visigothic church with the same concerns that dominate his writings: respect for the political authority of the Goths, incitation for increasing participation of the Hispano-Romans in the life of the church, and an overriding intellectual and moral commitment. A famous orator, he presided at the Council of Seville of 619 and at the Council of Toledo of 633. Mild and conciliatory, Isidore was a man of great human and Christian optimism; he struggled with his own strict education and with the intransigent atmosphere of the church after the triumph of catholic orthodoxy against the Arians, and over tensions with Jews after 614.

Isidore's writings, cataloged by his friend Braulio (d. 651), bishop of Zaragoza, may be grouped as follows:

1. biblical studies;
2. handbooks for clergy and monks: *Concerning the Ecclesiastical Offices, A Monastic Rule, Vademecum of the Catholic Faith for Use in Discussion with the Jews,* and *Catalog of Heresies;*
3. guides for personal and public spiritual development: *Synonyms* and *Sentences;*
4. works on civic education: *About the Universe,* an explanation of the system of the world and of natural phenomena for the purpose of preventing fear and superstition;
5. works extolling the national glory: *History of the Goths, Vandals, and Suevi; Praise of Spain; Chronicle of the World;* and *Catalog of Illustrious Men,* an innovation in this genre insofar as it introduces persons distinguished by their pastoral activity; and
6. works on general education, based largely upon linguistic or grammatical explanations: *Differences between Words,* his first writing, and *Etymologies,* on which he labored until his death and which was completed by Braulio.

He also wrote poems and letters, and he probably took part in preparing the *Collectio canonica Hispana* (Collection of Church Councils), covering both ecumenical and Spanish councils. Both Christian and non-Christian authors are cited in Isidore's writings with admiration and appreciation.

Isidore is best known through his *Synonyms* (known in manuscripts as "Soliloquies," a dialogue between man and his reason), which employed a new technique of parallel phrases with progressive variation of words. This work was simultaneously a source of practical vocabulary and a mechanism of catharsis that promoted in the reader a unified spirituality. It includes simple moral teaching and formulas for spiritual enlightenment. In three books, *Sentences* (*On the Greatest Good* in manuscripts) summarizes the spiritual organization of the human community by duties and obligations. It is in the form of easily memorized proverbs based upon Christian authors, and it combines moral knowledge with living experience. *Etymologies* (also named *Origines*), in twenty books, classifies and defines, according to a personal system of etymological interpretation, all the knowledge of Isidore's time as drawn from ancient sources through commentaries, glosses, and scholastic handbooks. In the Middle Ages it was considered the basic reference work for understanding texts and for coherently interpreting the world.

BIBLIOGRAPHY

An extensive critical introduction and systematic bibliography can be found in my introduction to *San Isidoro de Sevilla, Etimologías,* vol. 1, edited by José Oroz Reta, "Biblioteca de autores cristianos" (Madrid, 1982). See also J. N. Hillgarth's "The Position of Isidorian Studies," *Studi medievali* 24 (1983): 817–905. In French, see Jacques Fontaine's *Isidore de Séville et la culture classique dans l'Espagne wisigothique,* 2 vols. and suppl. (Paris, 1983), and "Isidore de Séville," in the *Dictionnaire de spiritualité,* vol. 7 (Paris, 1971).

MANUEL C. DÍAZ Y DÍAZ
Translated from Spanish by Maria Elisa Guirola

ISIS was one of the principal goddesses in the ancient Egyptian pantheon. She was the daughter of Geb and Nut ("earth" and "sky"), wife of Osiris, and mother of Horus. When Osiris was slain by his brother, Seth, Isis collected the dismembered parts of his body and with the help of Thoth was able to revive him at least partially and temporarily. Most important, she conceived and bore Osiris' son and avenger, Horus. Isis was a support for her husband both in this life and in the afterlife, and in this respect she was the perfect example of a devoted wife. She also shared Osiris' major role in the mortuary cult and became queen of the dead. As the nurturing mother of Horus she was the exemplar of motherhood, the patroness of childbearing, and the protectress of the child. In this connection she was also a role model for the queen of Egypt, who was generally "daughter of the god," "great wife of the king," and "mother of the god." The queen's role in the divine succession was just as important as that of her husband. In the Ramessid period, Isis bore the queenly title of Isis the Great, Lady of Heaven, Mistress of the Two Lands.

The name *Isis* means "seat" or "throne" (of Osiris), and like her sister, Nephthys, who was the spouse of Seth and whose name means "lady of the house," Isis seems to have owed her existence in the Egyptian pantheon primarily to the obvious need for a consort for Osiris. Very little is known of her early origin or of the cult that may have attached to her in the Old Kingdom. She is clearly well established but not adequately described in the Pyramid Texts. In later funerary texts and in *The Contendings of Horus and Seth,* her role is clear, but her position is somewhat ambivalent. She supports Horus, but not to the point of allowing him to destroy her evil brother, Seth. She is regarded as clever, even crafty, yet an enraged Horus can decapitate her for her supposed disloyalty.

Much of the early myth having to do with Isis, Osiris, and Horus was preserved best by Plutarch, and it was in the Ptolemaic and Roman periods that the cult of Isis really developed and spread. She assumed the symbolic emblems, representations, and characteristics both of Hathor, the true early mother goddess and goddess of love, and of Mut ("mother"), who was consort of Amun-Re in the later pharaonic periods. Among the many sites that had temples and shrines dedicated to Isis, certainly the most important was the island of Philae in Upper (southern) Egypt, with its numerous Ptolemaic and Roman buildings.

At the beginning of the Ptolemaic dynasty the cult of Isis, now the highest ranking goddess in Egypt, was already becoming widespread on the Greek mainland, in the Aegean islands, and in the Greek towns of Asia Minor. The cult of Serapis, a later development of Osiris, followed, and the two cults flourished throughout the Roman empire despite several attempts to repress Egyptian cults. These cults owed their appeal partly to their humaneness and partly to their mysteries, but it is also clear that they were no longer, strictly speaking, Egyptian, since the very nature of the gods and their attributes had changed. Isis became an earth goddess and a patroness of sailors. The *Isis-aretalogy* (a first-person account of the virtues and benefactions of the goddess) describes a goddess who was responsible for much of creation, ruled with great power, was patroness of both love and war, and was universally worshiped under different names. This text, preserved only in Greek, must have been largely of Greek origin and presents only a few epithets that can be traced to Egyptian sources.

In Egypt the cult of Isis was the last pagan cult to survive Christianity. Indeed, in part because the Blemmyes of Nubia concluded a peace with the Roman commander in Egypt in 451 AD guaranteeing them access to the temples of Philae, it was not until the sixth century that the temple of Isis was closed by Justinian. Philae was the last of the pagan temples to succumb to Egypt's conversion to Christianity, although it has often been suggested that the cult of Isis was not completely lost, having had considerable influence on the cult of the Virgin Mary.

BIBLIOGRAPHY

Bergman, Jan. *Ich bin Isis.* Acta Universitatis Upsaliensis, Historia Religionum, vol. 3. Uppsala, 1968.

Müller, Dieter. *Ägypten und die griechischen Isis-Aretalogien.* Sächsischen Akademie der Wissenschaften, Abhandlungen, Philologisch-historische Klasse, vol. 53, no. 1. Berlin, 1961.

Münster, Maria. *Untersuchungen zur Göttin Isis vom Alten Reich bis zum Ende des Neuen Reiches.* Münchner ägyptologische Studien, vol. 11. Berlin, 1968.

Witt, R. E. *Isis in the Graeco-Roman World.* London, 1971.

LEONARD H. LESKO

ISLAM. [*This entry consists of an overview of the origins and development of the classical Islamic tradition and historical surveys of Islam in ten geographical areas outside the core Middle East:*

An Overview
Islam in North Africa
Islam in Spain
Islam in Sub-Saharan Africa
Islam in the Caucasus and the Middle Volga
Islam in Central Asia
Islam in China
Islam in South Asia
Islam in Southeast Asia
Islam in Modern Europe
Islam in the Americas

In addition to the related articles referred to in this entry, see also the biographies of the principal figures mentioned herein.]

An Overview

The root *slm* in Arabic means "to be in peace, to be an integral whole." From this root comes *islām*, meaning "to surrender to God's law and thus to be an integral whole," and *muslim*, a person who so surrenders. It is important to note that two other key terms used in the Qur'ān with high frequency have similar root meanings: *īmān* (from *amn*), "to be safe and at peace with oneself," and *taqwā* (from *wqy*), "to protect or save." These definitions give us an insight into the most fundamental religious attitude of Islam: to maintain wholeness and proper order, as the opposite of disintegration, by accepting God's law. It is in this sense that the entire universe and its content are declared by the Qur'ān to be *muslim*, that is, endowed with order through obedience to God's law; but whereas nature obeys God's law automatically, humanity ought to obey it by choice. In keeping with this distinction, God's function is to integrate human personality, both individual and corporate: "Be not like those who forgot God, and [eventually] God caused them to forget themselves" (surah 59:19).

Origin and History

Muslims believe that Islam is God's eternal religion, described in the Qur'ān as "the primordial nature upon which God created mankind" (30:30). Further, the Qur'ān claims that the proper name *Muslim* was given by Abraham (22:78). As a historical phenomenon, however, Islam originated in Arabia in the early seventh century CE. Two broad elements should be distinguished in that immediate religious backdrop: the purely Arab background and the penetration of Judeo-Christian elements. The Qur'ān makes a disapproving reference to star worship (41:37), which is said to have come from the Babylonian star cult. For the most part, however, the bedouin were a secular people with little idea of an afterlife. At the sanctuaries (*ḥarams*) that had been established in some parts, fetishism seems to have developed into idol worship; the most important of these sites was the Ka'bah at Mecca. [*See* Ḥaram and Ḥawṭah *and* Ka'bah.]

The bedouin Arabs believed in a blind fate that inescapably determined birth, sustenance (because of the precarious life conditions in the desert), and death. These Arabs also had a code of honor (called *murūwah*, or "manliness") that may be regarded as their real religious ethics; its main constituent was tribal honor—the crown of all their values—encompassing the honor of women, bravery, hospitality, honoring one's promises and pacts, and last but not least, vengeance *(tha'r)*. They believed that the ghost of a slain person would cry out from the grave until his thirst for the blood of vengeance was quenched. According to the code, it was not necessarily the killer who was slain in retaliation, but a person from among his kin equal in value to the person killed. For reasons of economics or honor, infant girls were often slain, and this practice, terminated by the Qur'ān, was regarded as having had religious sanction (6:137).

In southwestern Arabia, a rather highly sophisticated civilization had existed since the Sabian period, with a prosperous economy and agriculture. The Sabian religion was, at the beginning, a trinitarian star cult, which was replaced, in the fourth century CE, by the monotheistic cult of al-Raḥmān (a term that appears to have traveled north and found a prominent place in the Qur'ān, where it means "the merciful"). In the sixth century CE, Jewish and Christian ideas and formulas were adopted, with the term *al-Raḥmān* applied to the first person of the Trinity. [*See* Arabian Religions.]

As for the Judeo-Christian tradition, it was not only present where Jewish and Christian populations existed (Jews in Medina—pre-Islamic Yathrib—in the south and in Khaybar in the north; Christians in the south, in Iraq, in Syria, and in certain tribes), but it had percolated in the air, generally speaking. Indeed, there had been Jewish and Christian attempts at proselytizing the Meccans, but these were unsuccessful because the Meccans wanted a new religion and scripture of their own, "whereby they would be better guided than those earlier communities" (35:42, 6:157). In the process, the Meccans had nevertheless come to know a good deal about Judeo-Christian ideas (6:92), and several people in Mecca and elsewhere had arrived at the idea of monotheism. Even so, they could not get rid of the "in-

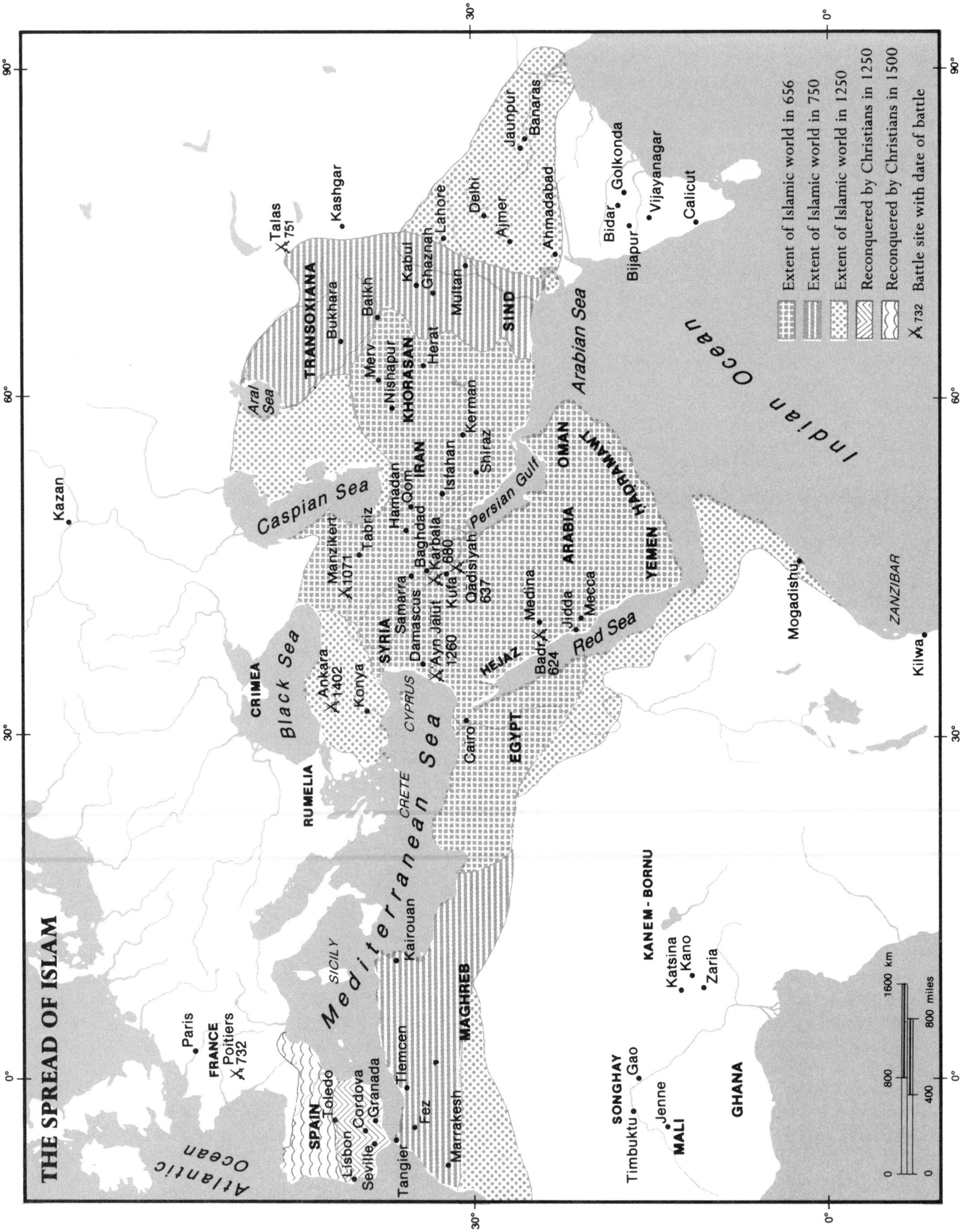
THE SPREAD OF ISLAM
Extent of Islamic world in 656
Extent of Islamic world in 750
Extent of Islamic world in 1250
Reconquered by Christians in 1250
Reconquered by Christians in 1500
732 Battle site with date of battle
0 800 1600 km
0 400 800 miles
90°
60°
30°
0°
Atlantic Ocean
Mediterranean Sea
Black Sea
Caspian Sea
Aral Sea
Persian Gulf
Red Sea
Arabian Sea
Indian Ocean
SPAIN
FRANCE
Paris
Poitiers 732
Lisbon
Seville
Toledo
Cordova
Granada
Tangier
Fez
Tlemcen
Marrakesh
MAGHREB
SICILY
Kairouan
CRETE
CYPRUS
RUMELIA
CRIMEA
Ankara 1402
Konya
Cairo
EGYPT
SYRIA
Damascus
Ayn Jalut 1260
Samarra
Baghdad
Karbala 680
Kufa
Qadisiyah 637
Manzikert 1071
Tabriz
Hamadan
Qom
IRAN
Isfahan
Shiraz
Kerman
HEJAZ
Badr 624
Medina
Jidda
Mecca
ARABIA
YEMEN
OMAN
HADRAMAWT
KHORASAN
Nishapur
Merv
Herat
TRANSOXIANA
Bukhara
Balkh
Kabul
Ghaznah
Talas 751
Kashgar
Kazan
SIND
Multan
Lahore
Delhi
Ajmer
Ahmadabad
Jaunpur
Banaras
Bidar
Golkonda
Bijapur
Vijayanagar
Calicut
Mogadishu
ZANZIBAR
Kilwa
SONGHAY
Gao
Timbuktu
Jenne
MALI
GHANA
KANEM-BORNU
Katsina
Kano
Zaria

termediary gods" for whom they had special cults, and there was still no cult for God, whom they called "Allāh," or "the God." In addition to these limitations, there was also a great disparity between the rich and the poor and disenfranchised in the thriving commercial community of Mecca. Both of these issues are strongly emphasized from the beginning of the Qur'anic revelation, making it clear that the primary background of Islam is Arab rather than Judeo-Christian, although the latter tradition has strongly influenced Islam. In its genesis, Islam grew out of the problems existing in an Arab Meccan society.

Early Development of the Community. During a twelve-year struggle in Mecca (610–622 CE), the prophet Muḥammad had gathered a devoted group of followers, largely among the poor but also among the well-to-do merchants. Yet his movement seemed to reach an impasse because of the unflinching opposition of the mercantile aristocracy, which saw in it a threat to both of their vested interests—their Kaʿbah-centered religion, from which they benefited as custodians of the sanctuary and recipients of income from the pilgrimage, and their privileged control of trade. After Muḥammad and his followers emigrated from Mecca to Medina in 622 (the beginning of the lunar Islamic calendar, called the *hijrī*, or "emigration," calendar), at the invitation of the majority of the Arab inhabitants there, he became the head of both the nascent community and the existing polity. However, while he gave laws, waged peace and war, and created social institutions, he never claimed to be a ruler, a lawgiver, a judge, or a general; he referred to himself always as a messenger of God. As a result, not only were Islamic "religious" doctrine and ritual in the narrower sense regarded as Islamic but so were the state, the law, and social institutions. Islam is thus the name of a total way of life and does not merely regulate the individual's private relationship with God.

In Medina, then, the Prophet was able to institute his social reforms through the exercise of the religious and political power that he had been denied in Mecca. After three battles in which Muslims gained the upper hand over the Meccans and their allies, Islam, now in rapid ascendancy, was able to take Mecca peacefully in AH 8/630 CE along with a large part, if not the whole, of the Arabian Peninsula. In Medina, too, the Muslim community *(ummah muslimah)* was formally launched in 2/624 as the "median community," the only community consciously established by the founder of a religion for a specific purpose, as the Qur'ān speaks of those "who, when we give them power on the earth, shall establish prayers and welfare of the poor and shall command good and forbid evil" (22:41). At the same time, the Qur'ān (22:40) provided this community with the instrument of *jihād* (utmost exertion in God's cause, including peaceful means but also cold and hot war). [*See* Jihād.] Finally, Mecca was declared to be the goal of annual pilgrimage for the faithful and also the direction *(qiblah)* for prayer instead of Jerusalem. Both the constitution and the anchoring of the community were complete. [*See also* Ummah *and the biography of Muḥammad.*]

After a brief lapse into tribal sovereignty following the Prophet's death, Arab resistance to the acknowledgment of Medina's central authority was broken by force. The tribesmen's energies were turned outward in conquests of neighboring lands under the banner of Islam, which provided the necessary zeal for rapid military and political expansion. Within a century after the Prophet's death, Muslim Arabs were administering an empire stretching from the southern borders of France through North Africa and the Middle East, across Central Asia and into Sind. Muslim rule in the conquered territories was generally tolerant and humane; there was no policy of converting non-Muslims to Islam. The purpose of *jihād* was not conversion but the establishment of Islamic rule. Nonetheless, partly because of certain disabilities imposed by Islamic law on non-Muslim subjects (mainly the *jizyah*, or poll tax—although they were exempt from the *zakāt*, or alms tax levied on Muslims, the *jizyah* was the heavier of the two, particularly for the lower strata of the population) and partly because of Islamic egalitarianism, Islam spread quickly after an initial period during which conversions were sometimes even discouraged. This was the first phase of the spread of Islam; later on, as we shall see, Muslim mystics, or the Ṣūfīs, were the main vehicles of Islamic expansion in India, Central Asia, and sub-Saharan Africa, although the role of traders in the Indian and Indonesian coastal areas and China must not be minimized. Even in the twentieth century, Turkish soldiers brought Islam to South Korea during the Korean War.

Several major developments in this early period affected the religious texture of the Muslim community as a continuing phenomenon. Less than half a century after the Prophet's death, political dissensions over succession led to civil war. A number of groups called the Khārijīs ("those who went out") declared war on the community at large because it tolerated rule by "unrighteous" men; they claimed that a Muslim ceased to be a Muslim by committing a reprehensible act without sincerely repenting, and that other Muslims who did not regard such a person as non-Muslim also became non-Muslim. In reaction to the Khārijīs and the ensuing civil strife, the community (both the Sunnī mainstream and the Shīʿah, or party of ʿAlī) generally adopted a religious stand that not only was tolerant of religious and political deviations from strict Islamic norms but was even positively accommodating toward them. The members of the community who took this stand were known as the Murji'ah (from *irjā'*, meaning "postponement," in the sense of not judging a person's religious worth, but leaving it to God's judgment on the Last Day). The net result of this basic development was that excommunication was ruled out so long as a person recognized the community as Muslim and professed that "there is no god but God and Muḥammad is his prophet."

This formula created or rationalized accommodation for an amazing range of different religious opinions and practices under one God and Muḥammad's prophethood. Oddly enough, the only systematically rigid and illiberal school of doctrine that persecuted its opponents, after it became state creed under the Abbasid caliph al-Ma'mūn in the first half of the ninth century, was the liberal rationalist school of the Mu'tazilah. The emergence of this school was largely the result of the impact on the Islamic religion of the wholesale translations of Greek works of science, philosophy, and medicine into Arabic on the orders of al-Ma'mūn. The Mu'tazilah tried to create necessary free space by insisting on freedom of human will and God's rational justice, but the Muslim orthodoxy, countering with doctrines of the inefficacy of human will and the absolutism of God's will and divine predeterminism, actually provided more accommodation for varying opinions and human actions and thereby halted the growth of the rationalist school.

With the advent of the Abbasids, there were other political, social, and religious changes as well, among them the improvement of the status of the Iranians, who, under Umayyad rule, were denied an identity of their own as "clients" *(mawālī)* of the Arab tribes; and the espousal and implementation of legal measures created by the religious leadership, which had been largely alienated from the Umayyads. All of these developments combined to facilitate the rapid spread of Islam.

Medieval and Later Developments. With the weakening of the central caliphal authority in Baghdad, the tenth century saw not only the virtual fragmentation of the Abbasid empire and the rise of *de facto* independent rulers (sultans and emirs) in the provinces but the almost ubiquitous rise of the Shī'ah. While Baghdad came under the political and fiscal "management" of the orthodox Twelver Shī'ah through the Persian Buyid family, Egypt and North Africa came under the rule of the Ismā'īlī Fatimids. But if the Buyids were able to influence Islamic practices in some ways—such as the observance of 'Āshūrā', the tenth of Muḥarram (the first month of the Islamic calendar) as the commemoration of the martyrdom of the Prophet's grandson Ḥusayn at the hands of the Umayyad troops—Fatimid rule, by and large, did not leave much of a trace on later Muslim thought and institutions, despite the fact that the Ismā'īlīyah had offered a revolutionary ideology claiming to usher in a new world order through the establishment of a universal religion. [*See also* Shiism.]

In purely religious terms, indeed, it was not so much Shiism as the rise and spread of Sufism that constituted the new and greatest challenge to Islamic orthodoxy, in terms of ideas and spiritual orientation, and indeed, it was Shiism that suffered most, in terms of following, as a result of the new movement. From modest beginnings as an expression of refined piety on the part of a spiritual elite in the eighth and ninth centuries, Sufism became a mass religion from the eleventh century onward. In its origins as a deepening of the inner "life of the heart," Sufism was largely complementary to the outer "life of the law," which was the domain of the *'ulamā'*, the religious scholars who functioned as custodians of the *sharī'ah* (sacred law) and never claimed to be pastors or custodians of the soul.

In its later development, however, through networks of brotherhoods that spread from the shores of the Atlantic to Southeast Asia, it practically took the place of "official" Islam, particularly in the countryside. Feeding on certain pantheistic ideas of eminent Ṣūfīs and generating latitudinarian, indeed protean, tendencies, it served to convert to Islam large populations in the Indian subcontinent, Central Asia, Africa, and Indonesia. A long line of orthodox Ṣūfīs, beginning in the eighth and ninth centuries and culminating in the monumental work of al-Ghazālī (d. 1111), struggled hard, with a good measure of success, to bring about a synthesis that would ensure a respectable place for Ṣūfī spirituality in the orthodox fold. After the advent of Sufism, and particularly after al-Ghazālī's success, the number of converts to Islam expanded dramatically, and the number of Shī'ah shrank equally dramatically, apparently because the demands for an inner life that Shiism had satisfied through its esoteric claims were now satisfied by Sufism. [*See also* Sufism.]

During the thirteenth and fourteenth centuries, Islam penetrated into the Malay archipelago largely through Arab traders, who went first to the coastal areas of Java and Sumatra and afterward to Malaysia. Shortly after the advent of Islam, however, these lands fell under western European domination. Because the structure of British power in Malaysia differed from Dutch colonialism in Indonesia, in that British overlordship was exercised through regional sultans whereas the Dutch ruled directly, Islam was inhibited in Indonesia: a large percentage of the population of the interior remained *abangans*, or "nominal Muslims," whose life is still based on ancient custom *('ādat)* under a thin Islamic veneer. Recently, however, a large-scale thrust of islamization has changed this picture considerably. In Djakarta, for example, a little more than a dozen years ago, there were only a few cathedral mosques for Friday services, but now the number has multiplied spectacularly; indeed, there is a mosque attached to every government department. This process of "consolidation in orthodox Islam," necessitated by the initial compromises made by Ṣūfīs with local cultures, has been going on for some decades in the Indian subcontinent as well.

In Africa south of the Sahara, Islam appears to have penetrated through both traders and pilgrims. Although, as noted above, Islam spread there through the influence of Ṣūfī orders, one unique feature of African Islam seems to be the combination of Sufism with militancy, the latter acclaimed as the result of the Islamic teaching on *jihād,* although it is also congruent with the spirit of local tribalism.

Africa is the only continent where Muslims are in the majority, while in Europe, Islam now constitutes the second largest religion, mainly comprising emigrants from Muslim lands but a few Western converts as well. In North America, Muslims are said to number around two million, most of whom are emigrants from Muslim countries. But there is also in the United States a significant phenomenon of conversion among local blacks, originating in the social protest movement against white ascendancy. The earliest group, known as the Black Muslims, called itself the Nation of Islam during the lifetime of its founder, Elijah Muhammad, and was a heterodox movement. After his death in 1973 it moved closer to the rest of the Muslim community, taking the new name of American Islamic Mission and receiving financial help from oil-rich Arab countries such as Saudi Arabia, Libya, and Kuwait. (The organization was dissolved in 1985.) There are also other numerous, though small, Afro-American Muslim groups scattered throughout the United States. [*See* Afro-American Religions *and the biographies of Elijah Muhammad and Malcolm X.*]

Arriving at a precise estimate of the Muslim population in China presents a serious problem. According to data collected unofficially by Chinese Muslims in 1939–1940 and extrapolations from these data in terms of population growth, Chinese Muslims might number close to one hundred million in the 1980s. The official Chinese figure given in the early sixties, however, was ten million, a figure revised to between fifteen and twenty million two decades later (religion is a factor not counted in the Chinese census). According to the 1979 United Nations statistics, the world Muslim population is just under one billion.

The Systematic Content of Islam

With the rise of Islamic legal and theological thought in the eighth century CE, a framework had to be articulated within which religious developments were to be set. The most basic sources in this framework were the Qur'ān and the *sunnah* of the Prophet.

The Qur'ān. The God of the Qur'ān is a transcendent, powerful, and merciful being. His transcendence ensures his uniqueness and infinitude over and against all other creatures, who are necessarily characterized by finitude of being and potentialities. Hence God is all-powerful, and no creature may share in his divinity (belief in such sharing is called *shirk* and is condemned in the Qur'ān as the most heinous and unforgivable sin). This infinite power is expressed, however, through God's equally infinite mercy. The creation of the universe, the fact that there is plenitude of being, rather than emptiness of nothing, is due solely to his mercy. Particularly with reference to humanity, God's creation, sustenance, guidance (in the form of revelations given to the prophets, his messengers), and, finally, judgment, are all manifestations of his power in mercy.

God created nature by his command "Be!" In fact, for whatever God wishes to create, "He says, Be! and there it is" (36:82). But whatever God creates has an orderly nature, and that is why there is a universe rather than chaos. God puts into everything the proper "guidance" or "nature" or laws of behavior to make each part fit into the entire pattern of the universe. "All things are measured" (e.g., 54:49), and only God is the measurer; hence he alone is the commander, and everything else is under his command. This command, which is a fact of automatic obedience in the case of nature (3:83), becomes an "ought" in the case of humans, for whom moral law replaces natural law. Nature is, therefore, a firm, well-knit machine without rupture or dislocations.

Here it is interesting and important to note that while the Qur'ān patently accepts miracles of earlier prophets (67:2–3), in response to pressure from Muḥammad's opponents for new miracles (e.g., 2:23, 10:38, 11:13), the Qur'ān insists that it is itself the Prophet's miracle, and one that cannot be equaled. [*For more on the nature of prophecy in Islam, see* Nubūwah.] As for supernatural miracles, they are out of date because they have been ineffective in the past (17:59, 6:33–35). Nature is, therefore, autonomous but not autocratic, since it did not bring itself into being. God, who brought nature into being, can destroy it as well; even so, although the Qur'ān, when speaking of the Day of Judgment, often invokes a cataclysm that strongly suggests destruction (see, for example, surah 81), in many verses it speaks instead of a radical transformation and a realignment of the factors of life (e.g., 56:60–63). Finally, the universe has been created for the benefit of human beings, and all its forces have been "subjugated" to them; of all creatures, only they have been created to serve God alone (e.g., 31:20, 22:65).

In its account of the human race, while the Qur'ān holds that humans are among the noblest of God's creatures and that Adam had indeed outstripped the angels in a competition for creative knowledge, a fact testifying to his unique intellectual qualities, it nevertheless criticizes them for their persistent moral failures, which are due to their narrowmindedness, lack of vision, weakness, and smallness of self. All their ills are reducible to this basic deficiency, and the remedy is for them to enlarge the self and to transcend pettiness. This pettiness is often represented by the Qur'ān in economic terms, such as greed, fraud, and holding back from spending on the poor (as was the case with the Meccan traders): "If you were to possess [all] the treasures of the mercy of my lord, you would still sit on them out of fear of spending [on the needy]" (17:100). It is Satan who whispers into people's ears that they would be impoverished by spending, while God promises prosperity for such investment (2:268). Instead of establishing usurious accounts to exploit the poor, believers should establish "credit with God" (2:245, 57:11, 57:18 et al.).

In its social doctrine and legislation, the Qur'ān makes a general effort to ameliorate the condition of the weak and often abused segments of society, such as the poor, orphans, women, and slaves. People are asked to free slaves on freedom-purchasing contracts, "and if they are poor, you give them from the wealth God has bestowed upon you" (24:33). An egalitarian statement concerning males and females is made, but the husband is recognized as "one degree higher" (2:228) because he earns by his strength and expends on his wife. Polygamy is limited to four wives with the provision that "if you fear you cannot do justice [among them], marry only one" (4:3), and the further admonition that such justice is impossible "no matter how much you desire" (4:129). Kind and generous treatment of wives is repeatedly emphasized; celibacy is strongly discouraged, although not banned outright. The basic equality of all people is proclaimed and ethnic differences discounted: "O you people, we have created [all of] you from a male and a female, and we have made you into different nations and tribes [only] for the purpose of identification—otherwise, the noblest of you in the sight of God is the one who is the most righteous" (49:13).

In the economic field, the widespread practice of usury is prohibited. The *zakāt* tax is levied on the well-to-do members of the community; it was meant as a welfare tax to be spent on the poor and the needy in general, but surah 9:60, which details the distribution of *zakāt*, is so comprehensive in its scope that it covers practically all fields of social and state life. In general, fair play and justice are repeatedly advised. Detailed inheritance laws are given (4:7ff.), the main feature of which is the introduction of shares to daughters, although these shares are set at half of what sons receive. Communal affairs are to be decided through mutual consultation (*shūrā baynahum*, 42:38), a principle that has never been institutionalized in Islamic history, however.

One noteworthy feature of the moral teaching of the Qur'ān is that it describes all wrong done against anyone as "wrong done against oneself" (*ẓulm al-nafs*, as in 2:231, 11:101, 11:118). In its teaching on the Last Judgment, the Qur'ān constantly talks of "weighing the deeds" of all adult and responsible humans (101:6–11, 7:8 et al.). This doctrine of the "weight" of deeds arises out of the consideration that people normally act for the here and now; in this respect, they are like cattle: they do not take a long-range or "ultimate" (*ākhirah*) view of things: "Shall we tell you of those who are the greatest losers in terms of their deeds? Those whose whole effort has been lost [in the pursuit of] this life [i.e., the lower values of life], but they think they have performed prodigies" (18:104). The rationale of the Last Judgment is to bring out the real moral meaning, "the weight" of deeds. But whereas the Last Judgment will turn upon individual performance, the Qur'ān also speaks about a "judgment in history," which descends upon peoples, nations, and communities on the basis of their total performance and whether that performance is in accord with the teaching of the divine messages brought by their prophets: many nations have perished because of their persistence in all sorts of disobedience and moral wrong, for "God gives inheritance of the earth [only] to good people" (21:105). [*See* Eschatology, *article on* Islamic Eschatology.]

The Qur'ān, therefore, declares unequivocally that God has sent his messages to *all* peoples throughout history and has left none without guidance (35:24, 13:7). These messages have been essentially the same: to reject *shirk* (associating anyone with God) and to behave according to the law of God. All messages have emanated from a single source, the "Mother of All Books" (13:39) or the "Hidden Book" (56:78) or the "Preserved Tablet" (85:22), and although every prophet has initially come to his people and addressed them "in their tongue" (14:4), the import of all messages is universal; hence it is incumbent on all people to believe in all prophets, without "separating some from the others."

For this reason the Qur'ān is severely critical of what it sees as proprietary claims upon God's guidance by Jews and Christians and rejects Jewish claims to special status in strong terms (62:6, 2:94–95, 5:18, et al.). Despite the identity of divine messages, moreover, the Qur'ān also posits some sort of development in religious consciousness and asserts that on the Last Day every community will be judged by the standards of its own book and under the witness of its own prophet(s) (4:41, 16:84, et al.). The Qur'ān protects, consummates, and transcends earlier revelations, and Muḥammad is declared to be the "seal of the prophets" (33:40).

Finally, the Qur'ān states five basic constituents of faith *(īmān):* belief in God, in angels, in revealed books, in God's messengers, and in the Last Day. Corresponding to these five items of belief, a fivefold practical doctrine was formulated very early on. These "Five Pillars" include (1) bearing witness in public at least once in one's lifetime that "There is no god but God and Muḥammad is his prophet"; (2) praying five times a day (before sunrise, early afternoon, late afternoon, immediately after sunset, and before retiring), while facing the Ka'bah at Mecca; (3) paying *zakāt;* (4) fasting during Ramaḍān (the ninth month of the Islamic lunar year), with no eating, drinking, smoking, or sexual intercourse from dawn until sunset, when the daily fast is broken; and (5) performing the annual pilgrimage to the Ka'bah at least once in one's adult lifetime, provided one can afford the journey and leave enough provisions for one's family. [*See also* Shahādah; Ṣalāt; Zakāt; Ṣawm; *and* Pilgrimage, *article on* Muslim Pilgrimage.]

The pilgrimage is performed during the first ten days of the last month of the Islamic year. One may perform the lesser pilgrimage *('umrah)* at other times of the year, but it is not a substitute for the great pilgrimage *(al-ḥajj al-akbar).* The pilgrimage has, through the centuries, played an important role, not only in strengthening general unity in the global Muslim community but also in disseminating religious ideas both orthodox and Ṣūfī, for it provides the occasion for an annual meeting among religious leaders and scholars from different parts of the Muslim world. For the past few decades, it has also served to bring together political leaders and heads of Muslim states. In recent years, too, because of new travel facilities, the number of pilgrims has vastly increased, sometimes exceeding two million each year. [*See also* Worship and Cultic Life, *article on* Muslim Worship, *and* Qur'ān, *articles on* The Text and Its History *and* Its Role in Muslim Piety.]

Sunnah. The word *sunnah* literally means "a well-trodden path," but it was used before Islam in reference to usage or laws of a tribe and certain norms of intertribal conduct accepted by various tribes as binding. After the rise of Islam, it was used to denote the normative behavior of the Muslim community, putatively derived from the Prophet's teaching and conduct, and from the exemplary teaching of his immediate followers, since the latter was seen as an index of the former. In the Qur'ān, there is no mention of the term *sunnah* with reference to the Prophet's extra-Qur'anic precepts or example, but the term *uswah ḥasanah,* meaning a "good model" or "example" to be followed, is used with reference to Muḥammad's conduct as well as the conduct of Abraham and his followers (33:31, 60:4, 60:6). The term *uswah* is certainly much less rigid than *sunnah* and does not mean so much a law to be literally implemented as an example to be matched.

Even so, there is clear evidence that the concept of *sunnah* was flexible in the early decades of Islam because, with hardly any written codifications of the *sunnah* (which was used in the sense of an ongoing practice rather than fixed formulas), there was no question of literal imitation. As political, legal, and theological dissensions and disputes multiplied and all kinds of positions sought self-validation, however, the opinions of the first three generations or so were projected back onto the Prophet to obtain the necessary authority, and the phrase *sunnat al-nabī* (the *sunnah* of the Prophet) gradually took the place of the term *sunnah.* [*See* Sunnah *for further discussion.*]

During the second and third centuries AH, the narration and codification of the *sunnah* into ḥadīth was in full swing. A report that claims to convey a *sunnah* (or *sunnah*s) is called a *ḥadīth.* It is reported that while earlier people used to accept a *ḥadīth* as genuine on trust alone, after the civil wars of the late first to early second centuries AH, a *ḥadīth* was accepted only on the basis of some reliable authority. From this situation emerged the convention of the *isnād,* or the chain of guarantors of *ḥadith,* extending from the present narrator backward to the Prophet. The *isnād* took the following form: "I, So-and-so, heard it from B, who heard it from C, who said that he heard the Prophet say so-and-so or do such-and-such." Then followed the text *(matn)* of the *ḥadīth.* A whole science called "principles of *ḥadīth*" developed in order to lay down meticulous criteria for judging the reliability of the transmitters of *ḥadith,* and the discipline stimulated in turn a vast literature of comprehensive biographical dictionaries recording thousands of transmitters' names, their lives, character, and whether a transmitter actually met or could have met the person he claims to transmit from. The canons for criticizing transmitters were applied rigorously, and there is hardly a transmitter who has escaped criticism.

The experts on *ḥadīth* also developed canons of "rational critique" alongside the critique of the chains of transmission, but they applied the former with far less rigor than they did the latter. Although the specialists divided *ḥadīth* into several categories according to their "genuineness" and "reliability," to this day it remains the real desideratum of the science to work out and apply what is called historical criticism to the materials of *ḥadīth.* The six authoritative Sunnī collections of *ḥadīth* date from the third century AH, while the famous Shīʿī collection of al-Kulīnī, *Al-kāfī* (The Sufficient), dates from the early fourth century. In modern times, the authenticity of *ḥadīth* and hence of the recorded *sunnah* of the Prophet (although not so much the biographies of the Prophet and historical works) has come under general attack at the hands of certain Western scholars and also of some Muslim intellectuals—and this is happening increasingly—but the *ʿulamāʾ* have strenuously resisted these attacks because a large majority of Islamic social and political institutions and laws are either based on *ḥadīth* or rationalized through it. [*See also* Ḥadīth.]

Law. The well-known dictum among Western Islamicists that, just as theology occupies the central place in Christianity, in Islam the central place belongs to law is essentially correct. Law was the earliest discipline to develop in Islam because the Muslims needed it to administer the huge empire they had built with such astonishing rapidity. Recent research has held that the early materials for Islamic law were largely created by administrators on the basis of *ad hoc* decisions and that, in the second stage, systematic efforts were made by jurists to "islamize" these materials and bring them under the aegis of the Qurʾān and the *sunnah.* (The content of the latter, in the form of *ḥadīth,* developed alongside this activity of islamization.) This picture is probably too simplistic, however, and it would be more correct to say that the process of subsuming administrative materials and local custom under the Qurʾān and the *sunnah* went hand in hand with the reverse process of deriving law from the Qurʾān and whatever existed by way of the *sunnah* in the light of new administrative experiences and local custom.

Although clarification of this issue requires further research, it is certain that up to the early third century AH the schools of law were averse to the large-scale use of *ḥadīth* in the formulation of law and that, in fact, some scholars explicitly warned against the rise of "peripheral *ḥadīth*" and advised the acceptance of only that *ḥadīth* that conformed to the Qurʾān. However, the need for the anchoring authority of the Prophet had become so great that in the latter half of the second century AH al-Shāfiʿī (d. 204/819) made a strong and subsequently successful bid for the wholesale acceptance of "reliable" *ḥadīth*—even if narrated by only one person. As a result, *ḥadīth* multiplied at a far greater rate after al-Shāfiʿī than before him. Nevertheless, the followers of Abū Ḥanīfah (d. 767) continued to reject a single-chain *ḥadīth* in favor of a "sure, rational proof derived from the *sharīʿah* principles," just as the followers of Mālik (d. 795) continued to give preference to the early "practice of Medina" over *ḥadīth.*

The final framework of Islamic jurisprudence came to recognize four sources of law, two material and two formal. The first source is the text of the Qurʾān, which constitutes an absolute "decisive proof"; the second is *ḥadīth* texts, although these can vary from school to school, particularly between the Sunnī and the Twelver Shīʿī schools. In new cases, for which a "clear text" *(naṣṣ)* is not available, a jurist must make the effort *(ijtihād)* to find a correct answer himself. The instrument of *ijtihād* is analogical reasoning *(qiyās),* which consists in (1) finding a text relevant to the new case in the Qurʾān or the *ḥadīth,* (2) discerning the essential similarity or *ratio legis* (called *ʿillat al-ḥukm*) between the two cases, (3) allowing for differences *(furūq)* and determining that they can be discounted, and (4) extending or interpreting the *ratio legis* to cover the new case. This methodology, although neatly formulated in theory, became very difficult to wield in practice primarily because of the differences of opinion with regard to "relevant texts," particularly in the case of *ḥadīth.*

The fourth source or principle is called *ijmāʿ*, or consensus. Although the concept of consensus in the sense of the informal agreement of the community (for Islam has no churches and no councils to produce formal decisions) has in practice an overriding authority, since even the fact and the authenticity of a Qurʾanic revelation are finally guaranteed by it, there is no consensus on the definition of consensus: it varies from the consensus of the *ʿulamāʾ*, through that of the *ʿulamāʾ* of a certain age, to that of the entire community. There is also a difference of opinion as to whether a certain consensus can be repealed by a subsequent one or not; the reply of the traditionalists is usually, though not always, in the negative, while that of modern reformers is in the positive. [*See* Ijmāʿ; Ijtihād; Maṣlaḥah; Qiyās; *and* Uṣūl al-Fiqh.]

A special category of punishments called *ḥudūd* (sg., *ḥadd*) was established by jurists and includes penalties specified in the Qurʾān for certain crimes: murder, theft, adultery, and false accusation of adultery, to which was later added drunkenness. The theory is that since God himself has laid down these penalties, they cannot be varied. But in view of the severity of the punishments, the jurists defined these crimes very narrowly (adultery, for example, is defined as the penetration of the male organ into the female) and put such stringent conditions on the requisite evidence that it became practically unattainable (for example, in order to prove adultery, four eyewitnesses to the sexual act itself were required). The legal maxim "Ward off *ḥadd* punishments by any doubt" was also propounded, and the term *doubt* in classical Islamic law had a far wider range than in any other known system of law. In addition, Muslim jurists enunciated two principles to create flexibility in *sharī'ah* law and its application: necessity and public interest. The political authority, thanks to these two principles, could promulgate new measures and even suspend the operations of the *sharī'ah* law. In later medieval centuries, the Ottoman rulers and others systematically promulgated new laws by invoking these particular principles of the *sharī'ah*.

After the concrete and systematic establishment of the schools of law during the fourth and fifth centuries AH, original legal thought in Islam lost vitality; this development is known as "the closure of the door of *ijtihād*." It was not that new thinking was theoretically prohibited but rather that social, intellectual, and political conditions were unfavorable to it. However, a procedure known as *talfīq* (lit., "patchwork") was introduced whereby, if a certain provision in one legal school caused particular hardship, a more liberal provision from another could be borrowed, without necessarily taking over its reasoning. Thus, given the impracticality of the Ḥanafī school's regulation that a wife whose husband has disappeared must wait more than ninety years before remarrying (according to the reasoning that the wife must wait until her husband can be presumed dead through natural causes), the Mālikī school's provision that such a wife may marry after four years of waiting (Mālik reasoned that the maximum period of gestation, which he had himself witnessed, was four years) was taken over in practice.

Of the four extant Sunnī schools of law, the Ḥanafī is prevalent in the Indian subcontinent, Central Asia, Turkey, Egypt, Syria, Jordan, and Iraq; the Mālikī school in North Africa extends from Libya through Morocco; the Shāfi'ī, in Southeast Asia, with a considerable following in Egypt; and the Ḥanbalī school, in Saudi Arabia. Within Shī'ī jurisprudence, the Ja'farī (Twelver Shī'ī) school prevails in Iran. At one time, the "literalist" (Ẓāhirī) school was represented by some highly prominent jurists, but it has practically no following now, while the Khārijī school is represented in Oman, and to a limited extent in East and North Africa. [*For more on the schools of Islamic law, see* Madhhab.]

It must finally be pointed out that when we speak of Islamic law, we mean all of human behavior, including, for example, intentions. This law is therefore very different from other systems of law in the strict sense of the term. Islamic law does not draw any line between law and morality, and hence much of it is not enforceable in a court, but only at the bar of conscience. This has had its advantages in that Islamic law is shot through with moral considerations, which in turn have given a moral temper to Muslim society. But it has also suffered from the disadvantage that general moral propositions have very often not been given due weight and have been selectively construed by jurists as mere "recommendations" rather than commands that must be expressed in terms of concrete legislation: the result has been an overemphasis on the specific dos and don'ts of the Qur'ān at the expense of general propositions. For example, the Qur'anic verse 4:3, permitting polygamy up to four wives, was given legal force by classical Muslim jurists, but the rider contained in the same verse, that if a person cannot do justice among co-wives, then he must marry only one, was regarded by them as a recommendation to the husband's conscience that he should do justice. [*See also* Islamic Law, *articles on* Sharī'ah *and* Personal Law.]

Theology. At an elementary level, theological speculation in Islam also began very early and was occasioned by the assassination of 'Uthmān, the third caliph (d. 665), but its rise and development was totally independent of the law, and the first great theological systems were constructed only in the third and fourth centuries AH. The first question to become the focal point of dispute was the definition of a true Muslim. The earliest political and theological schism was represented by the Khārijīs (from *khurūj*, meaning "secession"), who contended that a Muslim ceases to be a Muslim by the commission of a single serious sin such as theft or adultery, no matter how many times that person may recite the profession of faith, "There is no god but God and Muḥammad is his prophet," unless he or she repents sincerely. They held that 'Uthmān and 'Alī (the fourth caliph) had both become *kāfirs* (non-Muslims), since the former was guilty of serious maladministration, including nepotism, and the latter had submitted his claim to rule to human arbitration, even though he had been duly elected caliph. The Khārijīs, who were exemplars of piety and utterly egalitarian, and who believed that the only qualification for rule is a person's goodness and piety, without consideration of race, color, or sex, were mostly bedouin, which largely explains both their egalitarianism and their fanaticism. They were "professional rebels" who never united but always fought successive governments in divided groups and were almost entirely crushed out of existence by the middle of the second century AH. [*See* Khārijīs.]

While the Khārijīs were not a systematic theological school, a full-fledged school, that of the Mu'tazilah, soon developed from their milieu. These thinkers, who emerged during the second and third centuries AH, held that while grave sinners do not become *kāfirs*, neither do they remain Muslims. Their central thesis concerned what they called "God's justice and unity," which they defended to its logical conclusion. God's justice demands that human beings have a free and efficacious will; only then can they be the locus of moral responsibility and deserve praise and blame here and reward and punishment in the hereafter. They carried this belief to the point of holding that just as God, in his justice, cannot punish one who does good, neither can he forgive one who does evil, for otherwise the difference between good and evil would disappear. This position certainly offended religious sensitivities, since the Qur'ān repeatedly mentions that God will forgive "whom he will" (2:284, 3:129 et al.).

For the Muʿtazilah, God plays no role in the sphere of human moral acts, except that he gives man moral support provided man does good by himself; God's activity is limited to nature. All anthropomorphic statements in the Qur'ān were interpreted by the Muʿtazilah either as metaphors or as Arabic idioms. They rejected *ḥadīth* outright because much of it was anthropomorphic and refused to base law upon it on the ground that *ḥadīth* transmission was unreliable. They further held that good and evil in terms of general principles (but not the positive religious duties) were knowable by human reason without the aid of revelation but that revelation supplied the necessary motivation for the pursuit of goodness. In conformity with this view, they believed that one must rationally ponder the purposes of the Qur'anic ordinances, for in laying these down, God had a positive interest in furthering human well-being *(maṣlaḥah)*. This presumably means that law should be rationally grounded; there is, however, no evidence that the Muʿtazilah ever attempted to work out a legal system. [*See* Muʿtazilah *and* Free Will and Predestination, *article on* Islamic Concept.]

On the issue of God's unity, the Muʿtazilah rejected the separation of God's attributes from his essence, for this would entail belief in a multiplicity of eternal beings, amounting to polytheism. They did not deny that God is "living," "knowing," and "willing," as divine activities, but they denied that God is "life," "knowledge," and "will," as substantives. The development of this particular doctrine was possibly influenced by Christian discussions on the nature of the Trinity, and how and whether three hypostases could be one person, because the terms in which it is formulated are all too foreign to the milieu of pristine Islam. As a consequence of this doctrine, the Muʿtazilah also denied the eternity of the Qur'ān, the very speech of God, since they denied the substantiality of all divine attributes. [*See also* Attributes of God, *article on* Islamic Concepts.] When their credo was made state creed under Caliph al-Ma'mūn, they persecuted opposition religious leaders such as Ibn Ḥanbal (d. 855), but because of these very doctrines—denial of God's forgiveness and of the eternity of the Qur'ān—they became unpopular, and Caliph al-Mutawakkil (d. 861) brought Sunnism back to ascendancy.

What is in fact called Sunnism means nothing more than the majority of the community; it had its content defined in large measure as a reaction to the Khārijīs and the Muʿtazilah, for Sunnī orthodoxy is but a refined and sophisticated form of that popular reaction that crystalized against these groups. There, no small role was played by popular preachers and popular piety, which had already found its way into *ḥadīth*. In doctrinal form, this reaction can be described as Murji'ism (from *irjā'*, "postponement"), the belief that once adults have openly professed that there is no God but Allāh and Muḥammad is his prophet, if there is no reason to suspect that they are lying, mad, or under constraint, then such people are Muslims, irrespective of whether their deeds are good or whether their beliefs quite conform to orthodoxy, and that final judgment on their status must be "postponed" until the Last Day and left to God.

In conscious opposition to the Khārijīs and the Muʿtazilah, the Murji'ah were content with minimal knowledge of Islam and Islamic conduct on the part of a believer. On the question of free will, they leaned heavily toward predestinarianism, and some were outright predestinarians. There is evidence that the Umayyad rulers supported the Murji'ah, apparently for their own political ends, since they were interested in discouraging questions about how they had come to power and set up a dynastic rule that abandoned the first four caliphs' model and high moral and political standards. However, it would have been impossible for these rulers to succeed if popular opinion had not swung toward the Murji'ah, particularly in reaction against the Khārijīs. [*For more on the Murji'ah, see* Īmān and Islām.]

The chief formulator of the Sunnī creed was Abū al-Ḥasan al-Ashʿarī (d. 935), a Muʿtazilī who later came under the influence of the traditionists *(ahl al-ḥadīth)* and turned the tables on his erstwhile preceptor and fellows among the Muʿtazilah. For al-Ashʿarī, people cannot produce their own actions; rather, God does, and neither man nor nature has any powers or potencies before the actual act. At the time of the act, for example, when fire actually burns, God creates a power for that particular act. Thus God creates an action, while human beings "appropriate" or "acquire" *(kasaba)* it and thereby become responsible for "their" acts. The Ash'arī theologians are, therefore, atomists in terms of both time and space, and they reject causation and the entire idea of movement or process. God is under no obligation to do what human beings call justice; on the contrary, whatever God does is just. Justice involves reference to certain norms under which the agent works; since God has no norms to obey, there is no question of doing justice on his part. He also promised in the Qur'ān that he will reward those who do good and punish those who do evil, and this is the proper and only assurance we have of the fate of human beings; if he had chosen to do the reverse, no one could question him. It also follows that good and bad are not natural characteristics of human acts, but that acts become good or bad by God's declaration through the revelation that he has been sending since Adam, the first prophet. It is, therefore, futile to probe rationally into the purposes of divine injunctions, for these are the result of God's will.

On the question of divine attributes, al-Ash'arī taught that these are real, although they are "neither God, nor other than God." God has an eternal attribute of "speech," which al-Ash'arī called "psychic speech," manifested in all divinely revealed books. Although the Qur'ān as God's "psychic speech" is eternal, as something recited, written, and heard it is also created: one cannot point to a written copy of the Qur'ān or its recital and say "This is eternal." [*See also* Ash'arīyah *and* Creeds, *article on* Islamic Creeds.]

A contemporary of al-Ash'arī, the Central Asian theologian al-Māturīdī (d. 944), also formulated an "official" Sunnī creed and theology that in some fundamental ways was nearer to the Mu'tazilī stance. He recognized "power-before-the-act" in man and also declared good and bad to be natural and knowable by human reason. Whereas al-Ash'arī belonged to the Shāfi'ī school of law, which was based principally on *ḥadīth*, al-Māturīdī was a member of the Ḥanafī school, which gave greater scope to reason. Yet, in subsequent centuries, the former's views almost completely eclipsed the latter's, although in the Indian subcontinent such prominent thinkers as Aḥmad Sirhindī (d. 1624) and Shāh Walī Allāh of Delhi (d. 1762) criticized Ash'arī theology. The reason behind this sweeping and enduring success of Ash'arī theology seems to be the overwhelming spread of Sufism (particularly in its pantheistic form), which, in theological terms, was much more akin to Ash'arī thought than to that of Mu'tazilah or even the Māturīdīyah, in that it sought to obliterate the human self in the all-embracing and all-effacing self of God, the most important nodal point of this conjunction being al-Ghazālī.

In the intellectual field, as we shall see, Sufism grew at the expense of theology and utilized the worldview of the Muslim philosophers. On the moral and spiritual planes, however, the powerful corroboration of theology and Sufism stimulated the vehement reaction of the jurist and theologian Ibn Taymīyah (d. 1328). Struggling all his life against popular Ṣūfī superstitions, against worship of saints and their shrines, and against Ash'arī theology, he tried to resurrect the moral activism of the Qur'ān and the *sunnah*. He regarded the Mu'tazilī denial of God's role in human actions as an error but considered the Ash'arī denial of human free and effective will as extremely dangerous and, in fact, stated that pantheistic Ṣūfīs and the Ash'arī theologians were considerably worse than not only the Mu'tazilah but even the Zoroastrians. He held that the Zoroastrians' postulation of two gods was undoubtedly an error but argued that they had been forced into this belief by the undeniable distinction between good and evil that both Ash'arī theology and pantheistic Sufism virtually obliterated, leaving no basis for any worthwhile religion. (As we shall see, a similar argument was conducted within Sufism by a later Indian Ṣūfī, Aḥmad Sirhindī.) Ibn Taymīyah sought to solve the perennial problem of free will versus divine omnipotence by saying that the actual application of the principle of divine omnipotence occurs only in the past, while the *sharī'ah* imperatives are relevant only to the future. His teaching remained more or less dormant until the eighteenth century, when it inspired the Wahhābī religious revolution in the Arabian Peninsula. [*For further discussion of Islamic theology, see* Kalām *and* God, *article on* God in Islam.]

Sufism. The mainspring of Sufism lay in the desire to cultivate the inner life and to attain a deeper, personal understanding of Islam. Among the many proposed etymologies of the word *ṣūfī*, the most credible is the one that derives it from *ṣūf*, meaning "coarse wool," a reference to the kind of garb that many Ṣūfīs wore. The first phase of this spiritual movement was definitely moral, and the works of most early Ṣūfīs, those of the second and third centuries AH, show a preoccupation with constant self-examination and close scrutiny of one's motivation.

Ṣūfī doctrine. The dialectic of the trappings and self-deception of the soul developed by Ḥakīm al-Tirmidhī (d. 898) in his *Khatm al-awliyā'* (The Seal of the Saints) provides one extraordinary example of spiritual insight, but this strongly moral trend continues from Ḥasan al-Baṣrī (d. 728) through al-Muḥāsibī (d. 857) to his pupil al-Junayd (d. 910). The essence of their doctrine is moral contrition and detachment of the mind from the "good things" of the world *(zuhd)*. But from its very early times, Sufism also had a strong devotional element, as exemplified by the woman saint Rābiʿah al-ʿAdawīyah (d. 801). The goal of love of God led to the doctrine of *fanā'* or "annihilation" (that is, of the human self in God). There were definitely Hellenistic Christian influences at work here. But the annihilation ideal was soon amended into "survival *(baqā')* after annihilation," or (re)gaining of a new self, and this formula was given different interpretations.

Most Ṣūfīs taught that, after the destruction of the human attributes (not the self), mortals acquire divine attributes (not the divine self) and "live in" them. The firm view of the orthodox and influential Ṣūfī al-Junayd was that when a person sheds human attributes and these attributes undergo annihilation, that person comes to think that he or she has become God. But God soon gives that person the consciousness of otherness (not alienation) from God, which is extremely painful and is only somewhat relieved by God's also giving the consolation that this is the highest state attainable by human beings. Yet there were also Ṣūfīs who, most probably under the influence of Hellenistic Christianity, believed in human transubstantiation into God. In 922, al-Ḥallāj, a representative of this school, was charged with having uttered the blasphemous statement "I am God" and was crucified in Baghdad. Yet, a somewhat earlier mystic, al-Bisṭāmī (d. 874), who is said to have committed even graver blasphemies, was never touched by the law. It may be, as some contend, that the real reasons behind al-Ḥallāj's execution were political, or it may be related to the fact that al-Ḥallāj was in the capital, Baghdad, whereas al-Bisṭāmī lived in an outlying province.

This example of such divergent interpretations of a fundamental doctrine should warn us that with Sufism we are dealing with a truly protean phenomenon: not only do interpretations differ, but experiences themselves must differ as well. However, under pressure from the *ʿulamā'*, who refused to acknowledge any objective validity for the Ṣūfī experience, the Ṣūfīs formulated a doctrine of "spiritual stations" *(maqāmāt)* that adepts successively attained through their progressive spiritual itinerary *(sulūk)*. These stations are as objectifiable as any experience can be. Although the various schools have differed in the lists of these stations, they usually enumerate them as follows: detachment from the world *(zuhd)*, patience *(ṣabr)*, gratitude *(shukr)* for whatever God gives, love *(ḥubb)*, and pleasure *(riḍā)* with whatever God desires.

After the violent death of al-Ḥallāj, another important doctrine of the dialectic of Ṣūfī experience was developed by orthodox Ṣūfīs. According to this doctrine, the Ṣūfī alternates between two different types of spiritual states. One type is the experience of unity (where all multiplicity disappears) and of the inner reality. In this state the Ṣūfī is "absent" from the world and is "with God"; this is the state of "intoxication" *(sukr)*. The other state, that of "sobriety" *(ṣaḥw)*, occurs when the Ṣūfī "returns" to multiplicity and is "with the world." Whereas many Ṣūfīs had earlier contended that "intoxication" is superior to "sobriety" and that, therefore, the saints *(awliyā')* are superior to the prophets (who are "with the world" and legislate for society), the orthodox Ṣūfīs now asserted the opposite, for the goodness of saints is limited to themselves, whereas the goodness of prophets is transitive, since they save the society as well as themselves.

On the basis of this doctrine, al-Ḥallāj's famous statement was rationalized as "one uttered in a state of intoxication" and as such not to be taken at face value. But it was al-Ghazālī who effected a meaningful and enduring synthesis of Ṣūfī "innerism" and the orthodox belief system. A follower of al-Ashʿarī in theology and of al-Shāfiʿī in law, al-Ghazālī also studied thoroughly the philosophic tradition of Ibn Sīnā (known in the West as Avicenna, d. 1037), and although he refuted its important theses bearing on religion in the famous work *Tahāfut al-falāsifah* (The Incoherence of the Philosophers), he was influenced by it in important ways as well. He then adopted Sufism as his "way to God" and composed his *magnum opus, Iḥyā' ʿulūm al-dīn* (The Revivification of the Sciences of the Faith). His net accomplishment lies in the fact that he tried to infuse a new spiritual life into law and theology on the one hand and to instill sobriety and responsibility into Sufism on the other, for he repudiated the Ṣūfī *shaṭaḥāt* (intoxicated utterances) as meaningless.

Within a century after al-Ghazālī's death, however, a Ṣūfī doctrine based on out-and-out monism was being preached by Ibn al-ʿArabī (d. 1240). Born in Spain and educated there and in North Africa, Ibn al-ʿArabī eventually traveled to the Muslim East; he lived for many years in Mecca, where he wrote his major work, *Al-futūḥāt al-makkīyah* (The Meccan Discoveries), and finally settled in Damascus, where he died. Ibn al-ʿArabī's writings are the high-water mark of theosophic Sufism, which goes beyond the ascetic or ecstatic Sufism of the earlier period, by laying cognitive claims to a unique, intuitive experience (known as *kashf*, "direct discovery," or *dhawq*, "taste") that was immune from error and radically different from and superior to the rational knowledge of the philosophers and the theologians.

Ibn al-ʿArabī's doctrine, known as Unity of Being *(waḥdat al-wujūd)*, teaches that everything is in one sense God and in another sense not-God. He holds that, given God, the transcendent, another factor that in itself is not describable "either as existent or as nonexistent" comes to play a crucial role in the unfolding of reality. This factor is neither God nor the world; it is a "third thing," but it is God with God and world with the world. It is the stuff of which both the attributes of God (for God as transcendent has no names and no attributes) and the content of the world are made. It is eternal with the eternal and temporal with the temporal; it does not exist partially and divided in things: the whole of it is God, and the whole of it is the world, and the whole of it is everything in the world. This "third thing" turns out finally to be the Perfect or Primordial Human Being (who is identified with the eternal, not the temporal, Muḥammad), in whose mirror God sees himself and who sees himself in God's mirror. This immanent God and Human Being are not only interdependent but are the obverse and converse of the same coin. There is little doubt that Ibn al-ʿArabī represents a radical humanism, a veritable apotheosis of humanity.

This monistic Sufism found certain devoted and distinguished exponents in Ibn al-ʿArabī's school, in both prose and poetry, the most illustrious and influential representative of the latter being Jalāl al-Dīn Rūmī (d. 1273), whose *Mathnavī* in Persian has been hailed as the "Qur'ān in the Persian language." Through poetry, moreover, it has had a profound and literally incalculable influence on the general intellectual culture of Islam, in terms of a liberal humanism, indeed, latitudinarianism, and among the lower strata of Islamic society even antinomianism. A striking feature of this antinomianism, where orthodoxy was unashamedly scoffed at and ridiculed for its rigidity and narrow confines, is that it was tolerated by the orthodox only when it was expressed in poetry, not in prose. Also, because of the latitude and broad range of Ṣūfī spirituality, from roughly the twelfth century to the impact of modernization in the nineteenth century, the more creative Muslim minds drifted from orthodoxy into the Ṣūfī fold, and philosophy itself, although it remained rational in its methods, became mystical in its goals.

I have already noted the severe reaction against Ṣūfī excesses on the part of Ibn Taymīyah in the fourteenth century. It may be mentioned here that for Ibn Taymīyah the ultimate distinction between good and evil is absolutely necessary for any worthwhile religion that seeks to inculcate moral responsibility, and further, that this distinction is totally dependent upon belief in pure monotheism and the equally absolute distinction between man and God. He sets little value on the formal fact that a person belongs to the Muslim community; he evaluates all human beings on the scale of monotheism. Thus, as seen above, he regards pantheistic Ṣūfīs (and, to a large extent, because of their predestinarianism, the Ashʿarīyah as well), as being equivalent to polytheists; then come the Shīʿah and Christians because both consider a human being to be a divine incarnation; and last come Zoroastrians and the Muʿtazilah, since both posit two ultimate powers.

Later, the Indian shaykh of the Naqshbandī order, Aḥmad Sirhindī (d. 1624), undertook a similar reform of Sufism from within. His massive *Maktūbāt-i Aḥmad Sirhindī* (Letters), the main vehicle of his reform, besides the training of disciples, was twice translated into Ottoman Turkish and was influential in Turkey; in the Arab Middle East, his reformist thought was carried and spread in the nineteenth century. Sirhindī, who accepts Ibn al-ʿArabī's philosophical scheme at the metaphysical level, introduces a radical moral dualism at the level of God's attributes and, instead of identifying the temporal world with the stuff of divine attributes, as Ibn al-ʿArabī does, regards that world as being essentially evil, but evil that has to be transformed into good through the activity of the divine attributes. The basic error of the common Ṣūfīs, for him, is that instead of helping to transform this evil into good, as God wants to do through his attributes, they flee from it. The spiritual heights to which they think they are ascending are, therefore, a pure delusion, for the real good is this evil, "this earth," once it has been transformed. But this realization requires a constant struggle with evil, not a flight from it. It is a prophet, then, not a saint, who undertakes the real divine task, and the true test of a person's ascent to real spiritual heights is whether he or she reenters the earth in order to improve and redeem it. Despite the efforts of Ibn Taymīyah, Sirhindī, and other figures, however, Ibn al-ʿArabī's influence has been, until today, very strong in the Muslim world, not just on Sufism but on Islamic poetry as well.

Ṣūfī orders. Up to the twelfth century, Sufism was a matter of limited circles of a spiritual elite that might be aptly described as "schools" with different spiritual techniques and even different spiritual ideologies. From the twelfth century on, however, they developed into networks of orders, involving the masses on a large scale. Systems of Ṣūfī hospices—called variously *zāwiyahs* (in Arabic), *tekkes* (in Turkish), and *khānagāhs* (in Iran and the Indian subcontinent)—where the Ṣūfī shaykh lived (usually with his family in the interior of the building) and guided his clientele, grew up from Morocco to Southeast Asia. Although in some of the hospices orthodox religious disciplines such as theology and law were taught along with Ṣūfī works, orthodox education was generally carried on in the *madrasahs*, or colleges, while only Ṣūfī works were taught in the Ṣūfī centers. [*See* Khānagāh *and* Madrasah.]

Ṣūfī orders can be divided into those that are global

and those that are regional. The most global is the Qādirī order, named after ʿAbd al-Qādir al-Jīlānī (d. 1166), with branches all over the world that are tied only loosely to the center at Baghdad. Somewhat more regional are the Suhrawardī and the Naqshbandī orders. The latter, which originated in Central Asia in the thirteenth century, formulated an explicit ideology early in its career to try to influence the rulers and their courts, with the result that they have often been politically active. One of its branches, the Khalwatīyah, played a prominent role in modernizing reform in Turkey during the eighteenth and nineteenth centuries. Several of the Ṣūfī orders have been associated with guilds and sometimes, particularly in Ottoman Turkey, have been directly involved in social protests and political rebellions against official oppression and injustice.

Another broad and important division is that between urban and "rustic" orders. The former, particularly the Naqshbandī order and its offshoots, were refined and close to the orthodoxy of the *ʿulamāʾ*, with the result that an increasingly large number of the *ʿulamāʾ* gradually enrolled themselves in these urban Ṣūfī orders, particularly the orthodox ones. By contrast, many of the rustic orders were without discipline and law *(bī-sharʿ)*, especially in the Indian subcontinent, where they were often indistinguishable from the Hindu *sādhūs* (monks). With the spread of modernization, Sufism and Ṣūfī orders have suffered greatly; in Turkey, they were suppressed by Mustafa Kemal Atatürk in the 1920s, and their endowments were confiscated by the government. It is interesting to note, however, that since the mid-twentieth century some orders have experienced a revival in the industrial urban centers of Muslim lands, probably in reaction to the excessively materialistic outlook generated by modernization, while in Central Asia their underground networks are waging anti-Soviet activities in an organized manner. Correspondingly, in the West, several intellectuals, such as Frithjof Schuon and Martin Lings, have actively turned to Ṣūfī devotion to escape the spiritual vacuity created by their own overly materialistic culture. [*For more on the Ṣūfī orders, see* Darwīsh *and* Ṭarīqah.]

Sects. There are two broad divisions within the Muslim community, the Sunnīs and the Shīʿah. The theological views and the legal schools of the Sunnīs—the majority of the community—have been dealt with above. The Shīʿī schism grew out of the claim of the Shīʿah (a word meaning "partisans," in this context "the partisans of ʿAlī") that following the Prophet, rule over Muslims belongs rightfully only to ʿAlī, Muḥammad's cousin and son-in-law, and to his descendants. This doctrine, known as "legitimism," was opposed to the Khārijī view that rule is open to any good Muslim on a universal basis and to the Sunnī view, which was no more than a rationalization of actual facts, that "rulers must come from the Quraysh," the Prophet's tribe, but not necessarily from his clan or house.

The Shīʿah, in early Islam, were primarily sociopolitical dissidents, sheltering under the umbrella of "the house of the Prophet" but actually representing various elements of social protest against Umayyad Arab heavy-handedness and injustices. But it was not long before they began establishing an ideological and theological base for themselves. Until well into the third century AH, Shīʿī theology was crude and materialistic: it asserted that God was a corporeal being who sat on an actual throne and created space by physical motion. Hishām ibn al-Ḥakam (d. 814?), among the best known of the early Shīʿī theologians, is reported to have said that God was "a little smaller than Mount Abū Qabīs." There were several other early Shīʿī theologians who attributed some kind of body, including a physical body, to God, but beginning in the latter half of the ninth century, Shīʿī theology was radically transformed, inheriting and asserting with increasing force the Muʿtazilī doctrine of human free will against the Sunnīs.

In the thirteenth century CE, through the work of the philosopher, theologian, and scientist Naṣīr al-Dīn Ṭūsī (d. 1273), philosophy entered Shīʿī theology, a process that was further facilitated by Ṭūsī's student, the influential theologian al-Ḥillī (d. 1325). In his work on the creed, *Tajrīd al-ʿaqāʾid* (Concise Statement of the Creeds), which was subsequently commented upon by both Shīʿī and Sunnī theologians, Ṭūsī describes man as "creator of his own actions." Ṭūsī, however, rejects the philosophical thesis of the eternity of the world. Here it is interesting to compare this Shīʿī development with the Sunnī position that was articulated about three-quarters of a century earlier at the hands of Fakhr al-Dīn al-Rāzī (d. 1209), who expanded the official Sunnī theology by incorporating into it a discussion of major philosophical themes. But whereas the Shīʿah accepted many philosophical theses into their theology, al-Rāzī and other Sunnīs after him refuted all the philosophical theses point by point, thus erecting a theology that was an exclusive alternative to philosophy. Against this background is probably to be understood the fact that while philosophy was exorcized from the curricula in the Arab world from the thirteenth century on and declined sharply in the rest of the Sunnī world, it reached its zenith in Shīʿī Iran in the seventeenth century and continues unabated until today, although many of the orthodox Shīʿah continue to oppose it.

In law, the Twelver Shīʿī school has long been recognized as valid by the Sunnīs, despite differences, the most conspicuous being that Shīʿī law recognizes a temporary marriage that may be contracted for a fixed period—a year, a month, a week, or even a day. Among the Shīʿah, the nearest school to Sunnism, particularly in law, is that of the Zaydīyah in Yemen, whose founder Zayd ibn ʿAlī (d. 738), a brother of the fifth imam of the Shīʿah, was a theology student of the first Muʿtazilī teacher, Wāṣil ibn ʿAṭāʾ (d. 748).

But the most characteristic doctrine of the Shīʿah is their esotericism. This has a practical aspect called *taqīyah,* which means dissimulation of one's real beliefs in a generally hostile atmosphere. This doctrine, apparently adopted in early Islamic times, when the Shīʿah became a subterranean movement, as it were, in the wake of political failure, subsequently became a part of Shīʿī dogma. [*See* Taqīyah.] But in its theoretical aspect esotericism is defined by the doctrine that religion, and particularly the Qurʾān, has, besides the apparent, "external" meaning, hidden esoteric meanings that can be known only through spiritual contact with the Hidden Imam. In the early centuries of Islam, this principle of esotericism was probably unbridled and fanciful in its application, as is apparent from the ninth- to tenth-century Qurʾān commentary of al-Qummī. But as Shiism was progressively permeated by rational thought, esotericism became more systematic, even if it may often seem farfetched (as in certain philosophical interpretations of the Qurʾān). As pointed out earlier, the Ṣūfīs also patently practiced esotericism in understanding the materials of religion, particularly the Qurʾān; the ultimate common source of both Shiism and Sufism lies in gnosticism and other comparable currents of thought, and, indeed, Ibn al-ʿArabī's interpretations are often purely the work of his uncontrolled imagination.

Beginning from about the middle of the tenth century, when the Sunnī caliph in Baghdad came under the control of the Shīʿī Buyid dynasty, there were public commemorations of the martyrdom of Ḥusayn at Karbala on the tenth of Muḥarram (ʿĀshūrāʾ). These ceremonies caused riots in Baghdad and still do so in some countries such as Pakistan and India today. The commemoration is traditionally marked by public processions in which participants lamenting the death of the Prophet's grandson beat their breasts and backs with heavy iron chains. Scenes of Ḥusayn's death are recreated in passion plays known as *taʿziyahs*, and he is eulogized in moving sermons and poetry recitals. Fed from childhood with such representational enactments of this event, a Shīʿī Muslim is likely to develop a deep sense of tragedy and injustice resulting in an ideal of martyrdom that is capable of being manipulated into outbursts of frenzied emotionalism, like the spectacular events of the Iranian Revolution. [*See* ʿĀshūrāʾ *and* Taʿziyah.]

Shīʿī subsects. In the first and second centuries of the Islamic era, Shiism served as an umbrella for all kinds of ideologies, with a general social protest orientation, and the earliest heresiographers enumerate dozens of Shīʿī sects, several with extremely heretical and antinomian views. The main surviving body, the Ithnā ʿAsharīyah, or Twelvers, number probably between fifty and sixty million people. All other sects (except the Zaydīyah of Yemen) are regarded even by the Twelvers themselves as heretical extremists *(ghulāt).* The main one among these, the Ismāʿīlīyah, or Seveners, broke with the Twelvers in a dispute over which son of the sixth imam was to be recognized as the latter's successor: the Twelvers refused to recognize the elder son, Ismāʿīl, because he drank wine, while the Seveners did recognize him (thus the name Ismāʿīlī) and continue to await his return.

The Ismāʿīlīyah established a powerful and prosperous empire in North Africa and Egypt from the tenth to the twelfth centuries. Prior to this, the Ismāʿīlīyah had been an underground revolutionary movement, but once they attained political power, they settled down as part of the status quo. Since the late eleventh century, they have been divided into two branches: the Nizārīyah, commonly known by the name Assassins, who were active in Syria and Iran, and in recent years have been followers of a hereditary Aga Khan, and the Mustaʿliyah, who are mainly centered in Bombay. Ismāʿīlī philosophy, which is reflected in the *Rasāʾil Ikhwān al-Ṣafāʾ* (Epistles of the Brethren of Purity), produced by a secret society in the late ninth century, is essentially based on Neoplatonic thought with influences from gnosticism and occult sects.

The Ismāʿīlī sect, which was organized and propagated through a well-knit network of missionaries *(duʿāh),* adheres to a belief in cyclic universes: each cycle comprises seven Speakers, or Messengers, with a revelation and a law; each Speaker is followed in turn by one of the seven Silent Ones, or Imams. The last imam, when he appears, will abrogate all organized religions and their laws and will institute a new era of a universal religion. During the leadership of the third Aga Khan (d. 1957), the Ismāʿīlī community started drawing closer to the mainstream of Islam, a trend that seems to be gaining further strength at present under Karīm Aga Khan's leadership: Ismāʿīlī intellectuals now describe their faith as the "Ismāʿīlī *ṭarīqah* [spiritual order] of Islam." There are other "extremist" subsects within the Shīʿah, including the Druze, Nuṣayrīyah, and ʿAlawīyūn. Of these, the Druze are the most prominent. This sect arose in the eleventh century as a cult of the eccentric Fatimid ruler al-Ḥakim, who mysteriously disappeared in 1021. [*For more on the principal divisions of the Shīʿah, see* ʿAlawīyūn; Assassins; Druze; Ikhwān al-Ṣafāʾ; Qarāmiṭah; *and* Shiism, *articles on* Ismāʿīlīyah *and* Ithnā ʿAsharīyah.]

Later sects. In more recent times, there have been two noteworthy sectarian developments, one within Shīʿī Islam in mid-nineteenth-century Iran and the other within Sunnī Islam in late nineteenth-century India. During an anticlerical movement in Iran, a certain Muḥammad ʿAlī of Shiraz claimed to be the Bāb, or "Gate," to God. He was executed by the government under pressure from the *ʿulamāʾ* in 1850. After him, his two disciples, Subḥ-i Azal and Bahāʾ Allāh, went different ways, and the latter subsequently declared his faith to be an independent religion outside Islam. While the origin of the Bahāʾī religion was marked by strong eschatological overtones, it later developed an ideology of pacifism and internationalism and won a considerable number of converts in North America early in the twentieth century. In Iran itself, Bābīs and Bahāʾīs are frequent targets of clerical persecution, and many of them have been executed under the Khomeini regime. [*See* Bābīs *and* Bahāʾīs.]

The Sunnī sect called the Aḥmadīyah arose in the 1880s when Ghulām Aḥmad of Qadiyān (a village in East Punjab) laid claim to prophethood. He claimed to be at once a "manifestation" of the prophet Muḥammad, the Second Advent of Jesus, and an avatar of Kṛṣṇa for the Hindus. It is possible that he wanted to unite various religions under his leadership. After his death, his followers constituted themselves as an independent community with an elected *khalīfah* (successor; i.e., caliph). When the first caliph died in 1911, the Aḥmadīyah split in two: the main body carried on the founder's claim to prophethood under Aḥmad's son, Bashīr al-Dīn, while the other, the Lahore group, claimed that Ghulām Aḥmad was not a prophet, nor had he claimed to be one, but rather that he was a reformer or "renovator" *(mujaddid)* of Islam. Both groups have been active with missionary zeal, particularly in Europe and America. In 1974, the National Assembly of Pakistan, where the main body had established its headquarters after the creation of the state, declared both groups to be "non-Muslim minorities." [*See* Aḥmadīyah.]

Modernism. In the eighteenth century, against a background of general stagnation, a puritanical fundamentalist movement erupted in Arabia under Muḥammad ibn ʿAbd al-Wahhāb (1703–1792). The movement called for a return to the purist Islam of the Qurʾān and the *sunnah* and its unadulterated monotheism, uncompromised by the popular cults of saints and their shrines. Ibn ʿAbd al-Wahhāb married into the family of Saʿūd, a chieftain of Najd, who accepted his teaching and brought all Arabia under his ruling ideology. [*See* Wahhābīyah *and the biography of Ibn ʿAbd al-Wahhāb.*] At the same time, in the Indian subcontinent, Shāh Walī Allāh of Delhi, a highly sophisticated intellectual (said to have been a fellow student of Ibn ʿAbd al-Wahhāb during his stay in Medina), also advocated a return to pristine Islam although, unlike his Arabian contemporary, he was a Ṣūfī at a high spiritual level.

In the nineteenth century a reformist militant group called the Jihād movement arose out of Walī Allāh's school, and three more movements followed in Africa—the Sanūsī in Libya, the Fulbe in West Africa, and the Mahdists in the Sudan. Although these three movements emerged from different environments, common to all of them was a reformist thrust in terms of the recovery of the "true pristine Islam" of the Qurʾān and the Prophet, particularly emphasizing monotheism; an insistence upon *ijtihād,* that is, rejection of the blind following tradition in both theology and law in favor of an attempt to discover and formulate new solutions to Islamic problems; and finally, resort to militant methods, including the imposition of their reformist ideologies by force. In addition, these movements generally brought to the center of consciousness the necessity of social and moral reforms as such, without recourse to the rewards and punishments of the hereafter. In other words, all three were characterized by a certain positivistic orientation.

While these premodernist reform movements laid great emphasis on *ijtihād,* in practice their *ijtihād* meant that Muslims should be enabled to disengage themselves from their present "degenerate" condition and to recover pristine Islam. Also, it is a general characteristic of all fundamentalist movements that in order to "simplify" religion and make it practical, they debunk the intellectualism of the past and discourage the growth of future intellectualism. In such cases education becomes so simplified that it is virtually sterile, thus leaving little possibility for *ijtihād.* Of the fundamentalist groups I have described above, the progenitors of the Indian and Libyan movements were sophisticated and accomplished scholars, but the leaders of the other three had only a modicum of learning and were primarily activists.

Nonetheless, these movements signaled real stirrings in the soul of Islam and paved the way for the intellectual activity of the Muslim modernists—Muslims who had been exposed to Western ideas and who, by integrating certain key ones among them with the teaching of the Qurʾān, produced brilliant solutions to the crucial problems then faced by Islamic society. The influence of premodernist reformism upon the modernists is apparent from the fact that they keep the Qurʾān and the tradition of the Prophet as ultimate referents for reform while criticizing or rejecting the medieval heritage. Thus, although their individual views regarding, for example, the relationship between faith and reason differ, all of them insist on the cultivation of positive sciences, appealing to numerous verses of the Qur'ān that state that the entire universe has been made subservient to good ends of humankind and that we must study and use it.

In the political sphere, citing Qur'ān 42:38, which says that Muslims should decide all their affairs through mutual consultation (*shūrā*, actually a pre-Islamic Arab institution confirmed by the Qur'ān), the modernists contended that whereas the Qur'ān teaches democracy, the Muslims had deviated from this norm and acquiesced to autocratic rule. Similarly, on the subject of women, the modernists argued that the Qur'ān had granted equal rights to men and women (except in certain areas of economic life where the burden of earning and supporting the family is squarely laid on men), but the medieval practice of the Muslims had clearly departed from the Qur'ān and ended by depriving women of their rights. Regarding polygamy, the modernists stated that permission for polygamy (up to four wives) had been given under special conditions, with the proviso that if the husband could not do justice among his co-wives then he must marry only one wife, and that finally the Qur'ān itself had declared such justice to be impossible to attain (4:129). [*See* Modernism, *article on* Islamic Modernism.]

Of the half-dozen most prominent names in Islamic modernism, two were *'ulamā'*-trained along traditional lines: Jamāl al-Dīn al-Afghānī (1839–1897), a fiery activist with a magnetic personality, and his disciple, the Egyptian shaykh Muḥammad 'Abduh (1845–1905). Three were lay intellectuals with modern education: the Turk Namık Kemal (1840–1888) and the two Indians Ameer Ali (d. 1928) and Muhammad Iqbal (1877–1938), while the Indian Sayyid Ahmad Khan (1817–1898), the most radical of them all in theological views, was a premodern lay-educated scholar. Yet, despite their differences and the fact that none of them, except for al-Afghānī and 'Abduh, ever met any of the others, they shared the basic tenet—*à la* premodernist reform movements—that medieval Islam had deviated on certain crucial points from the normative Islam of the Qur'ān; this argument runs through all the issues that they discuss.

However, while these modernists sought reform within their own societies, they also waged controversies with the West on the latter's understanding of Islam, and some of them, particularly Iqbal, argued about the West's own performance on the stage of history. Iqbal bitterly and relentlessly accused the West of cheating humanity of its basic values with the glittering mirage of its technology, of exploiting the territories it colonized in the name of spreading humanitarian values, which it itself flouted by waging internecine wars born of sheer economic savagery, and of dewomanizing the women and dilapidating the family institution in the name of progress. Iqbal was an equally strong critic of the world Muslim society, which for him represented nothing more than a vast graveyard of Islam. He called the whole world to the "true Islam" of the Qur'ān and the Prophet, a living, dynamic Islam that believed in the harnessing of the forces of history for the ethical development of mankind.

Iqbal and others, such as the Egyptian Rashīd Riḍā (d. 1935), proved to belong to a transitional stage from modernism to a new attitude, perhaps best described as neofundamentalism, for unlike the fundamentalism of the premodernist reform movements, the current neofundamentalism is, in large measure, a reaction to modernism, but it has also been importantly influenced by modernism. This influence can best be seen on two major issues: first, the contention that Islam is a total way of life, including all fields of human private and public life, and is not restricted to certain religious rites such as the Five Pillars (to which the Islam of the traditionalist *'ulamā'* had become practically confined); and, second, that cultivation of scientific knowledge and technology is desirable within Islam.

Besides emphasis on technology (although Iran appears to pay only lip service to science and technology), neofundamentalists have, on the one hand, oversimplified the traditionalist curriculum of Islamic studies, and, on the other, embarked upon a program of "islamization" of Western knowledge. Besides these points, the most basic factor common to the neofundamentalist phenomena is a strong assertion of Islamic identity over and against the West, an assertion that hits equally strongly at most modernist reforms, particularly on the issue of the status and role of women in society. This powerful desire to repudiate the West, therefore, leads the neofundamentalist to emphasize certain points (as a *riposte* to the modernist, who is often seen as a pure and simple westernizer) that would most distinguish Islam from the West. Besides the role of women, which is seen to lie at home, the heaviest emphasis falls on the islamization of economy through the reinstitution of *zakāt* and the abolition of bank interest (which is identified with *ribā*, or usury, prohibited by the Qur'ān). No neofundamentalist government in the Muslim world—including Iran and Pakistan—however, has been successful in implementing either of the two policies, while the Libyan leader Mu'ammar al-Qadhdhāfī has declared that the modern banking institution is not covered by the Qur'anic prohibition of *ribā*.

Neofundamentalism is by no means a uniform phenomenon. Apart from the fact that there exist, particularly in the Arab Middle East, extremist splinter groups of neofundamentalists that are strikingly reminiscent of the Khārijīs of early Islamic times, on most crucial issues, such as democracy or the nature of Islamic legislation, even the mainstream elements are sharply divided. While in Libya, for example, Muʿammar al-Qadhdhāfī has taken a most radical stand on legislation, repudiating the precepts of *ḥadīth* as its source and replacing them with the will of the people, the current rulers of Pakistan and Iran show little confidence in the will of the people. The most interesting attitude in this connection is that of the religious leaders of Iran: while almost all reformers since the mid-nineteenth century—including Shīʿī thinkers such as Ameer Ali—have insisted that there can be no theocracy in Islam since Islam has no priesthood, the Iranian religious leaders are asserting precisely the opposite, namely, that Islam does have a priesthood and that this priestly class must rule, a position expounded even prior to the Islamic Revolution by Ayatollah Khomeini, the chief ruler of Iran, in his work *Vilāyat-i faqīh* (Rule of the Jurist, 1971). [*See also* Jamāʿat-i Islāmī *and* Muslim Brotherhood.]

Finally, the phenomenon of international Islamic conferences in modern Islam is also to be noted since, in the absence of political unity in the Muslim world, these help the cause of unity of sentiment, if not uniformity of mind. The beginnings of this phenomenon go back to the 1920s, when conferences were held in Cairo and Mecca to deliberate on the possibility of reinstituting the caliphate after Atatürk abolished it with the secularization of the Turkish state. But from the mid-1940s on, as Muslim countries gained independence from European colonial rule, the sentiment for international Muslim gatherings became progressively stronger. In the mid-1960s all the national and international private Islamic organizations became affiliated with the semiofficial Saudi-sponsored Muslim World League (Rābiṭat al-ʿĀlam al-Islāmī), headquartered in Mecca; the league finances Islamic causes both in the Muslim world and in Western countries, where large numbers of Muslim settlers are building mosques and Islamic centers and developing Islamic community life, including programs for education.

At the same time, since the 1969 Muslim Summit Conference held in Rabat, Morocco, an Islamic Secretariat has been set up in Jiddah, Saudi Arabia, as the administrative center for the Organization of Islamic Conferences (OIC) on the state level. Besides holding summit meetings, this organization maintains a developmental economic agenda through which interest-free development banks have been set up, financed principally by oil-rich Arab countries to help poorer Muslim countries (this is in addition to the aid given to non-Muslim countries). All these conferences, whether organized by the OIC or the World Muslim League, discuss political problems affecting the Muslim world and try to formulate a common response to them, through the United Nations and its agencies or through other channels.

Islam's Attitude to Other Religions. According to Qur'anic teaching divine guidance is universal, and God regards all peoples as equal. Every prophet's message, although immediately addressed to a given people, is nevertheless of universal import and must be believed by all humanity. Muḥammad himself is made to declare, "I believe in any book God may have revealed" (Qur'ān 42:15), and all Muslims are required to do likewise. This is so because God is one; the source of revelation is one, and humankind is also one. The office of prophethood is, in fact, indivisible.

Muslims, however, have, from earliest times, considered Muḥammad to be the bearer of the last and consummate revelation. Nevertheless, there is a tension within the Qur'ān itself on this issue. In keeping with its fundamental teaching that prophethood is indivisible, the Qur'ān, of course, invites Jews and Christians to Islam; it insists on the unity of religion, deplores the diversity of religions and religious communities, which it insists is based on willful neglect of truth, and denounces both Jews and Christians as "partisans, sectarians," with "each sect rejoicing in what itself has" (30:32).

On the other hand, it states that although religion is essentially one, God himself has given different "institutions and approaches" to different communities so that he might "test them in what he has given them," and that they might compete with each other in goodness (5:48), which implies that these different institutional arrangements have positive value and are somehow meant to be permanent. In fact, the Qur'ān categorically states that whether a person is a Muslim or a Jew or a Christian or a Sabian, "whosoever believes in God and the Last Day and does good deeds, they shall have their reward with their Lord, shall have nothing to fear, nor shall they come to grief" (2:62; see also 5:69). This tension is probably to be resolved by saying that it is better, indeed incumbent upon humankind to accept Muḥammad's message, but that if they do not, then living up to their own prophetic messages will be regarded as adequate even if it does not fulfill the entire divine command.

The organization of Muslims as a community—which was inherent in the message of the Prophet—set in motion its own political and religious dynamics. The Qur'ān itself, while strongly repudiating the claims of Jewish and Christian communities to be proprietors of divine truth and guidance, frankly tells Muslims also (for example, in 47:38) that unless they fulfill the message they cannot take God for granted. Soon after the time of the Prophet, however, the community came to be regarded as infallible, and a *ḥadīth* was put into currency that the Prophet had said "My community shall never agree on an error." This development was necessitated partly by intercommunal rivalry, but largely by the internal development of law, since the doctrine of legal consensus had to be made infallible.

In his last years, the Prophet decided on the policy of forcible conversion of Arab pagans to Islam and gave religious and cultural autonomy to Jews and Christians as "people of the Book" (although Jews were driven out of Medina by Muḥammad and later from the rest of the Arabian Peninsula by ʿUmar I). Muslims had to determine for themselves the status of Zoroastrians, Hindus, and Buddhists when they conquered Iran and parts of Northwest India. It was decided that these populations were also "people of the Book" since they believed in certain scriptures, and consequently they were allowed to keep their religion and culture, like the Jews and Christians, on payment of the poll tax *(jizyah)*. In contrast with their stance toward Jews and Christians however, Muslims were prohibited from having social intercourse or intermarrying with these other groups.

Indeed, when the community became an imperium, further developments took place that had little to do with the Qur'ān or the *sunnah* of the Prophet but rather were dictated by the logic of the empire itself. The law of apostasy, for example, which states that a Muslim apostate should be given three chances to repent and in the case of nonrepentance must be executed, has nothing to do with the Qur'ān, which speaks of "those who believed and then disbelieved, then once again believed and disbelieved—and then became entrenched in disbelief" (4:137; see also 3:90), thus clearly envisaging repeated conversions and apostasies without invoking any penalty in this world. It is, therefore, important to make these distinctions and to treat historic Islam not as one seamless garment but rather as a mosaic made up of different pieces.

There are numerous other laws that are the product neither of the Qur'ān nor of the Prophet's *sunnah*, but of the Islamic imperium, such as the inadmissibility of evidence of a non-Muslim against a Muslim in a criminal case. In this legal genre also falls the juristic doctrine that the world consists of three zones: the Abode of Islam *(dār al-Islām)*, where Muslims rule; the Abode of Peace *(dār al-ṣulḥ)*, those countries or powers with whom Muslims have peace pacts; and the Abode of War *(dār al-ḥarb)*, the rest of the world. This doctrine was definitely the result of the early Islamic conquests and the initial Islamic law of war and peace resulting from them. But during the later Abbasid period, the concept of *jihād* was formulated in defensive terms, because the task then was the consolidation of the empire rather than the gaining of further territory through conquest. To this general problem also belongs the consideration advanced by several Western scholars that Islam cannot authentically be a minority religion because the presumption of political power is built into its very texture as a religion. What is true is that Islam requires a state to work out its sociopolitical ideals and programs, but this does not mean that Muslims cannot live as a minority; indeed they have done so throughout history. The Qur'ān, in fact, envisages some sort of close cooperation between Judaism, Christianity, and Islam, and it invites Jews and Christians to join Muslims in such a goal: "O People of the Book! Let us come together on a platform that is common between us, that we shall serve naught save God" (3:64).

[*For further discussion of Islamic institutions, see* Caliphate; Imamate; Kaʿbah; *and* Mosque. *The philosophical tradition in Islam is discussed in* Falsafah. *For an account of the exegetical tradition in Islam, see* Tafsīr. *Among other related articles are* Iʿjāz; Islamic Religious Year; *and* Islamic Studies. Domestic Observances, *article on* Muslim Practices, *and* Folk Religion, *article on* Folk Islam, *should also be consulted.*]

BIBLIOGRAPHY

General Works. For a general survey of Islam, see *The Cambridge History of Islam*, vol. 2, *The Further Islamic Lands, Islamic Society and Civilization*, edited by P. M. Holt, Ann K. S. Lambton, and Bernard Lewis (Cambridge, 1970), and my own book entitled *Islam*, 2d ed. (Chicago, 1979). Richard C. Martin's *Islam: A Cultural Perspective* (Englewood Cliffs, N.J., 1982) gives a good description of Islamic religious practice. For a developmental view of Islam in a global setting, see Marshall G. S. Hodgson's *The Venture of Islam*, 3 vols. (Chicago, 1974). A collection of essays rarely matched for perspective interpretation of Islamic civilization is H. A. R. Gibb's *Studies on the Civilization of Islam* (Boston, 1962). Two other works of general interest are *The Legacy of Islam*, edited by Thomas W. Arnold and Alfred Guillaume (London, 1931), and *The Legacy of Islam*, 2d ed., rev., edited by C. E. Bosworth and Joseph Schacht (Oxford, 1974).

Topical Studies. For the general reader and the scholar alike, an excellent guide to the Qur'ān is *Bell's Introduction to the Qur'ān* (Edinburgh, 1970), W. Montgomery Watt's revised and enlarged edition of a work published in 1953 by Richard

Bell. My own study, *Major Themes of the Qur'ān* (Chicago, 1980), is a systematic presentation of the views of the Qur'ān on God, man, society, revelation, and so on. Among translations of the Qur'ān, three can be recommended: *The Meaning of the Glorious Koran*, translated and edited by M. M. Pickthall (New York, 1930); *The Koran Interpreted*, translated by A. J. Arberry (New York, 1955); and *The Message of the Qur'ān*, translated by Muhammad Asad (Gibraltar, 1980). Both Pickthall's and Arberry's translations have been frequently reprinted and are readily available, but Asad's painstaking and thoughtful translation is well worth seeking out.

Two works on *ḥadīth* that may profitably be consulted are Ignácz Goldziher's *Muslim Studies*, 2 vols., edited by S. M. Stern and C. R. Barber (Chicago, 1966–1973), and Alfred Guillaume's *The Traditions of Islam* (1924; reprint, Beirut, 1966).

Among the many works devoted to the Prophet's biography, none is entirely satisfactory. Alfred Guillaume's *The Life of Muhammad: A Translation of [Ibn] Isḥāq's "Sīrat Rasūl Allāh"* (1955; reprint, Lahore, 1967), an English translation of the first extant Arabic biography (second century AH), is the best guide one has at the present. W. Montgomery Watt's *Muhammad at Mecca* (London, 1953) and *Muhammad at Medina* (London, 1956) may be usefully read as secondary sources.

On Islamic theology the following works are recommended: *A Shi'ite Creed: A Translation of "Risālatu'l-I'tiqādāt" of Muhammad b. 'Alī Ibn Bābawayhi al-Qummī*, edited and translated by A. A. Fyzee (London, 1942); D. B. Macdonald's *Development of Muslim Theology, Jurisprudence and Constitutional Theory* (1903; reprint, New York, 1965); W. Montgomery Watt's *The Formative Period of Islamic Thought* (Edinburgh, 1973); and A. J. Wensinck's *The Muslim Creed: Its Genesis and Historical Development* (1932; reprint, New York, 1965).

For information on Islamic law the following works are useful: *Law in the Middle East*, edited by Majid Khadduri and Herbert J. Liebesny (Washington, D.C., 1955); J. N. D. Anderson's *Islamic Law in the Modern World* (New York, 1959); Noel J. Coulson's *A History of Islamic Law* (Edinburgh, 1971); and Joseph Schacht's *An Introduction to Islamic Law* (Oxford, 1974).

Numerous works on Sufism are readily available. Among them are Reynold A. Nicholson's *The Mystics of Islam* (1914; reprint, Beirut, 1966) and *Studies in Islamic Mysticism* (1921; reprint, Cambridge, 1977); A. J. Arberry's *Sufism: An Account of the Mystics of Islam* (London, 1950); J. Spencer Trimingham's *The Sufi Orders in Islam* (New York, 1971); and Annemarie Schimmel's *Mystical Dimensions of Islam* (Chapel Hill, N.C., 1975).

For Islamic political thought and education, the following works are useful: A. S. Tritton's *Materials on Muslim Education in the Middle Ages* (London, 1957); E. I. J. Rosenthal's *Political Thought in Medieval Islam* (Cambridge, 1958); Bayard Dodge's *Muslim Education in Medieval Times* (Washington, D.C., 1962); Ann K. S. Lambton's *State and Government in Medieval Islam*, vol. 1, *The Jurists* (London, 1981); Hamid Enayat's *Modern Islamic Political Thought* (Austin, 1982); and my own *Islam and Modernity: Transformation of an Intellectual Tradition* (Chicago, 1982).

The most important statements on Islamic modernism by Muslim modernists themselves are Syed Ameer Ali's *The Spirit of Islam: A History of the Evolution and Ideals of Islam*, rev. ed. (London, 1974), and Muhammad Iqbal's *Reconstruction of Religious Thought in Islam* (1934; reprint, Lahore, 1960). General writings on and critiques of Islamic modernism by modern Western scholars include H. A. R. Gibb's *Modern Trends in Islam* (Chicago, 1947); G. E. von Grunebaum's *Modern Islam: The Search for Cultural Identity* (Los Angeles, 1962); and Wilfred Cantwell Smith's *Islam in Modern History* (Princeton, 1957).

The following are important regional treatments: Charles C. Adams's *Islam and Modernism in Egypt* (1933; reprint, New York, 1968); Wilfred Cantwell Smith's *Modern Islam in India* (London, 1946); Albert Hourani's *Arabic Thought in the Liberal Age, 1798–1939*, 2d ed. (Cambridge, 1983); Bernard Lewis's *The Emergence of Modern Turkey* (London, 1963); Niyazi Berkes's *The Development of Secularism in Turkey* (Montreal, 1964), a mine of information despite its secularist bias; and J. Boland's *The Struggle of Islam in Modern Indonesia* (The Hague, 1971).

FAZLUR RAHMAN

Islam in North Africa

The term *North Africa* usually denotes the region that includes the countries of Libya, Tunisia, Algeria, Morocco, and Mauritania. Since this region corresponds to what Arab writers call the Maghreb (the "west"), I shall use both terms here with no distinction of meaning. The unity of this region originates in its continuous settlement: from the dawn of history it has been inhabited by Berbers who came mostly from the banks of the Red Sea and who were later joined by Europeans, Semites, and blacks. North Africa was in contact with all the great civilizations of antiquity and became an integral part of the Islamic world at the end of the seventh century CE. Although it has never become wholly arabized like Greater Syria and Egypt, it was totally islamized, with the exception of a Jewish minority that has always been in existence there. Moreover, from the twelfth century CE, the vast majority of the population has followed the Mālikī legal tradition *(madhhab)*.

In North Africa as elsewhere, Islam may be considered either as a religion or as a form of culture, and according to the point of view adopted, the same facts may be interpreted in quite different ways. In the following pages we refer to Islam not as a culture that has been more or less influenced by the Qur'anic message but as a religion. Discussion will center on the movements, the works, and the people who have formed the feelings and the religious behavior of the inhabitants of the Maghreb.

Pre-Islamic Religion. The message of the prophet Muḥammad itself bore the marks of Arab polytheisms, and

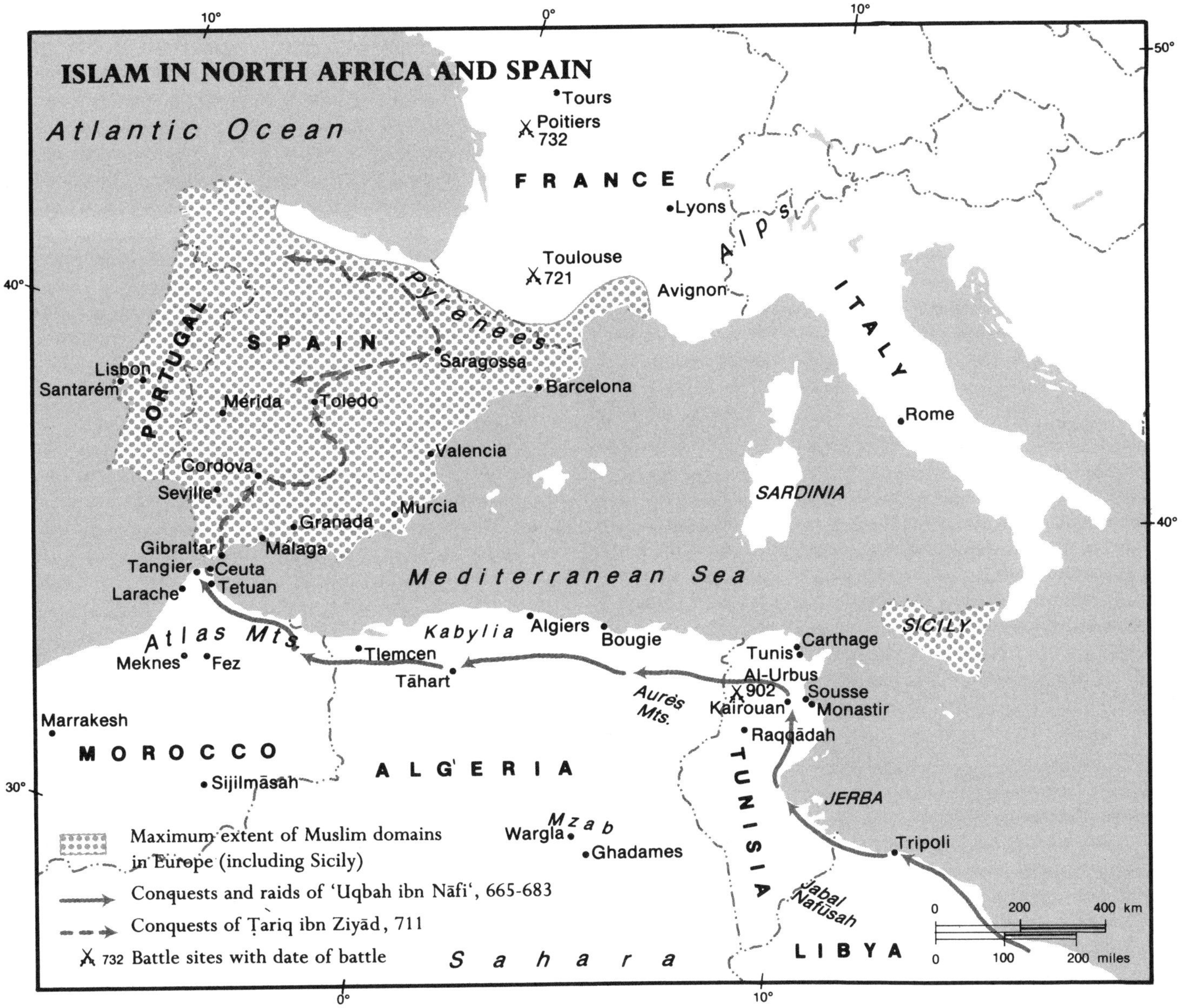

the islamization of North Africa was likewise influenced by the religious situation already present there.

The prehistoric substrate. The prehistory of the Berbers remains obscure. The Libyan inscriptions guard their secrets, and funerary monuments and rock drawings can be interpreted in diverse ways according to whether Egyptian, Mediterranean, or Saharan influences are discerned in them. Scholars do agree, however, on two points: the ancient Berbers did not differentiate between magic—a technique used to harness the powers of nature—and religion—the worship of a divinity with a more or less distinct identity. Later their divinities were exclusively local ones.

Thus, say the specialists, it is better to refer not to a Berber religion as such, but to a specific attitude toward the sacred, which the inhabitants of North Africa associate even today with caves, springs, certain trees, certain stones, and so on. This strategy of the sacred was aimed at satisfying basic needs, such as causing rain, curing an infertile woman, or guaranteeing victory. Its presence has been noted by writers as far apart in time and space as the Greek historian Herodotus (sixth century BCE), the Moroccan traveler Ibn Baṭṭūtah (fourteenth century CE), and the Finnish anthropologist Edward Westermarck (twentieth century). The notion of *barakah* (a polymorphous power linked to holiness), the institution of the *zāwiyah* (a brotherhood centered on a sanctuary), the *ziyārah* (cult of saints), the *shaṭḥ* (a ritual dance), and the *samāʿ* (ritual music) have all played an important role in the religious feeling of the Maghreb people until quite recently, despite the fact that official Islam has opposed them for centuries; many anthropologists maintain that such features can only be explained in terms of this fundamental attitude toward the sacred that had already colored the Phoenician religion, Roman polytheism, and Christianity well before the arrival of Islam.

The Phoenico-Punic influence. The Phoenicians reached the shores of North Africa at the beginning of the first millennium BCE, founded Carthage, and set up a large number of trading posts along the coast. A seafaring nation of traders, they did not venture far into the interior until well into the fifth century BCE. What was their influence on local culture? Historians differ in their assessments, but they all maintain that it was crucial, for the Berbers were also from the East. The punicization of Maghrebi culture did not coincide, however, with the period when Carthage was at the height of its power: it was only after the city was overcome and destroyed (146 BCE) that the *aquellids* ("kings") of Numidia and Mauritania adopted the most characteristic features of Carthaginian civilization. Both epigraphic and archaeological discoveries have shown that the cult was colored by the Phoenico-Punic religion, that the goddess Tanit was accorded an important position, and that child sacrifice, so loathsome to the Romans, was commonplace. This speeding up of the process of punicization seems to have been a deliberate challenge to imperial Rome. According to Stephane Gsell, the French specialist on ancient African history, it also prepared the population for islamization later on.

Romanization and christianization. Roman polytheism as it spread to the peoples of North Africa was inseparable from romanization, which had been, in many respects, quite remarkable. But, challenged by the Carthaginian divinities and soon undermined by Christian propaganda, the Roman religion never had time to gain a permanent foothold. Many studies have shown that it was profoundly africanized. Latin names only superficially mask pre-Roman divinities: Jupiter has been identified with Amun, Saturn—that most African of gods—with Baal-Hammon, Juno-Caelestia with Tanit, Asklepios with Eshmun, and so forth.

The problem of specific local characteristics also arises with reference to African Christianity. The new religion rapidly made converts, especially in the towns, as we can see from the number of followers affected by the persecutions of the third century CE. Nor can we forget the appearance of such great thinkers as the apologist Tertullian (d. after 220 CE), Cyprian, bishop of Carthage (d. 258), and Augustine the church father (d. 430). However, the most significant phenomenon during this period was undoubtedly the Donatist schism, which deeply divided Roman Africa throughout the fourth century. Whether this was an attempt to found a national church or a movement of social protest, the basic point is that it reveals a permanent aspect of the psychology of the Maghrebians. They seem to accept foreign cultures easily enough but select from them one element that they then transform into a symbol of their own identity. In this sense we can say the Donatists foreshadowed the Muslim Khārijīs of three centuries later.

Berber religiosity. North Africa was thus subjected in turn to Egyptian, Phoenician, Greco-Roman, and Christian influences, without any real alteration of its fundamental religious attitude. Foreign religions, which gave the appearance of being accepted without any difficulties, were in fact profoundly transformed on the day-to-day level. Professions of faith, institutions, and cults changed, but what remained intact was a type of religiosity: characterized by its vehemence, its extremism, and its tendency to intellectual simplification, it is to be found at each stage of the development of Maghrebi Islam.

Excessive intellectualism was linked with a strong attachment to the humblest of popular cults, as though the North Africans refused to see religion as a means of individual salvation: the social always took precedence over the individual, the concrete and useful over the purely spiritual. For them, religion was above all a communal ethic. The simpler and clearer the creed, the better it fulfilled its role. Both local cults and elaborate dogma, however far apart they might seem to be from a purely formal point of view, nevertheless tended toward the same end: holding the social body together.

A single religious consciousness expressed in diverse religious forms—this is a hypothesis of continuity that many specialists would be reluctant to accept. However, a number of historians have adopted it, at least as a starting point for their work, even if it has proved necessary to alter it later for a clearer explanation of how the Maghreb became Muslim. Islamization, in North Africa as elsewhere, was a dual process. Islam originated as a set of beliefs and behaviors indigenous to the Arabs of the Middle East, but the long and rich experience of the Maghrebi population that received it was also to determine its final form. Three centuries before the appearance of the first Muslim missionaries, the region, with the exception of Carthage, was totally free from foreign influence. Independent principalities, whose internal histories are relatively obscure, had come into being. Epigraphic evidence proves that the Punic religion and Christianity persisted, that Judaism was spreading, and that Donatism and Manichaeism were flourishing again. It was within this extremely complex situation, with its strange syncretisms, that Islam was to develop. The belief that North Africa went directly from Christian orthodoxy to Sunnī Islam is nothing but an illusion.

The Arab Period. This term, inadequate as it might seem, refers to the period from the second to the fifth Muslim centuries (seventh to eleventh centuries CE). With its own distinctive features, the period was Arab only in a very restricted sense. But under this rubric we shall consider first of all the conquest, or the taking of political power by the warriors from the Middle East; second, islamization, or the adoption of rites and beliefs defined by the Qur'ān; and finally, arabization, in its dual ethnic and cultural senses as a change in the actual makeup of the population and as the adoption of Arab language and customs. These three developments were far from identical.

The conquest. The first Arab armies arrived in Ifrīqiyā (formerly known as Byzacene) in AH 26/647 CE, but the conquest began only nine years later, when ʿUqbah ibn Nāfiʿ founded the city of Kairouan as a permanent base for his soldiers. ʿUqbah decided to skirt the northern towns that had been fortified by the Byzantines and to follow the inland route of the high plateaus, where the independent principalities had been set up. At first these tactics paid off, for the Arab general, after defeating the Berber chief Kusaylah, was able to cross the whole country as far as the Atlantic Ocean without meeting any further resistance. However, on his way back he found that the Berbers and the Byzantines had united to cut off his lines of communication, and his army, which he had misguidedly divided into small groups, was wiped out. Another leader of the conquest, Ḥassān ibn al-Nuʿmān, drew the logical conclusions from this defeat and decided to attack Carthage, which was the center of Byzantine power. He took it by storm in 691, lost it, then recaptured it definitively in 695. It was at that moment that the mountain people of the Aures, who had fought fiercely for their independence against the Vandals and the Byzantines during the past two centuries, rose up in revolt under the leadership of a woman the Arabs called al-Kāhinah ("the sorceress"). Since the conquerors are interested only in our wealth, al-Kāhinah reasoned, let us turn our land into a desert and they will leave. She then gave the order to cut down all the trees, thus causing a terrible deforestation with consequences that are still felt today. Is this truth or legend? In either case, this last-ditch effort did not have the anticipated results. The Arabs did not leave the devastated land, and al-Kāhinah, seeing how things were turning out and herself unable to surrender, advised her sons to go over to the enemy. Military operations continued for another ten years or so in the west of the country. The new general, Mūsā ibn Nuṣayr, returning to the policy of one of his predecessors, Abū al-Muḥājir, widely applied the system of *walā'* ("adoption") and took into the Arab aristocracy the sons of the vanquished leaders. This ethnic interpenetration was so rapid that the conquest of Spain, which began in 711, was led by a *mawlā* ("client") of Mūsā, the Berber Ṭāriq ibn Ziyād.

Unlike the centralized monarchies of Egypt, Persia, and Spain, whose destinies were sealed by the outcome of a single battle with the Muslims, the Maghreb was conquered definitively only after a half-century of fighting. There were several reasons for this. Mountainous, compartmentalized, and politically fragmented, the country was always difficult to conquer. The Arabs were faced with several different groups: Rūm (Byzantines), Afranj (Romans), Afāriq (punicized Berbers), nomad and sedentary peoples. Each of these groups had its own defense tactics and had to be countered by an appropriate attack. Berber resistance varied between the policy of Kusaylah and that of al-Kāhinah, and the Arab strategy also wavered between the rigor of ʿUqbah and the liberalism of Abū al-Muḥājir. Moreover, the conquering armies felt the repercussions of the crises that shook the Muslim caliphate from 660 to 694.

Some historians who are not specialists on Islam believe that the first Arab conquerors were nomads like the Banū Hilāl, who invaded the country more than three centuries later. This belief is wholly erroneous; they were in fact highly skilled horsemen, trained in the latest cavalry tactics. Most of them came from Syria and were the descendants of men who had been in contact with the Romans and the Byzantines for generations. Thus they came to the Maghreb as heirs of ancient civilizations. As time went on, the neo-Byzantine character of the Arab administration became more and more obvious.

Arabization. From an ethnic point of view, the process of arabization seems to have been very limited in scope. According to the most reliable historians, the number of Arabs settled in the country during the first Muslim century did not exceed fifty thousand. The local population, especially in Ifrīqiyā, was already fairly mixed; this characteristic was accentuated by the conquest, for the "Arab" armies in fact included Byzantines, Persians, and, very early on, Berbers, probably nomads, who were later known as Zanātah.

The adoption of Arab customs, habits, costume, and language was doubtless very rapid; the early Arab chroniclers all emphasize the Himyarite (Yemenite) origin of the Berbers, which suggests that a feeling of distant ethnic solidarity existed. The system of *walā'* meant that many Berber clans were linked with the

Qahtanites (southern Arabs). The word *berber* rapidly lost its original etymological meaning and came to designate the inhabitants of isolated mountain regions. Since islamization, the fundamental distinction in North Africa has been sociocultural rather than ethnicolinguistic.

Cultural arabization was naturally enhanced when political authority was in Arab hands. During the period under consideration the power of the Arabs was solidly established in what is now Tunisia and in that part of Spain bordering on the Mediterranean. These were populated, prosperous regions, easy to defend, where the Punic influence had been deep and lasting. Kairouan and Cordova, the capitals of the two provinces, maintained uninterrupted relations with the other Muslim metropoles and were the starting points for the spread of Arab culture and orthodox Islam.

After the conquest the Maghreb was governed by emirs appointed by the Umayyad caliphs in Damascus. With the Abbasid Revolution of 750, which saw the capital transferred to Baghdad, the empire became more Persian than Arab, more Asian than Mediterranean. The western provinces, which from then on would be more difficult to watch over, began to break away one after the other. In 755 an Umayyad prince who had fled to Spain founded an independent emirate there. In 787 Idrīs I, a descendant of ʿAlī ibn Abī Ṭālib, did the same in Morocco. Finally, in 800, Ifrīqiyā achieved autonomy under the Aghlabid dynasty, with the consent of the caliph.

In the ninth century, the Umayyad and Aghlabid emirates exercised military and commercial control over the whole of the western Mediterranean. Muslim Spain, which became a caliphate in 929, retained its preeminence right up to the great crisis of 1009; its capital, Cordova, was the equivalent of Baghdad or Cairo. The western half of the Maghreb lived in the sphere of Spain's cultural and political influence; the princes of Ceuta, Fez, Tlemcen, and elsewhere, whether Arabs or Berbers, were clients of the caliph of Cordova, and as such they spread Andalusian culture and Umayyad orthodoxy.

As for the Aghlabid emirate, it fell victim to the propaganda of the Shīʿī Fatimids, who maintained that only the descendants of ʿAlī and Fāṭimah, the cousin and daughter respectively of the prophet Muḥammad, could legitimately lay claim to the caliphate. One of their *dāʿīs* ("missionaries") who had come from the Yemen settled among the Kutāmah Berbers in the mountainous region of Little Kabylia. There, surrounded by a population favorable to the ʿAlids and out of the reach of Aghlabid power, he patiently bided his time. The Aghlabid army, weakened by the quarrels that split the reigning family, was crushed at al-Urbus (ancient Laribus) in 909, and the residence of the emirs, Raqqādah, was taken by storm. A year later the real pretender arrived and officially adopted the title of ʿUbayd Allāh al-Mahdī. But for the victorious Fatimids Ifrīqiyā was no more than a base for the conquest of the Abbasid empire. Once they had taken command of Egypt in 969, they abandoned Ifrīqiyā to their Kutāmah allies. Thus two dynasties were born: the Zirids in what is now Tunisia, and the Hammadids in the east of present-day Algeria; both were descendants of Zīrī ibn Manād, the army general who became regent after the departure of the Fatimid caliph, and both were to prosper until the mid-eleventh century.

Applied to this period, then, the term *Arab* is clearly inadequate. It was indeed princes from the East who founded states and created cities where the army, the administration, and the religious institutions spread Arab culture, but very early on political power was shared; without the Awribah, Idrīs I would never have reigned, and without the Kutāmah, ʿUbayd Allāh could never have laid claim to the caliphate.

There is no doubt that the process of arabization was very slow. Epigraphic finds have shown that Punic and Roman-Christian influences subsisted for a long time after the conquest, but the importance of such relics must not be exaggerated. The narratives that tell the story of the beginning of the Fatimid dynasty show clearly that the Kutāmah homeland, although it was far from the capital and isolated by its mountainous surroundings, was nevertheless open to the influence of the cities, which were themselves wholly given over to the distinctive values of Arab culture. Arabization was set in motion by Arab governors, but it did not cease when the power passed into Berber hands, as we can see from the behavior of the Zirid and Hammadid princes, who were direct descendants of the Ṣanhājah Berbers.

Islamization. In 660 a serious crisis split the eastern Muslim community. Two opposing clans were struggling for the caliphate: the supporters of Muʿāwiyah and the Umayyad family in general, and the followers of ʿAlī ibn Abī Ṭālib and, by extension, the Hashimites, the Prophet's clan. Later there appeared a more neutral faction who maintained that authority should be conferred by election and that the caliph could be non-Qurayshī and even non-Arab. The last mentioned were known as Khārijīs; the second were called Shīʿah; and the first, *ahl al-jamāʿah*, that is to say, the supporters of the majority, who were later to become the Sunnīs (orthodox ones). At first all three factions were similarly Arab; but when the conquering Umayyads set up a predominantly Qurayshī administration in Damascus, the Shīʿah and the Khārijīs turned toward the newly converted, and, confronted by Sunnism—an official, conservative, moderate Islam that was also an Arab Islam—they took up a non-Arab and sometimes even a frankly anti-Arab stance.

Islam spread more rapidly in North Africa than did the Arab language. This was a paradoxical result of the schismatic propaganda, for the autonomy movement, which was directed against the political power of the Arabs and their clients, endowed Islam with a profoundly national character.

After the death of al-Kāhinah in 701, the conquest was almost completed. The new rulers, seeking to reorganize the country, imposed a regular tax system. But since the decline of the Roman empire the population had become used to living in small, independent communities. As early as 720 the Berbers of Ifrīqiyā rose up and killed the emir, Ibn al-Ḥabḥāb. In 740 a more serious revolt broke out in northern Morocco and soon spread throughout the whole of North Africa. One of the main rebel chiefs, Maysarah, had lived in Kairouan, where he had come under the influence of the Ṣufrīyah, who were Khārijī extremists. Thus the Berbers rose up in the name of those values of justice, equality, and austerity that had been taught by Islam itself but that, in the Berber view, had been betrayed by the Umayyads. In 740, on the banks of the Chelif River, in the center of what is now Algeria, the flower of the Arab aristocracy fell in the Battle of the Nobles *(ghazwat al-ashrāf).* Thenceforth, the western half of the Maghreb was independent. The struggle continued to the east, but no decisive battle was won against the rebels. The new rulers of the empire, the Abbasids, despairing of a rapid victory over this distant province, delegated their authority to Ibrāhīm ibn al-Aghlab, a brilliant general who had defended Zāb, in the south of present-day Tunisia, against the insurgents; this event led to the birth of the Aghlabid dynasty within the frontiers of what had been Roman Africa.

The Khārijīs were now in command of the central and western Maghreb, but they soon proved to be incapable of establishing a great state. As proponents of absolute equality, they refused any form of hierarchy or discipline; they accepted without discrimination all those who shared their beliefs. They had a taste for theological controversies and, in case of disagreement over a point of dogma, they would depose their imams and, in some cases, kill them. The principalities that they founded after 754 had shifting frontiers and rudimentary structures. Entrepôt towns like Tāhart in western Algeria and Sijilmāsah in southwestern Morocco were situated at the junction of the important communication routes between east and west, between the Sahara and the Mediterranean, and as such were busy and prosperous despite their political instability. The state of Barghwāṭah, founded at the same period on the rich Atlantic plains, was just as prosperous, according to travelers in the tenth century; the fruit of the Khārijī revolt, it tended more and more toward a very broad syncretism. [*See* Khārijīs.]

After Khārijism, it was Shiism that dominated the political and religious history of the Maghreb. Indeed, the founding of the Idrisid kingdom was probably not fortuitous. There is some evidence for the existence of a real network of Shīʿī missionaries who took to the western routes from Medina or Iraq to spread their good word. They began by questioning students and pilgrims from the Maghreb about the state of mind of their countrymen. If the latter seemed to nurture some sympathy for the ʿAlids and if they were unhappy with their rulers, then a missionary was sent over to find out firsthand what the situation was and perhaps prepare the ground for the arrival of the ʿAlid pretender. The success of Idrīs I encouraged several of the descendants of Ḥasan ibn ʿAlī to follow his example. In the middle of the eleventh century, nearly a dozen Hasanid princes were established in the west of Algeria. Some confined themselves to the role of honored guests, while others were regarded as local chiefs, although their ambitions were limited by the fact that they had no armies. Owing to the presence of so many ʿAlid "guests," Shīʿī ideology was able to permeate Maghrebi society, sometimes replacing Khārijī thought, sometimes combining it with older beliefs to produce strange syncretisms. We find one example in the region of Ghumārah, south of Tetuan, where a pseudo-prophet called Hā' Mīm founded a separate cult in conjunction with his aunt, Tangīt. The victory of the Fatimids would be incomprehensible without the preliminary activity of the Shīʿī missionaries. The notion of Mahdi (messiah), the dispenser of justice who brings to a close an era of injustice, may or may not have sounded the echo of ancient beliefs, but henceforth it was to become a permanent aspect of the mentality of the Maghreb, before taking on official status with the Almohads. [*See* Shiism.]

The Islam that was spread among the Berbers by the schisms now seems to us to be very unorthodox, but can we really speak of orthodoxy in relation to that far-off time when no remotely hierarchical institution existed? As long as there was no strong state capable of imposing an official ideology throughout North Africa, there was room enough for different interpretations of dogma, and these ultimately deepened the impact of the Qur'anic message. The Fatimids were the first to attempt the political and ideological unification of the Maghreb; the Khārijīs were almost completely eradicated, with the exception of the Mzab region in southern Algeria and Jabal Nafūsah to the west of what is now Libya, where communities persist down to the present day. It was with the Almoravids that Mālikī Sunnism was to triumph, mainly because islamization had already been achieved through the activity of the schismatics.

Literary works. Berber literature has always been basically oral. Berber prophets like Ṣāliḥ of the Barghwāṭah or Hā' Mīm of the Ghumārah probably employed oral means of communication. Although the eleventh-century Andalusian geographer al-Bakrī asserts that the Barghwāṭah had a Qur'ān in Berber, no trace of this has been found so far.

If no written document exists to shed light on the syncretisms, this is not so for the Khārijīs. After the fall of Tā-hart, the survivors fled to Mzab with their sacred books, and in this way two important works were saved. The first, *Kitāb akhbār al-Rustumīyīn* (Memorable Events in the History of the Rustimid Imams), was written by Ibn al-Ṣaghīr (d. 894), who was alive at the time of the events he recorded; the second, *Kitāb al-sīrah wa-akhbār al-a'immah* (Lives and Works of the Imams), is a later work—its author, Abū Zakarīyā', lived in the eleventh century—although it remains with in the limits of the period under consideration. Both texts are concerned above all with enlightening the faithful; nevertheless they give us some historical information and clues to the psychology of the Khārijīs in the Maghreb.

The early Shī'ī movement did not leave behind comparable works; it is known only through the prehistory of the Fatimid dynasty as it was recorded by Qāḍī al-Nu'mān ibn Ḥayyūn (d. 974). This writer was the main ideologue of the Fatimids. In his major work, *Iftitāḥ al-da'wah* (Our First Missions), he describes, with remarkable objectivity and accuracy, the region that escaped the political control of the Aghlabids while remaining open to their cultural influence.

The most important works of this period, however, were conceived in Kairouan. Until the eleventh century, profane literature was dominated by émigrés from the East, but local writers won renown in the field of religious culture. At first Ifrīqiyā followed the example of Baghdad and adopted the legal tradition of Abū Ḥanīfah (d. 768), but it soon came to favor that of Mālik ibn Anas (d. 796). What was the reason for this preference? It seems that there were several. Students and pilgrims from the Maghreb went more readily to the Hejaz, Mālik's home, than to Iraq, where Abū Ḥanīfah was born. Since he had lived all his life in Medina, Mālik seemed to guarantee greater fidelity to the tradition of the Prophet. Many of the inhabitants of the Maghreb wished, perhaps unconsciously, to dissociate themselves from the East but without falling into the schisms. Finally, the Mālikī school, which was simpler than the Ḥanafī, was better suited to the society of Ifrīqiyā, which was still predominantly rural and thus relatively homogeneous.

But whatever the causes, the results were of major importance. The Mālikī school in Kairouan took decisive steps toward the ideological unification of the Maghreb. 'Abd al-Salām ibn Sa'īd, known as Saḥnūn (d. 854), set down in his *Mudawwanah* (a handbook of Mālikī law) the code of the civil society of the Islamic Maghreb. Doubtless many ancestral or even prehistoric customs persisted, but they were judged by reference to the model laid down in the *Mudawwanah*. From now on the Mālikī *faqīh* (jurisprudent) was one of the two most important figures in society. The other was the *'ābid* (man of God) who disdained any honors offered him, was always ready to criticize the powers that be, and thus was able to channel popular discontent. The master among these was Buhlūl ibn Rāshid (d. 799), who, along with others like him, was said to have prepared the blossoming of those brotherhoods *(zawāyā)* that were so characteristic of Berber religiosity. If Sunnism prevailed in the end, it was thanks to men like him, whose example suggested how to influence the government by means other—and better—than bloody rebellion. As the society became more urbanized and more stable, such an example found even greater echoes. These ascetics have not left any written works, but their attitude has been described in detail and their sayings recorded in the *manāqib* (hagiography) literature, beginning with the *Ṭabaqāt 'ulamā' Ifrīqiyā wa-Tūnus* (Biographies of the Religious Scholars of Ifrīqiyā and Tunis) by Abū al-'Arab Muḥammad ibn Tamīm (d. 944).

When, in the middle of the tenth century, the Kutāmah Berbers inherited a stable, prosperous state that soon gained its autonomy, they encouraged the growth of a genuinely local literature. The second Zirid emir, al-Manṣūr ibn Buluggīn (984–996), left Raqqādah, the former Aghlabid residence, and went to live in great luxury in Ṣabrā-Manṣūrīyah, where the court life, so typical of Islamic civilization, favored the development of *ādāb* (profane literature). Here we may mention the names of three men whose fame extended far beyond the frontiers of Ifrīqiyā. Ibrāhīm ibn al-Raqīq (d. 1027) was chancellery secretary and a committed Shī'ī; his vast historical work, *Ta'rīkh Ifrīqiyā wa-al-Maghrib*, served as a reference for all subsequent chroniclers, although very little of it has come down to us. Muḥammad ibn Sa'īd ibn Sharaf (d. 1067) was known as both a poet and a historiographer; his treatise of literary criticism, *Masā'il al-intiqād*, has been translated into several European languages. Ḥasan ibn Rashīq (d. 1064), a poet and anthologist, has left to posterity a book of rhetoric *(Kitāb al-ʿumdah)* that is remarkable for the depth of its analysis and the elegance of its style.

The mosques of Kairouan and Sousse, the remains of the palace in Raqqādah, the fortresses of Belezma and Baghā'ī, the citadels of Sousse and Monastir, all bear witness to the wealth of the reigning dynasties and the adaptation of Islamic art to North Africa. The architecture of this period resulted from a harmonious symbiosis of the Byzantine heritage, the influence of Abbasid Iraq, and a spirit of sobriety that was expressed in the asceticism of a man like Buhlūl.

The Berber Period. The culture of Ifrīqiyā reached its peak in the eleventh century and then spread throughout the Maghreb as a result of the unifying policies of the Almoravid, Almohad, and Marinid dynasties. For want of a better name, the three hundred years from the mid-eleventh to the mid-fourteenth century, when supreme power was in the hands of the Berber dynasties, is known as the Berber period, but the term is as unsatisfactory as the adjective *Arab* that I applied to the previous three centuries. Indeed, neither arabization nor islamization had been halted, and on the contrary, it was in this period that they reached the point of no return.

The three Berber dynasties practiced an imperial policy aimed at the unification of the Maghreb; although this attempt failed in the end, it left indelible traces. In the eleventh century there was an obvious difference between the eastern and western halves of the Maghreb. The former was Arab in culture and politically unified, while the latter was fragmented into numerous principalities that were fought over by the rulers of Cordova and Kairouan. Maghrāwah and Miknāsah, alternately serving the interests of one and the other, wore themselves out in a series of fruitless conflicts. Quite suddenly and for various reasons, the caliphate of Cordova disappeared in 1031, and the Zirid and Hammadid emirates in 1052; with this vacuum on the North African political scene, the time of the western Maghreb had come. The Almoravid Lamtūnah, starting from the Atlantic region of the Sahara, built an empire around Marrakesh (founded in 1062); this empire, which lasted until 1146, stretched from Andalusia to the Sahara and from Algiers to the Atlantic. The Almoravids were replaced by the Almohads, whose main strength came from the Maṣmūdah of the High Atlas; extending the empire they had inherited as far as Tripoli, they reigned in Marrakesh until 1276 and, under the name of the Hafsids, in Tunis until 1573. Then came the turn of the Zanātah shepherds from the borders of Algeria and Morocco, who, as the Marinids and then the Wattasids, reigned in Fez until 1550 and, as the Zayyanid-ʿAbd al-Wadids, in Tlemcen until 1554.

Unlike the Kutāmah, the Berber groups from the western Maghreb had not set out at the call of an Arab refugee. In both cases, however, the seizure of power by a Berber dynasty was accompanied by cultural arabization that owed its fast pace to the luxurious life of the court. Ethnic arabization was intensified too, since the Banū Hilāl Bedouins, who were responsible for the fall of the Zirid and Hammadid emirates, continued to emigrate to the Maghreb right up to the fifteenth century; the last to arrive, the Banū Maʿqil, arabized the province of Shangīṭ, which lies to the north of what is now Mauritania.

The Almoravid movement. One of the leaders of the Lamtūnah, on his way back from a pilgrimage to Mecca, attended the lessons given by Abū ʿImrān al-Fāsī, a famous man of law from Morocco. "My countrymen," he told the teacher, "know nothing of true Islam and have need of a guide. Who would you recommend?" Abū ʿImrān replied, "Go on my behalf to see Wajjāj, who knows your region well." Wajjāj in turn directed the Lamtūnah chief to a *faqīh* from Sijilmāsah called ʿAbd Allāh ibn Yāsīn. When they got back to the Sahara, the warrior chief and the missionary founded a *ribāṭ* (monastery) where the future leaders of the movement gathered together; for this reason they were given the name *al-murābiṭūn*, transformed by the Spanish into Almoravids. Later, under the leadership of Yūsuf ibn Tāshfīn, the disciples of Ibn Yāsīn set out to conquer a vast empire.

This story closely resembles that of Abū ʿAbd Allāh, the Fatimid *dāʿī*, apart from the fact that this time the missionary was Sunnī. The Almoravid movement in the West, like the Seljuk movement in the East, belonged to the vast counteroffensive launched by the Abbasids in the eleventh century to destroy Shiism and repel the Christian crusade. One of the spiritual fathers of the movement, the Mālikī *qāḍī* al-Bāqillānī (d. 1013), was Abū ʿImrān's teacher, and it was with the blessing of the grest jurisprudents of the East that Yūsuf ibn Tāshfīn overthrew the Andalusian princes and took the title of Amīr al-Muslimīn ("commander of the Muslims"), which symbolized his supreme authority in the Muslim West under the suzerainty of the Abbasid caliphs.

In the new Almoravid state the *faqīh*s held pride of place. Chosen from among the early adherents of the movement, they set out to defend and spread the official ideology. They gave advice to local emirs, kept a close watch on the verdicts of the courts, preached asceticism to the governed and austerity to the governing. Qāḍī ʿIyād of Ceuta (d. 1149) was the embodiment of this clerical caste. He left many works, two of which were of considerable importance. His *Shifā'* (Book of Healing), which draws a complete portrait of the Prophet, simultaneously gives readers an example to follow at every moment of their lives, thus proving that, contrary to Shīʿī thought, they had no need of an imam to guide them to the truth. In the *Kitāb al-madārik* (Book of Exploits), he drew up a long list of the celebrities of the Mālikī school. This book completed the work that Abū al-ʿArab had begun by putting together what can be considered a veritable patrology of Maghrebi Islam.

However, in spite of the wholehearted support of the state, Mālikī preeminence was short-lived, and with the coming of the Almohad dynasty the Maghreb was once more to experience a schism. Official Almoravid ideology seems to have lagged behind the sociointellectual evolution of the rest of the Islamic world. Whereas in the East, thanks to al-Ghazālī (d. 1111), Sunnism had succeeded in integrating dialectical theology *(kalām)*, logic *(manṭiq)*, and mysticism *(taṣawwuf)*; and while in Andalusia, Ibn Ḥazm (d. 1064) was pioneering new directions in juridical thought, the Mālikīyah of the Maghreb remained blindly attached to the school of Kairouan and refused any kind of reform. When in power they applied a reactionary policy in the true sense of the term, refusing to systematize the *fiqh* in the manner of al-Shāfiʿī (d. 820), condemning and burning all the works of al-Ghazālī, and declaring war on popular piety. They formed an isolated, activist minority that refused the spirit of the *sunnah*, that is, to choose the middle way and always seek the consensus of the majority. It was not until they had suffered bitterly from the persecution of the Almohads that they discovered the virtues of moderation.

The Almohads. From a political point of view, the Almohad century represented the apogee of North African history, but from a religious point of view it was simply an interlude. The official ideology, which from the very beginning had been opposed by the *ʿulamāʾ* and later was to be seen as schismatic by a majority of the population, was eventually repudiated by the descendants of those who had established it in the first place. How can we explain its appearance? Was it a belated offshoot of earlier schisms? An original creation stemming from the Berber mentality? A national religion comparable with what was to become Twelver Shiism in Persia? All of these remain questions without answers.

Muḥammad ibn Tūmart, the Almohad ideologue, unlike Ibn Yāsīn, was not the propagandist of a movement that was external to his native region. Toward 1107 he left southern Morocco for Cordova, where he immersed himself in the teachings of Ibn Ḥazm, then traveled on to Iraq where, according to some biographers, he may have met al-Ghazālī. About 1116 he began to return homeward, stopping off for a long time in Alexandria, Tunis, Bougie, Tlemcen, Fez, and Meknes. In each of these cities he set himself up as the arbiter of morals, antagonizing the local authorities but gaining disciples who, like ʿAbd al-Muʾmin al-Gūmī, became fanatical followers. When he arrived in the Almoravid capital of Marrakesh, he challenged the *faqīh*s and led them into theological controversies for which they were ill prepared. An advocate of strict monotheism *(tawḥīd)* who made no concessions to popular imagination, he accused his adversaries of anthropomorphism *(tajsīm)*. In fact, *Almohad* is a Spanish distortion of the Arabic *al-muwaḥḥid* ("unitarian").

Expelled from the capital in 1121, Ibn Tūmart took refuge in Tinmal in the High Atlas; there, surrounded by his followers, and with the support of the Hintātah Berbers, a clan of the Maṣmūdah, he put himself forward as a candidate for the imamate. He spent seven years organizing a veritable revolutionary army, then set out in 1128 to attack Marrakesh. The Almoravid empire was still in the prime of youth, and the attacking army was repelled with serious losses, although Ibn Tūmart's forces were able to regain a place of refuge without being pursued. Ibn Tūmart died soon after this defeat, but he left behind him a perfectly tuned instrument of warfare. His successor, ʿAbd al-Muʾmin, had only to choose tactics of attrition to overcome the power of the Almoravids.

Ibn Tūmart was closely involved in the ideological training of his disciples and for their benefit wrote a series of theological texts that have come down to us. Like the Khārijīs, he held that faith *(imān)* should not be passive, and he believed that he had to actively follow good and fight against evil. Like the Muʿtazilah, he defined the divine attributes in strictly rational terms, with recourse if need be to *taʾwīl* (allegorical interpretation). As the leader of an independent school, he applied *ijtihād*, following his own opinions without reference to a particular legal school. As a pretender to political power, he claimed ʿAlid ancestry and presented himself as the infallible imam *(maʿṣūm)*, the Mahdi whose coming had been so long awaited by the weak and the oppressed. Here we are far from the Mālikī school, but the only point that was really unacceptable to a Sunnī Muslim was the doctrine of infallibility, and this was to be abandoned in Marrakesh in 1229 and later in Tunis by the Hafsids. If Ibn Tūmart had contented himself with claiming the right to *ijtihād*, the *faqīh*s would have have been able to do no more than question his abilities, without ever going so far as to condemn him for heresy.

The arrival of a man like Ibn Tūmart in a region that was so far from the great cultural centers shows to what extent the Maghreb had been islamized; however, it would be a serious error to consider the Almohads a purely local phenomenon; their ideology expressed a general desire to go beyond the narrow legalism of the Mālikī school, to apply logic to both law and theology. This was in fact achieved in the following century. To the extent that there is today a homogeneous Maghrebi people, in spite of their internal diversity, this is the result of the policy of the Almohad caliphs. Ibn Tūmart owed his victory to the support of the Maṣmūdah in the Moroccan High Atlas, who were then to play a leading role in the empire. However, his successor, Caliph ʿAbd al-Muʾmin, came from western Algeria, and, according to the chroniclers, he brought forty thousand of his countrymen with him to Morocco in order to reinforce his personal power. During his later campaigns, when he came up against the Zanātah, arabized Berbers migrating along the Algerian-Moroccan borders, he moved them to the regions of Meknes and Taza; he likewise sent the Banū Hilāl, Arab Bedouins from Ifrīqiyā, to the Atlantic plains. He imposed military service on both groups and in return granted them *iqṭāʿ*s, tax farms for vast tracts of land. Thus there came into being a caste of soldiers who were superimposed on the local population and who brought with them their Arab culture and language. In this way the arabization of the plains and plateaus of the Maghreb was completed. Both toponymy and anthroponymy bear witness to the fact that the same groups were to be found everywhere.

This period also saw the development of a pietistic religious movement that had its origins in Almoravid times. Encouraged by the victory of the Almohads, it was nonetheless distinguished from them from the beginning by its aims and methods. Ibn Tūmart's intellectualism was permeated with great fervor, and yet its austerity left no room for the religious sentimentality that the people doubtless needed. Numerous ascetics left for the countryside to spread the word of God to the people in a colorful language that was simple enough to be understood by the least educated. Only a very few of them were real *faqīh*s, and some were even quite uneducated, but they were all men of God. They settled in lodges (*zāwiyah*s) far from any town, where they spent their days in prayer and meditation. For the scattered populations that still had no fixed homes, these lodges became centers where they could gather, and in fact they were the forerunners of what are today the *mawāsim* (annual fairs; sg., *mawsim*). The biographies of these men, the greatest of whom was ʿAbd al-Salām ibn Mashīsh (d. 1128), can be found in the *Tashawwuf* of Ibn al-Zayyāt. It was with this movement that Islam truly became the culture of the people of the Maghreb.

Two centuries later than Ifrīqiyā but on a larger scale, the western Maghreb in its turn witnessed a court life that was to familiarize it with Arab-Islamic civilization. By emulating the Andalusian émigrés, Moroccans such as Abū Jaʿfar ibn ʿAṭīyah (d. 1158), Ibn Ḥabbūs (d. 1174), and Aḥmad al-Jarāwī (d. 1212) distinguished themselves in the field of profane literature. A school of historiography also came into being, and through it we obtain our first glimpses of the interior of the western Maghreb. The most important authors in this field were Ibn al-Qattān, who lived during the reign of Caliph al-Murtaḍā (1248–1266), ʿAbd al-Wāḥid al-Marrākushī (d. 1230), and Ibn ʿIdhārī (d. after 1213). For the first time, too, a Maghrebi capital, Marrakesh, could be compared with Cordova or Cairo. The celebrated Andalusian philosophers and jurists Ibn Ṭufayl (d. 1185) and Ibn Rushd and Ibn Zuhr (who both died in 1198) lived there for many years and wrote some of their most important works there. During the Almohad period the art of the Maghreb reached the height of its greatness and harmony. Rigor, sobriety, and modesty were the characteristics ascribed to the ideology of Ibn Tūmart and to the collective psychology of the Maghrebi people.

The post-Almohad period. The Almohad empire, exhausted by its wars in Andalusia against the combined forces of Christendom, finally gave way to three dynasties that divided the North African territory among themselves. Under the descendants of Abū Ḥafṣ ʿUmar, one of the first disciples of Ibn Tūmart, Ifrīqiyā once more became autonomous within its former frontiers. The Hafsids remained loyal to Almohad ideas for a certain time, then dissociated themselves and were reconciled with the Mālikī *ʿulamāʾ*. The rest of the Maghreb was shared between two Zanātah groups: the Marinids in Fez and the Zayyanids in Tlemcen. The Marinids, who considered themselves the sole rightful heirs of the Almohads, attempted to rebuild the empire but failed, and after 1350 the three dynasties coexisted more or less peacefully.

The Maghreb of the fourteenth century was homogeneous. Various names were used for what was in fact the same political organization, the Almohad *makhzan* (state government) that had been directly inherited by some and copied by others. The army was dominated everywhere by the Banū Hilāl, the bureaucracy by the Andalusian émigrés who brought with them their refined system of etiquette. The retreat of the Andalusians from Spain marked the third step in the cultural arabization of the country. Fashions in dress or cooking, language, music, architecture, decoration, all the framework of a certain kind of middle-class existence, still bear witness to this cultural influence today. The same names, the same customs, the same way of speaking are to be found in Fez, Tlemcen, and Tunis.

The failure of Ibn Tūmart's extremism left the field clear for a renewed Sunnism that was both faithful to the heritage of the past and open to the new questions that the Almohad crisis had brought to light. The Marinids, who had no ideological pretensions, took the advice of the *'ulamā'* and, following the example of the Seljuks in the East, set up *madrasahs*, colleges where the Islamic disciplines were taught from an orthodox viewpoint. These were immediately copied by the Zayyanids and Hafsids. The teaching was organized by the authorities, but its content was defined by the consensus of the *'ulamā'*, based on a tradition that was nurtured by the vast body of biographical literature of the *ṭabaqāt*. The growing number of pupils led to a need for manuals; thus began the era of dry, hermetic summaries that soon required long commentaries *(shurūḥ)*. This was perhaps an inevitable development, but one that turned out to be negative in the long run.

Official Islam. As the reigning dynasties grew weaker, the *'ulamā'*, without ever becoming truly independent, gained more power and put the finishing touches on an official ideology that was characterized by moderation, simplicity, and positivity. For a long time Sunnī Islam had been faced with a precise problem: the rationalization of law, theology, and mysticism. The Ẓāhirī and Shāfi'ī jurists claimed that it was possible to reduce the various Qur'anic dictates to a few laws. The Mu'tazilī and Ash'arī theologians wanted to derive all the attributes of God from a single principle. The mystics of the school of Ibn 'Arabī (d. 1240) justified their metaphysical monism with the desire to be identified with God. The Mālikī *faqīhs*, taking a completely different viewpoint, considered this attempt at systematization useless methodological extremism. For them, Islam is above all a divine order *(amr)* that is self-evident. The duty of the Muslim is to obey this order; hence the cardinal importance of the notion of *bid'ah*, innovation in regard to ritual. The Prophet is by definition the perfect believer; why go beyond what he taught his followers? Does this not imply either that he was not perfect or that he did not transmit faithfully the message of God?

Since Islam is above all a *sharī'ah* (law; lit., "path"), *fiqh* is the central discipline in Islamic science. The community can always do without theologians and mystics, as in Medina at the epoch of the Prophet, but it cannot live without *faqīhs*, who form an integral part of the governing elite. And because *fiqh* fills a social need, it must be founded on a simple *'aqīdah* (profession of faith), that of the *salaf* ("ancestors"); any attempt to complete it or to clarify it would lead inevitably to endless dissension. *Fiqh*, the constitution of the Muslim community, is a positive element and must be accepted as such; it is justified by the will of God, which is itself inseparable from the final good of humanity.

Such an attitude is easy to understand in the light of the disastrous consequences that partisan rifts have had throughout the history of Islam, but it is impossible to ignore the fact that as this attitude became more widespread, it tended to discourage any form of intellectual curiosity. Indeed, the last achievements in the exact and natural sciences date from no later than the fifteenth century in the Maghreb.

The history of the Maghreb seems to come to a standstill at the moment when Islam assumed its definitive characteristics. Contemporary scholars were aware of this and attempted to record, in encyclopedic form, the knowledge handed down from past centuries. One such example in the field of law is the *Mi'yār* (Norm) of al-Wansharīsī (d. 1508). Ibn Khaldūn (d. 1406), the greatest thinker ever produced by the Islamic Maghreb, also endowed his famous *Muqaddimah* (Prolegomena) with an encyclopedic content. This work was the conclusion of a deep reflection on the history of the Maghreb, widened to include the entire Arab-Islamic past. The author, who had been a serious student of Greco-Arab philosophy and who was personally inclined toward mysticism, nevertheless remained absolutely faithful to Mālikī methodology. In two brilliant chapters of his main work, he contrasts the positivism of *fiqh* with the rationalism of *kalām* on the one hand, and the monism of mysticism on the other. More important, he reveals the sociological basis for such a contrast: universal history, according to him, had evolved from *'umrān badawī* (rural civilization) to *'umrān madanī* (urban civilization). In the Maghreb the two kinds of culture exist side by side, resulting in a structural dichotomy. In the city, society tends naturally toward a religion of reason, whereas rural society upholds a naturalist religion: the sultan (the political authority) plays the role of mediator between the two forms of social life; his official ideology, Mālikī *fiqh*, must necessarily remain at an equal distance from rationalism and naturalism, hence its qualities of positivism and moderation.

The Islam of the Zāwiyahs. During the fourteenth and fifteenth centuries the Maghreb underwent a general crisis. Nomadic life spread at the expense of a ruined agriculture; commerce languished and plunged the cities into profound inactivity. The Spanish and the Portuguese, masters of the seas, conquered many ports on the North African coasts. Faced with such unfavorable developments and already weakened by incessant wars, the three reigning dynasties collapsed.

The Ottoman Turks. This period began with the Portuguese seizure of Ceuta in 1415 and ended with the defeat of the Spanish in Tunis in 1574, and of the Portuguese in Wādi al-Makhāzin near Larache in 1578. Morocco was saved by an outburst of nationalism, the rest of North Africa by the Ottoman Turks.

Ottoman sovereignty theoretically persisted in Algeria until 1830, in Tunisia until 1881, and in Libya until 1911. However, from 1710 on, each of these provinces gained its autonomy. The official language was Turkish, but Arabic remained the language of culture. The Ottomans reintroduced Ḥanafī law into the Maghreb; the resulting competition with Mālikī law rekindled interest in long-neglected disciplines such as *uṣūl al-fiqh* (fundamental principles of law) and *kalām*. In Morocco, under the new Sa'did dynasty, the social and political scene was dominated by the Ṣūfī brotherhoods.

The marabout movement. Popular pietism, which had been launched under the Almoravids and the Almohads, covered the country with a network of *zāwiyahs* where ascetics lived—in theory at least—cut off from the world. In reality they taught children and even adults the rudiments of religion; they used the offerings they received from the population to help the poor and give shelter to travelers; in cases of conflict they served as mediators. The person who was called *ṣāliḥ* (man of good works), *walī* (man of God), *sayyid* (lord), and *shaykh* (leader) had become an indispensable figure. The last two terms indicate that he was endowed with a spiritual authority that the *qā'id* (representative of the central powers) could not easily ignore.

Up to this time the *zāwiyahs* fulfilled a social need and completed the work of the *makhzan*. When the latter turned out to be incapable of getting rid of the Portuguese who had settled on the coasts, the *zāwiyahs* were transformed into *ribāṭs*, rallying centers for warriors. (Here the word *murābiṭūn*—as with Almoravids earlier—yields *marabout* in French and English.) The man who symbolized this transformation was Muḥammad ibn Sulaymān al-Jazūlī, the author of a celebrated book of prayers concerning the Prophet called *Dalā'il al-khayrāt* (The Signs of Blessings); his *zāwiyah* was located in Afūghāl, near present-day Safi. He died in 1465, before the Portuguese occupation of the city, but his disciples, who later led the struggle for freedom, considered that he had prepared them spiritually for their task. All the *zāwiyahs* founded later were linked to al-Jazūlī and, through him, to 'Abd al-Salām ibn Mashīsh.

The marabout movement was based on the legacy of several centuries. To the tasks of education and moral reform it added a political program—the struggle against foreign domination—and this was its originality. The majority of its leaders prided themselves on being *sharīfs* (descendants of the Prophet through his daughter Fāṭimah); victory over the invaders gave them a social importance that was based on an assumption of holiness *(barakah)*. From this time on, being a marabout and being a *sharīf* were closely linked in the eyes of the people if not in reality.

From Brotherhood to Principality. The parent *zāwiyah*, which was a center for teaching and meditation, trained missionaries whose task was to spread the good word far and wide. The followers gathered in a special chapel, also known as a *zāwiyah*, to recite their *wird* ("litany"). Thus the *ṭarīqah* (brotherhood) came into being. With the weakening of the central power and the gradual splitting up of the country, the people turned more and more to the shaykhs of *zāwiyahs* who thus became, sometimes much against their will, the new political leaders. Similar circumstances surrounded the birth of the great North African brotherhoods: the Nāṣirīyah and Wazzānīyah in the mid-seventeenth century, and the Darqāwīyah, Tijānīyah, and Sanūsīyah during the nineteenth century. The *zāwiyah* thus took on diverse forms: it could be a monastery, brotherhood, or principality. On the one hand, it united the faithful over and above their traditional splits; on the other hand, it created new splits with its activism. In fact the *zāwiyah* competed with the political authority and the clerical institution on their respective grounds.

In the eyes of his disciples, the shaykh was in possession of a beneficial power that enabled him to work wonders *(karāmāt)*. When he died he became the object of a cult *(ziyārah)* because of his power of intercession *(shafā'ah)*. From the point of view of its organization, the brotherhood had something of a secret society or, at the very least, a private club about it. The principle of the brotherhood posed a problem for orthodoxy. However, until the beginning of the nineteenth century, every inhabitant of the Maghreb, literate or illiterate, was a member of one or several of them. Because it was a family affair, women and children were included in the brotherhood even if they did not usually participate in the ceremonies. The authorities and the clerics were unable to rise up openly against such a widespread practice.

The zāwiyah and the naturalist substratum. Each brotherhood produced a vast body of hagiographic literature listing the qualities that placed its successive leaders among the chosen and omitting any details of their behavior that were not quite orthodox. Nevertheless the official religious hierarchy remained suspicious. What was the true practice of the *zāwiyah*? Those who knew it from the inside were sworn to secrecy, while those who remained outside could say nothing with authority. Were the old pre-Islamic cults lingering on in the *zāwiyahs*? The Sunnīs insinuated that this was so but were unable to produce solid proof. And in any case, even if the naturalist cults were kept up in secret, they were reinterpreted in an Islamic language. The notions of *barakah, karāmah, shafā'ah,* and *sirr* ("secret") were directly linked to the teachings of the Prophet.

For three centuries the Islam of the brotherhoods, characterized by faith in hereditary grace, a supererogatory cult, and a hierarchical organization (which related it to the Shīʿī *daʿwah*), dominated the scene in the Maghreb so overwhelmingly that any outside observer took it for the true Islam, with the doctrine of the jurists being mere rationalization. Later history showed that this was not the case. From the mid-nineteenth century on, scriptural Islam returned in force; then began the long struggle against the *zāwiyah*s that finally brought them into disrepute. And yet one question remains: if the brotherhoods were so popular, was it not because they fulfilled an affective need that official Islam was unable to satisfy? Whatever the case, they gave rise to a renewal of literary expression. Whereas classical Arabic poetry (the *qaṣīdah*, "ode") was becoming bogged down in a welter of archaisms and stylistic artifices, the new emotionalism that emerged from the brotherhoods gave rise to *malḥūn*, poetry in the spoken language that was meant to be sung. Created by artists versed in the subtleties of classical prosody, *malḥūn* produced genuine masterpieces.

The Islam of the Salafīyah. Throughout the Maghreb, the second half of the eighteenth century was a period of recovery. The power of the central authority was reinforced, trade revived, and the cities prospered again. At the same time as did the Wahhābīyah of Arabia, the *faqīh*s of the Maghreb began to criticize the most absurd aspects of popular religiosity. Their movement claimed to continue the inspiration of the first Muslims *(salaf)*, hence the name Salafīyah conferred on it by historians.

Pre-Salafīyah and Salafīyah. The Salafīyah were not the first reformers to appear in the modern history of Islam, so how can they be distinguished, apart from chronology? The ʿAlawid sultans of Morocco, Muḥammad III (d. 1790) and Sulaymān (d. 1822), seeking to return to a simpler form of religion, criticized the subtleties of the jurists and the supererogatory practices of the brotherhoods. Muḥammad ibn al-Madanī Gannūn (d. 1885) spoke out vehemently against music and ritual dances. The book written by Ibn al-Hāj (d. 1336) against all kinds of innovation, *Al-madkhal* (The Introduction), was reprinted, and numerous clerics published summaries of it. Thus, from the mid-eighteenth century on normative Islam began to regain control, but it was in the minority and it attacked only the most aberrant aspects of the marabout movement, never its basic tenets. This phase is what we shall call the pre-Salafīyah.

The Salafīyah in the proper sense of the term appeared at the end of the nineteenth century, when several Arab countries, including Algeria (in 1830) and Tunisia (in 1881), came under the yoke of European imperialism. The movement expressed an awareness of the failure of traditional Islamic society in the face of foreign domination, as well as a desire for radical reform in the intellectual and social domains. From this standpoint the Islam of the *zāwiyah*s appeared as a distortion of true Islam, an alteration that lay at the origin of the decadence of the Muslims. The Salafīyah declared total war on maraboutic Islam.

The North African Salafīyah formed part of the movement that had been launched by the pan-Islamic leader Jamāl al-Din al-Afghānī (d. 1897) and his Egyptian disciple Muḥammad ʿAbduh (d. 1905). The review *Al-ʿurwah al-wuthqā* (The Strongest Bond), which they published for a short time in Paris, was widely read by enlightened Tunisians. ʿAbduh himself stayed briefly in Tunisia and Algiers in 1901/2. The Cairo review *Al-manār* (The Lighthouse), launched at ʿAbduh's instigation in 1898 by his disciple Rashīd Riḍā, had an immediate influence on the pupils of the *madrasah*s. It shaped the minds of such future leaders of Islamic reformism as the Tunisian Bashīr Ṣfar (d. 1937), the Algerians Ṭayyib al-ʿUqbī (d. 1962) and ʿAbd al-Ḥamīd ibn Bādīs (d. 1940), and, to a lesser extent, the Moroccans Abū Shuʿayb al-Dukkālī (d. 1940) and al-ʿArbī al-ʿAlawī (d. 1962).

The critique of the zāwiyahs. In 1937 the Algerian Mubārak al-Mīlī (d. 1962) published a pamphlet called *Risālat al-shirk wa-maẓāhirih* (Aspects of Polytheism), in which he summarized the main criticisms leveled by the Salafīyah against the brotherhoods. From the point of view of faith, he argued, the practices of the brotherhoods are tainted with *shirk* ("associationism"). Those who give offerings believe that this is the price to be paid for the intercession of the patron saint of the *zāwiyah*. However much the shaykh maintains that it is God alone who really intervenes, the donors still believe that it is the saint; they associate another being with God and thus commit the worst of sins.

From a legal point of view, the brotherhood is an innovation. Its members frequent a chapel, not a mosque, and this in order to recite prayers rather than the Qur'ān; they fast during periods other than the month of Ramaḍān and go on pilgrimages to places other than Mecca. According to the Salafīyah, this is a cult that has elements in common with Islam and yet is distinct from it. New *zāwiyah*s are created every day, and the Muslim community, instead of being united around the Qur'ān, is splitting up into sects that rise up against one another.

Finally, from a social point of view, the *zāwiyah* is a school of *taqlīd* (the act of following blindly) and *tawakkul* (fatalism). The disciple follows the shaykh in the belief that he can work wonders. Thus parasitism is encouraged. The *zāwiyah* is indeed active, but only in that it recruits people and takes them away from a productive life. In short, for the Salafīyah the *zāwiyahs* divide the Muslims, disarm them morally, impoverish them economically, and enslave them spiritually. They mark a reappearance of the paganism *(jāhilīyah)* that the Prophet had fought against. A return to the religion of the one God is a return to freedom, to a sense of action and solidarity, in other words, to the qualities responsible for the greatness of the ancestors.

From Salafīyah to nationalism. The Salafīyah were at work in a Maghreb that was dominated by European colonialism; they were not members of the *ʿulamāʾ*, even if they had been taught in such traditional institutions as the Zaytūnah in Tunis or the Qarawīyīn in Fez. They were fighting above all against the leaders of the *zāwiyahs*, but they also criticized the *faqīhs* who, prudently favoring middle-of-the-road solutions, had little liking for their vehemence. The Salafīyah drew their strength from the anticolonialist feelings harbored by the majority of the North African people. In response to the question "Why have we been colonized?" the Salafīyah gave a forceful answer: "Because we have been morally disarmed by the brotherhoods." The reply to this criticism came from Aḥmad ibn ʿAliwah (d. 1934) in Algeria and from Aḥmad Skīraj (d. 1944) in Morocco, but because it was purely religious in form it caused little stir.

The triumph of Salafīyah can be explained by the social and political environment of the time. As the cities became poorer, the Islam of the brotherhoods predominated. Then, during colonization, the cities recovered their prosperity and gave rise to a new merchant class whose lifestyle owed nothing to the practices of the *zāwiyahs*. It was from this class that Salafīyah drew the strength that enabled it to confront the colonial administration, the shaykhs of the brotherhoods, and the prudent *ʿulamāʾ*. However, since it was at once a religious and a sociopolitical movement, the Salafīyah had to follow the same evolution as the society, which, becoming ever more urbanized and politicized, obliged it to merge first with liberalism, then with nationalism, and finally with socialism. In this way the movement lost its specificity, as illustrated by the careers of ʿAbd al-ʿAzīz al-Thaʿālibī (d. 1937) in Tunisia and ʿAllāl al-Fāsī (d. 1974) in Morocco, who began as Salafī thinkers and wound up nationalist leaders.

Political Islam. In the present-day Maghreb, the state completely dominates both the society and the individual. Traditional institutions—*madrasahs*, *zāwiyahs*, *ḥabūs* (religious foundations)—are under the close supervision of their respective ministries. In Morocco the *ʿulamāʾ*, organized on a national level in a *jamʿīyat ʿulamāʾ al-Maghrib* (Moroccan ʿUlamāʾ Association) and in each province in a *majlis ʿilmī* (ʿUlamāʾ Council), are consulted on questions concerning dogma or the life of society in general, but they are allowed no say whatsoever in political affairs. In Algeria, the FLN (National Liberation Front), the sole political party, monopolizes public activity by law; in Tunisia, it is the dominant PSD (Destourian Socialist Party); in Libya, the people's committees, while the *ʿulamāʾ* are no more than civil servants.

The new dichotomy. After their liberation from the colonial yoke, the states of the Maghreb adopted the Salafī position as their official ideology. What has become of the Islam of the *zāwiyahs*? Scholars do not agree on this subject. The religious evolution of the Maghreb seems to have followed two quite separate paths. On the one hand, there are the Khārijī and Shīʿī schisms, which, containing elements of prehistoric polytheism, influenced the Almohads and the practices of the brotherhoods; on the other hand, there is strict monotheism, expressed at first through the Kairouan Mālikīyah, later redefined by the Sunnism of the thirteenth and fourteenth centuries and revived by the modern Salafīyah. This dichotomy could explain Ibn Khaldūn's opposition between rural and urban civilization. If so, the growing urbanization and industrialization of the independent Maghreb, which requires an increasingly rationalist religiosity, constantly reinforces the Salafīyah to the detriment of residual naturalist practices.

However, urbanization itself creates new needs. The city is never wholly middle class; it also contains a subproletariat that remains close to its peasant roots and an intelligentsia that is socially mixed and vulnerable to unemployment. The former group (the women in particular) indulges in magical practices, while the latter zealously seeks out mystical emotion or political activism. Under these circumstances, there could well be a revival of the *zāwiyahs*, but they would be used to fulfill a role that is defined more by present needs than by the legacy of the past. This fact is common to all the great cities in the world.

Political temptation. The Salafī ideology, which is spread among the masses by the machinery of the state, retains its original activist character. As the state is not always faithful, in practice, to Qurʾanic prescription, individuals who adopt this ideology find themselves on the horns of a dilemma: either they envisage it as a purely spiritual exercise or they derive a program of political reform from it. Now this dilemma is not confined to the Maghreb; it takes on a particular form only to the extent that religious experience in the Maghreb has distinct features.

North Africa has never produced intellectual mystics like the Andalusian Ibn ʿArabī, the Egyptian Ibn al-Fāriḍ (d. 1235), or the Persian Jalāl al-Dīn Rūmī (d. 1273); rather, it is a land of ascetics, educators, missionaries, and *mujāhids* (warriors of the faith), all of whom were close to the ordinary people and sensitive to the problems of the community. In the same way the great Mālikī *'ulamā'* were inclined to practicality and moderation, with little concern for methodological subtleties. It is most significant that the greatest author born in the Maghreb, Ibn Khaldūn, chose as his field of investigation the history and evolution of societies. In the Maghreb more than anywhere else, Islam seems to have been less individualist and intellectual, much more pragmatic and concerned with the community. We can also assume that it will retain these characteristics in the future, particularly in the absence of any opposing tendency thus far. The practice of the *zāwiyah*, wherever it remains in evidence, is increasingly purified by the *'ulamā'*. In people's minds Islam is above all a law *(sharī'ah)* that expresses the solidarity of the faithful, as can be seen in the way the majority is still attached to the fasting at Ramaḍān and the pilgrimage to Mecca. Islam as it is envisaged by the Society of Muslim Brothers (al-Ikhwān al-Muslimūn) does have a certain influence on official Salafī thought, but until now it has remained peripheral.

[*See also* Berber Religion; Christianity, *article on* Christianity in North Africa; Judaism, *articles on* Judaism in the Middle East and North Africa to 1492 *and* Judaism in the Middle East asnd North Africa since 1492; Rites of Passage, *article on* Muslim Rites; Ṭarīqah; Modernism, *article on* Islamic Modernism; *and the biographies of the principal historical personages mentioned herein.*]

BIBLIOGRAPHY

For a general historical introduction, see Jamil M. Abun-Nasr's *A History of the Maghrib* (Cambridge, 1971) and my *L'histoire du Maghreb: Un essai de synthèse* (Paris, 1970), translated by Ralph Manheim as *The History of the Maghrib: An Interpretive Essay* (Princeton, 1977). The problem of the pre-Islamic substrate is dealt with in François Decret and Muhammed Fantar's *L'Afrique du Nord dans l'antiquité: Histoire et civilisation des origines au cinquième siècle* (Paris, 1981). See also Marcel Bénabou's *La résistance africaine à la romanisation* (Paris, 1976) and W. H. C. Frend's *The Donatist Church: A Movement of Protest in Roman North Africa* (1952; reprint, Oxford, 1971). These are to be compared with ethnographical studies such as Edward Westermarck's *Ritual and Belief in Morocco*, 2 vols. (1926; reprint, New Hyde Park, N.Y., 1968), and Émile Dermenghem's *Le culte des saints dans l'Islam maghrébin*, 4th ed. (Paris, 1954).

Mohamed Talbi's *L'émirat aghlabide 184–296/800–909: Histoire politique* (Paris, 1966) summarizes and criticizes the literature concerning the beginnings of Islam. Roger Le Tourneau's *The Almohad Movement in North Africa in the Twelfth and Thirteenth Centuries* (Princeton, 1969) gives a brief survey of the work of Ibn Tūmart and his successors. The Almohad organization is described in J. F. P. Hopkins's *Medieval Muslim Government in Barbary until the Sixth Century of the Hijra* (London, 1958). For the *zāwiyahs* see T. H. Weir's *The Shaikhs of Morocco in the Sixteenth Century* (Edinburgh, 1904) and Jacques Berque's *Al-Yousi: Problèmes de la culture marocaine au dix-huitième siècle* (Paris, 1958).

The Salafī movement is studied in depth by Ali Merad in his *Le réformisme musulman en Algérie de 1925 à 1940: Essai d'histoire religieuse et sociale* (The Hague, 1967) and by Arnold H. Green in his *The Tunisian Ulama, 1873–1915: Social Structure and Response to Ideological Currents* (Leiden, 1978). The account given by 'Allāl al-Fāsi in *The Independence Movements in Arab North Africa*, translated by Hazem Zaki Nuseibeh (Washington, D.C., 1954), is an important one. A defense of maraboutism is presented in Martin Lings's *A Moslem Saint of the Twentieth Century: Shaikh Ahmad al-Alawi*, 2d ed. (Berkeley, 1973).

The anthropological point of view can be found in Clifford Geertz's *Islam Observed: Religious Development in Morocco and Indonesia* (New Haven, 1968), which uses Weberian concepts, and Ernest Gellner's *Muslim Society* (Cambridge, 1981), which is more structuralist. Dale F. Eickelman's *Moroccan Islam, Tradition and Society in a Pilgrimage Center* (Austin, 1976) is descriptive. Vincent Crapanzano's *The Hamadsha: A Study in Moroccan Ethnopsychiatry* (Princeton, 1973) is more limited in scope. To the list can be added the self-criticism of Paul Rabinow in *Reflections on Fieldwork in Morocco* (Berkeley, 1977). The present-day situation is analyzed acutely and competently by Elbaki Hermassi in *Leadership and National Development in North Africa* (Berkeley, 1972) and by Mohammed Arkoun in *La pensée arabe* (Paris, 1975).

ABDALLAH LAROUI
Translated from French by Glyn Thoiron

Islam in Spain

Not long after Ṭāriq ibn Ziyād landed in Carteya in 711, the Muslims became masters of a major portion of the Iberian Peninsula. Al-Andalus, as the Muslims refer to Spain, which had hitherto been ruled by the Christian Visigoths—converts from Arianism to Catholicism—now witnessed the introduction of a new religion, Islam, which was to coexist in Spain with Christianity and, to a lesser extent, Judaism for the next nine centuries. This essay will outline the religious achievement of the Muslims in Spain within the following general chronological schema:

- Period of the governors (711–756)
- The emirate (756–912)
- The caliphate (912–1031)
- The *ṭā'ifah* kings (1031–1091)
- The Almoravids in Spain (1091–1146) and their *ṭā'ifahs* (1146–1157)

- The Almohads in Spain (1157–1212) and their *ṭā'ifahs* (1212–1230)
- The Nasrids of Granada (1230–1492)
- The Moriscos (1492–1609)

The main outward religious concern of the Muslim conquerors was the affirmation both of the prophethood of Muḥammad and of his message, namely, that there is no god other than God, alone and without associate or compeer. In Spain, as in other predominantly Christian regions, this affirmation was essential in view of the skepticism of the conquered Christians in regard to Muḥammad's prophethood and in the light of the Qur'anic rejection of the Christian doctrines of the Trinity and the Incarnation (as well as of the death and resurrection of Christ). Maintaining this assertive stance, Spanish Islam moved rapidly into a broad spectrum of intellectual and spiritual literary activity elaborating on the profundity of the message of the faith. And while the Muslims had never reconciled themselves to the "polytheism" of the Christians, the polemics against Christianity and its teachings intensified only when the Muslims were provoked. At the same time, intermingling with Christian compatriots encouraged influences in literature and social practices, although not in matters of religious doctrine. Under Islam, Spain became the most culturally advanced country in medieval Europe. Its cities excelled in the various fields of learning as well as in arts, agriculture, industry, and commerce.

The Earliest Religious Documentation. Aside from the Qur'ān, the earliest "documents" to circulate in Spain containing a statement of the faith were coins issued by the Muslim rulers. The legends on the earliest of these coins proclaim God's oneness and uniqueness in compacted Latin (long before the translation of the Qur'ān became an issue)—"NONESTðSNISIIPSESOLCISN" for "Non est deus nisi ipse solus cui socius non est" ("There is no god but God, alone; he has no associate"). Later, the Arabic equivalent was used as well: "Lā ilāha illā Allāh waḥdahu lā sharīka lahu." After the numismatic reform of 696, an all-Arabic coin was introduced, on which a Qur'anic legend was inscribed that read "Allāh aḥad Allāh al-ṣamad lam yalid wa-lam yuwlad" ("God is one, God is everlasting; he has not begotten and has not been begotten," surah 112), a direct address against the doctrine of the Trinity. Other Arabic legends, affirming the prophethood of Muḥammad, read "Muḥammad is the apostle of God," or more emphatically, the verse described as the "prophetic mission": "Muḥammad is the apostle of God. He sent him with the guidance and the true religion" (surah 48:29 preceded by part of verse 28 or, with the later addition of "even though those who associate [the Christians] may be averse," surah 9:33 or 61:9).

The *kalimah* ("word" or "testimony"), "There is no god but God; Muḥammad is the apostle of God," and the prophetic mission continued to appear as legends on the coins of the subsequent Muslim rulers until the rise of the Almoravids. At that time, the prophetic mission on the earlier coins was replaced by a verse that appeared to declare the superiority of Islam: "Whoso desires another religion than Islam, it shall not be accepted of him, and in the next world he shall be among the losers" (3:85). To the Spanish Christians, this implied a change in the Muslim attitude toward non-Muslims.

During the period of Almohad predominance, the legends on these coins declared the Mahdist doctrine that the movement was attempting unsuccessfully to introduce into Spain: "God is our Lord, Muḥammad is our apostle (or prophet), the Mahdi is our leader." A new Qur'anic passage was now used, emphasizing the unitarian view of the Almohads: "Your God is one God; there is no god but he, the merciful, the compassionate" (2:158). The Nasrids of Granada used the same verse on their coins alongside another that reflected on their straitened situation: "O believers, be patient, and vie in patience; be steadfast; fear God; haply so you will prosper" (3:200).

Schools of Fiqh in Spain. Spain was influenced, to varying degrees, by most of the established Eastern schools of *fiqh* (jurisprudence). It was not long, however, before the Spanish Muslims developed their own identity in this sphere.

The Awzāʿī school. The first school *(madhhab)* of *fiqh* to prevail in Spain was that of the Syrian master al-Awzāʿī (d. 774). According to the Spanish Muslim biographer Ibn al-Faraḍī (d. 1013), this system was introduced in Spain by Ṣaʿṣaʿah ibn Salām (d. 808), who was the *muftī* (chief canon lawyer) of al-Andalus during the reigns of ʿAbd al-Raḥmān I (756–788) and Hishām I (788–796). In accordance with the teachings of this school, trees were planted in the courtyard of the Great Mosque of Cordova and subsequently in other Spanish mosques, a practice frowned upon by other schools. Ṣaʿṣaʿah is given credit for the introduction of *ḥadīth* literature *per se* into Spain.

The rival Ḥanafī school, which had extended its influence westward as far as Kairouan and even Morocco, failed to take root in Spain. True, there were individual adherents of this school, but it does not seem to have appealed to the religious conservatism that characterized Muslim Spain.

The Mālikī school. Throughout its history Muslim Spain was identified with the Mālikī school, which, in spite of its severity and strict adherence to orthodoxy, did not extinguish the flame of learning kindled by Islam. On many occasions scholars of this school attempted, sometimes successfully, to stop the dissemination of ideas, religious or otherwise, that they felt diverged from orthodoxy. But they, in turn, expressed that orthodoxy in an impressive form of discourse that constitutes a major part of the literary heritage of Muslim Spain. Lévi-Provençal is correct in stating that the strict controls applied by the Mālikī jurists protected Spain from the religious infighting that came to characterize the rest of the Muslim world. The scholarship of the Mālikī jurists was of such quality as to form a branch school of their own alongside the other branch schools of the Mālikī master Saḥnūn in Kairouan, by which they were influenced and from which they diverged, and the Mālikī school in Iraq, with which they had no major contact.

Mālikī law was introduced into Spain during the reigns of Hishām I and al-Ḥakam I (796–822). According to Ibn Khaldūn there were two reasons for its adoption there: the *ḥajj* (pilgrimage to Mecca) brought the Spanish Muslims in contact with the intellectual activity of Medina but not with that of Iraq (which was superior), and the prevalence of nomadism in the mentality of the people of al-Andalus and Morocco prompted them to prefer the ideas of the nomadic thinkers of the Arabian Peninsula to those of the more refined Iraqis. Its success in Spain, according to Ibn Ḥazm, was due to the influence exerted in the court by Yaḥyā ibn Yaḥyā al-Laythī and other early masters of the school, who saw that Mālikī scholars were appointed to judicial and other positions. Be that as it may, the Mālikīyah attracted the respect of the populace by their close adherence to Qur'anic stipulations in matters that directly concerned the public (taxation is but one example). Their jurisconsults acted as the defenders of orthodoxy and of the believing public in the face of the tyranny or corruption of some of the rulers.

Distinguished Mālikī scholars of Spain were legion, and Hispano-Arabic biographical literature abounds in references to them. Only a few of the more notable among them will be mentioned here. The rise of the Mālikīyah in Spain may be credited to Ziyād ibn ʿAbd al-Raḥmān al-Lakhmī, called Shabaṭūn, a disciple of Mālik. We are told that this *faqīh* (jurisconsult or religious scholar) lauded the piety and good government of Hishām I (al-Ḥakam, according to al-Maqqarī) to Mālik, the school's Medinese eponym, who responded by praising Hishām. As a result, the Spanish ruler favored the school and its scholars. Shabaṭūn was thus held in high esteem by the pious Hishām; on one occasion, for example, Hishām refrained from carrying out an order to cut off a servant's hand when Shabaṭūn cited Mālik on the matter.

A second prominent Mālikī *faqīh* (he was also a judge) was ʿĪsā ibn Dīnār, who arrived in Medina just after Mālik's death and then studied in Fusṭāṭ (Egypt) under Ibn al-Qāsim, a distinguished disciple of Mālik. Upon his return to Spain he was appointed *muftī* of Cordova, a position he held until his death in 827. His *Kitāb al-hidāyah* (Book of Guidance) is a compendium of Mālikī *fiqh* based on the work of his teacher and including his own extensive interpretations. His work contributed to the establishment of an autonomous Spanish school of Mālikī *fiqh* and is one of four major manuals of Mālikī religious law in Spain. Later in his life he became weary of the rigidity of the Mālikīyah, particularly resenting the near-veneration of Mālik's *Muwaṭṭa'* (his compendium of judicial, ritual, and other practices, which was based on the consensus of the Muslims of Medina) and its treatment by Mālikī scholars as an ultimate source of legal formulations. He wished to break away from the Mālikīyah and "return to the Qur'ān and the *sunnah*," but he died before achieving this goal.

Another important *faqīh* was Yaḥyā ibn Yaḥyā al-Laythī, a Berber disciple of Mālik. His *Kitāb al-ʿasharāt* (Book of Tens) was one of the major manuals of Spanish Mālikī law. He became prominent only after the death of ʿĪsā ibn Dīnār, when the pleasure-loving ʿAbd al-Raḥmān II (822–852) gave him full power to administer the affairs of the state.

One of the most prominent Mālikī scholars was ʿAbd al-Malik ibn Ḥabīb (d. 854), who was given the honorific title ʿĀlim al-Andalus ("the scholar of Spain"). His *Kitāb al-wāḍiḥah* (Book of the Evident) is one of the more important manuals of Mālikī *fiqh*. One of his disciples, Muḥammad ibn ʿUtbah (also known as al-ʿUtbī, d. 868), produced another of the major Mālikī manuals, entitled *Kitāb al-mustakhrajah* (Book of Excerpts) and, according to Ibn Khaldūn, the one most often used in Spain and Morocco. In it he brought together what he had learned from both Ibn Ḥabīb and Saḥnūn, the renowned Mālikī master of Kairouan.

The leading Mālikī *faqīh* of the period of the *ṭā'ifah* kings (the Muslim party kings who ruled a divided and warring Spain between the fall of the caliphate in 1031 and their removal by the Almoravids shortly after 1086) was Abū al-Walīd al-Bājī (1012–1081). A prolific writer on matters of *fiqh* and Qur'anic studies, he defended Islam with eloquence at a very difficult time in its history. This is evident from an epistle he wrote to a monk from France who had asked al-Muqtadir ibn Hūd of Saragossa (1046–1081) to convert to Christianity. It is also illustrated in the debate he had with Ibn Ḥazm, of the opposing Ẓāhirī school, as a result of which the latter was charged with unorthodoxy and suffered the humiliation of having his books burnt in public and banned.

Such Mālikī zeal, which tended to equate free inquiry with unorthodoxy, led Ibn Ḥamdīn, the *qāḍī* of Cordova and a leading *faqīh* during the period of the Almoravids, to counsel a ban on al-Ghazālī's work *Iḥyā' 'ulūm al-dīn* (The Revivification of the Sciences of Religion). The public burning of the book in 1113 prompted the jurisconsults of Almería to draw up a *fatwā* (legal opinion) condemning the action. Another leading Mālikī during this period was Abū al-Faḍl ʿIyāḍ (1083–1149), a native of Ceuta (in North Africa) and *qāḍī* of Granada. In addition to his biography of distinguished Mālikī scholars, *Kitāb tartīb al-madārik wa-taqrīb al-masālik* (Preparing the Way and Bringing Nigh the Means for Knowing the Masters of Mālik's School), he wrote several religious works, including *Kitāb al-shifā' bi-ta'rīf ḥuqūq al-Muṣṭafā* (Book of Healing through the Knowledge of the Rights of the Prophet), which is a meditation on the life of the Prophet, and *Kitāb qawā'id al-Islām* (Book of the Fundamentals of Islam), a systematic "catechism" that continues to exert its influence in religious education in Muslim North Africa.

The Shāfiʿī school. This school, which, unlike that of the Mālikīyah, emphasized the *ḥadīth,* was introduced in Spain by Qāsim ibn Sayyār of Cordova (d. 891), who studied the Shāfiʿī system in the East and became its most notable master in Spain. Among his works was a critique of the Mālikī master al-ʿUtbī, in which he attacked the Mālikīyah for their "blind" adoption of the *Muwaṭṭa'*. Ibn Sayyār was protected from his opponents by the sagacious Muḥammad I (852–886), who gave him the position of royal notary. In spite of this, the Shāfiʿī school did not succeed in establishing itself in Spain.

The Ẓāhirī school. Except for its brief adoption during the reign of the Almohad sultan Yaʿqūb al-Manṣūr (1184–1199), this school also had little success in Spain. It was present strictly through the activities of its individual adherents, some of whom achieved high positions in the state.

The Ẓāhirīyah was first introduced in Spain by the *qāḍī* Mundhir ibn Saʿīd al-Ballūṭī (d. 966) and was made prominent by Ibn Ḥazm, who gave the main exposition of its doctrines in his writings. His literary legacy covers a wide spectrum of creativity including literature, philosophy, and the religious sciences, to which he turned after he despaired of political activities. From his *Ṭawq al-ḥamāmah* (The Ring of the Turtle Dove), a work on courtly love (not without a religious foundation), we may obtain a picture of the rigorous education of a man of his caliber in Muslim Spain: the Qur'ān, *ḥadīth, fiqh,* and theology, as well as grammar, lexicography, philosophy, logic, rhetoric, and poetry. In his treatises *(rasā'il)* dealing with education he argues that only through the acquisition of such an education would the human cultural achievement be preserved and enhanced. He affirms that all fields of learning are interrelated and, following a Qur'anic dictum, that proper learning can be achieved only after the abandonment of the deceptive life of ease and pleasure (a reflection on his earlier life). [*See the biography of Ibn Ḥazm.*]

Independent scholars. Not every *faqīh* belonged to a specific school. A notable example was Baqī ibn Makhlad (817–889), who was a disciple of the Mālikī Ibn Ḥabīb and who also studied in the East with Ḥanbalī and Shāfiʿī scholars. If we are to accept Ibn Ḥazm's claim, he studied with the Ẓāhirīyah as well and introduced their method to Spain. Although it is sometimes said that he was a Shāfiʿī, he seems to have chosen a path independent of all schools, while utilizing their scholarship as his methodology permitted him. He is credited with a *tafsīr* (Qur'ān commentary), now lost, which, in Ibn Ḥazm's estimation, was superior to that of al-Ṭabarī. In *fiqh,* he rejected the Mālikī approach and the emphasis it placed on the *Muwaṭṭa'*. He favored the utilization of the *ḥadīth,* as did the Shāfiʿī scholars, and is credited for the introduction of Imām al-Shāfiʿī's *Uṣūl al-fiqh* (Foundations of *fiqh*) into Spain. He also introduced the *Musnad* (Book of Transmitted Traditions) of Ibn Abī Shaybah, which he commented on in his *Muṣannaf* (Book of Classified Traditions). This annoyed the Mālikīyah, who attempted to bring charges of unorthodoxy against him. To his fortune, he also was given the protection of the caliph Muḥammad I, who encouraged him to continue in his scholarship.

The Literary Heritage. There exists a large body of Hispano-Arabic literature covering nearly every area of human creativity. The biographical works of Ibn al-Abbār, Ibn al-Faraḍī, and others (published in the last century by Francisco Codera in the series *Biblioteca hispano-árabe*) shed some light on the extensive literary activity in Muslim Spain. Works dealing with the literary history of Muslim Spain, such as Ibn Bassām's *Kitāb al-dhakhīrah* (Book of Treasures) and Ibn al-Khaṭīb's *Kitāb al-iḥāṭah fī akhbār Gharnāṭah* (Book of Information about the Affairs of Granada), among many others, give us a glimpse into the richness of Spanish Muslim culture. A fascination with this culture led al-Maqqarī, a seventeenth-century Moroccan, to write an encyclopedic work entitled *Nafḥ al-ṭīb min ghuṣn al-Andalus al-raṭīb* (The Diffusion of Fragrance from the Tender Branch of al-Andalus), which, in spite of its breadth, covers only a portion of the literary works of the Spanish Muslims. One may also mention Ibn Ḥayyān's *Al-muqtabis* (Book of the Seeker of the Knowledge of the History of al-Andalus), of which only some fragments are extant.

Qur'anic literature. In addition to *fiqh*, other areas of the religious sciences received the attention of Muslim scholarship. In the field of *qirā'āt* (Qur'ān reading), Spanish Muslims initially employed the traditions of the East; then, toward the end of the period of the caliphate, Mujāhid (the well-versed slave of al-Manṣūr ibn 'Āmir and governor of Denia) displayed special interest in this science. It was under his patronage that Abū 'Amr al-Dānī (981–1053) established himself, with his *Kitāb al-taysīr* (Book of Facilitation), as the leading Spanish authority in this field. His contemporary Makkī ibn Abī Ṭālib (d. 1045) also distinguished himself in this genre with his *Kitāb al-tabṣirah* (Book of Enlightenment), said by al-Maqqarī to be the best work on the Qur'ān.

In *tafsīr*, Spanish Muslims were always well acquainted with the works of such leading exegetes as al-Ṭabarī, al-Zamakhsharī, al-Rāzī, and al-Bayḍāwī. However, the Qur'ān commentary of Yaḥyā ibn Salām al-Baṣrī, a Mālikī scholar of Kairouan (d. 815), triggered the beginning of an Andalusian exegetical tradition. A condensation of his work became the basis of the Qur'ān commentary of Ibn Abū Zamanīn of Elvira (936–1008), a work that continued to be employed in Spain until the end of the sixteenth century. One of the three surviving fragments of his work was written in Aljamiado, the romanized dialect used by the Moriscos (Muslims who came under Christian rule after the fall of Granada). Another important exegete was Ibn 'Aṭīyah al-Muḥāribī al-Gharnāṭī (1088–1151), a *qāḍī* of Almería, whose *Al-muḥarrar al-wajīz* (The Compendious Record) was highly acclaimed both in and outside of Spain. The tradition of religious learning continued into the difficult period of the fourteenth century, as is evident from the work of Abū Ḥayyān al-Gharnāṭī, who migrated to Cairo where he taught until his death in 1345. His Qur'ān commentary, *Al-baḥr al-muḥīṭ* (The Encircling Sea), is characterized by its emphasis on the linguistic analysis of the vocabulary of the Qur'ān.

Philosophical literature. Not only was philosophy late in coming to Spain (ninth century), but it had to encounter the stiff opposition of Mālikī scholarship. This difficulty, however, did not obstruct the development of influential philosophical schools. Thanks to the pilgrimage and travel in search of education *(ṭalab)*, Spanish Muslims came into close contact with philosophical developments in the Muslim East. Thus, Mu'tazilī ideas, for example, were introduced by such people as Khalīl ibn 'Abd al-Malik, whose personal library was burned by some Mālikī adherents after his death.

One of the earliest to engage in speculative thought was Muḥammad ibn Masarrah of Cordova (883–931). A philosopher and ascetic, he lived with some of his disciples in a "hermitage" in the mountains near Cordova. According to Ibn Ḥazm, he shared some of the views of the Mu'tazilah at a time when the difficult political situation in Spain led the Mālikī scholars to exercise very strict controls and censorship. As a result of a treatise against him by a distinguished Mālikī *faqīh* and ascetic who was no less outstanding than he was, Ibn Masarrah was accused of espousing the views of the pseudo-Empedocles and was even suspected of *zandaqah* ("heresy"), a capital offense. Little, if anything, is known of his *ṭarīqah* ("way" [of the Ṣūfī]), and none of his writings have survived; in fact, we know the titles of only two: *Kitāb al-tabṣirah* (Book of Enlightenment) and *Kitāb al-ḥurūf* (Book of Letters). We are indebted to Asín Palacios for his reconstruction of Ibn Masarrah's thought, drawn from the writings of Ibn Ḥazm and Ibn al-'Arabī, as well as from the development of his ideas by members of his "school" and from his influence on later Jewish and Christian mysticism.

Another notable philosopher was Ibn Bājjah (Avempace), who intermittently held high positions of power under the Almoravids but was occasionally imprisoned for his views. A poet and music theoretician, he was one of the earliest among the philosophers of the Peripatetic school in Muslim Spain. [*See the biography of Ibn Bājjah.*]

A philosopher influenced by Ibn Bājjah was Ibn Ṭufayl (1110–1185). In addition to his works on astronomy and medicine (he was physician of the Almohad ruler Yūsuf al-Manṣūr), he also wrote on moral philosophy. Nothing has survived of his work other than his celebrated *Ḥayy ibn Yaqẓān* (Alive, the Son of Awake), a treatise cast in narrative style.

There is no doubt, however, that the greatest philosopher of Muslim Spain was Ibn Rushd (Averroës), a contemporary and friend of Ibn Ṭufayl. He was encouraged in his philosophical pursuits by Yūsuf al-Manṣūr, the Almohad ruler who himself enjoyed a philosophical discourse. A complaint by this ruler that Aristotle's works were not clearly translated prompted Ibn Rushd to write his commentaries, for which he is widely known in the West, and which were translated into Latin and Hebrew but have not survived in Arabic. The school of philosophy that he founded in Spain had its influence not only on Islamic intellectual circles but also on Jewish and Christian thought. [*See the biography of Ibn Rushd.*]

The Ṣūfīs of Spain and their literature. Given the general tendency in Islam to meditation and the piety that characterized the life of the Muslims in Spain, those who chose to lead an ascetic life were favored by all levels of Spanish Muslim society. However, while in principle they were not a threat to orthodoxy, ascetics aroused suspicion when, in preaching their doctrine of *waḥdat al-wujūd* (the unity of all being), they appeared to espouse pantheism. While there is no doubt that individual ascetics existed from the earliest periods of Muslim history in Spain, the Ṣūfī tradition gained attention only as a result of the teachings of Ibn Masarrah.

A notable Ṣūfī who lived during the Almoravid period was Ibn al-ʿArīf (1088–1141). He received his traditional and Ṣūfī instruction in Almería, a center of Ṣūfī activity and of resistance to the severity of the Mālikī jurisprudence that had been receiving the unequivocal support of the Almoravids. In his work *Maḥāsin al-majālis* (Merits of the Assemblies) he outlines the qualities of the life of a Ṣūfī, who was to exercise asceticism in all pursuits (including asceticism itself) except in seeking the knowledge of the truth, which is God, and the boundless love for that truth.

A contemporary and close associate of Ibn al-ʿArīf was Ibn Barrajān of Seville, who was well trained in the sciences of Muslim theology, *ḥadīth, qirā'āt,* and Sufism. Like many of his ascetic contemporaries, he was influenced by the teachings of al-Ghazālī, which were quite unpopular in strict Mālikī circles. Because he did not interpret his asceticism to mean a total withdrawal from the affairs of the world where these touch on the well-being of the faithful, Ibn Barrajān agitated against the Mālikīyah and their Almoravid supporters. This activity led to his trial and execution, while his associate Ibn al-ʿArīf was exonerated and honored. It was Ibn Qasī, a member of this political-ascetic association and author of *Kitāb khalʿ al-naʿlayn* (Book of Taking Off Sandals), who led the 1145 rebellion that precipitated the downfall of the Almoravids in southern Portugal.

The most distinguished among the Ṣūfī masters who originated in Spain was Muḥyī al-Dīn ibn al-ʿArabī (1164–1240), most of whose works, however, were written outside Spain. He too was trained in the traditional studies of the Qur'ān, *ḥadīth,* and *fiqh* by one of the disciples of Ibn Ḥazm. His *Rūḥ al-quds* (Book of the Holy Spirit) and *Al-durrah al-fākhirah* (The Splendid Pearl) are brief biographical notes on contemporary Ṣūfī masters of Spain. In *Al-futūḥāt al-makkīyah* (The Meccan Revelations), he reports on his meeting with Ibn Rushd, who was displeased with Ibn al-ʿArabī's esotericism and lack of interest in rational speculation. [*See the biography of Ibn al-ʿArabī.*]

Religion and Government. The inseparability of religion from everyday life was closely observed in Mālikī Spain under the scrutiny of the *fuqahā'* (pl. of *faqīh*), who at times did not refrain from arousing public wrath against a ruler who deviated from orthodoxy. As a result, governmental institutions were identified more closely as religious than in the East. Three institutions touching on the daily lives of the Muslims of Spain illustrate this phenomenon.

The caliphate. Until 912 Muslim Spain acknowledged the sovereignty of the caliph, whether Umayyad (in Damascus) or Abbasid (in Baghdad). After the fall of the Umayyad caliphate in the East (750), ʿAbd al-Raḥmān I, an Umayyad who had survived the Abbasid massacre of his people, established himself as emir (prince) of Muslim Spain, tacitly recognizing the caliphal authority of the Abbasids of Baghdad. However, when the Abbasid caliphate had become too ephemeral and a Fatimid (Shīʿī) counter-caliph (a grave threat to orthodoxy) was established in North Africa, ʿAbd al-Raḥmān III (912–961), with the acquiescence of the religious authorities, declared himself caliph in Spain.

More than a century later, the Almoravids restored loyalty to the Abbasid caliphate as part of their fundamental reform. However, this loyalty was abrogated by the Almohads, by the end of whose reign the Abbasid caliphate had been destroyed by the Mongols (1258). Henceforth, the claim to the caliphate was common to any and all rulers of Muslim Spain.

The qāḍī. In Spain, the *qāḍī* ("judge") held a position of esteem second only to the caliph. In the hierarchy put forth by al-Nubāhī of Málaga (d. end of the fourteenth century), himself a judge, the *qāḍī* was preceded only by a just and righteous caliph and the prophets. While he had to be competent to sit alone in judgment, the Spanish Muslim *qāḍī* was often aided, especially in cases of appeal, by an advisory council *(shūrā)* composed of qualified *fuqahā'*. He was considered to be a leader of his community, as is evident from the fact that in times of crisis it was largely the *qāḍī* who took over the management of the affairs of a city.

The muḥtasib. Strictly speaking, *ḥisbah* ("reckoning") is the manner in which the individual fulfills the Qur'anic obligation of "bidding to honor and forbidding dishonor" (surah 3:104 and elsewhere) in all matters of conduct. *The muḥtasib* was the official entrusted with ensuring that individuals complied with the requirements of the codes of behavior and the law in their public dealings. Aside from their obvious application in the marketplace, rules of *ḥisbah* were also applied (to Muslims and non-Muslims alike) in the fulfillment of public religious obligations as well as public morality. However, little Mālikī *ḥisbah* literature (treatises outlining these rules and the manner of their application) has survived; three works from Spain are those of Ibn ʿAbdūn of Seville, al-Saqaṭī of Málaga, and Ibn Sahl of Jaén, all of the Almoravid period.

Popular Religious Practices. One subject that has received little scholarly attention is popular religion among the Muslims of Spain. In fact, for reasons of ethnicity, movements centering on pseudoprophecy found active support in some Berber circles. When, for example, Shaqyā ibn ʿAbd al-Walīd, a Berber of Miknāsah, claimed descent from the Prophet through ʿAlī and Fāṭimah (his own mother was named Fāṭimah), a rebellion ensued in 768 and posed a serious threat to the nascent regime of ʿAbd al-Raḥmān I. Another Berber pseudoprophet appearing toward the end of the reign of ʿAbd al-Raḥmān II gave a new interpretation to the Qur'ān and established new symbolic codes of religious behavior such as a ban on cutting one's hair or nails.

Parallel to the dictates of orthodoxy, there appear, here and there in the literature, references to astrology, magic, divination, visitation of the tombs of "saints" in pursuit of *barakah* ("blessing"), and speaking with the dead. Before the Battle of Zallaca in 1086, Ibn ʿAbbād of Seville consulted his astrologer, to the annoyance of the puritanical Yūsuf ibn Tāshfīn, the Almoravid prince. Ibn al-ʿArabī, for mystical reasons, consulted the dead. Several Arabic texts of "fortune" (manuals that instruct the user in ways and means of prediction and foretelling) have survived, and the practice continued among the Moriscos, for whom manuals for "fortune" were composed in Aljamiado.

Spanish Christians under Muslim Rule. The Christians of the peninsula, who, together with the Jews, were *ahl al-kitāb* ("people of the Book"; the term *ahl al-dhimmah* or *dhimmī*, "people of the trust or covenant," was also used but gradually came to be reserved for the Jews), were given the option of converting to Islam and thus enjoying the benefits (and responsibilities) that accrue to all Muslims, or of maintaining their religion subject to certain obligations, including the payment of the *jizyah* (tribute). Those who converted—and many did because of the poor treatment the ordinary classes had received under the Visigoths—came to be known as the *muwalladūn* (pl. of *muwallad; mollitis* in Christian texts), while those who maintained their Christian faith subject to treaty were called *musālimūn* ("peace-bound") or *mu'āhidūn* ("covenant-bound").

The terms that governed the relationship between the ruling Muslims and the governed Spanish Christians may be adduced from the treaty of Murcia, whereby the Muslims, under the guarantee of God and the Prophet, assured Theodemir, the vanquished Christian ruler of Murcia, that

> no harm shall befall him or his people; they shall not be taken into captivity nor would they be separated from their women or children; they shall not be killed; their churches shall not be burnt; they shall not be oppressed in regard to their religion [i.e., they shall not be forced into conversion]. . . . He and his people shall pay the *jizyah*.

The Christians were in fact entitled to keep their churches, although they were rarely permitted to build new ones (or rebuild ruined ones), except occasionally as compensation where the Muslims had taken over churches and converted them into mosques, such as in Cordova. Under Muslim rule, Toledo remained the see of the metropolitan of Spain while Cordova, Seville, and Mérida remained centers of major Christian concentrations. Bishops were appointed with the approval of the Muslim sovereign, and some, such as Rabīʿ ibn Zayd (Recemundu), enjoyed high esteem in the service of the court of ʿAbd al-Raḥmān III (he was sent on embassies to Byzantium and Germany). His *Kitāb al-anwā'* (Book of the Seasons) offers an interesting picture of the liturgical calendar of the Spanish Christians.

Many Spanish Christians became arabized (Mozarabs), but others did not accept Muslim predominance. A few went to the extent of provoking the Muslims by publicly insulting the Prophet and the Qur'ān, thus inviting capital punishment.

While conversion to Islam was encouraged, coercion was not practiced except when the faith was offered as an alternative to execution in cases of persistent public slander of the Prophet or the faith. On the other hand, Christian attempts to convert Muslims formed part of the mission of the Cluniac Benedictines in Spain and may have prompted a reaction on the part of the Almoravids, whose period of predominance witnessed some forced conversions.

Spanish Jews under Muslim Rule. Like their Christian counterparts in Spain and elsewhere, the Jews were also given the option of converting to Islam or retaining their religious autonomy while paying the *jizyah*. Unlike Spanish Christians, however, they achieved a very high degree of political, diplomatic, and economic power. More impressive were their works in the various areas of learning, in many cases written in Arabic. Rather than being a conquered people—as were the Spanish Christians—the Jews from the start were allies of Islam in its conquest of Spain.

The paucity of references to the Jews in textual sources makes it difficult to reconstruct a reliable picture of their daily life during the first four centuries of Muslim rule. It may be said, however, that except for sporadic moments to the contrary, especially in eleventh-century Granada (under the Zirids), the Jews of Muslim Spain enjoyed a relatively prosperous and secure life. It was not until the age of the Almohads—a period of successive military setbacks for Islam—that they were persecuted.

In the prevailing environment of prosperity and tolerance, Jewish religious (as well as artistic, literary, and scientific) creativity found fertile soil to flourish. Under the patronage of Ḥasday ibn Shaprūṭ, minister of the caliphs ʿAbd al-Raḥmān III (912–961) and al-Ḥakam II (961–976), Talmudic studies were quickly developed by Mūsā ibn Ḥānūk and his school. Influenced by the Muslims' concentration on the study of the language of the sacred scriptures, the Jewish scholar Yahūdā ibn Dāwūd (Ḥayyūj) developed the first work on Hebrew grammar, which he wrote in Arabic. He was followed by Marwān ibn Janāḥ of Cordova (Merinos), who wrote a similar work in Hebrew after having written his *Kitāb al-mustalḥiq* (Book of the Addendum) in Arabic.

In the eleventh century, Sulaymān ibn Yaḥyā ibn Gabirol (1021–1070) wrote his *Yanbūʿ al-ḥayāt* (The Font of Life), probably the earliest work on Jewish philosophy written in Spain. His contemporary Baḥyā ibn Fāqūdhā (Ibn Paqudah) also wrote in Arabic and, like Ibn Gabirol, was influenced by the ideas of al-Ghazālī, as may be seen from his book *Al-hidāyah ilā farāʾiḍ al-qulūb* (Guidance to the Duties of the Heart), a pietist, mystical work which contrasts sharply with that of Ibn Bājjah, his rationalistic Muslim contemporary. [*See the biographies of Ibn Gabirol and Baḥye ibn Paquda.*]

But the greatest of Spanish Jewish writers and religious thinkers was Mūsā ibn Maymūn (Maimonides) of Cordova (1135–1204). Writing in Arabic, he employed his philosophical and religious training to respond to the crises facing Judaism at that time. His *Risālah fī al-riddah* (Treatise on Apostasy) was written in response to the forced conversion of Jews in Morocco during the fanatical rule of the Almohads. Similarly, his *Risālat al-ʿazāʾ* (Epistle of Comfort) was addressed to the Jews of Yemen who had been forced to convert to Islam by the Fatimids. Among several other religious works he wrote in Arabic, the most notable is his *Dalālat al-ḥāʾirīn* (The Guide of the Perplexed), which remains by far the most important religious (and philosophical) work in Judaism. [*See the biography of Maimonides.*]

After the gradual retreat of Islam in Spain beginning in the eleventh century, the Jews, like many Mozarabic immigrants to Christian Spain, occupied important positions in political as well as intellectual circles. But two centuries later, their intellectual activity in their new environment rapidly degenerated to that of translation, notably in Christian Toledo, Catalonia, and Provence. Unlike Spanish Muslims, the Jews were allowed, as early as the middle of the eleventh century (the Council of Coyonca in 1050), to live in urban centers in Christian Spain. However, similar to their Muslim compatriots, they were not spared the choice between forced conversion to Christianity or exile, especially after the fall of Granada in 1492.

Spanish Muslims under Christian Rule. The Mudéjares, Muslims who found themselves under Christian rule, especially between the fall of Toledo and the fall of Granada (1085–1492), and the Moriscos, those who came under Christian rule after the fall of Granada and chose "baptism" rather than expulsion (1502–1609), endeavored to maintain their faith in the face of the rapidly growing pressure on them to convert. As they gradually forgot their language, they were unable to recite the Qurʾān in Arabic (a requirement of the faith). Consequently, Aljamiado translations of the scriptures were made by their scholars. The earliest was the one prepared by ʿĪsā ibn Jābir in 1456, and others were to follow.

Aljamiado works on *tafsīr* were also produced during this period. The work by ʿĪsā ibn Jābir, *El-alquiteb segobiano: Brebiario sunni, memorial de los principales mandamientos y debedamientos de nuestra santa ley y sunna* (The Book of Segovia: A Sunnī Breviary and Reminder of the Principal Matters and Requirements of Our Sacred Religion and *Sunnah*), was one that gained wide circulation. Equally widespread was the work of the anonymous author known only by the pen name of Mancebo de Arévalo ("young man of Arévalo"), in which the ideas of al-Ghazālī are evident. There were also Aljamiado translations of earlier Arabic works, including the *tafsīr* of Ibn Abī Zamanīn, to which we have already referred, and the non-Spanish work on Mālikī *fiqh*, *Kitāb al-tafrīʿ* (Book of Ramification) by Ibn al-Jallāb al-Baṣrī.

In addition to this literature, which is more imitative than creative, there existed a body of poetry that portrayed the piety of these Muslims. We do not know the author of the *Poema de José* or whether, indeed, it is of Muslim rather than Jewish origin. Significantly, however, it reproduces the story of Joseph as this is depicted in the Qurʾān. Another Aljamiado poem, a hymn in praise of the Prophet, depicts the tenderness with which the Moriscos addressed Muḥammad even in time of great duress.

As in the case of the Christians who came under Muslim rule in the eighth century, the well-being of the Mudéjares and the Moriscos was governed by treaty. According to the treaty of the surrender of Granada, the Muslims were guaranteed their freedom to remain Muslim, but in 1502 that treaty was abrogated and the Muslims were given the choice of conversion or expulsion. Because of their inability (or unwillingness) to assimilate into the mainstream of Spanish Christian society (culturally inferior to their own), and their rebellion in

1568–1570 (the rising of the Alpujarras), the majority of the descendants of those who converted to Christianity were forced into exile in 1609–1610 by order of Philip III, prompted by the unprincipled duke of Lerma (viceroy of Valencia). With that, the presence of Islam in the Iberian Peninsula came to an end.

BIBLIOGRAPHY

The student of Muslim Spain will be well advised to examine first James T. Monroe's *Islam and the Arabs in Spanish Scholarship, Sixteenth Century to the Present* (Leiden, 1970), where the major problems of scholarship in this field are cogently analyzed. Unfortunately, there is a paucity of material in English. To date, the standard history of Muslim Spain—extending only until the end of the period of the caliphate—is that of Evariste Lévi-Provençal, *Histoire de l'Espagne musulmane, 711–1031,* 3 vols. (Paris, 1950–1953). The third volume concentrates on the social and cultural history of Spain during the period of the caliphate. Lévi-Provençal's work supersedes the first two volumes of Reinhart Dozy's *Histoire des musulmanes d'Espagne* (1861), revised by Lévi-Provençal (Paris, 1932). Dozy's work has been translated by Francis Griffin Stokes as *Spanish Islam: A History of the Moslems in Spain* (1913; reprint, London, 1972). Coverage in Dozy's third volume extends only to the period of the *ṭā'ifah* kings. For the period of the Almoravids and Almohads see Jacinta Bosch Vilá's *Los Almorávides* (Tetuán, Morocco, 1956) and Roger Le Tourneau's *The Almohad Movement in North Africa in the Twelfth and Thirteenth Centuries* (Princeton, 1969). S. M. Imamuddin's *Muslim Spain, 711–1492 A.D.: A Sociological Study* (Leiden, 1981) is one of very few books that attempt to portray Muslim Spain in a manner other than that of a political survey. A well-written volume that is sympathetic to the cultural achievement of the Muslims in Spain is *A History of Islamic Spain* by W. Montgomery Watt and Pierre Cachia (Edinburgh, 1965). Titus Burckhardt's *Moorish Culture in Spain,* translated by Alisa Jaffa (London, 1972), is an interesting volume by a generalist, intended for the lay reader.

While some Arabic texts have been translated into French, and more into Spanish, the main sources remain untranslated. One important exception is al-Maqqarī's *Nafḥ al-ṭīb min ghuṣn al-Andalus al-raṭīb,* which has been edited by Reinhart Dozy and others as *Analectes sur l'histoire et la littérature des Arabes de l'Espagne,* 2 vols. (1855–1861; reprint, Amsterdam, 1967), and partially translated and edited by Pascual de Gayangos y Arce as *A History of the Mohammedan Dynasties in Spain,* 2 vols. (1840–1843; reprint, New York, 1964). Gayangos includes in the appendixes the translation of fragments other than al-Maqqarī's.

On the history of Christian Spain during the period under discussion, see Joseph F. O'Callaghan's *A History of Medieval Spain* (Ithaca, 1975), as well as Ramón Menéndez Pidal's *The Cid and His Spain,* a translation by Harold Sunderland (London, 1934) of the first of two volumes of the work of the master of Spanish historians. Thomas F. Glick's *Islamic and Christian Spain in the Early Middle Ages* (Princeton, 1979) is a successful attempt at a comparative analysis of the two contemporary societies of medieval Spain. Differing approaches to the issue of conversion are found in the chapter on Spain in Richard W. Bulliet's *Conversion to Islam in the Medieval Period: An Essay in Quantitative History* (Cambridge, Mass., 1979), pp. 114–127, and Thomas W. Arnold's *The Preaching of Islam: A History of the Propagation of the Muslim Faith,* 2d ed. (1913; reprint, Lahore, 1961), chap. 5.

On the history of the Jews in Muslim Spain, see Eliyahu Ashtor's *The Jews of Moslem Spain,* translated by Aaron Klein and Jenny Machlowitz Klein, 2 vols. (Philadelphia, 1973–1979), and, *inter alia,* volumes 4 and 5 of Salo W. Baron's *A Social and Religious History of the Jews,* 2d rev. ed. (New York, 1957).

There is a need in English for a work similar to A. González Palencia's *Historia de la literatura arábigo-española,* 2d ed. (Barcelona, 1945), which deals with all aspects of Spanish Muslim literature in an introductory fashion. Among the works of the distinguished D. Miguel Asín Palacios, attention must be drawn to his *Abenházam de Córdoba y su historia critica de las ideas religiosas,* 5 vols. (Madrid, 1927–1932), as well as his *Abenmasarra y su escuela: Orígenes de la filosofía hispanomusulmana* (Madrid, 1914), translated by Elmer H. Douglas as *The Mystical Philosophy of Ibn Masarra and His Followers* (Leiden, 1978). Among various English translations of Ibn Ḥazm's *Ṭawq al-ḥamāmah,* the latest is that of A. J. Arberry, *The Ring of the Dove: A Treatise on the Art and Practice of Arab Love* (London, 1953). For the work of Ibn Ṭufayl, see *Ibn Tufayl's Hayy Ibn Yaqẓān: A Philosophical Tale,* translated with introduction and notes by Lenn Evan Goodman (New York, 1972). Ibn al-ʿArabī's biography of the Ṣūfīs of Muslim Spain appears in English as *Ṣūfīs of Andalusia: The "Rūḥ al-Quds" and "al-Durrat al-Fākhirah" of Ibn ʿArabī,* translated with notes by R. W. J. Austin (London, 1971).

On the period of the Mudéjares and Moriscos see the ongoing work of Robert I. Burns (with special attention to the region of Valencia), such as his collected essays, *Moors and Crusaders in Mediterranean Spain* (London, 1978). See also (with reference to the kingdom of Aragon) John Boswell's *The Royal Treasure: Muslim Communities under the Crown of Aragon in the Fourteenth Century* (New Haven, 1977).

HANNA E. KASSIS

Islam in Sub-Saharan Africa

Our main sources for the study of the history of Islam in sub-Saharan Africa before the sixteenth century are works by Arab geographers and historians. Archaeological excavations (in Kumbi-Saleh, Awdaghust, Jenne, Niani, and Kilwa) provide new evidence for historical reconstruction. Oral traditions, if carefully interpreted, may offer the Africans' own perception of their history. From the sixteenth century on, writings in Arabic by African Muslims become of great importance. For this period oral traditions are somewhat more reliable, and ethnographic data is of greater relevance. Finally, external evidence can be drawn from European records.

Islam in the Sahara and the Sahel. The Arab conquerors of North Africa stopped on the fringes of the Sahara, and Islam was carried across the Sahara by traders rather than by warriors. Between the eighth and tenth centuries these traders were mostly members of Khārijī sects, who had their centers in the oases at the northern gates of the Sahara (Sijilmāsah, Tāhart, Wargla, and Ghadames). As trade developed they established towns in the southern Sahara (Awdaghust, Tadmekka, and Kawwar). These towns faced the African states of Ghana, Gao, and Kanem in the northern belt of the Sudan, which the Arabs called *sāḥil* (the "shore" of the desert).

The Fatimid conquest of North Africa, the migration of the Hilalian nomads, and the rise of the Almoravids all contributed to the decline of Khārijī influence in the tenth and eleventh centuries. The Mālikī scholars who arrived in North Africa at the beginning of the ninth century won adherents among the common people against the dominant schools supported by the rulers, first the Aghlabids, who favored the Ḥanafī school, and then the Fatimids, who were a Shīʿī sect. With popular support the Mālikī scholars survived ordeals by the rulers. The Almoravids, who were strict adherents of the Mālikī school, finally gave it official status, and it has dominated the Sahara and the whole of West Africa ever since. [*See also* Islam in North Africa.]

Three stages of islamization. By the eleventh century traders from North Africa had settled in the capitals of the African states of the Sahel. The role of Islam in three of those states may be inferred from the observations of the Andalusian geographer al-Bakrī, writing in

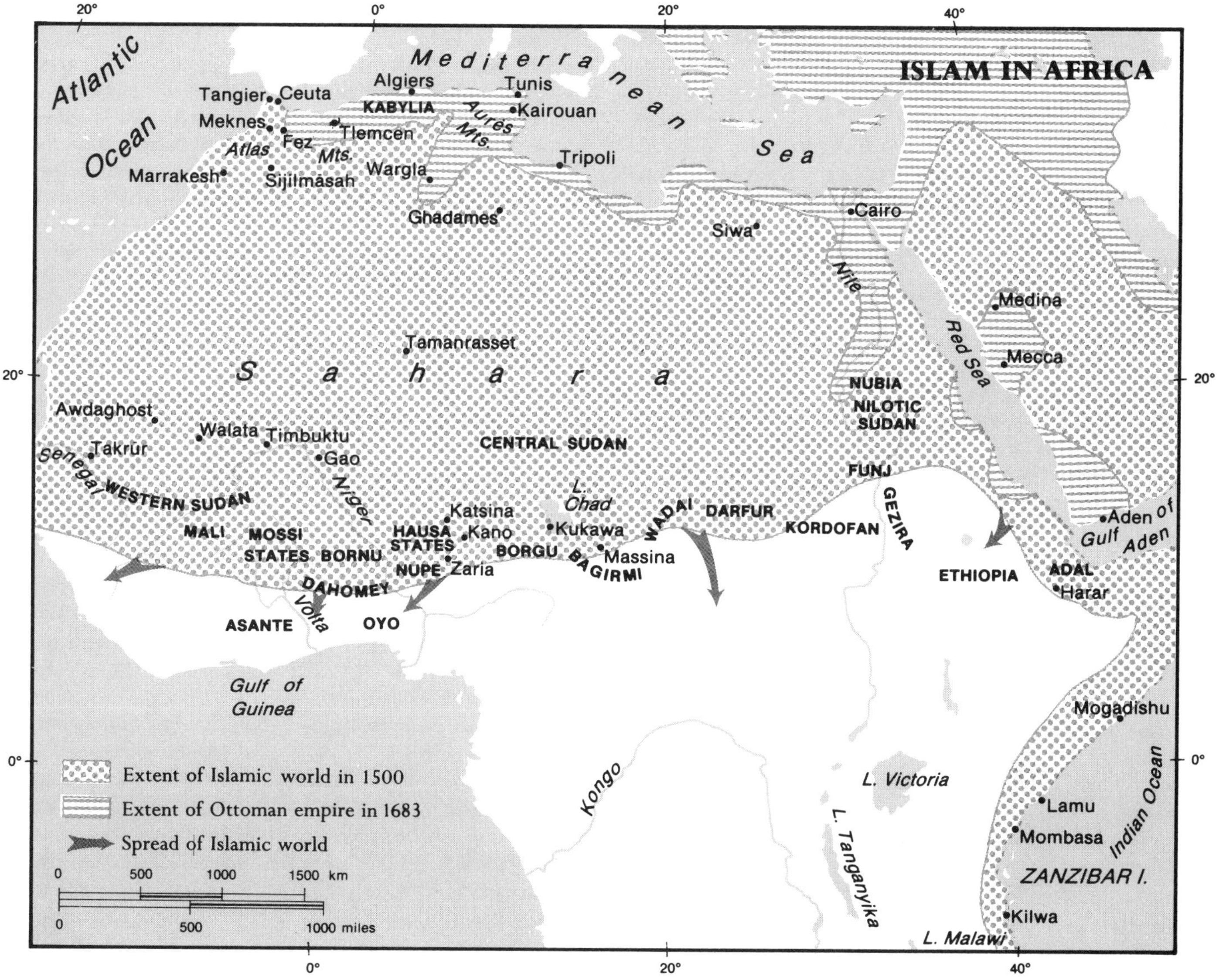

1067/8. In Ghana, he reports, Muslims lived in their own town, separate from the king's town. The king, though himself a non-Muslim, was praised for "his love of justice and generosity toward the Muslims." The majority of his ministers were Muslims. Gao, on the Niger east of the river bend, was also divided into Muslim and royal towns. The king of Gao, however, was considered Muslim, while his subjects adhered to their ancestral religion, and pre-Islamic customs continued at the court. In Takrūr, on the lower Senegal River, the Muslim king forced his subjects to accept Islam. He introduced Islamic law and waged a holy war against the infidels.

These three contemporary situations described by al-Bakrī may also be taken to represent three successive stages in the islamization of West Africa: first, the growth of a Muslim community under a non-Muslim king; second, the adoption of Islam as the court's religion; finally, the rise of Islamic militancy, entailing the imposition of Islamic law and the conversion of the common people. It was the second stage, represented by Gao, that was most typical of West Africa until the eighteenth century.

According to the evidence of the geographer al-Zuhrī, writing in 1137, the people of Ghana converted to Islam in 1076/7, under the influence of the Almoravids *(al-murābiṭūn),* a militant movement of the Berbers of the southwestern Sahara. In 1154 al-Idrīsī described Ghana as a Muslim state, still among the most powerful in the Western Sudan. But by the middle of the thirteenth century the power of Ghana had declined, the center of gravity had shifted southward, and Mali, on the Niger, emerged as the dominant power.

Mali: The West African pattern of islamization. From the tenth century on, political developments in West Africa were influenced by the extension of trade routes to new sources of gold farther to the south, which brought new territories and more peoples within an expanding commercial network. The traders who operated over these routes were Africans, mostly of Soninke origin (related to the rulers of Ghana), known in the Arabic sources as Wangara and in modern writings as Dyula. Through their dealings with North African traders they too were exposed to Islam, which they adopted more easily because they had abandoned the peasant way of life in which African traditional religions are rooted. In their wanderings they created trading communities that served as new solidarity groupings to replace old tribal loyalties. But as long as Islam was confined to traders it remained peripheral to African societies. The latter were penetrated only when Muslim clerics (rather than traders) succeeded in winning over the chiefs. An early account of such a process was recorded by al-Bakrī in the eleventh century:

> A small chiefdom of the Malinke was afflicted by drought. Prayers and sacrifices of the local priests were in vain. The king complained to a Muslim guest, apparently an itinerant cleric ("he used to read the Qur'ān and was acquainted with the *sunnah*"). The Muslim promised that if the king accepted Islam he would pray for his relief. When the king agreed, the Muslim "made him recite some easy passages from the Qur'ān and taught him religious obligations and practices which no one may be excused from knowing." On the following Friday, the king purified himself and was dressed in a white cotton robe (which still distinguishes Muslims from non-Muslims). The two set out for a nearby hill and stood in prayer for the whole night. At dawn God caused abundant rain to descend upon them. "The king ordered the idols to be broken and expelled the sorcerers from his country. He and his descendants as well as his nobles became Muslims, while the common people of his kingdom remained polytheists *(mushrikūn).*"

As al-Bakrī's account suggests, the Muslim succeeded by demonstrating the omnipotence of God: praying to Allāh saved the kingdom after the local priests had failed. Indeed, Islam made its earliest appeal in competition with African traditional religion. The chiefs were particularly inclined to seek the Muslims' prayers and amulets because of the great strains they underwent in the process of state-building: competition over the chieftaincy, fear of plots, wars with other states, and, above all, the responsibility for the welfare of the whole community. By contrast, the common people, even within the new states, did not experience radical social and economic changes that called for a readjustment of religious life. The traditional religion—fertility rites, ancestor worship, and the supplication of deities—remained compatible with their way of life. Also, chiefs, rather than commoners, came into physical contact with Muslims in controlling their commercial activities, in inquiring about conditions in other countries, and in employing the literati in the administration. Hence, they played an important role in the process of islamization as early recipients of Islamic influence. Indeed, a survey of the spread of Islam in West Africa indicates that Islam was not adopted by segmentary societies even when and where Muslim traders and clerics were present.

In this situation, Islam could have become a divisive factor between the chiefs, who came under Islamic influence, and the commoners, who remained attached to their ancestral religion. As a result, the chiefs, whose authority was rooted in the traditional system, chose to hold a middle position between Islam and tradition.

They behaved as Muslims in some situations while following the traditional etiquette in others. They patronized Muslim religious figures but referred also to traditional priests and shrines. Dynasties or individual rulers could opt for greater commitment to Islam or could fall back upon tradition. An examination of the particular case of Mali will serve to illustrate the historical circumstances underlying such choices.

Arabic sources and oral traditions agree that chiefs among the Malinke had come under Islamic influence before Sundiata, the founder of the empire of Mali. But Sundiata appears in the traditional lore as a great hunter and a magician, with little or no reference to Islam. Sundiata led his people to a war of liberation against the Soso, but in mobilizing the national resources of the Malinke, he turned to the traditional heritage, not to Islam. Later, when Mali expanded to the Sahel, it incorporated towns such as Walata and Dia that had already been important centers of trade and Islam, and through the Saharan trade came closer to the wider Muslim world. Three of its rulers even went to Mecca. As the small Malinke chiefdom became a vast multiethnic empire, its rulers' attachment to the ancestral religion shifted toward a more Islamic outlook.

Mali reached its zenith in the fourteenth century, when, as documented by Ibn Baṭṭūṭah, it had the appearance of a Muslim state, with many mosques, Muslim scholars, and official Islamic festivals. On his visit to the capital of Mali in 1352/3 Ibn Baṭṭūṭah attended these festivals. Noting that the presence of the king also attracted non-Muslims to the celebration, which had become a national feast, he condemned the persistence of pre-Islamic customs (the sources of the king's legitimacy), but he praised the people of Mali for their assiduous observance of the Friday prayer and their concern for the study of the Qur'ān from memory.

In the fifteenth century Mali lost control to the Tuareg and later to Songhay over the Sahel, where Islam had been more firmly established, and as a result, it was also deprived of direct communications with the wider Muslim world. As more ethnic groups escaped the domination of Mali, the state contracted to its original Malinke nucleus on the Upper Niger. Muslim divines continued to serve the chiefs' courts, but their patrons lost the Islamic commitment of their fourteenth-century predecessors.

Scholars and rulers: Timbuktu in Songhay. Traders, we have seen, opened new routes and established commercial towns, which became arteries and foci for the spread of Islam. But the carriers of Islam were the men of religion, the *'ulamā'* (sg., *'ālim*) in Arabic. In African languages they are variously known as *karamoro* in the Manding languages, *alfa* in Songhay, *tierno* in Fulfulde, or *mallam* in Hausa. These terms cover a whole range of religious personalities, from the scholars who are part of a worldwide body of the learned elite to the clerics who render magico-religious services to non-Muslim chiefs. The latter became integrated into African societies by playing religious, social, and political roles similar to those of traditional priests. Like these priests, Muslim clerics were peacemakers who pleaded for the wrongdoers, and their mosques, like the traditional shrines, served as sanctuaries. They were expected not to interfere in the political competition within African societies. Immunity of life and property, enhanced by their magico-religious role, was effective only as long as Muslims posed no threat to the existing sociopolitical order.

While some Muslims served in chiefly courts, others lived in autonomous market towns, such as Timbuktu. As a center of trade and learning, Timbuktu provided an important link between the Sudanic savanna and the Berber Sahara. In the fourteenth century, under the rule of Mali, its leading scholars were blacks. Mansā Mūsā, the most distinguished king of Mali (1312–1337), sent Malian scholars to study in Fez. In the fifteenth century, under the patronage of the Tuareg (Berbers of the central Sahara), Sanhājah scholars, who were their kin, became prominent in Timbuktu. They became known as the people of Sankore because they lived in the quarter of the Sankore mosque.

The Sanhājah scholars of Timbuktu seem to have been concerned, more than other West African *'ulamā'*, with the political content of Islam. They did not conform to the matrix that had helped Muslims to become integrated into African states. As spokesmen of the merchants of Timbuktu they guarded the autonomy of the city, and this situation led to a bitter conflict when Timbuktu was conquered by Sonni 'Alī in 1469. Sonni 'Alī turned the small kingdom of Gao into the extensive empire of Songhay. Like his predecessors in the kingship of Gao since the tenth century, he was a Muslim who remained attached to the traditional heritage. A ruthless ruler, he persecuted those scholars of Timbuktu whom he considered a threat but respected others who collaborated with him. This was perhaps the earliest case of mounting tensions between scholars and rulers in West Africa.

In 1493, following Sonni 'Alī's death, his son was overthrown by one of the generals who had allied himself with the discontented Muslim elements in the western provinces of Songhay. As Askiyā Muḥammad, this general became the founder of a new dynasty and consolidated the empire by pursuing a pro-Muslim policy in collaboration with the scholars of Timbuktu. Three years after his accession he went on the pilgrimage and returned with the title of *amīr al-mu'minīn* ("commander of the faithful"), which made him the politico-religious head of the Muslim community *(ummah)* in the Western Sudan.

Askiyā Muḥammad's conciliatory politics helped integrate even the Tuareg of the Sahara into the empire, a development that served the commercial interests of Timbuktu. The scholars of Timbuktu did not agitate for radical changes in the Songhay empire and seem to have rejected the militancy of al-Maghīlī, a visiting scholar from the oasis of Tuat in the northern Sahara. Al-Maghīlī's *Responses* (to questions supposedly put to him by Askiyā Muḥammad) represent the most severe denunciation of the religious and political situation in West Africa prior to the Islamic revolutions of the eighteenth and nineteenth centuries.

Intellectual life in Timbuktu was influenced by that of Egypt. In the late fifteenth and sixteenth centuries the Mālikī scholars from Timbuktu visited Cairo on their way to and from Mecca. In Cairo they studied under eminent scholars, most of whom belonged to the Shāfiʿī school of law. Hence what they acquired there was not legalistic erudition but the knowledge of *ḥadīth* (the prophetic traditions), *taṣawwuf* ("mysticism"), and *balāghah* ("rhetoric"). In this way, scholarship in Timbuktu was freed of the narrow parochialism of the Mālikī school that seems to have strangled intellectual life in the Maghreb at that time. At the end of the sixteenth century the excellence of one Timbuktu scholar, Aḥmad Bābā, was acknowledged when scholars from the major towns of Morocco came to hear his lectures in Marrakesh.

Aḥmad Bābā had not come to Marrakesh voluntarily: he was among the leading scholars of Timbuktu who were exiled following the Moroccan conquest of 1591. But when the formerly autonomous town became the seat of an oppressive military government, once again—as in the time of Sonni ʿAlī—the scholars led the resistance. The continued intellectual preeminence of Timbuktu is signaled by the two most important Arabic chronicles of West Africa, *Ta'rīkh al-Sūdān* (History of Sudan) and *Ta'rīkh al-Fattāsh* (The Researcher's History [of Takrūr]), both of which were written there in the middle of the seventeenth century.

Timbuktu, deteriorated, however, under the rule of the descendants of the Moroccan conquerors. Feuding factions struggled for power within Timbuktu, and Tuareg nomads harassed the town from the outside. In 1737 the Tuareg became the dominant power on the Niger bend. Islamic scholarship, so closely associated with the commerce of Timbuktu, also declined. When military and political ascendancy passed into the hands of the Tuareg, learning and spiritual leadership also departed from the town to the nomads' camp. By the middle of the eighteenth century the Kunta, a nomadic clan of Arab and Berber descent, wielded influence over the whole of Muslim West Africa.

In the segmentary societies of the Saharan nomads, the prestige of the religious leaders, known as *marabouts*, carried political influence through their mediation between warring groups. Clerical lineages in the Sahara were also engaged in trade, employing a network of disciples and followers. The conversion of religious prestige to economic resources and political assets explains the rise of the Kunta. Their leader, Sīdī al-Mukhtār al-Kabīr (1728–1811), was a learned scholar and a great mystic. He reinvigorated the Qādirīyah Ṣūfī order, which had played an indistinct role in the religious life of the Sahara for more than two centuries. He was venerated by the Tuareg and through his influence over them extended his patronage over Timbuktu. But his religious authority reached even farther as his disciples spread his Qādirī teachings among many Muslim groups in the savannah.

Islam in the savanna. In the savanna Islam suffered a setback as a result of the collapse of the imperial system in the Western Sudan, which had been sustained by the successive hegemonies of Mali and Songhay. Muslims had lost the patronage of great kings such as Mansā Mūsā and Askiyā Muḥammad, with their strong commitment to Islam, and by the seventeenth century they were living under the auspices of lesser chiefs who were strongly influenced by their traditional heritage. But what Islam had lost in intensity it gained in extent. Muslim traders now reached the fringes of the forest and opened up new areas to the influence of Islam. Moreover, in the age of the great empires Islam had been an urban phenomenon, restricted to merchants, scholars, and clerics. In the seventeenth and eighteenth centuries Muslims made inroads into the countryside and won adherents among peasants and fishermen who until then had hardly been influenced by Islam.

On the Middle Niger, in the central parts of present-day Mali, the Bambara, who had resisted islamization when they were subjects of imperial Mali, became more open to Islam when they entered a process of state formation of their own. Bambara chiefs began to practice rudimentary Islam without abandoning traditional rituals.

The role of Muslims as advisers to rulers and as masters of supernatural power was transmitted from the Middle Niger to the Volta Basin, where several patterns of islamization and integration evolved. East of the Black Volta River—in Gonja, Dagomba, Mamprusi, and

Wa (present-day northern Ghana)—Muslims of Dyula and Hausa origin adopted local languages and other cultural features. They became integrated into the sociopolitical system of these states. West of the Black Volta River (modern Ivory Coast) the Dyula preserved their cultural and linguistic identity either as residents of states such as Buna and Gyaman or as autonomous communities among stateless peoples. In Kong and Bobo-Dyulasso (formerly Upper Volta, now Burkina Faso) the Dyula created their own states.

Farther west, over an extensive area where the modern frontiers of the Ivory Coast, Guinea, and Mali meet, the Dyula lived among Malinke warriors and peasants, from whom they differed only in their commercial occupation and Islamic religion. The distinction between Malinke and Dyula thus corresponds to the dichotomy between warriors and Muslims that prevailed over the whole of the Western Sudan and the Sahara. Warrior who exercised political authority, shed blood, and indulged in drinking alcohol often professed Islam but were not committed Muslims. As chiefs they were in a religious category of their own, between Islam and tradition. Muslims accepted this as a divinely ordained order that should not be disturbed.

The early jihād movements. With the rise of Islamic militancy in the last quarter of the seventeenth century, a crisis came about. In the southwestern Sahara, where the Almoravid movement had originated more than six centuries earlier, a cleric challenged the political supremacy of the Ḥassānī warriors. Nāṣir al-Dīn, as he chose to call himself, was an ascetic scholar known for his emanating blessing *(barakah).* He called for repentance and, at the head of a body of devoted disciples, declared a *jihād* about 1675.

This was the first in a series of what are often referred to as *jihād* movements. For the militant Muslim leaders their wars were indeed conceived as *jihād* (war against unbelievers), with the legal and theological meanings of this concept. But the historical circumstances in West Africa were different from the classical model of *jihād* that was carried to extend the frontiers of *dār al-Islām* ("the abode of Islam") at the expense of *dār al-ḥarb* ("the abode of war"). In West Africa the *jihād*s brought about the political ascendancy of Islam not through conquest from the outside, but through the uprising of Muslim militants who lived within pluralistic societies including infidels as well as believers at different stages of islamization. West African *jihād*s were therefore revolutions that accomplished a long evolutionary process.

Nāṣir al-Dīn extended his preaching to the Senegal Valley among the Tokolor of Fūta Tōro and to the Wolof. As millennial expectations were raised, people shaved their heads as a sign of repentance and doubled their prayers. Chiefs of the Wolof and those in the Fūta Tōro area rejected the call for repentance because it meant for them not religious conversion, since they considered themselves Muslims, but adoption of a clerical way of life, the antithesis of their ethos as chiefs and warriors. The clerics were temporarily successful as leaders of a popular uprising, but by 1677 the warriors had recuperated and emerged victorious. Significantly, alignments of ruling warriors against Muslims crossed ethnic boundaries, in both the Sahara and the Senegal Valley.

The *jihād* of Nāṣir al-Dīn failed, but directly or indirectly, it inspired the eighteenth-century revolutionary movements. In Bundu in present-day Senegal (c. 1700), in Fūta Jalon in present-day Guinea (c. 1725), and in Fūta Tōro (c. 1776), clerics took arms and seized political authority. They all, like Nāṣir al-Dīn, adopted the title *al-imām* ("the imam," alternately *elimani, almamy*), which implied political and religious leadership. These clerics were Torodbe, members of clerical lineages in the Fūta Tōro. In Bundu, Mālik Sī led Tokolor migrants to a sparsely populated area and carved his own state out of the dominions of the Soninke ruler of Gadiaga. In Fūta Jalon, Torodbe and Malinke clerics offered ideological and organization leadership to Fulbe pastoralists in their conflicts with Susu, Jallonke, and other peasant societies. After about half a century of warfare the imamate of Fūta Jalon was consolidated. In Fūta Tōro, Torodbe clerics overthrew the Denianke dynasty that had ruled since the beginning of the sixteenth century, wavering between Islam and tradition.

In Fūta Jalon the post-*jihād* state was torn by internal conflicts. The office of the *almamy* rotated between two families, but its effective authority was circumscribed by the power of nine emirs, political rulers descended from the nine clerics who had proclaimed the *jihād.* Tensions arose between the emirs and the council of the *'ulamā'* as the latter, guardians of the ideals of the *jihād,* sought to guide the clerics' descendants. The non-Fulbe inhabitants of Fūta Jalon became serfs of the Fulbe aristocracy. Conversion to Islam among this subaltern group was discouraged, so that their religion could be used to justify their inferior status. Islam therefore was not an integrative factor in Fūta Jalon as it was to be, for example, in post-*jihād* Hausaland.

In Fūta Tōro, 'Abd al-Qādir, the first *almamy* of the post-*jihād* state (1776–1806), built mosques and appointed imams to strengthen Islam at the local level of the villages. But he and his successors could not establish the central authority that was necessary to implement radical reforms. The authority of the *almamy* was limited by the old landed aristocracy, which had not been dispossessed, and by the new oligarchy of Torodbe lineages, who had participated in the *jihād* and were granted land as fiefs. Fūta Tōro did not even have a permanent capital and each *almamy* ruled from his own village. For a reformer like ʿUmar Tāl (al-Ḥājj ʿUmar), Fūta Tōro represented an incomplete revolution. [*See* Fulbe Religion *for further discussion.*]

Kanem-Bornu and Hausaland to 1800. Kanem, in present-day Chad northeast of Lake Chad, was one of the earliest states mentioned in the Arabic sources, about the middle of the ninth century. But Islam was introduced into Kanem by Muslim traders from Tripoli and Fezzan (in present-day Libya) only at the beginning of the twelfth century, at least a century after it had gained a foothold in Takrūr and Gao.

Whereas in the Western Sudan the spread of Islam was aided by the gold trade, with its extensive network of routes leading to the goldfields, in the Central Sudan the slave trade to North Africa that dominated the economy inhibited the spread of Islam. Instead of an expanding network of routes, there was a boundary of enmity and violence, crossed only by raiding warriors, not by traders and clerics. During periods of military strength, Kanem, and later also Bornu, expanded northward into the Sahara, not to the south. It was only in the sixteenth century that Islam entered Baghirmi, the first islamized state south of Lake Chad.

Though Islam came late to Kanem, its impact seems to have been greater than in the states of the western Sudan. In the thirteenth century, under powerful rulers, Kanem expanded as far as Fezzan. Its kings went on pilgrimage, and in the 1240s a *madrasah* ("school") was built in Cairo for its students and scholars there. About the middle of the fourteenth century the Saifawa dynasty was forced to abandon Kanem and moved to Bornu in the southwestern corner of Lake Chad (present-day Nigeria). There, Bornu reached its zenith under Mai Idrīs Alawma (1570–1603), when all dignitaries of the state were Muslim and the capital, N'Gazargamu, was an important center of Islamic learning. As judges, imams, and teachers, scholars were influential in government and were granted privileges and exempted from taxation. Other scholars preferred to preserve strict piety by refusing any association with the political authorities, however, and they established autonomous Muslim communities in the countryside. In Bornu, more than in other African states, Islam also spread among the common people. But even in Bornu, perhaps the most islamized of all African states before the *jihāds*, pre-Islamic elements persisted on the symbolic and organizational levels. Early in the nineteenth century the survival of pre-Islamic cults were to be exploited as a pretext to justify the extension of the *jihād* from Hausaland to Bornu. Muhammadu Bello, son of Usuman dan Fodio, wrote in *Infāq al-maysūr* (p. 9): "We have been told that their rulers and chiefs today have places to which they ride where they offer sacrifices and then pour the blood on the gates of their towns. . . . They perform rites to the river. . . ."

Islam came to Hausaland only in the fourteenth century, the period when the Saifawa dynasty moved from Kanem to Bornu. Also at that time a direct trade route developed from Hausaland to Tripoli, and Wangara traders from Mali extended their commercial operations to Hausaland as well. The Wangara were accompanied by clerics, who offered their services to the rulers of the Hausa states as they had done in the chiefly courts of the Western Sudan. Traditions recorded in the Kano Chronicle (written in its present form in the nineteenth century) describe how Wangara clerics were appointed to different religious functions in the Kano court. Predictably, there was a reaction among the custodians of the traditional religion, and successive rulers of Kano oscillated between commitment to Islam and reliance on traditional resources.

At the end of the fifteenth century, King Rumfa of Kano attempted a reform with an order to cut down the sacred tree under which the first mosque had been built, thus eliminating a symbol of the symbiosis of Islam and prior tradition. He also appointed Islamic judges and encouraged the building of mosques. Rumfa's reformist thrust may have been influenced by al-Maghīlī, the militant North African scholar who visited Kano in 1493. Kano's traditions remember al-Maghīlī and suggest that he left a disciple there to continue the task of instructing the king. Katsina, the rival Hausa state north of Kano, also came under stronger Islamic influence at that time. Scholars from Timbuktu visited Kano and Katsina on their way to the pilgrimage and taught in these towns for some time, and their presence in turn contributed to the growth of a body of local Hausa scholars and clerics.

Since the sixteenth century Muslim clerics had served in the courts of the Hausa rulers, where they held official titles and participated in the election of the kings. These clerics became the target for the criticism of the reformers, who called them the "vile *ʿulamāʾ*" because of their commitment to the existing sociopolitical order. Along with the clerics in the chiefly courts, the scholars of Yandoto, the autonomous Muslim town in Hausaland, also opposed the *jihād.*

Revolution and reform in Hausaland and Bornu. Pious scholars avoided not only the chiefly courts but also the trading towns. They preferred to live in independent communities *(jamāʿāt)* with their disciples in the countryside, where they preached among the peasants and contributed to the radicalization of Islam.

Scholars who had previously been spokesmen of the merchants only began to articulate the grievances of the peasants in Islamic terms. In addition, by the eighteenth century religious treatises were being written in Hausa, which made them accessible to a wider public, not simply to the few scholars who knew Arabic.

Reformist ideas were in the air throughout the Muslim world in the eighteenth century. Ṣūfī orders, which had, since the thirteenth century, developed popular ecstatic practices and antinomian tendencies, became reoriented toward greater adherence to the *sharīʿah*. Speculative mysticism, which had encouraged otherworldly escapism, gave way to increased involvement in society and to political activism. Unlike the Wahhābī movement in Arabia, which rejected Sufism altogether, these movements insisted on reform within Sufism. The reformed Ṣūfī orders played an important role in eighteenth- and nineteenth-century West Africa. There were also some direct links with the general movement. Jibrīl ibn ʿUmar, the militant mentor of Usuman dan Fodio, was affiliated with the Khalwatī order, which contributed to the resurgence of Islam in Egypt, North Africa, and the Sudan. It is in this context that the political activism of the Kunta and the reinvigorated Qādirīyah they propagated may also be understood.

Usuman dan Fodio, the leader of the Fulbe *jihād*, belonged to the scholarly community of the Toronkawa, (the Hausa form of Torodbe), who lived in autonomous communities in the countryside and were not engaged in trade. Communicating with the Hausa rulers of Gobir from a distance, they avoided accommodation and integration and continued the scholarly tradition of Timbuktu with a high level of learning. They were affiliated with the Qādirīyah through the Kunta. They identified themselves as Fulfulde speakers, and though they were sedentaries and committed Muslims, they shared cultural values with the Fulbe pastoralists: in spite of their scholarly vocation they remained good horsemen and carried arms.

Usuman and his disciples also preached around the villages. Oppressed and exploited peasants responded to these holy men, who called for the removal of arbitrary government and for the creation of a new order governed by the law of God, in short, an alternative form of leadership for the common people. Tensions grew between Usuman and the king of Gobir, who had rejected the Shehu's reformist program. As Usuman's life was in danger, he moved from Degel to Gudu, some fifty kilometers to the northwest. This event became known as his *hijrah*, or "emigration," following the example of the prophet Muḥammad. It brought about the disengagement of committed Muslims from the rest of society, a preparatory stage for the *jihād*.

At that point the reformers adopted a more severe definition of unbelief *(kufr)*, which became political rather than theological. Those who collaborated with the enemy, or even those Muslims who stayed behind, became legitimate targets for the *jihād*. As a *jihād* may be waged only against infidels, anathematizing *(takfīr)*, which had hardly been known earlier in Sunnī Islam, became a living issue. There was no more place for the ambiguity that had prevailed for centuries. Rulers who held a middle position between Islam and tradition were declared infidels.

The Fulbe pastoralists, whose military support later proved crucial, joined the *jihād* only after Usuman had scored his first victories. They were motivated not by Islamic zeal but by their old antagonism with the Hausa rulers and by solidarity with the Toronkawa, to whom they were culturally related.

From Gobir the *jihād* spread to the other Hausa states, where a similar coalition of Toronkawa, Fulbe pastoralists, and discontented Hausa peasants revolted. Leaders of the local *jihād*s, some of them former disciples or associates of Usuman, recognized his authority, symbolized by the acceptance of a flag. After each of them had established his emirate they accepted Usuman and his successors as *amīr al-muslimīn* (Hausa, *sarkin musulmi*), the supreme religious and political leaders of the community. [*See also the biography of Dan Fodio.*]

In the Sokoto caliphate a serious attempt was made to govern according to the *sharīʿah*, but the political dynamics produced a gap between ideals and realities. The scholars who led the *jihād* and became rulers retained their religious titles (such as *shekhu* or *mallam*), but their successors adopted political titles (such as *sultan* and *emir*). Further, since the post-*jihād* states were created over the foundations of the former Hausa states, entrenched pre-*jihād* structures and practices came to the surface and interfered with the application of a purist Islamic model of government. The local interests of the emirates encouraged centrifugal tendencies within the caliphate. But the ideals and values of the *jihād*, even when not fully realized, remained normative and guided the rulers, because the essence of the revolution was the shift of Islam from its former peripheral role to that of the *raison d'être* of the state. Islamic institutions gradually transformed the life of the society as a whole and of the individuals within it. In the post-*jihād* states of West Africa, as in the central lands of Islam many centuries before, conversion to Islam occurred under Muslim political domination. Non-Muslims were permitted to practice their own faiths, but there was an unremitting process of conversion to the rulers' religion. There remained, however, into the twentieth century, non-Muslim Hausa-speaking communities known as Maguzawa.

Territorially the *jihād* extended beyond the former Hausa states to the politically fragmented regions of Adamawa and Bauchi in the southeast and to Nupe and the northern parts of Yorubaland in the southwest. The military thrust was arrested in the forest of western Nigeria, but Islam reached an advanced position from which impressive inroads were to be made among the Yoruba in the nineteenth and twentieth centuries.

Fulbe clan leaders on the southwestern frontiers of Bornu, following the example of their kinsmen in Hausaland, revolted against the king of Bornu. Although Bornu had been a Muslim state for many centuries, the Fulbe considered their fighting as an extension of the *jihād*. The cause of Bornu was defended by a scholar, Muḥammad ibn al-Amīn al-Kānimī, who succeeded in warding off the Fulbe and assumed effective authority although the king continued to reign. Under al-Kānimī, Bornu was accepted as a legitimate Muslim state, even by those leaders in Sokoto who had earlier justified a *jihād* against it. In 1846 Shekhu ʿUmar, al-Kānimī's son, deposed the last king of Bornu and put an end to the old Saifawa dynasty along with its traditional heritage.

The nineteenth-century jihāds in the Western Sudan. The success and consolidation of the reform movement in Hausaland and Bornu had already shaped the political contours of modern northern Nigeria early in the nineteenth century, but in the Western Sudan, there were still many upheavals to come.

In 1818 a Fulbe cleric, Shekhu Aḥmadu Lobbo, declared a *jihād* against Fulbe clan leaders practicing a mixed Islam in Massina, on the Middle Niger south of Timbuktu. Shekhu Aḥmadu's militancy exceeded his scholarship, and the theocratic state he created was distinguished by bigotry and parochialism. It was criticized by the more sophisticated Kunta shaykhs and leaders of the Sokoto caliphate. In 1862 this state, then ruled by Shekhu Aḥmadu's grandson, was conquered and destroyed by a rival *jihād* led by al-Ḥājj ʿUmar (ʿUmar Tāl), who accused Massina of collaborating with the non-Muslim Bambara.

Al-Ḥājj ʿUmar (1794/97–1864) considered the rulers of the post-*jihād* states of his time—with the exception of the Sokoto caliphate—unworthy successors to the leaders of the *jihād* movements. His main objective was to complete the unfinished revolution in his homeland, Fūta Tōro, but the road to Fūta Tōro was blocked by the French, who were protecting their interests on the Senegal River. Al-Ḥājj ʿUmar therefore turned eastward and conquered the Bambara states of Segu and Kaarta as well as Massina to form a state over large parts of the present republic of Mali. Although al-Ḥājj ʿUmar did not take over the Fūta Tōro area, he won the hearts of many thousands of Tokolor, who responded to his call, made the *hijrah*, and formed the core of his military force.

During his pilgrimage to Mecca (c. 1830) al-Ḥājj ʿUmar was appointed the leader *(muqaddam)* of the Tijānī Ṣūfī order in West Africa. The Tijānīyah was a new order, founded by Aḥmad al-Tijānī (1737–1815) as part of the more general Ṣūfī revival of the eighteenth century. Al-Ḥājj ʿUmar came back from the pilgrimage dedicated to the reform of Islam. He challenged not only the old West African pattern of mixed Islam but also other Ṣūfī orders, such as the Qādirīyah. The Tijānīyah, as propagated by al-Ḥājj ʿUmar, appealed to all strata of the population, which added to its radicalism; the expanding Ṣūfī order survived the state created by the *jihād*.

Al-Ḥājj ʿUmar was killed when fighting in Madina in 1864. For about thirty years the vast state he created was under the threat of the French, who exploited revolts of subjugated ethnic groups and rivalries among members of his family. Other *jihād* movements in the Western Sudan that started in the second half of the nineteenth century were also thwarted by advancing French colonialism, as in the case of Samori Touré (c. 1830/35–1900), who was in the process of building a powerful Muslim state among the southern Malinke, of Ma Ba (d. 1867) on the Gambia River, and of Mamadu Lamine (c. 1835/40–1887) among the Soninke in Bundu. [*See also* Jihād *and the biography of ʿUmar Tāl.*]

Modern West Africa. Al-Ḥājj ʿUmar and Samori are remembered in the nationalist lore of West Africa as symbols of resistance to the colonial conquest. Groups that had been historically associated with these two *jihād* leaders were later active in the radical anticolonial movements in present-day Guinea and Mali.

In Fūta Jalon the post-*jihād* polities survived until the end of the colonial period. But because the Fulbe ruling aristocracy had not integrated the non-Fulbe ethnic groups into the state through conversion to Islam (as did the ruling Fulbe aristocracy in northern Nigeria), Seku Turé, leader of the radical party of Guinea, succeeded in alienating the non-Fulbe and in eliminating the chieftaincies of Fūta Jalon.

The Sokoto caliphate was the only post-*jihād* state that survived into the postcolonial period. Under the banner of Islam, with commitment to the ideals of the *jihād*, traditional and modern politicians cooperated to secure the ascendancy of the Muslim north in the Federation of Nigeria, especially in the immediate postindependence era (1960–1966).

In Senegal, the decline of the traditional Wolof political authorities under the colonial occupation opened the way for Muslim clerics to present themselves as an alternative leadership. Within two or three decades almost all the Wolof became committed Muslims and affiliated themselves with one of two Ṣūfī orders, the Tijānīyah or the Murīdīyah. The latter was an ingenious Wolof contribution to Ṣūfism. The founder, Aḥmad Bamba (1850–1927), reorganized displaced Wolof peasants and warriors in new settlements for the cultivation of groundnuts. Emphasizing the spiritual importance of work and obedience to the shaykh, he elevated working in the fields to a religious duty. The shaykh took over responsibility for the spiritual well-being of the disciples, and religious prestige was converted to economic power as a large proportion of the income of the groundnut production reached the shaykhs, known in Senegal as marabouts. Tensions with the colonial authorities gave way to working understanding. Under colonial rule and after independence the Murīd marabouts acted as intermediaries between the government and their disciples, for which they gained material benefits and considerable political influence. Tijānī marabouts soon created similar structures.

The influence of the marabouts in Senegal is unique in West Africa. Nowhere else did holy men attain such religious, economic, and political influence, nor did the prestige of the Senegalese marabouts themselves spread elsewhere. Only one of them, Ibrāhīm Niass (1900–1975), gained international fame. Whereas the Murīdīyah had developed a particularistic "wolofized" Islam, Ibrāhīm Niass promoted universalistic Islam by emphasizing the teaching of Arabic and the Islamic sciences and by participating in international Muslim organizations. His branch of the Tijānīyah is the most widespread order in West Africa. In northern Nigeria it won adherents in Kano, and the old political tensions between Kano, the largest state, and Sokoto, the seat of the sultanate, took a new form as conflicts between the Tijānīyah and the Qādirīyah. These conflicts played an important role in the party politics of northern Nigeria.

Under the influence of the Salafīyah in Egypt and North Africa, a reform movement developed, mainly in French West Africa, during the 1930s. Its adherents, educated in Cairo and North Africa, were committed to purifying Islam and to combatting ignorance through the teaching of Arabic and Islam according to modern methods. They attacked the marabouts for exploiting the credulity of the common Muslims. The French colonial authorities supported the traditional religious leadership and restricted the activities of the reformers, whom they identified as "Wahhābīs." The reformers, already under the influence of the anti-Western ideology of Islamic fundamentalism, joined the radical anticolonial movements in Guinea, Mali, and Senegal.

Under colonial rule Islam spread rapidly to new areas opened by modern transportation and by urbanization. In the Sahel and the northern savanna, Islam at last reached all levels of society, so that 80 to 90 percent of the population of Senegal, Gambia, Guinea, Mali, Niger, and northern Nigeria became Muslim. In the southern savanna—Burkina Faso, the northern parts of the Ivory Coast, Ghana, Togo, Benin, and the "Middle Belt" of Nigeria—the resilience of the traditional religions and activities of Christian missions restricted the progress of Islam, and only 20 to 40 percent of the population is Muslim in this area. In southwestern Nigeria Islam won converts among the Yoruba of the forest, but elsewhere in the forest and on the West African coast Muslims were generally perceived as migrants from the north. Their quarters, known as *zongos*, became the melting pot for people from different regions and ethnic groups.

In the coastal towns of the former British colonies—Nigeria, Ghana, and Sierra Leone—the Aḥmadīyah movement was introduced after World War I by Indian missionaries. Membership in the Aḥmadīyah is counted in thousands in West Africa; most adherents had been Muslims before, however, and only very few converted to the Aḥmadīyah directly from traditional religion. The attraction of the movement was that it offered an Islamic way to modernization, largely through a pioneering Muslim-Western education. [*See* Aḥmadīyah.]

Ethiopia and the Horn of Africa. Because of longstanding economic, cultural, and political relations between Arabia and Ethiopia, which is just across the Red Sea, Muslims settled on the Ethiopian coast as early as the eighth century, and by the ninth century there were Muslim communities along the trade routes to the interior, where the Christian kingdom had survived many vicissitudes. Muslims were unable to proselytize within Christian Ethiopia, but farther south their influence resulted in the emergence of Muslim political units, the most important of which was the twelfth-century sultanate of Ifat. With the support of the Muslim rulers, Islam spread among the local people. This development marked the beginning of the long struggle between Islam and Christianity in Ethiopia.

The growing power of Ifat and other Muslim principalities threatened the Christian kingdom, which, in a series of military expeditions at the beginninig of the fourteenth century, defeated Ifat (1332). Ifat's successor as the leading Muslim power was Adal, which controlled Harar, the most important center of trade and Islam in the interior. In their conflict with Christian Ethiopia the rulers of Adal relied on the Somalis as an inexhaustible source of manpower and on the support of the sultanate of Mogadishu.

Somali traditions associate the founders of their clans with Muslim Arabs who settled on the coast and intermarried with the local people. The Somali nomads carried Islamic influence as they expanded along the coast and into the interior. Some coastal settlements developed into thriving towns. By the thirteenth century, according to the Arab geographers, Mogadishu was the most important town on the coast and a center of a sultanate.

At the end of the fifteenth century effective power in Adal was taken over by a general, Aḥmad ibn Ibrāhīm, who advocated a more aggressive policy toward Christian Ethiopia, which he articulated in religious terms. He won the support of religious leaders and himself adopted the politico-religious title of *imām*. Imam Aḥmad Grān, as he became known, incorporated Somalis and other Muslim people into a restructured Islamic state, which by 1527 was ready to launch a *jihād* against Ethiopia. As he penetrated deeper into Christian territories he met little or no resistance. In 1529 he won a decisive victory which completely broke the strength of the Christian kingdom. By 1535 he had appointed Muslim governors over most of the provinces, and it appeared that Islam had finally won the struggle. Christianity, however, was saved by the timely arrival of the Portuguese in the Red Sea. A Portuguese force joined with the Ethiopian emperor's army and together they defeated and killed Aḥmad Grān in 1543.

The devastation caused by the wars between Muslims and Christians opened the way for the Galla pastoralists, who were pressing northward. For some time Muslims and Christians were separated by the pagan Galla who invaded the plateaus. The Galla also invaded the Sidama principalities southwest of Christian Ethiopia, where they adopted the social and political institutions of the sedentary Sidama, and by the beginning of the nineteenth century several centralized Galla states had developed.

On the coast and along the routes leading from the coast Muslims followed the Shāfiʿī school as in Arabia. But in those parts of Ethiopia that came under Islamic influence from the Sudan, the Mālikīyah predominated, as in the Sudan.

Among the Somalis, resistance to Ethiopian and to British imperialism is associated with Muḥammad ibn ʿAbd Allāh, known as the Mad Mullah (1864–1920). Like al-Ḥājj ʿUmar he propagated the cause of a vigorous new order, the Ṣāliḥīyah, and challenged the established religious leadership. He became the symbol of a united Somali nationalism, of which Islam was an integral part. Islam was identified in turn with Arabism, and Somalia, though not an Arabic-speaking country, became a member of the Arab League in 1974.

East Africa. The East African coast and its interior were always sparsely populated. The first Bantu-speaking people had come there only in the sixth and seventh centuries CE, about the same time as the early migrants from Persia and Arabia. Over the centuries, there evolved a new civilization, known as Swahili, from the Arabic *sawāḥilah,* "people of the coast."

Islam reached East and West Africa at about the same time, but while Islam in West Africa had penetrated inland as far as the fringes of the forest by the end of the fifteenth century, in East Africa it remained limited to the coast, occurring only through a process of individual conversion. People from the interior who reached the coast, voluntarily or as slaves, were cut off from their ethnic groups and became integrated into the Muslim Swahili community; islamization implied swahilization. In such a process, fewer people converted, and there was no territorial expansion of Islam, as there was in West Africa.

The first Muslim period. By the thirteenth century the Indian Ocean was a Muslim sea, with Muslims controlling trade and establishing coastal settlements in India, Southeast Asia, and East Africa. Some of the earliest towns in East Africa were built on islands off the coast, which were better protected from attacks by people from the mainland. There was little trade with the interior except in Somalia to the north and Sofala, on the coast of Mozambique, to the south.

Sofala was the port for the gold trade with Zimbabwe. Because Sofala could not be reached from Asia in a single monsoon voyage, the island of Kilwa became a staging post, where the boats for Sofala spent the winter. The nature of life in Kilwa at the peak of its commercial success in the fourteenth century is recounted in the *Chronicle of Kilwa* (written in Arabic in the sixteenth century) and is also reflected in the mosques and palaces that have been unearthed by archaeological excavations there. Ibn Baṭṭūṭah, who visited the coast in 1332, left a record as well: praising the piety, generosity, and humility of the sultan of Kilwa, he wrote that in Kilwa, as well as in Mombasa and Mogadishu, he felt at home because he was traveling within the lands of Islam.

Colonial encounters. The Portuguese conquest in the sixteenth century put an end to the first Muslim period on the East African coast. At the end of the seventeenth century, the Portuguese were expelled from the coastal area north of Mozambique by a combination of local resistance and the rising power of Oman. Omani rule became effective, however, only in 1832, when the sultan moved his capital to Zanzibar in a determined effort to exploit the economic potentiality of East Africa.

It was at that period, in the eighteenth and nineteenth centuries, that Swahili society as it is now known developed. In the mainstream of this society there was no clear line between Arabs and Africans, although some people chose to maintain an Arab identity, especially the Ibāḍīyah (members of the old Khārijī sect) from Oman, whose distinct religious affiliation helped them to maintain racial (i.e., Arab) purity. Swahili, a Bantu language, testifies to the interpenetration of cultures with its large number of Arabic loanwords.

During the seventeenth and eighteenth centuries, trade was initiated not on the coast but by the people of the interior, and by the beginning of the nineteenth century the Nyamwezi were trading between the copper mines of Katanga (in modern Zaire) and the coast. During the 1830s Swahili Arabs, backed by Indian financiers, took over the trade, which was by that time mostly in slaves. They established trading centers in the interior, including Tabora and Ujiji. Their most important partners were the Nyamwezi and the Yao.

Among the Yao, in the area of Lake Nyasa, trade, slave raiding, and the supply of firearms contributed to the rise of powerful territorial chiefs. They employed Swahili clerics as scribes and as divines who offered amulets and prayers. Adoption of Islam helped the Yao chiefs to overcome tensions created in the process of state formation. Matrilineality did not inhibit islamization among the Yao; rather, chiefs consolidated their position by using Islam to avoid the system of uxorilocality, under which the man lived in his wife's matrilineal settlement. Also, the islamization of traditional ceremonies and initiation rites helped spread Islam to all levels of the Yao society.

There was little trade from the coast of Kenya into the interior. The first Muslim traders arrived in Buganda, north of Lake Victoria, through the central route to Lake Tanganyika. In the centralized state of Buganda, Islam could have been introduced only through the court. For a decade (1867–1876), the *kabaka* ("king"), Mutesa, was under Islamic influence and some Buganda nobles converted to Islam, but tensions were generated when the custodians of traditions discovered the threat of Islam, and even more so when aggressive representatives of Islam, Egyptian and Nubian troops, advanced from the north. The coming of Christian missionaries in 1877 opened a fierce competition between Islam and Christianity, which remained undecided until the British conquest helped Christians to gain the upper hand. Muslims, however, secured a foothold in the new system, which accommodated Protestantism, Catholicism, Islam, and traditional religion.

In the second half of the nineteenth century, much of the slave raiding took place west of Lake Tanganyika. That area, later to become the eastern provinces of the Congo, was politically fragmented, and the Swahili Arab warlords, the most famous of whom was Tippu Tip, created their own political and commercial organization. Displaced and uprooted people were drawn to the Swahili Arab centers and were recruited into their armed bands. Imitating the Swahili Arabs in customs, dress, and rituals, they remained the local representatives of Islam after the Swahili Arabs had been expelled from the Kongo Basin in the 1890s.

In the Nile-Kongo divide, Arab slave raiders and traders from the east coast met those from the northern belt of the Sudan and Chad; together they penetrated south among loosely organized peoples and established a network of settlements (*zarībah*s), where they were joined, as elsewhere, by Muslim clerics. Hunting for slaves and ivory wrought destruction, but around the *zarībah*s, as a result of the fusion of Arabs with their servants, slaves, and uprooted people, nuclei of local Muslim groups developed. These were the scattered Muslim communities of present-day northeastern Zaire and the Central African Republic.

Colonial conquest arrested the advance of the Arabs. But local people who had adopted Islam under the Arabs' influence remained and helped the diffusion of Islam under colonial rule. In Tanganyika, Swahili Arabs who served as agents of the German administration also contributed to the spread of Islam. Islam made progress in Tanganyika after the upheavals of the Maji Maji rebellion (1905–1907) and World War I. From the 1920s on there was a resurgence of Islam as a result of the activities of the Ṣūfī Qādirīyah.

Islam did not play a significant role in the political development of East Africa before independence, however. In the 1960s Muslims on the coast of Kenya failed to achieve any of their political demands in the face of growing domination by the Kikuyu people inland. The creation of Tanzania did not bring about the real integration of Zanzibar and Tanganyika that could have given Islam more weight in national politics. In the 1970s Idī Amīn tried to promote Islam in Uganda, which, with a population that was no more than 15 percent Muslim, became identified internationally as a Muslim state, but this effort was terminated with his overthrow in 1979.

The great majority of Muslims in East Africa are Sunnīs who follow the Shāfiʿī school of law. The non-Sunnīs are all descendants of migrants who retain their separate ethnic and cultural identity.

Cultural Dynamics. The islamization of Africa was greatly aided by the africanization of Islam. Only a few examples may be brought here to illustrate the cultural dynamics that explain not only the integration of Islam into African societies but also how African Islam remained an integral part of the Muslim world.

Arabic is the language of Islam, diffused and maintained through the educational system. Most Muslims can recite from the Qur'ān but have a very limited knowledge of Arabic, and only the scholars have acquired a good command of Arabic. Throughout history the latter had rich libraries and produced works in different fields of the Islamic sciences, in particular legal studies, commentaries on theological treatises, poems on the unity of God and in praise of the Prophet, and most important of all, biographies and historical chronicles. Significantly, Muslim historiography in Africa was equally influenced by general Muslim historiography and by African oral history traditions.

Some of the major African languages, such as Swahili, Hausa, Manding, and Fulfulde, which are also regional lingua francas, may be considered Muslim languages. They share at least two characteristics: about a third of their vocabularies are Arabic loanwords, and they were reduced to writing in the Arabic script. Thus, while comprehension of the Arabic language remained limited, knowledge of the Arabic script was common. With the introduction of the Arabic script for the writing of African languages, literacy became widespread. Since the eighteenth century religious poems, sermons, and litanies have been written in the Muslim languages of Africa, and legal manuals translated from Arabic to these languages.

During the early stages in the process of islamization the ritual rather than the legal aspects of Islam were prominent. The written word was more important for its magical qualities than for the message it carried, and the Qur'ān was a sacred object rather than a source for legislation. Islam won adherents, but at a price, insofar as it adopted the this-worldly orientation of African religions together with their tolerance. Traditional customs continued if they were not bluntly contradictory to the basic injunctions of Islam. Islamic notions were interpreted in traditional terms: the proscription of pork, for example, is explained by a taboo rendering the pig a sacred animal that cannot be eaten because the prophet Muḥammad was once saved by a pig.

In islamized societies the Muslim festivals replace most other feasts, except those closely associated with the seasonal cycle of the peasants. Yet only the few fully committed Muslims—clerics and traders—observe these festivals as prescribed. For others—chiefs and commoners—festivals have been transformed to the extent that the original Islamic features can hardly be recognized. The rites of passage combine Islamic and traditional ceremonies, and only in the case of funerals are the former clearly predominant.

Spirit possession cults survive in islamized societies because Islam does not deny the existence of those powers. Spirits and lesser deities may be islamized as *jinn* and angels.

From the viewpoint of Islam, symbiotic relations with traditional religions must be temporary. Premodern and modern reform movements called for the renunciation of traditional beliefs and customs and for closer adherence to the law of Islam. To this day Islam in Africa oscillates between accommodation and reform, particularism and universalism, quietism and political activism.

BIBLIOGRAPHY

The pioneering studies of Islam in the major regions of sub-Saharan Africa are those by J. Spencer Trimingham: *Islam in the Sudan* (Oxford, 1949), *Islam in Ethiopia* (Oxford, 1952), *Islam in West Africa* (Oxford, 1959), *A History of Islam in West Africa* (Oxford, 1962), and *Islam in East Africa* (Oxford, 1964). A new phase, of more detailed studies, has come in sight with a seminar at Zaria on *Islam in Tropical Africa,* 2d ed., edited by I. M. Lewis (Oxford, 1980). The introductory essay by the editor covers major issues from the viewpoint of an anthropologist. For broad historical outlines of the regions where Islam spread one may consult the relevant chapters in *The Cambridge History of Africa,* 8 vols. (London, 1975–).

The most important Arabic sources are now available in English or French translations; the more recent texts appear in the series "Fontes Historiae Africanae." The external Arabic sources before the sixteenth century are collected in the *Corpus of Early Arabic Sources for West African History,* edited by myself and J. F. P. Hopkins (Cambridge, 1981). Four chronicles from Timbuktu are now available in French: *Ta'rīkh al-fattāsh,* translated by O. Houdas and M. Delafosse (Paris, 1913); *Ta'rīkh al-Sūdān,* translated by O. Houdas (Paris, 1899); *Tadhkirat al-nisyān,* translated by O. Houdas (Paris, 1913–1914); *Tombouctou au milieu du dix-huitième siècle d'après la Chronique de Mawlāy al-Qāsim,* translated by M. Abithol (Paris, 1982). Al-Maghīlī's text has been translated by John O. Hunwick as *Sharī'ah in Sunghay: The Replies of al-Maghīlī to the Questions of Askiya al-Ḥājj Muḥammad* (London, 1985). On the *jihād* in Sokoto, see 'Abd Allah ibn Fūdī's *Tazyīn al-waraqāt,* translated by M. Hiskett (Ibadan, 1963), and Usuman dan Fodio's *Bayān wujūb al-hijrah,* translated by F. H. El-Masri. See also al-Ḥājj 'Umar's *Bayān mā waqa'a,* translated by M. Mahibou and J. L. Triaud (Paris, 1983).

On Islam in the early states of the Western Sudan, see my *Ancient Ghana and Mali* (London, 1973). This may be followed by John O. Hunwick's "Religion and State in the Songhay Empire," in *Islam in Tropical Africa,* cited above, pp. 296–317, and by Elias N. Saad's *Social History of Timbuktu: The Role of Muslim Scholars and Notables, 1400–1900* (New York, 1983). A new approach to the study of Muslim religious figures has been opened by Lamin O. Sanneh's *The Jakhanke: The History of an Islamic Clerical People of the Senegambia* (London, 1979). In *Muslim Chiefs and Chiefs in West Africa* (Oxford, 1968) I have analyzed patterns of integration of Muslims into the sociopolitical system of West African states.

On Islam in two south Saharan societies that influenced West African Islam, see H. T. Norris's *The Tuaregs: Their Islamic Legacy and Its Diffusion in the Sahel* (Warminster, 1975) and C. C. Stewart's *Islam and Social Order in Mauritania* (Oxford, 1973).

Bradford G. Martin's *Muslim Brotherhoods in Nineteenth Century Africa* (New York, 1976) underlines the importance of Sufism in the *jihād* movements. Essays on the precursors and leaders of the *jihāds* are presented in *Studies in West African Islamic History: The Cultivators of Islam,* edited by John R. Willis (London, 1979). For the major *jihād* movements, see Mervyn Hiskett's *The Sword of Truth: The Life and Times of Shehu Usuman dan Fodio* (New York, 1973); Murray Last's *The Sokoto Caliphate* (London, 1967); Louis Brenner's *The Shehus of Kukawa* (Oxford, 1973) on Bornu; David Robinson's *Chiefs and Clerics: Abdul Bokar kan and Futa Toro, 1853–1891* (Oxford, 1975); B. O. Ọlọruntimẹhin's *The Segu-Tokolor Empire* (London, 1972); and Yves Person's *Samori: Une révolution dyula,* 3 vols. (Nimes, 1968–1975).

On Islam in the modern politics of West Africa, see Donal B. Cruise O'Brien's *The Mourides of Senegal* (Oxford, 1971), John N. Paden's *Religion and Political Culture in Kano* (Berkeley, 1973), and Lansiné Kaba's *The Wahhabiyya: Islamic Reform and Politics in French West Africa* (Evanston, Ill., 1974), as well as Humphrey J. Fisher's *Ahmadiyya: A Study in Contemporary Islam on the West African Coast* (London, 1963).

In comparison with the West African material, there are fewer specialized studies on Islam in other parts of sub-Saharan Africa. Some of the best analyses of the development of Islam have appeared in historical studies of those regions as well as in anthropological studies of different peoples who came under Islamic influence, including Edward A. Alpers's "Towards a History of the Expansion of Islam in East Africa: The Matrilineal Peoples of the Southern Interior," in *The Historical Study of African Religion,* edited by T. O. Ranger and I. N. Kimambo (Berkeley, 1972); Aryeh Oded's *Islam in Uganda: Islamization through a Centralized State in Pre-Colonial Africa* (New York, 1974); and August H. Nimitz, Jr.'s *Islam and Politics in East Africa: The Sufi Order in Tanzania* (Minneapolis, 1980). An interpretative essay, illustrated by ninety-one plates that represent the best of Muslim artistry in Africa, is René Bravmann's *African Islam* (London, 1983).

NEHEMIA LEVTZION

Islam in the Caucasus and the Middle Volga

When the first Arab invaders appeared in eastern Transcaucasia in the seventh century, the Caucasus was a borderland between the nomadic world to the north and the old sedentary world to the south, and between the Greek civilization in the West and the Iranian world in the East. It had a highly sophisticated urban civilization where several world religions, including Judaism, Manichaeism, Zoroastrianism, and Christianity, were already well entrenched. Among the Christians, the Georgians and Alans were Orthodox, and the Armenians and Albanians were Monophysites. Unlike Central Asia, which has been characterized by religious tolerance, the Caucasus for centuries has been the fighting ground for three great monotheistic religions—Christianity, Judaism, and Islam.

Islam in the Caucasus

The spread of Islam was inhibited by powerful political rivals who reinforced religious rivalries. The Turkic Khazar empire in the north formed an effective barrier against the progress of the conquering Arabs north of Derbent; the Christian Georgian and Armenian principalities, backed by the Byzantine empire, presented an insuperable obstacle to Muslim progress westward.

The Slow Islamization of Dagestan. The Arabs penetrated into Azerbaijan in 639; local rulers agreed to become subordinate to the caliph but retained their Christian faith. In 643, the Arabs reached Derbent (which they called Bāb al-Abwāb) and in 652 attempted to move north of the city but were heavily defeated by the Khazars. For almost a century the territory of present-day Dagestan was disputed between the Khazars and the Arabs, as expeditions and counterexpeditions succeeded each other almost without interruption and without any decisive victory. Not until the governorship of Marwān ibn Muḥammad (734–744) were the Khazars decisively defeated in Arrān. Derbent, solidly held by an Arab garrison, became the northernmost bastion of Islam facing the world of the Turkic nomads. Several thousand Arab settlers from Syria and northern Iraq were established in northern Azerbaijan by the governor Maslamah ibn ʿAbd al-Malik.

First inroads. Notwithstanding several Khazar expeditions between 762 and 799, by the end of the eighth century Islam was already the dominant religion of Arrān and of the coastal plain south of Derbent. Even so, Christian and Jewish communities survived in the area. Indeed, in 1979 there were in northern Azerbaijan and southern Dagestan some 5,919 Monophysite Christian Udins, the last survivors of the Albanian church. There were also about 30,000 "Mountain Jews," or Dagh Chufut, the descendants of the Jewish military colonists established in the Caucasus by the Sasanid kings. In recent years, most of them have migrated to Israel.

The progress of Islam into the mountains was, by contrast, slow and difficult. According to Dagestani legends, Maslamah ibn ʿAbd al-Malik (r. 723–731), having conquered all Dagestan, imposed Islam on the local rulers. In reality, the submission of the indigenous chieftains was purely formal. As soon as the Arab control weakened, the local population reverted to their ancient

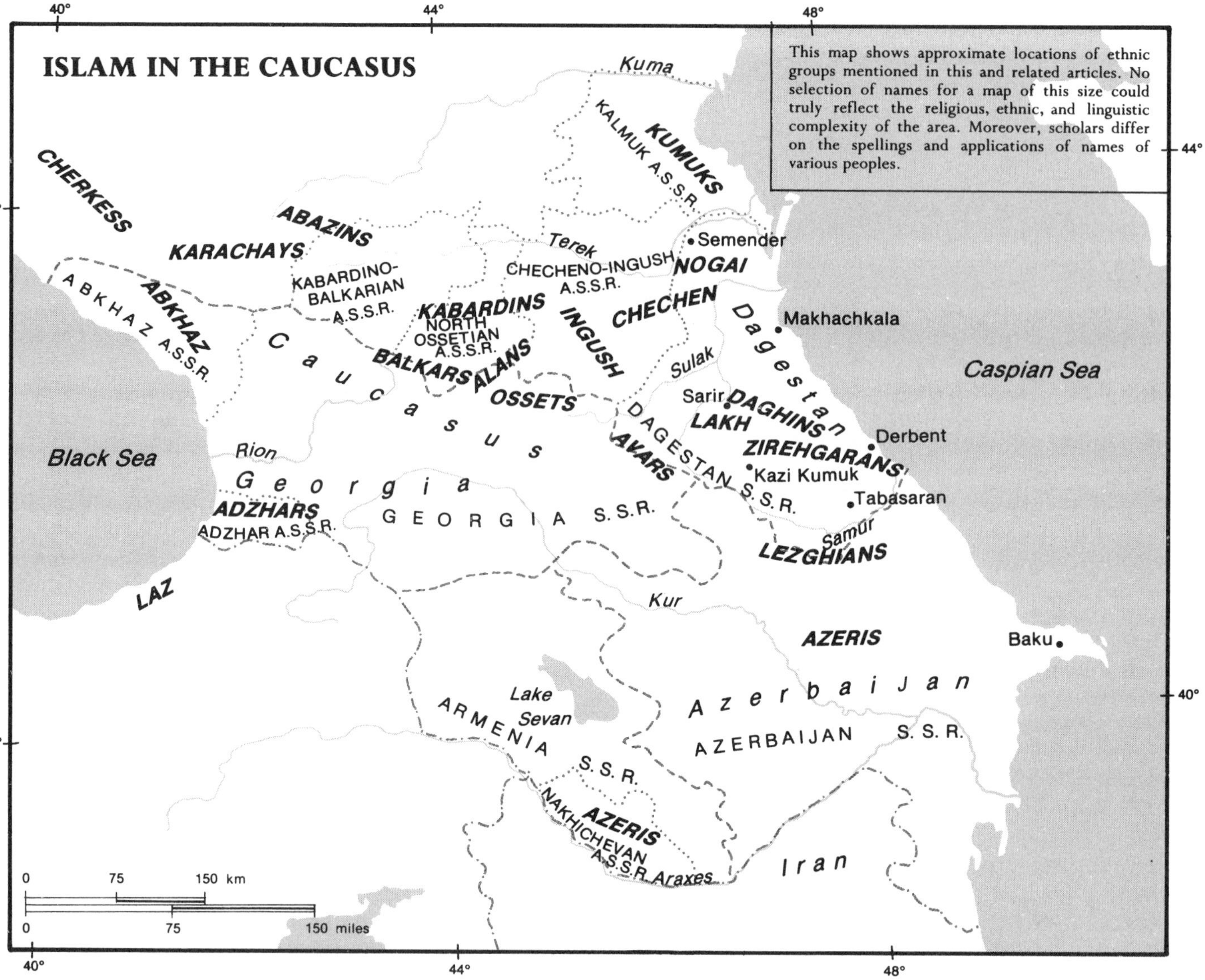

religion. In some instances, after Dagestani rulers embraced the new religion, their subjects remained Christian, Jewish, or animist. The northern Caucasian mountain area remained virtually untouched by Islam into the tenth century. In southern Dagestan, the ruler of Tabasaran professed Islam, Christianity, and Judaism simultaneously. All three religions were represented among the Zirīhgarāns of central Dagestan. The Lezghians of southern Dagestan were "infidels." Sarīr, in the Avar country of western Dagestan, had a Christian prince (Orthodox of Georgian rite), but his subjects were in the majority animist, with traces of Zoroastrianism. Samandar in northern Dagestan was governed by a Jewish prince related to the Khazar khagan, but all three religions were represented among his subjects. The majority of the Iranian Alans of the central Caucasus were Christian Orthodox of Byzantine rite, while the Kabardins and the Cherkess were animist, with a Christian minority. On the Black Sea coast the Abkhaz paid tribute to the Arabs but remained Christian. At the end of the tenth century, the borderline of the *dār al-Islām* ("abode of Islam") was still situated three miles north of Derbent. Islam was solidly rooted only in Derbent, which was an important fortress, a prosperous economic center, and one of the wealthiest cities of the Arab caliphate, and also in the Lakh country of central Dagestan. According to a local legend, a mosque was built in the Lakh capital, Kazi-Kumukh, in 777.

This first period of islamization of the Caucasus (through the tenth century CE) was marked by exceptional religious tolerance. Not only did the three monotheistic religions coexist peacefully, but there was toleration of those not originally included among the "people of the Book" *(ahl al-kitāb)*—Zoroastrians and animists. In short, Islam was only superficially superimposed on a deeply rooted set of pre-Islamic beliefs, customs, and rites.

Further expansion. In the eleventh century, a new phase of islamization began. The Khazar empire had been destroyed in 965 by the Russes, thus removing the main obstacle to relations between the Muslim Bulgar kingdom in the far north and the lands of the caliphate on the one hand, and to the islamization of the Turkic nomads beyond Derbent on the other. Meanwhile, in the south, the foundation of the Seljuk empire improved security along the trade routes and favored the peaceful penetration of Islam into the mountains. This movement was facilitated by two additional phenomena. First, in the tenth century, the old clanic formations were replaced by stronger feudal principalities in Dagestan: the Nutzal of Avar, the Ūsmīyat of Kaytāk in the Darghin country, the Shāmkhālat of Kazi-Kumukh (central Dagestan), and the Maʿṣūmat of Tabasaran in southern Dagestan (Lezghian country). By the end of the eleventh century the rulers of these principalities were already Muslim, and their vassals and subjects tended to follow the example of the suzerain. Second, there was a total disappearance of the old alphabets (Aramaic, Pahlavi, Albanian) formerly used to transcribe the local languages. These were replaced by Arabic, which became and remained henceforward the only literary language of the area.

In the eleventh and twelfth centuries, the majority of the Darghins and the Lakh of central Dagestan became Muslims, and Islam penetrated into western and northern Dagestan. By contrast, the more remote territories, bypassed by the main trade routes—in particular, the Chechen and Ingush countries—preserved a purely prefeudal (clanic) society and were resistant to Islam.

In the middle of the twelfth century, a visitor to Dagestan, Abū Ḥāmid al-Andalusī of Granada, discovered traces of Christianity and Zoroastrianism among the Zirīhgarāns; he also found many Christians and animists among the Avars.

Mongol era. The Mongol invasion did not modify the complicated religious situation of the northern Caucasus. As elsewhere, in Central Asia, in the Bulgar country, or in Iran, the first wave of Mongol invaders were animists, Nestorian Christians, or Buddhists, and generally hostile to Islam. But the destruction wrought by the expeditions of Sübetey and Djebe (1220) and of Batu (1239) were not followed by religious persecution. During the Mongol rule, Caucasian Islam ceased to be exclusively the religion of rulers and of elites and became more deeply rooted in the popular elements. The Caucasus was divided between two rival Mongol khanates, the Golden Horde in the north and the khanate of the Il-khanids in Iran. The third khan of the Golden Horde, Berke (r. 1257–1266), embraced Islam, and although his successors reverted to their ancestral religion, they remained tolerant and even favorable toward Islam.

In 1313, Uzbek Khan, a Muslim, became the ruler of the Golden Horde. His reign marked the final victory of Islam among the Turkic nomads roaming the immense steppe area between the Crimea and the Volga. One of the Turkic tribes, the Nogai Horde, played an important role in the islamization of the northern Caucasus during the fourteenth century. It was through the Nogais that Islam made inroads for the first time among the Cherkess, the Kabardins, and the Chechen. Also, in the first half of the fourteenth century, the Ṣūfī brotherhoods began to appear in the northern Caucasus as well. Shaykh Muḥammad al-Baṭāʾiḥī of the Rifāʿī *ṭarīqah* (order) founded a *khānqāh* ("lodge") in Māchar in the steppeland of the northern Caucasus. This *ṭarīqah* disappeared a century later, however.

Timurid rule. The final phase of islamization in Dagestan took place in the late fourteenth and early fifteenth centuries, during the reign of Timur (Tamerlane). The great conqueror led several expeditions into Azerbaijan and Dagestan between 1385 and 1395. He took a personal interest in the destruction of the last survivals of pre-Islamic religions, and Islam became henceforward the only religion of the Lakh of central Dagestan. In turn, the Lakh became the champions of Islam against those neighbors remaining animist or Christian. The city of Kazi-Kumukh, the capital of the principality of the Shāmkhālat Lakh, was the new center for the islamization of Dagestan and the lands beyond its western frontiers, and it was the Lakh missionaries who brought Islam to the Chechen and the Kumiks. Timur also dealt a deadly blow to the power of the Christian Alans of the north-central Caucasus (the ancestors of the Ossets). The Christian Alans had been the mightiest nation of the Caucasus, and their decline was followed by a new expansion of Islam in the northern Caucasus.

During Timur's period, the majority of the Kaytāks became good Muslims. Earlier, the Kaytāks were considered as "people without faith" *(bī-dīn)* or as a "people of bad faith." Subsequently, the Lezghians of southern Dagestan and the Avars turned Muslim as well.

It was in this high, mountainous territory that Christianity held out longest, and its survival was important to the Georgian kings' efforts to protect their coreligionists. The village of Karakh in the high Avar country did not adopt Islam until 1435. The Dido and the Andi tribes remained Christian until 1469, and Gidatl became Muslim in 1475 or 1476.

At the end of the fifteenth century, two new Muslim

powers appeared on the Caucasian scene, and their influence on the process of islamization became decisive. The Ottoman empire brought the spirit of *jihād* (religious war) to the Caucasus. The rulers of the Crimean khanate dominated the lowlands of the western and central Caucasus. The Ottoman advance was marked by the gradual conversion of the Laz of the southwestern Caucasus (they were formerly Christian) and of the Abkhaz of the Black Sea coast. At the same time the Crimean Tatars introduced Islam among the western and eastern Cherkess tribes. Derbent and Shirvan in eastern Transcaucasia were conquered by the Safavids in 1538. As a consequence, the Twelver Shīʿī rite of the Safavid rulers became the dominant form of Islam in Azerbaijan.

In the middle of the sixteenth century, Sunnī Islam of the Shāfiʿī rite was solidly established in Dagestan, while the Ḥanafī rite was making steady progress in the western Caucasus. The tribes of the central Caucasus, however—the eastern Cherkess, the Kabardins, the Ossets, the Balkars, the Karachays, the Chechen, and the Ingush—were for the most part Christian or pagan, and only the upper level of their feudal aristocracy had adopted Islam.

Battle with Muscovy. After 1556, the power of Muscovy appeared in the Caucasus. As a consequence, relations between Islam and Christianity were dramatically modified. Specifically, the era of religious tolerance came to an end, and the Caucasus entered a new period of religious confrontation. Both Moscow and Istanbul favored their coreligionists. Temrük, the great Kabardian prince (a Muslim), accepted Russian sovereignty and married his daughter, Maria (converted to Christianity), to Ivan the Terrible. The central Caucasus was thus opened to Russian influence. Christian missionaries were sent in great numbers, and churches were built in Kabardia, among the eastern Cherkess, and in Ossetia. In 1584, Muscovy began its military advance southward, and three years later, the Russians reached the Terek Valley. In 1590, their vanguards appeared on the Sunzha River, threatening Dagestan, but already the Crimean Tatars and the Ottomans were reacting vigorously. In the same year, the Ottomans, advancing from the south, occupied Derbent; in 1587 the Crimean khan had already invaded and ruined Kabardia, Moscow's principal ally in the northern Caucasus. In 1594, there was a major confrontation: on the banks of the Sulaq River in northern Dagestan, a Russian army was opposed by a joint force of Ottomans, Tatars, and Dagestanis. In a furious battle, with all the characteristics of a "holy war," the Russians were pushed back. They returned in 1604 and were once again heavily defeated. Thus, the first *jihād* in Dagestan and the religious competition in Kabardia between Christianity and Islam ended with a complete Muslim victory. Russian influence was pushed back as far as Astrakhan and the Lower Volga. Kabardia, strategically the most important area of the northern Caucasus, became a solid Muslim bastion.

In the seventeenth and eighteenth centuries, the Ottoman Turks and the Crimean Tatars continued their steady efforts to introduce Islam among the remaining Christian or pagan tribes of the northwestern Caucasus. These tribes included the Karachay, the Balkars, the western Cherkess, the Abazins, and the Abkhaz. In 1627, southwestern Georgia was conquered by the Turks, and a part of its population embraced Islam. The descendants of these Georgian Muslims, the Adzhars, totaled from 100,000 to 150,000 people late in the twentieth century.

The Period of the "Holy Wars." The Russian advance toward the Caucasus, suspended in 1604, was resumed in 1783 after the conquest of the Crimea and the occupation of the steppe areas north of the Kuban River.

Naqshbandīyah. The arrival of the Russians, this time with overwhelming force, coincided with the appearance of the Naqshbandīyah Ṣūfī brotherhood in the northern Caucasus. This was a Turkistani order founded in Bukhara by Muḥammad Bahāʾ al-Dīn Naqshband (1317–1389). For more than a century, the adepts of the Naqshbandīyah were the organizers of the "holy war" against the advancing conqueror. It was during the struggle against the "infidels" and the "bad Muslims" who served them that Islam became the dominant religion of the northern Caucasus and that its character was fundamentally modified. At the end of the eighteenth century, the superficially islamized communities were tolerant toward their neighbors who remained Christian. They also tolerated those who remained attached to numerous pre-Islamic beliefs and rites and followed various non-Muslim customary laws (*ʿādāt*). But a century later, Caucasian Islam, deeply rooted in the rural masses, was characterized by its rigorous conservatism, by its intolerance toward non-Muslims, and by its strict adherence to *sharīʿah* law. [*See* Jihād.]

The first Naqshbandī *jihād* against the Russians was led by Imam Manṣūr Ushurma, a Chechen who was probably the disciple of a shaykh from Bukhara. The movement began in 1785 in Chechnia and spread to northern Dagestan and the western Caucasus. But Manṣūr was captured in 1791 in Anapa and died two years later in the fortress of Schlüsselburg. It was a shortlived attempt to stop the advance of the invaders. Even so, during Manṣūr's rule Islam became deeply rooted in Chechnia, formerly only about one-half Muslim.

After Manṣūr's defeat, the Naqshbandīyah disappeared from the northern Caucasus for nearly thirty years, and during this period the Russians, almost unopposed, made substantial advances. The *ṭarīqah* reappeared in the 1820s in the province of Shirvan, however, with the Naqshbandī missionaries coming this time from the Ottoman empire. The second Naqshbandī *murshid* ("guide") to preach "holy war" was Shaykh Muḥammad of Yaraglar. He was the master of Ghāzī Muḥammad and Shāmil, the first and the third imams of Dagestan. The long and fierce resistance of the mountaineers lasted from 1824 to 1859, when Shāmil was finally defeated and captured. Despite its failure, this second Naqshbandī *jihād* left an indelible impact on northern Caucasian Islam. Shāmil liquidated forever the traditional customary legal system and replaced it with the *sharī'ah*. Moreover, in the nineteenth century, classical Arabic became the official written language of the imamate and also the spoken intertribal language of Dagestan and Chechnia. Thus, for the first time in history, the northern Caucasian population was united by a strong religious, linguistic, and cultural bond. Finally, the intense work of the Naqshbandī missionaries in the central and western Caucasus achieved the islamization of all Cherkess and Abazin tribes. During Shāmil's rule, Dagestan became an important center of Arabic culture. Its scholars, the so-called Arabists, were exported to the entire Muslim world.

Qādirīyah. After 1859 and the subsequent Russian occupation of the Caucasus, the Naqshbandīyah went underground. Its leaders migrated to Turkey or were deported to Siberia. Some became *abrek,* "bandits of honor," forming guerrilla groups in the mountains. Another Ṣūfī order, the Qādirīyah (or Kunta Haji *ṭarīqah*), replaced the Naqshbandīyah on the front line of religious resistance. This order appeared in the Chechen country in the 1860s, when "infidel" domination had become a fact of life. It was different, at least at the outset, from the militant Naqshbandīyah in that its ideology was inspired by the mystic search for God rather than by "holy war." Even so, it was rapidly outlawed by the authorities and was obliged to go underground. At that point, the Qādirīyah became another center of military resistance to the Russian presence. Both the Naqshbandī and the Qādirī *ṭarīqahs* played an active part in the anti-Russian revolt of 1877–1878 in Dagestan and Chechnia.

The Qādirīyah were vigorous missionaries. Because of their activities, the Ingush, who had remained animist until the fall of Shāmil, finally became Muslim. The last animist Ingush village was converted to Islam in 1864.

The Russian Revolution provided the Ṣūfī adepts with the opportunity to shake off Russian rule. During this period, the Naqshbandīyah surfaced and made one last attempt to expel the "infidels." They fought for four years—from 1917 to 1921—first against the White armies of Denikin, then against the Red Army. Their resistance was finally crushed in 1921, and after their defeat, both Ṣūfī brotherhoods were subjected to a long and bloody persecution. But they survived. In 1928, the Qādirīyah and the Naqshbandīyah joined together in a revolt in Dagestan and the Checheno-Ingush republic. This armed uprising was followed by similar revolts in 1934 and 1940–1942. The revolt during World War II was led by nationalists, but the Qādirīyah were numerous among the guerrilla fighters.

Caucasian Islam under the Soviets. Administratively, the Caucasus is now divided between two Muslim spiritual boards, the Spiritual Board of Dagestan and the Northern Caucasus, and the Spiritual Board of Transcaucasia.

The Spiritual Board of Dagestan and the Northern Caucasus is located in Makhachkala (Dagestan). Arabic is its administrative language, and it follows the Sunnī Shāfi'ī rite. Its authority covers all the northern Caucasian autonomous republics and regions (Adygei A.R., Karachayevo-Cherkess A.R., Kabardino-Balkarian A.S.S.R., North Ossetian A.S.S.R., Checheno-Ingush A.S.S.R., Dagestan A.S.S.R.). It also has administrative authority over the territories of Krasnodar and Stavropol. The Muslim population under its jurisdiction (about three and one-half million in 1983) is all Sunnī (Shāfi'ī in Dagestan and in the Checheno-Ingush republic, Ḥanafī elsewhere).

The Spiritual Board of Transcaucasia is located in Baku. It is chaired by a Shī'ī Shaykh al-Islām whose deputy is the Sunnī (Ḥanafī) *muftī.* The board uses Azeri Turkic as its administrative language. Its authority covers all the Twelver Shī'ī communities of the U.S.S.R., totaling about four million in 1983 (3,800,000 Azeris; 150,000 Tajiks and Uzbeks in Central Asia; around 20,000 Tātīs of Dagestan; and some 20,000 Baluchis of Turkmenistan). The board's authority also extends to the Sunnī Ḥanafī communities of the three Transcaucasian republics—Georgia (including the Abkhazian and the Adzhar A.S.S.R.s), Armenia, and Azerbaijan. Within these Transcaucasian republics, the Sunnīs consist of the Kurds (116,000 in 1979), the Abkhaz (probably about 25,000), the Laz (1,000), the Adzhars (roughly 100,000 to 150,000), and the Ingilois (thought to number about 5,000). In the early 1980s the Muslim population under the jurisdiction of the board totaled around 4,300,000 (4,000,000 Shī'ah and 300,000 Sunnīs).

The official Islamic establishment has been reduced to a skeleton framework. There are no religious schools, no religious endowments (*waqfs*) to administer, and no religious courts (forbidden by Soviet legislation). It is estimated that by 1982 the number of "working" mosques had been limited to no more than fifty for the entire northern Caucasus; known working mosques include twenty-seven in Dagestan, seven in the Checheno-Ingush A.S.S.R., and three in the Karachaevo-Cherkess A.R. There are probably fewer than thirty working mosques in Transcaucasia, of which sixteen (mixed Sunnī-Shīʿī) are in Azerbaijan.

The level of religious feeling among the Muslim population of the Caucasus is quite high, especially in Dagestan and in the Checheno-Ingush republic, where more than 80 percent of the population are considered "believers." The strength of Islam in the northern Caucasus is due, in part, to the intense activity of the Ṣūfī brotherhoods. The *ṭarīqah*s still control a network of clandestine houses of prayer and Qur'anic schools, where children are taught Arabic and receive the rudiments of the Muslim faith. The schools and underground mosques are often organized around the holy places of pilgrimage, generally tombs of Ṣūfī shaykhs.

Ṣūfī *ṭarīqah*s are especially active in the Checheno-Ingush republic and in northern Dagestan, while they are not represented in the central and western Caucasus. The Naqshbandīyah dominates Dagestan, northern Azerbaijan, and the western districts of Chechnia. In the northern Caucasus, the Qādirīyah, more popular and more dynamic, is divided into four sub-*ṭarīqah*s, called *wird*s. These are the Batal Haji, Bammat Giray Haji, Chim Mirza, and Vis (Uways) Haji. The Qādirīyah *ṭarīqah* is predominant in the Checheno-Ingush republic and is spreading into western Dagestan. According to Soviet sociological surveys from the 1970s, the total number of Ṣūfī adepts in the northern Caucasus may be estimated at about 150,000, an exceptionally high proportion, especially after sixty years of hard antireligious propaganda aimed mainly at the Ṣūfī orders.

Islam in the Middle Volga

As early as the fifth or sixth century a few Turkic tribes, the ancestors of the Volga Bulgars, began settling in the territory of the Middle Volga. These tribes were the first Turks to settle down and to abandon the nomadic way of life.

Islamization: Trade, Conquest, Sufism. The area—the Kama River and the Urals—was situated at the crossroads of two main trade routes during the Middle Ages. The fur route ran from northern Russia–Siberia (Arḍ al-Ẓulm, the "Land of Darkness" of the Arab geographers) to the Muslim Middle East, and the Silk Road linked northern and central Europe to China. The Turkic Bulgars were traders in furs, slaves, amber, and ivory. Accordingly, they traveled widely, some as far as Baghdad and Gurganj on the Amu Darya, coming into contact with Arab merchants as early as the ninth century. It is through such trade relations that Islam penetrated into the Middle Volga, initially from Khorezm, then from Baghdad farther west.

The Bulgar kingdom. In 921, the Bulgar king, Almas, received an embassy sent by Caliph al-Muqtadir and converted to Islam on 12 May 922. His example was followed rapidly by the ruling elite of the kingdom. At the end of the tenth century, most of the Bulgars were already Muslim, and there were mosques and schools in virtually every village. For three hundred years, the Middle Volga area remained a Muslim island—the northernmost vanguard of the *dār al-Islām*—completely surrounded by Christian or animist neighbors. Its ties with the faraway Muslim world were maintained through the Volga trade route.

In spite of, or perhaps because of, their isolation, the Bulgars were zealous Muslims from the beginning. They played a role in the conversion of some nomadic Turkic tribes, the Pechenegs and Cumans, to Islam. They also nursed hopes of spreading Islam to the Russians, who were at that time still animists. In 986 a Bulgar embassy was sent to Kiev with the aim of converting the grand prince, Vladimir. The Russian Primary Chronicle recounts that some time later, Vladimir, in search of a suitable religion, also received representatives of Western and Eastern Christianity and of Judaism and heard each speak in turn of the merits and tenets of his faith.

Little more is known about the cultural history of the Bulgar kingdom prior to the thirteenth century. We may assume that Islam remained the religion of the Turkic city-dwellers, the feudal elite, and the merchant class, while the rural population, of whom the majority was ethnically Finnic, remained animist.

The Golden Horde. The Bulgar kingdom was destroyed by the Mongols around 1236. This was a major disaster that left the country devastated and ruined. But its Islamic character survived. The economic and political center was transferred from the valley of the Kama River to the Volga, near what is now the city of Kazan. Subsequently, Kazan became one of the most prosperous trading centers of the Golden Horde. In this area there was a biological and cultural merging of the indigenous Muslim Turks and the invading Mongols, with the less numerous Mongols assimilated by the Muslim Turks. Even so, the new nation was called "Tatar," the name of a Mongol tribe.

During the period of the Golden Horde, Uzbek Khan (1313–1341) adopted Islam as the official religion of the Mongol rulers. This example was followed by all the Turkic and Mongol tribes roaming in the steppes between the former Bulgar kingdom and the Black and Caspian seas. Islam gained a firm footing in the Crimea as well.

Sufism. It was also during the period of the Golden Horde—between the thirteenth and fourteenth centuries—that Sufism was brought to the Volga region. It was introduced by adepts of a mystical Turkistani brotherhood, the Yasawīyah *ṭarīqah,* founded by the Turkic poet and mystic Aḥmad Yasawī (d. 1166?). Thanks to the efforts of the Ṣūfī preachers, Islam was no longer limited to being the religion of rulers and scholars: it became deeply rooted in the countryside among the rural populations and even among the nomadic tribes.

In 1445, with the weakening of the Golden Horde, Kazan became the capital of an independent Tatar khanate that lasted until 1552. It was a wealthy city, a world capital of the fur trade, and a brilliant cultural center famous for numerous mosques and *madrasahs*. In the late fifteenth and the early sixteenth century, a new Ṣūfī brotherhood became active in Kazan—the Naqshbandīyah *ṭarīqah,* which, as mentioned above, later opposed Russian advances in the northern Caucasus. An intellectual order representing the city elites, the Naqshbandīyah practiced the silent *dhikr,* or Ṣūfī prayer litany. In contrast, the Yasawīyah practiced the "loud" *dhikr* with songs and ecstatic dances reminiscent of old Turkic shamanistic rituals. The influence of the Naqshbandīyah on Tatar literature became predominant, and nearly all the Tatar poets from the sixteenth to the nineteenth century were adepts of the order, including Muḥammadiyar, the sixteenth-century author of *Tukhfat-i mardān* (The Gift for the Courageous) and *Nūr-u ṣudūr* (The Light of the Soul), Mawlā Qulī in the seventeenth century, Utyz Imānī al-Bukhārī (1754–1815), ʿAbd al-Manih Kargaly (1782–1826), ʿUbayd Allāh Ṣāḥib (1794–1867), and Shams al-Dīn Zakī Ṣūfī (1825–1865). [*See also* Ṭarīqah.]

Russian Rule. In 1552, the khanate was destroyed by the Russians and its territory was incorporated into the Muscovite state. In 1556 and 1598, two other Muslim remnants of the Golden Horde, the khanates of Astrakhan on the Lower Volga and of Sibir (or Tumen) in western Siberia, were conquered and annexed by Muscovy. Their inhabitants, whether Muslim or animist, were incorporated into the fabric of Russian Orthodox society. They were treated as Russian subjects, but were denied those rights reserved to Christians. Only by religious assimilation, that is, by their conversion to the Orthodox faith, could the Tatars become the equals of the Russians. Russia, except for Spain, was the only European power to attempt systematically to convert her Muslim subjects to Christianity. Missionary activity was begun in 1555 by Arkhiepiskop Gurii, the first archbishop of Kazan. This initial attempt at conversion was relatively liberal. Tsar Ivan the Terrible, who was tolerant in religious matters, advised the Kazan missionaries to work "through persuasion and not through compulsion." The effort was partly successful and resulted in the conversion of a large community of Christian Tatars—the Old Converts (Starokriasheny; Tatar, Taze Kryash). However, the majority of the converts were former animists, not Muslims.

The anti-Muslim campaigns. The campaign of conversions, interrupted during the seventeenth century, was resumed with a new vigor under Peter the Great and continued violently until the reign of Catherine II. Mosques were destroyed, Qur'anic schools were closed, and special schools were opened for the children of the converts. At the same time, Muslim counterproselytism was punishable by death. The climax was reached under the reign of Empress Anna (1730–1740), when some forty to fifty thousand New Converts (Novokriasheny; Tatar, Yeni Kryash or Aq Kryash) were added to those who had been converted during the sixteenth century.

To strengthen the religious pressure, civil and economic coercion was added. The feudal landed nobility, considered by the Russian rulers as their most dangerous adversary, was either physically liquidated or deprived of its feudal rights (Muslim landlords were forbidden to have non-Muslim serfs), dispossessed of its property, and ruined. Muslim urban dwellers, merchants, clerics, and artisans were expelled from Kazan. Tatar farmers were forced to leave the best agricultural lands along the river valleys and were replaced by Russians.

After more than a century of sustained pressure, the very existence of the Islamic civilization in the Middle Volga was in danger. But the pressure produced conflicting results. The landed nobility disappeared as a class; although some of its representatives became Christian, its most dynamic elements remained Muslim and became merchants, traders, and small industrialists. Expelled from the cities, the Tatars took refuge in the countryside. By the seventeenth century, Tatar Islam presented a curious and unique feature in the Muslim world: it had become a rural religion with its most famous mosques and *madrasahs* situated in small villages. In the same way, Tatar merchants expelled from the cities of the Volga-Kama area migrated eastward, where they formed trading colonies in Siberia, the Kazakh steppes, along the Lower Volga, in the Caucasus, in Turkistan, and as far as China. Already in the seventeenth century, the Tatar nation, reduced to a minority in its Volga homeland, had become a diaspora community led by a dynamic merchant class. Religious persecutions against Islam created a lasting hatred among all the Tatars—Muslim and Christian alike—against Russia and the Russians.

During the reign of Catherine II, the anti-Muslim campaign was halted and even reversed. The empress, who personally deemed Islam to be "a reasonable religion," succeeded in gaining the sympathies of the Tatars. She closed the schools for Christian converts and allowed the Tatars to return to Kazan and to build mosques and Qur'anic schools in the cities of the Middle Volga and the Urals. Religious persecution was stopped, and a *modus vivendi* was achieved between the Russian state and its Muslim subjects. The Russian authorities even helped Tatar "clerics" to build mosques in the Urals and in the Kazakh steppes. By a 1773 decree they were granted religious freedom, and in 1782, a Muslim spiritual board *(muftiat)* was established in Orenburg and invested with authority over all religious matters. The chairman of the board was appointed by the Ministry of the Interior in Saint Petersburg. Those Tatars who had been converted to Christianity began to return to Islam. Finally, the last decade of the eighteenth century was marked by a new phenomenon: the massive conversion to Islam of the indigenous Finnic tribes of the Middle Volga region. These tribes—Cheremiss, Mordvins, Udmurts—were formerly animist or superficially christianized; after conversion, there was rapid "tatarization."

The pressure against Islam was renewed under Nicholas I and Alexander II, however. By new methods, including education and propaganda, efforts were made to attract Tatars to Christianity. In 1854, a special anti-Muslim missionary department was organized by the Kazan Theological Academy. In 1863, a new educational policy was elaborated by Nikolai Il'minskii, a missionary and orientalist professor at the Religious Academy of Kazan. His aim was to create a new native Christian elite of Tatar intellectuals, educated along European lines but retaining the use of its native language. This Christian elite, which had not broken its links with the national past, was charged with missionary work among its Muslim brethren. As a result of this effort, assisted by an intense and brilliant propaganda campaign, more than 100,000 Muslims and almost all the remaining animists from the Volga area were converted.

The economic threat from Russia. Yet another danger threatened the Tatar nation: its economic prosperity was in jeopardy. During the late eighteenth century and the first half of the nineteenth, the Tatar merchant class had been allied with the young Russian capitalists and had acted as an intermediary between Russian industrial towns and the markets of Turkistan. But that fruitful cooperation was not to last: during the second half of the nineteenth century, after Russian armies had opened the gates of Turkistan to Russian enterprise, Russian capitalists were able to dispense with the Tatar middlemen. The two bourgeoisies had become rivals, and the Tatar bourgeoisie, as the weaker, appeared to be doomed. The economic threat, coupled with the resumption of the policy of religious and educational assimilation, produced a lively reaction among the Tatar bourgeoisie during the reign of Alexander III. The *jadid* reformist movement, which has been properly called "the Tatar renaissance" of the nineteenth century, was the direct consequence of this threat, as well as of the desire to unify all the Muslim and Turkic peoples on the basis of a religious, ethnic, and cultural ideology. The Tatar merchants, supported by the young intelligentsia and the modernist *'ulamā'*, or religious scholars, were aware that a successful resistance would involve confronting Russian imperialism with another imperialism. They knew that it would be necessary to extend their economic and cultural scope to all Muslim peoples of the empire, and that they would have to constitute themselves as the leaders of Russian Islam and, taking advantage of the linguistic similarity and of their common religion, propagate the notions of pan-Islam and pan-Turkism. [*See* Modernism, *article on* Islamic Modernism.]

The Jadid Renaissance. In the middle of the nineteenth century, the Tatar community was a curious element in the Muslim world. It had survived centuries of political and religious pressure, and, led by its merchant bourgeoisie, it had reached a high economic and cultural level. In the Middle Volga area, the proportion of literate Tatars was greater than among the Russians, especially among women. The Tatar bourgeoisie was aggressive and dynamic, able to compete successfully against its Russian counterpart. But at the same time, the Tatar elite lived intellectually in a conservative medieval world. Indeed, their strict conservatism had protected their community from contamination by a technically more advanced Russian establishment and preserved its Islamic character. But by the end of the nineteenth century, it had become obvious that "the Tatar oxcart" could no longer compete effectively with the Russian "steam engine." In order to survive in a modern world, it was necessary for the Tatars to modernize their intellectual *Weltanschauung* rapidly and thoroughly. Without questioning the religious foundation of Muslim society, Tatar reformers applied themselves to modernizing Islam by imitating the spirit of Western liberalism.

The reformist movement manifested itself in almost all the Muslim countries, from the Ottoman empire to Indonesia, but nowhere was it so dramatic and so deep as in the Tatar country. There, the problem facing the native elite was not merely how to regain its lost power; rather, it was concerned with survival itself.

Theological reform. The movement began in the early nineteenth century with an attempt by Tatar *'ulamā'*, educated in Bukhara, to break with the conservative Central Asian traditionalists who had dominated the spiritual life of Russian Muslims. The first to challenge their scholasticism was Abu Nasr Kursavi (1783–1814), a young Tatar teacher in a Bukhara *madrasah*. Accused of impiety by the emir of Bukhara and by the *muftī* of Orenburg, he was obliged to flee to Turkey. Later challengers included Shihabeddin Mayani (1818–1889), the greatest and the most respected among Tatar scholars, and a generation of modernist theologians including Ibrahim Khalfin, Husein Faizkhanov (1825–1902), Rizaeddin Fahreddin Öglu (1859–1936), and Musa Jarullah Bibi (1875–1945). Their action restored life and vigor to the Muslim religion in Russia and exercised an undeniable influence on the neighboring countries. Especially affected was the Ottoman empire, where the prestige of Tatar *jadid* thinkers was invoked by all those who sought to undermine the authority of medieval scholasticism.

By the turn of the century, Tatar Islam was endowed with a powerful religious establishment consisting of thousands of mosques and schools (*maktab*s and *madrasah*s) using the *jadid* system of teaching. It also included a brilliant new literature inspired by the challenge of the modern world and committed to religious and political reforms, along with a rich, diverse, and sophisticated periodical press in the Tatar language.

Language and literature. One figure dominated the literary scene of the Tatar world. The Crimean Tatar Ismail Gaspraly (Gasprinskii) (1851–1914) was a historian, philologist, novelist, and politician. Over a period of twenty-five years, he developed in his magazine, the celebrated *Terjüman*, published from 1883 in Bakhchisarai, the doctrine of a liberal modernist pan-Turkism summed up in its watchword, "unity of language, of thought, and of action" *(dilde, fikirde, işte birlik)*. Gaspraly called for the union of all the Turkic peoples of Russia and for a new Muslim culture, which would be in contact with the West through the medium of Russian and Ottoman models. To achieve this unity he elaborated and used in his *Terjüman* a common pan-Turkic language based on a simplified Ottoman Turkish that would be understood by all the Turks from the Balkans to China.

Gaspraly also reorganized the teaching system, and his model *madrasah* in Bakhchisarai was imitated throughout Russia, especially in the Volga Tatar country. Some of the reformed *madrasah*s—such as the Huseiniyeh of Orenburg, Aliyeh of Ufa, Rasuliyeh of Troitsk, and Mohammadiyeh of Kazan—were among the best educational establishments of the Muslim world.

At the turn of the century, in response to the great effort made by the people as a whole, the cultural level of the Volga Tatars had been raised to a remarkable degree. The cities, particularly Kazan, Orenburg, Ufa, Troitsk, and Astrakhan, had acquired the character of genuine intellectual centers.

Politics. After 1905, the reform renaissance passed beyond the confines of education, language, and theology and became a political movement, an attempt to shake the pressure of the West without abandoning the Islamic basis of the Tatar society. The defeat of Russia by Japan in 1905, revealing Russia's weakness and stirring the hope of revenge among the subject peoples of the empire, was the psychological shock that transformed cultural reformism into a political movement. For the Muslims, and particularly for the Tatars who at that time were playing the role of the unquestioned intellectual leaders of Russian Islam, this defeat demonstrated that the tsarist empire was not invulnerable and that a political struggle was possible.

Between 1905 and 1917, the Tatar political scene became highly diversified and sophisticated, with all political trends involved. At the extreme right were the ultraconservatives, represented by a puritanical Ṣūfī brotherhood, God's Regiment of Vaysī, a dissident offshoot of the Naqshbandīyah. Founded a half-century earlier, in 1862, the brotherhood rejected the authority of the Russian state and refused to pay taxes or perform military service. Moreover, it condemned all the other Muslims as "infidels" for their submission to Russian rule. The Vaysī brotherhood was persecuted by the Russian authorities and brought to trial several times. In 1917, its adepts sided with the Bolsheviks; their leader, Shaykh Inan Vaysov, was killed by the Tatar counterrevolutionaries while fighting alongside the Red Army. Less radical was the traditionalist *(qadim)* wing of the Tatar community, which dominated the official Islamic administration until the Revolution. Its representatives were conservative in religion and politics. They were law-abiding citizens, hostile to the reformist movement, loyal to the tsarist regime, and personally loyal to the Romanov monarchy.

The majority of Tatars belonged to the liberal and radical trends. The liberals, followers of Ismail Gaspraly, believed that open struggle against Russia would be impossible and ill-fated. They advocated peaceful cooperation between Russia and the Muslim world, arguing that this would be of great and lasting advantage to Islam. The liberals dominated the Tatar national movement until the Revolution, but even though they were culturally united, they were politically divided. A few liberals sought to satisfy their demands within the framework of the tsarist autocracy; the majority envisaged a more or less lasting cooperation with the Russian liberal bourgeoisie. After 1908, Tatar leaders convinced of the impossibility of achieving reforms and equality of rights with the Russians by legal methods within the framework of the tsarist regime began to migrate to Turkey. Alternatively, they moved nearer to various socialist-Marxist or non-Marxist parties, giving birth to an original cultural and political movement, Muslim socialism. After the Revolution, Muslim socialism became Muslim communism. From Russian (or European) socialism, Muslim communism borrowed its phraseology, certain features of its agrarian program, its methods of propaganda, and organization; even so, it remained deeply rooted in the Islamic tradition.

Until the Revolution, even the most radical left-wing Tatar group, the Uralchylar (officially controlled by the Russian Marxists), refused to break away from Islam and to follow the antireligious line of the Bolsheviks.

Tatar Islam under the Soviet Regime. For the majority of the Tatar *jadids*, the Russian Revolution provided an occasion to fulfill their century-long struggle for the modernization and the secularization of their society. They took advantage of the downfall of the Romanov monarchy in February 1917 to create an independent religious establishment. The first All-Russian Muslim Congress, held in May 1917 in Moscow, abolished the tsarist practice whereby the *muftī* of Orenburg was appointed by the Russian minister of the interior. At this congress they elected their own *muftī*, Galimjan Barudi, a *jadid* scholar. The first ten years of the new regime were relatively quiet for the Muslims of the Middle Volga. Local power belonged to the Tatar communists, former *jadids* who had joined the Bolshevik party without breaking completely with their Islamic background.

The leader of the Muslim communists was a Volga Tatar, Mīr Said Sultan Galiev (1880–1936?), a companion of Stalin and, in the 1920s, the highest-ranking Muslim in the Communist party hierarchy. Although Mīr Said Sultan Galiev was a dedicated Marxist and an atheist, he believed that "no antireligious propaganda may succeed in the East as long as it remains in the hands of the Russians"; he also believed that "the main evil threatening the Tatars [is] not Islam, but their political backwardness" ("Metody antireligioznoi propagandy sredi Musul'man," *Zhizn' natsional'nostei*, 14 Dec. 1921, 23 Dec. 1921). Sultan Galiev was denounced by Stalin as a bourgeois nationalist and was arrested in 1923; he reemerged briefly in 1925 but was arrested again in 1928. He and all his companions disappeared in the decade-long purge that followed.

The liquidation of Galiev and his followers marked the beginning of a full-scale government offensive against Islam. It began with the foundation of the Tatar branch of Sughushchan Allahsyzlar (the "union of godless militants") and the appearance in 1924 of an antireligious periodical press in Tatar, Fen ve Din ("science and religion"), replaced in 1928 by Sughushchan Allahsyzlar. By 1929 all religious institutions, such as religious schools, religious courts, and *waqfs*, had disappeared. During the 1930s most of the mosques were closed or destroyed. In 1931, 980 parishes with 625 "clerics" remained in the Tatar A.S.S.R. By comparison, in 1889 the *muftī* of Orenburg had 4,645 parishes (sg., *mahalle*), served by 7,497 "clerics," under his jurisdiction. In the mid-1930s the anti-Islamic campaign culminated with the massive arrest of Muslim clerics accused of counterrevolutionary activity and espionage for Japan. The *muftī* of Orenburg, Kashaf Tarjemani, was arrested and executed.

During World War II, in 1942, one of the few surviving *jadid* clerics, Abdurrahman Rasuli (Rasulaev), approached Stalin with a view toward normalizing relations between the Soviet government and Islam. Stalin accepted the proposal, and a concordate was established. Persecutions were suspended, anti-Islamic propaganda lessened, and the *muftiat* reestablished (in Ufa instead of Orenburg). Abdurrahman Rasuli was appointed *muftī* and occupied this post until his death in 1962.

The *modus vivendi* established in 1942 continues to be the basis for the legal position of the Volga Muslims. According to the 1979 census, the total Muslim population placed under the theoretical jurisdiction of the *muftī* of Ufa was around seven and one-half million (6,317,000 Tatars and 1,371,000 Bashkirs). Official Islam is represented by the executives of the Spiritual Board of European Russia and Siberia, located at Ufa. The head of the Spiritual Board is a *muftī*. In 1980, when a Volga Tatar was elected, there were some 250 to 300 "registered clerics." The number of "working mosques" controlled by the Spiritual Board of Ufa is unknown, but a reasonable estimate would be 200 (maximum). There are no religious courts, no *waqfs*, and no religious schools. Tatar clerics are trained in the two *madrasahs* of Central Asia, Mīr-i ʿArab in Bukhara and Imām Ismāʿīl al-Bukhārī in Tashkent. Half a dozen Tatar and Bashkir students graduate every year from these two institutions. In spite of the weakness of the official Islamic establishment and the absence of any active Ṣūfī brotherhoods, the level of religious belief of the Volga Muslims remains astonishingly strong. Sociological surveys conducted in the 1970s show that around 60 percent of the Tatar and Bashkir population may be considered "believers" (by personal conviction, by tradition, or by nationalism). Islam thus remains an important ingredient of their ethnic identity and protects them from biological symbiosis with the Russians.

Ayze-Azade Rorlich, in her noteworthy analysis of Tatar Islam under Communist rule (*Central Asian Survey*, vol. 1, 1982, p. 37), writes:

> Social segregation along ethnic lines still characterizes the Muslim attitude toward non-Muslims in the USSR, despite the Soviet Government's efforts to promote integration, "drawing together," and eventually assimilation. At the root of this attitude lies a set of sociocultural values and traditions, many derived in whole or in part from the behaviour of the Muslim and Russian communities toward one another for centuries. These attitudes are unlikely to change quickly under any circumstances.

BIBLIOGRAPHY

Abdullaev, M. A., and M. V. Vagabov. *Aktual'nye problemy kritiki i preodoleniia Islama.* Makhachkala, 1975. A biased but well-documented Soviet work on Islam in Dagestan.

Abdullin, Yahya. *Tatarskaia prosvetitel'naia mysl'.* Kazan, 1976.

Avksentiev, Anatolii. *Islam na Severnom Kavkaze.* Stavropol, 1973. Well-documented propaganda.

Bennigsen, Alexandre, and Chantal Lemercier-Quelquejay. *Les mouvements nationaux chez les Musulmans de Russie: Le Sultangalievisme au Tatarstan.* Paris, 1960.

Davletshin, Timurbek. *Cultural Life in the Tatar Autonomous Republic.* New York, 1953. In Russian.

Fisher, Alan. *The Crimean Tatars.* Stanford, 1978.

Ibragimov, Galimjan. *Tatary v Revoliutsii 1905 goda.* Kazan, 1926.

Ishmuhametov, Zinnat. *Sotsial'naia rol' i evoliutsiia Islama v Tatarii (Istoricheskie ocherki).* Kazan, 1979. One of the few Soviet works on Islam in the Tatar country.

Marjani, Shihabeddin. *Mustafadh ul-akhbar fi ahvali Qazan ve Bolghar.* 2 vols. Kazan, 1897–1900.

Minorsky, Vladimir. *The Turks, Iran and the Caucasus in the Middle Ages.* London, 1978.

Sattarov, Magsad. *Islam dini galyglary haggynda.* Baku, 1967. A biased but serious Soviet work on Islam in Azerbaijan.

ALEXANDRE BENNIGSEN and FANNY E. BRYAN

Islam in Central Asia

Central Asia (Turkistan) was already an ancient and prosperous center of civilization when penetrated by Islam in the seventh century. Its population, both sedentary and nomadic, was of Iranian stock. For several hundred years its rulers had controlled the two most important trade routes of the ancient world, the Silk Road linking the Mediterranean to China and the Spice Road to India. Despite its location and the resulting prosperity, however, Turkistan had not been the center of a mighty empire: the native principalities were too weak to mount a successful opposition to their more powerful neighbors to the east, north, and west.

Indeed, Central Asia had been invaded and conquered more than once, by the Achaemenid Persians, the Macedonians of Alexander, the Seleucids (who succeeded Alexander), the Sasanids, the Kushans (nomads from the north), the Hephthalites, the Türk (in the sixth century), and finally the Chinese, who had reached the zenith of their political power toward 620 under the T'ang dynasty. The Türk, who made their first appearance in Central Asia around 565, had displaced the Iranian nomads and established an immense empire from the frontiers of China to the confines of Sasanid Persia and Byzantium. On the eve of the Arab invasion, Turkistan was divided into a number of small principalities, the most important of which were the kingdoms of Samarkand, Ferghana, and Khorezm. As a result of its past history, the sedentary civilization of the area presented a unique picture of religious and cultural syncretism. Almost all the major organized religions were to be found there, coexisting in a climate of exceptional tolerance: Zoroastrianism, the religion of the ruling class of Khorezm and Bactria; Buddhism, especially in Bactria, Sogdiana (the capital of Samarkand), and Tokharistan; as well as Nestorian Christianity, Judaism, and Manichaeism among the urban trading communities of the Silk Road. When the Arabs penetrated into Turkistan, the various priesthoods played no part whatsoever in the warfare.

The Beginning of Islamization. In marked contrast to the rapid progress of the Arab conquerors in Iran or North Africa, the expansion of Islam in Transoxiana (Lat., "beyond the Oxus," like the Arabic name for the same territory, Mā warā'a al-Nahr, "what lies beyond the river") was a slow and lengthy matter. The earliest Arab expeditions beyond the Amu Darya (Oxus River) were motivated by the desire for booty and glory. In the main, religion was of as little importance to them as it was to the defenders of the land. Although the expeditions began in 649, it was not until a century later, after the Arabs' great victory over the Chinese at the battle of the Talas River in 751, that Islam prevailed in Turkistan. At this same time Arab victories over the Turkic nomads on the Syr Darya River (Jaxartes) brought about the final dismemberment of the Turkic khaganate. As a result, a new era of peace and prosperity came to the sedentary town lands of Transoxiana, and the ba-

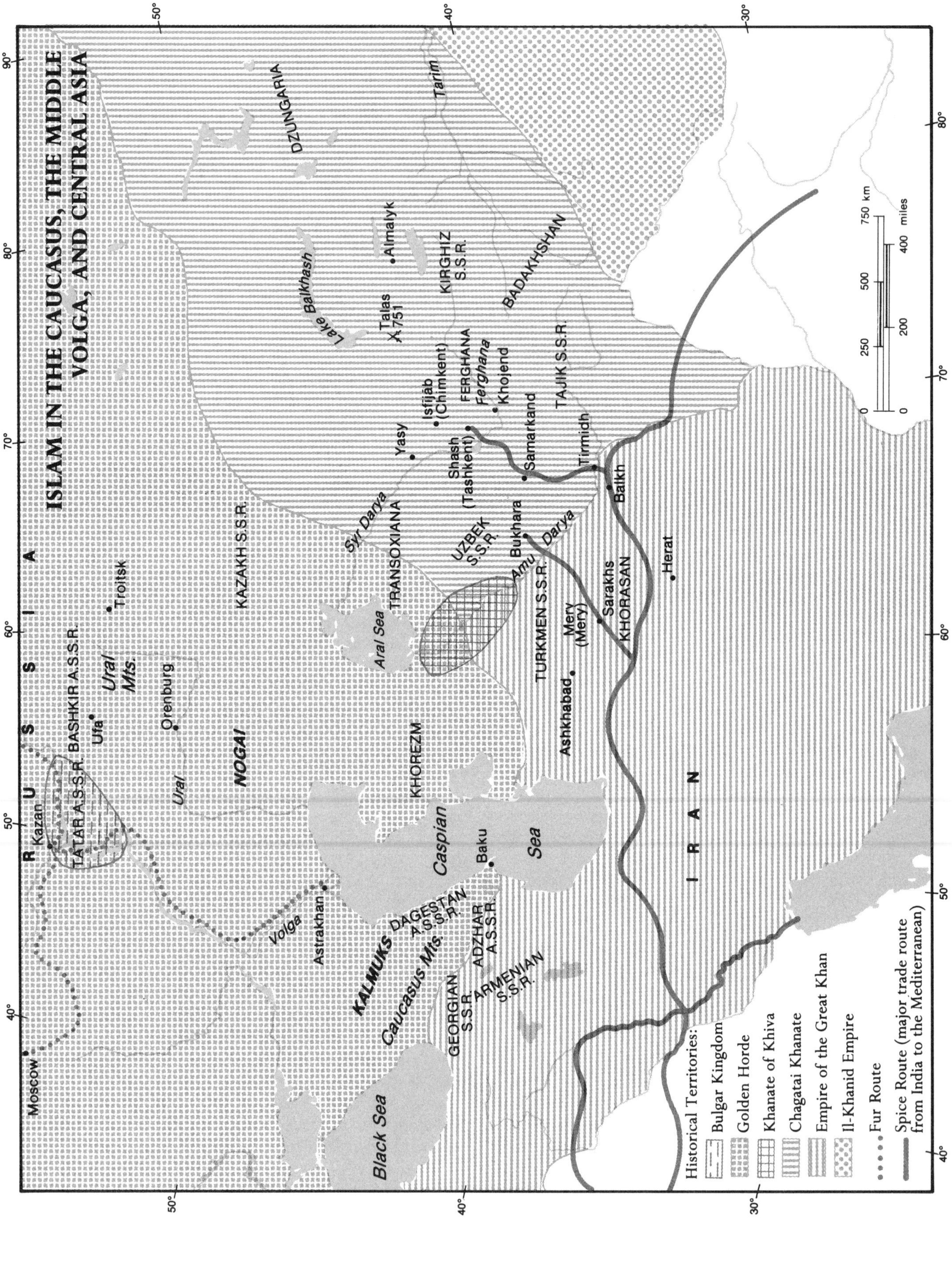
ISLAM IN THE CAUCASUS, THE MIDDLE VOLGA, AND CENTRAL ASIA
R U S S I A
I R A N
Moscow
Kazan
TATAR A.S.S.R.
BASHKIR A.S.S.R.
Ufa
Ural Mts.
Orenburg
Troitsk
Ural
NOGAI
KAZAKH S.S.R.
Volga
Astrakhan
KALMUKS
Caucasus Mts.
DAGESTAN A.S.S.R.
ADZHAR A.S.S.R.
GEORGIAN S.S.R.
ARMENIAN S.S.R.
Black Sea
Caspian Sea
Baku
KHOREZM
Aral Sea
TRANSOXIANA
Syr Darya
UZBEK S.S.R.
Amu Darya
Bukhara
TURKMEN S.S.R.
Ashkhabad
Merv (Merv)
Sarakhs
KHORASAN
Herat
Balkh
Tirmidh
Samarkand
Shash (Tashkent)
Yasy
Isfijāb (Chimkent)
FERGHANA
Ferghana
Khojend
TAJIK S.S.R.
BADAKHSHAN
KIRGHIZ S.S.R.
Talas 751
Lake Balkhash
Almalyk
DZUNGARIA
Tarim
0 250 500 750 km
0 200 400 miles
Historical Territories:
Bulgar Kingdom
Golden Horde
Khanate of Khiva
Chagatai Khanate
Empire of the Great Khan
Il-Khanid Empire
Fur Route
Spice Route (major trade route from India to the Mediterranean)

sis was laid for the "Golden Age" of the Samanids in the tenth century.

Legend has it that the first Arab incursion took place under the caliph ʿUthmān (r. 644–656), when 2,700 companions of the Prophet were said to have invaded Ferghana, and Muḥammad ibn Jawr led the companions to their death in battle against the "infidels." In fact, ʿAbd Allāh ibn Amīr, governor of Basra, conquered Merv and Sarakhs in present-day Turkmenistan in 649. Twenty-five years later the first Arab troops crossed the Amu Darya and defeated the ruler of Bukhara; this raid, under ʿUbayd Allāh ibn Ziyād, governor of Khorasan, was followed by several others north of the Amu Darya.

In 676 a cousin of the Prophet, Qutham ibn al-ʿAbbās, is said to have arrived in Samarkand together with Saʿīd ibn ʿUthmān ibn ʿAffān. Qutham became known to the Central Asians as Shah-i Zindah, the "living prince." During the reign of the Abbasids, and probably with their cooperation, Qutham's tomb in Samarkand—whether actual or alleged is not known—became the object of religious pilgrimage, and it is still one of the most holy places in Central Asia.

A successful campaign was waged against Khorezm between 681 and 683 by Salm ibn Ziyād, governor of Khorasan. He later advanced to Samarkand and became the first Arab governor to winter across the Amu Darya.

Other expeditions were conducted across the Amu Darya against Shahr-i Sabz and Tirmidh (Termez) in 697 and again at the turn of the century, but the real conquest of Turkistan began early in the eighth century. During the period between 704 and 715, Qutaybah ibn Muslim, governor of Khorasan, brought the definitive annexation of the lands north of the Amu Darya. He conquered Bukhara, where he built the first mosque (on the site of a former Buddhist temple), and Samarkand. Establishing an Arab garrison at Shāsh (Tashkent), he pressed forward to the north as far as Isfījāb. At his death in 715, Qutaybah was campaigning in Ferghana.

After Qutaybah's death, the Arabs suffered a considerable setback in Transoxiana. In 721 Khojend, the key of the Ferghana Valley, surrendered to them; three years later, however, a Muslim expedition on Ferghana was heavily defeated by the Türk.

Asad ibn ʿAbd Allāh al-Qaṣrī, governor of Khorasan, was the first to fortify the border of the Arab possessions. In 727 he built *ribāṭ*s (stations for cavalry troops) to defend the frontier against the attacks of the Türk. Asad also began the project of converting all the inhabitants of Transoxiana to Islam. Missionaries dispatched to Samarkand initially met with moderate success, but as taxes *(kharāj)* continued to be levied on all those who were formerly liable, a general revolt broke out. The whole of Sogdiana rose against the Arabs, and help was sought from the Türk. In 728, only Samarkand remained in Arab hands, but in 729 the Arabs reestablished their authority over Bukhara as well.

For over a decade the Arabs remained on the defensive, losing control of practically all their territories north of the Amu Darya, and in 737 the Turkic khagan was even able to make incursions south of the river. The following year, however, the Arab-Turkic competition for control of Transoxiana came to an end. The Türk were finally defeated, and their empire crumbled. Naṣr ibn Sayyār, the governor of Khorasan, once again pacified Transoxiana and reestablished Arab domination over the Syr Darya region. In 739 he established Arab governors in Shāsh and Fergana to rule the provinces side by side with the native (Iranian) princes.

The real islamization of Central Asia began at the time of the transfer of power from the Umayyads to the Abbasids around 750. A major role was played by Abū Muslim (ʿAbd al-Raḥmān ibn Muslim), an Abbasid missionary who succeeded in winning the support of the local feudal nobility and the rural population. Abū Muslim was able to effect a certain compromise between Islam and local beliefs. Although he was put to death in 755 by the caliph al-Manṣūr, he had a lasting influence on the people of Khorasan and Transoxiana. His memory was constantly revived in connection with various cults that made their appearance in later years, and series of proto-Shīʿī movements were also connected with his name.

During the same period, the T'ang emperor, still the nominal sovereign of Turkistan, sent a powerful Chinese expedition to reestablish his power. The Chinese entered the upper Syr Darya Valley but were heavily defeated in 751 at the Battle of Talas. This victory, led by Abū Muslim's general, Ziyād ibn Ṣāliḥ, put an end to Chinese pretensions of rule in Transoxiana and was soon followed by the final submission and the conversion to Islam of the rulers of the Turkistani principalities.

The islamization of Turkistan was accompanied by a singular renaissance of the Persian language and literature that V. V. Barthold (1956–1962) has called "the cultural triumph of the vanquished over the victors." This triumph was achieved at the end of the ninth century with the foundation of the Iranian Samanid dynasty by Ismāʿīl ibn Aḥmad (r. 892–907). From their capital in Bukhara, the Samanids ruled over the whole of Transoxiana. Ferghana and Khorezm, protected against the shamanist Turkic nomads by a line of frontier posts, were regarded as good Muslim countries, and their native populations began to take part in the battle for the faith against their infidel neighbors. There appeared at this time the first guilds of "warriors for the faith" (*ghuzāt* and *fityān;* sg., *ghāzī, fatā)* composed of urban volunteers. Sedentary Turkistan also began to be used as a base by the first Ṣūfī dervishes undertaking missionary work within the Turkic steppes. [*See* Dervishes.]

The Rooting of Islam. In the heyday of the Samanid dynasty (ninth and tenth centuries), Central Asia reached an exceptional level of political, cultural, and economic prosperity marked by the rise of cities and the expansion of international trade and industry. Bukhara and Samarkand in particular were important centers for the manufacture of rag paper (an art learned from Chinese prisoners captured at the Battle of Talas in 751) and textiles. Enterprises in these cities maintained close trade contacts with China, India, the kingdom of Bulgar and the rest of the Muslim world. The brilliant Samanid court made Bukhara one of the capitals of the Muslim world and, with the poet Rūdākī (913–943), the birthplace of Persian literature. The new order of centralized civil and military bureaucracy introduced by the Samanids brought autocratic rule and heavy taxation to their subjects, and their political structure came to supersede completely the old feudal regime of independent princes and landed aristocracy. Even so, the subject population retained some of its warlike habits and continued to carry arms; it was the urban masses who provided the bodies for the "warriors of the faith" defending the frontiers against the raids of the pagan nomads.

It was also under the Samanids that Sunnī Islam of strict orthodoxy was firmly established in Transoxiana. Islamic judges and religious leaders acquired great prestige. Among the most celebrated were Abū Ḥafṣ (d. 832), Abū Manṣūr al-Māturīdī of Samarkand (d. 944), and Abū Bakr al-Qaffāl al-Shāshī (d. 1114). By the end of the ninth century, Bukhara had a solid reputation as one of the main centers of Islamic theology.

The early spread of Islam. The Samanids were the first Central Asian rulers to conduct raids against the shamanist or Christian Turkic people of the steppes. In 893, under the leadership of Ismāʿīl ibn Aḥmad, the Samanids carried out a successful expedition to Talas and converted the main Nestorian church into a mosque. They also granted lands along the Syr Darya to Turkic settlers who agreed to embrace Islam and to defend the border against their shamanist kin. It was these sedentary people, together with Muslim merchants and the vagabond dervishes, who brought Islam to the steppes.

The Muslim rulers of Khorezm, vassals of the Samanids, and the merchants from Gurganj played the same missionary role vis-à-vis the steppes of the Lower Volga and the faraway Bulgar. But the Samanids never tried to mount a systematic religious propaganda campaign, nor did they attempt to convert the Turkic nomads by force. As Barthold points out, "The success of the Muslim trade was not always accompanied by the success of Islam as a religion. Muslims who traveled for commercial purposes did not get involved in religious propaganda" (*Four Studies on Central Asia,* vol. 1, p. 19). It was through example rather than through persuasion or force that Islam was spread among the nomads.

Thus, in the second half of the tenth century (955), Satuk Bughra Khan, the Karakhanid ruler, embraced Islam. The year 960 is considered to be the date of the first conversion of an entire Turkic horde (200,000 tents strong), without any mention of a "holy war." In 977, Sebüktigin, the Turkic slave who founded the Ghaznavid dynasty, was already a Muslim. In 980, Seljuk, the chief of a Türkmen tribe, crossed the lower reaches of the Syr Darya and became a Muslim.

Numerous non-Muslim colonies survived in Turkistan. Barthold remarks that Central Asian Christians and Manichaeans profited more in their proselytizing activities from the success of Muslim trade than did the Muslims themselves. In fact, the Christians and Manichaeans made their most important gains in Inner Asia (including Sinkiang and Mongolia) under Muslim rule during the tenth and eleventh centuries.

At the time of the Samanids, there were Nestorian Christian communities to the south of the Syr Darya on the border between the cultivated lands and the steppes; Nestorian communities were also to be found in and around Samarkand and Merv (the seat of a Nestorian bishopric). Monophysite Christians were numerous in Khorezm, and there were Jewish trading colonies and Manichaean communities in Samarkand, Bukhara, and Balkh. Traces of Zoroastrianism were to be found around Bukhara and in Khorezm. In the tenth century, a Zoroastrian temple was still in existence at Ramush in the neighborhood of Bukhara. At the periodic fairs held in the city of Bukhara, idols (probably Buddhist figures) were freely sold. Although all Buddhist temples were destroyed in the ninth and early tenth centuries, it is probable that heathen, Buddhist, or dualist beliefs persisted in the countryside. Indeed, these beliefs have survived to the present. Within Sufism, for example, the cult of saints includes some barely distinguished Zoroastrian or Buddhist deities.

At the end of the Samanid period, the northern frontier of Islam coincided broadly with the limits of the cultivated land: Islam did not penetrate deeply into the steppes. Even so, the Muslim base was sufficiently widespread that there was no important incursion of Turkic shamanists from the steppes into Transoxiana after 904. At that time, the invaders were driven back, and from then until the era of the Kara-Khitay, all the nomadic invaders entering Transoxiana from the steppes were already Muslim.

The eastern provinces of Wakhan, Shughnan, Darwaz, and Rushan were politically subject to the Muslims but were populated by shamanists. The city of Jarm in Badakhshan marked the extreme limit of Muslim dominion. Farther north, in the eastern part of the Ferghana valley, the city of Osh (formerly a Zoroastrian center) was a fortified frontier *ribāṭ*.

Ṣūfī influence. As early as the tenth century, Central Asian Islam had acquired features that distinguished it from Islam in the neighboring regions. The most important of these features was the Ṣūfī *ṭarīqah* (lit., "way"; brotherhood). As early as the ninth century, Abū ʿAbd Allāh Muḥammad ibn Karrām (806–869), a native of Sistan, founded the Karrāmīyah, a mystical sect that spread throughout Transoxiana, including Ferghana, Merv, and Samarkand, and lasted until the Mongol domination. Its adepts practiced pietism and extreme asceticism and were responsible for the conversion of a large number of Zoroastrians and Christians.

Another characteristic aspect of Central Asian Islam was the cult of saints, which combined the veneration of authentic *ghāzī*s and more or less historical Ṣūfī shaykhs with various pre-Islamic beliefs, including the ancestor cult and Zoroastrian or Buddhist deities. Holy places were particularly numerous in the Ferghana Valley near the border of the *dār al-Islām*. Among the most venerated was the tomb of the prophet Ayyūb (Job) near the city of Jalālābād; the tomb was known in the tenth century. Also important were the burial place of the legendary 2,700 companions of the Prophet in Ferghana; the *mazār* ("tomb") of Imam ʿAbd Allāh, the grandson of Imam Ḥusayn, in the city of Kokand; the tomb of Qutaybah ibn Muslim near the village of Kakh; and the tomb of the Ṣūfī shaykh Ḥakīm Abū ʿAbd Allāh Muḥammad ibn ʿAlī al-Tirmidhī in the city of Tirmidh.

With the fall of the Samanids in 1005, the Iranians were replaced by the Turkic dynasties—Karakhanids, Ghaznavids, Khwarizm-shahs, and Seljuks—but this change neither modified the profile of Central Asian Islam nor interrupted the development of Iranian culture. The general economic progress of the country continued as well. The new conquerors either were already Muslim when they crossed the fortified borderline or, as in the case of the Seljuks, embraced Islam as soon as they penetrated into the sedentary territory. They imitated the model of the Samanid court, protecting the frontiers against their barbarian brethren (Türk) or cousins (Mongols).

The new rulers were rapidly "iranized" and became zealous Muslims, allowing all recollection of their pre-Islamic past to fade. Their old Uighur alphabet was abandoned in favor of the Arabic script. Persian and Arabic became the only official languages of the court. All elements of earlier cultures—Manichaean, Chinese, Buddhist, and Nestorian Christian—were forgotten.

During the eleventh and twelfth centuries the brilliant literature flourishing in Central Asia was based exclusively on Muslim and Persian patterns. Among the distinguished scholars, writers, and philosophers of the era were the poet Abū Bakr Muḥammad ibn al-ʿAbbās al-Khwārizmī; the historian Maḥmūd al-Kāshghari, who gave a detailed account of the Turkic tribes and dialects of the Karakhanid kingdom in his *Dīwān lughāt al-Turk;* the Khorezmian Abū al-Rayḥān al-Bīrūnī; the philosopher Abū Sahl al-Masīḥī; Abū ʿAlī ibn Sīnā (Avicenna) from Khorezm, who wrote in Persian and in Arabic; and the great poet Firdawsī at the court of Maḥmūd of Ghaznah. [*See the biographies of al-Bīrūnī and Ibn Sīnā.*]

The Turkic rulers, especially the Karakhanids, were distinguished by great piety, but contrary to their Samanid ancestors, they honored Ṣūfī shaykhs and ascetics more than they honored representatives of the dogmatic religion. During their reign (and especially between 1131 and 1141 under Maḥmūd II ibn Sulaymān), several expeditions were undertaken against the shamanist nomads (Kipchaks) in order to impose Islam by force of arms, although more important in the spread of Islam was the preaching of the Ṣūfī missionaries in the Kipchak steppe.

The twelfth century was marked by the transformation of loose Ṣūfī communities into closely knit, well-organized brotherhoods with formal initiation rites. Two native *ṭarīqah*s were particularly active. The Kubrawīyah *ṭarīqah* in Khorezm was founded by Najm al-Dīn Kubrā (born in Khiva in 1145 and killed in Urgench in 1220 by the Mongols). The Yasawīyah *ṭarīqah* had a great influence in both eastern and western Turkistan and in the adjacent steppes. It was founded by the Turkic poet and mystic Aḥmad Yasawī (born in Isfījāb, present-day Chimkent, and died in 1166 in Yasy, present-day Turkistan in southern Kazakhstan). The Yasawīyah spread throughout Transoxiana, to Khorezm and as far as Bulgar. Its success was partly due to the fact that the brotherhood incorporated into its doctrine certain pre-Islamic (shamanistic) religious practices such as the "loud" *dhikr,* a vocal prayer ceremony in remembrance *(dhikr)* of God. [*See* Dhikr.]

The Period of Disasters. On 9 September 1141, the army of the Seljuk sultan Sanjar was routed in the Qaṭvān steppe to the north of Samarkand. The new invaders were the Kara-Khitay, a federation of Mongol tribes who had ruled northern China. The defeat by the Kara-Khitay was the greatest disaster ever suffered by the Muslims. Not only were as many as thirty thousand men said to have been killed, but the defeat had been inflicted by "infidels." All of Turkistan had been subjected to the power of a non-Muslim people. Kara-Khitay rule was not exceedingly harsh (especially compared with the Mongol invasion of the next century), but for the first time, a major sector of Islam was challenged by a rival ideology of equal or even superior military and political might. All Muslim chronicles of the time reflect the utter horror of the Islamic world in the face of this new and unexpected development. Indeed, the episode even became known in western Europe.

The Kara-Khitay in Central Asia. Kara-Khitay rule in northern China lasted from 916 to 1125, when their kingdom was overrun by the Jurchens, a Manchu people, and the remaining Kara-Khitay moved westward. The Kara-Khitay had been strongly influenced by Chinese culture and probably used Chinese as their official administrative language. There were some Nestorian Christians and Confucians among them, but the great majority were Buddhists who were particularly unyielding to Islam. The first Kara-Khitay ruler *(gürkhan)*, Yeh-lü Ta-shih, was Buddhist; his son and successor had a Nestorian Christian name, Yi-lieh (Elie). The Kara-Khitay penetrated into the steppes of present-day Kazakhstan in 1130; crossing the Syr Darya several years later, they inflicted a heavy defeat on the Karakhanid ruler near Khojent in 1136. Their victory at Qaṭvān in 1141 made them the masters of the whole of Central Asia with the exception of Khorezm.

Even Buddhist domination did not moderate the expansion of Islam, however. Instead, the brief period of peace established by the Kara-Khitay rule permitted Muslim merchants, Ṣūfī preachers, and men of learning to spread Islam farther north and east into the steppes. During the twelfth century, the Turkic rulers of the Ili valley and Almaligh became Muslim, and, according to legend, the Qādirīyah brotherhood began to penetrate into Turkistan.

The situation of Islam grew worse when the Kara-Khitay emperor was deposed by Küchlüg, head of the Mongol Naiman tribe, in 1211. Originally a Nestorian Christian like the majority of his tribe, Küchlüg later became "pagan" (probably Buddhist). He was an open enemy of the Muslims, and under his rule—for the first, and the last, time since Islam was introduced into Central Asia—the religion of the Prophet suffered persecution. Public Muslim worship was suppressed. Muslims were forced to embrace Christianity, to become "idolaters," or at the very least to exchange their Muslim clothing for the Chinese garb of the Kara-Khitay.

Central Asia under the Mongols. In the autumn of 1219, Mongol vanguards appeared in Central Asia. Less than two years later they had conquered Turkistan, Afghanistan, and the Caucasus. Chinggis Khan was tolerant in religious matters and had no personal animosity against Islam. Muslims, chiefly merchants, were his trusted counselors. Under his reign, Muslims and all other religious groups enjoyed complete religious freedom. His son and successor, Ögedei, was also kindly disposed toward Muslims and gave preference to Islam over other religions. Nonetheless, the destruction and slaughter wreaked on the major cities were so overwhelming that the Mongol conqueror became the symbol of the deadliest danger ever to threaten Islam. The brilliant Muslim civilization of Transoxiana and Khorezm suffered a major setback. For a century Turkistan was put under the administration of yet another "infidel" power. The first Mongol ruler of Turkistan (with the exception of Khorezm, which fell within the province of the Golden Horde) was Chinggis Khan's son Chaghatai. Unlike his father, he was personally hostile to Islam and rigorously punished the observance of certain Islamic prescriptions that infringed on Mongol law, such as performing ablutions in running water or slaughtering an animal by cutting its throat. Chaghatai died in 1241. The majority of his successors remained shamanists. Several, such as Khan Alu-ghu (1259–1266), were strongly inimical to Islam, while others were tolerant in religious matters, although some were more or less influenced by Buddhism or Nestorian Christianity.

This was an unhappy period for Central Asian Islam. A state religion for centuries, it had lost its predominant position and was obliged to share its prestige with other religions, including the hated Buddhism—the creed of the despised idolaters (Pers., *būt-parast*). In the thirteenth and fourteenth centuries there was an upsurge of Nestorian Christianity in Central Asia. Christians were allowed free rein to propagate their faith and to build churches. Orthodox Christians (Alans, Khazars, and Russians) are mentioned by late thirteenth-century European travelers in Urgench, and in 1329 Pope John XXII sent a Catholic bishop to Samarkand, a city where Christians were predominant, according to a Chinese source. There was a Nestorian bishop in Kashgar.

Even more significant was the deep change that took place within Central Asian Islam. The decline of urban culture was followed by the decline of the old Arab-Iranian Muslim religious establishment that had been deeply rooted in city life. Under the Mongols, Islam ceased to be the religion of the ruling elites and became the religion of the rural masses, both sedentary and nomadic.

In the early fourteenth century, according to Barthold, the Mongol rulers of the Chaghatai *ulus* ("appanage") made a decisive step toward the adoption of traditional Islamic culture, if not yet of Islam as a religion. The khan Kebek (1318–1326) renounced the nomadism of his ancestors and took up residence in Transoxiana; although he remained shamanist, he protected the Muslims. His brother and successor, Tarmashirin (1326–1344), was converted to Islam and maintained a climate of great religious tolerance.

Mongol rule witnessed the further development of the Ṣūfī *ṭarīqah* in Central Asia. The Kubrawīyah spread throughout Khorezm; the Yasawīyah was dominant in the Ferghana Valley and among the southern Türkmen tribes; the Qādirīyah developed mainly in the cities of Transoxiana. J. Spencer Trimingham has noted in *The Sufi Orders of Islam* that

> during this period, the Ṣūfīs became for the people the representatives of religion in a new way. . . . The shrine [of the holy *murshid*], not the mosque, became the symbol of Islam. The shrine, the dervish house, and the circle of *dhikr*-reciters became the outer forms of living religion for Iranians, Turks, and Tatars alike.

The Victory of Islam and the Era of Decadence. The character of Central Asian Islam changed once more in the fifteenth and sixteenth centuries under the Timurid dynasty and its Shaybanid successors. Though Timur followed the Mongol state and military traditions, Islam and Islamic culture were, as Barthold remarks, "cleverly exploited to justify his actions and enhance the splendour of his throne. . . ."

The great conqueror enjoyed the full support of the Muslim upper classes, the religious leaders, and the nomadic aristocracy, whose zeal for Islam was moderate. Timur was also supported by the Iranian population of the Transoxianan cities, those merchants and craftsmen who were more religious than the nomadic Turks. Timur himself was a pious Muslim and was personally interested in deepening the hold of Islam among the superficially islamized rural population and among the nomads. It was during Timur's reign that all traces of non-Muslim religion, with the exception of Bukharan Jews, disappeared from Central Asia. Among the first to disappear were the Nestorian Christians, so powerful under the Čagadai Mongols.

The ṭarīqahs. Ṣūfī brotherhoods played a dominant role in the expansion and intensification of Islam in Central Asia. They were active during Timur's reign and those of his successors. At this point the Naqshbandīyah and the Yasawīyah were particularly active.

The Naqshbandī *ṭarīqah* was founded in Bukhara by Muḥammad ibn Bahā' al-Dīn Naqshband al-Bukhārī (1317–1389). It is a highly intellectual order, practicing the silent *dhikr*. Although the order is mystical, it is permanently involved in worldly affairs, a dual character symbolized in the two well-known Naqshbandī rules: "Khalvat dar anjoman" ("Solitude in the society") and "Dast be-kār dil bā Yār" ("The hand at work and the heart with the Friend").

The Naqshbandīyah rapidly gained immense prestige throughout Central Asia on every social level. It penetrated the upper echelons among the administrative and military elite of the Timurid state, and also became a major factor on the popular level among the craftsmen of the cities. The tomb of the founder of the *ṭarīqah*, located in a village near Bukhara, is still one of the most popular centers of pilgrimage in Turkistan.

The adepts of the Yasawīyah, meanwhile, were active in spreading the teachings of Islam among the Turkic nomads. Ṣūfī saints whose cults were connected to the national traditions of nomads were particularly important for Timur. Significantly, Timur himself built the mausoleum of the order's founder, Shaykh Aḥmad Yasawī, who had been especially active among the nomads.

Under the Timurids, urban life in Central Asia experienced a new era of economic prosperity and cultural development. Samarkand under Ulugh Beg (1409–1449) and Herat under Ḥusayn Baykara (1469–1509) were brilliant centers of intellectual activity. In Herat, Central Asian poetry, especially in Turkic and Persian, reached its peak with Mīr ʿAlī Shīr Navā'ī, who wrote mainly in Čagadai Turkic, and ʿAbd al-Raḥmān Jāmī, the last of the great Persian poets, both of whom belonged to the Naqshbandī *ṭarīqah*. Against the background of this last Golden Age of Turkistan, it is difficult to agree with those historians (including Barthold) who characterize the era of Ulugh Beg by the emergence of "religious reaction," personified by the Naqshbandī *murshid* Khoja Aḥrār (1404–1490). [*See also* Ṭarīqah.]

Later dynasties. The sweeping Uzbek conquest of Central Asia in the early sixteenth century did not stop its cultural progress. The Shaybanid rulers, unlike their Mongol ancestors in the thirteenth century, were not "barbarians"; that is to say, they were already Muslims when they crossed the borders of Khorezm. Moreover, they protected the borderlands of Central Asia against their nomadic brethren; ʿAbd Allāh Khan (1559–1598), for example, led several expeditions into the interior of the steppes. Under their rule, their capital, Bukhara, and also Balkh became centers of cultural and social life. The Shaybanid khans, especially ʿUbayd Allāh (d. 1539), were regarded as ideal rulers in the spirit of Muslim piety. This was also true of the Astrakhanids (or Janids), another Chinggisid dynasty that succeeded the Shaybanids in the seventeenth century. They were great builders and protectors of the arts and literature, and a rich historical literature developed in Turkistan under their rule.

By the early sixteenth century, however, the first signs of decline were in evidence. One of the main reasons for the decline was the discovery and development of maritime routes between western Europe, India, and China, which rapidly undermined the Inner Asian caravan trade. By the eighteenth century the area had drifted into an era of economic, political, and finally cultural and intellectual decadence.

The emergence of the Safavid Shīʿī power in Iran and the conquest of Astrakhan by the Muscovites in 1556 established major barriers to the north and south of the Caspian Sea. As a result, the Sunnī world was cut into two parts, and the eastern Turkic peoples of Central Asia were permanently isolated from their brethren in the Ottoman empire to the west.

Finally, in the seventeenth and eighteenth centuries Central Asia suffered one of the most tragic disasters that had ever befallen Muslim Turkistan: the invasion of the "barbarians" from Inner Asia. This incursion, which was particularly detrimental to the northern areas, began in the early years of the seventeenth century, when a full tribe from western Mongolia, the Torgut Mongols, left Dzungaria. Crossing Central Asia from northeast to southwest, they settled in 1613 in the southern Volga region, where they took the name of Kalmuks. Militant Buddhists and adversaries of Islam, they remained an alien, hostile body in the midst of a Muslim Turkic environment.

For a century and a half the Volga Kalmuks and their cousins, the Oirats (who had remained in Dzungaria), systematically raided Central Asia. In contrast to the Mongols of Chinggis Khan, neither the Kalmuks nor the Oirats had the slightest intention of settling in Turkistan. Their interest was confined to plundering and destroying their hated enemies, and their expeditions brought all the ferocity of a religious war, a "Buddhist crusade." The imprint of horror they left behind them virtually erased the memory of all previous invaders, including the Kara-Khitay and the Mongols.

Salvation came to the Muslims only after 1757, when the Oirat kingdom of Dzungaria was finally destroyed by the Manchu armies. But the long struggle against the Buddhists had laid waste Central Asia, ruining its cities and breaking its unity. Toward the end of the eighteenth century three new Turkic dynasties were founded: the Mangit in Bukhara, the Qungrat in Khiva, and the Ming in the Ferghana Valley. However, none of them was strong enough to reunify Turkistan or to protect it from an exterior danger. When the last invaders, the Russians, appeared in Central Asia they encountered only a minimal resistance.

Russian and Soviet Domination. Once the Kalmuk and Dzungarian assault had reduced the mighty Turkic (Kazakh and Nogai) Muslim hordes to a state of total impotence, the Russian vanguard moving south from western Siberia was not only unopposed but welcomed. The Kazakh hordes, unable to resist the superior military power of the Oirats, invoked Russian help and asked for protection. After the destruction of the Dzungarians in the middle of the eighteenth century, there were no rivals to Russian rule. Nominal protection was gradually turned into virtual possession, and direct Russian administration displaced the old feudal systems exercised by the native rulers. All revolts led by the feudal aristocracy against the Russians were crushed, and by the middle of the nineteenth century, the power of the Kazakh khans had been liquidated.

In the Kazakh steppes, the Russians did not try to assimilate the natives. Instead, they adopted a policy that tended to favor the development of a purely Kazakh national, modernist, and secular culture. They hoped to turn such a structure to their own advantage, by setting the superficially islamized Kazakh nomadic nobility against the Tatar merchants and Turkistani clerics who represented Muslim civilization. Notwithstanding a few instances of spectacular success, by and large, this strategy met with failure, and the number of "westernized" Kazakhs remained limited. During the second half of the nineteenth century Islam, brought simultaneously by the Tatar reformers known as *jadid*s and the conservative Bukhara clerics, became more deeply rooted among the nomadic masses. [*See also* Modernism, *article on* Islamic Modernism.]

The Russian advance into Turkistan south of the Syr Darya began as soon as the Caucasian Wars were over in 1859 and met with only sporadic resistance. The three native principalities of Bukhara, Kokand, and Khiva, which had long ago lost their economic and political power, were unable if not unwilling to oppose the overwhelming might of the tsarist empire. Even so, it required half a century of military operations to complete the conquest, beginning in 1855 with the occupation of Chimkent and ending in 1900 with the occupation of the eastern part of the Pamirs. The khanate of Kokand was suppressed, and its territory was placed under direct Russian military administration as the governate general of Turkistan. Bukhara and Khiva became Russian protectorates.

In Turkistan, a country of overpopulated oases, rural colonization was impossible. Consequently, Russian presence remained minimal. There were a few officials and military garrisons, creating "white" colonies in quarters specially built for them. The natives were not considered Russian "citizens" and were not drafted into military service. Russians and Muslims formed distinct communities, coexisting but not mixing with each other. Central Asia as a whole was likewise cut off from any other outside influence. The aim of this simple strategy was to preserve the most archaic forms of Islamic culture in Central Asia. Proselytizing by the Russian Orthodox church was strictly prohibited, and the Tatar modernist *(jadid)* teachers were banned as well. In their place, Qur'anic schools, both *maktab*s and *madrasah*s, of the most conservative *(qadim)* type were favored by the Russians and protected from any modernist influence.

By fostering social, intellectual, and political backwardness, the Russian overlords sought to reduce the possibility of organized national resistance, and their strategy was partly successful. On the eve of the 1917 Russian Revolution, Turkistan was without a doubt one of the most conservative and least advanced areas of the entire Muslim world. But in spite of this limited "success," the dream of keeping the immense territory of Central Asia isolated and "protected" from all external influences was an illusion. Foreign influences—Tatar, Turkish, and Iranian—inevitably penetrated the territory, and while they were of diverse character, ranging from revolutionary to conservative, the common factor among all of them was Islam. As it turned out, these disparate ideas played an important role in the cultural and political awakening of Turkistan at the turn of the twentieth century.

In the same way, the attempts of the Russian authorities to win over the sympathies of the Muslim religious scholars *('ulamā')* were only partly successful. The Turkistani *'ulamā'* remained influential and prosperous through the maintenance of religious endowments. They did not participate in anti-Russian movements after the conquest; indeed, until the 1917 Revolution they remained politically inactive. But at the same time, the equally influential Ṣūfī brotherhoods, especially the militant Naqshbandīyah, played a leading role in virtually all uprisings against Russian rule. Particularly important were the Andijan revolt of 1898 led by a Naqshbandī, the *ishān* (shaykh) Madali, and the resistance of the Tekke Türkmen tribe at Gök-Tepe in 1861, led by another Naqshbandī shaykh, Kurban Murat. However, the Central Asian Naqshbandīyah did not succeed in transforming their revolts into a full-scale "holy war" on the model of the Caucasian Wars.

The 1917 Revolution and the Civil War provided Central Asian Muslims with an opportunity to shake off Russian rule. In 1918 a popular guerrilla movement started in the Ferghana Valley and spread to almost all of Turkistan. The revolt, known as the Basmachi movement (from Uzbek *basmach,* "bandit"), lasted for ten years and was finally crushed in 1928 after a long and difficult struggle. Like the earlier Naqshbandī revolts, the Basmachi movement did not have the characteristics of a holy war. Nonetheless, it was an attempt not only to regain independence but also to protect the purity and the glory of the faith. The Russian Bolsheviks were both alien and infidel rulers and "people without religion" *(bī-dīn).* Although it was not a holy war, Ṣūfī shaykhs and adepts, Naqshbandī and Yasawī, were numbered among the guerrilla fighters.

Islam in Central Asia Today. According to the 1979 Soviet census, the total Muslim population of Central Asia had reached 29 million, including about 27 million natives and about 2 million immigrants from the Caucasus, the Middle Volga, and the Urals. Crimean Tatars and Transcaucasian Turkic peoples (deportees rather than immigrants), and the remnants of former deportees, the Chechen and Ingush, probably constituted a little less than a million people. By early 1983 the total figure was estimated to have risen to nearly 32 million.

The Turkic peoples (native and immigrants) make up the overwhelming majority (around 90 percent) of the population. Non-Turkic peoples include the Tajiks, the Ironis (descendants of Persian prisoners taken in the seventeenth and eighteenth centuries), the Pamirians, the Chinese Muslims, or Dungans (immigrants of 1856), and an unknown number of Muslim gypsies.

The great majority of Central Asian Muslims are Sunnīs of the Ḥanafī rite. Non-Sunnīs include both Ismā'īlī and Twelver Shī'ah. The Ismā'īlīyah, numbering roughly 60,000 to 100,000, are made up of Pamirians in the Gorno-Badakhshan Autonomous Region; their ancestors were converted to Ismā'īlī Shiism in the eleventh century by the poet-philosopher Naṣīr-i Khusraw. The Twelvers include about 30,000 Ironis, approximately 20,000 Baluchis, and an unknown number (perhaps as many as 100,000) of Uzbeks and Tajiks. The Twelvers are scattered throughout the cities of Samarkand, Urgench, Tashkent, Ashkhabad, Bukhara, and Merv.

Administration. Sunnī Islam in Central Asia is endowed with an official administration, the Muslim Spiritual Board of Central Asia and Kazakhstan, created by the Soviets in 1943. Its headquarters are located in Tashkent. The Twelvers are placed under the authority of the Shaykh al-Islām of Baku. There is no officially recognized authority for the Ismā'īlīyah.

The spiritual board of Tashkent has under its control

all the registered clerics (e.g., *imām-khaṭīb,* muezzin) who alone are permitted to perform religious rites; these probably number less than 1,000. The number of working mosques is estimated at 150 to 200. It is believed that there are 4 mosques in Turkmenistan, 39 in Tajikistan, and probably about 100 in Uzbekistan. The greatest concentration of mosques is found in the cities of Uzbekistan, in southern Kirghizia (the eastern part of the Ferghana Valley), and in southern Kazakhstan along the Syr Darya Valley.

The U.S.S.R. is not only a secular state but is also officially an atheistic state; hence the church (mosque) is totally separated from the state and from the school. Religious activity outside the official working mosque is strictly forbidden. There are no *waqf*s ("endowments") to administer and no religious courts. Although religious education is banned from Soviet schools, two *madrasah*s administered by the Tashkent Spiritual Board are permitted to train Muslim clerics. One of these, Mīr-i ʿArab in Bukhara, is geared toward intermediate instruction, while the other, Imām Ismāʿīl al-Bukhārī in Tashkent, serves the higher level. The total number of students was estimated at about sixty in the 1980s. After graduation, the best students are sent to al-Azhar University in Egypt or to the Qarawīyīn in Morocco.

All religious publications are forbidden, with the exception of a quarterly periodical published by the Spiritual Board of Tashkent. This quarterly, *Muslims of the Soviet East,* appears in five languages: Arabic, Uzbek in Arabic script, Persian, English, and French. Significantly, there is no Russian edition, nor is there one in modern Uzbek; in other words, the periodical is only for foreign consumption, not for a domestic readership.

Faced with these restrictions, the official Islamic establishment appears to be unable to satisfy the spiritual needs of the population. Its meager resources have been dwarfed by the unrelenting and massive antireligious propaganda campaign to which the population has been subjected since 1928. Despite the inadequacies of official Islam and the ever-present propaganda, however, Soviet sociological surveys conducted in the Central Asian republics in the 1970s revealed that the level of the religious feeling of the Muslim population there was astonishingly high. According to these data, the "believers" constituted some 80 percent of the total population. Within the population, about 20 percent were "believers by conviction" (referred to as "fanatics" in Soviet literature); approximately 10 percent were "believers by tradition"; about 20 percent were "hesitants"; and roughly 30 percent were "unbelievers, who, even so, perform essential religious and custom rites." The "atheists" accounted for the remaining 20 percent of the population, but even among that group, the majority performed the three religious rites of circumcision, marriage, and burial that, to the population, represent adherence to Islam. By contrast, among former Christians in the U.S.S.R. about 80 percent were identified as atheists.

Ṣūfī organizations. In large part, the strength of Islam is due to the intense activity of the Ṣūfī brotherhoods. After a long period of decline in the nineteenth century, the Ṣūfī brotherhoods gained new prestige from the example of the Basmachi movement. Since the beginning of Soviet rule, Ṣūfī organizations have effectively replaced the official Islamic establishment. They have maintained a network of clandestine houses of prayer and Qur'anic schools (especially around the numerous holy places), and in the absence of "registered" clerics, their adepts are performing the religious rites. In fact, the level of the religious feeling is exceptionally high in those areas where official Islam has been weakened to the brink of total disappearance. Such is the case of the Türkmen Republic, where only four mosques have survived but the Ṣūfī brotherhoods are especially active. According to all Soviet surveys, Turkmenistan is the most religious territory of all Central Asia.

The Ṣūfī *ṭarīqah*s are especially active in the formerly nomadic areas, where the traditional infrastructure of tribes and clans has been preserved and the extended family or the clan serves as the basis for the *ṭarīqah.* One of these areas includes Turkmenistan and southern Kirghizia (in the eastern part of the Ferghana Valley); another consists of southern Kazakhstan and Tajikistan.

Four brotherhoods are prominent today in Central Asia: the Naqshbandīyah, the Yasawīyah, the Qādirīyah, and the Kubrawīyah. But in practice, the distinctions among the orders tend to disappear, and there are many examples of adepts belonging simultaneously to two or more *ṭarīqah*s.

The Naqshbandīyah is influential in the cities of Central Asia and in the rural areas of Turkmenistan, northern Uzbekistan, Karakalpakistan, in the Ferghana Valley, and in western Tajikistan. It is still the largest and probably the most popular Ṣūfī brotherhood of Central Asia.

The Yasawīyah is dominant in the Syr Darya area and in the Ferghana Valley. Until the 1917 Revolution the adepts of this brotherhood were involved in secular affairs, but in the 1920s many of the Yasawīyah took an active part in the Basmachi movement. Following the defeat and repression of the Basmachis, the Yasawīyah gave birth to a new sub-*ṭarīqah,* centered in the Ferghana Valley, the order of the "Hairy Ishan" (Kirghiz,

Chachtuu Eshander), which was a highly politicized secret organization. Soviet sources accuse the "Hairy Ishan" adepts of sabotaging the regime, of fanaticism, and of political terrorism.

The Qādirīyah is probably the second largest Ṣūfī order in the U.S.S.R. Founded in Baghdad in the twelfth century, it was introduced into Central Asia in the thirteenth, but as the more dynamic Naqshbandīyah expanded in the fifteenth and sixteenth centuries, the influence of the Qādirīyah declined. Around 1850, the Qādirīyah was brought to the northern Caucasus by a Dagestani, Kunta Haji Kishiev. After Kishiev died in a Russian prison, his *ṭarīqah* was divided into three suborders: Bammat Giray, Batal Haji, and Chim Mirza. In 1943, the deported northern Caucasian Chechen and Ingush brought the Qādirīyah back to Central Asia. In the 1950s the Chim Mirza brotherhood gave birth to a fourth Qādirī sub-*ṭarīqah*, Vis (Uways) Haji, which is the most puritanical of all the Ṣūfī orders. Its adepts practice rigorous endogamy within the brotherhood.

After the rehabilitation of the deported Caucasians in the late 1950s and their return to their homeland, the four Qādirī branches continued to survive in Central Asia. Vis Haji, with its followers concentrated in Kirghizia and southern Kazakhstan, seems to devote the most effort to proselytizing activities. The Kubrawīyah is apparently in the process of being absorbed by the Naqshbandīyah. It survives only in the Aral Sea area (northern Turkistan and Karakalpakistan).

All the Ṣūfī brotherhoods in Central Asia are conservative, traditionalist societies. Although they are clandestine, they are not really closed; indeed, they are involved in an unlawful (from the Soviet standpoint) but active religious proselytism. Their role in the preservation of Islam as a faith, as a way of life, and as an "ideology" has been and still is of capital importance. Without their day-by-day missionary work it is probable that the Muslim republics would have been swept off by a wave of atheism. The role of "preserver of Islam" played by the Ṣūfī brotherhoods under the Soviet regime may be compared to the similar role played by the same *ṭarīqah*s during the dark age of the Mongol invasion. But the role of the conservative Ṣūfī organizations is not limited to the preservation of religious belief and cult observance. For example, the Ṣūfī brotherhoods have also become the focal point of traditional opposition to the Russian presence.

[*For a survey of the Central Asian context into which Islam was introduced, see* Buddhism, *article on* Buddhism in Central Asia; Inner Asian Religions; *and* Shamanism, *article on* Siberian and Inner Asian Shamanism.]

BIBLIOGRAPHY

There is no special monograph on the religious history of Central Asia since its conquest by the Arabs. Information concerning the history of Islam is scattered in all of the historical works on Central Asia. Among the most important are the following.

Barthold, V. V. *Istoriia kul'turnoi zhizni Turkestana.* Leningrad, 1927.

Barthold, V. V. *Four Studies on the History of Central Asia.* 3 vols. Leiden, 1956–1962.

Barthold, V. V. *Turkestan down to the Mongol Invasion.* 2d ed. London, 1958. A classic, basic reference work.

Bennigsen, Alexandre, and Chantal Lemercier-Quelquejay. *Islam in the Soviet Union.* New York, 1961.

D'Ohsson, Mouradja. *Histoire des Mongols depuis Tchinguiz-Khan jusqu'à Timour bey ou Tamerlan.* 4 vols. Amsterdam, 1834–1835.

Grousset, René. *L'empire des steppes: Attila, Gengis-Khan, Tamerlan.* Paris, 1939.

Hayit, Baymirza. *Turkestan im 20. Jahrhundert.* Darmstadt, 1956.

Holdsworth, M. *Turkestan in the Nineteenth Century.* London, 1959.

Howorth, Henry H. *History of the Mongols from the Ninth to the Nineteenth Century.* 4 vols. 1876–1888; reprint, New York, 1927.

Klimovich, Liutsian I. *Islam v tsarskoi Rossii.* Moscow, 1936. A biased but well-informed Soviet work on Islam in the nineteenth century.

Rakowska-Harmstone, Teresa. *Russia and Nationalism in Central Asia: The Case of Tadzhikistan.* Baltimore, 1970.

Rywkin, Michael. *Moscow's Muslim Challenge.* New York, 1982.

Togan, A. Zeki Velidi. *Bugünkü Türkistan ve yakın tarihi.* Istanbul, 1947. A basic reference work on Turkistan under Russian rule.

Wheeler, Geoffrey. *The Modern History of Soviet Central Asia.* London, 1964.

Alexandre Bennigsen and Fanny E. Bryan

Islam in China

Islam arrived in China within a few decades after the death of the prophet Muḥammad. Yet the first Chinese Muslim writings on Islam date from the seventeenth century. The first detailed descriptions of early Islamic history, as well as the first Chinese translations of the Qur'ān, derive from that same era. Most of the earlier accounts derive from the works of Chinese Confucians and focus on the commercial roles of the Muslims without supplying much information on the social and religious life of the Islamic communities. Thus, knowledge of the trends in Chinese Islam before the seventeenth century is fragmentary.

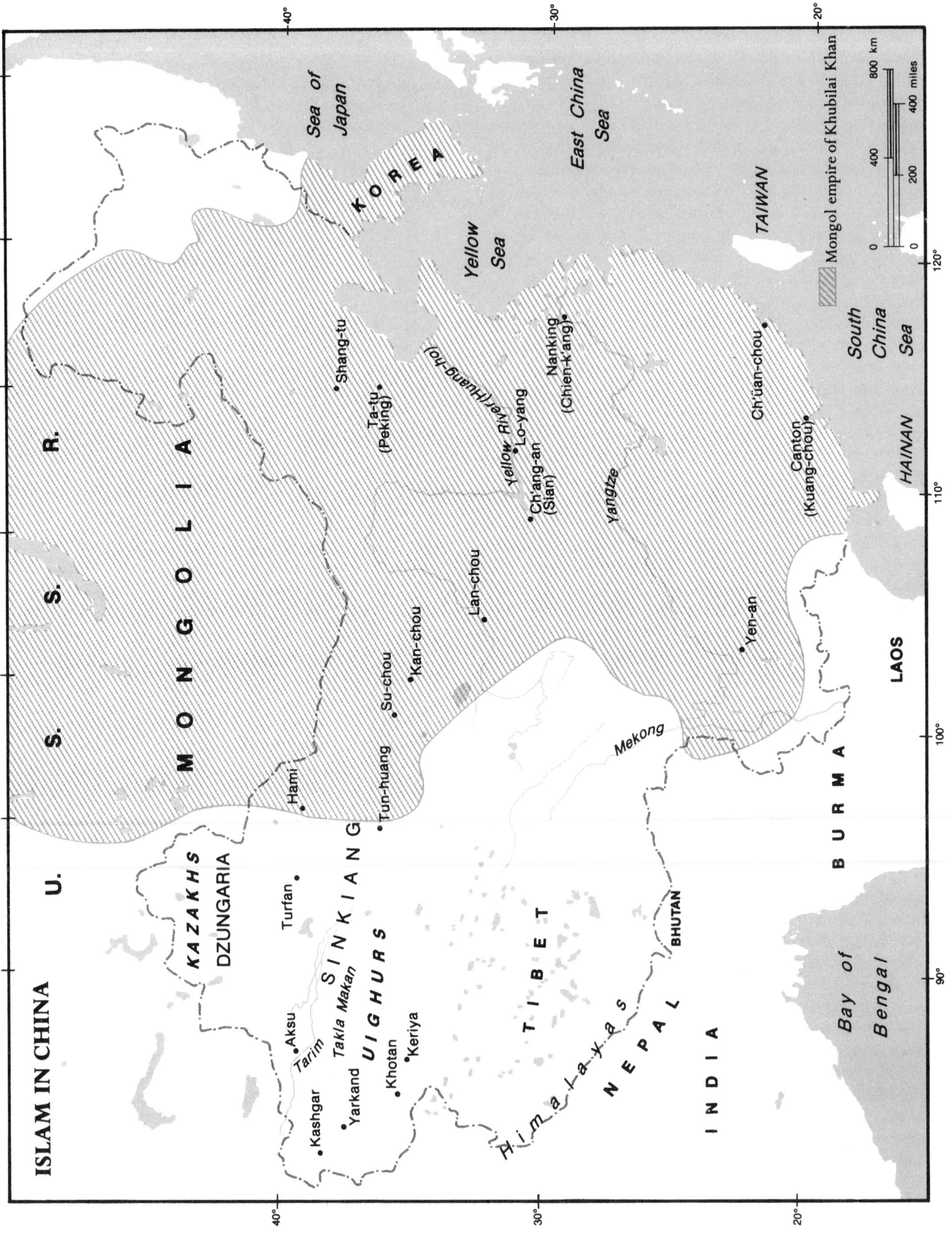
ISLAM IN CHINA
U. S. S. R.
M O N G O L I A
KAZAKHS
DZUNGARIA
SINKIANG
UIGHURS
Takla Makan
Tarim
Kashgar
Yarkand
Aksu
Khotan
Keriya
Turfan
Hami
Tun-huang
Su-chou
Kan-chou
Lan-chou
Shang-tu
Ta-tu (Peking)
Ch'ang-an (Sian)
Lo-yang
Yellow River (Huang-ho)
Nanking (Chien-k'ang)
Yangtze
Ch'üan-chou
Canton (Kuang-chou)
Yen-an
Mekong
TIBET
Himalayas
NEPAL
BHUTAN
INDIA
BURMA
LAOS
HAINAN
TAIWAN
KOREA
Sea of Japan
East China Sea
Yellow Sea
South China Sea
Bay of Bengal
Mongol empire of Khubilai Khan
0 400 800 km
0 200 400 miles
140°
130°
120°
110°
100°
90°
80°
40°
30°
20°

Arrival of the Muslims. Discounting the legendary accounts of the arrival of Islam in China, it seems clear that Middle Eastern and Central Asian traders introduced the new religion to the Chinese. By the late seventh century, Muslim merchants had reached China both by land and by sea. The land routes consisted of the old Silk Roads, which had connected China to the West as early as the time of the Roman empire. Winding their way from Persia through Samarkand and Bukhara, the Muslim caravans skirted the Taklamakan Desert either south via Khotan and Keriya or north via Turfan and Hami. They then headed into China proper, often halting at Tun-huang and Lan-chou, and concluded their travels at the capital in Ch'ang-an (modern Sian). China's northwest was thus exposed to the new religion, and some Chinese converted to Islam as early as the eighth century. The sea route was navigated by Arabs and Persians who set forth across the Persian Gulf to the Indian Ocean and eventually docked in the ports of southeast China. The cities of Canton, Hang-chou, and Ch'üan-chou were the principal destinations of these sailors and merchants.

Diplomacy and warfare. The first official contacts between the Arab rulers and the Chinese court were more bellicose. In 651 and again during the K'ai-yüan era (713–742), the caliphs, through their generals in the field, dispatched at least two embassies to the T'ang dynasty court. When the envoys in the second mission refused to perform the kowtow to the Chinese emperor, the Chinese elite, appalled by this discourteous behavior toward the Son of Heaven, perceived the Arab rulers as foes. The hostilities between the two empires culminated in the 751 battle of the Talas River in Central Asia, where an invading Arab army clashed with T'ang troops led by Kao Hsien-chih, a general of Korean descent. The Arabs won the battle but did not capitalize on their victory. Instead, most of them withdrew to return home and take part in the ongoing struggle for power within the Islamic empire, which had recently resulted in the establishment of the Abbasid dynasty (750–1256).

Official hostilities appear to have had scant effects on individual Muslims in China. They were not compelled to leave the country nor were they discriminated against in the Chinese communities where they chose to settle. A few even assisted the T'ang court in quelling a major rebellion: the T'ang dynastic histories report that Arab troops served in the foreign contingents that helped to crush the rebel leader An Lu-shan and to recapture the two capital cities of Ch'ang-an and Lo-yang in 757. The court surely recompensed them for their aid. According to Chinese Muslim tradition, these troops settled in China and became the ancestors of the Muslim communities in central and northwestern China.

The T'ang elite, which had a heightened sense of its own superiority, did not attempt to impose itself upon these Muslims. The Confucian ruling class believed that Chinese civilization was more advanced than any other culture. The sophisticated Chinese language, the carefully devised Confucian ethical principles, and the magnificently planned capital cities could not, in their view, be matched elsewhere. Impressed by China's superiority, foreigners would come to China to be "transformed" or "civilized" *(lai-hua)*. They would be converted into proper Confucian gentlemen and would eventually abandon their own cultural or religious heritage. During this transformation, the Chinese would not actively proselytize; foreigners would, of their own accord, accept and emulate Chinese practices, and until that time, the court would not restrict the foreigners' freedom of religious expression.

Communal life. As a result of these policies, the Muslim communities prospered, forming virtually self-governing enclaves in their areas of residence. The accounts of contemporary Arab travelers to China confirm the T'ang version of the Muslims' relations with the court. Though the report of Ibn Wahhāb, who reached China and had an audience with the emperor in 815, does not mention the presence of Muslim communities there, the anonymous traveler cited in *Akhbār al-Sīn wa-al-Hind* (Accounts of China and India) offers a description of his coreligionists in southeast China. Reaching China by sea in 851, he provides convincing evidence of the autonomy granted to the Muslim communities. He notes that

> there is a Mohammedan appointed Judge over those of his religion, by the authority of the Emperor of China, and that he is Judge of all the Mohammedans who resort to those parts. Upon several days he performs the public service with the Mohammedans. . . . The merchants of Irak who trade thither are no way dissatisfied with his conduct or his administration in the post he is invested with, because his actions . . . are conformable to the Koran, and according to Mohammedan jurisprudence. (Broomhall, 1910, pp. 47–48)

He also records, however, that he did not encounter Chinese Muslims; the communities he came across were composed of foreign Muslims residing in China.

The Muslims practiced their religion in China, but it appears that they did not erect a substantial structure as a house of worship during the T'ang period. According to one Muslim tradition, Sayyid [Ibn Abī] Wakkās, identified as a maternal uncle of Muḥammad, built the first mosque in Canton late in the sixth century or early in the seventh century. This chronology is clearly absurd because Muḥammad did not begin to expound the main tenets of Islam until the early seventh century, and his ideas could not have been known in China until the middle or later years of that century. The accounts concerning Sayyid Wakkās appear to be spurious, and the Huai-sheng Mosque and the adjacent Kuang-t'a minaret in Canton, which he is reputed to have built, doubtless derive from a later period. Similarly, the traditional dates of origin of the Great East Mosque and the Great West Mosque in Sian are questionable. Two stone inscriptions in these mosques, which were said to date from 742, have been shown to be later forgeries, probably originating no earlier than 1300, and the present buildings were either constructed or renovated in the early Ming dynasty (1368–1644). The Muslims may have prayed in small, unpretentious, and unprepossessing halls slowly built up over the years, but the more imposing mosques and minarets are of later origin.

Trade relations. While it is undeniable that the Muslims enjoyed great leeway in religious practices and self-governance, the Chinese were more hesitant in matters of trade. The court allowed the Arabs and Persians to offer tribute and to trade as long as they abided by Chinese regulations and controls on commerce. The Confucian elite, in theory, considered trade demeaning. Confucian scholars and officials were scornful of mercantile pursuits and considered merchants to be parasites who merely exchanged, rather than produced, goods. Since China was self-sufficient, there was no need, they reasoned, to trade with Muslim merchants, and such trade was permitted only because of the court's compassion, not because of its need for foreign goods. This official view was ingenuous. During the T'ang, mandarins kept an especially watchful eye on export goods to make sure that the government received its share of the profits. Although the government and its scholars and officials would not admit its value, commerce with the Muslims was lucrative.

Ordinary Chinese were not as unrealistic. Chinese merchants, innkeepers, and even some officials profited from this foreign trade and were grateful for the goods brought by the Muslims. They did not share the official disdain for trade and for the Muslim merchants. Yet inevitably commercial jealousies and disputes created rifts between the Muslim and the Chinese merchants, and animosity toward the Muslims and other foreigners surfaced in a ninth-century rebellion. According to the accounts of the Arab historian Abū Zayd (878–916), the Chinese rebel Huang Ch'ao massacred over 100,000 Muslims, Nestorians, and Jews in Canton in 878. The figure that Abū Zayd cites is an exaggeration, but the Chinese dynastic histories confirm the event (which they date to 879, owing to discrepancies between the Chinese and Muslim calendars). Nonetheless, this attack against the Muslims appears to have been an aberration, traceable to economic grievances rather than to religious discrimination, for foreigners generally seem to have been accepted in China.

Knowledge of the religious views and practices of the Islamic community in China is stymied by the attitudes of the Confucian literati, who wrote the principal histories of the time. Feigning a lack of interest in foreigners and foreign lands, they wished to portray foreign practices as infantile and "barbaric" so that the need for sinicization would be obvious. Thus their descriptions emphasized what they believed to be bizarre or exotic or "uncivilized." Similarly, reports on the foreign religions and foreign communities in China were not encouraged.

The Muslims continued to fare well even after the fall of the T'ang dynasty. Overland trade between the Muslim world and China decreased, but the seaborne commerce escalated dramatically. Arab and Persian seafarers arrived at the Chinese court in far greater numbers, bringing with them frankincense, myrrh, and sandalwood, among other commodities. During the Sung dynasty (960–1279), Chao Ju-kua, a superintendent of maritime trade, wrote a lengthy monograph describing the Islamic countries and the products that Muslim merchants imported into China. Toward the end of the dynasty, a Muslim of Arab origin named P'u Shou-keng even became the superintendent of maritime trade in the port of Ch'üan-chou. Yet once again, the Chinese chronicles yield pitifully few details about the religious life and concerns of the Muslims.

Islam and Mongol Rule. The invasions of the Mongols and the founding of the Mongol Yüan dynasty (1279–1368) brought China into closer contact with the Muslim world and resulted in an influx of Muslims into the Middle Kingdom. The Mongol conquerors did not have the administrative and financial skills to rule the country: they had only recently emerged from nomadic pastoralism and lacked experience in governing a vast sedentary empire. Nor could they rely upon the Chinese to provide the assistance they needed, for the Mongol khans were wary of depending upon the people whom they had just subdued. When Khubilai Khan took power in 1260, he sent Hao Ching to seek a peaceful accommodation with the still-unpacified southern Sung Chinese. Instead the Sung imprisoned the envoy and severed relations with Khubilai. Two years later, a Chinese named Li T'an rebelled against Mongol rule. Understandably enough, Khubilai became ever more suspicious of the Chinese.

Desperate for assistance, Khubilai imported Muslims from various parts of his domain to help govern China.

He assigned them to positions in the financial ministries of the government, though a few served in the Bureau of Astronomy and in the army. Many were employed as tax collectors, an occupation that did not endear them to the Chinese. Several Muslims supervised the government monopolies of salt, iron, tea, liquor, bamboo, and other vital commodities, and a few oversaw the foreign trade in the coastal cities of the southeast. These economic activities certainly damaged the Muslim image in the eyes of the Chinese. Khubilai also encouraged Muslims to engage in trade, making them even more vulnerable to Chinese hostility, and he accorded them special privileges, including exemption from regular taxation. The Muslims founded merchant associations, known as *ortaq,* to advance their commercial interests. Contemporary Chinese sources accused the *ortaq* of excesses, evasions, and exploitation. The Chinese histories assert that some of the Muslim merchants compelled soldiers to join and protect them on their travels, forced officials at the postal stations to provide them with lodging, and used improper and illegal methods to force borrowers to repay their loans promptly. These excesses contributed to the development of a negative image of the Muslims.

The Mongols' need for additional revenue imposed further burdens on their Muslim underlings. When Khubilai constructed new capitals in Ta-tu (modern Peking) and Shang-tu (Samuel Taylor Coleridge's "Xanadu"), extended the Grand Canal, and continued his military campaigns in Central Asia, Japan, and Southeast Asia, he turned to his Muslim administrators to raise the required revenue. His finance minister Aḥmad (fl. 1262–1282) imposed new taxes, added to the list of products monopolized by the court, and streamlined the collection of state revenues. Not surprisingly, his success provoked Chinese hostility, and the first serious stirrings of anti-Muslim sentiments surfaced. In this respect, the Muslims were a convenient buffer for the Mongols. Chinese animosity toward the rulers themselves was diverted somewhat to the Muslims, who began to be portrayed in Chinese sources as avaricious and unprincipled.

Yet neither the Mongols nor the Chinese could deny the Muslims' contributions to China. Persian doctors introduced new drugs and new kinds of hospitals. A Muslim architect helped to design the capital city at Ta-tu. In 1267 the Persian astronomer Jamāl al-Dīn built an observatory in the capital and provided new astronomical instruments for China. His successes prompted Khubilai to found an official Institute of Muslim Astronomy in 1271. Ismā'īl and 'Alā' al-Dīn, two Muslim engineers, constructed weapons to assist the Yüan armies. A Central Asian Muslim named Sayyid Ajall Shams al-Dīn imposed Yüan rule on China's southwestern province of Yunnan, which had been composed of autonomous tribes and kingdoms until the thirteenth century. After the Mongols conquered the region they assigned Sayyid Ajall to bring it into the Chinese orbit. He encouraged the development of an agrarian economy in part by promoting irrigation projects. He also prodded the local people to initiate trade with the rest of China and with the countries to the southwest. As a Muslim, Sayyid Ajall recruited an army composed primarily of his coreligionists, many of whom eventually settled in Yunnan and intermarried with the natives. Most of these families retained their identity as Muslims rather than assimilating into the local or into the Chinese culture, and they became the ancestors of the sizable modern Muslim community of Yunnan.

With the support of their Mongol patrons, it is no wonder then that the Muslims were found in all regions of China. The Muslims had settled in northwest China as early as the T'ang dynasty. Kan-chou, Su-chou, and Yen-an each had separate Muslim quarters, and by 1274 they had built a mosque in Kan-chou. The Muslims had their own leaders, known in Chinese as *ta-shih-man* (from the Persian *dānishmand,* "scholar"), and they maintained relations with their coreligionists in Central Asia. In northern China, Muslims built mosques in Shang-tu and Ta-tu, established their own schools in the province of Hopei, and took part in the horse trade in the province of Shantung. In southwest China, Muslims settled in Szechwan, which lay along the main trade routes to Burma and India. On the southeastern coast, Arabs and Persians continued to trade, and one-third of the thirty-six superintendents of maritime trade in Fukien during the Yüan were Muslims.

The Mongols adopted a *laissez-faire* policy toward the Muslims. In Ch'üan-chou, the community had its own leader, the Shaykh al-Islām (in Chinese, *hui-hui t'ai-shih*), who served as its intermediary with the Mongol authorities. The *qāḍī* ("judge"; in Chinese, *hui-chiao-fa-kuan*) interpreted Muslim laws and principles for the settlement. The Muslim section had its own bazaars, hospitals, and mosque, and many members of the community still spoke Arabic or Persian. The Yüan court generally permitted the Muslims to fast during Ramaḍān, to circumcise male infants, to recite the Qur'ān, and to slaughter animals in their own fashion. The fourteenth-century Arab traveler Ibn Baṭṭūṭah recorded that Muslim musicians in Hang-chou could perform songs in Arabic and Persian. Orchestras composed of three hundred to four hundred men played Middle Eastern music at banquets in his honor.

The Restoration of Native Chinese Rule. After the fall of the Mongol dynasty, the native Chinese Ming dynasty

(1368–1644) might have been expected to discriminate against the Muslims who had served their oppressors. The court did attempt to restrict or at least regulate relations with the Muslim states, and Chinese officials generally managed to prevent the Muslim envoys from mingling with ordinary Chinese. Yet Ming policy toward the Muslims in China was fairly tolerant. The court employed them as astronomers, calendar makers, and diviners in the Directorate of Astronomy. The Ming emperors also recruited them as envoys, translators, and interpreters. Chinese of Muslim backgrounds became renowned as explorers, philosophers, and military leaders.

Moreover, two of the Ming emperors were attracted by Islam. The Hung-wu emperor (i.e., the emperor of the Hung-wu reign era, 1368–1398), the first Ming ruler, had two Muslim cousins, and some sources claim that his wife was a Muslim as well. Three mosques were built, with imperial approval, during his reign; according to an inscription at one of these mosques,

> The emperor had proclaimed that each Muslim be given 50 *ting* of paper money and 200 bolts of silk and that mosques be built in two places. One [was to be built] in . . . Nanking, and the other in . . . [Hsi-an] Sian. . . . If there are dilapidated mosques, restoration is permitted. . . . The administration offices . . . will handle the purchases of all things needed in this restoration. If the transport of materials will involve the passing of ferries and barricades, no one is permitted to stop them. (Rossabi, "Muslim Inscriptions," p. 24)

The Cheng-te emperor (1506–1521), the second of these rulers, surrounded himself with Muslim eunuchs and advisers; he authorized the production of bronzes and porcelains for Muslim patrons, and he welcomed to his court ambassadors from the various Muslim lands. While some Chinese clearly despised and discriminated against the Muslims, and a few of the Ming emperors did not look with favor upon these "outsiders," official court policy encouraged toleration toward them.

Peaceful coexistence. The Muslims, in turn, abided by court regulations and pursued a policy of peaceful coexistence with the Chinese. They continued to practice their faith but in a way that did not offend the sensibilities of the Chinese. They did not actively proselytize nor were they aggressive or ostentatious in the performance of their religious duties. The Muslim communities in northwest and southwest China were by this time the most numerous, though there were Muslim groups scattered throughout China. Their numbers decreased in southeast China as fewer Arabs and Persians arrived by sea, and with more and more of the newer migrants originating from Turkic Central Asia, Turkic-speaking peoples began to constitute a larger percentage of the Muslims in China.

The Muslims in the northwest and southwest organized themselves in small communities and did not, at least during this period, unite and offer their allegiance to a single leader. The Chinese, pleased by this lack of unity, did not perceive the Muslims as a threat. The Muslims also compromised with Chinese regulations. After a century of the foreign, Mongol rule, the Chinese of the early Ming were determined to compel the foreigners residing in China to accept some Chinese ways. The Muslims thus adopted Chinese dress, erected tablets near their mosques pledging their loyalty to the Chinese emperor, and started to learn the Chinese language; the court demanded that they assume Chinese names as well. But the Ming was to be sorely disappointed in its hopes for their gradual assimilation. The Muslims retained their identity because they had their own leaders, their own educational system, and a strong feeling of their distinctiveness. They lived in separate areas, trained several of their members in Persian or Arabic in order to have access to Islamic texts, and encouraged pilgrimages to Mecca. Each community had its own mosque, which also served as a binding force. Their faith was, in addition, supported by their frequent associations with their coreligionists in Central Asia. In their work as merchants, interpreters, and camel and horse grooms, they had numerous opportunities to meet with Muslims from beyond the Chinese border. Such encounters kept them in touch with the wider Muslim world, enabling them more readily to maintain their faith in a non-Islamic environment.

Some Muslims intermarried with the Chinese. Most of these unions were between Muslim men and Chinese women. Contrary to the Ming court's expectations, however, their children were generally reared as Muslims. The Islamic community also grew as a result of adoptions. Wealthy Muslim families bought or "adopted" young Chinese boys, raised them as Muslims, and thus had mates for their daughters. The court's encouragement of intermarriage and assimilation paradoxically gave rise to Chinese converts to Islam, mostly in the northwest and southwest. These Chinese converts came to be known as "Hui," while the non-Chinese were identified with their ethnic group.

Negative images. The economic roles of the Muslims as intermediaries reinforced the popular stereotypes about them among the common people. Ordinary Chinese did not resent the Muslims' religious views or customs. They found some of the Muslims' practices (e.g., fasting during Ramaḍān, abstaining from liquor) strange, but they were unfazed by them. In fact, they were so uninterested in investigating these Islamic observances that they failed to distinguish between the Muslims and other religious groups, notably the Jews: they frequently lumped the Muslims and the Jews together because both wrote in "peculiar" scripts and refused to eat pork. Most of their negative images of the Muslims revolved around trade. They described Muslim merchants as not only shrewd but also conniving. Muslim traders could not be trusted. Their avariciousness on occasion led to deception and fraud. They did not even carry out their own religious practices unswervingly; if a specific belief interfered with commercial gain, it would be ignored as they pursued their profits. Chinese anecdotes emphasizing the Muslims' hypocrisy and deception began cropping up during this time, and such disagreeable epithets as *hui-i* ("Muslim barbarians") and *hui-tse* ("Muslim bandits") started to be applied to them.

Despite this developing negative image, the Ming court did not attempt to sever the Muslims' relations with their coreligionists in Central Asia. Mosque communities there, as elsewhere in the Muslim world, guaranteed Muslim travelers a friendly welcome and a place to stay; relations between Muslims in China and Central Asia were further strengthened by the occupations they pursued. Many of the Muslims in northwest China were involved in commerce as merchants, interpreters, postal station attendants, and camel and horse grooms; in short, their livelihood and their very survival was directly linked to trade with fellow Muslims from Central Asia.

Repression and a Muslim Renaissance. The apparent decline of trade with the deterioration of economic conditions in the late sixteenth and early seventeenth centuries was thus devastating to the Muslims of northwest China. The previously profitable caravan trade across Central Asia faced stiff competition from the oceangoing vessels from Europe; Muslim lands such as Persia and Turkey, which had earlier participated in trade, had declined; the expansion of the Russian empire into Central Asia disrupted commerce in that area; and the northwest had suffered from severe droughts. Economic distress led the Muslims to join in the rebellions against the Ming dynasty. Chinese rebel leaders in the northwest had contingents of Muslims in their detachments, and some scholars have even suggested that Li Tzu-ch'eng, one of the two most important rebel leaders, was a Muslim. Li was adopted at the age of ten by an old Muslim woman and was familiar with Islamic practices and beliefs, but it seems unlikely that he converted to Islam. Other rebel leaders, such as Niu Chin-hsing and Ma Shou-ying (also known as Lao Hui-hui or "Old Muslim"), were Chinese Muslims and played a vital role in the early successes of the Muslims in the northwest.

Ch'ing expansionism. The Manchus, who finally crushed the Ming and established the Ch'ing dynasty (1644–1911), did little to alleviate Muslim discontent and distress. In fact, the Ch'ing exacerbated the Muslims' difficulties with its policies. Contrary to the court's expectations, once again the Muslims did not assimilate. They survived as a distinct minority group and, through intermarriage with the Chinese, had increased in number. Together with their coreligionists in Central Asia, they had proved troublesome in the last years of the previous dynasty. The Ch'ing therefore sought to resolve its Muslim "problem" through an expansionist policy. Assuming that the Muslims of nearby Central Asia were inspiring the Muslims within China to engage in antigovernment activities, the Ch'ing advanced throughout the late seventeenth and eighteenth centuries into Central Asian territories that had never traditionally been part of China. Their first thrust was directed at Dzungaria in the northern region of the modern province of Sinkiang. By 1696, a Ch'ing army had routed the Dzungar Mongols, and the court began to order its forces to move south into the lands of the Muslim Uighur Turks. In 1758, an efficient and ruthless general named Chao-hui imposed Ch'ing rule on the Uighur oases in Central Asia. He occupied the towns of Kashgar, Yarkand, and Aksu in southern Sinkiang. With this military success, the Ch'ing court had now incorporated a new and sizable contingent of Muslims.

The Ch'ing court attempted to promote good relations with the Muslims within China and in the newly subjugated areas in Central Asia. It established an administration with a large measure of local self-rule for the Muslims, and it did not interfere with the Muslims' practice of their faith, though in the 1720s it did impose a temporary moratorium on the construction of mosques. It attempted to foster the economic recovery of the lands in northwest China and Central Asia that had been devastated during the Dzungar wars. Yet these policies were not properly implemented and ultimately backfired. In seeking to promote the economy of the northwestern regions, the Ch'ing court encouraged its Chinese subjects to migrate there to raise grain, fruit, and cotton and to extract the vast mineral and natural resources, including iron, gold, and copper. The Chinese peasants and merchants who moved into the Muslim areas tended to engage in bitter disputes with the local inhabitants and to exploit them, despite the good intentions of the government. Though the Muslim leaders had some degree of autonomy, the officials dispatched by the Ch'ing court still made the most critical decisions, and they often exercised their power in a capricious and oppressive manner. They occasionally imposed onerous taxes and other obligations on the Muslims and sporadically contravened the regulations of the court to impede the Muslims' practice of their religion.

Apologetic response. The Muslim reaction was predictable. Dissatisfaction with Ch'ing rule grew, and eventually such tensions gave rise to violence and revolts. Starting in the late eighteenth and continuing into the nineteenth century, the Muslims in both northwest and southwest China rebelled against the Ch'ing government. But the precursors to the rebellions were the writings of the Chinese Muslims, provoked by oppression and discrimination to define their faith and to assert their identity in the face of powerful opposition. Only in the seventeenth century had the Chinese Muslims produced their first works on the Islamic religion. Some of the early Muslim writers sought an accommodation with Confucian thought while the later, more radical Muslim authors insisted on a clear distinction between Islam and Confucianism and emphasized a pure, untainted form of Islam.

The Chinese Muslim Wang Tai-yü (1580–1650?) wrote the first important text in Chinese on Islam. As a youth, he had received a Muslim education in a mosque, but as an adult he devoted himself to a study of the Confucian classics. He wrote his principal work, the *Cheng-chiao chen-ch'üan* (Veritable Explanation of the True Religion), in 1642 in order to explain the fundamental tenets of Islam to the Chinese Muslims. By this time, many of the Muslims were Chinese converts who had scant detailed knowledge of Islam. Wang thus tried to expound the Islamic teachings in a style familiar to the Chinese. Using Confucian terminology and argumentation to explicate the major ideas of the foreign religion, he asserted that Confucianism and Islam shared common views with regard to personal virtue, brotherly love, and the ordering of social relationships, as between sovereign and ministers or fathers and sons. Even the dualistic concept of *yin* and *yang* was acceptable to him. He also appropriated the term for the five Confucian virtues of benevolence and wisdom, among others, to signify the five cardinal responsibilities of a Muslim, including the pilgrimage to Mecca and almsgiving. In effect, he appealed to the Chinese Muslims in terms and ideas they understood and showed them that Islam was not unremittingly hostile to Confucianism. The main critique he made of Confucianism was its lack of concern for and its unwillingness to accept monotheism. The concepts of God and of divine intervention were, Wang regretted to point out, omitted in Confucian thought. Yet even on this crucial point of Islamic doctrine he did not fault Confucius, attempting instead to establish some common grounds with that revered Chinese cultural figure. He found some shreds of monotheistic thinking in Confucius's use of the terms *t'ien* (heaven) and *Shang-ti* (God?). Wang clearly did not seek a break with Confucianism; he merely wished to clarify and champion Islamic beliefs.

Liu Chih (1662?–1736?), the most renowned of the Chinese Muslim authors of the late seventeenth and early eighteenth centuries, likewise focused on the similarities between Islam and Confucianism. In his familiarity with the two religions he resembled Wang, but his education was even more encompassing, for he also pursued studies on Buddhism and Taoism. He borrowed Confucian concepts and applied them to his definition of Islam. In his book *T'ien-fang hsing-li* (The Philosophy of Arabia), for example, he wrote that the Confucian term *li* (moral rectitude) was universal; Muslims too, he argued, strove to achieve this goal. In the same book, Liu repeatedly praised some of the Confucian cultural heroes. A contemporary Chinese official was so pleased with Liu's work that he noted in the preface that "although his book explains Islam, in truth it illuminates our Confucianism" (Ford, p. 150).

Liu nonetheless still perceived the Chinese Muslims as his prime audience, and in his books he tried to explain as concisely and simply as possible the main features of the Islamic tradition. In his biography of the Prophet *(Chih-sheng shih-lu)*, he wrote a sketch of the life of Muḥammad that gained wide circulation in the Muslim community. Basing himself on his researches in Arabic and Persian sources, he provided a straightforward, clear, and generally accurate account of the career and teachings of the founder of Islam. In *T'ien-fang tien-li* (Laws and Rituals of Islam), he offered a brief description of the basic ceremonies and laws associated with the faith. Though Liu was not a creative, innovative thinker, he undertook considerable research in the preparation of these books. His views accorded with those of the Ḥanafī school of law within Sunnī Islam, the principal mode of belief of most of the Chinese Muslims. Yet also noticeable in his works was a growing reliance on and interest in Sufism, which he employed to seek an accommodation with Confucianism.

The New Teaching. The principal Muslim thinkers of the later eighteenth century, however, were much more hostile to Confucianism. The mid-eighteenth-century repression of Islam by local Chinese officials and by private citizens prompted the development of a more fundamentalist form of Islam. The Chinese Muslim Ma Ming-hsin, a native of Kansu Province in northwest China, was the main exponent of a Ṣūfī order that challenged both Confucianism and the Ch'ing dynasty. After a period of study in the Middle East and Central Asia, Ma returned to China in 1761 to introduce the New Teaching *(Hsin-chiao)*, a different form of the Ṣūfī teachings that had reached northwest China as early as the seventeenth century. Like the earlier Ṣūfīs, Ma belonged to the Naqshbandī order and, also like them, stressed a personal, mystical expression of faith. Unlike the earlier Ṣūfīs, who were known as proponents of the so-called Old Teaching *(Lao-chiao)*, however, Ma's New Teaching emphasized chanting and a vocal remembrance of God *(dhikr-i jahrī)*, a characteristic of the Jahrīyah branch of the Naqshbandīyah, which differed from the more sober form of the Naqshbandīyah in India and Central Asia. The Old Teaching was less rambunctious and more solitary because it entailed a silent remembrance *(dhikr-i khafī)* of God, which was associated with the Khafīyah branch of the Naqshbandīyah, and the leaders of the entrenched Old Teaching viewed Ma as a subversive. He appears to have been a charismatic figure, and he reportedly engaged in faith healing. His disciples and supporters danced, bobbed their heads, chanted, and went into trances in their efforts to achieve union with God. Such public displays offended the leaders of the Old Teaching. His emphasis on the personal relationship between the master (shaykh) and his followers and on worship at the site of tombs of important shaykhs also challenged the Old Teaching hierarchy, which was organized into leading lineages *(men-huan)* with hereditary leaders who controlled landed estates and dominated the commercial networks among the Muslims. They resented the intrusion of Ma's New Teaching because it threatened their political and economic power.

The Ch'ing dynasty was to be even more perturbed by Ma's ideas and activities. He repeatedly denounced any doctrinal or ritual compromises with foreign religions or cults and advocated a return to the pure, untainted form of Islam. From the Ch'ing standpoint, such an uncompromising attitude might contribute to social unrest, and like the leaders of the Old Teaching, the Ch'ing authorities in the northwest perceived Ma to be a subversive. He had already challenged the power of the lineages of the Old Teaching by noting that "since religion belonged to all . . . why should it be made the private possession of one family?" Now Ma was inciting his followers to adopt a hostile stance toward Confucianism and, by extension, toward the Confucian Ch'ing state. The loyalty he demanded from these same followers was also worrisome to the Chinese and Manchu authorities, for the power that thus accrued to him could readily be translated into political authority. The Naqshbandī orders in general and Ma in particular were not hesitant to become embroiled in politics. In fact, Ma's uncompromising attitude necessitated involvement in politics in order to ward off the possibility of being engulfed or even tainted by the Confucian civilization that surrounded the Muslims in China.

Muslim Rebellions. The ultimate logic of Ma's views was the establishment of a Muslim state along China's borders, and the religious and economic hostilities that separated the Muslims and the Chinese soon resulted in actual rebellions. In 1781, Ma and his fellow Muslim Su Ssu-shih-san led a revolt against the Ch'ing authorities in the province of Kansu. The New Teaching forces were defeated only after the arrival of Ch'ing troops from other provinces. Ma was executed, but Muslim unrest did not wither away. A Muslim religious brotherhood descended from the Central Asian religious leaders known as Khojas, who were associated with the Naqshbandīyah, organized this popular discontent into violent outbreaks with the intent of establishing an autonomous Muslim theocratic state in northwest China. The first result of their efforts was a rebellion in 1784, and the Ch'ing needed an even greater effort to defeat the rebels. After the suppression of the revolt, the Ch'ing proscribed the New Teaching, prohibited the construction of new mosques, and barred the conversion of Chinese Confucians to Islam.

Resentment over these new Ch'ing policies grew and finally flared out into open rebellion. In 1815, a Muslim chieftain of non-Chinese descent named Ḍiyā' al-Dīn led a short-lived rebellion in the modern province of Sinkiang. Five years later, the religious leader Jahāngīr Khoja organized an insurrection against the Ch'ing government. Although he was defeated, the troops sent against him could not annihilate his forces; eight years elapsed before they finally captured him and disbanded his army. Even then his capture did not end China's difficulties in the northwest, for his relative success encouraged other Muslims to challenge Ch'ing rule. In 1832, his brother Khoja Muḥammad Yūsuf attacked several garrisons in Sinkiang before fleeing to the safe haven of western Central Asia. In 1847, seven Khojas from Central Asia led forays into Sinkiang and caused havoc there until the Ch'ing troops forced them to withdraw. One of these Khojas reappeared in 1857 to plague Sinkiang and occupied part of the region for some months.

The most devastating of the rebellions erupted in Shensi in 1862, provoked by a dispute between some Muslims and Chinese over the sale of bamboo poles. The Chinese Muslim Ma Hua-lung, the recognized leader of the New Teaching groups, quickly became a prominent figure. From his base in Kansu, he fostered anti-Ch'ing sentiment and encouraged his followers to seek independence from China. The rebel forces were successful, and within two years most of Shensi and Kansu were no longer under Ch'ing control. But the religious leadership was unable to establish its rule over the rebel troops. Instead a Muslim adventurer-soldier named Ya'qūb Beg ultimately took charge. His harshness, the corruption of some of his associates, and his increasingly oppressive secret police force alienated his people and disrupted the unity of the Chinese Muslims. The disunity among them enabled the Ch'ing government to move slowly to recapture the northwest. Under the able Chinese general Tso Tsung-t'ang, the Ch'ing gradually reconquered most of Shensi, Kansu, and Sinkiang. In 1877, Ya'qūb Beg died, and by early in the following year Tso had recovered all of the rebellious lands and had reimposed Ch'ing control.

As a result of these rebellions, Chinese views of the native and foreign Muslims again became increasingly unfavorable. Anecdotes about the Muslims, mostly apocryphal stories, portrayed them as profiteering, insincere, and faintly sinister. The moral of many of the stories was that Muslim merchants could not be trusted. They were avaricious, and crafty to the point of dishonesty. They were false Muslims, practicing their faith only when it suited them. They often ignored the taboos on pork and liquor, finding bizarre rationalizations for their transgressions. Stories such as the following manifested the Muslims' "cruel, evil natures":

> During the season of the Chinese New Year, Muslims, who do not observe the same festival, invited the Chinese in their caravan to make merry, while they would stand the night watch. After the Chinese were drunk, the Muslims rose up, pulled their tent down on them and beat them to death under it. Then, they threw the bodies into a dry well and made off with the silver. (Lattimore, 1929, pp. 165–166)

Muslim intermarriage with Chinese and their adoption of Chinese boys perturbed officials. They had counted on the gradual assimilation of foreigners and foreign ideologies. Here they faced a group that not only refused to abandon its religious heritage but gained a following among native Chinese as well.

The negative Chinese image of the Muslims in the late nineteenth and early twentieth centuries contributed to the tensions in western China, where there was much unrest. In the southwestern province of Yunnan, a Muslim rebellion erupted in 1855 and lasted until 1873. During these eighteen years, perhaps as many as five million of the eight million residents of the province died. Neither the Ch'ing victory in Yunnan in 1873 nor its suppression of the northwestern rebellions in 1878 quelled the turbulence in China's western domains. The New Teaching did not perish and continued to clash with the adherents of the Old Teaching. The internal conflicts among the Muslims complicated their relations with the Chinese. In the struggles that broke out after the suppression of the initial Muslim rebellions, Muslims of the Old Teaching occasionally cooperated with the Chinese against the adherents of the New Teaching. Some even advocated closer collaboration with the Chinese. In 1900, Ma Fu-hsiang, a Muslim warlord from the province of Kansu, urged his own people to integrate into Chinese society and he organized an Assimilationist Group to promote such an integration.

Autonomy for Sinkiang, 1911–1949. After the fall of the Ch'ing dynasty in 1911, a number of Chinese officials in the Muslim areas sought to ingratiate themselves with the Muslims and to encourage their assimilation into Chinese society. Yang Tseng-hsin, the most important military figure in the northwest, tried to prevent exploitation of the non-Chinese, in particular the Muslims, in his domain in Sinkiang. Maintaining an effective system of controls over the government, he imposed harsh sanctions on those who illegally alienated the Muslims. His economic policies were designed to reduce the tax burden on the Uighurs and Kazakhs, the majority of whom were Muslims, and the Chinese Muslims, now known as the Hui, and to win their support. Many of the Muslims responded to his benevolent policies, and by 1916 the tensions that had bedeviled relations between the Muslims of the northwest and their Chinese rulers had abated. Yang himself was virtually independent of any control of the various governments based in Peking. After the Bolshevik Revolution he became increasingly close to the Soviet Union, further limiting the Peking government's jurisdiction over him.

Yang's death in 1928 ended the somewhat less hostile relationship that had prevailed between the Chinese and the Muslims of Sinkiang. Chin Shu-jen and Sheng Shih-ts'ai, the succeeding warlords who ruled the province until 1943, were less sympathetic to Muslim interests. Instead they sought to reimpose Chinese controls, with scarcely any concern for the Muslims. The native people grew increasingly restive. In the waning years of Sheng's regime, local uprisings broke out and finally led to a full-scale rebellion by the Kazakh chieftain Osman (Usman) Bator. By the mid-1940s, several Muslim groups in Sinkiang were calling for autonomy; in January of 1945, they united to form the Eastern Turkistan Republic, an independent state free of Chinese control.

The Nationalist government of Chiang Kai-shek, which controlled most of China other than Sinkiang from 1928 to 1948, paid lip service to the ideals of equality for the Muslims within its domains. In fact, its policies did not differ significantly from those of many earlier Chinese governments. It still did not respect the Muslims' differences and uniqueness. But it also did not admit that its ultimate goal was the sinicization of the Muslims. Instead the government proclaimed the Muslims one of the five "great peoples" of China, alongside the Han (ethnic Chinese), the Mongols, the Tibetans, and the Manchus. A national flag composed of five symmetrical stripes represented the equality of the five different peoples in Chinese territory. Yet the Nationalists' own prejudices and the activities they sanctioned undermined their efforts to win over the Muslims. Many in the government regarded themselves as superior to the Muslim minorities and considered them lazy, slow, and "inexact." The Nationalists wanted to civilize these "barbarians."

The Muslim communities responded in different ways to the pressures exerted by the warlords in Sinkiang and by the Nationalists in other parts of China. The non-Chinese Muslims of Sinkiang retained their identities, continued to practice their Islamic faith, and repeatedly sought to establish independent states. The Hui, the Chinese Muslims, were not as separatist. They did not attempt to set up their own autonomous states, nor did they seek to impose barriers between themselves and their Chinese neighbors. Their knowledge of Islamic doctrine was becoming increasingly sketchy. Not only could they not distinguish between Sunnī and Shīʿī forms of Islam, but many had barely any acquaintance with the Qur'ān. Few of the Chinese Muslim communities had members who could read Arabic or Persian. Many of the Hui probably knew more about Confucianism and Buddhism than about the essential features of their own faith. Yet they considered themselves to be different from the Chinese. Although their conceptions of fundamental Islamic beliefs were hazy, they maintained some practices that bolstered their view of their uniqueness and set them apart from the Chinese. Thus they abstained from eating pork, for example, and occasionally practiced circumcision. The fact that they often lived in their own neighborhoods, clustered around a mosque, also promoted greater unity among them.

Islam under the People's Republic. When the People's Republic of China (PRC) was founded in 1949, the leadership needed to assert its authority over the Muslim areas in the northwest. No Chinese national government had truly governed Sinkiang since 1911, and since 1925, the Muslims of Sinkiang had maintained closer ties with the Soviet Union than with China. The main opposition to PRC rule came from the Sinkiang League for the Protection of Peace and Democracy, a group founded in 1948 and primarily composed of Muslims. After a mysterious airplane crash in 1949 killed many of the leaders of that organization, Burhan and Saifudin, the two succeeding Muslim leaders of non-Chinese origin, worked out an agreement with the government. The final effect of this compact was the creation in 1955 of the Sinkiang Uighur Autonomous Region, which by its name, at least, indicated a greater degree of independence for the Muslims of the region. Saifudin became the first governor of the newly constituted government, another indication of the autonomy pledged to the region by the central authority. In fact, it has imposed numerous controls on the Muslims of the region.

Sinicization and its limits. Consonant with its attitude toward all religions, the government has been condescending toward the Islamic faith. The traditional Chinese literati had believed that they possessed a unique ideology, Confucianism, and a sophisticated civilization superior to any other in the world. Like their forebears, the Communists have asserted that their unique form of Marxism would enable them to be a more productive and, by implication, superior civilization. Islam is, from this viewpoint, a conservative ideology that could not compete with Marxism. Like the "barbarians" of old, the Muslims need instruction from the Chinese. The state's ultimate goal for the Muslims still appears to be sinicization. Since the Muslims constitute a majority in some areas, particularly in Sinkiang, sinicization has proven difficult.

The government's eagerness to maintain good relations with the Islamic states also impeded sinicization. Some of the Islamic states outside of China had vast petroleum reserves, were located on the crossroads of Asia, Africa, and Europe, and could prove troublesome if they allied themselves with powers hostile to China. A few of their leaders (e.g., Nasser of Egypt, Sukarno of Indonesia) frequently acted as spokesmen for the Third World, a bloc of countries that the Chinese hoped to affect. Influence on the Muslim Middle East might also translate into influence in Africa, another area that the Chinese hoped to sway politically. The government could therefore not afford to impose Chinese culture on the Muslims within their own country. Nor could it appear to discriminate against Islam or to prevent the Muslims from practicing their faith. In effect, its general antireligious sentiments and policies had to be moderated in the case of Islam, for repressive policies would inevitably harm Chinese interests in the Islamic world.

Similarly, good relations with the Muslims were vital for the security of China's northwestern frontiers. The non-Chinese Muslims, including the Uighurs and the Kazakhs, inhabited the border regions adjacent to the U.S.S.R. Across the borders lived Muslims of Turkish background who shared the same language and ethnic derivations as those on the Chinese side. Such a community of interests might make the Muslims of China responsive to Soviet blandishments. With the growing rift between China and the U.S.S.R. after 1956, the Muslims residing along the Sino-Soviet border became increasingly important. Both the Soviet and the Chinese governments attempted to sway the Muslims and to recruit them to their side of the dispute. From the Chinese point of view, a hostile Muslim minority threatened to weaken border defense, increase the danger of Soviet attack, and perhaps even result in territorial losses.

Perhaps equally significant for the Chinese was the economic potentiality of the Muslim regions in the northwest. The mineral resources of these territories are virtually untapped; their lands offer a useful source of animals and animal products, and the so-called Autonomous Regions of Sinkiang and Ninghsia, inhabited mostly by Muslims, are relatively underpopulated and can absorb migrants from the more crowded eastern coast of China. The figures for Muslim population cited by the Chinese are unrealistically low. According to the 1980 estimates by the government, a total of thirteen million Muslims resided in China. Less biased experts on demography estimate that there are forty to fifty million Muslims throughout the country. Nonetheless, the regions in which the Muslims live are sparsely settled and are attractive to Chinese planners who face problems of tremendous overcrowding in most other regions of China.

Conflicting policies. It is not surprising then that the government has devoted considerable attention to the Muslim minority in China. But its policy toward the Muslims has been inconsistent, alternating between radical and conservative positions. The conservative approach, which was dominant from 1949 to 1957, 1962 to 1965, and again after 1976, emphasized the special characteristics of the Muslims and proposed a cautious, conciliatory policy. The Turkic Muslims were permitted to use their own languages and dialects in the schools and the mass media; the majority of Communist party cadres were recruited from the native peoples, not from Chinese migrants to the Muslim areas; in the Chinese Muslim, or Hui, areas as well, many party members were drawn from the Muslims; the native elites of the pre-1949 period were often granted important positions in local government; and the distinctive customs and practices of the Muslims, even if they occasionally impeded economic development or communization, were neither interfered with nor prohibited. The government, for example, often sidestepped the issue of equal rights for women in the Muslim areas, where Islamic practice accorded women a lesser role and lower status.

The radical approach, which informed government policy during the Great Leap Forward of the late 1950s and the Cultural Revolution from 1966 to 1976, posited that nationality and ethnic distinctions would disappear with the obliteration of class differences and contended that class struggle ought to be the cornerstone of policy toward the Muslims. Communist cadres replaced the traditional Muslim leadership and sometimes displayed scant consideration for Islam. The central government dominated the autonomous regions founded in Muslim areas. Some mosques were closed or destroyed or converted to other uses. The government insisted that the Chinese language be adopted in the schools and employed in the mass media. The Chinese Islamic Association, a quasi-governmental agency, supervised the mosques, decided how many copies of the Qur'ān were printed, and, in effect, controlled the religious hierarchy. The leaders would not permit Muslim customs to interfere with the economic and social changes promoted by the government. They also encouraged and, in fact, ordered non-Muslim Chinese to move into the Muslim regions, including Sinkiang, hoping in this way eventually to outnumber the Muslims in the northwest.

Despite their differences, both the conservatives and the radicals favor the integration and the assimilation of the Muslims into Chinese culture and society. They differ only in the tactics they employ rather than in their objectives: both seek a "common proletarian culture" for the Chinese and the Muslims. One means of promoting the assimilation of the Muslims has been by showing them a "better life," and indeed, the government has raised their living standards: they are better fed, clothed, and sheltered than before 1949 and have greater access to medical care. Yet the Muslims still consider themselves to be different from the rest of the population of China.

The negative images of Muslims entertained by the Chinese majority have exacerbated the difficulties of integration. Visitors to China in the 1980s reported that some Chinese they encountered expressed blatantly anti-Muslim sentiments. These Chinese asserted that only the elderly actually worship in the mosques. They told foreign visitors that religious Muslims sometimes do not abide by the dictates of their faith (e.g., by evading the taboo on liquor). Like the Chinese of earlier dynasties, they expressed the belief that the Muslims would assimilate, as was the case with other minorities such as the Manchus and the Mongols in the nineteenth and twentieth centuries (the Manchus no longer survive as a distinct population in China).

Muslim response. The Muslims' reactions to government policies since 1949 are difficult to gauge. Independent observers were until the late 1970s excluded from the minority areas. Since 1978, tourists and scholars have been permitted access to the Muslim regions, but they have not been granted sufficient time to observe conditions in these areas. Nor have specialists been allowed to conduct research on the Muslims. Consequently, knowledge of the Muslim communities is meager. Religious currents among the Muslims are even more difficult to fathom. It is impossible at the present time to find out about the various orders of Islam. Some of the Ṣūfī orders and Sunnī institutions that had such a profound influence in the eighteenth and nineteenth centuries probably survive, but reliable accounts of their beliefs and activities are currently unavailable.

In theory, the Muslims ought to be struggling for independence. There is no evidence, however, that the Chinese Muslims or the Uighurs, Kazakhs, and other non-Chinese have sought to rebel and establish their own independent states. Yet the Muslims have expressed their discontent with specific Chinese policies directed at them. In 1958, the Chinese leaders, wishing to hasten basic changes in the Kazakh economy and society, adopted a direct and radical approach to reach their objectives. They founded livestock communes, encouraged the development of agriculture to accompany livestock production, and required the Kazakhs to abandon their nomadic pastoralism for a more sedentary lifestyle. They also urged Chinese colonists to migrate to Sinkiang in order to counter the anticipated opposition of some Kazakhs. These policies heightened Kazakh fears of sinicization and resulted in even greater opposition to the Chinese. The drive toward communization and the arrival of the Chinese colonists alienated many Kazakhs. A few who had contacts with the Kazakhs on the Soviet side of the border were attracted by the higher standard of living enjoyed by their compatriots across the frontier. In 1962, approximately sixty thousand Kazakhs fled to the Soviet Union, a tangible indicator of the unrest and dissatisfaction among one group of Muslims.

Again during the Cultural Revolution of 1966 to 1976, the Muslim regions were turbulent. The government appeared to foster anti-Muslim acts, including the destruction of mosques and the harassment of fervent practitioners of the faith. It sanctioned antireligious propaganda and closed down many mosques. It limited the number of texts of the Qur'ān in circulation and demanded the use of Chinese rather than the native Turkic languages in Sinkiang. The results were predictable: hostilities between the Muslims and the radical Red Guard groups erupted, pitched battles ensued, and heavy casualties were suffered by both sides. Until 1969, the northwestern borderlands were extremely unsettled. After the extreme phase of the Cultural Revolution ended in that year, Chinese pressure on the Muslims abated.

Only since 1976 has the government taken positive steps to help the Muslims. The government provided funds for the rebuilding or restoration of mosques damaged during the Cultural Revolution. In 1980, it reprinted the Qur'ān, and that work was made widely available in mosques throughout the country. Antireligious propaganda was stifled, and the mullahs again came forward to become the leaders of many Muslim communities. Muslims were not prevented from attending services at the mosques. Muslim food stores, pastry shops, and restaurants were found throughout China from Peking and Canton in the east to Lan-chou and Turfan in the west. The government has been taking great pains to preserve, repair, or restore Islamic monuments. Many of the older mosques possess stone tablets on which information about the construction or restoration of the minarets, prayer halls, and grounds is provided. These inscriptions yield precise dates, names of prominent leaders in the Muslim community, regulations concerning the mosques, and the circumstances leading to the building projects. Over the centuries, the weather, natural disasters, and perhaps deliberate defacement have taken their toll. Quite a number of the inscriptions have been damaged and are unreadable. Starting in 1982, the government belatedly began an effort to prevent further damage to these tablets.

Toward the end of the twentieth century, at least, there is no active persecution of the Muslims. The mosques have once again become centers for the Muslim communities. Interest in the history and culture of the Muslims has revived both among the minorities themselves and among the Chinese. It is difficult to predict how long this moderate policy will persist. Similarly, it is difficult to ascertain whether the Muslim community can survive surrounded by a huge Chinese population whose leaders are still bent on the assimilation and sinicization of all foreign groups and religions in China.

The most remarkable aspect of Islam in China has been its ability to survive in the face of pressures to assimilate and occasionally hostile government policies. Its tenaciousness in a culture that has sinicized so many different religions and ethnic groups is truly noteworthy. Not only have the primarily Turkic-speaking Muslims survived, but they have also succeeded in converting numerous Chinese to Islam. The Chinese Muslims, or Hui, have not by and large been highly conversant with the tenets of Islam, but they still perceive themselves to be different from other Chinese and have often identified with the larger Islamic world community. Although the Muslims in China have not made any major contributions to Islamic doctrine, they have deviated from traditional Islam in trying to reconcile their doctrines with Confucian ideology. Yet this deviation has not led to a dramatic abandonment of Islam by the Muslims in China.

BIBLIOGRAPHY

General Works. Useful bibliographies on Islam in China include Claude L. Pickens, Jr.'s *Annotated Bibliography of Literature on Islam in China* (Hankow, 1950), Hajji Yusuf Chang's "A Bibliographical Study of the History of Islam in China" (M.A. thesis, McGill University, 1960), and Mark S. Pratt's "Japanese Materials on Islam in China: A Selected Bibliography" (M.A. thesis, Georgetown University, 1962). These works are now dated and are being superseded by the bibliographies produced by Donald D. Leslie, including "Islam in China to 1800: A Bibliographical Guide," *Abr-Nahrain* 16 (1976): 16–48; *Islamic Literature in Chinese* (Canberra, 1981); and, with Ludmilla Panskaya, *Introduction to Palladii's Chinese Literature of the Muslims* (Canberra, 1977).

The best and most detailed general survey of Islam in China is Tazaka Kōdō's *Chūgoku ni okeru koikyō no denrai to sono kōtsū*, 2 vols. (Tokyo, 1964), but it is primarily a compilation rather than an analytical study. Marshall Broomhall's *Islam in China* (London, 1910) is regrettably out of date, and Raphael Israeli's *Muslims in China: A Study in Cultural Confrontation* (London, 1980) and "Muslims in China," *T'oung pao* 63 (1977): 296–323, offer interpretative studies not totally based on the primary sources.

Historical Studies. Specific studies of the Muslims in the early dynasties include F. S. Drake's "Mohammedanism in the T'ang Dynasty," *Monumenta Serica* 8 (1943): 1–40; *Biography of Huang Ch'ao*, 2d rev. ed., translated by Howard S. Levy (Berkeley, 1961), pp. 113–121; and my own "The Muslims in the Early Yüan Dynasty," in *China under Mongol Rule*, edited by John Langlois (Princeton, 1981), pp. 257–295, and "Muslim and Central Asian Revolts," in *From Ming to Ch'ing*, edited by Jonathan D. Spence and John F. Wills (New Haven, 1979), pp. 169–199. Some prominent Muslims have been accorded fine biographies: for P'u Shou-keng there is Kuwabara Jitsuzo's exhaustive biography in the *Memoirs of the Research Department of the Tōyō Bunko* 2 (1928): 1–79 and 7 (1935): 1–104; for the Ming explorer Cheng Ho, a translation of one account of his travels can be found in *The Overall Survey of the Ocean's Shores*, edited by J. V. G. Mills (Cambridge, 1970); and on the late Ming philosopher Li Chih, two recent studies are Jean-François Billeter's *Li Zhi: Philosophe maudit, 1527–1602* (Geneva, 1979) and Hok-lam Chan's *Li Chih, 1527–1602, in Contemporary Chinese Historiography* (White Plains, N.Y., 1980).

Preliminary studies of the Muslim thinkers and writers of the seventeenth and eighteenth centuries can be found in J. F. Ford's "Some Chinese Muslims of the Seventeenth and Eighteenth Centuries," *Asian Affairs: Journal of the Royal Central Asian Society* 61 (June 1974): 144–156, and Joseph Fletcher's "Central Asian Sufism and Ma Ming-hsin's New Teaching," in *Proceedings of the Fourth East Asian Altaistic Conference*, edited by Ch'en Chieh-hsien (Taipei, 1975), pp. 75–96. An extraordinary analysis of the Muslim order in nineteenth-century China can be found in Joseph Fletcher's "Ch'ing Inner Asia c. 1800" and "The Heyday of the Ch'ing Order in Mongolia, Sinkiang, and Tibet," in *The Cambridge History of China*, vol. 10, *Late Ch'ing, 1800–1911, Part 1*, edited by John K. Fairbank (Cambridge, 1978), pp. 35–306, 351–408. The late nineteenth-century rebellions are covered in Chu Wen-djang's *The Muslim Rebellion in Northwest China, 1862–78* (The Hague, 1966), Immanuel C. Y. Hsü's *The Ili Crisis: A Study of Sino-Russian Diplomacy, 1871–1881* (Oxford, 1965), my own *China and Inner Asia: From 1368 to the Present Day* (London, 1975), and Jonathan N. Lipman's "Ethnicity and Politics in Republican China: The Ma Family Warlords of Gansu," *Modern China* 10 (July 1984): 285–316.

The PRC policy toward the minorities is analyzed in June Teufel Dreyer's *China's Forty Millions* (Cambridge, Mass., 1976). Their attitude and policy toward the Islamic countries is described in Bruce D. Larkin's *China and Africa, 1949–1970* (Berkeley, 1971) and Yitzhak Shichor's *The Middle East in China's Foreign Policy, 1949–1977* (Cambridge, 1979). Studies of the Chinese government's policies in Northwest China include Donald H. McMillen's *Chinese Communist Power and Policy in Xinjiang, 1949–1977* (Boulder, 1979) and George Moseley's *A Sino-Soviet Cultural Frontier: The Ili Kazakh Autonomous Chou* (Cambridge, Mass., 1966). Notable studies of the Muslims in contemporary China and in Taiwan include Barbara L. K. Pillsbury's "Being Female in a Muslim Minority in China," in *Women in the Muslim World*, edited by Lois Beck and Nikki R. Keddie (Cambridge, Mass., 1978); Pillsbury's "Factionalism Observed: Behind the Face of Harmony in a Chinese Community," *China Quarterly* 74 (1978): 241–272; and my "Muslim Inscriptions in China: A Research Note," *Ming Studies* 15 (Fall 1982): 22–26.

Morris Rossabi

Islam in South Asia

As Islam in South Asia has, in its twelve-hundred-year history, manifested most of the varieties of response to the proclamations of the Qur'ān and the life of the prophet Muḥammad that are found in other parts of the Islamic world, "South Asia" might appear to be merely geographers' shorthand for a physically distinct region inhabited by large populations (approaching 240 million) of professing Muslims. The temper of their religious responses has ranged, as elsewhere, from the violent, pietist, and assured to the pacific, introspective, and tentative; and the setting of those responses has been, as elsewhere, the individual conscience and conduct, the life of the sect, order, or community, the courts of kings, the councils of legislators, or the conferences of politicians.

But perhaps it is the very protean character of Islam in South Asia that constitutes its distinctive "South-Asian-ness." So too perhaps is the sense of disappointment and uneasy wariness among the Muslims of the region at having, after so many centuries, some witnessing great Muslim kingdoms and empires, still to live in close proximity with a majority of neighbors whose Hindu culture can be seriously assaulted but not seriously wounded. Muslims throughout the world have lived as minorities surrounded by eavesdropping neighbors, but only Muslims in South Asia have succeeded in registering successfully the claim that members of a minority Muslim culture must have their own state to protect their culture. This must be regarded as a distinctively South Asian Muslim contribution to world Islam; so too must the openness of the theological, ethical, and jurisprudential debates occurring among the Muslims

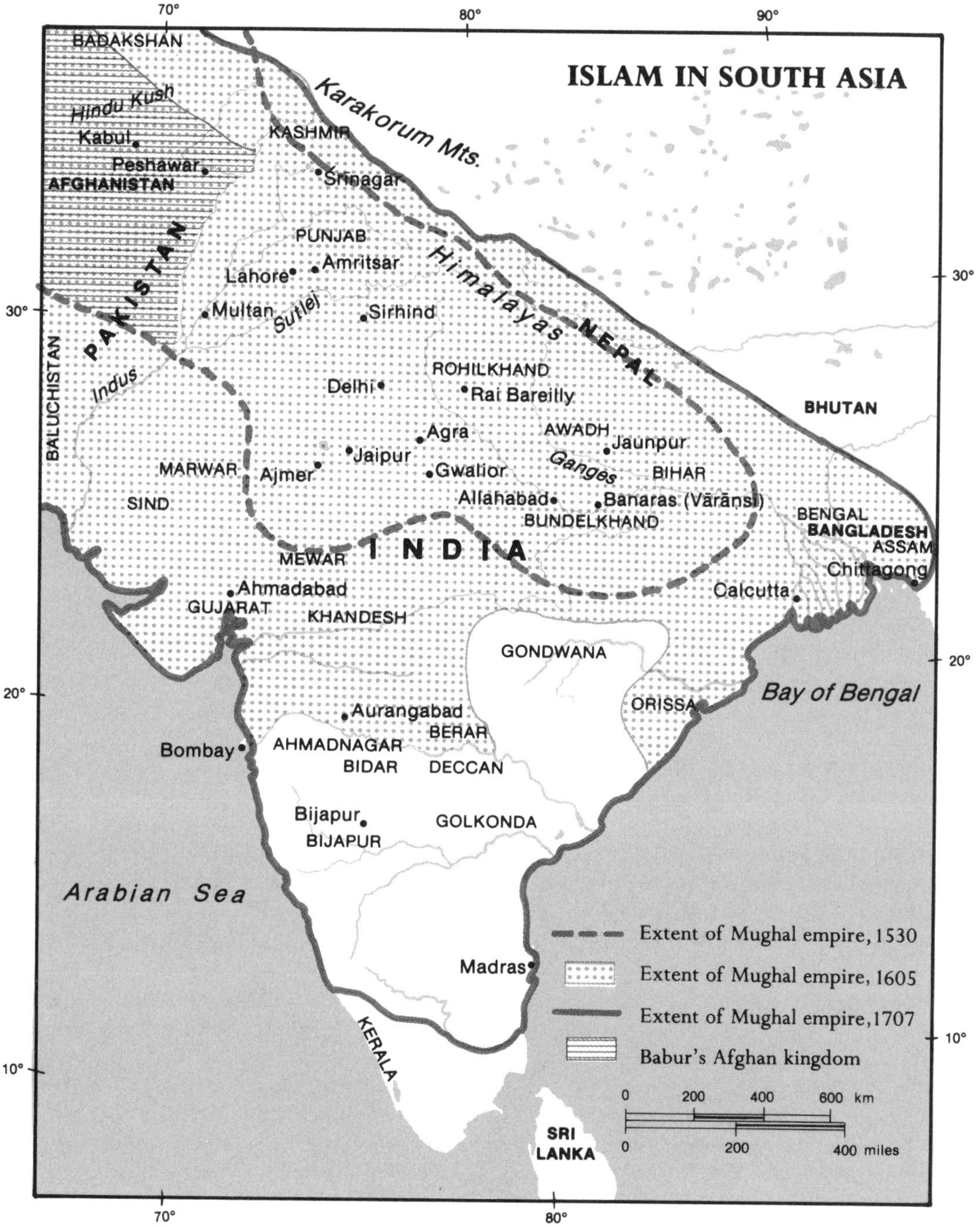

of the Republic of India on how best to obey God in their present situation. If a patterned and lively confusion is characteristic of Hinduism, so too is it characteristic of Islam in South Asia.

The Arrival of Muslims in South Asia. Muslims came to South Asia to earn a living, to conquer, to teach their religion, and to seek refuge. According to tradition, within a generation of the Prophet's death, the western coastal peoples first encountered Muslims as Arab settler-traders. In the following centuries, Arab Muslim traders were to be found in most of the ports on the east and west coasts of South India. By the tenth century (fourth century AH), Muslim merchants had settled in major cities of the Deccan and the North Indian plain. In the eleventh century, Ismāʿīlī missionaries from the Yemen were active in Gujarat. As raiders, then as conquerors, Muslims penetrated the Indo-European areas of western Afghanistan toward the end of the seventh century. The Arabs conquered Sind from 711 on. Ghaznah became the Muslim headquarters in 962 and from the time of Sebüktigin (977–997) Muslims from Central Asia were using force to penetrate the North Indian plain. Inland areas of Bengal were conquered at the beginning of the thirteenth century, and Muslims invaded Assam and Orissa about the same time. Muslim Turks were probably first seen in Kashmir in the eleventh century, while from the fourteenth century Muslims from northern India penetrated the Terai plain at the foot of the mountains of Nepal. Muslim settlements in the central and western areas of Nepal date from the seventeenth century. Major Muslim settlement in the interior of the Deccan and the south (as distinct from settlements of resident traders) began with raids by the forces of the sultan of Delhi between 1295 and 1323. There are traditional accounts of the penetration of parts of Bengal and Bijapur by Muslim saints before the main Muslim military thrusts occurred in those regions, but there is no scholarly consensus that such traditions represent actual historical events.

Islamic Education in South Asia. There has been no overarching framework or set of constraints in South Asia within which Islam has spread. Scholar, Ṣūfī, piously inclined ruler, creator of a *waqf* ("trust, inalienable endowment"), *qalandār,* or wandering holy man, Ismāʿīlī *dāʿī* ("propangandist"), and, in modern times, teacher of Islamic studies in a government college in Pakistan—all have remained remarkably free to make their own contributions as they wished. Certainly, in more modern times, coincident with Muslim loss of political supremacy, scholars have gathered under the umbrellas of such teaching institutions as Farangī Maḥall (founded 1694), Dār al-ʿUlūm at Deoband (founded 1867), and Nadwat al-ʿUlamāʾ (founded 1891) to follow a common syllabus for study and to award formal qualifications, but these began and continued as wholly voluntary associations of like-minded scholars. For the greater part of Islam's history in South Asia, the only hierarchy among religious communicators was one of esteem. Perhaps the most formal organization was to be found among members of the Ṣūfī *ṭāʾifahs*, or orders, with their formal ceremonies of initiation and successorship and their hierarchy of tyros, accepted disciples, and spiritual directors. But there was no bar to the introduction of orders new to South Asia and little inhibition of the formation of sub-branches of the main orders (as, for example, the Ṣābirīyah branch of the Chishtī order) with their own regional focuses and modified disciplines.

Sunnī scholars. Little is known of the coming of Sunnī Muslim *ʿulamāʾ*, or religious scholars, to the Muslim trading settlements on the southwest coast of India: the sixteenth-century Malayali author Zayn al-Dīn al-Maʿbarī suggests in his *Tuḥfat al-mujāhidīn* (Gift to the Holy Warriors) that missionaries from Arabia founded the first mosques in Kerala. In 1342, the Moroccan Arab traveler Ibn Baṭṭūṭah found mosques, *qāḍīs* ("judges") following the Shāfiʿī school of law, and students being supported by gifts from Muslim seamen and merchants. Sebüktigīn and Maḥmūd, the Ghaznavid rulers of eastern Afghanistan and the Punjab, patronized *ʿulamāʾ* of the Karrāmīyah sect (said by opponents to hold that God has a body). The Shāfiʿī school was strong under the later Ghaznavids and the Ghurids, but by the middle of the thirteenth century, the Ḥanafī school was dominant in northern India. The presence of the scholar-Ṣūfī Shaykh ʿAlī al-Hujwīrī in Lahore, where he died between 1072 and 1077, the travels of Fakhr al-Dīn al-Rāzī (1149–1209), the famous theologian and exegete, in the Ghurid territories, archaeological remains in Lahore from the eleventh and twelfth centuries, and the praises of Muslim historians for the Muslim rulers' zeal in founding mosques and encouraging scholars to move to India all indicate that the *ʿulamāʾ* were firmly established in the Punjab by the beginning of the thirteenth century. Under the Delhi sultan Iltutmish (1211–1236) and his successors, a considerable migration of scholars from the Mongol-devastated lands of Islam to India eased the task of appointing *qāḍīs* to the increasing number of strongholds of Muslim rule in the north. Gujarat and the Deccan drew scholars more from the Yemen and the Hejaz, but as Shīʿī ideas found rulers' favor from the middle of the fifteenth century, more scholars migrated to the Deccan from southern Iran.

Under the Delhi sultanate the teaching centers of the Sunnī *ʿulamāʾ* appear to have been informal schools attached to mosques rather than separate *madrasahs*, or religious colleges. Under the Bahmani sultanate in the Deccan, the Persian minister Maḥmūd Gāwān founded a *madrasah* at Bidar in 1472. In Bengal, inscriptions of the thirteenth to fifteenth centuries refer to *madrasahs* attached to mosques. But it was not until the last years of the rule of Awrangzīb (d. 1707) that *madrasahs* that were to acquire a far-reaching reputation made their appearance: in addition to the Farangī Maḥall already mentioned, Shāh ʿAbd al-Raḥīm, Shāh Walī Allāh's father, founded at Delhi the Madrasah-i Raḥīmīyah, which the son was to make famous. The nineteenth century was the age of the *madrasah* in South Asia, with foundations affiliated to Deoband being established at Muradabad, Saharanpur, and Darbhanga, for example. Colleges founded in such widely separated centers as Madras, Peshawar, and Chittagong regarded themselves as Deobandi. In this century, *madrasahs* have multiplied in Kerala.

The Sunnī *ʿulamāʾ* obtained material support from a variety of sources. All Muslim rulers in South Asia, sultans of Delhi, "provincial" sultans, and Mughal *pādshāhs* ("emperors") appointed *qāḍīs*, royal tutors, *khaṭībs* ("mosque preachers"), and *imāms* ("mosque prayer-leaders") and paid them in cash or by income from revenue-free land. Others received an income from *waqfs*. *ʿUlamāʾ* who did not enter service (and were often the more respected for that) lived from gifts from the faithful, from fees in money or kind for private tuition, or sometimes from cultivation or trade, though this was uncommon. Sometimes a noted scholar would accept a royal pension or a subvention from a government official, without the obligation to perform a public function. The *ʿulamāʾ* of the Dār al-ʿUlūm at Deoband broke new ground under British rule: they opened subscription lists and drew regular voluntary contributions from Muslims at all social levels, though chiefly from the better-off. Deoband today is a flourishing institution, while Farangī Maḥall, which drew much of its income from large landholders, is defunct.

The social status of the *ʿulamāʾ* was high. Indeed, at all times, though not in all places, a good proportion of them belonged to families with a record of high position under the rulers of the day. As sayyids and shaykhs, many claimed an ancestry reaching outside South Asia and back to seventh- or eighth-century Arabia. In the nineteenth century some *ʿulamāʾ* openly despised the indigenous convert. In later nineteenth-century Bengal, some disliked efforts to communicate Islam to rural Muslims in Bengali, partly because Bengali was not to them an "Islamic" language, but also partly because it was not an educated Muslim gentleman's language. The *ʿulamāʾ* maintained their status by marrying within the family or at least within the circle of the so-called *ashrāf*, the honorable, who claim descent from the Prophet, or from his companions, or from the former Pathan and Mughal ruling elite. But acceptance by other *ʿulamāʾ* through the following of a recognized course of study according to recognized methods could gain entry to the body of the *ʿulamāʾ* for the lowly, even for the recent convert to Islam. Such social mobility is more fully documented in modern than in medieval times: for example, the family of Sayyid Ḥusayn Aḥmad Madanī of Deoband was thought to have been weavers; Mawlānā ʿUbayd Allāh Sindhī, also a prominent Deobandi *ʿālim*, was born a Sikh. Of course, the high status of an *ʿālim* might have a very local recognition: the rural mullah and *mawlawī* in Bengal, Bengali-speaking and able only to imitate the sounds of the Qurʾān, would not be recognized outside his neighborhood as an equal of the scholar with Arabic, Persian, and Urdu at his command.

Shīʿī scholars. Although in South Asia reverent respect for the Prophet's family was strong, public communication of the Twelver Shīʿī tradition waited on favorable political and social developments, both in the outside Muslim world and in parts of South Asia. In the fifteenth century, following marked immigration to the Deccan Bahmani sultanate from the area of southern Iran, where Twelver Shīʿī sentiment was growing, the Bahmani sultan Aḥmad I (1422–1436) was himself "converted," but the dynasty's public position continued to be ambiguous. Of the successor sultanates to the Bahmanis, Bijapur supported the Twelver Shīʿī position from about 1510 to 1534 and again between 1558 and 1580; Golkonda's Quṭb-Shāhī dynasty was Shīʿī from its beginning under Qulī Quṭb al-Mulk (1496–1543); and from the reign of Burhān I (1509–1553), the sultanate of Aḥmadnagar supported Twelver Shiism. The establishment of Mughal rule made northern India a safer place for Shīʿī scholars. The Shīʿī Ṣafavid shah, Ṭahmāsp (1524–1576), helped Humāyūn to reestablish the Mughal position in eastern Afghanistan by 1550, and Shīʿī Persians formed an important proportion of the Muslim elite of the Mughal empire from its creation under Akbar. In the eighteenth century, under the nawabs of Awadh, Lucknow became the Twelver Shīʿī cultural and educational capital in South Asia.

The Ismāʿīlī Shīʿī communities in South Asia present, by contrast, a hierarchical model for conveying Islam as they understood it. Regarded as subversive by the Abbasid caliphs and by the Sunnī warlords who took effective control of the eastern Muslim world by the middle of the ninth century CE, they managed in the tenth century to establish a stronghold in the fringe area of Multan and, in the following century, a community in the Hindu-ruled area of Gujarat. In 1094, the Ismāʿīlīyah split, over the succession of the Fatimid imamate, into the Mustaʿlīyah and the Nizārīyah. In South Asia this split gave rise to the Bohora and the Khoja communities, respectively. Bohora communities were probably in existence in Gujarat by the middle of the twelfth century and certainly before the conquest of Gujarat by the Delhi sultan that began in 1299. The Khojas probably formed communities in Sind in the twelfth century and were well established in Gujarat by the fifteenth century. In the 1840s, the living imam of the Nizārīyah, the Aga Khan, Ḥasan ʿAlī Shāh, moved to India from Iran and asserted his leadership over the Khoja community. Among the Bohoras, the *dāʿī mutlaq*, or untrammeled summoner, acting for the imam believed to be in occlusion, has full religious knowledge and controls all activities of the community, assisted by shaykhs, mullahs, and *ʿāmil*s ("agents"), who are, however, only executive functionaries and do not participate in the formulation of doctrine and right conduct. Among the Khojas, the Aga Khan has an absolute power of decision over belief and practice, but in the running of the day-to-day affairs of the community, he is assisted by a hierarchy of central, provincial, and local councils. Among both Bohoras and Khojas, there have been opponents of the claims to supremacy of the *dāʿī muṭlaq* and of the imam, respectively.

The Ṣūfī Orders. The authority of the *ʿulamāʾ*, of whatever persuasion, as "mediums" of Islam flows from recognition of learning; the authority of the mystics, the spiritualists of Islam, the seekers of the wisdom of the heart, flows from recognition that they have had (or are preparing themselves and others to have) direct, intuitive experience of the divine realities, and that divine grace might endow them with special efficacies. These efficacies have often been believed to continue after physical death. By the twelfth century, seekers had developed distinct spiritual disciplines and formed themselves into fraternities organized around *khāngāh*s ("hospices") headed by a shaykh responsible for investing a successor, appointing deputies, admitting novices to full discipleship, and perhaps controlling a network of centers.

The arrival of the orders. Although Shaykh ʿAlī al-Hujwīrī, the Ṣūfī author of a textbook on Sufism, *Kashf al-maḥjūb* (The Unveiling of the Veiled), settled and died in Lahore, the arrival of members of orders in South Asia was broadly contemporary with the Ghurid invasions at the end of the twelfth century. Khwājah Muʿīn al-Dīn of the Chishtī order, founded in Afghanistan, settled in Ajmer (Rajasthan) in the 1290s. His successor, Quṭb al-Dīn Bakhtiyār Kākī (d. 1235) spread Chishtī influence to Delhi, while his successor Farīd al-Dīn, called Ganj-i Shakar ("store of sweetness," d. 1265), who left Delhi for Pākpattan by the Sutlej, consolidated a Chishtī position in the Punjab. During the lifetimes of the two great shaykhs of fourteenth-century Delhi, Niẓām al-Dīn Awliyāʾ (1238–1325) and Naṣīr al-Dīn Maḥmūd Chirāgh-i Dihlī ("lamp of Delhi," 1276–1356), the Chishtī order was spread to Bengal by Shaykh Sirāj al-Dīn (d. 1357), to Daulatabad by Burhān al-Dīn (d. 1340), and to Gulbarga by Sayyid Muḥammad Gīsū Dārāz ("of the long locks," 1321–1422). Other Chishtī mystics settled in Malwa and Gujarat. The other principal order in sultanate South Asia, the Suhrawardīyah, was strong in the southwest Punjab, at Multan in the person of Shaykh Bahāʾ al-Dīn Zakarīyāʾ (1182–1262), and, at Uchch, of Sayyid Jalāl al-Dīn Surkhpush ("red-dressed") Bukhārī (d. 1292) and his grandson Jalāl al-Dīn Makhdūm-i Jahāniyān ("lord of the mortals," 1308–1384). In Bengal a leading Suhrawardī saint was Shaykh Jalāl al-Dīn Tabrīzī (thirteenth century, dates uncertain). In Bihar, an offshoot of the Kubrawīyah order, the Firdawsīyah, attained fame through Sharaf al-Dīn ibn Yaḥyā Manērī (1263–1381). In Kashmir, the intellectually influential Kubrawīyah order gained a foothold through a visit by Sayyid ʿAlī Hamadānī between about 1381 and 1384.

From about the middle of the fifteenth century, other Ṣūfī orders made their appearance in South Asia, notably the Qādirīyah, the Shaṭṭārīyah, and the Naqshbandīyah. Muḥammad Ghawth (d. 1517), claiming to be tenth in succession to the founder ʿAbd al-Qādir al-Jīlānī (1077–1176), settled at Uchch, but before that, Qādirī Ṣūfīs had settled at Bidar about the time it became the capital of the Bahmani sultanate in 1422. The Bijapur sultanate later became a major center for the Qādirīyah. Another order that, as with the Qādirīyah, became influential in the Deccan as well as in North India, was the Shaṭṭārīyah, introduced from Iran by Shaykh ʿAbd Allāh al-Shaṭṭār (d. 1485). Under Muḥammad Ghawth of Gwalior (1485–1562/3), the order spread to Gujarat and caught the attention of the Mughal emperors Humāyūn and Akbar. A Central Asian order which, after its introduction into South Asia, was to challenge the direction which Sufism had hitherto taken was the Naqshbandīyah, principally introduced by Khwājah Bāqī Billāh (1563/4–1603), who initiated in his last years the most influential member of the order in South Asia, Shaykh Aḥmad Sirhindī (1564–1624).

The social role of the mystics. Members of the mystic orders in Islam have been, according to some scholars, "bridge-people" adjusting the demands and the proclamations of Islam to the psychology of different populations and, in the reverse direction, introducing new emphases and rites into the central tradition of Islam. Certainly, by the period that the orders came to South Asia, Sufism had become more a devotional than a mystical movement, embracing a collection of cult associations which centered on the pir or shaykh, a figure more approachable than that of the Arabian prophet or the *'ālim* for many in South Asia. Not that the Chishtī saints of the earlier period did not emphasize the grounding of their spiritual teaching in the scriptural and jurisprudential disciplines of the *'ulamā'*: they and their fellow Ṣūfīs of the Suhrawardī order preferred to reassure their followers that, as much as the *'ulamā'* and their pupils, they belonged to *dār al-Islām* (the "abode of Islam").

Discussions of more speculative and philosophical formulations of Sufism were not taken up until the middle of the fourteenth century. However, by the later fifteenth and early sixteenth centuries, possibly as an outcome of the growth of an indigenous Muslim convert population, the shaykh or the pir was being seen as a charismatic figure with special personal efficacies, rather than as a teacher and guide along a path to personal experience of the truths of God. The *dargāh,* or tomb, was beginning to supplant the *khāngāh* in the popular imagination. Membership in, or allegiance to, particular orders became less important—indeed some adepts now belonged to more than one order. Some orders gained in appeal; others diminished. Perhaps this was related to the way in which members of particular orders responded to the local environment. Traditionally, Mu'īn al-Dīn Chishtī is represented as having gained many followers after allowing music in his *khāngāh.* No doubt, too, willingness to use the local vernacular would enhance a shaykh's appeal. Ṣūfīs belonging to the *ṭā'ifah*s appear to have been more willing than the *'ulamā'* to found *khāngāh*s away from the principal centers of political power and thus to have drawn more of the rural and small-town populations to themselves. Certain orders, notably the Qādirīyah and Shaṭṭārīyah in Bijapur, were more urban-based. Rulers of the day early recognized the popular appeal of the shaykhs among Muslims and wished to turn that appeal to their own advantage. Shaykhs were offered pensions and revenue-free lands. The Chishtīyah would have none of this and relied upon voluntary offerings *(futūḥ),* while Suhrawardī saints were willing to accept royal largesse, and the Shaṭṭārī order cultivated Mughal rulers. In Bijapur in the seventeenth century, Qādirī and Shaṭṭārī Ṣūfīs accepted land grants. It is difficult therefore to accept fully the contention that the Ṣūfī orders represented an organized religious establishment in medieval India independent of the different Muslim political establishments.

Qalandārs. Closest to the common people as mediums of Islam were a variety of wandering mendicants distinguished from orthodox or "respectable" Ṣūfīs by scantiness of dress, the wearing of bizarre iron insignia, indifferent performance of prescribed religious obligations, and, sometimes, aggressive attitudes toward Ṣūfīs belonging to the mainstream orders. They went under a variety of names—*qalandārs*, Ḥaydarīs, Madārīs among them. Certain great shaykhs of the orders, notably the Chishtī, recognized men of genuine intuitive experience among these *qalandārs* and sometimes looked to them to reach those classes of Muslims that the regular orders did not reach. On the other hand, the Madārīs (so called after a Jewish convert, Shāh Madār, who migrated to South Asia from Syria), who sometimes went naked, smeared themselves with ashes, used hashish, and ignored the duty to fast and pray, and who possessed no property, went far toward Hindu religious idioms. Just because the *qalandārs* and others were footloose and so evidently outside the Muslim "establishment," it is possible to regard them as being important in communicating some identifiable Islamic religious motifs to the non-Muslim country-dweller.

Religious Thought before the Nineteenth Century. The extended register of relationships between Muslim and non-Muslim in South Asia, ranging from a wary and frigid intimacy to a warm and indulgent segregation, did not, in the premodern period, give rise to a body of religious thought dramatically different in its concerns from those of other regions of the contemporary Islamic world. True, in Bengal, the fifteenth- and sixteenth-century poems of Shaykh Zāhid and Sayyid Sulṭān express such Hindu ideas as creation through the union of the male and female principles and the human body as a microcosm of the cosmos, with descriptions of its psycho-physiological processes in a Nath idiom, but the Lord being sought is the God of Islam; the problem was to convey that Lord to would-be Muslims using a language and living in an environment charged with non-Islamic nuances. If the agenda of religious discussion among Muslims in South Asia is much the same as that elsewhere, the timing and emphases of discussion, however, appear related to the regional situation. For example, the emphatic discussion of the status of the shaykh and spiritual director (a general Muslim concern) among the Chishtīyah and by Sharaf al-Dīn Yaḥyā Manērī seems especially relevant for Muslims needing reassurance about the authority of their preceptors in a plural religious world.

No doubt the intuition that, in a colonial society, stability and self-assurance lay in adhering to the established religious and intellectual disciplines prompted the *'ulamā'* 's use of the works of the assured authorities of the parent culture: for *ḥadīth,* the selections called *Mashāriq al-anwār* (Lights of the East) by Mawlānā Rāzī al-Dīn Ḥasan Saghānī (from Badā'ūn, d. 1225); for Qur'anic commentary, the *Kashshāf* (Unveiler) by Abū al-Qāsim al-Zamakhsharī (d. 1143/4), and for jurisprudence, the *Hidāyah* (Guidance) by Burhān al-Dīn al-Marghinānī (d. 1197). Until the middle of the fourteenth century, the religious literature of the mystics points to the Chishtī and Suhrawardī orders' concentration, in partnership with the *'ulamā',* on the teaching of a basic piety that Muslim immigrants to South Asia would find acceptably Islamic.

The influence of Ibn al-'Arabī. From that time on, however, theoretical discussion was awakened by the reception, somewhat delayed, of the ideas of the Spanish Ṣūfī Ibn al-'Arabī (1165–1240), mediated to South Asia by the poet Fakhr al-Dīn 'Irāqī (d. 1287) in his *Lama'āt* (Flashes), a poetic interpretation of Ibn al-'Arabī's *Fuṣūṣ al-ḥikam* (Bezels of Wisdom). Ibn al-'Arabī's work provided, against the background of Islam's commitment to monotheism, a spiritually enriching statement of the experience of absorption in unity that finally overcame the seeker. At the end of the mystical path only God is found because only he, at the end, is there to be found: since creatures only exist as reflections of the divine attributes, and since God becomes a mirror in which humans contemplate their reality, and humans become a mirror in which God contemplates his names and qualities, there is but one substantively real being, namely God, with which the mystic becomes identical.

The doctrine of *waḥdat al-wujūd,* the unity of being (or rather the nonexistence of all other than God), has preoccupied Ṣūfīs and others in South Asia until modern times. Possibly drawing upon 'Alā al-Dawlah al-Simnānī of Khorasan (1261–1336), who argued that the being of God was an attribute distinct from his essence and that the final degree of reality attainable by the mystic was *'ubūdīyah* or servanthood, the Chishtī saint Gīsū Dārāz voiced his opposition; Sharaf al-Dīn Manērī, in his *Maktūbāt-i sadī* (One Hundred Letters), also disassociated himself from *waḥdat al-wujūd.* Shaykh Aḥmad Sirhindī in the Punjab, probably also indebted to 'Alā al-Dawlah al-Simnānī, offered a formulation of mystical experience which, Sirhindī claimed, was the correct interpretation of Ibn al-'Arabī's ideas. Sirhindī was concerned lest the mystics' experience of oneness should be so described as to put in question the distinction, essential to Islam, between the creator and the created. *Waḥdat al-wujūd* or, in Sirhindī's Persian terminology, *tawḥīd-i wujūdī,* is merely an intellectual perception. At the level of experience, with the sight rather than the knowledge of certitude, the mystic becomes aware that God is manifesting his Oneness *(tawḥīd-i shuhūdī),* but not that nothing else exists at that moment. In an image similar to one used by Manērī, Sirhindī argues that the light of the sun may blind one to the light of the stars, but they continue to exist nevertheless. In an effort to grant the world of phenomena a kind of independent but derivative existence, Sirhindī holds that the divine attributes are reflected in their opposite not-beings, and these reflections are the world as humans know it, a shadow of the perfections of the only Necessary Being, namely God.

The challenge to prophetic Islam. In the late fifteenth and sixteenth centuries, Muslims in South Asia appeared to be pushing the figure of the prophet Muḥammad into the background and to be challenging the principle that the *ijmā',* or consensus of the *'ulamā',* represented in practice the authoritative interpretation of divine command. Around this time in Gujarat, Sayyid Muḥammad of Jaunpur (1443–1505) claimed to be the Mahdi ("guided one") of Sunnī tradition, who will lead the world to order and justice before the day of resurrection. His followers claimed for him a rank equal to that of the Prophet and clustered around him as though around a pir. Bāyazīd Anṣārī (1525–1572/3), born at Jallandhar in the Punjab, was a Pathan who claimed to be the *pīr-i kāmil* ("perfect preceptor") in direct communication with God, who shone his divine light upon him. Bāyazīd himself combined the perfections of the paths of law, mysticism, and wisdom attaining to gnosis of God. In the last stage of his disciples' spiritual ascent, they might exempt themselves from some of the obligations of the *sharī'ah.* Gathering support from among the Pathan tribesmen of the northwest, he and his followers clashed with the Mughals.

Shaykh Aḥmad Sirhindī, too, claimed to enjoy some of the perfections of prophethood and not to need, as ordinary believers do, prophetic mediation in order to reach God. His disciples acclaimed him as *mujaddid-i alf-i thānī,* "renewer of the second millennium" (of Islam). The Mughal emperor Akbar's friend Abū al-Faẓl (1551–1602), in his *Akbar-nāmah* (Book of Akbar) and *Ā'īn-i Akbarī* (Institutes of Akbar), drew heavily upon Ṣūfī concepts of the perfect man as a microcosm of the divine perfections, indeed a divine epiphany; upon Illuminationist ideas of light, perhaps transmitted through a divinely illumined figure, making knowledge of the real possible; upon Twelver Shī'ī beliefs in inner spiritual meanings of the text of revelation and of the universe; upon Ismā'īlī theories of a secret knowledge communicated in each cycle of time by specially endowed people; upon philosophical ideas of the ruler maintaining an organic society, and upon Sunnī ideas of the caliph and the just sultan and all of this to present Akbar as the earthly homologue and symbol of God. The Prophet, where he appears at all, is limited to giving a name to one religion among many.

Sunnī Muslims reacted to this submergence of prophetic Islam with a reassertion both of Muḥammad's role and of the paradigmatic character of his companions' lives. ʿAbd al-Ḥaqq Dihlāwī (1551–1642) devoted himself to the study of *ḥadīth* and wrote on prophethood. Mindful of a strong Shīʿī presence among the Mughal elite by reason of immigration from Iran, where the Safavids had established Twelver Shiism as the state religion, Shaykh Aḥmad Sirhindī wrote his *Radd-i rawāfiḍ* (On the Refutation of the Shīʿah) against the Shīʿī practice of cursing some of the companions. In his *Najāt al-rashīd* (The Orthodox Way of Deliverence), written in 1591, the historian Badāʾūnī condemned innovation, idol worship, and time-serving *ʿulamāʾ*. He upheld the duty of the Muslim ruler to enforce the *sharīʿah* as understood by the consensus of the Sunnī scholars. But all these writers—together with the admiring commentator on Ibn al-ʿArabī, Shāh Muḥibb Allāh of Allahabad (1587–1648), and the emperor Shāh Jahān's eldest son Dārā Shikūh (1615–1659), a follower of the Qādirī order who attempted a comparative study of technical terms in Vedanta and Sufism, the *Majmaʿ al-baḥrayn* (Confluence of the Two Seas), and a Persian translation of fifty-two Upaniṣads, and who was executed on pretext of heresy by his brother and rival for the throne, Awrangzīb—treated *taṣawwuf*, the personal quest for God, as the fulfillment of Islam.

Shāh Walī Allāh. *Taṣawwuf* continued its hold over the Muslim religious imagination in South Asia into the eighteenth century, but in the encyclopedic scholarship of the Delhi *ʿālim* Shāh Walī Allāh (1703–1762), there are signs of a sea-change. Although he wrote much on mysticism, trying to show that the differences between *waḥdat al-wujūd* and *waḥdat al-shuhūd* are only verbal in that for both, God's imagination of himself is the only real existent, he believed himself called by God to demonstrate, over the whole range of the Islamic sciences, in *fiqh* (jurisprudence), *tafsīr* (Qurʾān commentary), *falsafah* (philosophy), that a harmony of apparently different views in fact exists, or could be achieved. In jurisprudence he is concerned to argue that more emphasis on rulings supported by *ḥadīth* from the Prophet which had been carefully examined for authenticity would tend to bring the four schools of Sunnī jurisprudence together, and that indeed it is permissible for rulings to be sought outside one's usual school. In theology he tries to reconcile doctrines of creation from nothing with those of the unity and changelessness of God by claiming an overflow of divine power which brings the universe into being from potential not-being (because the source of everything is not-being, there is no duality in the one divine being, and because potentiality was already an aspect of the divine being, there was no change in the divine being when that potentiality was manifested). In his *Ḥujjat Allāh al-bālighah* (The Mature Proof of God), Shāh Walī Allāh argues that, although the divine truths and commandments do not originate in a reason comprehensible to humans, nevertheless they are not an affront to that reason.

Concerned with the growing divisions between Sunnī and Shīʿī Muslims in his time (following, probably, more Shīʿī immigration in the 1740s and the growing influence of the Shīʿī nawabs of Awadh), Shāh Walī Allāh wrote a defense of the actual line of succession of the Sunnī caliphs after the Prophet's death, entitled *Izālat al-khafāʾ ʿan khilāfat al-khulafāʾ* (Clarification of Tenets Regarding the Successorship of the Successors). Furthermore, although Shāh Walī Allāh was an *ʿālim* writing mainly for *ʿulamāʾ* (indeed, he wrote much in Arabic), he did write a number of letters calling for political action by Muslim rulers to curb the power of non-Muslims by waging *jihād* (war for the supremacy of Islam). Shāh Walī Allāh's work provided an epitome of Sunnī scholarship for South Asia to which later generations of *ʿulamāʾ*, and indeed of other educated Muslims, have resorted for instruction and inspiration. But more than that, his work was an assertion that the individual commitment to Islam might now need widespread public action in its support.

The Vernacular Islam of the Regions: The Example of Bengal. In South Asia, Islam as commitment and praxis spread to those for whom Arabic, Persian, and Urdu (the new North Indian vernacular with a large Arabic and Persian vocabulary capable of conveying scriptural and Middle Eastern Islam) remained impenetrable. Only if Islamic values and cultural images were expressed in the regional languages would human beings with a nurture greatly removed from that in the Arabic- and Persian-speaking lands be able to make the Islamic perception of reality both meaningful and their own. In Bengal, where developed the second largest total (after Indonesia) of rural Muslims in the Islamic world, between the fifteenth and eighteenth centuries, many Muslim cultural mediators, writing in Bengali, expressed Islam in the local cultural idiom, an idiom greatly enriched in the same period by translations of the great Hindu epics, the *Rāmāyaṇa* and the *Mahābhārata*, into Bengali, and the expression of Nath and Vaiṣṇava teachings.

For example, in his *Nabīvamśa,* Sayyid Sulṭān (sixteenth–seventeenth centuries) depicted the prophet Muḥammad as an *avatāra* of God, as worshiped by members of the Hindu pantheon and as struggling against Hindu enemies in an Arabia portrayed as Bengal. He assimilated Hindu ideas of the four *yuga*s in a cosmogonical myth which treated the four ages as periods of gestation for the divine messenger, Muḥammad. Sayyid Murtaẓā (dates uncertain) identified stages and stations of *taṣawwuf* with the *cakra*s or nerve plexuses of Tantric yoga. Other Bengali Muslim writers apotheosize their preceptors as gurus. Muḥammad the Prophet is able to bring the blessings of *siddhi* (fulfillment) and *mukti* (liberation) to his devotees. The spiritual guide, guru, or pir should be served as the Lord himself. Folk literature endowed the pir, sometimes addressed as a historical figure and sometimes as a personified spirit, with supernatural and thaumaturgic powers. In the nineteenth century, the manifestations of such efforts to make Islam a religion of, as well as for, Bengali-speakers, were attacked by scripturalist-minded reformers drawing inspiration from outside Bengal.

Islamic Renewal. By 1800 an irreversible change in the temporal setting of Islamic faith and practice in South Asia first gradually, and then dramatically, transformed the assumptions of debate and action among the communicators of Islam. Marathas, Sikhs, and the English East India Company had overborne Mughal military power and become the effective rulers, even in the territory of Delhi itself. Muslim ruling elites were not rudely supplanted nor did they all immediately suffer hardship; indeed some of their members quickly made themselves, with personal profit, indispensable to the new masters. But they were no longer confidently in charge, under Muslim rulers, of their future. By 1803 the East India Company had occupied Delhi and Agra, the historical centers of Mughal imperial power, and had begun to control the application of Islamic law to Muslim society. In their savage repression of mutiny and rebellion in 1857–1858, the British demonstrated that any future Muslim success and prosperity must be on terms laid down by British rulers. Moreover, Muslims were obliged to live under censorious rulers who made it possible for Christian missionaries publicly to attack their religion and for anyone to allege that Muslims were behind in the race of progress because they were Muslim. Infidels had conquered Muslims before but had often surrendered to Islam later. Now Western imperialism, intellectual and moral as well as political, seemed to proclaim that either God was not omnipotent or that he was punishing his would-be servants for failing to be true and faithful servants.

Today, in South Asia, few openly claim that they are Muslim by culture only—"census Muslims." Most would-be Muslims proclaim the reality of Allāh, the authenticity of the Qur'ān as his revelation and of Muḥammad the Prophet as his messenger, and the truth of the existence of heaven and hell for which life on earth is a selective examination by continuous assessment. Some Muslims in South Asia (as in other regions of the Islamic world) have tried to restore strength and, sometimes, sincerity to their convictions by seeking in scripture—variously defined as the Qur'ān only or as the Qur'ān and the authentic collections of Muḥammad's *ḥadīth*—norms and the authority for norms appropriate to modern needs and situations in the belief that in scripture those needs and situations had been, if not foreseen, then provided for, in other words, that change is good and Islamic or could be rendered so. Other Muslims have wished instead to reproduce exactly the patterns of a past period of human life, a period deemed to be ideal, usually that of the Prophet's own lifetime and of that of his companions. Change, it is implied, has been for the worse, and should be reversed. Muslim debate over the future has swayed between these two positions.

Muslim experience and understanding of British rule and of intrusive Western cultures have shaped decisively such debate. Temporal success, associative social action, community identity, and intracommunity and group cooperation have moved to the center of Muslims' preoccupations. British assumptions that law was a corpus of rules made mandatory by a sovereign power, that in medieval times Muslims had been governed by such law, the *sharī'ah*, indeed had been defined as a community by such governance, and that their law was essentially a law directed to extraterrestrial ends, fostered, in some Muslims, convictions that without the ability to enforce such law upon themselves, they could not be true Muslims. As the *sharī'ah* was seen more as legal rules to be enforced and less as ethical and moral aspirations to be satisfied (it embraces, of course, both), so the issues of authoritative interpretation of the *sharī'ah* and of the identity and character of its enforcers grew more insistent.

Early revivalist movements. With the loss of ground in the eighteenth century, Muslims shifted their vision away from the pir in medieval South Asia to the Prophet in seventh-century Arabia. Khwājah Mīr Dard (1721–1785) places the spiritual perfections of Muḥammad above those of imam and saint. Shāh Walī Allāh's son, Shāh 'Abd al-'Azīz (1746–1824), depicts Muḥammad as a figure radiating light, of which all the protectors and teachers of Islam are but reflections. Shāh 'Abd al-'Azīz criticizes some of the practices of Sufism in South Asia as innovations without foundation in the Prophet's *ḥadīth*. Sayyid Aḥmad of Rai Bareilly (1786–

1831) led a militant movement, some of whose adherents migrated, in 1826, from British India to the Pathan borderlands, where they waged *jihād* against the Sikhs, creating an imitation of the first Muslim community of Mecca among the Pathans before being killed by the Sikhs at the Battle of Balakot. The ideology of the movement, expressed in *Ṣirāṭ-i mustaqīm* (The Straight Path) and *Taqwiyat al-īmān* (The Strengthening of Faith in God), compiled and written by Shāh Muḥammad Ismāʿīl (1779–1831), grandson of Shāh Walī Allāh, took the form of a *ṭarīqah-i muḥammadī* ("Muhammadan way"), a Sufism reformed of polytheistic practices (such as expecting the spirits of dead saints to grant boons). It was advocated that the Prophet should be regarded as the seeker's pir. The urge to recreate the earliest days of Islam is signaled by Sayyid Aḥmad's refusal to initiate *jihād* in British India without first making *hijrah* ("emigration"). (The hold of the Prophet's Hijrah over Muslim sentiment was to be further demonstrated in 1920 when, on the urging of mosque imams and pirs, about thirty thousand Muslims from Sind and the Frontier Province migrated to Afghanistan as their *dār al-Islām.*)

In Bengal, Ḥājjī Sharīʿat Allāh (1781–1840) founded the Farā'iḍī movement. He had earlier lived in the Hejaz for about eighteen years. He sought to teach Bengali Muslims to observe the obligatory duties *(farā'iḍ)* of Islam, to abandon reverence for pirs, and to forsake "hinduized" life ceremonies. On the ground that there were no properly constituted Muslim rulers and *qāḍīs* in nineteenth-century India, the Farā'iḍīs abandoned Friday and *ʿīd* ("holiday") prayers. Under Ḥājjī Sharīʿat Allāh's son Dudū Miyān (1819–1862) violence broke out between the movement's largely peasant following and the landlords. Throughout the nineteenth century, a variety of Sunnī scholars and teachers, including Mawlānā Karāmat Jawnpurī (d. 1873), a follower of Sayyid Aḥmad Barēlī willing to accept British rule, devoted themselves to trying to rid Islam in Bengal of polytheistic attitudes and practices, while disagreeing among themselves about the acceptability of *taṣawwuf,* or about which school of jurisprudence should be followed. In the far south, among the Māppiḷḷas, *ʿulamā'* such as Sayyid ʿAlawī (d. 1843/4) and his son Sayyid Faḍl (d. 1900), though creating no formal organization, perpetuated local Muslim traditions of *jihād* and martyrdom so that the violent Māppiḷḷa agrarian opposition to Hindu landlords, and to the British, which continued throughout the nineteenth century and during the Māppiḷḷa rebellion of 1921, was expressed in the idiom of a return to the earliest days of Islam.

The Deobandi ʿulamā'. But renewal of Islam by attempts to relive the believed patterns of a model era occurred mainly as a peaceful process of education by the *ʿulamā'*. They progressively took over the religious leadership of Muslims in South Asia under non-Muslim rule. Shāh ʿAbd al-ʿAzīz had begun to assert that leadership by delivering rulings (*fatwās*) to the many Muslims seeking assurance in a period of rapid change. The position of the *ʿulamā'* was strengthened in the course of Sunnī-Shīʿī controversy—Shāh ʿAbd al-ʿAzīz's *Tuḥfat al-Ithnā ʿAsharīyah* (An Offering to the Twelvers) was of major significance—and in public debate with Christian missionaries. After 1857, the *ʿulamā'* at Deoband proved adept at using the post, telegraph, railways, and the press to communicate their teachings to the Urdu-knowing Muslim public. Their leaders, Mawlānā Muḥammad Qāsim Nanawtawī (1832–1880) and Rashīd Aḥmad Gangohī (1828–1905) stood for the Ḥanafī school, subjecting local custom to a careful critique in the light of the model practice of the Prophet and seeking always to ensure that believers kept the divine *tawḥīd* (unity) before them. The Deobandi leaders assumed the status of Ṣūfī shaykhs and initiated disciples; but the special efficacies *(karāmāt)* that were attributed to them were depicted as being exercised to influence people to follow the *sunnah.* The Deobandis were opposed to treating the tombs of shaykhs as centers of worship or intercession. Since some leading Deobandis claimed initiation into all the main Ṣūfī orders in South Asia, Deoband encouraged comprehensiveness and consolidation of intellectual and experiential traditions. Although they accepted the British as rulers, the Deobandis (in *fatwās* sought by anxious Muslims) weighed their culture and usually found it wanting. Muslims were not to accept their contemporary world on its own terms.

Other groups. The Ahl-i Ḥadīth (People of the *Ḥadīth*) were another group of *ʿulamā'* aiming to reform custom and to purify convictions soiled by custom. Led by Ṣiddīq Ḥasan Khān (1832–1890) and Sayyid Nadhīr Ḥusayn (d. 1902), they derided the authority of the four schools of Islamic jurisprudence in favor of a literal interpretation of Qur'ān and *ḥadīth.* At the same time, they opposed the Sufism of the shrines. However, the Ahl-i Ḥadīth's treatment of the prophet Muḥammad's *ḥadīth* as an implicit revelation which elaborated authoritatively the explicit revelation of the Qur'ān exposed them to the charge of introducing a dualism into God's communication with humans. In reaction, the Punjab-based Ahl-i Qur'ān (People of the Qur'ān), founded in 1902 and led by ʿAbd Allāh Chakralawī, held that Muḥammad was the messenger for only the Qur'anic mode of revelation and that Muslims should treat as divine commandment only what was specifically and exclusively enjoined in the Qur'ān. Hence, for example, the Ahl-i Qur'ān regarded the call to prayer and the performance of *'īd* and funerary prayers as not essential Islamic obligations. But other *'ulamā'* accepted the customs and practices that had developed in medieval South Asia. Led by Aḥmad Riḍā Khān (1856–1921) with headquarters at Bareilly and Badā'ūn in Rohilkhand, they accepted a variety of mediators of Islam from the prophet Muḥammad to the saints and pirs of the shrines. The Barelwīs observed the birthdays of both the Prophet and the saints—a practice objected to by Deobandis and others on the ground that such celebrations implied that the dead were present. Some *'ulamā'* were less concerned with taking up militant stances toward the past of Islam in South Asia and devoted themselves to teaching a simple understanding of Islam to those whose knowledge was limited. In the later nineteenth century more *madrasah*s were founded in Bengal, and popular *naṣīḥat-nāmah*s (books of admonition) in Bengali were published. In the twentieth century, Mawlānā Muḥammad Ilyās (1885–1944) traveled in Mewar (southwest of Delhi) preaching and encouraging those who were not *'ulamā'* to uphold the basic articles of faith. This "mass-contact" campaign was conducted with a minimum of formal organization.

Sayyid Ahmad Khan. The first major figure to argue that the changes Muslims were experiencing in the nineteenth century were Islamic was Sir Sayyid Ahmad Khan (1817–1898). The British suppression of the mutiny and rebellion of 1857–1858 convinced him that Muslims must accept a future shaped by British power. As a totally believing Muslim, he wished to demonstrate that God was not being mocked when Muslims, in hope of advancement, were being taught in British-influenced schools and colleges a natural science that appeared to contradict divine revelation and indeed to give, in supposedly immutable laws of nature, partners to God. He wished to assure Muslims that they were not disobeying divine commandments in search of worldly gain when they acted as though they had abandoned even the ideal of a public and social life controlled by the norms of the *sharī'ah*. Briefly, Sayyid Ahmad Khan argued that the word of God and the work of God, revelation and nature as understood by nineteenth-century Western science, are wholly in harmony. God is the cause of causes; the laws of nature are divine attributes, and any apparent discrepancies between the Qur'ān's account of the natural world and that of Western scientists are to be attributed to misunderstandings of the language of the Qur'ān. As for the Muslims' belief that their social arrangements and behavior must be obedient to God's command, Sayyid Ahmad Khan did not disagree. Muslims have, however, wrongly taken to be divine command what is not. Although each prophet in history has communicated the same *dīn*, or set of human obligations toward God, each has brought to his age a different *sharī'ah*, or set of detailed prescriptions for performing those obligations. Islam, then, accommodates historical change. Muslims must realize that only the manifestly declared injunctions of the Qur'ān are the commandments of religion and that much of the reported dicta and behavior of the Prophet is of doubtful authenticity.

Muhammad Iqbal. The poet-seer Muhammad Iqbal (1877–1938) offered a conception of a God-human relationship which he intended to inspire Muslims to action with the confidence that they would be innovating, but in a distinctively Islamic fashion. Reality is not a given, but a becoming. Thought is a potency which forms the very being of its material. The life of the individual ego is that of actualizing in thought and deed the infinite possibilities of the divine imagination. Men and women explore servanthood in acting as God's assistants in creation, but in accordance with the principle of unity that is the godhead. Iqbal's philosophy of "humanism with God" was intended to inspire Muslims to act as an association of participants in a common enterprise and to advance beyond the individual cultivation of a pious but passive sensibility. Iqbal called for a free *ijtihād*, a striving to discover the demands of Islam in changing circumstances, and he pointed out that Muslims would not be collectively free to exercise that *ijtihād* and to implement it unless they had their own independent polity free from the interference of non-Muslim legislators. His call in 1930 for an autonomous Muslim state embracing the northwestern areas of India expressed his confidence in Islam's ability to inspire a new social order for the twentieth century.

Abū al-Kalām Āzād. Abū al-Kalām Āzād (1888–1958) began by proclaiming, immediately before and immediately after World War I, that Indian Muslims should assert their distinctive collectivity by rallying around the symbol of the *khilāfat* (an office held, so he argued, by the Ottoman sultan) and organizing themselves voluntarily to obey the *sharī'ah*. Later, in his *Tarjumān al-Qur'ān* (Interpretation of the Qur'ān), first published in 1930 and 1936, Abū al-Kalām offers a personal reaction to the Qur'ān when approached directly without any intermediate commentary. Revelation interprets correctly the inward moral convictions planted in humans by God, who exercises his benevolent lordship over nature to human advantage. God lays upon all humankind the same obligations to recognize the real nature of the world he has created; at the root of all apparently distinctive religions is the same *dīn* ("religion"). People have disguised this truth by their "groupism" and attachment to group rites and rituals. They should gradually abandon their distinctions and recognize that only one group fulfills their true destiny—the group comprised of all humankind. In effect, Abū al-Kalām Āzād modifies a classical position, that God fashions all people to be Muslims were they but aware of it; the inference he draws, however, is not that some should coerce others to become so aware, but that all should cooperate peacefully (especially Hindus and Muslims in South Asia) until all voluntarily come to acknowledge the Muslim-ness within them. (There is an interesting analogy here with the Upaniṣadic idea of recognition of the reality of *brahman-ātman* within each person.)

Ghulām Aḥmad. In the nineteenth-century Punjab a movement arose from within Islam expressing the motif of renewal under a mahdi, this time a mahdi who prohibited *jihād* and whose followers were willing to adopt modern methods of propaganda, economic organization, and education, especially of women. Mīrzā Ghulām Aḥmad (1839?–1908), son of a doctor in Qādiyān, claimed to be a mahdi or *masīḥ* ("messiah"). He claimed also the status of a minor prophet, reminding people of revealed scripture, but not bringing a new scripture. After Ghulām Aḥmad's death, his adherents, the Aḥmadīyah, formed themselves into an exclusive community for emulating the believed standards, but not the particular mores, of the time of the first four Sunnī caliphs. [*See* Aḥmadīyah.]

Islam in Contemporary South Asia. Developments since the gaining, in 1947, of political independence for the subcontinent demonstrate that plasticity is the most widely shared characteristic of an Islam located, since 1971, in three separate states: India, Pakistan, and Bangladesh.

In the Republic of India there is no method other than voluntary cooperation for Muslims to express their aspirations to live as an *ummah,* or community in obedience to divine law. The Deobandi *'ulamā'* have taken full advantage of constitutional guarantees of freedom to run their religious institutions as before. The Indian branch of Mawdūdī's Jamā'at-i Islāmī (Islamic Society) has continued work in hope that all Indians will turn to Islam. Although a decreasing majority of Indian Muslims continues to resist any replacement of Muslim law (as interpreted by the Indian courts) by a wholly secular code for all the Republic's citizens, writers such as A. A. Fyzee (1899–1981) and Muhammad Mujeeb have questioned whether religious belief must be complemented by religious law. Meanwhile the personal quest for the divine realities in a Ṣūfī idiom and the teaching of Islamic ideals of right conduct continue.

In Pakistan, the integral Islam visualized by Iqbal and, later, by such supporters of the Pakistan movement as Mawlānā Shabbīr Aḥmad 'Uthmānī (1887–1949) in their different ways, has not come to pass. The constitutions of 1956, 1962, and 1972 all left the character and the pace of islamization under the control of largely Western-educated political, military, and bureaucratic elements. The only major legislative outcome of their *ijtihād* has been the Family Laws Ordinance of 1961, which made polygamy and male-pronounced divorce more difficult (but not illegal) and conferred rights of inheritance from grandparents upon orphaned grandchildren.

Something resembling the medieval ideal of a partnership between a pious ruling institution and qualified scholars was advocated by Sayyid Abū al-A'lā Mawdūdī (1903–1979), founder of the Jamā'at-i Islāmī in British India in 1940. [*See* Jamā'at-i Islāmī.] Opposed before 1947 to the creation of Pakistan because he believed it would not be governed by true Muslims in a truly Islamic mode, he subsequently migrated to Pakistan and advocated the establishment of an Islamic state by elective assemblies and by representative government. A more codified form of the *sharī'ah* as interpreted by properly qualified scholars would become the law of Pakistan. Mawdūdī would not have enforced all rulings in existing books of *fiqh* and would have allowed some interpretative decisions to be arrived at by majority vote. He was prepared for modern legislation where the Qur'ān and *sunnah* were silent, provided that the general objectives of the *sharī'ah* were served and no infringement of divine commandment could occur. Mawdūdī appreciated, more perhaps than the *'ulamā',* the need for clarity, certainty, and effectiveness of action in a fast-changing world of rising Muslim expectations.

Under the martial law regime of General Ẓiyā al-Ḥaqq (Zia al-Haq), *sharī'ah* courts have been established, *zakāt* (prescribed alms levy) introduced, and the intention of enforcing the Qur'anic penalties for crimes against God proclaimed. Attempts are being made to introduce interest-free forms of banking and commercial enterprise. Such measures, even though devised and applied at the discretion of a regime seeking popular consent, may awaken Muslim minds and hearts in Pakistan to the servanthood of God or may nourish national sentiment for meeting worldly needs. Perhaps that ambiguity is inherent in the situation of Islam in Pakistan today. In Bangladesh, since 1971, there has been little attempt to assert that public life is shaped by the demands of Islam; it is sometimes maintained that how Bangladesh is being governed is not out of kilter with Islam.

Muslim Society in South Asia. Until the partition and mass migrations of 1947, which brought about vast Muslim majorities in what are now Bangladesh and Pakistan (85 percent and 97 percent respectively as of 1977), all the Muslims of South Asia lived embedded in a non-Muslim society. Muslim and non-Muslim alike had developed mutually dependent economic relationships—for example, in Calcutta Muslims paint images for Hindus, and in the villages, particularly, Muslims depend on Hindu astrologers, musicians, potters, and tinkers, whether by way of market exchange or through the traditional patron-client service relationship of *jajmani*. Before 1947 there were no distinct Muslim and non-Muslim economic orders. In patterns of social life, in kinship relationships, life cycles, forms of social stratification, and social avoidances, the surrounding non-Muslim environment has shaped Muslim behavior in modes that recent work has shown to be much more subtle than can be embraced by such concepts as filtration, syncretism, and synthesis.

The role of the sharī'ah. Despite the show by both *'ulamā'* and "modernist" Muslim thinkers that the *sharī'ah* displays Islam as a religion of total guidance for human relationships, Islamic law tends to curb and regulate those relationships rather than to define or command them in all their minutiae. Islamic law requires the individual to act or not to act in certain ways; it does not offer a reticulation for society. For example, Islamic law imposes modest limits on the degrees of relationship within which marriages are forbidden, but it does not forbid the principle of endogamy; indeed, in that it requires Muslim women to marry only Muslim men, it enjoins that principle. Through its rules of succession, its compulsory alms tax *(zakāt)*, and its rules for commercial partnerships, Islamic law takes individual property rights for granted, but it does not specify particular types of economic organization. The Muslim may lawfully take profit from an individual or from a collective enterprise so long as that profit is not usurious.

Reformist aspirations among the Muslims of South Asia in modern times have sometimes obfuscated comment on Muslim social behavior in South Asia by introducing the concept of "the spirit of Islam." Islamic law does not require a Muslim to marry any other lawfully available Muslim. Yet a strict regard for relative social position in the arrangement of a marriage is sometimes treated as a peculiarly South Asian infringement on Islamic norms perceived in the "egalitarian spirit of Islam." Again, although widows may remarry in Islamic law, they are not compelled to do so. Muslim behavior in South Asia, as doubtless elsewhere in the Islamic world, expresses an interplay between aspirations identifiable as Islamic and the experiences of daily life. Crucial is the aspiration: for example, Islamic authority for the matrilocal marriage and residence customs of the Māppiḷḷas of northern Kerala has been sought in the prophet Muḥammad's residing with his wife Khadījah's kin.

Succession is the principal area in Muslim social life in South Asia where *sharī'ah* requirements have often been ignored. Exclusion of women from inheritance of landed property is widespread. It is doubtful whether the Shariat Act of 1937 (and its subsequent extension in both India and Pakistan to cover succession to agricultural land), asserting the supremacy of Islamic law over custom, has had much effect. The Khojas may leave all their property by testamentary succession. Until the earlier years of the twentieth century, most Muslim Māppiḷḷas of northern Kerala lived in matrilocal joint family groups. Where joint family property was divided by common consent, shares devolved in the female lines. More recently, social change toward self-supporting patrilocal families and, since 1918, legislation by the Madras and Kerala legislatures empowering the courts to apply the Muslim rules of succession have weakened but not wholly removed the hold of customs so out of line with the *sharī'ah.*

Kinship and class systems. Muslim family and kinship systems in South Asia betray great variety within the general customs of endogamy and treating marriage as a form of social exchange between groups. Cross- and parallel-cousin marriages are common, sometimes within the male descent group as with some Punjabi Muslims, sometimes not, as with some Bengali Muslims. Others such as the Meos and certain North Indian artisan groups reject cousin marriage. Among matrilocal Māppiḷḷas, cross- but not parallel-cousin marriages occur. In Nepal, the exogamous patrilineal lineage has nothing like the depth of neighboring Hindu lineages.

Muslim society is highly stratified. The division between *ashrāf* ("honorable") and *ajlāf* ("ignoble"), between those of supposedly immigrant descent and those of convert descent, is related more to styles of education, occupation, and leadership and may have no relevance to status in a particular local situation. Subgroups of the *ashrāf*, namely, sayyids, shaykhs, Mughals, and Pathans, are more ready to intermarry than are respectable *ajlāf* groups. The latter follow specialized and mainly manual occupations, forming graded endogamous groups named after a hereditary calling which each member does not now necessarily follow: gardener, potter, carpenter, blacksmith. Below them are weavers, cotton carders, tailors, bracelet-makers; much lower, considered unclean but not untouchable, are the barbers, the *faqīrs* ("mendicants"), butchers, oil-pressers, and washermen. At the bottom are the descendants of former untouchables: musicians, dancers, tanners, sweepers, and cesspool-emptiers. It is these Muslim groups who can suffer discrimination in Muslim public life—refusal of the use of common burial grounds and denial of an equal place in the mosque as well as commensality on festive occasions. At these lower levels of Muslim society similarities with caste are most evident—more rigid hereditary occupational specialization and sharp hierarchical distinctions based on the dichotomy of pure and impure.

Rites of passage. Recent studies of Muslim social behavior in Nepal and Bengal suggest that that behavior may be, so to speak, an anagram of the behavior of the local Hindu society and that Hindu society, while magnetizing Muslim customs, does not dominate them completely. Life-cycle ceremonies in parts of Nepal and Bengal indicate the interplay that occurs. In Nepal, at birth, the *adhān* ("announcement of prayer") is shouted into the baby's ear. A period of impurity is then observed not only for the mother but for the whole patrilineage collectively—a deviation from scriptural Islam. The Cchaṭhī ("sixth day") ceremony follows, introducing the child to the community and placing it under the protection of the saint Shāh Madār, with singing and dancing by untouchable Hindus. The more canonical ceremony of *ʿaqīqah* (shaving of the child's head and animal sacrifice) is not performed. At six months the baby is fed solid food by unmarried girl relatives. The Islamic modes of initiation—circumcision and religious instruction—are followed. Forms of marriage are Islamic with *nikāḥ* ("marriage contract"), *mahr* ("bridal gift"), and officiating *qāḍī*. The accompanying ceremonies betray local attitudes: washing of the couple's feet by the bride's relatives and gifts from the bride's family suggest not the spirit of the canonical *nikāḥ* as a free exchange of consents, but the giving of a daughter to the bridegroom's kin-group. At death, burial ceremonies follow canonical rules, but the whole patrilineage of the deceased is affected by death-impurity, and ceremonies continue for forty days. In Nepal, rice balls used to be offered to the spirit of the deceased in the belief that if the death was not from old age or illness, the deceased would otherwise become an unquiet spirit speaking through a medium, usually a member of the deceased's patrilineage. In West Bengal, the placenta is buried in a clay pot for fear of attack by evil spirits, the mother's birth impurity lasts for forty days, and the mother's brother provides her with her first rice meal and the baby with its first solid food.

So a selective combination of canonical Islamic and local elements may occur: on the one hand, formal adherence to norms of Sunnī Islam, extending to ablutions and the killing of lawful animals in due form; on the other hand, extension of the Islamic rules for individual purity and impurity to a collectivity, the patrilineage. Local influence is betrayed in the role of young unmarried girls who are believed to be auspicious, in the emphasis on lineage solidarity (symbolized by the gifts of food by relatives and acts of deference by the bride's family toward the family of the bridegroom), and in the rites performed to pacify the spirit of the dead, which may otherwise wander.

South Asian Muslims present a truncated and reshuffled version of caste society, a simulacrum. The higher specialists, imam, *qāḍī*, and *ʿālim*, do not, as educated laymen, rank higher (as do the brahmans) than those who employ them; nor do they have ritual efficacy. The lower specialists who are essential to a Muslim way of life, the barbers who circumcise and the butchers who kill sacrificial animals, rank lower than those who employ them. The *faqīr* who receives *zakāt*, performs funeral ceremonies, officiates at shrines (notably at those dedicated to their patron saint Ghāzī Miyān), and organizes festivals dedicated to Ḥasan and Ḥusayn (the Prophet's grandsons), attended by both Sunnīs and Shīʿah, ranks low. Ṣūfī shaykhs, to whom some Muslims look for intercessory services and who rank high, are not analogous to brahmans, for they are made, not born, and their services are not indispensable. The proper ordering of Hindu society into functional classes, the maintenance of the dichotomy of ritual purity and ritual impurity, and the performance of rituals associated with the worship of gods, are necessary in Hinduism for the very functioning of the cosmos; for Islam, society is a situation in which individual Muslims perform acts of servanthood before their Lord; its proper ordering has no efficacy in the running of the world of the sacred.

Islamization in South Asia. Non-Muslims became Muslims more through slow acculturation by reason of a change in social belonging than through a dramatic individual change of attitude and conviction. Muslim rulers' need in South Asia for political brokers between them and the rural population discouraged proselytism of Hindu chiefs by kingdom-builders, while, having discovered that Muslim rulers would employ brahmans and leave Hindu society to itself as long as it paid revenue, brahmans usually preferred to remain brahmans. In a ritually stratified society, conversion of a ruler did not lead to all in his kingdom undergoing conversion too, although tribes freer of ritual hierarchy might follow their leader into Islam. Muslim political power did, however, create an urban milieu where the providers for Muslim garrisons of goods and services socially depressing in Hindu society might find turning Muslim convenient if not advantageous. Deracination and enslavement of captives, male and female, might lead to conversion in hope of better treatment and in search of companionship. As the depressed classes of Hindu society often remained depressed in Muslim society too, and as there are sometimes large numbers of untouchables in villages where Muslim landholders are dominant, the hypothesis of conversion in order to enjoy the greater equality of Islam is challengeable. Some conversion among landholding groups in order to ensure Muslim rulers' support probably did occur.

Ṣūfī shaykhs probably made more converts after death than in life—through pilgrimage to their tombs by those seeking successful exercise of the shaykhs' believed efficacies. Some shaykhs would accept disciples without prior conversion; advance along a spiritual path under Muslim guidance led to acceptance of Islam as a necessary condition of further advance. Attaching oneself to a *qalandār* might not bring one close to scriptural Islam, but it would take one away from previous associations and open the way to further education by revivalists in Islam for descendants. British census reports created the "census Muslim" in the nineteenth century, a Muslim for whom the perception that identification with the "great tradition" of Islam could bring advantages has often spurred greater study and practice of that tradition. Except for the Ismāʿīlīyah, Muslim missionary activity in South Asia has been directed more to awakening faith among those displaying some insignia of Islam than to converting adherents of another faith. It is interesting to speculate on the possible consequences for Islam in South Asia of the present, greatly increased opportunities for South Asian Muslims to acquire a knowledge of the language of the "great tradition" of Islam, namely Arabic. Large-scale migration to Arabia for employment and, especially in Pakistan, Arab aid for Arabic teaching, might transform existing structures of religious and cultural authority.

[*For further discussion of Sufism in India, see* Ṭarīqah *and the biographies of Khusraw, Niẓām al-Dīn Awliyā', and Sirhindī. For modern developments, see* Modernism, *article on* Islamic Modernism; Jamāʿat-i Islāmī; *and the biographies of Ahmad Khan, Ameer Ali, Iqbal, Mawdūdī, and Walī Allāh.*]

BIBLIOGRAPHY

The most comprehensive and scholarly handbook is Annemarie Schimmel's *Islam in the Indian Subcontinent* (Leiden, 1980), which has full bibliographies. Muhammad Mujeeb's *The Indian Muslims* (London, 1967) is a sensitive interpretation of Muslim responses to the South Asian setting. Sufism in South Asia has attracted much attention and some grinding of axes. Athar Abbas Rizvi's *A History of Sufism*, 2 vols. (New Delhi, 1978–1983), draws on rich material in an impressionistic way. Yohanan Friedmann's *Shaykh Aḥmad Sirhindī: An Outline of His Thought and a Study of His Image in the Eyes of Posterity* (Montreal, 1971) aims, successfully, to correct modern misconceptions. Monographs analyzing Shah Walī Allāh's thought in its full historical setting have yet to appear, but G. N. Jalbani's *Teachings of Shah Waliyullah of Delhi*, 2d ed. (Lahore, 1973), and Athar Abbas Rizvi's *Shāh Wali-Allah and His Times* (Canberra, 1980), the latter with an exhaustive bibliography, are useful compendia. Richard Maxwell Eaton's *Sufis of Bijapur, 1300–1700: Social Roles of Sufis in Medieval India* (Princeton, 1978) is a pioneer work in its field. Asim Roy's *The Islamic Syncretistic Tradition in Bengal* (Princeton, 1984) is an original demonstration of how the exogenous religion of Islam was remolded as an effective appeal in a region with a vigorous autochthonous culture.

For modern developments, Aziz Ahmad's *Islamic Modernism in India and Pakistan 1857–1964* (London, 1967) is the standard survey. Also recommended is Wilfred Cantwell Smith's *Modern Islām in India*, rev. ed. (New York, 1972). Christian Troll's *Sayyid Ahmad Khan: A Reinterpretation of Muslim Theology* (New Delhi, 1978) is authoritative and contains original translations from Sayyid Ahmad Khan's writings. Annemarie Schimmel's *Gabriel's Wing: A Study into the Religious Ideas of Sir Muhammad Iqbal* (Leiden, 1963) is the essential work of reference. Barbara Metcalf's fine effort of scholarly empathy, *Islamic Revival in British India: Deoband, 1860–1900* (Princeton, 1982), in fact covers more than the Deobandi scholars. For a sample of Mawdūdī's writing, see Syed Abul ʿAla Maudoodi's *The Islamic Law and Constitution*, 2d ed., translated and edited by Khurshid Ahmad (Lahore, 1960).

Significant advances in the study of Muslim social behavior are reflected in three works edited by Imtiaz Ahmad: *Caste and Social Stratification among Muslims in India*, 2d rev. ed. (New Delhi, 1973), *Family, Kinship and Marriage among Muslims in India* (New Delhi, 1976), and *Ritual and Religion among Muslims in India* (Columbia, Mo., 1982). Valuable new insights are provided in two articles by Marc Gaborieau: "Life Cycle Ceremonies of Converted Muslims in Nepal and Northern India," in *Islam in Asia*, vol. 1, *South Asia*, edited by Yohanan Friedmann (Jerusalem, 1984), pp. 241–262, and "Typologie des spécialistes religieux dans le sous-continent indien: Les limites de l'islamisation," *Archives de sciences sociales des religions* 55 (1983): 29–51.

PETER HARDY

Islam in Southeast Asia

Southeast Asia is in some respects a forgotten world of Islam, for much the same reasons as its counterparts in West and East Africa. Neither its arrival nor its development there was spectacular, and the local languages that were to be adopted by Muslim communities did not become vehicles for works of universal and commanding stature as had Arabic, Persian, Turkish, and some of the vernaculars of the Indian subcontinent. Yet, Islam in Southeast Asia has its own styles and its own temper and intellectual traditions. Its sacral practices and folk beliefs that color and live alongside the profession of Islam no more invalidate that basic allegiance than do the sacral practices and folk beliefs of Arab Muslims. Indeed, Southeast Asia is the home of almost one-third of the world's Muslims. Indonesia alone, with over 130 million Muslims, is the largest such community in the world.

Historical Geography

Southeast Asia is best described as a great archipelago, a huge land mass that juts southward between the Indian subcontinent and China and then fragments at its extremity into a complex of thousands of islands, the largest of which are Sumatra, Borneo, and Java, while the smallest hardly registers on the map. Today this region is identified with the modern nation-states of Burma, Vietnam, Laos, Kampuchea, Thailand, Malaysia, Singapore, Brunei, Indonesia, and the Philippines. All of these nation-states have Muslim communities. In Burma, Kampuchea, and Vietnam they are insignificant minorities. In Thailand, the Muslim community, though still a minority, has a distinct profile. In Malaysia, Indonesia, and Brunei, on the other hand, Islam has an imposing position. Farther to the east, in the Philippines, it constitutes a significant cultural minority that is in some respects a part of the Philippine nation, but in others, the nucleus of a distinct national entity.

Structures in Transition. In seeking to understand the historical evolution and contemporary significance of these communities, it is necessary to distinguish between the modern period of nation-states, on the one hand, which derive from the growth of local nationalisms, and, on the other hand, the traditional distribution of centers of power in Southeast Asia. With the creation of nation-states such as Indonesia and Malaysia, the establishment of capital cities in Jakarta or Kuala Lumpur has made these centers a focus of the national personality of the political entities in which they are set. They are the gateway, the immediate point of identification, the seat of government, to which their inhabitants turn. They have a status that defines the other parts of the country as provinces.

Nevertheless, and although it might seem, from a contemporary perspective, that these nations have always existed in some form or another and that their present role derives simply from the expulsion of colonial powers and the recovery of national sovereignty, the reality is far more complex and the results more radical. In fact, the creation of such states has turned the traditional world of Southeast Asia on its head. The role of capital cities with a strong central authority dominating the political, economic, and religious life of the region is very recent.

Traditionally, centers of political power in Southeast Asia were distributed among a wide range of focal points that served as harbors for the exchange and transshipment of goods; these points became the sites of port cities, which from time to time grew strong enough to wield an extensive political authority. Such sites were diverse, discrete, numerous, scattered, and largely unstable centers of activity; they had relations with each other on the basis of rivalry and self-interest, without the direct hegemony of a central authority or any stable and continuing point of reference. Unlike the great cities of the Middle East and South Asia, which enjoyed stability over centuries, if not millennia (one need only mention Cairo, Alexandria, Damascus, Baghdad, or Delhi), centers of power in traditional Southeast Asia rarely maintained their position for more than a century, and the authority they enjoyed was very different from that of the modern capital cities of, for example, Kuala Lumpur and Jakarta. The historiography of the region, in its many languages, reflects this character in the emphasis that it lays on genealogy in its accounts of the origins of settlements.

These circumstances have important implications for an understanding of Islam and the processes of islamization in the region. On the one hand, its origins need to be seen in the planting of numerous local traditions of Islam at focal points in the archipelago. In the course of time, these traditions coalesced and emerged for a while as Islamic city-states or fissiparated and disappeared as significant entities, to be succeeded by new ones. On the other hand, the establishment of modern nation-states with single centers of authority has laid the foundation for a new kind of Islamic tradition with a national character, and these centers in turn have exercised a normative influence on the development of such traditions.

The Diversity of Southeast Asia. From earliest times, Southeast Asia has been a region with a variety of peoples, social structures, means of livelihood, cultures, and religions. Denys Lombard, admittedly writing of the modern period, puts it this way:

> We are in fact dealing with several levels of mentality. . . . The thought processes of fringe societies in which "potlatch" is a prevailing custom (the Toraja); those of concentric agrarian societies (the Javanese states and their off-shoots at Jogja and Surakarta); those of trading societies (Malay towns, *pasisir* [Javanese coastal centers]); those of the societies living in large modern towns, and above all, the interplay of these various processes on each other, and their inter-relationships.

If the first broad distinction to be made is temporal and political, between the constellation of modern nation-states and that of the traditional period, another is geographical: between continental (excluding the Malay Peninsula) and insular Southeast Asia. The former includes the states of Vietnam, Kampuchea, and Thailand; the latter, the Malay Peninsula and the islands of what are now Indonesia and the southern Philippines.

To be sure, each has economic and social elements in common—settled rice cultivation, slash-and-burn shifting cultivation, fishing and seafaring, trading and piracy, gold mining, along with elements of megalithic culture, ancestor worship, and the numerous rituals and beliefs associated with rice cultivation. Yet they are separated by a division into two great language families—the Austronesian, of which the most important representatives are Malay and Javanese, and the Mon Khmer, of which the most important are Thai and Burmese—and the communications barrier between these families is much greater than that between related members within one family or the other. Equally important, although both parts of the great archipelago received a tincture of Hindu influence well before the birth of Islam, in continental Southeast Asia, Theravāda Buddhism became dominant, whereas Mahāyāna Buddhism in one form or another was practiced in the southern regions, in particular, Srivijaya (seventh to fourteenth centuries) based on South Sumatra, and Majapahit (thirteenth to fifteenth centuries) in East Java. These great divisions correspond to those regions in which Islam secured a dominant position and those in which it did not.

Southeast Asia in World Trade. The great archipelago of Southeast Asia lies across the sea routes between the Indian Ocean and the China Sea. In both divisions of the region there were some points open to a range of contacts with the outside world, and others where access was more difficult and where a lifestyle conditioned by such remoteness was preserved.

For centuries before the Christian era, the Indian Ocean had been dominated by the Yemenis, who traded in gold, gums, spices, rhinoceros horn, and ivory from the east coast of Africa. For this early period, it is not possible to identify place names accurately, but it is known that the Yemenis brought their goods to the land of gold, *suvarna bhumi,* the term by which Southeast Asia was referred to in some Sanskrit texts.

In the beginning of the Christian era, both continental and insular Southeast Asia reacted to, and in a remarkable way were fecundated by, contact with Indian cultural influences carried to the focal trading centers referred to earlier, which were to be creative for over a millennium. A constant succession of Hindu and Buddhist influences was established in particular regions, with various phases carrying the different traditions, schools, and artistic styles of these great religions and modifying each other as they were adapted to the new environment.

The Coming of Islam

Up to the tenth century CE there is very little evidence of the presence of Islam in Southeast Asia. Indeed, although the Portuguese conquerors of Malacca in 1511 give us some important information about the progress of Islam in the region, apart from a few archaeological remains, reports by Chinese merchants, and the records of individual travelers such as Marco Polo and Ibn Baṭṭūṭah, both of whom give descriptions of North Sumatra, there is little concrete documentation until the seventeenth century. By that time, however, with the appearance of the Dutch and British trading companies in the region, the evidence of widespread islamization becomes overwhelming. The territories of the Islamic commonwealth in Southeast Asia were so vast that the process of their creation has been called "the second expansion of Islam," alluding to the original expansion from Arabia into North Africa and the Fertile Crescent. Unlike that first period of extraordinary growth in the seventh century, however, the spread of Islam in Southeast Asia was hesitant, modest, and discreet: what was achieved in one century in the Middle East took virtually a millennium in Southeast Asia.

There is too little evidence to document the beginnings of this process, yet a reasonable working hypothesis may be formulated as follows: as soon as there were Muslim sailors aboard ships sailing under whatever flag in the Indian Ocean trading system and disembarking goods or individuals at points in Southeast Asia, there was the possibility of a Muslim presence at those points. This could have been as early as the end of the seventh century. Hardly anything is known of the history of trading settlements along the littoral of Southeast Asia during this period; however, reliable evidence for the presence of Muslims in China from the beginning of the eighth century, if not before, suggests that Muslim seamen and merchants were already breaking their long voyages at one or another of the numerous natural harbors along the coasts of Sumatra, the Malay Peninsula, Borneo, and northern Java. The unloading of goods to await transshipment with the change of the monsoon, the establishment of warehouses and semipermanent settlements, and trading and intermarriage—and other relationships—with the local peoples were all factors that combined to establish small but viable Muslim communities.

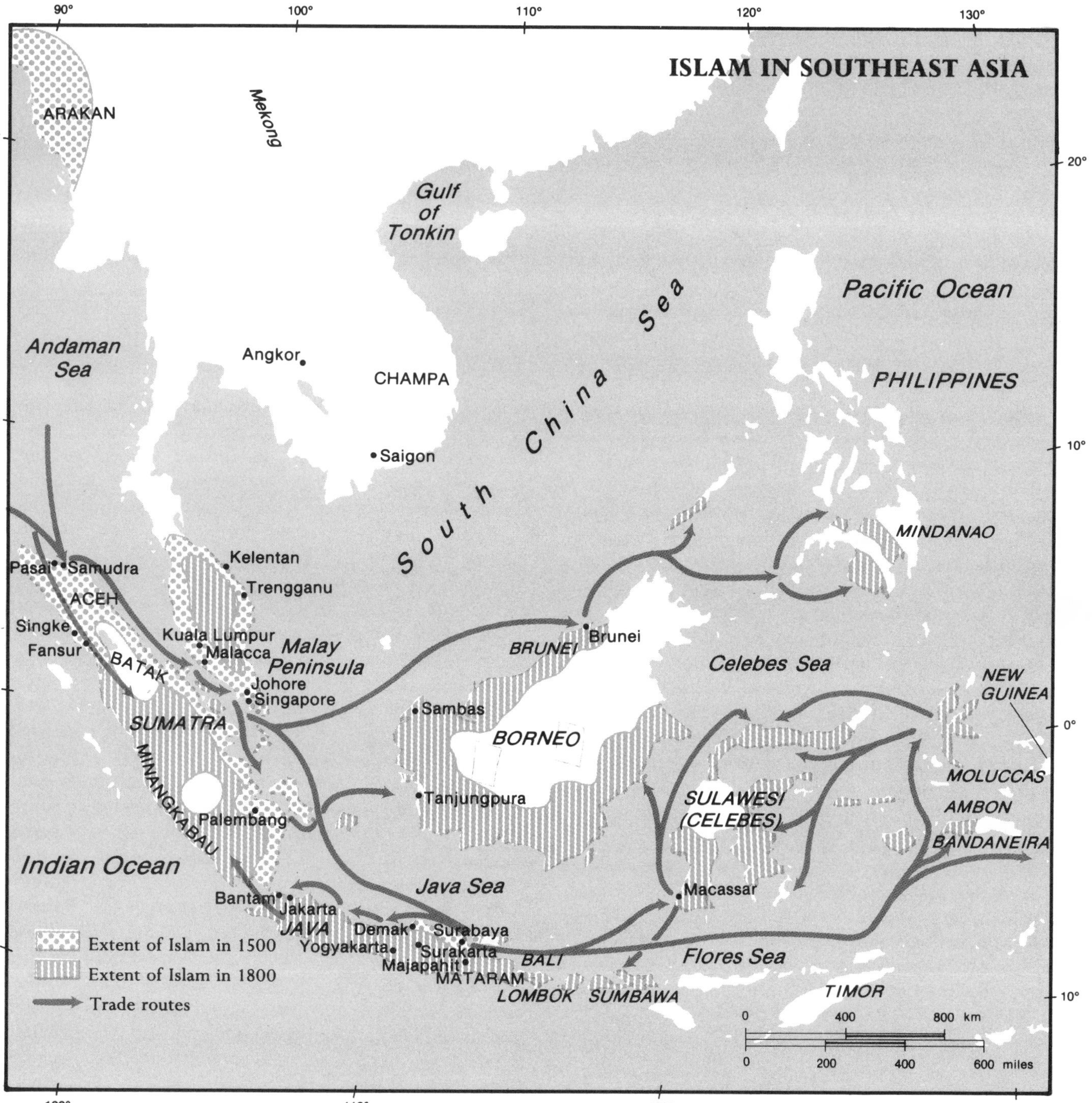

Given the diversity and discontinuities of the region, the provenance of Southeast Asian Islam is not a practical topic for discussion, although hypotheses have located it anywhere from Egypt to Bengal. One thing is certain: all movement of ideas and peoples from West and South Asia to Southeast Asia is related to the maritime history of the Indian Ocean (although it is still possible that communities made part of the journey by land across the Indian subcontinent, or even the "great circle" route via the Silk Road through Central Asia, and then by sea from Canton to the islands). The greater the number of Muslims involved in the trading system, the greater the diversity of the Muslim tradition that became diffused, and the greater the probability of Muslims coming together in sufficient numbers to generate a critical mass—a Muslim community that could become stable through intermarriage with local women and play a distinctive role among other communities on equal terms. This community may have already included Arabs in the early years of the Islamic commonwealth; from that era, no information has survived. But the process of consolidation was slow. It is not until the thirteenth century that Islamic communities appear with a political profile, as port city-states ruled by sultans. The earliest of these sultanates was that of Pasai, on the east coast of North Sumatra; it was succeeded by others. The appearance of such city-states must be seen as the culmination of a long period of Muslim presence with a rather lower profile, and a circumstance that has made the ethnic mix of the communities difficult to define.

Once Islam achieved a political presence in the region, further growth and the exercise of political power became possible. By this time the trading system of the Indian Ocean was largely in Muslim hands; this assured economic power to Muslims, and Muslim mercantile law served to generate business confidence. The power and self-confidence of the Muslim states gave them a position as power brokers and allies. Marriage alliances that required a profession of Islam doubtless had a role as well.

First Traces. The earliest archaeological evidence is slight: a lone pillar in the region of Phanrang on the mid-east coast of Vietnam, inscribed in Arabic and dating from the tenth century. The French scholar Ravaisse (quoted by S. Q. Fatimi in *Islam Comes to Asia*) believes it to indicate that

> there existed there in the eleventh century an urban population of whom we know little. They were very different from the indigenous people in race, belief and habits. Their ancestors must have come about a century earlier, and must have married native women. They were merchants and craftsmen living in a perfectly well-organized society mixing more and more with the natives. They asked one of themselves to act as their representative and defender with respect to the authorities of the place. He was called Shaikh al-Suq ["master of the market"], and was assisted by the Naqib (a merchant or craftsman in charge of the management of the community to which he belonged). Along with him were "notables who, enriched by their commerce, occupied an important place."

Another piece of evidence from roughly the same period suggests that there was some kind of Muslim presence at Leren on the north coast of Java. This is a tombstone marking the grave of a merchant's daughter. It provides no certain evidence of a Muslim community; even the date cannot be taken for granted since tombstones were frequently imported long after a burial.

In Trengganu, an east-coast state on the Malay Peninsula, a fragment of a stone pillar inscribed in Malay in Arabic script and dating from between 1321 and 1380, suggests the presence of a Muslim community. By the fifteenth century there is sporadic but more substantial evidence of Muslims in the East Javanese empire of Majapahit, again from gravestones. Probably they belonged to communities of merchants, but this too is hardly more than surmise. Just as there were Muslims in Java, there is evidence that there were Muslims in the great Buddhist empire of Srivijaya (seventh to thirteenth centuries) based on South Sumatra, an empire that thrived on trade and maintained close relations with China and India.

The earliest evidence that substantiates not simply the presence of Muslims in the region but the existence of an Islamic maritime sultanate dates from the thirteenth century. This is a tombstone of the first Muslim ruler of Pasai, in North Sumatra, and reports of foreign travelers confirm that his subjects were Muslims. What circumstances enabled the Muslim community to achieve a critical mass and generate a state in which the ruler could style himself sultan, and what processes led to this event, we cannot tell. Likewise there is little evidence as to the ethnic composition of this state: to what extent was it local, to what extent foreign? (And even the term "foreign" at this time begs a number of questions.) Many of the titles and names attributed to the personalities of this sultanate in a local chronicle have a South Indian ring to them.

Nonetheless, from this point on, the documentation of Islam at the political level is relatively straightforward, and it is possible to chronicle the emergence of states with Islamic rulers. Even though internal records are sparse and their human and cultural dynamics remain in darkness, at the very least their names are recorded by foreign visitors.

The Sultanates. I have posited Pasai as the earliest Muslim state in the Malay world and its ruler as the first sultan there. The only evidence of his life comes from his tombstone. But Pasai was at least referred to by Marco Polo and Ibn Baṭṭūṭah in the thirteenth and fourteenth centuries. Although the extent of its political authority is not known, it occupied a strategic position at the entrance to the straits of Malacca and was a convenient point for exchanging goods and taking on board supplies of water and firewood. Moreover, by making alliances with either pirates or nascent states on the other side of the straits, it was able to ensure that shipping did not go elsewhere, and that port taxes were paid.

Malacca. Malacca, on the west coast of the Malay Peninsula, inherited the mantle of Pasai. Far more is known of its history than that of Pasai, from both local and foreign sources. It became Muslim shortly after its foundation around 1400, and via its dependencies, both on the Malay Peninsula, where it established the dynasties of the Malay sultanates, and on the east coast of Sumatra, it served as a conduit for Muslim influence to other parts of the archipelago. Various factors were involved here: local traders from the neighboring islands were attracted to its emporium, Muslim traders from Bengal, India, and further afield found scope for business activities opened up in its trading partners and dependencies, and it attracted foreign *'ulamā'* (religious scholars; sg., *'ālim*), principally from India, although many of them may have had Arab blood and used this Arab descent to their advantage. Although Malacca held an important position, however, it was not unique. There were many smaller states that played an analogous role along the littoral of East Sumatra, the north coast of Java, Borneo, Sulawesi (Celebes), and later the Spice Islands (Moluccas) and the southern Philippines. In every case the same kind of processes that were illustrated at Malacca were taking place, perhaps on a smaller scale, perhaps on a larger scale, and they had been happening even before the birth of Malacca. It must be stressed that there is no "big bang" explanation for the coming of Islam to Southeast Asia; such claims as the Portuguese statement that Java was converted from Malacca must be regarded as hyperbole.

Smaller states. After Malacca fell to the Portuguese in 1511, it was such smaller states that were to grow to eminence: Aceh, Palembang, Banten, Ceribon, Demak, Surabaya, and Makassar, as well as smaller centers in the Spice Islands. Each of them became integrated into the Muslim trading system, each became a center of Islamic learning, and each, by a continuing process of osmosis, attracted people from the interior into contact with these cities. In every case, networks of family, Ṣūfī order (*ṭarīqah*), guild, and trade association relationships gradually served to diffuse Islam back into the interior, although it was transmitted at different levels of intensity and perceived in rather different ways according to the cultural backgrounds of the various communities.

Special attention should be drawn to Aceh, which first came to prominence in the 1520s and reached its apogee during the reign of Sultan Iskandar Muda (1607–1636). During the first half of the seventeenth century it was the dominant economic and political power of the region. It conquered the northern half of the Malay Peninsula and northern and parts of central Sumatra, gaining control of the pepper areas and enforcing a trading monopoly. Aceh was the first Muslim state in the region to have extended intercourse with Europe. It is also noteworthy for a surviving legacy of Islamic learning: for the first time we have historical information about a state in the region generating works of Islamic scholarship that remain accessible to us, some of which are used in schools throughout the Malay world even today. In addition, we are able to identify individual Acehnese scholars, both in Aceh and in the Arabian centers of Mecca and Medina, and the teachers with whom they studied. Indeed, of the great ministers of state between 1600 and 1630, Shams al-Dīn was a noted *'ālim*. There are eyewitness reports from British, Dutch, and French sailors on the celebration of the conclusion of the fast of Ramaḍān ('Īd al-Fiṭr) and the festival of the sacrifice marking the climax of the pilgrimage rites in Mecca. It is also possible to establish and describe some of the relations between Aceh, the Mughal court, and the Ottoman empire. [*See* Acehnese Religion.]

The Islamic history of Aceh during this period is better known than that of any of its neighbors, but analogous centers of lesser political power played a major role elsewhere in the region as Islam moved inland during the seventeenth century. In Sumatra, for example, the inland highlands of the Minangkabau region, territories rich in gold and pepper and which for centuries had established this part of the island in a network of trading systems, became Muslim. This area was to put a distinctive stamp on its interpretation and realization of Islam by maintaining a matrilineal social structure alongside a commitment to Islam that was among the staunchest in the archipelago.

Another inland region where Islam became established was the state of Mataram in Central Java, which was, until its defeat by the United Dutch East India Company in 1629, the largest single state on the island. Even after the defeat, it maintained this status, a status that added special significance to the fact that its ruler, Susuhunan Agung (1613–1645), assumed the title of sultan and in 1633 established the Islamic calendrical system in Java.

The Colonial Era. The expansion of the United Dutch East India Company as a political power in the region and its increasing monopoly of international trade severely dislocated the traditional rhythm of the rise and fall of states in the region as well as the economic life. Company power continued to grow to the point that it was not simply a state among states but was virtually invulnerable. During this period of colonial expansion from the seventeenth century on, Islam, according to conventional wisdom, was in decline. Decline, however, is a word that conceals more than it reveals. Throughout the region more people were gradually drawn into the new religion, to the basic recognition of transcendence implicit in the confession "There is no god but God." To be sure, numerous cults survived alongside this confession, together with practices and rituals and the use of spells and magical formulas that derived from the Indic and megalithic traditions. Nevertheless there was a continuing momentum toward the subordination and finally the subsuming of the spiritual concepts of such traditions into the terminology of Islam: thus numerous Javanese spirits were largely included within the Islamic category of beings, the *jinn.* Doubtless the intensity of response to the more exclusive demands of Islam waxed and waned, yet amid all these communities where Islam had been planted, some degree of formal recognition was given to Islamic law, particularly in relation to diet, to burial of the dead, to marriage, to circumcision, and to the fast, even where the performance of the daily prayer was lax. Indeed it is striking how the pre-Islamic cult of the dead reflected in the building of great mausolea for the Javanese god-kings, and the extravagant sacrifices of buffaloes still carried on today in non-Muslim areas such as the Torajas (Central Sulawesi), completely disappeared with the acceptance of Islam.

The pilgrimage too was important; some individuals stayed to study for years in the Middle East; The Ṣūfī orders also played their role, and religious teachers, keeping on the circuit, gave fresh life to communities and religious schools and held the ear of local rulers. The constant retelling of stories of the prophets and the heroes of Islam and their cultural adaptation to local conditions gradually created a unitary and universalistic frame of reference for local and world history and established Islamic concepts—of the creation, of the sending of God's messengers culminating in Muḥammad, of the community, and eventually of the resurrection of the body—as the norm and benchmark by which all competing systems of ideas were to be measured and into which they were largely to be assimilated.

The Era of Reforms. This spread of sensitivity to and identification with an Islamic ethos, although at times mixed and not totally unequivocal, rendered such communities responsive to movements that caught the imagination and fired the enthusiasm of Muslims in other parts of the Muslim world. One such movement was the Wahhābī uprising in Arabia during the last quarter of the eighteenth century. Inspired by the ideal of cleansing Islam from accretions and practices that were held to be incompatible with *tawḥīd,* the oneness of God, it resorted to force to put Islamic law and ritual observances into effect.

The Wahhābī legacy. The enthusiastic preaching of such doctrines by a group of scholars returning from Arabia in 1803 led to the rise of the Padri movement in the Minangkabau area of Sumatra. This movement set itself against the traditional elite, which it regarded as compromising with non-Islamic practices and values, whether reflected in the lifestyle of the traditional rulers or in the matrilineal descent system of the region. Their reaction was to lead to a civil war that gave the Dutch government an opportunity to intervene on the part of the traditionalists and to defeat the leader of the revolt, Imam Bondjol, in 1842.

It may well have been also that the Java War (1826–1830) between rival members of the royal court likewise took part of its energy from this ferment in Islam. It should not be imagined that the expansion of Islam was always peaceful, or that even the relationships among different traditions of Islam were without conflict. One need only recall the persecution and book burning in Aceh between 1637 and 1642, sometimes referred to as an attempt by the so-called Shuhūdīyah ("unity of witness") school of mysticism to suppress the Wujūdīyah ("unity of being") tradition; the wars waged by Sultan Agung's successor, Amangkurat I, in the 1660s against the legalistic Muslim communities of the north coast of Java; and the scatological diatribes written in Javanese to make fun of the professional *'ulamā'* in the nineteenth century.

The same channels that had brought the aftermath of the Wahhābī movement to the then-Dutch East Indies, were, about a century later, to bring the Islamic reformist movement to Sumatra, Java, and the Malay Peninsula, to be diffused from there to southern Thailand, and paradoxically, from Ḥadramī communities in Java back to southern Arabia.

The impact of 'Abduh and Rashīd Riḍā. In fact, appearance of the reform movement inspired by Jamāl al-Dīn al-Afghānī and pioneered by Muḥammad 'Abduh soon fecundated a vigorous counterpart in Southeast Asia. In particular, students from the Malay world in the Middle East, especially those studying at al-Azhar University in Cairo, were inspired by 'Abduh, Rashīd Riḍā, and their followers, and as they returned to Malaya and the Indies, they carried the new ideas with them. The effect that they had in their homeland was quite dramatic. 'Abduh's reformist program was based on four main points: the purification of Islam from corrupting influences and practices; the reformation of Muslim education; the reformation of Islamic doctrine in the light of modern thought; and the defense of Islam. The establishment of the reformist journal *Al-manār* (The Lighthouse), published between 1898 and 1936 under the editorship of 'Abduh and later that of Riḍā, directly inspired two counterparts in the Malay world. *Al-imām* (The Imam), published in Singapore between 1906 and 1908, transmitted the views of *Al-manār* and 'Abduh's earlier journal, *Al-'urwah al-wuthqā* (The Strongest Bond), and published translations of their articles into Malay. Its layout followed that of *Al-manār*. *Al-munīr* (The Radiant), established in the major West Sumatran port town of Padang, was published between 1911 and 1916; it too referred regularly to *Al-manār* and published translations from the Egyptian journal.

Al-manār in turn reflected the great interest that it generated in Southeast Asia: from the very year of its founding, it included articles, in Arabic, either written by Southeast Asian Muslims studying in Cairo or sent from a wide range of places in the Indies, including Singapore, Batavia, Malang, Palembang, Surabaya, and Sambas (Borneo). A 1930 communication from Sambas was particularly important, for it requested Rashīd Riḍā to put to the famous writer Shakīb Arslān certain questions relating to reasons for the backwardness of Muslims and the progress of other peoples. The response to this request, first published in three parts in *Al-manār*, was to become Arslān's well-known book *Limādhā ta'akhkhara al-Muslimūn wa-taqaddama al-ākharūn* (Why Do the Muslims Stay Behind and the Others Progress?), which was in due course to be translated into Malay. The episode is important because it indicates the seriousness and care of the response of Egyptian scholars to the queries and difficulties of their Southeast Asian coreligionists.

There is an interesting range of Southeast Asia–related topics raised in *Al-manār*. An 1898 article, for example, reports on a request by some Javanese Muslims to the Dutch colonial government for them to be allowed to acquire Ottoman citizenship; other articles address complaints of Dutch harassment of Muslims, problems of marriages between sayyids (the Muslim elite) and Muslim commoners, and the humiliations of quarantine regulations imposed on Muslims making the pilgrimage. A 1909 article from Palembang tells how *Al-manār* had inspired the Muslims of the region to form associations and financial unions to support Islamic schools to teach Arabic, the religious disciplines, and secular subjects. Two years later, another interesting entry praises the periodical for creating an intellectual movement among Muslims and describes how a school director had been inspired by *Al-manār* to introduce the Berlitz method of teaching foreign languages in his school. [*See also* Modernism, *article on* Islamic Modernism.]

The educational dimension of the reform program quickly made itself felt. Here a few examples will suffice. The work of To'Kenali (1866–1933), a scholar from Kelantan, an east-coast state of the Malay Peninsula, is representative of many, including some who became famous in Patani and Cambodia (Kampuchea) at the turn of the century. He went to Mecca at the age of twenty and stayed in the Middle East for twenty-two years before returning to Kelantan in 1908. In 1903 he traveled to Egypt to visit al-Azhar and other educational institutions. It is possible that he met ʿAbduh on this occasion. There is no doubt, however, that he had absorbed the educational ideals of the movement. He quickly became famous as a teacher was appointed assistant to the *muftī* in Kelantan with responsibility for Islamic education in the state, and set up a network of schools. He introduced Malay textbooks in religious knowledge and devised a system of graded instruction in Arabic grammar. Indeed, one of his students (born in Mecca of Malay parents in 1895), on returning to Kelantan in 1910, was inspired by him to compile an Arabic-Malay dictionary with entries and definitions in part based on the Arabic classic *Al-munjid;* published in 1927, the Malay work is still popular.

The reform, however, was reflected not only in textbooks, but also in classroom organization. The traditional method of teaching was known as the *ḥalaqah* ("study circle"), where students, irrespective of age, would sit in a circle around the teacher, who would present material to be learned by rote. The introduction of the classroom method, where the students sat in rows and used graded texts, together with the encouragement of active class participation, was a remarkable change of style. No less remarkable was the inclusion of secular subjects in the curriculum. Schools inspired by the reform movement multiplied in various parts of the archipelago, sometimes identified with individuals, sometimes initiated within the framework of an organization. Many sprang up and disappeared like mushrooms.

Of those founded by individuals, one that became important was the Sumatra Thawalib school founded in 1918. Another was the Sekolah Diniyah Putri in Padang Panjang, a religious school for girls founded in 1921 by a woman named Rahmah al-Yunusiyah. Designed to train students in the basic rules and practices of Islam and in the understanding of the principles and applications of Islamic law, particularly in matters of special concern to women, the school also set out to give girls an education in those matters that would enable them to run their homes efficiently and care for the health and education of their children. While from one standpoint the discipline of the institution was very strict and the scope for individual development narrow, it won the confidence of isolated village communities, and in fact, its students gained wider horizons than those girls who remained in the interior.

This school was a strikingly original institution (which was to inspire the founding of the Kullīyat al-Banāt within al-Azhar in 1957). Yet it was based on very simple premises: a universalistic interpretation of

Islam, and the founder's determination to establish an institution that would present itself in every respect as an alternative to the Dutch system, from curriculum to the yearly cycle of festivals and the Islamic calendar (Friday was the day off) to student dress. It guarded its independence and refused offers of subsidy from the Dutch government. It still flourishes today and during the 1930s had branches in Java and the Malay Peninsula.

The Muhammadiyah. The most famous and long-lived of all socioreligious reformist movements in the Indies was the Muhammadiyah, founded in 1912 in Yogyakarta (Central Java) by Kiyai Haji Dahlan. One of the goals of its founder was to inculcate the ideas of the reformists concerning the purification of Islam from traditional accretions, in particular from the animistic beliefs that were so much part of the worldview of the Javanese peasantry, and from the religious attitudes and values of the upper classes, for whom the Hindu-Buddhist traditions of the pre-Islamic period—traditions embodied in the Javanese shadow theater—were still very much alive.

One particular target was the cult of saints' tombs. The movement consciously adopted the institutional structures of the Dutch, and its members made a careful study of the techniques of Christian missionary organizations. Carrying on vigorous missionary activities, it expanded into journalism and publishing and established mosques, religious endowments, orphanages, and clinics. But its central role was in education, where it set up an entire system from primary school to teacher training colleges. Like To'Kenali in Kelantan, the Muhammadiyah carried on the impulse generated by Muḥammad ʿAbduh to reform the traditional Islamic educational system—by grading teaching materials and classes, by sitting students at desks faced by teachers with blackboards, and by assessing their progress with formal examinations and the award of individual marks that determined when they could move from one grade to the next.

The Muhammadiyah's strict and responsible methods of organization and financial management ensured its stability, and by the 1930s it had established branches as far afield as North, Central, and South Sumatra, Borneo, and Sulawesi, thus taking on a protonational character.

Another aspect of the reformist movement was its campaign against the Ṣūfī *ṭarīqah*. For the reformers the *ṭarīqah* represented the one element in traditional Islam that most contributed to the backwardness of Muslims and the lack of respect they had in the world. They held that the *ṭarīqah* promoted a passive other-worldliness, that it discouraged initiative, and that the dedication to the shaykh, the head of the branch, overshadowed devotion to the Prophet and God himself. In addition, the ascetic exercises of members and their fondness for reciting sacred formulas were considered intellectually harmful, often paving the way for the absorption of non-Islamic practices. In short, the reformists took over and applied all the arguments marshaled against the *ṭarīqah* by the *Al-manār* tradition. There is a reasonable documentation of debates between the two sides on the issue. In the Dutch East Indies, the Ṣūfī orders appeared to be almost a spent force by the 1930s, with their followers to be found only in the remoter rural areas. The qualification is important, for of religious life in these remoter rural areas little is known. On the Malay Peninsula they fared better and still maintain a social role there. Indeed, one of the leading figures of religious reform and revival in Kelantan was Wan Musa, who, when he studied in Mecca with his father, was introduced to the theosophy of Muḥyī al-Dīn ibn al-ʿArabī and inducted into the Shādhilīyah *ṭarīqah*. He introduced the reforms of ʿAbduh and Rashīd Riḍā into Kelantan and rejected *taqlīd*, or unquestioning acceptance of precedent, yet defended the institutional role of the *ṭarīqah* and preserved the content of Ṣūfī doctrine, stressing in his instruction the role of intellect, intuition, and emotion. [*See also* Ṭarīqah.]

Some idea of the residual role of the Indonesian *ṭarīqah* at a public level by 1955 can be gained from the fact that an attempt to obtain representation for these movements in the national parliament at the first general election resulted in the election of one member, a Naqshbandī. This, of course, need mean nothing more than that many *ṭarīqah* members did not see the national parliament as a place for *ṭarīqah* representation.

There was, however, a response to the reform movement in the Indies, and this was the Nahdatul Ulama (lit., "revival of the *ʿulamā*'"), founded in 1926. This movement was not designed to defend the *ṭarīqah*, or even the mystical tradition, although in practice it did so. It stood for the traditional role of the *ʿulamā'* and opposed the reformists' reliance on the Qur'ān and *sunnah* alone. Adherence to one or another of the four schools of law as the basis for the application of *fiqh* was basic, and in Indonesia this meant, in practice, the Shāfiʿī school.

Postwar politics. With the Japanese occupation, all Muslim associations were dissolved and then reconstituted into an umbrella organization encompassing both reformists and traditionalists, the Majlis Shura Muslimin Indonesia, or Consultative Assembly of Indonesian Muslims, known widely by its acronym Masyumi. After the war, the organization broke up into two main wings: the one that kept the name Masyumi became the political wing of the reformist movement and drew most of its strength from Sumatra and the large towns in Java, while the other, Nahdatul Ulama, now took a public role as a political party and derived most of its strength from the rural areas of East Java. An index to the standing of the parties, and therefore the distribution of attitudes, is furnished by the results of the 1955 elections, in which the Masyumi won 57 seats and the Nahdatul Ulama won 45 out of a total of more than 250. Even taking into account the seats held by minor religious parties, this meant that more than half of the Muslim electorate had cast its vote for nonreligious parties.

In Malaysia, up to the time of independence in 1957 religious parties did not have a high political profile: to be a Malay is, by definition, to be a Muslim, to live by Malay custom, and to speak the Malay language. In a country in which the native inhabitants were less than half the total population, had scarcely any urban presence or economic power, and could only manifest their identity in the persons and ceremonial role of the sultans and in the profession of Islam—a situation in which the Malay language and even survival of the Malay race was at stake—there was no scope for splitting up the components of the political package that became known as the United Malays National Organization into competing religious allegiances. Indeed, it is striking that with Malayan independence in 1957, Islam became a national religion without the creation of an Islamic state in Malaya (now Malaysia). The situation, however, is not quite what it seems, for this is at the national level. At the state level, under the rule of the hereditary sultans, Islamic law is enforced upon Muslims, and offenses such as breaking the fast are punishable by religious courts.

Islam in a Spiritual and Cultural Role

The modalities by which islamization established itself in the region and its subsequent cultural achievements are far richer in character than a purely political survey can communicate, although the political survey provides a necessary framework. Discussion of such issues must be based on the territories that are now Malaysia and Indonesia, the core Islamic areas of the region. Compared to these regions, and despite their intrinsic interest and importance, Thailand, the other mainland states, and the Philippines are fringe areas.

Let us consider in a little more detail the cases we have mentioned. The community at Phanrang lived and governed itself apart from its neighbors. Typologically this situation is difficult to account for. Thus the hypothesis that it was founded by descendants of a community of Shīʿī refugees who fled from a persecution by the Umayyad governor al-Ḥajjāj (d. 714) is plausible. It will be noted later that although today the region is Sunnī, there are some remnants of Shīʿī influence from the past, such as the commemoration of the martyrdom of Ḥasan and Ḥusayn in a coastal region of western Sumatra.

Processes of Islamization. The descriptions of the sultanate of Pasai referred to earlier make a clear distinction between the Muslim community of the city itself and those people of the hinterland who were still unbelievers. This distinction suggests that an originally foreign community became settled over a number of years, and that an individual with sufficient charisma at one point proclaimed himself sultan. The coastal port of Malacca on the other hand presents an example of a mercantile state whose ruler professed Islam soon after its foundation. The case of Aceh is different again, in that it appears to have arisen after the amalgamation of two small Muslim states in the north of Sumatra into a single state that was to dominate the straits of Malacca for the greater part of the seventeenth century.

The importance of Aceh cannot be overstressed. It was known in popular parlance as the gateway to the Holy Land (Arabia). Aspiring pilgrims and scholars from all parts of the archipelago would make the journey in stages over a period of years. Aceh was the last port of work and residence and study that they would encounter before leaving their own region of the world and heading out across the Bay of Bengal. It was also the first place of call on their return journey. And the intensity of religious education, debate, and teaching in Aceh, as well as the constant movement of peoples of diverse ethnic groups, ensured a wide dissemination of religious ideas and, to some extent, a normalization of religious life through the distribution of networks of religious affiliations. (From the early days, it should be noted, there is evidence of the presence of *ṭarīqah*s.)

The acceptance of Islam by Sultan Agung of Mataram (r. 1613–1646) is a special case. His kingdom was not a port-state but was located in the interior and was based on wet rice cultivation rather than on trade. It was the prestigious heir to the great Śiva Buddha tradition of East Java and included in its territories the sites of the great Buddhist stupa, the Borobudur, and other Hindu and Buddhist shrines built during the seventh, eighth, and ninth centuries. Yet for Agung, this history was not enough, nor was his title of *susuhunan.* To all this he added the title of sultan, purchased from Mecca; thus he assumed a dignity which, although largely symbolic, had a major role in elevating the status of Islam in Java (although this activity should not be confused with the conversion of Java to Islam).

As C. C. Berg points out in a seminal article (1955),

kings and princes operated as factors of acceleration and deceleration of the islamization process in Java. In this instance, Agung played a role of acceleration following his defeat by the Dutch East India Company in 1629. This event turned him toward whatever enemies of the Dutch could be found in the seas and islands of the archipelago: the Portuguese and communities of Muslim merchants. As a Muslim by profession, if not by passion, until 1629, he soon became a Muslim in search of authority and power. Whatever his psychological motivations, he changed the face of his kingdom and its cultural character by introducing the Muslim calendar with the announcement that from 1 Muḥarram 1043 AH, a date corresponding to 8 July 1633 CE, this calendrical system should operate in Java alongside the traditional Javanese system of Saka years. Symbolically this was an act of very great importance, because it meant that the advent of Islam became the event in relation to which other events in Javanese society were to be recorded.

In the last analysis, however, the creative achievement of a religion is to be seen in the lives of the individuals it inspires, the intellectual activity it generates, and the dimensions it adds to spiritual, cultural, and social life. But one of the difficulties in coping with the story of Islam in Southeast Asia is the absence of historical figures to whom one can attribute the early spread of the religion.

It is striking that, in the Malay texts at least, there are no historical figures to whom the primal conversion of a state to Islam can be attributed. The same holds true for the preaching of Islam in Java as presented by Javanese court chronicles. This is not to say that such figures are always nameless, or that they may not be based on individuals who did once exist, but certainly in the way they are presented, there is nothing that could be described as a personality base. In his contribution to Nehemia Levtzion's *Conversion to Islam* (1980), Jones gives an account of ten conversion myths from different parts of the archipelago. The account from the *Sejarah Malayu* (Malay Annals) is typical: the ruler of Malacca had a dream in which he saw Muḥammad, who ordered him to recite the Muslim Shahādah ("witnessing"): "There is no god but God, and Muḥammad is his Messenger." The prophet then told him that the following day, at the time of the afternoon prayer, a ship would arrive from Jidda with a religious teacher on board whom he was to obey. When the king awoke, he found he had been circumcised. At the time foretold on the following day the ship arrived, and the religious teacher came down from it. There and then he performed the afternoon prayer on the beach, and the bystanders gathered round asking: what is this bobbing up and down. The king, on hearing what was happening went down to the beach to welcome him, and together with all his courtiers and subjects embraced Islam.

An intriguing feature of this work is that most of the religious teachers described in its pages are presented as figures of fun. There is the eccentric who takes sling shots at kites flown over his house, and there is the religious teacher who is teased by a drunken court officer because he cannot pronounce Malay words correctly. There is also the mystically inclined teacher who refuses to accept the sultan as a religious disciple unless he leaves his elephant behind at the palace and comes humbly on foot.

Of these figures, one may possibly be identified: Sadar Jahan, the religious adviser to Sultan Ahmad Shah of Malacca. When Ahmad Shah came out on his elephant to face the Portuguese attack that destroyed the city in 1511, Sadar Jahan accompanied the sultan. Under a hail of musket shots he begged his master to retreat to a safer position with the words: "This is no place to discuss the mystical union." He has been identified with a scholar-jurist-diplomat Fayd Allah Bambari, known as Sadr-i Jahan, who was sent by King Ayaz from Gujarat via Jidda to negotiate a defensive wall from Hormuz to Malacca against the Portuguese incursion into the Indian Ocean. He arrived in Malacca by ship in 1509 to stiffen Malaccan resistance to the Portuguese and is presumed to have been killed during the sack of the city. The identification is not wholly certain. Nevertheless, the evidence is sufficient to show that as early as the fifteenth century, religious teachers from various parts of the Muslim world took part in the religious life of the Southeast Asian sultanates. It is also worth noting that the religious figures in the Javanese chronicles are presented without the lightness of touch and irreverence that characterize the Malay figures. They are sometimes identified as numbering eight, but more often nine, a total that has more to do with cosmology than arithmetic, since the number nine indicates the eight points of the compass and the center. Their spheres of influence are distributed among different regions of Java, and they are associated with the origin of elements of Javanese culture such as the Javanese shadow theater and gamelan orchestra, which existed long before Islam. All of them are presented as figures with a mystical insight into the reality of things; they have a role in the founding of dynasties and are not subject to the laws of nature. One of them, Siti Jenar, was executed for uttering words that claimed identity between himself and God. It seems likely that this event—if indeed it occurred—is a doublet of the al-Ḥallāj story.

It is only from the late sixteenth century that it becomes possible to identify individuals among religious teachers, and so to have the foundations for an intellectual and spiritual history of Islam in this region. However, since the information available about such figures is very sparse—biography and, even more, autobiography are undeveloped art forms in Southeast Asia—it is not possible to do much more than situate them within a general framework of the intellectual and spiritual life of the region, as far as this can be established.

Languages. Southeast Asia is an area of great linguistic diversity: there are over three hundred languages in the Indonesian area alone. Of these languages, Malay was known throughout Southeast Asia as a lingua franca as early as the sixteenth century. During the period already discussed, it had also been established as a vernacular of Islam and as a language of the court for areas as far afield and diverse as Malacca, Aceh, and Makassar. It is this very early diffusion of the language, with its religious, economic, cultural, and chancellery roles, that led to its adoption in the twentieth century, in slightly different forms, as the national language of Malaysia and Indonesia, where it became known as Bahasa Malaysia and Bahasa Indonesia, respectively. Of course, other languages related to Malay were to become vehicles of Muslim learning and culture, in particular Javanese, Sundanese, Madurese, and some of the languages of southern Sulawesi. But although some of these, notably Javanese, had a far richer literary tradition than did Malay, none rivaled its widespread authority.

Its role as a language of Islam was also made clear by the well-nigh universal use of a form of the Arabic script for its written transmission, supplanting a script of Indic derivation that was used for inscriptions before the coming of Islam. Other languages that accepted the Arabic script include Taosug and Maranouw from the southern Philippines, and it was also used alongside (but never supplanted) scripts derived from Indian syllabaries for writing Javanese and Sundanese.

There is only one example of the use of an Indic script for an already islamized Malay. This is found on a tombstone from Minye Tujuh in Aceh marking the grave of a Queen Alalah, daughter of a Sultan Malik al-Zahir, who was a khan and a son of a khan (the title suggests a foreign origin). Dated in the equivalent of 1389 CE, it is written in an Indian script, and possibly in an Indian meter; if this is so, it shows a remarkable skill, even at this early period, in using Arabic loanwords within the requirements of Indic meters. The Malay inscription on the Trengganu stone (1320–1380), it will be recalled, was written in the Arabic script. The fact that there is a gap of almost two centuries between this tombstone and the survival of manuscripts simply emphasizes how arbitrary are the constellations of chance that provide material for knowledge of the region.

By the seventeenth century Malay had absorbed a rich stratum of Arabic loanwords and the acceptance of Arabic structures, along with some elements of Arabic morphology, provides striking evidence of the permeation of the region by an Islamic ethos and its modulation to the expression of Islamic ideas. Many of these ideas relate to religious matters, for example, those relating to the ritual prayer, marriage, divorce, and inheritance. Some Arabic words have undergone a narrowing: that is to say, they have lost a general meaning and kept only a religious one. Others range from technical terms, relating to religious matters and the administration of religious law, or terms of medicine, architecture, and the sciences, to the most common everyday expressions. Sometimes the words are so thoroughly assimilated that they would pass unrecognized unless one were able to identify them as Arabic by following through the patterns of sound change that Malay imposes on the loanwords it absorbs. Most remarkable is the adoption of an Arabic word to refer to local systems of culture, law, and traditional usage: *adat* (Arab., *ʿādah*). In fact, the concept identified by the word is so characteristically Malay that it would not be recognized as an Arabic word unless its origin were pointed out. The number of Arabic words in Malay—whether borrowed directly from Arabic or indirectly from other languages such as Persian—is well over a thousand.

Nor is it only Malay that has received a large corpus of Arabic loanwords; the same is true of many of the Malay-related languages in Sumatra, Java, and Borneo, notably Javanese, Sundanese, Madurese, Acehnese, and Minangkabau. The establishment of Muslim communities in the Philippines likewise brought numbers of loanwords to various Philippine languages. In Tagalog the number is relatively small, but in the southern Philippines, where Muslim communities are concentrated, they are most numerous.

Local Scholarship. This absorption of Arabic words in large measure derived from the study of Arabic works on the fundamental Islamic disciplines of Qur'anic exegesis, traditions, and jurisprudence, as well as Sufism (i.e., *tafsīr*, *ḥadīth*, *fiqh*, and *taṣawwuf*). There is no documentation of the early stages of the development of these studies, although there is no reason to doubt that the seeds were planted at least as early as the thirteenth century. Indeed, it should be stressed again that there were Islamic communities in the region long before the earliest evidence for Islamic states.

It is only from the seventeenth century that manuscripts from these traditions survive, whether in Arabic (mostly representing key works from the Islamic tradition) or in Malay or other regional languages such as Javanese. The Arabic manuscripts, some doubtless copied on the instructions of, or at least the permission of, a teacher in the Muslim Holy Land are of various levels of difficulty. Of works of *tafsīr,* that known as *Al-Jalālayn* is the most popular. Van Ronkel (1913) lists a significant number of manuscripts from various parts of the archipelago, some with interlinear translations, or at least annotations, in Malay or Javanese, sometimes with a dedication to a local ruler. There may be a temptation to look down on *Al-Jalalayn.* In fact it contains *multum in parvo* and is an excellent work for early levels of study, ideally suited for students who, though trained in an Islamic school, are not native speakers of Arabic. After *Al-Jalālayn,* al-Bayḍāwī's *Anwār al-tanzīl* takes pride of place, followed by al-Khāzin's *Lubāb al-ta'wīl fī ma'ānī al-tanzīl.* There are in addition fragments of Ṣūfī commentaries, including al-Bayhaqī's *Kitāb al-tahdhīb fī al-tafsīr* copied in 1652, which for a manuscript with a Southeast Asian provenance is very early indeed. There is even a work by al-Dānī on the seven recitations *(qirā'at)* of the Qur'ān. It should be stressed that these manuscripts represent the tip of the iceberg in relation to the number of those unknown from that period, or simply lost.

Collections of *ḥadīth,* especially those of al-Bukhārī, are numerous, and with them commentaries; the same collections of forty *ḥadīth (Al-arbā'īn),* especially that of al-Nawawī, were also popular. To these may be added a selection of works on history and biography, jurisprudence, astronomy, and *taṣawwuf.* A very popular Ṣūfī text, on the basis of the number of surviving manuscripts, is *Al-ḥikam al-'Aṭā'īyah* of Ibn 'Aṭā' Allāh; this work too is often accompanied by commentaries. There are treatises on the Shādhilī, Naqshbandī, and 'Alawī orders and a sprinkling of works in the Ibn al-'Arabī tradition, both by Ibn al-'Arabī himself and by his great commentator, al-Kāshānī. Of such manuscripts, one of the most striking contains the introduction to the commentary on Ibn al-Fāriḍ's poem *Al-tā'īyah al-kubrā* by Sa'īd ibn 'Alī al-Farghānī (d. 1299).

Given how scattered and arbitrary this list is, clearly, manuscripts have only survived by chance. Nevertheless, the evidence is sufficient to show that many basic Arabic works were accessible to scholars in this region, and that a variety of traditions was represented.

Local Authors. We have already mentioned interlinear translations, glosses, and annotations on Arabic manuscripts. These represent in embryonic form the tradition of works in Malay and other regional languages on the religious disciplines. How early this tradition began it is not possible to determine, nor do the extant manuscripts allow us to establish the order in which works of different categories were written.

Ḥamzah Fanṣūrī. The earliest Malay author known is Ḥamzah Fanṣūrī (d. 1600). The details of his life remain few, but some of his writings have been preserved. These suggest that in Mecca he came into contact with a particular formulation of Ṣūfī theosophy, apparently an Arabo-Iranian one based on the Ibn al-'Arabī tradition as it was reformulated and extended by al-Jīlī. It may have included Shī'ī elements; at least this would be consistent with the stories of Shī'ī heroes in Malay versions that were discovered in Aceh from the beginning of the seventeenth century.

A verse from one of the *sya'ir* (poems made up of end rhyming quatrains) of Ḥamzah Fanṣūrī gives a good example of the ascetic theology of the Ibn al-'Arabī school of mysticism:

> Regard heat and cold as one and the same;
> Abandon greed and avarice;
> Let your will melt like wax in the flame
> So that you will gain your difficult goal.

It should not be supposed that this is the earliest instance of Islamic writing in Malay. The technical skill in which religious ideas are handled in his quotations suggests that he represents a culminating point in a long tradition.

Shams al-Dīn. The next figure to emerge is Shams al-Dīn, the guide and teacher of Iskandar Muda, sultan of Aceh from 1607 to 1636. Shams al-Dīn reflects a tradition from North India, in which the system of emanations so characteristic of the Ibn al-'Arabī tradition was reduced to a convenient seven, and this framework, which was rapidly adopted by the Naqshbandī, Shādhilī and Shaṭṭārī orders, soon became part of the stock-in-trade of the mystical tradition in all parts of the archipelago. An important figure of state, Shams al-Dīn was the author of a significant corpus of writings in both Arabic and Malay. The single most important work that he used as the basis for his teaching was a summary of the key ideas of Ibn al-'Arabī's system set out in a framework of seven grades of being ranging between the Absolute and the Perfect Human Being. This system appears to have been inaugurated by development of a North Indian tradition of Islam that replaced the tradition of al-Jīlī.

This tradition of scholarly works on Islam written in Arabic has continued even up to the present. Many such works are minor tracts devoted to issues that became shibboleths, for example, whether the commencement of the fasting month was to be decided by the sighting of the moon or by calculation, or whether the formulation of intention before beginning a ritual prayer should be made aloud or mentally. Such material has only a local and historical importance. Occasionally, however, a substantial work appears and wins an established position. One such text was *Marāḥ labīd* (Rich Pasture), a two-volume Qur'ān commentary of about one thousand pages by a scholar from Banten, on the north coast of West Java, Muḥammad Nawawī al-Jāwī. He was born in 1815, went to study in the Muslim Holy Land in 1830, and died early in the twentieth century. Published in Cairo by the well-known firm of Ḥalabī in 1887, *Marāḥ labīd* is still available in the Middle East and remains very popular as an intermediate-level work in religious schools in many regions of Malaysia and Indonesia. The Arabic style, it may be remarked, is fluent and lucid, and among the author's acknowledged sources, Fakhr al-Dīn al-Rāzī's *Mafātīḥ al-ghayb* has an important position. It is also worth drawing attention to a large (thousand-page) commentary on al-Ghazālī's *Minhāj al-ʿābidīn ilā jannat rabb al-ʿālamīn* by an East Javanese scholar from the region of Kediri, which was recently republished in Surabaya. In addition to these major works, there are hundreds of minor ones issuing from Arabic printing presses scattered over Sumatra, Java, the Malay Peninsula, and Borneo, where both private and public schools have also been established.

ʿAbd al-Ra'ūf. By the second half of the seventeenth century, ʿAbd al-Ra'ūf (1615–1690) had prepared a full rendering of the Jalālayn *tafsīr* in Malay. It was extended by one of his students, Dāwūd al-Rūmī, by selections from the *qirā'āt* literature and citations from the *tafsīrs* of al-Khāzin and al-Bayḍāwī. It is still reprinted with the cover title *Tafsīr al-Bayḍāwī.* The translation of this work into Malay means in effect that there was also a complete rendering of the Qur'ān in Malay before the end of the seventeenth century.

In addition to these works, others written in Malay include, for example, simple summaries of the Muslim creed, such as al-Sanūsī's *Umm al-barāhīn* (Mother of Proofs), and hundreds of works on topics such as the mystical practice of various *ṭarīqahs* (the Naqshbandīyah, Shaṭṭārīyah, and Shādhilīyah in particular), the twenty attributes of God, *tawḥīd* (the unity of God), the application of Islamic law on various topics, and eschatology. One example is a four-volume abridgement of al-Ghazālī's *Iḥyā' ʿulūm al-dīn* (The Revivification of the Religious Sciences) by an expatriate scholar, ʿAbd al-Ṣamad of Palembang, who compiled it around 1780 in Ṭā'if, Arabia. It is still reprinted in various parts of Malaysia and Indonesia, and although there are now more academically prepared translations of the work in Malay published in the Roman script, they have not yet supplanted the earlier version.

The process of development from an understanding and explication of traditional texts to the preparation of original ones developed to meet local needs was slow and has not yet attained a commanding stature in this part of the Islamic world; this is largely due, no doubt, to the dominance of the oral tradition in the transmission of knowledge. From this standpoint, there is no comparison between the intellectual achievements of Southeast Asia and those to be found in Turkish, Persian, or Arabic language areas. This is only to say, however, that the achievements of Southeast Asia are of a different character—as in fact is also the case with India and sub-Saharan Africa—particularly when one considers how different the human ecology of monsoon Southeast Asia is from that of the Middle East, and how wide was the range of traditions and forms of social organization that had their home there.

Historiography. The Arabo-Muslim tradition also contributed to the development of a historiography in Malay. Certainly there is an influence of both Arabic and Persian historiography on the writing of Malay court chronicles. Such works were given an Arabic flavor by the use of words derived from Arabic, such as *sejarah* (Arab., *shajara*[*t al-nasab*]), meaning family line, chronicle, or history, and *silsilah,* or lineage, in the titles to indicate a genealogy or succession of rulers. The Malay chronicle of the kingdom of Malacca that purports to give an account of the antecedents and genealogy of the Malaccan sultanate (1400–1511), for example, is known as the *Sejarah Melayu.* Although popularly known in English as *The Malay Annals,* the title really means a genealogy of the Malays, who are in this case the Malay rulers of Malacca. The work, it may be noted, although it spans a century and the careers of rulers, has no dates, and its division into chapters may be a result of Persian influence.

There are numerous histories of the Malay states of the peninsula; despite Arabic words in their titles, however, they are more representative of the Malay folk tradition than of Arabic historiography. In fact, up to the late nineteenth century only in a few cases did works of this kind develop with the concern for date and fact that characterizes Muslim historiography as a whole. One such example is found in the historical writings of Nūr al-Dīn al-Rānīrī, an itinerant scholar of Gujarati origin (thus illustrating the continuing role of expatriate *ʿulamā'* in the religious life of the region). Although only in Aceh between 1637 and 1642, he wrote copiously in Malay and compiled a universal history, including a book on the history of Aceh up to this day, but also contributed vigorously to polemics between adherents of different schools of Ṣūfī theosophy during this period. Another example is the *Tuḥfat al-nafīs* by Raja Haji Ali of Riau, written in the wake of an Islamic revival toward the end of the nineteenth century.

Literature. Works more literary in character, although based on figures of the prophets, of people around the prophet, and of the heroes of Islam, likewise are known from the seventeenth century. The early stories that have been discovered include Malay renderings of the story of Joseph and Potiphar's wife, possibly from a Persian source that was copied in 1604, and alongside it versions of the story of Iskandar Dhū al-Qarnayn (Alexander the Great) and other stories of the prophets of Islam. The 1612 rescension of *The Malay Annals* opens with a version of the story of Alexander's invasion of India and presents him as the ultimate ancestor of the Malacca dynasty. Thus the story was well known, and the name was popular. Iskandar, it may also be remarked, was the name of the greatest ruler of Aceh (Iskandar Muda, r. 1607–1636).

Other stories that became popular from this period centered on the Prophet's uncle Amīr Ḥamzah and the Shīʿī hero Muḥammad ibn al-Ḥanafīyah. *The Malay Annals* suggests that versions of these stories were preserved in the Malacca library and as of 1511 were held in great esteem. The reference to them may be apocryphal: it indicates that they were to be recited to the Malaccan soldiers to give them courage for battle against the Portuguese on the following day, a battle that was to end in the Portuguese occupation of Malacca. Nevertheless, their symbolic role was well known at the time that the 1612 rescension of *The Malay Annals* was compiled. Equally important, the popularity of such works suggests at least the presence of a Shīʿī flavor to Islam in Aceh during this period. Shīʿī or not, there is certainly a strong Persian flavor in the literary works that were rendered into Malay, the most outstanding of which at this early period is a version of the *Ṭūṭī-nāmah* (Book of the Parrot) known in Malay as *Hikayat bayan budiman* (Story of the Wise Parrot).

Popular storytelling. At the same time, a whole complex of the storytelling tradition of Islam has found its way into Malay and Javanese. Such stories derive more from the popular than the belletristic traditions, and more has come via the Indian subcontinent than directly from the Arab Middle East, although even here the distinction is not absolute. Arabic works have been recopied in India and transmitted, or passed through, a variety of Indian languages into the languages of the Indonesian archipelago.

It must be remembered that stories about the heroes of Islam, while having a role as religious instruction, were equally important as entertainment and became widely popular. As a result, these heroes became part of community education for all levels of society and all ages, and thus, by allowing popular audiences to share in the experience of other communities of these heroes, they served to create a general pan-Islamic consciousness. Manuscript catalogues include numerous copies of stories of Muḥammad ibn al-Ḥanafīyah and Amīr Ḥamzah; there are collections of stories of the prophets and tales of the individual prophets including Adam, Abraham, Noah, and Moses. In Java, the story of Joseph was especially popular.

To these, however, should be added stories quite divorced from these religious figures, but which derive from Islamic sources and which have an Islamic ethos. These include many tales that appear in collections such as *The 1,001 Nights,* and classics such as the *Ṭūṭī-nāmah* referred to earlier. Among other collections of stories are the *Kalīlah and Dimnah,* which was known as early as 1736, and the *Bakhtiyār-nāmah* (Book of Bakhtiyār), a kind of reversal of the *1,001 Nights* that is a grand story of a young prince who is accused by ten viziers of having an affair with a chambermaid, but who postpones his execution by telling stories until the truth is discovered. This theme, it may be noted, was famous in Persian and Turkish popular literature, as well as in medieval Latin.

How these tales were first rendered into Malay is not known: they may have been carried by the oral tradition and set down in writing by court scribes, according to established literary conventions, to be recited on royal occasions, or there may have been some kind of committee composed of reader, oral translator, and scribe. It is certain, however, that such stories were preserved in court libraries, that access to them was restricted to senior court officials, and that the sultan had the authority to declare which might be read.

This composite Islamic tradition, whether formed directly from Arabic sources or mediated through Indian vernaculars, remains popular throughout Muslim Southeast Asia in numerous retellings, adaptations, and even dramatizations. In West Java, a cycle of Amīr Ḥamzah stories has become part of the repertory of the puppet theater. Evidence of this past and present popularity, apart from observation, can be gleaned from the catalogues of Malay, Javanese, and Sundanese manuscripts, to mention only a few.

In view of this rich complex of traditions and wide popularity, it is striking that although some members of the Muslim educated elite pioneered the use of Malay in either its Malaysian or its Indonesian form, the greater part of the modern literary achievement has been produced by authors secular in orientation and secular in subject matter and theme.

Recent Times

With the proclamation of Indonesian independence on 17 August 1945, two days after the Japanese surrender, and with the transfer of sovereignty by the Dutch in 1950, Muslim groups exerted considerable pressure to have Indonesia declared an Islamic state, with the provisions of Muslims law binding on Muslims.

It was only after long and bitter debates between religious factions and the secular nationalists in the few months prior to the Japanese surrender that a compromise was reached, and the Pancasila ("five pillars"), a set of five principles devised largely by Sukarno, first president of the republic, were with certain qualifications accepted as the basis of the new state. Since the first of these principles was belief in one God, this formula made Indonesia a nonconfessional state without making it a secular one. A corollary of this charter was the establishment of a ministry of religion early in the republic's history. This ministry was to take care of the needs and interests of every religious community in the country (although later there were to be difficulties as to the terms under which the Hindu Balinese and the Javanese mystical groups might be included within its terms of reference).

Religious Revolts. The compromise, however, did not last long. After the proclamation of independence, the secular nationalists dropped the references to the position of Islam in the state agreed to in it. For the hard-line Muslims, this was a confirmation of their worst fears. The disillusion and bitterness generated on the Muslim side led to three major risings against the republican government. The first and most dangerous broke out before independence from the Dutch had been secured. After several months of guerrilla activity, Kartosuwirjo (1923–1962), a former medical student, proclaimed the establishment of the Islamic state of Indonesia on 7 August 1949 in the mountainous regions of West Java and was inaugurated as imam of the state. He and his movement conducted a guerrilla war, the Darul Islam revolt, against the government until 1962, when Kartosuwirjo was captured, and he and five of his associates were executed. The movement, while at first idealistic and attracting at least tacit support among some members of the Muslim political parties, gradually degenerated into a terrorist group that caused great human and material damage over West Java for more than ten years. It plundered and destroyed farms and peasant holdings to get financial resources and was behind several attempts to assassinate President Sukarno.

Two other major religious revolts inspired by the ideal of making Indonesia an Islamic state and realizing in it a *dār al-Islām* (Arab., "abode of Islam"; Indon., *darul Islam*) were to break out. One was on the island of Sulawesi in 1952, with the leader of the movement, Kahar Muzakkar, accepting a commission from Kartosuwirjo in West Java as commander of the fourth division of the Islamic army of Indonesia. With varying levels of success he managed to maintain his movement until early 1965, when he was encircled and shot by republican forces. The other revolt, in late 1953, was led by Daud Beureu'eh in Aceh, a region already referred to on several occasions for the strength of its Islamic traditions. This rising too was associated with the West Javanese movement. Daud Beureu'eh proclaimed an Islamic state of Aceh and styled himself "Commander of the Faithful" (Amīr al-Mu'minīn, the historic title of the Muslim caliphs), but after nine years of struggle he made his peace with the central government in 1962. The details of these struggles belong more to political history than to that of Islam. It is important to observe, however, that these three very serious uprisings, costly in human lives and property, were put down by Muslim soldiers under a Muslim president of a national state based on an ideology, the Pancasila, that did not recognize exclusive claims on the part of any one religious tradition.

Opposition Politics. On a predominantly political level, the years between 1950 and 1965 saw continued but decreasingly successful efforts by the Muslim parties to gain by political means the power required to make Indonesia an Islamic state. However they were never sufficiently strong to outnumber or wily enough to outmaneuver the alliance between the "secular" nationalists and the radical left-wing parties. In the last resort they could claim loyalty to the Indonesian state by recognizing the Pancasila as the state ideology. And this they did by claiming that only Muslims could supply an adequate content to its first principle: belief in one God.

The elimination of Sukarno as a political force in 1965 in the wake of an attempted communist coup, and the destruction of the Communist Party, led to a revival of Muslim expectations of a positive Islamic stance in government. These expectations were again disappointed, although Muslim mass action succeeded in blocking a proposed civil marriage law in 1973.

By the last quarter of the twentieth century, the Muslim parties, although under secular names, had assumed the role of a political opposition to what was essentially a secular government and offered the only form of organized dissent. If in the 1950s the Islamic parties set as their goal the ideal of Indonesia as an Islamic state, their role was now to demand social and economic justice and to protest against corruption in government, against secularism, consumerism, and an open economy.

It should be stressed, however, that far from a majority of Indonesian Muslims support Islamic political movements. The majority live and work within the status quo, Javanese dominated though it is, and with Islamic norms of behavior and forms of worship tacitly accepted as the majority cultural religious tradition of the nation in much the same way as the Church of England fulfills such a role in Britain, although, let it be stressed, Islam is a majority, not an established, religion.

This however is not the whole story. There are systems of Islamic education alongside the government system, and there are state institutes of Islamic training designed to produce graduates in Islamic law, education, and preaching. There is a large number of smaller institutions that teach in Arabic and graduate hundreds of students who travel overseas for higher learning; sometimes these students attend secular institutes in Australia, Britain, and Canada, for example, but of course they go more often to religious ones in India, Pakistan, Saudi Arabia, and Egypt. Indeed, students from Indonesia and Malaysia have a very high profile at al-Azhar in Cairo, and at the celebration of the millennium of al-Azhar in April 1983, Southeast Asian students were the most prominent community of foreigners studying at the institution, as indeed they are on the pilgrimage to Mecca. Nevertheless, the diffusion of graduates of these institutions is uneven, and there is a significant number of Muslim thinkers who have developed an intellectual interest in the role of religion in the modern world, outside of the traditional Islamic disciplines of *fiqh* and *kalām,* some under the influence of the minority Lahore Aḥmadīyah, who have a small presence in Indonesia.

The Continuum of Islamic Experience. There is therefore a great variety of intensity in the profession of Islam. To the superficial observer, many of the Javanese peasantry, for example, might not appear to be Muslims at all. Yet relatively few claim exclusive allegiance either to Buddhism, which is enjoying a revival, or to the mystical sects. For the great majority, what perception they have of transcendence is of Islamic transcendence. Even if this is the limit of their commitment, it is sufficient for them to be identified as Muslims. At the opposite extreme are groups of radical Muslims inspired by the ideals of Ḥasan al-Bannā', founder of the Ikhwān al-Muslimūn, or Muslim Brotherhood, and of Mawdūdī of Pakistan, or even by the Egyptian Takfīr wa-al-Hijrah ("denounce and abandon") groups. Despite internal differences, principally regarding tactics and strategy, they understand Islam as a revealed total way of life, with absolute demands. They reject the four schools of law and accept as their authorities the Qur'ān and *sunnah* alone. Theirs is a view that rejects the tradition of scholars who accept the authority of the four schools of law and the role of case law, precedent, and analogy.

Yet the divisions are not clear cut, and one has to do with a continuum rather than sharp discontinuities. For the ordinary members of the Muslim community, moreover, these issues do not arise. Community practice is as rhythmic as the act of breathing, whether the community places a high value on external observances such as the fast and the ritual prayer or a low one, and whatever the regional observances it chooses to decorate and enhance its Islamic practice. One cannot overstress, however, that for many, Islam is a matter of personal devotion, morality, marriage, divorce, and to an uncertain degree, depending on the region, inheritance.

The situation in Malaysia is complicated by the racial composition of the country. To be a Malay is to be a Muslim, and Islam is the means by which the Malays assert their identity and their rights against other races, the Chinese in particular; thus the danger of a kind of religious fascism is not altogether absent. There have been waves of Islamic enthusiasm since the early 1970s, and there is considerable pressure to islamize the government of the country. This has taken the form of moves to introduce Islamic banking; promulgation of rules for social behavior, especially in the form of *khalwat* laws, which prohibit situations of "suspicious proximity" between the sexes; and the imposition of conditions on the handling and selling of pork that virtually ban it from the menus of international hotels.

The government's response to these and various other pressures has been measured. To take the initiative away from extremists, it has committed itself to a policy of islamization, which, it explains, is directed exclusively toward making Muslims better Muslims. There are differences of opinion, however, on the degree to which non-Muslims should be made subject to the norms of an Islamic ethos. A minor crisis developed in the northern Borneo state of Sabah in 1985 because of the election of a Dyak Christian as chief minister.

Certainly during this period observers have noted a marked increase in religious fervor. This is particularly evident in the university campuses and among civil servants: it is reflected in the observance of daily prayers and the fast, in the numbers of Muslims making the pilgrimage to Mecca, and in women's dress. In addition, various religious associations have sprung up, all dedicated to spreading Islamic teachings, but with different emphases. Some have been infiltrated by Iranian or Libyan elements; others find their inspiration in Mawdūdī. One of particular interest is the Dār al-Arqam, an association that is establishing self-sufficient commune-type communities to which individuals and their families, often from the professional classes, can withdraw on a short- or long-term basis; there they are to live a life totally in accord with the *sunnah* of the Prophet and away from the distractions of the imperfect world, which, it is believed, will gradually learn from the fruit of their example.

To the superficial observer, there is little outward evidence of Southeast Asia's widespread Islamic allegiance. There is none of the exuberant architecture that so characterizes Muslim civilization in South and West Asia. Traditional forms of music and the dance, styles of dress, social structures, systems of inheritance, and personal and family law all suggest a complex of cultures that owes little to Islam. Observers coming from the Middle East, taking as a norm outward manifestations of Islam in the Arab world, where so much that was local custom at the time of the Prophet is now inseparable from the Islamic tradition, may be perplexed at the variety and distinctiveness of Southeast Asian Islam. They may even regard much of what they see as non-Islamic, forgetting that at one time much even in Middle Eastern Islam was non-Islamic.

Nevertheless, it has been shown that virtually every movement in the Islamic world and every emphasis and school has found a counterpart in Southeast Asia, and that there is a long tradition of expatriate local *'ulamā'* settling in the Middle East, either permanently or on a long-term basis, as well as a tradition of *'ulamā'* from the Middle East and South Asia becoming domiciled in Southeast Asia. Indeed, in the region today there is a strength and vitality in Islamic life expressed in a wide range of religious perceptions and enthusiasms both at individual and community levels. The potential is negative as well as positive. Either way, in the fifteenth century of the Hijrah, Islam in Southeast Asia can no longer be ignored, whether in the heartlands of Islam, where it still has an impact to make, or in the West.

[*For other perspectives on Islam in Southeast Asia, see* Javanese Religion *and* Southeast Asian Religions, *article on* Insular Cultures.]

BIBLIOGRAPHY

No single classic work on Islam in Southeast Asia exists, unfortunately. What follows should serve as a guide to the general reader and not as an exhaustive list. For the historical context within which Islam plays its various roles in Southeast Asia, John Sturgus Bastin and Harry J. Benda's exquisitely written and lucid *A History of Modern Southeast Asia: Colonialism, Nationalism, and Decolonization* (Englewood Cliffs, N.J., 1968) makes sense of the region as a whole, from Burma to the Philippines. D. G. E. Hall's *A History of South-East Asia,* 4th ed. (London, 1981), is still the basic work for a historical survey of Southeast Asia as a whole from the earliest times up to 1950. A very useful source book is *Readings on Islam in Southeast Asia,* edited by Ahmad Ibrahim (Singapore, 1985). See also Barbara Andaya and Leonard Andaya's *A History of Malaysia* (London, 1982) and M. C. Ricklefs's *A History of Modern Indonesia, c. 1300 to the Present* (Bloomington, Ind., 1981).

The Modern Period. C. van Dijk's *Rebellion under the Banner of Islam: The Darul Islam in Indonesia* (The Hague, 1981) is an admirably lucid analysis of revolts against the republican government in Indonesia between 1950 and 1965 directed toward the transformation of the nation into an Islamic state. Clifford Geertz's *The Religion of Java* (Chicago, 1976) is a masterpiece of sensitive ethnographic description, despite its somewhat mechanistic division of Javanese society into Santri (Muslim), *abangan* (peasant), and Prijayi (aristocratic bureaucrat), and its lack of depth in understanding the historical context of Javanese religion. Peter G. Gowing's *Muslim Filipinos: Heritage and Horizon* (Quezon City, Philippines, 1979), an excellent survey of the Muslim communities in the Philippines from the earliest days up to the 1970s, has a particularly useful bibliography. *The Crescent in the East: Islam in Asia Major,* edited by Raphael Israeli (London, 1982), includes chapters on Islam in Burma, Malaysia, Thailand, Indonesia, and the Philippines. *Islam in Public Life,* edited by John L. Esposito (New York, 1986), includes chapters on Islam in public life in Malaysia and Indonesia that give a reasonable account of the state of play in each nation. See also B. J. Boland's *The Struggle of Islam in Modern Indonesia* (The Hague, 1982); G. W. J. Drewes's "Indonesia: Mysticism and Activism," in *Unity and Variety in Muslim Civilization,* edited by Gustave E. von Grunebaum (Chicago, 1955), pp. 284–310; my "An Islamic System or Islamic Values?: Nucleus of a Debate in Contemporary Indonesia," in *Islam and the Political Economy of Meaning: Comparative Studies in Muslim Discourse,* edited by W. R. Roff (Berkeley, 1986); and Astri Suhrke's "The Thai Muslims: Some Aspects of Minority Integration," *Pacific Affairs* 43 (Winter 1970–1971): 531–547.

Specialized Studies. S. Q. Fatimi's *Islam Comes to Malaysia* (Singapore, 1963) is a short, provocative, but delightfully written book that elaborates a role attributed to Ṣūfīs in the preaching of Islam in Southeast Asia, with a particularly interesting analysis of the inscribed pillar discovered at Phanrang. *Islam in South-East Asia,* edited by M. B. Hooker (Leiden, 1983), a collection of seven essays that add up to a fresh and vigorous approach to Islam in Southeast Asia, brings together perspectives derived from studies in ethnography, Islamic philosophy and law, and literature. Christiaan Snouck Hurgronje's *The Achehnese,* 2 vols., translated by A. W. S. O'Sullivan (Leiden, 1906), is a classic work of description of what from many aspects is the single most important Muslim community in Southeast Asia. *Islam in Asia,* vol. 2, *Southeast and East Asia,* edited by Raphael Israeli and myself (Boulder, 1984), includes such topics as a sociological analysis of islamization in Java,

Qur'anic exegesis in Malaysia and Indonesia, and the reciprocal relationships between Islamic Southeast Asia and the heartlands of Islam. Clive S. Kessler's *Islam and Politics in a Malay State: Kelantan 1838–1969* (Ithaca, N.Y., 1978) is an excellent microstudy of a small town in a Malay state that has wide implications for all Malaysia. *Conversion to Islam*, edited by Nehemia Levtzion (New York, 1979), is a very useful collection of essays providing a foundation for a comparative study of conversion to Islam. *Kelantan: Religion, Society, and Politics in a Malay State*, edited by W. R. Roff (Kuala Lumpur, 1974), is a most useful collection of material on Islamic life and movements in Kelantan that also presents a convincing paradigm for other regions. See also Muhammed Abdul Jabbar Beg's *Arabic Loan-Words in Malay: A Comparative Study* (Kuala Lumpur, 1982); C. C. Berg's "The Islamisation of Java," *Studia Islamica* 4 (1955): 11–142; Christine E. Dobbin's *Islamic Revivalism in a Changing Peasant Economy: Central Sumatra, 1784–1847* (London, 1983); my "Islam in Southeast Asia: Reflections on New Directions," *Indonesia*, no. 19 (April 1975): 33–55; and Deliar Noer's *The Modernist Muslim Movement in Indonesia, 1900–1942* (Singapore, 1973).

Literature. For an introduction to Islamic writing in the regional vernaculars, C. C. Brown's *Sĕjarah Mĕlayu; or, Malay Annals* (Kuala Lumpur, 1970) is a somewhat mannered but readable translation of the 1612 rescension of the *Sejarah Melayu*. G. W. J. Drewes's *The Admonitions of Seh Bari* (The Hague, 1969) is an edition and translation of a manuscript of a Javanese Primbon (student notebook) brought back to Europe around 1598; his *Directions for Travellers on the Mystic Path* (The Hague, 1977) includes a very valuable index and bibliography. Richard Winstedt's *A History of Classical Malay Literature* (Kuala Lumpur, 1969) is a difficult book, but worthy of sympathetic, careful study. See especially those chapters dealing with Muslim legends, cycles of tales from Muslim sources, and Islamic theology, jurisprudence, and history. See also L. F. Brakel's *The Hikayat Muhammad Hanafiyyah* (The Hague, 1975).

A. H. JOHNS

Islam in Modern Europe

Medieval Europe did not generally tolerate the permanent settlement of Muslims in the West. Nineteenth-century colonialism displaced numerous individual Muslims to the metropolitan countries, but those were usually short-term immigrants, and the establishment of communities came about only very rarely.

In the first half of the twentieth century, Muslims came to western Europe primarily as colonial troops—Algerians and Senegalese to France, Indians to England, Tatars and other groups inhabiting eastern Europe to Germany, Bosnians to Austria, Moroccans to Spain. After World War II most of the Muslim immigrants were laborers, but there was also a steadily increasing number of students and professionals who remained after completing their education or advanced training. In addition there was a growing number of political refugees in the 1970s and 1980s, especially from Lebanon (mostly Palestinians), Eritrea, Pakistan, Iran, and Afghanistan.

The rapid growth of this postwar Muslim diaspora in the short span of twenty-five years meant that religious life could hardly develop at the same pace, and the immigrants soon reached a cultural identity crisis. There were almost no mosques in western Europe before the twentieth century; even by the early 1980s only isolated mosques had been built, and these were often showcases located far away from the centers where Muslim populations were concentrated. For the most part, services were still performed in makeshift surroundings—private homes, shops, garages. In 1985 there were nearly five thousand of these "private mosques" in western Europe.

Demography. Because of continuous immigration and the statistical problems created by illegal residencies, reliable figures for Muslim populations are hard to come by: the counts are usually too low and, in any event, obsolete one or two years after publication.

In 1985 the total Muslim diaspora in western Europe was estimated at seven million people, with roughly two million each in Germany and France and just over one million in England. The highest concentration in western Europe was found in West Berlin, where 300,000 Muslims constituted the second largest religious group, outnumbering the 260,000 Catholics. In France likewise, Islam has been the second largest religion since the 1970s; by the year 2000 Muslims are expected to make up 10 percent of the total French population. In each of these three countries the Muslim scene is dominated by a particular ethnic group—Turks in West Germany, North Africans in France, Pakistanis (along with Bangladeshis and Indians) in England—although the group lines tend to merge. In England there are also large Turkish communities (almost exclusively from Cyprus), and in Germany there is a fairly large Pakistani and an even larger Moroccan community. Muslims from sub-Saharan Africa are found primarily in France, followed by England and to a lesser extent Germany. Yugoslavian Muslims work mostly in West Germany and Austria but also in France, England, Holland, and above all, Sweden. While there have been only a few hundred Afghans in England, and a few thousand in France, their number may well have swelled to about seven thousand in Germany by 1985. Middle Eastern Arabs and Iranians are almost equally represented in Germany, France, and England. Twenty thousand Arabs in West Berlin, half of them Palestinians, represent one of the heaviest concentrations. In England and France there are smaller but long-established communities from Yemen. The Muslim community in France includes the greatest number who have become citizens and is also the most homogeneous. Since West African Islam (found in Mauritania, Mali, Niger, Senegal, Guinea, Ivory Coast, Burkina Faso, Nigeria, and Cameroon) derives from the Maghreb, there is relatively more harmony than in England or West Germany, where the diverse communities are highly polarized.

A growing Muslim diaspora, mostly from Eritrea and Somalia but also from North Africa and Mali, can be found in Italy as well as in Greece, which has an additional group of Pakistanis working the shipping industry. In Spain, where Muslims also outnumber the Protestant and Jewish minorities, Moroccan workers probably still predominated in 1985, although here as elsewhere, West Africans have followed in the wake of the North Africans. Spain also has large communities of wealthy Arabs and Iranians; the government had accepted the largest number of Iranian refugees after the revolution of 1978–1979, but when their number reached sixty thousand, planeloads of newcomers were diverted to Denmark.

By the mid-1980s there was no western European government that had not instituted some legal measures to stop further immigration or even to repatriate some of the Muslim minorities. Such actions were taken in response to national fears resulting from the grim employment situation, but so far the xenophobic argument that the immigrants are responsible for spreading unemployment remains largely psychological, since most Europeans are not yet ready to undertake the marginal, low-paying jobs that the immigrants have assumed. Nonetheless, the situation may change drastically once a European-born generation of Turks, Moroccans, and Pakistanis comes of age. Already in England in 1981 the number of Muslim doctors in the British Health Service was estimated at ten thousand, school teachers at fifteen thousand to seventeen thousand, and engineers and scientists at twenty thousand. The data are similar for France, and although the numbers are lower in West Germany, the general trend is the same.

The interconfessional situation: Sunnī and Shīʿī Muslims. In western Europe, as in the Americas, the Sunnī-Shīʿī ratio parallels that of the Muslim world as a whole, namely about 90 percent Sunnī and barely 10 percent Shīʿī. In France, because of the African predominance, the Shīʿī ratio is even smaller, and this in spite of the relatively heavy concentration of Iranians and a lesser number of Lebanese Shīʿah. In West Germany, on the other hand, the Shīʿī proportion approaches 20 percent if the Alevi sect, heavily represented among Turkish "guest workers," is included.

In England numerous Iranian Shīʿah are joined by what is probably an even greater number from India and Pakistan, so that here too the Shīʿī proportion may exceed 10 percent, particularly with the inclusion of the Ismāʿīlī followers of the Aga Khan, who are mostly Indians from East Africa.

Because of pressure in the diaspora, Sunnī and Shīʿī Muslims often draw closer to one another and frequently share mosques. At the same time, the situation may lend itself to continuing old quarrels. In comparison to Turkish or Pakistani police, those in England or Germany treat troublemakers with comparative leniency, so that extremists in the diaspora risk much less. In the English city of Rotherham, for example, with its four thousand Muslims, there were violent Sunnī-Shīʿī confrontations, and British police shut down a disputed mosque. In Germany Turkish parties of the extreme right have attempted to instigate Sunnī youth against the Alevis, who are usually members of the Kurdish national minority within Turkey and politically leftist.

Demographic anomalies and conversion trends. One of the serious social problems besetting the Muslim diaspora is that of sexual disequilibrium, which is not without religious ramifications. Islamic moral precepts prevent an equally heavy migration of women, since it appears difficult to guard their privacy in the uncertain living conditions of Europe. Girls are often sent back to the home country after attaining puberty so they will not "fall" into marriages with men from outside their community, particularly non-Muslims, or ruin their positions in their own community by adjusting too willingly to their liberal surroundings. Of the more than four hundred thousand Moroccans in France, for example, only about 25 percent are women. In West Germany the ratio is even smaller, and in Scandinavia it is as low as 16 percent. Among refugee groups such as the Afghans and Pakistanis (mainly in Germany), the ratio is likewise very low. It is larger among Turks in Germany but still far from equal.

Increasing concern with identity in the wake of "reislamization" has induced an increasing number of young men to "import" a bride from back home, a trend observable among students as well as workers. The upsurge in racism throughout western Europe has also had some effect in reducing the number of European women accessible to Muslims for marriage. Where mixed marriages do occur, however, the result usually adds to the ranks of the Muslim believers: the majority of non-Muslim female spouses tend to convert to Islam, at least nominally, and since Islamic law rules out marriage between a Muslim woman and a non-Muslim man, European men marrying Muslim women almost invariably convert as well.

Islam in western Europe has also grown from the approximately ten thousand converts who have embraced Sufism, or mystical Islam. In addition to those who fully converted, about twice their number remain affiliated more loosely with Ṣūfī communities, especially in Britain and Germany but also in the Netherlands, Italy, and even Greece. The existence of a chain of Ṣūfī centers or "homes" cannot be considered a fleeting phenomenon or merely off-track spiritualism. The Chishtī *ṭarīqah* (brotherhood), which plays an important role in Afghanistan and the Indian subcontinent, has opened western headquarters in Bradford-on-Avon (Wiltshire); at Saint Anne's Center in Baldshaw (Eastern Sussex), the organization's European director, Pīr Vilāyat 'Ināyat Khān, offers a program of "teachings, meditation, conversations with experienced healers about preventive medicine, dance, and universal prayer." An English poetess who adopted the name of Islam's most revered female mystic, Rābi'ah al-'Adawīyah, opened a branch in Tunis in 1980.

In addition to the nondenominational Ṣūfīs, there are others who have joined the Darqāwī *ṭarīqah,* which claims a spiritual link to the Moroccan city of Fez. The teachings of the Darqāwī disciples clearly point to the influence of the great European Ṣūfī masters René Guénon, Frithjof Schuon, and Titus Burckhardt, although they broke with this older generation at an early stage. The Darqāwīyah's militant interpretation of Sufism seems, on various counts, closer to fundamentalism than mysticism; indeed, this group of European and American converts, drawn solidly from the professional middle class, renounces every aspect of modern life for a return to the traditions of the early Middle Ages. Nonetheless, the major center for this group of converts, the Darqāwī Institute outside Norwich (Norfolk), operates with management experience and efficiency. On the local level, they maintain a society of Islam in England with an office in London that coordinates the activities of other religious branches. These include the Society for the Return of Islam to Spain, with centers in Málaga, Seville, Cordova, and Granada; the American subdivision, the Islam West Foundation, based in Tucson, Arizona, and the Center for the Unification of Native American Peoples (CUNAP), which operates a Muslim mission for Indians in Bolivia.

A very different group of converts, who are generally not even known as such, includes former student leaders of the independent Left. As such, they are deeply involved in international initiatives regarding human rights and are particularly committed to Third World liberation movements. These converts have a profound knowledge of Islamic teachings and are quite genuinely attached to their new faith, notwithstanding the many reservations they may have and the fact that their version of the faith is hardly that of the orthodox majority but rather that of the intellectual vanguard.

European converts to Islam have included a number of prominent figures, especially in academic life, and their humanist perspective has contributed to bridging the gap between cultural worlds. This group includes Baron Omar von Ehrenfels, the Austrian anthropologist (d. 1980); Vincent Monteil, the specialist on African and Islamic affairs; Michel Chodkiewicz, director of the French publishing house Éditions du Seuil; and Roger Garaudy, the French philosopher and former Communist Party member.

More generally, however, the relationship between converts from the West and their eastern coreligionists is often problematic. Newcomers frequently complain that there is no place where Islam is practiced authentically, not one country Muslims can choose as a model, no leader they can look up to. These converts, and especially the Darqāwīyah, usually regard the Muslims of the diaspora, be they students, diplomats, or workers, as an altogether bad example.

Public Recognition of Muslim Communities. From 1980 onward there were considerable complaints from groups within the Muslim diaspora in Europe that their representation had been unduly usurped by bodies mainly comprised of diplomats from Muslim countries and that these spokesmen tended to be out of tune with the issues besetting the immigrant communities. These grievances, not without foundation, reflect a basic difficulty in the diaspora situation. Islam, ideally at least, rejects the idea of priesthood and knows no church. One alternative to the assumption of European-style church organization would be the structures developed by the Jewish communities, whose rabbis function not unlike the Muslim *'ulamā',* or religious scholars. However, many Muslims resent any adjustment to European patterns, be they Christian or Jewish. Reactions differ widely, but successful acceptance of modern systems of community organization is usually found only in countries where the Muslim diaspora has existed for several generations.

In Britain, France, and Germany, a fairly large number of prominent Muslim academics and intellectuals—some of them now citizens of their host countries—are becoming increasingly active in community affairs. European Christians may not regard such "laymen" as appropriate representatives of a religious community, but Islamic tradition does shoulder such intellectuals with this responsibility, and the Muslim communities, by and large, take their cues from them.

Among international bodies, the Muslim World Congress has so far been the most successful in coping with the situation of diaspora communities. By appointing local representatives for each province or state, it has provided authorities in the host countries with Muslim officials to consult on matters of mutual interest. Such representation is essential for official recognition of Islam as a corporate body within the European legal framework. In France, recognition was announced in 1977 on the eve of the Prophet's birthday celebrations, and on that occasion French Interior Minister Michel Poniatowski declared that Muslims had now had equal rights to broadcast time in the media as well as a corresponding voice in the choice of school curricula. Austria and Belgium took similar steps, but by the mid-1980s West Germany was still lagging behind.

Options for the Future: Assimilation or Isolation? The numerous difficulties encountered in Muslim community life in the diaspora tend to foster obscurantism or religious and political extremism that impedes integration into the host society and even multiplies the problems of preserving Muslim identity. Quite often this situation becomes a vicious circle as isolation hinders the progress of Muslim youth, who then grow up educationally disadvantaged and without much hope of upward mobility in the host country that has become their home.

Where new arrivals are accepted into already existing larger communities, there is often an extreme isolation from the life of the host country, and the former way of life remains virtually intact. Orthodox Turkish communities, in particular, tend to create an atmosphere devoid of any sense of living in the diaspora. Indeed, Germany was for some time considered a congenial host country for the most conservative of these communities, a place where the lifestyle that was forbidden, or at least difficult to implement, in Kemalist Turkey might be maintained. Religious instructors (*hocas*), for example, who never attended teacher training courses instituted by the Turkish government and thus could not teach officially at home, converged upon Germany, where immigrant workers, fearing that their children might be led astray by the temptations of modern life, were often willing to pay their way.

By the beginning of the 1980s, the majority of North Africans in France had been born in the host country. Among this "second generation," as they are called, a trend toward re-islamization became unmistakable, with community interest mostly upheld by the younger members. Youthful participation in religious rituals of prayer and fasting greatly increased, although this often represented a defiant mood rather than piety in the traditional sense. North Africans frequently express the view that "through identification with Islam, which is the true revolutionary power of the Third World, we gain self-confidence and the respect of our neighbors." Others put it even more bluntly: "Without Islam we amount to nothing in France!" This pride in belonging to Islam has increased in the rest of the diaspora as well.

BIBLIOGRAPHY

The study of Muslim communities in the modern West has, not surprisingly, grown with the increasing visibility of the communities themselves. Even so, much of the available material appears in journals and other serials rather than in book form. Two research groups that regularly issue publications on the subject are the Institute of Muslim Minority Affairs at King Abdulaziz University, Jidda, Saudi Arabia, which has its own journal, and the Centre for the Study of Islam and Christian-Muslim Relations at Selly Oakes Colleges, Birmingham, England, which produces a variety of short monographs. The London-based journal *Impact International* contains a wealth of material on diaspora life. Further periodical references may be gleaned from my article "Die Problematik der muslimischen Diaspora in Europe und Amerika," *Orient* 23 (March 1982): 45–80.

An early attempt at providing an overview of the western diaspora is M. Ali Kettani's *Muslims in Europe and America*, 2 vols. (Beirut, 1976). Country studies include Zaki Badawi's *Islam in Britain* (London, 1981); M. S. Abdullah's *Geschichte des Islam in Deutschland* (Vienna, 1981); and Felice Dasseto and Albert Bastenier's *L'Islam transplanté* (Brussels, 1984), which deals with Turkish and Moroccan Muslim immigrants in Belgium. An excellent short study on France is Mahfoud Bennoune's "Maghribin Workers in France," *MERIP Reports*, no. 34 (January 1975): 1–12, 30; a complementary essay focusing on the difficulties faced by the immigrant communities there is Tahar Ben Jelloun's *Hospitalité française: Racisme et immigration maghrébine* (Paris, 1984).

The situation of Muslim women in Europe remains virtually unexplored, but see the work of Nermin Abadan-Unat, including her "Implications of Migration on Emancipation and Pseudoemancipation of Turkish Women," *International Migration Review* 11 (1977): 31–57.

CALID DURÁN

Islam in the Americas

The identity of the first Muslims to set foot on American soil is unknown. Evidence suggesting that Muslims from Spain and West Africa arrived before Columbus is ambiguous but cannot be discounted. It is recorded, for example, that in the mid-tenth century, Muslims of African origin who ruled Spain and adjacent North Africa sailed westward from Cordova into the "Ocean of Fog" and returned after a long absence with much booty from a "strange and curious land." Although people of Muslim origin are known to have accompanied Columbus and subsequent Spanish explorers to the New World, their religious affiliation at the time of the voyages was not recorded and thus is open to question. Granada, the last Muslim stronghold in Spain, fell to the Christians in 1492, just before the Spanish Inquisition was launched. Many non-Christians fled or embraced Catholicism to escape persecution. At least two documents imply the presence of Muslims in Spanish America before 1550. A decree issued in 1539 by Charles V, king of Spain, forbade migration to the West Indies of the grandsons of Muslims who had been burned at the stake. It was evidently ineffective, for when it was ratified in 1543, an order for the expulsion of all Muslims from overseas Spanish territories was published simultaneously.

Slave and Plantation Communities. Of the hundreds of thousands of slaves brought from West Africa by the Spaniards, Portuguese, Dutch, French, and British between 1530 and 1850 to work in mines or on plantations in the American colonies, about 14 to 20 percent were Muslims. Among them were Mande- and Wolof-speaking villagers from the Senegal coast and upper Niger River, Hausa peasants and artisans from the oasis towns south of the Sahara, and Fulbe herders from the western savannas of the Sudan. Many enslaved Muslims were highly educated and literate in Arabic. These Afro-Muslims were Sunnī and adhered to Mālikī legal interpretations. Though they spoke diverse, mutually unintelligible native languages, they could communicate with one another by reciting prayers and sayings in Arabic.

African slaves were taken to Peru and Mexico to extract precious minerals and ores until about 1680, after which they either died out or were absorbed into local Indian populations. Beginning in the seventeenth century, European immigrants settled in temperate zones of North and South America, but their small family farms and cattle ranches did not require a large supplementary labor force. Only in the warm, fertile lowlands of the Caribbean islands, northern South America, eastern Brazil, and the southeastern United States was the economy built upon slave labor. Here native populations were rapidly exterminated, necessitating the importation of workers, the vast majority of whom were captives from Africa.

After the influx of enslaved Africans into the southern United States during the eighteenth century, later generations of slaves were born in America. Thus, the ancestral traditions of U.S. slaves were not revitalized by a continuing stream of new arrivals from Africa. Vigorous proselytization by Anglo-Protestant missionaries pressured non-Christian slaves, including Muslims, to observe their faiths covertly and fragmentarily during the nineteenth century, and few Islamic practices survive from the slave period among U.S. blacks today. Yet Afro-Americans who trace their genealogies often encounter Muslim ancestors, and oral histories taken from elderly blacks through the 1940s contain occasional mention of Islamic customs. Extant texts in Arabic written by Muslim slaves before the Civil War and scattered references in travelogues by European authors of the same period further confirm the once greater visibility of Islam in the southern United States.

Replenishment from abroad until about 1860 kept the many religions of Caribbean blacks alive. In the early nineteenth century, Afro-Muslim men of Brazil wore the turban as a mark of learning, and Muslim women of Trinidad covered their breasts, in contrast to their non-Muslim sisters. Afro-Muslims of Port of Spain, Trinidad, operated their own schools and raised funds to buy the freedom of Muslims in bondage. After the abolition of slavery by the Portuguese in 1830, the British in 1833, the French in 1848, and the Dutch in 1863, countless blacks from the islands and nearby mainland returned to Africa. Though Islam has virtually disappeared among twentieth-century blacks of Brazil and many of the islands, small communities of rural blacks in Surinam, Guyana, and Trinidad and Tobago still cling tenaciously to the faith of their Muslim forebears.

Caribbean plantations suffered a drastic labor shortage when the emancipated slaves refused to continue working for the low wages offered them. The British solved the labor problem in their newly acquired colony of Guiana (Guyana) by indenturing servants from colonial India. From 1835 to 1917, over 240,000 East Indians, mostly illiterate, Urdu-speaking villagers, migrated to Guiana; 84 percent were Hindus, but 16 percent were Sunnī Muslims who followed Ḥanafī legal precepts. Given the opportunity to make down payments on land with their return passage money after their work contracts expired, 66 percent opted to stay, and their families came from India to join them. In the late twentieth century Guyana's population consisted of 48 percent East Indians, 34 percent blacks, and the remainder, small percentages of American Indians, Portuguese, Chinese, Creoles, and western Europeans. Most Afro-Guyanans are Christian; 54 percent of Guyana's urbanites are Protestant Creoles, largely professionals and government bureaucrats who play a dominant role in national life. Guyana's Muslims therefore are mostly rural and are far outnumbered by both Hindus and Christians.

Competition between blacks and East Indians for land in Guyana during the nineteenth century alienated the two peoples, who also were separated by a language barrier. These factors prevented Guyana's East Indian and Afro-Muslims from blending into a single ethnic group based on Muslim heritage. On the other hand, the shared hardships of plantation life weakened caste and religious boundaries among the East Indians. Today both Hindu and Muslim East Indians are divided into conservative and reformed factions. Conservative Muslims formed their own political party when Guyana achieved independence in 1964, keep women in purdah, and arrange the marriages of their children. Reformed Muslims, however, have relaxed the social segregation of the sexes; women are not veiled, and many young adults select their own spouses. Urban Muslim shopkeepers sell pork, cigarettes, and alcoholic beverages. Reformed Muslims and reformed Hindus attend one another's religious celebrations.

East Indian Muslims make up about 5.3 percent of the population in Trinidad and Tobago and 2 percent in Surinam. In the 1890s Javanese men came to Surinam to work on Dutch sugar plantations. Most were Mālikī Sunnīs of peasant origin. By 1901 they numbered 33,000, and by the 1970s, 50,000. Because of the scarcity of women among them, some married Christian Creole women, and many of the children of such couples have abandoned Islam.

Other Caribbean Muslims include a few thousand Chinese Sunnī families who arrived late in the nineteenth century and are now dispersed in the larger cities of Trinidad, Panama, Mexico, Ecuador, and Peru. Linked by business interests, they are a tightly knit, endogamous community that transcends national boundaries. Aḥmadīyah missionaries, members of a heterodox sect that originated in the nineteenth century in what is now Pakistan, and the Bilalians, Black Muslims and other Afro-Americans who embraced Sunnī Islam after 1976, have won many converts among Caribbean black Christians. Caribbean Sunnī Muslims of different origins have little contact with one another. Isolated in many separate communities, they do not form a unified religious body. In the 1970s a Muslim religious leader from Trinidad complained that East Indian Muslims in the Caribbean would rather marry Hindus than blacks of their own faith.

Ottoman Immigrants. During the nineteenth century Muslim dignitaries and Christian merchants from the Ottoman empire visited cities in the United States to attend trade fairs, and a handful of Turks and Arabs escorted two shipments of camels purchased by the U.S. government to facilitate travel in its Southwest Territory. One of them later became a scout for the U.S. Army. The 1871 Canadian census notes thirteen "Muslims" of unknown origin, but those of 1881 and 1891 list the number of Muslims as zero. A few white American Christians converted to Sunnī Islam in the 1870s and 1880s. Muhammad Alexander Webb, jeweler, newspaper editor, and diplomat, founded the American Islamic Propaganda Movement in 1893 after his conversion to Islam while visiting India. He lectured extensively in the United States, wrote three books on Islam, published a periodical called *The Moslem World,* and established seven circles of the Moslem Brotherhood in eastern and midwestern cities. He received financial support first from India, then from the Ottoman sultan, Abdul Hamid II. After Webb died in 1916, his movement evaporated.

Several hundred Ḥanafī Muslim Arabs from the Ottoman province of Syria appeared in North America between 1900 and 1914, with most arriving in 1908. A few Arabs from Morocco, the Sudan, and Yemen also came during these years. The overwhelming majority were uneducated village men, fourteen to forty years of age, who hoped to return to their homeland after making a fortune in America. Many began their careers as wholesale traders and peddlers for Arab Christian merchants who had settled in New York City, Boston, and Philadelphia about twenty years earlier. Arab Muslims dispersed throughout the Dakotas, Minnesota, Montana, Alberta, and Manitoba. After World War I, many purchased small farms, but others were drawn to the factories of Chicago, Gary, Pittsburgh, and Detroit, where an enterprising few opened grocery stores, restaurants, coffee houses, barber shops, and funeral parlors. The majority of the men never married, violating the ideals of Islam. They feared American Christian brides would not embrace Islam or adjust well to life in the old country when they returned. Men who had married before they emigrated often never saw their wives and children again, although they sent them money regularly. Of the handful who did marry, three-quarters either found Muslim brides in the United States or managed to import brides from abroad, and the rest wed North American Christian women. Many mixed and unmixed marriages were troubled, and some ended in divorce. Lacking access to a proper Islamic education, most of the tiny second generation converted to Christianity and were assimilated into the U.S. or Canadian mainstream.

Elsewhere in the Ottoman empire, some forty thousand Turks, Kurds, Albanians, and Bosnians who were Sunnī Muslims left the war-torn Balkan and eastern Anatolian provinces for the United States between 1900 and 1925. In sex ratio, age at entry, social class background, illiteracy rates, and reasons for emigrating, they resembled Arab Muslim immigrants of the same period. Before World War I they scattered across the continent to work as stokers, ditchdiggers, lumberjacks, railroad builders, and miners, and some migrated to Panama to help construct the canal. After 1920 many Albanians returned to their newly created nation in the Balkans, but most Turks, Kurds, and Serbian-speaking Bosnians found jobs in the industrial cities of the eastern seaboard and Great Lakes. Between the two world wars, a few thousand Turkish families joined their countrymen's urban enclaves or took up residence in small towns of western Pennsylvania, West Virginia, and Virginia.

Urban Life. Detroit, the second largest Muslim center in the United States, reflects the heterogeneous nature of Muslim settlements in North America. Founded in 1903 by a Turkish immigrant, metropolitan Detroit's Ottoman Sunnī community in the 1920s and 1930s boasted about two thousand persons, mostly Turks (45 percent) and Kurds (45 percent), plus a smattering of Arabs and Albanians (10 percent). They cohered as an ethnic unit despite language barriers. By 1912 they congregated to pray in the home of Detroit's first imam, an Arab from the Levantine coast. A Sudanese Arab Ford employee, the mosque's leading fundraiser, bought plots in a Detroit cemetery for the burial of Muslims who might die in Michigan. Before he returned to his homeland in the late 1920s, he organized a funeral association and established a local chapter of the Kızıl Ay, or Red Crescent, the Muslim wing of the International Red Cross. Red Crescent members received booklets issued from Ankara, the capital of Turkey, with regulations in Arabic script and spaces for the placement of stamps acknowledging monthly donations. Detroit's Sunnīs shunned the little group of southern Lebanese Shīʿī Muslims who gathered in the metropolitan area in the 1920s, preserving the most significant sectarian boundary within Islam. However, emerging nationalist loyalties periodically divided the Sunnīs after the establishment of the secular Turkish republic in 1923 in the heartland of the dismantled Ottoman empire. The Kurdish revolts of 1928 and 1936 in Turkey were echoed by schisms between Turks and Kurds in Detroit. Kurds spurned a Turkish-owned coffee house, the social hub of the entire Sunnī community, opened one of their own, and retained control of the Kızıl Ay. In retaliation, the Turks resigned from the Kızıl Ay, organized a separate funeral association, and founded the Türkiye Çocuk Esirgeme Kurumu (Turkish Orphans' Association). When the Kurdish wars subsided, Detroit Turks and Kurds frequented one another's coffee houses, attended one another's funerals, and belonged to both charitable societies.

Of the 5 percent of Detroit's Sunnī men who wed, three-quarters took American Christian or Jewish wives, while the rest found Sunnī Turkish or Albanian brides. While most American wives did not work outside the home, many Turkish women worked in their husband's store or found jobs elsewhere. American wives encouraged their husbands to become U.S. citizens but not to deny Islam, and they participated in the fundraising activities and holiday celebrations of the Red Crescent. Most Sunnī wives did not get involved in either of their charitable organizations.

Muslims from tsarist Russia, and later from the Soviet Union, also immigrated to the United States. During the first decade of the twentieth century, a few hundred Polish-speaking, Sunnī Tatars left Baltic Russia to make their homes in Brooklyn, New York, and some Turkic-speaking Crimean and Kazan Tatar families fled from southern Russia in the aftermath of the 1917 revolution. After World War II, Crimean Tatars who had fought in the Red Army and were captured by the Nazis came directly to America or migrated via Turkey. They clustered in New York City, adjacent New Jersey, and Chicago; elsewhere they were integrated into Turkish communities.

In the 1940s several thousand Sunnīs in metropolitan New York City annually celebrated the Day of Sacrifice (ʿĪd al-Aḍḥā) in Harlem with a dazzling parade. Men donned long robes and turbans or fezzes, and women bedecked themselves in brocades and jewels. Led by Shaykh Davud Ahmed Faisal, born on the Caribbean island of Grenada allegedly of Moroccan and Syrian parents, they included immigrants from many nations plus Afro-American converts. They intermarried freely, worshiped in private homes and rented halls, and held religious classes for children on Saturdays. Most of the year they wore ordinary clothing, and the men worked as bellboys, waiters, mechanics, janitors, factory workers, insurance agents, and businessmen.

Pre–World War II Muslim immigrants in North America were a beleagered minority in an alien, Christian world. Though they usually kept a low profile, most adhered to their faith. Albanian Muslims founded a religious association and built a mosque in Maine in 1915 and another in Connecticut in 1919. In the 1920s, Lebanese Sunnīs built a mosque in Ross, South Dakota, and in 1934, in Cedar Rapids, Iowa. Polish-speaking Sunnī Tatars constructed a mosque in Brooklyn in 1928 that is still in use today. Canada's first mosque opened in 1938 near Edmonton; it served twenty Lebanese families, who founded the Arabian Muslim Association.

Postwar Demography and Developments. Muslims who left Asia and Africa to live in the Americas and elsewhere after World War II were spurred by economic changes and political upheavals in their homelands and attracted by opportunities for economic betterment in the West. By the end of the twentieth century Muslims are found in virtually every country in the Western Hemisphere; they come from sixty different nations (mostly Middle Eastern) and include speakers of many Arabic dialects and numerous Turkic and Indo-European languages.

Very little is known about Muslims in Latin America except that they are predominantly Palestinian and Lebanese Arabs. Most of the former became refugees during the Palestine-Israel wars, have a stronger nationalist than religious identity, and tended to migrate in family units. They cluster in the larger cities of Brazil, Argentina, and Chile, where they work in factories or operate their own businesses. Lebanese migrants are largely from mountain villages and until about 1965 were mostly males. Many launched their careers by peddling textiles and sundry items, often for an already established relative, then opened tiny retail outlets which they subsequently expanded. Men who wed before emigrating were joined by their wives and children after a few years; bachelors either went home briefly to marry or sent for a bride from the old country.

Estimates of Muslims living in Anglo-America range from nine hundred thousand to three million. In 1951, Canada contained only two to three thousand Muslims, including descendants of former immigrants, newcomers, and native-born converts. By 1983, they numbered one hundred thousand, about .04 percent of the total population; 60 percent were foreign born. The United States, which has not conducted a religious census since 1936, is home to over two million Muslims, according to figures adjusted for the 1980s from a 1970 census taken by the Islamic Center of Washington, D.C., and the Federation of Islamic Associations. In both countries, large numbers of postwar Muslim immigrants arrived with student visas and remained after earning university degrees. Over 750,000 Muslim foreign students now attend universities in the United States and Canada, and many of them probably will not return permanently to their countries of origin. Some American women who marry Muslim students have converted to Islam. In addition, thousands of American-born former Black Muslims and Afro-Christians have embraced Sunnī Islam since 1976.

North American Muslims are ethnically diversified on the basis of national origin, language, and religious sect. Arabic-speaking Muslims form the biggest and most differentiated Muslim group in the United States (although only 10 percent of Arab-Americans are Muslims); they include Yemeni migrant farmworkers in California, factory workers from Lebanon, Palestine, and the two Yemens, prosperous Lebanese and Palestinian businessmen, and highly trained professionals of all Arab nationalities. Other large Muslim nationality groups in the United States are the Iranians (90,000), who cluster primarily in California, and the Turks (85,000). The Sunnīs outnumber the Shīʿah in both the United States and Canada, although proportionately more Shīʿah live in Canada than in the United States. Many Shīʿī sects and heterodox Islamic groups have also established communities in Anglo-America.

Though Islam can be practiced in the absence of a mosque, by 1983 Muslims in the United States owned 110 mosques or centers in 24 states and the District of Columbia; Bilalians have constructed 156 mosques in 39 states since 1976. Canadian Muslims have mosques in at least one city in every province. These mosques, some of which reflect traditional Islamic architecture, are sites of a broad spectrum of activities, from Friday or Sunday prayers, holiday celebrations, marriage and funeral rites, classes for children, and lectures for adults to informal social gatherings. Since the 1950s the governments of Egypt, Saudi Arabia, Iran, and Lebanon have allocated funds for the construction of mosques for Muslim communities in non-Muslim lands, including the United States and Canada. Nevertheless, many Muslims in Anglo-America still gather to pray in rented halls and private homes.

With few exceptions, imams serving the Sunnī communities in the United States and Canada were born abroad, the vast majority in Arab nations and the remainder in Albania, Pakistan, Yugoslavia, and Turkey. Most were educated at al-Azhar University in Egypt or in British universities. They ably meet the spiritual needs of the immigrant generation but often do not fully understand the sociocultural conflict experienced by the immigrants' children. North America lacks theological colleges where imams could be trained and encouraged to resolve the dissonance between Islam and the individualistic values and secular institutions that mold Anglo-American society. A council of Sunnī imams from the United States and Canada was formed in 1972, and a Shīʿī council of mosques was established shortly afterward.

National-level Islamic organizations first emerged in the United States and Canada in the 1950s. A Lebanese World War II veteran organized the Federation of Islamic Associations (FIA) in 1954; despite factional disputes arising in the 1980s, it owns buildings and extensive camp grounds, publishes *The Muslim Star,* and has a scholarship fund for college-bound high school graduates. The Muslim Students Association of the United States and Canada (MSA) was founded in 1963 to promote Islamic solidarity, preserve the Islamic way of life, and foster friendship with non-Muslims. It has over one hundred branches and has spawned the Islamic Medical Association, the Association of Muslim Social Scientists, and the Association of Muslim Scientists and Engineers. It operates an Islamic teaching center, a press, a book service, and missionizes in prisons in the United States.

Each Muslim ethnic group has its own religious and secular societies as well. In Canada, for example, some twenty thousand Nizārī Ismāʿīlīs, members of a Shīʿī sect originally from Northwest India who follow the Aga Khan, maintain district religious councils linked to regional, national, and international councils. They have built ten *jamāʿat khānah*s, or prayer houses, in Toronto and others in Vancouver, the two cities where they also maintain their own business information centers. Their children, boys as well as girls, benefit from the Aga Khan Fund for Higher Education.

Muslim ethnic communities are differentially integrated into the North American mainstream, depending on the social background of members in their homeland and opportunities and constraints in the localities where they live. Most recent Turkish immigrants, for instance, were born to families of government bureaucrats, high ranking military officers, and small town elites. Their North American communities are scattered in affluent suburbs and include women as well as men who are physicians, university professors, and engineers. Most of the six hundred Turkish families in Rochester, New York, however, are from the artisan and shopkeeper class of towns in southeastern Turkey. In Rochester, both men and women are skillful tailors who work for clothiers or have their own shops. Turks in Windsor, Canada, emigrated from villages and towns of Asian Turkey, and they became skilled laborers in auto plants in their new home. Husbands and wives both frequently work to increase the family income. Religious expression in each Turkish community varies. Among the professionals are many nominal Muslims who accept the unity of God and Muḥammad as his prophet, but they rarely pray, fast inconsistently during Ramaḍān, drink moderately, and eat pork on occasion. Women dress like their wealthy suburban American counterparts, and families allow their daughters to date. They stress their Turkish rather than their Muslim identity. Rochester Turks emphasize both identities. They renovated several old buildings on land they purchased, converting one into a mosque and another into a social hall with a cafeteria and classrooms where English language, Turkish history and heritage, and religious courses are taught. They hold weekly prayers led by a Turkish imam, fast during Ramaḍān, hope to make the pilgrimage to Mecca, and avoid pork. Windsor Turks share a mosque with other ethnic groups, utilizing it mainly for marriages and celebrating religious holidays in private homes. All families forbid their teenage girls to date and arrange the marriages of sons and daughters.

Islam has been practiced variably in the Americas at different times and in different places and is flexible enough to be adapted to local customs which do not violate its tenets. Contemporary Muslims in the Americas are developing appropriate standards of modesty for women in societies where female bodies are highly exposed, viable guidelines for interaction of men and women in a permissive cultural environment, new conjugal relationships when wives work outside the home, and ways to transmit Islamic values to the next generation.

[*See also* Afro-American Religions, *article on* Muslim Movements.]

BIBLIOGRAPHY

Publications by and about North American Muslims are discussed by Sulayman S. Nyang in "Islam in the United States of America: A Review of the Sources," *The Search: Journal for Arab and Islamic Studies* 1 (1980): 164–182. Excellent overviews of Islam in Anglo-America are Akbar Muhammad's "Muslims in the United States," in *The Islamic Impact,* edited by Yvonne Yazbeck Haddad, Byron Haines, and Ellison Findley (Syracuse, 1984), pp. 195–217, and Baha Abu-Laban's "The Canadian Muslim Community: The Need for a New Survival Strategy" and Emily Kalled Lovell's "Islam in the United States: Past and Present," in *The Muslim Community in North America,* edited by Earle H. Waugh, Baha Abu-Laban, and Regula B. Quereshi (Edmonton, 1983), pp. 75–92 and 93–110, respectively.

Studies of specific Muslim communities in the Western Hemisphere are reported in scattered articles in periodicals such as *al-Ittihad,* published by the Muslim Students Association of the United States and Canada; *The Arab Studies Quarterly,* published by the Association of Arab American University Graduates; *The Muslim World,* and various anthropological and sociological journals. Books containing informative articles about Arab-American Muslim groups include *The Arab World and Arab Americans: Understanding a Neglected Minority,* edited by Sameer Y. Abraham and Nabeel Abraham (Detroit, 1981); *Arabs in America: Myths and Realities,* edited by Baha Abu-Laban and Faith T. Zeady (Wilmette, Ill., 1975); *Arabic-speaking Communities in American Cities,* edited by Barbara C. Aswad (New York, 1974); *The Arab Americans,* edited by Elaine C. Hagopian and Ann Paden (Wilmette, 1969); and *Minority Canadians: Immigrant Groups,* edited by Jean L. Elliott (Scarborough, 1961). An analysis of the difficulties encountered by a group of Arab Muslim immigrant laborers is "Detroit's Yemeni Workers," by Nabeel Abraham, *MERIP Reports*, no. 57 (1977): 3–9. Abdo Elkholy's *The Arab Moslems in the United States* (New Haven, 1966) remains the only published book-length study of the adaptations of Muslim communities and transformations in their observance of Islam in the Americas. I have explored these and other facets of sociocultural life among Turkish Muslims in "Variations in Family Structure and Organization in the Turkish Community of Southeast Michigan and Adjacent Canada" (Ph.D. diss., Wayne State University, 1985) as well as in short articles on Turkic-speaking and other Detroit-area Muslim communities in *Ethnic Groups in Michigan*, edited by James M. Anderson and Iva A. Smith (Detroit, 1983).

BARBARA J. BILGÉ

ISLAMIC LAW. [*This entry includes a general survey of* sharīʿah, *or Islamic law, in historical and geographical context, followed by an examination of its most pervasive element, personal law.*]

Sharīʿah

Sharīʿah is an Arabic term used to designate Islamic law. It originally referred to a path trodden by camels to a water source, and the commonly used Arabic phrase *al-sharīʿah al-islāmīyah* may be translated as "the Islamic way." In the case of Islamic law, the way is one that leads the righteous believer to Paradise in the afterlife. The *sharīʿah* is not deemed a religious law by virtue of the subject matters it covers, for these range far beyond the sphere of religious concerns strictly speaking and extend to the mundane affairs of everyday life. Rather, its religious character is due to the Muslim belief that it derives from divinely inspired sources and represents God's plan for the proper ordering of all human activities. Although Muslims agree that they are bound by the *sharīʿah,* the interpretations of its requirements have differed historically according to sectarian and school divisions and, in modern times, also according to differing views of how the *sharīʿah* applies in the changed circumstances of present-day societies.

The interpretations of the requirements of the *sharīʿah* are contained in the *fiqh.* In a general sense, *fiqh* means "knowledge" or "understanding," but it is also used in the more specific sense of Islamic jurisprudence. *Sharīʿah* and *fiqh* are often treated as synonymous terms designating the body of rules constituting Islamic law. However, *fiqh* can also refer to the science of interpreting the *sharīʿah.*

Origins and Nature. The historical origin of the *sharīʿah* lies in the revelation that Muslims believe was given to the prophet Muḥammad by God through the vehicle of the archangel Gabriel in the last decades before the Prophet's death in 632 CE. This divine revelation was later recorded in a text known as the Qurʾān. Although only a small portion of the Qurʾān concerns strictly legal questions, it sets forth a number of general principles regarding how Muslims are to conduct themselves. The Qurʾān is replete with commands to believers to abide by God's limits, to obey God and his Prophet, and to judge according to what God has laid down. It contains many references to God's laws and commands. The prevailing view among Muslims is that the Qurʾān laid the underpinnings for a distinctively Islamic legal order and one that all Muslims are bound to follow as a token of their submission (*islām* in Arabic) to the will of God.

From this kernel the *sharīʿah* grew into a vast corpus of law. One of the great, challenging issues of Islamic intellectual history has been that of defining the relationship between the text of divine revelation and subsequent legal development, an effort that has entailed the working out of a theory of resources to provide an Islamic theoretical basis for resolving legal problems not explicitly addressed in the Qurʾān.

Sharīʿah rules were part of the positive law applied by the government of the early Muslim community, which was originally conceived as an entity where political and religious loyalties would be coterminous. At the same time, the *sharīʿah* was also understood as a system of moral guidance for the individual believer.

In the Islamic view, governments exist only to ensure that the *sharīʿah* is properly administered and enforced. Governments are subordinate to the *sharīʿah* and must execute its commands and prohibitions. In other words, what Islam envisages is a scheme of divine nomocracy, in which the law is the medium of social control—truly, a government of laws, not of men.

Should the government of a Muslim society fail in its obligation to uphold the *sharīʿah* as the positive law, or the judges of this world fail in their obligation to administer justice in accordance with the *sharīʿah,* the individual believer would still be held to the responsibility incumbent upon all Muslims to conform their behavior to the *sharīʿah.* On the Day of Judgment each Muslim will be held to account for any personal failures to comply with the commands and prohibitions of the *sharīʿah.*

Classification of acts. The dual nature of the *sharīʿah* as positive law and deontology, serving the combined functions of law and of what in some other religious systems might be moral philosophy, is reflected in the fact that Muslim jurists distinguish between two fundamentally different ways of classifying human acts.

One way is to assess the moral character of acts, an assessment that corresponds to the deontological quality of the *sharīʿah*. For this task there exists a fivefold scheme of classification, according to which an act may be mandatory, recommended, neutral (that is, entailing no moral consequences), blameworthy, or prohibited. Knowledge of this classification scheme enables pious Muslims to follow a meritorious course of conduct that will ensure their salvation on the Day of Judgment.

The second way of classifying acts reflects the fact that the *sharīʿah* is meant to be used as the positive law of Muslim societies. The fundamental distinction made by Muslim jurists in this connection is between acts that are legally binding and valid and those that are of no legal effect or invalid. They also distinguish between licit acts and illicit acts warranting the imposition of penalties or exposing the actor (and potentially persons in privity with the actor) to legal liability. The classifications in the two schemes are not correlated; from knowledge of how an act is to be evaluated from the ethical standpoint, one cannot draw any automatic conclusions about the legal validity or invalidity of an act or whether it is punishable or goes unpunished by worldly authorities. Likewise, one cannot safely make assumptions about how acts will be classified from an ethical standpoint based on whether they are legally valid or not or whether they entail penalties or legal liability.

The precise nature of the relationship between the *sharīʿah* and Islamic theology is not easy to delineate and has been the subject of disagreement among Muslim scholars of Islamic philosophy, theology, and law over the centuries. However, throughout the history of Islam there has been a tendency to emphasize the elaboration of exact standards for conduct rather than setting detailed standards for what Muslims should believe, and, by extension, to require adherence to the standards of orthopraxis rather than demanding orthodoxy of creed.

Principal divisions. The two principal divisions of the *sharīʿah* are based on the subject categories of legal rules. The first category is that of the *ʿibādāt*, or strictly religious obligations. These comprise the believer's duties vis-à-vis the deity. In this category one finds very extensive rules regarding precisely how to carry out the acts of worship and religious observances incumbent on the individual Muslim. The performance of daily prayers *(ṣalāt)*, the pilgrimage to Mecca *(ḥajj)*, the practice of fasting during the month of Ramaḍān *(ṣawm)*, and the payment of the alms tax *(zakāt)* are all regulated by the rules of *ʿibādāt*. These, along with the profession of faith *(shahādah)*, constitute the so-called pillars of the faith in Islam. Ancillary rules such as those for identifying sources of ritual pollution and setting forth the requirements for the ablutions necessary to achieve a state of ritual purity, the techniques for correct preparation of a corpse for burial, and the selection of a prayer leader in a given congregation are likewise included in the *ʿibādāt* category. [*See* Worship, *article on* Islamic Worship; Pilgrimage, *article on* Muslim Pilgrimage; Ṣalāt; Ṣawm; Shahādah; *and* Zakāt.]

The Islamic concern for orthopraxis in religious matters clearly emerges from any examination of the very exacting scheme of *ʿibādāt* rules. While some specific provisions of *ʿibādāt* rules vary according to sectarian and school divisions, one finds considerable agreement on the fundamental features of the *sharīʿah* in this area. Within a given sect, the rules of *ʿibādāt* have tended to remain relatively stable and uncontroversial over the centuries.

The other main category of *sharīʿah* rules is that of the *muʿāmalāt*, which regulate the conduct of interpersonal relations rather than the relationship of the believer to the deity. There is considerable diversity among the sects and schools regarding the *sharīʿah* rules in this category. Today there is also significant controversy about the degree to which these rules, originally formulated by medieval jurists, need to be updated and reformed in the light of modern circumstances.

Historical Development. The question of the historical development of the *sharīʿah* cannot be fairly discussed without acknowledging the deep and persistent cleavage between the views set forth in modern Western scholarship and the views of the majority of Muslim scholars. The positions that have been taken by Western scholars regarding the historical development of Islamic law challenge deeply held convictions of most Muslim scholars and are strongly reprehended by the latter. The nature of the differing views and their implications will be explained in what follows.

The relation of the Qurʾān to previous law. As already noted, the Qurʾān provided the original kernel of *sharīʿah* law. Most of the Qurʾanic verses dealing with legal questions were transmitted to the Prophet in the decade after the Hijrah, or flight from Mecca to Medina (622 CE).

An unresolved dispute in Islamic jurisprudence stems from the question of whether the rules set forth in the Qurʾān should be regarded as a break with the preexisting system of western Arabian customary law or whether the revelations came to modify and reform some aspects of that law while otherwise retaining it. Some Muslim scholars have concluded that the great unevenness in depth of coverage of different topics in Qurʾanic legislation should be taken to imply that the resulting gaps were intended to be filled by reference to those pre-Islamic customary laws that were not changed by the Qur'ān, while others see in it a fresh starting point for legal development.

The Sunnī-Shīʿī division. The death of the prophet Muḥammad in 632 CE marked the end of the period of Qur'anic revelation to the Muslim community. Until the Umayyad dynasty (661–750) came to power, the community was ruled by four leaders known as the Rāshidūn, or the "Rightly Guided [Caliphs]." The assumption of leadership by the Umayyads had great consequences for both sectarian and legal developments. Repudiating the Umayyads, the Shīʿī and Khārijī factions both broke away from the main body of Muslims, who came to be called Sunnīs, and their respective legal orientations thenceforth diverged. The Khārijīs (also known as the Ibāḍīyah) believed that the leadership of the Muslim community should be determined by elections and that Muslims had the right to rebel against an unqualified ruler. This Khārijī position has generally been regarded as heretical by other Muslims, and although small Khārijī communities have survived in remote areas of the Muslim world, Khārijī thought has been marginalized by the majority. The Shīʿī faction believed that the first three caliphs had usurped the rule of the community, which in their view should have passed to the fourth of the Rāshidūn, ʿAlī ibn Abī Ṭālib (d. 661), a cousin and son-in-law of the Prophet. While Sunnī Muslims subsequently looked to the pronouncements and examples of all of the Rāshidūn for authority on how the community should be governed and for guidance on questions of Islamic law, the Shīʿah repudiated the authority of all but the caliph ʿAlī.

Not only did the Shīʿah believe that the caliph ʿAlī had been the rightful successor of the Prophet, but they also believed that leadership of the community rightfully still belonged to Alī's blood descendants after the civil war that resulted in his death and the establishment of a hereditary monarchy by the victorious Umayyads. Those of the caliph ʿAlī's descendants who inherited his authority were known as imams, and like him they were believed by the Shīʿah to share the same divine inspiration that had enabled the Prophet, while himself not divine, to make authoritative pronouncements on *sharīʿah* law. That is, their imams were qualified to interpret the divine will for mankind and could thus serve as an ongoing link between God the Lawgiver and the community after the death of the Prophet. The Shīʿī community subsequently split into subsects over questions of who was entitled to succeed to the position of imam. The largest of the subsects, the Twelvers, believes that the last imam, who disappeared in 874, went into a state of occultation from which he is expected eventually to return, while the other subsects follow lines of imams whose descent has continued into the modern era.

The earliest stage of sharīʿah law. For Sunnīs the possibility of divine revelation and the making of new Islamic law ceased with the death of the Prophet. Subsequent generations of Muslims who were concerned with how to establish a legal system on an Islamic basis were thus faced with a problem of scarce source material. Although there is little information on the development of legal thought in the generations immediately following the death of the Prophet, it does not appear that this problem was initially of great concern to the leaders of the community, who were preoccupied with the challenges of meeting the military threats to the growing Islamic polity and administering its rapidly expanding territory. *Ad hoc* measures and a spirit of pragmatism appear to have characterized much of the decision making of the early political leaders, who also served as judges.

The view of Western scholarship is that as the new empire absorbed its early conquests of Syria, Iraq, Egypt, and Iran, it was also exposed to influences from the local civilizations, which included the very highly developed legal cultures of Romano-Byzantine law, Jewish law, Sasanid law, and the law of the Eastern Christian churches. The assumption generally made by Western scholars is that educated converts to Islam from these cultures perpetuated the legal traditions of the conquered civilizations, which, in a syncretic process, were assimilated into the nascent Islamic legal culture. According to such scholars, the ostensibly Islamic derivation of much of *sharīʿah* law is the product of later attempts to create Islamic pedigrees for legal principles actually borrowed from other legal traditions by linking them to Islamic sources. Most Muslim scholars absolutely reject this view and take the position that *sharīʿah* law owes no debt whatsoever to any non-Islamic tradition. In any event, it must be said that the historical and comparative legal research that would be needed to prove or disprove scientifically either of these two theses has never been undertaken, and the dispute about the relation of the *sharīʿah* to other legal traditions in the areas first conquered by the Islamic Empire cannot be resolved at present.

Ancient law schools. The jurisprudence of the Sunnī branch of *sharīʿah* law had its beginnings in what are called the ancient schools of law. Within a century of the Prophet's death there were prominent law schools in various cities in Iraq, Syria, and the Hejaz. It appears that the scholars in these ancient schools felt free to resort to ratiocination to develop legal rules for new situations and that they may also have been influenced in their approach to legal questions by the judicial practice of the tribunals set up by the Umayyad rulers. While individual scholars did attain renown in this period, what was viewed as the normative legal standard was the consensus of the scholars in a given locality, or the *sunnah*—roughly, "custom"—of the school. Some attempts were made to establish Islamic derivations for such local custom, which might be ascribed to early authorities in the first generation of the Muslim community, including the Prophet himself. [*See* Sunnah.]

The traditionist movement. Meanwhile, a second movement was under way, that of the traditionists, who began to make their influence felt in the course of the second century after the Prophet's death. The traditionists did not accept the authority of the *sunnah* of the ancient schools, nor did they accept the practice of the scholars of those ancient schools who relied on juristic opinion to resolve legal questions. Instead, the traditionists proposed that accounts relating the sayings and doings of the Prophet should be treated as legally binding statements of law. The traditionists collected traditions, known as *ḥadīth* (pl., *aḥādīth*), which purported to record the Prophet's sayings and his reactions to the different situations he had confronted.

Unlike the Qur'ān, the final version of which was written down in 653 and which most Muslims believe accurately represents God's speech, the authenticity of the *ḥadīth* literature was immediately challenged by Muslim scholars unsympathetic to the traditionists' thesis. The early traditionists tried to meet their opponents' criticisms by developing criteria for distinguishing sound *ḥadīth* from those that were not genuine, an effort that resulted in the development of an elaborate science of *ḥadīth* criticism. The dispute regarding the authenticity of the *ḥadīth* has persisted to the present and has meant that a substantial part of Islamic jurisprudence is and always has been a source of controversy among Muslims.

The genuineness of the *ḥadīth* literature is yet another point on which modern Western scholars tend to find themselves in disagreement with many of their Muslim counterparts. The prevailing view among Western scholars has been that most, if not all, of the *ḥadīth* are pious forgeries put into circulation by traditionists of the first and second Muslim centuries with a view to creating Islamic pedigrees for rules of law that had originally been the products of juristic reasoning or judicial practice, that were inherited from Arabian customary law, or that were borrowed from other legal cultures. Western scholarship has generally evaluated the traditional science of *ḥadīth* criticism as inadequate for differentiating historically accurate accounts from later fabrications. In the view of most Muslims, including those who have reservations about the genuineness of some of the *ḥadīth* and the adequacy of *ḥadīth* scholarship, these Western criticisms are excessively harsh. Wholesale dismissals of the *ḥadīth* literature as a product of later forgeries and of the traditional science of *ḥadīth* criticism as defective are rarely encountered in Muslim scholarship. [*See* Ḥadīth.]

The beginnings of the classical law schools. Despite the initial resistance that it encountered, the traditionists' position steadily gained ground at the expense of the influence of the ancient schools of law in the second century after the death of the Prophet. The ancient schools did not disappear but adapted in differing degrees to the new trends in legal thought. It is in the second century AH (ninth century CE) that the foundations were laid for the development of what were subsequently to become the classical *sharīʿah* schools. Each school came to be referred to by the name of an eponymous founder, but it should be noted that the views of the scholars who gave their names to schools did not always prevail among their immediate disciples, much less among their later followers.

The oldest of the classical Sunnī schools is the Mālikī, which originated in Medina and was named after the prominent legal scholar and traditionist Mālik ibn Anas (d. 795). Respect for the *sunnah* of Medina as the place most closely associated with the mission of the Prophet and the first Muslim community persisted in the legal thought of the Mālikī school.

The Ḥanafī school was meanwhile developing in the context of the legal community in Kufa in southern Iraq. Although the school was named after a prominent local jurist, Abū Ḥanīfah (d. 767), its followers actually often showed greater deference to the views of two of his disciples, Abū Yūsuf (d. 798) and al-Shaybānī (d. 805). The Ḥanafī school bore many traces of influences from the Iraqi environment in which it developed. Ḥanafī jurists attached great importance to systematic consistency in legal thought and the refinement of legal principles. They used juristic speculation to develop rules and characteristically resolved legal questions through formalistic approaches.

Muḥammad ibn Idrīs al-Shāfiʿī (d. 820), the founder of the school that bears his name, was associated with the city of Medina. He ranks among the foremost figures in the history of Islamic legal thought and was, more than any other person, responsible for the eventual triumph of the traditionist thesis in classical Islamic legal thought. According to al-Shāfiʿī, the *sunnah* of the Prophet as embodied in the *ḥadīth* totally superseded the *sunnah* of the ancient schools as a normative legal standard. Al-Shāfiʿī thus elevated the *sunnah* of the Prophet to the status of a source of law coequal with the Qur'ān. He articulated the view, which subsequently found widespread acceptance, that the *sunnah* of the Prophet explained the meaning of the Qur'ān.

Having established the Qur'ān and the much more extensive corpus of *ḥadīth* literature as the material sources of the *sharīʿah,* al-Shāfiʿī rejected the use of juristic opinion or speculative reasoning in formulating legal principles and insisted that jurists be restricted to the use of analogical reasoning *(qiyās),* to extend principles in the sources to cover problems not explicitly addressed in the texts of the Qur'ān and *ḥadīth.* In his view, only by insisting that jurists limit themselves to such careful, piecemeal extensions of principles in the texts could one be sure that the jurists were not injecting undue subjective elements into their interpretations of *sharīʿah* requirements or distorting the rules set forth in the sources. Al-Shāfiʿī also refused to accord any weight to juristic consensus and held that the only binding consensus would be one among all members of the Muslim community. Despite his great prestige, al-Shāfiʿī was unable to prevail on this last point even among members of his own school, who, like most Sunnī Muslims, came to believe that *ijmāʿ,* or the consensus of all the jurists in a given generation, could conclusively validate the correctness of a legal proposition and foreclose further debate. In general outlines, the jurisprudence developed by later members of the Shāfiʿī school has much in common with that of the Ḥanafī school.

The last of the classical Sunnī schools crystalized around Aḥmad ibn Ḥanbal (d. 855), a traditionist from Baghdad who traveled widely among different centers of learning. Subsequent members of the Ḥanbalī school have shared Ibn Ḥanbal's traditionist orientation and his concern for the consensus of the companions of the Prophet, but individual Ḥanbalī scholars have taken diverging opinions on questions of jurisprudence. The doctrines of the Ḥanbalī school, and particularly those of its more idiosyncratic members, are difficult to characterize, so that it is necessary to be wary of generalizations purporting to describe broad features of Ḥanbalī doctrine.

Other schools of law founded in the first centuries of Islam have not survived into the modern era. Perhaps the most influential of these was the Ẓāhirī school founded by Dāwūd ibn Khalaf (d. 884). It takes its name from the Arabic *ẓāhir,* meaning "that which is apparent" and referring to the insistence of this school that the *sharīʿah* required literal adherence to the words of the Qur'ān and the *sunnah.* In the Ẓāhirī school, human interpretations of their meanings were not binding.

The development of the legal doctrines of the early Shīʿī schools, aside from their shared doctrine regarding the imams' title to succeed to the leadership of the community, seems to have begun somewhat later. It is important to note that while sectarian disputes in Islam often led to the development of bitter intellectual antagonisms and sometimes took on political dimensions, within the Sunnī sect legal scholars generally demonstrated great tolerance of and even respect for divergent opinions on the part of members of the four classical schools, all four of which were regarded as equally orthodox.

The islamizing impetus in Islamic legal development that had been encouraged by the traditionist movement was also promoted by the official policies of the Abbasid dynasty, which justified its overthrow of the Umayyads in 750 on the basis of its greater claims to Islamic legitimacy and piety. The Abbasids manifested a desire that all persons in their domains, including the rulers, should follow the commands and prohibitions of the *sharīʿah.* They elevated the *sharīʿah* to the status of the official law to be applied in the courts by *qāḍīs,* or judges, who were required to be well versed in it. [*See* Qāḍī.] However, before many decades passed, it became abundantly clear that for the Abbasids, promoting the cause of the *sharīʿah* was entirely subordinate to the achievement of their dynastic political objectives. As a result, many jurists who were unwilling to readjust their idealistic views of the role that Islamic law should play in the governance of the Muslim community to the dictates of political expediency retreated from all contact with government and the administration of justice. It became common for great jurists to shun positions in courts and to retire to lives of scholarship and academic disputations. With this abjuring of political involvement, the basic elements in Sunnī law on the subject of how the Muslim community should be governed tended to remain fixed at the stage of elaborating models derived from the era of the Rāshidūn caliphs, despite the fact that the practical relevance of these models had been superseded by changed historical realities.

Uṣūl al-fiqh. With the development of the classical schools of Islamic law came the articulation of the principles of *uṣūl al-fiqh,* the roots or sources of jurisprudence. Although the *uṣūl* are often called sources of the *sharīʿah,* only the Qur'ān and the *sunnah* are material sources. Ultimately, the study of *uṣūl al-fiqh* is concerned with establishing a science of proofs of the Islamic derivation of substantive legal principles, thus enabling the jurist to discern which legal rules are correct statements of *sharīʿah* principles. The rules shown by this science to be authentically Islamic are known as the *furūʿ al-fiqh,* the branches of jurisprudence. The study of *uṣul* has been one of the major preoccupations of Muslim jurists over the centuries and continues to be so today. As the subsequent history of the development of the *sharīʿah* demonstrates, the influence of al-Shāfiʿī on the formulation of the classical Sunnī theory of *uṣūl al-fiqh*—a formulation that was basically complete by the ninth century—was considerable. [*See* Uṣūl al-fiqh.]

The first root of the *fiqh* is the Qur'ān. In the prevailing view, it is to be treated as the eternal and uncreated word of God, part of his essence. Although the Qur'anic revelation constitutes the starting point for the development of the *sharīʿah*, a relatively small portion of *sharīʿah* rules can be traced directly to the text of the Qur'ān. Aside from setting forth rules regarding acts of worship and the rituals that they entail, the Qur'ān includes extensive provisions on intestate succession, many on domestic relations and the status of women, a few criminal laws, and some rules of evidence and contracts.

Muslim jurists developed an elaborate methodology to interpret the Qur'ān, and, in fact, the legal significance of the Qur'ān cannot be properly understood without an appreciation of this methodology. Muslim jurists themselves have differed over the legal significance of many specific lines of the Qur'ān. Some differences in the legal principles derived from the Qur'ān relate to the sectarian divisions of Islam; perhaps the most striking example lies in the laws of intestate succession among the Sunnīs and the Twelver branch of the Shīʿah. From the same Qur'anic verses, which are more extensive on this subject than on any other legal topic, the two groups have derived markedly contrasting legal rules. In the Sunnī view, the Qur'ān meant to retain, with only limited modifications, the pre-Islamic Arabian scheme of agnatic succession, in which males inheriting through the male line got a major part of the estate. By contrast, the Twelver Shīʿī jurists held that, in designating inheritance shares for females and the children and parents of the deceased, the Qur'ān was implicitly repudiating the customary law of pre-Islamic Arabia and setting forth a completely different scheme of succession. As a result, Sunnī law favors inheritance by agnatic kinsmen, while that of the Twelvers favors the inheritance by the children and parents of the deceased, including females.

Al-Shāfiʿī succeeded in persuading subsequent jurists that the *sunnah* of the Prophet should be treated as the second root of Islamic jurisprudence and a source coequal with the Qur'ān. It is generally accepted among Muslims not only that the Prophet was a perfect human being and thus worthy of emulation, but also that he enjoyed divine inspiration and thus could make no error in matters of religion or *sharīʿah* law. As noted, challenges to the authenticity of the *ḥadīth* literature on which the understanding of the Prophet's *sunnah* rested generated a science of *ḥadīth* criticism to weed out unsound or dubious accounts. In addition, methodologies were worked out to reconcile seeming contradictions and inconsistencies in different *ḥadīth* and between *ḥadīth* and verses of the Qur'ān. As in the case of the Qur'ān, reading the *ḥadīth* literature without a grasp of how orthodox Islamic scholarship interprets the legal implications of the *ḥadīth* and the relevant jurisprudence can lead to erroneous conclusions.

Most Sunnī Muslims have taken the view that the *ḥadīth* assembled in certain classic collections, such as those of al-Bukhārī and Muslim, which date from the latter part of the third century AH, should be regarded as genuine, while members of the other sects rely on their own *ḥadīth* collections, which include many *ḥadīth* accounts that conflict with those in other collections and support their respective sectarian legal positions. Challenges to the authenticity of the *ḥadīth*, which have repeatedly arisen in various forms over the history of Islam, have important implications for the *sharīʿah*. Since the *ḥadīth* literature is very extensive (classical collections contain over four thousand reports) and covers a much wider range of topics than the legal verses in the Qur'ān, it has supplied the Islamic rationale for a major part of *sharīʿah* law, which would forfeit its Islamic legitimacy if the *ḥadīth* literature were discredited.

Qiyās, reasoning by analogy, is a method for expanding the rules in the Qur'ān and *sunnah* to cover problems not expressly addressed in the sources. Most Sunnīs accept *qiyās* as the third root of *fiqh*. *Qiyās* involves the application of a legal ruling from a case mentioned in the Qur'ān or *sunnah* to a subcase not mentioned in the text but sufficiently related to permit coverage by analogical extension. Even though many jurists insisted on the use of *qiyās* on the theory that extending the scope of principles in the Qur'ān and *sunnah* by analogical reasoning minimized the risk of distorting those principles, a number of Sunnī jurists remained critical of its limitations on the grounds of the subjective element it involved. The extension of rules through *qiyās* ultimately involves human judgment, since it is first necessary to identify the reason underlying the original rule set forth in the text. In practice, jurists have been far from unanimous in their identification of these underlying reasons, with the result that they have extended the rules of the Qur'ān and *sunnah* in different ways. The reliance on analogical reasoning meant that Sunnī jurists analyzed series of concrete instances of application of specific rules rather than trying to abstract general rules from the sources. As new issues arose and generated Islamic rules coined by the use of analogy, these rules were added to the earlier compilations without attempts to synthesize and codify the underlying legal principles.

Twelver Shīʿī jurists do not accept the Sunnī model of *qiyās*. Many of them use forms of juristic reasoning that are not limited to drawing analogies in order to construe the meaning of the Qur'ān and *sunnah*. Known as the Uṣūlīyah, Twelver Shīʿī jurists who believe that *sharīʿah* rules can be extended by human reason have historically been opposed by another faction of jurists, the Akhbārīyah, who insist that rules generated by human reason cannot be binding statements of *sharīʿah* law and argue that the Qur'ān and the *sunnah* of the Prophet and the Shīʿī imams alone provide trustworthy guidance. [*See* Qiyās.]

Ijmāʿ refers to the retroactive ratification of the correctness of an interpretation of *sharīʿah* requirements. Most Sunnīs treat *ijmāʿ*, which is constituted by the consensus of all the jurists of one generation, as the fourth root of *fiqh*. According to the majority Sunnī position, once a legal principle has won such unanimous endorsement, it becomes definitively established and cannot be challenged by subsequent generations. Al-Shāfiʿī's different view of *ijmāʿ* has already been noted. Prominent Ḥanbalī scholars have been among those who have rejected the binding force of *ijmāʿ* as defined by the majority; they claim that only the consensus of the companions of the Prophet could bind later Muslims. Also among the critics of the Sunnī view of *ijmāʿ* are the Twelver Shīʿah, who have historically taken a variety of positions on the significance of *ijmāʿ* and how it is constituted. [*See* Ijmāʿ.]

This bare summary of the basic principles of *uṣūl al-fiqh* does not begin to do justice to the tremendously complex and subtle analysis that Islamic legal scholarship is capable of bringing to bear on questions of the Islamic derivation of legal rules. Problems of *uṣūl al-fiqh* have attracted the attention of many of the finest Muslim scholars over the centuries and are still capable of generating controversy and provoking important intellectual developments.

In addition to the fundamental rules of *uṣūl al-fiqh*, there are subsidiary law-finding principles that are used to interpret the requirements of *sharīʿah* law. These principles provide the jurist with guidelines for resolving questions of *sharīʿah* law where the usual sources offer no unequivocal answer or where the facts of the case mean that the application of an otherwise dispositive principle will produce an unsatisfactory result. Predictably, these subsidiary principles vary considerably according to school and sectarian affiliations, and even within one school individual jurists may display different views on their use. An example of such a subsidiary principle is *maṣlaḥah* (considerations of public welfare), which was particularly emphasized in Mālikī jurisprudence. By reference to the criterion of *maṣlaḥah*, Muslim jurists can adjust their interpretations of *sharīʿah* requirements to promote the well-being of society. [*See* Maṣlaḥah.]

Jurists and the development of the sharīʿah. With the foundation of the classical schools of Islamic law and the formulation of the fundamental principles of *uṣūl al-fiqh*, the *sharīʿah* became a jurists' law, and exhaustive training in law and ancillary disciplines was essential for interpreting how the *sharīʿah* applied to a given problem. The jurist, or *faqīh* (pl., *fuqahā'*), came to enjoy great prestige as a result of his monopoly of expertise regarding the sacred law. The prominence and power of the *fuqahā'* as a class in Muslim societies has in some instances led to the misperception that Islam envisages a theocratic system of government. In fact, it is the *sharīʿah* itself that is supposed to be the instrument of social control, and the *fuqahā'*, in theory powerless to alter the law, are no more than its faithful interpreters. For the most part, the *fuqahā'* have eschewed direct participation in the affairs of government and an overt role in political life.

The task of interpreting the requirements of the *sharīʿah* is termed *ijtihād*, and the person performing the interpretation is termed a *mujtahid*. The exercise of *ijtihād* by the early jurists defined the basic contours of the *sharīʿah* by the start of the tenth century CE. It has been widely believed that at that point in Sunnī jurisprudence, the *fuqahā'* were held to be bound by the solutions to legal problems reached by jurists of earlier generations on the grounds that the latter, being closer in time to the prophet Muḥammad, were less likely to fall into error than scholars of later generations. This bar to reexamination of previously decided questions of *sharīʿah* law has been termed "the closing of the door of *ijtihād*." Never recognized by Twelver Shīʿī law, it may have inhibited innovative thought and retarded legal reform in Sunnī circles, although not in the Ḥanbalī school, where many jurists denied that they could be bound by the *ijtihād* of their predecessors. However, the common supposition that the corollary doctrine of *taqlīd*, or obedience to established legal authority, immutably fixed *sharīʿah* doctrines at an early stage and had a stultifying impact on the evolution of *sharīʿah* law has never been conclusively established; the necessary scientific examination of the actual historical effect of *taqlīd* on the ability of jurists to adjust legal doctrines and respond to the exigencies of the changing environment has not been undertaken. [*See* Ijtihād.]

Of course, even if Sunnī jurists did consider themselves bound in areas where there had been *ijtihād* by the jurists of the first centuries, they were free to resolve questions that had not been definitively settled by their predecessors. In Muslim societies, important new problems of *sharīʿah* law were traditionally referred for resolution to a qualified *mujtahid.* In Sunnī environments this function was exercised by scholars who had attained the status of *muftī,* meaning that they were able to issue *fatwās*, or binding legal rulings, on such problems. A *muftī* might act in a private capacity, advising individuals who came to him with inquiries about how the *sharīʿah* applied to a problem, but jurists were appointed as official or governmental *muftīs* by rulers. *Fatwās* that were widely respected and collected for further use and study could be incorporated in *fiqh* works and could acquire considerable currency and authority.

In contrast to the important role played by *fatwās* in the development of *sharīʿah* rules, only rarely were decisions rendered by *qāḍīs* in actual cases treated as authoritative in the *fiqh* literature. Most of the *fuqahāʾ* did not recognize judicial precedent as binding, perhaps because in the wake of the disenchantment with government after the first Abbasids many of the more eminent *fuqahāʾ* preferred to disassociate themselves from the court system and often declined to serve when offered judgeships. The one important exception in this regard occurred in Morocco, where *ʿamal,* or judicial practice, was considered authoritative.

The Mature Classical Law Schools. From the tenth century until the disruptive impact of European imperialism made itself felt in India in the eighteenth century, and in the other parts of the Muslim world in the nineteenth century, there was no major discontinuity in the development of doctrines of the classical law schools. Instead, one could say that this period was devoted to refining and amplifying the early treatments of Islamic jurisprudence.

As the schools matured, their doctrines became more elaborate—often, as already noted, deviating from the views of their eponymous founders. Although the schools did not require that all members adhere to precisely the same doctrines, within each school there tended to be a core of doctrines that enjoyed widespread acceptance and that embodied a distinctive approach to the resolution of legal problems. The jurists of the different schools wrote treatises on *fiqh* that were evaluated and reevaluated by their peers and successors. Some works gained particular renown and respect and were widely circulated and studied. The same work would often be recopied with added commentaries and supercommentaries in the margins by subsequent scholars. As the *fiqh* literature expanded, it was typical for the jurists in a given locality to select one of the more highly regarded treatises from what was the dominant legal school as the authoritative statement of legal doctrine in their jurisdiction. They also prepared summaries of the classical statements of a school's doctrine, which were meant to be easier to use and understand than the scholarly originals. Even so, works of *fiqh* were intelligible only to learned specialists. Institutions of higher learning were set up to train students in *fiqh* and related fields, the first and most enduringly influential of which was al-Azhar in Cairo, founded in 972.

One of the ancillary subjects essential for aspiring *fuqahāʾ* to master was classical Arabic, the language of God's speech in the Qurʾān and the language of the *ḥadīth.* Arabic has continued to be the essential language for the study of the *sharīʿah.* No translated versions of the Qurʾān or the *ḥadīth* are adequate for use in scholarly investigations. All of the classical *fiqh* works are also in Arabic. Although recently some have become available in translations, these are of very uneven quality and must be used with great caution.

The schools spread far from their original settings. Adherence to one school or another, as well as sectarian allegiances, changed in accordance with the many political upheavals and vicissitudes suffered by the different parts of the Muslim world over the centuries, and the patterns of school and sect distribution varied significantly at different eras of Islamic history. One of the prerogatives of the Muslim ruler was to select the law of a sect or, more commonly, of a Sunnī school that would become the official norm in his domains and would be applied by the courts. In some large cities, court staffs would include judges from different schools and sects, so that the law applicable in a given case could be selected to correspond to the affiliations of the parties.

It should be recalled that all of the four classical Sunnī schools are considered equally orthodox. Although concerns for doctrinal consistency and coherence mandated that a jurist follow the established doctrine of his school, it was not unusual for jurists to study the *fiqh* of other Sunnī schools or even to refer extensively to the opinions of other schools in treatises. This approach was less common, however, when *fiqh* principles of other sects were involved. The protracted polemics between the Sunnī and Twelver Shīʿī camps on the question of temporary marriage, which the former claim is prohibited and akin to prostitution and which the latter argue is clearly established in the Qurʾān and the *ḥadīth,* is an example of the hostile attitudes that were engendered by sectarian disputes about interpretations of the requirements of *sharīʿah* law. However, Sunnī jurists have been prepared to accord some deference to the *fiqh* of the Zaydī Shīʿah, since the Zaydīyah are considered to be more moderate and closer to Sunnīs in their views than the other Shīʿī sects.

Geographical distribution of the schools. The long sponsorship of Ḥanafī law by the Ottoman sultans meant that the Ḥanafī school came to predominate in most of their former territories in the eastern Mediterranean. As the major Sunnī school of the Indian subcontinent as well, the Ḥanafī school is by far the largest school of law.

The adherents of the Mālikī school tend to be concentrated today in the western portions of the Muslim world, particularly in North and West Africa, although one does find them in other parts of the Arab world, including the Hejaz and Kuwait. The distribution of members of the Shāfiʿī school tends to correspond to patterns of major trade routes, with Shāfiʿī communities mostly concentrated in coastal areas. One finds large numbers in East Africa, Ceylon, Malaysia, and Indonesia. The Ḥanbalī school has dwindled in size to such a point that its adherents are scarcely found outside central Saudi Arabia. The widely appreciated originality and intellectual distinction of some of its medieval *fuqahā'* has, however, allowed it to retain an influence entirely out of proportion to its numbers.

The Twelvers, by far the most numerous branch of the Shīʿah, claim the adherence of a majority of the people of Iran and, probably, Iraq, as well as sizable minorities in Pakistan, eastern Arabia, and Lebanon. Since 1501 Twelver Shiism has been the official religion of Iran, and it has come to be particularly identified with that country. As noted, a deep and important cleavage in Iranian Twelver Shīʿī legal thought has divided the Akhbārī and Uṣūlī subschools.

The followers of the Aga Khan belong to the Ismāʿīlī branch of Shīʿī Islam. His ancestors once ruled an Ismāʿīlī state, the powerful and intellectually influential Fatimid empire (969–1171), from their capital in Cairo, but today the Ismāʿīlīyah are everywhere in the minority and are widely scattered around the globe. Sizable communities remain in the Indian subcontinent and East Africa. The Zaydīyah are concentrated in the Yemen Arab Republic (North Yemen), which was ruled until the 1960s by a Zaydī imam.

A very small but intellectually significant group whose law cannot receive its due here is that of the Khārijīs or Ibāḍīyah, many of whom have managed to survive in the more remote parts of the Muslim world, such as the Berber areas of North Africa and in Oman.

Although a ruler is free to select the school of law that will apply on his territory, this selection binds only the formal legal system. In the absence of unusual external pressures mandating a change in allegiance, individual Muslims remain free to follow the school of their choice. Typically, Muslims consider themselves followers of the same school as their fathers, and even within the Sunnī sect, where all four schools are deemed equally orthodox, it is unusual for a Muslim to change school affiliation.

Comparisons of the rules of the classical fiqh. In detail the rules of the various Sunnī schools are often different enough to affect the outcome of a legal dispute. On the average legal question, the degree of doctrinal difference between a given Sunnī school and a Shīʿī school is often not much greater. Notwithstanding the different approaches that Sunnī and Shīʿī *fiqh* purport to have to the sources of law, aside from their differences regarding who should rule the Muslim community, one finds few major divergencies except on some points of religious ritual and worship, certain rules of marriage and divorce, and the laws of inheritance.

A comparison of the *muʿāmalāt* rules of the medieval *fiqh* literature with rules in other medieval legal systems of the Middle East and Europe, whether secular or religious, reveals many broad similarities. The single most distinctive accomplishment of the medieval *fuqahā'* from the standpoint of comparative legal history lies in their very sophisticated and complex schemes of intestate succession.

Principal figures. The founders of the schools of Sunnī law and the imams of the Shīʿī sects, who enjoyed the same capacity as the prophet Muḥammad to make authoritative pronouncements regarding the requirements of the *sharīʿah*, would have to be ranked in the forefront of the principal figures in the history of Islamic law. Given the vast corpus of writings on the *sharīʿah*, it is impossible to present any summary treatment without risking unfair omissions of outstanding figures. The following list must therefore be understood to be only a selection of persons who are representative of some of the important aspects of the Islamic legal heritage and suggestive of its variety and richness.

An early jurist who is notable for a conception of the role of the *sharīʿah* different from that of his more orthodox contemporaries was Ibn al-Muqaffaʿ (d. 756). He unsuccessfully urged the Abbasid caliph al-Manṣūr to end the confusion and disparities in the *sharīʿah* resulting from conflicting interpretations by the jurists of the early law schools by systematizing and codifying the *sharīʿah*. He argued that the *sharīʿah* should be enacted into uniform legislation that would apply throughout the caliph's domain; his failure to convince others of the correctness of his ideas meant that the *sharīʿah* continued to be viewed as a jurist's law independent from and untouchable by political authorities.

Before its extinction, the once-influential Ẓāhirī school enjoyed a flowering in Muslim Spain. The most famous and distinguished Ẓāhirī thinker was Ibn Ḥazm (d. 1065), a vigorous polemicist who made many enemies in the course of his harsh attacks on the doctrines of other law schools. He challenged the authenticity of much of the *ḥadīth* literature, rejected *qiyās* and the rules it produced, limited *ijmāʿ* to that of the companions of the Prophet, and insisted that, in the absence of explicit commands in the Qurʾān and *sunnah,* all conduct should be regarded as outside the concern of religious law.

One of the most eminent figures in Islamic intellectual history, al-Ghazālī (d. 1111) examined the teachings of the *sharīʿah* in relation to his own theological and philosophical views. Although he is best known for his searching inquiry into the theological fundamentals of Islam, al-Ghazālī also wrote a number of important books of Shāfiʿī *fiqh.* In his greatest work, *Iḥyāʾ ʿulūm al-dīn* (The Revivification of Religious Sciences), al-Ghazālī sought to achieve a synthesis of the teachings of Islam and to define the role of the *sharīʿah* in relation to other aspects of religion. His work may constitute the most accomplished statement of what passed for Sunnī orthodoxy in medieval Islam.

One of the most original medieval jurists was the Ḥanbalī Ibn Taymīyah (d. 1328), who had an influential disciple in Ibn Qayyim al-Jawzīyah (d. 1350). Ibn Taymīyah strongly attacked the doctrine of *taqlīd* that bound Muslims to the interpretations of the early jurists. He argued that qualified Muslim thinkers should be free to return to the Qurʾān, *sunnah,* and consensus of the companions of the Prophet and interpret them afresh. Muḥammad ibn ʿAbd al-Wahhāb (d. 1792), the leader of the puritanical Wahhābī reform movement that won many followers in Arabia and elsewhere, invoked Ibn Taymīyah's ideas in his rejection of the authority of the classical law schools and his insistence on fresh *ijtihād.*

Theories about the need to identify and follow the fundamental policies underlying *sharīʿah* provisions and to interpret these provisions in a manner responsive to social needs were developed by the Mālikī jurist al-Shāṭibī (d. 1388). Ibn Nujaym (d. 1562) was a Ḥanafī jurist who extracted what he saw as the fundamental *sharīʿah* principles from the specific instances of applications of rules set forth in the *fiqh.* While not himself a jurist, the Mughal emperor Awrangzīb ʿĀlamgīr (d. 1707) made his mark on Islamic legal history by ordering the composition of the famous *Fatāwā ʿĀlamgīrīyah,* a thorough compilation of Ḥanafī *fiqh.*

Muḥammad ʿAbduh (d. 1905) served as Grand Muftī of Egypt and in that capacity and in his writings on Islamic law proposed rationalist and liberal reformist interpretations of the *sharīʿah.* The influential Salafīyah movement inspired by ʿAbduh and led by his disciple Rashīd Riḍā advocated a return to a purified version of the *sharīʿah* meant to be more authentic than the versions developed in the course of the centuries devoted to the study of medieval *fiqh.* An example of ʿAbduh's approach may be seen in his famous argument that the *sharīʿah* prohibits polygamy. Dismissing traditional support for polygamy among the *fuqahāʾ,* ʿAbduh returned to the Qurʾān and offered a novel reading of two critical verses, which he claimed were to be taken together, although they had previously been held to apply to different issues. Surah 4:3 of the Qurʾān was traditionally interpreted to allow a man to wed up to four women at a time, with a moral injunction to marry only one if he could not treat additional wives justly. Surah 4:129, which says it is not possible for a man to deal equally with his wives, was traditionally interpreted as offering reassurance to the polygamous husband that he was not sinning if he felt stronger attraction to and affection for one of his wives. Treating the injunction to deal equally with wives in the earlier verse as a legally binding precondition for a valid marriage, ʿAbduh used the later verse as evidence that this precondition could not in practice be met, so that in the *sharīʿah,* no polygamous marriage could be valid. ʿAbduh's practice of interpreting *sharīʿah* rules to serve the ends of enlightened social policies had far-reaching intellectual repercussions. His ideas encouraged many Middle Eastern Muslims in the first half of the twentieth century to accommodate liberal political, economic, and social reforms in their interpretations of Islamic law.

Among the principal figures of Twelver Shīʿī jurisprudence, Muḥammad ibn al-Ḥasan al-Ṭūsī (d. 1067) wrote a number of works that became treated as classic statements of principles of Shīʿī *fiqh,* as were the writings of Muḥaqqiq al-Ḥillī (d. 1277). An important representative of the Akhbārī faction of Twelver Shiism was Muḥammad Bāqir al-Majlisī (d. 1699), who, in addition to producing an encyclopedic statement of *fiqh,* also served as a judge and became the most powerful judicial figure under the Safavids. After the Safavids made Twelver Shiism the state religion of Iran, he, like many major Shīʿī jurists, attempted to define the proper political relationship between the Shīʿī clergy and the state. Al-Majlisī conceived of a powerful, independent political role for the clergy. A jurist of similar eminence, but representing very different tendencies in Twelver thought, was Murtaḍā Anṣārī (d. 1864). A member of the Uṣūlī school, which predominated in Iran in the nineteenth century, he wrote a major treatise on the Uṣūlī theory of sources. His writings promoted the view that each layperson was bound to follow the legal interpretations of the most learned of living jurists, the *marjaʿ-i taqlīd*, whose *ijtihād* became absolutely binding on his followers. He took the view that public law was not a true concern of the *sharīʿah* and stressed instead its ethical dimensions. The single most important Ismāʿīlī jurist is Qāḍī al-Nuʿmān (d. 974), who served as the highest judge in the Fatimid empire and also wrote a great treatise of Ismāʿīlī law.

Principal subjects. Classical *fiqh* works have similar, although not always identical, subject divisions. They begin with a section on the very extensive *ʿibādāt*, the obligations of the individual to God discussed above. The remaining subjects belong to the *muʿāmalāt* category, including (in a representative, though not exhaustive, list) marriage, divorce, manumission of slaves, oaths, criminal penalties, relations between the Muslim community and non-Muslims, treasure troves, missing persons, partnership, religious trusts, sales, guarantee contracts, transfers of debts, rules for judges, evidence, legal claims, acknowledgments of legal obligations, gifts, hire, the purchase of freedom by slaves, the defense of compulsion, incapacity, usurpation and damage of property, preemptive purchases, partition, agency, contracts for cultivation of agricultural land, slaughter of animals (for food), animal sacrifice, hateful practices, cultivation of waste lands, prohibited drinks, hunting and racing competitions, pledge, personal injuries, blood money and fines, intestate succession, and wills.

Historically, the areas of *sharīʿah* law that were most developed in the classical *fiqh* corresponded to the areas where *qāḍīs* in the *sharīʿah* courts were best able to retain jurisdiction over disputes, while legal issues in other areas tended to be dealt with by secular tribunals with more flexible procedures and greater enforcement powers, such as the police tribunals. The *sharīʿah* rules of intestate succession and family law are the two most developed portions of the *sharīʿah*, and recourse to *sharīʿah* courts was very common for resolution of disputes on these subjects. The *sharīʿah* courts also had jurisdiction over pious endowments, *(awqāf;* sg., *waqf)*, which were very important legal institutions in traditional Islamic societies, allowing for the consolidation and protection of private property and often providing the financial basis for schools, hospitals, mosques, and other public institutions. *Waqf*s continued to serve such functions until the twentieth century, when they were generally abolished or significantly reformed. The *sharīʿah* law of contracts, and particularly of sales contracts, is also quite extensive. The difficulties of complying with some of the *sharīʿah* contract rules—such as the prohibition of interest—spawned an ancillary legal literature by some Ḥanafī and Shāfiʿī jurists on how to circumvent inconvenient rules by means of ingenious exploitation of legal technicalities (the so-called *ḥiyal*, or "legal tricks").

The Situation in Recent Times. The situation of the *sharīʿah* in recent times has two significant dimensions, corresponding to its dual nature as a positive law and a deontology.

Beginning in the nineteenth century, the *sharīʿah* was increasingly supplanted as a positive law in the legal systems of Muslim countries by borrowed European law. Historically, substantive *sharīʿah* rules survived in the legal systems of modern Muslim countries in rough proportion to the importance traditionally accorded to the subject area involved, but even in those areas where the *sharīʿah* was able to maintain itself, it was nonetheless subjected to some reforms. In the twentieth century, *sharīʿah* reform became one of the major legal problems faced by Muslim societies and provoked protracted political and intellectual controversies. Despite popular and clerical support for retention of the *sharīʿah*, governments have generally moved as quickly as political constraints permit in the direction of westernization. In the 1970s the political influence of forces favoring the retention and/or renewal of the *sharīʿah* began to make itself felt, and a process of abrogating westernizing reforms and reinstating *sharīʿah* law began in Libya, Iran, Pakistan, Egypt, Sudan, and Kuwait. How far the process of islamization will proceed and what the future role of the *sharīʿah* as a positive law will be are at present uncertain.

Also in the twentieth century, Muslim intellectuals concerned with questions of *fiqh* subjected the medieval versions of the *sharīʿah* to critical reexamination and brought new interpretive approaches to the *sharīʿah* sources. The variety in modern approaches to the *sharīʿah* is reminiscent of the situation prevailing in the first centuries after the death of the Prophet, before the doctrines of the classical schools coalesced. There are still many conservative thinkers who defend the validity of the medieval *fiqh*. Arrayed against them are many who support new interpretations of what the *sharīʿah* means. Adding to the fragmentation of legal doctrines is the fact that with the spread of educational opportunities and the increase in literacy, many Muslims who are educated but have not pursued a traditional course of study at a religious institution are contributing interpretations of the *sharīʿah*. In other words, laypersons who belong to the modern educated elite do not necessarily feel that they must defer to the specialized knowledge of the *fuqahāʾ* and are prepared to challenge the monopoly formerly enjoyed by the *fuqahāʾ* to make authoritative statements on *sharīʿah* law. As a result, it has become very difficult to make generalizations about contemporary *sharīʿah* doctrines.

The westernization of legal systems in the Muslim world. The westernization of the legal systems of Muslim countries began with the impact of European imperialism on Muslim societies in the eighteenth and nineteenth centuries. The legal systems of Muslim societies subjected to direct colonial rule underwent distinctive transformations in relation to the legal culture of the colonizing power. Thus, there developed in Muslim parts of India under British rule a peculiar blend of common law and elements of the *sharīʿah* that became known as Anglo-Muhammadan law. This unique, hybrid law was progressively reformed to eliminate what were regarded as the more archaic features of the *sharīʿah* elements, and it remained influential in the legal systems of India and Pakistan after they achieved independence in 1947. Algeria was part of France from 1830 until independence in 1962, and as a French colony, it also developed a hybrid legal system, known as *le droit musulman algérien,* which incorporated many French features.

Eager to strengthen their relatively backward and weak societies in the face of threatened European domination, most elites in the independent countries of the Muslim world tended to see the *sharīʿah* as an obstacle to the achievement of essential modernization. Governments first replaced those parts of the *sharīʿah* that were viewed as impeding economic transformation, such as *sharīʿah* commercial law, or those possessing features that seemed particularly archaic by modern standards, as in the cases of *sharīʿah* procedural and criminal law.

It was not always the substance of *sharīʿah* rules that troubled modernizers. Their arcane formulation and their diffuse mode of presentation in medieval *fiqh* treatises meant that only specialists with a mastery of medieval legal Arabic and an extensive traditional training could find answers to legal questions in a reasonably efficient manner. The cumbersome form of the *fiqh* works could be compared with the streamlined, systematized legal compendia to be found in nineteenth-century continental European codes. Growing impatience with the *fiqh* works encouraged a definite preference for codified law.

At the early stages of this legal reform process, one possibility for saving the *sharīʿah* from eclipse by Western law seemed to be that of vastly simplifying and systematizing its presentation. Attempts were made to codify the *sharīʿah* in the late nineteenth century, the most notable accomplishment being the promulgation of the Ottoman Majalla in 1877. Starting with some general principles of *sharīʿah* law taken from Ibn Nujaym, the Majalla presents a codification of the law of obligations derived from the views of various Ḥanafī jurists. The Majalla proved its utility, surviving for decades in former Ottoman territories well after they had obtained their independence from the empire. A later code, the Ottoman Family Rights Law of 1917, constituted an original attempt to codify *sharīʿah* law on that subject by reference to the doctrines of more than one Sunnī law school. This was the first important instance of the application of the technique of *takhayyur,* or picking and choosing the most apt principles from the doctrines of different schools and combining them in an arrangement that had no precedent in the classical *fiqh.* However, the preference for wholesale importation of Western law codes was ultimately so strong that there was soon little incentive to pursue projects for devising further codes on a *sharīʿah* basis.

Another factor mandating change from the old *sharīʿah*-based system of law was the international political setting. The rulers of Muslim states in the nineteenth and twentieth centuries were obliged to deal with a historical reality that was vastly different from what had been contemplated in early *sharīʿah* theory. The *sharīʿah* was originally conceived as a law whose application would be coextensive with religious affiliation. The world was to be converted to Islam, and there would result one community of believers with a common political allegiance and a common obligation to follow the *sharīʿah.* This conception did not envisage the appearance of obstacles in the way of the realization of this ideal, such as the fragmentation of the Muslim community into separate and mutually hostile political units, the development of national identities and the rise of modern nationalism, the failure of large non-Muslim communities within the Muslim world to convert, and the need to deal with non-Muslim countries possessed of greater economic and military resources.

The continued existence of non-Muslim communities had necessitated one legal adaptation at an early stage of Islamic history, namely, the allowance of separate religious laws and courts for minority communities. Members of the minority religious communities on Muslim territory were permitted to follow their own religious laws in matters of personal status and in transactions between themselves while remaining subject to the *sharīʿah* in their interactions with outsiders or in their public activities. This practice was highly developed under the Ottoman empire, where it was known as the *millet* system.

Under outside pressures, this system was further modified by a practice of according a special legal status to non-Muslims from the powerful European states: from the medieval period onward, certain states exacted from Muslim governments agreements, or "capitulations," according extraterritorial status to their nationals. Originally granted only by way of exception, capitulatory privileges were expanded apace with growing European influence. An example of the resulting system of extraterritoriality can be seen in the powerful Mixed Courts of Egypt, set up in 1875, expanded after the British occupation in 1882, and continuing until 1949. Originally established as alternatives to the "native courts" for cases involving foreigners, the Mixed Courts were able to extend their jurisdiction to a wide variety of cases, including those involving Egyptians, in instances where the courts detected some "foreign interest" in the outcome. One reason for the exaction of these concessions, the demands for which became increasingly onerous as Muslim power and wealth declined and that of the West grew, was the Western perception that the substantive provisions of the *sharīʿah* were "primitive" and "barbaric" by modern European legal standards, and that the justice meted out by the traditional courts was arbitrary. European powers also objected to the inferior legal status accorded to non-Muslims under the *sharīʿah* and exploited this as a pretext for political intervention. In attempts to forestall such intervention, the Ottoman sultan promulgated the Ḫaṭṭ-i Şerîf of Gülhane in 1839 and the Ḫaṭṭ-i Humâyûn of 1856, officially establishing the principle that Ottoman citizens regardless of their religion should be equal in terms of their legal rights and obligations.

Retention of *sharīʿah* law as the law of the land in these political circumstances thus presented obstacles to setting up a unified national legal system and entailed exposure to risks of compromising the sovereignty and national dignity of the Muslim states. The reluctance of governments to continue to make such sacrifices provided an impetus for law reform that would place legal systems in Muslim countries on a par with the emerging modern international standard.

The formation of modern nation-states in the Muslim world starting in the nineteenth century and the subsequent collapse of the Ottoman empire in World War I prompted Muslims to reassess the relationship between the *sharīʿah* law and the new political entities into which the Muslim world had been divided. Although the claims of the Ottoman sultans to be the legitimate successors of the Prophet had been based on tenuous legal and historical arguments, some Sunnīs saw in the sultan-caliphs an embodiment of the original *sharīʿah* notion that religious allegiance—not nationality—should determine political loyalties. With the ouster of the last of the Ottoman sultan-caliphs in 1924, there ended any real chance in the Sunnī world of preserving an Islamic caliphate, a government under which all Muslims would share a common political and religious allegiance.

Iran's *ʿulamāʾ* faced a momentous question at the turn of the twentieth century, when a growing movement favored the establishment of a democratic government, and the Constitutional Revolution of 1905–1909, led to the overthrow of the Qajar dynasty. To the *ʿulamāʾ*, accepting this revolution meant acknowledging the legitimacy of a government based on the principle of popular sovereignty and the lawmaking authority of the people's representatives. Such changes were seen by some as a challenge to the theoretical primacy of the imamate and the exclusive prerogative of the *ʿulamāʾ* to determine and declare the law. Other important jurists, such as Muḥammad Nāʾīnī (d. 1936), however, took the position that, pending the return of the Hidden Imam from the state of occultation, it was impossible to have a government that truly accorded with *sharīʿah* ideals and that it was therefore permissible for Iran to adopt a constitutional form of government in the interim.

The acceptance of the idea in the Sunnī and Shīʿī camps that laws should be enacted on a national basis by representatives of the people did not by itself entail a reduction of the role of the *sharīʿah*. However, the attendant pressures for systematic uniformity meant that statutes enacted by the state inevitably replaced the old, decentralized system of jurists' law. Thus, the realization that laws would henceforth be made by national governments encouraged the acceptance of the idea that there should be neutral, secular laws that could apply to all persons on the national soil. The typical pattern in Muslim countries in the nineteenth century, and more particularly in the twentieth century, was to abandon the *sharīʿah* in favor of imported European law save in matters of personal status and religious trusts, and occasional token provisions in other fields such as the law of contracts.

The timing of the adoptions of Western law was related to the chronology and extent of various countries' exposure to European imperialism. The Ottoman empire was therefore the first Muslim state to adopt Western laws, followed shortly by the semiautonomous province of Egypt. The first French-based codes to be introduced in the Ottoman empire were in the areas of commercial law (1850), penal law (1858), and commercial procedure (1861). The countries that remained most insulated from such influences—Afghanistan, the Yemen, and Saudi Arabia—were the last to undertake westernization of their legal systems. In most countries, legal westernization was largely completed by the 1950s. Alone among Muslim countries, Turkey, under the leadership of Kemal Atatürk after the collapse of the

Ottoman empire, abandoned the *sharīʿah* in favor of a completely secular legal system. At the opposite extreme, Saudi Arabia has retained the *sharīʿah,* or more specifically, Ḥanbalī *fiqh,* as the official norm, which has prevented the government from openly undertaking legislative activity, including the enactment of a constitution.

In contemporary Muslim countries the desire on the part of the governments for legal modernization combined with the need to show respect for the *sharīʿah* has resulted in various compromises. In the area of personal status, a number of reforms, by and large modest ones, have been enacted in Muslim countries with a view to improving the status of women in matters of marriage, divorce, support, and child custody. The boldest reforms in this area were enacted in the Tunisian Code of Personal Status of 1956, the Iranian Family Protection Law of 1967 (since abrogated by the revolutionary government), and the South Yemen Family Law of 1974. Only a few very cautious reforms of aspects of the *sharīʿah* law of intestate succession have been undertaken.

Even Muslim states with westernized legal systems generally enshrine Islam in the national constitution as the state religion and stipulate that the *sharīʿah* is a source of law or even the source of all laws. In some constitutions there are provisions stating that laws must accord with the *sharīʿah* or that they may be reviewed and nullified if they are found to violate the *sharīʿah.* In the past such provisions often had little more than symbolic significance, but as supporters of the *sharīʿah* gained political strength in the 1970s throughout the Islamic world, there was increasing pressure for reinstatement of *sharīʿah* rules and the abrogation of imported laws that conflict with *sharīʿah* principles. Thus, the *sharīʿah* is tending to be treated more and more as a fundamental law in the legal systems of Muslim countries.

The islamization campaign. The circumstances in which the replacement and reform of the *sharīʿah* took place resulted in political tensions between the westernized elites and other, more traditional segments of Muslim societies. The masses remained attached to the idea of the supremacy of *sharīʿah* law and were resentful of the importation of laws from Christian Europe, which they perceived to be hostile to Islam and the interests of Muslims. The *fuqahāʾ* continued to study and defend the *sharīʿah* and were offended by their displacement by the new class of lawyers and judges trained in Western law; as traditional guardians of the *sharīʿah* heritage, the *fuqahāʾ* also retained prestige and a popular following among the masses.

The political potency of the combination of these factors was illustrated in the 1978–1979 Iranian Revolution, which was inspired in part by the anti-Shah polemics of a prominent Twelver Shīʿī *faqīh,* Ayatollah Khomeini, who had as one of his goals the reinstatement of *sharīʿah* law. Khomeini had written prior to the revolution about the requirements for Islamic government in the absence of the imam and posited that the state should be ruled by the foremost *faqīh* of the era. Although many other Iranian *fuqahāʾ* disputed the correctness of Khomeini's views, his accession to power and the ability of allied *fuqahāʾ* to ensconce themselves in leading positions in the government meant that Iran became a quasi-theocratic state. Considerable abrogation of Western law and application of *sharīʿah* principles ensued, sometimes with variations on the traditional *sharīʿah* rules that reflected the politics of the revolutionary situation.

Elsewhere, secular regimes in the Muslim world have responded to the demonstrated popularity of islamization programs by enacting selected principles of *sharīʿah* law in statute form. Libya was the first country to undertake such initiatives in the 1970s, and its example was subsequently imitated in Pakistan, Algeria, Sudan, Kuwait, and Egypt. It is important to note that these measures did not mean that the governments were relinquishing control over the legal systems, which remained basically Western in structure. The major emphasis in such islamizing legislation tended to be on reenactment of Qurʾanic criminal laws that had previously fallen into desuetude outside Saudi Arabia. It is premature to predict the long-term consequences of the turnabout in the fortunes of the *sharīʿah,* but it is clear that the position of imported Western laws in the legal systems of the Muslim world is not secure and that the *sharīʿah* retains considerable potency as a countermodel.

Contemporary reformulations of the sharīʿah. At the same time that there is mounting pressure for the reinstatement of the *sharīʿah,* there is growing diversity of opinion on what the requirements of the *sharīʿah* are and how they should be applied in modern circumstances. Previously settled issues of Islamic law are being reopened and reexamined.

While some contemporary Muslims, particularly those educated in traditional Islamic institutions of higher learning, consider medieval *fiqh* treaties authoritative, there is a marked and growing tendency to treat such works as secondary legal sources that are useful but not conclusive guides on questions of *sharīʿah* science and substantive rules. The old hierarchies of sources and the established methodologies for interpreting them are also questioned by contemporary thinkers. Although the traditional techniques of legal reasoning from the sources are also rejected by many modern students of the *sharīʿah,* no consensus about what new methodology should replace the ones used by the traditional scholars is discernible.

Increasingly, Muslims turn directly to the Qur'ān and *sunnah* for guidance. The tendency has also mounted to give precedence to the Qur'ān over the *sunnah*—because of either a more critical appraisal of the reliability of the *ḥadīth* literature or a conviction that the Qur'ān was intended to serve as the primary source of *sharīʿah* principles. While it is rare for Muslims to reject the authenticity of the entire *ḥadīth* literature, it has become more common for them to evaluate negatively the traditional science of *ḥadīth* criticism. As a result, there has been a greater willingness to discard or discount the legal value of *ḥadīth* that are not demonstrably genuine.

A noteworthy development in contemporary Sunnī legal thought is that on questions of methodology and substance alike there is a tendency to disregard the former school divisions. When seeking enlightenment from past scholarship, modern Sunnīs commonly treat the views of all the classical Sunnī schools and also the extinct schools as deserving of consideration. Thus, the process of *takhayyur* exemplified in the Ottoman Family Rights Law of 1917 is now routinely utilized.

Many contemporary interpretations of the *sharīʿah* tend to reflect ideological visions of the social order that should result from the application of the *sharīʿah.* In these interpretations the *sharīʿah* does not function only as a criterion for the legal validity or permissibility and ethical character of human acts but as a blueprint for the perfect ordering of all social relations and the solution to the problems of achieving social harmony and justice. The latest ideologized versions of the *sharīʿah* reflect all the different ideological currents that are contending for the loyalties of peoples in the Muslim world from the most conservative to the most radical, so that this ideologization of Islamic legal thought has led to a polarization of opinions. Topics that have given rise to particularly important disagreements include remedies for maldistribution of wealth, the sanctity of private property, the nature of Islamic government, human rights, and the role of women.

Because the latest ideological perspectives characteristic of contemporary Islamic thought have few counterparts in the traditional *fiqh* and do not correspond to any of the traditional school or sectarian divisions of the *sharīʿah,* they have created new divisions and alliances along ideological lines. The willingness on the part of Sunnī and Shīʿī Muslims to utilize the economic and political theories presented by members of the other sect is growing. Thus, on the theoretical level, all the old doctrinal certainties are now challenged by modern attempts to understand the *sharīʿah* in relation to the great political, economic, and social questions confronting Muslim societies. It is premature to predict which of the many presently competing versions of the *sharīʿah* will ultimately find favor with the majority of Muslims, but it is clear that many Muslims believe that the answers to these questions must be sought by reference to the *sharīʿah.*

[*The two most important bases of the* sharīʿah *are discussed in more detail in* Qur'ān *and* Sunnah. *For further discussion of the classical schools of law, see* Ḥanābilah; Madhhab; *and the biographies of Abū Ḥanīfah, Abū Yūsuf, Mālik ibn Anas, and al-Shāfiʿī. The* fuqahā', *or jurists, are discussed in* ʿUlamā'. *See also the biographies of the historical personalities mentioned in the text.*]

BIBLIOGRAPHY

As a general reference with extensive indexes and bibliography, the most reliable and comprehensive scholarly work is Joseph Schacht's *An Introduction to Islamic Law* (Oxford, 1964). Another solid and very detailed reference work is *The Encyclopaedia of Islam,* 4 vols. and supplement (Leiden, 1913–1938), and its condensed version, the *Shorter Encyclopaedia of Islam* (1953; reprint, Leiden, 1974). A new edition of the larger version has been issued alphabetically in fascicles since 1960. To use these works it is necessary to know the Arabic terms for different aspects of Islamic law.

An outstanding bibliography of works in many languages is Erich Pritsch and Otto Spies's "Klassisches Islamisches Recht," in *Orientalisches Recht* (Leiden, 1964), pp. 220–343, suppl. vol. 3 of *Der Nahe und der Mittlere Osten,* first part of *Handbuch der Orientalistik.* An old but still usable general book is Nicolas P. Aghnides's *Muhammadan Theories of Finance* (New York, 1916), with a broader scope than the title suggests. A basic anthology is *Law in the Middle East,* vol. 1, *Origin and Development of Islamic Law,* edited by Majid Khadduri and Herbert J. Liebesny (Washington, D.C., 1955), but not all chapters are of equal quality.

Unparalleled in its depth of analysis and a uniquely valuable contribution to the comparative study of Islamic jurisprudence is Yvon Linant de Bellefonds's *Traité de droit musulman comparé,* 3 vols. (Paris, 1965–1973), covering aspects of contract and family law. A readable short historical survey of the development of the *sharīʿah* from the beginnings to the modern period is Noel J. Coulson's *A History of Islamic Law* (1964; reprint, Edinburgh, 1971). A useful general survey work by a modern Muslim scholar—one of the few that have been well translated into English—is S. R. Mahmassani's *Falsafat al-Tashrīʿ fī al-Islam: The Philosophy of Jurisprudence in Islam,* translated by Farhat J. Ziadeh (Leiden, 1961). A. A. Fyzee's *Outlines of Muhammadan Law,* 4th ed. (Bombay, 1974), combines a general introduction to the *sharīʿah* with a discussion of features of Anglo-Muhammadan law.

An exceptionally thorough and critical examination of the doctrines of the Mālikī school in comparison with the Shāfiʿī school can be found in David Santillana's *Istituzioni del diritto musulmano malichita*, 2 vols. (Rome, 1925–1938). It has no equal in Western languages for scope and detail of coverage of the doctrine of a classical Islamic law school. One of the great medieval encyclopedias of *fiqh* is that of the Ḥanbalī scholar Muwaffaq al-Dīn ibn Qudāmah, *Al-mughnī*, 12 vols., edited by Ṭāhā Muḥammad al-Zaynī (1923–1930; reprint, Cairo, 1968–), notable for its balanced treatment of the doctrines of the different Sunnī schools and still a standard reference work.

The most erudite and complete statement of the Western scholarly position on the early development of the *sharī'ah* is Joseph Schacht's *The Origins of Muhammadan Jurisprudence* (Oxford, 1950). A collection of original and provocative essays of high scholarly merit and importance is Robert Brunschvig's *Études d'islamologie*, 2 vols. (Paris, 1976). Useful chapters on the interrelationship of theology and law in Islam can be found in the short volume edited by G. E. von Grunebaum, *Theology and Law in Islam* (Wiesbaden, 1971). An older work on this topic by one of the major European scholars of Islam is Ignácz Goldziher's *Introduction to Islamic Theology and Law*, published in German in 1910 and now translated by Andras and Ruth Hamori (Princeton, 1981).

A thorough treatment of the legal position of non-Muslims in Muslim society is Antoine Fattal's *Le statut légal des non-musulmans en pays d'Islam* (Beirut, 1958). A careful comparative study of the doctrines of the different law schools regarding intestate succession is Noel J. Coulson's *Succession in the Muslim Family* (Cambridge, 1971). The best treatment of the administration of justice in the setting of traditional Islamic civilization is Émile Tyan's *Histoire de l'organisation judiciaire en pays d'Islam*, 2d ed. (Leiden, 1960). The *sharī'ah* law affecting relations of the Muslim state with the non-Muslim environment is examined in Majid Khadduri's *War and Peace in the Law of Islam* (Baltimore, 1955).

A number of informative chapters on Twelver Shī'ī law are in *Le shī'isme imāmite: Colloque de Strasbourg, 6–9 mai 1968*, edited by Toufic Fahd et al. (Paris, 1970). A very detailed examination of Twelver Shī'ī legal doctrines is Harald Löschner's *Die dogmatischen Grundlagen des shī'itischen Rechts* (Cologne, 1971).

A distinguished assessment of the liberal reformist thought is Malcolm H. Kerr's *Islamic Reform: The Political and Legal Theories of Muhammad Abduh and Rashid Rida* (Berkeley, 1966). A wide-ranging survey of the current situation of the *sharī'ah* in the legal systems of modern countries of the Muslim world is presented in J. N. D. Anderson's *Law Reform in the Muslim World* (London, 1976). Surveys of modern law in Egypt, Tunisia, Algeria, Morocco, and Turkey appear in *Orientalisches Recht*, cited above. An example of a modern, enlightened approach to interpreting the requirements of Islamic law is Fazlur Rahman's *Islam and Modernity* (Chicago, 1982). Chapters on Twelver Shī'ī law in the context of political developments since the Islamic revolution in Iran appear in *Religion and Politics in Iran*, edited by Nikki R. Keddie (New Haven, 1983), and Islamic institutions and the role of the clergy in Iran are examined in detail in Shahrough Akhavi's *Religion and Politics in Contemporary Iran* (Albany, N.Y., 1980). Both books are useful as illustrations of the connection between questions of *sharī'ah* interpretation and political developments in contemporary Muslim societies.

ANN ELIZABETH MAYER

Personal Law

The area of personal law is often considered to be the main bastion of Islamic law. One reason for this is that the Qur'ān devotes greater attention to subjects such as marriage, divorce, and inheritance than it does to any other legal topic. In this sense the law of personal status represents an entrenched part of the religion, and Muslims have by and large regarded adherence to its principles as a criterion of the religious propriety of individuals and governments. It is, therefore, not surprising to find that the *sharī'ah* law of personal status has remained largely applicable in Muslim countries today in spite of recent reforms that have adapted many aspects of the classical law to suit the requirements of modern life. Reform of the *sharī'ah* law is a phenomenon of the twentieth century and, because of the continuing relevance of the law of personal status to the Muslim community, has been concentrated mainly in that area. Other portions of the *sharī'ah*, such as criminal law, taxation, and constitutional law, have either fallen into abeyance or remained relatively untouched by modern reformist legislation. Under the renewed influence of Islamic movements in the 1970s and 1980s, however, these other areas of the law have also begun to attract the attention of reformers as the effort is made to revive their significance.

In modern-day Islam, the Ḥanafī school commands a greater following than any other school of law. This survey is, therefore, based on *sharī'ah* law as developed within the framework of the Ḥanafī school. Wherever Ḥanafī law diverges from the law of the other three Sunnī schools (Shāfi'ī, Mālikī, and Ḥanbalī), their differences are outlined. References to Shī'ī law generally relate to the Twelver Shī'ī school, which is mainly adhered to in Iran and has the largest following of all the branches of Shī'ī Islam.

Marriage. Like any other private contract, marriage under *sharī'ah* law is concluded by the mutual agreement, oral or written, of the parties or their representatives. The only formality required is the presence of two witnesses at the conclusion of the contract, and even this is not necessary under Shī'ī law. Formalities usually observed, such as ceremonies performed in the presence of a religious leader, are matters of customary practice and not a legal requirement.

The requirements of a marriage contract are basically the same in all *sharī'ah* schools. First, the parties or their representatives must be legally competent persons, and second, there must be no legal impediment to marriage. Sanity and majority are the basic requirements of the legal capacity to contract. Legal majority is established with physical puberty, which is attained upon proof of sexual maturity rather than at a specific age. Unless proven otherwise, a boy below the age of twelve and a girl below the age of nine are legally presumed to be minors. Similarly, both sexes are presumed to have attained majority with the completion of the fifteenth year. A boy or girl who has reached the minimum age of majority but is still below fifteen is permitted to marry provided he or she shows signs of puberty. A person who has attained majority *(bāligh)* and is of sound mind *(ʿāqil)* has rights and obligations, must fulfill religious duties, and incurs criminal responsibility. The minor *(saghīr)* and the insane *(majnūn)* are wholly capable of contracting marriage. The idiot *(maʿtūh)* and the imbecile, who are incapable of managing their own affairs, have the capacity only to conclude purely advantageous transactions, such as the acceptance of a gift, but they are not permitted to contract marriage. A major who is incompetent *(safīh)* may be subjected to interdiction *(ḥajr)* and placed under the supervision of the authorities, and this procedure could lead to restrictions on his capacity to contract. An adult woman has the capacity to contract her own marriage only in Ḥanafī and Shīʿī law. According to the other three Sunni schools, her marriage guardian *(walīy)* must conclude the contract on her behalf. All schools recognize, in principle, the compulsory power of the marriage guardian, which is known as *ijbār.* The guardian is accordingly authorized to contract his ward, whether the ward is male or female, in marriage at his discretion regardless of the ward's wishes. But the precise extent of this power varies among the schools. In Ḥanafī law, only minor wards are subject to *ijbār,* and the power is absolute only when exercised by the father or paternal grandfather. In all other cases, the ward has the right to repudiate the marriage on attaining puberty. This option of puberty *(khiyār al-bulūgh)* is, however, lost by the affirmative act of consummating the marriage. Guardianship in marriage is vested in the nearest male relatives in accordance with the order of priorities that is applied in inheritance, that is, the father, grandfather, brother, nephews, uncles, and cousins, and failing them, the female relatives.

Under the Ḥanafī doctrine of *kafāʾah* (equality), the guardian of an adult female may oppose the marriage of his ward on the ground that the prospective spouse is not her equal. This doctrine is, however, mainly applicable to the man, who is required to be the equal of his prospective wife in respect of lineage, religion, freedom (as opposed to slavery), piety, means, and profession. If, however, both the guardian and bride fail to raise the question of equality before the contract, neither can have the marriage annulled upon discovery that the husband is not the equal of his wife. In both the Shāfiʿī and Mālikī schools, the adult virgin is denied the right to conclude her own marriage; since the guardian himself is concluding the marriage, the doctrine of *kafāʾah* is not applicable under these schools.

Marriage is prohibited between close relatives. Relationships that constitute permanent impediments to marriage fall into three categories: (1) blood relationship *(garābah),* which implies that a man may not marry any of his lineal descendants, lineal ascendants, the offspring of his parents, or the immediate child of any grandparent; (2) affinity *(muṣāharah),* which creates a bar to marriage between a man and the ascendants or descendants of his wife, or the wife of any of his ascendants or descendants; (3) fosterage *(raḍāʿ),* which arises when a woman breast-feeds the child of someone else. Fosterage creates a bar to marriage not only between foster brothers and sisters, but also between the foster mother and all her relatives on the one side, and her foster children, their spouses, and descendants on the other.

In addition, difference of religion is a bar to marriage: a Muslim woman may not marry a non-Muslim man unless he professes Islam. A Muslim man is, on the other hand, allowed to marry a *kitābīyah,* that is, a woman who follows a religion that has a revealed scripture, such as Judaism or Christianity. The Qur'ān further prohibits both Muslim men and women from marrying polytheists or fire worshipers. Finally, a man may not marry a woman who is already married or who is observing *ʿiddah,* that is, the waiting period that a woman must observe following a divorce, with the exception of a divorce ending an unconsummated marriage. *ʿIddah* usually lasts for three menstrual cycles or, where the wife proves to be pregnant, until the delivery of the child. The main purpose of *ʿiddah* is to determine a possible pregnancy prior to marriage. A widow must observe a waiting period of four months and ten days following the death of her husband.

The marriage contract is classified into three types, namely valid *(ṣaḥīḥ),* irregular *(fāsid),* and void *(bāṭil).* A marriage contract is valid when it fulfills all the legal requirements. This contract brings about a fully effective union that renders intercourse lawful between the spouses, entitles the wife to dower and maintenance, obligates the wife to be faithful and obedient to the husband, and creates prohibited degrees of relations and mutual rights of inheritance between the spouses.

A void *(bāṭil)* marriage is one that is unlawful from

the outset and that does not create any rights or obligations between the parties. In such a marriage no illicit sexual intercourse *(zinā')* is considered to have been committed if the parties were unaware that the marriage was void. Marriage with a woman within the prohibited degrees and marriage that is brought about without the consent of the adult parties are void. The offspring of a *bāṭil* marriage is illegitimate.

An irregular *(fāsid)* marriage, on the other hand, is not unlawful in itself, but involves some irregularity of a temporary nature that could be rectified by means of a new contract. Marriage without witnesses, marriage with a fifth wife (the maximum limit being four), marriage with a non-*kitābīyah* (a woman who is neither Jewish nor Christian), and marriage with a woman undergoing *ʿiddah* are examples of *fāsid* marriages. Such a marriage may be terminated by either party or by a judge, should it come to his notice. A *fāsid* marriage has no legal effect before consummation, but when consummated, the wife is entitled to dower and maintenance, and the issue of the marriage is legitimate. A *fāsid* marriage does not create any right of inheritance between the parties.

Islamic law requires the husband to pay his wife a dower *(mahr)*. The amount of dower and the terms of its payment are matters of agreement between the parties. Anything that can be considered as goods *(māl)* may be given as a dower, but objects which are prohibited in Islam, such as wine and pork, are excluded from the definition of *māl*. If no dower is specified in the contract, the wife is entitled to a "proper" dower *(mahr al-mithl)*, that is, a dower that is equivalent to the dower usually received by women of similar status. A dower may be paid at the time of the contract, or it may be deferred, in whole or in part, subject to the agreement of the parties. A deferred dower remains a debt on the part of the husband and is payable upon the dissolution of the marriage by death or divorce. In the event of a divorce prior to consummation, the wife is entitled to half the specified dower; if no dower is specified in the contract, the wife is entitled to a gift *(mutʿah)*, which consists of a set of clothing.

The husband is bound to maintain his wife as soon as she cohabits with him. Should she refuse to cohabit or refuse herself to him, the husband is relieved of his duty, unless her refusal is for a lawful cause such as the husband's failure to pay the dower or unsuitability of the lodging for a person of her status. In such cases, the wife's refusal to cohabit does not relieve the husband of his duty of maintenance, which includes food, clothing, and accommodation. According to the majority of jurists, the wife is entitled to maintenance in a style that conforms to the husband's status, regardless of her own premarital position. Should the husband desert his wife without providing for her maintenance, a judge may authorize the wife to make the necessary arrangements at her husband's expense. The wife is not, however, entitled to a decree for past maintenance unless the claim is based on a specific agreement. Shāfiʿī and Shīʿī law, on the other hand, entitle the wife to claim her past maintenance. The general rule in maintenance is that no individual who is capable of maintaining himself is entitled to receive maintenance from others; the only exception is the wife, who is entitled to maintenance regardless of her own financial status. The father is bound to maintain his sons until they attain puberty, and his daughters until they are married; he is also responsible for the maintenance of a widowed or divorced daughter. The law entitles every blood relative to maintenance provided that, if male, he is a child and destitute, and if a female, she is destitute whether a child or an adult. A widow is not entitled to maintenance during the period of *ʿiddah* following her husband's death, since in this case she would be entitled to a share of the inheritance. The liability of a person to support these relatives is generally proportionate to his or her share of their inheritance.

The *sharīʿah* entitles the husband to discipline his wife lightly when she transgresses. The law is not precise as to how and when the husband is entitled to do so, nor indeed as to what amounts to a transgression *(maʿṣiyah)*. She must not dishonor him, refuse herself to him without lawful excuse, or cause him loss of property that is deemed unacceptable according to normal social usage. The wife is entitled to visit her parents once a week and other relatives once a year, even without the permission of her husband. She may also leave the husband if he refuses to pay her a dower. Similarly, unreasonable requests by the husband—that she should accompany him on long journeys, for example—may be refused by her. The wife retains her full capacity to enter contracts and transactions with regard to her own property as if she were not married. Indeed, the law recognizes no merger of either the personality or the property of the wife into that of her husband's. Separation of property is the norm in *sharīʿah* law and is presumed to apply unless the parties make a specific agreement to the contrary. If a man beats his wife without reason (even lightly), or beats her for cause but exceeds moderation, he is liable to punishment following her complaint to the court.

Islam allows a man to marry up to four wives simultaneously provided that he does not combine, as co-wives, two women so closely related that if either of them were a male, they would themselves be within the prohibited degrees of marriage. Each of the co-wives is entitled to a separate dwelling and to an equal portion of the husband's time and companionship.

Modern legislation in Muslim countries has either sought to restrict the practice of polygamy or to abolish it altogether. At the one extreme is the Tunisian law of 1957, which prohibits polygamy outright. At the other is the Moroccan law of 1958, which entitles the wife to seek judicial divorce if she has suffered injury as a result of polygamy. Syria, Iraq, and Pakistan have adopted a middle course by requiring official permission before a polygamous marriage is contracted. The modernists have generally justified their reforms by direct resort to the Qur'ān and a reinterpretation of the Qur'anic verse on polygamy (5:4), which permits polygamy but at the same time expresses the fear of injustice in polygamous relationships. Modern reformers have reasoned that the fear of injustice in a polygamous marriage is bound to be present in every case of polygamy and therefore have concluded that abolishing polygamy is consistent with the Qur'anic dispensations.

Marriage under Sunnī law is a lifelong union, and any stipulation that sets a time limit to it nullifies the contract. Shīʿī law, however, recognizes temporary marriage, known as *mutʿah*. This is a contractual arrangement whereby a woman agrees to cohabit with a man for a specified period of time in return for a fixed remuneration. *Mutʿah* does not give rise to any right of inheritance between the parties, but the issue of *mutʿah* is legitimate and entitled to inheritance. As the reader will note, *mutʿah* also signifies a gift of consolation to a divorced woman; the word appears in the Qur'ān in both senses (2:236, 4:24), hence the origin of its double legal meaning.

Modern legislation in most Muslim countries compels marriage registration, and failure to comply is usually liable to legal sanctions. The law similarly requires the express consent of the parties to a marriage in order for it to be valid. To facilitate meeting the consent requirement, parties to a marriage contract must be of marriageable age. This age is almost everywhere enacted at sixteen for females and eighteen for males. Modern reforms concerning the age of marriage have thus departed from the classical *sharīʿah*, which stipulated no specific age for marriage and only presumed the minimum and maximum ages of legal majority; the age of marriage established under the new codes also signifies the age of majority for all legal purposes. A marriage in which the parties have not reached the specified age is denied registration and may render the parties liable to statutory penalties. As a result of the enactment of a statutory age for marriage, child marriage has been effectively abolished in most Muslim countries. Similarly, the powers that the marriage guardian enjoys under classical *sharīʿah* law have, as a result of the age provisions, been either abolished or substantially restricted.

Divorce. Marriage under *sharīʿah* law may be dissolved either by the husband at his will, by mutual agreement of the spouses, or by a judicial decree. All the *sharīʿah* schools recognize the husband's right of unilateral repudiation, known as *ṭalāq*. Sunnī law requires no formalities as to the manner in which a *ṭalāq* may be pronounced. A husband of sound mind who has attained puberty may effect *ṭalāq* orally or in writing without assigning any cause. Any words indicative of repudiation may be used, and no witnesses are necessary for the pronouncement. In Shīʿī law, *ṭalāq* must be pronounced in the presence of two witnesses, and the exact term *ṭalāq* must be used. Whereas in Ḥanafī law *ṭalāq* pronounced by way of jest or in a state of intoxication is nonetheless valid, in both Shāfiʿī and Shīʿī law, *ṭalāq* is valid only when accompanied by a definite intention.

The husband can delegate his power of *ṭalāq* to his wife or to a third person who may then pronounce it according to the terms of the authorization *(tafwīḍ)*. Thus there can be a valid agreement between the spouses authorizing the wife to repudiate herself if the husband marries a second wife, and the wife can exercise the power when the occasion arises.

In Sunnī law, *ṭalāq* is classified as "approved" *(ṭalāq al-sunnah)* or "disapproved" *(ṭalāq al-bidʿah)*, according to the circumstances in which it is pronounced. The former is generally revocable, whereas the latter is irrevocable and terminates the marriage tie immediately upon pronouncement. The "approved" *ṭalāq* may consist of either a single repudiation pronounced during a clean period, that is, a period between menstruations, known as *ṭuhr*, followed by abstinence from sexual intercourse for the whole of the waiting period *(ʿiddah)*, or it may consist of three repudiations pronounced during three successive *ṭuhr*s. In the former case, *ṭalāq* becomes final after the expiration of the *ʿiddah*, whereas in the latter, it becomes final upon the third pronouncement. Until the *ṭalāq* becomes final, the husband has the option to revoke it, and this may be done either expressly or by implication, through the resumption of normal marital relations. The "disapproved" *ṭalāq* may consist of a single repudiation which is expressly declared to be final, or it may consist of three repudiations pronounced at once. Shīʿī law does not recognize the "disapproved" form of *ṭalāq*.

Divorce by mutual agreement may take one of two forms: *khulʿ*, in which the wife secures her release from the marital tie by offering the husband financial consideration, commonly the return of the dower, which is accepted by the husband; or *mubāra'ah*, which is a dissolution of marriage on the basis of mutual release of the spouses from any outstanding financial commitments arising from the marriage. In both cases, the divorce is final and extrajudicial, effected simply by the mutual agreement of the parties.

With respect to judicial dissolution, Ḥanafī law is the most restrictive of all the *sharīʿah* schools. This law allows a woman to seek a dissolution *(faskh)* of her marriage from a *qāḍī* (Islamic judge) under four specific conditions: if she was married at a young age by a guardian other than her father or grandfather, she can ask the *qāḍī* to dissolve the marriage upon attaining puberty; if insane, upon regaining her sanity; if the husband is sexually impotent; or if he is a missing person and ninety years have elapsed since the date of his birth. All the other schools, including the Shīʿī, authorize the *qāḍī* to grant a judicial divorce in cases where the husband is suffering a physical or mental disease. Whenever it is proved that the disease is incurable, the court is to order dissolution immediately, but if it is a disease that requires time to cure, the court must order a stay of judgment for one year. The Shāfiʿī and Ḥanbalī schools also consider a husband's willful refusal to support his wife and a husband's desertion as valid grounds for a judicial divorce. Even more liberal is the Mālikī school, which recognizes the husband's illness, his failure to maintain, desertion for more than one year for whatever reason, and injurious treatment *(ḍarar)* as valid grounds for judicial divorce. According to the last ground, the wife can demand a judicial dissolution by claiming that cohabitation with her husband is injurious to her in a way that makes the continuation of marital life impossible for a person of her status. A decree of divorce granted on any of these grounds is final, except in the case of failure to maintain, where the court's degree effects only a revocable divorce, and the husband can resume normal marital relations during the period of *ʿiddah* if he proves that he can support his wife.

And finally, apostasy from Islam by either of the spouses operates as an immediate and final dissolution of the marriage without any judicial intervention. If both spouses renounce Islam simultaneously, their marriage is permitted to endure. Conversion to Islam by the husband alone where both spouses were Jewish or Christian does not impair the marriage, and the wife may retain her religion. However, if a Christian or Jewish woman, married to a man of the same faith, becomes a Muslim, the marriage is dissolved unless the husband also adopts Islam.

A final divorce, whatever its mode may be, renders sexual intercourse unlawful and entitles the wife to remarry after completing the waiting period of *ʿiddah*. If the marriage is not consummated, she is free to marry immediately. A triple *ṭalāq* renders remarriage between the divorced couple unlawful until the woman marries another person; only after the dissolution of this latter marriage may she remarry her former husband. Upon a final divorce, mutual rights of inheritance cease between the parties, and any outstanding dower becomes immediately payable to the wife. She is entitled to maintenance only during her *ʿiddah*.

Modern reforms of divorce law in Muslim countries have been primarily directed at restricting the husband's power of unilateral divorce on the one hand, and at increasing the remedies available to the wife in cases of injurious circumstances on the other. The main restriction on the husband's power of unilateral *ṭalāq* comes from the abolition of the irrevocable forms of *ṭalāq*. The husband is thus no longer able to terminate his marriage immediately by pronouncing a final and irrevocable *ṭalāq*. Legislation in some Muslim countries also entitles the wife to financial compensation for any injury she may have sustained as a result of the husband's abuse of his power. In the traditionally Ḥanafī countries, the wife's position has been enhanced by legislative measures, which entitle her to a judicial divorce on grounds substantially the same as those recognized under Mālikī law. Modern legislation has also departed from the Ḥanafī position that ignores intention in *ṭalāq* by adopting provisions under which *ṭalāq* is only valid if accompanied by a definite intention. The Tunisian law of 1957 is the most far-reaching of the modern reforms in that it abolishes all forms of extrajudicial divorce, whether by *ṭalāq* or by mutual consent. By abolishing the husband's power of unilateral *ṭalāq*, the Tunisian law effects complete equality between the spouses in divorce.

Inheritance. In pre-Islamic Arabia, succession was purely tribal and agnatic, that is, the heirs were normally the closest male relatives, and women and minors were excluded. A fundamental reform that the Qur'ān brought about was to assign definite shares to female relatives. According to the Islamic scheme of inheritance, a female generally receives half the share of a male. The deceased fictitiously remains the owner of the estate until his obligations are fully discharged. The creditors can, therefore, only assert their claims against the estate and not against the individual heirs. All funeral expenses, debts, and bequests have to be paid in full before the estate can be distributed among the heirs.

An essential condition of inheritance is that the heir must survive the deceased. In doubtful cases, arising, for example, when persons who would inherit from one another have died without proof of who died first, neither can inherit from the other according to the majority, but Shīʿī and Ḥanbalī law entitle both to inherit from one another. Similarly, inheritance can only pass to an heir who exists at the time of the death of the deceased, except when a man leaves a pregnant widow, in which case the share of an unborn male child is reserved for the offspring. If the child is female, she will receive her normal share of inheritance, and the remainder of the reserved portion reverts back to the estate to be redistributed among the heirs proportionate to their normal shares.

The birth of a child, whether male or female, may affect the position of an heir in a variety of ways. He or she may be excluded from succession, have their share reduced, or in some circumstances, become entitled to a larger share. In all cases, the present heirs are, according to the majority view, entitled to take their minimal shares and reserve the largest share for the unborn child. This is the share of a male child under Ḥanafī law, whereas the Shāfiʿī, Ḥanbalī, and Shīʿī law assume that twin boys or twin girls will be born, and the other heirs are entitled to the share they would receive in one case or the other, whichever is less. In Mālikī law the distribution is completely suspended until the birth of the child. All schools are unanimous, however, in suspending the distribution of the estate in the event that all the other heirs would be totally excluded by the birth of the child. Excluded from succession are the following: one who has caused the death of the deceased; a non-Muslim as the heir of a Muslim and vice versa (a bequest, however, can be made to a non-Muslim), and a slave who, under classical law, is not capable of owning property.

The heirs are mainly divided into three groups: those who are entitled to a prescribed share, known as Qur'anic heirs *(dhawū al-furūḍ);* those who receive the remainder, known as agnatic heirs *(ʿaṣabah);* and distant kindred *(dhawū al-arḥām),* persons who are related to the deceased in the female line and fall into neither of the first two categories. In the absence of all three, the estate goes to the public treasury *(bayt al-māl).*

The Qur'ān allots shares to eight relatives, namely the daughter, mother, father, husband, wife, brothers, and sisters. But the rules regarding the daughter have been extended, by analogy, to the daughter of a son, and those regarding the parents, to the grandparents. In addition, a distinction has been made between a full sister, a half sister on the father's side, and a half sister on the mother's side. The total number of Qur'anic heirs has thus been raised to twelve.

A daughter who has no brothers is entitled to half the estate, and two or more daughters share equally in a portion of two-thirds. But if daughters inherit along with sons, they become *ʿaṣabah* and receive half the portion of the sons. A son's daughter without brothers inherits half the estate; if there are two or more son's daughters, their share is two-thirds. A son's daughter is excluded if that son has two or more sisters inheriting along with him. The father inherits one-sixth in the presence of a son, and in the presence of a daughter or a son's daughter, one-sixth plus any residue. In the absence of descendants, the father inherits as the nearest *ʿaṣabah.* The father's father inherits one-sixth, but he is excluded if the father is alive. The mother's portion is one-sixth if there are children and one-third if there are none. The mother's mother inherits one-sixth, but she is excluded if the mother is alive. One full sister in the absence of brothers inherits one-half, and two or more, two-thirds. A half sister on the father's side receives the same share as a full sister, but both are excluded in the presence of a son, or a son's son, or the father. Both a half brother and a half sister on the mother's side receive one-sixth, and two or more share a third among them, but they are excluded by descendants and male ascendants. The husband receives a quarter if there is a descendant, and in the absence thereof, a half. The wife inherits one-half of what the husband would receive under the same circumstances.

Sometimes the number of qualified Qur'anic heirs or the sum of their shares may be larger than the whole of the estate. In this case, their shares are reduced under the principle of proportionate reduction, known as *ʿawl.* For example, if the deceased is survived by a husband and two full sisters, their shares will be one-half and two-thirds respectively, which exceed unity. Hence, the share will be reduced to three-sevenths and four-sevenths respectively.

The agnatic heirs *(ʿaṣabah)* inherit the remainder of the estate after the Qur'anic heirs have received their shares. The *ʿaṣabah* are divided into the following classes, in order of priority: (1) the son and his descendants in the male line; (2) the father and his ascendants in the male line; (3) the male descendants of the father; (4) descendants of the paternal grandfather; and (5) descendants of the paternal great-grandfather. Any member of a higher class totally excludes any member of a lower class, except that the brothers of the deceased are not excluded by the grandfather. Among the relatives of the same class, the nearer in degree to the deceased excludes the more remote: in class three, for example, a nephew will be excluded by the deceased's brother. Among agnatic relatives of the same class and the same degree, germanes have priority over consanguines. Thus, for example, the germane brother of the deceased totally excludes the consanguine brother.

If there is no *ʿaṣabah* and the Qur'anic heirs do not

exhaust the estate, the remainder is proportionately distributed among the Qur'anic heirs under the principle of reversion, known as *radd.* For example, if the deceased is survived by his mother and a daughter, their shares will be one-sixth and one-half; since these are less than unity, they will be increased to one-quarter and three-quarters respectively.

Bequests. All the *sharīʿah* jurists agree that a person who is adult and sane has the capacity to make a bequest, while bequests made by a minor or a mentally defective person, a person acting under compulsion, or under temporary loss of reason (through, for example, intoxication) are void. A bequest may be oral or written, and any words, or even signs, may be used provided they clearly indicate the testator's intention. All free individuals, juristic persons, and fetuses in the womb, whether Muslim or non-Muslim, and irrespective of domicile, are capable of receiving a bequest. Any object of value that is considered as goods *(māl),* including income and usufruct arising out of the property owned by the testator, may be given in bequest. A bequest is invalid if made in pursuit of unlawful purposes, such as promoting a brothel. Further, no Muslim may bequeath more than one-third of the residue of his estate after the payment of debts and other charges. In Sunnī law, a bequest made in favor of a legal heir is void unless the other heirs consent to it. Similarly, a bequest which exceeds the bequeathable third does not take effect without the consent of the surviving heirs. In Sunnī law, such consent must be obtained after the death of the testator, whereas in Shīʿī law it may be obtained either before or after the testator's death. Shīʿī law also permits the testator to bequeath to any person, including a legal heir, within the limit of one-third. Without the consent of the surviving heirs, bequests amounting to more than one-third of the estate must be reduced to the maximum of one-third.

A testator may specify the order in which several of his bequests are to be executed, and this order will be observed until the bequeathable third is exhausted. If no order is specified and the limit of one-third is exceeded, the abatement will be proportionate in Sunnī law, whereas under Shīʿī law the first in chronological order prevails. A bequest is null and void if made in favor of a person who has caused the death of the testator. And finally, if the legatee predeceases the testator, the bequest lapses in Ḥanafī law, but passes on to the heir of the deceased legatee in Shīʿī law.

Paternity. Paternity is the legal relation between father and child that is created by a legitimate birth. The paternity of a child is normally established by marriage between its parents. Maternity on the other hand is not dependent upon marriage. In Sunnī law, the maternity of a child, whether the offspring of marriage or of adultery, is established in the woman who actually gives birth to the child. Thus if a man commits adultery and a child is born, it is considered to be the child of its mother and inherits from her and her relations. But the man is not considered to be the father of the child, for paternity is established only through marriage. In Shīʿī law, however, an illegitimate child has no legal relationship with either its father or its mother.

The law normally presumes that a child born to a married woman is the legitimate child of her husband. This presumption, however, operates within the limits of what the law recognizes as the minimum and maximum duration of the gestation period. According to all the *sharīʿah* schools, the minimum period of gestation is six months. The maximum period varies between nine months (Shīʿī), two years (Ḥanafī), four years (Shāfiʿī), and five to seven years (Mālikī). In Ḥanafī law, therefore, the paternity of the child is ascribed to the husband if it is born after not less than six months of marriage, and within not more than two years after the dissolution of marriage. The only method by which the husband can challenge the presumption of legitimacy and disown his child is to resort to the imprecation procedure, known as *liʿān.* According to this procedure, the husband must swear four oaths that the child is not his and then invoke the curse of God upon himself if he is lying. This effects an immediate and final divorce according to the majority view, whereas in Ḥanafī and Shīʿī law, the marriage subsists until the court orders the parties to separate. If the wife confesses to the adultery, the penalty is imprisonment according to Ḥanafī law, and death by stoning according to the other schools (Ḥanafī law forbids the enforcement of capital punishment for *zināʾ* unless it is proven by the testimony of four witnesses). Alternately, she may deny the charge by swearing four solemn oaths to plead her innocence and finally calling upon herself the wrath of God if she was in fact guilty. Regardless of whether the wife confesses or denies the charge, as a consequence of *liʿān* the child is disowned by the husband.

Either of the spouses, or failing this, the judge, may initiate the *liʿān* proceedings. The traditional law of *liʿān* does not, however, provide for the eventuality where the wife might initiate a charge of adultery against the husband. In the event that the wife accuses the husband of *zināʾ,* she would normally be required to prove the accusation by the testimony of four witnesses, in which case the husband would be liable to the capital punishment for *zināʾ.* But if she fails to provide the required proof, she would herself be liable to punishment for slanderous accusation *(qadhf),* which is eighty lashes. In neither case, however, would recourse be made to *li'ān*, for the latter is invoked only when the husband accuses his wife of *zinā'*, and not vice versa. If the husband accuses his wife of *zinā'* but fails to resort to *li'ān*, he too would be liable to the punishment of *qadhf*. Some jurists have held the view that the wife's unproven accusation of *zinā'* would provide sufficient grounds for judicial separation on the basis of injury *(ḍarar)*.

Where the paternity of a child cannot be proved by establishing a marriage between the parents at the time of conception, the law recognizes acknowledgment *(iqrār)* as a method whereby such a marriage and legitimate descent can be established. This method can be used only if real paternity is possible; thus the acknowledged child must be at least twelve and one-half years younger than the acknowledging parent, since this interval represents the minimum period of gestation added to the minimum age of puberty. In addition, one person may acknowledge the paternity of another on the following three conditions: the child is of unknown paternity; there is no definite proof that the child is the offspring of adultery; and the acknowledgment does not contradict another person's presumption of paternity. An acknowledgment need not be expressed in words, but may be implied by the deliberate conduct of one person who treats another as his legitimate offspring. Subject to repudiation by an acknowledgee who is adult and sane, an acknowledgment of paternity is binding for all purposes, and once effected, it is irrevocable.

The *sharī'ah* law of paternity has been criticized mainly for accepting gestation periods of two years (Ḥanafī law) or more, which has encouraged people to claim the paternity of illegitimate children for purposes of inheritance. In a 1929 law, the Egyptian legislature reduced the maximum period of gestation to one year. Consequently, no claim of paternity on behalf of a child born more than one year after the termination of the marriage can be heard in Egyptian courts. Furthermore, the Egyptian law provides that proof of nonaccess between the spouses since their marriage or for one year preceding the birth of a child would debar a claim of the legitimacy of such a child. Syria, Tunisia, and Morocco have also adopted these measures with minor variations, and one year represents the maximum period of gestation in these countries. It may be added that the modern law provision enabling a husband to prove that he had no physical access to his wife during the possible time of conception supersedes the procedure of *li'an*. In appropriate circumstances, therefore, the new rules of evidence will determine the disputed paternity of a child. Proof of nonaccess, under modern law, would also seem to defeat the claim to inheritance of a child in embryo, at least where the basis of such a claim is the legitimacy of the child, and would, in turn, overrule the provision of the traditional law concerning the reservation of a portion of the estate for such a child. The fundamental rules governing the custody of children *(ḥaḍānah)* are common to all the *sharī'ah* schools. Following the dissolution of a marriage, the custody of the young children belongs to the mother, but she loses this right if she remarries, in which case custody reverts to the father. The mother's right to custody terminates with the completion of seven years in the case of male children, and in case of female children, with the onset of puberty.

BIBLIOGRAPHY

An accurate exposition of the *sharī'ah* law of marriage and divorce can be found in al-Marghinānī's *Al-hidāyah*, a twelfth-century source book of Ḥanafī law, translated by Charles Hamilton as *The Hedaya, or Guide*, 4 vols., 2d ed. (Lahore, 1957). A source book on the law of inheritance is Sirāj al-Dīn al-Sajāwandi's *Al-sirājīyah*, the text and translation of which will be found in a modern work by al-haj Mahomet Ullah ibn S. Jung, *The Muslim Law of Inheritance* (Allahabad, 1934). The whole range of personal law is treated by D. F. Mulla's *Principles of Mahomedan Law*, 16th ed. (Bombay, 1968), a well-known Ḥanafī law text that is also informative on the application of this law in India and Pakistan. F. B. Tyabji's *Muslim Law: The Personal Law of Muslims in India and Pakistan*, 4th ed. (Bombay, 1968) is skillfully classified and comprehensive on all the major schools of *sharī'ah* law. A. A. Fyzee's *Outlines of Muhammadan Law*, 4th ed. (Bombay, 1974) is more informative on Shī'ī personal law, and its introductory chapter gives background information on the sources and history of the *sharī'ah*. The best single book on the law of inheritance and its modern reforms remains Noel J. Coulson's *Succession in the Muslim Family* (Cambridge, 1971). A useful collection of the statutory laws of various Muslim countries, with special reference to modern reforms, can be found in Tahir Mahmood's *Family Law Reform in the Muslim World* (Bombay, 1972). Herbert J. Liebesny's *Law of the Near and Middle East* (Albany, N.Y., 1975) is also very useful on the application of *sharī'ah* law in various Muslim countries. For the status of women, see John L. Esposito, *Women in Muslim Family Law* (Syracuse, N.Y., 1982).

There are many good books in Arabic on the subject. Muḥammad abū Zahrah's *Al-aḥwāl al-shakhṣiyah* (Cairo, 1957) is written in readable style and deals with the whole range of the *sharī'ah* personal law. 'Abd al-Raḥmān al-Sabūni's *Madā ḥurriyat al-zawjayn fī al-ṭalāq*, 2 vols., 2nd ed (Beirut, 1968) is most comprehensive on the *sharī'ah* law of divorce in its various schools. And finally, Muhammad Zayd al-Ibyāni's *Sharh al-aḥkām al-sharī'ah fī al-aḥwāl al-shakhṣīyah*, 3 vols. (Beirut, 1976), is a useful modern work on the whole range of the *sharī'ah* personal law.

M. Hashim Kamali

ISLAMIC PHILOSOPHY. *See* Falsafah.

ISLAMIC RELIGIOUS YEAR. The Islamic religious year is highlighted by two major events that are enjoined by the Qur'ān and that are celebrated all over the Muslim world. These are the pilgrimage, or *ḥajj*, which culminates in the ʿĪd al-Aḍḥā (Feast of Sacrifice), in the last lunar month, and Ramaḍān, the month of fasting, which ends with the celebration of the ʿĪd al-Fiṭr (Feast of Fast Breaking) on the first day of the next month, Shawwāl. Because the twelve-month calendar of Islam is based on a purely lunar year of 354 days, these events have no fixed relation to the seasons of the 365-day solar year. Over the course of years, they may occur in spring, summer, autumn, and winter. Thus, no connection with pre-Islamic solar feasts can be made, nor can any tradition of agricultural cults be traced. (Celebrations of the solar seasons do occur in various parts of the Muslim world, but they are not based on the Qur'ān or on *ḥadīth*.)

The beginning of each month of the Muslim calendar is reckoned from the appearance of the new moon, which must, according to tradition, be reported by at least two trustworthy witnesses. Because religious leaders in some Muslim countries do, in fact, rely on astronomical calculation of the first appearance of the crescent while others continue to follow the Qur'anic prescription of actually seeing the moon, differences of one day in reckoning the beginning or end of a month are common. The date may also vary according to local weather conditions.

Certain days of the week are considered to be endowed with good or bad qualities, as can be understood from relevant collections of *ḥadīth*. Friday, the day of communal prayer at noon, is always regarded as auspicious, and Monday and Thursday carry positive aspects, as do the "white nights" before and after a full moon.

The year begins with the month of Muḥarram. Its tenth day, ʿĀshūrā', was suggested as a fast day by the Prophet but subsequently became associated with the death of Muḥammad's grandson, Ḥusayn ibn ʿAlī, who was killed in the Battle of Karbala on 10 Muḥarram 81 / 10 October 680. Although this day is a time of mourning for all Muslims, it is the Shīʿah, the "party" of ʿAlī, who have attached very special significance to Ḥusayn's martyrdom and to the entire month of Muḥarram. Thus, Sunnī Muslims do not subscribe to the elaborate celebrations developed in later centuries, particularly in Iran and India, where commemorations extend through the first ten days of the month. During this period women wear subdued colors, preferably black, with no jewelry. Men and women hold separate gatherings *(majālis)* during which a male or female preacher reminds the audience of the suffering of Ḥusayn and the other imams. The preacher recounts legends of the events at Karbala; singers recite threnodies; and those present beat their breasts, call blessings upon the Prophet, and profusely shed tears. "Weeping for Ḥusayn opens the door to Paradise," it is said, and the tears themselves are collected for future use as a panacea.

During the first ten days of Muḥarram, special craftsmen prepare *taʿziyah*s, or *tābūt*s, tall, domed, wooden structures (up to thirty feet high) that represent the tombs of the imams. Beautifully carved and gilded or painted, they are carried in the ʿĀshūrā' processions along with colorful standards lofted in memory of Ḥusayn's standard-bearer, Jaʿfar. A lavishly caparisoned white horse is led as a symbol of Ḥusayn's mount, Dhū al-Janāḥ, and of the white horse on which the Hidden Imam is expected to ride when he finally reappears. During these processions many people flagellate themselves with chains from which hang small knives (wounds thus inflicted never become septic), and fire walking is sometimes performed. In some areas, such as the Deccan, ʿĀshūrā' processions at times assumed almost carnivalistic aspects, as eighteenth-century miniatures show. Late in the day the small *taʿziyah*s are buried in a place designated as "Karbala," while the more precious ones are stored, along with other implements, in *ʿāshūrā-khānah*s or *imām-bārah*s, large buildings for the meetings of the Shīʿī community. A special dish with numerous ingredients is cooked in remembrance of the mixed food in Karbala, prepared from whatever happened to be in the heroes' bags. In Turkey, sharing this *aşure* with neighbors is a custom among both Sunnī and Shīʿī families.

In nineteenth-century Lucknow, *taʿziyah* rites were continued until the tenth day of the following month of Ṣafar, thus marking forty days of mourning from the start of Muḥarram. Among the Shīʿah, no weddings are celebrated in Muḥarram, and the month has always been a time when communal or sectarian feelings run high. Not infrequently, rioting results. The Ismāʿīlī community, at least since the time of Aga Khan III (r. 1885–1957), does not participate in Muḥarram because it has a *ḥāẓir imām* ("present imam") in the Aga Khan and need not look back to Ḥusayn's death.

Various literary and dramatic genres have also developed around the events at Karbala. The genre of *maqtal Ḥusayn*, poetry or prose telling of Ḥusayn's suffering, has been known since the early Middle Ages, and the *marthiyah*, or threnody, began to be developed by Indian poets about the beginning of the seventeenth century. This latter genre, which originated in the Deccan and spread to northern India, found its finest expression at the Shīʿī court of Lucknow in the nineteenth century.

In Iran, and to a lesser degree in Iraq and Lebanon, the martyrdom of Ḥusayn came to be recreated in *ta'ziyah* plays interweaving numerous mythical elements to establish the martyrdom as the central event in the history of the universe.

In the month of Ṣafar, which follows Muḥarram, a sad mood used to prevail among Muslims because the Prophet once fell ill during this period. The last Wednesday of the month, when the Prophet felt better, was a day of rejoicing.

Rabīʿ al-Awwal ("first Rabīʿ"), the third lunar month, is marked by the Mawlid al-Nabī ("birthday of the Prophet") on the twelfth. The day is celebrated as the date of the Prophet's birth *(mīlād)* although it was actually the date of his death and is also widely commemorated in that connection. Nonetheless, the joyful celebration of Muḥammad's birthday began comparatively early; it was introduced on a larger scale in Fatimid Egypt, where the rulers, descendants of Muḥammad's daughter Fāṭimah, remembered the birthday of their ancestor by inviting scholars and by distributing sweets and money, a feature that has remained common. Ever since, the pious have felt that celebrations of the Mawlid have a special blessing power *(barakah)*.

The first major celebration of the Mawlid al-Nabī is described for the year AH 604/1207 CE in Arbalā' (modern Irbil, in northern Iraq), where the Ṣūfīs participated actively. The Mawlid became increasingly popular first in the western and then in the central Islamic lands. A special genre of poetry known as *mawlūd* developed in almost all Islamic languages. In Turkey the *mevlûd* by Süleyman Çelebi (d. 1409), telling in simple verse the miracles connected with the birth of the Prophet and describing his life, is still sung. In many countries, candles are lit—in Turkey the day is still called Mevlûd Kandılı (Lamp Feast of the Birth)—and the Mawlid provides an occasion for donning festive clothes, burning incense, and distributing sweets. Orthodox circles have traditionally taken issue with the use of candles because of the similarity to Christmas celebrations; likewise they have disallowed musical performances and deemed that only the recitation of the Qur'ān seems permissible on a day that also marks the Prophet's death. The stories that have been traditionally recited reflect the people's love and veneration of the Prophet, whose birth, according to some eighteenth-century writers, was "more important than the Laylat al-Qadr," the night when the Qur'ān was first revealed, for it meant the arrival of "mercy for the worlds" (surah 21:107). Lately, however, there is a growing tendency to demythologize the contents of Mawlid literature; the speeches and poems offered on that day, and throughout the month in many countries, are meant to remind people of the ethical and social role of the Prophet, the "beautiful model" (surah 33:21) of his community. Newspapers and television publicize this attitude.

The following month, Rabīʿ al-Thānī ("second Rabīʿ"), has no ritual justified by the Qur'ān or *ḥadīth*. However, in many areas, especially in India and Pakistan, the eleventh marks the anniversary of ʿAbd al-Qādir al-Jīlānī, whose Ṣūfī order, the Qādirīyah, is the most widespread fraternity. The month is therefore called simply Yārhīñ, meaning "eleven" in Sindhi. As on other saints' days, flags are flown, meetings are convened to recite eulogies for the saint, and food is cooked and distributed in his name.

No religious events, other than local saints' days, are noted for the following two months, Jumādā al-Ūlā ("first Jumādā") and Jumādā al-Ākhirah ("last Jumādā"), but the seventh lunar month, Rajab, is blessed by celebration of the Prophet's Miʿrāj, his heavenly journey, which took place on the night of the twenty-seventh. In Turkey, this is again a *kandıl*, or "lamp feast," on which people fast during daytime. In other areas, such as Kashmir, it used to be celebrated for a whole week. Although the celebration of the Miʿrāj cannot vie in popularity with the Prophet's birthday, the mystery of the Prophet's heavenly journey has deeply impressed Muslim piety and poetry. Other events commemorated in Rajab include the first nights of the month, *raghā'ib*, celebrated in some areas (notably Turkey) as the time when Āminah conceived the Prophet, as well as ʿAlī's birthday, celebrated by all Shīʿī communities on 13 Rajab.

In the following month, Shaʿbān, a non-Qur'anic but very popular feast is the Laylat al-Barā'ah (Pers., Shab-i Barāt), celebrated on the night of the full moon. Historically this is the night when the Prophet entered Mecca triumphantly, but in Muslim folklore it is considered to be the night when the "writing conferring immunity is written in heaven" or, more generally, the night during which the fates for the coming year are fixed. Therefore pious Muslims fast, pray, and keep vigils. On the whole, however, and especially in Indo-Pakistan, the night is celebrated with illuminations and fireworks. Orthodox critics object to such displays as symptoms of Hindu influence, even though the Shab-i Barāt is mentioned in a non-Indian environment as early as the twelfth century, in a poem by Sanā'ī of Ghaznah (d. 1131). The Shīʿī community celebrates the birthday of Imam Mahdi, the last of the twelve imams, on this day.

The month of Ramaḍān is the most demanding of the Islamic year, especially when it falls in the hot season.

Each day, Muslims must fast from the moment there is enough light to distinguish white from black threads until the sun has completely set. The order to abstain from food, drink, smoking, sex, and even from injections or intake of fragrance requires a strong intention *(nīyah)* of the fasting person. He or she will then break fast with an odd number of dates and some water before proceeding to the evening prayer. The problem of how to keep the fast in northern countries during the long summer days has aroused much controversy; one solution is to break fast at the time when the sun sets in the next Muslim country or on the forty-fifth degree of latitude. For every day that the fast is neglected, or cannot be performed because of illness, pregnancy, or menstruation, the observant Muslim is obliged to compensate either by fasting some other day or by feeding a number of the ever present poor.

The Laylat al-Qadr ("night of power"; surah 97), during which the first revelation of the Qur'ān took place, is one of the last odd-numbered nights in Ramaḍān, generally considered the twenty-seventh. In its honor people may spend the last ten days of Ramaḍān in seclusion, and those who do not fast otherwise will try to do it during that period. The pious hope for the vision of the light that fills the world during this blessed night. The Ismāʿīlīs pray all night in their Jamāʿat-khānah. Many people perform the *tarāwīḥ* prayers (a long sequence, including twenty to thirty-three *rakʿah*s of prayers and prostrations) after breaking the fast. Then they may enjoy the lighter side of life: the illumination of mosques and the activities of all kinds of entertainers that used to be a regular part of every Ramaḍān night. A second meal is taken before the first sign of dawn.

The ʿĪd al-Fiṭr (Feast of Fast Breaking), which brings release from the month-long abstinence at daylight, is called the "lesser feast," but it is most eagerly awaited as a celebration of the return to normal life. Its Turkish name, *Şeker Bayramı* ("sugar feast"), points to the custom of distributing sweets. After the morning prayer of 1 Shawwāl in the spacious *ʿīdgāh,* it is customary to put on new clothes and to visit friends. The sigh that one has no new clothes for the feast is a touching topic in Islamic love poetry.

After the ʿId al-Fiṭr there is no major feast in Shawwāl or in Dhū al-Qaʿdah. The later month is used for preparations for the pilgrimage *(ḥajj),* which takes place in Dhū al-Ḥijjah. [*See* Pilgrimage, *article on* Muslim Pilgrimage.]

On 10 Dhū al-Ḥijjah, the ʿĪd al-Aḍḥā, or ʿĪd al-Qurbān (Feast of Sacrifice), called the "major feast," is celebrated in the valley of Minā, near Mecca, with thousands, and now millions, of Muslims ritually slaughtering sheep or larger animals and thus reenacting the substitution of a ram for Ismāʿīl, whom Abraham was willing to sacrifice (surah 37:102). Because this is the only feast in which the community celebrates the memory of a mythical event, every Muslim is called upon to repeat the slaughter at home; theologians do not accept the substitution of money for the sacrificial animal, as some liberal Muslims have suggested. According to popular belief, the slaughtered animal will carry its owner across the Ṣirāṭ Bridge to Paradise. The meat of the animal sacrificed at home is distributed to the poor, and the hide is given to a charitable foundation. The Indo-Muslim designation of the feast as Baqar ʿĪd (Cow Feast) and the slaughtering of cows have often caused Hindu riots during these days. The return of the pilgrims is duly celebrated, as one can witness every year at the airports of Muslim countries. Later in the month, on 18 Dhū al-Ḥijjah, the Shīʿī community celebrates the ʿĪd al-Ghadīr (Feast of the Pond), the day on which Muḥammad invested ʿAlī as his successor near the pond Khumm.

Every place in the Islamic world has special celebrations for commemorating local saints. Some of these festivities, called *ʿurs* (spiritual "wedding"), attract tens of thousands of people. Almost all of them follow the rhythm of the lunar year. The *ʿurs* of Aḥmad al-Badawī in Tanta, Egypt, is celebrated, however, according to the solar year in early June, when the Nile is rising, and may be connected with pre-Islamic fertility rites. In Turkey, the anniversary of the birth of Mawlānā Rūmī is now celebrated on 17 December. Likewise, Ismāʿīlīs celebrate the Aga Khan's birthday according to the Christian, or common, era.

Some Muslim festivals are connected with the solar year. The most important is Nawrūz, the Persian New Year, which occurs at the vernal equinox. It is celebrated in a joyous way wherever Persian culture spread, even in Egypt. It is customary that seven items have to be on the table (in Iran, the names of these seven must begin with the letter *s*). Orthodox Muslims have often objected to the celebration of Nawrūz, but for most people the beginning of spring has always been too delightful to be neglected. The Bektashī order of Ṣūfīs in Turkey have explained Nawrūz as ʿAlī's birthday and have thus islamized it. Another Turkish celebration, Hıdrellez, combines the feasts of the saint-prophet Khiḍr and of Ilyās, associated with the biblical Elijah. The day falls on 6 May and is connected with a change of winds and weather.

An interesting way of depicting the sequence of the ritual year is found in a poetic genre of Indo-Pakistan called *bārahmāsa* ("twelve months"). It is derived from Hindu tradition and in its islamized forms describes the twelve months through the words of a lovesick young woman who experiences in Muḥarram the pain of seeing her beloved slain, celebrates his birthday in Rabīʿ al-Awwal, and finally meets him in Dhū al-Ḥijjah, when visiting either the Kaʿbah in Mecca or the Prophet's tomb in Medina.

Muslim mystics, as strictly as they might have adhered to ritual, have spiritualized the liturgical year. The Feast of Sacrifice—whether it be named ʿĪd al-Aḍḥā, ʿĪd al-Qurbān, or ʿId al-Naḥr—has meant, for them, to sacrifice themselves before the divine Beloved, and the true *ʿīd* has been to see the face of the Beloved whose very presence makes every day a feast for the lover.

[*See also* ʿĀshūrāʾ; Mawlid; Nawrūz; *and, for discussion related to the month of Ramaḍān,* Ṣawm. *For discussion of the events of the Islamic religious year in a broader context, see* Worship and Cultic Life, *article on* Muslim Worship.]

BIBLIOGRAPHY

Gustave E. von Grunebaum's *Muhammedan Festivals* (New York, 1951) gives a general survey of the Islamic festivals, mainly based on classical sources. See also the article "Muslim Festivals" in Hava Lazarus-Yafeh's *Some Religious Aspects of Islam* (Leiden, 1981), pp. 38–47. E. W. Lane's *An Account of the Manners and Customs of the Modern Egyptians,* 3 vols., 3d ed. (1846; reprint, New York, 1973) deals with the seasons as they were celebrated in early nineteenth-century Cairo, while Jaʿfar Sharif's *Islam in India, or the Qanun-i-Islam,* translated by G. A. Herklots and edited by William Crooke (1921; reprint, London, 1972), describes the Muslim year as celebrated in India, particularly in the Deccan. For the Muḥarram ceremonies, the best introduction is *Taʿziyeh: Ritual and Drama in Iran,* edited by Peter J. Chelkowski (New York, 1979), and the classic study of the *ḥajj* is still Christiaan Snouck Hurgronje's *Het Mekkansche feest* (Leiden, 1880).

ANNEMARIE SCHIMMEL

ISLAMIC STUDIES encompass the study of the religion of Islam and of Islamic aspects of Muslim cultures and societies. At the outset we must recognize that the word *Islam* itself is used in very different senses by faithful Muslims, for whom it is a norm and an ideal, and by scholars (Muslim and non-Muslim Islamicists), who refer to it as a subject of study or a kind of symbol for the focus of their inquiry, as well as by the larger public in the West who are outsiders and give different appreciations of what is felt by them to be "foreign." By extension, a sharp distinction must be made between normative Islam (the prescriptions, norms, and values that are recognized by the community as embodiments of divine guidance) and actual Islam (all those forms and movements, practices and ideas that have in fact existed in the many Muslim communities in different times and places). In other words, Islamic data sought for the sake of scholarly understanding are not the same as the ideals that Muslims as adherents of Islam attach to them, the meaning they attribute to them, or the truth they recognize in them.

This familiar distinction between practice and ideal, fact and (subjective) meaning of religious data must be maintained not only for the purpose of analysis and understanding but also for the making of valid comparisons. Practices may be compared with practices, ideals with ideals, but the practice of something in one religion should not be compared with the ideal of the same thing in another religion. From a scholarly point of view, moreover, we have no reason to say that any particular Muslim society represents Islam as a norm and an ideal better than another. We must proceed by reporting the various ideas and practices that prevail in one or another group and by trying to explain differences and discover their implications. Whatever the eternal truth of Islam at all times and places, its ideas and practices at different times and places are to be studied as they present themselves.

The Scope of Islamic Studies

On the basis of these distinctions, it is possible to identify three different enterprises that come under the general rubric of Islamic studies:

1. *The normative study of Islamic religion* is generally carried out by Muslims in order to acquire knowledge of religious truth. It implies the study of the Islamic religious sciences: Qurʾānic exegesis *(tafsīr),* the science of traditions *(ʿilm al-ḥadīth),* jurisprudence *(fiqh),* and metaphysical theology *(kalām).* Traditionally pursued in mosques and special religious colleges (*madrasah*s), it is now usually carried out in faculties of religious law *(sharīʿah)* and of religious sciences *(ʿulūm al-dīn)* at universities or special Islamic institutes in Muslim countries. It should be noted, however, that normative studies of Islam can also be undertaken by non-Muslims, such as Christians seeking to proselytize among Muslims or to develop a theology of religions in which a particular place is assigned to Islam.
2. *The nonnormative study of Islamic religion* is usually done in universities and covers both what is considered by Muslims to be true Islam (the Islamic religious sciences in particular) and what is considered to be living Islam (the factual religious expressions of Muslims). This nonnormative study of Islamic religion can be pursued by Muslims and non-Muslims alike, wherever they observe the general rules of

scholarly inquiry. This is the research that is generally called "Islamic studies."

3. *The nonnormative study of Islamic aspects of Muslim cultures and societies* in a broader sense is not directed toward Islam as such. It takes a wider context into consideration, approaching things Islamic from the point of view of history and literature or cultural anthropology and sociology, and not specifically from the perspective of the study of religion.

My focus in this essay is on the two nonnormative forms of study, which we may call Islamic studies in the narrower (2) and the wider (3) sense. In the narrower sense of Islamic studies, the focus is on Islamic religion as an entity in itself; the wider sense of Islamic studies deals with data that are part of given Muslim communities and are culled from the Islamic experience but that may or may not possess a religious (i.e., Islamic) significance for particular Muslim groups.

In the case of studies of particular Muslim communities, a further distinction can be made. On the one hand, some general concept of Islam may be held implicitly or explicitly by the researcher, even if the research is limited to one or to a few concrete situations. In research of this kind, notwithstanding its specialized character, Islam as a whole remains within the horizon of the researcher. On the other hand, there are studies dealing with Muslim communities of a specific area and period that do not take into consideration any general concept if Islam. Yet this research still belongs implicitly to Islamic studies in the wider sense to the extent that Islamicists may find it useful.

History of Islamic Studies in the Narrower Sense

The rise of scholarly interest in Islam as a religion represents in part a critical response to numerous images of Muḥammad and Islamic religion in general that were widespread in medieval Europe. Although Arab science and philosophy were appreciated and admired, Islam was projected as the great adversary of Christianity. The first effort to acquire a more scholarly knowledge of the Islamic religion on the basis of the sources was made by Peter the Venerable, abbot of Cluny (c. 1094–1156), who financed a team of translators working in Spain. One of the results was the first Latin translation of the Qur'ān, which was completed in 1143 by Robert Ketton.

Since the beginning of the sixteenth century, Arabic and other so-called Islamic languages (notably Persian and Turkish) have been studied in European universities; language competency was the first prerequisite for the investigation of Islam. Another prerequisite was a serious study of Islamic history, carried out first (from the sixteenth century) as a history of Muslim peoples, especially the Turks, and later (from the eighteenth century on) as a history of Islamic religion, which, thanks to the Enlightenment, could be appreciated more adequately. Noteworthy indeed is the objective description of Islamic religion, based on Muslim sources, presented by Adrian Reland in his *De religione mohammedica libri duo* (1705; 2d ed., 1717). Such approaches were to lead to the rise of Islamic studies as a discipline based on textual criticism and historical analysis with a view to the writing of a history of Islamic religion and culture. As a modern field of scholarship, Islamic studies emerged around the middle of the nineteenth century, with the publication of biographies of Muḥammad by Gustav Weil (1843), William Muir (1861; rev. ed., 1912), and Aloys Sprenger (3 vols., 1861–1865). Early studies of the Qur'ān were Weil's *Historisch-kritische Einleitung in den Koran* (1844; 2d ed., 1878) and Theodor Nöldeke's *Geschichte des Qorans* (2 vols., 1860; 2d rev. ed., 1909–1938). Alfred von Kremer's *Geschichte der herrschenden ideen des Islams* (1868) and *Culturgeschichtliche Streifzüge auf dem Gebiete des Islams* (1873) were the first attempts to present the history of Islam as an integrated whole.

Islamic Studies as Part of Oriental Studies. The development of Islamic studies in the nineteenth century was part of the general development of Oriental studies, commonly called "Orientalism." This effort was the first serious intellectual encounter between Europe and another civilization, albeit a unilateral encounter and one in which current cultural images of the "Orient" unavoidably played a role. Oriental studies were largely patterned after the classical studies that had arisen in the sixteenth century; they were based on philology in the broad sense of the term, that is, the study of a particular culture through its texts. Islamic studies in this sense lead to nonnormative accounts of Islamic religion as described under (2), above. The field has always been a demanding one, presupposing an intensive study of Arabic and other "Islamic" languages, on the basis of which text editions can be prepared and textual studies, including textual criticism and literary history, can be carried out. Familiarity with the texts, in its turn, is a prerequisite for the further study of history. Supplemented by the study of other Islamic expressions in art and architecture and in present-day religious life, textual, historical, and anthropological research together prepare the way for the study of Islamic culture and religion.

Within the Orientalist tradition, Islamic studies were conceived of as a cultural discipline and exhibited certain assumptions of European civilization of the time, notably the superiority of Western civilization and the excellence of its scholarship. Stress has generally been laid on the differences between Islamic civilization and European culture, with an ethnocentric bias toward the latter. Beyond the interest in its origins, a certain predilection can be discerned for the "classical" period of Islamic civilization, a preference that can also be observed in other branches of Oriental studies. Specialization increasingly led to detailed studies, and the ideal of a comprehensive view of Islam often came down simply to mastering an extraordinary mass of facts. Just as the preponderance of facts in Oriental studies has given Islamic studies a rather "positivist" orientation, the approach to Islamic religion too has been essentially based on establishing historical facts with little attention being paid to the problem of the meaning of these facts, which is a problem of interpretation.

The Nonnormative Study of Islamic Religion. The history of Islamic religion has been approached in three basic ways. A great number of historians, following the example set by Julius Wellhausen (1844–1918) in his various studies on the early Islamic period, have focused on the external history of Islam. Later historians such as Claude Cahen and Bernard Lewis have shown how much light can be thrown on particular Muslim institutions and movements by viewing them against the background of economic, social, and political history.

Another kind of historical research concentrates rather on what may be called the inner developments in Islamic religion and culture. This approach was introduced by one of the major figures in the field, Ignácz Goldziher (1850–1921), who tried to establish the basic framework of an intellectual history of Islam. Another scholar working along these lines was Helmut Ritter (1892–1971), who revealed the inner connections among a great number of religious concepts, mainly theological and mystical, as they developed in history.

Somewhere between the general historians and the historians of religion are cultural historians of the medieval period such as Carl Heinrich Becker (1876–1933), Jörg Kraemer (1917–1961), and Gustav Edmund von Grunebaum (1909–1972), all of whom set religious developments within wider cultural frameworks, which were related in turn to political and military history. The name of Marshall G. S. Hodgson (1921–1968) should also be mentioned here because of his efforts to situate the total history of Islam within a culturally oriented world history.

These three types of historical study are also reflected in the vast number of specialized historical researches on particular Muslim communities of the past, as well as in studies dealing with the contemporary history of Muslim societies. Here I must limit myself to indicating the major points of the history of research into broad topics, mentioning some names but omitting many others of no less significance. (The categories that follow are those set out by Charles J. Adams in his 1976 survey, "Islamic Religious Tradition.")

Muḥammad. Various approaches have developed since the mid-nineteenth-century biographies mentioned earlier. In a two-volume biography, *Mohammed* (1892–1895), Hubert Grimme gave an account of the social factors in Muḥammad's life and stressed the Prophet's aspect as social reformer; Frants Buhl assembled all historical materials available at the time for a substantial biography of Muḥammad in *Das Leben Muhammed* (1930; 2d ed., 1955). Tor Andrae studied later Muslim views of Muḥammad as a prophet and paradigmatic figure in his *Die person Muhammeds in lehre und glauben seiner gemeinde* (1918). A breakthrough in establishing the context of Muḥammad's life and work is W. Montgomery Watt's two-volume study, *Muhammad at Mecca* (1953) and *Muhammad at Medina* (1956), which focuses attention on the social and economic changes in Arabia (Mecca) that Muḥammad tried to address in his prophetic activity. Maxime Rodinson's thought-provoking biography, *Mohammed* (1961; Eng. trans., 1971), interprets historical data from a similar perspective but adds a psychological dimension. An era in which Western scholarship recognizes the originality of Muḥammad's achievements seems to have dawned, following a period during which stress was placed by Jewish scholars on the Jewish influences on Muḥammad and by Christian scholars on Christian influences. Biographies of Muḥammad written by Muslims are too numerous to be treated here in full. The classic one is that by Ibn Isḥāq (d. 767?), translated by A. Guillaume as *The Life of Muhammad* (1955). E. S. Sabanegh studied some modern Egyptian biographies of Muḥammad in his *Muhammad b. Abdallah "le Prophete": Portraits contemporains, Egypte 1930–1950* (1982).

The Qur'ān. After the important translation into English by George Sale (1697?–1736), published in 1734 with a famous "preliminary discourse," a great number of translations of the Qur'ān have seen the light. I may mention those by Richard Bell (1937), A. J. Arberry (1955), and Marmaduke Pickthall (1930), this last being recognized by Muslims. The classic study of the Qur'anic text remains that of Theodor Nöldeke in its three-volume second edition (1909–1938), enlarged and revised with the help of colleagues. Arthur Jeffery published two important studies, *The Textual History of the Qur'ān* (1937) and *The Foreign Vocabulary of the Qur'ān* (1938). Rudi Paret's conscientious German translation (1962) was subsequently accompanied by his important commentary (1971). Important is Angelika Neuwirth's

Studien zur Komposition der mekkanischen Suren (1981). John Wansbrough's *Quranic Studies* (1977) has brought the accepted theory on the early collation of the Qur'anic text into question.

It is noteworthy that while great progress has been made with regard to the textual-critical, linguistic, and literary aspects of the Qur'ān, the study of its contents, concepts, and worldview—that is, its meaning—has only started to take off. In this connection Toshihiko Izutsu's semantic analyses of the Qur'ān, *The Structure of the Ethical Terms in the Qur'ān* (1959; rev. ed., 1966) and *God and Man in the Koran* (1964), have played a pioneering role. Needless to say, critical studies of the Qur'ān and of Muḥammad have offended some Muslim sensibilities in much the same way that source criticism of the Bible has offended some biblicist Christians.

The study of the Qur'ān implies that of Muslim commentaries (*tafsīrs*) of the Qur'ān. See Helmut Gätje's *Koran und Koranexegese* (1971) and compare Mohammed Arkoun's *Lectures du Coran* (1982).

Ḥadīth. Goldziher's critical stand in *Muhammedanische Studien*, vol. 2 (1890; Eng. trans., 1971), with regard to the historical dating of *ḥadīth*s ("traditions") that were ascribed to Muḥammad or his companions but were in fact later creations, was carried further by Joseph Schacht (1902–1969) in *The Origins of Muhammadan Jurisprudence* (1950) and led to a debate on their authenticity not only among Muslims but also in Western scholarship. Later work by Fuat Sezgin in the first volume of his *Geschichte des arabischen Schrifttums* (1967) has led to a reconsideration of the extreme criticism by Goldziher and Schacht, although the falseness of many of the attributions to Muhammad remains acknowledged. Since the *sunnah* (consisting of *ḥadīth*s) is the second source, after the Qur'ān, of religious knowledge and law in Islam, here too Muslims are particularly sensitive to scholarly criticism from outside. See G. H. A. Juynboll's *The Authenticity of the Tradition Literature: Discussions in Modern Egypt* (1969).

Law. The structure of religious law (*sharī'ah*) in Islam, its ideal character, and the rules of juridical reasoning by Muslim jurists were first elucidated by Goldziher and by Christiaan Snouck Hurgronje (1857–1936), who also studied its application, side by side with customary law, in Indonesia. Further studies in depth were carried out by Éduard Sachau (1845–1930), Gotthelf Bergsträsser (1886–1933), and especially Joseph Schacht, who summarized his findings in *An Introduction to Islamic Law* (1964). Current trends toward islamicization in Muslim countries are again arousing interest in its juridical aspects. Among the scholars who have worked on changes in the application of the *sharī'ah* in modern Muslim states, the names of J. N. D. Anderson and Noel J. A. Coulson deserve particular mention.

Metaphysical theology. It has been only in the course of the twentieth century that Islamic theological speculation (*kalām*) has been revealed in its originality. An important study on early Muslim creeds is A. J. Wensinck's *The Muslim Creed* (1933). Georges Anawati and Louis Gardet's *Introduction à la théologie musulmane* (1948) demonstrates the structural similarity of medieval Islamic and Christian theological treatises. Here and in other works these authors stress the apologetic character of Islamic theology. On the other hand, Harry A. Wolfson, in *The Philosophy of the Kalam* (1976) is attentive to parallels between Islamic, Christian, and Jewish theological thought. Important are recent studies by Richard M. D. Frank and J. R. T. M. Peters on Mu'tazilī theology.

Islamic philosophy. In the wake of T. J. de Boer's handbook on the subject, *The History of Philosophy in Islam* (1901; Eng. trans., 1903; reprint, 1961), philosophy in Islam was taken to be the continuation of Aristotelian philosophy with Neoplatonic overtones. Important work on this philosophical line appears in Richard Walzer's *Greek into Arabic* (1962). Subsequently, however, it has become clear that there are other old philosophical traditions of a more gnostic nature in Islam. They can be found in Shī'ī intellectual circles, both Iranian Twelvers and Isma'īlī Seveners. We owe this discovery mainly to the investigations of Henry Corbin (1903–1978), whose works, such as *En islam iranien* (4 vols., 1971–1972), revealed hidden but still living spiritual worlds. See also Heinz Halm's *Die islamische Gnosis: Die extreme Schia und die 'Alawiten* (1982).

Mysticism. Muslim mystical thought and experience have attracted serious scholarly attention in the West only in the course of the twentieth century, especially through the work of Reynold A. Nicholson (1868–1945) and Louis Massignon (1883–1962). The former concentrated on certain major works and their authors, such as *The Mathnawī* of Jalāl al-Dīn Rūmī; the latter focused on the development of mystical terminology and produced a four-volume biography of the tenth-century mystic al-Ḥallāj (1922; Eng. trans., 1982). This line of study has been pursued for mystical poetry by A. J. Arberry (1905–1969) and later by scholars such as Annemarie Schimmel in *Mystical Dimensions of Islam* (1976). Muslim mystical orders have also received considerable attention, for instance by J. Spencer Trimingham and F. de Yong.

Islamic art and architecture. This field deserves a separate status among the disciplines making up Islamic studies, since it deals with materials other than texts and is linked with art history in general. Among scholars who deserve mention are K. A. C. Creswell (1879–1974), and Richard Ettinghausen (1906–1979), and at present Oleg Grabar and Robert Hillenbrand. The study of this field is now becoming more integrated into the broader cultural history of Islam.

Religious institutions. In recent decades important breakthroughs have been made in the understanding of the relationships between Islamic religious institutions and the societies in which they function. In *La cité musulmane* (1954), Louis Gardet attempted to sketch the outline of the ideal society in terms of orthodox Islam, while H. A. R. Gibb and Harold Bowen addressed the eighteenth-century Muslim "religious structure," especially with regard to processes of modernization in parts 1 and 2 of *Islamic Society and the West* (1950–1957). Considerable attention has been paid to religious authorities (*'ulamā'*, Ṣūfī shaykhs) with their different roles in society. *Scholars, Saints and Sufis*, edited by Nikki R. Keddie (1972), reflects much of this research through the early 1970s. Important in this respect is A. C. Eccel's study *Egypt, Islam and Social Change: Al-Azhar in Conflict and Accommodation* (1984). See also Michael Gilsenan's *Recognizing Islam: An Anthropologist's Introduction* (1982) and *Islamic Dilemmas: Reformers, Nationalists and Industrialization*, edited by Ernest Gellner (1985).

Living Islam. Travelers, civil servants such as Christiaan Snouck Hurgronje, and anthropologists such as Edvard A. Westermarck (1862–1939) had already in the nineteenth century given descriptions of actual Muslim life, and this kind of research has increased considerably in the twentieth century, mainly through the efforts of anthropologists. Rudolf Kriss and Hubert Kriss-Heinrich, for example, wrote a handbook of popular Islam, *Volksglaube im Bereich des Islams* (2 vols., 1960–1962); Klaus E. Müller dealt with current beliefs and practices among sectarian groups in Islam in his *Kulturhistorische Studien zur Genese pseudoislamischer Sektengebilde in Vorderasien* (1967); and Constance Padwick has studied prayer manuals in actual use in Egypt in *Muslim Devotions* (1961).

Since the 1960s several important studies of living Islam in the broader context of society and its structure have been published by social scientists, among them Clifford Geertz, who, in *Islam Observed* (1968), compares Moroccan and Javanese Islamic structures. Other books in this vein, focusing on Ṣūfī structures, are Michael Gilsenan's *Saint and Sufi in Modern Egypt* (1973) and Ernest Gellner's two works on Morocco, *Saints of the Atlas* (1969) and *Muslim Society* (1981). To this same category belong the numerous writings by Jacques Berque that deal with Arab society and the role of Islam within it. The literature on the status of women in Muslim societies is growing rapidly. See for instance *Women in the Muslim World*, edited by Lois Beck and Nikki R. Keddie (1978).

Modern developments in Islam. Scholarly surveys of modern developments in Muslim countries commenced with a 1932 volume edited by H. A. R. Gibb, *Whither Islam? A Survey of Modern Movements in the Moslem World*, which was followed by the same scholar's *Modern Trends in Islam* (1947) and by Wilfred Cantwell Smith's *Islam in Modern History* (1957). It has since become clear that recent developments should be described according to the country within which they occur and that although certain patterns can be established as valid for nearly all Muslim countries, in each country various groups, including the government, have their own articulation of Islam. A major contribution to this formulation is *Der Islam in der Gegenwart*, edited by Werner Ende and Udo Steinbach (1984). Events in revolutionary Iran have shown, moreover, that Islamicists in the Orientalist tradition simply have not been adequately equipped to interpret what happens in Muslim countries. On the other hand, *Religion in the Middle East: Three Religions in Concord and Conflict*, edited by A. J. Arberry (2 vols., 1969), may be mentioned here as an example of objective and impartial information about the three major religions that coexist in the Middle East, in an environment ridden with political tensions, where religions can be abused for all kinds of purposes, and where good relations among the three traditions have been hampered by claims of exclusivity.

Present-Day Islamic Studies in the Wider Sense

As in other scholarly fields and disciplines, new issues have come under discussion in Islamic studies, whether through the internal development of scholarly research or through current developments in Muslim countries, which developments demand interpretation.

Methodological Issues. Intense epistemological debates seem to have been absent from Islamic studies until the 1960s, chiefly because of the inherited pattern established by the scholarly tradition. Yet there have been other currents in Islamic studies too, and with the incorporation of textual research within a larger cultural and even religious perspective, scholars such as Louis Massignon, Gustav E. von Grunebaum, Wilfred Cantwell Smith, and Clifford Geertz have been able to see the Islamic universe in new ways. We shall point here to three matters of paramount importance: (1) the questioning of Islamic identities, (2) the increased assertion of Islamic identities, and (3) Islam as a living religion and faith.

Questioning Islamic identities. Among Western scholars who have reevaluated accepted readings of the Islamic tradition, John Wansbrough has opened up critical research with regard to the text of the Qur'ān in the aforementioned *Quranic Studies* and has extended this inquiry to early Islamic history in *The Sectarian Milieu* (1978). In an even more controversial work, *Hagarism: The Making of the Islamic World* (1977), Patricia Crone and Michael Cook have argued that the historical formation of Islamic religion and civilization can be explained in terms of a complex network of Jewish-Arab relations. While their argument has found little favor, it may well lead other scholars to reconsider the role of historically falsified material in their research.

Asserting Islamic identities. The growing participation of Muslim scholars in the field of Islamic studies has had the opposite effect to that mentioned above. An intention to assert Islamic identities becomes evident in books such as *Islamic Perspectives: Studies in Honor of Sayyid Abul Ala Mawdudi*, edited by Khurshid Ahmad and Zafar Ishaq Ansari (1979), and *Islam and Contemporary Society*, edited by Salem Azzam (1982). One important contribution of Muslim scholars is that of making Muslim forms of understanding available to other Islamicists; their work should lead, moreover, to discussions within the Muslim community. Noteworthy, for instance, is Mohammed Arkoun's semiotic approach in *Lectures du Coran* (1983) and Fazlur Rahman's studies on the history of Islamic thought, for instance in his *Prophecy in Islam: Philosophy and Orthodoxy* (1979).

Islam as a living religion. Recent methodological and epistemological concerns have been stimulated in large part by a growing interest in Islam as a living religion and faith, which is connected with certain political solidarities and social and economic issues. As a result, the meaning of events and processes in Muslim countries is studied more and more in their contemporary cultural and Islamic framework. Three questions are paramount in these Islamic studies in the wider sense:

1. Which kinds of groups support and transmit various particular interpretations of Islam, and who are the leaders of these groups?
2. How do particular changes occurring in the religious institutions (or in institutions legitimized by religion) relate to changes in society at large, and what are the consequences of such social changes for the institutions concerned (and vice versa)?
3. What general social functions do various Islamic ideas and practices perform within particular Muslim societies, apart from the specifically religious meaning they are meant to have?

Such questions can also be asked about Muslim societies of the past, provided that historical data are available to answer them. Indeed, it is a mark of epistemological progress that subjects excluded from investigation fifty years ago for lack of methodological tools can now come under the purview of Islamic studies. We can think of the distinctions that can be made now between religious and other (e.g., political) meanings of Islamic data, and of our better insight in the appeal that particular Islamic ideas and practices can have for specific groups.

Tradition in a wider sense. The notion of tradition, too, has attracted new attention in Islamic studies among both historians and anthropologists, who recognize that successive generations of Muslims have interpreted their lives, their world, and history through the religious and cultural framework, or "tradition," of the society into which they have been born. On the one hand, we have the normative "great" tradition with elements ranging from the Qur'ān and parts of the *sharī'ah* to particular creeds, practices of worship, and paradigmatic figures and episodes in Islamic history. On the other hand, for each region we must add numerous elements of the local "little" tradition, including legendary events in the history of the region, miracles and blessings of particular saints, the meritorious effect of particular practices, and so on, all of which constitute local, popular religion.

New Topics of Research. As a result of these and other methodological issues, new topics of research have come within our horizon, of which the following may be mentioned as examples.

Revitalization of Islam. Different forms of Islamic revitalization have been signaled by both Muslim and non-Muslim observers in a number of countries. While the media have addressed the political and "exotic," even abhorrent dimensions of this revitalization, scholarly investigation is needed to distinguish various sectors of life and society in which such revitalization takes place (as well as its religious from its nonreligious aspects) according to both Islamic criteria and criteria developed by the scientific study of religion. Preceding movements of reform and renewal should be taken into account.

Ideologization of Islam. During the last hundred years a great number of Islamic ideologies have developed; what for centuries was considered a religion based on revelation seems to have evolved in certain quarters into an Islamic system or ideology of a cognitive nature, in which the dimension of faith and religious knowledge seems to have given place to a definite set of convictions and values. This ideologization responds to a need for rationalization and may serve apologetic purposes, against criticism from the West, for instance, or against secularizing trends within society. Often the predicate "Islamic" suggests that a correspondence is sought between the older cultural and religious tradition and the solutions proposed for the problems of the present.

Islam, political action, and social and economic behavior. After a period of Western domination in which a political articulation of Islam was mostly impossible, Islam has again come to play various political roles, in both more conservative and more progressive quarters, usually bypassing the authority of those schooled in religious law (the *'ulamā'*). So the question arises: what are the possibilities and the limits of the political, social, and economic use and abuse of Islam? Islam has permitted very different economic systems (including a form of capitalism) as Maxime Rodinson (1966) has demonstrated. We may go on to ask in what ways Islam can be related positively or negatively to economic development, and to determine what basic values economic development is subordinated to within the Islamic framework. That Islam is articulated basically as a way of life and as social behavior has become evident again, for instance, by the recurrence of the veil and by expressions of solidarity with Muslims in other parts of the world.

Muslim self-interpretations. In the course of the history of Islamic studies, serious hermeneutical mistakes, that is, errors of interpretation, have been made. Western scholars for instance tended to reify Islam, forgetting that "Islam" in itself does not exist, that "Islam" is always Islam *interpreted,* and that Muslims keep this interpretive process going. Much more attention should be paid to what Muslim authors, speakers, groups, and movements actually mean when they express themselves in particular situations, free from interpretations or explanations imposed from outside. Carrying out study in collaboration with Muslim researchers is appropriate here as in many fields.

Interaction and image formation. It is perhaps a sign of renewal of Islamic studies that Islam is no longer studied only as an isolated culture, tradition, and religion that may have assimilated outside influences, but that more attention is given to the spread of Islam, processes of interaction with other communities, and Muslim images of other religions and of the non-Muslim world generally. This direction of inquiry is evidenced first by works of Arab scholars like Albert Hourani, Abdallah Laroui, and others, as well as by publications like Bernard Lewis's *The Muslim Discovery of Europe* (1982) and *Euro-Arab Dialogue: Relations between the Two Cultures,* edited by Derek Hopwood (1985). This area of study has been opened up as a consequence of the recognition of Islamic religion and culture as an autonomous partner in international religious and cultural relations, which are linked, in turn, to political and other relationships. The recent establishment of considerable Muslim communities living side by side with a non-Muslim majority in a number of Western societies may also have made both North America and Western Europe more sensitive to the plurality of religions and cultures in daily life.

Study of Religion in Islamic Societies. The study of religion as a focus of Islamic studies has received considerable attention in the work of Wilfred Cantwell Smith, especially in his *On Understanding Islam* (1980). The major epistemological problem in Islamic studies is still apparently the difficulty involved in correlating scholarly categories of description, analysis, and interpretation with the adequate "reading," conceptualization, and translation of the raw data of Islamic realities. Since "Islam" is not an empirical datum in the same way as is an actual text, a practice, or even an ideal, the way in which Islam is "thematized" and what is held to be the "reality" of Islam largely depend on the concepts and categories with which a particular scholar is working. It is only logical that certain sets of concepts will lead to Islam being denied any "reality," or at least to the denial of the possibility of scholarly knowledge of any such reality. This does not mean that such a position precludes important work in Islamic studies but rather that, in this case, the concept of "Islam" makes little scholarly sense.

How should we then approach and study religion in the context of Islamic studies? Our starting point must be the recognition that Islam is always linked to persons, to societies, and to the Muslim community at large. Whereas texts, monuments, social practices, and so on, be they sacred or profane, somehow exist in themselves, this is not the case for "Islam," which exists first of all as a meaning for people, both Muslims and outsiders (including non-Muslim Islamicists). The subjective meaning of a particular datum, however, may be different for each person; in abstract terms, religious meanings are not inherent in particular facts. If we are interested in such meanings, accurate scholarly study of the religious aspects of Islam should avoid using general terms derived from Western parlance, such as *religion, worldview, ideology, faith,* and so on, and should instead start by looking at those data that possess significance for groups of Muslims—data that can be said to have a semiotic or symbolic value for Muslims.

Islam as a *religion,* in the strict sense of the word, can probably best be called a network of signs, or a semiotic system; when such signs are internalized, they become symbols. Interestingly enough, the Qur'ān hints at this process. Indeed, Islam constitutes the right human response to the *āyāt* ("signs," sometimes translated as "symbols") that have been provided mankind in the

Qur'ān, in nature, and in history. The *āyāt* are nexus points of divine revelation and human reflection. Making full use of reason, Muslims are enjoined to draw right conclusions from these *āyāt* for their lives on earth, for the life and order of society, and for eternal bliss. Muslims are called upon to abandon themselves to the God who sent the *āyāt* and to obey his will as communicated through them. They should appeal to others to follow and understand the signs as well. They should, before all else, understand the Qur'ān itself as a "sign" revealed to humankind. Religion in the Islamic sense is faith (in God), knowledge (of the God-given signs), and a way of life accordingly.

Insofar as this interpretation corresponds with the Islamic notion of what religion is, it avoids stamping Islamic data with Western-coined concepts that are part of ideals, views, ideologies, and faiths fundamentally alien to Islam as Muslims see it. Paralleling the Muslim's focus of interest, this approach discovers the sense of the universe, humanity, and society, and the rules of right behavior and correct thinking, by means of the study of the *āyāt* that are recognized as providing meaning, orientation, and guidance. A study of Islam as a network of signs will reveal certain permanent vehicles of religious meaning, which permit communication between Muslims despite varying circumstances of place and time. By approaching Islam as a communicative, religious sign system, we avoid the one extreme of reifying Islam (and the concomitant search for an eternal essence), as well as the other extreme of denying any reality to Islam as measured against the material world.

BIBLIOGRAPHY

Full bibliographic data for the literature referred to in the section on the history of Islamic studies, above, can be found in Charles J. Adams's "Islamic Religious Tradition," in *The Study of the Middle East*, edited by Leonard Binder (New York, 1976), pp. 29–96. For further bibliographic data, see *A Reader's Guide to the Great Religions*, 2d ed., edited by Charles J. Adams (New York, 1977), pp. 407–466.

Islamic Studies: A Tradition and Its Problems, edited by Malcolm H. Kerr (Malibu, Calif., 1983), deals admirably with the full scope of Islamic studies. On the history of Islamic studies, see Maxime Rodinson's "The Western Image and Western Studies of Islam," in *The Legacy of Islam*, 2d ed., edited by Joseph Schacht with C. E. Bosworth (Oxford, 1974), pp. 9–62. Rodinson has elaborated his views in his *La fascination d'Islam* (Paris, 1980).

My own study, *L'Islam dans le miroir de l'Occident*, 3d ed. (Paris, 1970), focuses on five prominent Islamicists: Goldziher, Snouck Hurgronje, Becker, Macdonald, and Massignon. This work may be supplemented with my essay "Changes in Perspective in Islamic Studies over the Last Decades," *Humaniora Islamica* 1 (1973): 247–260.

The following works treat the development of Islamic studies in particular European countries. England: A. J. Arberry's *Oriental Essays: Portraits of Seven Scholars* (New York, 1960). France: Claude Cahen and Charles Pellat's "Les études arabes et islamiques," in *Cinquante ans d'orientalisme en France, 1922–1972*, a special issue of *Journal asiatique* 261 (1973): 89–107. Germany: Rudi Paret's *The Study of Arabic and Islam at German Universities: German Orientalists since Theodor Nöldeke* (Wiesbaden, 1968) and Johann Frick's *Die arabischen Studien in Europa* (Leipzig, 1956). Netherlands: J. Brugman and F. Schrödder's *Arabic Studies in the Netherlands* (Leiden, 1979). Spain: James T. Monroe's *Islam and the Arabs in Spanish Scholarship, Sixteenth Century to the Present* (Leiden, 1970).

Islamic studies in the West have not escaped criticism by Muslim Islamicists. See, for instance, A. L. Tibawi's *English-Speaking Orientalists: A Critique of Their Approach to Islam and Arab Nationalism* (Geneva, 1965) and *Second Critique of English-Speaking Orientalists and Their Approach to Islam and the Arabs* (London, 1979). The following works also deserve mention in this connection: Anouar Abdel Malik's "Orientalism in Crisis," *Diogenes* 44 (1963): 103–140; Abdallah Laroui's *The Crisis of the Arab Intellectual* (Berkeley, 1976); Edward Said's *Orientalism* (New York, 1978); and Sadiq al-Azm's "Orientalism and Orientalism in Reverse," *Hamsin* 8 (1981): 5–26.

Finally, I have discussed methodological issues at greater length in "Islam Studied as a Sign and Signification System," *Humaniora Islamica* 2 (1974): 267–285; "Islamforschung aus religionswissenschaftlicher Sicht," in *XXI. Deutscher Orientalistentag, 24–29. März 1980 in Berlin: Ausgewählte Vorträge*, edited by Fritz Steppat (Wiesbaden, 1982), pp. 197–211; and "Assumptions and Presuppositions in Islamic Studies," *Rocznik Orientalistyczny* 43 (1984): 161–170. For an application, see *Islam: Norm, ideaal en werkelÿkheid*, edited by me (Weesp, Netherlands, and Antwerp, 1984).

JACQUES WAARDENBURG

ʿIṢMAH ("infallibility") is a Muslim theological concept associated with the prophet Muḥammad and, among Shīʿī Muslims, with the imams as well. As a prophetic religion, Islam teaches a revelation that comes from a transcendent God and is transmitted by prophets to humankind to serve as reliable guidance. Clearly, this revelation should be authentic at its inception and maintain its authenticity and integrity throughout the centuries.

Within this framework, two distinct problems appear in relation to the *ʿiṣmah:* (1) the infallibility of the Prophet, which concerns the authenticity of the divine message, and (2) the infallibility of the consensus of the community *(ijmāʿ)* and that of the infallible imam, which concern the transmission of this message and its preservation from error among later generations within the community. In addition, the two great branches into which Islam is divided (albeit unevenly), the Sunnīs and the Shīʿah, hold diametrically opposed positions on the *ʿiṣmah*. These must also be studied separately.

The Infallibility of the Prophet. The issue of prophethood is common to both Sunnī and Shīʿī Muslims. Prophethood is essentially an investiture granted by God to certain people. For the Ashʿarīyah, God, by decree, predetermines freely who is to receive from him the mission of prophet and envoy. The prophet is the "warner," the faithful echo of the divine words who must show an absolute sincerity *(ṣidq)* in the strict accomplishment of the mission. It is for this reason that the prophetic *ʿiṣmah* is ascribed to that person.

Neither the Qur'ān nor the *ḥadīth* (prophetic traditions) discusses this question, however; rather, it is a product of later elaboration. The Qur'ān itself speaks of the errors committed by the prophets, of the admission of their errors, and of their repentance (surahs 8:23; 21:87). Even Muḥammad is not exempt from this general rule (9:43, 118; 33:37), and the Qur'ān affirms his fallibility (47:21). The prophet is a person like all others (18:110). Nor do the first professions of faith mention this *ʿiṣmah* of the prophets; it is apparently affirmed for the first time with the tenth-century *Fiqh akbar II* (The Greater Understanding II). Ibn Saʿd (d. 845) and al-Ṭabarī (d. 923) show a clear tendency to safeguard Muḥammad from any risk of polytheism, both to guarantee the authenticity of his mission and to honor him.

In the Iranian milieu, meanwhile, the old cults of Oriental demigods had left "traces" on the popular consciousness, and it is not impossible to believe that they influenced the Shīʿah in their concept of the perfect imam and in their quasi-deification of the ʿAlids. Muḥammad was thus invested with extraordinary privileges, and from the admixture of Neoplatonic philosophy and Iranian myths there developed a form of "illuminative theophany" that saw Muḥammad as the eternal Logos and spoke of the "Muhammadan Light" *(nūr muḥammadī)*. From such Ṣūfī quarters these concepts passed slowly to the people at large, who were always ready to attribute to the Prophet, the Messenger of God *par excellence*, the most extraordinary privileges.

Leaving aside the scholastic discussions, one can state, on the basis of the *Fiqh akbar II* (art. 8 and 9), those positions that are more or less universally accepted, namely that all the prophets are free of major and minor errors, and of all unbelief or evil act, apart from involuntary minor errors. This principle applies to Muḥammad at every instant during his life.

For the Shīʿah, sinlessness is a "hidden grace" *(luṭf ghā'ib)* that God accords to the imams and the prophets. For the *falāsifah*, the Muslim philosophers, it belongs to the prophets by nature; it is a faculty *(malakah)* that finds its purpose in the prophets' knowledge *(ʿilm)* of the good and evil nature of things, and of acts of obedience and disobedience. For the *mutakallimūn*, the scholastic theologians, *ʿiṣmah* is explained by the fact that God does not create moral sins in those he freely and openly chooses to be his prophets and apostles. For each act God places his prophet in a status *(ḥukm)* of sinlessness.

The Infallibility of the Community. Sunnī Muslims hold that *ʿiṣmah* is manifested in the general concensus *(ijmāʿ)* of the community. *Ijmāʿ* means literally "unanimous agreement"; thus it can be seen as a kind of generalized inspiration, the equivalent of *vox populi vox Dei*. This agreement concerns essential questions; on many secondary matters a certain tolerance is accepted in accord with the *ḥadīth* that "the variety of opinions is a mercy of God."

The qualified interpreters of *ijmāʿ* were originally the companions of the Prophet and their immediate successors, with subsequent recourse to the *ʿulamā'*, or "men of science." *Ijmāʿ* is not the result of a wide consultation; it is rather the tacit approbation given by the *ʿulamā'* to decisions made by a group of their colleagues. The infallibility of *ijmāʿ* exists to a certain extent after the fact, in the sense that it only legitimates what has already been adopted by the community. It is not in itself a principle of renewal, but one of stability.

The Infallibility of the Imam. In contrast to the Sunnīs, who represent what can be called a community of *ijmāʿ*, the Shīʿah, from the beginning, professed their doctrine of the infallible imam: the imam is a special man, chosen by God to guide the believers, both spiritually and temporally, on the right path. The imam is designated by the hereditary transmission of a divine right. Shīʿī doctrine adds to the five pillars of Muslim faith a sixth, *wilāyah*, or adherence to the imams and, by implication, rejection of their enemies.

Because of his personal qualities, which are themselves gifts of God, the infallible Shīʿī imam is the guide and teacher of Islam. He is the heir of the Prophet; he commands and teaches in the name of God. Thus the infallible divine revelation manifests itself through the imam of the age. This phenomenon cannot occur, however, unless he is raised above ordinary humanity by superhuman qualities coming from his very substance. Shīʿī thinkers would go very far in this vein, speaking of a divine light that passes from one generation to the next until it reaches the imam of the age and endows him with the highest possible level of clear knowledge, namely, complete infallibility. Nor is this clear knowledge limited to the religious domain, for the imams also possess a secret knowledge that passes from one to the other. They are inspired and can only proclaim the truth. For the Shīʿah, the imam is the last criterion of truth in interpreting the will of God and of the Prophet.

BIBLIOGRAPHY

For a more technical study of *'iṣmah*, the articles "'Iṣma," "Idjmā'," and "Idjtihād" in *The Encyclopaedia of Islam*, new ed. (Leiden, 1960–), are useful. The subject is thoroughly treated in Henri Laoust's *Essai sur les doctrines sociales et politiques de Takī-d-Dīn Aḥmad B. Taimīya* (Cairo, 1939); see note 1 on page 187 for a valuable bibliography on *'iṣmah*. Other works dealing with *'iṣmah* include Louis Gardet's *La cité musulmane* (Paris, 1954), esp. pp. 119–134, and his *Dieu et la destinée de l'homme* (Paris, 1967), esp. pp. 181–192. My article on "Le problème de l'infaillibilité dans la pensée musulmane" in *L'infallibilità: L'aspetto filosofico e teologico*, by Enrico Castelli and others (Padua, 1970), pp. 505–514, and Tor Andrae's "Die Unfehlbarkeit (*'iṣma)* der Propheten" in *Die person Muhammeds in lehre und glauben seiner gemeinde* (Stockholm, 1918), pp. 124–174, should also be consulted. More general works dealing with the subject include Ignácz Goldziher's *Le dogme et la loi de l'Islam* (Paris, 1920), esp. pp. 175–180, and Dwight M. Donaldson's *The Shi'ite Religion* (London, 1933), esp. chaps. 29–31.

GEORGES C. ANAWATI
Translated from French by Richard J. Scott

ISMAILIS. *See* Shiism, *article* on Ismā'īlīyah.

ISRAEL. *See* Jacob; *see also* Jewish People *and, for a different perspective,* Zionism.

ISRAEL BEN ELIEZER. *See* Besht.

ISRAELITE LAW. [*This entry consists of five articles on the law of the ancient Israelites:*

An Overview
Personal Status and Family Law
Property Law
Criminal Law
State and Judiciary Law

For discussion of postbiblical Jewish law, see Halakhah.]

An Overview

Law is generally defined as the principles, regulations, and policies of a society that are recognized and enforced by judicial decision, thus constituting a system of social control. This definition recognizes that social norms in order to be deemed legal must be regularly enforced in fact or in threat by physical power applied by privileged authority. Since little is known of the adjudication and administration of justice in ancient Israel, it is difficult to distinguish Israelite legal norms from other Israelite social norms. Furthermore, any description of Israelite law must be viewed as a hypothetical construct based upon the interpretation of inherently complex biblical data, therefore giving rise to certain methodological considerations.

Methodological Considerations. Since no contemporary evidence for the actual practice of Israelite law has been preserved or unearthed, one can undertake only the study of the law of the Hebrew Bible. At best, biblical law can only mirror facets, and at times conflicting facets, of ancient Israelite law and indeed may even contain features that were never part of the real legal world of ancient Israel. Furthermore, one must always be mindful of the heterogeneous nature of the biblical legal data. The modern scholar must disentangle the accounts of legal practice and procedure that are embedded in the historical narratives, prophetic messages, religious poetry, and wisdom literature that emanate from various schools of thought and tradition in ancient Israel and may reflect distinct traditions of monarchical, prophetic, priestly, or tribal law. Even the legal material of the Pentateuch, or Torah, which constitutes the basic source of our knowledge of biblical law, is not monolithic. Three major law corpora exist within the Torah: the laws of *Exodus*, including the Covenant Code in *Exodus* 20:19–23:33; the Priestly laws, mainly in *Leviticus* and *Numbers*, including the Holiness Code in *Leviticus* 19–26; and the laws of *Deuteronomy*, including the Deuteronomic Code in chapters 12–27. Each with its own distinguishing features and traits presents the student of biblical law with the following fundamental problems, which cannot be answered simply and must be kept in mind always.

1. One must consider whether the dates of composition assigned to each of the law corpora are also valid for the legal material incorporated therein or whether certain provisions reflect older material.

2. One must question the relationship of the various law corpora to one another and consider whether they should be viewed as representing different evolutionary stages in the development of biblical law or as independent crystallizations of biblical law stemming from different schools of transmission.

3. One must question the relationship of the law corpora to the legal references mentioned in the nonlegal literature of the Bible. One must consider also how those references in the historical, prophetic, or wisdom books that contradict the legal provisions of the Torah law corpora may be interpreted and whether they may be used as criteria for dating the law corpora.

These questions are integrally bound to the problem of the nature of the Torah law corpora and their status in preexilic Israelite society. Only if the provisions of these corpora represent the binding statutory law of ancient Israel can contradictions from other sources, such as the historical narratives, be marshaled as evidence for the nonexistence of these provisions at a given time in Israelite history. If, on the other hand, the law corpora are viewed primarily as a literary work of a small circle within Israel whose provisions were ideal didactic pronouncements of justice, little of these biblical data can be used for the reconstruction of ancient Israelite law as reflected in the historical narratives.

The nature of the responses to these problems will form the basic underlying suppositions implicit in the discussions below of specific aspects of ancient Israelite law as reconstructed from a study of all the relevant biblical legal data.

Conception and Character of Law. Since law is an aspect of culture, biblical law must be in consonance with the basic cultural postulates inherent within the biblical worldview. The dominant cultural postulate that distinguishes the biblical worldview from those of other ancient Near Eastern cultures is the radically different theological conception of the nature of the biblical godhead. The essence of the biblical theological conception, usually termed monotheism, is not merely the belief in the existence of one God. Rather, it is the idea that the deity is transcendent and sovereign over all. It differs fundamentally from paganism in the absolute freedom of the godhead. Unlike the ancient Near Eastern gods who are born into a primordial realm of natural and supernatural forces that precede them in time and transcend them in power, the biblical God is there from the beginning, and the forces of the universe are all inherent within him. Thus the biblical deity acts in total freedom, unrivaled either by the wills of other gods or by the cosmic forces of the universe.

This theological conception forms the basis of a series of philosophical and cultural postulates that are consistent with it. These postulates are not operative only in the realm of religion and cult, but they pervade the very fabric of biblical thought, including its conception of law. Biblical thought cannot accept the Mesopotamian conception of the ultimate sanction of law as rooted in a primordial cosmic principle that transcends both the gods and humanity: to the biblical mind, God is the ultimate sanction of law, and law is conceived as the expression of his will. Thus the most common designations for law in the Bible are references to God's *mitsvah* ("commandment"; *Dt.* 11:13), *torah* ("instruction"; *Gn.* 26:5), *davar* ("utterance"; *Dt.* 4:13), and various nominal forms of *ḥoq* ("decree"; *Lv.* 33:3) in addition to the term *mishpaṭ* ("norm"; *Ex.* 21:1). From this postulate flows the corollary that any violation of law, even when it involves property or family law, is not only an offense against society but also a sin—a violation of God's command, an absolute wrong for which the wrongdoer is held accountable to the deity (e.g., *Gn.* 20:6, *Lv.* 19:20–22, *Nm.* 5:5–8). Thus biblical law does not distinguish fundamentally between religious and secular offenses. The fact that the biblical law corpora contain an intermingling of both civil and cultic matters is best understood in this context; for in terms of its ideological orientation, it would not be meaningful for biblical law to draw such distinctions in its legal structure.

Although the biblical God is unrivaled and omnipotent, he is not indifferent to the universe he created. The biblical conception is that of a God who is intimately concerned with the welfare of his creation, and to this end, he communicates his will to man. Law, therefore, is conceived as revealed instructions by which every element in the universe, including man, must abide in order to secure well-being (*Gn.* 2:16–17, 9:1–7). Such a conception accounts for the didactic tone and the frequency with which motive clauses are found in the biblical law corpora. In keeping with this postulate, God addresses the law directly to the entire community of Israel. Moses' intermediary role as a messenger relaying God's utterances to the people is viewed as a divine concession to the request of the people (*Ex.* 20:18–20, *Dt.* 5:23–31). As a result of this direct communication between God and people, every Israelite had some cultic status (*Ex.* 19:6, *Nm.* 16:3), which imposed upon the people the observance of certain ritual laws and cultic taboos (cf. *Ex.* 22:31, *Lv.* 22:8). Of greater consequence is the fact that the entire people were held responsible both individually and communally for the observance of the law (*Dt.* 11:13–28), the maintenance of justice (*Dt.* 16:18–20), and the punishment of offenders (*Dt.* 17:2–7). Communal responsibility is most explicitly stated with regard to offenses of sexual immorality (*Lv.* 18:26–28), homicide (*Nm.* 35:31–34, *Dt.* 21:1–9), and idolatry (*Dt.* 13:6–18).

Another important corollary to this postulate is that the law is conceived as the basis of a covenantal relationship between God and Israel. Both the Sinaitic covenant and the covenant of the Plains of Moab center on a book of law (*Ex.* 24:4, 24:7; *Dt.* 29:11, 29:13, 29:20) that contains divinely dictated legislation. This law also contains elements of vassalship, formulated as covenant stipulations, demanding undivided loyalty and allegiance to God. Explicit is the affirmation that God and Israel are bound in contract whereby faithful observance of the law guarantees prosperity and divine protection, while violation of the law results in dire calamity and misfortune to both the individual and the nation (*Lv.* 26:3–45, *Dt.* 28). This conception of a covenant of law remains a dominant theme throughout Israelite history and is reaffirmed in the covenants of Joshua (*Jos.* 24), Josiah (*2 Kgs.* 23), and Ezra (*Neh.* 9–10).

Despite their ideological differences as reflected in their cultural postulates, it must be remembered that the bearers of the biblical tradition were members of the interrelated cultural complex known as ancient Near Eastern civilization. Biblical law has many similarities to the ancient Near Eastern law corpora both in legal substance and formulation. These shared features represent the aspects of ancient Near Eastern legal thought that were not inimical to the biblical worldview.

Law and Morality. A secular society tends to differentiate between law and morality, relegating them to two different spheres: law is considered to be a social creation enforced by judicial authority, while morality is considered to be a personal phenomenon based on a sense of individual obligation. Thus law is viewed primarily as regulations governing the violation of existing obligations and rights that are operative only after the violation has occurred. On the other hand, a religious society bases its jurisprudence upon theological conceptions in which law and morality are closely intertwined. According to the biblical worldview, God in the absolute freedom of his godhead is not only the source of law but also the source of morality. In his concern for man, God has mandated the law as a blueprint for the conduct of human society in accordance with moral and ethical ideals. For this reason, legal and moral norms are not distinguished in the Bible. Noncompliance with the law even in property matters represents a religious offense that affects humanity's relationship with God. Thus, for example, the commandment to return lost property (*Ex.* 23:4–5, *Dt.* 22:1–4) represents a legal obligation to fulfill a religious-moral duty. Hence biblical law is conceived as a positive prescriptive code of ethical behavior rather than as a reactive redress of violated rights.

This unity of morality and law, which distinguished the biblical from other ancient Near Eastern legal-moral systems, created a new basis of authority for the observance of social ethics by placing ethics above political and economic interests. Similarly the biblical conception of law as the basis of a covenantal relationship between God and Israel heightened moral responsibility by making obedience to the covenantal imperatives not merely a personal concern but a national obligation. The covenant clearly made individual as well as national prosperity and well-being dependent upon the observance of ethical and moral norms.

Biblical ethics are founded in the belief that humanity was created in the image of God; the realization of the concept becomes a legal imperative. God enjoins his people to be like him (*Lv.* 19:2) and to walk in his ways (*Dt.* 10:12, 26:17). This concept is the consistent motivation for the commandments to love the stranger and treat the widow and orphan justly (*Dt.* 10:18–19), to be gracious to the poor (*Ex.* 22:26), and to judge righteously (*Dt.* 1:17). Thus while man must never forget his status as a creature of the Creator or abrogate to himself God's prerogatives, man is nevertheless commanded to be godlike in his behavior.

[*See also* Law and Religion, *overview article.*]

BIBLIOGRAPHY

Boecker, Hans J. *Recht und Gesetz im Alten Testament und im alten Orient.* Neukirchen, West Germany, 1976. Translated by Jeremy Moiser as *Law and the Administration of Justice in the Old Testament and Ancient East* (Minneapolis, 1980). A presentation of legal materials found in the Pentateuchal law corpora and in the cuneiform law collections, with greatest emphasis placed upon the code of Hammurabi and the covenant code.

Greenberg, Moshe. "Some Postulates of Biblical Criminal Law." In *Yehezkel Kaufmann Jubilee Volume,* edited by Menaḥem Haran, pp. 5–28. Jerusalem, 1960. An appreciation of biblical law as an expression of the underlying cultural values of ancient Israelite society.

Greenberg, Moshe. "Crimes and Punishments." In *The Interpreter's Dictionary of the Bible,* edited by G. A. Buttrick, vol. 1, pp. 733–744. Nashville, 1962. An excellent survey of biblical criminal law, discussing the biblical concept of crime and punishment as well as the methodological problems inherent within the biblical sources.

Hoebel, E. Adamson. *The Law of Primitive Man: A Study in Comparative Legal Dynamics* (1954). New York, 1968. Offers anthropological insight into the cultural background of law and the distinction between legal and social norms.

Jackson, Bernard S. "Reflections on Biblical Criminal Law." *Journal of Jewish Studies* 24 (Spring 1973): 8–38. A reaction to recent studies that attempt to distinguish biblical law from the legal culture of the ancient Near East on the basis of different cultural postulates.

Kaufmann, Yeḥezkel. *Toledot ha-emunah ha-Yisra'elit.* Tel Aviv, 1955. Translated and abridged by Moshe Greenberg as *The Religion of Israel* (Chicago, 1960). A comprehensive study of the history of Israelite religion, its character, and basic theological conceptions.

McCarthy, Dennis J. *Old Testament Covenant: A Survey of Current Opinions.* Richmond, Va., 1972. A presentation of scholarly contributions to the biblical concept of covenant as it relates to law, cult, kingship, and theology, with extensive bibliography.

McCarthy, Dennis J. *Treaty and Covenant: A Study in Form in the Ancient Oriental Documents and in the Old Testament.* Rome, 1978. A completely revised and rewritten edition of the author's previous study, offering a close analysis of the ancient Near Eastern and biblical textual evidence and extensive bibliography.

Mendenhall, George E. *Law and Covenant in Israel and the Ancient Near East*. Pittsburgh, 1955. An overview of biblical law in light of the ancient Near East, with special emphasis on covenant forms in Israelite tradition.

Paul, Shalom M. *Studies in the Book of the Covenant in the Light of Cuneiform and Biblical Law*. Leiden, 1970. Annotations to the laws of the Book of the Covenant, stressing the parallel cuneiform legal materials. Also contains an excellent bibliography of biblical and cuneiform law.

Silberg, Moshe. "Law and Morals in Jewish Jurisprudence." *Harvard Law Review* 75 (1961): 306–331. A discussion of the relationship of morality and religion as reflected in Jewish law.

Barry L. Eichler

Personal Status and Family Law

Biblical laws concerning personal status may relate to individuals as members of larger segments of society (slaves, poor, aliens, women), or they may govern relations between persons in a household, as in laws governing the treatment of slaves, and those stipulating the relations between members of the family. These categories are followed in the discussion below.

Personal Status. One of the essential characteristics of Israelite law is that there are no legally defined social classes among free Israelites. This contrasts with the laws of Hammurabi, which assume two classes of free men, the *awilum* ("man," the higher class) and the *mushkenum* (a poorer class, perhaps only partially free, partially in royal service), with notable differences in the treatment of each, as, for example, in the prescription of penalties for assault by a member of one group against a member of the other. In Israelite society the economic differences between rich and poor never resulted in differences in their treatment before the law. Nevertheless, there are clear distinctions between free Israelites and slaves, between men and women, between adults and minors, and, to a lesser extent, between Israelites and foreigners, and between king and subjects.

Slaves. Israelite law distinguishes between foreign and Israelite slaves and, to a lesser extent, between male and female slaves. Foreign slaves could be bought or, theoretically, acquired as prisoners of war. Once acquired, they were expected to be slaves permanently (*Lv.* 25:46). Israelites, however, could not be slaves permanently. The law allowed a free man to sell his children into slavery or to sell himself in order to escape poverty or debt (*Lv.* 25:39); he is required to sell himself if he cannot otherwise pay the penalty for having committed a robbery (*Ex.* 22:2). An Israelite would also be a slave if he or she were born to slaves (*Ex.* 21:4). But the male Israelite "slave" (almost certainly the meaning of *ʿeved ʿivri*) was to be set free in the Sabbatical (seventh) year unless he chose to make his status permanent, which decision was formalized in a ceremony in which his ear was pierced. According to *Exodus* 21:7–8, female slaves were not freed according to the laws that freed male slaves; this may be because a woman was sold as an *amah*, a term which may imply concubinage, for she was to be set free if her master's sons denied her matrimonial rights (*Ex.* 21:11). In *Deuteronomy* 15:12–17 female slaves were treated like male slaves, possibly an indication that by this time it was written (no later than the seventh century BCE) Hebrew women were not sold into concubinage. Foreign women could be taken as concubines in war; they could subsequently be divorced but not sold (*Dt.* 21:10–14). *Deuteronomy* 15:12–17 requires that freed slaves be given substantial provisions. According to *Leviticus* 25:40, debt-slaves were to be released in the Jubilee (fiftieth) year. Yet there is some indication in *Jeremiah* 34:8–16 that people in ancient Israel were not punctilious about obeying the laws regarding manumission.

Although a fully recognized institution, slavery was considered an undesirable state of existence. There was a death penalty for kidnapping free Israelites to use or sell as slaves (*Ex.* 22:15, *Dt.* 24:7). Israelites discovered to be slaves of non-Israelites were to be redeemed (*Lv.* 25:47–54), and fugitive slaves (Israelite or foreign) were not to be given up to their masters (*Dt.* 23:16–17). Israel was to ameliorate the condition by treating slaves well and treating Israelite slaves as if they were hired laborers (*Lv.* 25:40, 25:53). The law adjured these efforts on the slaves' behalf in the remembrance that the Israelites had been slaves in Egypt (*Dt.* 15:15) and that they continued to be the slaves of God, who had redeemed them (*Lv.* 25:55). Slaves were to be considered members of the household: they were to be circumcised (*Gn.* 17:23) and could thereupon eat the Passover sacrifice (*Ex.* 12:44); priest's slaves could eat of the holy offerings (*Lv.* 22:11). Slaves shared in sacrificial meals (*Dt.* 12:11–12, 12:18) and in feasts (*Dt.* 16:11, 16:14) and observed the Sabbath (*Ex.* 20:10, 23:12; *Dt.* 5:14–15). Slaves could be beaten; but if they died of a beating, their death would be avenged (*Ex.* 21:20), and if they were permanently injured, they were to be set free (*Ex.* 21:26–27). Slaves could acquire their own property and might ultimately be able to redeem themselves (*Lv.* 25:29).

The poor. Although there were no formal classes in Israelite society, there were distinctions between wealthy and poor. The "book of the covenant" stipulates that one should not impose usury on loans to the poor (*Ex.* 22:25), that cloaks taken as pledges be returned by sundown (*Ex.* 22:26–27; cf. *Dt.* 24:12–3), and that poverty not result in mistreatment before the law (*Ex.*

23:6). *Deuteronomy* further stipulates that a hired worker be paid immediately (*Dt.* 24:14–15) and prescribes the giving of charity to the poor even when the Sabbatical is near (*Dt.* 15:7–11), at which time the produce was to be left for the poor (*Ex.* 23:11). The seventh year was to some extent a time for the redistribution of wealth, in that debts were to be canceled (*Dt.* 15:1). The difference between rich and poor may have increased after the development of the monarchy, and the unequal distribution of wealth is an important theme of the prophets, who condemned the accumulation of capital by the rich.

Resident aliens. Immigrants to Israel and the original inhabitants of the land were considered *gerim* (sg. *ger,* "resident alien"). This designation also extended to the Levites, who had no tribal territory of their own, and, in the early days, to an Israelite outside the territory of his own tribe. *Gerim* are often grouped with the poor, widows, and orphans, who were to be allowed to collect fallen fruit and olives and glean at harvest time (*Lv.* 19:10, 23:22; *Dt.* 24:19–21) and to share in the tithe of the third year (*Dt.* 14:29) and the produce of the Jubilee (*Lv.* 25:6). The Israelites were to treat them well, remembering that they too had been *gerim,* in Egypt (e.g., *Ex.* 22:20); the laws that apply to them, thus, are generally found within law addressed to the free Israelites. *Gerim* had equal status with Israelites in civil and criminal law; in religious law the one recorded difference is the statement in *Deuteronomy* 14:21 that a *ger* may eat a dead carcass; *Leviticus* 17:15, however, forbids this. *Gerim* observed the Sabbath (*Ex.* 20:10, *Dt.* 5:14) and the Day of Atonement (*Lv.* 16:29); they offered sacrifices (*Lv.* 17:8, e.g.) and participated in religious festivals (*Dt.* 16:11, 16:14); and they observed the laws of purity (*Lv.* 17:8–13) and, if circumcised, could partake of the Passover sacrifice (*Ex.* 12:48–49).

Minors. A person was considered a fully adult member of Israel, counted as such in the census, at age 20 (*Ex.* 30:14); this was also the age above which the Israelites who had come out of Egypt were condemned to die in the desert without reaching the promised land (*Nm.* 14:29). At least in theory, children below that age were under the jurisdiction of their father, who could contract marriages for them and even sell them into slavery to pay his debts and to whom they owed allegiance. A rebellious son could be accused by his parents and thereupon stoned (*Dt.* 21:18–21). There are no specific regulations relating to minors. They were, however, treated as individual persons before the law in matters of punishment, for, unlike the ancient Near Eastern codes, biblical law did not allow the punishment of children for the crimes of their parents. For example, the death of a victim who was a minor son did not entail the execution of the minor son of the offender in biblical law as it did in Babylonian law (*Ex.* 21:31; cf. laws of Hammurabi 229f.).

The king. The king in Israel occupied a special intimate relationship with God: as God's appointed and anointed, his person was inviolable (*2 Sm.* 1:14), and cursing the king was tantamount to cursing God and was punishable by death (*2 Sm.* 19:21–22; *1 Kgs.* 21:10, 21:13). The Israelite king was not regarded as divine, and his close relationship with God, expressed as sonship (*2 Sm.* 7:14), was understood to arise from adoption (cf. *Ps.* 2:7) rather than divine paternity. The king was not a lawgiver but his role in the legal system was twofold: to uphold the laws in his capacity as judge and to obey fully the laws of God, who is Israel's only legitimate lawgiver. A king who disobeyed God's laws might lose all of his kingdom, as did Saul (*1 Sm.* 13:13) and Jeroboam (*1 Kgs.* 14:7–11), or part of his domain, as did David. The divine promise of a dynasty to the House of David made the rulers of the southern kingdom of Judah less concerned with the possibility of losing the throne. However, the deeds or misdeeds of a king could influence the fortunes of the land, for God could bring pestilence, military defeat (as under David, *2 Sm.* 24:13), or drought as a consequence or royal apostasy (as under Ahab, *1 Kgs.* 17:1).

Two passages deal with royal prerogative. In one, in his effort to discourage the people from establishing a monarchy, Samuel warns them that a king will take their sons as soldiers and their daughters as domestics, that he will tithe their property, and that he will appropriate their fields to give to his servants (*1 Sm.* 8:11–18). The other passage, *Deuteronomy* 17:14–20, sets limits to the grandiosity of the monarch, declaring that the king should not acquire many horses or wives or much wealth and that he should copy a book of the Law, keep it with him, and read it so that he learns to keep the law and not act arrogantly toward his people. Despite Samuel's warning that a king would appropriate fields, the kings did not simply commandeer property. David bought a threshing floor (*2 Sm.* 24:24); Omri bought the hill of Samaria (*1 Kgs.* 16:24); and even Ahab did not feel free to simply commandeer the vineyard of Naboth (*1 Kgs.* 21). Kings did, however, confiscate the land of those who had committed treason: David took Mephibosheth's land to give to Ziva after Ziva reported that Mephibosheth was planning to take the throne (*2 Sm.* 16:1–4) and Ahab set out to take Naboth's vineyard after Naboth was falsely convicted and executed for having cursed the king (*1 Kgs.* 21:13–16). Nor did the kings of Israel exercise unrestrained power over their subjects' lives: Jezebel made sure that Ahab was convicted and executed by the courts, and David maneuvered Uriah so that he would be killed in battle (*2 Sm.* 11)—neither king killed the inconvenient subjects outright. [*See also* Kingship, *article on* Kingship in the Ancient Mediterranean World.]

Women. The laws present a picture of women as socially inferior to men. In terms of family life, a woman was expected to be subordinate first to her father and then, when married, to her husband. This subordination also found expression in economic matters. Women did not normally hold property, though they could inherit if there were no male heirs. This right of inheritance is presented in the Bible as a special divine decree to answer the needs of the daughters of Zelophehad (*Nm.* 27:1–11), which was soon modified to require daughters who inherited their father's property to marry within the "family of the tribe of their father" in order to keep the ancestral holdings in the paternal estate (*Nm.* 36:1–9). A comparison with near Eastern law shows that the laws of Lipit-Ishtar, written in Sumerian about 1900 BCE, contain a proviso whereby if a man had no sons, his unmarried daughters could inherit his property.

The inferior economic position of women is also indicated by the fact that when a person took a vow to dedicate members of his family (to temple service?) or to donate their monetary worth, an adult male was valued at fifty shekels and a woman at thirty (*Lv.* 27:3–4). It is also clear that women did not have equal right of disposition of the family property, for the male head of the household could annul the vows of women under his authority if he did so the day that he heard them (*Nm.* 30:5–8). Nevertheless, there is no hint that women could be considered thieves if they took or sold family property (as is the case in the Middle Assyrian laws, according to which the wife who took something and gave it to another is labeled a thief, and the receiver, a fence); on the contrary, the "woman of valor" of *Proverbs* 31 is particularly praised for her commercial ability and independent enterprise.

Some of the laws of sexual purity were applicable to both men and women. After sexual intercourse, both partners had to bathe in water and were considered impure until the evening (*Lv.* 15:16–18). In case of genital discharges (as in gonorrhea), both men and women were isolated until seven days after the discharge stopped and were then to bring an offering of two birds (*Lv.* 15:1–15, 15:25–29). In addition, women were instructed to remain isolated during menstruation (*Lv.* 15:19–24) and childbirth (*Lv.* 12:1–8). The impurity of menstruation was contagious: a man would become impure by having sexual relations with a menstruating woman (for which he could also expect divine punishment). Furthermore, he would become impure by touching her, sitting on a seat on which she sat, or eating food that she had cooked. This resulted in total isolation, although it is not known whether women were isolated in their own homes or spent the week in women's hostels (to which there is no textual reference). The "impurity" of the menstruating woman was not believed to bring danger to others (as is the case in many other cultures). Nevertheless, it became a metaphor for contamination (*Jer.* 13.20, *Lam.* 1.9, *Ez.* 36.17) and clearly was used to the denigration of women. [*See* Menstruation.]

Despite the image portrayed by the legal documents, the biblical narratives indicate that women did not have a particularly weak position with respect to their husbands. The Shunammite woman entertained Elijah without prior consent from her husband (*2 Kgs.* 4:8–17), and Abigail commandeered large amounts of her husband's supplies to bring them to David (*1 Sm.* 25). The legal documents may, therefore, be affirming ideals rather than prescribing reality.

Women were generally expected to fit into a domestic niche, as wife and/or mother. However, there were also nondomestic roles. The queen had a powerful position, and might, as Jezebel and Athaliah did, exercise the power of the throne (*1 Kgs.* 18–19; *2 Kgs.* 9:30–37, 11:1–16); the position of queen-mother also seems to have had some importance, as may be inferred from the fact that Asa removed his mother Maacah from that position (*1 Kgs.* 15:13). "Wise women," who are mentioned in the time of David (*2 Sm.* 14, 20:16–22), may have been some sort of village elders. Deborah was a political and judicial leader (*Jgs.* 4–5); Deborah, Miriam (*Nm.* 12:2), Huldah (*2 Kgs.* 22:14–20), and Noadiah (*Neh.* 6:14) are recorded as prophetesses.

Family Law. Our picture of family law is incomplete: the law corpora were not intended to be comprehensive, and frequently they omit matters that were well known in that culture or were not of concern to the writers. The picture can be filled in to some extent with details from the few narrative accounts of family life contained in the historical books. Important information also comes from the law collections of the ancient Near East, since it is clear that there was a common jurisprudential tradition in the area.

The Bible reveals two social systems. The first, the older system, is the extended family of the patriarchal period. The male head of the family had great power over his children, both male and female, in that he could contract marriages for them. Girls would leave their father's house in order to enter the dominion of the head of the family into which they were marrying.

In the event of the husband's death, the woman stayed in her new family, either as the mother of children or, if there had been no children, by being given in marriage to her deceased husband's brother through the institution of the levirate. In such a system women were completely dependent on the kindness and attentiveness of the males in their lives and could affect events only by influencing them, as through persuasion or trickery. If a man were abusive, a woman had no recourse, and the principle of male disposition of women lent itself to such abuses as Lot's offer of his daughters to the men of Sodom (*Gn.* 19:8), the Levite's offer of his concubine to the men of Gibeah (*Jgs.* 19:24), and Jephthah's sacrifice of his daughter (*Jgs.* 11).

The other major social pattern is the monogamous family depicted in *Genesis* 3:6. This was the dominant pattern during the history of the biblical state (apart from the royal family, which continued the patriarchal pattern). At marriage, the girl moved from her father's house to that of her husband, and was thereafter under her husband's (rather than her father's or father-in-law's) domination. Polygyny was possible, but certainly not the norm. The ancient Near Eastern law collections also envision polygyny, or rather *bigyny* (having two wives), but severely limit the circumstances under which a man could take a second wife.

Marriage. The stages by which a marriage was contracted are not detailed in the biblical laws, but information is available, from both biblical narrative and the Near Eastern legal compilations, and the close agreement between these sources indicates that they reflect a biblical and Near Eastern reality. A preliminary agreement was reached between the fathers (or between the groom and the bride's parents), and then the groom or, frequently, the groom's father, paid a sum, the "bride-price," to the girl's father. There was also a dowry, though this does not seem to have been essential, and there was another custom, not universally observed, in which the father of the bride returned the bride-price to the couple at the completion of the marriage (unlike Lagan, who did not; *Gn.* 31:15). The bride-price was not a purchase, for the girl was not considered property, but it did guarantee the groom certain rights over the girl. At this point, once the bride-price was paid, the girl was "betrothed," which was an inchoate form of marriage. The marriage could still be canceled by either party (with appropriate financial penalties). Nevertheless, the bridegroom at that point owned the girl's sexual and reproductive capacity, and any sexual relations with a betrothed girl was considered adultery. The betrothed girl would stay in her father's house until the groom came to call for her (which could be a duration of years if she had been betrothed very young). At that point he would bring her to his house, and the marriage was complete.

Divorce. The details of divorce are also not clearly defined in the Bible. The laws in *Exodus* do not mention divorce; *Deuteronomy* does not describe the procedure but does mention the requirement of a bill of divorce (*Dt.* 24:1) and the stipulation of the two occasions on which the husband cannot divorce his wife: when he has acquired his wife after rape (*Dt.* 22:28–29) or when he has falsely accused his wife of not having been a virgin as a bride (*Dt.* 22:13–21). These laws prevented men, to some extent, from divorcing unloved brides who would have been at a great disadvantage in the Israelite socioeconomic system. Since the details are not provided, we cannot be certain that divorce was always at the prerogative of the husband; the laws of Hammurabi indicate that a woman could apply to the court for divorce (with the risk that her case would be investigated; and if she were found to have been a bad wife, she would be executed). There is evidence that early Jews on Elephantine (in Egypt) and in Palestine believed that the Bible allowed female-initiated divorce. In the postbiblical period it has been taken for granted that only husbands could initiate divorce proceedings.

Extramarital relations. A woman's sexual capacities were under the control of the head of the household. Girls were expected to be virgins at marriage. If a bridegroom accused his bride of not being virginal, their bedsheets were to be examined: if there was no blood on the sheets, she would be stoned; if she was proved innocent, her husband could never divorce her (*Dt.* 22:13–21). If a nonbetrothed girl was seduced, the seducer had to pay the full virgin's bride-price to her father, who decided whether to give her in marriage (*Ex.* 22:16–17). *Deuteronomy* provides that the seducer must pay the bride-price, take the girl as his wife, and never divorce her (*Dt.* 22:28–29); it is possible that the Deuteronomic rule concerned rape, but it may also have applied to any illicit sex with a virgin. The penalty for adultery was death for the married woman and her lover (*Lv.* 20:10); the extramarital relations of a married man were not considered adultery. If a man suspected his wife of adultery, he had the right to accuse her, and she would then undergo a solemn oath procedure (drinking the "bitter waters"). If, innocent, she suffered no ill effects, she could return to her husband. If she were guilty, she would ultimately be punished by God, who could cause her belly to swell and her thigh to fall; that is, some disaster to her fertility could occur, possibly a prolapsed uterus (*Nm.* 5:11–31). Even if she did not suffer these dire consequences and, moreover, demonstrated her fertility by later bearing a child, her husband could not be penalized for making a false accusation.

BIBLIOGRAPHY

Boecker, Hans Jochen. *Law and the Administration of Justice in the Old Testament and Ancient East.* Translated by Jeremy Moiser. Minneapolis, 1980.

Driver, G. R., and John C. Miles, eds. and trans. *The Babylonian Laws.* 2 vols. Oxford, 1952–1955.

Falk, Ze'ev. *Hebrew Law in Biblical Times: An Introduction.* Jerusalem, 1964.

Frymer-Kensky, Tikva. "The Strange Case of the Suspected Sotah." *Vetus Testamentum* 34 (January 1984): 11–26.

Vaux, Roland de. *Ancient Israel,* vol. 1, *Social Institutions.* 2d ed. Translated by John McHugh. London, 1965.

Whitelam, Keith W. *The Just King: Monarchical Judicial Authority in Ancient Israel.* Journal for the Study of the Old Testament Supplements, no. 12. Sheffield, 1979.

TIKVA FRYMER-KENSKY

Property Law

Like Israelite law in general, Israelite property law is marked by a concern for the rights of the individual. In particular an attempt is made, at least in theory, to safeguard the rights of the less fortunate (the poor, widows, orphans, etc.). As will be seen in this article, Israelite property law shares many points of contact, both in actual detail and in terminology, with property laws found elsewhere in the ancient Near East.

Conveyance of Property. As expressed ideally in the laws of the Hebrew Bible, the only transference of property in ancient Israel should be through inheritance. Every Israelite family was allocated a plot of land at the original apportionment, traditionally held to have been in the time of Moses and Joshua (*Nm.* 26:52–54, 33:54; *Jos.* 13–22), and it was believed that this ancestral plot should remain, if not in the family's possession, then at least in the possession of the clan. Thus there really should be no sale of land. Theological justification for this point of view is given in *Leviticus*: "But the land must not be sold beyond reclaim, for the land is Mine; you are but strangers resident with Me" (*Lv.* 25:23). This view regards God as owner of all property and the Israelites as only temporary tenants who may not buy or sell land. The duty of redemption and the institution of the Jubilee year (for both, see below) tend to corroborate this point of view, as does the complete absence in the Bible of laws concerning the renting of property.

Sale of land. While there is some evidence that this view of the inalienability of property was current in monarchical times (as can be gathered from Naboth's response to Ahab in *1 Kings* 21:3), there can be little doubt that the very emergence of the monarchy and the growth of the cities led to sweeping sociological changes as far as land ownership was concerned. Because of debt, many small farmers were forced to sell their farms to a new landed aristocracy. The situation became so serious that by the time of the eighth century the old Israelite society based on the small farmer had been destroyed. This was the situation that attracted the opposition of the prophets who denounced the land-grabbing practices of the new aristocracy. For example, Isaiah complains, "Ah, those who add house to house and join field to field, till there is room for none but you to dwell in the land!" (*Is.* 5:8). Similarly, Micah condemns those who "covet fields, and seize them; houses and they take them away. They defraud men of their homes, and people of their land" (*Mi.* 2:2).

Contracts of sale. The Bible records a number of property transactions, including Jacob's purchase of land at Shechem (*Gn.* 33:18–20), David's purchase of the threshing floor from Araunah (*2 Sm.* 24:24), Omri's purchase of the hill of Samaria, site of his future capital, from Shemer (*1 Kgs.* 16:24), and Boaz's purchase of a field from Naomi (*Ru.* 4:9). Two transactions are recorded in detail: when Abraham purchases the Cave of Machpelah (*Gn.* 23:3–20) and when Jeremiah, fulfilling his duty as near kinsman, redeems (purchases) the land in Anathoth from his impoverished cousin Hanamel (*Jer.* 32:6–15). In these two transactions there are elements which conform to standard ancient Near Eastern real estate documents.

In Abraham's purchase, one can discern the strict attention that is paid to ensure that the transaction conforms to all the details of ancient Near Eastern law. Thus, as required by early Mesopotamian law, two stages in the transfer of the property can be seen: payment of the price by the transferee to the transferor and taking possession of the property by the transferee. Hence it is twice said that the field was transferred to Abraham, once after Abraham weighed the silver for Ephron, that is, after payment of the price (*Gn.* 23:17), and then again after he buried Sarah (*Gn.* 23:20), that is, after he took possession of the field.

Another reflection of Mesopotamian law may be seen in the passage about Jeremiah's redemption of land which describes in detail the writing of a real estate contract (*Jer.* 32:6–15). Two copies of the deed of sale are made and witnessed, all "according to rule and law" (*Jer.* 36:11). Both are kept in the archives, but one is sealed as the official permanent record, and the other is unsealed for consultation when necessary. This reflects the Mesopotamian practice of enclosing a contract in a clay envelope that shows a copy of the same contract on the outside.

Redemption of Hereditary Land and the Jubilee Year. In accordance with the principle, expressed above, of the inalienability of land, a person's patrimony should ideally never be sold. However, should a man, due to economic straits, have to sell his land, then the law provides relief for its retrieval in two ways. First, the debtor's nearest family member is given the option of first refusal to the property (redemption). Second, in the absence of a family redeemer, the property ultimately reverts back to the debtor in the Jubilee year.

Redemption. Among the Israelites, the redemption of property from indigent family members was regarded not only as a moral obligation but also as a noble form of social action (*Lv.* 25:25–34). Two examples in the Bible of family members redeeming property (already mentioned) are Jeremiah redeeming his cousin's field at Anathoth (*Jer.* 32:6–9) and Boaz redeeming the field belonging to Naomi (*Ru.* 4:1–10). Note that in these cases the land is not restored to the impoverished kinsman but becomes the property of the redeemers. (For a contrary opinion, see Levine, 1983). Under the laws of the Jubilee, however, the land reverts back to the original owner. In both cases, the clan is protected from the alienation (loss) of the property.

The Jubilee year. The law of the Jubilee year *(shenat ha-yovel)* is set out in *Leviticus* 25. Three regulations concerning property ought to be mentioned here:

1. Anybody who is forced to sell ancestral lands may reclaim them every fiftieth year, pointing to the principle that land cannot be irrevocably sold (*Lv.* 25:10, 25:13, 25:28).
2. Since land cannot be irrevocably sold, what can be sold is only so many harvests (*Lv.* 25:15–16). Consequently every sale of land becomes a kind of lease for a number of years before the next Jubilee.
3. Town houses, other than those belonging to Levites, are not subject to the Jubilee law. If they are not redeemed within one year of purchase, then the seller can never reclaim them (*Lv.* 25:29–30).

The terminology used to describe property that cannot be reclaimed is *tsemitut* ("beyond reclaim"), a term that has both semantic (*tsamit*, "beyond reclaim") and functional parallels in real estate documents from Ugarit in the thirteenth century BCE.

The original intention of the Jubilee law is much debated. There are two major schools of thought. One holds that in the Jubilee law the old tribal principle of inalienability of the land was affirmed, but because of the new social realities, the land laws were relaxed. Hence when the new economic order, which was not tied to the land or to patrimony, came into being, irrevocable sales in the cities were permitted (Weinfeld, 1980). The other school believes that the law is a later (postexilic) reworking of the Sabbatical year (on which all agree it is patterned) by the Priestly school. The principle here is that of *restitutio in integrum*, "a restoration to an original state": the land has to be returned to its original owner and thereby effect a restoration of the structure of Israelite society as it had been divinely ordained in ancient days (Noth, 1977).

Scholars also differ on the question of whether the Jubilee law was ever actually put into effect. The problem is aggravated because of the paucity of references in the rest of the Bible. The Jubilee is not referred to in any historical text, not even in postexilic ones. Outside of *Leviticus* 25, it is mentioned only in *Leviticus* 27:17–25 and briefly in *Numbers* 36:4 and *Ezekiel* 46:17. The protests of the prophets concerning land monopoly may indicate that the Jubilee law was not observed in preexilic times, and, because Nehemiah makes the people promise to observe the Sabbatical year but says nothing about the Jubilee year (*Neh.* 10:32), the same may probably be said for postexilic times as well.

Rights of Inheritance. The norm in ancient Israel was that a man's property was inherited by his sons, the firstborn receiving a double share (*Dt.* 21:15–17). In the event that a man had no sons, the line of inheritance was transferred through a scale of family members: from daughters to brothers to uncles and, ultimately, to the nearest kinsman of the deceased (*Nm.* 27:8–11). It is noteworthy that there is no provision in this list for a man's widow (see below). While the principle of primogeniture was the rule, there are numerous cases recorded in which the firstborn did not get the preferential share. Indeed, a significant motif in the narrative sections of the Bible is that the younger son eventually supplants the older both in cases where property is concerned (e.g., Ishmael and Isaac, Esau and Jacob, Reuben and Joseph, and Manasseh and Ephraim) and in cases of succession to the throne (e.g., Eliab and David and Adonijah and Solomon).

Rights of daughters. According to *Numbers* 27:1–11, daughters originally were not eligible to inherit any part of the family estate. Only after the case of the daughters of Zelophehad was provision made for daughters to inherit on a limited basis: they could inherit providing the deceased had no sons (*Nm.* 27:8) and they married within the clan, so that the patrimony would not be transferred to another tribe (*Nm.* 36:6–9). There is a reference in the *Book of Job* to Job's daughters inheriting alongside their brothers (42:15). However, because of the fact that *Job* is set in a non-Israelite locale, scholars generally do not regard this as standard Israelite practice.

Rights of widows. As already indicated, the line of inheritance in *Numbers* makes no provision for the widow, not even for the usufruct of her husband's property. This is unusual since in most ancient Near Eastern law collections (e.g., the code of Hammurabi and Hittite and Assyrian laws) the widow is appropriately provided for. This omission is usually explained by the supposition that it was incumbent on the eldest son, who receives a preferential share of the estate, to provide for his mother and the unmarried female members of the family. It is also pointed out that widows, although not specifically mentioned in the line of inheritance, were provided with some degree of protection in the laws concerning the levirate.

The laws of the levirate state that should a man die without leaving a son, the brother of the deceased must marry the widow. The first child of this marriage is to be considered the heir of the deceased (*Dt.* 25:6). By this device, the estate of the deceased would be preserved, since his inheritance would pass to the child. However, there are indications that these laws were not widely observed (e.g., in the story of Judah and Tamar; see *Gn.* 38), and the penalties for nonobservance were insignificant (*Dt.* 25:7–10, *Ru.* 4:7–8). There was no incentive other than moral duty for the brother to perform what may well have been regarded as a most onerous and unwelcome task (Davies, 1981). For by assuming the duty, the brother not only lost his claim to his own brother's estate—since if there were no heir, he and his brothers would be next in line (*Nm.* 27:9)—but in certain cases performance of the levirate could actually be damaging to his own estate (by having to take responsibility for the widow as well as managing his dead brother's land). Performance of the levirate must therefore have been considered a magnanimous act by the brother: he was assuming obligations without necessarily deriving any corresponding benefits.

Childless couples. In the ancient Near East, having an heir was of paramount importance. Should a wife remain childless, her husband could marry another woman. To forestall this, the woman might give her own personal slave to her husband to bear the children for her. Children born of such unions were thought of symbolically as the wife's. Examples of barren women giving maids to their husband include Sarah, who gives Hagar to Abraham (*Gn.* 16:3), Rachel, who gives Bilhah to Jacob (*Gn.* 30:3), and even Leah, who, not barren but no longer bearing children, gives Zilpah to Jacob (*Gn.* 30:9–13). Children of such marriages had the same rights of inheritance as natural children (e.g., Ishmael in *Gn.* 17:18, 21:10).

Another method that was very common in the ancient Near East, and to which childless couples often resorted, was adoption. Although there are no laws of adoption in the Bible, the institution may underlie some of the patriarchal narratives, for example, in Abraham's complaint that since he was childless, Dammesek Eliezer would inherit from him. (*Gn.* 15:2–4).

BIBLIOGRAPHY

There is as yet no work exclusively dealing with Israelite property laws of ownership and inheritance. Material on this subject can be garnered from general works on Israelite law and institutions. Still the classic among these is the chapter "Economic Life" by Roland de Vaux in his *Ancient Israel*, vol. 1, *Social Institutions*, 2d ed. (London, 1965), pp. 164–177. Particularly useful is the survey of Israelite law by S. E. Loewenstamm in his article "Law" in *The World History of the Jewish People*, edited by Benjamin Mazar, vol. 3, *Judges* (Tel Aviv, 1971), pp. 231–267.

On specific topics, Edward Neufeld's article "The Emergence of a Royal-Urban Society in Ancient Israel," *Hebrew Union College Annual* 31 (1960): 31–53, is helpful for understanding the changing economic conditions in Israel at the time of the monarchy. Baruch A. Levine's study "Late Language in the Priestly Source: Some Literary and Historical Observations," in *Proceedings of the Eighth World Congress of Jewish Studies . . . , Bible Studies and Hebrew Language* (Jerusalem, 1983), pp. 69–82, deals with the terminology of land tenure. Robert North's *Sociology of the Biblical Jubilee* (Rome, 1954) is a full-length treatment of most aspects of the Jubilee, which may be supplemented by the relevant sections in Martin Noth's *Leviticus* (Philadelphia, 1977), pp. 181–193, and in Moshe Weinfeld's *Mishpaṭ u-tsedaqah be-Yisra'el uva-'amim* (Jerusalem, 1985), pp. 104–106. Articles dealing with different aspects of rights of inheritance are Zafrira Ben-Barak's "Inheritance by Daughters in the Ancient Near East," *Journal of Semitic Studies* 25 (Spring 1980): 22–33; Eryl W. Davies's "Inheritance Rights and the Hebrew Levirate Marriage," *Vetus Testamentum* 31 (1981): 138–144, 257–268; and Tikva Frymer-Kensky's "Patriarchal Family Relationships and Near Eastern Law," *Biblical Archeologist* 44 (Fall 1981): 209–214.

DAVID MARCUS

Criminal Law

Criminal law is a modern legal concept that relates to punitive actions taken by society when confronted by conduct that is considered socially harmful, morally offensive, or a threat to fundamental values or norms. Crimes are public offenses because the community, often acting through its authoritative representation, punishes the offender. The claims of any injured individual are submerged into the public actions of the community; society as a whole reacts as if it were the injured party. The punishment imposed on the criminal offender is often corporal: death, mutilation, or beating. Punishment might also be exile, imprisonment, or public humiliation. Sometimes monetary fines are imposed as well, but these go to the state, not to an injured individual.

In modern times, crimes are to be distinguished from torts, which belong to the category of civil law. Torts are offenses that society is satisfied to leave private. To redress a tort, the injured individual either acts alone or seeks the aid of kinfolk or powerful allies (self-help). In more developed societies, the king or government might help the individual enforce his claims. But the injured individual acting privately in civil law can exact only indemnity or monetary compensation from the offending party.

Biblical Concepts. The literary books that constitute the Hebrew Bible only partially reveal the legal practices of ancient Israelite society. One can, however, discern elements of criminal law among the stated commandments or prohibitions and casuistic legal formulations as well as in the details of narrative elements. All of this ancient evidence must be considered, although, to be sure, one does not know the extent to which it reflects the ancient realities or actual practices.

One cannot tell whether the ancient Israelites articulated a conscious distinction between criminal and civil law. Clearly, the lines between private and public offenses were drawn differently from those of modern, Western societies. Some offenses like battery (*Ex.* 21:18–19 [verse citations unless otherwise specified are to the Eng. version]) and theft (Masoretic text *Ex.* 21:37, 22:3), which today are criminal or public, were still considered to be private torts in the Bible. Conversely, offenses like witchcraft (*Ex.* 22:18, *Lv.* 20:27, *1 Sm.* 28:3), adultery (*Lv.* 20:10; *Dt.* 22:20–24; *Ez.* 16:38–41, 23:45–49), and violation of the Sabbath (*Ex.* 31:14–15, 35:2; *Nm.* 15:32–36), which in modern secular societies are either private torts or nonactionable, were in the Bible considered serious public offenses or crimes.

There are no special Hebrew terms for *crime* and *criminal;* the same words, *sin, transgress,* and so forth, are used to describe both human offenses against other people and those against God. Religious and secular concerns are commingled, and most of the extant criminal laws are presented as God's own pronouncements. In this sense, all crimes are offenses against God. But one cannot assert that all sins are crimes. God may punish all sins, but the term *crime* is here reserved to describe only those public offenses that were punished by Israelite (i.e., human) society.

Crimes against King, Parents, and Civil Authorities. The biblical narratives relate that the death penalty was meted out by the king for treason (*1 Sm.* 22:13–19; *1 Kgs.* 1:50–53, 2:23–24), regicide (*2 Sm.* 1:14–16, 4:9–12; *2 Kgs.* 14:5–6), cursing God or king (*2 Sm.* 19:21–23; *1 Kgs.* 2:46, 21:9–16; cf. *Ex.* 22:28, *Lv.* 24:10–16), "treasonous" prophecy against the state (*Jer.* 26:8–24, *2 Chr.* 24:19–21), and witchcraft (*1 Sm.* 28:9–10). These executions were carried out by the king's men; at other times, by mass actions like stoning, preceded by a public trial. "Treasonous" prophecy was sometimes treated as a minor crime, punished by imprisonment, beating, or exile (*1 Kgs.* 22:13–27; *Jer.* 20:2, 32:2–3; *Am.* 7:9–13).

There was a stated duty to obey both parental and civil authority. The death penalty was prescribed for those who rebelled against the courts (*Dt.* 17:8–13) as well as against the ruler (*Jos.* 1:18). There are similar provisions for striking a parent (*Ex.* 21:15), cursing a parent (*Ex.* 21:17, *Lv.* 20:9), or rebelling against parental commands (*Dt.* 21:18–21).

Sexual Offenses. The death penalty was also prescribed for a variety of sexual offenses: adultery (in addition to the references cited above, see *Gn.* 20:3, 38:24; *Dt.* 22:22–24), sexual relations of a man with his father's or son's wife (*Lv.* 20:11–12) or with his mother or daughter (*Lv.* 20:14), rape of a married or even a betrothed woman (*Dt.* 22:25–27), bestiality (*Ex.* 22:19, *Lv.* 20:15–16), male homosexuality (*Lv.* 20:13), and prostitution engaged in by the daughter of a priest (*Lv.* 21:9).

Idolatry. The biblical laws reflect the long conflict with idolatry and polytheism that came to a climax at the end of the monarchy. The death penalty is prescribed for a variety of idolatrous acts (*Lv.* 20:2–5, *Dt.* 17:2–7) as well as for promoting idolatry to others (*Dt.* 13:1–5, 13:6–11, 18:20–22; cf. the general slaughter of idolaters in *Exodus* 32:27). *Deuteronomy* 13:12–18 assigns the death penalty to an entire city and its livestock; all other possessions and goods were considered *ḥerem,* that is, to be dedicated to God and burned by fire (cf. *Ex.* 22:20).

Homicide and Manslaughter. The biblical response to homicide hovers between the spheres of private and public law. The relatives and allies of the victim retained the right to take action; society allowed them to slay the offender or to accept monetary compensation for the death of kin. Their choice of action, however, depended upon whether death was due to negligent homicide, involuntary manslaughter, or murder; the free or unfree status of the victim was also a factor to be considered. The negligent owner of the ox that fatally gored a person (*Ex.* 21:28–32) only owed compensation for a dead slave but was subject to the death penalty if the victim was a free man. The owner, however, was allowed to negotiate compensation in that case, too; but the ox was put to death in either case. A man who committed involuntary manslaughter could rightfully be slain by the relatives of the victim; but the civil authorities could intervene to grant the manslayer asylum (a form of exile) in a "city of refuge" (*Ex.* 21:12–13, *Nm.* 35:1–34, *Dt.* 19:1–13). The normal penalty for murder was death (*Gn.* 9:6, *Ex.* 21:14). In most cases, vengeance was taken by kin or allies of the victim (*Gn.* 4:11–15, *2 Sm.* 14:4–11; cf. the case of wrongful vengeance, *2 Sm.* 3:26–30, *1 Kgs.* 2:5–6). Public outrage could sometimes boil over into community action against the slayer (*Ex.* 21:14; *Dt.* 19:11–12; *Jgs.* 20:12–13; *Ez.* 16:38–41, 23:45–49).

The giving of compensation in cases of murder is strongly condemned in *Leviticus* 24:21 and *Numbers* 35:31–34 (cf. *Lv.* 24:18), since biblical law generally considers murder a public, not private, offense. Glimpses of that practice, however, may be seen in *2 Samuel* 21:1–4 and *1 Kings* 20:39. There is evidence that compensation was given for a number of other offenses where the death penalty was prescribed. Compensation for adultery is suggested in *Proverbs* 6:30–35 (in *Leviticus* 19:20–22 the slave status of the female obviates punishment). Compensation replaces the death penalty for breaking a solemn oath in *1 Samuel* 14:24–46 but not in *Judges* 11:30–40. One may also note the institution of *'erekh* ("monetary equivalents"), which could be offered in place of a dedicated object, including persons (*Lv.* 27:1–33), except in the case of *ḥerem* (*Lv.* 27:29). *'Erekh* is offered in order to redeem potential victims of exile or death in *2 Kings* 23:35.

Theft. Even more than the response to homicide, the responses to theft hover between public and private law. Kidnapping and sale of a person was punished by death (*Ex.* 21:16, *Dt.* 24:7), but the theft of animals was settled by compensation (MT *Ex.* 21:37, 22:3). There are, nevertheless, hints of capital punishment in the outbursts of King David in *2 Samuel* 12:5–6 (cf. *1 Sm.* 26:16) and of Jacob in *Genesis* 31:32. A thief caught stealing during the day was not to be killed, but a thief caught in the night could be slain without penalty (*Ex.* 22:2). This same distinction, between daytime and nocturnal theft, also appears in the Babylonian laws from Eshnunna (modern-day Tell Asmar, Iraq; sections 12–13). The taking of property belonging to God *(ḥerem)* was punished by death (*Jos.* 7:1, 7:18–26).

Multiple Penalties. One encounters the actual commingling of private and public concerns in cases where a criminal penalty was imposed in addition to the payment of compensation. The man who brought a false charge of adultery against his betrothed wife was punished on two levels: the father of the woman received monetary compensation, and the man was beaten (*Dt.* 22:13–19). Beating could apparently also be added, as a criminal penalty, to the settlements reached in civil or private disputes (*Dt.* 25:1–3).

Talion. Battery, as noted above, was normally a private offense. But battery became a criminal or public matter if it caused serious, permanent injury or death (*Ex.* 21:20–23). The criminal penalties varied according to the injuries sustained; one finds repeated expression of this principle of *lex talionis* (*Ex.* 21:23–25, *Lv.* 24:19–20; for false accusation, see *Dt.* 19:15–21). The harshness of the talionic rules has led some interpreters, both ancient and modern, to question their literal application, especially in noncapital cases. One could compare the offering of compensation in place of the death penalty for homicide, discussed above. Yet there are instances where talion was literally imposed: the cutting off of thumbs and toes in *Judges* 1:6 and mutilation for battery leading to serious injury in *Deuteronomy* 25:11 (there is no exact talionic parity between male and female in this case).

There is some textual evidence that the harsher practices of earlier times were gradually modified or eased in later times. This is reflected, for example, in the discontinuation of the practice of assigning collective guilt for crimes committed by one individual (*Dt.* 24:16, *2 Kgs.* 14:5–6; cf. *2 Sm.* 21:1–9, *2 Kgs.* 9:24–26). Similarly, for the change in the treatment of the corpses of the executed, one may contrast *2 Samuel* 21:9–14 with *Deuteronomy* 21:22–23.

Criminal Law and Sacred Law. Divine as well as human punishment was expected for some criminal offenses, such as cursing a parent (*Dt.* 27:16), bestiality (*Dt.* 27:21), sexual relations of a man with his son's or father's wife (*Dt.* 27:20, 27:23), Sabbath violation (*Ex.* 31:14). These mark points of overlap between criminal and sacred law. Sacred law involved God and man, and it transcended the human agencies of court, judge, and so forth. It has been noted that the Decalogue (*Ex.* 20:2–17, *Dt.* 5:6–21) addresses areas of concern that are also treated in the criminal laws; similarly, *Leviticus* 18:8–23 promises divine punishment for offenses that are given societal penalties in *Leviticus* 20:10–21. (Jewish commentators of late antiquity came to consider offenses lacking societal penalty to be a category of lesser crime, punishable by beating; see Mishnah *Makkot* 3.1–10 and Maimonides' *Mishneh Torah*, Sanhedrin 18–19.)

[*For further discussion of how punishment was enacted, see the following article on* State and Judiciary Law.]

BIBLIOGRAPHY

Diamond, A. S. *Primitive Law, Past and Present.* London, 1971. A good general historical introduction to ancient law.

Greenberg, Moshe. "Some Postulates of Biblical Criminal Law." In *Yehezkel Kaufmann Jubilee Volume,* edited by Menahem Haran, pp. 5–28. Jerusalem, 1960.

Haase, Richard. "Körperliche Strafen in den altorientalischen Rechtssammlungen." *Revue internationale des droits de l'antiquité* 10 (1963): 55–75. A comparative study of corporal punishments in ancient Near Eastern law collections. This work adds useful perspective to the consideration of biblical materials.

Jackson, Bernard S. "Reflections on Biblical Criminal Law." In his *Essays in Jewish and Comparative Legal History,* pp. 25–63. Leiden, 1975. Contains a thoughtful critique of earlier studies.

Phillips, Anthony. *Ancient Israel's Criminal Law.* Oxford, 1970. Useful for its bibliography and scope; Phillips approaches the subject from a viewpoint different from Diamond's.

SAMUEL GREENGUS

State and Judiciary Law

In ancient Israel, laws were regarded as divinely ordained. The upholding of the laws, therefore, devolved upon the state, the religious establishment, and the people. Although the state could, presumably, impose sanctions for breaches of law, most cases were decided on the local level, and punishment was executed by the people as a whole (as in stoning), by the family of the victim (as in cases of murder), and by God.

Jurisdiction. There were several different strands of jurisdiction and authority in ancient Israelite law. Priests were in charge of religious matters, which included the important determination of secular and profane, pure and defiled (*Lv.* 10:10, *Ez.* 44:23; cf. *Dt.* 33:10). They oversaw the expiation of those misdeeds that could be expiated (*Lv.* 5:1–13; see below); they were involved in the trial of false witnesses; and they were members of the superior court envisioned in *Deuteronomy* (*Dt.* 17:8–13) and in the judicial reform under Jehoshaphat (*2 Chr.* 19:11). Alongside this priestly jurisdiction was a secular legal system that included the elders of the towns, the king, and judges and their officers.

Trials were usually held in the villages before the local elders. The typical procedure for such trials has been reconstructed by Donald A. McKenzie (1964). The adversaries would come before the elders (normally at the town gate) to lay out their case. The elders would take their seats; the defendant would be given a prominent place (*1 Kgs.* 21:9) with the plaintiff on his right (*Zec.* 3:1). The witnesses would be sitting and later would rise to bear testimony; if the case were very important, citizens would be summoned to attend (*1 Kgs.* 21:9). The plaintiff would state his case; then the defendant would state his, after which the witnesses would rise to bear witness (*Dt.* 19:16. *Ps.* 35:11). The elders would discuss the matter and rise to give their verdict (*Ps.* 3:8, 35:2), declaring the defendant innocent or guilty. In the case of a guilty verdict, they would then oversee an immediate punishment. The informality of such procedures is indicated in chapter 4 of *Ruth,* in which Boaz waits at the gate for his kinsman and then convenes a court with what seems to be a random ten of the elders of the town.

Alongside this local system was the jurisdiction of the kings. There is a strong tradition, shared by Israel and Mesopotamia, that the kings were responsible for upholding justice. The kings of Israel, however, were not lawgivers, for Israel's laws were held to come directly from God. They were, however, responsible for judging fairly, for seeing that justice was done, and for upholding the cause of the powerless. From the revelation of the Law, biblical narrative depicts Israel's leaders as arbiters of justice: Moses is seen as a judge (*Ex.* 18:13); the charismatic leaders of the premonarchical period (the "Judges") are said to have judged Israel; Samuel rode a justice circuit (*1 Sm.* 7:15–16); and both David and Solomon are shown making judicial decisions (*2 Sm.* 15:2, *1 Kgs.* 3:16–28). However, there is no instance in which a case was referred from the elders to the king, nor is there any case in which a king overrode the decision of a local court. The royal system seems to have operated separately and may have been open to any citizen.

The stories of the decisions of the king, moreover, do not show formal trials. In the two phony disputes that David "decided," the parables of Nathan (*2 Sm.* 12:1–6) and of the wise woman of Tekoa (*2 Sm.* 14:4–7), only one party is heard—an outsider (Nathan) or a pleader. Similarly, when the woman whose son Elisha had restored to life comes before the king to reclaim her lands, nothing is heard of or from whoever is presently working those lands (*2 Kgs.* 8:1–6). The impression we get from these stories is that individuals would come to plead their case before the king in order to convince him—without formal process—and thus have the king become their advocate. It is in this sense that Absalom tells the Israelites coming to David for justice that they will find no "hearer" from the king (*2 Sm.* 15:2–6), that is, that the king will not grant them a sympathetic audience and act on their requests. Similarly, Josiah is said to have judged the case of the poor (*Jer.* 22:15–16). The only case we know of in which the king heard from both litigants is that of the two prostitutes before Solomon (*1 Kgs.* 3:16–28). The kings do not appear to have instituted trials at which they would preside. Even in the case of Naboth, where the charge was treason (cursing the king), Jezebel and Ahab did not preside: Jezebel went through the regular channels of the elders and nobles of the city in order to have Naboth convicted (by perjured testimony) (*1 Kgs.* 21:8–14).

At some time during the monarchy, most probably under Jehoshaphat, the system of trial by elders or by king was either augmented or superseded by the appointment of judges and their executives throughout the land and by the establishment of a superior court in Jerusalem to which the local elders and judges could bring cases that they could not decide. In the organization of the judiciary under Jehoshaphat (*2 Chr.* 19:5–11), the superior court had a dual composition: matters relating to God were referred to the priest in charge, Amariah; the "king's matters," to Zebadiah. This system of installing royally appointed judges throughout the land, as well as a superior court to which they could refer, is also envisioned in *Deuteronomy* (*Dt.* 16:18–9, 17:8–13).

Decision Making. Israelite trials were based on an accusatorial system in which the plaintiff bore testimony against the defendant. In effect, there was no difference between an accuser and a witness. This system is inherently vulnerable to the subverting of justice by false witnesses. Two mechanisms act to minimize this danger: the requirement of two (male, free, Israelite) witnesses for conviction and the institution of retributive punishment for bearing false witness or making a false accusation. *Deuteronomy* 19:15–21, as the laws of Hammurabi in Mesopotamia, requires the false witness or accuser to receive the punishment that the accused would receive if convicted: payment of equivalent damages if the case was pecuniary, and forfeiture of life if the case was capital. This provision is a change from the Sumerian system, which prescribed a fine for false witnesses, but is similar to the laws of Hammurabi. These precautions were not entirely sufficient; they did not prevent Jezebel from finding two witnesses willing to commit perjury (*1 Kgs.* 21:10), nor the two elders in *Susanna* from perjuring themselves; the Pharisaic insistence on intense cross-examination of witnesses in capital cases was meant to increase the safeguards against false conviction by means of witnesses.

In the absence of two witnesses, the courts did not have the authority to decide a case. This is the reason for the indictment of someone who hears the *alah* (here a judicial curse meant to call out witnesses) but does not speak up (*Lv.* 5:1). Certain cases could not be left undecided, and recourse would be had to divine intervention, either through divination, an oracle, or an oath procedure. Two types of divination used in Israel were lots and the Urim and Tummim. Lots could be used to determine whether an accused person was guilty, as in the case of finding the culprit who took booty from Jericho (*Jos.* 7:14–15). They would not be sufficient to convict; for after Achan was selected by the lots, his tent was searched, and even after the goods were found, he was asked to confess (*Jos.* 7:22–25). The Urim and Tummim were in the hands of the priests and also functioned to determine whether an accused were guilty (*1 Sm.* 14:38–42). Neither method of divination is heard of after the full establishment of the monarchy. Solomon's willingness to decide the case of the two prostitutes (in which there were no witnesses) may be an indication that the monarchy now considered itself strong enough not to need divine legitimation for its decisions; the recorded feeling of the people was that "the wisdom of God was in him to do judgment" (*1 Kgs.* 3:28).

Decision by oracle is heard of in such cases as blasphemy (*Lv.* 24:12) and Sabbath offenses (*Nm.* 15:34); the accused would be put under guard until a divine decision was heard. Such matters may have continued to be decided by divine oracle even under the monarchy, for *2 Chronicles* records that people might come to the superior court for the argument of a case or for God's judgment (*2 Chr.* 19:8).

God could also be involved in the judicial process by means of an exculpatory oath by the accused, in which the accused placed himself under God's jurisdiction in affirming his innocence (*Ex.* 22:7–10, *Lv.* 5:20); the court would believe him under the supposition that he would not risk divine retribution for commiting a falsehood. A particularly solemn form of exculpatory oath is the procedure for the suspected adulteress (*Soṭah*): the woman accused by her husband stood "before the Lord" and drank a potion that contained dust from the sanctuary and the dissolved words of the oath in which she affirmed her innocence and her belief that the waters would not harm her if she was innocent but would cause infertility if she was guilty (*Nm.* 5:11–31). After drinking the potion, the woman was free to go and would "bear her penalty" (that is, she would await divine retribution). If she was guilty, "her belly shall distend and her thigh shall fall," which may indicate a prolapsed uterus and certainly indicates future infertility. If she was innocent, she would ultimately be totally vindicated by becoming pregnant, and her husband would not be penalized for making a false accusation. Although this procedure is sometimes called an ordeal, it differs from true ordeals in two ways: (1) no divine decision is immediately apparent and (2) God himself rather than the human court is expected to punish the woman.

Execution of the Decision. There are several different kinds of penalties. Fines might be exemplary, multiple payments such as the repayment of double, fourfold, or fivefold damages for theft (*Ex.* 22:1–4). Or, specific penalties could be prescribed, such as the guilt offering *(asham)* of a ram imposed for violating a slave woman designated to marry (*Lv.* 19:20–21) or the payment of the standard bride-price to the father of a deflowered virgin (*Ex.* 22:16–17). In certain cases the amount of the penalty is determined by the family of the injured party. Thus, after an ox had gored someone to death, its owner was to pay whatever was demanded of him in order to ransom his own life (*Ex.* 21:30), and after having caused a woman to miscarry, one was to pay whatever the woman's husband and the judge decided (*Ex.* 21:22).

There is little corporal punishment in the Bible. The most common instance of it is scourging, or flogging, limited by law to forty lashes (*Dt.* 25:1–3). A woman who touched a man's genitals while protecting her husband in a fight could have her hand cut off (*Dt.* 25:11–12). This was the only specific mutilation prescribed in the Bible, in contrast to Babylonian and Assyrian law (e.g., Laws of Hammurabi 192, 193, 194, 205, 218, 282; Middle Assyrian Laws 4, 5, 8, 9, 15, 18, 20, 44, 52).

A question is raised by the law of talion *(lex talionis)* which requires equal retaliation in cases of assault and battery (*Lv.* 24:19–21). Given the lack of mutilation practiced in Israel, it has been suggested that talion is a statement of judicial principle rather than a concrete description of practice and that the actual penalty was the payment of compensation money computed by talionic principles. This is almost certainly the case with the other two statements of the talionic principle in the Bible, the accidental injury to a pregnant woman (*Ex.* 21:23–25) and the penalty for false witnesses (*Dt.* 19:19–21): if there were no judicial penalties of mutilation, then the mention of talionic mutilations must have been a judicial maxim to express the principles of equivalent retaliation. Equivalent retaliation stopped with the accused. In Mesopotamia the child or wife of a perpetrator could be punished for a misdeed against the child or wife of the injured party. In Israel this was not allowed (*Ex.* 21:31, *Dt.* 24:16), although a belief that God would punish and reward the children (*Ex.* 20:5) was held until the days of Jeremiah and Ezekiel (*Jer.* 31:30, *Ez.* 18).

Capital Punishment. Death by burning is prescribed for two sexual offenses (*Lv.* 20:14, 21:9, cf. *Gen.* 38:24). Death by the sword is prescribed for an idolatrous city (*Dt.* 13:15; cf. *1 Kgs.* 18:40, *2 Kgs.* 23:30). The most common penalty mentioned in capital cases is stoning. The stoning was to be held before the judges; the witnesses cast the first stone, followed by the rest of the people (*Dt.* 17:7), who were thus collectively acting to rid themselves of the guilt of the misdeed. There is a difference of opinion as to whether stoning was in fact the common mode of execution (Phillips, 1970), or whether it is specifically mentioned only for those cases in which it was used, cases in which there had been a major offense against the hierarchical order of the universe (J. J. Finkelstein, 1981; Tikva Frymer-Kensky, 1983).

In cases of murder, the agent of execution was the "blood redeemer" *(go'el ha-dam)*, who was obligated to avenge the murdered party. He was to chase the culprit, who could escape to one of the cities of refuge, set up to be places where a person who had accidentally killed someone could go for a trial. If the person was found to be an intentional murderer, he was handed over to the blood redeemer; if found to be an accidental murderer, he stayed in the city of refuge (a kind of quarantine) until the death of the priest. If he left before that, the blood redeemer was charged with executing him. The reason for this law is explicit: the blood of the slain pollutes the Land of Israel; thus accepting money as restitution for murder or even allowing an accidental murderer to leave the city of refuge would pollute the Land of Israel (*Nm.* 35:9–34, *Dt.* 19:1–12). The blood redeemer is normally taken to mean the closest male relative of the slain, whose job it would be to protect the family. Anthony Phillips (1970), however, has argued that the blood redeemer was, on the contrary, the appointed representative of the local court, whose job it was to carry out the court's instructions.

Expiation. Despite the fact that Israel's law had a fundamentally religious base, there was little expiation in the legal system. Someone who ignored the charge for witnesses and did not come forth, who swore a false oath, or who touched impurity might bring a conscience sacrifice, the *asham* (*Lv.* 5:1–13, traditionally translated as "guilt offering"). In the case of the discovery of a murdered corpse when the murderer cannot be found, the elders of the city were to perform the ritual of the heifer whose neck is broken, attesting to their lack of culpability, averting the blood pollution of their land, and expiating the failure of the legal system (*Dt.* 21:1–9).

BIBLIOGRAPHY

Falk, Ze'ev. *Hebrew Law in Biblical Times: An Introduction.* Jerusalem, 1964.

Finkelstein, J. J. *The Ox That Gored.* Transactions of the American Philosophical Society, vol. 71, pt. 2. Philadelphia, 1981.

Frymer-Kensky, Tikva. "Tit for Tat: The Principle of Equal Retribution in Near Eastern and Biblical Law." *Biblical Archeologist* 43 (Fall 1980): 230–234.

Frymer-Kensky, Tikva. "Pollution, Purification and Purgation in Biblical Israel." In *The Word of the Lord Shall Go Forth*, edited by Carol L. Meyers and M. O'Connor. Winona Lake, Ind., 1983.

Frymer-Kensky, Tikva. "The Strange Case of the Suspected Sotah." *Vetus Testamentum* 34 (January 1984): 11–26.

Greenberg, Moshe. "Crimes and Punishments." In *The Interpreter's Dictionary of the Bible*, edited by George A. Buttrick, vol. 1, pp. 733–744. Nashville, 1972.

McKenzie, Donald A. "Judicial Procedure at the Town Gate." *Vetus Testamentum* 14 (1964): 100–104.

Milgrom, Jacob. *Cult and Conscience: The Asham and the Priestly Doctrine of Repentance*. Leiden, 1976.

Phillips, Anthony. *Ancient Israel's Criminal Law: A New Approach to the Decalogue*. Oxford, 1970.

Ploeg, J. P. M. van der. "Les anciens dans l'Ancien Testament." In *Lex Tua Veritas: Festschrift für Hubert Junker*, edited by Heinrich Gross and Franz Mussner, pp. 175–191. Trier, 1961.

Ploeg, J. P. M. van der. "Les juges en Israel." *Populus dei: Studi in honore del card. Alfredo Ottaviani per il cinquantesimo di sacerdozio*, vol. 1, pp. 463–507. Rome, 1969.

TIKVA FRYMER-KENSKY

ISRAELITE RELIGION. This discussion of the religion of Israel pertains to the religion as presented in the literary sources of the Hebrew scriptures. These sources constitute a selection guided by certain normative principles and therefore do not always reflect the real circumstances of daily life. The religion of Israel described in the Hebrew Bible represents the view of the elite circles of the society of ancient Israel, such as priests, prophets, and scribes, who shaped the image of the ideal Israel. Furthermore, as will be shown below, even this ideal image of the religion of Israel underwent a process of development. However, despite this idealization, a continuous line of development of the religion of ancient Israel can be discerned, and it is this development that I shall attempt to delineate.

General Features

Unique in many ways, Israelite religion is most remarkable for its monotheism. The difference between monotheism and polytheism is not only in number—one god versus a plurality of gods—but in the character and nature of the deity. In contradistinction to the polytheistic system according to which gods are subject to biological rules (the existence of male and female in the divine sphere, which means procreation, struggle for survival, etc.), the God of Israel is transcendent, that is, beyond the sphere of nature and therefore not subject to physical and biological principles. In the biblical descriptions of the deity we never encounter any sexual feature, procreation, struggle for survival, or gaining of status. Theogony (genealogy of the gods) and theomachy (strife among the gods), which are almost indispensable in any polytheistic religion, are completely absent from the religion of Israel.

In what appears to be an exception, we are told that God subdued Rahab, the monster, during the creation period (*Is.* 51:9, *Ps.* 89:11, *Jb.* 26:12; verse citations are to the Masoretic text). However, this does not mean that Rahab existed outside the domain of the creator. Rahab could have been created by God, as were the other creatures, but in contrast to others he rebelled and therefore was crushed and defeated (cf. *Ps.* 74:12-14).

The transcendence of God explains the absence of mythology in the religion of Israel. Mythology, here defined as storytelling about gods and their life, activities, and adventures, is inconceivable in the monotheistic sphere. God's relation to men may be described in an anthropomorphic manner, but nothing is told about God's own self or body or about his personal activities and adventures. His actions, when depicted, are always presented in the framework of God's relationship to people or to his nation.

The transcendent character of the God of Israel explains, too, the objection of Israelite religion to magic, which was so prominent in polytheistic religions. The pagan prophet, according to ancient Israelite perception, resorts to various media in order to reveal the will of gods or to coerce them to do something for men. But the Hebrew scriptures express the Israelite belief that God's will cannot be revealed unless he himself wishes to do so; his will cannot be revealed through magic, which draws its power from mystic powers not subordinated to the deity. Indeed, the Israelite legislator, speaking about pagan diviners and the prohibition against pagan mantic devices (*Dt.* 18:9–12), adds an important explanation: "You must be wholehearted [*tamim*, "sincere"] with the Lord your God. Those nations that you are about to dispossess do indeed resort to soothsayers; to you, however, the Lord your God has not assigned the like" (*Dt.* 18:13–14). The use of magic presupposes reliance on ungodly forces, and that means "insincerity" toward God.

It is true that the biblical stories as well as the biblical cult contain magical elements. There are many allusions to the marvelous transformation of objects: the staffs of Moses and Aaron become serpents (*Ex.* 4:2–4, 7:9–10); Moses divides the sea with his staff (*Ex.* 14:16); Elisha's staff is supposed to revive the Shunammite's son (*2 Kgs.* 4:29); and the three arrows that Joash, the king of Israel, drove into the ground gave him three victories over Aram (*2 Kgs.* 13:14–19). However, all these acts are considered wondrous signs from God. The wonder is seen as "the hand" and power of God and not as originating in the action itself or in the power of the sorcerer, as was the case in pagan religions (cf. *Ex.* 4:1–4, 7:8–10, et al.). Thus, for example, Elisha's staff performs wonders only when accompanied by prayer (contrast *2 Kgs.* 4:29–31 with 4:32–35).

Another transcendent feature of Israelite monotheism is the prohibition against representing God by visual symbol or image: "You shall not make for yourself a sculptured image [*pesel*] or any likeness" (*Ex.* 20:4, *Dt.* 5:8, et al.). This is explained in *Deuteronomy* 4:15: "Be most careful [not to make for yourself a sculptured image], since you saw no shape when the Lord your God spoke to you at Horeb out of the fire." The god which is beyond nature and cosmos cannot be represented by anything earthly and natural.

It is this feature which makes the Israelite religion philosophical, as conceived by the Greeks. For example, it was the observation of Theophrastus (c. 372–287 BCE), a disciple of Aristotle, that "being philosophers by race, [the Jews] converse with each other about 'the Divine' [*to theion*]" (Menachem Stern, *Greek and Latin Authors on Jews and Judaism,* vol. 1, 1974, p. 10). "The Divine" denotes here the philosophical concept of the one force that governs the world in contrast to the popular belief in various mythical deities.

Historical Development until the Temple Cult

It is hard to know how and under what concrete circumstances the monotheistic belief crystallized and whether at its emergence the religion of Israel was already characterized by the negation of mythology as well as of magic and iconic representation of the deity. According to Yeḥezkel Kaufmann in *History of the Religion of Israel* (trans. Moshe Greenberg, 1972), the sudden emergence of monotheism cannot be understood unless we suppose a radical revolutionary move under the leadership of Moses. Kaufmann compares this to the emergence of Islam, which, under the aegis of Muḥammad, succeeded in taking control of the whole Middle East in the course of twenty-five years. One must agree with Kaufmann that there is no clear evidence of an evolutionary process in the Israelite religion. The evolutionary approach of the last century supposes that monotheism developed gradually from polytheism through henotheism (belief in one national god while not excluding the existence of gods of other nations) to monotheism. Real monotheism—according to this opinion—crystallized in Israel only during the times of the prophets, in the eighth century BCE. [*See* God, *article on* God in the Hebrew Scriptures.]

However, this supposition has little support in the literary-historical sources of the Bible. The documents and sources of the Bible, which represent a very broad spectrum of opinions and beliefs rooted in various historical periods, do not show any trace of such polytheistic concepts as the origin of God (theogony), God's consort and family, or the gods' battle for survival (theomachy). By the same token, we do not find anything in these sources which alludes to the official religious use of magical devices for mantic purposes—as, for example, hepatoscopy (inspecting an animal's liver) or augury (deriving inferences from the behavior of birds and other omens), which was so prevalent in pagan religions.

It should be stressed that this article is concerned with the offical religious trend and not with popular religious life. In the popular religion, cultic practices prevailed that reflected pagan beliefs, especially beliefs connected with a divine power of fertility that was represented by the female characteristics of the deity. Archaeological excavations in Palestine revealed numerous female figurines that were used as amulets for securing fertility (see J. B. Pritchard, *Palestinian Figurines in Relation to Certain Goddesses Known through Literature,* London, 1943). Similarly, it was found that the Israelites worshiped the female goddess Asherah and the goddess of fertility Astarte (cf. *Jgs.* 2:13, 3:7; *1 Sm.* 7:4, 12:10; *1 Kgs.* 15:13; *2 Kgs.* 21:7, 23:6). In recent years inscriptions that date back to the ninth century BCE were discovered in Kuntillet ʿAjrud (in southern Palestine) in which YHVH is being blessed next to Asherah—a positioning that suggests syncretic religious worship. Moreover, the worship of the Queen of Heaven (Ishtar?) was widespread in Judah during the end of the monarchic period (*Jer.* 7:18, 44:18). [*See* Astarte.]

All of these tendencies toward syncretism were strongly condemned by the prophets of the northern kingdom of Israel and the southern kingdom of Judah, who considered them aberrations from the pure monotheistic faith.

More complicated is the problem of the aniconic characteristics of Israelite religion. Although erection of images is prohibited in the legitimate Israelite cult, as attested in the various legal codes of the Hebrew scriptures (*Ex.* 20:20, 23:24, 34:14, 34:17; *Lv.* 19:4, 26:1; *Dt.* 4:15ff., 5:8; et al.), the practice as such was not unheard of in ancient Israel. It is not the worship of the golden calf as told in *Exodus* 32 and in *1 Kings* 12:28ff. which we have in mind, because, as investigation has shown, this worship cannot be considered idol worship. The iconic art of the ancient Near East shows that the calf or bull usually represented the pedestal of a god and not the deity itself. The latter was usually carved in human form. Indeed, the most appropriate place for an image of the deity, should this have existed, would have been the throne or the chariot of God, both represented by the Ark of the Covenant (cf. especially *Nm.* 10:35–

36). The Ark, which together with the cherubim represented the throne and the footstool of the deity (see Menahem Haran: "The Ark and the Cherubim: Their Symbolic Significance in Biblical Ritual," *Israel Exploration Journal* 9, 1959, pp. 35ff.), actually constitutes an empty throne: the god sitting on it is invisible, which attests to the antiquity of the aniconic principle in the religion of Israel.

On the other hand, the practice of image making in ancient Israel is described in the stories in *Judges* about Gideon and Micah. Gideon, the great judge of Israel, made an ephod (some sort of image) of gold and set it up in his town (*Jgs.* 8:27), and, similarly, the mother of Micah consecrated silver to make a sculptured image *(pesel)* and a molten image *(massekha)* to YHVH (*Jgs.* 17:3). However, it has been suggested that these events might be seen as deviations from the pure legitimate worship, as were other incidents in the history of Israel caused by Cannaanite influence (cf. the worship of Baal during the period of King Ahab [c. 874–853], *1 Kgs.* 19:18 et al.) and should not be considered a reflection of genuine Israelite religion. Indeed, as will be shown below, new evidence about the tribal setting in Sinai, the cradle of Israelite monotheism, tends to confirm the view that Israelite monotheism was aniconic from its beginning.

The Religion of the Patriarchs. Tradition considers Abraham the father of Yahvistic monotheism but this has no basis in the Bible itself. On the contrary, the biblical documents show an awareness of a gap between the religion of the patriarchs and the Yahvistic national religion of Israel. The name of God, *Yahveh* (preserved only unvocalized in the texts, i.e., *YHVH*) is not known before Moses (*Ex.* 3:13f., 6:2ff.), and the nature of the patriarchal creed is completely different from that of Moses and later Israelites. The god of the patriarchs is tied to person and family; the god is called God of Abraham, Isaac, or Jacob or "the God of the father" (*Gn.* 26:24, 28:13, 31:42, 32:10, 46:3, 49:25), as is appropriate to a wandering family. When *El*, the generic designation of the god, occurs in the patriarchal stories, it is not of a national or universal character, as in later Israel; the name *El* is always bound to the place where the patriarch stays. In Jerusalem God's name is El-ʿElyon (*Gn.* 14:18f.); in Beersheba the name of the deity is El-ʿOlam (*Gn.* 21:33); in Bethel, El-Beit-El (*Gn.* 31:13); and in Shechem, El-elohei Yisra'el (*Gn.* 33:20). The names of the patriarchal family do not contain the Yahvistic component, and there is no trace in the patriarchal religion of an established cult or of official cultic objects. It must be admitted, then, that the national concept of "Yahveh the god of Israel" does not apply to the patriarchal period. The very term *patriarchal period* has to be used with great caution, since Israel as such did not yet exist, and the descriptions of this period are based on anachronisms. At any rate, according to the descriptions themselves, the national creed and cult were still nonexistent.

Historical Circumstances of the Birth of Monotheism. According to the stories of *Exodus*, Mount Sinai or Horeb, which became the mountain of God's revelation to Israel, was hallowed before the revelation to Moses (*Ex.* 3:1; cf. Zeer Weisman, "The Mountain of God," *Tarbiz* 47, 1978, pp. 107–119). It is designated as Mountain of God, a geographical appellation, prior to any connection to Yahveh's theophany (*Ex.* 4:29). Furthermore, it was known as the Mountain of God to Jethro, the Midianite priest, Moses' father-in-law, and he went to this mountain in order to offer sacrifices and to celebrate (*Ex.* 18:12), which points to the fact that the Mountain of God was known to other nomadic tribes of the Sinai area. This is corroborated by the divine epithet "the god of the Hebrews" which occurs only in the stories of *Exodus* discussed here (*Ex.* 3:18, 5:3). This epithet refers to the god to whom the Hebrew tribes paid allegiance before their crystallization into Israel under Moses.

As is well known, the term *Hebrews ('Ivrim)* is associated with the term *Habiru*, which designates the nomadic population in the ancient Near East during the second millennium BCE. The "god of the Hebrews" was worshiped by all sorts of nomads in the area of Sinai and the Negev: the Midianites and Kenites, as well as the Israelites. Most important in this respect is the new, extrabiblical evidence which came to light in the last decades. In the Egyptian topographical lists of King Amenhotep III (1417–1379 BCE) discovered in the temple of Amon at Soleb in Nubia as well as in the list of King Ramses II (1304–1237 BCE) discovered at Amarah West, we find "the land of nomads [of] Yahveh," along with "the land of nomads [of] Seir" (see Raphael Gibeon, *Les bédouins Shosu des documents égyptiens*, Leiden, 1971, nos. 6a, 16a). A land of nomads associated with Yahveh alongside the land of Edom (Seir) reminds us of the old traditions of Israel, according to which Yahveh appeared from Sinai, Edom, Teman, Paran, and Midian (*Dt.* 33:2, *Jgs.* 5:4, *Hb.* 3:3–7). The fact that Yahveh's revelation is associated with places scattered over the whole Sinai Peninsula as well as over the Edomite territory east of Sinai seems to indicate that Yahveh was venerated by many nomads of Sinai and southern Palestine and that "the land of nomads of Yahveh" refers to the whole desert to the east of the delta. To be sure, the god revealed to Moses and adopted by the Israelites reflects a unique phenomenon. Monotheism did come out of Israel and not out of Edom or Midian. However, in the light of the new evidence, one must consider the existence of some kind of proto-Israelite belief in Yahveh in the wilderness region of Sinai and Edom (cf. S. Herrmann, "Der Name Jhw in den Inschriften von Soleb." *Fourth World Congress of Jewish Studies,* vol. 1, Jerusalem, 1967, pp. 213–216; B. Mazar, "Yahveh came out from Sinai," *Temples and High Places in Biblical Times: Proceedings of the Colloquium in Honor of the Centennial of Hebrew Union College–Jewish Institute of Religion, Jerusalem, 14–16 March 1977,* ed. A. Biran, 1981, pp. 5–9). The Egyptian inscriptions which speak about nomads living in the land of Yahveh make it easier for us to understand the biblical traditions about the connections between the Israelites, the Kenites, and the Midianites during their wanderings in Sinai. Moses marries the daughter of Jethro, the Midianite priest (*Ex.* 2:16ff., 3:1f.), and it is during his stay with Jethro that he visits the Mountain of God. According to *Exodus* 18:11, Jethro gives full recognition to the god Yahveh and even helps Moses to organize the judicial institutions of Israel (*Ex.* 18:14–27). On another occasion we find Moses proposing to his father-in-law to join him and serve as a guide for the Israelites in the wilderness (*Nm.* 10:29–32). In *Judges* 1:16 we hear that the Kenites of the clan of Jethro settled together with the tribe of Judah in the Negev.

All this shows that there were close relations between the Israelites and other nomads in the desert, and, as we have indicated above, Yahveh's appellation in *Exodus,* "the god of the Hebrews," seems to support this notion. Another important contribution to the problem discussed here is the archaeological findings in the area. Excavations at Timna, some 30 kilometers (19 miles) north of the Gulf of Aqabah, have shown that the Midianites who built a shrine on the top of an Egyptian sanctuary mutilated the statue of the Egyptian goddess Hathor and reused many objects from the original structure. According to the excavator, Benor Rothenberg, there is evidence of a tent-sanctuary the Midianites erected on the place of the Egyptian shrine, and this brings to mind the tabernacle of the Israelites in the desert (B. Rothenberg, "Timna," in *Encyclopedia of Archaeological Excavations in the Holy Land,* ed. Michael Avi-Yonah and Ephraim Stern, vol. 4, 1978).

In this Midianite sanctuary a copper snake was found, which reminds us of the copper serpent made by Moses and mounted on a standard (*Nm.* 21:4–9). This was the only votive object found in the sanctuary. The Egyptian representations of the goddess Hathor were effaced, and the central niche was left empty. All this should be interpreted as a reaction of the Midianite nomads against Egyptian religion and culture, not unlike the Israelite reaction against pagan idols. Israelite monotheism is described in *Exodus,* as emerging out of a wrestling with Egyptian religion and magic (cf. *Ex.* 7:8ff., 8:12f., 12:12). Indeed, the aniconic tendency of Israel's religion is characteristic not only of ancient Israel but also of other nomadic tribes in the wilderness of Sinai and southern Palestine and seems to have persisted down to the period of the Nabateans in the third to second century BCE.

The affinity of Israel's faith with the faith of their nomadic confederates is clearly expressed in the episode about Jehu, the king of Israel (c. 842–815 BCE) who, by his zeal for Yahveh and his opposition to the Canaanite Baal, asked Jehonadab the son of Rechab to cooperate with him (*2 Kgs.* 10:15–16). The Rechabites, who were associated with the Kenites (*1 Chr.* 2:55: cf. 4:12 [Septuagint]), preserved their nomadic way of life for hundreds of years (cf. Diodorus Siculus 9.9 on the first Nabateans). They were persistent in their zeal for Yahvism (see *2 Kgs.* 10:16), which was the faith of their ancestors, the nomads who lived in the land of Yahveh, according to the Egyptian inscriptions. In this connection it should be noted that the ninth-century BCE prophet Elijah who, like Jehu, opposed the Baal worship, made a pilgrimage to Sinai to express his zeal for Yahveh (*1 Kgs.* 19), and, as will be shown below, reestablished the cult of Mount Carmel according to the Mosaic principles and Sinaitic traditions. The trend in the ninth century against Baal stirred a movement which strove for a return to the old Mosaic worship.

Exodus from Egypt. Among the nomadic tribes in the land of Yahveh (that is, the Sinai Peninsula), the Israelites were under Egyptian control, and, as I have indicated, the religion of Israel actually took shape in the course of a struggle with Egyptian religion and culture. As shown above, the Midianites, who were close in their religion to the Israelites, also fought Egyptian cult and religion. The struggle of the Israelite tribes with the Egyptians comes to full expression in the story about the liberation of Israel from "the house of bondage"—that is, the Exodus, which became the hallowed Israelite epic.

Historical background. Egyptian documents tell us about constant movements of nomads from Edom and other eastern regions into Egypt as well as of movements from Egypt into the desert. In one of these documents (Papyrus Anastasi VI) we read about the entrance of nomads into the pasturage of the delta: "We have finished letting the Shosu nomads of Edom pass the fortress . . . to keep them alive and to keep their cattle alive," (James B. Pritchard, *Ancient Near Eastern Texts relating to the Old Testament,* 3d ed., Princeton, 1969, p. 259), and in another we are told about the pursuit of runaway slaves (ibid.). This calls to mind the biblical traditions about the Israelite tribes entering Egypt in order to survive a famine (*Gn.* 45:7) and about their subsequent escape from slavery (*Ex.* 13–14). The Exodus stories may perhaps be traced back to a clash between a group of enslaved Hebrew nomads and the Egyptian authorities.

Biblical account. According to biblical traditions, the leader of the Israelites was Moses, an Egyptian-born man (cf. *Ex.* 2:19) who was at odds with the Egyptian authorities and had been forced to flee to the desert. There he found shelter amongst the Midianites and married the daughter of the Midianite priest Jethro (compare the Egyptian prince Sinuhe, who fled Egypt and found shelter in the house of one of the leaders of an Asiatic tribe). His acquaintance with the Midianites and his previous associations with Egypt enabled him to conceive his plans for the liberation of his brethren from Egyptian slavery. Moses availed himself of his ties with the Midianites and Kenites in order to find his way in the wilderness of Sinai (cf. *Nm.* 10:29–32), and these ties were remembered for hundreds of years among the tribes of Israel (cf. 1 *Sm.* 15:6). Furthermore, according to *Exodus* 18:12, Moses and Aaron and the elders of Israel participated in the common sacrificial meal prepared by Jethro, the Midianite priest, and learned from him how to administer justice, which procedure Moses initiated among the Israelite tribes.

Religious meaning ascribed. The successful flight of the Israelites and their interpretation of it as divine salvation turned into the main vehicle of national-religious education. The God of Israel was always hailed as the one who redeemed the people from "the house of bondage" (see the prologue to the Ten Commandments, *Ex.* 20:1 and *Dt.* 5:6), and the events of the Exodus were recited to the children of Israel, especially during the festival of Passover, in order to teach them loyalty to God (*Ex.* 12:26–27, 13:8, 14–16; *Dt.* 6:20–25). The events of the Exodus were also recited during religious gatherings of the tribes when they recounted their glorious past and the divine help given them (*Dt.* 29:1–5; *Jos.* 24:5–7; *1 Sm.* 12:6–8; etc.). Individual thanksgiving also opened with praises of God for his deliverance of Israel from Egypt (*Dt.* 26:5–9).

The liberation from Egyptian slavery was the reason behind the divine command for the abolishment of slavery within Israel—"For they are my servants, whom I freed from the land of Egypt, they may not give themselves over into slavery" (*Lv.* 25:22)—and was similarly used as motivation for not oppressing the stranger—"You shall not wrong a stranger or oppress him, for you were strangers in the land of Egypt" (*Ex.* 22:20; cf. *Ex.* 22:9); "You shall love the stranger, for you were strangers in the land of Egypt" (*Dt.* 10:19; cf. *Lv.* 19:34). The liberation from "the house of bondage" was considered an act of grace by the God of Israel for which the people were to express their gratitude by being loyal to God, that is, by keeping his commandments. This loyalty had to be endorsed by a solemn act: a covenant between God and Israel.

Early Cultic Worship. According to Pentateuchal sources, God revealed himself to the people on a specific mountain called Sinai or Horeb. However, ancient poems hail several places in the Sinai Desert as places of theophany. For example, *Deuteronomy* 33 speaks of YHVH coming from Sinai, Seir, and Mount Paran (33:2; cf. *Jgs.* 5:4-8). In *Habakkuk* 3 we read that God comes from Teman and from Mount Paran, and in the continuation of this poem Cushan and Midian are also mentioned. In all of these instances God sets out from his holy abode (on the mountain) to save his people, not to give laws as in the later prosaic sources. Furthermore, in these poems the deity sets out not from a single hallowed place (e.g., Sinai or Horeb) but from various places scattered throughout the Sinai Peninsula and the northwestern Arabian Desert. It seems that there were several holy mountains in this area that served the nomads who venerated YHVH.

This supposition can be supported by the excavations at Mount Karkom in the Negev (see Emmanuel Anati, "Has Mt. Sinai Been Found," *Biblical Archaeology Review* 11, 1985, pp. 42–57). This mountain constituted a sacred site for nearly a thousand years (3000 BCE to 2000 BCE) and displays features that characterize Mount Sinai as it is presented in the Pentateuchal tradition. At the foot of this mountain twelve standing stones were discovered. These stones are placed next to a structure that looks like an altar (cf. *Ex.* 24:4). A cleft was discovered in the mountain that is similar to the cleft in the rock, described in *Exodus* 33:22, in which Moses hides himself.

Such excavational findings suggest that the Sinai Desert was the site of a long tradition of cultic practices; Mount Sinai was only one of many cultic sites. The elaborate biblical descriptions of the cultic practices at Mount Sinai may reveal aspects of worship at such sites throughout the desert. The center of the tribal worship was the Mountain of God, ascent to which was allowed only to the priesthood and the elders (*Ex.* 24:1–2, 24:9, 24:14). Access to the godhead was the privilege of the prophet Moses alone (*Ex.* 3:5, 19:9–13, 19:20–22, 24:15, 33:21–23, 34:2ff.). Beneath the mountain stood an altar and twelve pillars (*Ex.* 24:4), where sacrificial rites were performed.

A reflection of this procedure may be found in the stories of the prophet Elijah, who tried to revive the old nomadic religion in defiance of that brought in by the

Phoenicians (*1 Kgs.* 18–19). Like Moses, Elijah ascends Mount Horeb (*1 Kgs.* 19), and the divine revelation to him is similar to God's revelation to Moses in *Exodus* 33. Both stand at the opening of a cave or rock with their face hidden or wrapped (*Ex.* 33:22; cf. *Ex.* 3:6; *1 Kgs.* 19:13) while seeing God's "back" pass (*Ex.* 33:23, 34:6; *1 Kgs.* 19:11). Both fast forty days and forty nights before or during their encounter with the deity (*Ex.* 24:18, 34:28; *Dt.* 9:9ff.). They demonstrate their zeal toward God in a similar manner: Moses commands the killing of the men who violated the covenant and worshiped the golden calf (*Ex.* 32:37–38); Elijah slaughters the prophets of Baal out of zeal for Yahveh and his covenant with the children of Israel (*1 Kgs.* 18:40, 19:10, 19:14).

More instructive is the parallel of the cultic establishment by Moses at Sinai and by Elijah at Mount Carmel. Like Moses, who builds an altar at Sinai and erects twelve stone pillars there in order to mark the bond between God and Israel, Elijah restores the altar of Yahveh at Carmel with twelve stones, which represent the tribes of Israel, and performs the sacrificial rite, which symbolizes the presence of God and the reestablishment of the relationship with him (*1 Kgs.* 18:30ff.). Just as the people at Sinai confirm their bond with God by a solemn declaration of loyalty ("The people declared unanimously: 'Whatever Yahveh commanded we shall do,'" *Ex.* 24:3, 24:7; cf. *Ex.* 19:5), so the people gathered at Mount Carmel declare, "Yahveh alone is God" (*1 Kgs.* 18:39). Furthermore, the establishment of Yahveh's cult at Mount Carmel is strikingly similar to its establishment at the Tabernacle at Sinai. In the Priestly account of the dedication of the Tabernacle (*Lv.* 9:24), we read that when the people saw that the fire of Yahveh consumed the burnt offering, they fell on their faces and shouted (that is, they proclaimed in a hymnic way the praise of God). Similarly, we read of the ceremony at Mount Carmel that when all the people saw the fire of Yahveh consuming the burnt offering, and so on, they fell on their faces and said, "Yahveh alone is God, Yahveh alone is God" (*1 Kgs.* 18:39).

Though not all of these features may be traced to the time of Moses, it seems that most of them are rooted in the ancient nomadic reality of the Israelite tribes reflected in Mosaic tradition. In the Elijah stories there is a conscious tendency to reshape the religion as it was in the Mosaic period, which means that there was a strong awareness in Israel of the period of the Sinai revelation and its importance for the faith of the nation. In the light of the adduced parallels we may say that the Mosaic religion as presented in the Pentateuch was already a living tradition in the northern kingdom of Israel in the ninth century BCE. This implies that the kernel of this tradition goes back to premonarchic times, when tribal religion was fresh and dominant in the life of Israel and historically close to the Mosaic period.

Covenant between God and Israel. The covenant of Sinai, which became so central in the religion of Israel, denotes not a bilateral agreement between the deity and the people but rather a commitment by the people to keep the law of YHVH as it is inscribed on tablets and found in the "Book of the Covenant" (*Ex.* 24:3–8). The word *covenant* (Heb., *berit*) means a bond or obligation that is accompanied by a pledge or oath and that is validated by sanctions, dramatized curses, threats, and the like performed in specific cultic rites.

A very old Mosaic cultic rite not repeated in later periods is the blood covenant as described in *Exodus* 24:3–8. After Moses builds an altar at the foot of Mount Sinai and erects twelve stone pillars, he prepares sacrifices and uses the blood of the animal sacrifices for the covenantal ceremonies. Half of the blood he sprinkles on the altar (and, apparently, on the stone pillars), and the other half he puts into basins in order to sprinkle it over the people. Then he declares: "This is the blood of the covenant that the Lord [YHVH] has cut with you" (*Ex.* 24:8).

Blood covenantal ceremonies are attested in ancient nomadic societies. Herodotus (3.8), writing in the fifth century BCE, tells about covenantal procedures of the ancient Arabs. We read that the covenant was performed by taking blood of the participants' thumbs and smearing it on the holy stones which stood between them. A closer analogy to the Sinaitic blood ritual is found in a Ramesside ostracon of the twelfth century BCE. Here we read about a father reproaching his son for associating himself with the Semites of the delta by eating bread mixed with blood, that is, by making a pact with them (see Jaroslav Ćerny, "Reference to Blood Brotherhood among Semites in an Egyptian Text of the Ramesside Period," *Journal of Near Eastern Studies* 14, 1955, pp. 161–163). The fact that the blood ritual is found only in the Sinaitic ceremony may teach us that it belongs to the ancient nomadic reality and therefore reflects a Mosaic background.

Revelation at Sinai. In the description of the Sinaitic cult we find a clear distinction between the place of revelation on Mount Sinai and the place of worship below the mountain. This situation is reflected in the tradition about the tent of meeting *(ohel mo'ed)* at Sinai. According to *Exodus* 33:7–11, Moses pitches the tent of meeting outside the camp, and there it serves as a place of encounter between God and Moses. This contrasts with the later description of the Tabernacle by the Priestly source, which conceives the tent of meeting as the sanctuary in the middle of the camp, where Moses meets

God (cf. *Ex.* 29:42–43; 40:34–35). The two phenomena, revelation and cult, which previously existed separately, amalgamated here, a situation which prevailed in later times when prophecy and cult joined hands in the Israelite and Judahite temples.

The place of revelation, be it the top of the mountain or the tent outside the camp, was out of bounds to the people. Indeed, according to the Sinaitic tradition it was Moses alone who received the words of God (the Decalogue), and as mediator, he delivered them afterward to the people. Literary criticism shows that gradually the notion developed that all Israel witnessed the theophany at Sinai and received with tremor the Ten Commandments. The rest of the laws were given indirectly; that is, they were transmitted through Moses (*Ex.* 24:3, *Dt.* 5:28ff.). But the distinction between two kinds of divine legislation, a short one written on tablets *(luḥot)* and a longer one written on a "book" *(sefer)*, always prevailed. As described in *Exodus* 32, the Ten Commandments, the basic constitution of Israel, were written by God on the tablets, which were put into the Ark, which represented the footstool of the deity, as described above. As holy documents they were deposited, as it were, beneath the feet of God, a procedure known to us from other ancient Near Eastern cultures.

That the words written on the tablets of the covenant are identical with the commandments of *Exodus* 20 is explicitly said in *Deuteronomy* 5:19, 9:10, and 10:4, and there is no reason to suppose that this was differently understood in former times. A series of cultic commandments in *Exodus* 23:10–19 (paralleled in *Exodus* 34:10–26) has been considered the original Decalogue by some scholars, who see the traditional Decalogue (*Ex.* 20:1–14) as a later ethical decalogue inspired by prophetic circles. But there is no warrant for this supposition. The division of the series of laws in *Exodus* 23:10–19 and 34:10–26 into ten discrete commandments is highly controversial, and the idea that a "cultic decalogue" should be more ancient than an "ethical" one has no basis at all. There is nothing specifically prophetic in the ethical decalogue; on the contrary, one can show that the prophets drew upon it (see *Hos.* 4:2, *Jer.* 7:9) and not vice versa. The "ten words" written on the tablets (cf. also *Ex.* 34:27) should be seen as identical with the commandments in *Exodus* 20:2–17 (and *Dt.* 5:6–18), while the series of cultic laws in *Exodus* 23:10–19 and 34:10–26 belongs to the Book of the Covenant.

The Ten Commandments: Their Essence and Function. From the point of view of content and form there is no difference between the Ten Commandments and other laws. The various law codes of the Bible contain the same injunctions which are attested in the Decalogue in both its versions. The prohibitions against idolatry and swearing falsely, the observance of the Sabbath, the honoring of parents, and the prohibitions against murder, adultery theft, and false witness—all these appear again and again in the various laws of the Pentateuch. The only exception is the injunction against coveting a neighbor's property, and this is indeed indicative of the particular nature of the Decalogue.

Let me state the five most particular and most characteristic features of the Decalogue.

1. *Universality.* In contrast to the ordinary laws whose enactment depends on particular personal or social circumstances such as sacrifices offered in various conditions (e.g., priestly dues dependent on income; civil laws dependent on ownership of property; laws of matrimony dependent on family status, etc.), the ordinances of the Decalogue apply to everybody regardless of circumstances. Every Israelite is committed not to practice idolatry and not to swear falsely, to observe the Sabbath and honor his or her parents, not to murder, not to commit adultery, not to steal, not to give false witness, and not to covet, no matter what his or her personal status is or in what society or in which period he or she lives. The commandments have thus universal validity.

2. *Restrictive conditionality.* The commandments are for the most part formulated in the negative, and even the positive, such as observance of the Sabbath and honoring one's parents, are in fact prohibitions. The observance of the Sabbath is explained by way of a prohibition: "Six days you shall work but the seventh day is a Sabbath . . . you shall not do any work" (*Ex.* 20:9–10). Similarly, the object of the commandment to honor one's parents is to prevent offense or insult to them, as implied by the various other laws concerning parents (cursing and beating in *Exodus* 21:15, 21:17, and in *Leviticus* 20:9; rebellion and disobedience in *Deuteronomy* 21:18–21). These negative conditions determine the moral obligations or restrictions demanded of every member of this special community governed by the Decalogue.

3. *Instructability.* The commandments are concisely formulated and contain a typological number of units (ten) easy to inculcate. Biblical scholarship long held that the original Decalogue was even shorter than the present version and was approximately like this:

1. I am the Lord your God, you shall have no other god beside me.
2. You shall not make for yourself a sculptured image.
3. You shall not swear falsely by the name of the Lord your God.
4. Remember to sanctify the Sabbath day.
5. Honor your father and your mother.

6. You shall not murder.
7. You shall not commit adultery.
8. You shall not steal.
9. You shall not bear false witness against your neighbor.
10. You shall not covet your neighbor's house.

That the present form of the Decalogue is expanded may be learned from the fact that the explanation of the Sabbath commandment in the version of the Decalogue in *Deuteronomy* is completely different from that in the version in *Exodus*. This shows that both authors had before them a short commandment which they expanded, each in his own way. The author of the *Exodus* version added an explanation of a sacral-cosmogonic nature, while the author of *Deuteronomy* added an explanation of a sociohumanistic nature. The terse structure and short form of the Decalogue, the typological number ten divided into two (commandments concerning man versus God and commandments concerning man versus his neighbor), enabled their engraving on two stone tablets and their learning by heart. This intimates that these commandments make up a set of fundamental conditions which every Israelite was obliged to know and to inculcate.

4. *Covenantal, nonlegislative nature.* The commandments are, as indicated, essentially categorical imperatives of universal validity; they are beyond a specific historical time and place and independent of circumstances. Therefore no punishment is prescribed, and no detailed definition of each crime is given. One might ask what kind of theft is meant in the eighth commandment and what would be the thief's punishment, but these questions are irrelevant since the commandments are not intended to represent legislation as such; rather, they constitute the formulation of God's decrees set as conditions for being part of the covenantal community. The tenth commandment, not to covet, is irrelevant for any court legislation since no court could enforce punishment for mere intention (cf. Bernard S. Jackson, *Essays in Jewish and Comparative Legal History*, Leiden, 1975, pp. 212ff.). It is a principle employed by God's justice for the holy community and not by jurisprudence of man. Only under the terms of a covenant with God could man be punished for violation of such a commandment. The commandments are given to the people and not applied to the court. Anyone who does not observe these commandments excludes himself from the community of the faithful.

5. *Personal, apodictic nature.* The commandments are formulated in the second person singular, as if they were directed personally to each and every member of the community. This formulation of "I and thou" is not found in the legal corpora in the ancient Near East and indeed looks strange in human jurisprudence. The latter is usually formulated in casuistic style, that is, stating the objective case (in the third person) and giving the terms of punishment for the violation. On the contrary, in the Decalogue we find the apodictic style, which addresses the listener in the second person and does not mention punishment at all. This bears the character of instructions given by a master to his pupils or by a lord to his vassals. Indeed, this style is prevalent throughout the Bible in the various instructions and adjurations of the highest king to his subjects. (See my "The Origin of the Apodictic Law," *Vetus Testamentum* 23, 1973, pp. 63–75.) It is rooted in the covenantal assembly, where the God of Israel confronts his subjects and addresses them personally.

The Decalogue is, then, distinguished by its concisely worded basic obligations directed at every member of the Israelite community and is an aspect of a special covenant with God. It is an Israelite creed similar to the Shemaʿ declaration (*Dt.* 6:4), which also consists of an easily remembered verse containing an epitome of the monotheistic idea and serving as an external sign of identification for monotheistic believers. It is no accident that both the Decalogue and the Shemaʿ were recited together in the Temple (*Tam.* 5.1). In *Deuteronomy* the whole Decalogue pericope (chap. 5) precedes the Shemaʿ passage (*Dt.* 6:4f.), which opens Moses' discourse, so that the combination of both in liturgy has its roots in the tradition of *Deuteronomy* itself.

Though we do not have clear evidence of when the Decalogue was crystallized and accepted, it seems to be very old. It is referred to by the eighth century BCE prophet Hosea (*Hos.* 4:2) and later by Jeremiah (*Jer.* 7:9) and is cited in two ancient psalms (*Ps.* 50:7, 50:18–19, 81:9–11), and one cannot deny that it might date from the beginning of Israelite history; it may even be traced back to Moses, the founder of Israel's religious polity.

A clear parallel in the ancient world to such a phenomenon as Moses, the prophet who reveals divine commands to the people, is to be found in a Greek document of the Hellenistic period. In a private shrine of the goddess Agdistis in Philadelphia (modern-day Alaşehir), in Asia Minor, an oath inscribed in a foundation stone of the sanctuary was found which contains injunctions similar to the ethical part of the Decalogue: not to steal, not to murder, not to commit adultery, and so on. These were revealed in a dream by the goddess Agdistis to the prophet Dionysius, who inscribed them on the stela of the sanctuary (see F. Sokolowski, *Lois sacrées de l'Asie Mineure*, 1955, no. 20, ll. 20ff.). It is also said in the inscription that whoever will violate one of the mentioned commandments will not be allowed to enter the shrine. Although this document is of late origin (first century BCE), it undoubtedly reveals ancient religious practice which is typologically similar to that of the Decalogue: a concise set of commandments revealed by a god to his prophet, who is to transmit them to the believers.

The tablets containing the Decalogue thus constituted a kind of binding foundation-document for the Israelite community. With the disappearance of the Ark of the Covenant and the tablets of the covenant sometime during the existence of the First Temple, the Decalogue was freed from its connection to the concrete symbols to which it was previously attached. At sacred occasions and every morning in the Temple, the Decalogue was customarily read, and all who were present would commit themselves to the covenant by oath *(sacramentum)* (cf. Pliny's epistle on the Christians who make an oath [*sacramentum*] every morning not to steal, commit adultery, etc., which is, no doubt, an allusion to the Decalogue).

Despite the similarity in background between the Decalogue tradition and the oath of the worshipers at the temple in Philadelphia, there is a decisive difference between them: the basic religious demands that are included in the first pentad of the Decalogue are not found and are not expected to be found in the Philadelphia oath. The first five commandments have a peculiarly Israelite nature: the name *YHVH* is mentioned in each commandment, whereas the last five commandments are of a universal nature and do not mention the name *YHVH*.

The Law. Biblical law consists of different literary types, indicating varying backgrounds of formation. In the oldest Israelite law corpus, *Exodus* 21–23, referred to in the Bible as *sefer ha-berit* ("book of the covenant"), we can recognize three types of law: civil law (*Ex.* 21:1–22:16), sociomoral law (22:17–23:9), and cultic ordinances (23:10–19). However, this distinction blurs in the later law corpora, where the laws mingle and blend, leaving little possibility of distinguishing between the various types. Furthermore, civil laws, which account for over half of the Book of the Covenant and make up the larger portions of Mesopotamian law codes, gradually diminish and disappear in the later law codes of the Bible, because the religious legislator in Israel is no longer concerned about them.

This blurring of borders between types of laws is also discernible in the form and formulation of the laws. While in the Book of the Covenant the civil laws use a style known as casuistic ("if . . . then"), which is predominant in the ancient Near Eastern law corpora, and the cultic and moral-ethical laws use primarily an imperative apodictic style ("you shall," "you shall not," "do not," etc.,), in the late collections the styles are mixed. A law commencing casuistically switches in midstream to the apodictic, and no distinction can be made between them (e.g., *Lv.* 22:18–22; *Dt.* 22:23–24).

Furthermore, the later codes, and especially the Deuteronomic code, crystallized in the seventh century BCE, tend to free themselves of their legalistic character and become humanistic, sermonizing, and rhetorical. Thus, explanations given add a moral motivation for obedience to the law, for example:

> You shall not oppress a stranger, for you know the feelings of the stranger, having yourselves been strangers in the land of Egypt. (*Ex.* 23:9)

> Six days you shall do your work, but on the seventh day you shall cease from labor in order that your ox and your ass may rest and that you bondman and the stranger may be refreshed. (*Ex.* 23:12)

> You shall not rule over [your servant] ruthlessly, you shall fear your God. (*Lv.* 25:43)

> You shall not take bribes, for bribes bland the eyes of the discerning and upset the plan of the just. (*Dt.* 16:19; cf. *Ex.* 23:8)

Furthermore, the "laws" themselves sometimes lose their legal character because of their moralistic, sermonizing nature:

> You shall not hate your kinsfolk in your heart . . . . Love your fellow as yourself. (*Lv.* 19:17–18)

> Do not harden your heart and shut your hand against your needy kinsman. Rather, you must open your hand and lend him sufficient for whatever he needs. (*Dt.* 15:7–8)

Such demands, which are directed to one's heart, are in fact moralizing discourses and cannot be considered legislative. Even cultic-ritual laws are explained and motivated by inner religious and moral reasons. For example, the obligation to sprinkle the blood of the sacrifice is explained by the necessity to atone for the shedding of blood (*Lv.* 17:1–7). The prohibition against eating carcass is motivated by the notion of the holiness of Israel (*Dt.* 14:21), and the same motivation is given for the command to ban the Canaanites and to destroy the pagan cultic installations in the Land of Israel (*Dt.* 7:5).

Covenant between God and Israel. The obligation of Israel toward God to keep his law equals the pledge to show loyalty to him. Besides the Mosaic covenant, which is based on the promise to observe the laws, we find in *Joshua* 24 a covenant which stipulates exclusive loyalty to the one God. Joshua's covenant, which took place in Shechem, modern-day Nablus (cf. *Dt.* 27 and *Jos.* 8:30–35), is mainly concerned with the choice of the God of Israel and the observance of strict loyalty toward him: "He is a jealous God. . . . if you forsake the Lord and serve alien gods, . . . he will make an end of you" (*Jos.* 24:19–20). This covenant, which was concerned with loyalty and made at the entrance to the Promised Land, was especially necessary because of the exposure to Canaanite religion and the danger of religious contamination.

In fact, the Shechemite covenant described in *Joshua*, which is associated—as indicated—with the foundation ceremony between mounts Gerizim and Ebal (cf. *Dt.* 27, *Jos.* 8:30–35), is close in its character to the covenant of the plains of Moab, presented in *Deuteronomy*. This covenant takes place before the crossing into the Promised Land and is defined as an act of establishing a relationship between God and Israel (*Dt.* 26:17–19, 27:9–10, 29:12; see expecially *Dt.* 27:9: "This day you have become a people belonging to the Lord your God").

The two covenants presented in the Pentateuch, the one at Sinai (*Ex.* 19–24) and the other at the plains of Moab in *Deuteronomy*, were patterned after the type of covenant prevalent in the ancient Near East between suzerains and vassals. Thus we find treaties or, rather, loyalty oaths between the Hittite suzerain and his vassals that contain the following elements:

1. Title and name of the suzerain,
2. Historical introduction, in which the suzerain tells about the graces he bestowed upon his vassal which justify the demand for the vassal's loyalty,
3. The basic stipulation of allegiance,
4. Stipulations of the covenant,
5. Invocation of witnesses,
6. Blessings for keeping loyalty and curses for disloyalty,
7. The deposit of the cofenantal tablets in the sanctuary,
8. The recital of the covenant before the vassal and his subjects.

All these are reflected in the Pentateuchal covenants. First comes God's introduction of himself, then a historical introduction (*Ex.* 19:4, *Dt.* 1–11; cf. *Jos.* 24:2–13), the statement of the basic postulate of loyalty (*Ex.* 19:5–6, *Dt.* 6:4–7:26, 10:12–22; cf. *Jos.* 24:19–24), covenantal stipulations (*Ex.* 21–23, *Dt.* 12–26), invocation of witnesses (*Dt.* 4:26, 30:9, 31:28; cf. *Jos.* 24:22, 24:27), blessings and curses (*Ex.* 23:16–28, *Dt.* 28), the deposit of the tablets of the covenant and the Book of the Covenant (*Ex.* 25:21, *Dt.* 10:1–5, 31:24–26; cf. *Jos.* 24:26), and the recital of the covenant before the people (*Ex.* 24:7, *Dt.* 31:9–13).

The forms which served a political need in the ancient Near East came then to serve a religious purpose in Israel. The religious use of a political instrument was especially suitable to Israel because the religion of Israel was the only religion that demanded exclusive (monotheistic) loyalty; it precluded the possibility of multiple loyalties, such as were found in other religions where the believer was bound in diverse relationships to many gods. The stipulation in political treaties demanding exclusive loyalty to one king corresponds strikingly to the religious belief in one single, exclusive deity. The political imagery applied to the divine being also helped crystallize the concept of the kingship of God so that in Israel the relations between the people and their God were patterned after the conventional model of relations between a king and his subjects. Thus, for example, political loyalty was generally expressed by the term *love* (see my article, "The Loyalty Oath in the Ancient Near East," in *Ugarit Forschungen* 8, 1976: 383–384). The emperor demanding loyalty of his subjects enjoins: "Love the king of Assyria as you love yourselves" (see Donald. J. Wiseman, *Vassal Treaties of Esarhaddon*, London 1958, p. 49). Similarly, the worldly emperor demands love "with the whole heart and soul," thus placing in context *Deuteronomy* 6:5: "and you will love the Lord your God with all your heart and with all your soul." *Love* here, as in the treaties, means loyalty and absolute devotion.

The notion of exclusive loyalty that is characteristic of the monotheistic belief has been dressed not only in the metaphor of the relationship between suzerain and vassal but also in the metaphor of the relationships between father and son and husband and wife. Just as one can be faithful only to one suzerain, to one father, and to one husband, so one can be faithful only to the God of Israel and not to other gods as well. The prophets elaborated the husband-wife metaphor in describing the relations between God and Israel (*Hos.* 3, *Jer.* 3:1–10, *Ez.* 16, 23).

Spiritual Transformation of Cultic Rituals. Cultic acts in pagan religions were performed in order to reenact events of the divine sphere, such as the celebration of the divine marriage *(hieros gamos)*, the dramatization of the death of the young god (Tammuz) and his annual resurrection, the ceremonies of awakening the god, and so forth. These are not attested at all in Israelite religion. By the same token, no magic procedure is applied in Israel's ritual. The priest never used spells in order to drive out evil spirits, and no incantations were used in the Israelite cult. It is true, sacrifices and purification rituals were very common in ancient Israel, and the techniques of sprinkling blood and burning incense before the deity were practiced like in the pagan religion. We even find the scapegoat ritual on the Day of Atonement (*Lv.* 16). However, in contrast to the pagan cult, all these are not accompanied by spells and magical formulas, save the confession of sin (*Lv.* 16:21).

The festivals and rituals of the Israelites, many of which derived from the customs and celebrations of ancient Near Eastern peoples, especially those of Hittite-Hurrian origin (cf. Moshe Weinfeld, 1983), underwent a transformation when adapted to the religion of the Israelites. As opposed to the mytho-theogonic explanations of the ancient Near Eastern festivals, the Israelite festivals are given historical explanations. The harvest festival as well as the ingathering festival are, for example, associated with the Exodus (*Ex.* 23:15, *Lv.* 23:42–43). [*See* Sukkot]. Even the first-fruit ceremony, in which one would expect to hear about the god who fertilizes the earth and provides the crops, consists only of a thanksgiving prayer in which the liberation from Egypt and the grant of land by God are hailed (*Dt.* 26:5–10). [*See* Shavu'ot].

The New Year signifies the creation of the world by God, as in other Near Eastern religions; but in contrast to the latter, the New Year festival in the religion of Israel does not commemorate the combat of the supreme god with his rivals, as we find in the Babylonian epic *Enuma elish,* which was recited in the New Year ritual. The New Year in Israel serves as a day of "rememberance before the Lord," indicating the beginning of God's rule over the world. It is called "day of acclamation" (*yom teru'ah, Nm.* 29:1; cf. *Lv.* 23:24) because of the blowing of the horn, which signifies the coronation of a new king. This is the day of God's ascent to the throne and of his salutation as king (cf. *Ps.* 47, 96–99) and therefore bears a cosmic character. In the liturgy of this day there comes to expression the hope that all the nations will recognize the sovereignty of Israel's god-king and will abandon idolatry (see Sigmund Mowinckel, *The Psalms in Israel's Worship,* vol. 1, Oxford, 1962, pp. 101–189).

The severance of the cult from its mythological and magical background transforms the ritual into a series of actions symbolizing spiritual values. The tenth day of the New Year festival, Yom Kippur, whose main purpose was the purification of the sanctuary (cf. the *kuppuru* rites in the Mesopotamian New Year festival Akitu), becomes the Day of Atonement for the sins of the individual. The ceremony of purification itself (*Lv.* 16) has much in common with Hittite and Assyro-Babylonian purification ceremonies (see Weinfeld, 1983, pp. 111–114); however, the distinct feature of the Israelite atonement ceremony is the confession of the sins of the children of Israel (*Lv.* 16:30) and the injunction associated with it to fast on this day (*Lv.* 16:29; cf. *Lv.* 23:27–32). [*See* Ro'sh ha-Shannah and Yom Kippur.]

A similar transformation from a cultic aspect to a spiritual-moral one may be recognized in the Sabbath (Heb., Shabbat), which was originally seen as a reenactment of God's rest during creation (*Gn.* 2:1–3, *Ex.* 20:11, 31:17). However, the institution of the Sabbath in Israel became a covenantal sign that attested to the establishment of an external relationship between God and his people (*Ex.* 31:16–17). Elsewhere we find a moral-humanistic interpretation of the institution of the Sabbath: it was instituted in order to give rest to the enslaved and deprived (*Ex.* 23:12) and was motivated by the liberation of Israel from Egyptian slavery (*Dt.* 5:15). The idea of resting every seventh day undoubtedly has roots in the ancient world, where certain days (connected with the lunar cycle) were considered unfit for human activities. In Israel, however, these days were dissociated from their ancient magical background and became sanctified days endowed with deep moral-religious meaning. [*See* Shabbat.]

Other rituals, too, underwent similar transformations. Circumcision, an initiation rite known among various peoples, was explained in Israel as a sign of God's covenant with Abraham and as signifying the bond between God and Israel (*Gn.* 17:7ff.). The act of circumcision was gradually spiritualized and was applied to the heart, as, for example, in *Jeremiah* 4:4: "Circumcise your hearts to the Lord and remove the foreskins of your hearts" (cf. *Dt.* 10:16). Circumcision of heart means repentance, as becomes clear from *Deuteronomy* 30:6: "The Lord, your God, will circumcise your heart . . . so that you will love him with all your heart and soul."

Two more ancient Near Eastern symbols were transformed within Israelite religion. The amulets worn on the forehead (phylacteries) by the peoples of ancient Egypt and Syria were considered protective symbols of the deity with whom the believer was associated (see O. Keel, "Zeichen der Verbundenheit: Zur Vorgeschichte und Bedeutung der Forderungen von Deuteronomium 6, 8f. und Par.," *Orbis Biblicus et Orientalis* 38, 1981, pp. 159–240). In Israel the signs on the forehead and on the arm were conceived as a reminder of the belief in the uniqueness of God (*Dt.* 6:4–8) and in the gracious act of Exodus from Egypt (*Ex.* 13:9, 13:16). In the same way that these symbols developed into the *tefillin* (a pair of small boxes containing scriptural passages), the tassels of the garments that were worn by aristocratic people in the ancient Near East became the four-cornered *tsitstsit,* a sign of holiness in Israel. Like these two fundamental symbols of the faith, most of the rituals and customs of ancient Israel were explained in a similar manner and thus were freed of their primitive connotations.

Centralization of the Cult: The Great Turning Point

Although there had existed in Israel a central shrine since the times of the Judges (cf. the temple at Shiloh, *1 Samuel* 1–2), small chapels and altars were also allowed. We hear about the patriarchs building altars in various places in the land of Canaan (*Gn.* 12:7–8, 13:18, 26:25), and we also find that during the time of the judges altars were built in the fields and on rocks (*Jgs.* 6:24, 13:19; *1 Sam.* 19:35). These other shrines were not prohibited; on the contrary, from Elijah's words at his encounter with God at Horeb (*1 Kgs.* 19:10, 19:14), we learn that the destruction of an altar dedicated to Yahveh is tantamount to killing a prophet of Yahveh. Elijah himself is praised because of his restoration of an altar to Yahveh on Mount Carmel (*1 Kgs.* 18). We first hear about the liquidation of provincial sites and altars and worship on the one altar in Jerusalem in the time of Hezekiah, king of Judah (715–686 BCE). It was he who destroyed all the altars in the country and commanded the people to offer sacrifices only at the Temple of Jerusalem (*2 Kgs.* 18:4, 18:29). It was this same king who dared to smash the bronze serpent which Moses made in the desert and to which people had burned incense up to that time (*2 Kgs.* 18:4; cf. *Nm.* 21:8–9).

The act of Hezekiah was actually the culmination of a process which started in the northern kingdom of Israel in the ninth century. That was the period of the struggle initiated by the prophets against the Tyrian god, Baal (*1 Kgs.* 17–19, *2 Kgs.* 9–10). From this struggle emerged the polemic against the golden calves erected in Dan and in Bethel (*1 Kgs.* 12:28ff.) and, finally, an iconoclastic tendency which affected the high places and altars all over the country, developing further a tendency to purge Israelite religion of pagan elements. The Canaanite cult involved worship at high places which contained pillars *(matstsevot)* and wooden symbols *(asherot)* next to the altar. Such cultic objects were seen as idolatrous by Hezekiah and Josiah (r. 640–609) and were therefore prohibited for use in Israelite worship. The legal basis for their acts is found in *Deuteronomy,* the only book of the Pentateuch which demands centralization of worship in a chosen place and prohibits erection of altars, pillars, and wooden symbols (see *Dt.* 12, 16:21–22).

The abolition of the provincial sites created the proper atmosphere for the spiritualization of worship as reflected in *Deuteronomy*. Even the Temple in Jerusalem was now conceived not as the physical house of the Lord but as the house in which God establishes his name (*Dt.* 12:11, 12:21, et al.). Furthermore in the reform movement of Hezekiah and Josiah, which is reflected in *Deuteronomy,* there is a shift from sacrificial ritual to prayer. The author of *Deuteronomy* is not concerned with the cultic activities in the Temple, such as daily offerings, burning incense, kindling the lamp, and so on. On the other hand, he is very interested in worship that involves prayer (*Dt.* 21:7–9, 26:5–10, 26:13–15), because he sees in liturgy the most important form of worship. Indeed, the historiographer of *Kings,* who worked under the influence of *Deuteronomy,* describes the Solomonic Temple not as a place for sacrifices but as a place for prayer (*1 Kgs.* 8:30, 8:34, 8:36, 8:39, et al.). This anticipated the institution of the synagogue, which developed during the Second-Temple period.

The Religion of the Book: Scribes and Wise Men. Hallowed as the "book of the *torah*" *(sefer ha-torah)* written by Moses (*Dt.* 31:9), *Deuteronomy* became the authoritative, sanctified guidebook for Israel. It was the first book canonized by royal authority and by a covenant between God and the nation, established by the people gathered in Jerusalem in 622 BCE, under the auspices of King Josiah (*2 Kgs.* 23:1-3). Only after other books were appended to *Deuteronomy* did the term *Torah* refer to the whole Pentateuch.

The canonization of holy scripture which started with *Deuteronomy* turned the Torah into an object of constant study. The Israelites were commanded to occupy themselves constantly (day and night) with the written book of the Torah and to teach it to their children (*Dt.* 31:11–13, *Jos.* 1:8, *Ps.* 1:2). It is not by accident that *Deuteronomy* is the only book in the Pentateuch which uses the verb *lamad/limed* ("teach, educate"). The verb is most characteristic of wisdom literature, which was studied in the schools of ancient Israel, and thus reveals the scribal-educative background of *Deuteronomy. Deuteronomy* is indeed the only book of the Pentateuch which enjoins the people to act "according to the written *torah*" (cf., e.g., *Dt.* 28:58). This implies that it is not enough to do the will of the Lord; one must comply with the Lord's will as it is written in the book. Hence the importance of studying the written word, which became so important in Judaism, Christianity, and Islam.

The sanctification of the holy writ brought with it the need for scribes and scholars who had the ability to deal with written documents. It is in the period of the canonization of *Deuteronomy* that we hear about scribes *(soferim)* and wise men *(ḥakhamim)* preoccupied with the written Torah (*Jer.* 8:8). After the return to Judah of many Jews from exile in Babylonia, the man who brought with him the book of the Torah and disseminated it in Judah was Ezra the scribe (*Ezr.* 7:6, 7:11).

Since the scribes and wise men were preoccupied with education in general, they did not limit themselves to sacred literature but also taught wisdom literature. The latter consists of didactic instructions on the one hand and speculative treatises on justice in the world (e.g., the *Book of Job*) and the meaning of life (e.g., *Ecclesiastes*) on the other. It is true that wisdom literature is cosmopolitan in nature and therefore addresses man as such and does not refer at all to Israel or to other sacred national concepts. However, this did not deter the scribes and wise men in Israel from incorporating this literature into their lore.

Wisdom literature was canonized and turned into an integral part of the holy writ. Furthermore, it was identified with the revealed Torah (cf. *Sir.* 24). *Deuteronomy,* in which the subject of education plays a central role, defines *torah* as wisdom (*Dt.* 4:6), and as has been shown (Weinfeld, 1972, pp. 260ff.), contains a great many precepts borrowed from wisdom tradition. The amalgamation of the divine word of Torah with the rational values of wisdom turned the law of Israel, especially the Deuteronomic law, into a guide of high moral and humane standards. For example, rest on the Sabbath is explained here as including rest for the slave as well as for his master; similarly, the seventh year *(shemiṭṭah)* in *Deuteronomy* is not just for letting the land lie fallow but, also, for the release of the debts of the poor.

The Impact of Prophecy upon Israelite Religion. Prophecy was an indispensable tool for any monarchic society in the ancient world. No independent ruler could go out to war or initiate an enterprise of national character without consulting a prophet. Israel was no different in this respect from other nations. The only major difference between Israelite and pagan prophecy was in the way of obtaining the oracle. In the pagan societies the prophets resorted to mechanical devices such as hepatoscopy or augury, whereas in Israel these were forbidden and only prophecy by means of intuition was legitimate.

The prophets were thus serving political and national needs, which is why it is no wonder that most of them were furthering in their prophecies the interests of the king and the people (e.g., *1 Kgs.* 22:12, *Jer.* 14:13–14, et al.). However, the classical prophets, as idealists, managed to free themselves from the professional group (see *Am.* 7:14) and proclaimed, when necessary, messages unfavorable for the king and the people. This made them unique in the ancient world. In their drive for justice and morality, they predicted punishment for the violation of justice, and their words were preserved since their predictions were understood to have been borne out. In their messages the classical prophets came in conflict with popular tradition. They rejected the accepted mode of formal divine worship (*Am.* 5:21, *Is.* 1:13, *Jer.* 7:21–22) and spoke sarcastically and cynically about its conventional institutions (*Am.* 4:4, 5:5; *Hos.* 4:15). They even predicted the destruction of the Temple, which the people considered blasphemous (*Jer.* 26).

However, the prophets also foresaw a new concept of an ideal future in their eschatological visions. Israel was seen as bearing a universal message destined to obliterate idolatry and to bring the gentiles to the one true God, the God of Israel (*Is.* 2:17–18; *Jer.* 3:17, 16:19–21; *Is.* 45:20–25, 56:1–8; *Zep.* 3:9; *Zec.* 2:15, 8:20–23; et al.). In the language of the anonymous prophet ("Second Isaiah") who was active during the Babylonian exile, Israel is designated to become a "light for the nations" so that God's salvation "may reach the ends of the earth" (*Is.* 49:6; cf. *Is.* 42:1–4, 51:4–5). During the same period another prophet envisions that many peoples shall come to seek the Lord in Jerusalem, and "ten men from nations of every tongue will take hold . . . of every Jew by a corner of his cloak and say: 'Let us go with you, for we have heard that God is with you'" (*Zec.* 8:20–23). These idealistic universal visions marked the beginning of a process which culminated in the spread of monotheism through the agencies of Judaism, Christianity, and Islam. They stood in conflict to a particularistic trend which developed during the return from the Babylonian exile in the times of Ezra and Nehemiah (the middle of the fifth century BCE) and which led to Ezra's expulsion of gentile women from the community of Israel (*Ezr.* 9–10).

The particularistic tendency, which expressed a national/ethnic fear of assimilation, was based on scripture enjoining Israel's separation from gentiles (*Ex.* 23:31–33, 34:12–16; *Lv.* 20:26; *Dt.* 7:3–4). These verses refer only to the Canaanite nations, but they were interpreted as being directed against all foreign nations (*Ezr.* 9:12, *Neh.* 13:1–3), and an ideology was based on the idea that the new congregation should represent "the holy seed" (*Ezr.* 9:2), uncontaminated by foreign blood. If this attitude had prevailed, no proselytism would have been possible. Thanks to the universalistic "prophetic" movement, which aspired to admit as many nations as possible into the sphere of Jewish religion (*Zec.* 2:15, 8:23), the particularistic trend was neutralized and proselytism became possible.

An anonymous prophet of this period ("Third Isaiah") even polemicizes with the isolationists and says, "Neither let the foreigner . . . say: 'The Lord will separate me [*navdel yovdilani*] from his people'" (*Is.* 56:3). The prophet employs the same words used by Ezra when revealing his isolationist tendencies: "And the seed of Israel separated themselves [*vayibadlu*] from all foreigners" (*Neh.* 9:2; cf. *Ezr.* 9:1–2). The Judaism of the Second-Temple period managed to reach a synthesis between the two opposing tendencies. Proselytizing was subject to the obligation to keep the law: a gentile could become an Israelite the moment he agreed to take upon himself the precepts of the Israelite religion as embodied in the Torah, especially circumcision (for men) and observance of the Sabbath (see *Isaiah* 56:4: "the eunuchs who keep my Sabbaths, . . . and hold fast to my covenant [through circumcision]").

The Crystallization of Judaism: The Postexilic Period. The period of exile and restoration left its deep marks on the people and changed their spiritual character. The severance of the exiles from their land made it easier for them to get rid of the cultic habits associated with the land, such as high-place worship, the burning of incense on the roofs (*Jer.* 7:17–19, 44:15–19), child offering (*2 Kgs.* 23:10; *Jer.* 7:31, 19:5; et al.), and other customs rooted in the Canaanite culture. After the exile, pagan worship never returned to Israel.

Because the exiles were deprived of sacrificial worship as a result of the principle of centralization of worship in Jerusalem, the spiritual, abstract nature of the religion was enhanced. The shift from sacrifice to prayer was facilitated by the very act of centralization, as shown above; however, as long as sacrifice was being practiced in the chosen place in Jerusalem, religion was still tied to the Temple. In the religious vacuum created following the destruction of the First Temple, stress came to be laid on the spiritual side of religion, and thus the way was paved for the institution of the synagogue, which is based on prayer and the recital of holy scripture. We do not know how this institution developed; it is clear, however, that in the times of Ezra and Nehemiah (end of fifth century and beginning of the fourth century BCE) it started its existence in Jerusalem. In *Nehemiah* 8–9 we find all the components of synagogue worship:

1. The recital of scripture with all the pertinent procedure, such as the reader standing on the pulpit (*Neh.* 8:4) displaying the scroll to the people while they stand up (*Neh.* 8:5), the recitation of blessings before the start of the reading (*Neh.* 8:6), and the use of the Targum (an Aramaic translation and explanation of the Torah; *Neh.* 8:8).
2. The reading of the Torah on each one of the holy days (*Neh.* 8:18).
3. The summoning of the people to bless the Lord before starting the prayer (*Neh.* 9:5).
4. Communal prayer (*Neh.* 9:6–14), which contains the elements of the Sabbath and festival conventional prayer.
5. The confession of sin and supplication (*taḥanun*; *Neh.* 9:16–37).

All this leaves no doubt that the synagogue service was already taking shape in the fifth century BCE. Since the service as described in *Nehemiah* 8–9 was sponsored by the leadership of the exilic community, it is likely that the exiles brought with them the liturgy as it had crystallized in Babylonia. This suggestion might be supported by the fact that the whole pericope of *Nehemiah* 8–9, which describes in detail the service of the congregation during the first month, the month of the High Holy Days, does not allude at all to Temple worship, which was undoubtedly quite intensive in this season of the year. The author does not refer to the Temple worship (the Second Temple was in existence since 516 BCE) or comment on this omission since its procedure was performed by priests according to ancient conventional principles.

The relatively newly established synagogal liturgy contained a great deal of edifying material: the doctrines of creation and election (*Neh.* 9:6, 9:7), sin and repentance, and the observance of the Sabbath and the Torah (*Neh.* 9:13–14); thus the liturgy turned into an instrument for the education of the people. Second-Temple Jewry was dominated by the Babylonian returnees who, as descendants of the preexilic Judahite aristocracy, managed to preserve the genuine tradition of classical Israel.

Another important factor which shaped the character of Second-Temple Judaism was the impact of prophecy. The fact that prophets of the First-Temple period had predicted the return to Zion after a period of exile added to the glorification of the prophets and to the trust in their words. People began to believe that the prophecies about Jerusalem as the spiritual center of the world would also be realized and that the nations would recognize the God of Israel and finally abandon their idolatrous vanities. This was supported by the exiles' physical encounter with idol worshipers in Babylonia. Convinced of the futility of idol worship (cf. *Is.* 54:6ff.), the exiles apparently tried to persuade their neighbors of it. Some of the enlightened foreigners seem to have been attracted by the peculiar but reasonable faith of the Jews and joined the Jewish congregation (*Is.* 56:1–8; see above), a first step in the spreading of monotheism, and one which prepared the ground for later proselytism and for Christianity. It was during these several centuries that the fundamental elements of Judaism were settled.

Observance of the Torah. The exiles took seriously not only the demand for exclusive loyalty to the God of Israel, which meant complete abolition of idolatry and syncretism, but also the positive commands of God embodied in the law of Moses. They felt obliged not only to fulfill the law in a general sense but to do exactly as written in the book. This demanded expert scribes and exegetes to investigate scripture and explain it to the people (see *Neh.* 8:8).

At this time the Tetrateuch, the first four books of the Pentateuch, was added to the "Book of the Torah," or *Deuteronomy,* which had been sanctified before the exile, with the reform of Josiah in 622 BCE. The Tetrateuch was composed of ancient documents that had already been codified in literary sources, such as the Yahvistic-Elohistic source and the Priestly code. After adding these sources to *Deuteronomy,* the name "Book of the Torah" was extended to the whole of the Pentateuch, namely, the Torah, which was thus also taken as comprising the "Book of Moses."

The Pentateuch, then, comprised various codes representing different schools or traditions and different periods which sometimes contradicted each other. However, all of them were equally obligatory. How then would one fulfill two contradictory laws? According to the Priestly code, for example, one has to set aside a tenth of his crop for the Levites (*Nm.* 18:21f.), while the Deuteronomic code (written after centralization of the cult) commands one to bring the tithe to Jerusalem and consume it in the presence of the Lord (*Dt.* 14:22ff.). These laws reflect different social and historical circumstances, but since both were considered to belong to the law of Moses, both were authoritative; therefore, in the Second-Temple period two types of tithe were introduced: the so-called first tithe, which was given to the Levites, and second tithe, which was consumed in Jerusalem.

No less a problem was the exact definition of the ancient law in order to apply it to life circumstances. Thus, for example, the commandment "you shall not do any work on the seventh day" (*Ex.* 20:9) is quite vague. What does *work* mean? Is drawing water from the well considered work (as in *Jubilees* 50.8)? Interpretation of the law split the people into sects; the most practical were the Pharisees, who fixed thirty-nine chief labors forbidden on the Sabbath (*Shab.* 7.2), and thus tried to adjust the law to life. The Essenes, however, were much more stringent in their understanding of work forbidden on the Sabbath. Before the Maccabean Revolt (166–164 BCE), making war was forbidden on the Sabbath; in the Maccabean times, when the nation fought for its existence, the people learned that it could not survive without permitting themselves to fight on the Sabbath.

The struggle for the correct interpretation of the Torah was actually the struggle to fulfill the will of the Lord, and in this goal all Jews were united.

The fate of the individual. The problem of individual retribution and the fact of the suffering righteous is mainly dealt with in wisdom literature: *Proverbs, Job,* and *Ecclesiastes.* In *Proverbs* the optimistic view prevails: everybody receives his reward in accordance with his deeds. If one sees a righteous man suffering and a wicked man succeeding, this perception is only an illusion. In the long run the righteous will be vindicated, and the evil will fail (*Prv.* 23:18, 24:14–20, et al.). The wisdom traditions of *Psalms* express this idea most explicitly:

> though the wicked sprout like grass
> though all evildoers blossom
> it is only that they may be destroyed forever.
> (*Ps.* 92:8; RSV 92:7)

> Do not be vexed by evil men;
> do not be incensed by wrongdoers;
> for they soon wither like grass,
> like verdure fade away.
> (*Ps.* 37:1–2)

A similar solution is reflected in the prosaic narrative of *Job*: Job, the righteous one, is restored to his former happiness after long suffering (1–2, 42:7–17).

A different philosophical solution is offered in the poetic section of *Job* (3:1–42:6). In this section the point is made that no one can understand the ways of God and that one should not expect any reward for his deeds. The true faith is one that is independent of material interest. A more skeptical, cynical solution to the problem is found in *Ecclesiastes,* in which everything is said to be predestined by God, and nothing can be changed by man. Hence, one should not complain but enjoy life as long as one can; otherwise everything in life is vanity.

A somewhat mystical response to the problem of seemingly unjust rewards is found in the religious lyrics of *Psalms,* especially in Psalm 73. The Psalmist is perplexed by the problem of the evildoers, "the ever-tranquil who amass wealth" (*Ps.* 73:12), but finds the answer in God's dwelling. Through his trust in God he feels completely secure:

> My body and my mind came to end,
> but God is my portion forever.
> They who are far from you are lost. . . .
> As for me, nearness to God is good.
> I have made the Lord God my refuge.
> (*Ps.* 73:26–28)

The eternal portion (*ḥeleq*) which the pious finds in God reminds one of the expression of later Judaism about the portion in the world to come. That there was in ancient Israel some belief in immortality or blessed posthumous existence may be learned from Psalm 16.

The Psalmist opens his prayer with a declaration that he seeks refuge in God, a declaration found also at the end of Psalm 73. Then he speaks about the holy in the earth (the ghosts, *Ps.* 16:3), and in this connection he mentions that he will have no part of their bloody libations, a procedure well attested in the ancient world in connection with necromancy (cf. Theodor H. Gaster, *Myth, Legend, and Custom in the Old Testament*, vol. 2. 1975). Afterward we hear an exclamation, similar to the one in Psalm 73:26–28: "You, Lord, are my alloted portion [*ḥelqi*]. . . . Delightful is my inheritance." (*Ps.* 16:5–6). He expresses his hope that his body will rest secure and that God will not let him down into She'ol and will not cause him to see the pit (*Ps.* 16:10); on the contrary, he hopes that God will let him see his presence (literally, "face") in perfect joy (*Ps.* 16:11). Most instructive here is comparison of the concept of She'ol with that of the portion of the Lord. She'ol, "the world of shades" *(refa'im)*, is here understood in a negative manner, not unlike the Geihinnom (Gehenna) of the Second-Temple period, and is actually the opposite of God's portion and inheritance, which is reserved for the pious. That such ideas prevailed in ancient Israel may be deduced from *Proverbs* 15:24, where we read: "For the knowledgeable [in God's knowledge] the path of life leads upward, in order to avoid She'ol below." This view is supported by *Ecclessiastes* 3:21, whose author questions the generally accepted premise by asking: "Who knows if the man's spirit does rise upward and if a beast's spirit does sink down into the earth?"

Human nature and destiny. The prevalent outlook in the Hebrew Bible is that "man's thoughts and inclinations are always evil" (*Gn.* 6:5); "his inclination is evil from his youth onwards" (*Gn.* 8:21). Yet the fact that man was created in the likeness of God (*Gn.* 1:27, 5:1; cf. *Ps.* 8:6) makes him potentially good. God implanted in him the striving toward good or the good inclination (cf. *yetser ṭov* in rabbinic literature) which complements the evil one (cf. the tree of the knowledge of good and evil in *Gn.* 2–3). Indeed, the prophets envisioned in the ideal future a type of man who is naturally good and, consequently, who will do no evil.

Isaiah describes the ideal man in the framework of his vision of eternal peace (*Is.* 11:1–9). A world of peace between man and animal will be filled with knowledge of the Lord as water covers the sea (*Is.* 11:9). Jeremiah predicted that in the days to come, when the new covenant *(berit ḥadash)* will be established with Israel, there will be no need for teaching one another because every man and child will know the Lord, that is, will know how to behave:

> I will put my law into their inmost being
> and inscribe it upon their hearts. . . .
> no longer will they need to teach one another
> and say to one another: "Know the Lord,"
> for all of them, from small to great,
> shall know me. (*Jer.* 31:33–34)

Obedience to God and respect for one another will be part of human nature, and force will not be needed to impose God's law.

Transformation to Second-Temple Judaism. The canonization of the Torah during the time of Ezra brought with it scribal activity and exegesis that marked the beginning of a new period. Over time, the religion gradually shifted away from the domain of the Temple and its functionaries. The will of God, expressed in holy scripture, could now be interpreted not only by the priests but by trained sages *(ḥakhamim)* and scribes *(soferim)*. This shift was due in part to the fact that after the destruction of the First Temple exiles in Babylonia had begun to base their worship on prayer and the recital of the Torah. Furthermore, Jews living outside the Land of Israel were not subject to many of the purity laws and taboos connected with the land of YHVH (see *Hos.* 9:3–5, *Am.* 7:17b; cf. *Jos.* 22:19, *1 Sm.* 26:19). What had been the Israelite religion became less dependent on the physical reality. For Jews living outside the land and for those who had returned, the spiritual dimension of Jewish religious life intensified as stress was laid on institutions of a spiritual nature that were unrelated or only symbolically related to Land and Temple—the Sabbath, synagogal service, religious ethical obligations, and the other fundaments of Judaism as it was to evolve.

[*Related articles include* Biblical Temple; God, *article on* God in the Hebrew Scriptures; Israelite Law; Priesthood, *article on* Jewish Priesthood; *and* Prophecy, *article on* Biblical Prophecy.]

BIBLIOGRAPHY

Albright, William F. *Yahweh and the Gods of Canaan.* London, 1968.

Alt, Albrecht. *Der Gott der Väter: Ein Beitrag zur Vorgeschichte der israelitischen Religion.* Stuttgart, 1929.

Cross, Frank Moore. *The Ancient Library of Qumrân and Modern Biblical Studies.* Rev. ed. Garden City, N.Y., 1961.

Cross, Frank Moore. *Canaanite Myth and Hebrew Epic: Essays in the History of the Religion of Israel.* Cambridge, Mass., 1973.

Eissfeldt, Otto. *The Old Testament: An Introduction.* Translated from the third German edition by Peter R. Ackroyd. Oxford, 1965.

Fohrer, Georg. *History of Israelite Religion.* Translated by David E. Green. Nashville, 1972.

Gaster, Theodor H. *Myth, Legend, and Custom in the Old Testament.* New York, 1969.

Kaufmann, Yeḥezkel. *History of the Religion of Israel* (in Hebrew). 8 vols. in 6. Jerusalem, 1937–1956. Translated by Moshe Greenberg as *The Religion of Israel: From Its Beginnings to the Babylonian Exile.* New York, 1972.

Mowinckel, Sigmund. *The Psalms in Israel's Worship.* 2 vols. Translated by D. R. Thomas. Oxford, 1962.

Noth, Martin. *Gesammelte Schriften zum Alten Testament.* Munich, 1960.

Pedersen, Johannes. *Israel: Its Life and Culture.* 4 pts. Translated by Aslaug Møller and Annie I. Fausbøll. Oxford, 1926–1947; reprint, Oxford, 1959.

Rad, Gerhard von. *Gesammelte Studien zum Alten Testament.* Munich, 1958.

Rad, Gerhard von. *Old Testament Theology.* 2 vols. Translated by D. M. G. Stalker. New York, 1962–1965.

Vaux, Roland de. *Les institutions de l'Ancien Testament.* 2d ed. Paris 1961. Translated by John McHugh as *Ancient Israel: Its Life and Institutions.* London, 1965.

Vaux, Roland de. *Histoire ancienne d'Israel* (1971). Translated by David Smith as *The Early History of Israel.* Philadelphia, 1978.

Weinfeld, Moshe. "The Covenant of Grant in the Old Testament and in the Ancient Near East." *Journal of the American Oriental Society* 90 (April–June 1970): 184–203.

Weinfeld, Moshe. *Deuteronomy and the Deuteronomic School.* Oxford, 1972.

Weinfeld, Moshe. "Social and Cultic Institutions in the Priestly Source against Their Ancient Near Eastern Background." In *Proceedings of the Eighth World Congress of Jewish Studies,* pp. 95–129. Jerusalem, 1983.

Wellhausen, Julius. *Prolegomena to the History of Israel.* Translated by J. Sutherland Black. Edinburgh, 1885. Reissued as *Prolegomena to the History of Ancient Israel.* New York, 1957.

Zimmerli, Walther. *Gottes Offenbarung: Gesammelte Aufsätze zum Alten Testament.* Munich, 1963.

MOSHE WEINFELD

ISRAEL MEIR HA-KOHEN. *See* Kagan, Yisra'el Me'ir.

ISSERLES, MOSHEH (c. 1520–c. 1572), known by the acronym RaMa (Rabbi Mosheh); Polish rabbi, halakhist, and scholar. Isserles was born in Cracow to one of the most powerful families of the Jewish community of sixteenth-century Poland and rose very rapidly to a position of prominence in the rabbinical world of Ashkenazic Jewry. Isserles's wealth and social status, as well as his ties by marriage to other prominent intellectual and communal figures in Polish Jewry, allowed him to wield substantial authority at a young age, primarily through the important *yeshivah* that he established in Cracow. His contributions to Jewish law and learning were vastly influential, and he was one of the few eastern European rabbis of his age to be venerated as a saintly leader for centuries after his death.

Isserles was trained in the Talmudic academy of Shalom Shakhna of Lublin, where he imbibed a fundamental commitment to the Ashkenazic traditions brought to Poland from Germany in the fifteenth century. He returned to his native Cracow to take up the position of its chief rabbi and remained in this post in the Polish capital until his death. The Rama synagogue in Cracow, which he built with his own wealth in 1553 as a memorial to his first wife, stands to this day as one of the most significant emblems of Jewish religiosity and learning in eastern Europe.

Isserles's prowess in Jewish law was revealed in his *responsa,* first published in Cracow in 1640, that displayed a distinctive synthesis of rigor and flexibility. While adhering to the Ashkenazic tradition of conservative interpretation, the Rama's rulings argued for a considerable degree of leniency in situations of severe economic or social stress and emphasized his belief in the importance of local customs in determining law. One *responsum* also detailed Isserles's controversial dedication to the study of philosophy: taken to task by his senior colleague Shelomoh Luria for citing Aristotle as an authority of note, Isserles proclaimed his commitment to the Maimonidean view of the relation between philosophy and theology while explaining that he had only read Aristotle through the medium of medieval Hebrew texts. Isserles opposed the contemporary practice of teaching mysticism to the young and untried. However, in a number of quasi-philosophical works, the most important of which was *Torat ha-'olah* (The Doctrine of the Offering; 1570), a symbolic analysis of the commandments concerning the ancient Temple in Jerusalem, he attempted to demonstrate the confluence of Jewish philosophy and Qabbalah.

Isserles also published a large number of commentaries and glosses on various parts of the Bible, the Talmud, and other rabbinic literature. But his major scholarly accomplishment and claim to fame was his participation in one of the crucial legal enterprises in Jewish history, the creation of the *Shulḥan 'arukh.* As a leading but relatively inexperienced jurist, Isserles recognized the need for a guide to Jewish law that would collate the rulings of recent scholars with classic interpretations and traditions. He had only begun to prepare such a compendium when he learned that the great Sefardic sage Yosef Karo of Safad had just published his *Beit Yosef,* an exhaustive code of Jewish law. Isserles revised his plan and produced his *Darkhei Mosheh,* which abridged Karo's work yet differed from it by insisting on the authority of local custom and recent precedents in determining correct rulings. Ten years later, Karo himself issued an abridgement of his original work, now entitled the *Shulḥan ʿarukh*—the "set table." Isserles responded by writing his *Mappah*—the "tablecloth"—which was an extensive commentary on Karo's work that argued for the pertinence of Ashkenazic customs and recent rulings. Immediately accepted as a critical amplification of Karo's work, Isserles's glosses were incorporated into the now collaborative *Shulḥan ʿarukh,* which became the authoritative codification of Jewish law and the object of continuous scholarly interest and debate.

[*For further discussion of Isserles's importance in the context of Jewish law, see* Halakhah.]

BIBLIOGRAPHY

There exists no critical scholarly study of Mosheh Isserles or his works. The most successful reverential treatment is Asher Siev's *Rabbi Mosheh Isserles* (New York, 1972), in Hebrew. A useful summary of Isserles's legal works can be found in the standard, if dated, history of Jewish law, Haim Chernowitz's *Toldot ha-posqim,* vol. 3 (New York, 1947), pp. 36–73. An excellent description of Isserles's role in composing the *Shulḥan ʿarukh* is available in Isadore Twersky's elegant essay "The *Shulhan ʿAruk:* Enduring Code of Jewish Law," reprinted in *The Jewish Expression* (New Haven, 1976), edited by Judah Goldin. Chapters 4–6 of Moses A. Shulvass's *Jewish Culture in Eastern Europe: The Classical Period* (New York, 1975) may also be consulted.

MICHAEL STANISLAWSKI

IŠTAR. *See* Inanna.

ĪŚVARA. The epithets *īśa, īśvara,* and *īśāna* (all translatable as "lord" or "possessor of power," from the Sanskrit verbal root *īś,* "have power") were applied to Hindu deities from early Vedic times but are especially employed in the *Bhagavadgītā* and post-Vedic sectarian literature as designations of the supreme god, variously named. *Īśvara* was also used by Patañjali in his system of Yoga as the denotation of the god who assists yogins in their spiritual endeavors.

The significance of the verbal form *īś* is clearly indicated in the *Ṛgveda,* where it is frequently used to indicate the powers of specific deities or their dominion over parts of the cosmos and the processes of nature. The Vedic gods are together declared to "have power over the whole world" (*Ṛgveda* 10.63.8); here absolute lordship is not yet ascribed to any single deity. The term *īśāna* ("the master, the ruling one") is applied to several deities in the *Ṛgveda* (including Indra, Mitra, Varuṇa, Soma, and Savitṛ) in recognition of particularized sovereignty, extraordinary powers, remarkable accomplishments, or the ability to bestow desired gifts of one kind or another, including immortality. Of particular significance is the use of the term in reference to the god Rudra (*Ṛgveda* 2.33.9), who is given the name Īśāna in the *Atharvaveda* and who in later Vedic texts, in the form of Rudra-Śiva, is called Great God (Mahādeva) and Great Lord (Maheśvara), as well as Īśāna, such appellations suggesting the rise of a theistic cult attached to this god. Certainly from the time of the *Atharvaveda Saṃhitā* and the *Taittirīya Brāhmaṇa,* Īśāna is the name of a distinctive deity—"the lord, the master" of the universe; this terminology reflects an understanding of the sacred that likely fed into the Upaniṣadic conception of the one Lord, from whom the cosmos emanates. He is the ruler of the cosmos, and spiritual knowledge of him bestows immortality.

The term *īśvara* appears only in the Saṃhitā of the *Atharvaveda* and not in the Saṃhitās of the other Vedas. It is used both as a general designation of the Vedic deities as "lords" or presiding powers (e.g., *Atharvaveda* 7.102.1) but also (as in *Atharvaveda* 14.6.4) as the specific designation of the cosmic being, Puruṣa, by whose sacrifice the cosmos came into existence (*Ṛgveda* 10.90). Puruṣa is called Lord *(īśvara)* of Immortality, an expression which, like the term *īśāna,* was to be developed more fully in the Upaniṣads, particularly the *Śvetāśvatara,* where the immortal and imperishable Lord *(īśa)* is the source of the cosmos that he rules *(īśate).*

In the Upaniṣads all three terms—*īśa, īśāna,* and *īśvara*—are employed to denote the Supreme Lord, the source and very being of the cosmos, with whom the individual soul is in some sense identical and spiritual knowledge of whom brings liberation from time-space existence. The *Īśa Upaniṣad* opens with the words "By the Lord enveloped *(īśāvāsyam)* must this all be." In the *Śvetāśvatara* a theistic note is struck by the identification of ultimate reality *(brahman),* the great lord and ruler *(īśāna)* of the cosmos, with Rudra. It is in the *Bhagavadgītā,* however, that the understanding of the nature of the cosmic lord is fully developed. Here "the lord of all creatures" *(bhūtānām īśvaraḥ)* is referred to as the "highest Person," the supreme self, and the object of loving devotion *(bhakti).* A "portion" of the Lord *(īśvara)* becomes the incarnate soul of the human individual and indwells the phenomenal world as its "inner controller" *(antaryāmin).* As in the *Śvetāśvatara,* so in the

Bhagavadgītā the Great Lord *(parameśvara)* is the wielder of the power of cosmic manifestation *(māyā)*, a dynamic deity who is yet the Lord beyond all other deities. This Great Lord is thus the object of personal worship as well as all-embracing reality and the very ground of being, the sacred in both its manifest and its unmanifest forms.

In the later Vedantic philosophies *Īśvara* is the designation of the Absolute *(brahman)* only in its relationship to the phenomenal universe but not in its ultimate nature. In Patañjali's Yoga, *Īśvara*, although God, is neither the efficient nor the material cause of the universe. His role is to serve as an object of concentration for the yogin, to represent a spirit *(puruṣa)* freed from the bonds of phenomenal existence and the very model of absolute freedom and liberation. For Patañjali, devotion to Īśvara *(īśvarapraṇidhāna)* is an intellectual act, and Īśvara is the ideal of spiritual existence.

BIBLIOGRAPHY

Banerjea, Jitendra. *The Development of Hindu Iconography.* 2d ed. Calcutta, 1956.

Daniélou, Alain. *Hindu Polytheism.* New York, 1964.

Eliade, Mircea. *Yoga: Immortality and Freedom.* 2d ed. Princeton, 1969.

Gonda, Jan. *Change and Continuity in Indian Religion.* The Hague, 1965.

Gonda, Jan. *Viṣṇuism and Śivaism: A Comparison.* London, 1970; New Delhi, 1976.

Keith, Arthur Berriedale. *The Religion and Philosophy of the Veda and Upanishads* (1925). 2d ed. 2 vols. Westport, Conn., 1971.

H. P. SULLIVAN

ITHNĀ' ʿASHARĪYAH. *See under* Shiism.

ITŌ JINSAI (1627–1705), Japanese *kangakusha* (Sinologist), educator, and Confucian philosopher. In 1681 Jinsai opened a private school, the Kogidō, in Kyoto and thus founded the Kogakuha, the school of Ancient Learning, a school of thought opposed to the Shushigakuha and the Yōmeigakuha, based on the thought of the Chinese thinkers Chu Hsi and Wang Yang-ming, respectively. The Kogidō, where Jinsai educated hundreds of students from the upper classes, continued uninterruptedly under Itō family management until 1871, when it gave way to the modern curriculum adopted from the West.

Jinsai, known for his personal modesty, forgiving nature, and broadmindedness toward other convictions, such as Buddhism, deserves credit not only as an outstanding moral teacher of the Tokugawa period but also as a scholar whose interests lay beyond his country's boundaries. Unlike the *kokugakusha*, the scholars of National Learning (Kokugaku), he prepared Japan for the assimilation of Western ideas in the mid-nineteenth century. He was highly appreciated by the Imperial House, and his main works were presented to the Throne. His achievements were publicly recognized by the Meiji emperor in 1907, and those of his gifted son Tōgai (1670–1736), by the Taishō emperor in 1915. Jinsai's grave can still be seen at the Nison'in, a Buddhist temple in the Saga district, northwest of Kyoto.

Based on two books, the *Analects* of Confucius and the *Mencius*, Jinsai's thought has several features that are rare, if not unique, for a Japanese Confucianist. Jinsai resolutely discards all Buddhist and Taoist accretions to authentic, pre-Han Confucian doctrines. His cosmogony ascribes the origin of all things to a single cosmic yet anthropomorphous force. He honors the classic *yin-yang* theory, which explains change and motion, but sees the origin of both *yin* and *yang* in one supreme ultimate, in turn equivalent to the moral concept of a supreme law governing all things. This law is benevolent and free from defects. Jinsai takes his monism one step further in his definition of Heaven, whom he calls ruler, conserver, supreme judge, and benefactor of mankind. Heaven is personified, although it is not always clear whether it is distinct from nature. In daily life, Jinsai showed the utmost respect for spiritual beings. With great forbearance he trusted in Heaven as a witness to his sincerity.

Jinsai's moral system flows from his anthropomorphic cosmology: man is originally good and bent toward perfection. There is no need for Taoist or Zenlike abstention and meditation. There is balance between intellect and will, although freedom remains undefined beyond the pregnant phrase "Will means directedness toward good." Practically, virtue is manifest in the four cardinal virtues: humaneness or love, justice, propriety, and wisdom. These are reducible to two, humaneness and justice, whose apex unites in the supreme virtue, humaneness.

Jinsai's life was a paean to that virtue, even though he stood, with the dignity befitting a scholar, somewhat aloof from his surroundings. His educational principles paralleled his character, holding the middle between an exaggerated intellectualism and an unenlightened voluntarism. He was confident that a pupil, launched on his own way, runs no risk of being swept off his feet as long as he stands on the bedrock of classical learning and takes to heart the great lessons of history.

Among Jinsai's works, the following are best known and have gone through several editions: *Dōjimon* (1707), a question-and-answer presentation condensing his philosophical doctrines for classroom use; *Go-Mō jigi* (1683), a commentary on the *Analects* and *Mencius;* and the *Kogakusensei bunshū* (1717), an anthology prepared by Tōgai from his father's unpublished papers. Jinsai's originality has been challenged, but without success. Whether he came in contact with Ricci's *T'ien-chu shih i*, written to prove the existence of a unique God, remains a moot point.

The measure of Jinsai's influence must be found not only in his life and writings; even more, it lies in the lives and work of his many pupils. He imparted to them a critical spirit, for he doubted where others blindly believed, and he formed his own conclusions when it was still fashionable to follow the Sung masters. His philosophy has a peculiar human appeal. The moral order is not a mere haphazard rule, but a providential guide, based upon the inherent nature of things.

Jinsai's legacy is still highly regarded in Japan, because he penetrated to the very core of the national spirit. To no mean extent, Jinsai could claim to be an educator of his people. Not only did he stir in his followers something that they felt was deeply embedded in their national way of life, but he impressed on them that Confucianism is inherently associated with the good that lies between two extremes. Jinsai's lasting success is explained by the fact that, in his efforts to accomplish the ideal that he contemplated, he found a way to blend two seemingly paradoxical qualities: equanimity of mind and passionate devotion to a cause. In this, he found a way that is Japan.

BIBLIOGRAPHY

The only monograph available in English is my own, *Itō Jinsai: A Philosopher, Educator and Sinologist of the Tokugawa Period* (1948; reprint, New York, 1967).

JOSEPH J. SPAE

IZANAGI AND IZANAMI, in Japanese mythology, are the universal parents and creators who produced the land, mountains, rivers, waves, trees, fields, wind, fog, and the deities ruling these things. According to the early written chronicle of Japan called the *Kojiki*, they appeared on the Takama no Hara, or High Plain of Heaven, as brother and sister. Standing on the Bridge of Heaven, they churned the ocean's water with a jeweled spear, then drew the spear up. The brine that dripped from the tip of the spear became the first Japanese island, Onogoro. Izanagi and Izanami descended onto the island, erected there a high pillar and a hall, then circled the pillar in opposite directions. When they met, they were united, and thus the islands of Japan were born.

After the birth of the islands, various other deities were born of the two creator-parents. But when the fire god Kagutsuchi was born, the mother goddess Izanami was burned to death by the heat. Like the Greek Orpheus, Izanagi descended to the land of Yomi (the underworld) to bring back his wife. His attempt ended in failure when he peered into a dark room with his torch against Izanami's wishes, only to find there her decaying corpse. Pursued by the enraged Izanami and her subordinate demons, Izanagi fled. Finally, the two deities stood face to face at the entrance of the underworld and agreed upon a divorce. It was decided that Izanagi should rule the living and Izanami the dead (a motif paralleling that of Tane and Hina in Polynesia). Izanagi then returned to the earth, where he purified himself in a stream. From his purified eyes and nose appeared three great deities: Amaterasu (the sun goddess), Tsukiyomi (the moon god), and Susano-o (the violent god). These deities were appointed rulers of heaven, night, and the ocean. Izanagi thereupon returned to the celestial abode, where he remained.

Somewhat different versions of the creation myth are recorded in the other ancient Japanese chronicle, the *Nihonshoki*. In it, the three great deities are born of both Izanagi and Izanami, not of Izanagi alone. There is no descent to the underworld by Izanagi, who retires permanently to a hidden palace on the island of Awaji in the Inland Sea. Since ancient times, there has been an Izanagi shrine on Awaji, and the divine couple have been worshiped by the fishermen and divers of this and neighboring islands. The myth of *kuni-umi* ("birth of the islands from the sea") seems to have originated with the Awaji fishermen. In the most primitive form of the story the divine couple created only Awaji and its tiny neighboring islands, but the myth must eventually have grown in scale to include the creation of all the islands of Japan.

The *Kojiki* as well as the *Nihonshoki* record that the two deities gave birth first to Awaji. According to another account in the *Nihonshoki*, the fifth-century emperors Richū and Ingyō went hunting on this island, and through mediums were given oracles by Izanagi, Awaji's guardian deity. Then, as the fishermen migrated to or traded with other areas, their myths and formal worship were diffused. The tenth-century *Engishiki* records several shrines dedicated to Izanagi and Izanami in the Kinki area (the area enclosed by Kyoto, Osaka, and Kobe). The oldest manuscript of the *Kojiki* describes the worship of Izanagi at the Taga shrine in Ōmi (now Shiga Prefecture). In later ages the Taga shrine became the most famous and popular shrine for the worship of the divine couple.

BIBLIOGRAPHY

Aston, W. G., trans. *Nihongi: Chronicles of Japan from the Earliest Times to A.D. 697* (1896). Reprint, 2 vols. in 1, Tokyo, 1972.

Chamberlain, Basil Hall, trans. *Kojiki: Records of Ancient Matters* (1882). 2d ed. With annotations by W. G. Aston. Tokyo, 1932; reprint, Rutland, Vt., and Tokyo, 1982.

Matsumae Takeshi. *Nihon shinwa no shin kenkyū*. Tokyo, 1960.

Matsumoto Nobuhiro. *Nihon shinwa no kenkyū*. Tokyo, 1971.

Matsumura Takeo. *Nihon shinwa no kenkyū*, vol 2. Tokyo, 1955.

Philippi, Donald L., trans. *Kojiki*. Princeton, 1969.

Matsumae Takeshi

J

JACOB, or, in Hebrew, Ya'aqov, also called Israel; the son of Isaac and grandson of Abraham. The name *Ya'aqov* is generally regarded as an abbreviation of *ya'aqov el,* which probably means "God protects" and is attested among the Babylonians in the early part of the second pre-Christian millennium. The Bible relates it to forms of the Hebrew root *'qv,* meaning "heel" and "supplant," pertaining to Jacob's ongoing rivalry with his twin brother, Esau. That struggle originated in the womb, leading their mother Rebecca to seek a divine oracle from which she learned that the younger Jacob would rule over his brother. Esau was born first, with Jacob grasping at his heel *('aqev).* The theme of fraternal rivalry continued when, as a young man, Jacob exploited Esau's hunger in order to buy his birthright *(bekhorah)* and then stole his brother's blessing *(berakhah)* by taking advantage of his father Isaac's blindness during Esau's absence.

A second period in Jacob's life was spent in Haran in northern Mesopotamia, where he fled to escape his brother's wrath. On the way, he had a vision of a stairway with angels climbing from earth to heaven and back again while God promised that his descendants would be numerous and possess the land all around. Jacob thus recognized the spot as God's house (Bethel), the gateway to heaven. In Haran, Jacob worked for his uncle Laban in order to obtain Rachel as a wife. After the stipulated seven years, Laban deceived Jacob by substituting Rachel's older sister Leah under cover of darkness, just as Jacob had exploited his father's inability to see in order to obtain the blessings intended for his older brother Esau. [*See* Rachel and Leah.]

During his return to Canaan, Jacob engaged in physical conflict with an apparently supernatural being (see *Hos.* 12:4), after which his name was changed to *Israel* (Heb., *Yisra'el*). Although the historical etymology of this name is uncertain, the Bible explains it as meaning "he who has struggled with divine beings."

The final period of Jacob's life consists of various journeys and focuses primarily on the story of his son Joseph. Jacob eventually died at the age of 147 in Egypt, where he was embalmed before being brought back to Canaan to be buried in the family tomb at Machpelah.

Jacob's role as the third of Israel's patriarchs is central to the biblical account. The proper historical setting for all of the patriarchs is, however, currently a matter of scholarly disagreement. Although a wide range of possible dates have been proposed, most who accept the fundamental historicity of these figures date them to the middle or late Bronze Age on the basis of cultural similarities between the biblical descriptions and what is known of those periods from archaeological and epigraphic discoveries. One striking characteristic of these narratives is the way God is identified with individual patriarchs, as in the title *avir ya'aqov* (the "strong one" or perhaps "bull" of Jacob).

Many modern scholars consider the various patriarchal traditions to have come from different tribal groups. Some even regard Jacob and Israel as two originally separate figures, in which case Jacob probably comes from Transjordan (Gilead) and Israel from central Canaan (the region near Bethel and Shechem). These traditions were merged with those relating to Abraham and Isaac as the various tribes of biblical Israel coalesced. As his changed name attests, Jacob symbolizes the northern kingdom as well as the entire people of Israel, a perspective reflected also in the fact that his sons are named for the twelve tribes. Indeed, many actions, such as his entrance into the land and journey to Shechem and Bethel, foreshadow events involving the people as a whole.

Many interpreters have been troubled by the devious ways in which Jacob obtained his position of preeminence. Rabbinic tradition, in which he represented all of Israel even as his rival Esau came to stand for Rome, sought to minimize these negative traits, which seem so evident in the Bible. It must be recognized that from the biblical point of view these actions, whatever their moral character, serve primarily to ensure the fulfillment of God's design indicated even prior to Jacob's birth. Moreover, the Bible clearly describes how Jacob paid for his behavior: he was forced to leave his home, he was deceived by his uncle, he found his daughter raped, his favorite wife died in childbirth, and her son was kidnapped.

BIBLIOGRAPHY

An excellent survey of modern scholarship on the patriarchs is Nahum M. Sarna's *Understanding Genesis* (New York, 1972); more recent historical information relating to the date and historicity of these figures is provided by Roland de Vaux's *The Early History of Israel*, translated by David Smith (Philadelphia, 1978). Rabbinic traditions on Jacob are collected in Louis Ginzberg's *The Legends of the Jews*, vol. 1 (Philadelphia, 1909), pp. 311–424, with notes in vol. 5 (1925), pp. 270–323. An insightful description of the Jacob story's literary characteristics is contained in Michael A. Fishbane's *Text and Texture: Close Readings of Selected Biblical Texts* (New York, 1979).

FREDERICK E. GREENSPAHN

JACOB BEN ASHER. *See* Ya'aqov ben Asher.

JACOB TAM. *See* Tam, Ya'aqov ben Me'ir.

JADE. Today jade is universally admired for its beauty and durability as a precious stone, for its inexhaustible riches of color, and for its variety of grain and texture. In earlier times, however, in cultures as diverse as those of ancient China, Central America, and Polynesia, jade also had a religious value. This is most clearly the case in ancient China.

During the Chou dynasty (c. 1122–256 BCE), a large variety of jade objects played important symbolic roles in a religious and political system focused on sacred kingship. As symbols of political sovereignty, the jade insignia worn by the emperor and his officials were equally symbols of religious sanction. Ruling as the Son of Heaven, the emperor stood at the head of an elaborate ritual system, a sacral economy that found symbolic embodiment in a whole series of jade emblems. The emperor himself had the privilege of wearing ornaments of white jade, in particular the "large tablet" and the "tablet of power" that he wore as he offered the annual spring sacrifice to the Lord on High (Shang-ti). His officials were given jade emblems that varied in size, shape, and color according to their rank.

The *Chou li* (Rites of Chou) mentions six jade tablets that the *ta-tsung po* ("master of religious ceremonies") used in paying homage to Heaven, Earth, and the four cardinal points. Heaven was represented by a flat, doughnut-shaped jade disk called *pi*, while Earth was represented by a hollow jade tube, squared on the outside, called *ts'ung*. The jade *pi* in particular has remained one of the most important symbols in the Chinese religious tradition.

Jade was also used as a sacrificial substance. Round blue pieces of jade were offered to the Lord on High, and square yellow pieces were offered to Sovereign Earth. Several stories recount the offering of a jade ring to the god of the river in order to assure a safe crossing.

Jade played a particularly important role in funeral practices. This was undoubtedly due to the belief that jade, as the embodiment of the power of Heaven, would prevent the decay of the body after death. Accordingly one finds all manner of jade objects in the coffin of the deceased, often blocking the natural openings of the body so as to prevent putrefaction. Especially common were jade tablets placed upon the tongue and carved in the likeness of cicadas, perhaps as symbols of renewed life. One also finds full body-sized funeral masks made of jade.

Among the Taoists, the religious symbolism of jade was given a more precise focus. The Taoists believed that jade embodied the principle of cosmic life and could thus ensure immortality if used in connection with certain alchemical practices. These practices included the actual ingestion of jade, since it was believed that jade could not only prevent the decay of the body after death but actually regenerate it while alive. The importance of jade in Taoist thought is reflected in the name of the Taoist supreme being, the Jade Emperor.

Although ancient China presents the most numerous and most striking examples of the use of jade as a religious symbol, we also find very similar practices in ancient Mesoamerica. There are especially striking parallels in the use of jade in connection with burial. Among the Maya, for instance, small pieces of jade were placed in the mouth of the dead, while in the tomb under the Temple of the Inscriptions in Palenque, a funeral mask has been found that is a mosaic of small pieces of jade.

There is also evidence of the use of jade as a sacrificial substance. For instance, dredging operations at the sacred well at Chichén Itzá in Yucatán, a traditional site of pilgrimage and sacrifice, have turned up many pieces of jade from all periods.

The Aztec appear to have shared with the Chinese a belief in the medicinal properties of jade. In particular, jade seems to have been prescribed for relief from gastric pain. Such medicinal uses of jade, together with its use in burial and sacrifice, clearly point to a fundamental belief in its life-giving powers.

Finally, the importance of jade in the ritual garments of priests and princes should be noted. This importance is reflected in the mythology of the Aztec goddess Chalchihuitlicue, whose name means "she of the jade skirt."

Jade also seems to have attained a certain religious significance among the Maori of New Zealand, whose neck pendants, called *hei-tiki*, are made of jade. These are passed down from generation to generation, in the process becoming symbols of the ancestors.

BIBLIOGRAPHY

The classic study of jade in ancient China remains that of Berthold Laufer, *Jade: A Study in Chinese Archaeology and Religion* (Chicago, 1912). To this may be added the more wide-ranging and less technical work of Louis Zara, *Jade* (New York, 1969), and Adrian Digby's *Maya Jades* (London, 1964).

DAVID CARPENTER

JAʿFAR AL-ṢĀDIQ (AH 83–148/702–765 CE), properly Abū ʿAbd Allāh Jaʿfar ibn Muḥammad al-Ṣādiq; sixth imam of the Twelver (Imāmīyah) Shīʿah or fifth imam of the Ismāʿīlīyah, and a preeminent spiritual chief from the family of the prophet Muḥammad.

Life. Jaʿfar stood in direct male line of descent from Muḥammad's daughter Fāṭimah and his first cousin ʿAlī ibn Abī Ṭālib through their son Ḥusayn. Active in scholarly circles in Medina, where he was born, Jaʿfar transmitted his family's views on the events of the original Muslim community and a wide variety of legal and religious issues. His house was frequented by Muslims of different ideological persuasions, and he held disputations with exponents of other religions, pagan theosophers, and gnostics (Daysanite and Manichaean).

After the death of his father, Muḥammad al-Bāqir, about 733, Jaʿfar became the spiritual leader (imam) of a significant wing within the wider Shīʿī movement. While he advocated his family's rights as the divinely appointed leaders of the Muslim community, he remained politically disengaged among competing Shīʿī currents. He gathered around himself a personal following centered in Kufa in lower Iraq that included a high proportion of non-Arab clients (Aramaic, Persian, and Syrian). They formed a rudimentary organization under his designated agents, who acted as his intermediaries and collected the religious tax due him as imam. Jaʿfar promoted solidarity among his partisans in the face of government-sponsored oppression by encouraging, for example, the ritual mourning observances at Karbala, the site of Ḥusayn's martyrdom. The sustained efforts of his companions and their followers led to a process of doctrinal development that produced a coherent body of juridical and speculative traditions underlying Twelver Shiism, as well as Fatimid Ismailism, although the early stages of this process remain obscure.

Teaching. The center of gravity of Jaʿfar's thought is his doctrine of the imamate. As God's agent in creation, the imam serves as the exemplary witness *(ḥujjah)* who testifies for God against mortals in their covenantal relation. The spiritual authority *(wilāyah)* of the imam, as the only authoritative source of knowledge and guidance to whom obedience was obligatory, is understood to be part of a universal process of salvation in history (cf. the Qur'anic theme of successive revelations). This process begins with the pre-creation moment of being (the Qur'anic *yawm al-mithāq,* or "covenant day") and is manifested temporally through the universal chain of the prophets and their legatees and continuators, the imams. Prophethood and the imamate arose from the Light of Muḥammad (*nūr Muḥammadī,* also termed *al-ʿaql,* the noetic mind), which is behind all creation and shared equally by prophets and imams and to a lesser degree by their faithful elect. Owing to his primordial origin in the realm of God's throne, the imam enjoys impeccable moral purity *(ʿiṣmah)* as possessor of the sanctified spirit *(rūḥ al-qudus),* being "spoken to" by the Holy Spirit, and as recipient of a special form of eschatological knowledge. This cosmic scheme of salvation is perceived to be moving toward its culmination in the eschatological event to be heralded by the Qā'im or Mahdi (the Muslim messianic savior). Finally, the faithful are ranked hierarchically according to the perfection of their knowledge of the imam *(maʿrifat al-imām).*

Jaʿfar also pronounced original views on central theological issues of his day, although the concerns of later schools have shaped their presentation in the traditions. On the question of determinism, he taught a middle position that preserved God's autocracy yet allowed for human responsibility. He encouraged a certain use of rational speculative powers in religious discourse and preferred knowledge (*ʿilm,* or "gnosis") over mechanical pious observances, but he opposed the unhindered application of personal opinion and analogy *(qiyās)* as a source for legal rulings in religious practice.

His esoteric interpretation of the Qur'ān *(ta'wīl)* provided a rereading of scripture in the light of his partisans' ideological circumstances (much in the manner of the apocalyptic exegesis of earlier eschatological communities) and was presented as fresh authoritative guidance for a salvific remnant. The interpretation of key Qur'anic verses and tales of the prophets as paradigms for the interior experiences of his personal followers anticipated the later Ṣūfī *ta'wīl.*

Ja'far was a prime mover in the elaboration of specific themes intended to enhance the understanding of Islam in the nascent Muslim world. These include a pervasive dualism in cosmogony and history as well as among humans; an emphasis on the Adam, versus the Iblīs, cycle of legends and on the Sethian race; and the integration of current scientific notions into a religious psychology grounded in the Qur'ān. Several of his epistles to his leading companions have survived. Various wisdom discourses and collections of spiritual maxims are attributed to him, although they bear marks of later literary arrangement by Shī'ī gnostic schools or Ṣūfī circles.

Legacy. Attempts have been made to connect features of Ja'far's teaching, and of early radical Shiism, with older traditions of the Middle East, yet much of what is taken to be foreign importations within his teaching may only reflect the cultural pluralism of Islam's early centuries. In any case, there remains the part played by Ja'far himself in capitalizing on these unique conditions.

He provided the impetus for the ultimate emergence of the Twelver Shī'ah as an independent juridico-theological school; even among Sunnī jurists, the Ja'farī or Twelver rite is now recognized as a fifth law school. He is no less important for the radical Shī'ah (Ismā'īlī and Nuṣayrī), who have relied more on his esoteric teachings than on his jurisprudence. Shī'ī theosophers in medieval Iran considered aspects of his teaching to have anticipated key philosophical insights of later Muslim philosophy. His name is persistently linked with several major arcane disciplines, such as alchemy, the science of letter-number correspondences termed *jafr,* the occult arts (the *Fāl-nāmah* genre of alphabetic divination tables, physiognomy, and theurgic use of Qur'anic verses), as well as folk medicine.

Ja'far surfaces in early Ṣūfī tradition as a pillar of mystical precedents, earning a special place of honor over time, especially with the Turks, and he figures in the chains of transmission of some Ṣūfī orders. Aspects of his theory of the imamate, as well as some specific motifs and technical terms, may have had an impact on the formulation of parallel Ṣūfī doctrines.

BIBLIOGRAPHY

Many aspects of Ja'far's life and thought still await critical appreciation, owing to historical questions concerning the rise of the early Shī'ah and the literary-doctrinal problems presented by the mass of early Shī'ī traditions. For the former, see S. Husain M. Jafri's *Origins and Early Development of Shī'a Islam* (London, 1979), a somewhat apologetic survey with an adequate bibliography and a discussion of Ja'far's role. The traditional Twelver picture of him can be glimpsed in Shaykh al-Mufīd's *Kitāb al-irshād, The Book of Guidance into the Lives of the Twelve Imāms,* translated by I. K. A. Howard (London, 1981), pp. 408–435. Henry Corbin frequently dealt with al-Ṣādiq's mystical and philosophical legacy; see, for example, his *En Islam iranien,* vol. 1, *Le shī'isme duodécimain* (Paris, 1971). Paul Nwyia's *Exégèse coranique et language mystique* (Beirut, 1970) contains a useful treatment of Ja'far's Qur'anic exegesis in Ṣūfī tradition.

DOUGLAS S. CROW

JAGUARS. The jaguar occupies a place of considerable importance in the myths, beliefs, and shamanic rituals of South American Indians. There is the widespread belief that eclipses are caused by a huge celestial jaguar attacking the sun and the moon.

Symbolically, the jaguar is associated especially with fire and water. According to the Tucano Indians of the Amazon, the jaguar was created by the sun to be its main representative on earth. As the sun is fire in heaven, the jaguar is fire on earth; it represents the sun's fertilizing energy on earth, and so dominates fecundity. In Caingang mythology the twin culture heroes Kamé and Kayurukré created jaguars out of ashes and coals. The Indians of the Gran Chaco portray the jaguar as the original owner of fire, and the rabbit as the hero who stole it; while it is believed in eastern Brazil (among the Kayapó, the Timbirá, the Apinagé, and the Xerente) that a deserted boy obtained fire for Indians from the benevolent jaguar. Tobacco originated from the ashes made out of its burned body.

The jaguar is also associated by its roar with thunder, rain, and water. According to the Tucano, thunder, the jaguar's voice, is a gift from the sun; and lightning, a fertilizing force through its association with rain, is a glance of the sun. In eastern Brazil (e.g., among the Tembé) there is the widespread belief that the jaguar instructed people in how to celebrate the honey festival.

Shamanism is closely connected with the jaguar. The shaman claims to be able to transform himself into a jaguar. The curing shaman of the Taulipáng, a Carib tribe, invokes the jaguar to cure swellings caused by eating certain game (such as tapir, deer, and peccary) because the jaguar can eat all these animals and still not suffer swellings.

BIBLIOGRAPHY

There is much valuable information on the myths and symbols of the jaguar in Claude Lévi-Strauss's *The Raw and the Cooked* (New York, 1969), as well as in his *From Honey to Ashes* (New York, 1973). See also a brilliant study by Gerardo Reichel-Dolmatoff, *Amazonian Cosmos: The Sexual and Religious Symbolism of the Tukano Indians* (Chicago, 1971).

MANABU WAIDA

JAINISM (or Jinism) is the name given to the religious movement of the Jains, whose community follows the religious path established by Vardhamāna Mahāvīra, a prophet also known as the Jina, or "Victor." Born in northern Bihar, India, Mahāvīra is alleged to have preached in the sixth century BCE. Thus, according to tradition, he lived in the same area, and at approximately the same time as the Buddha. The earliest developments of Buddhism and Jainism are comparable to some extent. In later centuries, however, their destinies diverged. While Buddhism was progressively suppressed in India, the Jains remained in their homeland where, today, they form an admittedly small but nonetheless influential and comparatively prosperous community of 2,604,837 people (1981 census).

History. There remains no objective document concerning the beginnings of Jainism. The date of Mahāvīra's death ("entry into *nirvāṇa*"), which is the starting point of the traditional Jain chronology, corresponds to 527/526 BCE, but some scholars believe it occurred about one century later. In any case, the Jain community was probably not "founded" solely by Mahāvīra. Rather, his adherents merged with the followers of a previous prophet (Pārśva); reorganizations and reforms ensued and a fifth commandment was added to the older code, as was the practice of confession and repentance; nakedness came to be recommended to those among the believers who took the religious vows, although apparently it was not imposed on Pārśva's disciples.

Some differences in the monks' behavior were accepted, but disputes appear to have arisen at the end of the fourth century BCE, allegedly after a famine forced several religious groups, led by the eminent patriarch Bhadrabāhu, to migrate south. Finally, in 79 CE, the community split into two main churches—the Digambara, "sky-clad" (and thus naked), and the Śvetāmbara, "white-clad." By the time of the separation, however, the doctrine had been fixed for the whole community; this accounts for the fundamental agreement in the main tenets professed by the Śvetāmbaras and the Digambaras. On the other hand, epigraphic and literary records prove that religious "companies" *(gaṇa)* already existed, subdivided into *śākhās* ("branches") and *kulas* ("families" or "schools"). The remarkable organization of Mahāvīra's church has proved a firm foundation for the welfare and survival of his followers. The community of the monks and nuns is said to have been entrusted by Mahāvīra to eleven chief disciples, or *gaṇadharas* ("company leaders"). The chief among them was Gautama Indrabhūti, while his colleague Sudharman allegedly taught his own pupil Jambū the words spoken by the Jina. Thus the canon of the Śvetāmbaras goes back to Sudharman through uninterrupted lines of religious masters *(ācāryas)*.

The history of the sacred texts is further marked by the efforts made to preserve them from oblivion. To this effect, about two centuries after Mahāvīra, a synod was held in Pāṭaliputra (modern-day Patna). A great role was then played by Bhadrabāhu—whom the Jain traditions unanimously consider to be the last person who knew the Pūrvas (the "ancient" texts).

Other councils were later held by the Śvetāmbaras. The most important met in the middle of the fifth century in Valabhī (in Kathiawar, Gujarat), and at its close numerous manuscripts of the authoritative texts were copied and widely distributed in the community. However, the Digambaras deny the authenticity of this corpus and instead recognize the authority of "procanonical" treatises.

After Mahāvīra's time the Jain community spread along the caravan routes from Magadha (Bihar) to the west and south. They claim to have enjoyed the favor of numerous rulers. Notwithstanding possible exaggerations, they probably were supported by a number of princes, including King Bimbisāra of Magadha (a contemporary of the Jina), and later the Maurya emperor Candragupta Maurya (who, they say, fasted unto death on one of the hillocks overlooking the village of Śravaṇa Beḷgoḷa, following Bhadrabāhu's example). By the fifth century (or earlier), the Digambaras were influential in the Deccan, especially in Karnataka. Under the Gaṅga, Rāṣṭrakūṭa, and other dynasties Jain culture undoubtedly flourished. Numerous sects were founded, among them the brilliant Yāpanīya, now extinct. In the tenth century, however, Vaiṣṇavism and Śaivism crushed Jainism in the Tamil area, and in the twelfth century they triumphed over Jainism in Karnataka as well.

As for the Śvetāmbaras, they were especially successful in Gujarat where one of their famous pontifs, Hemacandra (1089–1172), served as minister to the Cālukya king Kumārapāla (1144–1173) and enforced some Jain rules in the kingdom. Decline was to follow soon after his death, which was hastened by the Muslim invasions. Jain activities did not cease with his demise, however. Elaborate sanctuaries were erected, such as that on Mount Abu, now in Rajasthan. The rise of several reformist sects testifies to the vitality of the Śvetāmbaras, who even succeeded in interesting the Moghul emperor Akbar (r. 1555–1605) in the Jain doctrine. Some of those sects have survived: the Sthānakvāsins (founded 1653) and Terāpanthins (founded 1761), who are known for their strong opposition to idols and temple worship, and the present Anuvrata movement, which was founded in 1949 by the Terāpanthin monk Acarya Sri Tulsi.

Although the Jain community never regained its former splendor, it did not disappear entirely; nowadays, the Digambaras are firmly established in Maharashtra and Karnataka and the Śvetāmbaras in Panjab, Rajasthan, and Gujarat. Jain businessmen are generally active in all the main cities of India, and many also outside India.

Literature. From early times the Jains have been engaged in a variety of literary activities. Their works, whether intended for their own adherents or composed with rival groups in view, generally have an edifying, proselytizing, or apologetic purpose. The languages used vary to suit the audience and the epoch.

All of the oldest texts are composed in varieties of Prakrits (i.e., Middle Indo-Aryan), more or less akin to the languages in current use among the people of northern India at the time of the first sermons. Later, the Jains turned to local vernaculars such as Old Gujarati in the North, and Tamil and Kannaḍa in the Dravidian South. In the Middle Ages, however, they also adopted the use of Sanskrit (i.e., Old Indo-Aryan), which had become the normal idiom for all scholarly debates.

The Jain traditions, while considering that the fourteen Pūrvas have been lost, contend that part of the material they included was incorporated into later books. The Digambaras boldly assert that some sections are the immediate basis of two of their early treatises (c. first century CE) whereas, according to the Śvetāmbaras, the teachings of the Pūrvas were embedded in the so-called twelfth Aṅga of their canon, now considered lost. The earliest extant documents are the canonical scriptures of the Śvetāmbaras and the systematic treatises *(prakaraṇas)* of the Digambaras.

The Śvetāmbara canon (variously called *āgama,* "tradition," *siddhānta,* "doctrine," etc.) is composed of forty-five treatises (according to the Sthānakvāsins, only thirty-two) grouped in six sections: the Aṅgas ('limbs"), Upāṅgas ("sub-*aṅgas*"), Prakīrṇakas ("miscellanea"), Chedasūtras ("treatises on cutting" [partially] religious authority; these mostly concern disciplinary technicalities), Cūlikāsūtras ("appendixes"; two propaedeutic texts), and Mūlasūtras ("basic" texts). As systematic as this arrangement appears to be, the canon is in fact mostly a compilation of texts of different origin, age, and importance, focusing on a wide range of topics; an entire subculture is reflected in its books. The oldest parts are written in a Prakrit characterized by several eastern (i.e., Gangetic) features, whereas a westernized idiom prevails in the later portions. Moreover, the preservation and traditional interpretation of the canonical texts has been ensured by an enormous mass of scholastic exegesis, written first in Prakrit and later (beginning with Haribhadra in the mid-eighth century) in Sanskrit.

The Digambaras rely on *prakaraṇa*s, of which the oldest are written in a third variety of Prakrit. Their authors, who lived around the first century of the common era, are: Vaṭṭakera, author of the *Mūlācāra* (Basic Conduct; approximately 1,250 stanzas); Kundakunda, a prolific writer and much admired mystic, and author of *Samayasāra,* (Essence of the Doctrine) and of *Pravacanasāra* (Essence of the Teaching); and Śivārya, who wrote *Ārādhana* (Accomplishment), which has more than 2,000 stanzas.

These books mark the beginning of an important literary genre that was also cultivated by the Śvetāmbaras. One of the fundamental treatises in this category is by Umāsvāti (c. second century; most likely a Śvetāmbara): with small variants, both churches accept the authority of his *Tattvārthādhigama Sūtra* (Sūtra for Attaining the Meaning of the Principles), a doctrinal synthesis composed of 350 aphorisms written in Sanskrit. This linguistic selection shows that the Jains were prepared to engage in polemics with other schools of thought and to engage the brahmans with Brahmanic terminology and words of discourse.

At this stage, the canonical collections and procanonical writings have been supplemented by many new compositions, often termed *anuyoga,* or "exposition." From the first to the fifteenth century CE an enormous mass of literature was produced, covering a wide range of topics: dialectics and logic, politics and religious law, grammar, scientific subjects, epico-lyric poems devoted to "universal history," *dharmakathā*s ("narratives on the [Jain] law"), *kathānaka*s ("short stories" illustrating the doctrinal teachings), gnomic poetry, and hymns. Although Jain literary activity has never ceased, since the fourteenth and fifteenth centuries it has often lacked its earlier force and originality.

Religious Practices. The practices observed among the Jains are dependent on two main factors: specific Jain convictions and the general Indian environment. They reflect, in fact, many parallels with the rules and observances of Brahmanic ascetics and Buddhist monks.

All Jains are members of the four-fold congregation *(saṃgha)*, composed of monks and nuns, laymen and laywomen. They share a common belief in the *triratna* ("three jewels"): *samyagdarśana* ("right faith"), *samyagjñāna* ("right knowledge"), and *samyakcaritra* ("right conduct"). Observance of the "three jewels" provides the conditions for the attainment of the goal, that is, liberation from bondage. Deliverance can be attained only by the *nirgrantha*, the Jain monk "free from bonds" both external and internal. The ideal practices therefore are those in force in the (male) religious community. Nevertheless, householders are permitted certain ceremonies (such as the worship of images, a practice borrowed from Hinduism), though they do actually break some of the restraints clearly accepted by all. Both the lay and the monastic followers must take solemn vows (*vrata*s), which form the basis of Jain ethics and will guide the pious believers' lives.

The monks and nuns take the five "great vows" *(mahāvratas)*, pledging to abstain from (1) injuring life, (2) false speech, (3) taking what is not given, (4) unchastity, and (5) appropriation. A sixth *vrata* ("vow") consists of abstaining from taking food and drink at night: it is evidently aimed at avoiding injury to insects, which might go unnoticed in the darkness, and thus is a consequence of the first *mahāvrata*.

The life of Mahāvīra is regarded as an ideal model. But despite the fact that he is depicted as living in solitude, ordinary monks and nuns live in a "company" *(gaṇa, gaccha)*, where they benefit from the advice of their superiors and from the active solidarity of their brethren. The *gaṇa* is further subdivided into smaller units.

Religious age and hierarchy play a great role: elders look to the material and spiritual welfare of the company; the *upādhyāya* is a specialist in teaching the scriptures; the *ācārya* acts as spiritual master. Full ordination takes place after a short novitiate that lasts approximately four months. Admission as a novice is subject to prior examination. At his departure from home, the novice abandons all property and his head is shaved. He then receives the equipment of a monk (alms bowl, broom, napkin, loincloths), and is taught the basic formulas or "obligations" *(āvaśyaka*s). Full admission entails taking the five great vows mentioned above. The *nirgrantha*s (monks) are also called *bhikṣu* ("mendicant") or *sādhu* ("pious"); the *nigranthī*s (nuns) are called *bhikṣuṇī*, or *sādhvī*. Monks and nuns must observe the utmost reserve. The nun's status, however, is always inferior to that of the monk.

Right religious conduct is minutely defined, giving rules for habitation and wandering, begging, study, confession, and penances. During the four months of the rainy season the religious groups remain in one locality; nowadays fixed places of shelter (*upāśraya*s) are prepared for them, often near a temple, where householders visit, ask advice, and listen to teachings. During the rest of the year members of the order wander from place to place, walking with circumspection indefatigably on the long Indian roads. Day and night are each divided into four equal parts *(pauruṣī*s) with prescribed occupations: the first and fourth *pauruṣī*s of both day and night are reserved for study, the second of both day and night for meditation, the third of the night for sleep, and the third of the day for alms-begging (*Uttarajjhāyā* 22.11–12; 17–18).

The begging tour is important in a community where the religious members have no possessions: it is therefore minutely codified. As always in India, the prescriptions concerning food are rigorous: to be "pure and acceptable," food should not be prepared especially for the monk and should contain absolutely no living particle. The monk—and the layman—are thus constrained to be strictly vegetarian, to the point that they should take only sterile water. Because of the importance attached to food, many of the "external" ascetic practices (which include difficult postures, etc.) consist of restrictions in the number, abundance, and seasoning of the meals. Fasting can even be prolonged unto death *(saṃlekhanā)*, which is regarded as "the wise man's death."

Begging and fasting must be conducted with great care and preceded by confession *(ālocanā)* and repentance *(pratikramaṇa)*, which are deemed essential activities. These two also take place at regular intervals (each fortnight), and, ideally, every day. They are prominent in the list of the ten penances which, together with good education, service, study, mental concentration, and abandonment, form the six "internal" austerities. These have been specified since the earliest tradition and are so perfectly integrated in the doctrine that the intellectual and spiritual aspirations of Jainism cannot be doubted.

Called *śrāvaka*s ("listeners") or *upāsaka*s ("servants"), the lay believers also take five main vows, similar to (but milder than) the *mahāvrata*s, and hence termed *aṇuvratas* ("lesser vows"). These include *ahiṃsā* ("nonviolence") and *satya* ("truthfulness"). They are complemented by three "strengthening vows" and four "vows of spiritual discipline," of which the last, but not the least, is *dāna* ("charity"). *Dāna* has a wide range of connotations; in its more restricted sense the term naturally refers to almsgiving—which ensures the ascetics' existence, and therefore the transmission of the doctrine; the laity should further visit and venerate the mendicant teachers. Following the example set by monks, householders observe the six "obligatory" duties, cultivate the right state of mind (often by taking part in pilgrimages to holy places), regularly practice meditation, observe fasts on the eighth and fourteenth days of the moon's waxing and waning periods, and confess their faults: a popular ceremony is the Sāṃvatsarī ("the annual"), performed for an eight- to ten-day period during the rainy season, when a general admission of sins and pleas for forgiveness are directed toward all.

These practices are evidently relevant in a doctrine that emphasizes individual exertion, and that considers the Jinas to be inaccessible, liberated souls. On the other hand, the Jain church has not been able to ignore the devotional aspirations of the laity, who are also attracted by Hindu ritual. Hence, although temple worship (with the burning and waving of lamps, plucked flowers and fruit, preparation of sandal paste, etc.) implies violence, cultic practices are tolerated, being considered ultimately of help to the worshiper's progress. Most sects (though not the Sthānakvāsins) allow the *upāsaka* to visit the temples and participate in rituals, including solemn celebrations such as the Digambara anointing of the head of Bāhubali's statue in Śravaṇa Beḷgoḷa, which every twelve years attracts enormous crowds. (Bāhubali was the son of the prince who later became the first *tīrthaṃkara* of the present *avasarpiṇī* period.) All these practices are believed to lead the soul to achieve its own "perfection" *(siddhi)*, acting as vehicles through which one crosses the stream of the innumerable rebirths one must face in the immensity of the cosmos during the course of many eons.

Mythology and Cosmology. The Jain representation of the cosmos *(loka)* is akin to (though not identical with) the standard Brahmanical descriptions. [*See* Cosmology, *article on* Hindu and Jain Cosmologies.] The cosmos is composed of three main parts: the lower, middle, and upper worlds. It is often represented as a colossal upright human figure, the enormous base of which is formed by seven hells (populated by beings whose past actions were violent and cruel and who consequently suffer terrible torments).

Compared with the other two, the "middle world" (Madhyaloka) is extremely small and resembles a thin disk. Though small, it has a great importance: there, in a few circumscribed areas, time and the law of retribution prevail, different kinds of men live (among them the civilized *āryas*), and spiritual awakening and perfection can be achieved. This is possible in some of its innermost parts, especially in the circular *dvīpa* ("island") situated in the middle of the Madhyaloka: this is Jambūdvīpa ("continent of the rose-apple tree"), with Mount Mandara (or Meru) rising exactly in its center and Bhārata (India) in its southern part. It is surrounded by numerous alternating rings of oceans and island-continents.

Occasionally, divinities come from the other two worlds to visit the Madhyaloka. Others belong to it: at various heights far above its surface those stellar gods (suns, moons, planets, constellations, and stars) who overlook the two and a half inner continents revolve around Meru. In twenty-four hours the suns and moons accomplish half the circuit, so that there are two of each, at a distance of 180 degrees from one another.

Beginning far above the stars, the upper world appears as a gradually purer and purer counterpart of the lower world. Finally, near the top of the *loka* lies the place, shaped like an inverted umbrella (or the crescent moon) where the *siddhas* ("perfected ones," i.e., liberated souls) are assembled.

Divinities are found in the three worlds, and fall into four main classes. Only mankind, however, can give birth to the Jain prophets, who are called *tīrthaṃkaras*, literally, "ford-makers" across the ocean of rebirths.

Like other Indian systems, Jainism compares the cyclic course of time *(kāla)* to the movement of a wheel, and divides it into recurring periods called *kalpas* ("eons"). Each *kalpa* has two phases, each further divided into six eras. In the first, descending phase *(avasarpiṇī)* a progressive decline leads from great prosperity to utter misery, which in the second, ascending phase *(utsarpiṇī)* progressively recedes until great prosperity is reached again. The first Jina of each phase is born in the course of the third era, which is characterized by prosperity mixed with sorrow. We are at present in the fifth era of an *avasarpiṇī* whose first Jina was Ṛṣabha and whose next twenty-three *tīrthaṃkaras* lived in the fourth era, which ended seventy-five years and eight and one-half months after the death of Mahāvīra (i.e., according to the Jains, 527/526 BCE).

Doctrine. The tenets of Jainism are well delineated in the Śvetāmbara canon and the Digambara procanonical books, and are systematically presented in the *Tattvārthādhigama Sūtra*. Jain logic (for the most part elaborated somewhat later, probably to meet the needs of controversy) will here be sketched first, together with the Jain theory of knowledge.

Knowledge *(jñāna)*, of which the Jains distinguish five kinds, is an essential attribute of the soul *(jīva)*. It culminates in *kevala-jñāna*, absolute and perfect omniscience. [*See also* Jñāna.]

The Jain system of logic is characterized by the complementary theories of *syādvāda* ("[different] possibilities") and of *nayavāda* ("[method of] approach"). The first affirms that a statement about an object is valid not absolutely but under one of "several conditions" (hence its other name, *anekāntavāda*); considering that an object "can be" *(syād)* such, not such, and so forth, seven modes of assertion are distinguished. The *nayavāda* defines seven main points of view (generic, specific, etc.) from which to consider an object. The Jains adopt an empirical standpoint.

Jainism is a pluralist substantialism that insists on the reality of change. The world and non-world are basically constituted from five *astikāyas* ("masses of being"): the *jīva* ("life" or soul, a real, spiritual monad), and, on the other hand, the inanimate substances: matter, space, movement, and rest. To these, several schools add time. All these factors are eternal and infinite in number. Matter furnishes to the souls a body in which to be incorporated and the possibility of corporeal functions. There are five kinds of bodies, each having different functions. All corporeal beings possess at least two of them, the "karmic" and the "fiery" (the latter for digestion). The karmic body results from previous actions; it is intimately attached to the *jīva,* for whom it causes servitude: hence arise incarnation and transmigration, that is, the law of the universe. [*See also* Karman, *article on* Hindu and Jain Concepts.]

Bondage occurs because the subtle matter resulting from anterior intentions and volitions is attracted to the soul through the vibration of its "soul-points"; this attraction (called *yoga*) is exercised by means of the material elements of speech, body, and mind. The subtle matter that has been so attracted becomes *karman* when entering the soul. The pious Jain strives to rid the latter of these material extrinsic elements. When life ends, the *jīva,* if it has recovered its essential nature, immediately rejoins the other *siddhas* at the pinnacle of the universe. If not, it passes to its new place of rebirth (determined by its *karman*); there are four "ways" of destiny: human, divine, animal, and infernal.

The process of bondage and liberation, then, may be summarized in the following table of seven categories: (1) *jīva;* (2) *ajīva;* (3) influx of karmic matter into the *jīva;* (4) bondage; (5) stoppage of karmic influx *(saṃvara);* (6) expulsion *(nirjarā)* of previously accumulated karmic matter; and (7) total liberation, to which (8) merit and (9) demerit are sometimes added. This table is both ontological and moral, thus leading to Jain ethics.

Ethics. The essentials of Jain ethics are contained in the sets of vows to be taken by the monks and nuns on the one hand, and by the lay believers on the other. Monks and householders further observe other series of prohibitions and engagements that are meant to favor spiritual progress.

The monks cultivate *saṃvara,* the spiritual path defined by the cessation of karmic influx, by means of established ethical and behavioral practices that are usually enumerated in stock lists, as follows:

1. the triple "supervision" of mental, verbal, and bodily activities
2. the fivefold "care" not to hurt living beings when walking, acting, speaking, begging, or performing excretory functions
3. the "tenfold righteousness," or *daśa-dharma:* patience, humility, uprightness, purity, truthfulness, restraint, austerity, renunciation, voluntary poverty, and spiritual obedience
4. the twelve mental "reflections," or *anuprekṣās,* including reflection on the impermanence of things, the helplessness of man, the course of transmigration *(saṃsāra),* the unmitigated solitude of each being in this cycle, the fundamental difference between body and soul, the impurity of the body, the presence of karmic influx, the means by which such influx may be stopped, the ways in which one may rid oneself of karmic matter, the fact that each person is responsible for his own salvation without the assistance of a deity, the rarity of enlightenment, and the truth (i.e., of the teachings presented by the Jinas, especially that of *ahiṃsā*)
5. the twenty-two "trials" (ranging from hunger to confusion) imposed by the pains inherent in religious life.

The monk finally sheds the residues of *karman* by means of steadfast and thorough asceticism *(tapas).*

Lists of the virtues required of the householder have received much attention in Jain tradition and literatures. Some lists include as many as thirty-five ethical imperatives incumbent on the nonclerical Jain, but all include five *aṇuvratas* ("small vows," as opposed to the monks' *mahāvratas,* or "great vows"): *(ahiṃsā),* truthfulness and honesty in all business affairs *(satya),* that material wealth be gained only through legitimate transactions (*asteya,* lit., "non-stealing"), restraint from all illicit sexual activities *(brahma),* and renunciation of one's attachment to material wealth *(aparigraha).* Moreover, the householder or business person should progress through the higher stages of renunciation involving increasingly complete performance of these vows. Thus, he can come closer and closer to fulfilling the monk's vows as well, and ultimately can attain the purity of the "wise man's death," the fast-unto-death *(saṃlekhanā).*

The actual path to liberation *(mokṣa)* is described by Jains as one that includes fourteen "stages of qualification" *(guṇa-sthāna)*. Leaving the state characterized by "wrong views," the path leads ultimately to the elimination of all passions and culminates in omniscience. [*See also* Mokṣa.]

Cultic Structures. It is a specific aspect of the householder's religious life that he is allowed to take part in temple rituals and to worship temple images. In fact, abundant amounts of money are spent on the construction of new temples and in the restoration or reproduction of ancient monuments, a source of prestige as well as a meritorious act.

The structure of the Jain temple is on the whole similar to the Hindu temple. [*See* Temple, *article on* Hindu Temples.] The distinctive feature of the Jain shrine is the image of the *tīrthaṃkara* to whom it is dedicated and the idols of the prophets who flank him or occupy the various surrounding niches. Secondary divinities are frequently added (and are very popular); there are also auspicious and symbolic diagrams: the wheel of the Jain law, and the "Five Supreme Ones": *arhat*s, *siddhas*, *ācārya*s, *upādhyāya*s, and *sādhu*s. There are also conventional representations of continents, of holy places, and of the great festive congregation *(samavasaraṇa)* in the middle of which the Jina is said to have delivered his sermon for the benefit of all creatures. In effect, the Jain temple is often said to be a sort of replica of this assembly. The offerings placed on the offering plates or planks by the faithful with the rice grains he has brought to the shrine are symbols of the three jewels (three dots), which provide escape from the cycle of bondage (the *svastika*) and lead to *siddhi* (a crescent at the top of the figure).

The example set by great men other than the *tīrthaṃkaras* is also commemorated: homage is paid to the "footprints" (*pādukās*) in stone of the great teachers. Above all, Bāhubali is a source of inspiration to the Digambaras: "sky-clad" on the crest of the Indragiri hill in Śravaṇa Beḷgoḷa, his colossal monolithic statue (fifty-seven feet high, erected c. 980) attracts streams of pilgrims, and has been reproduced at several other sites.

The two main churches differ on some other points of varying importance, such as the lists of auspicious objects and the cognizances of certain *tīrthaṃkara*s. The question of nudity has been controversial for centuries: nowadays in the Śvetāmbara shrines the *tīrthaṃkaras* are partly clothed and even decorated, with silver inlay in their eyes.

Iconography. As is to be expected, Jain art is essentially religious. The earliest preserved specimens apparently date back to the age of the Mauryas (third century BCE), and though the Jains' artistic activities have never ceased, their most impressive masterpieces date from the fifth to the fifteenth century CE. These were produced in central and southern India, and above all in the west and in Karnataka.

Stupas were among the first monuments erected by the Jain community, but very soon the Buddhists alone continued this tradition, so that in effect, the Jains have two main types of architectural masterpieces: rock-cut and structural temples. Caves had been used as habitations for monks from very early times in many parts of India. Many were altered, particularly in the Deccan and Tamil Nadu, to make them suitable as shrines. Some are comparatively simple, as, for example, in Sittanavasal. In the Cāḷukya kingdom caverns have been elaborately carved in the cliffs of Vātāpi (Badami) and in Aihole, where the carvings date to the seventh century; under the Rāṣṭrakūṭas (eighth to tenth centuries) the activity shifted to Ellora, where the Jains chiseled out of the rock a monolithic shrine called the Choṭā ("little") Kailāsa.

Structural temples are the most common. The earliest were probably made of wood; later, brick and masonry were used. Building in stone became extremely popular, and thus many architectural monuments have been preserved from as early as the sixth and seventh centuries. The general structure of the Jain temple resembles that of the Brahmanic shrine. The basic ground plan is comparatively simple: several halls in an axial line lead to the sanctum; the number of these *maṇḍapa*s can be increased and the decorative features multiplied. On the other hand, the Jains have favored a variant of the axial hall plan, the so-called *catur-mukha* ("four-faced") type, with a pivotal square at the center and four doors opening in the four directions giving access to a quadruple *tīrthaṃkara* image. Many of the shrines are built in an enclosed courtyard.

Some sites are famous: in the Deccan, Śravaṇa Beḷgoḷa and Aihole (from the ninth century); in southern Karnataka, Mudbidri ("Jain Kāśī," fourteenth century); in Tamil Nadu, Tirupparuttikkunram ("Jain Kāñcī," eleventh century). In the North, temple building began early in Osia near Jodhpur in Rajasthan (from the seventh century onward). In central India, Deogarh has comparatively simple shrines (beginning in the seventh or eighth century), whereas in Khajuraho several temples (such as Pārśvanāth temple, constructed in 954) rival the Brahmanic monuments.

It is probably in western India, however, that the Jain temples are the most numerous and impressive. Many have contributed to the fame of the "Caulukyan style." A number are in Mount Abu, where one of the earliest was erected in 1032, and several are built of delicately polished white marble. Another celebrated complex is in the Aravalli hills, at Ranakpur, where the main shrine (constructed in 1439) is of the *catur-mukha* type. Finally, in the Kathiawar Peninsula famous temple cities have been built in holy pilgrimage places: on the Girnar hill (900 meters above sea level), and south of Palitana, where, 600 meters above sea level, they cover two ridges, each some 320 meters long, of the Śatruñjaya mountain (from the sixteenth century onward).

For all these monuments a large quantity of statues and bas-reliefs (sometimes of enormous dimensions) was prepared in various sorts of stone and metal. Metal casting was well developed in the Caulukya period; a statue of the first *tīrthaṃkara* in one of the Abu temples weighs more than 4,000 kilograms. Smaller pieces have been constantly and abundantly carved and molded for home shrines and temples. For poorer people terracotta has been used.

The most characteristic carvings are the hieratic sculptures of the *tīrthaṃkara*s (and Bāhubali); they conform to strict canons that probably came into existence around the beginning of the common era (though two torsos found near Patna are older and are perhaps Mauryan). The Jains have also represented lesser divinities, whose carvings are not as hieratic as those of the *tīrthaṃkara*s. Moreover, decorative pillars, ceilings, brackets, friezes, and panels adorn many shrines (in Khajuraho, Abu, and Ranakpur) and contrast by their exuberance with the mystic concentration, renouncement, and serenity of the prophets. The *tīrthaṃkara* figures (sitting or standing erect in meditation) are now renowned worldwide: innumerable statues are installed in the shrines, and bas-reliefs are carved on the walls of a number of caves and cells. Many carvings of all sizes can also be seen in the open, chiseled on cliffs and boulders. Perhaps some of the best known are the huge images engraved in rows on the Gwalior cliffs; others, on the contrary, are extremely delicate.

Though only a few mural paintings have been well preserved there is no doubt that many shrines were embellished by painted panels. Nevertheless it is owing to the numerous illustrated manuscripts left by the Jains that their painting has come to be appreciated. The earliest miniatures are on palm leaves (Śvetāmbara, 1060 CE; Digambara, c. 1110); the largest dimensions of paper manuscripts afforded new facilities to the Śvetāmbara artists of Gujarat, especially in the fourteenth and fifteenth centuries. They popularized a typical "western Indian style," with many stereotypes and conventional figures (characterized by protruding eyes). The manner is linear, the colors bright (red, blue, white, green), placed directly beside one another. Altogether, in the five centuries preceding Akbar's reign, the quantity of Jain miniature painting was considerable: in this field no Indian community has matched the profuseness of the Śvetāmbaras.

The Jains have also been very successful in woodcutting, as can still be seen in Rajasthan and Gujarat: this artistic technique flourished particularly from the seventeenth to the nineteenth century. In and around Patan (Gujarat) it is not rare to see window frames and door lintels carved with *tīrthaṃkara* images or auspicious signs, as well as screen doors, lattice windows, and decorated pillars supporting the upper stories in private homes. Other masterpieces of which the preserved specimens are comparatively recent (from the fifteenth century onward), although the first models are certainly older, are the fine wooden temples (whether public or home shrines), still numerous in Gujarat. Given by wealthy individuals of the middle class, these sanctuaries are of modest proportions but exquisitely carved and decorated, sometimes with motifs influenced by the Mughal style. Built on the same pattern, the home shrines of the Gujarati Jains (some dating from the fifteenth century) are also elegantly embellished, as were the homes of the wealthy householders of such centers as Ahmedabad, Patan, Palitana, and Cambay. Though not as widespread as those mentioned earlier, these include perfect masterpieces of Jain art.

Prominent Jain Personalities. Jain achievements are due to the energy and courage of a comparatively united community. Certain brilliant and outstanding individuals, however, have influenced the movement, such as Devarddhi, president of the Valabhī council, or Haribhadra (eighth century), a great Śvetāmbara commentator and writer, in both Prakrit and Sanskrit. Others, such as Kundakunda and Hemacandra, embodied some or most of its tendencies or brilliantly represented it, as did Hīravijaya at Akbar's court. More recently, Mohandas Gandhi himself paid homage to the Jain jeweller and poet Raychandrabhai Mehta (1868–1901). [*See also the biography of Mohandas Gandhi.*] This is the epoch when, after two to three centuries of relative stagnation, a reawakening took place thanks to enlightened monks and householders. Among those who took part in this renewal, Vijaya Dharma Suri (1868–1922) is one of the best known, both in India and in the West. Among the many others who deserve mention are two Digambara scholars, Hiralal Jain (1898–1973) and A. N. Upadhye (1906–1975), or, on the Śvetāmbara side, those whose collaboration made the foundation of the Lalbhai Dalpatbhai Institute of Indology in Ahmedabad possible: the Muni Puṇyavijaya (1895–1971), Kasturbhai Lalbhai, and Pandit D. M. Malvania (a pupil of the philosopher Sukhlalji, 1880–1978).

Through the ages the Jains, though a minority, have clearly occupied a major place in Indian history. Their culture is both original and influenced by the Brahmanic society surrounding them. Conversely, their presence has probably encouraged certain tendencies of Hinduism, perhaps the most outstanding of which are the high value set on asceticism, and, certainly, the faith in *ahiṃsā*.

[*For further discussion of specific Jain topics, see* Tīrthaṃkaras *and the biography of Mahāvīra. For the Jain influence on Hindu and Buddhist thought, see* Ahiṃsā.]

BIBLIOGRAPHY

Interest in Jainism was awakened and placed on a sound basis by the pioneering works of Albrecht Weber and Ernst Leumann, editors of *Indische Studien*, vols. 16–17 (1883; reprint, Hildesheim, 1973), and Hermann Jacobi, editor of *The Kalpasūtra of Bhadrabāhu* (Leipzig, 1879) and translator of four basic canonical books in the series "Sacred Books of the East," vols. 22, 45 (1884, 1895; reprint, Delhi, 1968), all preceded by very important introductions in English.

Excellent presentations of Jainism are Helmuth von Glasenapp's *Der Jainismus* (1925; reprint, Hildesheim, 1964) and Padmanabh S. Jaini's *The Jaina Path of Purification* (Berkeley, 1979), the latter emphasizing (somewhat unusually) the Digambara point of view. A comprehensive Hindi dictionary of Jainism is Jinendra Jaini's *Jainendra Siddhānta Kosá*, 4 vols. (New Delhi, 1970–1973). A social survey has been presented by Vilas A. Samgave, *Jaina Community*, 2d rev. ed. (Bombay, 1980). The history of Jainism in the different parts of India is the object of numerous monographs; a more general account is given in Jyoti Prasad Jain's *The Jaina Sources of the History of Ancient India, 100 B.C.–A.D. 900* (Delhi, 1964).

Given the considerable literature of the Jains, philological studies are of prime importance. Ludwig Alsdorf has provided a general survey of the scholarly achievements and desiderata in this field in his *Les études jaina: État présent et tâches futures* (Paris, 1965); the same scholar has made many other illuminating contributions.

The doctrine is presented in a masterly book by Walther Schubring, *Die Lehre der Jainas, nach den alten Quellen dargestellt* (Berlin, 1935), based mostly, but not exclusively, on the Śvetāmbara canon (with an important bibliography up to 1935); it has been translated into English from the revised German edition by Wolfgang Beurlen as *The Doctrine of the Jainas, Described after the Old Sources* (Delhi, 1962), but the abovementioned bibliography is not included. Schubring has also edited and translated several canonical texts and is the author of basic monographs; see his *Kleine Schriften*, edited by Klaus Bruhn (Wiesbaden, 1977).

The fifth Aṅga can be regarded as a summary of Jainism: it is very well analyzed in Jozef Deleu's *Viyāhapannatti (Bhagavaī): The Fifth Aṅga of the Jaina Canon. Introduction, Critical Analysis, Commentary, and Indexes* (Brugge, 1970). It is impossible to quote all the editions (critical or uncritical) and translations of the original books. A convenient edition of the canon is the two-volume version published in Gurgaon (1954; being by Sthānakvāsins, it includes only thirty two texts). Important editorial series have also been created in recent years, the edited texts being often preceded by important introductions, and specialized journals have been published. Excellent English translations of selected Jain texts by A. L. Basham are included in *Sources of Indian Tradition*, compiled by Wm. Theodore de Bary et al. (New York, 1958).

Specialized studies are numerous. Several catalogues of manuscript collections (in India and in Europe) have been published, and contribute to our knowledge of Jain history, literature, and "manuscriptology" (a very important activity of the community); the most recent by Chandrabhāl Tripāṭhī, is the *Catalogue of the Jaina Manuscripts at Strasbourg* (Leiden, 1975), scrutinizing the systematic collection assembled there by Ernst Leumann.

Jain polemics against other schools of thought (as well as the commentators' methods) are studied in Willem B. Bollée's *Studien zum Sūyagaḍa: Die Jainas und die anderen Weltanschauungen vor der Zeitwende* (Wiesbaden, 1977). Monastic discipline is examined in Shantaram Bhalchandra Deo's *History of Jaina Monachism from Inscriptions and Literature* (Poona, 1956), and by many other scholars. The rules laid down for the laity are well analyzed in R. Williams's *Jaina Yoga* (London, 1963; reprint, Delhi, 1983). Jain cosmology is one of the three main parts of Willibald Kirfel's *Die Kosmographie der Inder* (1920; reprint, Bonn, 1967). See also my *La cosmologie jaïna* (Paris, 1981), which has been translated into English by K. R. Norman as *The Jain Cosmology* (Basel, 1981).

For the history of Jain literature (apart from good contributions in Hindi) reference can be made to Maurice Winternitz's *History of Indian Literature*, vol. 2 (Calcutta, 1933; reprint, Delhi, 1963). Attention has rightly been focused on some of the literary genres cultivated by the Jains; see, for example, Jagdishchandra Jain's *Prakrit Narrative Literature* (in fact, more or less completely Jain; New Delhi, 1981); see also the proceedings of the International Symposium on Jaina Canonical and Narrative Literature (Strasbourg, 1981), an edited version of which can be found in *Indologica Taurinensia* 11 (Turin, 1984).

Many books on Jain art and architecture have been published as a contribution to the celebration of the twenty-five hundredth anniversary of Mahāvīra's *nirvāṇa*. A comprehensive survey, edited by Amalananda Ghosh, is *Jaina Art and Architecture*, 3 vols. (New Delhi, 1974–1975), and very good monographs are collected in *Jaina Art and Archaeology*, edited by Umakant Premanand Shah and M. A. Dhaky (Ahmedabad, 1975).

Iconography is the subject of Brindavan Chandra Bhattacharyya's *The Jaina Iconography*, 2d rev. ed. (Delhi, 1974), and has inspired numerous important studies by Umakant Premanand Shah, whose *Studies in Jaina Art* (Varanasi, 1955) should also be mentioned. Illustrated manuscripts have been studied by W. Norman Brown in *A Descriptive and Illustrated Catalogue of Miniature Paintings of the Jaina Kalpasūtra* (Washington, D.C., 1934); on this subject, there exist many books, by Umakant Premanand Shah, for example, *Treasures of Jaina Bhaṇḍāras* (Ahmedabad, 1978), as well as Moti Chandra, Sarabhai Manilal Nawab, and others; they include many plates.

Colette Caillat

JALĀL AL-DĪN RŪMĪ. *See* Rūmī, Jalāl al-Dīn.

JAMĀʿAT-I ISLĀMĪ (The Islamic Society), a Muslim religio-political organization in the Indian subcontinent, was founded in August 1941 on the initiative of Abū al-Aʿlā Mawdūdī, who had issued a public invitation to all who were interested to meet in Lahore. In his earlier life Mawdūdī had worked as a journalist, but in 1932 he became editor of the religious monthly *Tarjumān al-Qurʾān,* which later served as the principal organ of the Jamāʿat. During the 1930s Mawdūdī participated in the debates about India's political future and opposed both the united Indian nationalism of the Indian National Congress and the Muslim nationalism of the Muslim League. All nationalism he thought contrary to Islam and insisted that the identity of Muslims derives from Islam alone.

In 1940 the Muslim League passed its famous Lahore Resolution calling for the creation of Pakistan as a homeland for Indian Muslims. Mawdūdī later said that the Lahore Resolution triggered his long-cherished plan to establish a society for the promotion of Islam. Earlier he had concentrated on criticism and reform of individual Muslim life; now, however, there was need for organized activity. At the initial meeting a constitution was adopted, and Mawdūdī was elected the first *amīr,* or leader. The Jamāʿat-i Islāmī has ever since been inseparably wedded to its founder. Not only was he its leader from the beginning until he retired in 1972, but his writings have provided the Jamāʿat's interpretation of Islam and its political beliefs.

The period between 1941 and 1947 was one of intense activity devoted to promoting the Jamāʿat. The organization's activities remained at the level of individual persuasion, however, and it had almost no influence in India. Although Mawdūdī opposed the nationalist view of Pakistan held by the Muslim League, and bitterly criticized their leadership, when India was partitioned in August 1947, he opted for Pakistan. He moved from East Punjab to Lahore with a portion of his followers, leaving another part of the Jamāʿat to remain in India. Since that time the Indian and Pakistani branches have been entirely separate, and the Indian one has been relatively less important.

History. In Pakistan the Jamāʿat first worked to assist the refugees pouring into the country from India. In early 1948, however, it leapt into political prominence by espousing the cause of the Islamic state and becoming the focal point of nationwide agitation. Pakistan, Mawdūdī reasoned, had been won in the name of Islam; it was, therefore, imperative that a truly Islamic system be established in the country. Since this position evoked a wide public response, it was troublesome for the liberal leadership of the Muslim League government, who could afford neither to reject the Islamic state nor to embrace it in the form demanded by the Jamāʿat-i Islāmī.

The Jamāʿat quickly came into confrontation with the government. Four things drew government wrath: (1) strident criticism of the leadership, (2) statements by Mawdūdī that the war against India over Kashmir was not a proper *jihād* ("war in the way of God"), (3) Mawdūdī's stand against oaths of unconditional loyalty to the government, and (4) a prepartition stand of the Jamāʿat against recruitment in the army. Mawdūdī and other leaders were arrested and held in jail for more than a year, but the campaign for the Islamic state continued.

When the Objectives Resolution of the Pakistan Constituent Assembly was passed in 1949, it was acclaimed by the Jamāʿat as Pakistan's declaration of intent to be an Islamic state; the issue then became election of a leadership to implement the Islamic ideal. Thus the way was opened for the Jamāʿat's active participation in elections. This decision to seek political office would subsequently, in 1957–1958, become the cause of a major rift in the Jamāʿat that would lead to the resignations of several important members.

In 1951 Mawdūdī reached the peak of his prominence in Pakistan and enjoyed respect even among the *ʿulamāʾ* ("religious scholars"), with whom he often differed. He was the principal figure at the conference of *ʿulamāʾ* convoked in Karachi in January 1951, in response to the controversial report of the Basic Principles Committee of the Constituent Assembly. The twenty-two points describing an Islamic state upon which the *ʿulamāʾ* agreed were largely due to his influence.

In 1952 and 1953 there was widespread agitation in Pakistan against the Aḥmadīyah sect, resulting in riots, loss of life, and destruction of property. Although the Jamāʿat did not officially sanction the "direct action" against the Aḥmadīyah, much of what happened had its tacit approval. Mawdūdī published a pamphlet entitled *Qādiyānī Masʾalah* condemning the group as non-Muslims. When martial law was declared in March 1953, he was again arrested, along with numerous Jamāʿat leaders, and was condemned to death. The sentence, however, was commuted, and he was released from prison in April 1955. During Mawdūdī's several imprisonments, others, such as Amīn Aḥsan Iṣlāḥī and Sulṭān Aḥmad, served as temporary *amīr*s of the Jamāʿat.

When the 1956 Pakistani constitution was promulgated, the Jamāʿat-i Islāmī welcomed it as meeting most of the requirements of an Islamic state. It did so even though the constitution did not declare Islam the official religion of Pakistan, did not make the *sharīʿah* the law of the land, and did not make the specifically Islamic provisions enforceable in the courts. Acceptance of the constitution robbed the Islamic state issue of its viability, and the Jamāʿat turned to a campaign for "true democracy" in Pakistan centered upon a demand for separate electorates for Muslims and antisecularist propaganda.

In 1958 a military coup brought Field Marshal Muḥammad Ayyūb Khān to power in Pakistan. The Jamāʿat-i Islāmī fell under the ensuing martial law banning political parties and was thus not allowed to function until the promulgation of a new constitution in March 1962. The Jamāʿat bitterly opposed Ayyūb, whom it saw as a dictator who had frustrated democracy to keep the Islamic forces in check. It rejected the political system established by the new constitution but nonetheless worked within it. The Jamāʿat's ire was especially stimulated by the Muslim Family Law Ordinance, which introduced changes into Muslim personal law. Its activities led Ayyūb to ban the Jamāʿat and to arrest Mawdūdī once again in early 1964. The courts, however, declared the ban and the arrest illegal. During Ayyūb's time the Jamāʿat first adopted the policy of allying itself with other parties in combined opposition to the government. In the 1965 elections it supported Fāṭimah Jinnāḥ for president, despite its teaching that Islam disapproved a woman as head of state, and following the brief India-Pakistan war of 1965, it added its voice to the protests against the Tashkent Declaration. In the 1970 elections the Jamāʿat joined other right-wing groups in opposing both the socialism of Ẓulfiqār ʿAlī Bhutto and the demands of Mujīb al-Raḥmān's Awami League; these elections, however, were a crushing defeat for the Jamāʿat throughout the country. When Yaḥyā Khān launched military action against East Pakistan in March 1971, the Jamāʿat supported the actions of the government and the army and thereby lost the little support it had in Bengal. After Bhutto's rise to power it posed a demand for the Niẓām-i Muṣṭafā ("prophetic system") against the socialist tendencies of the People's Party. When Bhutto was overthrown by General Ẓiyā al-Ḥaqq (Ziya al-Haq), the Jamāʿat was at first favored by the new government by several appointments to cabinet posts, but it was soon reduced to impotence by the government's interdiction of all political activity.

Organization. The Jamāʿat's constitution has been amended several times to compensate for changing circumstances. It provides for a highly centralized organization. Most power rests with the *amīr*, who is elected for a five-year term but who may hold office for life. Seven different central offices function under his direct supervision. He is assisted by a *majlis-i shūrā*, or consultative body, whose opinions, however, are not binding on him, and by a *majlis-i ʿumalāʾ*, or executive committee. There is also an executive assistant, the *qayyim*, who acts as secretary general. Duplicated at the district, circle, and provincial levels, this central organization is of great significance, for it is precisely that detailed for the ideal Islamic state. It was plainly the Jamāʿat's intention that it should become the government in the event of its political success. Membership in the organization, sharply restricted to persons meeting high standards of Islamic knowledge and personal conduct, has never been large. The majority of the Jamāʿat's associates are *muttafiqīn*, or sympathizers, who provide its principal political support and much of its finances. It is not uncommon for members to be expelled for misconduct or disinterest, and a number of the full members work full time for the Jamāʿat. Great attention is paid to training, and regular training sessions are held. Other activities include publication, including journals and newspapers, the maintenance of reading rooms, mobile clinics, disaster relief, and work with labor unions. There are also associated organizations, the principal one of which is the Islāmī Jamīʿat-i Ṭulabāʾ, a militant student group with powerful influence in Pakistani universities.

Ideology. The Jamāʿat-i Islāmī holds Islam to be an ideology comprising a complete set of principles for human life. Just as nature acknowledges the sovereignty of its creator by obedience to natural laws, so also should humans submit to the divine law for their existence. That law is known primarily through the Qurʾān and the *sunnah* of the Prophet. The Jamāʿat lays great emphasis on the all-inclusiveness of its ideology; Islam is not merely a matter of the relationship between the individual and God but must also govern social, economic, and political life. True Islamic faith demands that Muslims hold political power and that the state be ruled according to Islamic principles. There can be no political parties and no opposition in such a state since there is only one correct Islamic viewpoint. Neither can the state make law. Sovereignty belongs to God alone and all legitimate law must derive from his expressed will. Thus, the Jamāʿat insisted that policy-forming offices must be held by pious Muslims whose duties include suppression of rival ideologies. Non-Muslims have a protected status in the Islamic state but are treated as second-class citizens who must live under certain restrictions. The Jamāʿat envisages a totalitarian state united in obedience to a single ruler whose word prevails so long as it accords with the divine law. Such a state was considered democratic, however, since the ruler was elected and could be removed; it was also a welfare state obligated to meet the basic needs of its citizens. Despite the implicit authoritarianism of the ideology, the Jamā'at has consistently held revolutionary violence to be illegitimate and the way to the Islamic state to lie in peaceful democratic methods.

[*See also the biography of Mawdūdī.*]

BIBLIOGRAPHY

The role of the Jamā'at-i Islāmī in the early phases of Pakistani history is treated fully by Leonard Binder in *Religion and Politics in Pakistan* (Berkeley, 1963) and by Keith Callard in *Pakistan: A Political Study* (London, 1957). The only full-length treatment of the organization in English is Kalim Bahadur's *The Jamā'at-i-Islāmi of Pakistan* (New Delhi, 1977). I have discussed the society's ideology and teachings in "The Ideology of Mawlana Mawdudi," in *South Asian Politics and Religion*, edited by Donald Smith (Princeton, 1966), and "Mawdudi's Conception of the Islamic State," in *Voices of Resurgent Islam*, edited by John Esposito (Oxford, 1983). There are also two accounts of the Jamā'at's history by its founder: *Jamā'at-i Islāmī, uskā maqsad, ta'rīkh, awr lā'ih-i 'amal* (Lahore, 1952) and *Jamā'at-i Islāmī kē 29 sāl* (Lahore, 1970).

CHARLES J. ADAMS

JAMĀL AL-DĪN AL-AFGHĀNĪ. *See* Afghānī, Jamāl al-Dīn al-.

JAMES, E. O. (1888–1972), English academic anthropologist, folklorist, and historian of religions. Edwin Oliver James was born in London on 30 March 1888. He was educated at Exeter College, Oxford, where he took a diploma in anthropology under R. R. Marett, and at University College, London. From 1911 to 1933 he served as a priest of the Church of England, chiefly in parishes in London and Oxford, while maintaining a scholarly interest in anthropology, comparative religion, and folklore. During the 1920s and 1930s he was associated with the diffusionist school of Elliot Smith and William James Perry, and with the "myth and ritual school" that emerged out of it. Thus he became one of the earliest British "myth and ritual" writers, contributing to the school's first two symposia. For *Myth and Ritual*, edited by S. H. Hooke (London, 1933), he wrote "Initiatory Rituals," and for its sequel, *The Labyrinth*, also edited by Hooke (London, 1935), "The Sources of Christian Ritual." Although he had published several books on anthropology, his first major work was *Christian Myth and Ritual* (1933), in which he applied the methods of the myth and ritual school to questions of Christian origins and to later Christian ceremonies.

In 1933 James became professor of the history and philosophy of religion at the University of Leeds, and in 1945 he moved to a similar post at the University of London (King's College), where he remained until his retirement in 1955. From 1960 until his death on 6 July 1972 he was chaplain of All Souls' College, Oxford. Throughout his active life he was a member of numerous learned societies, including the Folklore Society, of which he was president from 1930 to 1932, and in 1954 he was instrumental in founding the British section of the International Association for the History of Religions.

James published a large number of books and articles on a wide variety of subjects connected with anthropology and comparative religion. The best known were perhaps *Origins of Sacrifice* (1934), *Introduction to the Comparative Study of Religion* (1938), and *Prehistoric Religion* (1957). He was not, however, an original writer or theorist, being content for the most part to have assimilated, and to reproduce, the findings of others. In matters of controversy he habitually took a mediating position, which left him without a strong profile of his own. In theology he was an Anglo-Catholic; in anthropology he was initially an evolutionist but at a later stage was prepared to modify his views in response to changes of emphasis. He was not, for instance, despite his theological position, disposed to accept all the findings of the school of Wilhelm Schmidt concerning "high gods." Thus, although he wrote that "High Gods do in fact stand alone, head and shoulders above all secondary divinities," he insisted that "the belief in High Gods among low races cannot be described as a true monotheism" (*Prehistoric Religion*, pp. 206–208).

James's significance lay in his capacity to assimilate and interpret a vast body of material about comparative religion and to present it for a wider public. At a time when the study of religion in Britain was at a fairly low ebb, he served as an admirable interpreter, and as a mediator between positions that were often polarized internationally. His best work was done in the 1930s, for some of his later works were little more than compilations of material readily available elsewhere.

BIBLIOGRAPHY

A full bibliography of James's writings up to 1963 can be found in *The Saviour God: Comparative Studies in the Concept of Salvation, Presented to Professor E. O. James to Commemorate His Seventy-fifth Birthday*, edited by S. G. F. Brandon (Manchester, 1963). See also D. W. Gundry's "Professor E. O. James, 1888–1972," *Numen* 19 (August–December 1972): 81–83.

ERIC J. SHARPE

JAMES, WILLIAM (1842–1910), American psychologist and philosopher. William James was the eldest son of Henry James, Sr. (1811–1882), a writer on social and religious subjects esteemed in his day, but never famous. William was born in New York City on 11 January 1842. His early education at his father's hands was supplemented by much travel abroad and some schooling in Boulogne and at the University of Geneva, where his scientific bent developed. Later, he attended lectures at the University of Berlin and elsewhere in Germany. He was from youth a voracious reader of philosophy and particularly concerned with the question of science and materialism. Plagued by illness and "neurasthenic" by temperament, he was long uncertain about a career. He tried his hand at painting, with fair success, but after joining the zoologist Louis Agassiz on an expedition of fifteen months to Brazil, James studied chemistry and medicine at Harvard, receiving his medical degree in 1869.

He soon decided against medical practice and began to teach anatomy and physiology at the university. The work of the new German school of physical psychology attracted him, and he prepared himself to teach the subject, establishing for it the first laboratory in the United States (and perhaps in the world). After a few years productive of noted papers, he seized the opportunity in 1878 to add to his teaching a course in philosophy—later famous as Phil. 3. The rest of his life was spent teaching philosophy at Harvard and lecturing widely at home and abroad. He died in Chocorua, New Hampshire, on 26 August 1910.

James's *Principles of Psychology*, which appeared in two volumes in 1890, was hailed as the *summa* of current knowledge, much of it based on his own previously published research. The work also contains the main elements of Jamesian philosophy and is a literary masterpiece besides. When it was reissued in the 1950s, reviewers in journals of psychology called it still able to inspire and instruct.

James next published *The Will to Believe* (1897). Its title essay, first published in 1879, was his first mature statement on the nature of faith, including religious faith. His later volumes, *Pragmatism* (1907), *A Pluralistic Universe* and *The Meaning of Truth* (both 1909), and the posthumous *Some Problems of Philosophy* (1911) and *Essays in Radical Empiricism* (1912), rounded out his philosophic vision.

But between the *Psychology* and these works, James delivered as Gifford Lectures in Edinburgh *The Varieties of Religious Experience* (1902). This full-scale treatise may be considered volume 3 of the *Psychology*, for James took the daring step of presenting to an audience known for its piety and conservatism a naturalistic view of the facts of religion.

His venture was a success at the time and the book has never been out of print since, one of the reasons being James's disclaiming any intention to "explain away" any part of his subject. On the contrary, he attacked what he called "medical materialism," the reductivism that attributes religious despair to a bad digestion, and the like. James's philosophy was rooted in the acceptance of experience as it comes, without preconceptions as to what is real and what is "mere" appearance. The recently published reconstruction of lectures James gave in 1896 on *Exceptional States of Mind* (1983) makes the same point.

James's contribution in *The Varieties* can be listed under a few main heads. (1) Religion is a universal phenomenon in mankind, therefore not an aberration due to disease or any other abnormality; this, despite the abnormal character of some religious leaders and followers. (2) The religious life and its tendencies are not uniform but various, sometimes contradictory. The "sick soul" contrasts with the "healthy minded"; the religious emotion embraces, the moral impulse divides; other features of faith—the sense of sin and of being saved, conversion, saintliness, asceticism, mystical union with God—all of these are recognizable manifestations of faith, yet they differ in frequency and repute within one and the same religion. There is even an atheistic religion, Buddhism. But (3) all religions, besides prescribing forms of conduct and worship, point to a transcendent world unlike the one perceived through the senses. A "higher law" governs that other world and should influence our aims and acts here below. (4) The right to believe rests on the principle that if belief can cause desirable alterations in behavior, then waiting for final evidence before believing is not a neutral act but one that negatives a possible result. (The garbling of the argument by careless critics has distorted the meaning of "the will to believe"; as a psychologist, James knew, like Augustine, that believing embodies an act of will, though nobody can believe at will.) (5) As for the truth of the diverse religious formulations, the Jamesian philosophy of experience and analysis of belief lead to a perspectivist view: truth is a species of the good and beliefs must submit to the test of consequences, the widest possible. Where no agreed standard is available, the assessment of results will vary—as the religions do. But the principle at work here does not differ from the scientific. Science also devises terms and categories to isolate parts of experience, ascertains relations, and then proves itself by pointing to results. (6) As a sidelight only, James offered the suggestion that the sense of transcendence comes from the subliminal. Knowledge about it was growing at the turn of the century, and James was inclined to view it as a vast sea of inarticulate awareness from which individuality and conscious mind are extracts and constructs: experience is wider than the senses alone can encompass.

For his own part, James said, he "lacked the germ" of explicit belief. In his Ingersoll Lecture on Human Immortality at Harvard (1898), he declared his inadequacy to his assignment and used the opportunity to deprecate the scientific orthodoxy, which opposed the study of religious and psychic phenomena. James had helped to found the American branch of the Society for Psychical Research and he devoted a good deal of time to investigating mediums. Some were shown to be frauds; others seemed to perform inexplicable feats; but none, James concluded, provided evidence of spirit return or of assured extrasensory powers. His last word on the subject was "I remain uncertain and await more facts."

The reader interested in antecedents should also consult the sympathetic monograph on his father's theology that James wrote as an introduction to *The Literary Remains of the Late Henry James* (1884).

BIBLIOGRAPHY

The Works of William James have been published by the Harvard University Press (Cambridge, Mass., 1975–). The letters are in preparation; an early selection in two volumes appeared in 1920. The best biography is Gay Wilson Allen's *William James* (New York, 1967). A large body of sources and comments was woven together by Ralph Barton Perry as *The Thought and Character of William James*, 2 vols. (Boston, 1935). J. S. Bixler dealt with *Religion in the Philosophy of William James* (Boston, 1926), and James's relation to the various departments of modern thought is treated in Jacques Barzun's *A Stroll with William James* (Chicago, 1983).

JACQUES BARZUN

JANUS. According to most linguists, the word *ianus* seems to be based upon the root *iā*, which constitutes an extension of the Indo-European root *ei-* ("to go"). This abstract term, signifying "passage," alternates between the stem form *-u-* and the stem form *-o-*. From the first are formed the derivatives *Ianuarius* ("January"), *ianu-al* (a biscuit reserved for Janus), and *ianu-a* ("door"). From the second comes *iani-tor* ("porter"), *Iani-culum* (Janiculum Hill), and *Iani-gena* (daughter of Janus). In the Roman pantheon Janus is an original figure who has no Greek homologue (Ovid, *Fasti* 1.90). The Etruscan name *Ani*, which appears on the sculpture of an augur's liver found at Piacenza, is a borrowing from either Latin or an Italian dialect. Since, as Cicero emphasizes (*De natura deorum* 2.67), the god embodies the motive of "passage," it is characteristic of him to be at the beginning, in line with the scholar Varro's definition cited by Augustine (*City of God* 7.9): "To Janus comes everything that begins, to Jupiter everything that culminates" ("Penes Ianum sunt prima, penes Ioven summa").

This primacy is verified in the liturgy: Janus is invoked first in ceremonies. On the same basis he is patron, along with Juno (whence his epithet *Iunonius*), of all the calends. The first member of the priestly corps, the *rex sacrorum* ("king of the sacrifices"), offers him a sacrifice at the beginning of each month (Macrobius, *Saturnalia* 1.15.10). In the same way, the first official sacrifice of each year, the Agonium of 9 January, is directed to Janus. Sculpted images of him with two faces—corresponding, according to the interpretations, to opening and closing or to past and future—gained for him the names of Janus Bifrons ("with double forehead"), Janus Biceps ("two-headed"), and Janus Geminus ("twin").

Other qualificatives have functional value. Thus tradition points to Janus Curiatius, who must have presided over a rite of passage of young men into the tribal subgroups called *curiae*, and to Janus Quirinus, mentioned in the "royal laws" as associated with the time when the third share of the *spolia opima* was allotted to the god Quirinus (Festus, ed. Lindsay, 1913, p. 204 L.). This last is the most ancient title given to Janus, who sits in the old Forum in the "ancient sanctuary provided with an altar" (Ovid, *Fasti* 1.275). According to whether its doors were shut or open, he "indicated the state of peace or war" (Livy, 1.19.2). Augustus, who restored this cult to a place of honor, boasted of having closed the temple on three occasions (*Res gestae* 13). This explains the appellation of Janus Quirinus: he is the god who presides over the passage from war to peace. This is the poet Horace's interpretation when he illustrates the "Quirinal" orientation of Janus by the expression "Ianus Quirini" (*Odes* 4.15.9), which he takes up elsewhere in a more prosaic and explicit phrase, "Janus, the guardian of peace" (*Epistles* 2.1.255).

BIBLIOGRAPHY

Dumézil, Georges. *Archaic Roman Religion.* 2 vols. Translated by Philip Krapp. Chicago, 1970.

Gagé, Jean. *Augustus, Emperor of Rome, 63 B.C.–14 A.D.: Res Gestae divi Augusti.* Paris, 1977.

Schilling, Robert. *Rites, cultes, dieux de Rome.* Paris, 1979. See pages 220–262 on Janus.

Wissowa, Georg. *Religion und Kultus der Römer.* 2d ed. Munich, 1912. See pages 103–113.

ROBERT SCHILLING
Translated from French by Paul C. Duggan

JAPANESE RELIGION. [*This entry provides an introduction to the religious traditions of Japan. It consists of four articles:*

An Overview
Popular Religion
Mythic Themes
Religious Documents

For treatment of specific religious traditions, see also Shintō; Buddhism, *article on* Buddhism in Japan; *and* Confucianism in Japan.]

An Overview

Like many other ethnic groups throughout the world, the earliest inhabitants of the Japanese archipelago had from time immemorial their own unique way of viewing the world and the meaning of human existence and their own characteristic rituals for celebrating various events and phases of their individual and corporate life. To them the whole of life was permeated by religious symbols and authenticated by myths. From this tradition an indigenous religious form, which came to be designated as Shintō, or "the way of *kami*," developed in the early historic period. Many aspects of the archaic tradition have also been preserved as basic features of an unorganized folk religion. Meanwhile, through contacts with Korea and China, Japan came under the impact of religious and cultural influences from the continent of Asia. Invariably, Japanese religion was greatly enriched as it appropriated the concepts, symbols, rituals, and art forms of Confucianism, Taoism, the Yin-yang school, and Buddhism. Although these religious and semireligious systems kept a measure of their own identity, they are by no means to be considered mutually exclusive; to all intents and purposes they became facets of the nebulous but enduring religious tradition that may be referred to as "Japanese religion."

It is worth noting in this connection that the term *shūkyō* ("religion") was not used until the nineteenth century. In Japanese traditions, religious schools are usually referred to as *dō*, *tō*, or *michi* ("way"), as in Butsudō ("the way of the Buddha") or Shintō ("the way of *kami*"), implying that these are complementary ways or paths within the overarching Japanese religion. Various branches of art were also called *dō* or *michi*, as in *chadō* (also *sadō*, "the way of tea"). This usage reflects the close affinity in Japan between religious and aesthetic traditions.

Prehistoric Background. The Japanese archipelago lies off the Asian continent, stretching north and south in the western Pacific. In ancient times, however, there were land connections between the continent and the Japanese islands. Animal and human populations thus were able to reach present Japan from different parts of the continent. Although we cannot be certain when and how the first inhabitants migrated to the Japanese islands, general agreement traces Japan's Paleolithic age back to between ten and thirty thousand years ago, when the inhabitants of the islands were primitive hunters and food gatherers who shared the same level and kinds of religious and cultural traits with their counterparts in other regions of the world.

Japan's prehistoric period is divided into two phases, (1) the Jōmon period (*jōmon* literally means "cord pattern," referring to pottery decoration) extending roughly from the fifth or fourth millennium to about 250 BCE, and (2) the Yayoi period (so named because pottery of this period was unearthed in the Yayoi district of present Tokyo) covering roughly the era from 250 BCE to 250 CE. Further subdivisions of both the Jōmon and Yayoi periods, as proposed by various archaeologists, are not relevant for our purpose. Archaeological evidence reveals a gradual development in people's use of fishing and hunting tools, but in the artistic qualities of pottery making and designs and in the living patterns of the Jōmon people we still have few clues regarding their religious outlooks or practices. Thus, we can only infer that the practice of extracting certain teeth, for example, indicates a puberty rite and that female figurines must have been used for fertility cults.

There is no clear-cut date for dividing the Jōmon and the Yayoi periods, because the Yayoi culture emerged in western parts of Japan while the Jōmon culture was still developing in the eastern parts. Nevertheless, the transition between these cultural forms was sufficiently marked so that some scholars even postulate the migration during the early third century BCE of a new ethnic group from outside. Yayoi pottery is more sophisticated in design and manufacturing techniques and more utilitarian than Jōmon ware; Yayoi jugs, jars, and pots were used for cooking as much as for preserving food. Moreover, Yayoi culture was based on rice cultivation, employing a considerable number of hydraulic controls. Evidently, communities were established in places of low altitude, and many farmhouses had raised floors, the space beneath them serving as storehouses for grain. As the Yayoi period coincided with the Ch'in (221–206 BCE) and the Han (206 BCE–220 CE) dynasties in China, and as Chinese political and cultural influence was penetrating the Korean peninsula, some features of continental civilization must have infiltrated into western Japan. This infiltration may account for the development in the Yayoi period of spinning and weaving and the use of iron, bronze, and copper. We can only speculate, however, whether and to what extent new features of the Yayoi culture such as bronze mirrors,

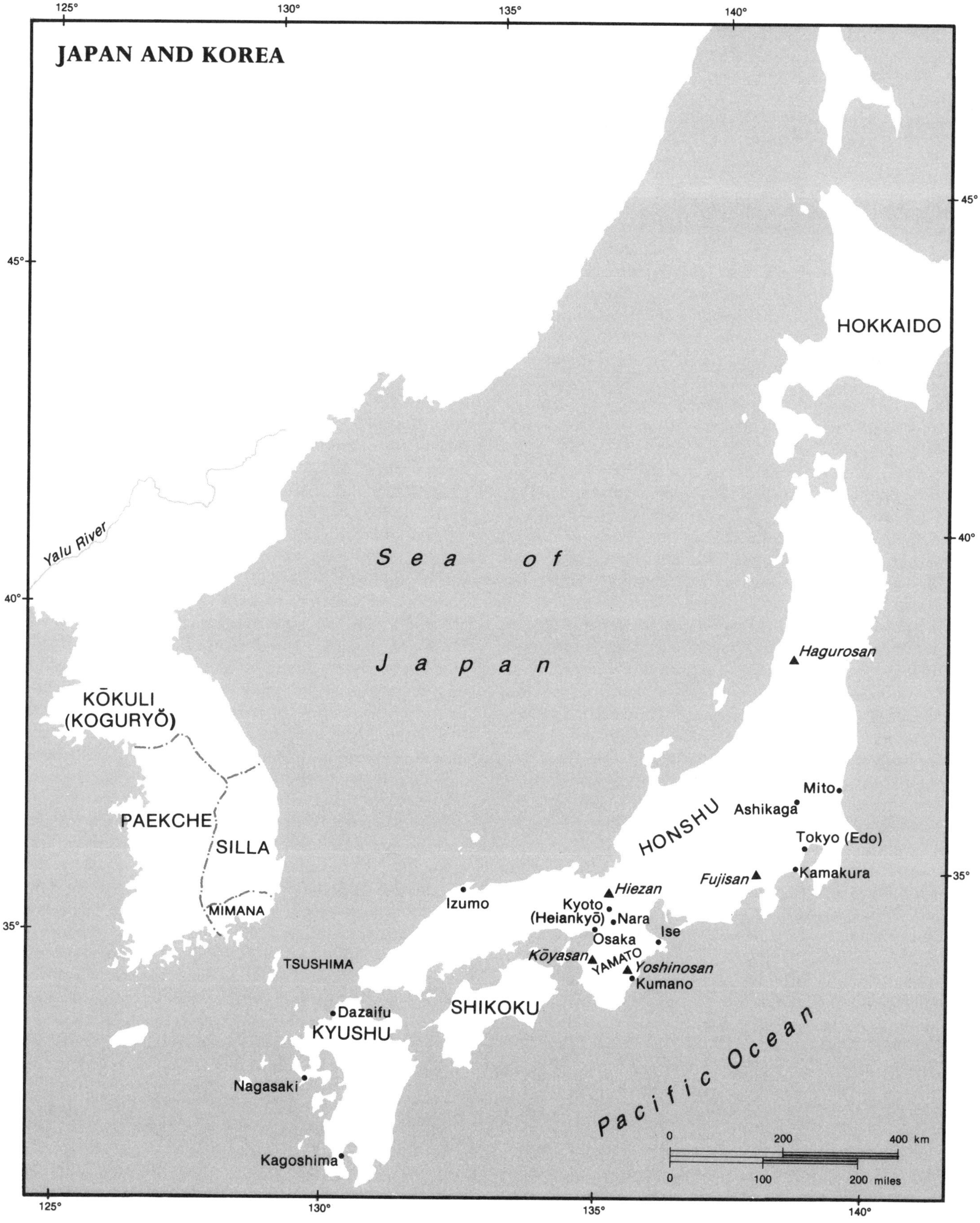
JAPAN AND KOREA
125°
130°
135°
140°
45°
40°
35°
HOKKAIDO
Yalu River
Sea of
Japan
Hagurosan
KŌKULI
(KOGURYŎ)
PAEKCHE
SILLA
MIMANA
Mito
Ashikaga
HONSHU
Tokyo (Edo)
Fujisan
Kamakura
Hiezan
Izumo
Kyoto
(Heiankyō)
Nara
Osaka
Ise
Kōyasan
YAMATO
Yoshinosan
Kumano
TSUSHIMA
Dazaifu
SHIKOKU
KYUSHU
Nagasaki
Kagoshima
Pacific Ocean
0
200
400 km
100
200 miles

bronze bells, dolmens, and funeral urns had religious meaning.

The Ainu controversy and a culture-complex hypothesis. Although it is safe to assume that migrations of people to the Japanese islands were only insignificant parts of larger movements of archaic peoples from Eurasia to North America, it is extremely difficult to determine the ethnic identity of the first settlers in Japan. In this connection a heated controversy has been carried on in recent decades as to whether or not the Ainu—who have lived on the Hokkaido, Sakhalin, and Kurile islands but who throughout history have never been assimilated into the cultural life of the Japanese—were indeed the original inhabitants of the Japanese islands. Current scholarly opinion holds that the Ainu lived in northern Japan as early as the Jōmon period, but that there has never, at least until the last century, been any significant amount of intermarriage between them and other inhabitants of the Japanese islands. [*See* Ainu Religion.]

Although the exact identity of the Jōmon people still remains unsettled, it is widely assumed that a number of ethnic groups came to the Japanese islands from various parts of the Asian continent during the prehistoric period, bringing with them various religious and cultural elements. A comprehensive culture-complex hypothesis proposed by Oka Masao in 1933 suggests that there were five major typological components in late prehistoric and early historic Japanese culture, mythology, religion, and social structure. According to Oka, various ethnic groups from South China and Southeast Asia with Melanesian, Austroasian, and Austronesian (Micronesian) cultural and religious traits—the "secret society" system; "horizontal cosmology"; female shamans; mythical motifs of brother-sister deities; initiation rites; cultivation of taro, yam, and rice; and so forth—provided the foundation for the agricultural society and culture of the Yayoi period. A Tunguz group originally from Siberia or Manchuria, on the other hand, contributed a "vertical cosmology," exogamous patrilineal clan system, and the belief in deities *(kami)* who descend from heaven to mountaintops, trees, or pillars. Finally, an Altaic pastoral tribe that had subjugated other tribes in Manchuria and Korea migrated to Japan toward the end of the Yayoi period or the early part of the historic period, establishing itself as the ruling class over the earlier settlers. This group, which had an efficient military organization, shared with the Tunguz group similar religious and cultural traits such as a "vertical cosmology," Siberian-type shamanism, and a patriarchal clan *(uji)* system. Its most powerful family emerged as the imperial house in the historic period. Oka carefully avoids the question of the origin and development of the Japanese people and culture in a chronological sense. Although his hypothesis has been criticized by other scholars, his proposal still remains one of the most all-embracing efforts to explain the pluralistic nature of Japanese social structure, culture, and religion. Despite the lack of agreement concerning the details of the culture-complex thus developed, it is widely agreed that by the end of the Yayoi period those who inhabited the Japanese islands had attained a degree of self-consciousness as one people sharing a common culture.

The Yamatai controversy. One of the age-old controversies regarding Japan in the Yayoi period centers around the geographical location of the state of Yamatai (Yamadai), an important state in the Japanese islands and one that is mentioned in such Chinese dynastic histories as the record of the Eastern (Latter) Han dynasty (25–220) and that of the kingdom of Wei (220–265). We learn from these documents that there were more than one hundred states in Japan and that they acknowledged a hereditary ruler who resided in the state of Yamatai. It is also recorded that the first Japanese emissary was dispatched to the Chinese court in 57 CE. A series of similar diplomatic missions followed in the second and third centuries. These same accounts reveal that during the second half of the second century political turmoil developed in Japan owing to the absence of a ruler. An unmarried female shamanic diviner, Pimiko or Himiko, who "occupied herself with magic and sorcery, bewitching people," then became the ruler, and order was restored. She was offered by the Chinese court the title "Queen of Wo (Wa) Friendly to Wei." Evidently she lived in seclusion in a palace, protected by armed guards. She was attended by a thousand female servants, whereas only a single male, a "younger brother," transmitted her instructions and pronouncements, presumably utterances she made in a state of trance. When she died, a great mound was raised, and a hundred attendants followed her to the grave. After her death a king was placed on the throne, but since the people did not obey him, a young girl of thirteen, Iyo, was made queen, and order was once again restored. From these Chinese records we learn, among other things, that political stability in prehistoric Japan depended heavily on magico-religious authority. The intriguing question still remains, however, whether or not the state of Yamatai was located in the western island of Kyushu, as many scholars now believe, or in the central part of the main island where the so-called Yamato kingdom was established in the early historical period.

Early Historical Period. The early historical period of Japan corresponds to what archaeologists call the Kofun ("tumulus") period (c. 250–600 CE), so named because of the gigantic mausoleums constructed during this period for the deceased of the ruling class in the present Nara and Osaka prefectures. These great tombs are the visible remains of the early Yamato kingdom. It is significant that Japan was not mentioned in Chinese records between the mid-third and the early fifth century. Many scholars conjecture that during this shadowy period, the Yamato kingdom was established in the present Nara Prefecture. Japan also gained a foothold on the southern tip of the Korean peninsula. During the fourth century, according to Korean sources, Japan became an ally of Paekche, one of the Korean states, and Korean artisans and scholars migrated to Japan, introducing new arts and techniques in weaving, ironwork, and irrigation, as well as the Chinese script and Confucian learning. In 391 Japanese expeditionary forces crossed the sea and fought against the north Korean state, Koguryŏ, but were badly defeated. Following the military defeat in Korea, Japan turned to the Chinese court to secure Chinese recognition and support for her claim of suzerainty over Korea. In fact, the *Sung shu* (History of the Liu Sung Dynasty; 420–479) mentions the names of five Japanese rulers who sent emissaries to the Chinese court. During the sixth century Japan continued her effort to restore her influences on the Korean peninsula. In this connection Buddhism was introduced officially from Paekche to the Yamato court in 538 or 552.

Prior to the introduction of Sino-Korean civilization and Buddhism, Japanese religion was not a well-structured institutional system. The early Japanese took it for granted that the world was the Japanese islands where they lived. They also accepted the notion that the natural world was a "given." Thus, they did not look for another order of meaning behind the natural world. Yet their religious outlook had a strong cosmological orientation, so that early Japanese religion might be characterized as a "cosmic" religion. Although the early Japanese did not speculate on the metaphysical meaning of the cosmos, they felt they were an integral part of the cosmos, which to them was a community of living beings, all sharing *kami* (sacred) nature. The term *kami,* a combination of the prefix *ka* and the root *mi,* signifies either a material thing or an embodied spirit possessing divine potency and magical power. The term *kami* thus refers to all beings that are worthy of reverence, including both good and evil beings. Early Japanese religion accepted the plurality of *kami* residing in different beings and objects, but their basic affirmation was the sacrality of the total cosmos. [*See* Kami.]

Equally central to the early Japanese outlook was the notion of *uji* ("lineage group, clan"), which provided the basic framework for social solidarity. Although the *uji* was not based on the strict principle of consanguinity, blood relationship, real or fictitious, was considered essential for communal cohesion. Each *uji* had clansmen *(ujibito),* groups of professional persons *(be)* who were not blood relations of the clansmen, and slaves *(nuhi),* all of whom were ruled by the *uji* chieftain *(uji no kami).* Each *uji* was not only a social, economic, and political unit but also a unit of religious solidarity centering around the *kami* of the *uji (ujigami)* who was attended by the *uji* chieftain. Indeed, sharing the same *kami* was considered more important to communal cohesion than blood relationship.

As far as we can ascertain, the early Japanese religion did not have fixed liturgies. Most religious functions took place either at home or around a sacred tree or sacred rock, in the paddy field, or on the seashore. Because the *uji* group tended to reside in the same locality, the *kami* of the *uji* often incorporated the quality of regional *kami.* Also, there were numerous other spirits that controlled the health, fortune, and longevity of people. They were variously called *mono* ("spiritual entities") or *tama* ("souls") and were believed to be attached to human and other beings or natural things. Equally prevalent was the notion of "sacred visitors" *(marebito)* or ancestral spirits who came from distant places to visit human communities. Celestial bodies (the sun, moon, and stars), meteorological phenomena (wind and storms), and awe-inspiring natural objects (mountaintops, tall trees, forests, the ocean, and rivers) were also considered sacred and thus were venerated. Not surprisingly, then, a variety of persons—fortunetellers, healers, magicians, sorcerers, and diviners—served as intermediaries to these divine forces.

Religion and government. The early Yamato kingdom was a confederation of semiautonomous *uji,* each of which owned and ruled its respective members and territories. The Yamato rulers paid tribute to China and in return received a monarchical title from the Chinese imperial court. Within Japan, the Yamato rulers solidified their influence over other *uji* chieftains with their military power and with their claims to genealogical descent from the sun deity. They thus exercised the prerogatives of conferring such court titles as Ō-muraji ("great magnate," conferred upon heads of the hereditary vassal families of the imperial *uji*) and Ō-omi ("chief of chieftains," conferred upon heads of the imperial *uji*'s former rival *uji* that had acknowledged the imperial authority); granting sacred seed at spring festivals to all *uji* groups; and establishing sacred sites for heavenly and earthly *kami,* as well as regulating *matsuri* (rituals) for them. The term *matsuri* has the connotation "to be with," "to attend to the need of," "to entertain," or "to serve" the *kami,* the soul of the deceased, or a person of high status. Prior to a *matsuri,* the participants were expected to purify themselves and to abstain from certain foods and from sexual intercourse. It was understood that the most important duty of the Yamato emperor *(tennō)* was to maintain close contact with the sun deity—who was at once the imperial family's tutelary and ancestral *kami*—and other heavenly and earthly *kami* by attending to their needs and following their will, which was communicated through oracles, dreams, and divinations and which concerned government administration *(matsurigoto).* Thus, in principle, there was no line of demarcation between the sacred and the profane dimensions of life or between religious rituals *(matsuri)* and government administration *(matsurigoto).* Both were the prerogatives of the sovereign, who was by virtue of his solar ancestry the chief priest as well as the supreme political head of the kingdom. The sovereign, in turn, was assisted by hereditary religious functionaries and hereditary ministers of the court. This principle of the unity of religion and government *(saisei-itchi)* remained the foundation of Japanese religion when it later became institutionalized and acquired the designation of Shintō in contradistinction to Butsudō (Buddhism).

Impact of Chinese civilization and Buddhism on Japanese religion. With the gradual penetration of Chinese civilization—or, more strictly, Sino-Korean civilization—and Buddhism during the fifth and sixth centuries, Japanese religion was destined to feel the impact of alien ways of viewing the world and interpreting the meaning of human existence. Sensing the need to create a designation for their hitherto unsystematized religious, cultural, and political tradition, the Japanese borrowed two Chinese characters—*shen* (Jpn., *shin*) for *kami,* and *tao* (Jpn., *tō* or *dō*) for "the way." Inevitably, the effort to create almost artificially a religious system out of a nebulous, though all-embracing, way of life left many age-old beliefs and practices out of the new system. Those features that had been left out of Shintō have been preserved in the Japanese folk religious tradition. At any rate, the adoption of the name Shintō only magnified the profound tension between the indigenous Japanese understanding of the meaning of life and the world—authenticated solely by their particular historic experience on the Japanese islands—and the claims of Confucianism and Buddhism that their ways were grounded in universal laws and principles, the Confucian Tao (the Way) and Buddhist Dharma (the Law).

There is little doubt that the introduction of Chinese script and Buddhist images greatly aided the rapid penetration of Chinese civilization and Buddhism. As the Japanese had not developed their own script, the task of adopting the Chinese script, with its highly developed ideographs and phonetic compounds, to Japanese words was a complex one. There were many educated Korean and Chinese immigrants who served as instructors, interpreters, artists, technicians, and scribes for the imperial court and influential *uji* leaders of the growing nation. The Japanese intelligentsia over the course of time learned the use of literary Chinese and for many centuries used it for writing historical and official records. Poets, too, learned to express themselves either in Chinese verse or by utilizing Chinese characters as a form of syllabary for Japanese sounds. The Japanese accepted Chinese as a written, but not a spoken, language. Even so, through this one-sided medium, the Japanese gained access to the rich civilization of China, and Chinese culture became the resource and model for Japan.

Through written media the Japanese came to know the mystical tradition of philosophical Taoism, which enriched the Japanese aesthetic tradition. The Japanese also learned of the Yin-yang school's concepts of the two principles *(yin* and *yang),* the five elements (metal, wood, water, fire, and earth), and the orderly rotation of these elements in the formation of nature, seasons, and the human being. The Yin-yang school thus provided cosmological theories to hitherto nonspeculative Japanese religion. It was also through written Chinese works that Japanese society, which had been based on archaic communal rules and the *uji* system, appropriated certain features of Confucian ethical principles, social and political theories, and legal and educational systems. [*See* Yin-yang Wu-hsing *and* Onmyōdō.]

The introduction of Buddhist art equally revolutionized Japanese religion, which despite its aesthetic sensitivities had never developed artistic images of *kami* in sculpture or painting. Understandably, when Buddhism was officially introduced to the Japanese court in the sixth century it was the Buddha image that became the central issue between the pro- and anti-Buddhist factions in the court. Anti-Buddhist leaders argued that veneration of a "foreign *kami*" would offend the "native *kami.*" After this initial controversy regarding statues of the Buddha, however, the chieftain of the powerful Soga *uji* secured imperial permission to build a temple in order to enshrine Buddha images. Soon, thanks to the energetic advocacy of the Soga, Buddhism was accepted by other aristocratic families, not because the profound meaning of Buddhist law (the Dharma) was appreciated but probably because Buddhist statues were believed to have magical potencies that would bring about mundane benefits. Thus the statues of Shaka (Śākyamuni),

Miroku (Maitreya), Yakushi (Bhaiṣajyaguru), Kannon (Avalokiteśvara), and Amida (Amitābha) were venerated almost indiscriminately in the *uji*-based Buddhism of sixth- and early-seventh-century Japan.

Prince Shōtoku. The regency of Prince Shōtoku (573–621), who served under his aunt, Empress Suiko (r. 592–628), marks a new chapter in the history of Japanese religion. By that time the bankruptcy of Japan's Korean policy had resulted in the loss of its foothold on the southern tip of the Korean peninsula, while the powerful Sui dynasty had unified China after centuries of disunity. To protect Japan's survival in the precarious international scene, Shōtoku and his advisers attempted to strengthen the fabric of national community by working out a multireligious policy reconciling the particularistic Japanese religious tradition with the universal principles of Confucianism and Buddhism. Clearly, Shōtoku's mentor was Emperor Wen (r. 581–604) of the Sui dynasty, who unified the races, cultures, and diverse areas of vast China by utilizing Confucianism and Buddhism, and Taoism to a lesser degree, as the arms of the throne, and whose claim to semidivine prerogative was sanctioned and authenticated by various religious symbols.

Shōtoku himself was a pious Buddhist and is reputed to have delivered learned lectures on certain Buddhist scriptures. Yet his policies, as exemplified in the establishment of the Chinese-style "cap-ranks" of twelve grades for court ministers or in the promulgation of the "Seventeen-Article Constitution," represented an indigenous attempt to reconcile Buddhist and Confucian traditions with the native Japanese religious tradition. Shōtoku envisaged a centralized national community under the throne, and he advocated the veneration of Buddhism as the final refuge of all creatures. Moreover, he held the Confucian notion of *li* ("propriety") as the key to right relations among ruler, ministers, and people. [*See* Li.] Shōtoku was convinced that his policy was in keeping with the will of the *kami*. In his edict of 607 he states how his imperial ancestors had venerated the heavenly and earthly *kami* and thus "the winter [*yin*, negative cosmic force] and summer [*yang*, positive cosmic force] elements were kept in harmony, and their creative powers blended together," and he urged his ministers to do the same.

Prince Shōtoku took the initiative in reestablishing diplomatic contact with China by sending an envoy to the Sui court. He also sent a number of talented young scholars and monks to China to study. Although Shōtoku's reform measures remained unfulfilled at his untimely death, the talented youths he sent to China played important roles in the development of Japanese religion and national affairs upon their return. [*See the biography of Shōtoku Taishi.*]

The Ritsuryō synthesis. Prince Shōtoku's death was followed by a series of bloody power struggles, including the coup d'état of 645, which strengthened the position of the throne. The Taika reforms of 645 and 646 attempted to consolidate the power of the centralized government by such Chinese-style measures as land redistribution, collection of revenues, and a census. During the second half of the seventh century the government, utilizing the talents of those who had studied in China, sponsored the compilation of a written law. Significantly, those penal codes (*ritsu;* Chin., *lü*) and civil statutes (*ryō;* Chin., *ling*), which were modeled after Chinese legal systems, were issued in the name of the emperor as the will of the *kami*. The government structure thus developed during the late seventh century is referred to as the Ritsuryō ("imperial rescript") state. Although the basic principle of the Ritsuryō state was in a sense a logical implementation of Prince Shōtoku's vision, which itself was a synthesis of Buddhist, Confucian, and Japanese traditions, it turned out to be in effect a form of "immanental theocracy," in which the universal principles of Tao and Dharma were domesticated to serve the will of the sovereign, who now was elevated to the status of living or manifest *kami*. [*See* Kingship, *article on* Kingship in East Asia.]

It should be noted in this connection that the government's effort to consolidate the Ritsuryō structure was initially resisted by the former *uji* chieftains and provincial magnates who had residual power in the court. Ironically, after usurping the throne from his nephew, Emperor Temmu (r. 672–686) managed to bring new elements into the rank of court nobility and reorganize the government structure. Emperor Temmu ordered the compilation of two historical writings, the *Kojiki* (Record of Ancient Matters) and the *Nihongi* (or *Nihonshoki*, the Chronicles of Japan), which were completed during the eighth century. Temmu is also credited with canonizing Amaterasu, the sun deity, as the ancestral *kami* and with making her Grand Shrine of Ise the tutelary shrine of the imperial house. [*See* Amaterasu Ōmikami.]

One characteristic policy of the Ritsuryō state was to support and control religions. Thus, the government enforced the Sōniryō (Law Governing Monks and Nuns), which was modeled after a Chinese code, the Law Governing Taoist and Buddhist Priests, of the Yung-hui period (640–655). The government also elevated the Office of Kami Affairs (Kanzukasa) to a full-fledged Department of Kami Affairs (Jingikan), charged with supervising all officially sponsored Shintō shrines and overseeing the registers of the entire Shintō priesthood and other religious corporations. The Jingikan was given equal rank with the Great Council of State (Dajōkan).

Nara Period. During the eighth century Japanese religion reached an important stage of maturity under Chinese and Buddhist inspirations. It was a golden age for the Ritsuryō state and the imperial court. Thanks to the newly acquired Chinese script, the two mytho-historical writings—the *Kojiki* and the *Nihonshoki*—as well as the *Fudoki* (Records of Local Surveys), the *Man'yōshū* (Anthology of Myriad Leaves), and the *Kaifūsō* (Fond Recollection of Poetry) were compiled. Also in this century the Yōrō Ritsuryō (Yōrō Penal and Civil Codes), the legal foundation of the Ritsuryō state, were fixed in writing.

The immanental theocratic principle of the Ritsuryō state undoubtedly was based on the myth of the solar ancestry of the imperial house. Similarly, as mentioned earlier, the compilation of the *Kojiki* and the *Nihonshoki* was ordered by Emperor Temmu in 673 in order to justify his accession to the throne. Thus, although the format of these chronicles was modeled after Chinese dynastic histories, their task was to sort out myths, legends, and historical events in such a way as to establish direct genealogical connections between the contemporary imperial house and the sun deity. With this objective in mind, the chroniclers worked out a smooth transition from the domain of myths, which were classified as the "age of *kami*," to the "historical" accounts of legendary emperors, who were presumed to be direct ancestors of the imperial house. Although the chronologies in the *Kojiki* and *Nihonshoki* were obviously fabricated, these mytho-historical writings provide a rich source of myths in which the ethos and meaning-structure of early Japanese religion unfold before us. Not surprisingly, these two chronicles came to be regarded as semicanonical scriptures of Shintō.

As important as the chronicles for our understanding of early Japanese religion is the *Man'yōshū*, which betrays amazingly little influence from the continent even though it was compiled two centuries after the introduction of Chinese civilization and Buddhism. In its literary form, the *Man'yōshū* utilized Chinese characters only for their sound value, disregarding their lexical meaning. Many of the poems in this anthology portray an interpenetration of what we now call religious and aesthetic values. The *Man'yōshū* also reveals an enduring feature of Japanese religion, namely, the poet as expert in sacred matters. The poet, as was also true in ancient Greece, was a maker and interpreter of sacral reality, and poems that addressed natural phenomena as *kami* were indeed sacred songs. [*See* Poetry, *article on* Japanese Religious Poetry.]

In contrast to earlier periods, when Korean forms of Buddhism influenced Japan, early eighth-century Japan felt the strong impact of Chinese Buddhism. In 710 the first capital, modeled after the Chinese capital of Ch'ang-an, was established in Nara, which was designed to serve as the religious as well as the political center of the nation. During the Nara period the imperial court was eager to promote Buddhism as the religion best suited for the protection of the state. Accordingly, the government established in every province state-sponsored temples *(kokubunji)* and nunneries *(kokubunniji)*. In the capital city the national cathedral, Tōdaiji, was built as the home of the gigantic bronze statue of the Buddha Vairocana. The government sponsored and supported six schools of Chinese Buddhism. Of the six, the Ritsu (Vinaya) school was concerned primarily with monastic disciplines. The other five were more like monastic schools based on different philosophical traditions than sectarian groups. For example, the two Hinayanistic schools—the Kusha (deriving its name from the *Abhidharmakośa*) and the Jōjitsu (deriving its name from the *Satyasiddhi*)—were devoted to cosmological and psychological analysis of elements of the universe, whereas the Sanron (Mādhyamika) school specialized in dialectic analysis of concepts in order to suppress all duality for the sake of gaining perfect wisdom. The Kegon school (deriving its name from the *Avataṃsaka Sūtra*) was a form of cosmotheism, and the Hossō (Yogācāra), probably the most influential system during the Nara period, stressed analysis of the nature of things and a theory of cause. Only those who had taken vows at one of the three official ordination platforms were qualified to be official monks. With government subsidy the monks were able to devote their lives to the study of the doctrinal intricacies of their respective schools, subject, of course, to the Sōniryō. [*See also* Mādhyamika; Yogācāra; *and* Hua-yen.]

Despite such encouragement and support from the government, Buddhism did not have much impact on the populace. More important were three new religious forms that developed out of the fusion between the Japanese religious heritage and Buddhism.

The first new form was the Nature Wisdom school (Jinenchishū), which sought enlightenment by meditation or austere physical discipline in the mountains and forests. Those who followed the path, including some official monks, affirmed the superiority of enlightenment through nature to the traditional Buddhist disciplines and doctrines. The indigenous Japanese acceptance of the sacrality of nature was thus reaffirmed.

Second, a variety of folk religious leaders, variously called private monks *(shidosō)* and unordained monks *(ubasoku;* from Skt. *upāsaka)*, emerged. Many of them were magicians, healers, and shamanic diviners of the mountain districts or the countryside who came under nominal Buddhist influence although they had no formal Buddhist training and had only tenuous connections to Buddhism. Their religious outlook was strongly influenced by the shamanistic folk piety of Japanese religious traditions and Taoism, but they also appropriated many features of Buddhism and taught simple and syncretistic "folk Buddhism" among the lower strata of society. [*See* Hijiri.]

A third new form grew out of the trend toward an interpenetration between, and amalgamation of, Shintō and Buddhism, whereby Shintō shrines found their way into the compound of Buddhist temples and Buddhist chapels were built within the precinct of Shintō shrines. The construction of Tōdaiji was enhanced by the alleged encouragement of the sun deity of the Grand Shrine of Ise and of the *kami* Hachiman of Usa Shrine, Kyushu. In fact, Hachiman was equated with a Buddhist *bodhisattva*. This Shintō-Buddhist amalgamation, which began in the eighth century and later came to be called Ryōbu ("two aspects") Shintō, remained the institutional norm until the late nineteenth century.

Because of the excessive support of religion and culture by the court, which benefited only the aristocracy, the capital of Nara during the second half of the eighth century was doomed by political corruption, ecclesiastical intrigue, and financial bankruptcy. Therefore the capital was moved in 794 from Nara to a remote place and then ten years later to the present Kyoto.

Erosion of the Ritsuryō Ideal. The new capital in Kyoto, Heiankyō ("capital of peace and tranquillity"), was also modeled after the Chinese capital. Although Kyoto remained the seat of the imperial court until the nineteenth century, the so-called Heian period covers only that time, in the ninth to the twelfth century, when political power was concentrated in the capital. Freed from ecclesiastical interference, the leaders of the Kyoto regime were eager to restore the integrity of the Ritsuryō system, and they forbade the Nara Buddhist schools to move into the new capital. Instead, the imperial court favored, side by side with Shintō, two new Buddhist schools, Tendai (Chin., T'ien-t'ai) and Shingon (Chin., Chen-yen), introduced by Saichō (767–822) and Kūkai (774–835), respectively. Both Saichō and Kūkai had been disillusioned in their youth by the formalism and moral decadence of the Buddhist schools in Nara, both had studied in China, and both were to exert great influence on the further development of Japanese religion.

Saichō, also known by his posthumous name, Dengyō Daishi, established the monastic center of the Tendai school at Mount Hiei, not far from Kyoto, and incorporated the doctrines of the *Saddharmapuṇḍarīka* (Lotus of the Good Law) *Sūtra*, Esoteric (i.e., Tantric) mysticism, Zen (Chin., Ch'an) meditation, and monastic discipline (Vinaya) into his teachings. He was conciliatory to Shintō, and his form of Shintō-Buddhist (Tendai) amalgam came to be known as Sannō Ichijitsu ("one reality") Shintō. Shortly after Saichō's death the Tendai school stressed its Esoteric elements to the extent that it came to be called Taimitsu (Tendai Esoterism). It should be noted that the Tendai monastery at Mount Hiei remained for centuries a most powerful institution and produced many prominent religious figures during the medieval period. [*See also* Tendaishū *and the biography of Saichō.*]

Kūkai, known posthumously as Kōbō Daishi, established the Shingon monastic center at Mount Kōya, not far from present-day Osaka, but also served as the head of the prestigious Tōji (Eastern Temple) in Kyoto. As a result, Kūkai's teachings are often referred to as Tōmitsu (Eastern Esoterism). Kūkai was noted for his unusual erudition. His scheme of the ten stages of spiritual development included teachings from all the major Buddhist schools and also from Hinduism, Confucianism, and Taoism. Moreover, he taught that the essential truth of Esoteric teaching could be revealed in art, thus affirming the mutual penetration of aesthetic and religious experiences. The Shingon school provided the theoretical basis for Ryōbu Shintō, as mentioned earlier. [*See also* Shingonshū *and the biography of Kūkai.*] According to both the Tendai and Shingon traditions of the Shinto-Buddhist amalgam, Shintō *kami* were believed to be manifestations *(suijaku)* of the Buddhas who were the original realities *(honji)*. [*See* Honjisuijaku.]

Meanwhile, in an important step toward restoring the Ritsuryō system, the government sponsored the *Shinsen shōjiroku* (New Compilation of the Register of Families), completed in 815. It divided the aristocracy into three arbitrary categories: (1) descendants of heavenly and earthly *kami (shinbetsu)*, (2) descendants of imperial and other royal families *(kōbetsu)*, and (3) descendants of naturalized Chinese and Koreans *(banbetsu)*. The preface to this register acknowledged that provincial records had all been burned. Thus there were no reliable documents. Many commoners then pretended to be scions of noblemen, and children of naturalized Chinese and Koreans claimed to be the descendants of Japanese *kami*. Despite such a frank admission of the impossibility of the task involved, the *Register* presented the genealogies of 1,182 families as an "essential instrument in the hands of the nation."

Nearly a century after the compilation of the *Shinsen shōjiroku* the government undertook the ambitious enterprise of collecting all supplementary rules to previously promulgated edicts and ceremonial rules known during the Engi era (901–922). Of the fifty books that comprise these documents, the *Engishiki,* the first ten are devoted to minute rules and procedures of dealing with various aspects of Shintō, such as festivals, the Grand Shrine of Ise, enthronement ceremonies, ritual prayers *(norito),* and a register of *kami.* Of special importance to the understanding of Japanese religion are the ritual prayers, some of which might be traced back to the mid-sixth century when ritualized recitation of prayers, inspired by the Buddhist example of reciting scriptures (*sūtras*), developed. [*See* Norito.] The remaining forty books of the *Engishiki* are detailed descriptions of rules and regulations of all the bureaus under the Grand Council of State (Dajōkan), including numerous references to affairs related to Shintō. It is interesting to note that the section on the Bureau of Yin-Yang (Onmyōryō), book 16, mentions the duties of masters and doctors of divination and astrology in reciting the ritual prayers *(saimon)* addressed to heavenly and earthly *kami.* The underlying principle of the *Engishiki,* which epitomized the Ritsuryō ideal, was that the imperial court was the earthly counterpart of the heavenly court. Just as the court of the sun deity included various functionaries, the imperial court included religious and administrative functionaries, and the stylized daily rituals of the court, properly performed, had great bearing on the harmonious blending of the *yin* and *yang* elements in the cosmos as well as on the welfare of the people. The *Engishiki,* which was completed in 927, was not put into effect until 967. When it was finally implemented, the document was no longer taken seriously. This was true not only because the rules of procedures of the *Engishiki* were excessively cumbersome but also because the very ideal of the Ritsuryō system was eroding by that time.

The foundation of the Ritsuryō system was the sacred monarchy, authenticated by the mytho-historical claim that the sun deity had given the mandate to her grandson and his descendants to "reign" and "rule" the world, meaning Japan, in perpetuity. Ironically, during the Heian period the two institutions that were most closely related to the throne, namely, the Fujiwara regency and rule by retired monarchs *(insei),* undercut the structure of the Ritsuryō system.

The regency had been exercised before the ninth century only by members of the royal family and only in times when the reigning monarch needed such assistance. But from the late ninth century to the mid-eleventh century the nation was actually ruled by the regency of the powerful Fujiwara family. The institutionalization of the regency implied a significant redefinition of the Ritsuryō system by the aristocracy. The aristocratic families acknowledged the sacrality of the throne, but they expected the emperor to "reign" only as the manifest *kami* and not to interfere with the actual operation of the government. The latter was believed to be the prerogative of the aristocratic officials. Moreover, the Fujiwaras, who had managed to marry off their daughters to reigning monarchs, thus claimed added privileges as the titular sovereigns' maternal in-laws.

The custom of rule by retired monarchs began in the eleventh century, when ambitious monarchs abdicated for the purpose of exercising power from behind the throne with the claim that they were still legitimate heads of the patriarchal imperial family. This institution of *insei,* which also compromised the Ritsuryō principle, lost much of its influence by the end of the twelfth century owing to the growth of political power held by warrior families.

The Heian period witnessed the phenomenal growth of wealth and political influence of ecclesiastical institutions, both Shintō and Buddhist, equipped with lucrative manors and armed guards. However, among the lower strata of society, which were neglected by established religious groups, magico-religious beliefs and practices of both indigenous and Chinese origins prevailed. In addition to healers, diviners, sorcerers, and the practitioners of Onmyōdō (Yin-yang and Taoist magic), mountain ascetics *(shugenja)*—heirs of the shamanistic folk religious leaders of the Nara period—attracted followers in places high and low. In the course of time, mountain ascetics allied themselves with the Tendai and Shingon schools and came to be known as the Tendai-Shugendō and the Shingon-Shugendō, respectively. [*See* Shugendō.] Such literary works as the *Genjimonogatari* (Tale of Genji) by Lady Murasaki and the *Makura no sōshi* (Pillow Book) by Lady Sei-shōnagon also reveal that during this period all calamities, from earthquake, fire, floods, and epidemics to civil wars, were widely believed to have been caused by the vengeance of angry spirits *(goryō).* Some of these spirits were venerated as *kami,* and Shintō shrines were built in their honor. Moreover, festivals for angry spirits *(goryō-e),* with music, dance, wrestling, archery, and horse racing, as well as Shintō, Buddhist, and Yin-yang liturgies, were held in order to pacify the anger of *goryō.*

Frequent occurrences of natural calamities during the Heian period also precipitated the widespread belief that the apocalyptic age of the Latter Days of the Law *(mappō)* predicted in Buddhist scripture was at hand. [*See* Mappō.] This may account for the growing popularity of the Buddha Amida (Skt., Amitābha, the Buddha of Infinite Light, or Amitāyus, the Buddha of Infinite Life), who had vowed to save all sentient beings and had promised rebirth in his Pure Land to the faithful. As we shall see presently, Amida pietism became a powerful spiritual movement in the subsequent period. [*See* Amitābha.]

The Heian period, and the elegant culture it produced, vanished in the late twelfth century in a series of bloody battles involving both courtiers and warriors. Then came a new age dominated by warrior rulers.

Religious Ethos during the Kamakura Period. That the nation was "ruled" by warrior-rulers from the thirteenth to the nineteenth century, even though the emperor continued to "reign" throughout these centuries, is a matter of considerable significance for the development of Japanese religion. There were three such feudal warrior regimes (*bakufu* or shogunates): (1) the Kamakura regime (1192–1333), (2) the Ashikaga regime (1338–1573), and (3) the Tokugawa regime (1603–1867). Unlike the Ritsuryō state, with its elaborate penal and civil codes, the warrior rule—at least under the first two regimes—was based on a much simpler legal system. For example, the legislation of the Kamakura regime consisted of only fifty-one pragmatic principles. This allowed established Shintō and Buddhist institutions more freedom than they had under the cumbersome structure of the Ritsuryō state. It also set the stage for the development of new religious movements, many with roots in the folk tradition.

Of course the emergence of warrior rule signified the further weakening of the already battered Ritsuryō ideal. For example, unlike the Fujiwara noblemen and retired monarchs, who had wielded power from within the framework of the imperial court, the Kamakura regime established its own administrative structure consisting of three bureaus—military, administrative, and judiciary. The warriors for the most part were not sophisticated in cultural and religious matters. Many of them, however, combined simple Buddhist piety with devotion to the pre-Buddhist indigenous tutelary *kami* of warrior families rather than those of the imperial Shintō tradition. The cohesion of the warrior society, not unlike the early Yamato confederation of semiautonomous clans, was based on the *uji* and the larger unit of *uji* federation. Accordingly, the tutelary *kami* of warrior families (for example, Hachiman, the *kami* of war of the Minamoto *uji,* founder of the Kamakura regime) escalated in importance. At the same time, the peasantry, artisans, and small merchants, whose living standard improved a little under the Kamakura regime, were attracted to new religious movements that promised an easier path to salvation in the dreaded age of degeneration (*mappō).* On the other hand, the Zen traditions, which had been a part of older Buddhist schools, gained independence under the influence of the Chinese Ch'an movement and quickly found patronage among the Kamakura rulers.

Significantly, all the leaders of new religious movements during this period had begun their careers at the Tendai headquarters at Mount Hiei but had become disillusioned by the empty ceremonialism, scholasticism, and moral corruption that characterized the monastic life of their time. Three of these leaders altered their religious resolutions when they found certitude of salvation in reliance on the compassionate Amida by *nembutsu* (recitation of the Buddha's name). They then became instrumental in the establishment of the three Pure Land (Amida's Western Paradise) traditions. They were Hōnen (Genkū, 1133–1212) of the Jōdo (Pure Land) sect, who is often compared with Martin Luther; Shinran (1173–1262) of the Jōdo Shin (True Pure Land) sect, a disciple of Hōnen, who among other things initiated the tradition of a married priesthood; and Ippen (Chishin, 1239–1289) of the Ji (Time) sect, so named because of its practice of reciting hymns to Amida six times a day. [*See* Jōdoshū; Jōdo Shinshū; *and the biographies of Hōnen, Shinran, and Ippen.*]

On the other hand, Nichiren (1222–1282), founder of the school bearing his name and a charismatic prophet, developed his own interpretation of the *Hokekyō* (Lotus Sutra), the *Saddharmapuṇḍarīka Sūtra,* as the only path toward salvation for the Japanese nation. [*See* Nichirenshū *and the biography of Nichiren.*]

In contrast to the paths of salvation advocated by the Pure Land and Nichiren schools, the experience of enlightenment *(satori)* was stressed by Eisai (Yōsai, 1141–1215), who introduced the Rinzai (Chin., Lin-chi) Zen tradition, and Dōgen (1200–1253), who established the Sōtō (Chin., Ts'ao-tung) Zen tradition. Zen was welcomed by Kamakura leaders partly because it could counterbalance the powerful and wealthy established Buddhist institutions and partly because it was accompanied by other features of Sung Chinese culture, including Neo-Confucian learning. The Zen movement was greatly aided by a number of émigré Ch'an monks who settled in Japan. [*See* Zen *and the biography of Dōgen.*]

Despite the growth of new religious movements, old religious establishments, both Shintō and Buddhist, remained powerful during this period; for example, both gave military support to the royalist cause against the Kamakura regime during the abortive Jōkyū rebellion in 1221. On the other hand, confronted by a national crisis during the Mongol invasions of 1274 and 1281, both Shintō shrines and Buddhist monasteries solidly supported the Kamakura regime by offering prayers and incantations for the protection of Japan.

A short-lived "imperial rule," 1333–1336, followed the

decline of the Kamakura regime. This rule aided the Ise Shintō movement, which tried not very successfully to emancipate Shintō from Buddhist and Chinese influences. Ise Shintō influenced the royalist general Kitagatake Chikafusa (1293–1354), author of the *Jinnō shōtōki* (Records of the Legitimate Succession of the Divine Sovereigns). The imperial regime was also instrumental in shifting the centers of Zen and Sung learning, established by the Kamakura regime in the Chinese-style Gozan ("five mountains") temples, to Kyoto. [*See* Gozan Zen.]

Zen, Neo-Confucianism, and Kirishitan during the Ashikaga Period. Unlike the first feudal regime at Kamakura, the Ashikaga regime established its *bakufu* in Kyoto, the seat of the imperial court. Accordingly, religious and cultural development during the Ashikaga period (1338–1573, also referred to as the Muromachi period) blended various features of warrior and courtier traditions, Zen, and Chinese cultural influences. This blending in turn fostered a closer interpenetration of religious and aesthetic values. All these religious and cultural developments took place at a time when social and political order was threatened not only by a series of bloody power struggles within the *bakufu* but also by famines and epidemics that led to peasant uprisings and, further, by the devastating Ōnin War (1467–1478) that accelerated the erosion of Ashikaga hegemony and the rise of competing daimyo, the so-called *sengoku daimyō* ("feudal lords of warring states"), in the provinces. In this situation, villages and towns developed something analogous to self-rule. Merchants and artisans formed guilds *(za)* that were usually affiliated with established Buddhist temples and Shintō shrines, whereas adherents of Pure Land and Nichiren sects were willing to defend themselves as armed religious societies. Into this complex religious, cultural, social, and political topography, European missionaries of Roman Catholicism, then known as Kirishitan, brought a new gospel of salvation.

Throughout the Ashikaga period established institutions of older Buddhist schools and Shintō (for example, the Tendai monastery at Mount Hiei, the Shingon monastery at Mount Kōya, and the Kasuga shrine at Nara) remained both politically and economically powerful. However, the new religious groups that had begun to attract the lower strata of society during the Kamakura period continued to expand their influence, often competing among themselves. Some of these new religious groups staged a series of armed rebellions—such as Hokke-ikki (uprisings of Nichiren followers) and Ikkō-ikki (uprisings of the True Pure Land followers)—to defend themselves against each other or against oppressive officialdoms. The Order of Mountain Ascetics (Shugendō) also became institutionalized as the eclectic Shugenshū (Shugen sect) and promoted devotional confraternities *(kōsha)* among villagers and townsmen, competing with new religious groups.

Zen and Neo-Confucianism. By far the most influential religious sect during the Ashikaga period was Zen, especially the Rinzai Zen tradition, which became *de facto* the official religion. The first Ashikaga shogun, following the advice of his confidant, Musō Soseki, established a "temple for the peace of the nation" *(ankokuji)* in each province. [*See the biography of Musō Soseki.*] As economic necessity compelled the regime to turn to foreign trade, Soseki's temple, Tenryūji, sent ships to China for this purpose. Many Zen priests served as advisers to administrative offices of the regime. With the rise of the Ming dynasty (1368–1644), which replaced Mongol rule, the third Ashikaga shogun resumed official diplomatic relations with China, again depending heavily on the assistance of Zen priests. After the third shogun regularized two Gozan (the five officially recognized Zen temples) systems, one in Kyoto and the second in Kamakura, Gozan temples served as important financial resources for the regime. Many Zen priests earned reputations as monk-poets or monk-painters, and Gozan temples became centers of cultural and artistic activities.

Zen priests, including émigré Chinese Ch'an monks, also made contributions as transmitters of Neo-Confucianism, a complex philosophical system incorporating not only classical Confucian thought but also features of Buddhist and Taoist traditions that had developed in China during the Sung (960–1127) and Southern Sung (1127–1279) periods. It should be noted that Neo-Confucianism was initially conceived in Japan as a cultural appendage to Zen. Soon, however, many Zen monks upheld the unity of Zen and Neo-Confucian traditions to the extent that the entire teaching staff and students of the Ashikaga Academy, presumably a nonreligious institution devoted to Neo-Confucian learning, were Zen monks. [*See* Confucian Thought, *article on* Neo-Confucianism.]

The combined inspiration of Japanese and Sung Chinese aesthetics, Zen, and Pure Land traditions, coupled with the enthusiastic patronage of shoguns, made possible the growth of a variety of elegant and sophisticated art: painting, calligraphy, *renga* (dialogical poetry or linked verse), stylized *nō* drama, comical *kyōgen* plays, flower arrangement, and the cult of tea. [*See also* Drama, *article on* East Asian Dance and Theater.] Some of these art forms are considered as much the "way" *(dō* or *michi)* as the "ways" of *kami* or the Buddha, implying that they are nonreligious paths to sacral reality.

The coming of Kirishitan. When the Ōnin War ended in 1478 the Ashikaga regime could no longer control the ambitious provincial daimyo who were consolidating their own territories. By the sixteenth century Portugal was expanding its overseas empire in Asia. The chance arrival of shipwrecked Portuguese merchants at Tanegashima Island, south of Kyushu, in 1543 was followed by the arrival in Kyushu in 1549 of the famous Jesuit Francis Xavier. Although Xavier stayed only two years in Japan, he initiated vigorous proselytizing activities during that time.

The cause of Kirishitan (as Roman Catholicism was then called in Japanese) was greatly aided by a strongman, Oda Nobunaga (1534–1582), who succeeded in taking control of the capital in 1568. Angry that established Buddhist institutions were resisting his scheme of national unification, Nobunaga took harsh measures; he burned the Tendai monastery at Mount Hiei, killed thousands of Ikkō (True Pure Land) followers, and attacked rebellious priests at Mount Kōya in order to destroy their power. At the same time, ostensibly to counteract the residual influence of Buddhism, he encouraged Kirishitan activities. Ironically, this policy was reversed after his death. Nevertheless, by the time Nobunaga was assassinated, 150,000 Japanese Catholics, including several daimyo, were reported to be among the Japanese population.

The initial success of Catholicism in Japan was due to the Jesuits' policy of accommodation. Xavier himself adopted the name *Dainichi* (the Great Sun Buddha, the supreme deity of the Shingon school) as the designation of God; later, however, this was changed to *Deus*. Jesuits also used the Buddhist terms *jōdo* ("pure land") for heaven and *sō* ("monk") for the title *padre*. Moreover, Kirishitan groups followed the general pattern of tightly knit religious societies practiced by the Nichiren and Pure Land groups. Missionaries also followed the common Japanese approach in securing the favor of the ruling class to expedite their evangelistic and philanthropic activities. Conversely, trade-hungry daimyo eagerly befriended missionaries, knowing that the latter had influence over Portuguese traders. In fact, one Christian daimyo donated the port of Nagasaki to the Society of Jesus in 1580 hoping to attract Portuguese ships to the port, which would in turn benefit him. Inevitably, however, Jesuit-inspired missionary work aroused strong opposition not only from anti-Kirishitan daimyo and Buddhist clerics but from jealous Franciscans and other Catholic orders as well. Furthermore, the Portuguese traders who supported the Jesuits were now threatened by the arrival of the Spanish in 1592, via Mexico and the Philippines, and of the Dutch in 1600.

Meanwhile, following the death of Oda Nobunaga, one of his generals, Toyotomi Hideyoshi (1536–1598), endeavored to complete the task of national unification. Determined to eliminate the power of Buddhist institutions, he not only attacked rebellious monastic communities, such as those in Negoro and Saiga, but also conducted a thorough sword hunt in various monastic communities. Hideyoshi was interested in foreign trade, but he took a dim view of Catholicism because of its potential danger to the cause of national unification. He was incensed by what he saw in Nagasaki, a port that was then ruled by the Jesuits and the Portuguese. In 1587 he issued an edict banishing missionaries, but he did not enforce it until 1596 when he heard a rumor that the Spanish monarch was plotting to subjugate Japan with the help of Japanese Christians. Thus in 1597 he had some twenty-six Franciscans and Japanese converts crucified. The following year Hideyoshi himself died in the midst of his abortive invasion of Korea. [*See also* Christianity, *article on* Christianity in Asia.]

The Tokugawa Synthesis. The power struggle that followed the death of Toyotomi Hideyoshi was settled in 1600 in favor of Tokugawa Ieyasu (1542–1616), who established the *bakufu* in 1603 at Edo (present Tokyo). The Tokugawa regime, which was to hold political power until the Meiji restoration in 1867, was more than another feudal regime; it was a comprehensive sixfold order—political, social, legal, philosophical, religious, and moral—with the shogun in its pivotal position.

1. *Political order.* The Tokugawa form of government, usually known as the *baku-han,* was a national administration *(bakufu)* under the shogun combined with local administration by daimyo in their fiefs *(han).*

2. *Social order.* Japan under the Tokugawas was rigidly divided into warrior, farmer, artisan, and merchant classes, plus special categories such as imperial and courtier families and ecclesiastics. Accordingly, one's birth dictated one's status as well as one's duties to nation and family and one's role in social relations.

3. *Legal order.* The Tokugawas formulated a series of administrative and legislative principles as well as rules and regulations *(hatto)* that dictated the boundaries and norms of behavior of various imperial, social, and religious groups.

4. *Philosophical order.* The Tokugawa synthesis was based on the Neo-Confucian principle that the order of Heaven is not transcendental but rather is inherent in the sacrality of nation, family, and social hierarchy.

5. *Religious order.* In sharp contrast to the Ritsuryō system, which was based on a principle of sacred kingship that authenticated the immanental theocratic state as the nation of the *kami,* the Tokugawas looked to the throne in order to add a magico-religious aura to their own version of immanental theocracy. They grounded this notion in what they felt were the natural laws and natural norms implicit in human, social, and political order. It is interesting to note in passing that the first shogun, Ieyasu, was deified as the "Sun God of the East" (Tōshō) and was enshrined as the guardian deity of the Tokugawas at Nikkō. According to the Tokugawas, all religions were to become integral and supportive elements of the Tokugawa synthesis. However, the Tokugawas tolerated no prophetic judgment or critique of the whole system.

6. *Moral order.* Running through the Tokugawa synthesis was a sense of moral order that held the balance of the total system. Its basic formula was simple: the Way of Heaven was the natural norm, and the way of government, following the principle of benevolent rule *(jinsei),* was to actualize this moral order. This demanded something of each person in order to fulfill the true meaning of the relations *(taigi-meibun)* among different status groups. Warriors, for example, were expected to follow Bushidō ("the way of the warrior"). [*See* Bushidō.]

Kirishitan under Tokugawa rule. The religious policy of the Tokugawa regime was firmly established by the first shogun, who held that all religious, philosophical, and ethical systems were to uphold and cooperate with the government's objective, namely, the establishment of a harmonious society. Following the eclectic tradition of Japanese religion, which had appropriated various religious symbols and concepts, the first shogun stated in an edict of 1614: "Japan is called the land of the Buddha and not without reason. . . . *Kami* and the Buddha differ in name, but their meaning is one." Accordingly, he surrounded himself with a variety of advisers, including Buddhist clerics and Confucian scholars, and shared their view that the Kirishitan religion could not be incorporated into the framework of Japanese religion and would be detrimental to the cause of social and political harmony. Nevertheless, the Tokugawa regime's initial attitude toward Catholicism was restrained; perhaps this was because the regime did not wish to lose foreign trade by overt anti-Kirishitan measures. But in 1614 the edict banning Kirishitan was issued, followed two years later by a stricter edict. A series of persecutions of missionaries and Japanese converts then took place. Following the familiar pattern of religious uprising (such as Hokke- and Ikkō-ikki), armed farmers, fishermen, warriors, and their women and children, many of whom were Kirishitan followers, rose in revolt in 1637 in Shimabara, Kyushu. When the uprising was quelled, Kirishitan followers were ordered to renounce their faith. If they did not do so, they were tortured to death.

The regime also took the far more drastic measure of "national seclusion" *(sakoku)* when it cut off all trade and other relations with foreign powers (with the exception of the Netherlands). Furthermore, in order to exterminate the forbidden religion of Kirishitan, every family was required to be registered in a Buddhist temple. However, "hidden Kirishitan" groups survived these severe persecutions and have preserved their form of Kirishitan tradition even into the present century.

Buddhism and the Tokugawa regime. The Tokugawa regime's anti-Kirishitan measures required every Japanese citizen to become, at least nominally, Buddhist. Accordingly, the number of Buddhist temples suddenly increased from 13,037 (the number of temples during the Kamakura period) to 469,934. Under Tokugawa rule a comprehensive parochial system was created, with Buddhist clerics serving as arms of the ruling regime in charge of thought control. In turn, Buddhist temples were tightly controlled by the regime, which tolerated internal doctrinal disputes but not deviation from official policy. Since Buddhist temples were in charge of cemeteries, Buddhism was highly visible to the general populace through burial and memorial services. Understandably, the combination of semiofficial prerogatives and financial security was not conducive to the clerics' spiritual quest. The only new sect that emerged during the Tokugawa period was the Ōbaku sect of Zen, which was introduced from China in the mid-seventeenth century. [*See the biography of Ingen.*]

Confucianism and Shintō. Neo-Confucianism was promoted by Zen Buddhists prior to the Tokugawa period. Thus, that Neo-Confucian scholars were also Zen clerics was taken for granted. Fujiwara Seika (1561–1619) first advocated the independence of Neo-Confucianism from Zen. By his recommendation, Hayashi Razan (1583–1657), one of Seika's disciples, became the Confucian adviser to the first shogun, thus commencing the tradition that members of the Hayashi family served as heads of the official Confucian college, the Shōheikō, under the Tokugawa regime. Not surprisingly, Razan and many Neo-Confucians expressed outspoken anti-Buddhist sentiments, and some Confucian scholars became interested in Shintō. Razan, himself an ardent follower of the Shushi (Chu Hsi) tradition, tried to relate the *ri* (Chin., *li,* "reason, principle") of Neo-Confucianism with Shintō. Another Shushi scholar, Yamazaki Ansai (1618–1682), went so far as to develop a form of Confucian Shintō called Suika Shintō. The Shushi school was acknowledged as the official guiding ideology of the regime and was promoted by powerful members of the Tokugawa family, including the fifth shogun. Especially noteworthy was Tokugawa Mitsukuni (1628–1701), grandson of the first shogun and the daimyo of Mito, who gathered together able scholars, including Chu Shun-shui (1600–1682), an exiled Ming royalist. He thereby initiated the Mito tradition of Confucianism. The *Dainihonshi* (History of Great Japan), produced by Mito scholars, subsequently provided the theoretical basis for the royalist movement.

The second tradition of Neo-Confucianism, Ōyōmeigaku or Yōmeigaku (the school of Wang Yang-ming), held that the individual mind was the manifestation of the universal Mind. This school also attracted such able men as Nakae Tōju (1608–1648) and Kumazawa Banzan (1619–1691). Ōyōmeigaku provided ethical incentives for social reform and became a pseudo-religious system. Quite different from the traditions of Shushi and Ōyōmei was the Kogaku ("ancient learning") tradition, which aspired to return to the classical sources of Confucianism. One of its early advocates, Yamaga Sokō (1622–1685), left a lasting mark on Bushidō, while another scholar of this school, Itō Jinsai (1627–1705), probed the truth of classical Confucianism, rejecting the metaphysical dualism of Chu Hsi.

Throughout the Tokugawa period, Confucian scholars, particularly those of the Shushigaku, Ōyōmeigaku, and Kogaku schools, exerted lasting influence on the warriors-turned-administrators, who took up Confucian ideas on the art of governing and on the modes of conduct that were appropriate for warriors, farmers, and townspeople, respectively. Certainly, such semireligious movements as Shingaku ("mind learning"), initiated by Ishida Baigan (1685–1744), and Hōtoku ("repaying indebtedness"), championed by Ninomiya Sontoku (1787–1856), were greatly indebted to Confucian ethical insights. [*See the biographies of the principal Neo-Confucian thinkers discussed above.*]

Shintō revival and the decline of the Tokugawa regime. With the encouragement of anti-Buddhist Confucianists, especially those of Suika Shintō, Shintō leaders who were overshadowed by their Buddhist counterparts during the early Tokugawa period began to assert themselves. Shintō soon found a new ally in the scholars of Kokugaku ("national learning"), notably Motoori Norinaga (1730–1801), whose monumental study of the *Kojiki* provided a theoretical basis for the Fukko ("return to ancient") Shintō movement. Motoori's junior contemporary, Hirata Atsutane (1776–1843), pushed the cause of Fukko Shintō even further. [*See* Kokugaku *and the biographies of Motoori and Hirata.*] The nationalistic sentiment generated by the leaders of the Shintō revival, National Learning, and pro-Shintō Confucians began to turn against the already weakening Tokugawa regime in favor of the emerging royalist cause. The authority of the regime was threatened further by the demands of Western powers to reopen Japan for trade. Inevitably, the loosening of the shogunate's control resulted in political and social disintegration, which in turn precipitated the emergence of messianic cults from the soil of folk religious traditions. Three important messianic cults developed: Kurozumikyō, founded by Kurozumi Munetada (1780–1850); Konkōkyō, founded by Kawate Bunjirō (1814–1883); and Tenrikyō, founded by Nakayama Miki (1798–1887). [*See* Kurozumikyō; Konkōkyō; *and* Tenrikyō.]

Modern Period. The checkered development of Japanese religion in the modern period reflects a series of political, social, and cultural changes that have taken place within the Japanese nation. These changes include the toppling of the Tokugawa regime (1867), followed by the restoration of imperial rule under the Meiji emperor (r. 1867–1912); the rising influence of Western thought and civilization as well as Christianity; the Sino-Japanese War (1894–1895); the Russo-Japanese War (1904–1905); the annexation of Korea (1910); World War I, followed by a short-lived "Taishō Democracy"; an economic crisis followed by the rise of militarism in the 1930s; the Japanese invasion of Manchuria and China followed by World War II; Japan's surrender to the Allied forces (1945); the Allied occupation of Japan; and postwar adjustment. The particular path of development of Japanese religion was, of course, most directly affected by the government's religious policies.

Meiji era. Although the architects of modern Japan welcomed many features of Western civilization, the Meiji regime was determined to restore the ancient principle of the "unity of religion and government" and the immanental theocratic state. The model was the Ritsuryō system of the seventh and eighth centuries. Accordingly, sacred kingship served as the pivot of national policy *(kokutai)*. Thus, while the constitution nominally guaranteed religious freedom and the historic ban against Christianity was lifted, the government created an overarching new religious form called State Shintō, which was designed to supersede all other religious groups. In order to create such a new official religion out of the ancient Japanese religious heritage an edict separating Shintō and Buddhism *(Shin-Butsu hanzen rei)* was issued. The government's feeling was that the Shintō-Buddhist amalgam of the preceding ten centuries was contrary to indigenous religious tradition. After the abortive Taikyō Sempū ("dissemination of the great doctrine") movement and the compulsory registration of Shintō parishioners, the government decided to utilize various other means, especially military training and public education, to promote the sacred "legacy of the *kami* way" *(kannagara):* hence the promulgation of the Imperial Rescript to Soldiers and Sailors (1882) and the Imperial Rescript on Education (1890). Significantly, from 1882 until the end of World War II Shintō priests were prohibited by law from preaching during Shintō ceremonies, although they were responsible—as arms of the government bureaucracy—for the preservation of State Shintō.

Furthermore, in order to keep State Shintō from becoming involved in overtly sectarian activities, the government created between 1882 and 1908 a new category of Kyōha ("sect") Shintō and recognized thirteen such groups, including Kurozumikyō, Konkōkyō, and Tenrikyō, which had emerged in the late Tokugawa period. Like Buddhist sects and Christian denominations, these groups depended on nongovernmental, private initiative for their propagation, organization, and financial support. Actually, Kyōha Shintō groups have very little in common. Some of them consider themselves genuinely Shintō in beliefs and practices, whereas some of them are marked by strong Confucian features. Still others betray characteristic features of folk religious tradition such as the veneration of sacred mountains, cults of mental and physical purification, utopian beliefs, and faith healing.

Buddhism. Understandably Buddhism was destined to undergo many traumatic experiences in the modern period. The Meiji regime's edict separating Shintō and Buddhism precipitated a popular anti-Buddhist movement that reached its climax around 1871. In various districts temples were destroyed, monks and nuns were laicized, and the parochial system, the legacy of the Tokugawa period, eroded. Moreover, the short-lived Taikyō Sempū movement mobilized Buddhist monks to propagate Taikyō, or government-concocted "Shintō" doctrines. Naturally, faithful Buddhists resented the Shintō-dominated Taikyō movement, and they advocated the principle of religious freedom. Thus, four branches of the True Pure Land sect managed to secure permission to leave the Taikyō movement, and shortly afterward the ill-fated movement itself was abolished. In the meantime, enlightened Buddhist leaders, determined to meet the challenge of Western thought and scholarship, sent able young monks to Western universities. Exposure to European Buddhological scholarship and contacts with other Buddhist traditions in Asia greatly broadened the vista of previously insulated Japanese Buddhists.

The government's grudging decision to succumb to the pressure of Western powers and lift the ban against Christianity was an emotional blow to Buddhism, which had been charged with the task of carrying out the anti-Kirishitan policy of the Tokugawa regime. Thus, many Buddhists, including those who had advocated religious freedom, allied themselves with Shintō, Confucian, and nationalist leaders in an emotional anti-Christian campaign called *haja kensei* ("refutation of evil religion and the exaltation of righteous religion"). After the promulgation of the Imperial Rescript on Education in 1890, many Buddhists equated patriotism with nationalism, thus becoming willing defenders and spokesmen of the emperor cult that symbolized the unique national polity *(kokutai)*. Although many Buddhists had no intention of restoring the historic form of the Shintō-Buddhist amalgam, until the end of World War II they accepted completely Buddhism's subordinate role in the nebulous but overarching super-religion of State Shintō.

Confucianism. Confucians, too, were disappointed by the turn of events during the early days of the Meiji era. It is well to recall that Confucians were the influential guardians of the Tokugawa regime's official ideology but that in latter Tokugawa days many of them cooperated with Shintō and nationalist leaders and prepared the ground for the new Japan. Indeed, Confucianism was an intellectual bridge between the premodern and modern periods. And although the new regime depended heavily on Confucian ethical principles in its formulation of imperial ideology and the principles of sacred national polity, sensitive Confucians felt that those Confucian features had been dissolved into a new overarching framework with heavy imprints of Shintō and National Learning (Kokugaku). Confucians also resented the new regime's policy of organizing the educational system on Western models and welcoming Western learning *(yōgaku)* at the expense of, so they felt, traditionally important Confucian learning (Jugaku). After a decade of infatuation with things Western, however, a conservative mood returned, much to the comfort of Confucians. With the promulgation of the Imperial Rescript on Education and the adoption of compulsory "moral teaching" *(shūshin)* in school systems, Confucian values were domesticated and presented as indigenous moral values. The historic Chinese Confucian notion of *wang-tao* ("the way of true kingship") was recast into the framework of *kōdō* ("the imperial way"), and its ethical universalism was transformed into *nihon-shugi* ("Japanese-ism"). As such, "nonreligious" Confucian ethics supported "super-religious" State Shintō until the end of World War II.

Christianity. The appearance—or reappearance, as far as Roman Catholicism was concerned—of Christianity in Japan was due to the convergence of several factors. These included pressures both external and internal, both from Western powers and from enlightened Buddhist leaders who demanded religious freedom. Initially, the Meiji regime, in its eagerness to restore the ancient indigenous polity, arrested over three thousand "hidden Kirishitan" in Kyushu and sent them into exile in various parts of the country. However, foreign ministers strongly advised the Meiji regime, which was then eager to improve its treaties with Western nations, to change its anti-Christian policy. Feeling these pressures, the government lifted its ban against the "forbidden religion." This opened the door to missionary activity by Protestant as well as Roman Catholic and Russian Orthodox churches. From that time until 1945, Christian movements in Japan walked a tightrope between their own religious affirmation and the demands of the nation's inherent immanental theocratic principle.

The meaning of "religious freedom" was stated by Itō Hirobumi (1841–1909), the chief architect of the Meiji Constitution, as follows:

> No believer in this or that religion has the right to place himself outside the pale of the law of the Empire, on the ground that he is serving his god. . . . Thus, although freedom of religious belief is complete and exempt from all restrictions, so long as manifestations of it are confined to the mind; yet with regard to external matters such as forms of worship and the mode of propagandism, certain necessary restrictions of law or regulations must be provided for, and besides, the general duties of subjects must be observed.

This understanding of religious freedom was interpreted even more narrowly after the promulgation of the Imperial Rescript on Education; spokesmen of anti-Christian groups stressed that the Christian doctrine of universal love was incompatible with the national virtues of loyalty and filial piety taught explicitly in the Rescript. Some Christian leaders responded by stressing the compatibility of their faith and patriotism. Although a small group of Christian socialists and pacifists protested during the Sino-Japanese and Russo-Japanese wars, most Christians passively supported the war effort.

Another burden that the Christian movement has carried from the Meiji era to the present is its "foreignness." The anti-Kirishitan policy and all-embracing, unified meaning-structure of the Tokugawa synthesis that had lasted over two and a half centuries resulted in an exclusivistic mental attitude among the Japanese populace. A new religion thus found it difficult to penetrate from the outside. However, during the time of infatuation with things Western, curious or iconoclastic youths in urban areas were attracted by Christianity because of its foreignness. As a result, Westernized intellectuals, lesser bureaucrats, and technicians became the core of the Christian community. Through them, and through church-related schools and philanthropic activities, the Christian influence made a far greater impact on Japan than many people realize.

Christianity in Japan, however, has also paid a high price for its foreignness. As might be expected, Christian churches in Japan, many of which had close relationships with their respective counterparts in the West, experienced difficult times in the 1930s. Under combined heavy pressure from militarists and Shintō leaders, both the Congregatio de Propaganda Fide in Rome and the National Christian Council of the Protestant Churches in Japan accepted the government's interpretation of State Shintō as "nonreligious." According to their view, obeisance at the State Shintō shrines as a nonreligious, patriotic act could be performed by all Japanese subjects. In 1939 all aspects of religion were placed under strict government control. In 1940 thirty-four Protestant churches were compelled to unite as the "Church of Christ in Japan." This church and the Roman Catholic church remained the only recognized Christian groups during World War II. During the war all religious groups were exploited by the government as ideological weapons. Individual religious leaders who did not cooperate with the government were jailed, intimidated, or tortured. Christians learned the bitter lesson that under the immanental theocratic system created in modern Japan the only religious freedom was, as stated by Itō Hirobumi, "confined to the mind."

Japanese religion today. In the modern world the destiny of any nation is as greatly influenced by external events as by domestic events. As far as modern Japan was concerned, such external events as the Chinese Revolution in 1912, World War I, the Russian Revolution, and the worldwide depression intermingled with events at home and propelled Japan to the world stage. Ironically, although World War I benefited the wealthy elite, the economic imbalance it produced drove desperate masses to rice riots and workers to labor strikes. Marxist student organizations were formed, and some serious college students joined the Communist party. Many people in lower social strata, benefiting little from modern civilization or industrial economy and neglected by institutionalized religions, turned to messianic and healing cults of the folk religious tradition. Thus, in spite of the government's determined effort to control religious groups and to prevent the emergence of new religions, it was reported that the number of quasi religions *(ruiji shūkyō)* increased from 98 in 1924 to 414 in 1930 and then to over one thousand in 1935. Many of them experienced harassment, intervention, and persecution by the government, and some of them chose for the sake of survival to affiliate with Buddhist or Kyōha Shintō sects. Important among the quasi-religious groups were Ōmotokyō, founded by Deguchi Nao (1836–1918); Hito no Michi, founded by Miki Tokuharu (1871–1938); and Reiyūkai, founded jointly by Kubo Kakutarō (1890–1944) and Kotani Kimi (1901–1971). After the end of World War II these quasi-religious groups and their spiritual cousins became the so-called new religions *(shinkō shūkyō)*. [*See* New Religions, *article on*

New Religions in Japan; Ōmotokyō; *and* Reiyūkai Kyōdan.]

The end of World War II and the Allied occupation of Japan brought full-scale religious freedom, with far-reaching consequences, to Japanese religion. In December 1945 the Occupation force issued the Shintō Directive dismantling the official structure of State Shintō; on New Year's Day 1946 the emperor publicly denied his divinity. Understandably, the loss of the sacral kingship and State Shintō undercut the mytho-historical foundation of Japanese religion that had endured from time immemorial. The new civil code of 1947 effectively abolished the traditional system of interlocking households *(ie seido)* as a legal institution, so that individuals were no longer bound by the religious affiliation of their households. The erosion of family cohesion greatly weakened the Buddhist parish system *(danka)* as well as the Shintō parish systems *(ujiko)*.

The abrogation of the ill-famed Religious Organizations Law (enacted in 1939 and enforced in 1940) also radically altered the religious scene. Assured of religious freedom and separation of religion and state by the Religious Corporations Ordinance, all religious groups (Buddhist, Christian, Shintō—now called Shrine Shintō—and others) began energetic activities. This turn of events made it possible for quasi religions and Buddhist or Sect Shintō splinter groups to become independent. Sect Shintō, which comprised 13 groups before the war, developed into 75 groups by 1949. With the emergence of other new religions the total number of religious groups reached 742 by 1950. However, with the enactment of the Religious Juridical Persons Law (Shūkyō hōjin hō) in 1951, the number was reduced to 379—142 in the Shintō tradition, 169 Buddhist groups, 38 Christian denominations, and 30 miscellaneous groups.

In the immediate postwar period, when many people suffered from uncertainty, poverty, and loss of confidence, many men and women were attracted by what the new religions claimed to offer: mundane happiness, tightly knit religious organizations, healing, and readily accessible earthly deities or divine agents. It is worth noting in this connection that the real prosperity of the new religions in Japan came after the Korean War, with the heavy trend toward urbanization. Not only did the urban population increase significantly, but the entire nation assumed the character of an industrialized society. In this situation some of the new religions, especially two Buddhist groups, namely, Sōka Gakkai and Risshō Kōseikai, gained a large number of followers among the new middle class. Some of these new religions took an active part in political affairs. For example, as early as 1962, Sōka Gakkai scored an impressive success in the elections of the House of Councillors, and its own political wing, Kōmeitō, now enjoys a bargaining power that no other religiously based group has achieved in modern Japanese politics. Other groups have also attempted to gain political influence by campaigning for their favorite candidates for political offices. [*See* Sōka Gakkai *and* Risshō Kōseikai.]

It has not been easy for older Buddhist groups to adjust to the changing social situation, especially since many of them lost their traditional financial support in the immediate postwar period. Also, religious freedom unwittingly fostered schisms among some of them. Nevertheless, the strength of the older Buddhist groups lies in their following among the intelligentsia and the rural population. Japanese Buddhological scholarship deservedly enjoys an international reputation. Japanese Buddhist leaders are taking increasingly active roles in pan-Asian and global Buddhist affairs while at the same time attending to such issues as peace and disarmament at home.

Christian churches, which had experienced hardship and mental anguish before and during World War II, rejoiced over their religious freedom after the war. They showed determination as they confronted many neglected problems, repairing church buildings damaged during the war, regrouping their scattered adherents, and training young leaders for the ministry. However, the popular interest in Christianity that developed in the immediate postwar years waned quickly. Furthermore, the massive support Christian churches expected from abroad never materialized, largely owing to the erosion of missionary incentive among Western churches except in Roman Catholic and fundamentalist groups. Christianity in Japan still suffers from its foreignness, its theological conservatism, and the lack of grass-roots participation in rural areas. On the other hand, church-related educational institutions are growing, and younger Christians are cooperating with other religionists in dealing with social and political issues.

It is difficult to feel the pulse of Japanese religion in the late twentieth century because the external signs are too contradictory. In the midst of their highly technological industrial society, the Japanese people still feel close to nature, still love poetry and the arts, and still observe numerous traditional rituals. A significant part of Japanese religious life continues to focus on family values and on observances performed in the home. [*See* Domestic Observances, *article on* Japanese Practices.] In addition, in spite of high literacy and scientific education, many men and women of high and low social status still subscribe to fortune telling, geomancy, and healing cults. The Japanese are avid global travelers, and yet their world of meaning is still strongly tied to their land, language, custom, and tradition. Furthermore, one is amazed by the quick recovery of Shintō, which smoothly transformed itself from State Shintō to Shrine Shintō almost overnight during the Allied occupation. Millions of pilgrims and worshipers continue to visit large and small Shintō shrines. Understandably, all these contradictory features are difficult for the Japanese to resolve. It may well be that with the redefinition of the once-divine monarchy and the loss of an overarching religious form, the character of the nebulous but deep-rooted Japanese religion has been transformed into a new framework that accommodates a genuine coexistence of different religious forms in the name of religious freedom.

BIBLIOGRAPHY

General Introduction

Anesaki, Masaharu. *History of Japanese Religion.* 2d ed. Rutland, Vt., 1963.

Earhart, H. Byron. *Religion in the Japanese Experience: Sources and Interpretations.* Encino, Calif., 1974.

Hori, Ichirō, ed. *Japanese Religion.* Tokyo and Palo Alto, Calif., 1972.

Kitagawa, Joseph M. *Religion in Japanese History.* New York and London, 1966.

Kitagawa, Joseph M. "The Religions of Japan." In *A Reader's Guide to the Great Religions,* 2d ed., edited by Charles J. Adams, pp. 247–282. New York, 1977. This bibliographic essay includes an appendix listing reference works, published bibliographies, and periodicals relevant to the religions of Japan.

Nakamura, Hajime. *Ways of Thinking of Eastern Peoples: India, China, Tibet, Japan.* Honolulu, 1964.

Sansom, George B. *Japan: A Short Cultural History.* New York, 1931.

Sansom, George B. *A History of Japan.* 3 vols. Stanford, Calif., 1958–1963.

Tsunoda, Ryūsaku, Wm. Theodore de Bary, and Donald Keene, comps. *Sources of Japanese Tradition.* New York and London, 1958.

Prehistoric Background

Groot, Gerard J. *The Prehistory of Japan.* New York, 1951.

Haguenauer, Charles M. *Origines de la civilisation japonaise,* pt. 1. Paris, 1956.

Kidder, Jonathan Edward, Jr. *Japan before Buddhism.* Rev. ed. New York, 1966.

Kitagawa, Joseph M. "Prehistoric Background of Japanese Religion." *History of Religions* 2 (Winter 1963): 292–328.

Komatsu, Isao. *The Japanese People: Origins of the People and the Language.* Tokyo, 1962.

Oka, Masao. "Kulturschichten in Alt-Japan." Ph.D. diss., Vienna University, 1933.

Early Historical Period. Basic textual sources are two mytho-historical writings, *Kojiki,* translated by Donald L. Philippi (Princeton and Tokyo, 1969), and *Nihongi: Chronicles of Japan from the Earliest Times to A.D. 697,* translated by William George Aston (Rutland, Vt., and Tokyo, 1972). Other important textual sources available in English are *The Manyōshū: One Thousand Poems,* translated by the Nippon Gakujutsu Shinkōkai (1940; reprint, New York and London, 1965); *Kogoshūi: Gleanings from Ancient Stories,* translated by Genchi Katō and Hikoshiro Hoshinō, 3d ed. (1926; reprint, New York and London, 1972); and *Izumo Fudoki,* translated by Michiko Y. Aoki (Tokyo, 1971). Regarding the development of the early historic Japanese society and nation, see *Japan in the Chinese Dynastic Histories,* translated and compiled by Ryūsaku Tsunoda, and edited by L. Carrington Goodrich (South Pasadena, Calif., 1951); Robert Karl Reischauer's *Early Japanese History, c. 40 B.C.–A.D. 1167,* 2 vols. (Princeton, 1937); Paul Wheatley and Thomas See's *From Court to Capital* (Chicago and London, 1978); Kan'ichi Asakawa's *The Early Institutional Life of Japan: A Study in the Reform of 645 A.D.*, 2d ed. (New York, 1903); and Richard J. Miller's *Ancient Japanese Nobility: The 'Kabane' Ranking System* (Berkeley and London, 1974).

Historical Period. Most of the books available in Western languages on the historical development of Japanese religion focus on particular religious traditions, primarily Shintō and Buddhism.

For translations of primary texts, see *Norito: A New Translation of the Ancient Japanese Ritual Prayers,* translated by Donald L. Philippi (Tokyo, 1959), and *Engi-Shiki: Procedures of the Engi Era,* 2 vols., translated by Felicia Bock (Tokyo, 1970–1972), which give us a glimpse of the Shintō foundation of the Ritsuryō state and its immanental theocracy.

Important studies of Shintō are Karl Florenz's *Die historischen Quellen der Shintō-Religion* (Leipzig, 1919); David Clarence Holtom's *The National Faith of Japan* (1938; reprint, New York, 1965); Genchi Katō's *A Study of Shintō* (Tokyo, 1926); and Tsunetsugu Muraoka's *Studies in Shinto Thought,* translated by Delmer M. Brown and James T. Araki (Tokyo, 1964). Holtom's *The Japanese Enthronement Ceremonies* (1928; reprint, Tokyo, 1972) and Robert S. Ellwood, Jr.'s *The Feast of Kingship* (Tokyo, 1973) portray an important aspect of the "Imperial Household" Shintō.

Works on Japanese Buddhism are numerous, including denominational histories, biographies of important Buddhist figures, and expositions of their writings. Among them, those that deal with Japanese Buddhism as a whole are Masaharu Anesaki's *Buddhist Art in Its Relation to Buddhist Ideals, with Special Reference to Buddhism in Japan* (1915; reprint, New York, 1978); Sir Charles Eliot's *Japanese Buddhism,* 2d ed. (London, 1959); Alicia Matsunaga's *The Buddhist Philosophy of Assimilation: The Historical Development of the 'Honji-Suijaku Theory'* (Tokyo, 1969); E. Dale Saunders's *Buddhism in Japan* (Philadelphia, 1964); Emile Steinilber-Oberlin and Kuni Matsuo's *The Buddhist Sects of Japan,* translated by Marc Logé (London, 1938); Marinus Willem de Visser's *Ancient Buddhism in Japan,* 2 vols. (Leiden and Paris, 1935); and Shōkō Watanabe's *Japanese Buddhism: A Critical Appraisal,* rev. ed. (Tokyo, 1968). On the eclectic Mountain Priesthood, see H. Byron Earhart's *A Religious Study of the Mount Haguro Sect of Shugendō* (Tokyo, 1970).

Books in Western languages on Japanese Confucianism are few and mostly dated. However, mention should be made of Robert Cornell Armstrong's *Light from the East: Studies in Japanese Confucianism* (Tokyo, 1914); Kaibara Ekken's *The Way of Contentment*, translated by Ken Hoshino (1904; reprint, New York, 1913); Olaf G. Lidin's translation of Ogyū Sorai's *Distinguishing the Way: Bendō* (Tokyo, 1970); Warren W. Smith, Jr.'s *Confucianism in Modern Japan* (Tokyo, 1959); and Joseph John Spae's *Itō Jinsai* (1948; reprint, New York, 1967). For the nebulous but persistent influence of Taoism and the Yin-yang school on Japanese religion, see Bernard Frank's *Kata-imi et kata-tagae* (Paris, 1958) and Ivan I. Morris's *The World of the Shining Prince: Court Life in Ancient Japan* (1964; reprint, New York, 1979).

The standard work on Japanese folk religion is Hori Ichirō's *Folk Religion in Japan: Continuity and Change*, edited by Joseph M. Kitagawa and Alan L. Miller (Chicago, 1968). Various aspects of folk religion are discussed in Geoffrey Bownas's *Japanese Rainmaking and Other Folk Practices* (London, 1963), U. A. Casal's *The Five Sacred Festivals of Ancient Japan* (Tokyo, 1967), and Cornelis Ouwehand's *Namazu-e and Their Themes* (Leiden, 1964).

Regarding Christianity in Japan, see Otis Cary's *A History of Christianity in Japan*, 2 vols. (1909; reprint, New York, 1971), and Richard Henry Drummond's *A History of Christianity in Japan* (Grand Rapids, Mich., 1971). On the Catholic church in Japan, see Joseph Jennes's *History of the Catholic Church in Japan: From Its Beginnings to the Early Meiji Period, 1549–1873* (Tokyo, 1973). On its development in the sixteenth and seventeenth centuries, see Charles Ralph Boxer's *The Christian Century in Japan, 1549–1650* (1951; reprint, Berkeley, 1967) and George Elison's *Deus Destroyed* (Cambridge, Mass., 1973). For Protestant Christianity in Japan, see Charles W. Iglehart's *A Century of Protestant Christianity in Japan* (Rutland, Vt., and Tokyo, 1959) and Charles H. Germany's *Protestant Theologies in Modern Japan* (Tokyo, 1965).

The most helpful introduction to Japanese religion in the modern period is *Japanese Religion in the Meiji Era*, edited and compiled by Hideo Kishimoto and translated by John F. Howes (Tokyo, 1956). For the guiding ideologies of the prewar Japanese government, see *Kokutai no Hongi*, edited by Robert King Hall and translated by John Owen Gauntlett (Cambridge, 1949), and Hall's *Shūshin: The Ethics of a Defeated Nation* (New York, 1949). Charles William Hepner's *The Kurozumi Sect of Shintō* (Tokyo, 1935), Delwin B. Schneider's *Konkō kyō: A Japanese Religion* (Tokyo, 1962), and Henry van Straelen's *The Religion of Divine Wisdom* (Tokyo, 1954) discuss the three so-called Sect (Kyōha) Shintō groups. Daniel Clarence Holtom's *Modern Japan and Shintō Nationalism* (Chicago, 1943) deals with the way Shintō was used for political purposes before and during the war.

As to the religious development after World War II, William P. Woodard's *The Allied Occupation of Japan, 1945–1952, and Japanese Religions* (Leiden, 1972) gives us the Occupation army's religious policy and its implications for Japanese religions. Those who want to read of the postwar religious ethos in Japan will find the following works informative: Robert J. Smith's *Ancestor Worship in Contemporary Japan* (Stanford, Calif., 1974), Joseph John Spae's *Japanese Religiosity* (Tokyo, 1971), Fernando M. Basabe, Anzai Shin, and Federico Lanzaco's *Religious Attitudes of Japanese Men* (Tokyo, 1968), and Fernando M. Basabe, Anzai Shin, and Alphonso M. Nebreda's *Japanese Youth Confronts Religion: A Sociological Survey* (Tokyo, 1967). Concerning numerous "new religions" *(shinkō shūkyō)*, which have mushroomed since 1945, consult H. Byron Earhart's *The New Religions of Japan: A Bibliography of Western Language Materials*, 2d ed. (Ann Arbor, 1983).

JOSEPH M. KITAGAWA

Popular Religion

In this article "popular religion" will be taken to include both "folk religion"—by which is meant the diverse and at most only locally organized attitudes, beliefs, and practices that together constitute a people's customary observance—and popular or lay aspects of ecclesiastical bodies whose organization and solidarity transcend local boundaries. What is not included, then, is the religion promoted by elites such as priests, monks, and nuns, as well as by governments upon occasion, including the rites, beliefs, and theoretical systematizations that such elites officially promulgate or defend. It should be understood that in practice often no sharp line can be drawn between any of these categories. Even religious elites often exhibit "folk" behavior and attitudes not justified by official doctrines; similarly, mutual diffusion can occur between official doctrines and folk attitudes and practices. These distinctions, however, are presented for the convenience of the student of religion and culture; they are usually not a part of the thought patterns of religious practitioners themselves.

For the purposes of this article, Japanese history will be divided into the following periods:

Prehistoric and protohistoric	?–645 CE
Classical (Asuka, Nara, Heian)	645–1185
Medieval (Kamakura, Ashikaga)	1185–1600
Premodern (Tokugawa or Edo)	1600–1868
Modern (Meiji, Taishō, Shōwa)	1868–present

Popular religion in Japan is composed primarily of elements that can be assigned Shintō or Buddhist origins, although elements deriving from Chinese folk religion—usually labeled Taoist—are also important, along with those of an elite Chinese tradition, Confucianism, and, more recently, aspects of Christianity. In addition, the term *Shintō* must be understood in its most inclusive sense, namely, as denoting all of the indigenous religious attitudes and practices of the Japanese people prior to the influence of Chinese civilization (roughly beginning in the sixth century CE), as well as those that evolved from these native traditions in later centuries. Shintō itself reached the more complex status of an elite tradition only at the beginning of the classical period, with the establishment of an official cult with imperial patronage and the eventual promulgation of an official mythology, codification of rituals, and establishment of a priestly hierarchy. Even during this time, however, popular Shintō continued largely unaffected by these elite events; further, official Shintō itself clearly was derived from the vast reservoir of folk practices that had regulated the religious lives of the Japanese people from time immemorial.

Indigenous Folk Religion. The fundamental religious concept of Shintō past and present is *kami,* a widely inclusive term embracing the notion of sacred power from a *mana*-like impersonal force inherent in all things and concentrated in the unusual, to personal and therefore godlike beings such as culture heroes, the geniuses of particular places or things, species deities, and ancestors. [*See* Kami.] Originally there were two major ways of interaction with *kami:* through *matsuri* ("rituals") that sought either to receive the blessings of the sacred powers or to turn aside their wrath, or through shamanic séances using the method of *kami* possession *(kamigakari),* by which the will of the *kami* could be made known through the oracular utterances of the shaman. Intermediate forms such as divination, omen reading, and oath swearing were also common. Although imperial recourse to *miko* (female shamans) is well documented in the legendary period, this element was largely lost to elite Shintō in the course of its development. *Miko* flourished among the common people, however, and have declined only in the modern period. On the other hand, public rituals, which take place at the thousands of Shintō shrines and mostly at regularly scheduled times throughout the year, have continued at all levels of Shintō.

An important class of *kami* were the *ujigami,* or ancestral deities of the large clans that came to dominate Japanese social, political, and religious organization in the protohistoric period; in modern times the *ujigami* survive at the village level, although without their former importance, as *dōzokushin.* Indeed, the *ujigami* was probably the most important *kami* to the early Japanese; as high priest, the clan head needed the shamanic services of his wife to ensure that the will of this *kami* was carried out for the weal of all.

Probably the most important *kami* of popular religion has been Inari, the rice deity, whose shrines are found everywhere, even in modern urban settings. Although not a part of the official mythology, Inari became associated in later classical times with such mythic *kami* as Ugatama, the female *kami* of food and clothing; Sarutahiko, the monkey *kami,* whose special province was fecundity; and Ame no Uzume, the goddess who, through exposing her genitals in an ecstatic dance, wielded the feminine *kami* power to bring back the lifegiving sun to a darkened and dying world. Such associations illuminate both the character of the folk deity Inari and the process by which popular religious elements were engrafted to the elite strata in Japan. Inari shrines still are places where farmers go to pray for abundant crops, but they are also places where both rural and urban dwellers pray for aid in conception, childbirth, and child rearing, as well as more generally for success in any endeavor.

The most famous Inari shrine is at Fushimi in the city of Kyoto, where the elaborate main shrine dedicated to the official cult is almost shouldered aside by the many popular shrines flanking the paths that meander about the mountain. Typical of the etiological tales associated with many shrines and temples is the legend that tells of the founding of Fushimi Inari shrine. In 711, many years before the founding of the capital at Kyoto, a nobleman was practicing archery by shooting at a ball of cooked rice tossed into the air. All at once the rice was transformed into a white bird that flew away and alighted at the peak of Mount Fushimi. There the nobleman built the shrine to the rice god.

Virtually all Inari shrines have statues of a pair of foxes flanking the main place of worship, a fact that illustrates syncretistic tendencies of popular religion. These foxes, now popularly understood to be the messengers of the rice god, or sometimes even identified with the god himself, were probably derived from popular Chinese lore concerning fox spirits. Certainly there exists in Chinese a large body of folk tales depicting the dangers of fox spirits, who usually take the form of a beautiful woman in order to seduce and ruin unsuspecting or weak-willed men. That these tales also have become naturalized in Japan discloses a much more general pattern of popular acceptance of Chinese cultural and religious elements; it also suggests the association of the fox as a symbol of sexual desire and Inari as a deity of fecundity and plenty. [*See also* Foxes.]

Impact of Chinese Culture and Religion. At the beginning of the classical period Japan experienced a cultural revolution brought about by the assimilation of Chinese technical, philosophical, aesthetic, and religious elements. Buddhism took its place as a more or less equal partner with Shintō in the official structure of government and in the religious practice of the aristocracy. Confucianism was adopted as a theory of government and a guide to personal conduct. Taoism was used to provide a ritual structure and to assist both Shintō and Buddhist efforts to ensure the well-being of the nation. To be sure, this revolution began among the Japanese elite and for many years was largely confined to it. By the Nara period, however, despite the government's attempts to control its spread, Buddhism had begun to reach the common people. The famous Buddhist tale collection, *Nihon ryōiki,* which used the folktale genre as a means of converting the masses and of inculcating Buddhist virtues, was produced by a monk for use by popular Buddhist preachers. The Nara period also saw the paradoxical rise of the *hijiri,* or holy men, who were popular preachers and miracle workers whose activities were proscribed by the government on the grounds that they "misled" the people. While not all *hijiri* were Buddhist, most combined a Buddhist understanding of a *bodhisattva*'s compassion with a sometimes indiscriminate mixture of magico-religious practices in attempting to ameliorate the physical as well as the spiritual condition of the masses. The most famous of the *hijiri* was Gyōgi, whose elevation to the head of the official Buddhist hierarchy by Emperor Shōmu in 745 expressed not only the pious emperor's desire to unify the nation under the banner of Buddhism, but also the growing recognition on the part of the elite of the popular forms of that religion.[*See* Hijiri *and the biography of Gyōgi.*]

Another result of Buddhist penetration at the popular level was reinforcement of native belief in malevolent spirits, known in the classical period as *goryōshin.* Buddhism gave such beliefs a strongly moralistic tone; previously, it was believed that *kami* power was concentrated in many kinds of beings, some of which were by their nature destructive. Now, however, destructive supernatural power could be understood as justified by human events. Just as motivation was discovered in the Buddhist psychology and its expression ensured by the law of *karman,* so did Buddhism present a new problem to the people. *Goryōshin,* as particularly the ghosts of humans who had been wronged in life, had to be propitiated or exorcised by Shintō rites and saved from their suffering by Buddhist prayers and priestly magic.

Medieval Popularization of Buddhism. The collapse of the classical social and political order, completed by the year 1185, not only brought on the medieval period of Japanese history but also resulted in the virtual destruction of official Shintō. To be sure, the imperial court continued to perform some of the old Shintō rituals in the name of the emperor and for the benefit of all the nation, but in fact these rites increasingly became the private cult of the imperial family and the ever more impoverished old aristocracy. But the relative decentralization of the times allowed a number of popular forms of Buddhism to become institutionalized independently of the old Buddhist schools. Among these, the Pure Land schools are especially noteworthy. These schools combined elite elements derived from monastic cults of the savior Buddha Amida (Skt., Amitābha) and popular practices of using Buddhist chanting to overcome evil influences. The so-called *nembutsu hijiri* had been at work among the common people throughout much of the classical period in healing and exorcising demons by chanting the Sino-Japanese phrase "Namu Amida Butsu" ("Hail to the Buddha Amitābha"). The Pure Land movement of the medieval period tended to convert this immediate concern for this-worldly problems to a concern for the ultimate salvation of the individual who, by complete faith in the power of Amida and by chanting of the Nembutsu, could be reborn at the end of this earthly life into the Buddhist paradise (the Pure Land). [*See* Amitābha *and* Nien-fo.]

It seems clear that neither major figure in the Pure Land movement, Hōnen (1133–1212) or his disciple Shinran (1173–1262), sought to found an independent Buddhist school. Instead, they were largely apolitical figures who intended to extend to the common people a share of Buddhist salvation hitherto reserved for monks. The result was a radical democratization and simplification of Buddhism—in short a truly popular form of that religion. In these schools, monasticism was abolished, priests were expected to marry, and the old elite Buddhism—what they called the Holy Path *(shōdōmon)*—was rejected as selfish and arrogant. This popular Buddhism had become a religion of lay participation, congregational worship, and acceptance of the social and political status quo. The elite quest of sanctification, of personal transformation, and of enlightenment was out of reach of the ordinary person; instead of working toward the transformation of self as in the Holy Path, the Pure Land schools (called, by way of contrast, *jōdomon,* or Path of Pure Land) brought about the transformation of Buddhism into an instrument of salvation open to all. [*See the biographies of Hōnen and Shinran.*]

Another way in which Buddhism accommodated itself to the popular mind can be seen in the rise of the *yamabushi,* or mountain ascetics, whose tradition goes back to the classical period. Both of the dominant schools of Buddhism in the Heian period, Tendai, headquartered on Mount Hiei, and Shingon, headquartered on Mount Kōya, established adjunct orders of *yamabushi.* Of these, one that was allied to Shingon, Shugendō, has survived into the modern age. The members of the *yamabushi* orders were differentiated by their varying degrees of initiation into the group's mysteries. In addition, the *yamabushi* did not follow the Buddhist monastic rules: they were laymen who lived ordinary lives except for certain times of the year when they would gather to go on pilgrimages and conduct their own secret rites deep in their sacred mountains. A famous *nō* play by Zeami *(Taniko)* depicts one of the Shugendō pilgrimages. [*See* Shugendō.]

Belief in sacred mountains appears to be a native Shintō phenomenon in Japan, although both Taoism and Buddhism brought from China their own traditions of encountering the sacred among mountains, traditions that served to strengthen and sometimes modify indigenous attitudes. Mountains were the special abodes of the Taoist *hsien* (Jpn., *sennin*), or immortals, as well as the saints and recluses that the personalistic side of that tradition promoted. [*See* Hsien.] These traditions, especially in the form of popular tales, were brought to Japan, where they found ready acceptance, mixing with the native *hijiri* tradition. In the Heian period, the Buddhists, themselves influenced by the Taoist tradition, especially sought out remote mountains as sites for monasteries as well as for retreats and hermitages for meditation. In addition, several mountains, such as Ontake and Fuji, were thought by the laity to be the special abodes of *bodhisattva*s or the entryways to the afterlife. All these cases show traces of the old Shintō notion that austerities practiced in mountains were especially efficacious for gaining spiritual power. The *yamabushi* demonstrate this connection by their habit of making long and arduous hikes through the mountains and by ritual bathing in icy mountain streams. Many sacred mountains in Japan were gathering places for *miko*, who served the common people by contacting the spirits of the dead or of Shintō, Taoist, or Buddhist saints and deities who were believed to inhabit such places.

The association and even amalgamation of Shintō and Buddhism among the people was aided by the *honjisuijaku* ("essence-manifestation") theory first promulgated in the classical period by Buddhist monks using Chinese models. Almost from the beginning of the Buddhist presence in Japan the people had assumed that Buddhist figures—saints, *bodhisattva*s, celestial Buddhas—were related in some way to native Shintō deities. The *honjisuijaku* theory simply gave official sanction to this popular view by stating that specific native figures were but the manifestation of certain Buddhist figures who were their true essence. This tendency to amalgamation can also be recognized in the practice, documented from the Nara period, of building small Buddhist temples within the confines of Shintō shrines, and vice versa. Thus the Shintō *kami* (deities) could be served by Buddhist rites, while Buddhist figures could be worshiped through Shintō rites. Sometimes the Buddhist rites were understood as attempts to bring the *kami* to Buddhist enlightenment; alternatively, they were thought of as a Buddhist accommodation to the parochial Japanese mentality, which often preferred native forms. By the medieval period, many local shrines and temples were served by priests who were both Shintō and Buddhist, performing the rites according to the figure addressed. Often, *yamabushi* would marry *miko* and carry on local priestly functions as a team within this popular amalgamation of religions. [*See* Honjisuijaku.]

Domestic Piety and Ancestor Reverence. Even today most Japanese families have within the home both a Shintō *kamidana* ("god-shelf") and a Buddhist *butsudan* ("Buddhist altar"). At both, offerings of flowers and food are made from time to time and prayers are recited. Ancestral tablets will be found within the home, placed either in a special shrine or within the *kamidana* or *butsudan* according to the emphasis of the particular family. Theoretically, the Buddhist prayers are offered for the benefit of the departed, to aid them in their continuing postmortem quest for salvation in various hells or heavens or in rebirths in this world, while the Shintō prayers are acts of filial piety that address the spirits of the dead as present in the tablets, as still present family members who require service in death as in life. In practice, however, the popular mind often does not make such sharp distinctions.

An important example of attitudes toward the dead can be seen in the Obon festival, traditionally from the thirteenth to the sixteenth day of the seventh lunar month. Although its origins can be traced back even to pre-Buddhist Hindu ancestral cults, it clearly shows its folk Buddhist as well as Shintō colorations in Japan. [*See* Buddhist Religious Year.] Preparations for the festival include cleaning and decorating the *butsudan* and preparing special offerings there. Usually this is an occasion for the full cooperation of the *dōzoku* in honoring its common ancestors. Fires are lit the first night before the door of each house as well as along the roads to the village to light the way of the dead, who are thought to return to the land of the living for these few days. The spirits are entertained in the home with food, gifts, and prayers, while in the village the entertainment takes the form of graceful dancing, the famous *bon odori*, of Shintō origin. During this time graves are visited and finally the sprits are sent off again with beacon fires.

Attitudes toward death among the Japanese people have been characterized by considerable ambivalance. On the one hand, the Shintō association of death with pollution or contamination has been strong from the first: touching, being in the presence of, or being kin to one who has just died make a person ritually unclean, requiring seclusion and ritual purification. A part of a larger and very ancient belief in the contagious nature of misfortune, this fear of the dead has resulted in a near monopoly of Buddhism in the conducting of funerals. On the other hand, much evidence, from prehistoric burial mounds as well as old Japanese poetry, attests to the continuing ties of affection and duty that the people maintained with the departed even in ancient times, while the continuing popularity of the Obon festival and of ancestral reverence in the home show that even today the continued presence of the dead, if properly handled through ritual, is still valued.

It should also be noted that Confucianism, another import from China, has played an important though amorphous role in promoting both ancestral reverence and family cohesion. From the beginning of the classical period the values of Confucian "familyism" were promoted by the government as the proper basis for a harmonious and prosperous nation. By the Tokugawa period Confucianism once again became an important philosophy of both government and personal life. Loyalty to the nation was one part of a value system that took the family as the model for all values. The native Japanese reverence for ancestors as well as for all *loci* of authority was thereby greatly reinforced. [*See* Confucianism in Japan.]

Folk deities, often of mixed Shintō, Buddhist, and Taoist heritage, continue to be accorded some degree of reverence among the people. *Kami* of hearth, privy, and yard are still known, and, curiously in the modern world, deities or nameless powers of good or ill fortune remain popular. Some examples of these are Ebisu, the *kami* of good luck, having its origin among fishermen, Dōsojin, the *kami* of roads and gates and protector of children and of marital harmony, and Kōshin, a rather malevolent deity of Taoist origin whose calendar days, occurring once every sixty days throughout the year, are considered unlucky. Belief in lucky and unlucky days was greatly stimulated in classical times by *onmyōji* ("*yin-yang* masters"), who popularized Taoist ideas and promoted themselves as expert diviners and ritualists and who could discover in their books of astrology times and directions to avoid or to welcome in order to ritually protect one from the consequences of ill-considered actions. Modern fortune tellers continue this tradition and Shintō shrines usually have booths where fortunes are told and charms can be bought. These charms, or *omamori,* are usually blessed by the priests of a particular shrine. [*See* Onmyōdō.]

Folk Tales as Expressions of Popular Religion. One important and often neglected expression of popular religion everywhere is the folk tale. Although in Japan as elsewhere this literary genre resists reduction to narrowly religious categories, in Japan especially many scholars have noted the close association of folk tale and popular religious sentiments. Many folk tales express deeply felt religious attitudes and values at variance with official codes set by ecclesiastical and governmental elites, yet many also reflect these more official views. Indeed, examples abound in which priests have made use of existing tales, either to create an official orthodoxy as in the construction of a mythology, or to teach certain religious values and behavior. In this latter category, the Buddhist use of folk tales in the *Nihon ryōiki* is an early example; later Shintō priests helped to invent the *okagura* dramas, which in part taught the old mythology to the masses at shrine festivals; similarly, the medieval Shintō-Buddhist world of ghosts and karmic retribution was combined with Zen-inspired aesthetics to create the famous *nō* dramas from folk tales and historical legends. In the Tokugawa period, popular pilgrimages, especially those to the great shrine dedicated to the sun goddess Amaterasu at Ise, spawned new tales of wonder, miracles, and divine retribution.

The well-known tale *Hagoromo* (The Feather Cloak), known in the West as *The Swan Maiden,* contributed significantly to the official mythology of Amaterasu, as well as to the Daijōsai ritual, in which a new emperor is enthroned. Again, tales of Buddhist piety as found in the *Konjaku monogatari* collection of late classical times indicate both the power of Buddhist faith and charms sanctioned by elite religion—one notes especially the long section depicting rewards both in this life and in lives to come for those with faith in the *Hokekyō* (Lotus Sutra)—and also an antinomian tendency that criticizes the faults and foibles of worldly clergy. A more purely folk phenomenon contained in these tales is the rejection of official unworldly values for such mundane goals as sexual fulfilment and the pursuit of wealth.

The greater portion of those folk tales that treat of supernatural phenomena have little to do with any official mythology, theology, or value system. To be sure, many promote such pan-Japanese values as loyalty, gratitude, and curbing of the appetites. However, the greatest number of tales as collected by professional folklorists in the twentieth century may be described as vaguely animistic in tone. The list of extrahuman powers and intelligences told of in such tales is very long and ranges from the ghosts of human beings to traditional *kami,* including many more fanciful entities such as the long-nosed *tengu,* hag-witches called *yamauba,* and mischievous fox-spirits. Not unusual are tales in which plants, especially trees, are endowed with powers that can cause much suffering among humans if insensitively treated. Perhaps the greatest error told of in these animistic tales is simply that of impiety: this world is a crowded place inhabited by myriads of powers, each of which the "good" man or woman treats with awe and respect, while the "bad" person ignores them to his or her peril.

Pilgrimage and Popular Drama. The rise of the pilgrimage as a popular form of religious expression can be traced to the sixteenth century, although the earliest Japanese literature shows that the aristocracy were wont to make journeys into sacred mountain fastnesses at least as early as the seventh century. It was not until the medieval period, however, that journeys to sacred sites, especially to Shintō shrines, became mass movements. The Ise Shrine, main cult center of Amaterasu, was the primary goal for the millions, mostly peasants, who undertook the often dangerous journey at the peak of the popularity of this phenomenon in the late eighteenth and early nineteenth centuries. [*See* Amaterasu Ōmikami.] A kind of frenzy, characterized by some as mass hysteria, caused many to drop their tools, abandon their domestic and economic responsibilities, and seek the abode of the *kami.* To be sure, motives were mixed, and nonreligious reasons such as a desire to break out of monotonous existence of toil must be considered. Still, popular tales of amulets mysteriously falling from the sky, of healings, of misfortune to those who resisted or preached against the urge to participate in the pilgrimage, all powerfully reinforced the prevailing notion that it was the will of the *kami* that the people should pay their respects in this way. [*See also* Pilgrimage, *article on* Buddhist Pilgrimage in East Asia.]

It should also be pointed out that in the case of the Ise Shrine, these mass pilgrimages mark the last stage in a long history of slow democratization of the worship of Amaterasu. Originally, she was the *ujigami* of the imperial family and thus admitted only their exclusive worship. Apparently, her status as a national deity, always implied by her position as progenitor of the imperial lineage, had made of her a direct object of veneration for all in the course of a thousand years or more. It must also be noted that the outer shrine of Ise is dedicated to Toyouke, goddess of food and fertility, basic existential concerns of those close to the subsistence level of economy. From this point of view, the ritual pilgrimage, with its set forms of dress and gesture, its taboos and sometimes ecstatic dances, can be seen as a new means of carrying out village rites of cosmic renewal. The dangerous and rigorous journey was a long ascetic rite of abstinence and purification. The dancing *(okage odori)* is homologizable to the dances that accompany village festivals such as *bon odori,* in which the deities and spirits of the dead are entertained, or again to the ecstatic trance-inducing dances of the *miko* who communicate with the deities in shamanic rites. Prayers at the shrine of destination, and the distribution of amulets by the attending priests, are also a part of village shrine festivals.

The rise of popular drama can be seen to some extent as a part of the same movement toward popularization of what had been the exclusive property of official Shintō, namely the mythology as set down in the early eighth century in the *Kojiki* and *Nihonshoki. Okagura* dramas enacted with music and dance the creation of the world by the primordial parents Izanagi and Izanami, the struggle between Amaterasu and her impetuous brother Susano-o, the descent to earth of the imperial grandchild Ninigi, and many other official mythic themes. As such, they represent a successful attempt on the part of the local Shintō priesthood to keep alive the old traditions by bringing them to the common people. The *okagura* became a part of many village festivals in the medieval period and gave rise to other dramatic forms, most notably the *nō* drama, which in particular achieved a high level of artistic sophistication. But *okagura* have remained popular phenomena, and still may be viewed today. Indeed, they offer a valuable opportunity to observe the blending of folk values and forms with classical elite forms and themes. There is a good deal of humor and even ribaldry in *okagura,* as well as a clear infusion of universal folk concerns that blend with the more solemn and particular mythic motifs. [*See* Drama, *article on* East Asian Dance and Theater.]

Institutionalization of Popular Religion. It can be said with some confidence that by the middle of the Tokugawa period the pattern of folk religion that can still be observed in village Japan had been established. The pattern bears two features that may at first sight seem contradictory: first is the high degree to which religious elements of disparate origin have become intermixed; second is the conspicuous division of labor among various religious institutions. This latter is expressed in the common formula that the Japanese are born and married by Shintō rites, buried by Buddhist rites, and live their everyday lives by Confucian principles. Yet both these features seem to stem from a single source, namely, a very pragmatic tendency among the Japanese people: they take those elements that seem immediately useful, employing them in a contextual framework all their own.

Another pattern that has emerged with special clarity—probably the result of Japan's relative isolation—is the process of interaction between elite and popular levels of religion. Within the long history of religion in Japan modern scholarship has been able to document much of the process through which elite elements are imposed upon or otherwise assimilated by the folk. Less well known is the reverse, in which folk elements are taken up into existing elite cultural strata or are institutionalized into what are often intermediate forms. Such popular movements often become church-like institutions with more or less clear hierarchical organization and geographical boundaries that go beyond the local arena. Beginning perhaps with the *yamabushi* movements of the Heian period, continuing in the medieval popular Buddhist movements of the Nichiren and Pure Land schools, and still continuing into the modern period with the celebrated burgeoning of the so-called "new religions" *(shinkō shūkyō)*, the religious institutions that have resulted have tended to combine simplified versions of old elite traditions—especially of monastic Buddhism and court Shintō—with popular values that center upon social interaction in this world and the maintenance of domestic health and prosperity. [*See* New Religions, *article on* New Religions in Japan.]

The Shintō new religion Tenrikyō was founded in the nineteenth century by Nakayama Miki after she was possessed by several *kami*, who, in the old way of Japanese shamanism, spoke through her while she was in a trance. In the course of these possessions a new mythology was revealed that, while similar in many respects to the old classical Shintō cosmogonic myth, shows striking differences from it. Present are the familiar primordial parents, and many lesser episodes concerning the creation of life are common to both; conspicuous by their absence, however, are references to Amaterasu and her brother, the central characters of the old mythology. Also absent is the entire mythic apparatus that supported the imperial institution. The classical mythology was a seventh-century creation that took many fragmented clan traditions and worked them into a drama of the establishment and legitimization of the classical religious and political order. Nakayama is more concerned, however, with domestic values. The *kami* of Tenrikyō are called divine parents; humans are their children. The good and correct life is led in humble recognition of this most fundamental relationship; hence the cardinal virtues are loyalty, obligation, and gratitude. Diseases and all other misfortunes are caused by insensitivity to this basic parent/child *(oya-ko)* relationship. Specific cultic duties consist largely of participation in ritual dancing and in group activities such as shrine building and works of charity. [*See* Tenrikyō.]

Another example, this time from the Buddhist tradition, can be seen in Sōka Gakkai (Value Creating Society), founded in 1937 by Makiguchi Tsunesaburō (1871–1944) and Toda Jōsei (1900–1958). [*See* Sōka Gakkai.] Makiguchi was a schoolteacher who, during the difficult decades of economic hardship and increasing totalitarian repression in the twenties and thirties, developed a philosophy of life he called *sōka*, meaning "value creation." Initially his views seem to have been largely secular, although they borrowed heavily from Buddhist metaphysics in their fundamental insight into the relativity of all values (at least in the mundane sphere) and the necessity of overcoming dependence upon false absolutes. Only gradually did this view take on a more traditional Buddhist coloration. Eventually, however, through the efforts especially of Toda, Sōka Gakkai became affiliated with Nichiren Shōshū, one of the smaller branches of Nichiren Buddhism. Toda admired much of the Nichiren tradition, especially its unusual intolerance of other religions, its simple and straightforward rituals, its demand of absolute faith in ritual objects, in its founder, and in its sacred text (the *Lotus Sutra*), and, perhaps more than anything else, the quasi-military hierarchical organization of the sect.

Sōka Gakkai calls itself a lay organization of Nichiren Shōshū; technically, it has no priests, its leaders remaining laymen. The society has been a tremendous success, with membership numbering in the millions. Typical of the new religions, and consistent with its origins, it stresses immediate attainment of all worldly goals and interprets the ancient Buddhist goal of enlightenment as something closely akin to "happiness." The mental culture of such a worldview is maintained through intense small group meetings that are partly testimonials, partly study sessions. Its very simplicity, as well as its emphasis on mundane problems and upon group solidarity, all have contributed to the success of this popular religion in meeting the needs of many Japanese in the modern industrial world, which constantly threatens to overwhelm them with anomie and rootlessness. Salvation is here and now, and the conviction of it is strongly reinforced by group rituals.

[*See also* Shintō; Buddhism, *article on* Buddhism in Japan; Domestic Observances, *article on* Japanese Practices; *and* Ancestors, *article on* Ancestor Cults.]

BIBLIOGRAPHY

Benedict, Ruth. *The Chrysanthemum and the Sword: Patterns of Japanese Culture.* Boston, 1946.

Blacker, Carmen. *The Catalpa Bow: A Study of Shamanistic Practices in Japan.* London, 1975.

Casal, U. A. *The Five Sacred Festivals of Ancient Japan.* Tokyo, 1967.

Earhart, H. Byron. *A Religious Study of the Mount Haguro Sect of Shugendō: An Example of Japanese Mountain Religion.* Tokyo, 1970.

Hearn, Lafcadio. *Glimpses of Unfamiliar Japan.* New York, 1894.

Herbert, Jean. *Shintō: At the Fountainhead of Japan.* London, 1967.

Hori Ichirō. *Wagakuni minkan shinkōshi no kenkyū.* 2 vols. Tokyo, 1953–1955.

Hori Ichirō. *Folk Religion in Japan.* Edited and translated by Joseph M. Kitagawa and Alan L. Miller. Chicago, 1968.

Kitagawa, Joseph M. *Religion in Japanese History.* New York, 1966.

McFarland, H. Neill. *The Rush Hour of the Gods: A Study of the New Religious Movements in Japan.* New York, 1967.

Philippi, Donald L., trans. *Norito: A New Translation of the Ancient Japanese Ritual Prayers.* Tokyo, 1959.

Seki Keigo. *Nihon mukashi-banashi shūsei.* 6 vols. Tokyo, 1950–1958.

Seki Keigo, ed. *Folktales of Japan.* Translated by Robert J. Adams. Chicago, 1963.

Yanagita Kunio, ed. *Japanese Folk Tales.* Translated by Fanny Hagin Mayer. Tokyo, 1954.

Yanagita Kunio, ed. *Japanese Folklore Dictionary.* Translated by Masanori Takatsuka and edited by George K. Brady. Lexington, Ky., 1958.

ALAN L. MILLER

Mythic Themes

In general, the tales recorded in such eighth- and ninth-century documents as the *Kojiki* (712), *Nihonshoki* (720), and *Kogoshūi* (807) are today considered "Japanese mythology." Of course, a long period of oral tradition preceeded the appearance of such literary works. Japanese mythology is the product of the early indigenous religion, Shintō, or "way of the *kami*" (Shintō deities). Its origin and development is to a large degree coextensive with that of early Shintō. Details of the most primitive forms of early Shintō are unknown; however, through such scientific methods as philology, archaeology, and comparative folklore these early forms can be conjectured to some extent.

The Development of Shintō. Early Shintō may be classified into five developmental stages. The first stage was that of the primitive beliefs of the peoples of the Jōmon and Yayoi periods. The Jōmon people were food gatherers; the Yayoi people, cultivators of rice. Animistic nature worship prevailed among both these peoples and provided the roots for the development of later Shintō. Some tales similar to that of the West Ceramese story of the maiden Hainuwele, such as *The Killing of the Food Goddess,* found in the *Kojiki* and *Nihonshoki,* may be the products of this period. In the second stage (fourth and fifth centuries CE), characteristically Shintō features began to appear. Animistic spirits were personified and individualized to some degree and assigned specific places of worship, such as sacred rocks or trees in mountain precincts. Most were nature deities: sun, moon, and thunder. Some were adopted as the tutelary deities of provincial clans that had begun to be powerful; however, their sanctuaries had no shrine structures as yet. Often, these deities were regarded as the ancestors of certain clans, but ancestor worship was not popular in this period. Ōmonomushi, the great deity of the Miwa Shrine in Yamato, exemplifies this developmental stage. In his sanctuary there is no main hall for his worship even today. Instead, the sacred rocks on Mount Miwa are regarded as the seat of Ōmonomushi. In several myths in the *Kojiki* and *Nihonshoki* he is said to take sometimes a human and sometimes a serpent shape. One of the myths concerning his mystic marriages with human maidens relates the origin of the Miwa clan. In this way the deity came to be regarded as the ancestor of the clan.

In the third stage (sixth and seventh centuries) the Yamato court began to use Shintō to support its claim to authority over the provincial clans and to centralize its power. The concomitant extension of the court's religious authority meant that the local clans lost much of their own religious authority. Their rituals, myths, and practices were also considerably modified or changed. Prior to this period there were numerous local sacred kings or chieftains in many districts of the Japanese islands. It seems likely that they each once had their own traditions regarding the divine origin of the clans. These myths were chanted by the *kataribe,* or storytellers, on the occasion of the enthronement of the local kings. However, with the formation of the Yamato kingdom most of them lost power owing to the confiscation of their own sacred regalia by the Yamato nobility. Their ancestral deities came to be regarded as subordinates who served the great Yamato deity Amaterasu. Local nature deities such as the moon god, sea gods, mountain gods, and so forth were also combined in the theogony of the imperial family. It was probably in this period that the mythic couple Izanagi and Izanami came to be regarded as the parents of Amaterasu, the ancestral goddess of the imperial family.

In the fourth stage (late seventh and eighth centuries, including the Nara period), the adoption of Chinese political and cultural systems changed the old forms of the state, but at the same time Shintō mythology completed its development as a legitimizer of centralized power. It was in this period that these traditions were recorded by government decree in the *Kojiki, Nihonshoki, Fudoki,* and other works. Although the imperial institution was modeled after that of the Chinese empire, Shintō beliefs and cosmology prevailed in the thinking of the court nobility during the Nara period. Thus, the emperor was called Akitsukami, or "living deity," because he was identified as the incarnation of the solar goddess Amaterasu, who was raised to the rank of a sovereign in the pantheon. The tutelary or ancestral deities of some powerful clans were also raised by the court to the rank of national hero-gods. Huge structures were constructed for their worship, and the sacred emblems *(shintai)*, mirrors, swords, jewels, and other such objects, were enshrined and worshiped there. In the collection of poems known as the *Man'yōshū*, a famous court poet Kakinomoto Hitomaro contributed various songs praising Empress Jitō and her son as "the descendants of Amaterasu shining in heaven."

In the last stage of development (from the later Nara to the early Heian period), Shintō was greatly changed under the influence of Buddhism, which became a national religion at this time. Some aspects of the aboriginal beliefs, rituals, and architecture of Shintō amalgamated into a syncretic religion. At some sites *jingūji* ("shrine-temples") served both traditions, but were presided over by Buddhist monks. Shintō deities came to be regarded as subordinate to Buddhas and *bodhisattvas* and as weak sentient beings seeking salvation. The *Nihon ryōiki*, written by the Buddhist monk Kyōkai at the beginning of the ninth century, tells how the great deity of Taga Shrine in Ōmi asked a monk to chant the *Lotus Sutra* for the sake of his salvation. During this period it became a common practice to chant Buddhist *sūtra*s in front of altars of Shintō deities. The deities who accepted salvation by Buddhist ritual and doctrine were believed to become the guardians and protectors of *dharma*. It was in this period that wooden images of Shintō deities, patterned after the images of Buddhas, first appeared. It was these images, rather than the *shintai*, that were worshiped in the inner halls of the shrine. This synthesis of Shintō and Buddhism continued until the end of the Tokugawa period.

Written Sources. Japanese myths were recorded in the following literary works: the *Kojiki* and the *Nihonshoki*, both of which were compiled under the auspices of the imperial court in Nara; the *Kogoshūi*, written by Imibe no Hironari; the *Fudoki*, or provincial records, also recorded and compiled under imperial orders of 713; the *Engishiki* of 927, which contains *norito*, or ceremonial prayers chanted in front of the altars on the occasion of festivals, and rites of the imperial court and the more important shrines; the *Man'yōshū*, a collection of early poems compiled toward the end of the Nara period; and the *Sendai kuji hongi*, which was compiled around the beginning of the ninth century. The most systematic traditions can be found in the *Kojiki*. The original plan of this compilation was made by Emperor Temmu (r. 673–686). He collected many old records of royal succession and old traditions from various clans and adopted some of them to further his own theological justifications for political power. A nebulous figure, Hieda no Are, was set by the emperor to read these sources. Temmu also planned to compile a book on the history of the Yamato state with these same texts. However, the plan was suspended with his death in 686. In 711, Empress Gemmei ordered Ō no Yasumaro to record and compile the semihistorical and legendary sources that Hieda no Are once learned. Yasumaro finished the work in 712 and presented it to the empress. Meanwhile, Prince Toneri and Ō no Yasumaro compiled the *Nihonshoki* in Chinese style and presented it to Emperor Genshō in 720. The *Kogoshūi* (Gleanings of Ancient Tales) was written and presented to the throne in 807 by Imibe no Hironari to protect against the oppression of his own clan by the more powerful Nakatomi clan. It contains many tales unknown to the compilers of the *Kojiki* and the *Nihonshoki*.

The above-mentioned literary sources contain a variety of mythical themes including the beginning of the universe and creation of the Japanese islands, the descent to the underworld, the origin of death and birth, the invention of cereal cultivation, and the inception of kingship. The most systematized form of Shintō mythology can be seen in the chapters on the divine age in the *Kojiki* and the *Nihonshoki*, both of which were compiled to justify the authority of the imperial court to rule all of Japan. The *Kojiki*, in particular, weaves various independent myths and legends into a long narrative that relates logically and systematically events from the beginning of the cosmos to the establishment of the dynasty. It seems likely that this construction reflects the intentions of Emperor Temmu, the original planner of the work. The *Nihonshoki*, for its part, includes many different versions of each myth, and thus lacks the narrative coherency and ideological consistency of its companion history.

Both texts strongly emphasize the absoluteness and eternity of the sovereignty of the imperial family as descendants of the solar goddess Amaterasu. Political as well as ethical and theological concepts lie at the core of the myths in this form. Such myths, embellished and modified to relate the story of "the children of the sun controlling the country," clearly support the Yamato court's efforts to establish its rule over the whole of Japan. It is the same in the *norito*, or "ceremonial prayers," found in the *Engishiki*. In the *Kogoshūi*, too, such sequential arrangement of myths reflects the presuppositions of the author, himself a noble in the imperial court. However, the *Kogoshūi* also includes strong assertions made for the benefit of the author's own clan, the Imibe.

In the *Fudoki*, provincial records from Hitachi, Harima, Izumo, Hizen, and Bungo are preserved. In addition, many fragments of the records from other provinces are cited in some medieval documents. But only in the *Izumo fudoki* can a systematized mythology and a pantheon be found. Although such famous deities as Susano-o and Ōnamuchi sometimes appear among the animistic deities in the myths and legends of the *Fudoki*, they often bear no connection to the theology of the Yamato court. In the *Fudoki* almost all of the myths and legends concerning these divinities are explanatory tales providing information about the names of districts and various local customs. Within this genre the *Izumo fudoki* stands as a unique work. Unlike the other four records that were compiled by provincial officials appointed by the central government, the *Izumo fudoki* was compiled in 733 by Izumo no Omi Hiroshima, chief of the Izumo clan, with the help of his friends. Accordingly, the *kuni no miyatsuko* of Izumo, "the chieftain of the Izumo clan," had his own personal theology and theogony, in which Ōnamuchi appears often as the Kunitsukuri no Ōkami, or "the grand creator of the land." Ōnamuchi seems to have been the principal deity in the Izumo pantheon. Other Izumo divinities, such as Susano-o and Ajisuki, appear naive when compared to their descriptions in the *Kojiki* and *Nihonshoki*.

The Mythology of the Kojiki. According to the cosmology of the *Kojiki*, in the beginning three supreme divinities appeared on the plain of high heaven. These invisible divinities, Ame-no-minaka-nushi ("heaven central lord"), Takamimusubi ("high producing"), and Kamimusubi ("divine producing"), represent the generative power for the creation of the world. Later, two other divinities sprang up like reeds from the primeval chaos and hid themselves. Thereafter, seven generations of male and female divinities appeared, ending with Izanagi and Izanami. This couple was ordered by the supreme deities to consolidate and fertilize the earth from the chaotic primordial ocean. Standing on the "floating bridge of heaven," they stirred the waters of the ocean with a jewelled spear. When the water began to coagulate, they gathered it up, letting a drop fall to form the island of Onogoro ("self-curdling island"). The two deities descended to this island and erected a hall and a high pillar, which they ritually circumambulated from opposite directions.

When they met the two deities had sexual intercourse, the product of which was the "grand eight islands," or the Japanese archipelago, and the various nature divinities, including the gods of wind, water, mist, and mountains. Thereafter, they decided to produce someone who would rule these islands. The firstborn, the deformed "leech-child," was abandoned in a reed boat in a stream. The goddess Izanami was burned to death by giving birth to their last child, Kagutsuchi, the fire god. Izanagi followed Izanami to the Land of Yomi, the underworld of the dead, to beg her to come back to the land of the living. She replied that she had already taken the "food of the dead" and thus her return was impossible.

In order to consult the Yomi divinities, Izanami then entered an inner room, begging her husband not to look. After a long time, Izanagi became impatient and looked in. Finding her putrefied and worm-filled, Izanagi fled in horror. Izanami, angry with Izanagi's disregard for his promise and his breach of her taboo, pursued him accompanied by her subordinate ogresses. At the entrance of the underworld the two divinities stood face to face on the slope of Yomi and swore their divorce. Thereafter, Izanagi ruled the land of the living and Izanami that of the dead. Upon his return to the terrestrial world Izanagi purified himself in a stream. From his eyes were born the solar goddess, Amaterasu, and the lunar god, Tsukiyomi; from his nose was born the violent god Susano-o. This version of the birth of Amaterasu, Tsukiyomi, and Susano-o is unique to the *Kojiki;* the *Nihonshoki* relates that these deities were the product of the union of Izanagi and Izanami.

Izanagi entrusted the rule of the heavenly world to Amaterasu, the night to Tsukiyomi, and the ocean to Susano-o. However, Susano-o did not obey his father's order and did nothing but weep bitterly. When Izanagi tried to expel Susano-o to the Land of Ne (the netherworld), Susano-o went up to the heavenly world to say farewell to his sister Amaterasu. She was amazed at her brother's thunderlike noise and his shaking of the mountains. Amaterasu's fears that the purpose of his visit was to execute an evil plan to deprive her of her sovereignty were quelled by Susano-o's vow that he had no evil intentions toward her. Nevertheless, Susano-o became more and more violent, ravaging Amaterasu's domain, destroying her rice fields, and polluting her sacred ceremonial hall. Finally, struck by fear, Amaterasu hid in a rock grotto, thrusting the entire world into a darkness from which evil demons arose. Eight hundred deities employed various devices to lure her out of the grotto—the comical goddess Uzume performed obscene dances and Ame no Koyane chanted prayers. When at last Amaterasu reappeared and light was restored to the world, Susano-o was punished and driven to Izumo. Upon his descent he rescued the maiden Kushi-inada-hime from an eight-headed serpent who threatened to kill her for his annual human sacrifice. Susano-o presented Amaterasu with a strange sword he retrieved from the serpent's tail. The sword later became one of the "three imperial regalia." Susano-o married the maiden and lived in Suga in Izumo Province.

The hero god Ōnamuchi, or Ōkuninushi, was the successor of Susano-o in Izumo. His myth retells the many trials, perils, and adventures his evil brothers forced him to endure in his youth. After Ōnamuchi was killed and resuscitated several times he took refuge in Ne, the land of the dead, which Susano-o governed. Susano-o, however, presented him with even greater trials. Finally, Ōnamuchi married Susano-o's daughter Suseri-hime (Suseri) and fled with her, stealing Susano-o's magical treasures. In the end, Susano-o recognized their marriage and permitted Ōnamuchi to keep the treasures and become the sovereign of the terrestrial world. In this way Ōnamuchi, with the help of a dwarf god Sukunabikona, ruled the Japanese islands.

At the same time, Amaterasu wished to send her grandson Ho-no-ninigi (Ninigi) to the terrestrial world to rule as a new sovereign. Twice her messengers failed to persuade Ōnamuchi to cede his sovereignty to her grandson. Finally, she sent the powerful god Takemikazuchi and another deity, Ame-no-torifune (Futsunushi in the *Nihonshoki* version). Ōnamuchi and his children consented to Amaterasu's demand, extracting Amaterasu's promise to establish a grand temple in his honor. Amaterasu bestowed upon Ho-no-ninigi the three divine regalia (i.e., the mirror, sword, and jewels), and sent him, with his attending deities, to earth. The party descended onto the summit of Mount Takachiho in Hyūga Province. Prince Ho-no-ninigi married the maiden Ko-no-hana-sakuyabime ("princess of the blossoms of the blooming trees"). When her father, Grand Mountain God, sent two other daughters, Iwanagahime ("rock-long princess") and her younger sister Ko-no-hana, to be his brides, Ho-no-ninigi rejected the elder sister because of her ugliness and married the younger princess. It is said that since that time emperors have not been as long-lived as rocks, because Ho-no-ninigi rejected Rock-long Princess.

Hiko-hohodemi, one of Ho-no-ninigi's three sons, once visited the dragon-king's palace at the bottom of the sea in search of a lost fishhook. When he married the dragon-king's daughter, Toyotama, the dragon-king returned the lost fishhook that had been recovered from the throat of a fish. He also bestowed upon Hiko-hohodemi magical jewels to control the tides. Returning to his terrestrial home, Hiko-hohodemi used the magical jewels against his ill-natured elder brother, who surrendered his sovereignty to him. Later, because he broke his promise not to look at her during childbirth (when she would take on the physical form of a dragon), Toyotama divorced Hiko-hohodemi and returned to her native marine home. Her baby, Ugaya-fuki-aezu, remained in his father's palace and eventually became sovereign of the country. Prince Kammu-yamato-iwarebiko, one of Ugaya-fuki-aezu's children, was the first emperor, Jimmu, founder of the Yamato dynasty. He and his brothers, accompanied by many generals and soldiers, traveled eastward along the Inland Sea in search of the most fertile land. After numerous trials and battles they arrived at the Nara Plain, where Jimmu acceded to the imperial throne in the Kashiwara Palace in Yamato.

The Structure of Japanese Mythology. The foregoing outline of the *Kojiki* mythology may be divided into the following cycles: (1) Cosmogony cycle, (2) Izanagi and Izanami cycle, (3) Amaterasu cycle, (4) Susano-o cycle, (5) Ōnamuchi cycle, (6) Ho-no-ninigi's Descent cycle, (7) Hiko-hohodemi cycle, and (8) Jimmu's Expedition cycle. The sixth and eighth cycles seem to be the most important kernels of the story, for they explain the divine origin of kingship. It is very likely that the other cycles were combined to form the foundation of an origin myth. [*See also* Kingship, *article on* Kingship in East Asia.]

The concept of a triad of supreme deities as related in the first cycle may have been influenced by the three supreme deities (the Three Pure Ones) in Taoist theology. [*See* Taoism, *overview article.*] It seems that the nobility of the imperial court worshiped Takamimusubi and Kamimusubi as male and female fertility deities. Later, they were worshiped in the Eight-Deity Shrine as the guardian deities of the imperial family. The successive generations of male and female deities produced after the appearance of this triad is a mythological representation of the creation of the world from chaos to cosmos. This genealogical or evolutionary form of the creation myth has many parallels among the Polynesians (Dixon, 1916; Matsumoto, 1971). [*See* Polynesian Religions, *article on* Mythic Themes.]

Although the appearance of Izanagi and Izanami are outlined in the final stage of the first cycle, the account of their creation and descent to the underworld is fully explicated in the second cycle. Originally the guardian deities of Awaji Island and vicinity, Izanami and Izanagi were worshiped by fishermen. The influence of these fishermen is evident in the motif of the creation of Onogoro from the chaotic ocean and that of Izanami's island-birth. Again, Polynesian mythology contains similar accounts of island-births. The story of the descent to the underworld by Izanagi and Izanami has many parallels in mythology throughout the world (e.g., Orpheus and Euridice, Demeter and Persephone in Greece). It is particularly noteworthy that the Polynesian myth of Hine and Tane, with its story of the birth and death of humankind, has much in common with the Japanese myth (Dixon, 1916). The entire cycle may have been of southern origin. Although the *Nihonshoki* tells of Amaterasu's birth from Izanagi and Izanami, there originally seems to have been no blood relation between them. The third cycle, which includes the Heavenly Rock-Cave myth, centers on the story of Amaterasu. There is clear evidence that Amaterasu originally was-not considered an ancestor deity of the Yamato family but rather was a local solar deity worshiped by the fishermen of Ise Province. The Heavenly Rock-Cave myth has strong parallels among the Miao tribes of southern China and the Southeast Asian peninsula, who hold that when the hidden sun reappeared at the crowing of a cock the whole world became light.

Cycles four and five are generally called the Izumo myth, because most of the activity of the deities and heroes takes place in Izumo Province and neighboring districts. The central figure in cycle four is Susano-o and in cycle five, Ōnamuchi. Both were worshiped widely in Izumo. According to the *Izumo fudoki,* Susano-o was not related to Amaterasu. Originally, he was a local fertility god, the term *susa-no-o* meaning "the male deity of Susa [a district in Izumo]." In this work it is said that Susano-o settled in Izumo, establishing his own spirit in the village. The depiction of Susano-o's character in the *Kojiki* is quite different from that of the *Izumo fudoki.* In the *Kojiki,* Susano-o, the violent, cruel god, is said to be Amaterasu's brother. A local legend in Izumo, that of Susano-o's rescuing a maiden from the eight-headed serpent, presents a motif that enjoys popularity throughout the world, as seen in the myth of Perseus and Andromeda. Most likely, the eight-headed serpent was also a fertility spirit in Izumo. Some elements of serpent worship are still popular today in Izumo. In the small shrines to the fertility god Kōjinsama, children shape huge serpents out of rope, coil them around sacred trees, and present offerings of various foods and wine. The artificial serpent is believed to be Kōjin himself (Higo, 1938). One of the versions of this myth in the *Nihonshoki* depicts this serpent as a terrible *kami* who is served sake by Susano-o. The victim maiden, whose name is Kushi-inada-hime ("wonderful rice field"), represents another element of folk origin associated with fertility rites in Izumo. The negative characterization of Susano-o as the storm god and the maker of evil seems to have been included to serve the political purposes of the Yamato nobility in the seventh century.

The fifth cycle describes Susano-o's son-in-law (or his son according to the *Nihonshoki*), Ōnamuchi, or Ōkuninushi. Although he was worshiped in the Izumo Great Shrine and is regarded as the most significant deity in the Izumo pantheon, there is extensive evidence that Ōnamuchi and his comrade, the dwarf god Sukunabikona, were once worshiped as the guardian deities of medicine and magic in areas extending beyond Izumo Province. According to most sources, including the *Fudoki, Engishiki,* and *Man'yōshū,* sanctuaries were built in their honor in many parts of Japan. Worship of these deities was common among shamans and medicine men, who regarded them as tutelary deities. The tales of Ōnamuchi's various trials and adventures and his death and resurrection reflect the initiation rituals held in shamanistic secret societies. Izumo and its neighboring districts seem to have once been a religious kingdom, governed by a priest-king and chieftain of many clans called the *kuni no miyatsuko* of Izumo. It is said that he possessed magico-religious power, served Ōnamuchi as his highest priest, and behaved as a living god. He was enthroned as a priest-king in a special rite of succession performed by every generation, even after the Taika Reforms in the mid-seventh century.

The significance of Izumo deities such as Susano-o, Ōnamuchi, and Sukunabikona in the *Kojiki* may be the result of the efforts of both the Izumo *kuni no miyatsuko* and his clansmen and of the shamans and medicine men to promote their mythology. The Yamato nobility, impressed by these groups, incorporated Izumo theology and myths into the central mythology, wherein Izumo deities were regarded as the *kunitsukami,* or the terrestrial deities, as opposed to the *amatsukami,* or the celestial deities (Matsumae, 1970).

Cycle six relates the tales of Ōnamuchi's surrender and Ho-no-ninigi's descent. The former tale originally belonged to the Ōnamuchi cycle, but, in the process of compilation and systematization by the imperial court in the seventh century it was separated from the original text and placed before the tale of Ho-no-ninigi's descent. Since Izumo, the site of Ōnamuchi's tale, and Hyūga, the site of Ho-no-ninigi's descent, were separated by a great distance, this unnatural combination of the tales was most likely prompted by the political needs of the Yamato court. Originally associated with the founding of the Izumo Great Shrine, Ōnamuchi's myth describes the negotiations leading to his surrender to the heavenly grandson, his retirement into the unseen world, and the establishment of the great shrine in Ōnamuchi's memory. The failures and eventual success of Amaterasu's mediators reflect the historical incidents that occurred in Izumo between the Izumo clans and the Yamato court. In the *Nihonshoki* version, Ame-no-hohi, who is regarded as the ancestor of the Izumo clans, is said to have received a heavenly decree ordering him to serve the retired Ōnamuchi as priest. It seems likely that in the original version Ame-no-hohi pacified Ōnamuchi's spirit and began his cult.

The myth of Ho-no-ninigi's descent is very similar to the foundation myths of the old Korean kingdoms. A thirteenth-century Korean work, the *Samguk yusa,* includes the myth in which Hwan-woong, the son of the heavenly king, descends onto the summit of a mountain carrying the three regalia and accompanied by three thousand attendants. His son Tangun is regarded as the founder of the ancient Korean kingdom of Old Chosun. The motif of the descent from heaven onto a mountain is especially popular. Owing to the striking similarities between the Korean and Japanese myths of descent, some scholars, including Egami Namio, Oka Masao, Matsumura Takeo, and Gari Ledyard, have hypothesized the invasion of Japan by horsemen from Korea. This theory, however, lacks sufficient historical and archaeological evidence. The existence of Korean elements in the Japanese myth, such as the decree of the heavenly deity, the three regalia, the numerous attendants, and the five-division system (in which the five principal deities responsible for successfully pulling Amaterasu out of the cave in which she had hidden herself became first her subordinates and later the chieftains of each clan, a system that is also found in the Korean kingdoms of Koguryŏ and Paekche), is not due to the sudden invasion of Korean warriors but, rather, to the later adoption and accretion of the Korean motifs into the original Japanese myth. The most primitive of the Japanese myths of descent is found in the *Nihonshoki*. Here, Ho-no-ninigi is depicted as having descended to earth as a baby wrapped in a coverlet. He did not carry regalia and was not accompanied by subordinates. In the *Kogoshūi*, Ho-no-ninigi, whose name means "abundant rice-ears," is depicted as the figure who carries the sacred ears of rice to earth. He is the deification of the essence of rice. Among the aboriginal tribes of the Malay Peninsula, there is the tale of a "rice-child," who, in the form of a bundle of ears of rice, is brought to a bed in a farmer's house, where it is treated as a newborn baby (Skeat, 1972). In Japan, during the ancient harvest festival, the Niinamesai, a sacred bed with a coverlet was prepared for hospitality to the *kami*. The descent myth of Ho-no-ninigi had a close relation with the Niinamesai (Origuchi, 1955; Matsumae, 1983).

Both parts of cycle seven have numerous parallels in the myths of other traditions. The first part of this myth belongs to the "lost fishhook" type and can be found in the myths of Okinawa, Kei, Sulawesi (Celebes), Palau, and so forth (Matsumoto, 1971; Matsumura, 1958, pp. 678–688). The earliest form of this tale seems to have originated in the south with the ancestral heroes of the Hayahito tribes of southern Kyushu. These tribes, once called the Kumaso ("land spiders"), were regarded as savage aborigines by the Yamato nobility. When they submitted to the imperial court in the early fifth century some were appointed to serve the emperor as guards and actors. They often performed their native dance, the *hayahitomai*, which included a comical mime of a struggle in the water that was, most likely, rooted in the myth of the lost fishhook. The second part of this myth-cycle, describing Hiko-hohodemi's breach of his promise not to observe his supernatural wife in childbirth, belongs to the Melusina motif, which enjoys wide popularity in both Europe and Asia. This motif provides a link between local rulers, thought to possess powers to control rain and water, and the water deities who also possessed such powers. By combining these two tales the Yamato nobility were able to shape the myth of their ancestral heroes. The imperial family identified the Hayahito hero Hiko-hohodemi as one of their ancestors. Therefore, as descendents of the dragon-king they were able to claim possession of the magical ability to control all rain and water. Strikingly similar tales are told about the legendary ancestral heroes of the Koryŭ kingdom in Korea and the Pagan kingdom in Burma.

Cycles one through seven, which appear in the first chapter of the *Kojiki*, entitled "The Age of the *Kami*," were compiled and systematized to explain the divine origin of the Yamato kingship. The historian Tsuda Sōkichi maintained that the construction of Japanese myths was made in the sixth or seventh century by minor nobility with political intentions (Tsuda, 1948). While the date of construction may be correct, it should be noted that most of the motifs of the systematized mythology prevailed in earlier folk traditions. Tales of the same or similar motifs can be found in the folk tales of modern Japan, China, Korea, Southeast Asia, and Oceania. Tsuda also maintained that the great deities who appear in the *Kojiki* (e.g., Amaterasu, Izanagi, Susano-o, and Ōnamuchi) were the political creations of the Yamato nobility, and that these figures were neither the subjects of folk belief nor enshrined as deities. In an attempt to redress this imbalance toward rationalism, recent Japanese scholarship has acknowledged the existence of the actual worship of these deities.

Finally, cycle seven, which is found in the first part of the second chapter of the *Kojiki*, relates Jimmu's expedition and enthronement as the first emperor of the Yamato dynasty. Many modern historians, however, suspect his historicity. Some, as noted earlier, hypothesize the invasion of a tribe from Korea; others point to the similarity of Jimmu's expedition to the actual immigration of some Kyushu clans to Yamato (Inoue, 1960). The tale of Jimmu's expedition seems to have been created in order to infuse the heroic traditions of Hyūga into the Yamato court. The second chapter of the *Kojiki*, called "The Heroic Age," narrates the legendary tales of the successive generations of human emperors and heroes beginning with Jimmu. This chapter includes descriptions of supernatural beings, such as deities and spirits; legends about the mystic marriages between human maidens and Ōmonomushi, the great deity of Mount Miwa; the legend of Prince Yamato Takeru, a typical

Japanese hero; and the tale of Empress Jingū (Jingō) who journeyed to the Korean kingdom of Silla. Although high heavenly deities, such as Amaterasu and Takamimusubi, sometimes appear in these tales, they always play a secondary role. While the third chapter of the *Kojiki* tends toward more historical and human tales, there are also descriptions of supernatural beings, including the great deity Hitokotonushi of Mount Katsuragi, who appeared before Emperor Yūryaku (r. 457–479).

Although there are many different versions of each cycle, in the *Nihonshoki* the fundamental structure of mythology is almost the same as that of the *Kojiki*. The first chapter narrates the myths of "the age of *kami*," and the second chapter begins with Jimmu's expedition. The descriptions and expression in the *Nihonshoki* often betray a Chinese influence. At the same time, however, this work includes more primitive versions of the myths in each cycle as well as tales that are not found in the *Kojiki*. For example, in the *Nihonshoki* there is the tale about Tsukiyomi, the moon god, who was sent by his sister Amaterasu to earth to meet the food goddess, Ukemochi. Ukemochi served him various foods that she had produced from her mouth. Tsukiyomi, furious with her behavior, killed her. Later, Amaterasu found Ukemochi dead. Cows and horses had sprung from her head and silkworms from her eyebrows; millet grew from her forehead and rice from her stomach. Amaterasu was so angered by the murder that she separated herself from her brother. This tale, which relates the cause of the separation of the sun and moon, belongs to Jensen's "Hainuwele type" and must have been of southern origin (Obayashi, 1973). A similar version found in the *Kojiki* replaces Tsukiyomi with Susano-o as the murderer.

Shintō Cosmology. In the classical myths the universe was divided into various territories. The heavenly world was occupied by numerous *amatsukami*, or celestial deities, arranged in a pantheon. The two sovereigns, Amaterasu and Takamimusubi, governed the entire universe with the exception of the dragon king's marine world and Yomi, the underworld. The middle world, or earth, was inhabited by *kunitsukami*, or terrestrial deities, including the deities of mountains, valleys, rivers, fields, slopes, human beings, and animals. The terrestrial deities could take on both human and animal forms and were generally believed to be of lower rank than the celestial deities. Beneath the earth there existed the land of Yomi, or the world of the dead, where the Yomi deities, demons, ogresses, thunder gods, and so forth lived. The goddess Izanami, who ruled there as a queen, would send her messengers to earth to pull the souls of humans into her territory. At the entrance of Yomi there was a slope called Yomotsu-hirasaka. Since all manner of diseases and evils were believed to arise from this world, an annual grand purification ceremony was held in many districts throughout Japan. Unlike the Christian notion of hell, Yomi was not regarded as a place of punishment. All beings went to Yomi after death. Some poems of the *Man'yōshū* give evidence to a later belief that the members of the imperial family, as the children of the sun, ascend to the heavenly world after death.

After the introduction of Buddhism into Japan, Yomi, which had been simple and innocuous, was transformed into a terrible place of punishment for the souls of the sinful persons. Such hells are described in the *Nihon ryōiki*. Another territory of classical cosmology was the ocean bottom, known as Watatsumi, the land of marine deities. Here, the dragon-king, who had the power of controlling the tides and water, and his family governed over all marine creatures who lived in his dragon place. Beyond the sea there was Tokoyo-no-kuni, the land of eternal life, which was inhabited by deities and some human heroes. The humans were initially visitors to Tokoyo-no-kuni, but when they returned to earth they found that what had appeared to be a short visit was indeed aeons. In addition to these territories, there was the Land of Ne, located beyond the sea. It seems likely that this world was at one time thought to be the original homeland of the Japanese people but later became confused with Yomi.

Among the many hypotheses concerning the origin of this worldview, some maintain that the concept of a vertical construction of three territories—upper, middle and subterranean—was derived from North Asian shamanism (Torii, 1921). Others argue that the belief in Tokoyo, the land beyond the sea, was influenced by Chinese Taoism (Shimode, 1975). Still others insist that notions of a dragon palace were of South Asian origin (Matsumoto, 1968). There is, however, a general consensus that the divinities, such as the solar, lunar, thunder, and mountain deities, were derived from early forms of nature worship and that in the early stages of development there was no ancestor worship. Later, divinities were adopted as the ancestors of the particularly powerful clans. However, it was not until the beginning of the Heian period (794–1192) that human heroes and ancestors, such as Princess Inoe (717–775), the wife of Emperor Kōnin, and Sugawara Michizane (849–903), the minister of Emperor Uda, were deified and worshiped in Shintō shrines. The deification and enshrinement of human heroes and ancestors who were killed or exiled during periods of political intrigue served to console and pacify their vengeful spirits. This addition to Shintō theology is evident in the cases of the great governor Toyotomi Hideyoshi (1536–1598) and Tokugawa Ieyasu (1542–1616), the founder of the Tokugawa shogunate, both of whom were deified (of their own volition) after they died. The Toyokuni Shrine in Kyoto and the Toshogu Shrine in Nikko were established in their memory.

[*See also* Shintō; Izanagi and Izanami; Amaterasu Ōmikami; Ōkuninushi no Mikoto; Susano-o no Mikoto; Yamato Takeru; Jingō; Ame no Koyane; Kunitokodachi; *and* Jimmu.]

BIBLIOGRAPHY

Dixon, Roland B. *Oceanic Mythology* (1916). New York, 1964.

Higo Kazuo. *Kodai denshō kenkyū.* Tokyo, 1938.

Inoue Mitsusada. *Nihon kokka no kigen.* Tokyo, 1960.

Jensen, Adolf E. *Das religiöse Weltbild einer frühen Kultur.* Stuttgart, 1948.

Ledyard, Gari. "Galloping Along with the Horseriders: Looking for the Founders of Japan." *Journal of Japanese Studies* 1 (Spring 1975): 217–254.

Matsumae Takeshi. *Nihon shinwa no keisei.* Tokyo, 1970.

Matsumae Takeshi. "Origin and Growth of the Worship of Amaterasu." *Asian Folklore Studies* 37 (1978): 1–11.

Matsumae Takeshi. "The Myth of the Descent of the Heavenly Grandson." *Asian Folklore Studies* 42 (1983): 159–179.

Matsumoto Nobuhiro. *Tōa minzoku bunka ronkō.* Tokyo, 1968.

Matsumoto Nobuhiro. *Nihon shinwa no kenkyū.* Tokyo, 1971.

Matsumura Takeo. *Nihon shinwa no kenkyū,* vol. 4. Tokyo, 1958.

Ōbayashi Taryō. *Inasaku no shinwa.* Tokyo, 1973.

Oka Masao, Egami Namio, and Yawata Ichirō. *Nihon minzoku no kigen.* Tokyo, 1958.

Origuchi Shinobu. *Kodai kenkyū,* vol. 3, *Koku bungaku hen.* Tokyo, 1955.

Shimode Sekiyo. *Dōkyō to nihonjin.* Tokyo, 1975.

Skeat, Walter William. *Malay Magic.* New York, 1966.

Torii Ryūzo. *Jinruigaku yorimitaru waga jodai bunka.* Tokyo, 1921.

MATSUMAE TAKESHI

Religious Documents

[*This article treats the major literary, religious, and historical texts of early Japan, those instrumental in establishing the ideology of the Japanese state. For an overview of the literatures of the sectarian traditions, see especially* Buddhism, *article on* Buddhism in Japan.]

The oldest extant writings of the Japanese, apart from brief inscriptions, date from the eighth century CE. The major texts of this century include: *Kojiki* (Record of Ancient Matters; 712) and *Nihonshoki* (or *Nihongi;* Chronicle of Japan; 720), both of which are compilations of myth and history; *Izumo fudoki* (completed 733), a gazetteer of Izumo Province in western Honshu; *Kaifūsō* (751), an anthology of poetry in Chinese; and the epochal *Man'yōshū* (Collection of a Thousand Leaves; c. 759), an accumulation of more than forty-five hundred poems in the native, Japanese language. Except for *Kaifūsō,* which is only marginally important to an understanding of the age, these works as a group inform us of the nature of the ancient Japanese state, its society, and its beliefs as they emerged during a period of protracted cultural borrowing from China that began in the middle of the sixth century.

Japan in the Chinese Dynastic Histories. An important source of written knowledge about Japan that predates the eighth century is the accounts of Japan in the sections treating "barbarians" in the dynastic histories of China. The earliest references to Japan in these texts date from about the first century BCE, the time of the Former Han dynasty (206 BCE–8 CE); but the fullest account of Japan—known as the Land of Wa—in the early dynastic histories dates from the middle of the third century CE (during the Wei dynasty, 220–264, of North China).

The ancient state of Japan first took shape in the third century, and we can discern what are probably the origins of this state in the discussion in the *Wei chih* (History of the Wei Kingdom) of a territorial hegemony or "country" of Wa called Yamatai, which was then ruled by a queen named Himiko (or Pimiko). Himiko was a shaman. Remaining unmarried and served only by women, she lived in an isolated palace and devoted herself to magic and sorcery. She had no direct contact with the mass of her subjects, but instead allowed her younger brother to handle the actual rule of the country. [*See* Himiko.] The *Wei chih* provides information about customs of Yamatai that are strikingly similar to those of the Japanese of later times. For example, the people clapped their hands in worship, they showed respect toward others by squatting or kneeling with both hands on the ground, and they purified themselves in water after a funeral.

The Yamato State. Historians have been unable to make a precise connection between Yamatai, whose exact location and size cannot be determined, and the state that gradually evolved in Japan from the third through the sixth centuries with its seat in the central provinces or the region of the present-day cities of Nara and Kyoto. Interestingly, however, this state became known as Yamato, a name close in sound to *Yamatai.*

Yamato made the transition from prehistory to history in the late sixth century, when the *Nihonshoki,* the only native written source treating this time, becomes generally reliable as a factual record. Beginning about the mid-sixth century, Yamato embarked upon a course of centralization and expansion of its territory under the stimulus of cultural borrowing from China. By the early eighth century, the country—also called Nihon (land of the "sun's source")—had attained a high level of civilization, perhaps best symbolized by the construction of the capital city of Nara in 710.

The government of Yamato or Nihon (Japan) that had evolved by the Nara period (710–784) was structured on the model of China and was headed by an emperor or empress *(tennō)*, who was assisted by a corps of courtier ministers. An effort was made to adopt the Chinese principle of ministerial advancement on the basis of merit, but it was not successful. As before, the rulers of Japan (i.e., the imperial and courtier families) constituted an aristocracy whose members claimed their positions solely on the basis of birth and traced their genealogies back to deities or to mythical or semimythical emperors of the remote past.

Kojiki and Nihonshoki. History writing in traditional China was regarded as virtually a function of government, inasmuch as study of the past was thought to be essential to proper governance in the present. Under Chinese influence, the Japanese also began writing histories by at least the early seventh century. But no such writings have been preserved from that time, and the project of historical compilation that resulted in the issuance of the *Kojiki* in 712 and the *Nihonshoki* in 720 was begun by Emperor Temmu (r. 673–686) in the late seventh century. According to the preface of the *Kojiki*, Temmu lamented that the records of the "various houses" (presumably the imperial and courtier houses) had been altered and falsified, and ordered a man at court named Hieda no Are, who possessed a fabulous memory, to memorize an imperial genealogy and a collection of ancient narratives. We do not know why Temmu ordered the genealogy and the narrative collection to be memorized, although perhaps it was a reflection of the continuing importance of the oral transmission of literary and other writings at this early period of Japanese history. In any case, the genealogy *(teiki)* and collection of narratives *(kyūji)* appear to have been source materials, whether in oral or written form, that dated back possibly to the early sixth century. Although little else is known about Temmu's history project, the *teiki* and *kyūji* seem indeed to have served as the basis for the *Kojiki* and the *Nihonshoki*.

The *Kojiki* and the first part of the *Nihonshoki* both contain the mythology of Japan. It is a richly textured mythology, including tales from various parts of the country as well as from other civilizations, such as China and Korea, Polynesia, Southeast Asia, and perhaps even Greece and Rome. The central sequence of myths recounts the story of the installation of the sun goddess, Amaterasu Ōmikami, as the supreme ruler in heaven, the descent of her grandson, Ninigi, to earth (Japan), and the establishment of a ruling dynasty by Ninigi's grandson, Jimmu (the first emperor), in 660 BCE. [*See* Amaterasu Ōmikami *and* Jimmu.]

When Ninigi departed from heaven, Amaterasu bestowed upon him the three sacred objects—mirror, sword, and jewel (or necklace of jewels)—that became the regalia of emperorship, and decreed that his family should rule Japan eternally. Although archaeological and other evidence indicates that, in fact, the historical ruling dynasty of Japan probably dates from only the early sixth century CE, the record of an unbroken imperial line beginning with Jimmu as found in the *Kojiki* and the *Nihonshoki* became the basis for the great myth of *bansei ikkei*, "one dynasty to rule for a myriad generations [i.e., forever]." Whereas in China there were frequent dynastic changes, justified by the theory of the mandate of Heaven (i.e., that Heaven both mandated emperors to rule and withdrew their mandates when they or their families proved unworthy), in Japan it was established from early times that rulership had been given unequivocally and forever by Amaterasu to a single line of her descendants. (The present emperor of Japan is held, according to *bansei ikkei*, to be the 124th sovereign in direct descent from Jimmu.)

The writers of "history" at the early Yamato court thus shaped and adapted a body of myths to give primacy to the sacred and preeminent origins of the imperial family and to its exclusive right to reign over Japan. Although the court did not accept the mandate of Heaven notion, it was nevertheless strongly influenced by traditional Chinese political ideas and practices. For example, sometime in the late sixth or seventh centuries it adopted the title, taken from China, of *tennō* ("heavenly sovereign") to give an exalted—indeed transcendent—status to its office of national ruler.

While the genealogy of the imperial family is central to the mythology as presented in the *Kojiki* and *Nihonshoki*, the pasts of the leading courtier families are also woven conspicuously into it. A good example is the Nakatomi (later, Fujiwara) family, whose founder, according to the mythology, was Ame no Koyane, one of five deities *(kami)* deputized by Amaterasu to accompany Ninigi on his descent from heaven. [*See* Ame no Koyane.] The importance attached to genealogy in the mythology is a manifestation of the highly aristocratic character of the ruling class at court in the late seventh and eighth centuries in Japan. Since status depended almost entirely on birth, the ruling families, headed by the imperial family, had a powerful interest in making sure that the "histories" revealed their lines to be of as great antiquity and sacredness (through lineage from the gods or from the imperial family) as possible. During the Heian period (794–1185), when the Fujiwara rose to dominance at court as imperial regents, they referred to the *Kojiki* and *Nihonshoki* and claimed that their right to "accompany" and "assist" in rule was as ancient and unassailable as the imperial family's right to rule.

The *Kojiki*, whose editing was completed in 712 by the courtier Ō no Yasumaro (d. 723), is a book in three parts. Part one deals with the age of the gods from the time when the first deities appeared, as heaven and earth took shape, up to the birth of the future emperor Jimmu. Part two covers the period from Jimmu through Emperor Ōjin, the fifteenth sovereign in the traditional chronology; part three traces the imperial succession from Nintoku, Ōjin's son, through Empress Suiko, a historical figure who reigned from 592 to 628. But the narrative content of the *Kojiki* comes to an end about a century before Suiko (the late 400s), and the last century of its coverage gives only a listing of sovereigns with biographical data.

Although the final part of the narrative portion of the *Kojiki* (the section treating the fifth century) may be regarded as protohistory, the work as a whole is mythology. It is written mainly in Japanese with some Chinese interspersed. But the Japanese of the *Kojiki* is transcribed in an exceedingly complex manner, utilizing Chinese characters for their rebus—phonetic—value. So difficult is the *Kojiki* to read that little attention was paid to it for more than a thousand years, until the great scholar Motoori Norinaga (1730–1801) spent some thirty-five years in translating it into vernacular Japanese. [*See the biography of Motoori Norinaga.*]

Historians can only speculate why the *Nihonshoki*, which in its first part covers the same "history" as the *Kojiki*, was produced a scant eight years after the *Kojiki*, in 720. In any case, the *Nihonshoki* is a substantially different book from the *Kojiki*. For one thing, it is more than twice the *Kojiki*'s length, its later portions dealing in considerable detail with the events of the sixth and seventh centuries (the *Nihonshoki* ends with the abdication of Empress Jitō [645-720], in 697). Second, the *Nihonshoki* is written in Chinese, and for this reason has always been relatively easy for educated Japanese to read.

An interesting feature of the first part of the *Nihonshoki*, covering the age of the gods, is its inclusion of variant myths. While the *Kojiki* gives only one version of each of the stories that constitutes the sequence of myths in the age of the gods, the *Nihonshoki* often provides three, four, or more versions of a story, such as the birth of Amaterasu and her elevation to rulership over heaven or the descent of Ninigi to earth.

A later record states that the *Nihonshoki* was compiled chiefly by Prince Toneri (676–735), although it is thought that Fujiwara no Fubito (659–720), the leading statesman of his day at the Nara court, also played an important role in producing it. The work was clearly intended to be a more public, official "history" than the *Kojiki*. By composing it in Chinese, the written language *par excellence* of traditional East Asia, its authors no doubt wished it to be universally respected as literature. They also wanted the *Nihonshoki* to be like the Chinese dynastic histories, even though they chose to organize it chronologically rather than in the topical manner (imperial annals, records of the great families, essays, etc.) of the Chinese histories. In fact, the *Nihonshoki* became the first of six national histories *(rikkokushi)*, the last of which ends with the death of Emperor Kōkō (r. 884–887).

One of the most distinguishing features of the *Nihonshoki* is the great attention it devotes to international affairs. The sixth and seventh centuries were an especially dynamic age in East Asia. After more than three centuries of disorder, China was once again unified under the Sui (589–618) and T'ang (618–906) dynasties; Korea was united in the late seventh century under the kingdom of Silla; and the Yamato state of Japan achieved considerable centralization and a high civilization under both Chinese and Korean influence. The international order of East Asia at this time was centered, of course, upon China, which under the T'ang dynasty became the most far-reaching and powerful country in the world. Japan in the *Nihonshoki* was vitally interested in clarifying its status vis-à-vis the other lands of East Asia, and it is a remarkable fact that Japan became the only country in a region extending around much of China to reject the Chinese tributary system—a system whereby other countries acknowledged their subordination and sent periodic tribute-bearing missions to China, the "Middle Kingdom"—and asserted its national independence. Perhaps the most vivid proof of this assertion of independence is the account, recorded in the history of the Sui dynasty, of a message sent in 607 by the Japanese court to China that began: "From the sovereign of the land of the rising sun to the sovereign of the land of the setting sun. . . ." The emperor of China was not pleased with this salutation, and indeed it was rude. But it was also clearly an attempt by Japan to establish a relationship in which the ruler of one country directly, and on a basis of diplomatic equality, addressed the ruler of another.

If Japan sought internationally to establish equality with China (an equality that the mighty Middle Kingdom disdainfully ignored), internally the Japanese—for example, in the *Nihonshoki*—frequently spoke of their country as the "land of the gods" and thus implied that Japan was superior to other countries. It is fascinating to observe how, in this way, small and remote Japan, even in an age when it appeared to be importing the entirety of Chinese culture and civilization, asserted its own national uniqueness and superiority. Here is the complete *bansei ikkei* myth: the concept of Japan as a land created by and therefore "of" the gods, and as a land superior to all others both because of its sacred origins and because it was to be ruled always by a single family descended from the sun goddess. This myth remained an unchallenged orthodoxy in Japan until the end of World War II.

The *Nihonshoki* is a fairly impressive work of history for its time. Its authors especially deserve to be commended for the range of their sources. Although this range cannot be known precisely, it included not only the *teiki* and *kyūji* (upon which the *Kojiki* was almost entirely based) but also such foreign documents as the *Wei chih* of China and the chronicle of the Korean kingdom of Paekche *(Paekche ki)*.

Although I have discussed the *Kojiki* and *Nihonshoki* in terms of mythology and history, both are clearly also religious texts, and have at different times and in different ways served as the scriptures of Shintō. The first great flourishing in the study of the *Nihonshoki* occurred during the medieval age (the late twelfth through the late sixteenth centuries), when scholars devoted their attention almost exclusively to the examination of and research into the book's first section, the "age of the gods." This study of the *Nihonshoki* was part of a larger Shintō revival in medieval times that focused on three major concepts: (1) that Japan was a divine land protected by the gods of Shintō (in opposition to the belief, prevalent since at least the late seventh century, that the country was primarily under the heavenly guard of the deities of Buddhism); (2) that Japan was unique and superior among countries because it was ruled by a single dynasty, a concept that was fundamental, of course, to the *bansei ikkei* myth but that had been relatively ignored or deemphasized during the Heian period, when centralized Buddhism was in the ascendant; and (3) the syncretic concept that Buddhism, Confucianism, and Shintō complemented each other and were, indeed, the "root [Shintō] and the branches and blossoms [Buddhism and Confucianism] of the same tree."

The *Kojiki*, as noted, was scarcely comprehensible until translated by Motoori Norinaga in the eighteenth century. Norinaga's work on the *Kojiki*, the *Kojikiden*, was part of the National Learning (Kokugaku), or Neo-Shintō, movement that began in the late seventeenth century. This movement, which embraced philological, literary, and political as well as religious concerns, was essentially motivated by the desire to investigate the origins of the Japanese national tradition. Members of the movement were interested in the *Kojiki* because it was written in Japanese and was thus thought to be more reliable than the *Nihonshoki* as a source for the study of the beginnings of Japan and the Japanese people. [*See also* Kokugaku.]

In 807 the Imbe family of court ritualists produced a book that came to be called *Kogoshūi* (Gleanings from Ancient Stories) containing stories, not found in the *Kojiki* and *Nihonshoki*, that date as far back as the time of the founding of Japan by the gods Izanagi and Izanami. Most significant is the fact that many of the stories deal with the history of the Imbe. The main purpose of the Imbe in compiling the *Kogoshūi* nearly a century after the *Kojiki* and *Nihonshoki* was their desire to combat the ascendancy at that time of the rival Nakatomi family in Shintō affairs at court.

The Izumo fudoki. In 713 the newly established Nara court issued a decree to all the provinces of Japan, calling upon each to compile a report on its geography, natural resources, local traditions, and the like. The idea of requesting such reports was evidently taken from the practice of gazetteer-writing in China, and was intended primarily as a means for the Nara government to extend its control more fully over the provinces. Of these reports, called *fudoki*, only one has survived intact: the *Izumo fudoki*. Four others—the reports of Harima, Hizen, Bungo, and Hitachi provinces—have been preserved in fragments. The *Izumo fudoki* is written primarily in Chinese, with some passages composed in Japanese using Chinese characters as rebus symbols as in the *Kojiki*. It is mainly a collection of data, and possesses very little merit as literature.

Izumo is a region situated in western Honshu on the coast of the Japan Sea. Relatively isolated by mountains, it seems to have maintained its independence for a considerable period during the time when the Yamato state was evolving, from about 300 CE. The final conquest of Izumo was apparently one of the most important steps taken by the Yamato state in its march to national hegemony. Indeed, so significant was this conquest that it was written prominently into the mythology contained in the *Kojiki* and *Nihonshoki*. According to the mythology, Izumo, governed by the earthly deity Ōkuninushi (or Ōnamuchi) and representing the earth (Japan), opposed repeated attempts by heaven to force it to submit to heavenly rule. Finally, however, Ōkuninushi and Izumo were persuaded to give in (*kuniyuzuri*, "to cede the land"), thereby setting the stage for the dispatch of Ninigi to earth to found a ruling dynasty. [*See* Ōkuninushi no Mikoto.]

Completed and submitted to the Nara court in 733, the *Izumo fudoki* was compiled mainly under the direction of one Hiroshima, an official and high priest of

Izumo. The work comprises nine sections, each treating one of the nine districts into which Izumo was then divided. The sections are subdivided into passages on the various communities, post stations, Shintō shrines, mountains, rivers, and islands of the districts. Interspersed throughout are local tales and legends that collectively constitute the mythology of Izumo. When the Yamato rulers assumed control of the province they took only those legends that could be used to explain how Yamato conquered Izumo for inclusion in the *Kojiki* and *Nihonshoki*.

A distinctive aspect of the *Izumo fudoki* is the explanation of the etymologies of place-names. This may in part reflect the traditional Japanese preoccupation with such etymologies, but it is also the result of an order from the Nara court directing the compilers of the *fudoki* to assign auspicious Chinese characters for the writing of all place-names. Perhaps the court wished by this means to reduce local associations with the names.

The Man'yōshū. The *Kojiki* contains more than one hundred archaic songs, which constitute the oldest body of written poetry in Japan. But the Japanese poetic tradition truly began with the compilation of the *Man'yōshū* about 759. This is a large anthology of more than 4,500 poems, the vast majority of which (4,200) are in the *tanka,* "short poem," form. (The term *waka,* "Japanese poem," is often used interchangeably with *tanka.*) The *Man'yōshū* was edited chiefly by Ōtomo no Yakamochi (d. 785); although its earliest poems are attributed to an empress of the fourth century, it is a collection of verse mainly of the century from about the mid-600s to the mid-700s.

Like the *Kojiki* and passages from the *Izumo fudoki,* the *Man'yōshū* is written in Japanese primarily by the use of Chinese characters according to the rebus principle. In the case of the *Man'yōshū,* the writing system is called *man'yōgana,* or the *Man'yō* syllabary, and became a forerunner of *katakana* and *hiragana,* the two syllabaries that were developed by the tenth century and that enabled the Japanese for the first time to write their own language with some ease. Since the creation of *katakana* and *hiragana* Japanese has been transcribed principally by means of a mixture of Chinese characters (for their meanings) and syllabic symbols (for their sounds).

In 751 the *Kaifūsō,* an anthology of poems by Japanese in Chinese, was completed. From that time on, throughout the premodern period and even into modern times, the Japanese have continued periodically to write poetry in Chinese. Significantly for their own cultural history, however, the Japanese in the early age with which we are dealing retained a sharp distinction between foreign (Chinese) poetry and their own native (Yamato) verse. Until the *Man'yōshū,* this verse was preserved largely in oral form; even though the Japanese of the eighth century could devise no better writing system to transcribe Yamato poetry than the cumbrous *man'yōgana,* they were able to minimize its being "tainted" by the Chinese language. They maintained the vocabulary of Yamato poetry as a purely native language, eschewing the Chinese loanwords that were incorporated into Japanese in increasingly large numbers from at least the late sixth century on.

The greatest poet of the *Man'yōshū* was Kakinomoto no Hitomaro, who flourished in the late seventh century. A low-ranking courtier, Hitomaro was a true "court poet" in the sense that he was engaged by the court to compose poems on important public occasions, such as imperial hunts and other excursions, and the deaths of sovereigns. This function of poetic composition for public occasions was a distinctive feature of the age of the *Man'yōshū.* Later court poetry (that is, poetry written by members of the courtier class) became exclusively private verse, devoted especially to the subjects of nature and romantic love. Hitomaro was also a splendid composer of private poetry. Here are lines he wrote to express longing for his wife:

> Oh, does my wife
> See my sleeves
> As I wave them
> Amid the trees
> On Tatsuno Mountain in Iwami?
> (*Man'yōshū,* no. 132)

Like the *Kojiki,* the *Man'yōshū* was also greatly admired by the National Studies, or Neo-Shintō, scholars of the late seventeenth and eighteenth centuries. For the *Man'yōshū* too was believed to be imbued with the primitive spirit and sentiments of the Japanese when they were still relatively "unpolluted" by Chinese culture. In fact, many of the most prominent poets of the *Man'yōshū* were well steeped in the culture of China, including Confucianism, Taoism, and Buddhism. Nevertheless, compared to the overly refined court poetry from the ninth century on, *Man'yōshū* poems on the whole contain a youthful vigor, spontaneity, and breadth of emotion that sets the anthology apart from all later collections of verse.

Part of the fundamental "spirit" of the ancient Japanese that is supposed to be found in poetry of the *Man'yōshū* is the *kotodama* or "spirit of words." One manifestation of the *kotodama* were the *makura-kotoba* ("pillow words") of classical Japanese poetry, epithets that were evidently first employed for liturgical purposes. A good example of a pillow word is *hisakata no* (far-reaching), as used in such phrases as "far-reaching heaven," "the far-reaching clouds," or even "the far-reaching capital." Here again we see the great importance attached by the early Japanese to the native—Yamato—language, whose cadences were thought to possess both religious and magical qualities that belonged only to Japan and that needed to be zealously guarded against destruction by foreign influences. Another illustration of the use of the *kotodama* are the sacred verse and prose pieces known as *norito*. Some *norito* purportedly date from the seventh century, but most are to be found in *Engishiki* (Supplementary Regulations of the Engri Era), compiled in 927. In any case, all *norito* are based on seventh-century diction, and thus are thought to retain the primitive spirit of the Yamato language. [*See also* Norito *and* Poetry, *article on* Japanese Religious Poetry.]

The major writings of eighth-century Japan, the *Kojiki*, *Nihonshoki*, and *Man'yōshū*, constituted a great literary base for the subsequent development of Japanese civilization. One of the most interesting features of these writings taken collectively is the tension we find in them between native and foreign culture, between wholesale borrowing on the one hand and nativistic protectionism on the other. This is something we do not see in, for example, the visual arts, sculpture, and architecture, where continental (largely Buddhist) modes and tastes swept all before them. The rapid development of civilization in Japan in this ancient age was indeed a complex and dynamic process.

[*See also* Shintō. *For further discussion of the imperial mythology of Japan, see* Kingship, *article on* Kingship in East Asia.]

BIBLIOGRAPHY

Akashi Mariko et al., trans. "Hitachi Fudoki." *Traditions* 1 (1976): 23-47 and 2 (1977): 55-78.

Aston, W. G., trans. *Nihongi: Chronicles of Japan from the Earliest Times to A.D. 697* (1896). Tokyo, 1972.

Bock, Felicia, trans. *Engi-shiki: Procedures of the Engi Era*. Tokyo, 1972. A translation of books 6–10.

Brower, Robert H., and Earl Miner. *Japanese Court Poetry*. Stanford, 1961.

Chamberlain, Basil Hall, trans. *Kojiki: Records of Ancient Matters* (1882). 2d ed. Tokyo, 1932; reprint, Rutland, Vt., and Tokyo, 1982.

Kato Genchi and Hoshino Hikoshiro, trans. *The Kogoshūi: Gleanings from Ancient Stories*. Tokyo, 1926.

Kato Shuichi. *A History of Japanese Literature: The First Thousand Years*. Translated by David Chibett. Tokyo, 1981.

Konishi Jin'ichi. *A History of Japanese Literature*, vol. 1, *The Archaic and Ancient Ages*. Translated by Aileen Batten and edited by Earl Miner. Princeton, 1984.

Levy, Ian Hideo, trans. *Hitomaro and the Birth of Japanese Lyricism*. Princeton, 1984.

Miller, Richard J. *Ancient Japanese Nobility*. Berkeley, 1974.

Philippi, Donald L., trans. *Norito*. Tokyo, 1959.

Philippi, Donald L., trans. *Kojiki*. Princeton and Tokyo, 1969.

Sansom, George B. *A History of Japan to 1334*. Stanford, 1958.

Tsunoda, Ryusaku, et al., comps. *Sources of the Japanese Tradition*. 2 vols. New York, 1958.

Varley, H. Paul. *Japanese Culture*. 3d ed. Honolulu, 1984.

H. Paul Varley

JASPERS, KARL (1883–1969), one of the most influential German thinkers of the twentieth century and one of the founders of modern existential philosophy. Born in Oldenburg, Jaspers studied law and medicine. After writing several works on psychopathology, he turned to philosophy, and in 1920 he became a professor at Heidelberg. He was dismissed from that position by Nazi authorities in 1937; after 1948 he taught at Basel, where he died.

For Jaspers, philosophizing is an effort to understand and to express the authentic experience of realities that can never be conceptually explained and are not objectifiable; therefore it cannot pretend to be knowledge in the same sense as scientific knowledge. Jaspers accepts the Augustinian maxim "Deum et animam scire cupio" (I want to know God and the soul), but neither God nor the soul are possible positive objects of metaphysical speculation. Their place is taken respectively by "the all-encompassing" (*das Allumgreifende*), or transcendence, and existence. The latter, even though it reveals itself in one's empirical being (*Dasein*), is not a psychological subject, not an empirically accessible reality, and the former is not God in the sense of any mythological tradition. Still, both realities are known not only negatively, not only as a realm of the unknown beyond knowledge, but they are inseparably linked with each other: the transcendence is there only for existence; it opens itself to me insofar as I am able radically to experience my freedom. The presence of the transcendence cannot be described in metaphysical or scientific language; in other words, we do not hear God's voice in the empirical word. It speaks to us through ciphers we can meet in all forms of being: in nature, in history, in art, in mythology. Yet ciphers are untranslatable. Therefore, in vain do we try to grasp God in metaphysical doctrines or in the dogmas of an institutionalized religion. The language of mythology, too, is a way that mankind has tried to commune with the transcendence, but this language is *sui generis*, it cannot be converted into a philosophical system. Therefore, Jaspers totally opposed Bultmann's project of "demythologization," which, he argued, implied that myths are theories in disguise, that they could be translated into a profane tongue so that a theologian could salvage elements that are acceptable to scientifically trained "modern man" and discard the "superstitious" rest.

Myths, according to Jaspers, are the means by which people gain access to ultimate reality, and although they have no empirical reference, they are an indispensable part of culture. All attempts of positive theology to reach God in metaphysical categories are useless; so are efforts to express the transcendence in the dogmatic formulas of one or another confession. But a personal existence, in an effort of self-illumination, is able to meet the transcendence as a pendant of its own reality. Existence is not a substance within the empirical word and it cannot survive death; it nevertheless reaches eternity as moments of timelessness within empirical time. Therefore, existence cannot avoid the ultimate defeat; our death cannot be given a meaning. Still, the radical awareness of one's own finitude is not necessarily a reason for discouragement: in the very acceptance of inevitable defeat we find the way to being. While existence and the transcendence become real only in an encounter which is expressible in ciphers, and not in any scientific or theological knowledge, this encounter does not make our communication with other people or our living participation in historical processes unimportant. We can never isolate ourselves entirely from empirical realities, from history, and from our fellow human beings; quite the contrary, it is only from within, not by a kind of mystical detachment, that we can understand our relationships with infinity; and yet, this understanding can never take the form of "objective" knowledge.

Jaspers tried, in his historical studies, positively to assimilate the entire history of European philosophy which, from various angles, supported his intuition. Both those who stressed the radical irreducibility of personal existence to "objective" reality (Augustine, Kierkegaard, Nietzsche) and those who attempted, however awkwardly, to grasp unconditional being conceptually (Plotinus, Nicholas of Cusa, Bruno, Spinoza, Schelling, Hegel) represented in his view the human effort to cope with the eternal tension between our life among things and our desire to reach the ultimate.

In interpreting religious phenomena Jaspers rejected all positivist or scientific attempts to reduce them to needs that might have an anthropological, social, or psychological explanation. On the other hand, he refused to believe that a rational theological or metaphysical enquiry might elucidate them. Both institutionalized Christianity and the tradition of the Enlightenment were unable, in his view, to express properly the relationship between existence and transcendence.

BIBLIOGRAPHY

Works by Jaspers

Allgemeine Psychopathologie. Berlin, 1913. Translated by J. Hoenig and Marian W. Hamilton as *General Psychopathology* (Chicago, 1963).

Die geistige Situation der Zeit. Berlin, 1931. Translated by Eden Paul and Cedar Paul as *Man in the Modern Age* (London, 1933).

Philosophie. 3 vols. Berlin, 1932. Translated by E. B. Ashton as *Philosophy* (Chicago, 1969).

Vernunft und Existenz. Groningen, 1935. Translated by William Earle as *Reason and Existenz* (New York, 1955).

Der philosophische Glaube. Zurich, 1948. Translated by Ralph Manheim as *The Perennial Scope of Philosophy* (New York, 1949).

Vom Ursprung und Ziel der Geschichte. Zurich, 1949. Translated by Michael Bullock as *The Origin and Goal of History* (New Haven, 1953).

Die Frage der Entmythologisierung. Written with Rudolf Bultmann. Munich, 1954. Translated as *Myth and Christianity* (New York, 1958).

Works about Jaspers

Bollnow, O. F. *Existenzphilosophie und Pädagogik*. Stuttgart, 1959.

Piper, Klaus, ed. *Offener Horizont: Festschrift für Karl Jaspers*. Munich, 1953.

Saner, Hans. *Karl Jaspers in Selbstzeugnissen und Bilddokumenten*. Reinbek bei Hamburg, 1970.

Saner, Hans, ed. *Karl Jaspers in der Diskussion*. Munich, 1973.

Schilpp, Paul A., ed. *The Philosophy of Karl Jaspers*. New York, 1957.

LESZEK KOLAKOWSKI

JASTROW, MORRIS (1861–1921), American Semitist, Assyriologist, and historian of religions. Born in Warsaw, Morris Jastrow moved to the United States in 1866 with his father Marcus Jastrow, the eminent rabbinic scholar. Philadelphia was his home and, apart from student years and later vacations, he spent his life there as a librarian and professor at the University of Pennsylvania.

Although active in Hebrew studies and as a writer of commentaries on several books of the Old Testament Jastrow devoted himself to the synthesizing of the new knowledge about Mesopotamia, its civilization and in particular its religion. His works catalogued and classified the deities of the various pantheons, described temples and cults, provided translations and discussions of religious texts, and increasingly emphasized the role of divination, especially hepatoscopy.

The general study of religion as an academic subject was also close to Jastrow's heart. He favored an approach that he called "historical" (but that seems now to be rather philosophical in character), which was nourished by his wide reading in the Western and Near Eastern cultural heritage. His approach was historical in the sense that it avoided the "intolerant" assumption that one religion was exclusively right, and insisted instead on a full description of any religion in detail as a prerequisite of its evaluation. However, it also rejected the "cynical" view that all religion was bogus. Himself religious, Jastrow believed that religion was based in something essential to the nature of man, that is, the power to seek for perception of the infinite. This was a wide humanistic approach. It was no accident that his biblical commentaries were on books that could be seen in this light: *Ecclesiastes, Job,* and *Song of Songs.*

Jastrow shared many of the attitudes toward religion that were widespread in his time, but the way he presented them was moderate and conciliatory. He believed that there had been an evolution in religion and that increasing cultural experience had led to "higher" forms; yet he also held that there is a unity between primitive and advanced forms of faith. The supreme achievement of Judaism, he thought, is not monotheism per se but spiritual and ethical monotheism. Evolutionist principles, however, were applied only gently by Jastrow. Similarly, he accepted the general trends of contemporary biblical criticism but softened its impact into something vaguer: ancient texts came into being, he thought, by a process of accretion, with one layer of a text being overlaid by another that expressed a different set of ideas. Criticism, properly understood, presented no threat to true religion. The note of contrast and conflict is muted in Jastrow's religious world. He was able to accept the many evident similarities between Mesopotamian and Hebrew religion while remaining confident of the eventual great distinctiveness of the Hebrew development.

The weakness of his work may be that too many of the connections and interpretations he offered, however reasonable, rested on his own reasoning rather than on actual textual evidence. Thus, for example, it may be reasonable to suppose, as Jastrow did, that hepatoscopy was based upon the idea that the liver of the sacrificial animal was itself an exact reflection of the mind of a god, but the question remains whether the texts actually say this.

Through his writings and his organizational work, Jastrow played an important part in the establishment of the study of religion as an academic subject in the United States.

BIBLIOGRAPHY

Jastrow's basic ideas about the study of religion are found in his early work *The Study of Religion* (London, 1901). His earlier *Religion of Babylonia and Assyria* (Boston, 1898) was greatly expanded, especially in respect of divination and hepatoscopy, in its German edition, *Die Religion Babyloniens und Assyriens,* 2 vols. in 3 (Giessen, 1905–1912). His Haskell Lectures, *Hebrew and Babylonian Traditions* (New York, 1914), deal with the problem area that most obviously arises from his approach. Jastrow's biblical commentaries include *A Gentle Cynic* (on *Ecclesiastes*), *The Book of Job,* and *The Song of Songs* (Philadelphia, 1919, 1920, 1921). See also the memoir by James A. Montgomery in the *American Journal of Semitic Languages and Literatures* 38 (1921): 1–11; as well as those by Julian Morgenstern, George A. Barton, and Albert T. Clay in the *Journal of the American Oriental Society* 41 (1921): 322–336 and 337–344.

JAMES BARR

JĀTI. *See* Varṇa and Jāti.

JAVANESE RELIGION. The Javanese occupy the central and eastern parts of Java, a moderately sized island over twelve hundred kilometers long and five hundred kilometers wide. The island constitutes only about 7 percent of the total land area of the Indonesian archipelago, which now constitutes the Republic of Indonesia. Javanese peasants have migrated to other islands in Indonesia and, because Dutch colonialists had for two centuries prior to Indonesia's independence moved Javanese unskilled laborers overseas, there are also Javanese communities in Cape Town, South Africa; in Surinam, Latin America; and in New Caledonia, Melanesia. They have in general retained the original Javanese culture and language.

Nearly all Javanese (i.e., about 97.3 percent) are Muslim, with the remainder either Roman Catholics, Protestants, Buddhists, or, in South Central Java, recent converts to Hinduism. The Javanese themselves recognize two variants of Javanese Islam: the one with the greatest number of adherents is syncretistic, incorporating Muslim, Hindu, Buddhist, and local religious elements; the other is more dogmatic and puritan. The first is called Agami Jawi ("Javanese religion") and the other, Agami Islam Santri ("Santri Islam religion"). Adherents of both variants are to be found in all Javanese communities, although in certain regions, one of the forms will predominate. In his study of Javanese religion, Clifford Geertz calls the first variant Abangan, and the second, Islam Santri.

Javanese Religious History. Early Javanese religion must have been based on local forms of ancestor worship, and the belief in spirits, magical power in natural phenomena, and sacred objects in the human environment. Hinduism probably came to Java during the fourth century of the common era through the trade routes from South India, although the earliest traces of a Hindu-Javanese civilization can only be dated to the eighth century. During that period Javanese Buddhism also developed, and the remnants of ancient religious structures such as the Hindu Prambanan and the

Buddhist Borobudur seem to indicate that Javanese Hinduism and Javanese Buddhism coexisted peacefully.

Although, initially, Hinduism and Buddhism had been spread along the trade routes, they were further disseminated by Indian brahmans and *bhikṣus*, who had quite likely been invited by Javanese rulers to act as consultants. Indian civilization was promoted and developed in the court centers of the ancient empires, first in Central Java during the eighth to tenth centuries, and later, during the eleventh to fifteenth centuries, in East Java, where it took on a specific Javanese character. Many elements of this Hindu-Javanese court civilization subsequently influenced Javanese folk culture.

Islam also came to Java through the trade routes, via North Sumatra and the Malay Peninsula between the fourteenth and seventeenth centuries. Islam in Java exhibits an emphasis on mystical ideas. Indeed, Islamic mysticism seems to have found fertile ground in Java because of the existing mystical elements in Javanese Hinduism: Muslim literary works written during the early period of Javanese islamization show the importance of mystical Islam, or Sufism (Arab., *taṣawwuf*). Dogmatic, puritan Islam, reformed Islam, and so forth arrived later, when Javanese devotees returned from making the pilgrimage *(ḥajj)* to Mecca.

As a new religion, Islam initially influenced the port towns and harbor states of Java's north coast, which subsequently became prosperous and powerful and undermined the declining power of the Majapahit empire of East Java. In the following period zealous Muslim missionaries who became holy men, called *wali* (Arab., *walī;* "saint, guardian") in Javanese folklore, spread Islam through the interior regions of East and Central Java. The Muslim religion, preached by the imam, included many mystical elements, a fact that probably facilitated the contact between the missionaries and the population, to whom mystical concepts and ideas had long been familiar. During the sixteenth and seventeenth centuries, students and disciples recorded notes of these teachings, which, presented as magical songs, have been compiled in books called *suluk.*

The court center of the Central Javanese empire, Mataram, traditionally resisted the penetration of Islam from the interior of Java. During the second half of the eighteenth century, however, Islam reached the heartland of the ancient Central Javanese civilization, although not always through peaceful means. The centers of the Hindu-Buddhistic civilization in Central Java merely had to accept the presence of Islam, and thus developed the syncretistic Agami Jawi variant of Javanese Islam.

Agami Jawi. The Agami Jawi belief system includes an extensive range of concepts, views, and values, many of which are Muslim in origin: the belief in God Almighty *(Gusti Allah),* the belief in the prophet Muḥammad *(kanjeng nabi Muhammad),* and the belief in other prophets *(para ambiya).* The Javanese consider God Almighty to be the creator and ultimate cause of life and the entire universe. They believe that there is but one God ("gusti Allah ingkang maha esa"). All human actions as well as important decisions are done "in the name of God" *(bismillah),* a formula pronounced many times a day to inaugurate any small or large endeavor.

Divine beings. The Javanese literary tradition has elaborated extensively on the nature of God and man. The most important source for this subject is the seventeenth-century work, the *Dewaruci,* written in Javanese prose. In the mystical, pantheistic view of the *Dewaruci,* God is conceptualized as the totality of nature: he is a tiny divine being, so small that he can enter any human heart, yet in reality as wide as the oceans, as endless as space, and manifested in the colors that make and symbolize everything that exists on earth. Between the sixteenth and eighteenth centuries this religious concept of God was interwoven with Islamic concepts by the spiritual leaders and intellectuals who wrote the Agami Jawi literature, which includes voluminous books such as the *Serat centhini* and the magico-mystical *suluk* mentioned earlier.

In addition to the belief in God and the prophets, the Agami Jawi Javanese also believe in saints. Included among these holy persons are the nine semihistorical "apostles" *(wali sanga),* or first missionaries of Islam, religious teachers, and certain semihistorical figures who were known to the people through the Babad literature. The belief in these saints is usually kept alive by the veneration of their sacred graves *(pepundhen).* Local saints are also venerated, and many regions have their locally acknowledged sacred places. In certain village communities, one social class often associates itself with a particular legendary figure in order to obtain an exclusive status. Famous village leaders, *wayang* puppeteers *(dhalang),* healers *(dhukun),* or religious leaders *(kiyai)* may become holy men even while they are still alive, and their graves may turn into *pepundhen* and objects of veneration.

Many other elements, such as the belief in a great number of deities *(dewata),* are of Hindu-Buddhist origin, as one can see from their Sanskritic names. However, the roles and functions of several of the deities are different from those of the original ones. Dewi Sri, for instance, who originated from Śrī, the wife of the Hindu god Viṣṇu, is in Javanese culture the goddess of fertility and rice. Bathara Kala was derived from the Hindu concept of time *(kāla),* and this destructive aspect of Śiva the creator is in Javanese culture the god of death and calamity.

An indigenous pre-Hindu element is the divine trickster Semar. The Javanese believe that Semar has the power to act as an intermediary between the world of mortals and the divine. In the dramatic *wayang*, the Javanese shadow-puppet play, he is a clown figure who acts as both the servant and guardian of the heroes of the *Bratayuda*, the Javanese version of the Hindu *Mahābhārata* epic.

Indigenous Javanese beliefs are primarily concerned with spirits, in particular, ancestral spirits *(ruh leluhur)*, guardian spirits who care for the individual's well-being and are usually conceived of as the soul's twin *(sing ngemong)*, and guardian spirits who oversee places such as public buildings, old wells, spots in a forest, turns in a river, old banyan trees, caves, and so forth. They also believe in a number of ghosts *(lelembut)*, spooks *(setan)*, and giants *(denawa)*, who are frightening and malevolent creatures *(memedi)*, and in fairies *(widadari)* and dwarfs *(thuyul)*, who are considered benevolent.

The Agami Jawi has a cosmogony *(kang dumadi)*, a cosmology *(bawanagung)*, an eschatology *(akhiring jaman)*, and messianic beliefs *(ratu adil)*. While these are principally of Hindu origin, the Agami Jawi concepts of death and afterlife *(akherat)* have been influenced by Islam. Originating in pre-Hindu religious systems is their concept of magic, which imparts magical powers to certain people, parts of the human body, objects, certain plants, and rare animals.

Cultic life. The Agami Jawi ceremonial and ritual system differs essentially from the dogmatic teachings of Islam. The second pillar *(rukn)* of Islam, the *ṣalāt*, or ritual prayer performed five times daily, is considered unimportant and is often ignored. Instead, various kinds of sacred communal meals *(slametan)* are central to its ceremonial system. The family hosting the ceremony usually invites friends, neighbors, and important members of the community. A sacred meal consisting of particular, customary dishes is served after being blessed by a religious official from the mosque who recites of verses *(āyāt)* from the Qur'ān. A *slametan* ceremony often includes the *dhikr*, a monotonous chant of the phrase "La ilāha illā Allāh" ("There is no god but God"). This is repeated in chorus by all of the participants and may last for more than an hour without interruption.

The size, elaborateness, and cost of a *slametan* ceremony depend on the importance of the occasion and the financial resources of the host. The occasion may vary from celebrations of events associated with the individual's life cycle, of which circumcision and weddings may be considered the most important, to mortuary rites held on the day of the funeral and on the seventh, the fortieth, one-hundredth, and one-thousandth day after death. The *slametan* meals held as part of the funerary rites include elaborate *dhikr* chants. [*See also* Rites of Passage, *article on* Muslim Rites.]

Among the rural peasants, periodic *slametan* are held in connection with the stages of the agricultural cycle, whereas both rural and urban Javanese hold *slametan* meals on religious holidays of the Javanese Muslim calendar. Seasonal, community-sponsored *slametan* ceremonies, the *bersih dhusun*, are meant to purify the community. Intermittant *slametan* ceremonies are held in connection with disturbing events in the individual's life, such as a serious illness, accident, or bad dreams. More secular *slametan* are held to celebrate the move to a new house, the changing of one's name, the start of a long journey, an occupational promotion, or academic graduation, and the anniversaries of clubs and fraternal organizations, professional, functional, and recreational associations.

An equally important practice of the Agami Jawi is the veneration of the dead and ancestors, through visits to the graves of deceased relatives and ancestors *(nyekar)*. Also indispensable to Agami Jawi observance are the numerous offerings *(sajen)* that appear in nearly all the ceremonies and may be performed independently as well. The latter type of offering, held at specific times, such as Thursday evenings, consists of bits of food (including tiny rice cones and an assortment of cookies), spices, and a variety of small items that are decoratively arranged on small trays of plaited bamboo. A careful analysis of the items reveals some consistency in their symbolic meanings, which relate to their names, appearance, colors, or use.

Fasting is not only practiced during the Muslim month of the fast, Ramaḍān, but on many other occasions as well. Other religious practices include deliberately seeking hardship *(tirakat)*, asceticism *(tapabrata)*, and meditation *(samadi)*. The attainment of a state of trance is an integral aspect of a number of religious and semireligious folk dances, songs, and plays. Performances of certain *wayang* puppet dramas and religious concerts on sacred *gamelan* sets also accompany religious concepts and activities. [*See* Drama, *article on* Javanese Wayang.]

Agami Islam Santri. The Agami Islam Santri belief system of both rural and urban Javanese is composed of puritanical Islamic concepts about God, the prophet Muḥammad, creation, personal ethics, death and afterlife, eschatology, the day of resurrection, and so forth. These concepts are all clearly determined by dogmatic creed. Peasant Santri Javanese generally take these for granted and are indifferent about their interpretation. The urban Santri, however, are usually quite concerned about the moral and ethical backgrounds of the doctrine. In addition to having memorized certain parts of the Qur'ān, many have also been exposed to the exegetical literature *(tafsīr)*, and prophetic tradition *(ḥadīth)* during their education in more advanced religious schools *(pesantren)*. The Muslim belief system is organized and systematized in the *sharīʿah* (Islamic law); the dominant legal school *(madhhab)* in Java, and throughout Indonesia, is that of al-Shafiʿi (d. 820).

The Santri Javanese practice a ceremonial and ritual system that follows the dogmatic rules of the Five Pillars *(arkān*, pl. of *rukn)* of Islam. The second pillar, the daily and Friday *ṣalāt* (Jav., *sembahyang*), is the central ceremony. *Ṣalāt*, often incorrectly translated as "prayer," is a series of religious acts of worship and prostration, accompanied by incantations that are fixed in form and content. The obligatory performance of the *sembahyang* is done individually five times a day and communally once a week, at noon on Friday. The Javanese also have voluntary personal prayers to God called *ndonga*, which may be performed at any time, using the Javanese vernacular rather than the prescribed Arabic. The third pillar is the gift to the poor, called *jakat* (Arab., *zakat*); the fourth is the fast (Jav., *siyam;* Arab., *ṡawm*); and the fifth, of great import to Javanese Santri Muslims, is the *ḥajj*, or pilgrimage.

Most of the Islamic calendrical ceremonial celebrations are observed by the Santri Javanese. Unlike the adherents of the Agami Jawi religion, the Santri do not prepare *slametan* meals on those holidays. They do, however, perform special *ṣalāt* rituals, recite verses from the Qur'ān throughout most of the night, listen to stories about the life of the Prophet, and attend *slawatan* performances consisting of religious songs accompanied by drums and tambourines.

Santri Javanese also perform rites to celebrate certain events in the life cycle of the individual. However, unlike the Agami Jawi Javanese, who hold numerous *slametan* ceremonies, they prefer to give *sedhekah* sacrifices in accordance with the *sharīʿah*. Their funerary ceremonies do not differ significantly from those of the Agami Jawi. The *ṣalātu 'jjināzah*, absent in the Agami Jawi, is a mortuary *ṣalāt* that is preceded by the act of cleansing oneself, and is performed in front of the body of the deceased person by those who come to show sympathy.

Javanese Spiritual and Religious Movements. There have always been adherents of Agami Jawi for whom recurrent *slametan* rituals, *sajen* offerings at fixed periods, and routine visits to graves represent a superficial, meaningless, and unsatisfactory religious life. Therefore, they search for a deeper understanding of the essence of life and spiritual existence. One response to the demand for a more spiritually meaningful life are the numerous *kebatinan kejawen* spiritual movements, which have emerged and disappeared, but have retained a constant following in the course of Javanese history. The term *kebatinan* refers to the search for truth, *batin* (Arab., *bāṭin*). Since the late 1960s, the number of these movements has increased significantly.

Most of the Javanese *kebatinan* movements have a local base with only a limited number of followers (usually not more than two hundred), and are officially called "small movements" (Indonesian, *aliran kecil*). Others, however, have thousands of followers, and are called "large movements" (Indonesian, *aliran besar*). The four largest are Susila Sudi Darma (SUBUD), Paguyuban Ngesti Tunggal (PANGESTU), Paguyuban Sumarah, and Sapta Darma. Although *kebatinan* movements are to be found throughout the Javanese area, the most important ones are located in Surakarta. In 1983 there were nineteen such organizations in that city, with a total of approximately 7,500 members. At the end of 1982, the entire province of Central Java listed ninety-three movements, with a total of over 123,570 members. While most of the movements are based on mystical ideas, at least five other types can be distinguished: movements that focus on mysticism; moralistic and ethical movements that focus on the purification of the soul; messianic Ratu Adil ("just king") movements; nativistic movements, focusing on the return to original Javanese culture; and movements focusing on magical practices and occultism.

There are also movements with Santri orientation. These are usually based on a particular Islamic religious school *(pesantren)*. Unification with God is the central objective of most of those Santri movements. In Indonesia, and particularly in Java, as in the rest of the Islamic world, Ṣūfīs are organized into movements called *tarekat* (Arab., *ṭarīqāt*). The *tarekat* are led by a charismatic teacher called *kiyai* in Javanese. Many Santri Javanese belong not only to these local *tarekat* movements, but also to various international Ṣūfī orders, such as the Qādirīyah, Wāḥidīyah, Naqshbandīyah, Shaṭṭārīyah, and Ṣiddiqīyah. In addition to spiritual movements with a mystical orientation, Javanese Santri have also initiated puritan religious reform movements. In the early twentieth century K. H. Achmad Dehlan (b. 1868) from Yogyakarta, brought Muslim reformist ideas to Java. Influenced by the Islamic modernist Muḥammad ʿAbduh of al-Azhar University in Cairo, Dahlan founded the Muhammadiyah in 1912 in his home city. Preaching the return of Islam to its two basic sources, the Qur'ān and the *ḥadīth*, Dahlan not only attacked the syncretistic Agami Jawi Islam, but also Islam Santri scholasticism and mysticism. The Muhammadiyah developed into a nationwide movement, which applied itself not only to religious reform and modernization but also to education and social welfare.

[*See also* Southeast Asian Religions, *articles on* Insular Cultures *and* Modern Movements in Insular Cultures, *and* Islam, *article on* Islam in Southeast Asia.]

BIBLIOGRAPHY

Alfian. *Islamic Modernization in Indonesian Politics: The Muhammadijah Movement during the Dutch Colonial Period, 1912–1942.* Madison, Wisc., 1969. An excellent description of the history of the Javanese Muhammadiyah modern reform movement, initiated by K. H. Achmad Dahlan in 1912.

Dhofier, Zamaksyari. *The Pesantren Tradition: A Study of the Role of the Kyai in the Maintenance of the Traditional Ideology of Islam in Java.* Canberra, 1980. A good description of a Javanese Muslim religious school community.

Geertz, Clifford. *The Religion of Java.* Glencoe, Ill., 1960. A description of the two variants of Javanese Islam. The author has ignored the written indigenous religious literature; nevertheless, this book has dominated the literature on Javanese culture and society for more than twenty years.

Hien, Hendrik A. van. *De Javaansche Geestenwereld en de Betrekking, die Tusschen de Geesten en de Zinnelijke Wereld Bestaat: Verduidelijkt door Petangan's of Tellingen bij de Javenen in Gebruik.* 4 vols. Semarang, 1896. An extensive description of the Javanese supernatural world, including lists of over one hundred names with brief annotations of Javanese deities, spirits, and ghosts.

Poensen, Carl. "Bijdragen tot de Kennis van den Godsdienstigen en Zedelijken Toestand des Javaans." *Mededeelingen Vanwege het Nederlandsche Zendeling Genootschap* 7 (1863): 333–359 and 10 (1866): 23–80. An early description of two variants of Javanese Islam.

Soebardi. "Santri Religious Elements as Reflected in the Book of Tjĕntini." *Bijdragen tot de Taal-, Land- en Volkenkunde* 127 (1971): 331–349. A historical description of the absorption process of Muslim religious elements in the Hindu-Buddhist-Javanese syncretistic religion of the sixteenth and seventeenth centuries.

Zoetmulder, P. J. *Pantheïsme en monisme in de Javaansche soeloek-litteratuur.* Nijmegen, Netherlands, 1935. An analysis of the ancient Javanese mystical religious literature of the seventeenth and eighteenth centuries.

R. M. KOENTJARANINGRAT

JAYADEVA (late twelfth century?), Indian poet-saint who composed the dramatic lyrical poem *Gītagovinda.* Dedicated to the god Kṛṣṇa, the poem concentrates on Kṛṣṇa's love with the cowherdess Rādhā during a rite of spring. To express the complexities of divine and human love, Jayadeva uses the metaphor of intense earthly passion. The religious eroticism of the *Gītagovinda* earned sainthood for the poet and a wide audience for his poem.

There are conflicting traditions about Jayadeva's place of birth and region of poetic activity. Modern scholars of Bengal, Orissa, and Bihar have claimed him for their regions, but the most convincing evidence associates him with the Jagannātha cult of Puri in the latter half of the twelfth century. Although the poem originated in eastern India and remains most popular there, it spread throughout the Indian subcontinent in the centuries following its composition. As early as the thirteenth century it was quoted in a temple inscription in Gujarat (western India). Established commentatorial traditions and manuscripts exist in every part of India. The songs of the *Gītagovinda* are an important part of Vaiṣṇava devotional music and are still sung in temples from Orissa to Kerala. Its text represents one of the major subjects of Rajput painting.

Jayadeva is a name that the poet shares with Kṛṣṇa, the divine hero of his poem, whom he invokes in a song with the refrain "Jaya jayadeva hare" ("Triumph, God of Triumph, Hare!"). All versions of the legend of Jayadeva's life agree that he was born in a brahman family and became an accomplished student of Sanskrit and a skilled poet. However, he abandoned scholarship at a young age and adopted an ascetic life, devoting himself to God. As a wandering mendicant, he would not rest under any one tree for more than a night for fear that attachment to the place would violate his vow. His ascetic life ended when a brahman of Puri insisted that Jagannātha, Lord of the World, himself had ordained the marriage of Jayadeva with the brahman's daughter Padmāvatī, who was dedicated as a dancing girl in the temple. Padmāvatī served her husband, who in turn shared her devotion to Jagannātha. As Jayadeva composed, Padmāvatī danced—and so the *Gītagovinda* was composed. In the process of composing the poem, Jayadeva conceived the climax of Kṛṣṇa's supplication to Rādhā as a command for her to place her foot on Kṛṣṇa's head in a symbolic gesture of victory. But in deference to Kṛṣṇa the poet hesitated to complete the couplet. He went to bathe, and in his absence Kṛṣṇa himself appeared, disguised as Jayadeva, and wrote down the couplet; the god then ate the food Padmāvatī had prepared for Jayadeva and left. When the poet returned, he realized that he had received divine grace by exalting Kṛṣṇa's love for Rādhā.

The poem's emotional drama unfolds in twelve movements of Sanskrit songs (*padāvalīs*) composed in recitative verses. The songs are meant to be sung with specific melodic patterns (*rāgas*) and rhythmic cycles (*tālas*). They are sung by Kṛṣṇa, Rādhā, and Rādhā's friend, who acts as an intermediary between the lovers.

Critical acclaim of the poem within the Indian literary and religious culture has been high, but its frank eroticism has led many Indian commentators to interpret the love between Rādhā and Kṛṣṇa as an allegory of the human soul's love for God. Through the centuries learned and popular audiences alike have appreciated the emotional lyricism expressed by the *Gītagovinda* in its variations on the theme of the passion felt by separated lovers.

BIBLIOGRAPHY

Miller, Barbara Stoler, ed. and trans. *Love Song of the Dark Lord: Jayadeva's Gītagovinda.* New York, 1977.

Sandahl-Forgue, Stella. *Le Gītagovinda: Tradition et innovation dans le kāvya.* Stockholm, 1977.

Siegel, Lee. *Sacred and Profane Dimensions of Love in Indian Traditions, as Exemplified in the Gītagovinda of Jayadeva.* London, 1978.

BARBARA STOLER MILLER

JEHOVAH'S WITNESSES. Along with the Mormons, the Christian Scientists, and perhaps a few other groups, Jehovah's Witnesses is one of the few truly American expressions of religion. Like these others, Jehovah's Witnesses developed from a humble start into a worldwide religious movement. From its inception in 1872 with a handful of believers, it had increased by the 1980s to a membership of more than two million people in about two hundred countries. Powered by distinctive biblical beliefs, made effective by an efficient social organization, and fired by the conviction that the end of the historical era is at hand, the movement has maintained its distinctive appeal.

The organization's name is based on the assumption that the proper name for the Judeo-Christian deity is Jehovah. In their *New World Translation of the Holy Scriptures* (Brooklyn, N.Y., 1961), the Witnesses render as *Jehovah* the more than six thousand references in the Hebrew scriptures to the deity. Employing a variety of scriptural references (such as *Isaiah* 42:8, 43:10–11; *John* 18:37; and *Hebrews* 12:1), the Witnesses also conclude that the proper term for the followers of Jehovah is not *Christians* but *Witnesses.*

History. Jehovah's Witnesses was founded in Allegheny, Pennsylvania (now a suburb of Pittsburgh), by Charles Taze Russell, born in Pittsburgh in 1852 as the second son of Joseph L. and Eliza (Birney) Russell. Brought up as a Presbyterian, Russell came under the influence of the adventist teachings of William Miller (founder of the "Millerites") and others. Russell was prevented from obtaining an extensive education because of responsibilities in his father's chain of clothing stores, but he possessed a keen appreciation of the Bible and an engaging manner, which helped him in forming a small group to study the Bible from the perspective of the second coming of Christ. Russell's group grew, and in time other groups were formed and a publication was organized, *Zion's Watch Tower and Herald of Christ's Presence* (later called simply *The Watchtower).* The watchtower theme, appearing in various forms, has been central to the Witnesses' nomenclature. By 1884 the Zion's Watch Tower Tract Society was formed, later to become the Watch Tower Bible and Tract Society. By 1888 about fifty persons were working full-time to spread Russell's views on the Bible and the anticipated end of the age. Within a few years, groups arose throughout the United States and in a number of other countries. In 1909, finding increased acceptance, the Witnesses moved its headquarters to Brooklyn, New York, from which its international operations have been directed ever since. Russell ably led in the development of the movement despite several setbacks, including the divorce action of his wife Maria Ackley Russell in 1913. He died en route to Kansas on 31 October 1916.

Russell was succeeded by Joseph Franklin Rutherford. Born into a farm family in Morgan County, Missouri, in 1869, Rutherford was admitted to the Missouri bar at twenty-two after having been tutored in the law by a local judge. He joined the Jehovah's Witnesses in 1906 and soon shared public platforms with Russell. At a time when the Witnesses were increasingly involved in litigation, Rutherford's talents became ever more valuable. Two months after Russell's death, Rutherford was elected president of the society. He and other Witnesses believed that the "gentile times" had ended in 1914, ushering in Christ's millennial rule. Since that time, the movement has believed that Satan is the ruler of the nations and that it is therefore proper to assume a neutralist (not pacifist) stance. During World War I, Rutherford and seven other Witnesses were convicted under the Espionage Act and sent to prison, where they organized Bible studies. They were released when wartime emotions subsided.

Rutherford was an able organizer, and he persuaded the movement to use modern methods of advertising and communicating. Under his leadership the Witnesses greatly expanded their membership, the volume of their publications, the number of their full-time workers, and their international scope. In the last twelve years of his life Rutherford grew increasingly aloof from the organization, spending his time in a mansion in San Diego, California, that the society had built to house Abraham and the prophets upon their return to earth. He died at the age of seventy-two in 1942 and was interred in Rossville (Staten Island), New York.

The third president of the society was Nathan Homer Knorr, born in Bethlehem, Pennsylvania, on 23 April 1905. In his youth Knorr attended a Dutch Reformed church, but at sixteen he was attracted to the Witnesses and soon thereafter became a full-time worker. He worked in the printing plant in Brooklyn, was promoted to a higher position in the shipping department, and shortly thereafter became head of all printing operations. In 1935 he became vice-president of the society. Under his leadership, the Jehovah's Witnesses grew even more rapidly. Knorr was an indefatigable worker, an effective preacher, a world traveler for the cause, and an able administrator. He died in June 1977.

Organization and Financing. Although Knorr was succeeded by Frederick W. Franz as president, administrative leadership shifted to the Governing Body, in which no one person enjoys supreme authority. The Governing Body consists of six central committees and the lower administrative units, the branch committees. A new and more bureaucratic era had arrived. Since 1927 the society's voluminous literature has been produced in an eight-story factory building in Brooklyn, New York. The international headquarters there includes six additional buildings as well as nearby homes to house the workers needed for the printing and other activities of the society. Near Wallkill, New York, a combination farm and factory produces the two principal magazines *(The Watchtower* and *Awake!)* and food for the society's full-time workers. Aside from room and board, these workers receive a small monthly allowance for incidental expenses. The backbone of support for the society in all its activities is the voluntarism of its members.

Beliefs and Practices. Although the Witnesses' beliefs appear to be based upon the Judeo-Christian Bible and within that context seem to represent an American fundamentalist outlook, they are indeed distinctive. All that they believe is based on the Bible. They "proof text" (that is, supply a biblical citation to support) almost every statement of faith, taking for granted the authority of the Bible, which entirely supplants tradition.

For the Witnesses, God, properly addressed as Jehovah, is the one supreme and universal deity. Jesus is thought to be God's son, but he is held as definitely inferior to Jehovah. Yet Christ holds a special place in Witness theology: he is the first of God's creations; his human life was paid as a ransom for salvation; he died on a stake (not a cross), was raised from the dead as an immortal spirit person, and is present in the world as a spirit. He is the focus of congregational gatherings; the Witnesses pray to Jehovah only through Christ.

Witnesses believe that history has run its course and that the "time of the end" is very close. Until that end, Satan rules the world. For several decades various of the society's publications have used the same title: *Millions Now Living Will Never Die.* The end is that close. Until the end, a Witness must keep apart from the world and must obey only those secular laws and follow only those practices of faith that are in conformity with the society's understanding of the Bible. In this regard, several negative requirements must be upheld. Images must not be used in worship. Spiritualism must be shunned. Witnesses must not participate in interfaith movements. Taking blood into the body, through the mouth or by transfusion, is contrary to Jehovah's laws. A clergy class and distinctive titles are prohibited. No national flag is to be saluted and no pledge of allegiance to a nation is permitted. In maintaining these requirements, the Witnesses in some countries have been prosecuted by civil authorities and at times martyred. Adherence to their beliefs in opposition to the laws of various countries has won admiration from a wide spectrum of civil libertarians, although the society does not aim at extending human freedom, but rather at expressing its own deeply held religious convictions.

Although the Witnesses uphold the doctrine of the virgin birth of Jesus, they refuse to celebrate Christmas, believing that the holiday is of pagan origin. They say that the Bible nowhere teaches that Christ's birth, or indeed, anyone's birthday, should be celebrated. (Actually, the Witnesses believe that Christ was born on 1 October, 2 BC.) They also recognize neither Lent nor Easter. They do, however, have a Lord's Meal ceremony, which takes place once a year.

Witnesses believe that baptism by immersion symbolizes dedication. They deny the obligation of Sunday worship, asserting that the observance of the Sabbath day was pertinent to Old Testament religion only and that this requirement ended with the fulfillment of Mosaic law in Jesus. The Witnesses do, however, conform to social norms in accepting Sunday as a day of rest and worship. They meet in "kingdom halls" for study and worship, as well as in members' homes.

The Witnesses believe that the end of history will begin with a great battle (which the Witnesses call Har-Magedon) between the forces of good and evil. Historical circumstances as heretofore known will be destroyed and a new order created. Satan will be vanquished and wicked human beings eternally destroyed; hell is humankind's common grave. But although human death is a consequence of Adam's sin there is hope of resurrection. Those whom Jehovah approves will receive eternal life. But only a small flock of 144,000 true believers from the whole of history will be born again as spiritual children of God and will go to heaven to rule with Christ.

On earth, however, Christ will establish a new kingdom and will rule in righteousness and peace. Ideal living conditions will be established and the earth will be environmentally restored to perfection, never again to be destroyed or depopulated. In effect, heaven will be established on earth; those who inhabit it will enjoy all good. In the meantime, the Witnesses must give public testimony to the truth of the movement's teachings. This they do through a voluminous publishing program, worldwide efforts at conversion, a variety of weekly meetings and mass celebrations, and—as they have become known to countless non-Witnesses—through door-to-door visitations.

BIBLIOGRAPHY

Of prime importance in understanding Jehovah's Witnesses is the organization's literature, the annual *Yearbook of Jehovah's Witnesses* (Brooklyn, N.Y.), and the many publications of the movement, especially *The Watchtower*, a semimonthly magazine. A number of general accounts have been published, including William Whalen's *Armageddon around the Corner: A Report on the Jehovah's Witnesses* (New York, 1962), a popular overview written in journalistic style, and Chandler W. Sterling's *The Witnesses: One God, One Victory* (Chicago, 1975), a generalized report by a retired Episcopalian bishop. An early and comprehensive study is my own work, *The Jehovah's Witnesses* (1945; reprint, New York, 1967). A more recent one is James A. Beckford's *The Trumpet of Prophecy: A Sociological Study of Jehovah's Witnesses* (New York, 1975). Barbara G. Harrison's *Visions of Glory: A History and a Memory of Jehovah's Witnesses* (New York, 1978) is a vivid, personal account by a woman who was a Witness between the ages of nine and twenty-one. George D. McKinney, Jr., offers a critical analysis of the Witnesses' beliefs in *The Theology of the Jehovah's Witnesses* (Grand Rapids, Mich., 1962). Of course, the Witnesses have their critics, and a few of them are in print. William J. Schnell's *Thirty Years a Watch Tower Slave: The Confessions of a Converted Jehovah's Witness* (Grand Rapids, 1956) tells its story in the title. Albert Muller's *Meet Jehovah's Witnesses: Their Confusion, Doubts, and Contradictions* (Pulaski, Wis., 1964) reflects Roman Catholic perspectives.

HERBERT HEWITT STROUP

JEN AND I are basic terms in Confucian moral philosophy. In the *Lun-yü* (Analects) of Confucius, *i* is what one morally ought to do. One who does not do what one should, or who lacks the disposition to do so, is said to "lack *i*." Thus, *i* comes also to be a virtue. Common translations of the term include "righteousness" (Legge) and "dutifulness" (Lau). In the ordinary ancient language of China *i* meant "honor": a man of "high *i*" would not brook an insult. *Jen* has more prominence throughout the Chinese tradition. It is often translated "benevolence," following the usage of James Legge, who borrowed the term from Bishop Joseph Butler (1692–1752). In the *Lun-yü*, *jen* and *i* are not linked. Here, *jen* too is a virtue, and appears to be the quality, or sum of the qualities, of an ideally good man. It often has the specific sense "kindliness." In the *Meng-tzu* and in much of later Confucian ethics, however, the two words are often linked. Indeed, in *Meng-tzu* the binom *jen-i* appears simply to mean "morality" (Lau). When Meng-tzu notices the two separately, however, a distinction between *jen* as virtue and *i* as norm is evident: "*Jen* is man's heart; *i* is man's path" (6A.11). At other times, Meng-tzu also treats *i* as a virtue, and makes *jen* and *i* the first two (and most basic) of man's four innate moral qualities. Here, *jen* refers to the virtue that grows out of a person's *hsin* (innate "heart, mind," i.e., disposition) of spontaneous compassion for others in trouble, and *i* refers to the virtue that grows out of a person's innate "heart" of distaste or shame for doing something wrong or disgraceful (2A.6, 6A.6). Elsewhere, Meng-tzu characterizes *jen* as the maturation, and redirection toward all men, of the natural affection a child feels toward his parents, and *i* as the fruition of the natural respect the child feels for elders in the household (7A.15). Thus, Meng-tzu meets the danger of an amoral subjectivity inherent in an other-regarding ethic *(jen)* by positing an independent awareness of what is objectively right *(i)*, which, although in need of being "nourished," is nonetheless innate.

The etymology of the two words gives further insight into their meaning. *Jen*, the name of the virtue, is cognate with *jen*, "man." This relationship was commonly understood by the early Chinese philosophers, leading modern scholars to experiment with translations such as "human-heartedness," or even "manhood-at-its-best." The graph for *i* contains the element *wo* for "I, myself." Here too, the words are probably cognates. Ancient idiom gave *jen* the sense "other people," as contrasted with *wo*, or "me." Thus, perhaps, *jen* came to mean the ideal qualities of man as such, but also specifically concern for others, while *i* came to be used for my proper regard for myself, my sense of honor, my unwillingness to do what would bring blame or shame upon myself.

Another interpretive perspective is offered in *Lun-yü* 4.15, where Confucius's disciple Tseng-tzu interprets his teacher's remark that there is "one thread" running through his *tao* to refer to the moral qualities *chung* and *shu*. If *jen* is perfect virtue for Confucius, what we are offered here, in effect, is an analysis of the concept. *Shu* is the virtue of consideration for others (Confucius's "golden rule," *Lun-yü* 12.2 and 15.23). The dominant commentarial tradition makes *chung* (cognate with *chung*, "inside") the inner virtue and *shu* its practice. However, a more likely contrast is probably that suggested by *Lun-yü* 5.19, where *chung* (commonly, "loyalty") is shown to be the disposition to impose on oneself the responsibilities one would expect of others, just as *shu* is the disposition to extend to others the consideration one would want for oneself. It is regard for others that is essential to *jen.* This is explicitly put by the eleventh-century philosopher Chang Tsai (1020–1077), who says (in a comment on the Confucian "golden rule"), "If one loves others with the same disposition one has to love oneself, then *jen* is fully realized."

In his essay *Yüan-tao* (Inquiry into the Tao), the ninth-century writer Han Yü (768–824) defines *jen* as "wide-loving" and *i* as "acting accordingly and taking this [i.e., action] as what we ought to do." In later Confucianism, *i* retains its basic sense as "norm" and is often conjoined with *li,* or "moral principles," as in the binom *i-li* ("norms and principles," in effect, philosophy). On the other hand, *jen* is said to be the disposition of the ideal moral man (the sage) to expand the sensitivity of the self to include everything. For example, Ch'eng Hao (1032–1085) wrote that "medical books use the term 'unfeeling' [*pu-jen,* "not *jen*"] for numbness in the hands and feet." Similarly, he notes, "by benevolence *(jen)* Heaven and earth and the innumerable things are regarded as one substance, so that nothing is not oneself, and when this is recognized there is nothing one will not do for them" (Graham, 1958, p. 98). This concept of *jen* is important in the thought of Wang Yang-ming (1472–1529), whose personal name, Shou-jen, means "cherishing *jen.*" Since Wang's awakened moral man is able to apprehend any problem from the viewpoint of all things, he sees directly what ought to be done. Thus, a perfectly other-regarding *(jen)* "heart" exhibits in effect perfect *i;* its intuitions are perfect *li.* This concept of pan-sympathetic *jen* is imaginatively developed by T'an Ssu-t'ung (1865–1898) is his major philosophical work, *Jen-hsüeh* (Science of Jen). T'an adopts the concept of the ether of pre–twentieth-century science, identifying it with electricity (his transcription for ether is *i-t'ai,* "transcendent"). For T'an, a physical organism is a sensitory unity because of the operation of this ether-electricity pervading everything. Likewise, the entire universe in an ideal moral condition would be a mutually responsive whole. T'an thus gives his political utopianism a metaphysical basis, and sees the moral insights of the great religions as all pointing to the same idea.

[*See also the biographies of Confucius and Meng-tzu.*]

BIBLIOGRAPHY

Boodberg, Peter A. "The Semasiology of Some Primary Confucian Concepts." *Philosophy East and West* 2 (1952): 317–332.

Fingarette, Herbert. "Following the 'One Thread' of the *Analects.*" *Journal of the American Academy of Religion* 47, suppl. (September 1979): 373–405.

Fung Yu-lan. *A History of Chinese Philosophy,* vol. 2, *The Period of Classical Learning.* 2d ed. Translated by Derk Bodde. Princeton, 1953.

Graham, Angus C. *Two Chinese Philosophers: Ch'êng Ming-tao and Ch'êng Yi-ch'uan.* London, 1958.

Lau, D. C., trans. *Mencius.* Harmondsworth, 1970.

Legge, James, ed. and trans. *The Works of Mencius,* vol. 2 of *The Chinese Classics.* 2d ed. Oxford, 1895.

Waley, Arthur, trans. and ed. *The Analects of Confucius.* London, 1938.

Wang Shou-jen. *Instructions for Practical Living, and Other Neo-Confucian Writings, by Wang Yang-ming.* Translated, with notes, by Wing-tsit Chan. New York, 1963.

David S. Nivison

JENSEN, ADOLF E. (1899–1965), German ethnologist and historian of religions. Adolf Ellegard Jensen was born 1 January 1899 in Kiel, the city in which he also grew up. After World War I, he studied mathematics, natural science, and philosophy at the universities of Bonn and Kiel. He received a doctorate in 1922 with a dissertation on the writings on natural philosophy of Ernst Mach and Max Planck.

In the following year, Jensen took a position as research assistant at Leo Frobenius's newly founded Institute for Cultural Morphology in Munich. This position proved to be a turning point in Jensen's scientific ambitions, which from then on were directed toward the ethnological perspectives of Frobenius. When the institute was removed to Frankfurt in 1925, Jensen became a recognized lecturer at the university there. His thesis, "Beschneidung und Reifezeremonien bei Naturvölkern" (Circumcision and Puberty Rites among Primitive Peoples), was completed in 1933.

After the death of Leo Frobenius in 1938, Jensen was named director of the Institute for Cultural Morphology, which was eventually renamed for its founder. Also in 1938, Jensen succeeded Frobenius as director of the Municipal Ethnological Museum in Frankfurt, where he had served as curator since 1936. In 1946 Jensen received a chair in the University of Frankfurt's newly established department of cultural and ethnological studies. Jensen directed research expeditions to South Africa (1928–1930), Libya (1932), Ethiopia (1934–1935, 1950–1951, and 1954–1955), and the Moluccan island of Ceram (1937). The works that grew out of these research trips proved decisive in influencing the structure of cultural history and morphology studies in the tradition founded by Frobenius.

In his work *Das religiöse Weltbild einer frühen Kultur* (1948) Jensen presented an array of complex cultural factors that, although widely dispersed, create the impression of sharing elements common to one central myth. The content of this myth reveals information about human existence as well as about the formation of essential cultural elements. According to this myth complex, which relates the activities of a tribe of *dema* (ancestral) deities, the body of a murdered deity was, in primeval times, transformed into the first useful plants. The present order of existence, in which man became a reproductive and a mortal being, was then established. In this myth and its cultic form of expression, Jensen saw the nucleus of a worldview that was the ancient predecessor of that of the more advanced cultures, in which tubers were planted as a food crop. He maintained that contemporary "primitive" cultures could be viewed as living an earlier phase of human development, a fact that facilitates a reconstruction of the rise of culture.

Jensen's description of the *dema*-deity complex, based on his research in Ceram, has been cited widely by students of mythology. However, the difficulty that arises in understanding this evidence relates to the fact that we are divorced from the original motives for the formation of these cultures. Contact with older cultures occurred during a relatively advanced stage of civilization in which attention had shifted from the original essence of cultural unification to the secondary, that is, the functional or practical benefits that can be derived from cultural development. If one were to reconstruct the evidence in an ordered fashion, placing it within its original cultural context and intellectual framework, one could discover an explanation that would be comprehensible even within our own sociocultural milieu. In Jensen's opinion (which he shared with Leo Frobenius), all meaningful cultural creations owe their existence not to the practical advantages they confer but to an independent drive toward enlightenment that found outward expression in the mythology of primitive people. Myths and cults form an inseparable unit. In cults, which are dramatic presentations of mythical events, humans reenact the process of their creation as perceived and maintained within "true" myths.

Often honored for his work, Jensen was a member of various scholarly societies and was an honorary fellow of the Royal Anthropological Institute of Great Britain and Ireland. He died at his retirement home in Mammolsheim on 20 May 1965.

BIBLIOGRAPHY

Two books resulted from Jensen's expeditions to Ethiopia: *Im Lande des Gada* (Stuttgart, 1936) and *Altvölker Süd-Äthiopiens* (Stuttgart, 1959). The results of Jensen's expedition to the Moluccas are recorded in *Hainuwele: Volkserzählungen von der Molukken-Insel Ceram,* whose authorship Jensen shared with Heinrich Niggemeyer (Frankfurt, 1939), and *Die drei Ströme: Züge aus dem geistigen und religiösen Leben der Wemale* (Leipzig, 1948). Jensen's ideas on the history of religions are collected in his major work, *Mythos und Kult bei Naturvölkern* (Wiesbaden, 1951), which has been translated as *Myth and Cult among Primitive Peoples,* 2d ed. (Chicago, 1969).

OTTO ZERRIES
Translated from German by John Maressa